MW01133989

The Herbaceous Layer in Forests of Eastern North America

THE HERBACEOUS LAYER IN FORESTS OF EASTERN NORTH AMERICA

SECOND EDITION

Edited by Frank S. Gilliam

OXFORD
UNIVERSITY PRESS

OXFORD

UNIVERSITY PRESS

Oxford University Press is a department of the University of Oxford.
It furthers the University's objective of excellence in research, scholarship,
and education by publishing worldwide.

Oxford   New York
Auckland   Cape Town   Dar es Salaam   Hong Kong   Karachi
Kuala Lumpur   Madrid   Melbourne   Mexico City   Nairobi
New Delhi   Shanghai   Taipei   Toronto

With offices in
Argentina   Austria   Brazil   Chile   Czech Republic   France   Greece
Guatemala   Hungary   Italy   Japan   Poland   Portugal   Singapore
South Korea   Switzerland   Thailand   Turkey   Ukraine   Vietnam

Oxford is a registered trademark of Oxford University Press
in the UK and certain other countries.

Published in the United States of America by
Oxford University Press
198 Madison Avenue, New York, NY 10016

© Oxford University Press 2014

Library of Congress Cataloging-in-Publication Data
The herbaceous layer in forests of eastern North America / edited by Frank S. Gilliam.—2nd ed.
p. cm.
Includes bibliographical references. ISBN 978-0-19-983765-6 (alk. paper)
1. Forest ecology—East (U.S.)   2. Forest ecology—Canada, Eastern.   3. Forest plants—East
(U.S.)   4. Forest plants—Canada, Eastern.   5. Forest plants—Ecology—East (U.S.)
6. Forest plants—Ecology—Canada, Eastern.   I. Gilliam, Frank S., 1954–
QK115.H47 2014
577.30974—dc23
2013025753

9 8 7 6 5 4 3 2 1
Printed in the United States of America
on acid-free paper

I am humbled and honored to dedicate this second edition to the memory of my dear parents, Sara Dee Rainey Gilliam and M. Randolph Gilliam. Words will always be insufficient in conveying the dimensions of their love for me and their importance to both my personal and professional life, and equally insufficient in expressing my love and gratitude to them for all that they meant to me and our entire family.

F.S.G.

Contents

Preface to the Second Edition

The occasion of the publication of this second edition of *The Herbaceous Layer in Forests of Eastern North America* merits a bit of storytelling about the genesis of the first edition, which Mark Roberts, formerly of the University of New Brunswick (UNB), Canada, and I assembled and edited for its 2003 publication. Although Mark and I were officemates at Duke University for four years and were essentially soulmates during that time, our specific doctoral research was quite divergent in most respects. His focused on successional aspen forests of northern lower Michigan, whereas mine examined biogeochemical and herb layer response to fire in Coastal Plain South Carolina.

Upon successful completion of our respective Ph.D.s, we went our separate ways, both geographically and in terms of academic positions. He was able to land a tenure-track assistant professor position right out of the gate, so to speak, at UNB, from which he retired in 2009. In stark contrast, I began a post-doctoral meandering, first at Kansas State University, then University of Virginia, then University of North Carolina-Greensboro, before attaining a tenure-track assistant professor position here at Marshall University in 1990. I mention all of this because, in retrospect, it seems that the farther away we became, the more we endeavored to collaborate on research-related projects, whether they were manuscripts or organizing special sessions at meetings. These have long added immeasurably to my career as a plant ecologist and professor. Indeed, many are mentioned in the preface to the first edition, but they merit brief repetition here.

Our first success was convening a symposium for the 1993 Annual Meeting of the Ecological Society of America (ESA) ("Effects of Forest Management on Plant Biodiversity: Patterns and Mechanisms in Forest Ecosystems"), leading to the 1995 publication of a special section, "Plant Diversity in Managed Forests," in *Ecological Applications*. Shortly after we published an article in the *Journal of Vegetation Science* in 1995 based on Mark's herb layer data from successional forests in Michigan, I thought that the time was right to convene another ESA symposium—one that focused solely on the herb layer. Although I had not met him by that time, my initial invitation to Fakhri Bazzaz to contribute a paper to this gathering was energetically accepted by him. All others seemed to fall easily in line, with Fakhri as my "blue chip recruit." This led to the 1998 ESA symposium "Ecology and Dynamics of the Herbaceous Layer of Forest Communities of Eastern North America," which, of course, formed the basis for the first edition of this book. In 2002, during initial work on the book, we organized the session "Response of Understory Plant Diversity to Forest Practices" for the Second North American Forest Ecology Workshop, which led to a special issue of *Forest Ecology and Management* ("Forest Ecology in the Next Millennium: Putting the Long View into Practice") later that year.

A decade in the sciences can be like a century in other academic fields, with scientific advances appearing at ever-increasing rates. Plant ecology is no exception to this generalization. Thus, I felt that the time had come to update the 2003 volume with a second edition. This was not only to provide current literature and concepts for the original chapters, but also to add important topics that were missing from the first edition. Thus, although a few chapters remain unchanged, most have been substantially added to, in terms of both literature updates and conceptual content. In addition, eight new chapters appear in this second edition, including an overview of reproductive strategies among herb species, a rigorous examination of herb layer diversity in the southeastern United States, and an in-depth analysis of effects of a variety of disturbances on forest herb communities: overbrowsing by deer, timber harvesting, agricultural practices, excess nitrogen deposition, and climate change.

As I have tried to quantify in chapter 1, this has been an exciting time for vegetation scientists investigating the dynamics of the herb layer of forests, with an unprecedented increase in research efforts, as evidenced by publications on this topic. For example, the number of papers published on the herb layer in the first decade of the new millennium far exceeds—by as much as 50 percent more—the total number of papers published on the topic in the entire 20th century. One can only speculate why this has developed this way. The more cynical among us might simply claim that there are more journals and more plant ecologists; certainly, those factors contribute to some unknown extent. However, I am convinced that such growth has been due primarily to an increasing awareness of how significant the herbaceous layer is to the structure and functions of the very forest ecosystems that are vital to the sustainability of the biosphere. It is my hope that this second edition can be a worthy addition to the growing literature, and I look forward to a future of more research to be done.

I am deeply grateful to a great many people for the successful completion of this second edition. I must first thank Mark on both professional and personal levels, for without him, the first edition would have been impossible. He was always an image of scholarly discipline for me at a time during my graduate training when I needed it most; upon reflection, I suppose that image has stayed very much with me. He was also the best friend anyone could want, as running partner, sounding board, fellow Duke basketball fan, and source of requisite comic relief.

I want to thank the original authors who contributed to the first edition, and especially the majority of them who agreed to undertake the arduous task of revising their respective chapters, not only updating the voluminous current literature, but also further and more deeply developing new concepts that appropriately demonstrate the vibrancy of this exciting ecological field. In addition, of course, I am particularly grateful to the "new" authors for filling in the gaps inherent in the first edition. Although I am understandably biased, I think that these individuals complement the others in making this a truly state-of-the-science volume. I also want to convey a general expression of gratitude to a great many colleagues, whether I know you personally or solely through your published work, for interactions and insights regarding our field.

Clichéd though it may sound, not enough words of gratitude can be conveyed to Jeremy Lewis, executive editor at Oxford University Press, for this second edition. Due to a great many—mostly personal—unforeseen developments, it was difficult to stay on schedule throughout the publication process. Jeremy was the epitome of patience and understanding throughout all of it. I hope that the result of our collective efforts is a book of which he can be deeply proud. I would also like to acknowledge the critical contributions of Erik Hane, Jeremy's assistant at OUP, and Mary Jo Rhodes of Newgen North America, who served as Production Manager.

Financial support for professional indexing, always a necessary challenge in adding to the utility of a book such as this, was provided from numerous sources here at Marshall University, and greatly facilitated by several individuals. Thus, I would like to thank David Mallory (chair, Department of Biological Sciences), Donna Spindel (dean, Graduate College), and Chuck Somerville (dean, College of Science) for their respective roles in securing needed funds.

I have always thought that each of us is a magnum opus, the synthesis of a great literal body of work, such that all aspects—including all interactions with other people—of our lives make us who we are. And so, equally important to me are the not-necessarily-ecology people in my life. Although they are already in my dedication, I must begin by thanking my parents for, among so many other things, allowing me the intellectual freedom to pursue both the figurative and actual paths I have followed. My siblings (and their spouses, children, and grandchildren) have long been essential to me for their love and spiritual support, especially lately, now that it is "just the four of us." So, thanks, Dee, Bryan, and Grace, for all you have meant to me.

I am the grateful father of two children, Rachel and Ian, who never cease to amaze me. They were small children at the time of publication of the first edition. At the time of this publication, Rachel is a graduate student at the Duke University Divinity School and Ian is a Midshipman at the United States Naval Academy. So, it is quite obvious that they have made so much more of those 10 years than I have. I thank them for so many things, but especially for the unmerited joy in my life and for making life worth the living. And finally, my wife and best friend, Laura. Who would have thought that a pickup line at the beach would have led to two souls melding the way ours have? Thank you for your love, my happiness, and our children—and the journey we are on together.

F.S.G.
Huntington, West Virginia

Contributors

Wendy B. Anderson
Environmental Programs
Drury College
Springfield, MO 65802

Fakhri A. Bazzaz*
Department of Organismal and
    Evolutionary Biology
Harvard University
Cambridge, MA 02138

Susan W. Beatty
College of Liberal Arts and Sciences
Dean's Office
Portland State University
Portland, OR 97207-0751

Jesse Bellemare
Department of Biological Sciences
Smith College
Northampton, MA 01063

Yves Bergeron
NSERC-UQAT-UQAM Industrial
    Chair in Sustainable
Forest Management,
445 boul. de l'Université,
Rouyn-Noranda, Québec J9X 5E4
Canada

Catherine Boudreault
Universite du Quebec a Montreal
Centre d'Etude de la Foret
PO Box 8888, Stn. Centre-Ville
Montreal, Quebec
Canada, H3C 3P8

*deceased

Walter P. Carson
Department of Biological Sciences
University of Pittsburgh
Pittsburgh, PA 15260

Norman L. Christensen
Nicholas School of the Environment
Duke University
Durham, NC 27708-0328

Nicole J. Fenton
NSERC-UQAT-UQAM Industrial
    Chair in Sustainable
Forest Management,
445 boul. de l'Université,
Rouyn-Noranda, Québec J9X 5E4
Canada

Kathryn M. Flinn
Department of Biology
Franklin and Marshall College
Lancaster, PA 17604-3003

Lisa O. George
7938 Clarion Way
Houston, TX 77040

Frank S. Gilliam
Department of Biological Sciences
Marshall University
Huntington, WV 25755-2510

Carol Goodwillie
Department of Biology
East Carolina University
Greenville, NC 27858

Louis De Grandpré
Ressources naturelles Canada
Service canadien des forêts
Centre de foresterie des Laurentides
1055, rue du P.E.P.S., PO Box
  103800
Stn. Sainte-Foy, Québec G1V 4C7
Canada

Pierre Grondin
Ministère des Ressources naturelles
  du Québec
Direction de la Recherche forestière
2700 rue Einstein
Sainte-Foy, Québec G1P 3W8
Canada

Claudia L. Jolls
Department of Biology
East Carolina University
Greenville, NC 27858

James O. Luken
Graduate Studies
Coastal Carolina University
Conway, SC 29526-6054

Brian C. McCarthy
Department of Environmental and
  Plant Biology
Ohio University
Athens, OH 45701-2979

David A. Moeller
Department of Plant Biology
University of Minnesota
St. Paul, MN 55108

Robert N. Muller
Santa Barbara Botanic Garden
1212 Mission Canyon Road
Santa Barbara, CA 93105

Howard S. Neufeld
Department of Biology
Appalachian State University
Boone, NC 28608

Kyle A. Palmquist
Curriculum for the Environment and
  Ecology
University of North Carolina
Chapel Hill, NC 27599-3275

Robert K. Peet
Department of Biology
University of North Carolina
Chapel Hill, NC 27599-3280

Chris J. Peterson
Department of Plant Biology
University of Georgia
Athens, GA 30602-7271

Mark R. Roberts
Faculty of Forestry and
  Environmental Management
University of New Brunswick
Fredericton, NB E3B 6C2
Canada

Alejandro A. Royo
United States Department of Agriculture
Forest Service
Northern Research Station
Irvine, PA 16329

Miles R. Silman
Department of Biology
Wake Forest University
Winston-Salem, NC 27109

Samantha M. Tessel
Curriculum for the Environment and
  Ecology
University of North Carolina
Chapel Hill, NC 27599-3275

Thuy Nguyen
NSERC-UQAT-UQAM Industrial
  Chair in Sustainable
Forest Management,
445 boul. de l'Université,
Rouyn-Noranda, Québec J9X 5E4
Canada

Contributors

Donald M. Waller
Department of Botany
University of Wisconsin
Madison, WI 53706

Dennis F. Whigham
Smithsonian Environmental Research
  Center
Box 28
Edgewater, MD 21037

Julie L. Wyatt
Arts and Sciences Division
Gaston College
Dallas, NC 28034

Donald R. Young
Department of Biological Sciences
Virginia Commonwealth
  University
Richmond, VA 23284-2012

The Herbaceous Layer in Forests of Eastern North America

1 Introduction

The Herbaceous Layer—The Forest between the Trees

Frank S. Gilliam

Forest ecosystems have always been an integral part of human existence, whether as a source of food, fiber, and habitat, as an essential component in maintaining the atmospheric balance of O_2 and CO_2, or as a source of musical, artistic, or poetic inspiration. Yet, our image of forests often comes from the broad brush of a landscape perspective, whereby we see only the grandeur of the predominant vegetation—the trees. Such a distortion figuratively and literally masks the vegetation that, though of lesser prominence, contains the most spatially and temporally dynamic assemblage of forest plants. Often called the *herbaceous layer* (other synonyms are discussed later in this chapter), this stratum of forest vegetation carries with it an ecological significance to the structure and function of forest ecosystems that belies its diminutive stature.

Indeed, it has often been generalized—correctly, to be sure—that the herbaceous layer is the stratum of highest plant biodiversity in forests. To quantify this assertion, I surveyed the literature for studies in North America that quantified both overstory and herb layer richness on the same vegetation sample units, varying from plots to watersheds to an entire basin (the Coweeta Hydrologic Laboratory in Georgia) (Gilliam 2007). The ratio of herb layer species to woody overstory species generally ranged from ~ 3 to 10 (representing a range of relative richness in the herb layer of 75 to 91 percent), with the exception of a fire-maintained longleaf pine stand with its species-rich ground cover and overstory monoculture of *Pinus palustris* Mill., which had a ratio of ~ 250 (Platt et al. 2006; Gilliam et al. 2006). Indeed, conifer stands tend to have higher ratios, likely the result of lower overstory richness (Gilliam 2007). In addition, there was a significant positive relationship between herb layer richness and overstory richness, suggesting that site factors, such as soil fertility, may play an important role (fig. 1.1). The mean across all studies and sites (~ 30 in number), excluding the *P. palustris* study, was 5.6 ± 0.9 (95 percent confidence interval), suggesting that the herb layer generally represents 82–87 percent of plant diversity in forests (Gilliam

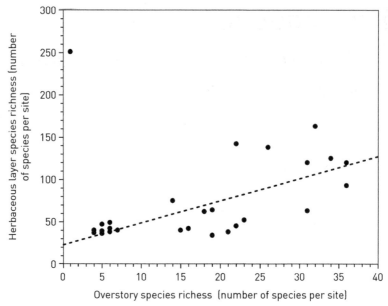

FIGURE 1.1 Herbaceous layer species richness versus overstory species richness across forest sites in North America.

2007), an impressive range considering that relative biomass of the herb layer is far less than 0.5 percent of aboveground biomass (Welch et al. 2007; chapter 2, this volume).

The purpose of this chapter is to introduce this second edition by documenting patterns of change in research interest in the herb layer, and by summarizing our general knowledge and understanding of the ecology and dynamics of forest herb layers. Because the literature contains numerous terms used synonymously with *herbaceous layer*, I begin with a discussion of the terminology and definitions that have been commonly applied to the herbaceous layer. Next, I document the increasing number of papers in the literature over the past several decades. I then develop a simple conceptual framework for understanding the spatial and temporal dynamics of the herbaceous layer. Finally, I describe the organization of the book.

TERMINOLOGY

A survey of the ecological literature reveals numerous synonyms for the term *herbaceous layer* used by ecologists, presenting a challenge to both experienced and beginning researchers. Whereas the term *herbaceous layer* has been adopted for the title of this book (and I will use it interchangeably with the more abbreviated *herb layer*), other authors use such terms as *herbaceous* (or *herb*) *stratum, herbaceous understory, ground layer, ground vegetation,* and *ground flora*. In addition, foresters and others interested in forest management sometimes refer to it as the *regeneration layer* (e.g., Waterman et al. 1995; Baker and van Lear 1998). This latter term arises from both an interest in patterns of regeneration of overstory dominant species and awareness that successful regeneration of such species can be determined largely by interactions among plant species in this stratum (chapter 14, this volume). Some terms even have a pejorative connotation. When I was a graduate student at Duke University, I once asked the professor of the summer dendrology course about a particular forest herb while walking through the Duke Forest, to which he replied, "Oh, that's just a *step-over*." Such a dismissive term emphasizes the lack of importance given to the herb layer by some foresters, at least in the late 1970s, as comprising plants unworthy of study and thus to be "stepped over" while focusing on trees. There are likely other synonyms to be encountered in the literature, so this is not intended to be an exhaustive list. Rather, the goal is to provide some idea of the diversity of terms one should expect to find in the literature.

Gilliam (2007) summarized the results of a search of Ecological Abstracts initially reported in the first edition of this book for citations from the 20-year period of 1980 to 1999 that have the herb layer synonyms mentioned either in the title, as key words, or in the abstract. The search represented articles from some 3,000 journals and 2,000 other publications, including books and monographs, and thus provided an indication of the frequency with which one might expect to encounter the various terms in the literature. The number of occurrences was not necessarily mutually exclusive among terms. That is, it is possible that one article may have used, for example, *herbaceous layer* in the title, and *ground layer* as a key word; this would result in one occurrence in each of the two synonym categories.

Clearly, *herbaceous/herb layer* and *ground vegetation* have been the more commonly used terms in the ecological literature, receiving 34.0 and 31.1 percent frequency of use between 1980 and 1999, respectively. For reasons that are not immediately apparent, North American studies have tended to use *herbaceous/herb layer*, whereas non-North American (particularly European) studies tend to use *ground vegetation*. Given these observations, I am not suggesting that a single consensus term be used. In fact, as editor of this volume, I have avoided requiring that all authors use identical terminology. The main point is that, particularly for researchers just beginning in this field, there are several terms that one must expect to encounter in the ecological literature. Accordingly, from a practical standpoint, those performing searches for herb layer studies (e.g., using Web search engines—see below) would be strongly advised to either use several terms (but especially *herbaceous/herb layer* and *ground vegetation*) or focus the appropriate term toward the geographical area of interest.

TEMPORAL CHANGE IN RESEARCH INTEREST IN HERB LAYER ECOLOGY

One of the better metrics of research interest in a particular scientific discipline or topic can arise from documenting patterns of change over time in the number of citations in the pertinent literature. Of the many Internet search engines, Google Scholar© (hereafter GS) provides one of the more effective means of reaching a wide variety of publications, including peer-reviewed journals, doctoral dissertations, master's theses, government white papers, and other scholarly documents. A further advantage of GS over the previous analysis used in the first edition is that GS searches text, in addition to simply searching titles, key words, and abstracts. Accordingly, I have performed GS searches on the two more common terms encountered in the literature: *herbaceous layer* and *ground vegetation*. As GS allows Internet searches to be broken down into set time periods, I have performed these by decade, beginning with the 1950s and extending to the present. In addition, GS allows searches on these terms exclusively, so that the results can be displayed for each term separately, as well as together.

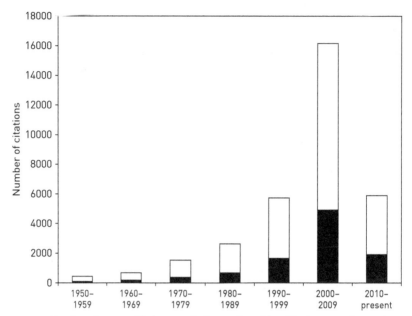

FIGURE 1.2 Number of papers with the terms *herbaceous layer* (closed bar) or *ground vegetation* (open bar) by decade, as searched by Google Scholar™.

In contrast to what was reported in the first edition of this book, *ground vegetation* is used more commonly than *herbaceous layer*, likely the result of the geographic distinction already discussed and the history of herb layer studies (i.e., because *ground vegetation* is used more among European studies and because such studies began earlier in Europe than in North America). More important than this distinction in use of terms, it is clear from such analyses that research interest in the ecology of forest herb layers has increased exponentially (fig. 1.2). Indeed, citation frequency has grown from < 400 in the 1950s to > 16,000 in the first decade of the new millennium. Furthermore, the number of citations in the current, incomplete decade (2010 to present) already exceeds that of the 1990s (fig. 1.2).

DEFINITIONS

The more commonly used definitions of the herbaceous layer emphasize its physical aspects as an assemblage of forest vegetation, with the focus on height, rather than on growth form. Commonly, the herb layer is defined as *the forest stratum composed of all vascular species that are ≤ 1 m in height*. The maximum height limit, however, varies among studies, as do the exclusion and inclusion of non-vascular plant species. In one of the earlier quantitative studies of the herb layer, Siccama et al. (1970) used 0.5 m as an upper limit for the Hubbard Brook Experimental Forest. Yorks and Dabydeen (1999) used 1.37 m to delimit the herb layer in clearcut hardwood stands of western Maryland. Using the terms *understory* and *inferior layer* interchangeably, Rogers (1981) defined this stratum as comprising vascular plants < 2 m in height for mature mixed mesophytic stands from Minnesota, Wisconsin, and Michigan.

Although it is rarely immediately evident why different studies use different height limits, the variation likely results from a combination of research inertia (i.e., "Well, that's the way we've always done it in this lab") along with true variation among forest types in the structure of vegetation. For example, mature second-growth hardwood stands, such as those found in Watershed 6 of Hubbard Brook, often lack a prominent shrub component, so the use of 0.5 m as the upper height limit by Siccama et al. (1970) was certainly justified. Yorks and Dabydeen (1999) used the term *vascular understory* along with a height limit of 1.37 m. Although they provide no reason for such a distinct height limit, it corresponds to the "breast height" often used in conjunction with DBH (diameter at breast height). Other studies include non-vascular plants in their definition (e.g., Bisbee et al. 2001). Although such studies are relatively uncommon, they generally occur in forests where bryophyte cover can be prevalent (e.g., boreal forests; chapter 12, this volume). Still other studies fail to specify a maximum height to distinguish the herb layer from other forest vegetation strata.

Just as no consensus on a single term was sought for use in studies of the herb layer of forest ecosystems, it is similarly not the intention of this book to establish a uniform definition of the herb layer. For the very reasons discussed here (and particularly the great inter-site differences in the physical structures of forest vegetation), vegetation scientists should feel free to adapt their definitions appropriately. However, it is imperative that researchers (1) fashion their definitions around key biological and physical characteristic of the forest system, and (2) state clearly their working definitions of the herb layer, along with an appropriate justification, especially if it departs greatly from the typical height range of 0.5 to 1.0 m.

CONCEPTUAL FRAMEWORK FOR STUDIES OF THE HERBACEOUS LAYER

Because the plant kingdom comprises species of an impressive array of physical growth forms, life history characteristics, and patterns of resource use, botanists and plant ecologists have long endeavored to group plant species into categories based on shared characteristics. This serves the dual purpose of decreasing the complexity and increasing the understanding of the ecological significance of those characteristics. One of the earliest such attempts was made by the Danish botanist Christen Raunkiaer, whose pioneering work was published originally in Danish in the early 20th century and later translated into English in the classic book *The life forms of plants and statistical plant geography* (Raunkiaer 1934). As the title implies, he classified plants into life forms (also called *growth forms*), a classification he based on the location of the structure that allows a plant to exist from one growing season to the next (i.e., the perennating structure—buds, rhizomes, and seeds). Still in use today, Raunkiaer's life forms represent one of the more successful endeavors placing plant species into ecologically meaningful categories.

Categories such as these are essentially groups of plant species based on common ecological functions. Appropriately, then, in more recent literature, they are often referred to as *plant functional groups*, and their ecological relevance has been expanded to include such phenomena as maintenance of biodiversity and stability of ecosystems, and effects on nutrient cycling (Huston 1994; Hooper and Vitousek 1998; Díaz and Cabido 1997). Other terms in the literature synonymous with *functional groups* include *guilds* and *functional types* (Wilson 1999). Körner (1994) discussed criteria for determining levels of organization within functional groups, and suggested that such levels represent a gradient of integration from sub-cellular structures up to ecosystems, and that ecological relevance increases along this spatially expanding gradient at the expense of precision.

Resident versus Transient Species

I have proposed a simple conceptual framework for the forest herbaceous layer, comprising two functional groups: *resident species* and *transient species* (Gilliam et al. 1994). *Resident species* are those with life history characteristics that confine them to aboveground heights of 1–1.5 m. These species would include, for example, annuals, herbaceous perennials, and low-growing shrubs. *Transient species* are plants whose existence in the herb layer is temporary (i.e., transient) because they have the potential to develop and emerge into higher strata (e.g., shrub, understory, and overstory layers). This group would include larger shrubs and trees. Juveniles (i.e., seedlings and sprouts) of regenerating overstory species must pass through this layer and compete as transient species with resident species (Morris et al. 1993; Wilson and Shure 1993; chapter 13, this volume). Because resident species play an important role in competition among themselves (Muller 1990) and with seedling and sprouting individuals of potential forest canopy dominants (Maguire and Forman 1983; Davis et al. 1998, 1999), the herb layer is a dynamic assemblage of these two groups.

Note that the term *transient* has a specific temporal and physical connotation that should not be confused with Grime's (1998) classification of plant species into dominant, subordinate, and transient species. His classification is based on the different roles species have in linking plant diversity to ecosystem function. Thus, his *transient* species are so called because they are transient in abundance and persistence, not in the strata of forest vegetation. In this sense, Grime's (1998) transient species are closely analogous to the *satellite* species of Hanski's (1982) core and satellite species hypothesis (see Gibson et al. 1999 for an excellent synthesis of both Grime's and Hanski's concepts).

As transient species emerge from the resident species, they become members of the other, overlying forest strata. These higher strata interact with the herbaceous layer through shading and utilization of moisture and nutrients (Maguire and Forman 1983). In addition, higher strata affect substrates for the herbaceous layer through inputs of litter and creation of tip-up mounds (chapter 8, this volume). Thus, it is important to understand the interactions between the herbaceous layer and other forest strata (chapter 9, this volume). Although Parker and Brown (2000) called into question the usefulness of applying the term *stratification* to forest canopies, there appears to be considerable ecological justification for it, considering the widely contrasting height-growth strategies seen among plant species of forest communities. Indeed, there may be a large number of forest strata, including several canopy layers, epiphytes and lianas within the tree canopy, shrubs, the herbaceous layer, and the thallophyte (non-vascular plant) layer (Harcombe and Marks 1977; Kimmins 1996; Oliver and Larson 1996).

The dynamic balance of resident and transient species in forest herbaceous layers, in terms of both numbers of species (i.e., richness) and cover, is mediated by (1) competitive interactions, (2) responses to disturbances, such as windthrow of canopy trees, herbivory, and harvesting, and (3) responses to environmental gradients, such as soil moisture and fertility, and other factors that vary spatially and temporally. Working in mature mesophytic stands from Minnesota to Michigan, Rogers (1981) found that the ratio of transient species cover to resident species cover in stands with high *Fagus grandifolia* Ehrh. Co-dominance in the overstory was nearly twice that in stands with little or no *F. grandifolia* (0.78 versus 0.40, respectively). Gilliam et al. (1995) found that relative cover of resident species was significantly higher in early successional stands than in mature stands of central Appalachian hardwood forests (71 percent versus 54 percent, respectively).

Resident versus Transient Species: Reproduction and Dispersal

Among the unique aspects of the herbaceous layer, then, is the intimate spatial and temporal coincidence of resident and transient species, which are two otherwise-disparate plant groups. The distinction between them is manifested not only in the more obvious differences in growth form, but also in the factors that determine their distribution and patterns of reproduction. Transient (in particular, tree) species are generally limited in their distribution by various combinations of disturbance patterns (Loehle 2000), and indeed have the potential for rapid migration (Clark 1998). In contrast, the distribution of resident species (predominantly woodland, or forest, herbs) is determined more by availability of suitable habitats, the likelihood of seeds to be dispersed to those habitats, and the successful germination (and subsequent growth) of seeds that reach them (Ehrlén and Eriksson 2000; Verheyen and Hermy 2001). Seed size can be an important variable in these latter two factors. Ehrlén and Eriksson (2000) found that seed size was negatively correlated with the likelihood of reaching suitable habitat, but positively correlated with the probability of successful germination. Furthermore, a disproportionate number of resident species are cryptophytes and hemicryptophytes (chapters 5 and 6, this volume) with the capability of asexual (clonal) reproduction (especially in the absence of disturbance), whereas far fewer transient species use this reproductive mode in the absence of disturbance. Singleton et al. (2001) found that only seven of 50 forest herb taxa from central New York lacked clonal expansion. McLachlan and Bazely (2001) suggested that knowledge of dispersal mechanisms of understory herbs could be applied to their use as indicators of recovery of deciduous forests following disturbance.

There are also sharp contrasts between transient versus resident species in their respective mechanisms of seed dispersal. For transient species (again, tree species in particular), the predominant mechanisms are wind and vertebrate herbivores (e.g., birds and rodents) (Cain et al. 1998; Clark et al. 2001). In contrast, the predominant dispersal vectors for resident species are invertebrates, particularly the phenomenon of myrmecochory, or seed dispersal by ants (Handel et al. 1981; Kalisz et al. 1999). Pakeman (2001) examined an additional dispersal vector for woodland herbs—large mammalian herbivores—and distinguished between endozoochory (seeds consumed and passed through the gut) and ectozoochory (seeds carried externally) as mechanisms for dispersal. He concluded that endozoochory could be an important mechanism for long-distance dispersal of herb species. Two mammalian herbivore species he considered, white-tailed deer (*Odocoileus virginianus* Zimmermann) and moose (*Alces alces* L.), have particular relevance for the herb layer of eastern North American forests (chapters 13, 16, and 17, this volume).

Based on a recent survey of literature, Cain et al. (1998) concluded that most wood-land herbaceous species are substantially limited in their seed-dispersal capabilities (chapter 5, this volume). Whitney and Foster (1988) cited poor colonizing ability (based largely on limited dispersal) as one of several factors that lead to the uniqueness of regional herb layer floras. Matlack (1994b) also demonstrated both slow clonal growth (asexual reproduction, e.g., via rhizomes) and low rates of plant migration via seed dispersal for forest herbs in hardwood forests of the Delaware/Pennsylvania Piedmont.

In conclusion, these numerous differences in resident versus transient species in the herbaceous layer of forest ecosystems create a forest stratum with impressive spatial and temporal variability, the very dynamic nature of vegetation originally articulated by Cowles (1899). Some of the substantial increase in herb layer research documented in fig. 1.2 (see also fig. 14.1 in chapter 14 for similar data on literature focused on the response of the herb layer to disturbance) has likely arisen from an increasing awareness among plant ecologists of the excitement and challenge of understanding the complex ecology of this important vegetation stratum, and of the urgency of applying this knowledge toward the wise, sustainable use of forest resources that will conserve herb layer species. Such complexity can be seen at all levels of ecological organization, from species-specific differences in light and nutrient use to the response of herb communities to disturbances to the forest canopy, which is the hierarchy of organization generally used in this book.

ORGANIZATION OF THE SECOND EDITION

The 1998 symposium that led to the first edition of this book had the term *forest communities* in its title. It is not surprising, then, that this book has a decidedly community-level orientation in its approach to examining the ecology of the herb layer within this broad region. As already discussed, however, the herb layer comprises plant species with widely varying responses to environmental factors and with widely varying population dynamics. Although seemingly inconsequential in biomass relative to trees (Gilliam 2007; chapter 2, this volume), the herb layer has several important roles in maintaining the structure and function of forest ecosystems. Accordingly, it is important to address the herb layer on all levels of ecological organization, from ecophysiological and population levels to community and ecosystem levels, much as one would find in a college ecology course. Ecologists with noted expertise in each of these fields were sought to contribute to this second edition.

The book is divided into five major sections. Part One addresses aspects of the environment in which plants of the herbaceous layer grow, including nutrient relations and light in chapters 2 (Robert Muller) and 4 (Wendy Anderson), and ecophysiological adaptations of herbaceous species to the environment in chapter 3 (Howard Neufeld and Donald Young). Part Two focuses on population biology of herb species, with chapter 5 (Carol Goodwillie and Claudia Jolls) providing an extensive review of reproductive strategies. Chapter 6 (Claudia Jolls and Dennis Whigham) discusses population dynamics with a particular focus on conservation ecology and rare species. Community dynamics of the herbaceous layer is the subject of Part Three. Chapters 7–9 in this section deal with mechanisms of herbaceous layer dynamics, with emphasis on old-growth forests (Brian McCarthy), habitat heterogeneity (Susan Beatty), and linkages between the herbaceous layer and the overstory (Frank Gilliam and Mark

Roberts). Chapters 10–12 are syntheses of studies of community dynamics in widely contrasting forest types, forests and woodlands of the southeastern United States (Robert Peet et al.), oak-hickory forests of the North Carolina Piedmont (Robert Peet et al.), and the boreal forest of Québec (De Grandpré et al.). The focus of Part Four is community dynamics of the herbaceous layer and the role of disturbance, beginning with an overview of the interactions of the herbaceous layer with disturbance (chapter 13, Mark Roberts and Frank Gilliam), followed by more specific discussions of disturbance vectors/mechanisms of herb response to disturbance, including competitive interactions between the herbaceous layer and tree seedlings (chapter 14, Lisa George and Fakhri Bazzaz), impacts of invasive species (chapter 15, James Luken), effects of deer herbivory (chapter 16, Don Waller), interactive effects of catastrophic windthrow and deer browsing (chapter 17, Carson et al.), impacts of timber harvesting (chapter 18, Julie Wyatt and Miles Silman), long-lived (legacy) effects of agricultural practices (chapter 19, Kathryn Flinn), impacts of excess nitrogen (chapter 20, Frank Gilliam), and responses of the herb layer to climate change (chapter 21, Jesse Bellemare and David Moeller). Finally, in Part Five, chapter 22 (Frank Gilliam) assesses our state of knowledge with respect to the herbaceous layer in eastern forests, summarizing and synthesizing some of the key ideas presented in previous chapters.

PART ONE
THE ENVIRONMENT OF THE HERBACEOUS LAYER

2 Nutrient Relations of the Herbaceous Layer in Deciduous Forest Ecosystems

Robert N. Muller

The contributions of deciduous forest herbs to ecosystem-level processes are frequently ignored due to low the contribution of this stratum to overall biomass. Thus, we are familiar with studies that treat the herbaceous layer as a dependent variable, responding to light and throughfall (R. C. Anderson et al. 1969), soil and biotic influences on nutrient availability (Snaydon 1962; Crozier and Boerner 1984), and local patterns of topographic variation (e.g., windthrow pits and mounds; Beatty 1984; chapter 8, this volume). Studies treating deciduous forest herbs as independent agents influencing community and ecosystem processes are less common and frequently focus on isolated circumstances in which processes, such as control of pollinators (Thompson 1986), allelopathy (Gliessman 1976; Horsley 1977b), or exploitative competition (Meekins and McCarthy 1999) can be demonstrated. Yet, in considering ecosystem-level influences of the herbaceous layer, we need only look at the effectiveness of understory removal on increasing wood production in plantation forestry to appreciate the importance of the herbaceous layer. For instance, a 12-year study of loblolly pine seedling response to herbaceous weed control demonstrated a 30–99 percent increase in growth (volume) over the period (Glover et al. 1989). Clearly, in these early successional stands, there are important competitive relationships among strata of mesic forests. In considering the potential for deciduous forest herbs to influence ecosystem-level processes, and the limitations of that influence, it is important to focus on the unique characteristics of the herbaceous layer that distinguish it from the overstory. Aside from size and the reduced proportion of woody tissues, these characteristics include differing tissue chemistry, phenology, and proportional allocation of fixed carbon to ephemeral tissues.

The importance of the herbaceous layer in nutrient cycles of temperate forests has its roots in the life histories of individual species and interactions of those species with site and environment. In this chapter, I discuss the attributes of deciduous forest herbs that significantly contribute to ecosystem-level nutrient dynamics. I attempt to distinguish among characteristics that are unique to some or all herbaceous species. Nutrient content and seasonal patterns of nutrient accumulation are compared among groups of deciduous forest herbs and with overstory species. I consider site quality (nutrient availability) as a determinant of herbaceous nutrient accumulation and discuss patterns of internal cycling (retranslocation) and decomposition of ephemeral materials. Finally, a fresh outlook on the influence of herbaceous populations on ecosystem-level nutrient cycling is discussed. In particular, I discuss the idea that spring ephemerals function to retard nutrient loss during spring runoff (a vernal dam; Muller 1978) with regard to its potential use and limitations in understanding the complex nature of deciduous forest ecosystems.

HERBACEOUS NUTRIENT CONCENTRATIONS

Most forest ecosystems are nutrient limited (i.e., exhibit growth response to increased nutrient availability). Thus, in the context of Chapin (1980), plants of forested ecosystems might be expected to exhibit a suite of attributes consistent with survival on infertile soils, including slow growth rate, low rate of nutrient absorption by roots, long root life, and low tissue concentration of mineral nutrients. However, nutrient limitation within forests is not static, and both temporal and spatial gradients of nutrient availability exist. Thus, plant adaptations to the nutrient environment of forests must be considered in the context of varying intensities of nutrient limitation. Nutrient concentrations of forest herbs exhibit distinct differences from woody components of the vegetation, suggesting that, within the fertility level of a given site, life form or position in the canopy may play an important role in mineral nutrition and, hence, in ecosystem relations. It has been commonly observed that concentrations of some foliar nutrients of forest herbs are higher than in woody vegetation from the same site (Bard 1945, 1949; Scott 1955; Gerloff et al. 1964; Likens and Bormann 1970; Henry 1973; Garten 1978; Lapointe 2001). Whereas variation certainly exists among studies, data from Hubbard Brook, New Hampshire, are reasonably representative (fig. 2.1; Likens and Bormann 1970). Potassium is consistently two to three times more concentrated in foliage of herbs than of trees (fig. 2.1). Similarly, magnesium concentrations of herbaceous foliage can be up to two times as high as in woody foliage (Likens and Bormann 1970). These patterns are less consistent for nitrogen, phosphorus, and calcium. However, spring ephemeral herbs appear to have significantly greater concentrations of foliar nitrogen than trees and other herbaceous groups. Among herbaceous life forms, there appears to be a greater concentration of calcium in summer-green herbs than in either spring herbs or cryptophytes. Among micronutrients, foliar concentrations of iron are consistently higher in herbs than in woody species (fig. 2.1; Likens and Bormann 1970; Henry 1973), whereas manganese is lower.

Siccama et al. (1970) noted that among herbaceous layer species, cryptophytes appear to have lower concentrations of phosphorus, calcium, potassium, zinc, and iron than summer-green herbs, but also have higher concentrations of sodium. However, inclusion of spring ephemerals in the analysis (data of Likens and Bormann 1970) suggests a more complex pattern. Relative to summer-green herbs, spring ephemerals

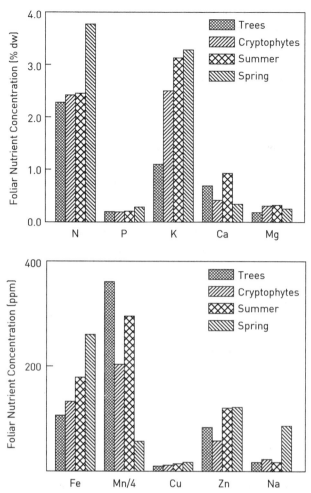

FIGURE 2.1 Average nutrient concentration in foliage of trees, cryptophytes (ferns), summer-green herbs (completing photosynthesis during the summer growing season), and spring herbs (completing photosynthesis before canopy development) in the northern hardwood forest at Hubbard Brook, New Hampshire. Foliage was collected in mid-growing season for the respective phenological groups. Data from Likens and Bormann (1970). Nitrogen data for spring ephemerals is from a single species, *Erythronium americanum* (Muller 1978).

have marginally higher phosphorous concentrations, considerably lower calcium and manganese concentrations, and much higher sodium and iron concentrations.

The biochemical and physiological role of the mineral constituents of plants is the subject of an extensive literature (Marschner 1995). However, some comments concerning the ecological ramifications of these patterns are important in understanding the role of herbaceous species in ecosystem relations. The strikingly high potassium concentrations suggest an important role in the fitness of herbaceous species. Potassium plays a number of roles in the biochemistry and physiology of plants; one of its more significant roles is in the osmoregulatory maintenance of cell turgor and especially the function of stomatal guard cells (Marschner 1995). High foliar concentrations of potassium in experimental settings have been found to result in better water relations and greater growth of herbaceous species (see Grewal and Singh

1980). The rooting volume of forest herbs is generally limited to surficial soils (Bauhus and Messier 1999) and, though many forest herbs are mycorrhizal (Brundrett and Kendrick 1990; DeMars 1996; Widden 1996), their access to water supplies is limited to those surface soil volumes. In contrast, trees have much more extensive rooting volumes (Stone and Kalisz 1991) and can tap deeper water sources. Herbaceous foliage, especially that of forbs, is frequently poor in structural polysaccharides (lignin; Melin 1930; Taylor et al. 1989; Wise and Schaefer 1994), which provide structural stability during periods of water stress. Additionally, limited studies of leaf ultrastructure suggest that vascular bundle extensions, which provide additional structural stability, are limited or nonexistent in herbaceous species (McLendon 1992).

In the forest floor environment, three primary resources for herbaceous growth—light, nutrients, and moisture—exist in limited supply. In the allocation of limited supplies of fixed carbon, the energetic costs of lignin production and construction of vascular bundle extensions to support leaf structure may be excessive. Consequently, alternative mechanisms of maintaining leaf structure, such as utilizing potassium to promote leaf turgor, may be favored. The known capacity of sodium to substitute for potassium in a variety of functions, but especially in maintaining water status, further suggests that leaf structure is maintained primarily by osmotic mechanisms. The rather succulent tissue of several spring ephemerals is suggestive of *Commelina benghalensis* L., in which the replacement of sodium for potassium in water relations has been demonstrated (Raghavendra et al. 1976). To the extent that structural compounds (lignin and cellulose) are reduced by the use of an alternative mechanism to maintain leaf structure (improved cell turgor as conferred by increased potassium and sodium concentration), the foliage of forest herbs would be expected to decompose at more rapid rates, thereby turning over nutrients more rapidly than other organic materials.

The relatively high concentrations of iron in foliage of all herbaceous species may well reflect its function in photosynthesis in low-light environments (Marschner 1995). However, it is notable that the highest iron (as well as nitrogen) concentrations are observed in spring ephemeral species, which are active during the spring period when light is greatly increased relative to summer. The apparent discrimination against manganese by forest herbs, especially spring ephemerals, is also notable. Newell and Peet (1998) found a positive correlation between soil manganese and diversity and abundance of the herbaceous layer. The implications of that correlation remain a mystery; however, manganese may be an indicator of general soil fertility, which may support greater biomass and species diversity.

SITE-TO-SITE VARIATION

Foliar nutrient concentrations of vascular plants frequently vary in response to environmental nutrient availability. Numerous studies in controlled laboratory or cropland situations have demonstrated a close relationship between foliar nutrient concentration and soil nutrient availability (Barber 1995). However, this relationship is less obvious in forest herbs growing in uncontrolled wildland settings. Some work (Tyler 1976; Gilliam 1988) has found correlations between foliar nutrient concentrations of forest herbs and soil nutrient availability. Fertilization studies have also found some, but limited, response of foliar chemistry (Eickmeier and Schussler 1993; Anderson and Eickmeier 1998). Additionally, a growing body of work has demonstrated that forest herbs recolonizing abandoned agricultural fields may respond positively to legacies of increased phosphorous (chapter 19, this volume; Baeten et al. 2010, 2011). To the extent that foliar chemistry responds to site quality, the influence of the herbaceous layer on ecosystem properties will be a function of both foliar concentration and herbaceous abundance, both of which would be enhanced on nutrient-rich sites. However, Chapin (1980) noted that enhanced growth response of wildland plants on fertile sites will effectively dilute foliar nutrient concentration, and a number of other studies have suggested that foliar nutrients of forest herbs vary little in relation to site quality. Gagnon et al. (1958) concluded that the lack of variation occurs because individual herbaceous species are site-specific and consequently are not exposed to widely varying soil characteristics. In a precursor to contemporary views of positive feedbacks between vegetation and site quality, Gagnon et al. (1958) also suggested that forest plants, including herbaceous species, influence soil fertility such that little relationship would be observed between foliar chemistry and site quality. However, Bard (1949) found that even in herb species common to three distinct soils in central New York, little variation in average foliar nutrient concentrations occurred (fig. 2.2). Foliar potassium showed the greatest variation among sites, but was unrelated to soil-available potassium. Foliar concentrations of other elements showed little variation among sites. Whether the distribution of individual species is restricted to particular sites or not, the relative constancy of foliar quality suggests that the influence of the herbaceous layer on ecosystem properties is primarily a function of abundance (and, consequently, total nutrient content) on the site.

The mechanisms accounting for the apparent lack of relationship between foliar chemistry and site quality remain unclear. Gilliam and Adams (1996b) suggested that foliar chemistry was strongly related to soil resources in early successional stands, but not later in succession. They suggested that in late successional stands, light becomes the limiting resource, thus eliminating the foliar chemistry–soil nutrient availability

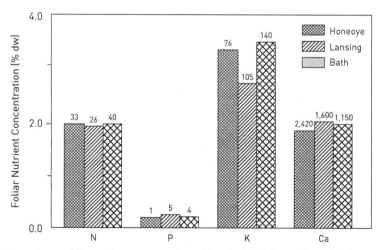

FIGURE 2.2 Average foliar nutrient concentrations of three herbs (*Galium triflorum* Michx., *Smilacina racemosa* [L.] Desf., and *Arisaema triphyllum* [L.] Torr.) common to three differing soil types in central New York. Values above bars are concentrations of soil extractable nutrients (μg/g). Soil pH varied from 5.00 (Bath), to 5.92 (Lansing), to 6.01 (Honeoye). Data from Bard (1949).

relationship. However, apparently consistent relationships among mineral cations in the foliage of a wide range of vascular and nonvascular plants (Garten 1976, 1978) suggest that wildland species have fixed nutrient requirements, both as individual ion concentrations and in proportion to other chemical constituents.

Luxury consumption has not been intensively studied in spring herbs but appears to be limited in wildland settings (Anderson and Eickmeier 1998; but see Baeten et al. 2010, 2011). Boerner (1986) has suggested that varying mycorrhizal infection with soil fertility may account, in part, for the seemingly fixed chemical composition of many forest herbs. Mycorrhizal infection of *Geranium maculatum* L. and *Polygonatum pubescens* Pursh. declined over a gradient of increasing soil fertility. Boerner (1986) suggested that forest herbs face a tradeoff in allocation of fixed carbon to mycorrhizal support or plant growth. Under conditions of nutrient limitation, fixed carbon is allocated to mycorrhizal support, thereby enhancing nutrient uptake and meeting plant nutrient demands. Under conditions of nutrient abundance, fixed carbon is allocated to plant growth, thereby diluting accumulated nutrients and limiting apparent luxury consumption. Similarly, Crick and Grime (1987) noted plasticity in allocation of resources to root systems of forest herbs and concluded that increased allocation on nutrient-poor sites enabled increased "foraging," which supported uniform foliar nutrient concentrations.

SEASONAL NUTRIENT DYNAMICS

It is well-recognized that nutrients in tissues of forest herbs are dynamic and change seasonally in response to phenological development and physiological demand. Most forest herbs are perennial, and these seasonal changes are frequently interpreted in the context of changing physiological demand created by fluctuating sinks of biomass (Chapin 1980). Within this framework, nutrient concentration should remain reasonably constant, and patterns of uptake should reflect immediate physiological need. An alternative interpretation considers physiological need in relation to environmental availability (Chapin 1980; Hommels et al. 1989; Lipson et al. 1996). Long-term success of plants that are beginning a period of active growth in a resource-limited environment may depend on uptake of an abundance of nutrients during periods of less limited availability. Subsequent internal reallocation meets the demands of changing tissue requirements, and tissue nutrient concentration may vary widely, whereas total nutrient content remains reasonably constant.[1]

Limited data seem to fit the latter interpretation. During early growth, foliar concentrations of most essential nutrients are high, followed by a gradual decline throughout the remainder of the leaf's life (Ferguson and Armitage 1944; Muller 1978; Grigal and Ohmann 1980; Whigham 1984). This pattern is most recognizable for nitrogen and is seemingly independent of phenological adaptations of species, as shown for a

[1] Such an interpretation would seem to argue for a reevaluation of earlier comments on luxury consumption (in the previous section). However, seasonal patterns of nutrient accumulation are probably well-synchronized from one site to another. Most analyses of luxury consumption involve collections of material from contrasting sites at the same time. Thus, it is not surprising that strong seasonal patterns of nutrient uptake (indeed, a different form of luxury consumption) may exist, while luxury consumption in the traditional sense is not apparent in populations from sites of different nutrient regimes.

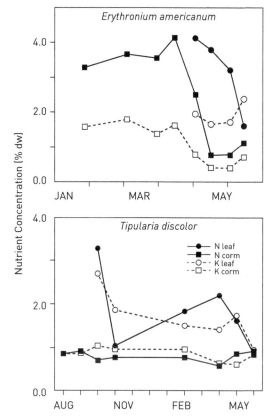

FIGURE 2.3 Seasonal patterns of nutrient concentrations in foliage and belowground organs of *Erythronium americanum* (top) and *Tipularia discolor* (bottom). Legend in the bottom panel applies to the top panel as well. Data from Muller (1978; top) and Whigham (1984; bottom).

spring ephemeral (*Erythronium americanum* Ker.) and a winter-green herb (*Tipularia discolor* Nutt.) in fig. 2.3. The almost immediate reduction of foliar nutrient concentration after leaf emergence is simply a dilution due to rapidly increasing biomass. Thus, most of the nitrogen used for photosynthesis is translocated into the young leaf early in development, rather than later when an increasing biomass sink might be viewed as creating additional demand. Phosphorus, potassium, and, to a lesser extent, magnesium show similar concentration patterns. However, calcium concentration (and content) increases throughout the foliar period, apparently in response to increasing biomass, reflecting the well-known structural function of this element in cell wall binding (Marschner 1995).

Subsequent patterns of allocation among plant parts and physiological function vary depending on nutrient and species. In *Allium tricoccum* Ait., total plant content of nitrogen, phosphorus, potassium, and magnesium remains reasonably constant after an initial spring increase (fig. 2.4; Nault and Gagnon 1988). Internal retranslocation, however, shifts these elements among plant parts, such that much of the nitrogen, which had been contained in leaves, is translocated to bulb and reproductive biomass upon foliar senescence. In contrast, calcium is concentrated in foliar biomass. As a less mobile element, its total plant content reflects seasonal biomass patterns and peaks as foliar biomass peaks. DeMars and Boerner (1997) showed similar patterns of

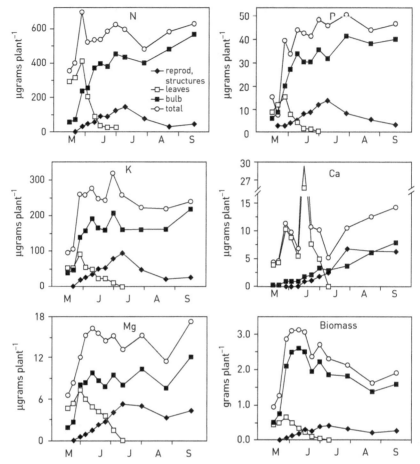

FIGURE 2.4 Seasonal nutrient and biomass accumulation in *Allium tricoccum*. Redrawn from Nault and Gagnon (1988), with permission. Letters along X-axis indicate the months May, June, July, August, and September.

resorption of nitrogen and phosphorous from senescing foliage of woodland herbs and also demonstrated a life history relationship with a spring ephemeral (*Cardamine concatenata*) exhibiting greater resorption than either a spring herb (*Trillium flexipes*) or a summer-green herb (*Smilacina racemosa*). Holub and Tůma (2010) found significant nutrient resorption in a winter deciduous fern (*Athyrium distentifolium*) and noted that resorption was much more efficient for phosphorous than for nitrogen. It seems that, as a group, spring ephemerals are particularly efficient in nutrient resorption during leaf senescence (Lapointe 2001).

Two important patterns of mineral nutrition of forest herbs emerge from these studies. First, retranslocation of stored nutrients is an important aspect of survival in the nutrient-poor and highly competitive environment of forest soils (Chapin 1980). Retranslocation, of course, reduces dependence on root absorption of nutrients in an environment in which supply is unpredictable. Second, absorption of nutrients is responsive to availability. Thus, rapid uptake occurs in spring and fall when nutrients are most available (reduced uptake by trees or increased decomposition of recently released organic material) and leads to an apparent luxury consumption at the beginning of the growing season (but see W. B. Anderson and Eickmeier 1998). The balance between translocation and absorption (Whigham 1984) varies by species and environment. However, no species is completely efficient in its utilization and retranslocation of nutrients among plant parts. Uptake at the beginning of the growing season and release with decomposing plant parts at the end of the season create the potential for impacts on ecosystem-level nutrient cycles.

Chapin (1980) has suggested a strong dichotomy between crop plants and plants of resource-rich, ruderal environments on the one hand and wildland plants of limited resource environments on the other hand. In this dichotomy, wildland plants are presumed to be slow growing, with slow rates of nutrient absorption and little evidence of luxury consumption. However, these infertile sites may also be characterized by reasonably predictable nutrient flushes in the spring and, to some extent, in the fall. The rate of nutrient absorption in wildland plants is slow and does not change in response to changing availability of nutrients during flushes. Thus, plants of resource-poor environments should be expected to exhibit greater total uptake of nutrients during a flush. The evidence presented in figs. 2.3 and 2.4 suggests that woodland herbs do respond in this manner to spring increases in nutrient availability. However, Anderson and Eickmeier's (1998) finding of limited response to fertilizer application suggests that there are limits to the amount of nutrients that can be taken up during this period.

BIOMASS/PRODUCTIVITY

In considerations of ecosystem dynamics (energy flux and nutrient transfers), the herbaceous layer of deciduous forests is frequently ignored because of its small contribution to the overall biomass of the system. The aboveground living biomass of a number of mature forests of the temperate zone of the northern hemisphere has been summarized by DeAngelis et al. (1981; table 2.1). Although widely varying in absolute amount, herbaceous-layer standing biomass is never > 1 percent of the total aboveground living biomass and, as a component of energy flow, the herbaceous layer is usually < 5 percent of aboveground net primary productivity. There are no strong trends in these patterns with latitude within the temperate zone, and biomass and productivity distribution among forests at latitudes of 40–60° N are similar to those of forests at 30–40° N latitude (table 2.2).

Biomass is not a singular material. In terms of the dynamics of energy flow and nutrient release, the biotic material produced in forested ecosystems is variably resistant to decomposition. Herbaceous layer biomass is important because it is a component of the much smaller pool of transient materials that decompose and return nutrients to available nutrient pools quickly. One measure of this, albeit a coarse one, is to consider herbaceous biomass as a component of annual foliar litter fall (table 2.1). Most herbaceous species of temperate forests are deciduous and, with some exceptions, aboveground stem and foliar biomass of all herbaceous species is replaced at least annually. As a component of annual foliar litter fall, herbaceous species may account for as much as 20–25 percent of the total, although on average, this is 10–15 percent and can be considerably less (table 2.2).

When the rapid decomposition of herbaceous litter is taken into account (see below), it is appropriate to consider herbaceous biomass as part of a labile pool of biological materials that decompose readily. The proportion of biotic material that can be considered to be labile varies with the origin of that material. As a generalization, the labile component of tree foliage is in the range of 20–45 percent ($\bar{x}$ =

Table 2.1 Aboveground living biomass and foliar litter fall of northern temperate zone forests.

Location	Forest type	Aboveground living biomass			Overstory foliage g/m^2	Annual foliar litter fall $g/m^2/year$	Page
		Overstory g/m^2	Understory g/m^2	Herbaceous g/m^2			
Ontario	Spruce	46,223	1	3	2,122	229	578
Ontario	Spruce	16,908	1	16	1,002	158	579
Denmark	Beech	21,570	540	16	210	285	581
Japan	Larch	16,43	403[a]	96	359	455	600
Poland	Oak	22,599	3,549	100	201	392	609
Romania	Beech-fir	29,470	0	20	1,410	375	613
Spain	Pine-holly	19,269	1,122	22	1,148	267	615
Sweden	Oak-birch	7,892	743	67	161	240	616
Sweden	Beech	32,390	0	10	390	367	617
Sweden	Beech	22,530	0	1	330	241	619
Sweden	Oak	15,500	4,510	20	300	346	620
Sweden	Beech	31,380	0	90	480	365	621
Russia	Oak	29,953	617	70	360	446	627
Great Britain	Oak	11,243	1,480	72	269	396	647
New Hampshire	Maple, birch	10,110	21	7	315	349	651
Oregon	Douglas-fir	76,230	870	7	1,329	224	656
Tennessee	Y-Poplar	13,117	853	28	323	401	657
Wisconsin	Oak	26,470	86	18	386	429	663
Germany	Beech	27,423	0	1	308	299	666

Annual foliar litter fall has been adjusted to include herbaceous litter, which is usually not accounted for in litter collectors. Data from Woodlands Data Set of De Angelis et al. 1981. Page number references specific data source.
[a]Includes standing dead.

32.5 percent; Currie and Aber 1997), whereas bark and wood have only trace amounts of labile extractives. Using the Hubbard Brook ecosystem as a model, aboveground net organic return (Gosz et al. 1973) has been partitioned by stratum into labile and non-labile pools (table 2.3). Also shown in table 2.3 is the amount of material that could be expected to decompose in the first year after entry into the dead organic pools of the forest. The comparison assumes that the labile component of wood is of little significance and that herbaceous material is entirely labile. Whereas the herbaceous layer accounts for 3.2 percent of the total organic matter return of the forest, it is 15 percent of the labile fraction of that material. Calculation of the amount of material decomposed during the first year after entry into the ecosystem suggests a similar significance. The important point in this analysis is that, whereas the herbaceous layer represents a small fraction of total biomass and annual energy fixation in a forest, it

Table 2.2 Distribution of biomass and productivity in cold and warm temperate zone forests.

	Forest biomass distribution				Forest productivity			Herbaceous litter as a component of total litter Fall	
	Biomass (g/m²)	Overstory (%)	Understory (%)	Herbs (%)	Total NPP (g/m²/year)	Herbaceous NPP (g/m²/year)	Herb %	(Percent)	(Range)
Northern temperate zone forests (40–60° N lat)	24,432	96.3	3.5	0.2	1050	41	3.9	15.9	0.4–28.8
Southern temperate zone forests (30–40° N lat)	21,145	96	3.8	0.2	863	36	4.2	9.1	1.8–20.2

Data are averages of values from DeAngelis et al. (1981). NPP, net primary productivity.

Table 2.3 Vertical distribution of the origin of aboveground litter fall within the northern hardwood forest at Hubbard Brook, New Hampshire (from Gosz et al. 1973).

	Litter fall		Labile fraction		1st Year decomposition	
	g/m²/year	%	g/m²/year	%	g/m²/year	%
Overstory						
Foliage	341.9	57.5	111.1	83.9	79.9	65.8
Wood	216.9	36.5	trace	trace	20.6	17.0
Understory						
Foliage	5.1	0.8	1.7	1.3	1.2	1.0
Wood	1.5	0.2	trace	trace	0.1	0.1
Herbs	19.6	3.2	19.6	14.8	19.6	16.1
Total	595.0		132.4		121.4	

The labile fraction was calculated using average labile fractions from Currie and Aber (1997). Wood was assumed to have only a trace of labile material in its biomass, and herbaceous materials were assumed to be 100% labile. First-year decomposition was calculated using a weighted average decay constant (k) for hardwood foliage from Gosz et al. (1973) and an average 10-month decay constant for woody material. The latter was chosen because dramatic weight losses during the following two months were reported to have come from the physical loss of buds and bark. Herbaceous material was assumed to completely decompose within the first year (see table 2.4).

can account for an important component of turnover of senesced materials returned to the forest floor each year. This is increasingly important in forests with large herbaceous populations relative to overstory litter fall (table 2.1).

ECOSYSTEM NUTRIENT DYNAMICS

Whatever influences the herbaceous layer may have on nutrient dynamics of forests, they are the product of the biology of the species involved, their interactions with other species, and their seasonal and spatial place in the ecosystem. As already noted, herbaceous foliage frequently contains higher concentrations of nutrients than foliage of woody species. Additional influences on ecosystem nutrient dynamics include uptake decomposition, influences on throughfall, and phenological patterns of growth and senescence.

UPTAKE

Patterns of nutrient absorption by deciduous forest herbs vary depending on phenological character and phylogenetic relationships of individual species (DeMars 1996; Lapointe 2001). Many deciduous forest herbs are mycorrhizal (DeMars 1996), which likely benefits both nutrient and water uptake in cold soils (Lapointe 2001). However, those species that are not mycorrhizal have long root hairs that may provide compensation (Brundrett and Kendrick 1988, 1990). In spite of its mycorrhizal status throughout the winter, nutrient absorption in *Erythronium americanum* (a spring ephemeral) is slow and occurs primarily in the spring (Muller 1978; Lapointe 2001), reflecting the influence of winter-chilled soils. Nutrient accumulation in *Allium tricoccum* (also a spring ephemeral) is slow as well, but occurs throughout the winter (Rothstein and Zak 2001). In contrast to these conclusions, analysis of understory plants of an oak forest in Sweden have shown levels of nitrate reductase activity (NRA) considerably above overstory species, suggesting that nutrient uptake and utilization may be relatively high among the shaded plants of the understory (Olsson and Falkengren-Grerup 2003). Clearly, patterns of nutrient absorption in deciduous forest herbs are highly variable and will strongly influence conclusions regarding ecosystem-level nutrient cycling processes.

Decomposition

Whereas the majority of decomposition studies have focused on the foliage and wood of trees, limited work on herbaceous materials has addressed rapidity of decomposition, interactions with soil organisms, and possible stimulatory effects of mixed litters on decomposition. However, cursory observation of herbaceous materials (foliage and stems) during the fall and winter in a deciduous woodland suggests rapid disappearance from the forest floor after senescence. In one of the first analyses of decomposition, Melin (1930) used CO_2 evolution in laboratory incubations to evaluate patterns of decomposition in fresh foliar litter of herbs and trees and noted variable rates of decomposition over the first 27 days of incubation. He attributed this variation to initial litter quality (nitrogen concentration), although this relationship was imperfect. In this study, decomposition of *Aralia nudicaulis* L. was more rapid than *Acer saccharum* Marsh. and *Fagus grandifolia* Ehrb., but not faster than *Fraxinus americana* L. It is likely that the rapid decomposition exhibited by all species reflected CO_2 evolution from decomposition of labile materials. These details of the very first stages of the decomposition process do not emerge from more conventional litter-bag studies.

More recent work, however, suggests that decomposition of foliar materials can be readily classified into materials whose decomposition is completed in less than a year and those that require longer than a year for completion. Most tree foliage has a decomposition constant $(k) < 1$. Whereas foliage of some tree species approaches $k = 1$, most are in the range of 0.3–0.8 (table 2.4). A clear exception to this trend has been observed in foliage of *Cornus florida* L. (Cromack and Monk 1975), whose calcium-rich foliage decomposes rapidly $(k \cong 1)$. In contrast, decomposition constants for herbaceous material (including stems) are generally > 1, and in some cases considerably greater (table 2.4). An apparent exception occurs in the bulked herbaceous litter of a 29-year-old mixed hardwood stand in New Brunswick, Canada $(k = 0.43–0.41;$ MacLean and Wein 1978). However, this stand was dominated by *Pteridium aquilinum* L. and *Vaccinium* L. sp., whose lower decomposition rates may have modified those of other herbaceous species in the bulked sample.

Thirty years of intense analysis of decomposition has amply demonstrated that, holding site variables and microclimate constant, decomposition is controlled most directly by litter quality, including principally concentrations of inorganic nutrients, lignin, and cellulose (Melillo et al. 1989). The higher concentrations of inorganic nutrients observed in herbaceous litters (fig. 2.1) and the apparently low concentrations of lignin and cellulose in those tissues (Dwyer and Merriam 1984) would certainly explain their rapid turnover. Most studies of decomposition of herbaceous species note that herbaceous material is fully decomposed within six months (or less) after senescence. The combination of initial leaching of nutrients after senescence and rapid decomposition of any remaining organic material leads to rapid disappearance and incorporation of inorganic nutrients and soluble organic materials into the forest floor. An extreme case is observed in *Erythronium americanum*, where leaf cells lyse during senescence, beginning at the leaf apex and moving basipetally (Muller 1978). This lysing pattern not only appears to enhance resorption of nutrients into the

Table 2.4 Decomposition constants (k) and half-life of foliar litter from herbs and trees from a number of sites in temperate zone forests.

Species	Location	Forest Type	Duration (months)	k/year	Half-life (years)	Reference
Cornus canadensis L.	Washington, USA	23-year Abies amabilis	12	1.02	0.68	Vogt et al. (1983)
			24	0.72	0.96	
Clintonia uniflora (Schult.) Kunth.		180-year Abies amabilis	12	3.31	0.21	
			24	1.96	0.35	
Bulked herbs	New Brunswick, Canada	7-year mixed hardwoods	11	1.25	0.55	MacLean and Wein (1978)
Bulked herbs		29-year mixed hardwoods	12	0.61	1.10	
			24	0.43	1.60	
Aralia nudicaulis			4	1.39	0.50	Melin (1930)
Anemone nemorosa	Germany	Fagus sylvatica	12	1.55	0.45	Wise and Shaefer (1994)
Mercurialis perennis			12	2.03	0.34	
Ash-maple			17	0.97	0.71	
Beech			17	0.31	2.23	
Allium tricocum	Ottawa, Canada	Beech-maple	6	1.90	0.36	Dwyer and Merriam (1984)
Caulophyllum thalictroides (L.) Michx.			6	1.08	0.64	
Beech-maple			6	1.04	0.67	
Acer saccharum	New Hampshire, USA	Northern hardwoods	12	0.51	1.36	Gosz et al. (1973)
Fagus grandifolia			12	0.37	1.87	
Betula lutea Michx. f.			12	0.85	0.82	
Quercus montana Wild.	North Carolina, USA	Oak forest		0.61	1.14	Cromack and Monk (1975)
Quercus alba L.				0.72	0.96	
Acer rubrum L.				0.77	0.90	
Cornus florida				1.26	0.55	

perennating organ but also encourages subsequent leaf decomposition. With the first rains after lysis all vestiges of the foliar material are lost.

Throughfall

The influence of the herbaceous layer on throughfall chemistry, as on other nutrient processes, is heavily dependent on its density. In dense, well-developed understory layers, the herbaceous stratum may have a leaf area index of 0.5–2 (one side: Werger and van Laar 1985; Kriebitzsch 1992c; Gratani 1997), providing an important surface for chemical exchange with incident rainfall as it passes through the canopy to the forest floor. Analyses are limited, but existing studies suggest that the herbaceous layer can significantly modify the characteristics of throughfall. The nature of this modification appears variable, depending on species composition of the understory and time of year.

Carlisle et al. (1967; data also presented in Brown 1974) present annual throughfall estimates for an oak woodland (*Quercus petraea* [Matt.] Liebl.) with a dense understory of *Pteridium aquilinum* (L.) Kuhn (table 2.5). The herbaceous layer, which accounted for 27 percent of total foliar litter fall, added as much as 37 percent of the potassium and < 1 percent of the calcium contributed by both layers to throughfall. The high potassium contribution would seem to be a consequence of its higher concentrations in herbaceous foliage, as well as its greater mobility in organic tissues than other elements. In contrast, the reduced contributions of the herbaceous layer to calcium cycling reflect its role in cell wall structure and binding, and in maintaining leaf form in the absence of the structural materials of lignin and cellulose. For all elements other than potassium, the proportionate impact of the herbaceous layer was reduced over what might be expected from its contribution to litter fall alone. The herbaceous layer accounted for 14 percent and 15 percent, respectively, of the total vegetation contribution to throughfall of phosphorus and magnesium. Similarly, the herbaceous layer accounted for only 9 percent of the organic nitrogen contributed by vegetation to throughfall and also accounted for 21 percent of the removal of inorganic nitrogen from incident precipitation. The absorption of inorganic nitrogen would seem to be

Table 2.5 Canopy and herbaceous layer modifications of throughfall in an oak woodland, Lancashire, England (after Carlisle et al. 1967)

	Litter fall	Inorganic N	Organic N	Total N	P	K	Ca	Mg	Na
				Precipitation and throughfall quality					
Incident rainfall	—	6.65	2.07	8.71	0.28	2.84	6.72	6.10	50.76
Canopy throughfall	4032.1 (73.3%)	4.32 (−78.7%)	5.49 (90.7%)	9.60 (145.9%)	0.55 (85.9%)	18.86 (63.0%)	19.01 (99.4%)	11.70 (85.5%)	82.78 (94.9%)
Herbaceous throughfall	1470.0 (26.7%)	3.69 (−21.3%)	5.84 (9.3%)	9.32 (−46.0%)	0.92 (14.1%)	28.26 (37.0%)	19.08 (0.6%)	12.65 (14.5%)	84.49 (5.1%)

The canopy was dominated by *Quercus petraea*; the herbaceous layer was a monospecific stand of *Pteridium aquilinum*. Data present annual foliar litter fall from the canopy and herbaceous layer (kg/ha/year), and nutrient content of water in incident rainfall, throughfall from the forest canopy and throughfall from the herbaceous layer canopy (kg/ha/year). Values in parentheses are contributions of each vegetation layer to the net change in incident precipitation reaching the soil surface.

responsive simply to the amount of foliar biomass in the herbaceous layer. However, the proportionately reduced contribution of herbs to throughfall modification for all other elements, except potassium, would seem to reflect more conservative cycling of those elements in this stratum.

The idea of conservation of nutrients within the herbaceous layer is supported by other studies suggesting a seasonal aspect to the relative influence of canopy and understory on throughfall. Andersson (1992) suggested a strong tendency for foliar absorption by an understory of *Mercurialis perennis* L. in a *Quercus robur* L. woodland. During late summer/early fall, the herbaceous layer reduced throughput of calcium by 27 percent, magnesium by 33 percent, potassium by 27 percent, and nitrogen by 39 percent. The cations in this analysis also showed a seasonal influence, with greatest absorption during the growing season and no apparent net influence during the period of foliar senescence. Yarie (1980) suggested similar trends in coniferous forests (*Tsuga mertensiana* Carr. and *Abies amabilis* Dougl. ex J. Forbes) of coastal British Columbia. Though significant only for phosphorus and nitrogen, the general trend was for absorption of all elements during the growing season and release of cations during senescence.

Conservation of nutrients with respect to throughfall and, indeed, absorption of nutrients from throughfall have several implications for the herbaceous layer. Regardless of origin of nutrients in canopy throughfall (leaching versus washoff), the potential for absorption of throughfall nutrients suggests a mechanism of direct cycling, which reduces the need for extensive root systems to locate and exploit nutrients. Further, to the extent that potassium contributes to positive water balances of forest herbaceous species, foliar absorption of this element also reduces dependence on extensive root systems to tap limited water supplies. The case can be made that the forest understory is a strongly resource-limited environment in which light, moisture, and nutrients are all in short supply. In considering the allocation of fixed carbon, any process that reduces the apparent limitations of one or another resource enables increased allocation to obtain another resource that continues to be limited. Hence, conservation and potential capture of nutrients in canopy throughfall by the herbaceous layer reduce the demand for extensive root systems and support greater shoot growth, thereby enhancing energy capture and increased foliar absorption of nutrients as well (Andersson 1992). Plants of shaded conditions (e.g., forest herbs) generally have low root:shoot ratios (Simonovich 1973; Zavitkovsky 1976; Bloom et al. 1985; Chapin et al. 1993; Andersson 1997).

From an ecosystem standpoint, the role of the herbaceous layer in modification of throughfall may strongly influence the amount of nutrients returned to the forest floor through this vector. Subsequent influences on microbial populations and uptake by roots of other species have not been examined.

THE VERNAL DAM REVISITED

In the northern hardwood forest, a suite of circumstances occurs that has suggested that one component of the herbaceous layer may play an important role in reducing nutrient loss during a period of high mobility. Snowmelt, which may account for as much as 30 percent of annual stream flow (Likens et al. 1977), occurs during the spring months of March–May. Nutrient removal from these forests is most directly related to the volume of water in stream flow. Hence, elevated stream flow during the spring snowmelt creates a time of significant nutrient loss. Overall biotic activity during this same period is much reduced compared to midsummer. Yet, some elements of the biota are active during the spring between snowmelt and canopy leaf-out. Among the herbs, the vernal component completes its entire aboveground lifecycle during this six-week period (Mahall and Bormann 1978; Muller 1978), and rising soil temperatures enhance microbial activity at this same time (Zogg et al. 1997).

The concept of the vernal dam (Muller and Bormann 1976; Muller 1978) builds upon this juxtaposition of high stream flow, rapid biomass accumulation by spring herbs, and subsequent senescence and decomposition of the non-perennating biomass of those species. During the spring period of high runoff, biomass accumulation by spring herbs, which represents the total net annual productivity of those species, involves the uptake and fixation of nutrients that might otherwise be lost in stream flow. Aboveground senescence of these species coincides with canopy closure of the overstory, and release of nutrients from the vernal species by mineralization occurs when stream flow levels are considerably reduced and activity of summer-green species (including the overstory) is high (fig. 2.5). Thus, vernal herbs may serve as a temporary biotic dam that retards the loss of nutrients and enhances internal biogeochemical cycling. At the Hubbard Brook Experimental Forest in New Hampshire, the spring flora (most of which is *Erythronium americanum*) appears to serve in this capacity, taking up and releasing potassium and nitrogen at the same order of magnitude as that lost in spring stream flow (table 2.6).

Since first proposed, the concept of the vernal dam has received some scrutiny, exploring the validity of the concept, its limitations, and potential ramifications. Blank et al. (1980) and Peterson and Rolfe (1982) verified the concept in two Midwestern forests and found that, because of significantly increased production of the spring flora of those ecosystems, the potential impact was as much as an order of magnitude greater than in New Hampshire (table 2.6). In both of these studies, the greater diversity and

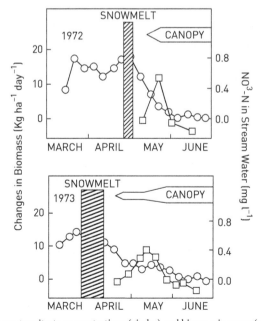

FIGURE 2.5 Stream water nitrate concentrations (circles) and biomass increase (squares) in *Erythronium americanum*. Biomass increase was calculated as the rate of biomass change between any two consecutive harvest dates. Redrawn from Muller and Bormann (1976), with permission.

Table 2.6 Net primary productivity (g/m^2/year) and nutrient uptake (kg/ha/year) by the spring herbaceous community in three regions of the deciduous forest of the eastern United States.

	New Hampshire[a]	Indiana[b]	Illinois[c]	Tennessee[d] Unfertilized	Fertilized
NPP	5.1	66.8	68.5	21.1	74.5
N	0.9 (1.1)	5.5	10.6	0.8	3.8
P	nd	0.1	1.6	0.1	0.5
K	0.6 (0.7)	4.5	18.9	nd	nd
Ca	0.1 (3.6)	1.8	3.9	nd	nd
Mg	0.1 (0.8)	0.6	1.7	nd	nd

For comparison, gross spring stream water losses of nutrients (April and May; kg/ha) in New Hampshire are provided. Similar data from the other sites are not available. In the Tennessee study, weekly additions of aqueous fertilizer solutions totaled annual inputs of 30 g N/m^2/year and 29 g P/m^2/year. NPP, net primary productivity; nd, not determined.

[a]Data from Muller and Bormann (1976) and Muller (1978).
[b]Data from Blank et al. (1980).
[c]Data from Peterson and Rolfe (1982).
[d]Data calculated from W. B. Anderson and Eickmeier (1998).

productivity of the spring herbs were attributed to the significantly richer soils of central Indiana and Illinois. Eickmeier and others (Eickmeier and Schussler 1993; W. B. Anderson and Eickmeier 1998, 2000) have evaluated the contribution of plasticity to the magnitude of the vernal dam. Increased productivity and tissue nutrient concentrations in *Claytonia virginica* L. that had been artificially fertilized suggested that a degree of plasticity would enable this and perhaps other species to respond to annual variation in spring nutrient availability (Eickmeier and Schussler 1993). However, W. B. Anderson and Eickmeier (1998) found that this plastic response had limitations such that, above certain levels of nutrient availability, no further increase in total spring ephemeral nutrient pool size was observed. Nonetheless, they found a potential maximum vernal nutrient pool size significantly greater than had been previously reported (table 2.6).

Further analyses of the vernal dam, particularly the interactions of spring ephemeral herbs and soil microbial populations, have raised important questions concerning the significance of the contributions of the spring vascular flora to the conservation of nutrients in deciduous forests. Zak et al. (1986) noted a close correlation in the distribution of herbaceous species in deciduous forests to rates of nitrogen cycling. Diversity and abundance of spring herbs were consistently related to nitrification potential of soils on a microscale. However, potential nitrate utilization by two prominent herbaceous species of the spring flora in those forests was strikingly low (Zak and Pregitzer 1988). *Allium tricoccum* and *Asarum canadense* L. demonstrated particularly low NRA, implying limited ability to utilize the ionic form of nitrogen most susceptible to leaching during the spring period. In addition, analysis of the soil microflora during the spring has suggested a dynamic system with considerable potential for microbial immobilization of nitrogen in addition to that utilized by plants (Groffman et al. 1993). Indeed, Groffman et al. (1993) suggested a competitive environment in which microbial populations are significantly more important than plants as nitrogen immobilizers. Tracer studies using 15N suggest that on sites with abundant spring herbaceous growth, uptake of nitrogen by microbial biomass is significantly greater than uptake by active plants (table 2.7). Zak et al. (1990) suggested that spring ephemeral herbs and spring microbial populations are competing for soil nitrogen resources, and that both may play a role in nitrogen retention during that period. These results suggest that spring microbial populations may serve an even more important function than plants in reducing nutrient losses during the spring when water movement is high and before the principal period of summer growth. As competitors, the net influences of herbs and microbes are not necessarily additive, and the absence of herbs may not necessarily imply a net reduction in retention of nutrients.

In an experimental test of the vernal dam hypothesis, Rothstein (2000) concluded that the influence of spring ephemerals in limiting nutrient loss from deciduous forests is less important than originally envisioned. Removal of *Allium tricoccum* Ait. in a sugar maple-basswood forest resulted in no observable increase in nitrate loss during the vernal period. Rothstein (2000) suggested that microbial populations dominate spring nitrogen dynamics such that any nitrogen that might be utilized by spring ephemerals would otherwise be absorbed by the soil microflora. Thus, if increased hydrologic movement during the spring does represent a time of potential loss, the vernal dam may in fact be important but may be moderated by immobilization in increasing microbial biomass rather than in the biomass of spring herbs. In this study, the reciprocal experiment (removal of microbial influence) was not conducted.

In a further analysis of the vernal dam hypothesis, Tessier and Raynal (2003) evaluated nutrient retention patterns of spring herbaceous communities and microbial populations in the acidic soils of an *Acer rubrum, A. saccharum, Fagus grandifolia*, and *Betula alleghaniensi* forest of the Catskill Mountains. Spring ephemeral species are

Table 2.7 Percent recovery of ^{15}N in soil pools in two forests of southern Michigan.

	Acer saccharum, Tilia americana, Allium tricoccum[a]		*Fagus americana, Acer saccharum, Quercus rubra, Claytonia virginica*[b]	
	$[^{15}N]NH_4^+$	$[^{15}N]NO_3^-$	$[^{15}N]NH_4^+$	$[^{15}N]NO_3^-$
Herbaceous biomass	1	3	<1	<1
Microbial biomass	22	32	21	20
Soil organic N	6	13	40	28
NH_4-N	3	2	10	0
NO_3-N	5	5	7	15

Applications and recovery of ^{15}N were made shortly after the spring ephemeral species had reached peak leaf area in mid-April.

[a]Data from Zak et al. (1986).

[b]Data from Groffman et al. (1993).

limited in these forests; however, the herbaceous layer dominants (*Dryopteris inter-media, Lycopodium lucidulum, Oxalis acetosella*, and *Acer* spp. seedlings) are pheno-logically active during the spring runoff period. In this system, while soil microbial biomass held a greater pool of nutrients, understory vegetation represented a greater net sink during the spring phenological period. Significant annual variation occurred in microbial and herbaceous layer nutrient uptake. However, this was not directly reflected in stream water nutrient flux, leaving open the possibility that other mecha-nisms may mediate spring nutrient flux in stream water. This study confirmed that non-ephemeral components of the herbaceous layer may play a significant role in springtime nutrient retention in deciduous forests (Tessier et al. 2001; Tessier and Raynal 2003). Similar conclusions were drawn from an independent analysis of NRA in an oak forest in Sweden (Olsson and Falkengren-Grerup 2003). Higher NRA per unit biomass was found among understory plants than among overstory species. The observed high NRA was consistent among all phenological groups (spring, early sum-mer, late summer) suggesting that the presence of a well-developed understory may be important in nitrogen dynamics throughout the active growing season.

In an interesting twist, Jandl et al. (1997) suggested that rich spring herb assem-blages may actually enhance nutrient loss from forest ecosystems. In a beech forest dominated by a spring herbaceous layer of *Allium ursinum* L. (net primary produc-tivity [NPP] = 200–300 g/m/year), the presence of senescent *Allium* foliar tissue in early summer is a nutrient-rich (particularly nitrogen) substrate for mesofauna graz-ing on the forest floor. Significantly enhanced populations of mesofauna (primarily collembolans) were observed on microsites dominated by *Allium*. Fragmentation of leaf litter by large and diverse mesofauna populations stimulated mineralization by soil microorganisms, creating even more favorable environments for soil mesofauna. Peak concentrations of soil solution nitrate, calcium, and magnesium coincident with *Allium* decomposition in early summer suggest that the synergism between mesofauna and microbial populations that has been initiated by *Allium* litter has fostered greater losses of nutrients than might otherwise occur in the absence of *Allium*. Wise and Schaefer (1994) also suggested that the rapid decomposition of other herbaceous species (*Anemone nemorosa* L. and *Mercurialis perennis* L.), due to high nitrogen concentration and low content of structural polysaccharides, served to enhance decomposition of overstory litter. Wolters (1999) suggested that the readily available source of carbon provided by *Allium ursinum* litter may partially overcome a deficit of carbon available to microbes in early summer, whereas Scheu (1997) argued that the potential for nutrient export is enhanced by the rapid decomposi-tion of *Urtica dioica* L. litter in the fall when uptake by vegetation is low. Regardless of mechanism, phenological relationships are clearly important in understand-ing the role of herbaceous populations in ecosystem nutrient dynamics. Similarly, temporal relationships of microbial populations appear to have strong impacts on internal nutrient cycles of a wide range of ecosystems (Schmidt and Lipson 2004; Schmidt et al. 2007).

Much remains to be determined about the role of herbaceous species, in particular spring ephemerals, in nutrient cycling of forested ecosystems. The dynamics of nutri-ent acquisition by herbs and microbial populations requires more analysis to deter-mine whether their relations are competitive (Zak et al. 1990) or additive. The relative nutrient cycling strengths of these groups may depend strongly on the character of the snowpack and may vary geographically from regions of continuous snowpack to areas of intermittent snow cover (Brooks et al. 1998). The possibility that spring ephemerals may facilitate nutrient loss raises new questions about the interactions of decomposition processes with herbaceous communities. Further complicating clear understanding of these relationships is the more recent recognition of the impact of mycorrhizal infections on the ability of deciduous forest herbaceous species to access soil N in its various forms (Kaye and Hart 1997; Lapointe and Molard 1997; Chapman et al. 2006, McFarland et al. 2010). It is important to recognize that there will be no single answer to any of these questions. Apparently competitive relations among herbs and microbes may become additive in more northerly ecosystems where continuous snow cover serves to separate phenology. Facilitated nutrient loss may occur only on those sites whose nutrient-rich qualities support highly productive spring herbaceous communities. Finally, if the vernal dam hypothesis is a meaningful mechanism of nutrient retention in deciduous forests, it should not be surprising to find similar relationships occurring in other ecosystem types with characteristic nutrient pulses, such as deserts (Chen et al. 2009), grasslands (Bilbrough and Caldwell 1997), and alpine tundra (Mullen et al. 1998).

SUMMARY

Although nutritional aspects of the herbaceous layer of deciduous forests have received considerably less attention than the overstory, available evidence suggests that this synusium is characterized by several unique features. Foliar concentrations of potassium are consistently two to three times higher among herbs than in woody overstory species. Similarly, magnesium concentrations can be up to two times higher than in the overstory. Although not true for all phenological groups, spring ephemerals appear to have significantly higher concentrations of nitrogen than either overstory species or herbaceous species from other phenological groups. It may be that the higher potassium concentrations in the foliage of herbaceous species play an important role in maintaining leaf structure through enhanced turgor pressure. Foliar nutrient concentrations, however, show surprisingly little variation among contrasting sites. Mechanisms accounting for this are unclear but may involve shifting carbon sinks from enhanced foliar growth on nutrient-rich sites or increased mycorrhizal support on nutrient-poor sites. Seasonal patterns of nutrient concentration suggest that herbaceous species absorb nutrients during periods of high availability and that subsequent retranslocation supports growth during periods of active biomass accumulation. Thus, although herbaceous species do not exhibit luxury consumption in the traditional sense of site-to-site variation, they do exhibit seasonal patterns of luxury consumption that support growth in seasons of limited nutrient availability.

As a component of forest ecosystems, the herbaceous layer contributes < 5 percent of aboveground net primary productivity. However, several possible roles of the herbaceous layer in nutrient cycling have been proposed and debated. Some studies have indicated that herbaceous species are capable of absorbing nutrients from throughfall. Such a mechanism would reduce dependence on extensive root systems in a low-energy environment and, given the fairly extensive herbaceous leaf area in some forests, would also contribute to a conservation of nutrients at the ecosystem level. Other analyses have suggested that spring ephemerals play a particular role in nutrient conservation by absorbing nutrients during high soil moisture periods before the break of winter dormancy by deciduous trees and then releasing those nutrients through rapid decomposition during the early season of tree growth. The spring ephemerals, then, contribute to a vernal dam by retarding nutrient loss at a time of low biotic activity and high soil moisture movement. Further studies of microbial activity during the spring, however, have found that this effect is essentially swamped out by concurrent microbial growth. Thus, the vernal dam would appear to be mediated more by microbial populations than by the herbaceous layer. Yet other work has suggested that a rich spring herb assemblage may actually stimulate nutrient loss by serving as a nutrient-rich substrate for soil mesofauna. Enhanced fragmentation of overstory leaf litter by large mesofaunal populations was observed to stimulate mineralization by soil microbial populations, resulting in higher concentrations of nutrients in the soil solution. It is clear that the interactions among herbaceous populations, soil biota, and overstory species are undoubtedly more complex than currently recognized.

ACKNOWLEDGMENT

This manuscript was revised under the auspices of the Santa Barbara Botanic Garden.

Soil Mesofauna —

3 Ecophysiology of the Herbaceous Layer in Temperate Deciduous Forests

Howard S. Neufeld and Donald R. Young

Light availability is the primary limiting resource for understory plants of eastern deciduous forests, and their long-term persistence in these habitats depends on adaptations that enable photosynthesis sufficient to maintain a positive annual carbon balance (Goryshina 1972; Pearcy et al. 1987). However, in addition to low light, understory plants may also be limited by water stress (Masarovičová and Eliáš 1986), nutrient deficiencies (chapter 2, this volume), and pollinator availability (chapter 5, this volume; also Motten 1986). Release of CO_2 from the forest floor by decomposition and root respiration may elevate concentrations in the understory (Sparling and Alt 1966; Koyama and Kawano 1973; Garrett et al. 1978; Baldocchi et al. 1986; Bazzaz and Williams 1991) and improve the photosynthetic efficiency of understory plants (Lundegardh 1921), particularly during sunfleck occurrences (Naumburg and Ellsworth 2000).

While plants in all habitats face some resource limitations, the limitations imposed on understory herbs have resulted in a suite of adaptations that distinguish them from plants that do not grow beneath forest canopies, and from plants that are only temporary residents of the understory, such as the seedlings of canopy trees or shrubs. The floras of deciduous forest understories are highly adapted to these habitats, distinctive in terms of their species composition, with close taxonomic affinities worldwide (Kawano 1970; Goryshina 1972; Boufford and Spongberg 1983; Cheng 1983; Ying 1983; Lapointe 2001) and high degrees of evolutionary convergence toward similar physiologies and morphologies (Goryshina 1972; Parkhurst and Loucks 1972; Givnish and Vermeij 1976; Shugart 1997). Yet direct physiological comparisons between herbaceous understory plants and tree seedlings are few. Adaptive responses to the environment can be both physiological and morphological (Givnish 1986) and exist at multiple scales of organization ranging from the subcellular, to the leaf, whole plant, and ecosystem levels (Ehleringer and Werk 1986; Givnish 1986; Küppers 1994; Pearcy and Sims 1994). This chapter focuses on the major ecomorphological and ecophysiological adaptations that characterize understory herbs and relates these features to the dynamic and limiting light environment in temperate deciduous forests. We begin our discussion by first characterizing the light microclimate within temperate deciduous forests, and then move on to physiological and morphological adaptations at increasing scales of organization. Surprisingly, relatively few studies of herb physiology have been conducted in eastern North American forests, so we are drawing on the literature for temperate deciduous forests from across all similar geographic regions in order to make global generalizations.

Our analytical approach is to utilize life-form analysis for scaling from the individual leaf or species to the ecosystem level. We use the concept of plant functional groups (Smith et al. 1997) to extrapolate general trends among species, using phenological strategies (Uemura 1994) as our grouping variable. As we will show, generalizations can be made concerning species functioning within specific phenological groups that pertain to temperate deciduous forests across the globe (Kawano 1970; Goryshina 1972; Lapointe 2001).

How woody seedlings cope with the understory environment as compared to understory herbs is not clearly understood. Certainly differences and similarities exist among these groups in terms of both their morphological and physiological attributes. For example, most, but not all, understory herbs are perennials, with large underground storage organs (Hicks and Chabot 1985) that are used to store carbohydrates for future growth and reproduction (Zimmerman and Whigham 1992; Pfitsch and Pearcy 1992; Tissue et al. 1995). Under conditions where rates of photosynthesis are low, such as during cloudy years or when substantial amounts of foliage are removed by herbivory, carbohydrates can be mobilized from belowground reserves to maintain dormancy and to sustain leaf emergence in the spring (Goryshina 1972; Lubbers and Lechowicz 1989; Lapointe 2001). However, this often comes at the expense of both vegetative and sexual reproduction (Pitelka et al. 1980, 1985; Lubbers and Lechowicz 1989; Pfitsch and Pearcy 1992). Tree seedlings can also mobilize belowground reserves for maintenance and leaf emergence, but generally do not reproduce when they are in the herb strata; thus, they do not face the exact same carbon allocation dilemma. Both woody seedlings and herbs may "idle" for years in a light environment near their photosynthetic light compensation point until a gap in the canopy occurs and the light environment improves (Crawford 1989). Each year, however, the tree or shrub is putting on secondary growth in the aboveground stem, with the ultimate strategy of growing up and out of the herbaceous layer. Thus, a commitment to mechanical stability via secondary woody tissue is an allocation priority for these plants. In contrast, herbs have no secondary growth of the aboveground stem, and replacement each year comes at great cost in terms of carbon and nutrients.

THE UNDERSTORY LIGHT ENVIRONMENT

Many authors have emphasized the dynamic nature of the understory light environment (Anderson 1964; Reifsnyder et al. 1971; Baldocchi et al. 1984; Chazdon 1988; Canham et al. 1990; Chazdon and Pearcy 1991; Baldocchi and Collineau 1994; Parker 1995; Küppers et al. 1996; Pearcy 1999; Vierling and Wessman 2000; Miyashita et al. 2012), and in particular, the role of sunflecks with respect to plant carbon gain (Chazdon 1988;

Chazdon and Pearcy 1991; Pearcy and Pfitsch 1995; Pearcy 1999; Way and Pearcy 2012). Although we focus here mainly on temperate deciduous forests, many of the conclusions we reach are common also to temperate and tropical rainforests, where much of this research has been concentrated (Becker and Smith 1990; Rich et al. 1993; Turnbull and Yates 1993; McDonald and Norton 1992; Clark et al. 1996; de Castro 2000).

Total Available Light in the Understory

In all forests, both the quantity (Anderson 1964; Reifsnyder et al. 1971; Hutchison and Matt 1977; Chazdon and Fetcher 1984; Brown and Parker 1994; Canham et al. 1994) and quality (Olesen 1992; Brown et al. 1994; Grant 1997) of light are modified by passage through the canopy of overstory trees and shrubs (Clinton 1995). Beneath forest canopies, the spatial and temporal patterns become highly variable and stochastic (Evans 1956; Reifsnyder et al. 1971; Chazdon and Pearcy 1991; Pearcy et al. 1994; Rich et al. 1993). This variability is caused by a number of factors, including overstory composition, leaf characteristics such as size, orientation, density, clumping, and fluttering (Hutchison et al. 1986), and gaps in the canopy due to branch or tree falls (Lawton 1990). In addition, there are penumbral influences (when canopy openings less than the diameter of the solar disk [0.5°] cause a shadow to develop along the edge of the sunfleck), topographical influences, changes in seasonal phenology, as well as daily and seasonal variations due to the weather and the solar path (Baldocchi and Collineau 1994).

The heterogeneity of the understory light environment means that an adequate sampling scheme for characterizing the photosynthetic photon flux density (PFD) of a particular locale necessarily involves a large number of sensors spread out over a substantial portion of the forest floor. Reifsnyder et al. (1971), working in Connecticut, estimated that it would take at least 18 sensors to adequately characterize the instantaneous direct radiation patterns in a deciduous forest (to within a standard error of 7 W/m^2), but only two to characterize the diffuse radiation pattern. However, just one or two sensors were adequate to characterize the *daily* or integrated radiation pattern, due to temporal averaging of the instantaneous values. The total daily PFD within a particular forest can be estimated from instantaneous measures of diffuse light, particularly on overcast days around noon, because the two are highly correlated in a diversity of forests (Koizumi and Oshima 1993; Parent and Messier 1996; Oshima et al. 1997; Machado and Reich 1999). Such measures can serve as good estimators of the relative amount of light available to understory plants over the course of a season, thus reducing the need for continuous measurements.

Site variation within a single forest stand is well illustrated by data from an oak forest in Tennessee, where correlations among light sensors became insignificant at distances greater than 3.0 m, and about 70 percent of all sunflecks were less than 0.5 m in diameter (Baldocchi and Collineau 1994). Since canopy widths of most understory herbs are often much smaller than 0.5 m, plants spaced more than 3 m apart would almost never experience identical light environments. For example, Pfitsch and Pearcy (1992) reported that the number of sunflecks received per day by individuals of the understory herb *Adenocaulon bicolor* Hook.˙ in a redwood forest ranged over two

---

˙ Appendix 3.1 lists all species mentioned in this chapter with their nomenclature as originally cited and the currently accepted nomenclature if changed.

orders of magnitude, from less than 10 to over 400. Similar analyses in eastern deciduous forests are lacking.

The concept of grain size has been useful in ecology for characterizing patchy habitats and for describing how organisms are adapted to dealing with different size patches (Levins 1968). The patchy distribution of herbs that is common in eastern forests (Rogers 1983a; Bratton 1976) results not only from variations in soil characteristics such as nutrients, water contents, and soil depths, but also because understory herbs are responding to the heterogeneous distribution of light on the forest floor (Pitelka et al. 1985), as well as disease occurrence (Warren and Mordecai 2010), ant-mediated dispersal (Warren et al. 2010), and the interaction of both biotic and abiotic factors (Warren and Bradford 2011). As Pearcy (1999) has noted, if the patch size encompasses an entire plant (e.g., sun versus shade habitats), the environment is perceived by the plant as coarse-grained. Spending its entire life in just one patch, the plant must be well adapted to the local conditions, or else it will be extirpated. If, on the other hand, the canopy of a plant extends beyond the edge of a patch, or is subject to patches of varying quality, the environment is perceived by the plant as fine-grained. In this case, acclimation to changing conditions (greater plasticity) would be most adaptive, since the plant will not complete its growth entirely within a single patch. How a plant copes with a fine-grained environment depends on whether it has indeterminate or determinate growth. Plants with indeterminate growth can produce successive leaves differing in anatomy and physiology based on the conditions present at the time of formation, thereby increasing efficiency of resource utilization (Jurik and Chabot 1986). Plants with determinate growth do not have that option, and tolerance to a variable environment is limited by the degree of acclimation possible among existing leaves (Pearcy and Sims 1994; Rothstein and Zak 2001).

Background Levels of Diffuse PFD

When the leaf area index (LAI) of a temperate deciduous forest is at a maximum of about 6 m^2/m^2 in late summer (Hutchison and Matt 1977), light levels near the forest floor are very low, ranging from 0.7–7 percent of the PFD incident above the canopy, with the most commonly reported values centering around 1–3 percent (Chazdon and Pearcy 1991; Brown and Parker 1994; Canham et al. 1994; Pearcy et al. 1994; Constabel and Lieffers 1996). This range represents a 10-fold difference in PFD, and even though the absolute values are very low, the variation is more than enough to influence species distributions and biomass (Reid 1964; Sparling 1967; Pitelka et al. 1985; Washitani and Tang 1991; Tang et al. 1992). Much higher light penetration values have been recorded for some forests, with values ranging from 9–25 percent (see Baldocchi and Collineau 1994 and references therein), but most of these are from studies done prior to 1972, and forest conditions were often not specified. Truly higher PFDs (up to 20 percent) however, are commonly found in riparian forests (Oshima et al. 1997) because of abundant side light. These edge effects can have large impacts on the abundances of understory vegetation and may extend great distances even into non-riparian forests (Ruben et al. 1999; Gehlhausen et al. 2000). Forests with minimal edge-to-area ratios (square or circular in shape) have less sidelight penetration than more irregularly shaped forests (Forman and Godron 1986).

Seasonal Patterns of Light Penetration

In temperate deciduous forests, light penetration to the herb layer is influenced most strongly by seasonality because of changing solar elevation and canopy phenology. The combination of these two factors results in several distinct phenoseasons (Hutchison and Matt 1977): winter/spring leafless, spring/summer leafing out, summer fully leafed, autumn partially leafed, and autumn/winter leafless. Many understory plants have phenological strategies that directly correspond to these demarcations (fig. 3.1) and can be grouped into several major categories (chapter 9, this volume; Robertson 1895; Seybold and Eagle 1937; Sparling 1964, 1967; Taylor and Pearcy 1976; Mahall and Bormann 1978; Chabot and Hicks 1982; Uemura 1994). These are discussed in detail later in this chapter.

Solar radiation striking the forest floor is greatest in the spring leafless period (rather than in winter) because the solar angle is higher relative to the winter minimum (Hutchison and Matt 1976). At this time of year, diffuse radiation penetration

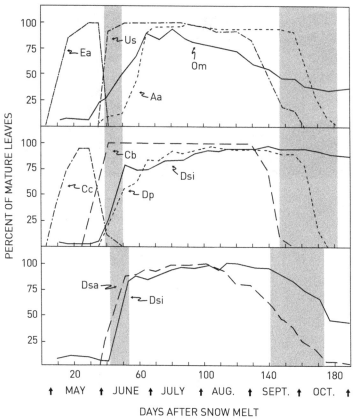

FIGURE 3.1 A comparison of the percentages of leaves in the mature stages for nine different taxa throughout a year. Shaded areas indicate periods of time when leaves are expanding or falling off the canopy. Species: Ea, *Erythronium americanum*; Us, *Uvularia sessilifolia*; Om, *Oxalis montana*; Aa, *Aster acuminatus*; Cc, *Claytonia caroliniana*; Cb, *Clintonia borealis*; Dp, *Dennstaedtia punctilobula*; Dsi, *Dryopteris spinulosa* var. *intermedia*; Dsa, *Dryopteris spinulosa* var. *americana*. Data from 664 m in Hubbard Brook, New Hampshire, except for the lower panel, which are from 782 m. Reprinted with permission from Mahall and Bormann (1978). Note: nomenclature as originally cited.

can range from 10–60 percent of the radiation incident above the canopy (Hutchison and Matt 1977; Baldocchi et al. 1984; Curtis and Kincaid 1984). At the Walker Branch Forest in Oak Ridge, Tennessee, 90 percent of the incident irradiance was contributed by direct beam radiation (Hutchison and Matt 1976, 1977). During this time of the year, PFDs may range up to full sun values of approximately 2,000 $\mu mol\ m^{-2}\ s^{-1}$ and are more than sufficient to allow herbs that are physiologically active in the leafless seasons to carry on some gas exchange (Hicks and Chabot 1985; Yoshie and Kawano 1986; Willmot 1989; McCarron 1995). As much as 20 percent of the annual irradiance can be received at the forest floor during just the spring months (Hutchison and Matt 1977).

As summer approaches, the solar angle continues to rise, but understory PFD drops to a minimum because of attenuation by the fully leafed canopy (fig. 3.2). For example, mid-day PFDs can range between just 2–10 $\mu mol\ m^{-2}\ s^{-1}$ and on an annual basis, only 13 percent of the total irradiance in a Tennessee oak-hickory forest falls in the 150-day period when the canopy is fully closed (Hutchison and Matt 1977). Once leaf fall begins in late summer, PFD again begins to rise, even though the solar angle is now declining

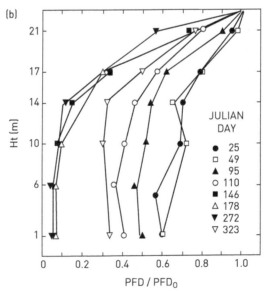

FIGURE 3.2 (Top) Hemispherical photographs through the canopy of a deciduous forest in North Carolina at different seasons and levels of openness (photos by Craig Brodersen). (Bottom) Seasonal variation in the vertical distribution of photon flux density (PFD) through the canopy normalized against that above the canopy (PFD$_o$). Reprinted with permission from Baldocchi et al. (1984).

(Hutchison and Matt 1976). At equivalent solar angles, light penetration is greater in the spring than the autumn, due to the persistence of leaves in the autumn canopy.

Successional Influences on Light Penetration

It is often assumed that as forests age, light penetration to the forest floor monotonically decreases due to increasing LAI and greater bole and branch size (Horn 1971; Waring and Schlesinger 1985). But Brown and Parker (1994), working in southern Maryland, have shown that after an initial period of maximum light penetration prior to canopy closure, light transmittance peaks in 50-year-old stands before dropping in older ones (fig. 3.3a). Light penetration in the younger stands is low because of high stem densities and foliage clumping. Over time, self-thinning reduces stem densities, and foliage density declines due to bole elongation, allowing greater light penetration (fig. 3.3b). Lower light penetration in older stands arises because of a greater preponderance of shade-tolerant canopy species, such as beech, sugar maple, and hemlock, all

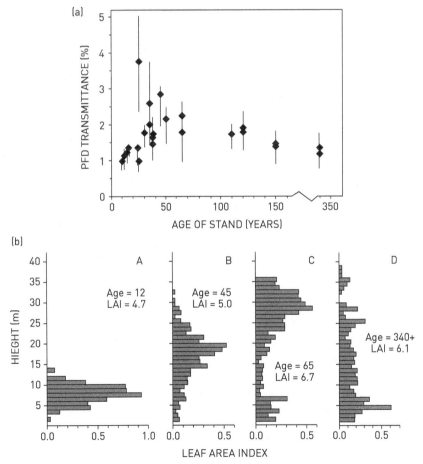

FIGURE 3.3 (Top) Percent transmittance of PFD through forest stands of various ages. (Bottom) Vertical distribution of leaf area index (LAI) for stands of various ages. Forests are in Maryland. Reprinted with permission from Brown and Parker (1994).

of which have deeper crowns and intercept more light than shade-intolerant species such as red oak and white ash (Canham et al. 1994).

Successional changes in light availability and other associated resources, following disturbance such as water and nutrients, have important implications for the distribution of understory plants (Whitney and Foster 1988; Meier et al. 1995; Singleton et al. 2001; but see Gilliam et al. 1995). If light was *the one* overriding limiting resource, we would expect greater diversity and biomass of herbs in mid-successional forests, rather than in early or late successional forests. Many eastern deciduous forests are young, second-growth stands (Whitney 1994), with relatively higher light levels compared to more mature stands, but herb abundances are actually reduced because of past disturbances (Meier et al. 1995; Singleton et al. 2001). Studies now suggest that recovery of the herb layer after logging, and particularly after conversion to agriculture, may take decades to centuries (chapter 14, this volume). Brown and Parker (1994) remarked on the near lack of an understory in the youngest stands they surveyed, but did not determine the causes. Other studies suggest that recolonization of disturbed forests may take 75 or more years, due to a variety of factors such as prior use for agriculture (Singleton et al. 2001), dispersal limitations (Cain et al. 1988; Beattie and Culver 1981), and canopy influences, such as the abundance and distribution of safe sites (Beatty 1984). Other studies have found conflicting results for herb diversity over successional time. Bossuyt et al. (1999) found no differences in herb abundance or diversity between old and young forests in Belgium, although herbs associated with the older forests were poor colonizers of younger forests. Similar results for herb diversity were found for forests in West Virginia by Gilliam et al. (1995).

Most likely, successional trends in herb abundances and diversity interact with the type and extent of the disturbances initiating this process (chapter 14, this volume). As forests age, and light levels decrease, colonization should result in increases in species diversity, but the counteracting effects of lower PFD might slow or reduce vegetative and reproductive success of some herbs, particularly the shade-adapted summer-greens, which grow and reproduce better in more open sites beneath the forest canopy (Pitelka et al. 1985).

Constabel and Lieffers (1996) noted that more open aspen stands had better developed shrub layers, which intercepted so much of the incoming PFD that percent penetration to the forest floor did not change as compared to more closed stands that had a less well-developed shrub layer. Oshima et al. (1997), working in a fragmented riparian forest in Japan, found that light availability in the spring above the herbaceous layer strongly correlated with light near the ground, but after canopy closure, the relationship turned negative, which they attributed to more vigorous growth of herbaceous species in sunnier sites. These studies suggest that the amount of PFD available to low-growing herbs may be fixed for various forest types independent of whether light interception occurs in the tree canopy or lower down in the shrub layer. However, even if the total PFD remains the same, a low canopy creates a substantially different light microclimate from a tall one, due to penumbral effects (Smith et al. 1989) and changes in the mean duration of sunflecks, which become shorter as canopy height decreases (Pearcy 1988; Pearcy et al. 1990). In undisturbed old-growth forests, maximum canopy heights have been estimated to be in the range of 20–37 m (Whitney 1994), while they may be only half that in second-growth forests; thus, sunfleck dynamics may be strikingly different between these two types of forests.

Periodic disturbances, such as windstorms, tornados, and hurricanes, contribute to the formation of canopy gaps that temporarily raise light levels in forest stands (Canham et al. 1990; de Freitas and Enright 1995; Tang et al. 1999), but have a reoccurrence frequency of perhaps only once every 1,000–2,000 years (Whitney 1994). Tree and branch death, due to disease, insects, or old age, occur much more frequently; gaps created by these processes enhance the growth of herbs within old-growth stands (Tang et al. 1999), as well as contribute to their patchy distribution (Rogers 1982; Bratton 1976). Many perennial herbs live for decades (Antos and Zobel 1984), and some clonal plants may be hundreds of years old (Tamm 1956). Most will certainly encounter some form of canopy disturbance that substantially increases the incoming PFD during their lifetime, and that will contribute to a period of rapid growth and enhanced reproduction (Cook 1979). The average return rate for gaps in eastern forests is approximately once a century (Runkle 1982), which represents a spatially averaged maximum number of years that an understory herb has to endure the lowest light levels in a particular forest.

Topographic Influences on Light Penetration

A number of topographic variables can affect the amount of light received in the forest understory, including position with respect to surrounding topography, slope, aspect, latitude, longitude, and time of day (Cantlon 1953; Frank and Lee 1966; Nuñez 1980; Flint and Childs 1987). Forest community types may vary depending on topography (Cantlon 1953), which in turn can exert strong influences on the understory environment (Helvey et al. 1972; Warren 2008). These complex interactions have important implications for the distribution of understory plants. In New Jersey, south-facing slopes have greater herb diversities and higher abundances than north-facing slopes. Certain species are primarily restricted to one slope or the other; *Asarum canadense* L., *Aralia nudicaulis* L., and *Actaea racemosa* L. are found on north-facing slopes, while *Viola palmata* L., *Lespedeza violacea* L. Pers., and *Eupatorium sessilifolium* L. occur on south-facing slopes (Cantlon 1953). On southwest-facing slopes in the southern Appalachians of Virginia, forests are dominated by evergreen pines, whereas deciduous oak forests prevail on northwest-facing slopes (Lipscomb 1986). Daily irradiance above the canopy is greater on southwest slopes, but interestingly, is nearly the same in the shrub layer beneath both canopies (Lipscomb and Nilsen 1990a), the result of differences in canopy structure between the pine and oak forests. However, there are differences in temperature between the two slopes, with maximum temperatures higher on southwest slopes, minimum temperatures higher than valley temperatures, and southwest ridge tops warmer than slope bottoms (Lipscomb and Nilsen 1990b). In other locations, north-facing slopes are generally cooler than south-facing slopes (Cantlon 1953; Stoutjesdijk 1974). Warren (2008) has shown that understory evergreen herbs were less abundant and reproduced less on south-facing slopes in the southern Appalachians. The main correlates with this distributional pattern were winter light and heat loads. Evergreens on south-facing slopes face seasonal stresses that include possible photoinhibition in winter and low soil moisture and high temperatures in summer. Vapor pressure deficits (Δw) are also lower on north-facing slopes, and the improved water status may favor ferns and bryophytes, which are more common on these slopes (Cantlon 1953).

Ridgetop forests tend to be shorter in stature, with more widely spaced trees and open canopies (Whittaker 1956; Hicks and Chabot 1985). They are highly prone to disturbances such as wind, ice, and defoliating insects (e.g., gypsy moths, *Lymantria dispar* L., prefer chestnut oak, *Quercus prinus* L., which is primarily a ridgetop species). If the surrounding hills are lower in elevation, then sidelight, particularly in the morning and afternoon, would be more abundant than in cove forests or in forests with little topographic relief. As a consequence, these forests would be expected to have higher understory PFDs. In some cases, this could lead to greater herb abundances, while in other cases, they could be lower because these forests might be situated on shallow, nutrient-poor soils (Whittaker 1956) that are more prone to drought stress in the summer. Much of the understory in these latter sites is composed of ericaceous shrubs and evergreen herbs that are conservative in their water use (Hicks and Chabot 1985; Givnish 1986; McCarron 1995).

Overstory Compositional Effects

Many temperate forests contain a mixture of both deciduous and evergreen species (Braun 1950). Mixed conifer/hardwood forests often have intermediate understory PFDs during the summer compared to deciduous forests (Constabel and Lieffers 1996), but lower PFDs in the winter because the evergreen species retain their leaves all year. Mixed species forests also have more patchy distributions of light because the conical geometries of the conifer crowns permit more light to penetrate between trees (Baldocchi and Collineau 1994).

The Contribution of Sunflecks

No matter what type of forest or successional stage, sunflecks are an important source of light for understory herbs. Sunflecks are transitory increases in PFD above the background diffuse PFD (Chazdon 1988; Pearcy et al. 1994) and are most often empirically defined as those periods of time when the PFD is above 50 or 100 μmol m^{-2} s^{-1}, which are typical background levels in temperate deciduous forests. However, as Chazdon (1988) and Smith et al. (1989) both point out, the criteria for defining a sunfleck are vague and imprecise. For example, Chazdon (1988) notes that the background PFD for a Wyoming forest (Young and Smith 1979) is nearly the same as that defined as a sunfleck for a tropical rainforest in Costa Rica (Chazdon and Fetcher 1984). Smith et al. (1989) proposed that openings in the canopy be categorized based on the duration and proportion of time each patch is in penumbra or numbra (direct beam radiation).

In temperate forests, most sunflecks last from seconds to minutes (Canham et al. 1990; Chazdon and Pearcy 1991; Horton and Neufeld 1998; Tang et al. 1999). Mean sunfleck durations for hardwood forests in the eastern United States are about seven minutes (Canham et al. 1990), while in a closed stand in Cades Cove, Great Smoky Mountains National Park (fig. 3.4), nearly 80 percent of the sunflecks were one minute or less in duration (Horton and Neufeld 1998). Sunfleck lengths in a temperate forest in Japan varied during the day, with the longest flecks around noon (12–18 minutes) and the shortest ones (6–10 minutes) occurring at 10 a.m. and 2 p.m. (Koizumi and Oshima 1993).

Larger sunflecks usually have higher PFDs than smaller ones due to penumbral effects (Reifsnyder et al. 1971; Koizumi and Oshima 1993) that proportionally increase

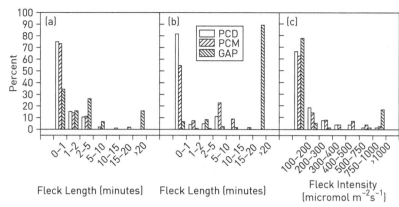

FIGURE 3.4 Frequency histograms for (A) sunfleck duration, (B) percentage of total daily PFD contributed by sunflecks of specific duration classes, and (C) sunfleck maximum intensity. Sites were sampled over three consecutive days and include a partially closed canopy dry site (PCD), a partially closed canopy moist site (PCM), and an open canopy gap site (GAP). Histograms represent combined data from 10 sensors per site. Reprinted with permission from Horton and Neufeld (1998).

the amount of diffuse radiation, thereby lowering the total PFD. The proportion of a sunfleck that is in penumbra depends on both the height and size of the canopy opening (Smith et al. 1989). For a gap with a diameter-to-height ratio of 0.01, the entire sunfleck would be in penumbra, whereas if the ratio was 0.04, 80 percent of the sunfleck would be numbra. In temperate forests, most short duration sunflecks are dominated by penumbra and consequently have PFDs of 250 $\mu mol\ m^{-2}\ s^{-1}$ or less (Chazdon 1988). In the Smokies, more than 60 percent of the sunflecks had PFDs less than 200 $\mu mol\ m^{-2}\ s^{-1}$ (Horton and Neufeld 1998). Vierling and Wessman (2000) measured sunfleck frequency, duration, and intensity in a Congolese forest as a function of canopy depth. Frequency and duration decreased with depth in the canopy, while sunfleck duration increased. At 34 m above the ground, > 80 percent of total PFD was supplied by sunflecks longer than 48 s, but only 6 percent for those less than 12 s. Despite their transitory nature, sunflecks contribute a substantial amount to the total daily energy budget of forest understories. Values range from 21 percent in a Connecticut forest (Reifsnyder et al. 1971) to 45–68 percent in eastern North American and Japanese forests (Hutchison and Matt 1977; Weber et al. 1985; Koizumi and Oshima 1993). In the Smoky Mountains and in Japan, nearly 80 percent of incoming PFD can be contributed by sunflecks (Horton and Neufeld 1998; Miyashita et al. 2012). Sunfleck contributions may be greater in the spring and autumn months due to the lower LAIs at those times (Koizumi and Oshima 1993), but the proportional contributions of sunflecks are greater in forests with lower background diffuse PFD (Chazdon 1988).

Even though sunflecks make up a substantial portion of the radiation budget in an understory, their total cumulative duration is quite brief. Values ranging between 12 and 25 percent of the daylight hours are common (Weber et al. 1985; Koizumi and Oshima 1993). In the study by Koizumi and Oshima (1993), sunflecks were more frequent in the morning and late afternoon, and less common around solar noon due to the changing solar path through the canopy.

In mountainous areas, it might be expected that ridgetop forests would have substantial sunfleck activity when the solar elevation is low because there would be a shorter optical path into the understory and less obstruction by adjacent trees. In cove forests, the opposite situation would predominate. Here, sidelight is almost entirely obliterated by slopes and other trees, and most sunflecks would occur near mid-day when the solar angle was high. North-facing slopes would have the shortest cumulative sunfleck durations because the sun drops below the horizon sooner than for a south-facing slope.

There are relatively few data on the temporal distribution of sunflecks. Since photosynthetic induction responses are dependent on closely spaced exposures to high light within a certain length of time (Chazdon 1988; Pearcy et al. 1994; Pearcy 1988, 1999), quantifying this parameter is important for modeling plant responses to sudden changes in PFD. Pearcy (1988) reported that 70 percent of sunflecks in a rainforest in Queensland occurred within one minute of the preceding sunfleck and only 5 percent were preceded by low light periods greater than one hour in length. In the Congo, nearly half of all sunflecks were separated by less than 30 s of low light, while a substantial number of sunflecks, particularly those close to the ground, were separated by low light intervals of greater than 32 mins (Vierling and Wessman 2000). These patterns may have strong influences on the induction and de-induction states of photosynthesis for understory herbs (see Way and Pearcy 2012) that occupy the lowest layer in the forest, and are discussed later in this chapter. Curiously, there do not appear to be any similar analyses of sunfleck clumping in temperate deciduous forests.

PLANT STRATEGIES FOR COPING WITH THE VARYING LIGHT ENVIRONMENT IN THE UNDERSTORY

Temperate understory herbs employ a combination of both physiological and morphological adaptations that gives them a selective advantage in low-light habitats. Besides general adaptations to the prevailing light conditions (typical sun/shade responses; see table 3.1), these herbs must also contend with cold temperatures for a large portion of the year. The combination of light and cold stress has resulted in the evolution of at least six distinct phenological strategies, whereas overstory trees have adopted primarily just the winter deciduous and evergreen habits (Uemura 1994), although other strategies do exist. For example, one shrub in Japan, *Daphne kamtschatica* Maxim. var. *jezoensis* (Maxim.) Ohwi, is shade deciduous (Lei and Koike 1998) but maintains overwintering leaves. In the eastern United States, the understory tree *Aesculus sylvatica* W. Bartram behaves similarly to a spring ephemeral; it leafs out early before the overstory does, begins to lose its leaves once the canopy closes, and is completely defoliated by the end of August (dePamphilis and Neufeld 1989). Vegetative phenologies also appear to be tightly linked to reproductive phenologies, and Kudo et al. (2008) have categorized forest herbs into three major syndromes of co-occurring lifecycle events: those that (1) leaf out, flower, and fruit early in the season before canopy closure, (2) leaf out before canopy closure, flower during closure, and fruit after closure, and (3) late summer plants that flower and fruit after canopy closure. The fact that herbs with contrasting phenologies coexist in the same communities, albeit to different degrees, suggests that there may be more than one evolutionarily stable strategy in these environments. In addition, by determining patterns of abundance among the different types of herbs, we may gain insight into the major selective factors that have resulted in the mix of herbs that populate deciduous forests.

Table 3.1 General Differences between Sun and Shade Leaves for Leaves of Plants Adapted to High and Low Light Intensities.

Characteristic	Sun Leaves	Shade Leaves
Morphological Features		
Leaf Area	-	+
Leaf Thickness	+	-
Palisade Parenchyma Thickness	+	-
Spongy Parenchyma Thickness	similar	similar
Specific Leaf Weight	+	-
Cell Abundance	+	-
Cuticle Thickness	+	-
Density of Stomata	+	-
Cell Ultrastructural Features		
Cell Size	-	+
Cell Wall Thickness	+	-
Chloroplasts per Area	+	-
Chloroplast Orientation	vertical	horizontal
Proportion of Stacked Membrane	-	+
Thylakoids per Stroma Volume	-	+
Thylakoids per Granum	-	+
Starch Grains in the Chloroplasts	+	-
Chemical Features		
Caloric Content	+	-
Water Content of Fresh Tissue	-	+
Cell Sap Concentration	+	-
Lipids	+	-
Anthocyanins, Flavonoids, Xanthophylls	+	-
Chlorophyll per Chloroplast	-	+
Chlorophyll per Area	similar	similar
Chlorophyll per Unit Dry Mass	-	+
Chlorophyll a/b Ratio	-	+
Light Harvesting Complexes per Area	-	+
Electron Transport Components per Area	+	-
Coupling Factor (ATPase) per Area	+	-
RUBISCO per Area	+	-
Nitrogen per Area	+	-
Physiological Functions		
Photosynthetic Capacity per Area	+	-
Dark and Photorespiration per Area	+	-
Photosynthetic Capacity per Dry Mass	similar	similar
Dark and Photorespiration per Dry Mass	similar	similar
Carboxylation Capacity per Area	+	-
Electron Transport Capacity per Area	+	-

(Continued)

Table 3.1 *(Continued)*

Characteristic	Sun Leaves	Shade Leaves
Quantum Yield	- (or similar)	+ (or similar)
Light Compensation Point	+	-
Light Saturation Point	+	-
Photoinhibition Likely	-	+
Transpiration	+	-

Source: Table derived from Nilsen and Orcutt (1996) and Lambers et al. (1998) and includes generalizations from Boardman (1977).

Phenological Strategies of Understory Herbs

The six common phenological strategies employed by understory herbs (Uemura 1994) include (i) spring ephemerals; (ii) summer-greens; (iii) winter-greens; (iv) heteroptics (Kikuzawa 1984) (i.e., species with two types of leaves: summer-green and overwintering, each lasting less than one year), and two types of evergreens; (v) those whose leaves last just over one year, called biennial-leaved by Uemura (1994); and (vi) those whose leaves last for more than two years (Mahall and Bormann 1978; Chabot and Hicks 1982; Uemura 1994; Tessier 2008). Parasitic and saprophagous (often mycotrophic) herbs constitute two additional groups, but their phenological correlation with the overstory canopy has not been well documented. Species that are hemi-parasites can perform some photosynthesis while holo-parasites apparently have no photosynthetic activity (dePamphilis et al. 1997). Carbon for non-photosynthetic herbs (such as *Monotropa uniflora* L.) probably comes from mycorrhizae that are themselves connected to other photosynthetically capable host plants, although one species of *Monotropa* appears to be able to perform non-photosynthetic carbon fixation via PEP carboxylase (Malik et al. 1983).

Spring ephemerals leaf out prior to canopy development when light levels are at their highest, but exhibit little tolerance to the deep shade that develops later in the season. In more northerly latitudes, they may even leaf out in the winter or very early spring, when, despite the lack of a canopy, total daily PFDs may be relatively small due to the low solar angle at these times of the year. Leaf senescence in this group begins once canopy closure occurs, and most species become dormant before mid-summer (Kawano et al. 1978; Tessier 2008). Rothstein and Zak (2001) have termed these plants *shade avoiders*. In contrast, summer-green species leaf out during or after canopy closure *(shade tolerators)* but retain their leaves for less than one year. Senescence usually occurs in late summer or the autumn. These species gain most of their carbon prior to the completion of canopy closure, but are able to continue some carbon assimilation under the low-light conditions that ensue later in the season. Winter-green species, as defined by Uemura (1994), form overwintering leaves in late summer or autumn, but which detach early the next summer. The difference between heteroptic and winter-green species is that the former have some type of leaf on the plant at all times during a year, whereas leaf lifespans of true winter-greens are less than one year, and plants are often without leaves during the summer. Heteroptic plants can be considered a special case of evergreenness. True evergreen species retain their leaves for more than one year, and sometimes for up to three or four years (Chabot and Hicks 1982; Koizumi 1985, 1989; Koizumi and Oshima 1985; McCarron 1995).

In cool temperate forests in Japan (Uemura 1994) and most likely in all temperate deciduous forests, the vast majority of understory species are summer-greens (69 percent) followed by evergreens (19 percent). Spring ephemerals constitute just 6 percent of the flora, winter-greens 3 percent, while least abundant are parasitic and saprophagous herbs (2 percent) and heteroptic species (1 percent). Some of the more common species in each of these phenological categories and their physiological characteristics are listed in table 3.2.

Based on abundances only, it appears that evolution has favored those species that grow during the warmer portions of the season when temperatures are more favorable for photosynthesis and nutrient uptake. Evolving the ecophysiological mechanisms necessary for carbon gain when the canopy is leafless may be either more difficult or the species pool from which the necessary adaptations could be obtained is limited, thereby curbing the number able to take advantage of these times of the year. In certain portions of northeastern England though, where the winters are relatively mild and have little snow cover, a number of ephemeral species have evolved to leaf out in late winter, such as *Ranunculus ficaria* L. and *Hyacinthoides non-scripta* (L.) Chouard ex Rothm. (Davison, pers. comm.).

Deciduousness is most likely a derived condition and probably evolved in response to alternating periods of unfavorable conditions arising from either cold or drought stress, or more likely, some combination of the two (Axelrod 1966; Stebbins 1974). Chabot and Hicks (1982) proposed several general hypotheses regarding the evolution of evergreen leaves that can be distilled down to two major themes: (1) Evergreen leaves are more advantageous on low nutrient soils and (2) evergreen leaves are an adaptation to drought or herbivory. Regarding the first hypothesis, Chabot and Hicks (1982) argue that longer leaf lifespans lower the carbon construction costs per unit of nutrient uptake, resulting in higher nutrient use efficiencies and a moderation of nutrient recycling rates (Monk 1966). In order to maintain functional leaves for more than one year, particularly through the harsh winters of temperate forests, these leaves need to be tough and resistant to injury. Such leaves are often sclerophyllic, with large amounts of lignin and other structural compounds that confer resistance to either abrasion or herbivory. These leaves also require a greater investment in carbon, which takes longer to pay back in terms of photosynthetic carbon gain. Evergreenness in herbs might also result from an inability to adapt to the low PFD during the summer, and hence their periods of peak photosynthetic activity are shifted to the colder portions of the year when light is more available. In more northerly locations, where the growing season is much shorter, evergreenness confers an advantage by allowing species to begin carbon gain in the early spring as soon as temperatures become warm enough without incurring leaf construction costs that would delay the time when net photosynthesis becomes positive. In the autumn, evergreen leaves could continue photosynthesizing until temperatures become too cold, thus extending the season of carbon gain as much as possible during times when the canopy is absent and light levels are highest. A similar argument applies to winter-greens and heteroptic species.

We also speculate that the proportion of evergreen herb species should increase toward the southern end of the distribution of temperate forests because in these locations, temperatures are more favorable when the canopy is leafless than in more northern forests. For example, certain species are summer-green in colder areas but evergreen in warmer areas (Sato and Sakai 1980). Landhäusser et al. (1997) report that the evergreen *Pyrola asarifolia* Michx. has higher rates of photosynthesis in the summer

Table 3.2 Summary of Gas Exchange Characteristics for a Sampling of Understory Herbs Grouped by Phenological Class.

Species	Light Compensation Point ($\mu mol\ m^{-2}\ s^{-1}$)	Light Saturation Point ($\mu mol\ m^{-2}\ s^{-1}$)	Apparent Quantum Yield ($\mu mol\ CO_2\ /\ \mu mol\ photons$)	Light Saturated Photosynthesis ($\mu mol\ CO_2\ m^{-2}\ s^{-1}$)	Dark Respiration ($\mu mol\ CO_2\ m^{-2}\ s^{-1}$)	Leaf Lifespan (weeks)	References
Spring Ephemerals							
Allium monanthum	5	700	.041	6.4	1.1	11	Kawano et al. 1978
Allium tricoccum	10; 22	400; 1800		13.1; 15.4	1.3; 1.4	10	Sparling 1967; Rothstein and Zak 2001
Anemone raddeana	23	600	.042	14.0	1.3	6	Yoshie and Yoshida 1987
Cardamine diphylla	8	76				10	Sparling 1967
Claytonia caroliniana	36	300				11	Sparling 1967
Dicentra canadensis	36	600				9	Sparling 1967
Dicentra cucullaria						7	Harvey 1980
Erythronium americanum	14–20	326–1000	.046	20.0; 14.7	1.2	11	Taylor and Pearcy 1976; Hicks and Chabot 1985; Hull 2001
Erythronium japonicum	20	>700[c]	.051	6.9	0.7	9	Kawano et al. 1978
Mertensia pulmonarioides						11	Harvey 1980
Mean	**20**	**592**	**.045**	**11.8 (16.5)[d]**	**1.1**	**10**	
Summergreens							
Adoxa moschatellina	17	700	.048	7.2	0.6	17	Kawano et al. 1978
Allium victorialis ssp. platyphyllum	6	200	.124[a]	5.9	0.6	17	Kawano et al. 1978

Species							Reference
Aralia nudicaulis		185		6.0			Landhäusser et al. 1997
Arisaema triphyllum	5	133	.044	5.6	0.4		Hull 2001
Asclepias exaltata	5	400	.056	20.6	1.1	16	Souza and Neufeld, unpubl. data
Cardiocrinum cordatum	22	700	.053	6.4	1.0	20	Kawano et al. 1978
Caulophyllum thalictroides	20	600				20	Hicks and Chabot 1985
Dryopteris filix-mas						32	Willmot 1989
Dryopteris dilatata						32	Willmot 1989
Dryopteris marginalis	4	60				30	Hicks and Chabot 1985
Hydrophyllum appendiculatum	20	420		5.7			Hicks and Chabot 1985
Jeffersonia diphylla						17	Harvey 1980
Maianthemum canadense	2	50				22	Sparling 1987
Maianthemum dilatatum	4	500	a	18.9	1.3		Koyama and Kawano 1973
Maianthemum racemosum	4	212	.041	8.5	0.9		Hull 2001
Mercurialis perennis	2–30	300	.060	8.0	0.05–1.3		Kriebitzsch 1992a
Microstegium vimineum	15	800	.037–.048	19.1	0.9	~28	Horton and Neufeld 1998
Oclemena acuminata	17–74	301–862	.051	7.9–11.5	0.4–0.9		Pitelka and Curtis 1986
Podophyllum peltatum	10–11	50–117	.036	11.5		18	Hicks and Chabot 1985
Rubus pubescens				4.6	0.8		Landhäusser et al. 1997
Sanguinaria canadensis	4	100				20	Hicks and Chabot 1985
Smyrnium perfoliatum				24.0			Olah and Masarovicova 1997
Solidago flexicaulis	10	240		11.0		28	Hicks and Chabot 1985
Trientalis borealis				3.2			Adams 1975
Trillium erectum	10	50				20	Hicks and Chabot 1985

(Continued)

Table 3.2 [Continued]

Species	Light Compensation Point ($\mu mol\ m^{-2}\ s^{-1}$)	Light Saturation Point ($\mu mol\ m^{-2}\ s^{-1}$)	Apparent Quantum Yield ($\mu mol\ CO_2\ /\ \mu mol$ photons)	Light Saturated Photosynthesis ($\mu mol\ CO_2\ m^{-2}\ s^{-1}$)	Dark Respiration ($\mu mol\ CO_2\ m^{-2}\ s^{-1}$)	Leaf Lifespan (weeks)	References
Trillium grandiflorum	10	280–460		10.3		11–22	Hicks and Chabot 1985
Viola pubescens	8	700		12.1	0.8	23	Rothstein and Zak 2001
Mean	**12**	**352**	**.056 (.048)**	**10.4**	**0.8**	**22**	
Winter-greens							
Cornus canadensis				5.5			Landhäusser et al. 1997
Dryopteris filix-mas						~52	Willmot 1989
Dryopteris dilatata						~52	Willmot 1989
Heuchera americana			.080			26	Skillman et al. 1996
Tipularia discolor	10–20	550	.040–0.059	8.5	0.8	~24	Tissue et al. 1995
Mean	**15.0**	**550**	**.065**	**8.5**	**0.8**	**39**	
Evergreens							
Dryopteris carthusiana	4	50				54	Hicks and Chabot 1985
Fragaria vesca	12–50[b]	400–600[b]		3.9[b]		14–20[b]	Hicks and Chabot 1985
Galax urceolata	4	400	.025	4.3	0.5	114	McCarron 1995
Hexastylis arifolia	4–30	480	.070	11.0		52	Hicks and Chabot 1985
Mitchella repens	8	140				120	Hicks and Chabot 1985
Pachysandra terminalis	8	200	.023–.080	9.0	0.8	182	Yoshie and Kawano 1986

Polypodium virginianum	20–33	.028–.033	120–175	2.5	0.7–1.4		Gildner and Larson 1992
Pyrola asarifolia			125	4.2			Landhäusser et al. 1997
Pyrola elliptica	8		140			54	Hicks and Chabot 1985
Tiarella cordifolia	9		330	6.8	0.3		Rothstein and Zak 2001
Mean	**10.7 (10.5)[b]**	**.044**	**291 (224)[b]**	**6.0 (6.3)[b]**	**0.7**	**85 (96)[b]**	

Calculation of means: Where multiple values exist for a single parameter, the average of those values was used for that species. Maximum seasonal values reported for photosynthesis. Other parameters correspond to this same time for comparative purposes. Readers are encouraged to consult cited references for details regarding measurement conditions. Some values were obtained from potted plants, some from the field, and others from detached leaves. When PFD was reported as Klux, a value of 100,000 Klux was taken as the best estimate of full sunlight.

[a] Mean in parentheses does not include value reported by Kawano et al. (1978), which seems unusually high.

[b] Although this plant is technically evergreen, it differs from the others in this category in that its leaves do not last for more than one year. The value in parentheses is the mean if this plant is deleted from the calculations.

[c] For determination of light saturation point, 700 μmol m^{-2} s^{-1} was used, even though the actual value is probably somewhat higher.

[d] Value in parentheses calculated excluding the two values from Kawano et al. (1978), which for this group appear anomalously low. Measurements were made on detached leaves.

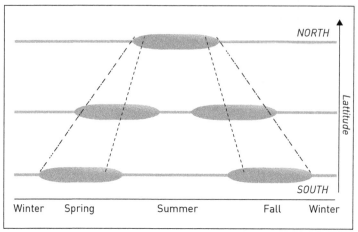

FIGURE 3.5 Model of phenology for an evergreen plant as a function of latitude. Dashed and dotted lines represent changes in date of last frost in spring and first frost in autumn; short-dashed lines represent dates when canopies are fully leafed out or fully leafless. Gray areas represent photosynthetic activity of evergreen herbs; width of gray area is proportional to activity. As latitude increases, the period for favorable carbon gain is shifted more toward the summer, and time available to take advantage of high light in spring and autumn is greatly reduced.

and does not take advantage of the higher light in the spring and autumn to raise assimilation rates. In fact, this plant behaves photosynthetically as a summer-green, with a lower compensation point than congeneric summer-green herbs. Yet in other studies of *Pyrola* species (*P. japonica* Klenze ex Alef.) from more southerly climates (southern Japan), plants acclimate to the high-light periods in spring and autumn and perform little photosynthesis in the summer when PFD is low (Koizumi 1989). We postulate that as the growing season shortens at more northerly latitudes, the windows of opportunity for appreciable carbon gain in the spring and autumn shrink in length because of later frosts in the spring and earlier frosts in the autumn, coupled with more rapid canopy leaf-out in the spring (fig. 3.5). If so, there could be a shift in photosynthesis more toward the summer as latitude increases, until at the most northern locations, it becomes more advantageous to gain carbon in the summer when temperatures are at their peak even if PFD is low. Finally, phenology may also be a function of plant size. *Dryopteris filix-mas* (L.) Schott, an understory species characteristic of British woodlands, switches from being winter-green when small to summer-green when large, presumably because smaller plants need more light during the leafless seasons to bolster carbon gain (Willmot 1989).

Leaf Morphology of Understory Herbs

Light strongly alters the leaf anatomy of a plant. Plants in low light environments tend to have larger but thinner leaves, with reduced palisade layer development, or in some cases, an absence of palisade tissue altogether (Boardman 1977, table 3.1). The two understory herbs *Hydrophyllum canadense* L. and *Asarum canadense* each have only a single layer of photosynthetic cells (DeLucia et al. 1991). Shade leaves are most commonly hypostomatous, with a greater preponderance of stomata on the abaxial surface. This helps distribute CO_2 within the leaf to those tissues receiving the most light, thus maximizing photosynthetic efficiencies when PFD is limiting (Evans 1996, 1999; Smith et al. 1997; Smith and Hughes 2009). Shade leaves also produce more widely spaced stomata than sun leaves (Salisbury 1928), which may reflect lower mean leaf temperatures and transpirational demands in the understory. However there is a suggestion that spring ephemerals may also have low stomatal densities (< 160 stomata/mm^2), and these plants may be either hypo- or amphistomatous (Eliáš 1981).

Another strategy for increasing light absorption is for leaves to increase internal light scattering and, as a consequence, reduce light transmission through the leaf. One way to do this is to produce more spongy mesophyll cells, because these irregularly shaped cells scatter light more so than palisade cells. When leaves of *H. canadense* or *A. canadense* are infiltrated with mineral oil (which nearly eliminates refraction from cell wall–air interfaces), light absorption is reduced nearly twofold, potentially lowering photosynthesis by 20 percent (DeLucia et al. (1996).

Shade leaves frequently have more reflective lower surfaces (Smith et al. 1997) that direct light back into the leaf that otherwise would not be captured, while upper surfaces are less reflective due to fewer intercellular spaces in the palisade layer (Lee and Graham 1986). Other species contain deeply pigmented abaxial epiderms that may enhance absorption of PFD, particularly among tropical understory plants (Lee and Graham 1986, Hughes et al. 2008). This latter phenomenon appears to be less prominent in temperate forests, perhaps because light levels are not quite as low as in tropical forests (Baldocchi and Collineau 1994), but *Oxalis sp.*, *Glechoma sp.*, and *Tipularia discolor* (Pursh) Nutt. are notable exceptions. Hughes et al. (2008) suggest that abaxially located anthocyanins in understory herbs may absorb primarily green light and prevent backscatter into the mesophyll layer. By being located on the lower leaf surface, absorption of PFD by the anthocyanins is minimized in the deep shade of the understory, allowing photosynthesis to proceed under light-limited conditions yet still protecting against photoinhibition during high light sunflecks.

Leaves of a number of evergreen herbs (e.g., *Galax urceolata* [Poir.] Brummitt) accumulate anthocyanins when exposed to high PFD and turn bright red in winter (McCarron 1995; Hughes et al. 2005, Hughes and Smith 2007; Hughes 2011). In most plants, the anthocyanins accumulate just below the adaxial epiderm, but in *G. urceolata*, they can also occur on the abaxial surface under high light stress. Leaves that are shaded remain green. The adaptive value of this reddening has been debated (Chalker-Scott 1999; Gould and Quinn 1999; Gould et al. 2000; Manetas 2006; Zeliou et al. 2009), but in many instances, it is clear that anthocyanins act as a light shield to protect against photoinhibition (Powles 1984; Hughes et al. 2005; Hughes and Smith 2007; Grace et al. 2002) caused by sunflecks during cold periods.

Some understory plants have glabrous leaves and lack trichomes and hairs that might reflect light that could otherwise be used for photosynthesis (Ehleringer and Mooney 1978). Cells in the adaxial surface are often shaped as concave lenses that may direct light more efficiently to those tissues within the leaf that contain the chloroplasts (Haberlandt 1914; Vogelmann 1993; Vogelmann et al. 1996). Palisade cells also act as light pipes, since the chloroplasts are often appressed against the anticlinal walls, which allow light to penetrate deeper into the leaf, reducing self-shading effects. However, palisade light piping does not appear to work in the diffuse light conditions that are typical most of the time in the understory, but may be of primary use during sunflecks, when direct beam radiation strikes the leaf surface (Pearcy 1998; Brodersen et al. 2008). Furthermore, shade-adapted leaves do not discriminate between the absorption of either direct or diffuse light (Brodersen et al. 2008; Brodersen and Vogelmann 2010). If epidermal cells in shade plants are more spherical than in sun plants, light would focus more shallowly within the leaf, and light intensities would peak directly within the palisade and spongy mesophyll cell layers where most of the chlorophyll resides. Using micro-fiber optic probes, light intensities as high as 3X full sunlight have been measured at the focal points inside leaves (Vogelmann 1993; Vogelmann et al. 1996), with concomitant reductions in transmitted light and increases in light use efficiencies.

Understory Plant Forms

Approximately 94 percent of the understory herbs in deciduous forests in North America are perennials; nearly two-thirds of these are hemicryptophytes (with perennial buds or shoots close to ground level), and slightly less than one-third are cryptophytes (with buds belowground on bulb or rhizome) (Buell and Wilbur 1948; Cain 1950; Struik and Curtis 1962). Only 6 percent are annuals (Hicks and Chabot 1982). Many of the perennial herbs are clonal, and production of ramets that explore the forest floor is an efficient means for vegetatively reproducing, as well as buffering individual ramets against localized resource deprivation. Several studies have shown that carbon (Ashmun et al. 1982; Alpert and Mooney 1986; Silva 1978; Stuefer et al. 1994), water (Lau and Young 1988; de Kroon et al. 1996), and nutrients (Birch and Hutchings 1994) are transferred among ramets, and that severing connections among ramets can be detrimental to survival (Lau and Young 1988).

The degree of integration among ramets and the length of time they remain functionally integrated varies by species (Ashmun et al. 1982). For example, *Oclemena acuminata* (Michx.) Greene rhizomes decay within two years of formation, whereas those of *Clintonia borealis* (Sol.) Raf. last many years. There is little or no inter-ramet translocation of ^{14}C in *O. acuminata* but there is in *C. borealis* (Ashmun et al. 1982). *Clintonia borealis*, which produces leaves early in the season prior to canopy closure, may be subjected to large extremes in resource availability at this time of year (Ashmun et al. 1982), and selection pressures to maintain physiological integration may be more intense than for the later-growing *O. acuminata*. In sites with extreme microhabitat heterogeneity, selection for maintenance of physiological integration may be favored (Zhang et al. 2009), whereas in more homogeneous sites, little translocation of resources may occur even though ramets remain connected (Silva 1978). Finally, disturbances that disrupt resource availability may result in reestablishment of physiological integration among connected ramets, improving survival of the genet as a whole (Ashmun et al. 1982; Lau and Young 1988; de Kroon et al. 1996).

Height of Forest Herbs

Tall plants are better competitors for light (Jahnke and Lawrence 1965; Horn 1975), and competition between herbs and tree seedlings depends, in part, on the maximum height that herbs can attain. Fig. 3.6 shows maximum heights for a variety of herbs of differing phenology. Using data obtained from the flora of the Carolinas (Radford et al. 1968), we show that spring ephemerals and evergreens are the shortest and summer-greens the tallest ($p < 0.05$) forest herbs. The former two groups are active in those portions of the year when light availability is highest and other resources such

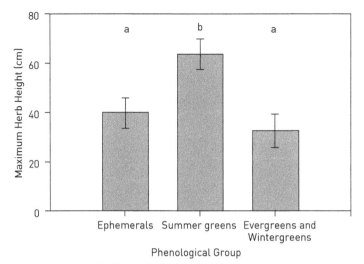

FIGURE 3.6 Mean maximum height ($\pm$ SE) of herbs as a function of phenological class. Means with the same letter are not statistically different at $p = .05$ ($N = 11$–15 among the group). Data from Radford et al. (1968).

as nutrients and water are less limiting, so there may be fewer selective pressures to grow tall (Reid 1964; Givnish 1982; Sakai 1994). In the summer, competition for light becomes more intense as leaf area coverage by summer-green herbs and woody plants increases and as a consequence, selection for height growth is intensified in order to maximize light interception (Givnish 1982, 1986; Sakai 1994).

The maximum heights that herbs achieve represent a compromise between allocation to support structures and allocation to leaves for photosynthetic carbon gain (Givnish 1982, 1986; Sakai 1994). For each unit increase in height, there is a proportionally greater investment in support rather than leaf tissue, due to the high costs of maintaining mechanical integrity. For competing plants, there is some maximum height at which the advantage in terms of carbon gained no longer warrants any further increase in height. Givnish (1986) has shown that each 7 percent increase in leaf coverage in a Virginia forest roughly results in a doubling of leaf height (fig. 3.7). The consequences of this for tree regeneration are great, since the habitats with the greatest light availability are often the most conducive to seedling growth, but also those in which competition against herbs for light will be greatest.

Givnish (1982) suggested that evergreen species are restricted to infertile, open sites because of the conflict between maintaining warm leaves in the winter and competition for light in the summer. Species active in the colder portions of the year may position their leaves close to, or directly on, the ground in order to obtain heat thermally re-radiated from the soil. Leaf temperatures will be elevated above cold air temperatures and significant photosynthesis may occur in the winter months. This would exclude them from more resource-rich sites, where they would be easily overtopped. However, evergreen herbs on open sites may be susceptible to high light and cold stress in the winter and high temperatures and drought stress in the summer (Warren 2008).

Christmas fern (*Polystichum acrostichoides* [Michx.] Schott) is an evergreen that prefers north-facing nutrient-rich slopes instead of more xeric, sterile sites. In spring, fronds are produced in an erect posture that is maintained throughout the

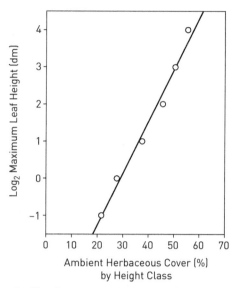

FIGURE 3.7 Maximum leaf height versus ambient cover for all species or seasonal morphs falling into a given height class. The least mean squares regression line is $y = -4.03 + 0.138x$, indicating that leaf height roughly doubles with each 7% increase in herbaceous cover. Redrawn from Givnish (1982) with permission.

summer. But after the first frosts, they reorient to lie flat on the ground. Givnish (1982, 1986) showed that prostrate leaves can be up to 5°C warmer when in contact with the ground compared to fronds raised to their summer erect position. This would theoretically enhance photosynthetic rates by 22 percent, although no actual measurements of photosynthesis have been done in the field. Neufeld (unpublished data) has shown that for the same species on north-facing slopes in the southern Appalachians, exposed leaves could be up to 6°C colder in the morning and 6°C warmer in the afternoon, compared to leaves lying below the litter. Thus, topography, because of the slope-orientation effects on light and temperature, could play a major role in determining the carbon balance of evergreen herbs.

Crown Architecture of Forest Herbs

Plants in shady habitats tend to form crowns that are monolayers, with minimal leaf overlap (Horn 1971; Valladares 1999). Light interception is maximized by maintaining large horizontally oriented leaves (Pons 1977; DeLucia et al. 1991; Menges 1987; Muraoka et al. 1998; Leach and Givnish 1999). If there are openings in the canopy from gaps or trails where sidelight can enter the forest, leaves will orient toward the direction of higher diffuse irradiance (Björkman and Demmig-Adams 1995; Muraoka et al. 1998). Under closed canopies, however, most of the light on the forest floor comes from within 20–40° of vertical (Canham et al. 1990), so most leaves will be horizontally oriented.

A horizontal leaf orientation, though, can pose a problem during periods of prolonged high light such as occur in long sunflecks or canopy gaps after a disturbance. During those times, high radiation amounts can cause overheating, increased transpiration rates, and photoinhibition (Young and Smith 1979; Oberhuber and Bauer 1991; Pearcy and Sims 1994; Björkman and Demmig-Adams 1995; Muraoka et al. 1998). To avoid overexposure, some plants (mainly in the families *Fabaceae* and *Oxalidaceae*) actively reorient their leaves parallel to the direction of incoming radiation (Björkman and Demmig-Adams 1995), which reduces the flux density of radiation by the cosine of the angle of incidence (Kriedeman et al. 1964) and allows species like *Oxalis oregana* Nutt. to avoid photoinhibition (Björkman and Demmig-Adams 1995). *Arisaema heterophyllum* Blume folds its leaves along the main vein when growing in high light situations (Muraoka et al. 1998). Other species passively reorient their leaves through changes in turgor pressure brought about by water loss when exposed to high PFD. Leaves of *Impatiens capensis* Meerb., *I. pallida* Nutt., *Rudbeckia laciniata* L., and *Eurybia macrophylla* (L.) Cass., to name but a few, wilt rapidly when exposed to sunflecks, causing the leaves to droop to a more vertical position (Schulz and Adams 1995; Schulz et al. 1993). In the case of *E. macrophylla*, short sunflecks of just a few minutes resulted in higher g_s, whereas prolonged sunflecks caused leaf overheating and increased the Δw, causing stomata to close (Schulz and Adams 1995). It must be noted though, that the majority of plants in the understory show no active leaf movements. Raven (1989) in a theoretical exercise suggests that when sunflecks are of long duration and separated by an interval long enough to allow for any repair of photodamage, avoiding incident PFD by reorienting leaves (pulvinar leaf folders) is energetically favored over simply repairing the injury (repairers, no reorienting of leaves). However, if flecks are of short duration and close together, leaf folding is the more costly option. Since the majority of plants in understories do not possess the pulvinar leaf-folding mechanism, the sunfleck regimes therein may be such that repairers are generally favored over leaf folders, or there is some phylogenetic constraint against species that are leaf folders.

Phyllotaxy can also be adjusted to maximize light interception and to reduce self-shading. Distichous and spiral leaf arrangements ensure that no leaf is fully shaded by an upper one and are common among plants in shady habitats (Leach and Givnish 1999; Valladares 1999). In a tropical forest understory in Panama, computer simulations showed that such arrangements could limit mutual shading to approximately 10 percent (Pearcy and Yang 1996). Tani and Kudo (2006) comment that giant (up to 2 m tall) understory summer-green herbs in northern Japan have a small light gradient from the top leaves to the bottom ones, helped along by the fact that most of the light in that layer of the forest is diffuse. This enables even the lowest leaves on these plants to carry out positive photosynthesis at the low PFDs in these forests.

Topographic relief may also influence crown architecture. Some herbs, such as *Maianthemum racemosum* (L.) Link., *Prosartes lanuginosa* (Michx.) D. Don, and *Polygonatum biflorum* (Walter) Elliott, have stems with distichous leaves that arch downslope. In the Smokies, the compass orientation of these species matches that of the slope on which they are growing (Givnish 1986) so that they arch out over other species lower down on the slope. Although this architectural strategy is more expensive (in terms of the carbon costs for gaining height) than those incurred by building an erect umbrella crown, the marginal gain in height on steep slopes presumably gives these species a competitive edge in these habitats (Givnish 1982, 1986).

PHYSIOLOGICAL ADAPTATIONS OF UNDERSTORY HERBS

Photosynthetic Pathways of Understory Herbs

Most understory herb species employ the C_3 pathway of photosynthesis, although there are a few representatives from the C_4 and CAM pathways (Leach and Givnish

1999). *Microstegium vimineum* (Trin.) A. Camus and *Muhlenbergia sobolifera* (Muhl.) Trinius are shade-tolerant C_4 grasses that can become prevalent in forest understories (Winter et al. 1982; Smith and Stocker 1992; Smith and Wu 1994; Williams 1998). *Microstegium vimineum* is an annual exotic that has spread throughout the eastern United States and may be displacing native forest herbs (Williams 1998, Warren et al. 2011). *Sedum ternatum* Michx. grows on rocky soils and shaded outcrops in southern Appalachian forests. It performs C_3 photosynthesis when well watered, but switches to CAM cycling if water-stressed (Gravatt and Martin 1992), which may moderate photoinhibitory effects (Luettge 2000). Although plants with the C_4 and CAM pathways have the potential to adapt to low light conditions (Pearcy 1983; Sage et al. 1999), their success in shaded habitats may ultimately be constrained by inherently higher ATP requirements (von Caemmerer and Furbank 1999), as well as by large interveinal distances in the leaves, which are inversely correlated with shade tolerance in C4 grasses due to effects on quantum yield (Ogle 2003).

Carbon Gain by Herbs before and after Canopy Closure— Leaf Lifespan

Data on the relationship between mean maximum photosynthetic rate and leaf lifespan can be seen in table 3.2. Leaves of spring ephemerals live on average only 10 weeks, while leaves of some evergreen species may last for up to 120 weeks. Mean maximum assimilation rates (A_{max} ± standard error) vary threefold among the phenological groups, ranging from 16.5 ± 1.8 µmol m^{-2} s^{-1} among spring ephemerals, down to 6.0 ± 1.2 µmol m^{-2} s^{-1} for evergreens. When mean assimilation rates are plotted against mean leaf durations (from table 3.2), a negative but highly significant nonlinear relationship is found (fig. 3.8). The curvature shows that as leaf lifespans increase beyond one growing season, there are diminishing costs in terms of decreased photosynthetic rates. Extending leaf lifespans from the mean for spring ephemerals to that for summer-greens (a 13-week increase) results in a drop in A_{max} of 0.44 µmol m^{-2} s^{-1} wk^{-1} of extended lifespan, whereas going from summer-greens to evergreens the decrease

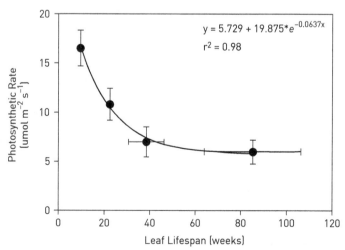

FIGURE 3.8 Mean maximum photosynthetic rates (± SE) as a function of mean leaf lifespan (± SE) for herbs from various phenological classes. Data from table 3.1.

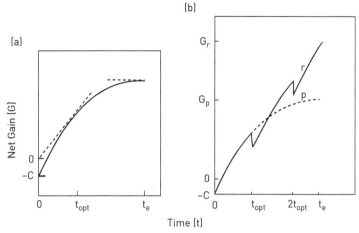

FIGURE 3.9 Schematic representation of net gain of carbon per leaf (G) to time (t) curve. (a) Net gain at time zero is minus construction cost ($-C$) and increases rapidly at first and then gradually because of decrease in photosynthetic rate with time due to aging. Net gain is maximized by replacing leaves when tangent line from origin touches curve (t_{opt}). Waiting until net gain is zero does not maximize gain. (b) Comparison of net gain for a plant that continually replaces leaves (r) and one that has persisting leaves. The net gain for the plant that replaces leaves (G_r) at time t_{opt} exceeds that of one with persisting leaves (G_p) that retains leaves to time t_e. Reprinted with permission from Kikuzawa (1991).

is only 0.08 μmol m^{-2} s^{-1} wk^{-1} of extended lifespan over a mean of 63 more weeks. Extended lifespans are necessary to pay back the costs of construction when rates of photosynthesis are low. Interestingly, construction costs on a per unit mass basis are similar between sun and shade leaves, but higher for sclerophylls due to their higher lignin contents (Poorter 1994; Pearcy 1999).

The variety of leaf phenologies among understory herbs can be understood within the context of cost-benefit models (Chabot and Hicks 1982; Williams et al. 1989; Kikuzawa 1991; Kikuzawa and Ackerly 1999). According to Kikuzawa's econometric model (Kikuzawa 1991), leaf longevities are short when initial photosynthetic rates are high, the decline of photosynthesis over time is rapid, and construction costs are low. If the costs for maintaining a leaf through an unfavorable period exceed the benefits of the preceding favorable period, the leaf should be dropped (fig. 3.9). The optimal time for a leaf to be replaced is when its net carbon gain per unit of time over its lifespan is maximum (i.e., when the marginal gain is maximized). The utility of this model is that it takes into consideration temporal and spatial variations in resource availability to explain patterns of leaf longevity among disparate groups of plants. In high resource sites, where nitrogen, water and light are freely available, rates of photosynthesis can be high, and as a consequence, leaf lifespans are short. In low resource sites, the acquisition of these resources takes more time; hence, leaf lifespans are longer.

Spring Ephemerals

Table 3.2 (updated from Hicks and Chabot 1985) shows gas exchange characteristics and leaf lifespans among a large number of forest understory herbs. Spring ephemerals, such as *Erythronium americanum* Ker Gawl., *Allium triccocum* Sol., *Anemone flaccida* Fr. Schmidt, and *A. raddeana* Regel, are the first deciduous herbs to leaf out after winter, and they complete their leaf growth either prior to or just after the overstory develops (Goryshina 1972; Kawano et al. 1978; Koizumi and Oshima 1985; Lapointe 2001; Tessier 2008). Average leaf lifespans are ~10–11 weeks, but can be as short as six weeks in more northerly latitudes (Yoshie and Yoshida 1987). Taylor and Pearcy (1976) noted that shaded leaves of *E. americanum* senesced earlier than unshaded leaves, presumably because of a lack of carbon gain. In *A. flacida*, leaf senescence actually begins prior to full canopy closure, suggesting that leaf lifespan may be genetically fixed (Koizumi and Oshima 1985), but more recent work by Lapointe and colleagues suggests that leaf lifespan in spring ephemerals is controlled more by sink limitations belowground than by changes in light availability (Lapointe 2001; Gutjahr and Lapointe 2008). Conditions favoring more rapid filling of the belowground reserves will result in feedback inhibition of *A* and earlier leaf senescence. Generally for most species in this group, senescence is complete by the time of full canopy development.

Many spring ephemerals produce typical sun-type leaves, with high A_{max} on a per unit area basis, high light compensation points (LCP), high light saturation points for photosynthesis (L_{sat}), and high dark respiration (R_d) rates (Taylor and Pearcy 1976; Boardman 1977; Kawano et al. 1978; Björkman 1981; Koizumi and Oshima 1985; see table 3.2). They also have thicker leaves than shade-tolerant summer-green herbs, a better developed palisade mesophyll with one or possibly two layers of cells, higher specific leaf mass (SLM, g/m^2), and higher chlorophyll a/b ratios (Sparling 1967; Taylor and Pearcy 1976; Rothstein and Zak 2001). Photosynthetic rates peak at or near full leaf expansion, but remain high for only one to two weeks before declining sharply (Taylor and Pearcy 1976; Kawano et al. 1978; Koizumi and Oshima 1985; Constable et al. 2007). Maximum rates of assimilation average nearly 17 $\mu mol\ m^{-2}\ s^{-1}$, but individual values can range between 13 and 20 $\mu mol\ m^{-2}\ s^{-1}$ (table 3.2).

High rates of assimilation in spring ephemerals result from a large investment in electron transport capacity (ET) and in enzymes associated with photosynthetic carbon reduction (PCR), particularly ribulose-1,5-bisphosphate carboxylase/oxygenase (RUBISCO) (Taylor and Pearcy 1976; Rothstein and Zak 2001). These high fixation rates require substantial amounts of leaf nitrogen (N) because much of the leaf protein N is allocated directly to RUBISCO (Poorter and Evans 1998). Additional N fractions are associated with the light harvesting complexes and processes related to N reduction (Evans 1986; Pearcy 1999). Although data are limited, it appears that spring ephemerals have the highest leaf N contents (nearly 4 percent in *E. americanum*; chapter 2, this volume) among the various phenological groups of herbs. Leaf N concentrations of summer-green herbs are generally lower (~ 2.5 percent), and those of evergreens (1.4 percent) the lowest (McCarron 1995). Nitrogen is more readily available for a short period in spring because of mineralization due to increasing soil temperatures and plentiful soil moisture, whereas later in the season, N becomes more limiting due to uptake and immobilization. With their high rates of photosynthesis and generally greater metabolic activity, spring ephemerals are able to accumulate high concentrations of N, whereas the slower-growing evergreens cannot, even though they too are active in the early spring. The dichotomy in response can best be explained by viewing spring ephemerals as ruderal-type species in the sense of Grime (1979) and evergreen species more as stress-tolerators, with inherently slower growth rates and reduced abilities to take up nutrients even when supplied in excess.

As is typical of many shade-intolerant plants, spring ephemerals exhibit little down regulation of photosynthetic capacity in response to a lowering of the prevailing PFD once the overstory closes (Pearcy and Sims 1994; Constable et al. 2007). Adaptations that confer a significant advantage in high light appear to be incompatible with persistence under low light conditions. For example, greater leaf thickness means more light attenuation within the leaf tissues, and cells near the abaxial surface may be at or below their LCP at the PFDs beneath a closed canopy. High investments in leaf N and enzymatic processes require substantial amounts of ATP and carbon that are not available once the canopy closes, and it becomes a liability to maintain these sun-type leaves under low light conditions (Smith and Hughes 2009).

Some studies have suggested that the absorbed quantum yield (φ) of shade plants (μmol CO_2/μmol *absorbed* photon) is higher under low PFD than it is for sun plants (Nilsen and Orcutt 1996; but see Björkman 1981), while Singsaas et al. (2001) conclude that it is relatively invariant among C3 plants, with an operational value of 0.081. However, more recent studies show that the more commonly measured *apparent* φ (μmol CO_2/μmol *incident* photon) varies considerably and is influenced by physiological and environmental conditions. Apparent φ among four understory herbs is only slightly lower in the spring ephemeral *E. americanum* (0.045 μmol CO_2/μmol photons) than that for several shade-tolerant summer-green herbs (0.048 μmol CO_2/μmol photons), while in other studies, the apparent φ depends strongly on A_{max} (Yoshie and Kawano 1986; Yoshie and Yoshida 1987; Hull 2001). In *Anemone raddeana* Regel, apparent φ varies seasonally in concert with A_{max}, ranging from ~ 0.020 to ~ 0.040 μmol CO_2/μmol photons. Spring ephemerals, for example, have both the lowest and highest values (0.029 μmol CO_2 μmol^{-1} photons in *Allium ursinum* L. to a maximum of 0.071 μmol CO_2 μmol^{-1} photons in *Arum maculatum*) among the herbs surveyed by Kriebitzsch (1992a). The complexity of responses and the large number of factors affecting φ make generalizations among phenological groups suspect, and it is not possible at this time to conclude that any significant differences exist (table 3.2).

Spring ephemerals achieve high rates of photosynthesis early in the season in part because of their ability to carry on gas exchange when temperatures are still quite low. This suggests that these plants might have lower temperature optima (T_{opt}) than summer-greens. Winter-greens and evergreens, in contrast, might adjust their T_{opt} to the prevailing temperatures over the year. However, the patterns found in the field are more complex and less distinguishing than hypothesized. Kawano (1970) and Koyama and Kawano (1973) have noted that the T_{opt} for understory herbs is quite broad, in some cases ranging up to 10–15°C. Kriebitzsch (1992b) defined the T_{opt} as the range of temperature over which photosynthesis is 90 percent of A_{max}. Working in Germany, he found no large differences among the phenological groups, despite large differences in prevailing air temperatures when the species were photosynthetically active. In spring, the T_{opt} for six species spread among most of the phenological groups ranged from 8–10°C at the lower end, to 16–26°C at the upper end, with, surprisingly, a spring ephemeral (*Arum maculatum* L.) having the highest T_{opt}. Over the season and across species, the T_{opt} shifted upward only about 2–4°C before going back down toward spring values in the autumn (Kriebitzsch 1992b). Over most of the season, the T_{opt} ranges were broad and averaged 8–10°C for all species. For those species persisting into the summer, the T_{opt} tended to shift upward as the canopy closed, probably because of lowered respiratory costs.

Winter-green and Heteroptic Species

Other species active in the early spring are the winter-green/evergreen and heteroptic species, plus summer-greens that produce leaves prior to canopy closure. Although winter-greens and evergreens have leaves present at the same time as spring ephemerals, they have a much lower A_{max} (table 3.2) with values more similar to summer-greens after canopy closure. The highest A_{max} reported in this group is 11 μmol m^{-2} s^{-1} for *Hexastylis arifolia* (Michx.) Small in North Carolina (Gonzalez 1972), but nearly half of the reported values for these species are below 6 μmol m^{-2} s^{-1}. While there may not be any inherent physiological reason why these plants could not attain higher rates of photosynthesis (Chabot and Hicks 1982), factors associated with evergreenness, such as lignification, defense against herbivores, lower mesophyll conductances, and perhaps drier and more nutrient deficient soils, appear to constrain photosynthesis in this group to lower mean values (Smith and Hughes 2009).

Winter-green species, such as *Tipularia discolor*, take particular advantage of the spring and autumn seasons. This species produces a single new leaf in the autumn that then overwinters prior to senescing in late spring. Photosynthetic rates are highest in the autumn and continually decline through the winter until just before senescence, when A_{max} is only 39 percent of that in the autumn (Tissue et al. 1995). Despite this dramatic decrease in photosynthetic potential, actual assimilation rates in the field decline by only 30 percent from autumn to spring because of compensating changes in light and temperature. Because the T_{opt} for this species is invariant and remains at about 26°C throughout the year, warm air temperatures and high light in the spring contribute to higher-than-expected rates of carbon uptake (Tissue et al. 1995). This differentiates *T. discolor* physiologically from another winter-green orchid, *Aplectrum hyemale* (Muhl. ex Willd.) Nutt., which can change its T_{opt} by nearly 10°C in response to changing air temperatures (Adams 1970). In essence, *T. discolor* behaves much like a spring ephemeral by making use of those periods when the canopy is absent, while avoiding the deep shade of the summer months by senescing its leaves. In contrast, *A. hyemale* has higher assimilation rates when preconditioned at low temperatures (T_{opt} is 15°C), and plants are able to obtain 75 percent of their A_{max} at 5°C and nearly 90 percent at 10°C. Below 5°C, photosynthesis declines markedly, suggesting that little carbon uptake occurs during the winter, especially when plants are snow covered.

Heteroptic species produce specialized leaves that maximize carbon gain during those times of the year when each leaf type is present. These species are both developmentally and physiologically more plastic than evergreen species that only produce leaves at one time during the year (Skillman et al. 1996). *Heuchera americana* L. produces leaves in both the autumn and spring, each of which only lasts about six months. Based on laboratory measurements, leaves produced in the winter have a much higher A_{max} (by 250 percent) than summer leaves, while the T_{opt} for summer leaves is higher by about 8°C. A_{max} increases over the winter for autumn-produced leaves, such that they are able to take immediate advantage of the high light and favorable temperatures in the spring prior to senescing as the canopy closes (Skillman et al. 1996). Given the higher prevailing air temperatures in summer, the higher T_{opt} for summer leaves allows for reasonable carbon gain, even though the PFD is low because of the tree canopy overhead.

Shifts in the way N is apportioned within leaves appear to be responsible for the different assimilation abilities of the two types of leaves. Nitrogen per unit leaf area does not differ between summer and winter leaves, but is much higher on a per unit chlorophyll basis in the winter for autumn-produced leaves. The ratio of A_{max}/N is low for this species, but within the range found for shade-tolerant tropical understory plants (Skillman et al. 1996). This suggests that much of the N has been diverted away from the photosynthetic apparatus to defensive compounds, although no systematic studies have been done that relate this ratio to secondary chemical concentrations in leaves of understory herbs. There appears to be little or no chronic photoinhibition (as measured by fluorescence) in *H. americana* leaves over the winter. Summer leaves allocate approximately 31 percent of their leaf N to the light harvesting complexes in the thylakoid membranes compared to only 17 percent for overwintering leaves, which enables this species to gain substantial carbon in the summer even though the PFD can be quite low (Skillman et al. 1996).

Evergreen Species

True evergreen species (leaf lifespans > 1 yr) utilize both the autumn and spring leafless periods to obtain much of their carbon gain (Koizumi 1985; Koizumi and Oshima 1985; Graves 1990; McCarron 1995; Rothstein and Zak 2001). They may also gain additional carbon during the summer in contrast to winter-greens that are dormant at this time of the year. Many evergreen species have leaves with some characteristics typical of shade plants, such as low photosynthetic rates and low LCPs (table 3.2). When exposed to high light and favorable temperatures, A_{max} remains low and in fact is sometimes inhibited by prolonged exposure to high light, as in *Galax urceolata* (McCarron 1995; Hughes et al. 2005; Hughes and Smith 2007) and the summer-adapted (shade) leaves of *Pachysandra terminalis* Siebold & Zucc. (Yoshie and Kawano 1986). Koizumi (1989) showed that *Pyrola japonica* was able to acclimate to rising temperatures in the summer but was not able to lower the T_{opt} to match air temperatures when they fell below 15°C, indicating only partial temperature acclimation.

Taken as a group, evergreens gain most of their carbon in the spring and the autumn, when light levels are the highest (Yamamura 1984; Koizumi 1989). The highest rates of assimilation for both *G. urceolata* and *P. terminalis* are found in the spring and autumn when temperatures are moderate; the lowest rates occur in the summer, due to extreme shade, and in the winter, when air temperatures are low and soils are frozen (Yoshie and Kawano 1986; McCarron 1995). There is some indication that populations at more northern latitudes have a higher A_{max} than more southerly populations that presumably compensates for the shorter growing season (Yoshie and Kawano 1986).

Rates of photosynthesis in evergreens also progressively decline with leaf age (Koizumi and Oshima 1985; McCarron 1995). A_{max} in *Pyrola japonica* drops from near 2.3 μmol m^{-2} s^{-1} in current year leaves to 1.6 μmol m^{-2} s^{-1} in one-year-old leaves, down to only 0.6 μmol m^{-2} s^{-1} in two-year-old leaves. Similar decreases in A_{max} have also been found in *Pachysandra terminalis* and *Galax urceolata* (Yoshie and Kawano 1986; McCarron 1995). These decreases represent losses of photosynthetic capacity and are not due to greater stomatal limitations to the diffusion of CO_2. While stomatal conductances (g_s) do decrease as leaves age, they do so in concert with decreases in A_{max} such that the ratio of internal to external CO_2 remains constant throughout the season (Koizumi and Oshima 1985). Losses in photosynthetic capacity with aging result from natural senescence processes, redistribution of resources (Tissue et al. 1995), or a combination of these events, but the actual biochemical/physiological factors causing age-related declines in A_{max} are not well understood. By analogy with the woody understory shrub *Rhododendron maximum* L., loss in A_{max} may be due to progressive deterioration of thylakoid membranes in the photosynthetic apparatus after prolonged exposure to high light during the winter (Nilsen et al. 1988; Bao and Nilsen 1988) and declines in RUBISCO activity and ET (Ethier et al. 2006; Warren 2006). In the evergreen *Viola hondoensis* W. Becker & H. Boissieu, winter leaves are shed in the spring as new leaves are produced, and shading from summer leaves and redistribution of N from old to new leaves appear to be the proximate causes of this senescence (Hikosaka et al. 2010).

Respiratory Demands of Spring Ephemerals

Spring ephemerals as a group possess high rates of R_d (Sparling 1967; Taylor and Pearcy 1976; Koizumi and Oshima 1985; Hull 2001; Rothstein and Zak 2001), which may be due to the large metabolic costs of sustaining and repairing PCR enzymes, maintaining the protein integrity of the light harvesting complexes, and processing carbohydrates that are present in higher concentrations than in shade leaves (Risser and Cottam 1968; Lambers 1985). Rates are dramatically higher during leaf formation when construction costs are high, but then drop significantly afterward. In *Anemone raddeana*, R_d was 1.5 μmol m^{-2} s^{-1} during leaf expansion but just 0.8 μmol m^{-2} s^{-1} once leaves matured (Yoshie and Yoshida 1987). The end result is that spring ephemerals as a group have a 40 percent higher R_d, an LCP nearly twice as high, and a L_{sat} of photosynthesis 250 μmol m^{-2} s^{-1} higher than more shade-tolerant summer-green herbs (table 3.2).

One of the big unknowns for spring ephemerals is how much assimilated carbon is translocated belowground and then lost via respiration by tissues such as roots and storage structures. Noda et al. (2007) studied *Primula sieboldii* E. Morren, a spring ephemeral, and found that during the foliar period early in the season, respiration of aboveground parts was 2.5X that of belowground organs. During the flowering period though, which followed leaf senescence in early summer, the reverse was true: Belowground respiration greatly exceeded (6.5X) that aboveground. Like other spring ephemerals, this species becomes relatively dormant during the warm summer and absolute rates of respiration in *P. sieboldii* decrease to just one-fifth of those in the spring, allowing this species to maintain an annual positive carbon balance (Noda et al. 2007; Lapointe and Molard 1997). On an annual basis, *P. sieboldii* consumes about 87 percent of its photosynthate in respiration, of which 70 percent occurs during leaf-out, 24 percent is consumed during the summer dormancy period, and 6 percent is lost in the autumn as the plant makes new roots and mycorrhizal connections (Noda et al. 2007).

Respiratory Demands of Winter-green and Evergreen Species

There are some methodological problems associated with making comparisons among phenological groups in terms of whether they differ in R_d. For example, most measurements of R_d are derived from light response curves at 0 PFD; but these measurements may be inappropriate for making comparisons among species that grow in habitats that differ greatly in the background levels of PFD. As Pearcy (1999) correctly cautions, measurements of R_d for sun plants obtained in this manner may be overestimates of the actual rates in the shade because of the dependency of R_d on carbohydrate processing. R_d is typically a function of the previous day's net photosynthesis (Syvertsen and Cunningham 1979) and is lowest just before dawn, by which time most carbohydrate reserves have been consumed. Thus, distinctions in R_d among the different phenological groupings as reported in most of the literature may reflect the different rates of carbohydrate processing rather than inherent differences in maintenance R_d among sun- and shade-type leaves. More accurate comparisons could be obtained if measurements of R_d were made after a standardized period in the dark to eliminate the influence of carbohydrate concentrations. This being said, R_d for winter-green and evergreen herbs, taken at the time of A_{max}, does not differ greatly from those of summer-green herbs (table 3.2).

Physiological Adaptations to the Light Environment after Canopy Closure Strategies to Maximize Light Use Efficiency

The persistence of herbs in the understory after the canopy has leafed out requires physiological, biochemical, and morphological changes in leaves that maximize photosynthetic efficiency under light-limited conditions, as well as leafing strategies that maximize whole plant carbon gain (Ida and Kudo 2009, 2010). Most plants adopt a strategy for coping with decreasing PFD by shifting resources away from the processes associated with fixation to those involved with light harvesting (Pearcy and Sims 1994; Rothstein and Zak 2001). This is accomplished in a variety of ways, including maximizing light absorption and the φ of photosynthesis, and by minimizing R_d. Not all species are equally effective in adjusting photosynthetic parameters to the decreasing light. In particular, spring ephemerals and evergreen species appear incapable of much adjustment. For example, evergreens have trouble adjusting φ in response to low PFD beneath a closed canopy, which may reflect pre-adaptation to the high light conditions of the leafless seasons. Quantum efficiencies in one-year-old *Pachysandra terminalis* leaves are highest in the spring and autumn (~0.073 and 0.080 μmol CO_2/μmol photons, respectively) but much lower in the summer (0.043 μmol CO_2/μmol photons), suggesting little acclimation to the shade (Yoshie and Kawano 1986). Insignificant change is observed for the evergreen *Asarum maculatum* Nakai in Europe during the spring-to-summer transition (Kriebitzsch 1992a). In contrast, the φ in summer-green species increases from spring to summer and is positively correlated with increases in total chlorophyll (Kriebitzsch 1992a). Together, these two changes contribute to more efficient photosynthesis by summer-green herbs at low PFD. The failure of the evergreen species to adjust suggests they are pre-adapted to the periods of high light before and after canopy closure, but can carry on a small amount of photosynthesis after canopy closure.

In addition to light, temperature strongly influences φ (Kriebitzsch 1992a). In the spring, φ is positively related to temperature when temperatures are below 15°C, but above this point, it begins to decline sharply with rising temperature. This pattern is consistent among species from different phenological groupings, and there is no suggestion that one group or another has a higher or lower φ.

Changes in Nitrogen Use Efficiency in Low Light

On a per unit mass basis, chlorophyll amounts in sun and shade leaves are reported to be similar (Björkman 1981), but shade leaves do shift chlorophyll away from the light harvesting complexes of PSI to those associated with PSII core proteins (LHCII). The end result is a lowering of the chl a/b ratio, because chl b is primarily found only in

LHCII, while the core protein complex contains only chl a. This reallocation increases light harvesting at the expense of ET, but raises the nitrogen use efficiency of photosynthesis because there is less N per unit chl-protein complex in LHCII (Evans 1986). Such a shift in chl a/b ratios has been documented in a number of European herbs, including both spring ephemerals and summer-greens (Kriebitzsch 1984; Eliáš and Masarovičová 1986a, b). During canopy closure, total chl (a+b) amounts in the summer-green *Mercurialis perennis* L. rise by nearly 2.5X, while the chl a/b ratio drops by ~ 3X, the result of a substantial (~ 5X) increase in chl b (Kriebitzsch 1984). A similar, albeit smaller response in total chl (1.5X) occurs for *Viola pubescens* Aiton in a hardwood forest in Michigan (Rothstein and Zak 2001), but no changes in total chl were observed for the evergreens *Tiarella cordifolia* L. or *Galax urceolata* (McCarron 1995). In contrast to these trends, Harvey (1980) found that the evergreen *Hepatica acutiloba* DC. actually increases its chl a/b ratio after canopy closure by 25 percent, mainly the result of large (84 percent) increases in chl a production.

Changes in Dark Respiration during and after Canopy Closure

Respiration is consistently lower in shade leaves and, in fact, may be the predominant factor that determines shade tolerance in plants (Pearcy 1999). Low rates of R_d result in a lower LCP and a more positive balance between photosynthesis and respiration, and hence a greater ability to photosynthesize at the PFDs typically found in forest understories. On a seasonal basis, R_d decreases after canopy closure because of lowered construction and maintenance costs, the cessation of leaf growth, and a decrease in activity of the PCR cycle. Large decreases in R_d are characteristic of all herbs that make the transition from spring to summer (Kawano et al. 1978; Kriebitzsch 1992a; Rothstein and Zak 2001, Constable et al. 2007; Noda et al. 2007; Ida and Kudo 2010). The drop in rates can span an order of magnitude (from 39 to 400 percent), but absolute differences are much smaller for winter-green/evergreen herbs because of their overall lower gas exchange rates (Kriebitzsch 1992a; Rothstein and Zak 2001; Isogai et al. 2003). After canopy closure, rates of R_d in the shade are so low that differences among groups of species can no longer be distinguished (table 3.2).

Because of the temperature dependency of R_d, static measurements in the laboratory do not provide a clear picture of the dynamic nature of respiratory processes in field situations. Kriebitzsch (1992a) made an extensive series of measurements of the temperature dependence of R_d in a variety of understory herbs. He showed that not only did R_d increase with temperature, but the response to temperature varied seasonally, with the greatest sensitivity during the transition from high to low light. As a result, the LCPs increased with increasing temperature. Despite this strong temperature dependency (nearly tripling every 10°C in the spring, but only doubling in summer and autumn), carbon losses in the summer were greatly moderated because canopy closure reduced the range of understory air temperatures. Similar results were obtained for the evergreen herbs *Pyrola japonica* (Koizumi 1989) and *P. incarnata* (DC.) Freyn (Isogai *et al.* 2003). Respiration rates were highest in leaves and flower organs in early spring, and low and constant the rest of the year. Rhizome respiration peaked in midsummer and then declined the rest of the year. Only new buds showed an increasing trend into the autumn and winter, presumably due to construction costs associated with maturation for the next growing season (Koizumi 1989). One conse-quence of these trends is that across a group of species representing spring ephemerals to evergreens, maintenance R_d values in the field are within a few percent of each other most of the season, particularly when the canopy is closed (Kriebitzsch 1992a). Similar field studies of R_d in North American woodland herbs have not yet been done.

Seasonal Timing of Carbon Gain with Respect to Canopy Closure

Both summer-green and evergreen/winter-green herbs often produce leaves prior to canopy closure and use this time of high light availability to gain much of their annual carbon (Blackman and Rutter 1946; Koizumi 1985; Koizumi and Oshima 1985; Pitelka et al. 1985; Graves 1990; Chazdon and Pearcy 1991; Kriebitzsch 1992c; Rothstein and Zak, 2001; Isogai et al. 2003). There is usually a short window of time before canopy closure when temperatures rise enough to permit appreciable carbon gain (Graves 1990). In Michigan, *Viola pubescens* accumulates 66 percent of its annual biomass increment in the six weeks prior to canopy closure, while the remaining 34 percent takes another 20 weeks (Rothstein and Zak 2001). If we assume that sunflecks can enhance carbon gain after canopy closure by an average of 30–40 percent (Weber et al. 1985) but occupy only about 10 percent of that time (Chazdon and Pearcy 1991), then *V. pubescens* could potentially accumulate 80 percent of its annual carbon in only 30 percent of the season (~ 10 percent per week). Over the remaining 18 weeks, accu-mulation would average only 1 percent per week, suggesting that for much of this time, the plant is barely above its LCP. Kriebitzsch (1992c) calculated that *Mercurialis perennis* gained 73 percent of its yearly carbon gain in just 44 days, with the remain-ing 27 percent taking an additional 168 days. Isogai et al. (2003) calculate that *Pyrola incarnata* gains 68 percent of its annual carbon prior to leaf-out in the spring, with the remaining 32 percent spread out over the summer and autumn. This suggests that car-bon gain is substantially lower in the autumn high light season than in the spring high light season, probably due to lower light resulting from protracted leaf fall dynamics in autumn, as well as leaf age effects. In some stands in Europe, total shoot carbon balances for *M. perennis* and *Geum urbanum* L. are actually negative for much of the summer after canopy closure (Graves 1990).

Changes in A_{max} after Canopy Closure

Once the canopy has fully leafed out, A_{max} drops sharply in a wide spectrum of summer-green species, with rates declining by nearly half over this period (Taylor and Pearcy 1976; Koizumi and Oshima 1985; Graves 1990; Kriebitzsch 1992a; Rothstein and Zak 2001; Ida and Kudo 2010). In contrast, little or no acclimation is found in boreal hardwood forests in Canada for either *Rubus pubescens* Raf. or *Aralia nudi-caulis* L. (Landhäusser et al. 1997). These species may not be able to take advantage of the higher light in the spring because of the cold temperatures and instead wait for the warmer temperatures of summer to gain carbon, which obviates the need to down-regulate A_{max}.

Declines in A_{max} result primarily from reduced mesophyll conductances to CO_2 and not greater limitations on the diffusion of CO_2 because of lowered g_s (Taylor and

Pearcy 1976; Yoshie and Kawano 1986; Yoshie and Yoshida 1987). Lower mesophyll conductances result from a loss of RUBISCO (Taylor and Pearcy 1976; Rothstein and Zak 2001) and decreases in the activation state of this and associated enzymes (Pearcy 1999). These processes serve to bring fixation processes in line with reduced ET capabilities.

Many summer-green herbs, such as *Asclepias exaltata* L., *Fragaria virginiana* Duchesne, and *Parasenecio auriculatus* (DC.) J.R. Grant (Ida and Kudo 2010), produce cohorts of leaves well after canopy closure. Strawberry (*F. virginiana*) continually replaces leaves throughout the season with those more suited to the prevailing environmental conditions (Jurik and Chabot 1986), thus maximizing whole plant carbon gain over the season. *Parasenecio auriculata* (DC.) J.R. Grant, in contrast, maintains a positive carbon budget all through the deep shade of summer by continually producing new shade-adapted leaves that persist throughout the summer, gaining as much as 80 percent of its total carbon during this period (Ida and Kudo 2010). Species that produce a single flush of leaves appear to depend more on the brief high light period prior to canopy closure for most of their annual carbon gain, whereas those that retain their leaves are able to establish a positive carbon budget during the low light period in summer, even gaining the major portion of their carbon at this time. The biennial *Hydrophyllum appendiculatum* Michx. is a species that exhibits the former strategy (Morgan 1968).

Interestingly, *Viola pubescens*, a summer-green that produces leaves prior to canopy closure, has the ability to decrease specific leaf mass during the transition to low light to a degree not observed in other species (Rothstein and Zak 2001). This morphological adjustment, which occurs presumably through continued leaf expansion after canopy closure, allows the leaf to take on characteristics more typical of shade leaves and contributes to shade acclimation.

Photosynthetic Responses to Sunflecks

Once the canopy closes, sunflecks represent the main supply of PFD and may provide up to 80 percent of total daily PFD (Horton and Neufeld 1998). Herbs depend on these brief periods of high light to gain the bulk of their carbon after canopy closure, which may constitute up to 60 percent of their total carbon gain in some cases (Chazdon 1988). The importance of sunflecks for the growth of understory herbs varies, however, depending on a number of factors, including prevailing forest conditions such as background levels of diffuse PFD, intensity and duration of sunflecks, temporal patterns of sunflecks (morning or afternoon, in rapid succession, or spaced widely apart), and interactions of sunflecks with vapor pressure, temperature, and drought. Together, the myriad combinations make it difficult to determine how a species will respond to sunflecks unless detailed modeling and field measurements are made (Pearcy and Way 2012; Porcar-Castell and Palmroth 2012; Way and Pearcy 2012).

Among the studies of understory herbs that we reviewed, only two, one by Pfitsch and Pearcy (1989a, 1989b, 1992) and another by Koizumi and Oshima (1993) have attempted to determine the contribution of sunflecks to carbon gain in *temperate* understory herbs. Using shadow bands that were designed to eliminate sunflecks, Pfitsch and Pearcy (1992) found that *Adenocaulon bicolor*, a common herb in redwood forests, became smaller and had less reproductive biomass. Plants receiving sunflecks did not increase in size, perhaps due to other effects associated with sunflecks, such as water stress and high leaf temperatures. However, the shadow bands also reduced the incoming diffuse radiation, which may have confounded interpretation of whether the growth effects were due solely to removal of the sunflecks, even though this factor was accounted for statistically. Nearly 70 percent of the carbon gain in the field may have been due to sunflecks. Koizumi and Oshima (1993) compared sunfleck responses of a summer-green herb (*Syneilesis palmata* Thunb. Maxim) to an evergreen herb (*Pyrola japonica*) in a warm temperate forest in Japan. Using steady-state light curves of photosynthesis combined with detailed analyses of the sunfleck dynamics at their site, they concluded that sunflecks contribute at most 7–10 percent of the carbon gain from May through July for *S. palmata*, and only 2–3 percent for *P. japonica*. The summer-green *S. palmata* is able to respond to sunflecks more dynamically because of its higher L_{sat} and A_{max}. In reality, though, these estimated contributions due to sunflecks may be too high. Calculations derived from steady-state responses of photosynthesis to PFD most likely overestimate expected carbon gain (sometimes by as much as 42 percent) due to the failure to take into account the dynamics of photosynthetic induction and de-induction (Pearcy 1990; Sims and Pearcy 1993; Pearcy et al. 1994, Porcar-Castell and Palmroth 2012, Way and Pearcy 2012), as well as possible photoinhibition under prolonged sunflecks. Furthermore, in the work reported by Koizumi and Oshima, high background levels of diffuse PFD may have reduced the relative impact of the sunflecks (Chazdon 1986).

In a study of tropical understory herbs, Watling et al. (1997) showed enhanced growth for two Australian understory species under fluctuating versus constant light of similar daily total PFD. In some cases, biomass was two to three times greater in fluctuating light. Aside from these studies, we know of no other attempts to quantify the importance of sunflecks for the growth of understory herbs. Whether differences exist among the phenological groups in their response to sunflecks, therefore, is still a very open question. However, given the much lower rates of photosynthesis and the potentially longer induction times of evergreen leaves (see below), we suspect that evergreen/winter-green species may respond less to sunflecks than either spring ephemerals or summer-greens.

Factors Affecting Utilization of Sunflecks—Induction and De-Induction Times

The induction state of a leaf is its photosynthetic capacity upon sudden exposure to high PFD after a prolonged period of low PFD, relative to steady-state rates at saturating PFD (Chazdon and Pearcy 1986a, 1986b). Induction involves light-induced increases in g_s, increases in amounts of enzymes responsible for RuBP regeneration, and RUBISCO activation (Chazdon and Pearcy 1986a; Sassenrath-Cole and Pearcy 1992; Sage 1993; Sage and Seemann 1993). Usually, changes in g_s lag behind those of photosynthesis, since activation times for RUBISCO and other enzymes can be on the order of just 1–2 minutes (Pearcy 1999), while changes in stomatal aperture may require 5–20 minutes. In very short flecks, g_s may even reach a maximum after the fleck has passed (Pearcy 1987).

The induction state is affected by prior environmental conditions, such as the length of the preceding low light period and the temporal sequence and intensity of those sunflecks (Chazdon and Pearcy 1986a, 1986b; Tang et al. 1999; Pearcy 1999). Induction velocity, or change in induction per unit of time after being exposed to a sunfleck, also depends on sunfleck intensity and the physiological status of the plant, such as whether it is drought-stressed or suffering from temperature limitations.

A number of researchers have suggested that shade-tolerant plants induce faster and maintain induction longer than shade-intolerant plants after a return to low light (Paliwal et al. 1994; Küppers et al. 1996), but a meta-survey by Vico et al. (2011) found that shade tolerance was less important than plant functional group and drought tolerance. In a survey of both woody and herbaceous plants from shady and sunny habitats, Ögren and Sundin (1996) found that the mean induction time to reach 90 percent of A_{max} for shade plants was only about 7 minutes, whereas fast-growing and slow-growing sun plants took 18 and 32 minutes, respectively. Yanhong et al. (1994) found faster induction in leaves of *Quercus serrata* Murray seedlings grown in low light (50 µmol m^{-2} s^{-1}) compared to leaves grown in high light (500 µmol m^{-2} s^{-1}). A more recent review of rates in woody species, however, found no clear patterns among sun or shade plants, except that gymnosperms take longer to induce (Naumburg and Ellsworth 2000). In the C_4 grass *Microstegium vimineum*, leaves showed no induction differences when grown in either 25 percent or 50 percent light, with leaves from both treatments reaching 90 percent maximum induction in 10–13 minutes (Horton and Neufeld 1998). Failure of the low light leaves to induce faster may have been because leaves were already partially induced at the lower light level.

Hull (2001) found that the spring ephemeral *Erythronium americanum* and the summer-green species *Podophyllum peltatum* L. both required higher light to maintain induction than did the summer-green species *Maianthemum racemosum* (L.) Link. and *Arisaema triphyllum* L. Schott. The spring ephemerals were more clearly delineated from the summer-green herbs by the minimum PFD necessary for maintaining induction, rather than induction velocity itself. Since typical background diffuse PFD in temperate forests is similar to the levels required by the summer-green species, they are likely to be in a moderate to high induction state throughout the day and primed to take advantage of an initial series of sunflecks (Hull 2001).

Among a group of tropical understory plants, Kursar and Coley (1993) observed that plants with shorter-lived leaves (~ 1 year) induced more quickly than plants with longer-lived (> 4 years) leaves. Induction times to 90 percent A_{max} were only 3–6 minutes for plants with short-lived leaves compared to 11–36 minutes for plants with long-lived leaves. Using oxygen electrodes, they found that induction of O_2 production was also faster in short-lived leaves, suggesting that slower induction times in longer-lived leaves were caused by slower activation of RUBISCO rather than a delay in the induction of ET. Thus, mean induction times may be longer for evergreen/winter-green herbs, and if there is seasonal adjustment to changing light conditions, activation times may vary accordingly.

Loss of photosynthetic induction begins once the PFD drops below the minimum level necessary to maintain an induced state. This occurs in two phases: an initial fast component, thought to be associated with deactivation of PCR enzymes, especially RUBISCO (Sassenrath-Cole and Pearcy 1992), followed by a progressive loss of g_s, which occurs more slowly (Chazdon 1988). Typical time constants for deactivation of associated enzymes are in the range of 3–5 minutes, while g_s may continue to change over longer periods of up to an hour or more. Species that maintain induction for longer periods of time will be better able to utilize subsequent sunflecks, including those that occur widely spaced apart, than species that de-induce rapidly. At present, there are no clear patterns with regard to which types of plants maintain induction for longer periods of time. Poorter and Oberbauer (1993) found that an understory tree maintained induction longer than a pioneer species, whereas Hull (2001) found no correlation of induction loss rate with phenological grouping among the understory herbs he studied. Induction losses may be more rapid in high light grown plants (Tinoco-Ojanguren and Pearcy 1993a, 1993b; Poorter and Oberbauer 1993; Horton and Neufeld 1998), suggesting that under these conditions, the emphasis is on maintaining water use efficiency at the expense of carbon assimilation. In addition, time of day may influence induction losses. Limitations on g_s can be brought about by increasing Δw in the afternoon, but also possibly because biochemical limitations change from morning to afternoon (Tinoco-Ojanguren and Pearcy 1993a; Poorter and Oberbauer 1993).

Direct comparative studies of induction/de-induction times between trees and herbs have not been done. Among the limited data that do exist, there is some evidence that graminoids and plants from arid habitats may have slightly faster induction times (Vico et al. 2011). It has not yet been demonstrated that either understory herbs or trees might gain a competitive advantage because of more efficient utilization of sunflecks.

Photoinhibition and Sunflecks

In a fraction of a second, a sunfleck can expose the leaf of an understory herb to over 100 times the background PFD (Chazdon and Pearcy 1991). This sudden rise in PFD is often utilized effectively for photosynthesis, but when fixation processes are overwhelmed, the leaf is unable to dissipate this excess energy without harm to the photosynthetic reaction centers, resulting in photoinhibition (Björkman and Demmig-Adams 1995). Leaves adapted to shady habitats, and with low rates of photosynthesis, have a reduced capacity to process excess light. While sunflecks contribute substantially to carbon gain beneath the closed canopy, there is also a potential for sunflecks to be injurious should they have too high intensity or too long duration (Pearcy et al. 1994).

Photoinhibition in temperate herbs can occur when high light coincides with low temperatures, as in the spring, autumn, or winter, or in the summer when shade-tolerant herbs are suddenly exposed to long sunflecks with high PFD. The dissipation of this excess energy can be accomplished by conversion into chemical compounds through fixation processes or other metabolic pathways, by re-emission through fluorescence, or lastly, by conversion to heat in the pigment beds (thermal dissipation). Once metabolic pathways are saturated, however, the only two viable alternatives are fluorescence and thermal dissipation. The latter is thought to be more important because fluorescence can at most dissipate only about 3–4 percent of the energy (Björkman and Demmig-Adams 1995). Development of a trans-thylakoid pH gradient in the presence of reduced ascorbate optimizes the conversion of the carotenoids violaxanthin and antheraxanthin to zeaxanthin, which plays a major role in the thermal dissipation of excess light energy away from the harvesting antennae (Demmig-Adams et al. 1996; Watling et al. 1997). The end result is that the excess energy is liberated as heat, preventing the deleterious formation of triplet excited chlorophyll and singlet oxygen. Sun leaves accumulate greater amounts of xanthophyll cycle intermediates than shade leaves (Königer et al. 1995), and leaves of plants exposed to sunflecks also show enhancement of the pigment concentrations (Watling et al. 1997; Schiefthaler et al. 1999). Low temperatures can also stimulate the formation of large amounts of zea-xanthin, which may prepare a leaf for subsequent exposure to high light in order to reduce the amount of potential photoinhibition that might occur (Oberhuber and Bauer 1991).

Low Temperature Photoinhibition

Spring ephemerals, early leafing summer-greens, and winter-green/evergreens are most at risk from low temperature photoinhibition, but relatively few studies have been done on these plants. Germino and Smith (2000) found small amounts of low temperature photoinhibition in *Erythronium grandiflorum* Pursh (a close relative of the spring ephemeral *E. americanum*) on sunny days following nights with frost, but photosynthetic capacity recovered by sunset of the same day. Appreciable carbon gain was possible even though temperatures were quite low at this time of year in large part because low temperature photoinhibition was not a serious problem. A similar lack of cold temperature photoinhibition has been reported for *E. americanum* by Gandin et al. (2011a). It is likely that most spring ephemerals have mechanisms to avoid low temperature photoinhibition, but no other studies are known of at this time.

The situation with regard to evergreen/winter-green species is more problematic. These species maintain functional leaves for a much longer time, are exposed to the greatest temperature variations on a seasonal basis, and can potentially be subject to both low and high temperature photoinhibition. Skillman et al. (1996) suggest that tradeoffs exist between the frequency of leaf production and the balance between photosynthetic acclimation and photoinhibition. The winter-green *Hexastylis ari-folia*, which produces one flush of leaves per year, suffers greater low temperature photoinhibition than the heteroptic *Heuchera americana*, which produces new leaves in the spring and autumn. In northern Japan, overwintered leaves of *Pachysandra ter-minalis* do not show any low temperature photoinhibition in early spring, although they do show high temperature photoinhibition later in the summer when exposed to prolonged high light (Yoshie and Kawano 1986). In Europe, east-facing leaves of the evergreen vine *Hedera helix* L. show substantial photoinhibition in the autumn after being exposed to high light, but north-facing leaves do not (Oberhuber and Bauer 1991).

Many evergreens produce anthocyanins when exposed to cold and high light (Chalker-Scott 1999; Hughes et al. 2005; Hughes and Smith 2007; Hughes 2011). The leaves of *Galax urceolata* turn red in the autumn after the onset of cold weather, and Hughes et al. (2005) have shown that such leaves are better protected against pho-toinhibition than green leaves upon sudden exposure to high light. These antho-cyanins, which can be located on both the adaxial and abaxial surfaces, protect the leaf primarily from excess green light, which can be especially detrimental to cells in the lower mesophyll layers of a leaf (Neill and Gould 2003). Anthocyanins may also act as antioxidants, which in cold conditions would function more efficiently than temperature-sensitive enzymatic antioxidants (Hughes 2011).

In conclusion, low temperature photoinhibition is probably not a major problem for spring ephemerals, but it can cause significant depressions of A_{max} in some, but not all, evergreens. Heteroptic species with specialized overwintering leaves may be less prone to such injury. However, production of anthocyanins can partially alleviate this by intercepting excess green light and/or by acting as temperature-insensitive antioxidants.

High Temperature Photoinhibition

Summer-green herbs growing in the shade beneath a closed canopy will suffer photo-inhibition if exposed to high light for a prolonged time (Critchley 1998), and a most interesting question is whether or not they do so when exposed to natural sunflecks. The negative impacts of photoinhibition may be ameliorated by either avoiding or tol-erating high PFDs. Avoidance is best illustrated by *Oxalis oregana*, which grows in very shady habitats below redwood trees (background PFD ~ 3–4 μmol m^{-2} s^{-1}). During sunflecks, the PFD can quickly rise to 1,800 μmol m^{-2} s^{-1}, and within six minutes, leaves reorient nearly parallel to the solar beam, lowering the intercepted radiation by 90 per-cent. If the leaves are immobilized, severe photoinhibition can occur within 30 minutes (Björkman and Powles 1981; Björkman and Demmig-Adams 1995). Banner (1998) has shown a similar phenomenon in *O. acetosella* L., but leaf folding only proceeds to 60 degrees, which attenuates PFD by just 50 percent, which is still above L_{sat} for this species. However, if sunfleck durations were short, little photoinhibition was detected. *Xanthoxalis grandis* (Small) Small, which is common in rich woods and beneath hem-locks in the eastern United States, does exhibit leaf folding movements in response to light, but the relationship to photoinhibition has not yet been elucidated (Levy and Moore 1993). Muraoka et al. (1998) have shown a similar behavior in *Arisaema hetero-phyllum*. This species displays leaves horizontally in intact forest understories, but in disturbed forests with higher PFD, it folds them along the main vein so that the blades are parallel to the incoming light, which apparently prevents photoinhibition in this species. We do not know of any similar studies on active leaf orientation changes in tree seedlings, although it is well known that leaf angles decline with depth through the canopy for overstory trees (Kinerson 1979; McMillen and McClendon 1979; Pickett and Kempf 1980).

Studies of photoinhibition in temperate forest herbs under natural sunfleck condi-tions are scarce, and the majority of studies have been done on tropical understory species (Königer et al. 1995; Logan et al. 1997; Schiefthaler et al. 1999; Watling et al. 1997). Pearcy et al. (1994) concluded that most sunflecks have too low PFD or are too short to cause lasting photoinhibition, but sensitivity does increase at higher tem-peratures. For example, in *Alocasia macrorrhizos* (L.) G. Don., injury does not occur at a leaf temperature of 40°C under a nearly saturating PFD of 375 μmol m^{-2} s^{-1} while it does at a similar PFD once leaf temperatures pass this critical point (Pearcy et al. 1994). Banner (1998) similarly found little evidence for photoinhibition in *Oxalis ace-tosella* L. after sunflecks of up to 1,000 μmol m^{-2} s^{-1}, but some inhibition was recorded after sunflecks of 2,000 μmol m^{-2} s^{-1}. Even so, nearly complete recovery occurred after about 30 minutes, suggesting that lasting effects were minimal. However, prolonged exposure to high light resulted in photodamage and leaf loss in this species, which may explain its restriction to shady sites.

Leaves exposed to a series of high light flecks may show a capacity for acclima-tion through increased resistance to further photoinhibition, most likely by increas-ing the pools of xanthophyll cycle intermediates that are used to thermally dissipate the excess energy. This may be particularly important for herbs with evergreen or winter-green leaves, which are exposed to many more episodes of high light. For summer-greens that are suddenly exposed to high light through formation of a gap in the canopy, increased resistance to photoinhibition may occur by production of new leaves better adapted to high light conditions (Pearcy et al. 1994). Finally, it should be noted that increased resistance to photoinhibition is not necessarily associated with increases in A_{max}. In fact, A_{max} is often reduced by sudden exposure to high light. Rather, increased resistance may be a mechanism to maintain some carbon gain in response to the change in the light environment until either new leaves are produced or the older ones have a chance to acclimate, which may take several days in some species (Pearcy et al. 1994).

WATER RELATIONS OF UNDERSTORY HERBS

Although there is no pronounced drought season in temperate deciduous forests, understory herbs may be limited by insufficient water at times, particularly in the summer, but also in the winter when soils are frozen. Competition for soil water between herbs and trees is evidenced by the large increases in biomass in the understory seen after trenching experiments (see extensive review by Coomes and Grubb 2000). However, despite the importance of water for the productivity of understory plants, less attention has been paid to the water relations of understory herbs as compared to photosynthesis and respiration.

Stomatal Conductance Patterns

Stomatal conductance will vary among understory herbs because of differences in stomatal densities, sizes, sensitivity to Δw, and responses to PFD. In most studies, g_s responds strongly to PFD, increasing sharply in the morning as PFD rises, and then dropping in the afternoon as PFD decreases. Eliáš (1983) found that g_s for a variety of understory herbs peaked between 9 and 11 a.m., but that sunflecks had a strong influence on rates, even among leaves on the same plant. For *Mercurialis perennis*, PFD and Δw were the two variables most responsible for variations in g_s (Kriebitzsch 1984). Schulz and Adams (1995) found that extended periods of high light caused leaf temperatures of *Eurybia macrophylla* to quickly rise, increasing the Δw and causing large (50 percent) decreases in g_s. Such decreases effectively reduced E even when Δw was large, although not enough to prevent a measurable drop in leaf water potentials (ψ_w). After the high light event was over, recovery of g_s often took several hours, even after ψ_w had fully recovered to pre-high light values. On a diurnal basis, PFD beneath the canopy drops substantially by early afternoon and as a consequence, g_s often declines earlier in the forest understory than outside (pers. obs.).

Maximum values for g_s among understory herbs are generally low (table 3.3), with values ranging between 0.050 and 0.350 mol H_2O m^{-2} s^{-1} (Körner et al. 1979; Eliáš 1983; Kriebitzsch 1992b; Schulz and Adams 1995; Gandin et al. 2011a) but occasionally higher (Davison et al. unpubl. data, 0.600 mol H_2O m^{-2} s^{-1} for *Asclepias exaltata*). Since g_s often scales with A_{max} in a variety of plants (Yoshie and Kawano 1986; Pearcy et al. 1987; Yoshie and Yoshida 1987), spring ephemerals should have the highest g_s followed in turn by summer-greens and then winter-green/evergreen species. While spring ephemerals do appear to have somewhat higher g_s, inspection of table 3.3 shows nearly identical values for g_s among summer-greens and winter-green/evergreens. Kriebitzsch (1992b) showed a moderate dependency of g_s on Δw among several

Table 3.3 Maximum Values for Stomatal Conductance (gs) among Phenological Groups of Herbs.

Phenological Grouping	Maximum g_s (mol H_2O m^{-2} s^{-1})	Reference
Spring Ephemerals		
Allium ursinum	0.100	Kriebitzsch 1992b[#]
Allium tricoccum	0.204	Taylor and Pearcy 1976[+*]
Anemone raddeana	0.310	Yoshie and Yoshida 1987[*]
Arum maculatum	0.166	Kriebitzsch 1992b
Erythronium americanum	0.187	Taylor and Pearcy 1976
Mean	**0.193**	
Summer-greens		
Aralia nudicaulis	0.160	Landhäusser et al. 1997[*]
Asclepias exaltata	0.600	Davison et al. (unpubl.)[#]
Geum urbanum	0.058	Eliáš 1983
Glechoma hirsuta	0.067	Eliáš 1983
Hordelymus europaeus	0.060	Kriebitzsch 1992b
Lamium galeobdolon ssp. galeobdolon	0.092	Eliáš 1983[+#]
Melica uniflora	0.069	Kriebitzsch 1992b
Mercurialis perennis	0.083; 0.105	Eliáš 1983; Kriebitzsch 1992b
Microstegium vimineum	0.100	Horton and Neufeld 1998[*]
Podophyllum peltatum	0.250	Taylor and Pearcy 1976
Polygonatum latifolium	0.075	Eliáš 1983
Rubus pubescens	0.075	Landhäusser et al. 1997
Solidago flexicaulis	0.129	Taylor and Pearcy 1976
Trillium grandiflorum	0.092	Taylor and Pearcy 1976
Viola mirabilis	0.100	Eliáš 1983
Mean	**0.132**	
Winter-greens/Evergreens		
Asarum europaeum	0.100	Kriebitzsch (1992b)
Cornus canadensis	0.100	Landhäusser et al. 1997
Galax urceolata	0.140	McCarron 1995[*]
Pachysandra terminalis	0.160	Yoshie and Kawano 1986[*]
Pyrola asarifolia	0.153	Landhäusser et al. 1997
Mean	**0.131**	

\# Values from field measurements.

* Values from laboratory measurements.

+ Values converted from cm s^{-1} or mm s^{-1} using a correction factor of 1 mm s^{-1} = 0.0416 mol m^{-2} s^{-1}.

species of herbs. The steepest declines in g_s in response to increasing Δw were found in the spring ephemerals, with lesser dependencies among the other species. *Mercurialis perennis* showed little response to Δw in summer, leading to high transpiration rates and low water potentials. Across groups, one might expect that species resistant to cavitation (most likely the evergreens) would show the least sensitivity to Δw since they could better maintain open stomata in response to increased drought stress.

Water Potentials of Understory Herbs

Few studies have followed diurnal and seasonal patterns of ψ_w in understory herbs. Early studies by Eliáš (1981) showed a range of minimum ψ_w from -0.32 to -0.63 MPa among several spring ephemerals and summer-greens, with an occasional reading as low as -0.90 MPa. Masarovičová and Eliáš (1986) showed that water saturation deficits (a surrogate for ψ_w) increased when plants were exposed to sunflecks, as did Schulz and Adams (1995). Kriebitzsch (1993) followed changes in minimum ψ_w over two growing seasons among six herbs in a beech forest in Germany. The two spring ephemerals (*Allium ursinum* and *Arum maculatum*) showed high ψ_w in both years due to low temperatures and Δw and the fact that soil water contents were high in the spring. The summer-green herbs and grasses developed very low ψ_w by midsummer, ranging between -2.0 and -3.0 MPa, respectively. Because understory herbs have the majority of their roots concentrated between 5 and 15 cm in depth (Plašilová 1970) where soil water deficits can rapidly develop, the occurrence of low ψ_w in these herbs is not unexpected, even at the low irradiance levels typical beneath the canopy. In the evergreen *Galax urceolata*, McCarron (1995) found that ψ_w were highest in midsummer (minimum ψ_w of -0.40 MPa), most likely because of the low PFD then, and lowest in winter (minimum ψ_w of -0.80 to -1.2 MPa). On one particular date in February, the air warmed considerably while the soil remained frozen, and PFD was quite high because of the lack of a canopy. As a result, ψ_w dropped as low as -1.6 MPa (McCarron 1995). In summary, spring ephemerals will exhibit the least water stress because of abundant soil moisture in early spring, summer-greens should exhibit greater water stress in midsummer due to warm temperatures and competition with trees and other understory plants for limited soil moisture, and winter-green/evergreens should have the lowest ψ_w in winter, when cold soils prevent the movement of water from roots to leaves.

Hydraulic Conductances in Understory Herbs

The ability to conduct water from the roots to the leaves is a major determining factor of the water balance of plants. For understory herbs, almost nothing is known concerning their hydraulic conductivities (K_h). Sobieraj (2002) worked on characteristics of K_h in petioles of the evergreen *Galax urceolata*. Xylem elements in this species are very small (80 percent of diameters < 30 μm) and may enhance tolerance of cold-induced embolisms, an important feature for an evergreen. *Galax urceolata* is also extremely drought-tolerant. Embolisms in the petioles do not appear until water potentials drop below -2.0 MPa, and even at water potentials as low as -4.0 MPa, K_h is still near 50 percent of maximum (fig. 3.10). This pattern is more typical of that found in desert plants (Pockman and Sperry 2000), and suggests that *G. urceolata* periodically experiences

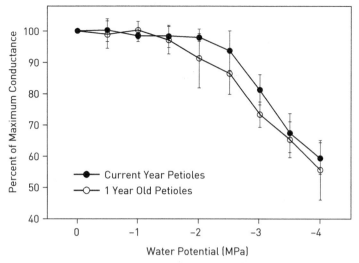

FIGURE 3.10 Vulnerability curve for mean hydraulic conductance (± SE) in *Galax urceolata* petioles. There were no statistically significant ($p < .05$) differences between petiole age classes ($n = 5$ for each age class). A pressure sleeve was used to induce embolisms, and conductances were measured using a Sperry apparatus (Sperry et al. 1988). Data from Sobieraj (2002).

severe water stress, perhaps because it is shallowly rooted in soils that can substantially dry out between rainfalls. Since the lowest ψ_w found in the field were only −1.6 MPa, *G. urceolata* may rarely embolize in response to typical droughts. But soil water potential values as low as −2.5 MPa can occur during severe droughts in the upper soil layers of deciduous forests in Tennessee (Wullschleger, pers. comm.) and are low enough to possibly induce at least a minimal number of embolisms. Maximum K_hs in *G. urceolata* are also quite low and may restrict g_s in this species to low values, which in turn prevents water deficits from building up rapidly. We suspect that other evergreen understory herbs may display similar hydraulic properties. Spring ephemerals should have higher K_hs associated with their higher g_s, but some aspects of their morphology, such as a lack of an aboveground stem, make determination of K_h in this group technically difficult. As a group, there is some evidence that herbs might have higher K_hs than woody plants, due in part to the differences in physical structural of the xylem between these two groups (Camacho-B et al. 1974).

COMMUNITY LEVEL CARBON AND WATER EXCHANGE

Carbon Exchange

Herbs generally make up less than 3 percent of the total biomass of temperate forests and contribute nearly the same proportion toward aboveground net primary productivity (ANPP). In the northern hardwood forests at Hubbard Brook, New Hampshire, ANPP is 2.7 percent of the ecosystem total (Bormann and Likens 1979); evergreens and summer-greens comprise 2.2 percent of that amount, with spring ephemerals (mainly *E. americanum*) contributing the remaining 0.5 percent. In a Tennessee forest, herbs constitute 3.1 percent of the standing crop, but take up 7 percent of the net photosynthetic carbon gain (Harris et al. 1975). Early estimates of the actual values for ANPP by understory herbs ranged between 10 and 100 g m^{-2} yr^{-1} (Ovington 1962), but later studies by Bazzaz and Bliss (1971) and Kriebitzsch (1992c) have extended the upper limit to between 135 and 175 g m^{-2} yr^{-1} although values fluctuate from year to year, depending on variation in light, temperature, and drought.

The relative contribution of herbs to ANPP does not always correlate directly with leaf level measures of carbon exchange. For example, despite high assimilation rates, grasses contribute relatively little to total understory ANPP in beech forests in Germany because of their low LAI. In contrast, *Mercurialis perennis* and *Allium ursinum* have more moderate gas exchange rates but high LAI and dominate in terms of ANPP (Kriebitzsch 1992c).

How much of the carbon assimilated aboveground is lost to belowground processes is poorly understood. Schulze (1972) estimated that belowground respiration in *Oxalis acetosella* constituted 28 percent of aboveground assimilation, while Kriebitzsch and Regel (1982) estimated losses of 26 percent for *Mercurialis perennis*. After reviewing the literature in this area, Kriebitzsch (1992c) concluded that the best estimates ranged between 20 and 30 percent of aboveground assimilation. In the spring and autumn, when there is still considerable aboveground activity by herbs, belowground respiration rates will be limited by cold soil temperatures. Appreciable soil warming can occur during the day, though, because of the lack of a canopy, which could stimulate respiration rates (Kawano 1970). Once the canopy closes in the spring, and once a snow cover is established in the winter, diurnal variations in soil temperature are greatly reduced, and estimates of belowground respiration are easier to model.

The translocation of carbon from above to belowground storage organs has been shown repeatedly to be important for growth and reproduction of understory herbs. Tissue et al. (1995) showed that 62–76 percent of $^{14}CO_2$ given to plants was stored in the corms and then later used to support the growth of reproductive structures and new leaves, roots, and corms. This confirmed earlier studies showing the high dependency of growth and reproduction on stored reserves (Whigham 1990; Zimmerman and Whigham 1992). A substantial portion of the translocated carbon was assimilated late in the season, even as photosynthetic rates declined and leaves began to senesce. Similar findings were reported by Hutchings and Barkham (1976) who suggested that carbon assimilated in the shade of summer was then transported to rhizomes in *Mercurialis perennis*. Muller (1979) showed that cormlet weights of *Erythronium albidum* Nutt. increased over 100 percent during leaf senescence due to translocation of carbohydrates from above to belowground tissues. In another spring ephemeral, *Adonis ramose* Franch., up to 25 percent of current photosynthates were translocated belowground (Horibata et al. 2007), while in *Corydalis ambigua* Cham. & Schltdl., up to 50 percent was translocated to the tubers, mainly late in the season as light levels began decreasing due to canopy closure (Kudo and Ida 2010). Ida and Kudo (2008) found that ~ 94 percent of recent photosynthate was retained in leaves and stems of *Trillium apetalon* Makino during flowering in the early spring, while after flowering during the summer, most recent photosynthates were shunted to the rhizome. Considering the substantial proportion of biomass belowground for understory herbs, the importance of these processes in determining carbon mass budgets for ecosystems cannot be underestimated. Studies similar to those of Kudo and colleagues have contributed greatly to understanding the variety of carbon allocation strategies available to understory herbs, but there are relatively few similar studies done on North American forest herbs, especially for summer-green and evergreen species.

Among the species Kriebitzsch (1993) tested, a spring ephemeral, *Arum maculatum*, had the highest transpiration rates, although the maximum values obtained for the grasses *Hordelymus europaeus* (L.) Jessen ex Harz and *Melica uniflora* Retz. and the herb *Mercurialis perennis* were similar. The evergreen *Asarum europaeum* L. and the spring ephemeral *Allium ursinum* both had the lowest water loss rates. The single most important factor in determining transpiration rates was PFD, while Δw played an important secondary role. For example, 1983 was a sunnier year than 1982, and transpiration was enhanced in 1983 between 60–200 percent over that in 1982. In concordance with the community-wide patterns of ANPP, Kriebitzsch (1993) calculated that *M. perennis* and *A. ursinum* achieved the highest water loss rates per unit ground area because of their higher LAIs, while the grasses and *A. maculatum*, with their lower LAIs, had much lower loss rates.

Kriebitzsch (1993) integrated water loss rates across the species groups in his extensive studies in Germany over two seasons. Using empirical models to predict leaf level water loss over the season, he scaled up to the community level by multiplying those rates by the LAI of each species and found that understory herbs could transpire between 20–40 mm of water per year, which is ~ 10 percent of the total water lost from the system.

ECOPHYSIOLOGICAL RESPONSES OF UNDERSTORY HERBS TO VARIOUS ASPECTS OF GLOBAL CHANGE

Global increases in atmospheric CO_2 concentrations, warming of air and soil temperatures, elevated nitrogen deposition (chapter 20, this volume), and high tropospheric ozone (O_3) are all potentially serious threats to understory herbs. The multitude and complexity of interactions among these factors makes predicting long-term outcomes for forest herbs exceedingly difficult, especially when one considers that few multi-factorial experiments have been done (Beier 2004; Baeten et al. 2010). Furthermore, poor dispersal abilities (chapter 5, this volume; Whigham 2004) and fragmentation of forests into isolated patches may limit the ability of forest herbs to migrate to more suitable habitats in the face of climate change (chapter 18, this volume). We conclude this section of our chapter by examining climate change impacts on forest herbs from an ecophysiological perspective, with the goal of providing mechanistic explanations for both observed and predicted responses to climate change (see Popović and Lindquist 2010).

Ecophysiological impacts of global change on understory herbs can be both direct, which includes abiotic factors such as soil and air temperatures, altered precipitation patterns and amounts, and elevated CO_2, nitrogen, and O_3; and indirect, which includes modifications of the understory microclimate and habitat resulting from the responses of the overstory vegetation to climate change. Such indirect changes would involve phenological shifts by both under- and overstory plants, as well as changes in LAI and soil moisture, along with potentially more intense competition from neighboring plants (Belote et al. 2003; Souza et al. 2010).

Indirect Effects through Warming-Induced Changes in Phenology

Warming from rising CO_2 concentrations is predicted to reduce the number of cold episodes in the winter and to cause more rapid increases in minimum night temperatures rather than higher daytime maxima. Although this would result in smaller diurnal temperature amplitudes (IPCC 2007), the global trend for decreasing amplitudes has ceased, and there is now considerable evidence that it varies geographically (Trenberth et al. 2007). Warming results in earlier leafing out of the overstory (Menzel and Fabian 1999; Schwartz and Reiter 2000; Richardson et al. 2006; Schwartz et al. 2006), delayed senescence in the autumn (Jeong et al. 2011; Dragoni and Rahman 2012), and a general lengthening of the growing period (Cleland et al. 2007; Jeong et al. 2011), although this can be quite species-specific (Juknys et al. 2012). In the United States, leaf fall was delayed anywhere from 17 to 40 days over the period of 1989 to 2008 (Dragoni and Rahman 2012) and was correlated with decreases in cooling degree days, more so for southern than northern forests. The lack of an effect in the southern Appalachians is most likely due to the absence of any discernible temperature or precipitation trends in this region (Warren and Bradford 2010). Warming also induces earlier leaf-out and flowering in a broad range of understory herbs (Rogers 1983b; Fitter and Fitter 2002; Fitter et al. 1995; Miller-Rushing and Primack 2008; Liang et al. 2012), but it is not yet clear whether the advancement in herb phenology is synchronized with that of the overstory.

A lengthening of the leaf season will affect understory herbs differently depending on their phenological strategy, but in most cases will have negative consequences for growth and flowering because it will extend the periods of low light and impair photosynthetic carbon gain (Noda et al. 2007). As noted earlier in this chapter, most spring ephemerals and early leafing summer-green forest herbs rely heavily on high PFD prior to canopy closure to obtain the majority of their annual carbon uptake (Goryshina 1972; Pearcy and Taylor 1976; Lapointe 2001; Constable et al. 2007). Evergreen and winter-green herbs, in addition, also depend on high light in the autumn after the overstory senesces (Yamamura 1984). Some summer-green herbs, such as *Parasenecio auriculata* (Ida and Kudo 2010) and the giant summer-green herbs found in the far eastern forests of Asia (Tani and Kudo 2006) might be better able to acclimate to an extended low light period because they continually produce shade-adapted leaves after canopy closure, which allows these plants to maintain a positive whole plant carbon balance. In fact, some of these plants accumulate the majority of their carbon *after* canopy closure. An extended leaf-out period could result in selection against summer-green herbs that produce only one flush of leaves in the spring (e.g., mayapple [*Podophyllum peltatum*] or bloodroot [*Sanguinaria canadensis*]), compared to those with continuous flushing throughout the summer.

Because overstory trees and understory herbs respond to different environmental cues (Rich et al. 2008; Liang et al. 2012), their current phenologies could become desynchronized in response to warming. Spring ephemerals, for example, respond strongly to snow melt and the subsequent increase in soil temperatures (Muller 1978; Takashi and Kudo 2008; Yoshie 2008), whereas overstory trees are more responsive to photoperiod and air temperatures (Richardson et al. 2006; Polgar and Primack 2011). If canopy trees leaf out too early, the ability of spring ephemerals to utilize the brief period of high light before canopy closure will be compromised unless they too are able to accelerate their phenology to match that of the overstory.

Routhier and Lapointe (2002) tested this idea by comparing the growth of *Trillium erectum* L. plants beneath sugar maple canopies along a north-to-south gradient. Sugar maple trees at the northern sites leaf out at cooler temperatures than those at southern sites, while *T. erectum* sprouted at all sites once temperatures reached ~ 7°C. As a result, the period of time between leaf expansion of *T. erectum* and canopy closure was shorter for the northernmost population, and those plants were smaller and allocated less carbon to rhizomes and fruits than plants at the southern sites. Ida and Kudo (2008) took this a step further and conducted a shading study with *T. apetalon* in a deciduous forest in Japan. Neutral density filters (83 percent shade) were placed over one set of plants from flowering (nearly coincident with overstory leaf-out) until fruit maturation (early July). Shaded plants translocated less carbon to the rhizomes and as a consequence, flowering was reduced the next year compared to unshaded plants. It is clear from these two studies that phenological shifts in the overstory can have adverse effects on understory herbs, but more studies are needed on additional species to be able to make better generalizations concerning the impacts of overstory/understory phenological asynchronization.

Winter-green and evergreen species, in contrast, would need to adjust their phenologies to utilize high light later in the autumn to cope with delayed overstory senescence. But even if these understory species successfully adjust their phenologies to coincide with the timing of these new high light periods, this would not bring them back to equivalent prewarming conditions, because an earlier spring leaf-out or a later leaf fall shifts the high light periods to times when the photoperiod is shorter and the maximum zenith angle is lower. Combined, these changes would reduce the total daily PFD available for photosynthesis and would therefore lower annual carbon uptake.

Shifting the leaf-out period to either earlier or later in the season also places plants at greater susceptibility to intermittent frost events (Hufkens et al. 2012), the long-term consequences of which are unknown for understory herbs. Although some spring ephemerals respond positively to shorter photoperiods, due to a more balanced source-sink relationship (Gandin et al. 2011a), the early leaf-out of the overstory would decrease irradiation levels before the full benefits of an extended leaf lifespan could be realized, and result in smaller plants with fewer stored carbohydrate reserves. Repeated over several consecutive seasons, this could potentially lead to the extirpation of spring ephemerals from these forests. Goryshina (1972) suggested that the relative paucity of spring ephemerals in western European forests, which leaf out earlier than eastern European forests, was for this very reason.

Direct Effects of Warming on Understory Herbs

Direct effects of warming on forest herbs can be studied by growing plants under highly controlled conditions in growth chambers or greenhouses (De Boeck et al. 2012; Souther et al. 2012), using latitudinal or elevational transplants as surrogates for *in situ* warming (De Frenne et al. 2011), by directly warming plants or soils in the field using IR lamps (Aronson and McNulty 2009), or by imposing open-top chambers (OTCs) over plants in the field (De Frenne et al. 2010b). Each methodology has limitations (Aronson and McNulty 2009; Amthor et al. 2010; Kimball 2011; Souther et al. 2012), but viewed in context, they all provide insights into the potential impacts of warming on plants in the herbaceous layer of forests.

At the same time, there is also a need for more *in situ* temperature monitoring conducted at or just below the soil surface, because it is at this microhabitat location where the relevant temperature cues are sensed by the dormant belowground structures of understory herbs and later on by the leaves, which for spring ephemerals and many evergreen species are located close to the ground. Most climate monitoring sensors, in contrast, are located 1 or 2 m above the forest floor, where the air temperatures can be substantially different, sometimes by as much as 10°C warmer or 5°C cooler (Graae et al. 2012), and disconnected from those that are sensed by the herbs themselves.

Impacts of warming depend not only on the magnitude of the warming but also on seasonality. For example, winter warming reduces the cooling degree days that primarily affect the timing and degree of budbreak of rhizomes, bulbs, and corms in the spring. It will also increase the number of days suitable for photosynthesis by evergreen and winter-green herbs, while at the same time raising respiration rates of both above and belowground structures. Summer warming, in contrast, will increase heating degree days and affect the timing of phenological events such as leaf-out, reproduction, senescence, and the induction of autumn dormancy. It too would raise respiration rates and lead to potentially negative carbon balances during the low light period in the summer, particularly for single-flushing summer-green herbs. Warming would also induce drier atmospheric conditions, which cause stomatal closure that can lower assimilation rates (Schulz and Adams 1995) and severely curtail growth of forest herbs (Lendzion and Leuschner 2009).

Effects of Warming on Release from Dormancy

Few studies have addressed the environmental cues releasing understory herbs from winter dormancy, or how this may be affected by global warming. Such studies are crucial to modeling changes in phenology of understory herbs caused by climate warming. Plant dormancy is a complex phenomenon controlled by external physical factors like moisture, temperature, and light and is also intimately linked to internal physiological mechanisms (such as innate dormancy, hormones, and enzymatic activities) that ensure the proper timing of lifecycle events (Anderson et al. 2001). Warming could possibly result in inappropriate temporal release from dormancy or a failure to be adequately released from dormancy, even if at the correct time of the year. The latter possibility may be more important at the southern geographical limits of a species, where the amount of cooling required is already limiting. Warming may also not affect all lifecycle processes similarly; flowering and leaf-out, for example, may have different release requirements (Woycicki 1945; Fukai et al. 2006).

Studies on dormancy release requirements in forest herbs have been carried out largely in a horticultural context (Yeh et al. 2000; Maqbool et al. 2004; Yun et al. 2011), although some have focused on native understory herbs (Gail 1966; Martin 1966; Risser and Cottam 1967; Takagi 2005). Both sets of studies are congruent with the fact that dormancy is more effectively broken following longer and colder periods of chilling, although some species may show ecotypic variation along latitudinal and possibly elevational gradients (Kauth et al. 2011). Temperatures of snow-covered soils remain nearly constant at 0°C or 1°C (Muller 1978), whereas after snow melt, the upper layer warms substantially and under certain conditions can even exhibit temperature inversions

(Vézina and Grandnter 1965). Many spring ephemerals and summer-green herbs begin sprouting once soil temperatures reach 0°C (Vézina and Grandtner 1965), and they develop more quickly after a longer and colder winter period (Risser and Cottam 1967; Muller 1978; Yoshie 2008). For example, *E. americanum* exhibits earlier leaf-out and matures more quickly after a late snow melt, which allows it to more effectively utilize what high light still remains prior to canopy closure (Muller 1978). This gives rise to the conundrum that while winter warming adversely affects release from dormancy in the spring, once an herb species is released, subsequent warming can enhance growth and flowering later on. This may cause unexpected effects though: Kudo et al. (2004) found that when spring ephemerals flowered early due to a warm spring, bee-pollinated ephemerals had low seed set because of a discordance between flowering times and bee activity; bees lagged behind peak flowering time. In contrast, fly-pollinated herbs suffered no such losses because peak flowering and fly activity times were more coincident.

Direct Effects of Warming on Aboveground Processes

Souther et al. (2012) carried out a growth chamber study on *Panax quinquefolius* L. (ginseng) to compare growth and physiology of populations originating from high and mid-elevation sites in West Virginia to changes in growth temperatures. They grew plants at the mean temperatures typical of the originating populations plus a high treatment that bracketed future warming predictions for that area. The results contradicted their *a priori* hypothesis that plants would be adapted to local conditions and respond better to conditions that mimicked temperatures in their natural habitat. When plants were grown at the high temperature, they produced fewer seeds, and those seeds were of lower mass than for plants grown at low temperature. Photosynthetic rates of plants from both populations were higher at low rather than high temperature, but plants from mid-elevation sites showed a sharper decrease in rates when tested at high temperatures than did those from high elevations sites, contrary to expectations.

Effects of Warming Deduced from Field Experiments: Heating Experiments

Only a few empirical warming studies have been carried out under field conditions. Farnsworth et al. (1995) performed one of the first such studies nearly 20 years ago, using heating cables to raise soil temperatures by ~ 5°C. The two dominant herbaceous species, *Maianthemum canadense* Desf. and *Uvularia sessilifolia* L., exhibited accelerated leaf-out early in the season in the heated plots, but neither photosynthetic rate nor the timing of flowering and fruiting were affected.

As a phenological group, spring ephemerals may be particularly sensitive to warming since they are highly dependent on the brief period of high light prior to canopy closure and are therefore restricted to carrying out the bulk of their aboveground growth while conditions are still fairly cold. *Erythronium americanum*, *Allium tricoccum*, and *Crocus vernus* (L.) Hill all grow better at lower day/night temperatures than higher (Lapointe and Lerat 2006; Badri et al. 2007; Lundmark et al. 2009; Gandin et al. 2011b; Bernatchez and Lapointe 2012). These species are also able to maintain positive water relations at very low temperatures (Goryshina 1972; Lapointe 2001), although if exposed to extended periods of high light and high Δw, symptoms of water stress can develop

(Sawada et al. 1997). During the brief period after snow melt and before canopy closure, *E. americanum* uses a high rate of photosynthesis to replenish carbohydrate reserves in the bulb that were depleted from root growth the previous autumn and epigeous growth in the spring. This species does not store starch in the leaf, so when the sink is filled, soluble sugars (most likely hexoses) build up (Gandin et al. 2011a) and induce a feedback inhibition of photosynthesis that eventually leads to leaf senescence (Lapointe 2001).

With higher temperatures, starch accumulates at faster rates and enzymatic reactions proceed at higher rates, leading to more rapid bulb filling and earlier leaf senescence (Gandin et al. 2011b). Lower temperatures lead to larger bulbs because the duration of filling is extended by lower metabolic rates and a delay in leaf senescence because sink limitations take longer to develop. These physiological responses to temperature appear to be common to many spring ephemerals (Yoshie 2008) and, therefore, herbs with similar physiologies will likely be at a competitive disadvantage in warmer climates because this will reduce carbohydrate reserves.

De Frenne et al. (2010b) placed small (1.15 m²) passively heated OTCs over individuals of *Anemone nemorosa* L., a spring ephemeral, in deciduous forests in Belgium. These chambers heated the air and soils by ~ 0.4°C and ~ 1.2°C, respectively, but only before canopy closure. The OTCs caused only minor changes in the microclimate, but did exert some effects on growth (e.g., greater height growth) while other parameters, such as specific leaf area, N, and leaf C, were unaffected. The authors concluded that this was a promising technology (at least for spring ephemerals) and should be expanded to other species.

Effects of Warming Deduced from Field Experiments: Transplant Experiments

De Frenne et al. (2010a) used latitudinal transplants as surrogates for warming and concluded that *A. nemorosa* plants in warmer sites had higher reproductive outputs than those at cooler (i.e., more northerly) sites. Phillip and Petersen (2007) also reported that higher temperatures stimulated greater rhizome growth in this species, which is different from the responses found by Lapointe's colleagues for *E. americanum*. It is possible that clonal spring ephemerals with spreading rhizomes may respond to temperature and other climatic variables quite differently from those with bulbs.

Van der Keken et al. (2012) transplanted four understory herbs varying distances north of their northern natural limits and assessed their survival over a period of seven years. They found that the farther away a species was planted from its natural boundary, the lower the survival rate, which possibly indicates that the transplant site was in a location where the climatic tolerance of the species was exceeded. It would be informative to conduct a similar series of transplant experiments but in the opposite direction to test whether the southern limits of forest herbs are constrained by biotic factors, such as competition with neighboring plants, or abiotic factors, such as extremely warm temperatures. It is quite possible that the northern and southern limits of herbaceous species are controlled by entirely different factors.

Few experiments have investigated the impacts of climate warming during the summer, when spring ephemerals and heteroptic species are dormant, or during the autumn, when ephemeral species produce new roots and mycorrhizal connections for the next spring. Warming could deplete the stored carbohydrate pool necessary for root production and establishment of mycorrhizal connections, which could later impact the capacity of these herbs to absorb water and nutrients the following spring (Lapointe and Molard 1997; Lerat et al. 2002).

Effects of Elevated CO_2 on the Ecophysiology of Understory Herbs

Atmospheric CO_2 concentrations are currently going up at a rate of about 2 ppm/yr, and in 2013, the mean annual concentration exceeded 400 ppm, which is a 43 percent increase over pre-industrial concentrations of ~ 280 ppm (IPCC 2007). By 2050, CO_2 concentrations will be above 500 ppm and could reach between 769 to 1,088 ppm by the end of the 21st century (IPCC 2007). Studies of the responses of herbaceous plants to elevated CO_2 (eCO_2) under the light limiting conditions of the forest understory are infrequent. Even so, photosynthetic rates would still be expected to increase with eCO_2, but acclimation through anatomical, morphological, or physiological changes could greatly modify this response. For example, eCO_2 has reportedly caused stomatal densities to decrease in a large number of understory herb species over the latter half of the 20th century (Beerling and Kelly 1997), and eCO_2 often causes stomatal closure (Leakey et al. 2009). In addition, increased leaf production by overstory trees could reduce PFD to levels below the LCP of plants even when exposed to eCO_2, as well as reduce the number and intensity of sunflecks, which would limit assimilation under conditions of relatively high PFD.

Are Forest Herbs Already Exposed to Chronically Elevated CO_2 in the Understory?

If herbaceous plants are already exposed to eCO_2 in the forest understory, there may be little further enhancement of photosynthesis as atmospheric CO_2 continues to rise. Reports about whether forest herbs are currently exposed to eCO_2 concentrations in the forest understory appear to conflict on this point. Although respiratory and decomposition processes below the canopy and in the soil can elevate the CO_2 in the first centimeter above the ground to as high as 1,800 ppm (Fuller 1948), most of the buildup in CO_2 near the forest floor occurs at night, when there is less wind and more vertical stratification. Once the sun rises, convection currents quickly dissipate the CO_2 gradient (Fuller 1948; Sparling and Alt 1966; Würth et al. 1998; Wu et al. 2012). However, other studies find that higher CO_2 concentrations near the ground can persist well into the afternoon hours (Bazzaz and Williams 1991; Skelly et al. 1996). An eCO_2 of ~ 50 ppm in midsummer has been reported in forests in Massachusetts, which then decreased in either spring or autumn (Bazzaz and Williams 1991), probably because of higher mixing rates prior to leaf-out and after leaf fall. Low-lying cove forests can experience ground level eCO_2 well into the afternoon hours as a result of nocturnal drainage of cold air from surrounding slopes (de Araújo et al. 2008). In tropical forests, Holtum and Winter (2001) found CO_2 concentrations at 10 cm as high as 494 ppm, which were high enough to stimulate photosynthesis in a late successional understory tree species. When small chambers were placed over seedlings in this same forest and exposed to eCO_2 of 700 ppm, there was an increase in growth of 25–76 percent among five tropical forest seedlings, despite the low light of the forest understory environment (Würth et al. 1998). By analogy, eCO_2 near the ground may be sufficiently high enough to stimulate photosynthesis of understory herbs too.

Indirect Effects of Elevated CO_2 on Understory Herbs

Indirect effects of CO_2 on forest herbs can occur because of changes in the growth and phenology of the overstory trees as they respond to rising atmospheric CO_2. Such changes can include a greater LAI and reduced PFD in the understory, fewer and lower intensity sunflecks, and a longer leaf season due to delayed autumnal senescence (Taylor et al. 2008; but see Asshoff et al. 2006 and references therein). At the Aspen FACE site in Rhinelander, Wisconsin, artificial forests of aspen, aspen/birch, and aspen/maple were exposed to eCO_2 and eO_3, and after several years of exposure, understory biomass was greatest in the aspen/maple and eO_3 plots, which were the ones with the most open canopies and higher light penetration (Bandeff et al. 2006; Awmack et al. 2007). eCO_2 by itself had little effect on understory biomass since those plots had denser canopies and less light penetrated to the understory. Perkins (ms. in prep.) found a similar response pattern for corticolous lichen coverage on the trunks of the aspen trees. Coverage was lower on trees exposed to eCO_2 (lowest light) compared to trees in ambient plots and was higher on trees exposed to eO_3 (highest light).

At the Oak Ridge FACE site, Souza et al. (2010) found that understory biomass (both herbaceous and woody) was enhanced by ~ 25 percent in the eCO_2 plots compared to the ambient plots. Continued exposure to eCO_2 accelerated successional processes, and the understory community shifted from being dominated by herbaceous species to being dominated by woody species after 10 years of exposure. Between 2001 and 2003, understory herbs made up 94 percent of the biomass, but by 2008, this had dropped to 33 percent, just over half that in the ambient plots (61 percent). The authors suggest that eCO_2 can accelerate succession in forest understories and give a competitive advantage to woody species, since the latter can accumulate more aboveground biomass each year and eventually overtop the herbs.

Exotic species may greatly influence the response of herb layer communities to global change. At the Oak Ridge site, two invasive species, *Lonicera japonica* Thunb. and *Microstegium vimineum*, dominated the annual productivity, and their responses to eCO_2 differed depending on rainfall: In the wet year of 2001, *M. vimineum* produced nearly twice the biomass in the ambient plots, whereas in the drier year, production was the same in both plots (Belote et al. 2003), showing that the effects of eCO_2 may be contingent on soil water availability and photosynthetic pathway. Although photosynthetic rates in C4 plants are already saturated at eCO_2, they can profit from improved water status caused by eCO_2-induced stomatal closure. Vine species respond very strongly to eCO_2 and will become stronger competitors in a high CO_2 world (Mohan et al. 2006), which could lead to the decline of certain understory herbs.

Direct Effects of Elevated CO_2 on Forest Herbs

Responses of forest herbs may differ depending on their phenological grouping. For example, the spring ephemeral *E. americanum* responds to eCO_2 in complex and unexpected ways, but all related to the early leafing strategy for plants in this grouping. eCO_2 stimulates leaf photosynthesis in this species, as well as bulb respiration (Gutjahr and Lapointe 2008; Gandin et al. 2009) but not leaf respiration (Gandin et al. 2009). High assimilation rates, coupled with low respiration rates, lead to high net photosynthetic rates. Because this species is sink-, rather than source-limited, the excess C gained is shunted to the bulb where it is metabolized away through upregulation of the alternative oxidase pathway (Gandin et al. 2009). This restores a more equitable carbon balance between source and sink and thereby prevents the formation of excess reactive oxygen species, which could be damaging to cells. The diversion of C away from bulb filling also prevents the initiation of premature leaf senescence from feedback inhibition and as a consequence, eCO_2 surprisingly does not result in a change in either leaf longevity or plant size (Gutjahr and Lapointe 2008). This suggests that spring ephemerals, or at least those with bulbs or corms, may not exhibit detectable changes in biomass under conditions of eCO_2.

Teskey and Shrestha (1985) found that CO_2 efficiency (unit change in photosynthesis per unit change in CO_2 concentration) was greater for shade-tolerant understory tree seedlings such as *Fagus grandifolia* Ehrh. than for intermediate or shade-intolerant species, leading one to posit that the same may be true for forest herbs. If so, this leads to the hypothesis that summer-green species, especially those with recurrent leaf flushing and the most shade-adapted leaves, would respond proportionately more to eCO_2 than other herbs, since they are the most active at the time when forest floor CO_2 exhibits the greatest enhancement.

Studies of Artificially Elevated CO_2 on Herbaceous Species beneath a Forest Canopy

The most comprehensive (and the only) investigation of the effects of eCO_2 on summer-green herbaceous species in the understory of a deciduous forest was carried out by Osborne et al. (1997) as part of a four-year experiment to investigate the responses of forest understories to rising atmospheric CO_2. The study was conducted at the Smithsonian Environmental Research Center in mixed, deciduous woodland and used large OTCs to raise the CO_2 to approximately 670 ppm compared to control OTCs that had a mean concentration of 380 ppm. The researchers investigated the responses of Indiana strawberry (*Duchesnea indica* [Andrews] Focke), a summer-green perennial with indeterminate clonal growth and the dominant herbaceous perennial on site to eCO_2. After several years of exposure to eCO_2, leaves of *D. indica* had increased their φ_{abs} (true quantum yield) by 22 percent and lowered their LCP by 42 percent. Lowering the LCP more so than the φ_{abs} suggested that other factors must be contributing to the increased efficiency of photosynthesis with eCO_2 in the light-limited conditions of the understory. Further analysis showed that eCO_2 resulted in a lowering in the amount of RUBISCO by 16 percent, as well as a 14 percent decrease in chlorophyll content, both well-documented responses (Leakey et al. 2009). Photorespiration was lowered by eCO_2, since under limiting light a higher ratio of CO_2/O_2 would favor carboxylation over oxygenation. But the reduction in photorespiration was not sufficient to fully account for the much larger decrease in the LCP, and the authors postulated a concomitant reduction in mitochondrial respiration to make up the difference. In other studies, eCO_2 has been found to stimulate respiration in plants, but the matter is far from settled (Leakey et al. 2009). So it is plausible that a lower investment in RUBISCO and associated proteins reduced maintenance costs that would explain the lower mitochondrial respiration in this study. This in turn means that positive rates of photosynthesis can be achieved at lower light levels in the presence of eCO_2. The reduced allocation to RUBISCO and chlorophyll also improves nitrogen use efficiencies of these leaves, another common response to eCO_2 (Leakey et al. 2009). The consequences of eCO_2 for altering the nitrogen dynamics of forest understories as a result of higher photosynthetic nitrogen use efficiencies is worthy of further study.

Finally, meta-analyses suggest that eCO_2 will result in lower g_s for most plants (Leakey et al. 2009), which in turn will reduce transpiration rates. As noted earlier, the herbaceous layer is disproportionately important for moving water through the system, due mainly to high g_s and a high LAI. However, it is difficult to predict whether eCO_2 will substantively change the water balance of forests, since there could be compensating effects arising from greater leaf area production from both understory and overstory plants.

Effects of Elevated O_3 on Forest Herbs

Ozone is the most phytotoxic gaseous pollutant and is projected to continue to increase over the next several decades (Vingarzan 2004), and the percent of temperate forests affected by high O_3 is expected to increase to nearly 50 percent by 2050 (Fowler 1999). Ozone is absorbed primarily through the stomata and causes stippling, cell death, and premature leaf senescence. Because of its high reactivity, O_3 is also scavenged quite effectively as it travels through the forest canopy, and concentrations in the herbaceous layer can be substantially lower than above the forest canopy. Neufeld et al. (1992) reported O_3 levels at 0.5 m above the forest floor that were ~ 50 percent lower than those above the canopy in hardwood cove forests, while in ridgetop forests, the depletion was less than 20 percent. Skelly et al. (1996) also reported lower O_3 (13 percent) near the forest floor in deciduous forests in Pennsylvania. Despite lower O_3 concentrations in the herbaceous layer, several investigators (Chappelka et al. 2003; Davison et al. 2003; Burkey et al. 2006; Souza et al. 2006; Neufeld et al. 2012), working in Great Smoky Mountains National Park, were able to find abundant stipple and premature leaf senescence in several woodland herbs, including cutleaf coneflower (*Rudbeckia laciniata*), crownbeard (*Verbesina occidentalis* [L.] Walter), and tall milkweed (*Asclepias exaltata*). How these plants will respond to further increases in O_3 in the context of rising atmospheric CO_2 and warmer temperatures is unknown at this time. There is some evidence that eCO_2 can ameliorate the impacts of O_3 (Karnofsky et al. 2003), particularly if temperatures increase (Leakey et al. 2009), and thus future adverse impacts may be lessened.

SUMMARY

The presence of herbs in the understory of temperate deciduous forests depends in large part on their ability to grow in an environment where resources like light, nutrients, and water are highly heterogeneous on both temporal and spatial scales. Light penetration to the forest understory herb layer is the highest during the spring overstory leafless period, reaches a minimum once the canopy leafs out, and then rises again after the overstory leaves senesce in the autumn. Spatial variations in irradiance can drive differences in other microclimatic factors, especially temperature, humidity, and water availability, all of which can have large influences on the herb layer. Adaptations to this dynamic environment can be both physiological and morphological and exist at multiple scales from subcellular to leaf, to whole plant, and with implications at population, community and ecosystem levels.

The presence of seasonality, coupled with distinct periods when the overstory canopy is present or absent, results in a suite of phenological strategies among herbs, including spring ephemerals, summer-greens, winter-greens, evergreens, heteroptics, and parasitic and saprophytic plants. It appears that evolution has favored species that are physiologically active during the warmer portions of the years when temperatures are more favorable for photosynthesis and nutrient uptake, although some evergreen species can take advantage of warm periods in the winter to carry on photosynthesis and enhance carbon gain. The proportion of evergreen herb species in the understory should increase toward the southern latitudinal limits of the distribution of temperate forest due to more favorable temperatures when the canopy is leafless.

Strategies to increase light absorption in the forest understory include a well-developed spongy mesophyll to scatter light, a reflective lower leaf surface to direct light back into the leaf, and adaxial surface cells that are concavely shaped to direct light toward cells containing chloroplasts. Selection for height growth and a monolayer canopy are intensified to maximize light interception during the light-limiting summer months.

Spring ephemerals have photosynthetic characteristics similar to sun-adapted plants and maximize carbon gain prior to development of the overstory canopy. These species are also well adapted to low temperatures. In contrast, winter-green and heteroptic herbs have much lower photosynthetic rates but are also much more plastic in response to seasonal variations in both temperature and light. Although evergreens are similar, these herbs obtain most of their carbon during the autumn and spring leafless periods. There is a strong inverse relationship between photosynthetic rate and leaf lifespan; evergreens have the lowest photosynthetic rate and the longest leaf lifespan.

For herbs that persist after canopy closure, physiological, biochemical, phenological, and morphological changes are required to maximize photosynthetic efficiency under light-limited conditions. Summer-green species with continuous leaf flushing produce leaves adapted to the low light conditions and can gain most of their carbon while the overstory is fully leafed out, whereas summer-green species that produce only a single flush of leaves are more dependent on the high light prior to canopy leaf-out to gain the majority of their annual carbon uptake. For both groups of summer-green herbs, resources are shifted from processes associated with carbon assimilation to those involved with light harvesting after canopy closure. Sunflecks represent the primary source of light after canopy closure and many species utilize light-induced increases in g_s, RuBP regeneration, and RUBISCO to enhance carbon gain at this time of the year. However, the high intensity irradiance of sunflecks may also lead to photoinhibition and stomatal closure, especially for species adapted to extremely shaded environments, although the durations of most sunflecks are not long enough to cause lasting injury. The vast majority of sunfleck work has been done in tropical forests, and understory herb responses in temperate deciduous forests have not been well documented.

Clearly, more morphological, biochemical, and physiological processes involved in the response of herbs to the dynamic light environment of the deciduous forest understory remain to be thoroughly investigated. The water relations of understory herbs have not been comparatively examined across the phenological strategies, but there is a suggestion that maximum hydraulic conductivities are higher, as a group, in herbs as compared to woody seedlings. The contribution of understory herbs to forest community-level carbon gain, production, and both CO_2 and H_2O exchange with the atmosphere is proportionately greater than what one would expect based on their relatively small contribution to the biomass of the forest. How the herbaceous layer will respond to climate change is still relatively unclear given the multiplicity of interacting factors and the paucity of experimental studies. But, given their poor dispersal abilities coupled with increasing habitat fragmentation, changes in climate could exceed their physiological capacities to adapt to local conditions, leading to their extirpation from some habitats, particularly those at the extremes of their current ranges. Further studies of herb layer ecophysiology are needed to deepen our understanding of how these species will respond to global climate change.

ACKNOWLEDGMENTS

The authors would like to acknowledge the guidance and assistance of the editor, Frank Gilliam, toward improving this chapter. In addition, several colleagues reviewed the manuscript, including Drs. Alan Davison, Jonathon Horton, and Erik Nilsen, who helped greatly to improve it, and to whom we express our most sincere thanks. Thanks also to Dr. Beverly Moser for translating several articles from German, Catherine Coleman for a much-needed translation of an article written in French, and Derick Poindexter and Alyssa Teat for kindly reviewing all scientific names. Authorities for scientific names came from either Weakley's Flora of the Southern and Mid-Atlantic States (2012) or The Plant List (2010).

APPENDIX 3.1

Species names for all understory herbs mentioned in chapter 3. Old names are those used in the originally cited literature, while new names are the currently recognized names according to either The Plant List (2010) at: http://www.ThePlantList.org (accessed 11-16-12) or Weakley's Flora of the Southern and Mid-Atlantic States (working draft, 9-28-12; http://herbarium.unc.edu/flora.htm (accessed 11-16-12).

Old Names	New Names
Actaea racemosa L.	
Adenocaulon bicolor Hook.	
Adonis ramosa Franch.	
Adoxa moschatellina L.	
Aesculus sylvatica W. Bartram	
Allium monanthum Maxim.	
Allium triccocum Aiton	*Allium triccocum* Sol.
Allium ursinum L.	
Allium victorialis L. ssp. *platyphyllum*	
Alocasia macrorrhiza Schott	*Alocasia macrorrhizos* (L.) G. Don.
Anemone flaccida Fr. Schmidt	
Anemone nemorosa L.	
Anemone raddeana Regel	
Aplectrum hyemale (Muhl. ex Willd.) Torrey	*Aplectrum hyemale* (Muhl. ex Willd.) Nutt.
Aralia nudicaulis L.	
Arisaema heterophyllum Blume	
Arisaema triphyllum (L.) Schott	
Arum maculatum L.	
Asarum canadense L.	
Asarum europaeum L.	
Asarum maculatum Nakai	
Asclepias exaltata L.	
Aster acuminatus Michx.	*Oclemena acuminata* (Michx.) Greene
Aster macrophyllus L.	*Eurybia macrophylla* (L.) Cass.
Caulophyllum thalictroides (L.) Michx.	
Cardiocrinum cordatum (Thunb.) Makino	
Cimicifuga racemosa Nutt.	*Actaea racemosa* (L.)
Claytonia caroliniana Michx.	
Clintonia borealis (Aiton) Raf.	*Clintonia borealis* (Sol.) Raf.
Cornus canadensis L.	
Corydalis ambigua Cham. & Schltdl.	
Crocus vernus (L.) Hill	
Daphne kamtschatica Maxim. var. *jezoensis* (Maxim.) Ohwi	
Dentaria diphylla Michx.	*Cardamine diphylla* (Michx.) Alph. Wood
Dicentra canadensis (Goldie) Walp.	
Dicentra cucullaria (L.) Bernh.	
Disporum lanuginosum (Michx.) Nicholson	*Prosartes lanuginosa* (Michx.) D. Don
Dryopteris dilatata (Hoffm.) A. Gray	
Dryopteris filix-mas (L.) Schott	
Dryopteris marginalis (L.) A. Gray	
Dryopteris spinulosa (Muell.) Watt	*Dryopteris carthusiana* (Vill.) H. P. Fuchs.

(Continued)

Old Names	New Names
Duchesnea indica (Andrews) Focke	
Erythronium albidum Nutt.	
Erythronium americanum Ker	*Erythronium americanum* Ker Gawl.
Erythronium japonicum Decne.	
Erythronium grandiflorum Pursh	
Eupatorium sessilifolium L.	
Fagus grandifolia Ehrh.	
Fragaria virginiana Duchesne	
Fragaria vesca L.	
Galax urceolata (Poir.) Brummitt	
Galeobdolon lutrum Huds.	*Lamium galeobdolon* spp. *galeobdolon*
Geum urbanum L.	
Glechoma hirsuta Waldst. & Kit.	
Hedera helix L.	
Hepatica acutiloba DC.	
Heuchera americana L.	
Hexastylis arifolia (Michx.) Small	
Hordelymus europaeus Jessen ex Harz	*Hordelymus europaeus* (L.) Jess. ex Harz
Hyacinthoides non-scripta L. Chouard	*Hyacinthoides non-scripta* (L.) Chouard ex Rothm.
Hydrophyllum appendiculatum Michx	
Hydrophyllum canadense L.	
Impatiens capensis Meerb.	
Impatiens pallida Nutt.	
Jeffersonia diphylla (L.) Pers.	
Lespedeza violacea Ell.	*Lespedeza violacea* (L.) Pers.
Lonicera japonica Thunb.	
Maianthemum canadense Desf.	
Maianthemum dilatatum (Alph. Wood) A. Nelson & J. F. Macbr.	
Melica uniflora Retz.	
Mercurialis perennis L.	
Mertensia virginica (L.) Pers. ex Link	*Mertensia pulmonarioides* Roth.
Microstegium vimineum (Trin.) A. Camus	
Mitchella repens L.	
Monotropa uniflora L.	
Muhlenbergia sobolifera (Muhl. ex Willd.) Trinius	*Muhlenbergia sobolifera* (Muhl.) Trinius
Oxalis acetosella L.	
Oxalis grandis Small	*Xanthoxalis grandis* (Small) Small
Oxalis oregana Nutt.	
Pachysandra terminalis Siebold & Zucc.	
Panax quinquefolius L.	

Old Names	New Names
Parasenecio auriculata	*Parasenecio auriculatus* (DC.) J. R. Grant
Podophyllum peltatum L.	
Polygonatum biflorum (Willd.) Pursh or *P. latifolium* Pursh	*Polygonatum biflorum* (Walter) Elliott
Polypodium virginianum L.	
Polystichum acrostichoides (Michx.) Schott	
Primula sieboldii E. Morren	
Prosartes lanuginose (Michx.) D. Don	
Pyrola asarifolia Michx.	
Pyrola elliptica Nutt.	
Pyrola incarnata (DC.) Freyn	
Pyrola japonica Klenze	*Pyrola japonica* Klenze ex Alef.
Quercus prinus L.	
Quercus serrata Thunb.	*Quercus serrata* Murray
Ranunculus ficaria L.	
Rhododendron maximum L.	
Rubus pubescens Raf.	
Rudbeckia laciniata L.	
Sanguinaria canadensis L.	
Sedum ternatum Michx.	
Smilacina racemosa (L.) Desf.	*Maianthemum racemosum* (L.) Link.
Smyrnium perfoliatum	
Solidago flexicaulis L.	
Syneilesis palmata Maxim	*Syneilesis palmata* (Thunb.) Maxim
Tiarella cordifolia L.	
Tipularia discolor (Pursh) Nutt.	
Trientalis borealis Raf.	
Trillium apetalon Makino	
Trillium erectum L.	
Trillium grandiflorum (Michx.) Salisb.	
Uvularia sessilifolia L.	
Verbesina occidentalis (L.) Walter	
Viola hondoensis W. Becker & H. Boissieu	
Viola mirabilis L.	
Viola palmata L.	
Viola pubescens Ait	*Viola pubescens* Aiton

4 Interactions of Nutrient Effects with Other Biotic Factors in the Herbaceous Layer

Wendy B. Anderson

The intent of this chapter is to elucidate the importance of both nutrients in forest herb physiology and community interactions, and of forest herbs in regulating the nutrient environment of their ecosystem. Although plants in the herbaceous layer account for only a small proportion of deciduous forest biomass, they perform many important functions in intra-system nutrient cycling. Understanding the physiological processes that occur in individuals provides insight into how herbaceous species interact with other species and function in the environment as individuals and functional guilds. Most physiological studies of forest herbs have focused on responses to light as the primary limiting resource (chapter 3, this volume); however, nutrients are also potentially limiting and may be as important as light in determining physiological, growth, and reproductive parameters for forest herbs.

The herbaceous species of eastern deciduous forests experience a spatially and temporally dynamic nutrient environment (chapter 9, this volume). Nutrient availability changes seasonally, peaking in the early spring and declining throughout the summer, and the phenology and physiology of the various herbaceous species reflect these patterns. Nutrient availability is also spatially heterogeneous, varying across spatial scales from centimeters to kilometers, and can alter physiological and community interactions within and among species. I focus first on the physiological responses that plants in the herbaceous layer of deciduous forests exhibit in response to variability in their nutrient environment. Then I address the effects of nutrient availability on community-level interactions between herbaceous species and their mycorrhizal associates, and between herbs and their herbivores. Finally, I summarize the possible ecosystem-level responses that these physiological and community processes may induce in a changing environment.

PHYSIOLOGICAL RESPONSES OF FOREST HERBS TO NUTRIENT AVAILABILITY

Interactions between Light and Nutrients

Many of the physiological studies addressing the relationship between nutrients and the herbaceous layer focus on the interaction between light and nutrients. As a general pattern across biomes, shading lessens the demand for soil nutrients via reduced photosynthesis rates and biomass accumulation (Cui and Caldwell 1997). For the herbaceous layer of forests, this pattern may explain variation in carbon acquisition rates between spring and summer herbs. In the following paragraphs, I highlight some representative studies from deciduous forests that show the relationships between light and nutrients for forest herb physiology.

In a classic study by Taylor and Pearcy (1976), spring ephemeral herbs that actively photosynthesized prior to canopy closure exhibited high light-saturated photosynthesis rates, high respiration rates, and high light compensation points, followed by negative net photosynthesis rates and ultimately senescence upon canopy closure. This time period is also associated with extremely high nutrient availability as freeze-thaw cycles lyse microbes that formerly immobilized nutrients (Zak et al. 1990; DeLuca et al. 1992), nutrients continue to leach from warming, decomposing leaf litter, and competition with woody plant species is minimized (Bormann and Likens 1979). Those available nutrients facilitate the high metabolic rates of spring ephemeral herbs. In contrast, summer herbs from the same deciduous forest site in New York exhibited low light-saturated photosynthesis rates, low respiration rates, and low compensation points, but could acclimate to increased irradiance in gaps and from sunflecks with slight increases in those rates (Taylor and Pearcy 1976). Nutrients are much less available in the summer as microbes and woody plants immobilize greater quantities; hence the shade plants of the forest floor in the summer must maintain low metabolic rates, even when light is occasionally available.

Two experimental studies of *Claytonia virginica* L. further illustrated the importance of light-nutrient interactions for spring ephemerals in a deciduous forest in Tennessee (Eickmeier and Schlusser 1993; W. B. Anderson and Eickmeier 1998). In the earlier study, additions of an NPK fertilizer enhanced carboxylation by ribulose-1,5-bisphosphate carboxylase/oxygenase (RUBISCO) and increased vegetative and reproductive biomass of plants growing in full sunlight. However, plants growing under shade treatments did not exhibit the same increases. In the latter study, both shaded and unshaded plants responded to nutrient additions with increased biomass, but shaded plants did not respond to the same degree as unshaded plants (fig. 4.1). Further, root:shoot biomass ratios decreased with nutrient additions when plants were in full sun, but did not respond to nutrient additions when shaded (fig. 4.1).

In addition to the growth responses described above, nutrient (nitrogen and phosphorus) concentrations of *C. virginica* increased with increasingly greater nutrient additions up to a point where the plants became saturated with nutrients (Anderson and Eickmeier 1998). The shaded plants reached this saturation point at a lower nutrient addition level than the plants in full sun. The shaded plants maintained internal

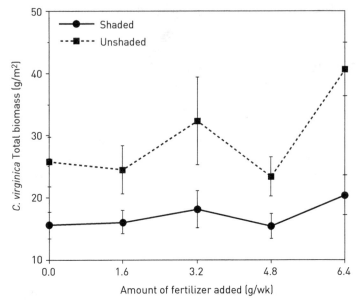

FIGURE 4.1 Total biomass of *Claytonia virginica* in response to shade and Peter's NPK fertilizer addition treatments. Data from three years are combined and presented as mean ± SE. N = 12 samples per treatment combination. (Reprinted from Anderson and Eickmeier 1998 with permission from the *Canadian Journal of Botany*.)

nutrient concentrations that were slightly higher than those of plants in full sunlight because of their lower total biomass. However, the nitrogen and phosphorus content (concentration x biomass) in shaded plants was significantly lower than those pools in unshaded plants (fig. 4.2; W. B. Anderson and Eickmeier 1998). These studies show that shaded plants have a lower demand for nutrients and may not be able to respond to higher nutrient availability when they are shaded.

Nutrient Availability and Nutrient Resorption

Nutrient availability in deciduous forests can also affect herbaceous species' ability to reabsorb nutrients prior to leaf abscission. Nutrient resorption is a metabolically expensive process that breaks down nutrient-rich organic molecules in senescing leaves and transports the nutrients into perennating organs to be stored until the next growing season. As a general pattern, plants growing in less fertile sites resorb greater proportions of nutrients than plants growing in more fertile sites, although this may not apply to herbaceous plants (Chapin 1980; Vitousek 1982; Shaver and Melillo 1984; but see Bridgham et al. 1995 and Pastor and Bridgham 1999 for conceptual and empirical alternatives). Measuring nutrient resorption rates in herbaceous plants provides information on the length of time nutrients reside in that compartment of the ecosystem, and what proportions are stored in that compartment versus returned to the soil (W. B. Anderson and Eickmeier 2000).

In an Ohio forest, *Smilacina racemosa* L., a summer herb, *Cardamine concatenata* (Michx.) O. Schwarz, an early spring herb, and *Trillium flexipes* Raf., a late spring herb, each resorbed greater proportions of P at lowland sites with low P availability than at upland sites with higher P availability (DeMars and Boerner 1997). The resorption

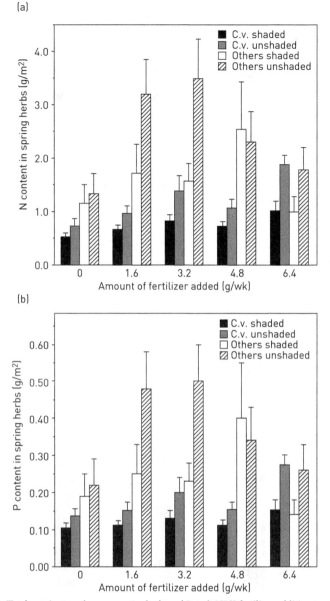

FIGURE 4.2 Total nutrient pool responses to shade and Peter's NPK fertilizer addition treatments for (a) N in *Claytonia virginica* (C.v.) and other herbs and (b) P in *Claytonia virginica* and other herbs. Data for three years are combined and presented as mean ± SE. N = 12 samples per treatment combination. (Reprinted from Anderson and Eickmeier 1998 with permission from the *Canadian Journal of Botany*.)

patterns for N in these species were less clear, in that all species on slope sites with intermediate N resorbed less N than in upland or lowland sites where N was more or less available, respectively. An interaction between nutrient availability and soil moisture might have confounded that resorption pattern (fig. 4.3).

DeMars and Boerner (1997) also made comparisons among summer and spring species to address resorption in terms of temporal variability in nutrient availability.

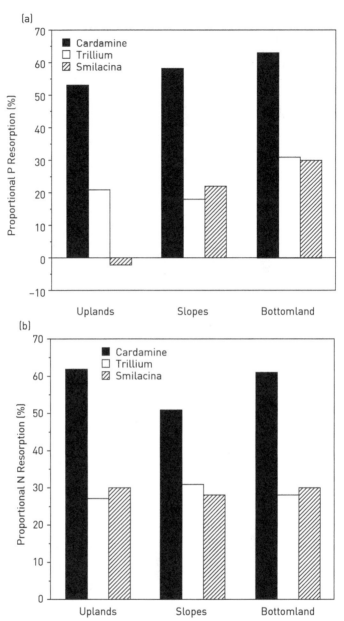

FIGURE 4.3 Overall proportional P (a) and N (b) resorption by species and topographic position. Each bar represents mean P or N for all years and sites. Data were pooled because P or N resorption did not differ significantly among years or sites for any topographic position. (Reprinted from DeMars and Boerner 1997 with permission from *Castanea*.)

They found that both *S. racemosa* and *T. flexipes* resorbed proportionally less P and N than *C. concatenata* (fig. 4.3). They provided two possible explanations to address this. First, although nutrients may be most available during *C. concatenata*'s peak months and least available during *S. racemosa* and *T. flexipes*'s peak months, the shade-tolerant physiology of the later spring and summer species may not allow for the high energy expenditure required by the process of resorption. In contrast, the *C. concatenata*'s high photosynthesis rates in full sun may afford that species the requisite energy for high proportions of resorption. Second, *C. concatenata*, like most early spring ephemerals, maintains relatively high green leaf nutrient concentrations, so even with high proportional resorption rates, it may still maintain relatively high concentrations in its senescent tissues.

W.B. Anderson and Eickmeier (2000) found that nutrient resorption in the spring ephemeral herb *C. virginica* was less efficient when plants were grown with higher nutrient availability. This was particularly true for nitrogen resorption and less so for phosphorus resorption. *C. virginica* growing under ambient nutrient conditions resorbed up to 80 percent of green leaf nitrogen and 86 percent of phosphorus, while *C. virginica* growing in fertilized conditions resorbed 47 percent of N and 56 percent of P, which is in the normal range of nutrient resorption efficiencies of many other spring ephemeral species (Muller 1978; DeMars and Boerner 1997) and other species across several biomes (Aerts 1996).

Another way to consider nutrient resorption is nutrient resorption proficiency, which is the lowest concentration to which a plant draws down its nutrients in senescing tissues (Killingbeck 1996). It reflects the adaptation of species to specific nutrient environments such that species adapted to typically high nutrient environments tend to retain higher nutrient concentrations in senescing tissues (low proficiency) than do species adapted to low nutrient environments (high proficiency). According to Killingbeck (1996), complete resorption would reduce senescent tissue concentrations to 0.3 percent for nitrogen and 0.01 percent for phosphorus. In *C. virginica*, resorption proficiency was relatively low, particularly when fertilized (W. B. Anderson and Eickmeier 2000). For *C. virginica*, resorption efficiency could be average or even high while proficiency was low because green leaf tissues contained extremely high concentrations of nitrogen (3.5–6 percent), and their senescent tissues, although 47–80 percent lower, still had 2.0–4.2 percent nitrogen. Although efficiency and proficiency results initially suggest conflicting conclusions about resorption, they show that *C. virginica*, which is the dominant spring herb species at this and many other study sites, can take up large quantities of nutrients during its short growing season, but will also return to the soil a large quantity of nutrients from its senescent leaves.

Physiological Effects of Pollution on Forest Herbs

Nutrient-based pollutants exert a range of effects on herbaceous species in deciduous forests. Although low levels of many pollutants can stimulate many plant growth responses, moderate levels can inhibit growth responses, and high levels can be fatal (W. H. Smith 1981). A more recent series of fumigation studies in Europe demonstrated this for forest herbs by focusing on the physiological responses of herbs exposed to increased nutrients and acid deposition (Fangmeier 1989; Steubing et al. 1989). These studies, summarized below, provide models of how herbaceous species in eastern deciduous forests of North America might respond to similar pollutants.

Fumigation with SO_2, NO_2, and O_3, either individually or in combination, reduced the leaf area index, chlorophyll contents, and glutamatedehydrogenase (GDH) activity of *Allium* L., *Anemone* L., *Viola* L., and *Arum* L. species, but not *Melica* L., *Milium* L., *Hedera* L., *Lamium* L., *Oxalis* L., or *Galium* L. However, responses varied across forest sites and across years, and some species, but not all, were more sensitive to combinations of pollutants than to a single source (Fangmeier 1989). Single or mixed fumigation also corresponded to a breakdown of cuticular waxes in all species, and lower transpiration and photosynthesis rates in most species, particularly at ambient PFD (appendix 3.1). Combinations of gases also increased the starch content of leaves (Steubing et al. 1989). Antagonistic interactions among the pollutants were also common. For example, the sulfur content of some leaves reflected the fumigation levels of SO_2 when it was applied alone, but when it was combined with O_3, leaf sulfur content decreased as O_3 leached sulfates from plant tissues. Finally, fumigation also increased the numbers of soil fungi and decreased the bacteria/fungi ratios of the soil (Steubing et al. 1989). These results indicate that herbaceous species are particularly sensitive to inputs of airborne pollutants, and these inputs can be as important as the light environment in altering photosynthesis rates and other growth and nutrient-related responses.

THE INFLUENCE OF NUTRIENTS ON THE RELATIONSHIPS BETWEEN FOREST HERBS AND MYCORRHIZAL FUNGI OR HERBIVORES

Mycorrhizal Associations and Nutrients

The nutrient environment can have profound effects not only on the physiology of species in the herbaceous layer, but also on the relationships that herbaceous species maintain (or avoid) with other organisms in their environment. As a general pattern, the frequency of vesicular-arbuscular (V-A) mycorrhizal associations in plants varies among sites depending on availability of nutrients, particularly phosphorus (Mosse and Phillips 1971; Menge et al. 1978; Chapin 1980). Individuals or species that grow in sites with higher phosphorus availability are usually less likely to facilitate mycorrhizal associations than those in lower phosphorus areas, and thus can maintain higher levels of carbon for growth and reproduction (Snellgrove et al. 1982). However, the lack of mycorrhizal associations could inadvertently increase water stress and possibly limit nitrogen uptake for those individuals or species.

For example, mycorrhizal associations are quite expensive for the carbohydrate reserves of *Erythronium americanum* Ker Gawler, but they may alleviate water stress during the spring growing season and enhance nutrient uptake in the autumn (Lapointe and Molard 1997). Although soils in the spring are usually not as dry as summer soils, water limitation could still occur in spring herbs because they maintain high light saturation points and photosynthesis rates (Taylor and Pearcy 1976) that would require that their stomates remain open longer, thus allowing plants to potentially become water-stressed. Summer herbs growing in the shade may be less likely to experience water stress, but may also be more likely to form mycorrhizal associations because of the increased nutrient limitation.

Mycorrhizal associations in two summer herbs in an Ohio forest, *Geranium maculatum* L. and *Polygonatum pubescens* (Willd.) Pursh., exhibited the general pattern of higher V-A infection rates in sites with lower P availability (Boerner 1986). Foliar P concentrations were positively correlated with V-A infection rates; however, proportional nutrient resorption was lower in individuals with high infection rates. Although general patterns (described earlier in this chapter) suggest that nutrient resorption should be higher in less fertile sites, this may not be true for species with mycorrhizal associations. The energy expenditure to maintain the fungal association may preclude the expense of resorbing nutrients prior to leaf abscission. However, Boerner (1986) suggested that shade-tolerant individuals with mycorrhizal associations growing in canopy gaps might be able to accumulate carbon at a high enough rate to support both the fungal symbiont and the energy-demanding process of resorption.

Herbivory and Nutrients

Invertebrate and mammalian herbivory of both spring and summer herbs occurs frequently and can substantially impact individuals and populations of forest herbs (Lubbers and Lechowicz 1989; Knight 2003; chapter 16, this volume). In the spring herbs *Jeffersonia diphylla* (L.) Pers., *Sanguinaria canadensis* L., *E. americanum*, and *Trillium sessile* L., experimental or natural defoliation of greater than 50 percent reduced reproductive performance, but often not until the following year (Rockwood and Lobstein 1994). Whigham (1990) showed that defoliation affected both reproduction and belowground storage in *Tipularia discolor* (Pursh.) Nutt., a winter-green perennial. Corm biomass dwindled each year following 50 percent and 100 percent annual defoliations over a period of three years. However, reproduction was diminished only in the second and third year of the 100 percent defoliation treatment, and only in the third year of the 50 percent defoliation. Apparently, translocation of stored carbon and nutrients from the corm could replace lost aboveground tissue for only one or two years.

Similarly, the timing of herbivory on perennial herbs impacts subsequent year growth and reproduction (Knight 2003). Deer herbivory of reproductive individuals of *Trillium grandiflorum* in the early season led to a higher likelihood of regression to non-reproductive states in the following year or two, or to declines in total plant biomass than deer herbivory happening later in the growing season. This was most likely a response to the fact that deer consume the entire aboveground biomass of the plant, which does not regenerate within that season. Given the importance of the current year's carbon assimilation and nutrient uptake for replenishment and storage for future years' growth and reproduction, loss of an entire season's growth and nutrients embodied aboveground would certainly set back biomass and reproduction for subsequent years, compared to losses later in the season after substantial accumulation of carbon and nutrients in rhizomes had occurred (Knight 2003).

The nutrient environment may influence the severity of herbivory and the ability of herbaceous species to recover from it. In a boreal forest in the southern Yukon, John and Turkington (1995) found that many herbaceous plants responded to both fertilization and protection from herbivores. *Festuca altaica* Trin. and *Mertensia paniculata* (Aiton) G. Don. increased in biomass in response to nutrients, while *Anemone parviflora* Michx. and *Arctostaphylos uva-ursi* (L.) Sprengel. decreased in abundance when fertilized. *F. altaica*, which is highly preferred by snowshoe hares, the predominant herbivores, was less abundant in fertilized plots open to herbivory than in hare exclosures. In contrast, *A. uva-ursi* was less preferred by the hares and performed better in open plots. Overall, herbivory had less of an impact on the total abundance of herbaceous species than fertilizer additions in this nutrient-limited environment. However, the interaction between nutrients and herbivory can alter the community structure of the herbaceous layer by increasing abundance or susceptibility of individual species.

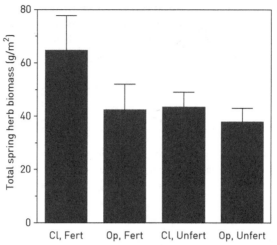

FIGURE 4.4 Biomass of spring herbs at Radnor Lake State Natural Area, Davidson County, Tennessee, USA, subjected to herbivore exclosures (Cl), open, control plots (Op), 6.4 g/wk. Peter's NPK fertilizer (Fert) and no fertilizer (Unfert).

An interaction between nutrient availability and herbivory was also found in a community of spring herbs in a Tennessee forest (W. B. Anderson 1998). Total biomass of all herbaceous species was greater in herbivore exclosures than in open, control plots, but these differences were much more striking in fertilized treatments than unfertilized treatments (fig. 4.4). This suggested that fertilized plants not protected by an exclosure were more susceptible to herbivory than unfertilized plants that were equally unprotected. However, this was not true for every species in the community. *Claytonia virginica*, which had lower concentrations of nitrogen and phosphorus than other species in all treatment combinations, had greater biomass in fertilized control plots than in fertilized exclosures, possibly because it was not preferred by herbivores or it was released from interspecific competition for light.

APPLICATION TO ECOSYSTEM PROCESSES

Species in the herbaceous layer of deciduous forests play an important role in nutrient cycling at the ecosystem level, particularly in the spring when many other species are still dormant (Muller 1978; Bormann and Likens 1979; chapter 10, this volume). Anthropogenic alterations of the nutrient environment (e.g., atmospheric deposition, burning and harvesting regimes) could have significant impacts not only on the physiological and community dynamics of the herbaceous layer, but on all forest species that interact directly or indirectly with the herbaceous layer. These effects could translate into changes in how nutrients cycle within deciduous forests.

The ability of spring herbs, which are sun plants (Taylor and Pearcy 1976), to photosynthesize, assimilate biomass, create large, thick sun leaves, and take up large quantities of nutrients in proportion to their biomass is dependent on both the light and nutrient environment (W. B. Anderson and Eickmeier 1998). Increased nutrient availability increases photosynthesis rates, biomass, and nutrient uptake by herbs, but only in full sun, and only up to a certain growth threshold and nutrient saturation point (Taylor and Pearcy 1976; W. B. Anderson and Eickmeier 1998). In the shade, these thresholds are lowered. If forests are invaded by evergreen or semi-evergreen shrub species (e.g., *Juniperus* or exotic species of *Lonicera*; chapter 15, this volume), or if the timing of canopy closure is sped up by global climate change (chapter 21, this volume), light availability will be reduced, which will reduce the ability of spring herbs to grow, store nutrients, and reproduce. Summer-green species may have inherently lower growth thresholds and nutrient saturation points than spring species because of their lower photosynthesis rates. In both spring and summer herbs, either light or nutrient limitation on growth will reduce the total amount of nutrients that flow through the herbaceous layer and increase the probability of nutrients leaching into streams (W. B. Anderson and Eickmeier 1998).

Increased nutrients also reduce nutrient resorption rates prior to senescence and potentially increase decomposition rates of the senescing tissues (Shaver and Melillo 1984). Senescence under these conditions could release more nutrients for uptake by other plant or microbial species. These mineralized nutrients might also be susceptible to being leached from the system. Higher levels of nutrients could also alter interactions between several herbaceous species and their mycorrhizal associates and could increase some herbaceous species' susceptibility to herbivory. In both cases, these interactions could alter the competitive relationships among herbaceous species and ultimately alter the species composition and diversity of the entire forest community.

Physiological and community-level responses of herbaceous species to the nutrient environment vary among species, sites, and seasons. Overall, though, an increase in nutrient availability could increase short-term nutrient uptake and growth, decrease resorption and mycorrhizal associations, and increase herbivory in the herbaceous layer, which would all increase the rate at which nutrients cycle through that layer and decrease the time that nutrients actually reside in that compartment of deciduous forest ecosystems.

SUMMARY

Although the nutrient environment of the herbaceous layer of deciduous forests may be relatively rich, light x nutrient interactions may affect herbaceous species' ability to exploit available nutrients. Shading may lessen the demand for soil nutrients, as the uptake of nutrients may be limited by the biomass accumulation of individual plants and their specific nutrient saturation points. Nutrient resorption may also occur less efficiently or proficiently in species or individuals that experience relatively high nutrient availability. Physiological responses of herbaceous species to fumigation by various pollutants vary depending on the species and the combinations of pollutants.

Nutrient availability may mediate interactions between herbaceous species and members of other kingdoms. Mycorrhizal associations are more common when nutrients are limited, and may indirectly mediate water stress for some species, although the associations have a high carbon cost. Nutrients may also increase susceptibility of herbaceous species to invertebrate or vertebrate herbivores. Finally, natural or anthropogenically altered nutrient environments may shift physiological responses and community patterns in such a way that nutrients reside in the herbaceous layer for shorter periods of time and possibly become more susceptible to being leached from forest ecosystems.

PART TWO
POPULATION BIOLOGY OF THE HERBACEOUS LAYER

5 Mating Systems and Floral Biology of the Herb Layer

A Survey of Two Communities and the State of Our Knowledge

Carol Goodwillie and Claudia L. Jolls

The herbaceous understory represents most of the biodiversity of forested eastern North America at its most threatened (Jolls 2003; Gilliam 2007). Empirical and theoretical understanding of sexual modes, including breeding biology, phenology, floral display, pollination, and mating systems, is central to our knowledge of the understory, both in ecological and evolutionary time. Understanding of, generalizations about, and conservation of the herb layer require basic biological information that we lack (Whigham 2004), including fundamental data on mating systems.

The herb layer is a distinctive flora in that populations can persist under a relatively long-lived and stable climax overstory, with infrequent and typically small disturbances associated with branch and tree fall gaps. Light, water, and nitrogen can be major limiting factors for understory herbs and function as important ecological drivers of the biodiversity of this stratum (McEwan and Muller 2011). Others have reviewed aspects of the reproductive ecology of the herbaceous understory in this ecological context (Schemske et al. 1978; Bierzychudek 1982a; Motten 1986; Jolls 2003; Whigham 2004; chapter 6, this volume). All agree that the data are limited relative to the diversity of the flora and that methodologies for characters such as reproductive effort are not standardized, making generalizations and comparisons difficult (Bierzychudek 1982a). Understory herbs have been characterized as largely perennial (Bierzychudek 1982a), relatively long-lived (Ehrlén and Lehtila 2002), and clonal, and as a result, populations can persist for extended periods with reliance on vegetative modes (Jolls 2003; Whigham 2004; Honnay et al. 2005). Despite the dominance of clonality, Bierzychudek (1982a) noted that species "flower and produce fruit regularly" (p. 760). Generalizations about breeding and mating systems of forest floor herbs are limited to observations that most species are hermaphroditic, with equal representation among self-compatible, self-incompatible, and partially self-incompatible systems (Bierzychudek 1982a; Whigham 2004; Honnay et al. 2005). It has been concluded that forest herbs are largely insect-pollinated (Bierzychudek 1982a), paralleling trends in most angiosperms (Wilcock and Neiland 2002). Seed dispersal is generally limited to a few meters (Jolls 2003; Whigham 2004), although there are some notable exceptions (Cain et al. 1998; > 1 km for *Trillium grandiflorum* (Michx.) Salisb. in Vellend et al. 2003). These reviews are largely from an ecological perspective, with emphasis on population biology, ecophysiology, species interactions, and nutrient dynamics. The distinctive longevity and potential for long-term persistence through clonality (Kudoh et al. 1999; Lezberg et al. 2001) of most forest herbs may have eclipsed focus on other aspects of mating systems.

Previous authors of reviews of woodland herbs have considered the literature on specific taxa and summarized what we know; most inferences are based on no more than a few dozen taxa. We have taken a somewhat different approach. Instead, we have sampled understory floras from a forest habitat and compiled available information for those taxa. Further, while previous surveys have focused on breeding systems, pollen limitation, and reproductive modes, a novel added contribution of our study is to characterize aspects of the floral biology of understory herbs as they relate to the reproductive and pollination ecology of the community. To gain further insights on forest herbs of eastern North America, we also use regional and global datasets for plant reproductive biology (Goodwillie et al. 2005, 2010) and compare data for forest herbs to those global trait distributions. Throughout this chapter, we summarize the reproductive traits of woodland plants of this region and interpret them in the context of the particular challenges and opportunities of woodland habitats for the reproduction of herbaceous plants.

SAMPLING WOODLAND HERBS

To sample from the large and diverse flora of the woodlands of eastern North America, we used species included in complete floras of two exemplar woodland communities. The communities chosen were matched roughly for spatial area and species richness: Harvard Forest, Massachusetts, and Crabtree Creek, North Carolina. Our intent was not to contrast these floras directly, given limitations of the data (discussed below), but rather to include two forests that differ in latitude and topographic diversity, as well as in species composition, with fewer than 20 percent of the total species occurring at both sites.

Harvard Forest (hereafter HF) is a transition hardwood-white pine-hemlock forest and a Long-Term Ecological Research Network site in the New England Upland Region. The site lies at 220–420 m elevation over granite, gneiss, and schist bedrock, with moderately to well-drained acidic soils of sandy loam glacial till and some alluvial and colluvial deposits. The climate is cool, moist temperate, with July and January mean temperatures of 20°C and –7°C, respectively; total precipitation averages 110 cm annually, distributed fairly evenly throughout the year. The area is described in detail by Jenkins et al. 2008; Jenkins and Motzkin 2009; and Barker Plotkin and Tomlinson

2010. Floristic data collection began in the early 1900s and is archived at the Harvard Forest Herbarium. Updated surveys were conducted in 2004–2005 and 2006–2007 (http://harvardforest.fas.harvard.edu). We used the flora for the approximately 1,200 ha area of the Prospect Hill (375 ha), Tom Swamp (475 ha), Slab City (200 ha), Simes (125 ha), and Schwarz (15 ha) tracts, and compiled a list of herbs occurring in forest, rich forest, or open forest habitats found there.

Crabtree Creek forest (hereafter CC) is 931 ha of southern Appalachian wide ridgetops, steep slopes, and wide floodplains along Crabtree Creek and Long Branch in Mitchell and Yancey Counties of western North Carolina. Elevations range from 792–1,195 m. The tract is one of the largest undeveloped properties in the region and is recommended for natural area designation. Vegetation types include chestnut oak forest, rich cove forest, and montane oak-hickory forest. The area is underlain by quartz diorite, patches of meta-ultramafic rock, and gneiss with stony, occasionally loamy or sandy soils. The climate is cool, moist temperate, with July and January mean temperatures of 15.8 to 27.2°C and –3.4 to –6.1°C, respectively, at nearby Mt. Mitchell and Spruce Pine. Total precipitation averages 114–147 cm annually, distributed fairly evenly throughout the year. Buchanan and Padgett (2007) of the NC Natural Heritage Program surveyed the area during three trips between August and November 2007 and recorded 394 vascular plant taxa.

We chose to focus our characterization and discussion of woodland herbs specifically on forbs, given more limited information on the breeding biology of the graminoids. From each floristic survey, we constructed a list of all forbs using scientific nomenclature and family designations as listed in the USDA Plants Database (USDA, NRCS 2012; www.plants.usda.gov). We eliminated a number of weedy species in both communities that were described in regional floras as occurring in waste areas and roadsides (Radford et al. 1968; Gleason and Cronquist 1991). We note that our analyses of the forest communities do not incorporate phylogenetic information. Thus, data points are not phylogenetically independent, and observed trends in reproductive biology of forest herbs might in some cases reflect multiple species belonging to the same genus or family that share features by common descent (Felsenstein 1985).

The final HF dataset comprises 95 species with representatives of 29 families; the CC community includes 167 species from 45 families, a comparable level of family diversity given the larger sample size. Forty species occur in both communities, yielding a total sample of 222 species. The two most common families in both communities are Asteraceae (20 species in HF, 45 species in CC) and Liliaceae (broadly circumscribed as in USDA Plants Database; 12 species in HF, 13 species in CC). For each species, we gathered information on flower color and shape (bilateral versus radial symmetry), corolla and inflorescence size, flowering phenology, breeding system (e.g., hermaphrodite, dioecious, cleistogamous), and other life history attributes (e.g., annual versus perennial, hemiparasitic, mycoheterotrophic) from the Manual of the Vascular Flora of the Carolinas (Radford et al. 1968), the Manual of Vascular Plants of the Northeastern United States and Adjacent Canada (Gleason and Cronquist 1991), or the USDA Plants Database. Additional information on vegetative reproduction was gathered from the Illinois Plant Information Network (Iverson et al. 1999; http://nrs.fs. fed.us/data/il/ilpin/list). Details on how data were recorded for individual analyses are given as results are presented below. We then sought additional information on the reproductive biology of each species in published literature in the Web of Science. We searched for research articles using each taxonomic name (including synonyms when appropriate) and a number of key words relating to various aspects of reproductive biology (e.g., flower, pollinator, mating system). At least one relevant research article was found for 43 (43 percent) of the species in the HF flora and for 58 (33 percent) of species in the CC flora (appendix 5.1).

BREEDING AND MATING SYSTEMS

The extraordinary diversity of plant mating systems has been a focus of a large literature in evolutionary ecology. Before presenting our findings on the mating systems of understory herbs, we provide a brief review of concepts and terminology from this literature. A small proportion of higher plants are dioecious (Renner and Ricklefs 1995), ensuring cross-fertilization, and a bewildering array of relatively uncommon breeding systems also exists, such as gynodioecy (separate female and hermaphrodite individuals) and andromonoecy (production of both male and hermaphrodite flowers on the same plant). The majority of plant species, however, are hermaphroditic with both male and female organs in the same flower; thus, the potential exists for self-fertilization (selfing) to occur. While some hermaphroditic plant species do reproduce primarily by selfing, others have evolved mechanisms to promote cross-fertilization (outcrossing). These include spatial separation of stigma and anthers (herkogamy), temporal separation of male and female function in flowers (protandry, when pollen is presented before stigmas become receptive, or protogyny, the reverse), and self-incompatibility, a genetically-based mechanism by which a plant can recognize and reject its own pollen.

Self- and cross-fertilization confer different benefits to plants. Outcrossing might allow a plant to produce higher fitness offspring when inbreeding results in the expression of deleterious recessive alleles (inbreeding depression, Charlesworth and Charlesworth 1987). However, autonomous selfing (self-fertilization that occurs without the assistance of a pollinating vector) can be beneficial in assuring reproduction in environments where pollinators or potential mates are scarce (Darwin 1876; Jain 1976). In delayed selfing, autonomous selfing occurs late in anthesis. Such mechanisms have been viewed as adaptations that allow opportunities for cross-fertilization yet still provide reproductive assurance, creating flexibility in the reproductive strategy (Lloyd 1992; Kalisz et al. 1999). Other species produce both cleistogamous (closed) flowers that are obligately selfing, as well as open, cross-pollinated flowers, and plants can often vary the allocation to each flower type in response to environmental cues (Schemske et al. 1978; Albert et al. 2011). In these examples, and in any hermaphrodite species without self-incompatibility, the outcrossing rate (the proportion of seeds produced by cross-fertilization) of a population at a given time will be determined by both floral mechanisms and the rate of pollinator visitation, often resulting in mixed mating systems (Brunet and Sweet 2006). Even in species with protandry, protogyny, or separation of stigma and anthers, self-fertilization can occur through geitonogamy, transfer of pollen among flowers on the same plant (de Jong et al. 1993). To characterize the mating systems of forest herbs of eastern North America, we used two approaches. First, we compared the distribution of genetically-based outcrossing rate estimates for understory forbs of eastern North America to a global plant distribution. We then examined the breeding systems (e.g., dioecy, monoecy) and qualitative information on mating systems (degree of self- versus cross-fertilization), when available, of species in the two study communities.

We searched for understory forbs of eastern North America in a comprehensive database containing all known outcrossing rate estimates for seed plants published to 2005 (Barrett and Eckert 1990; Vogler and Kalisz 2001; Goodwillie et al. 2005; Goodwillie et al. 2010). All estimates in the database were derived from genetic marker analysis of progeny arrays. This approach to the measurement of plant mating systems results in a continuum of outcrossing rates (t) ranging from 0 (completely selfing) to 1 (obligately outcrossing; Clegg 1980). The distribution of outcrossing rates for the global sample of 345 species was compared to the small subset of 21 forb species that occur in woodlands of eastern North America (five of which occur in one or both the HF and CC communities; fig. 5.1). Perhaps the first notable aspect of this analysis is the small number of woodland forb species for which quantitative outcrossing rates have been estimated from genetic data. In an attempt to expand the sample, we searched the Web of Science for more recently published data (2006 to 2011) and found no outcrossing rate estimates for woodland herbs of eastern North America published during this time interval. In the small sample of species that has been studied (N = 21), we found that the overall shape of the distribution was qualitatively different from the global pattern in that the frequencies of the highly selfing ($t = 0$ to 0.2) and highly outcrossing ($t = 0.8$ to 1) taxa were reduced. As has been shown for the broader distribution of outcrossing rates, there is likely to be a bias against estimating outcrossing rates for species that are known to be self-incompatible from crossing experiments (Igic and Kohn 2006) or species presumed to be highly selfing based on small flower size (Goodwillie et al. 2010). Nevertheless, we can think of no reason that such biases would affect the woodland herb sub-sample of flowering plants most strongly. Interestingly, in spite of a low proportion of species in the most extreme mating system classes, the distribution of outcrossing rates for this sample of forest herbs remains strongly bimodal, as predicted by theoretical models (Lande and Schemske 1985). It has been argued that the bimodality of the overall distribution can be attributed largely to wind-pollinated species (Aide 1986), with animal-pollinated species showing a continuous distribution (Vogler and Kalisz 2001, fig. 5.1). Yet, distinct peaks for largely outcrossing and largely selfing taxa can be seen in the woodland herb sample comprising only animal-(mostly insect-) pollinated species (see Floral Design and Pollination Biology below), suggesting the presence of two largely distinct mating strategies in this habitat. The equal proportion of predominantly outcrossing and predominantly selfing taxa was somewhat surprising given previous reports of a high incidence of outcrossing in the understory (Bierzychudek 1982a). However, annuals are overrepresented in the small sample of woodland herbs used for outcrossing rate estimates (40 percent of the 21 understory species in the outcrossing rate dataset are annuals versus 12 percent of the 222 exemplar community species), perhaps because of the convenience of annual plants as study organisms. Given the known association between the annual habit and selfing, the number of outcrossing rate estimates in the lower half of the distribution (fig. 5.1) might be inflated somewhat by this sampling bias.

The distribution of published outcrossing rates, though represented here by only a few species, suggests that predominant outcrossing or selfing are both effective means of reproduction in the understory, but obligate self- or cross-fertilizations are less successful. Other forms of data on mating and breeding systems for species in HF and CC, though also limited, were largely consistent with the patterns suggested by the outcrossing rate distribution.. A number of florl mechanisms that promote outcrossing were reported for species at HF and CC. Self-incompatibility, as typically inferred from

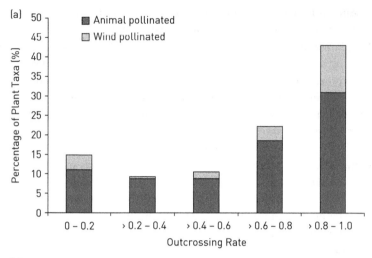

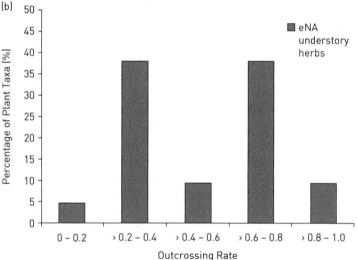

FIGURE 5.1 A comparison of the distribution of outcrossing rates between a global dataset of outcrossing estimates from genetic marker analysis of progeny arrays for seed plants (Barrett and Eckert 1990; Vogler and Kalisz 2001; Goodwillie et al. 2005, 2010; N = 345) with a subset of the data for herbaceous understory forbs of eastern North America (N = 21). All understory forbs sampled are insect-pollinated. Outcrossing rates were averaged when multiple population estimates were available for a species. Outcrossing rates are shown in intervals of 0.2, as is consistent with previous literature on the topic (Schemske and Lande 1985; Goodwillie et al. 2005).

studies in which hand self-pollination yields a reduced fruit set, was reported in 17 of the 30 species at HF and 14 of the 40 species at CC for which information on this trait was available. As pointed out by previous authors, methodologies differ among studies, and results are sometimes equivocal (Bierzychudek 1982a). In particular, low seed set after hand self-pollination could indicate extreme inbreeding depression, rather than a genetic mechanism for self-pollen recognition. Nevertheless, in both cases, a high rate of cross-fertilization might be inferred, since the magnitude of inbreeding depression has often been positively associated with the outcrossing rate (Husband and Schemske 1996). Protandry was reported for several species, including *Sabatia angularis* (L.) Pursh (Spigler and Chang 2009) and two species of *Monarda* at CC (Whitten 1981), and four species are listed as protogynous (e.g., *Clintonia borealis* and *Sanguinaria canadensis*, each of which is present in both communities). Information on herkogamy was rarely available; however, four species at CC are heterostylous (*Oxalis grandis* Small in the Oxalidaceae, *Houstonia purpurea* L., *H. serpyllifolia* Michx., and *Mitchella repens* L. in the Rubiaceae). In this type of breeding system, reciprocal herkogamy of two or three floral morphs and a physiological incompatibility system promote cross-fertilization between morphs (Barrett 1990).

Consistent with the pattern seen in the distribution of outcrossing rates for woodland herbs, we found relatively few examples of species at the extremes of the selfing to outcrossing spectrum. Obligate outcrossing can be enforced by dioecy or by strong self-incompatibility. Although 17 species at HF had some form of self-incompatibility, in 11 of these, the mechanism was described as weak or variable among individuals, resulting in a mixture of selfing and outcrossing. Similarly, in eight of 14 species with self-incompatibility in the CC community, the system was reported to be only partially effective in preventing self-fertilization. Dioecious species (e.g., *Urtica dioica* L., *Chamaelirium luteum* (L.) A. Gray, *Thalictrum revolutum* DC., and *Aralia racemosa* L.) comprised only 5.3 percent and 4.2 percent of species at HF and CC, respectively. At the other end of the distribution, we found a limited number of reports of highly selfing mating systems in those species for which qualitative information on the outcrossing rate was available: two of 30 species at HF and six of 40 species at CC. The relatively low number of highly selfing species in the woodland communities might be related to the predominance of perennial species there. A positive association between annual life history and self-fertilization has been well documented in other surveys (Barrett et al. 1996; van Kleunen 2007). Mechanisms of reproductive assurance are expected to be advantageous in the variable pollination environment of the understory, and indeed we found many examples among the species and habitats included in our analysis. Information on autonomous selfing, as tested using bagging experiments to exclude pollinators, was available for 10 species at HF and 15 at CC. The majority, seven and ten, respectively, were found to be capable of selfing without the aid of a pollinator. Cleistogamy, which assures seed set through closed, self-fertilized flowers, was common at HF and CC. Of the total 222 species sampled, 6 percent were cleistogamous (nine species at HF and eight at CC). These include *Amphicarpaea bracteata* (L.) Fernald, *Dalibarda repens* L., *Epifagus virginiana* (L.) W. Bartram, *Impatiens capensis* Meerb., *Polygala paucifolia* Willd., *Ruellia caroliniensis* (J. F. Gmel.) Steud., and several species of *Viola*. When last reviewed, cleistogamy had been reported in 693 species (Culley and Klooster 2007), only 0.2 percent of some 300,000 angiosperm species worldwide (Prance et al. 2000). Thus, even taking into consideration the fact that forbs of temperate North American forests are better studied than are plants in other regions of the world, we suggest that cleistogamy may be particularly adaptive for assuring seed set in the variable pollination environment of the understory.

Vegetative reproductive is common in the understory herb community (Bierzychudek 1982a; Jolls 2003; Whigham 2004; Honnay et al. 2005) and might also serve as a form of reproductive assurance (Vallejo-Marin and O'Brien 2007; Vallejo-Marin et al. 2010) in that asexual propagation allows species to persist in the face of limited pollinator service. Our sampling of two communities of eastern North America also shows this trend; 76 percent and 66 percent of the species at HF and CC, respectively, had some mechanism for vegetative reproduction, including clonal spread by rhizomes, stolons, and corms. The hypothesis that clonality confers reproductive assurance is supported by the finding of a significant association between vegetative reproduction and self-incompatibility in a combined analysis of the two communities (Fisher's exact test, $P = 0.04$). Of those species with vegetative reproduction, slightly fewer were found to be self-compatible (21) than self-incompatible (24). In contrast, in species without vegetative reproduction, the number of self-compatible species (18) was three times as high as the number of self-incompatible species (six), suggesting that vegetative reproduction and selfing represent alternative methods to ensure persistence. Our results parallel the finding of a similar association between clonality and self-incompatibility in the genus *Solanum* (Vallejo-Marin and O'Brien 2007). Finally, we found that at least three species of Asteraceae in the understory (*Antennaria plantaginifolia* 9 (L.) Richardson, *Erigeron strigosus* Muhl. ex Willd., *Eupatorium rotundifolium* L.) were capable of apomictic (asexual) seed production, which has also been argued to serve as a form of reproductive assurance (but see Hörandl et al. 2011).

FLORAL BIOLOGY OF THE UNDERSTORY HERB COMMUNITY

Floral and Inflorescence Architecture

The wide variety of reproductive strategies in angiosperms is accompanied by spectacularly diverse floral structures, driven largely by their breeding biology (Richards 1997). As we look at the array of angiosperm species, we might first notice that species differ dramatically in the size of their floral displays. Of the resources allocated to sexual reproduction, plants that reproduce primarily by animal pollination are expected to allocate relatively more to structures for attraction than are those that produce seeds largely by autonomous self-fertilization. This pattern has been documented within species and genera (e.g., Wyatt 1984; Armbruster et al. 2002) and also across the broad spectrum of angiosperms (Goodwillie et al. 2010). Another level of design concerns how resources are partitioned among flowers in an inflorescence. While some plants attract pollinators with one or a few large flowers, others present a large inflorescence of many small flowers. With finite resources to dedicate to reproduction, a tradeoff is expected between the number and size of flowers. The finding of a negative correlation between these two traits among both related species and broad samples of taxa provides support for a tradeoff (Goodwillie et al. 2010), although some studies have failed to find such evidence. While many small or a few large flowers may be equivalent in resource costs and pollinator attraction, the number of flowers on an inflorescence has additional consequences. The potential for transfer of pollen among flowers on the same plant by a vector increases with the number of flowers presented simultaneously (Harder and Barrett 1995; Ishii and Harder 2006). In self-compatible species, this can result in high rates of geitonogamous self-fertilization, which can incur a cost if inbreeding depression is substantial.

We first determined the distribution of flower and inflorescence sizes of species from the two study sites and examined it to seek insights into the reproductive biology of the species, given demonstrated relationships between floral architecture and mating systems. To further characterize the floral biology of the forest herb community, we compared the distributions of floral display sizes in species at our study sites to

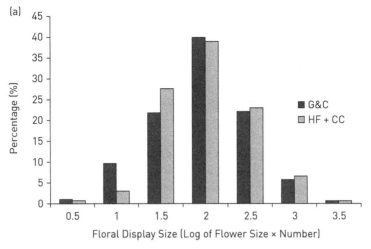

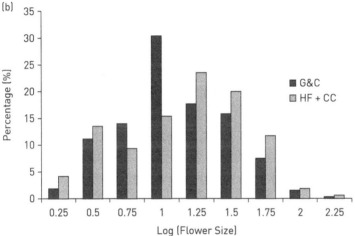

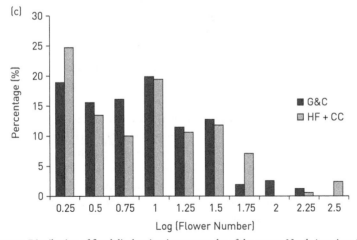

FIGURE 5.2 Distribution of floral display sizes in two samples of the eastern North American flora. Floral display (top panel) calculated as the log of the product of flower diameter and number of open flowers per inflorescence (see text for details). Flower size (middle panel) calculated as the log of corolla diameter or length in mm (see text for details). Flower number (bottom panel) calculated as the log of the number of open flowers per inflorescence (see text for details). G&C: 323 species from Gleason and Cronquist (1991) sampled evenly across habitats and plant forms. HF+CC: 170 species from the combined herbaceous floras of Harvard Forest and Crabtree Creek forest communities.

those in a previously published dataset of eastern North American species that samples evenly across the full spectrum of habitats and plant forms (Goodwillie et al. 2010).

For species at HF and CC, we recorded information on flower size, color, and symmetry from published floras (Radford et al. 1968 or Gleason and Cronquist 1991) using methods employed in Goodwillie et al. (2010). The most appropriate measure of flower size is biomass allocation, but this information is not available for most forest forbs. From the point of view of a pollinator, flower size might best be quantified as the diameter of the corolla, and we used this measure for the majority of the species sampled. When petal length was the only information provided for a radially symmetrical flower, we doubled the value as an estimate of flower diameter. In species with tubular flowers, we used corolla length as an estimate of flower size. We also attempted to quantify inflorescence size from a pollinator's viewpoint by counting the number of open flowers per inflorescence. Data on inflorescence size were rarely available in floras, except in cases of single-flowered inflorescences, so we estimated data from online photographic images in many cases, using only reputable botanical sources (e.g., USDA Plants Database; websites of herbaria and botanical societies). The previously published dataset of species used for comparison was constructed by sampling every sixth non-graminoid taxon listed in Gleason and Cronquist (1991); see Goodwillie et al. 2010 for details. We excluded members of the Asteraceae from the analysis because it is difficult to define the appropriate level of inflorescence structure for analysis or make meaningful comparisons to other taxa for flower size.

As with mating systems, we found diverse strategies for floral and inflorescence size in the understory community. Flower size ranged by nearly two orders of magnitude, from one to over 100 mm in diameter (fig. 5.2). Of the five largest-flowered species at each study site, all except one belong to the same three genera, though only two occurred at both sites: *Trillium erectum* (L.) (Liliaceae), *T. undulatum* Willd., *Lilium philadelphicum* L. (Liliaceae), *Cypripedium acaule* Aiton (Orchidaceae), and *Sanguinaria canadensis* L. (Papaveraceae) at HF; *Trillium erectum*, *T. catesbaei* Elliott, *Lilium superbum* L., *Cypripedium acaule* and *C. parviflorum* Salisb. at CC. At the small-flowered end of the spectrum, eight species at HF and 13 at CC produce flowers less than 2 mm in diameter (fig. 5.2). These include members of the Apiaceae (*Sanicula marilandica* L., *Zizia trifoliata* (Michx.) Fernald, *Cryptotaenia canadensis* (L.) DC), Araliaceae (*Aralia racemosa* L., *Panax quinquefolius* L., *P. trifolius* L.), Polygonaceae (*Polygonum scandens* L., *P. cilinode* Michx., *P. virginianum* L.), and Urticaceae (*Urtica dioica* L., *Pilea pumila* (L.) A. Gray, *Boehmeria americana* (L.) Sw). As in other surveys, we found a significant negative relationship between flower size and number (Pearson correlation coefficient, $r = -0.612$, $P < 0.001$, combined data from HF and CC), consistent with the idea of a tradeoff in resources between flower number and size.

The species that produced the largest flowers at both sites had either a single flower (*Trillium*, *Cypripedium*, *Sanguinaria*) or present relatively few flowers at a time (*Lilium* spp.). In contrast, the mean number of open flowers per inflorescence was 44 for the 17 species with flowers less than 2 mm (totaled across the two study sites). Hermaphrodite plants with many flowers are expected to experience high rates of geitonogamous self-pollination. Consistent with that prediction, the list of 20 species at CC that had the highest number of flowers per inflorescence included four of the six species in the community reported to be highly selfing, including *Conopholis americana* (L.) Wallr. (Orobanchaceae) and *Phytolacca americana* L. (Phytolaccaceae). Conversely, nine of the 20 many-flowered species were dioecious or subdioecious (separate males and female plants, with only occasional hermaphrodite flower production) and therefore not subject to a cost of self-fertilization by geitonogamy. This trend also was found in HF forbs, where four out of five dioecious species were among the 20 species with the greatest number of flowers per inflorescence. Interestingly, then, the display of many small flowers in woodland herbs may represent two distinct mating strategies: predominantly selfing or obligate outcrossing.

At the other extreme, many of the largest-flowered species had variable mating systems. While *Lilium philadelphicum* is self-incompatible, *Trillium erectum* has a mixed mating system, and *Asarum canadense* L., which had the eighth largest corolla at HF, was reported to be highly selfing. Goodwillie et al. (2010) found that the product of flower size and number was more strongly correlated with the outcrossing rate than is either factor alone (Goodwillie et al. 2010). Accordingly, among the top 20 species based on this multiplicative measure of display size, six out of nine for which mating system information was available at HF and six out of eight at CC were either partially or fully self-incompatible or described as highly outcrossing and unable to self autonomously. Interestingly, eight of the 20 species with large displays at HF had some form of trophic association with plants or fungi (e.g., *Pedicularis canadensis* L., *Pyrola chlorantha* Sw.). Perhaps reliance on another food source allows these plants to allocate more to reproduction than non-parasitic plants that face the challenges of resource limitation in the low light environment.

How does the distribution of floral display traits in the herb communities that we examined compare to plants from all life forms and habitats in eastern North America? We found that the relatively small number of forest herbs in our analysis (170 species after exclusion of Asteraceae) encompassed the entire range of values for flower size and number that are represented in the larger sample (323 species) that spans all life forms and habitats (fig. 5.2). In fact, relative to the larger comprehensive sample, we found a higher proportion of extreme values in the forest understory: more than expected single-flowered species; a slightly longer tail of the distribution toward many-flowered species, and an excess of large-flowered species in the woodland herbs. For floral display (the product of flower size and number), the mean of the comprehensive sample and the two forest communities did not differ statistically ($t = 0.611$, $df = 491$, $P = 0.54$), and the distributions were quite similar. However, we found fewer species at the low end of the floral display size distribution in the two sites that we sampled (fig. 5.2). We interpret this as further evidence that highly selfing species are relatively uncommon in woodland habitats.

Floral Design and Pollination Biology

The form and design of structures that play a role in pollinator attraction are shaped by the major pollen vectors that contribute to a species' reproductive success. Pollen transfer has been generalized into pollination syndromes, the "harmonic relationships of pollinators and blossoms" (Faegri and van der Pijl 1979, at p. 97): by insects (entomogamy/entomophily) or specifically bees (mellitophily/hymenophyly), beetles (cantharophily), flies (myophily), butterflies (psychophily), moths (phalaenophily), by birds (ornithogamy/orthophily), by mammals (therogamy), by bats (chierogamy/chiropterophily), by wind (anemogamy/anemophily), and by water (hydrogamy, hydrophily) (Faegri and van der Pijl 1979; Wyatt 1983). Flowers of different pollination syndromes have been described in terms of their color and shape for more than a century and perhaps overzealously (Köelreuter 1761–1766; Sprengel 1793; Knuth 1906–1909; Wyatt 1983). For example, red tubular flowers often are bird-pollinated and dish-shaped corollas of brown or white are associated with fly, wasp, or beetle pollination (Faegri and van der Pijl 1979). More recently, red flower color has been interpreted not as an attractant for birds, but rather as an escape from bees, allowing rewards for other specialized visitors. Faegri and van der Pijl (1979) themselves stressed that there were exceptions (e.g., visitors that are nectar or pollen thieves), thus generalizations about such relationships should not become a "mental straightjacket," to use their term (p. 98). One component of floral shape is its pattern of symmetry: radial versus bilateral. Certain types of radially symmetrical floral shapes (e.g., dish, bell) or bilateral shapes (e.g., flag, tube) have been associated with particular pollinators, but more generally, bilateral floral symmetry has been shown to be related to greater pollinator specialization (Sargent 2004; Fenster et al. 2004). One explanation offered for this pattern is that complex floral shapes promote more precise pollen placement on visitors and require more learning on the part of pollinators, thus resulting in greater fidelity in visitation to a single plant species (Laverty 1980).

How do the species of the understory meet the challenges of the pollination environment and accomplish reproductive success? For species at our two study sites, we collected data on flower visitors, or on pollinators when available, from the published literature and from the Illinois Wildflowers Flower-Visiting Insect Database (http://www.illinoiswildflowers.info/). Such information is incomplete, and studies to test pollinator effectiveness and distinguish between visitors and effective pollinators are rare (Motten et al. 1981; Thomson 1986; McKinney and Goodell 2010; Willmer 2011). To characterize the floral biology of the communities that is relevant to pollination, we report information on flower color, symmetry, and flowering phenology from regional floras (Radford et al. 1968; Gleason and Cronquist 1991). We expressed flowering phenology as the month of the midpoint of the flowering period reported by the appropriate regional flora for the site. Using the visitor information available for a subset of the species, we tested for expected associations between floral traits and pollinating vectors, and then used information on floral form, available for all taxa, to gain insights into the broad trends in pollination biology, including seasonal patterns.

Color and Phenology

Flowering phenology, the seasonal presentation of flowers, has implications in short-term ecological and long-term evolutionary time, although qualitative measures such as "midpoint of flowering month" are less useful than quantitative measurements such as "flowering curves" that quantify the number of flowers or inflorescences presented versus a date of census (Kearns and Inouye 1993). Nevertheless, even qualitative measures can provide cues about the proximate and ultimate factors that shape flower presentation and their associated visitors, including development and plant size, climate, and competition among pollinators for floral resources.

Certainly, flower color data also have their limitations. For one, flower color is highly anthropocentric and subjective (Arnold et al. 2009). Our perception of flower display is different from organisms like insects (particularly bees) that are able to detect other parts of the electromagnetic spectrum, as well as chemical cues. Assignment of floral color to any given plant taxon is complex (white, green, whitish-green, or greenish-white?), not only among scientists, but also within plant species. Some flowers are multicolored (e.g., *Aquilegia* spp.), and some species bear flowers of different colors on the same individual plant. Still others change color as they age, among microsites, or as a genetically based polymorphism. Most botanists would agree that any statement of the distribution of flower color in the angiosperms is, by necessity, limited in scope, and at best, a slightly educated guess. White and yellow flowers are very common, perhaps red and then blue less so. In contrast, green may be the most common flower color in nature, particularly if other growth habits, including trees and graminoids, are considered (Joe Marcus, Lady Bird Johnson Wildflower Center, the University of Texas at Austin, http://www.wildflower.org/expert/show.php?id=1456, unpubl. pers. comm.). Attempts to quantify and confirm such abundances and then associate them with patterns in space or time are limited and conflicting (see reviews in Willmer 2011).

There were two general peaks of flowering across taxa at HF and CC (fig. 5.3), first in May, representing the spring ephemerals that flower before canopy closure, and a second one in July, perhaps associated with taxa tolerant of lower light or those that flower in clearings (Proctor et al. 1996). This bimodality of forest understory herbs may be distinctive. In contrast, in the Rocky Mountain subalpine, few species flower near the beginning and end of the flowering season; most flower toward the middle (Morales et al. 2005). Most statistical comparisons of flowering within communities show aggregation or random patterns in phenology (Rathcke and Lacey 1985).

In our sample, most months were dominated by yellow and white flowers, typical of the distribution of floral color in angiosperms in general. Although very few woodland forbs have brown flowers, the few that do flower in early spring. Brown flowers are typically fly-pollinated, and flies can be some of the earliest insects out foraging in the early spring months (Schemske et al. 1978; Willmer 2011). A somewhat distinctive increase in green-flowered taxa occurs in early midsummer, seen at the more northern HF but not at the CC site in North Carolina to the south. Similar patterns of colorful, non-green flowers in May to early June, and then later in August, have been observed in the prairie flora (Kay Havens Young, Chicago Botanic Garden, pers. comm.). This so-called "green lull" in later June and July may represent the dominance of some taxa or simply the gap between flowering by more showy taxa (i.e., the dominance by spring ephemerals in early spring and then by summer taxa after canopy closure).

Floral Visitors and Phenology

Insect visitation data also must be viewed with caution, given the limited amount of quantitative information available, as well as the distinction between mere visitors and true pollinators. Seasonal patterns in insect abundance occur, although community-level changes relative to flowering phenology are difficult to document and are rarely reported quantitatively (Pyke et al. 2011).

The changes in the numbers of species with flower visitor data (heights of the bars in figs. 5.4 and 5.5) are driven largely by the flowering phenology of fig. 5.3. Most of the understory herbs are associated with insect visitors, a pattern seen for flowering plants as a whole. There have been very few reports of understory herbs being visited by hummingbirds. Species for which hummingbird visitations have been documented at our two study sites were *Aquilegia canadensis* L. (HF, CC), *Impatiens capensis* Meerb. (CC), *Lobelia cardinalis* L. (CC), *Monarda didyma* L. (CC), *Polygonatum pubescens*

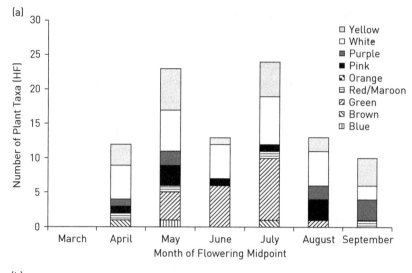

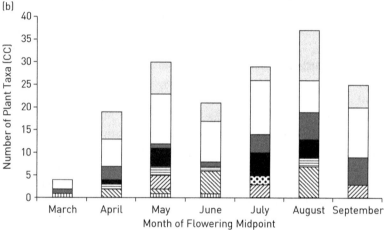

FIGURE 5.3 The phenology of floral color for the herbaceous understory flora of Harvard Forest (top panel) and Crabtree Creek (bottom panel).

(Willd.) Pursh (HF), and *Silene virginica* L. (CC). Only four taxa at the two sites have been identified as anemophilic (e.g., *Urtica dioica* at HF, and *Pilea pumila*, *Boehmeria cylindrica*, and *Laportea canadensis* (L.) Weddell at CC). Associated with the flowering sequences shown in fig. 5.3, there were two flushes of flower presentation among these herbaceous understory taxa. Most months at HF and CC were dominated by yellow and white flowers, and the dominant types of visitors (bees, flies, beetles, birds, wasps, butterflies, and moths) changed over the months. Proctor et al. (1996) found a similar pattern that we observed at both sites with many species completing flowering before late May and with open flowers visited by unspecialized bees, flies, and small Hymenoptera. There are documented changes in bumblebee seasonal abundances in temperate climates. In general, the number or density of foraging bumblebees generally increased from spring to summer (Gurel et al. 2008; Colla and Dumesh 2010), and sometimes an "early trough" occurred in bumblebee numbers following emergence of the spring queens (Teras 1983). Our data pool includes both short- and long-tongued bees, yet there still does appear to be a midsummer decline in flowering, as well as a

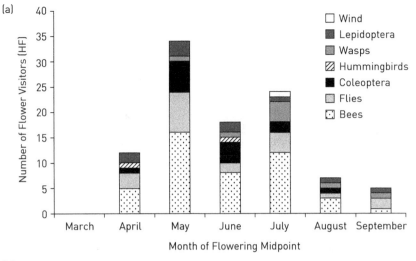

(a)

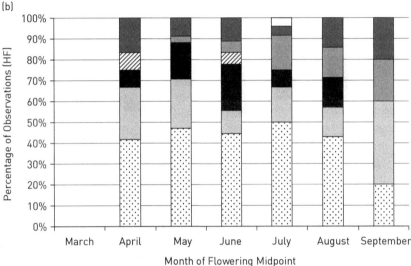

(b)

FIGURE 5.4 The phenology of flower visitors for the herbaceous understory flora of Harvard Forest, based on counts of plant taxa (top panel) and percentage of observations (bottom panel).

decline in the relative number of reports of flowers visited by bees in June (figs. 5.4 and 5.5, top panels). Proportionally, however, bees overall still dominate the insect visitors in June, with Diptera and other flies represented more in early spring and late summer (figs. 5.4 and 5.5, lower panels). There is a slight increase in the presentation of flowers visited by Lepidoptera from July onward at both the Massachusetts HF and North Carolina CC sites.

As noted above, any description of plant pollinators must be taken with caution given that the information available was incomplete and not available for all species at each site. Clearly this limited dataset may not be representative of patterns of abundance in either plant or insect taxa, and the observations include visitors that were not true pollen vectors. We conclude that there are still too few data to determine if there are any striking trends in the diversity of vectors that result in successful pollination of forest herbs.

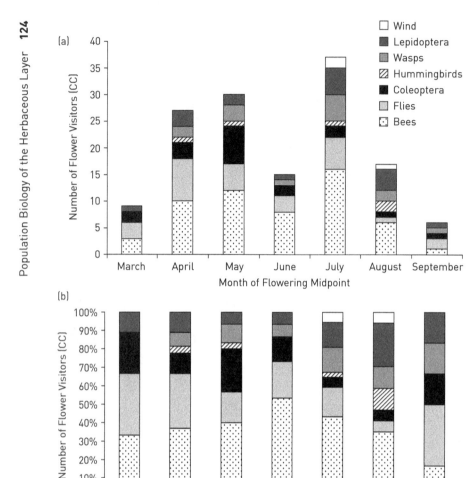

FIGURE 5.5 The phenology of flower visitors for the herbaceous understory flora of Crabtree Creek, based on counts of plant taxa (top panel) and percentage of observations (bottom panel).

Symmetry and Visitor Diversity

The understory woodland herbs of North Carolina and Illinois have been reported to be dominated by open, radially symmetrical flowers and unspecialized pollinators, perhaps a result of competition for limited pollinator abundance in early spring (Schemske et al. 1978; Motten 1986). In our sample, a substantial proportion of the HF and CC taxa have been reported to be visited by three, four, or even five major pollinator taxa (e.g., bees, beetles, flies, wasps, and butterflies), but reports of single pollinator groups (e.g., bees only) are also common (fig. 5.6). Consistent with other surveys (Fenster et al. 2004), we found an association between floral symmetry and specialization; nearly all of the bilaterally symmetrical flowers were pollinated by a single pollinator taxon, while radial flowers were often generalists (fig. 5.6). If this relationship is consistent, and if the understory at our two study sites is indeed dominated by plant species with generalist pollination syndromes, we might have expected

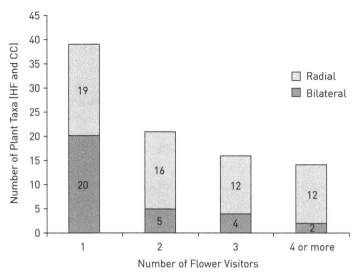

FIGURE 5.6 The distribution of floral symmetry (bilateral or radial) with the number of different types of floral visitors (major taxa, e.g., bees, flies, beetles) for the Harvard Forest and Crabtree Creek herbaceous understory floras combined, by counts.

to find a high proportion of open, radially symmetrical flowers. In contrast, approximately one-third of the species had bilateral floral symmetry, a value that was representative of the global distribution of symmetry types (Neal et al. 1998). Thus, we do not find compelling evidence for a dominance of true generalized pollination in the understory. We note, however, that even those plant species for which a single pollinator taxon was reported might well be visited by multiple and diverse members of an order and therefore would not be true specialists. Nevertheless, several plant species at each site were pollinated exclusively by bumblebees (e.g., *Pedicularis canadensis*, Macior 1968), long-tongued bees (*Goodyera pubescens*, Kallunki 1981), and hummingbirds (*Monarda didyma*, Whitten 1981), representing relatively specialized systems. Notably, all of these show bilateral symmetry.

The Special Case of Mycoheterotrophs and Hemiparasites

Trophic associations with other plants or fungi are a common feature of understory herbs and might have implications for their pollination and breeding biology. At HF, at least 14 of the 95 species engaged in some form of parasitism. *Epifagus virginiana* and *Orobanche uniflora* L. (both in the Orobanchaceae) are achlorophyllous root parasites on oaks, beeches, and various herbaceous plants. Mycoheterotrophs (achlorophyllous plants forming obligate trophic associations with fungi) at HF were *Monotropa hypopithys* L. and *M. uniflora* L. (Monotropacaeae), *Corallorhiza maculata* (Raf.) Raf. (Orchidaceae), and *Orthilia secunda* (L.) House (*Pyrola secunda* L., Pyrolaceae). Additionally, a number of hemiparasites were present (e.g., *Aureolaria pedicularia* (L.) Raf., *A. virginica* (L.) Pennell, *Pedicularis canadensis*, and *Melampyrum lineare* Desr. in the Scrophulariaceae). Parasitic plants were less common at CC; four occurred there, including the parasite of oak roots, *Conophilis americana* (Orobanchaceae), and three species also found at HF. Plants that form specialized relationships with trophic partners and as a result generally have small population sizes and narrow habitat requirements might be expected to avoid further specialized mutualisms with pollinators and reproduce either by self-fertilization or a generalist pollination syndrome (Bidartondo 2005; McCormick et al. 2009; Shefferson et al. 2011). Contrary to this expectation, however, in one of the only detailed studies of reproductive biology in mycoheterotrophic plants, Klooster and Culley (2009) found three species in the Monotropaceae (including two present at HF) to be largely outcrossing and pollinated nearly exclusively by *Bombus* species. We found some similar trends in the limited data available for the other parasitic plants at our study sites; of seven parasitic species for which pollinator information was found, five were pollinated exclusively by bees and one by wasps. The limited mating system information available indicated that parasitic plants at HF range from outcrossing to selfing. Strikingly, however, of the three obligate root parasites present in our sample, one has been reported to be highly selfing (*Conopholis americana*, Baird and Riopel 1986) and another reproduces almost entirely by cleistogamous flowers (*Epifagus virginiana*, Thieret 1969), providing some support for the idea that self-fertilization is an adaptive strategy for species with these unusual trophic relationships.

Pollen Limitation

We have examined the mating systems, inflorescence architecture, floral form, and natural history of understory herbs in the context of the challenges of the understory habitat for pollination. To what extent does pollen deposition limit reproduction in the understory, despite the presence of adaptations to cope with this potentially low visitation environment? For over two decades, pollen limitation of reproduction has been a topic of considerable interest in plant evolution and ecology (reviewed in Knight et al. 2005) because it links floral traits, breeding systems, and pollination biology to the demography of plant populations. The fundamental question addressed is whether population growth is limited primarily by seed set, and if so, what limits the number of seeds produced? In many plant species, only a fraction of ovules mature to produce seeds (Sutherland 1986; Charlesworth 1989); this has often been interpreted as evidence for pollen limitation. Alternatively, however, other resources such as light or nutrients might limit the number of seeds or fruits that can be provisioned. The classic experimental test for pollen limitation compares seed set from unmanipulated flowers in a natural pollination environment to seed set in flowers in which pollen has been deposited by hand (Zimmerman and Pyke 1988). If seed set increases with pollen supplementation, reproduction is inferred to be pollen-limited. Some methodological considerations have been raised, including the finding that seed set in supplemented flowers can draw resources from other fruits or future reproduction. As a result, whole-plant and lifetime estimates of pollen limitation often yield smaller effect sizes (Knight et al. 2006).

Pollinator visitation in the understory is expected to be constrained by temperature in the early spring and light availability after canopy closure, reflecting the thermoregulatory limitations of insects (Schemske et al. 1978; Herrera 1995). Low visitation suggests that pollen limitation of seed set should be common in the understory. Accordingly, a trend (though not statistically significant) toward greater pollen limitation in wooded, compared to open, habitats was found in a broad survey of angiosperms (Larson and Barrett 2000). Moreover, some of the first classic experiments demonstrating pollen limitation focused on forest herbs of eastern North America, including *Arisaema triphyllum* (L.) Schott (Bierzychudek 1981) and *Tipularia discolor* (Pursh) Nutt. (Whigham and McWethy 1980; Snow and Whigham 1989).

As a final component of our exploration of plant reproduction in the understory, we present the results of a literature survey on pollen limitation in forest herbs. We searched the primary literature in Web of Science for experimental research on pollen limitation in herbs that occurred at our two study sites. Because this yielded relatively few studies, we searched again for pollen limitation studies on any woodland herb of eastern North America. Our search yielded pollen limitation studies for 34 forest herbs of eastern North America (21 of which were at our study sites) that employed some variant of the classic pollen supplementation approach to quantify pollen limitation (appendix 5.1). Reproduction was consistently pollen-limited in 14 species, while in 11 species, pollen supplementation did not increase seed or fruit set. Consistent with the idea that visitation can be unreliable in the understory, spatial or temporal variation in pollen limitation was found in eight additional studies. The remaining studies were equivocal; for example, pollen limitation was detected for fruit but not seed set. Thus, in general agreement with previous characterizations, the majority of understory forbs in our survey (23 of 34 total) were pollen-limited in at least some sites and seasons and for some measure of reproductive success. Moreover, an additional seven species in our exemplar communities were reported to have low seed or fruit set in natural populations, which is suggestive of pollen limitation.

Pollen limitation in the plant taxa we surveyed was associated with several different factors. In *Campanulastrum americanum* (L.) Small, pollen limitation was found to be higher in shaded than in open habitats (Kilkenny and Galloway 2008) and in *Impatiens capensis*, pollinator visitation increased with light availability (Walters and Stiles 1996). This provides some support for the hypothesis that pollinator activity is limited generally by light in the understory. The effects of plant population size, another factor that might limit visitation in the understory, are less clear; pollen limitation in *Panax quinquefolius* was negatively associated with population size (Hackney and McGraw 2001), suggesting that visitation was reduced at low plant densities. In contrast, large populations of *Sabatia angularis* were more critically limited by pollen than small ones, which was interpreted as evidence for pollinator competition at high densities (Spigler and Chang 2009). In *Trillium grandiflorum*, both effects were seen, with pollen limitation increasing at both very high and very low densities of flowering plants (Steven et al. 2003). Finally, in *Impatiens capensis*, visitation did not vary with population size. Thus, we do not find much evidence in our survey that plant density in the understory is a consistent factor limiting visitation.

We have argued that multiple mechanisms of reproductive assurance allow understory plants to cope with inconsistent pollination. In broad surveys, pollen limitation has been shown to be lower in self-compatible than self-incompatible species, suggesting that selfing provides reproductive assurance when pollinator visitation is variable (Burd 1994; Larson and Barrett 2000). Similarly, in our survey of understory species, pollen limitation was somewhat more common in self-incompatible species (5 out of 6 were pollen-limited) than in self-compatible species (5 out of 11 were pollen-limited), although the association was not significant (Fisher's exact test, $P = 0.3$). Does a generalist pollination system alleviate pollen limitation? Again, our small sample provided little power to test this hypothesis, but a trend was suggested. Of the 10 insect-pollinated species for which pollen limitation was not detected (one additional species was wind-pollinated), half were reported to have a generalist pollination system. In contrast, the majority of the species with consistent pollen limitation were pollinated by a single insect group, and only one (*Amianthium muscitoxicum* (Walter) A. Gray) was reported to be a generalist. Thus, again, we find that the understory herbaceous species has an array of adaptations for reproductive assurance to reduce pollen deposition limitations on reproduction.

CONCLUSIONS

Our study differs from previous reviews on forest herbs in that we present a quantitative survey of reproductive and floral characteristics in a complete understory flora at two sites in eastern North America and comparative data from other studies. One of the potential advantages of this approach over a survey based only on species featured in the published literature was that we avoid the potential problem of bias in choice of study organisms. For some traits in our analysis, such as flower shape, color, and size, we were able to provide a comprehensive characterization of the forb communities at the two study sites. Yet, for many important aspects of the reproductive biology of the understory, such as outcrossing rate and pollination biology, our analysis nevertheless was constrained by the small, and perhaps biased, sample of species for which information is available.

Indeed, the common, as well as the rare, taxa of the forest herbaceous layer (chapter 6, this volume) are understudied, particularly with regard to their mating systems and reproductive ecology. While publications on the topic of the herbaceous layer of forests have increased in the past two decades (Gilliam 2007; chapter 1, this volume), marker-based research on mating systems for these taxa has declined in the past decade, despite the greater availability of genetic tools. Others have noted that research on pollination biology, mating systems, and other aspects of reproductive ecology and evolution has become increasingly specialized, possibly at the expense of synthetic, interdisciplinary understanding (Holsinger 1996; Mitchell et al. 2009). Of the 222 taxa of our two exemplar understory communities, only slightly more than 100 had information on pollination biology available, and just 80 had published research on any other aspect of reproductive biology. Of the 80 species, studies of 57 species contained information on self-incompatibility; 26 studies provided qualitative information on the degree of outcrossing; and genetically based estimates of outcrossing rates are available for a mere five taxa. Detailed studies of floral and pollination biology (e.g., on the timing of self- and cross-fertilization or the effectiveness of individual pollinator species) have been carried out for only a handful of the taxa.

Despite incomplete data on many aspects of floral and pollination biology, a picture emerges from the combined information of a flora with diverse reproductive traits. As in previous work, we found that understory herbs were mostly perennial and hermaphroditic. The limited genetic data suggested two distinct mating systems, not just largely outcrossing, as previously reported, but to a lesser extent, predominantly selfing as well. Qualitative information on autonomous selfing and floral outcrossing mechanisms in species of the exemplar communities supported this pattern. In agreement with previous authors, we found that a large proportion of the understory forbs is reported to have partial or complete self-incompatibility. Despite evidence for divergent strategies, we argue that the extremes—obligate self- and cross-fertilization—are relatively rare in understory taxa. Flexible mating systems appeared to be common, in which partial self-incompatibility, cleistogamy, or delayed selfing confer reproductive assurance when pollinator visitation was low. We noted that there were few species with small floral displays (the product of flower size and number), which also was suggestive of a low frequency of obligately selfing species. Strong self-incompatibility, although rare in the understory, was found to be accompanied by vegetative reproduction in most cases, which might allow the species to persist in the face of low visitation. We also found a diverse variety of floral displays, from the single large-flowered *Trillium* spp. to the myriad of small flowers in *Thalictrum*. Yet this diversity in inflorescence design appeared to be unlinked to mating systems, as species at both ends of the many-small, single-large flower spectrum were found to be both predominantly selfing and predominantly outcrossing. The pollination syndromes represented among these species are varied, despite limitations of historic classifications. Most were insect-pollinated, visited by several animal taxa, making them generalists by definition (Fenster et al. 2004); there were, however, a few distinctive specialists.

Pollinator data were limited and limiting; there have been few tests of effective pollinators for understory herbs. The lack of dominance of radial floral symmetry offered no real evidence in support of a generalist pollinator syndrome within the understory. We also found that many taxa appeared to be visited by a single pollinator type ($\sim$ 54/113 = 47 percent). This category, however, may have represented several species of short- and long-tongued generalist bees and flies. The prevalence of white and yellow flower color in the understory paralleled that of other communities and of angiosperms in general as had been suggested to reflect bee, beetle, or butterflies, and thus generalist pollination (Faegri and van der Pijl 1979). The association with flower color and pollinators as "syndromes" has been criticized as an overestimation of specialization (Waser et al. 1996). Our human bias also has associated pollinators with colors we can see, rather than those the animal visitor perceives; spectral reflectances (300–700 nm) have been used as a solution to this bias, at least for bee species (Kevan 1978; Kevan and Baker 1983; Chittka et al. 1994; Arnold et al. 2009, 2010; Willmer 2011). The few quantitative studies done for regional floras suggest no statistical preference for flower color by some insects, yet they do report trends of flies and beetles visiting human-perceived white flowers (bee blue-green) and large bees and butterflies visiting more human-perceived blue/pink/purple/violet (bee UV-blue) (Waser et al. 1996; Arnold et al. 2009; Willmer 2011). Trophic associations are common in the understory, but again, information on mating systems and pollination biology in these species is rare. We found no pattern of selfing or strong association with generalist pollinators for mycoheterotrophs or hemiparasites, but again, there was too little information to draw conclusions. Flower color, phenology, and other characteristics also can reflect evolutionary history and phylogenetic constraints, as well as selection for pollination (Ollerton and Lack 1992; Fox and Kelly 1993). It is also cautioned that these floral traits (size, color, symmetry, as well as presentation of rewards) operate in concert, not in isolation (Willmer 2011). As others have noted, these mixed forests, largely dominated by deciduous taxa, present two distinct seasons of high- and low-light environments, two distinct floras we know as the spring ephemerals and the later season forbs, flanking "the green lull" and perhaps a decline in bee activity. Yet, Arnold et al. (2009) reported a quantitative study using reflectance data and found no statistical support for changes in the frequency of flower color throughout the year, nor any evidence for a shift between early spring and later spring/summer after leaf-out in two woodland habitats.

There is a real need for comprehensive, quantitative studies, both of individual taxa and for the herbaceous understory as a community or ecosystem, for basic and applied approaches, and for integration of tools from ecology and population genetics (Cheptou and Schoen 2007). Promising work on some model taxa offers insights into how we can integrate reliable estimates of mating systems with experimental pollination biology (*Aquilegia canadensis*: Eckert and Schaefer 1998; Griffin et al. 2000; Herlihy and Eckert 2002, 2004, 2005; Eckert and Herlihy 2004; Kliber and Eckert 2004; *Sabatia angularis*: Dudash 1990; Spigler et al. 2010; *Silene virginica*: Dudash and Fenster 2001; *Trillium erectum*: Broyles et al. 1997; Irwin 2000, 2001; Sage et al. 2001).

More knowledge of mating systems and other aspects of reproductive ecology is needed, given the ecological and evolutionary importance of sexual modes in herbs, and increasing threats to populations and habitats of understory herbs (Jolls 2003; chapter 6, this volume). Habitat loss and fragmentation, species extinctions, and introductions can disrupt plant-pollinator associations (Eckert et al. 2010). Climate change has been documented to impact plant and insect phenology, with potential for disruption of mutualisms (Bartomeus et al. 2011; although see Rafferty and Ives 2011). The relatively long-lived, clonal, insect-pollinated, outcrossing taxa of the herb understory may be acutely sensitive to fragmentation; however, their decline may be slow. Such taxa are said to suffer a larger "extinction debt" (the delayed extinction of species after environmental perturbation, Tilman et al. 1994; Loehle and Li 1996; Honnay and Bossuyt 2005). How extinction debt plays out is species-specific and not always predictable (Aizen et al. 2002; Verheyen et al. 2003). Yet, the long duration of the herb understory extinction debt, even a century after forest clearing, may afford time to prevent further local extinction (Vellend et al. 2006). Our understanding of mating systems and sexual reproduction of the forest understory becomes biological knowledge that is critical for conservation, management, and restoration.

ACKNOWLEDGMENTS

Thanks for technical assistance, helpful comments, insightful discussion, and unflagging support are extended to Chelsea Barbour, Monica Burton, Frank Gilliam, John Kartesz, Jeff McKinnon, Andrew Morgan, Bob Peet, Kay Havens Young, Dennis Whigham, and to other researchers whose efforts make reviews possible. Nancy Tuchman, Kay Havens Young, and the Chicago Botanic Garden were gracious hosts to CLJ during the writing of this review.

APPENDIX 5.1

A list of some notable studies providing information on reproductive ecology used in construction of our datasets. Superscripts indicate that information used related to (a) mating or breeding systems, (b) pollinators, and/or (c) pollen limitation. One representative study is listed per taxon; multiple studies may have been published. Species shown in bold did not occur in the exemplar communities but were included in the pollen limitation survey. Note that a few of the studies providing information on mating and breeding systems were conducted outside of North America.

Taxon	Study of reproductive ecology
Achillea millefolium	Lofgren 2002 [a,b]
Actaea rubra	Pellmyr 1985 [a,b]
Agalinis strictifolia	**Dieringer 1992** [c]
Allium tricoccum	Nault and Gagnon 1987 [a,b,c]
Amianthium muscitoxicum	**Travis 1984** [c]
Amphicarpaea bracteata	Callahan and Waller 2000 [a]
Apios americana	Bruneau and Anderson 1988 [a,b]
Aquilegia canadensis	Eckert et al. 2009 [a,b]
Aralia nudicaulis	Flanagan and Moser 1985 [b,c]
Arisaema triphyllum	Barriault et al. 2010 [a,b]
Asarum canadense	Wildman 1950 [a,b]
Asclepias exaltata	Wyatt and Broyles 1994 [a,b]
Astilbe biternata	Olson 2001 [a,c]
Campanulastrum americanum	**Kilkenny and Galloway 2008** [c]
Caulophyllum thalictroides	Hannan and Prucher 1996 [a,b]
Chamaecrista fasciculata	Lee and Bazzaz 1982 [a,b,c]
Chamaecrista nictitans	Lee 1989 [a]
Chamaelirium luteum	Meagher 1986 [b]
Cleistes divaricata	Gregg 1991a [b,c]
Clintonia borealis	Galen et al. 1985 [a,b,c]
Coeloglossum viride	Willems and Melser 1998 [a,b]
Collinsonia canadensis	Albrecht and McCarthy 2006 [a,b]
Collinsia verna	Kalisz and Vogler 2003 [a,b,c]
Conopholis americana	Baird and Riopel 1986 [a,b]
Cryptotaenia canadensis	Williams and Guries 1994 [a,b]
Cypripedium acaule	Primack and Hall 1990 [a,b,c]
Cypripedium parviflorum	Case and Bradford 2009 [b]
Cypripedium reginae	**Edens-Meier et al. 2010** [c]
Desmodium nudiflorum	Schaal and Smith 1980 [a,b]
Epifagus virginiana	Thieret 1969 [a]
Erythronium americanum	Harder et al. 1993 [a,b]
Eupatorium resinosum	**Byers 1995** [c]
Eupatorium rotundifolium	Montgomery and Fairbrothers 1970 [a]
Eupatorium sessilifolium	Montgomery and Fairbrothers 1970 [a]
Fragaria virginiana	Case and Ashman 2009 [a,b]
Geranium maculatum	Ågren and Willson 1992 [b,c]
Geranium robertianum	Bertin 2001 [a,b]
Goodyera pubescens	Kallunki 1981 [a,b]
Goodyera repens	Neiland and Wilcock 1995 [a,b]
Goodyera tesselata	Kallunki 1981 [a,b]
Hepatica acutiloba	Murphy and Vasseur 1995 [b,c]
Heuchera villosa	Wells 1979 [a]
Houstonia purpurea	Glennon et al. 2011 [a]
Impatiens canadensis	Walters and Stiles 1996 [a,b,c]

(Continued)

Taxon	Study of reproductive ecology
Iris cristata	Motten 1986 [a,b]
Iris fulva	**Wesselingh and Arnold 2003** [c]
Laportea canadensis	Menges 1990 [a,b]
Lilium philadelpicum	Edwards and Jordan 1992 [a,b]
Linnaea borealis	Barrett and Helenurm 1987 [a,b]
Lobelia cardinalis	Johnston 1991 [a,b,c]
Lobelia inflata	Simons and Johnston 2000 [a]
Lobelia siphilitica	**Johnston 1991** [c]
Lysimachia asperulifolia	**Franklin et al. 2006** [c]
Lysimachia quadrifolia	McCall and Primack 1985 [a,b,c]
Maianthemum canadense	Wheelwright et al. 2006 [a,b,c]
Melampyrum lineare	Cantlon et al. 1963 [a,b]
Mimulus ringens	Karron et al. 1997 [a,b]
Mitchella repens	Hicks et al. 1985 [a,b,c]
Monarda clinopodia	Whitten 1981 [a,b]
Monarda didyma	Whitten 1981 [a,b]
Moneses uniflora	Knudsen and Olesen 1993 [a,b]
Monotropa hypopithys	Klooster and Culley 2009 [a,b]
Monotropa uniflora	Klooster and Culley 2009 [a,b]
Oenothera fruticosa	Silander and Primack 1978 [a,b,c]
Orthilia secunda	Knudsen and Olesen 1993 [a,b]
Osmorhiza claytonii	Williams and Guries 1994 [a,b]
Oxalis acetosella	Berg and Redbo-Torstensson 1998 [a,b]
Panax quinquefolius	Hackney and McGraw 2001 [a,b,c]
Pedicularis canadensis	Macior 1968 [b]
Phytolacca americana	Armesto et al. 1983 [a]
Pilea pumila	Cid-Benevento 1987 [a,b]
Platanthera hyperborea	Sheviak 2001 [b]
Podophyllum peltatum	Whisler and Snow 1992 [a,b,c]
Polemonium vanbruntiae	**Hill et al. 2008** [c]
Pyrola chlorantha	Knudsen and Olesen 1993 [a,b]
Ruellia caroliniensis	Long 1971 [a,b]
Sabatia angularis	Spigler and Chang 2009 [a,b,c]
Sanguinaria canadensis	Schemske 1978 [a,b]
Silene virginica	Dudash and Fenster 1997 [a,b,c]
Smilax herbacea	**Sawyer and Anderson 1998** [c]
Solidago canadensis	Robson 2008 [b]
Solidago odora	Elliott and Elliott 1994 [b]
Thalictrum dioicum	**Steven and Waller 2007** [c]
Thalictrum fendleri	**Steven and Waller 2007** [c]
Tipularia discolor	Snow and Whigham 1989 [a,b,c]
Trientalis borealis	Anderson and Beare 1983 [a,b]

(Continued)

Taxon	Study of reproductive ecology
Trillium erectum	Irwin 2000 [a,b,c]
Trillium grandiflorum	**Steven et al. 2003** [c]
Urtica dioica	Taylor 2009 [b]
Uvularia perfoliata	Whigham 1974 [a,b]
Viola canadensis	Culley 2000 [a,b]
Viola pubescens	Culley 2002 [a,b]

6 Populations of and Threats to Rare Plants of the Herb Layer

Still More Challenges and Opportunities for Conservation Biologists

Claudia L. Jolls and Dennis F. Whigham

Nature provides exceptions to every rule.
—Margaret Fuller (1810–1850)

Nature goes on her way, and all that to us seems an exception is really according to order.
—Johann Wolfgang von Goethe (1749–1832)

In 1982, Paulette Bierzychudek presented a seminal review on population biology of shade-tolerant herbs of temperate deciduous forests. Her focus was largely on life histories, demography, and processes occurring at the population level, inspired in part by Harper's (1977) treatise. In her opinion, our knowledge of herbs of particular forests was incomplete, particularly for coniferous forests, floodplains, rocky ledges, forested dunes, savannas, and subtropical forests. Particular taxa were underrepresented in the literature as well. For example, at the time, no life history study had yet been done on many shade-tolerant herbs that flower in later summer (Newell and Tramer 1978; Bierzychudek 1982a). Bierzychudek concluded that inadequate information existed for making generalizations about life histories of deciduous forest herbs, particularly their population growth rates or the temporal stability of their population sizes or structures. In 2004, Whigham stressed in his review of woodland herbs in temperate deciduous forests that these taxa are increasingly threatened by human activities, and we lack important knowledge of their basic ecology for conservation and restoration.

THREATS TO AND CONSERVATION OF HERBS OF FORESTED EASTERN NORTH AMERICA

Our ability to understand the ecology of herbs of forests of eastern North America is complicated by declining abundances and increasing risks of extinctions, particularly for rare taxa. Major causes for global declines in biodiversity have been attributed to the so-called Four Horsemen of the Environmental Apocalypse or "the evil quartet" (Diamond 1989; Pimm and Gilpin 1989). These threats are habitat loss, the presence of alien species, overexploitation, and secondary (or indirect) effects resulting from impacts of other taxa. In addition, the consequences of the many ramifications associated with global change have the potential of becoming yet another major cause of the decline in biodiversity (Vitousek et al. 1996). We use the framework of threats and global change to review major challenges to the diversity of herbs associated with forests of eastern North America, especially taxa listed as endangered or threatened. Using Bierzychudek (1982a) as a timeline for comparison and Jolls (2003) as a format, we consider what progress has been made in the understanding of the ecology of the herbaceous flora of eastern North American forests.

We limit the volume of literature to be reviewed by following Bierzychudek's lead and define a member of the herb layer as any vascular herbaceous taxon (forb, grass, grass-like plants such as sedges and rushes) growing in an upland habitat under a wooded (largely forested or rarely shrubby) overstory. We excluded floating or emergent aquatics. Geographically, we limit the review to temperate deciduous and boreal coniferous forests east of the Mississippi River, including associated Canadian provinces. In instances where the information is critical for the review we also consider examples from other parts of the world where temperate forests occur.

HABITAT LOSS AND FRAGMENTATION

Anthropogenic influences are responsible for major loss of habitat for herbs of the forest understory. In addition to direct habitat destruction, human activities in forests and other ecosystems can dramatically alter habitat, including natural disturbance regimes. Although some taxa are dependent on natural disturbance for persistence (e.g., *Aster acuminatus* Michx., Hughes et al. 1988; *Chrysopsis floridana* Small, Lambert and Menges 1996; *Hydrastis canadensis* L., Sinclair and Catling 2004; *Pedicularis furbishiae* S. Wats., Menges 1990), current forest management practices are impacting many species (chapter 14, this volume). Fire-dependent forests such as those of the southeastern coastal plain are losing species as a result of fire suppression (Gray et al. 2003). Rare habitats (scrub, scrubby flatwood, southern ridge sandhills) and their associated species have been lost in Florida, a biodiversity hotspot in the southeast (Peroni and Abrahamson 1985). Fire suppression and changes in the densities of native herbivores (i.e., white-tailed deer, *Odocoileus virginianus* Zimmerman) also have been shown to have an effect on the diversity of herbs in more mesic forests in eastern North America (Royo, Collins et al. 2010; chapter 16, this volume).

Forest herbs can be more sensitive over the short term and may be more at risk than other co-occurring growth forms or life histories. Others report that forest herbs may respond more rapidly (in as little as three to six years) and to a more complex suite of environmental factors than do woody taxa (Chandy and Gibson 2009), yet are slower to recover from disturbance (Duffy and Meier 1992; Wyatt and Silman 2010). Our methodologies also may underestimate the extinction risk of forest herbs. Quintana-Ascencio and Menges (1996) used a metapopulation model to suggest that herbs suffer higher risk of extinction than do woody plants as patch size decreases.

Some forest herbs may be more sensitive than other taxa to human-induced disturbance, such as logging (Gilliam and Roberts 1995; Meier et al. 1995; chapter 18, this volume) and conversion of forests to open (i.e., cultivation and pasture) habitats followed by subsequent succession; however, species-specific responses make generalizations difficult (Van Calster et al. 2008; Jenkins and Webster 2009; Dyer 2010). For example, vernal herbs associated with more mesic habitats of the Susquehanna River corridor occupied a more limited range of habitats and were less tolerant of disturbance than upland taxa (Bratton et al. 1994). Thus, the optimal sites for spring wildflowers may be most vulnerable to disturbance, demonstrating the need for a larger view to conserve the broadest range of woodland herbs (Bratton et al. 1994).

At the more local scale, direct human habitat destruction also can include trampling (Rossi et al. 2009; Rusterholz et al. 2009). Experimental studies of effects on rare plants from trampling are not numerous; however, work with other taxa suggests reduction in reproductive potential and declines in genetic diversity (Maschinski et al. 1997) for *Astragalus cremnophylax* var. *cremnophylax* Barney, and (Rusterholz et al. 2009) for *Anemone nemorosa* L.

HABITAT FRAGMENTATION

Management practices can directly destroy and fragment forest habitats, resulting in increased risk of extinction. Small populations of rare species may be at higher risk for extinction due to direct effects of demographic stochasticity (Ives et al. 1998; Matthies et al. 2004), edge effects (Jules and Rathcke 1999; Honnay and Jacquemyn 2007; Aguilar et al. 2008), and alteration of critical processes such as pollination, dispersal, and herbivory (Spira 2001; Franklin et al. 2006; Hill et al. 2008; Ness and Morin 2008; Schmucki and de Blois 2009a; Herrera et al. 2011). While rare species may be at greater risk, responses can be highly species-specific (Kolb and Diekmann 2005; Schmucki and de Blois 2009b). Fragmentation requires that conservation efforts be based on a firm knowledge of the dynamics of local populations and the linkages among them throughout the landscape, particularly if they function as a metapopulation.

The impact of fragmentation, specifically edge effects, may be specific to particular phases of the lifecycle. For example, edge effects reduced recruitment of *Trillium ovatum* Pursh. in coniferous forests of western North America through impact on some but not all phases of the lifecycle. Fragmentation can also have genetic consequences, both among and within populations. Recent molecular techniques have improved our ability to assess the role of genetics in the ecology of rare forest herbs. Independent of population size, taxa that have small populations and limited distributions suffer from reduced genetic diversity and gene flow (Cole 2003; Dolan et al. 2004; Godt et al. 2004; Gonzales and Hamrick 2005; Baskauf and Burke 2009; Vandepitte et al. 2010). Habitat fragmentation can promote increased selfing and subsequent decreased genetic diversity, especially in rare taxa with more pronounced impacts on recently rare, self-incompatible, and outcrossing animal-pollinated or dispersed plants

(Aguilar et al. 2008). Yet, the relationships among habitat fragmentation, population size, and genetic diversity are not always clear (Young et al. 1996; Gitzendanner and Soltis 2000; Leimu et al. 2006; Honnay and Jacquemyn 2007). Not all rare species have limited genetic variability. *Marshallia mohrii* Headle & F. E. Boynton (Watson et al. 1991), *Helianthus verticillatus* Small (Ellis et al. 2006), and *Sarracenia rubra* ssp. *alabamensis* (Case & Case) D. E. Schnell (Godt and Hamrick 1998a) had relatively high genetic diversity. In contrast, genetic diversity for *S. oreophila* Wherry, *Helonias bullata* L., and *Schwalbea americana* L. was extremely low (Godt et al. 1995, 1996; Godt and Hamrick 1996, 1998b). Many herbaceous understory taxa have more genetic diversity among populations; in some cases, more so for quantitative traits than allozymes (Hamrick et al. 2006). Increasing fragmentation of forest herb habitats demands an even greater knowledge of genetic differences among populations.

Corridors have been proposed as ways to restore connectedness among fragments; however, the spatial configuration of remaining habitat and low migrations rates may be unable to compensate for overall loss of habitat and fragmentation (Harrison and Bruna 1999; Schmucki and de Blois 2009a,b). Recent investigations suggest that the effectiveness of pollen flow through corridors may be highly species- and habitat-specific (Kirchner et al. 2003; Townsend and Levey 2005; Gardner and Engelhardt 2008; Winter et al. 2008; Van Geert et al. 2010). Van Dorp et al. (1997) argued that seed and propagule transplantation, rather than the promise of dispersal through corridors, may be the best way to conserve endangered plants. Similarly, woodland herbs may be infrequent in fencerows and forest edges that can serve as corridors (Fritz and Merriam 1994). Thus, corridors may not provide effective links between forest fragments due to limited dispersal of many forest herbs, particularly rare taxa (Whitney and Foster 1988; Cain et al. 1998).

SPECIES INTRODUCTIONS

Herbs of forested eastern North America are threatened by nonnative invaders (Mack et al. 2000). Such invasives can alter competitive regimes (chapter 15, this volume), compete with native taxa for regeneration opportunities in response to disturbance (Horvitz et al. 1998), alter environmental conditions, and produce impacts at the population, community, and ecosystem levels in forests (Gordon 1998; Horvitz and Koop 2001; Sakai et al. 2001; Lynch et al. 2009; Leicht-Young et al. 2010). As an example, invasion of dune habitat by *Robinia pseudoacacia* L., a nitrogen-fixing tree, limited native herbaceous species, increased soil nitrogen, and facilitated the non-indigenous grass *Bromus tectorum* L. (Peloquin and Hiebert 1999).

The phenology of invasives relative to that of native taxa also can affect their impact. The exotic shrub *Lonicera maackii* (Rupr.) Herder reduced survival and fecundity of native annual and perennial herbs by producing leaves earlier and shading species that are shade-intolerant and species that are spring ephemerals such as *Allium burdickii* (Hanes) A. G. Jones (Gould and Gorchov 2000; Miller and Gorchov 2004). Other invasives such as *Microstegium vimineum* (Trin.) A. Camus negatively impact forest herbs by being able to grow over a wide range of light levels and forming dense patches that limit light availability to native species (Callaway et al. 2006; Cheplick 2008). Rare taxa are at greater risk from invasives, given their smaller ranges and population sizes, typically lower genetic diversity, and often higher habitat specificity (Miller et al. 2010). Twenty-five of the 100 threatened and endangered taxa of forests of eastern North America are noted in their recovery plans to be at risk from invasive plants (appendix 6.1), a more than 50 percent increase since the first edition of this chapter (from species USFWS Five Year Reviews; COSEWIC Species-at-Risk (SARA) assessments and research; Colautti et al. 2006; Menges et al. 2011). While it seems clear that invasive species most often negatively impact native herbs in forests, our ability to design effective management can be limited by our understanding of the mechanisms by which invaders affect rare species (Thomson 2005; Allen et al. 2009).

Threats from introduced and native (e.g., white-tailed deer) animal species are extensive and can operate in concert with other factors to negatively impact forest herbs (Knight et al. 2009a,b; Leege et al. 2010; Goetsch et al. 2011; Kain et al. 2011). Damage from the introduced aphid-like hemlock woolly adelgid (HWA), *Adelges tsugae* Annand, from Asia creates canopy gaps, increasing light availability and promoting opportunistic understory herbaceous species (*Erechtites hieracifolia* Rafin. ex DC. and *Phytolacca americana* L.) and exotics (*Ailanthus altissima* Swingle and *Microstegium vimineum*) at the expense of native herbs (Orwig and Foster 1998). Recent invasions of temperate forests by earthworms mostly from Europe and Asia are of concern given the extensive earthworm ecosystem engineering on soil texture, chemistry, and composition of flora and fauna (Bohlen et al. 2004; Hale et al. 2005; McCormick et al. 2013; Szlavecz et al. 2011). Herbivores, both native and exotic, interact with invasive plant species and can have both positive (Royo, Collins et al. 2010) and negative (e.g., deer and invasive honeysuckle on *Trillium* spp., Leege et al. 2010) impacts on understory herbs. Introduced slugs feed preferentially on native species, resulting in greater competitive pressure from the plant exotic garlic mustard, *Alliaria petiolata* (M. Bieb.) Cavara and Grande (Hahn et al. 2010). Plant invaders like *Microstegium vimineum* may be met with increasing use of biological control agents for management; the impacts on forest herbs, particularly rare herbs, are largely unknown (Louda et al. 1997; Ewel et al. 1999; Louda, Arnett et al. 2003; Louda, Pemberton et al. 2003; Louda and Stiling 2004). Chapter 16 (this volume) provides further examples of changes in the herbaceous layer following disturbance by animal invaders.

Unfortunately, our richest sites for forest herbs may be at greatest risk from alien species (Allen et al. 2009; chapter 15, this volume). Although there is some suggestion that areas of low species richness are more readily invaded than areas of high plant species richness, Stohlgren et al. (1999) concluded that "hot spots" of plant biodiversity were prone to alien introductions. They suggested that this high risk of alien invasion might reflect resource availability rather than species richness. Either way, the herbaceous understory faces substantial threats from invasions by exotic plants and animals, but the interactions between alien species and native herbs are not always negative, and the outcomes of the interactions are influenced by many factors (Surrette and Brewer 2008).

OVEREXPLOITATION

Shortsighted harvesting of declining populations results in increased risk of extinction, in addition to other indirect effects. Nantel et al. (1996) used previously published transition matrices (Charron and Gagnon 1991) and data from confiscated harvests to compute extinction thresholds and minimum viable population sizes for American ginseng (*Panax quinquefolius* L.) and wild leek (*Allium tricoccum* Ait.). Illegal harvests of 3,600 wild leek bulbs per person and estimates as high as 25,000 ramets total per park have occurred. Even relatively modest harvesting of large American ginseng plants in Canada was sufficient to bring population growth rates below equilibrium (Nantel et al. 1996). Subsequent recent research suggests that size selection by humans and lack of legal compliance still contribute to the unsustainability of ginseng harvest (Mooney and McGraw 2007, 2009; McGraw et al. 2010). Exploited populations of American ginseng have lower genetic diversity and more small, nonreproductive plants compared to areas protected from harvest (Cruse-Sanders and Hamrick 2004). A recent study by Farrington et al. (2009) demonstrated that deer browsing, a factor that would normally depress ginseng populations, can have a positive impact because browsed plants are more difficult for harvesters to find.

At the community level, overexploitation of forest canopy resources, notably clearcutting, promotes early successional, shade-intolerant species (chapter 18, this volume) and often results in the establishment of invasive species that can have a negative effect on understory herbs. Ground flora diversity declined in cove hardwoods and mixed-oak hardwoods 16 years following cutting, with increases in *Erechtites*, *Solidago*, *Eupatorium*, *Panicum*, and *Aster* spp. Late successional, shade-tolerant understory taxa such as *Viola*, *Galium*, *Sanguinaria*, *Uvularia*, and *Veratrum* spp. also are known to decline following clearcutting (Whigham 1974; Elliott et al. 1997). Such a response, however, can be highly site-dependent, and modified harvest techniques may not necessarily be incompatible with rare species persistence (MacDougall 2001; Meyer and Parker 2003; chapter 14, this volume). Still, studies in North America and Europe demonstrate that there are long-term effects of logging on recovery of areas from which forests had been removed and that the diversity of understory plants may never return to pre-logging levels or that recovery will take more than a century (Wyatt and Silman 2010; De Frenne, Brunet et al. 2011; chapter 18, this volume).

SECONDARY EFFECTS AND POPULATION REGULATION

Impacts on native herbs may be mediated by indirect effects on other taxa such as loss of keystone species or alteration of competitive effects through extinction of one population or species, such as predators of generalized herbivores or pollinators. Loss of pollinators through habitat loss, fragmentation, or competitive displacement from species introductions can impact seed set and genetic diversity of forest herbs. Yet, some plants with specialized floral morphology may survive outside the range of specialist pollinators with the help of opportunistic flower foragers (e.g., *Corydalis cava* Schweigg. & Kort. in Kansas, Oleson 1996). Invasions from exotic earthworms can reduce abundance genera *Aralia*, *Botrychium*, *Osmorhiza*, *Trillium*, *Uvularia*, and *Viola* in the understory. Earthworm-associated changes in soil conditions and plant species can then alter competitive relationships and promote subsequent *Rhamnus cathartica* establishment and further affecting changes in vegetative composition (Frelich et al. 2006).

Changes in interactions between herbivores and their food plants are a major influence on changes in forest composition in temperate deciduous forests (chapter 16, this volume), notably, extreme browsing by overabundant populations of native herbivores. *Eurybia divaricata* (L.) G. L. Nesom (= *Aster divaricatus* L.), threatened in Canada and without status in the U.S., is preferentially browsed by white-tailed deer and has been proposed as a possible indicator of browsing intensity (Williams et al.

2000). Declines in species richness because of direct and indirect effects of herbivory by species of deer are suggested at the community level (Taverna et al. 2005; Suzuki et al. 2009; Goetsch et al. 2011) and at the plant and population levels for individual species (e.g., *Trillium*, Jenkins et al. 2009; *Anemone*, Mårell et al. 2009). Heckel et al. (2010) demonstrated indirect effects of deer herbivory on palatable understory species, including smaller size and male-biased sex ratios in *Arisaema triphyllum* (L.) Schott. Deer browse also suppressed the size of unpalatable species by decreasing soil quality and litter accumulation. Artificially high densities of herbivores have greater impact on plant species composition and abundance; however, at more typical levels of herbivory, productivity of the forest may play a larger role in determination of understory in boreal forests (John and Turkington 1997). Deer at moderate levels of abundance in recovering forests may promote herb diversity through preferential browsing of faster-growing pioneer species (Royo, Collins et al. 2010).

The impact of herbivores is highly variable and can be secondary to internal factors such as demography, population structure, and population dynamics (*Lathyrus vernus* Bernh., Ehrlén 1996). Grazing or simulated grazing have been shown to affect plant size and thus indirectly impact probability of flowering and survival to the next year for some perennial herbs (Whigham and Chapa 1999; Huber et al. 2004; Brys et al. 2011). Some have argued that our understanding of the role of herbivores on population-level processes is inadequate (Ehrlén 2002), particularly relative to our knowledge at the level of the individual and community.

GLOBAL CHANGE

Global change, particularly that mediated by anthropogenic effects (e.g., acid deposition, ozone effects, climate change), will significantly impact the herbaceous forest understory (Lovett et al. 2009; chapters 3 and 21, this volume). Dramatic declines in surface soil pH result in lower species diversity and a shift to acid-tolerant flora, such as the common forest herbs *Maianthemum canadense* Desf. and *Eurybia divaricata* (Greller et al. 1990). Forest herbs, however, will undoubtedly differ in their responses to global change. *E. divaricata* was less sensitive to ozone damage than *Rudbeckia laciniata* L. (Evans et al. 1996a,b). We could find no published accounts of the effects of ozone on rare herbs of forests; however, the limited data suggest forbs may be more sensitive than grasses (Rinnan and Holopainen 2004; Timonen et al. 2004).

Global warming could alter phenology of forest herbs more so than other growth forms of other habitats (Whigham 2004). Of 12 herbaceous, six shrub, and eight tree species, the herbs *Maianthemum canadense* and *Uvularia sessilifolia* L. were most sensitive to soil warming, with potential influences on carbon and nutrient acquisition dynamics (Farnsworth et al. 1995). In a report documenting earlier responses in spring (Bradley et al. 1999), only five of the 23 (22 percent) herbaceous understory plants showed a significant "increase in earliness." Subsequent work confirms that many species of herbaceous understory have significantly earlier phenologies in the past few decades (Walther 2004; Miller-Rushing and Primack 2008; Tooke and Battey 2010; Beaubien and Hamann 2011; McEwan and Muller 2011; McEwan et al. 2011). Some studies, however, indicate that understory plants may display divergent plasticity in response to global change, resulting in future changes in the species composition of herb communities in forests that might be considered both positive and negative (Graae et al. 2009; Baeten, Vanhellemont, De Frenne, Schrijver et al. 2010; De Frenne, Brunet et al. 2011).

Threats to plant populations and declining biodiversity make studies of the population biology of plants of forested eastern North America timely and critical. Of particular concern are rare taxa that have been given legal protection as threatened and endangered. Historically, studies of the population biology of rare woodland taxa were rare in the published literature. In Bevill and Louda's (1999) review of 38 studies comparing rare and more common plant taxa, herbaceous taxa of wooded habitats of eastern North America were conspicuously absent. They also reported profound inconsistencies in the variables studied; most of the attributes appeared in only one or two studies. In addition to the species included in Bevill and Louda, there have been a few studies of rare herbaceous taxa of eastern forests. Banks (1980), Morley (1982), and Pleasants and Wendel (1989) reported on *Erythronium propullans* A. Gray and *E. albidum* Nutt.; Fritz-Sheridan (1988) on *Erythronium grandiflorum* Benth.; Mehrhoff (1983) on *Isotria*; Primack (1980) on *Plantago* spp.; and Snyder et al. (1994) and Baskin et al. (1997) on *Echinacea tennesseensis* (Beadle) Small, *Iliamna corei* Sherff, and *Solidago shortii* Torr. & Gray. For this revision, we compiled more recent information on the population biology of threatened and endangered understory herbs of eastern North America.

The results of our compilation are provided in appendices 6.1 and 6.2. Appendix 6.1 lists 100 threatened and endangered vascular taxa of forests of the eastern United States and Canada, compiled from a variety of sources described in the appendix heading. Only herbaceous vascular taxa east of the Mississippi River associated with habitats at least partially dependent on shade from a forested overstory were included. Vascular plants of forests in the eastern U.S. were compiled using the United States Fish and Wildlife Service Environmental Conservation Online System (ECOS) (http://ecos.fws. gov/ecos/indexPublic.do) to search for threatened or endangered vascular plants for the 26 states east of the Mississippi River. Information on habit, distribution, habitat, and research needs was obtained from the species accounts and/or recovery plans, including the Center for Plant Conservation (www.centerforplantconservation.org). For the few taxa without accounts online or with data-deficient accounts, habitat information came from Gleason and Cronquist (1991) or the appropriate flora for the southern plants. We searched Canadian taxa using the Canada Species at Risk Program (SARA) Public Registry (http://www.sararegistry.gc.ca). We used this search engine for all vascular plants of Canada listed as endangered or threatened, confined to areas west of the Mississippi River (British Columbia, Alberta, Saskatchewan, and parts of Manitoba were eliminated). Nomenclature, including common names, follows that of the USDA Natural Resources Conservation Service Plants Database (www.plants.usda. gov).

Only taxa listed as endangered or threatened were used in appendix 6.1. We did include taxa that occurred in a variety of forest habitats, such as canopy openings and forest edges. We also included species of woodlands along closed canopy forest, such as shrublands, riparian forests, shaded stream banks, cedar glades, open woodlands, forest-river or forest-prairie ecotones, boggy areas in coniferous forests, and rosemary scrub or prairie-like oak savannas.

We then used the Institute for Scientific Information Science Citation Index from 1945–2011 to search for each taxon by its binomial. We chose to avoid discussions of the pollination biology of these taxa, given a limited literature (but see chapter 6, this volume), and defer to other important reviews of the genetics of rare plants (e.g., Falk and Holsinger 1991; Gitzendanner and Soltis 2000; Cole 2003). We eliminated articles on chromosome counts, vegetation composition and community associates, new accounts, horticulture, physiology, phytochemistry, or systematics.

Since the 2003 version of this chapter, two U.S. taxa have been delisted and eight have been added. Other than *Carex lutea* LeBlond, these additions are from Canadian listings (*Asclepias quadrifolia* Jacq., *Camassia scilloides* (Raf.) Cory, *Enemion biternatum* Raf., *Frasera caroliniensis* Walter, *Sida hermaphrodita* (L.) Rusby, *Symphyotrichum praealtum* (Poir.) G.L. Nesom, and *Symphyotrichum prenanthoides* (Muhl. ex Willd.) G. L. Nesom), largely upgraded from special concern to threatened or endangered status (new listings for *A. quadrifolia* Jacq. and *S. hermaphrodita* (L.) Rusby). In the U.S., the only status change since 2003 has been the recovery of *Echinacea tennesseensis* (Beadle) Small and *Helianthus eggertii* Small and the downgrade of *Scutellaria montana* Chapm. from endangered to threatened. Whorled sunflower, *Helianthus verticillatus* Small of woodland openings in Alabama, Georgia, and Tennessee, is currently a candidate for federal listing. In the 2003 edition of this chapter, 254 articles were retrieved for 94 taxa, and just over 150 articles dealt with the ecology or genetics of these rare herbs of forests of eastern North America. In searching for articles to include in this version, our list expanded to 100 taxa. Since 2000, a search for (plant* AND rar* AND forest* or wood*) resulted in 2,168 articles, a mere 136 of which dealt with North America systems; only 17 of those (12.5 percent) dealt with the herbaceous understory, rare or common, in any way, suggesting few peer-reviewed publications on rare taxa in the past decade.

Conservation of the rare herbs is further challenged by the lack of biological knowledge critical for recovery, notably basic biology, population dynamics, and critically important relationships between woodland herbs and mycorrhizal fungi (McCormick et al. 2009, 2012). Characterization of the attributes of rare species is summarized in appendix 6.2. While the majority of recovery plans contain excellent information on aspects of distribution and habitat of species of concern, less than half of more than 300 plans reviewed had information on fecundity, survivorship, or age structure (Tear et al. 1995). Thanks to digital access, important information housed in technical reports and theses is increasingly available. We had access to recovery plants for all of the 68 U.S. taxa. Virtually all 32 Canadian taxa had status reports and assessments. We here review what is known about aspects of the population biology of more common herbs of forested eastern North America and present our knowledge (or lack thereof) for the listed rare taxa of appendix 6.1 relative to the traits outlined by (Bierzychudek 1982a).

REPRODUCTION AND LIFE HISTORY CHARACTERISTICS

Modes of Reproduction

Despite the extensive use of fast-growing, short-lived weedy taxa in population studies, forest herbs have also contributed significantly to our understanding of plant reproductive strategies and resource allocation. Typically, reproduction of shade-tolerant forest herbs is by vegetative propagules and seed. Recruitment by seed is generally believed to be infrequent and limited (Abrahamson 1980), a pattern also suggested for listed rare taxa of forest systems (appendix 6.2). This generalization, however, was not supported by Bierzychudek's (1982a) and Whigham's (2004) reviews. In at least half of the 26 taxa listed by Bierzychudek, for example, sexual reproduction played a major role in population persistence as successful reproduction by seed was at least sufficiently frequent to balance mortality. Similar results have been found for reproduction of forest herbs in Europe (e.g., Jacquemyn et al. 2010a)

The life histories of forest herbs are varied, but for rare taxa, perennials dominate (appendix 6.2). Annuals are few, accounting for only nine of the 100 taxa (9 percent); similarly, 5–6 percent of Wisconsin forests' taxa were annuals (Struik 1965, cited by Bierzychudek 1982a); "pseudoannuals" adopt a year-long persistence of ramets (Whigham 2004). In deciduous forest understory, the infrequency of the annual habit may be related to resources and growth rates (McKenna and Houle 2000b). K-selected perennial species such as *Trillium flexipes* and *Dicentra canadensis* can be more frequent in richer, mature forest stands compared to younger ones (Bratton et al. 1994). Most of the taxa (88 percent) listed in appendix 6.2 are iteroparous perennials, in addition to the monocarpic *Frasera caroliniensis* of Canada. Annuals and biennials typically are associated with more open woodland habitats, such as *Agalinis gattineri* (Small) Small, *Agalinis skinneriana* (Alph. Wood) Britton, *Arabis serotina* Steele, *Geocarpon minimum* Mack., *Lesquerella lyrata* Rollins, *Polygala smallii* R. R. Smith & Ward, *Polygala lewtonii* Small, *Tephrosia virginiana* (L.) Pers., *Thalictrum cooleyi* H.E. Ahles, *Warea amplexifolia* (Nutt.) Nutt., and *Warea carteri* Small.

Phenology

The rare flora of forested eastern North America is too diverse to allow generalizations about timing of lifecycle events except within similar habits (annual, biennial, or perennial) and habitats (temperate, subtropical, deciduous, coniferous, fire-adapted, etc.). Shade-tolerant herbs of eastern temperate deciduous forests are often typified by leaf loss or formation of flower initials the previous autumn, leaf persistence in winter, leaf emergence in spring, and flowering before or after canopy closure (Bierzychudek 1982a; Whigham 2004). Seed set in shade-tolerant herbs of eastern forests occurs by mid- to late summer, concurrent with aboveground senescence. Seed germination occurs in autumn of the same year in some cases, but more often the following spring or autumn (e.g., *Trientalis borealis* Raf., Anderson and Loucks 1973; Bierzychudek 1982a). A number of woodland herbs (e.g., *Trillium* and *Uvularia* spp.) have a double dormancy syndrome for seed germination that requires two cold periods (i.e., two winters) for complete seed germination (Thompson and Leege 2011).

Increasing recent focus on plant functional traits has stimulated a promising body of work on leaf function and general phenological responses (Tessier 2008). Yet, even within a group of similar life forms in similar forests, phenological responses can be modified by extrinsic and intrinsic factors, including linkage of genetic architecture with sensitivity to environment (Whigham 2004; Wilczek et al. 2009; chapter 3, this volume). For example, flowering asynchrony in the common woodland herb *Actaea spicata* L. may be a response to seed predation by a geometrid (Eriksson 1995). For taxa with mixed mating systems, chasmogamous flowers are typically produced in spring followed by cleistogamous ones later in summer (Bierzychudek 1982a); this is also true for federally threatened pigeon wings, *Clitoria fragrans* Small, of Florida scrub (appendix 6.2). Another intrinsic factor affecting phenology of forest herbs may be the reproductive status of the individual in the previous growing season. Although few long-term studies provide sufficient data, shade-tolerant perennials rarely flower in consecutive years (e.g., *Allium tricoccum*, Nault and Gagnon 1993), suggesting a cost to sexual reproduction. Another factor that affects phenology and life history trad-eoffs is that some woodland herbs, especially species of orchids, go through periods of dormancy; this results in one to several years during which individuals remain alive belowground (Shefferson 2009).

Protracted organ development after preformation, however, is typical of many perennial herbs (Geber et al. 1997a) and may help limit the costs of flowering and fruiting. Reproduction in mayapple (*Podophyllum peltatum* L.) had little effect on branching but had marked effects on shoot type. Branch determination begins the year before and is completed by early spring of the subsequent year, and thus does not incur costs to fruit production (Geber et al. 1997a). Geber et al. (1997b) reviewed the taxonomic and ecological distribution of organ preformation in temperate forest herbs using the work of Randall (1952) for Wisconsin. These authors found a phylogenetic association of phenological traits of forest herbs, in addition to the strong phylogenetic component of their geographic ranges. They noted that the impacts of timing of development on population dynamics have been largely unexplored.

The timing, periodicity, frequency, and extent of plant processes such as flowering, fruiting, dispersal, and ecesis will be particularly sensitive to global change; however, responses of species will be highly varied (Primack et al. 2009; Miller-Rushing et al. 2010; DeFrenne, Brunet et al. 2011; De Frenne, Graae et al. 2011). Rare taxa in particular may be at risk, particularly those that lack genetic variability and have narrow ecological tolerances, limited plasticity, or even fleshy fruits sensitive to water availability (Bradley et al. 1999; Ting et al. 2008; Augspurger 2009). Again, as for other aspects of the biology of rare plants, long-term phenological data are some of the best tools to study and predict impact of climate change. Herbarium specimens can be useful supplements (but not alternatives) to long-term monitoring (Bolmgren and Lönnberg 2005; Lavoie and Lachance 2006; Miller-Rushing et al. 2006; Case et al. 2007).

Longevity

Long-term studies of individuals are understandably rare, confounded by the difficulties of aging herbaceous angiosperms (Werner 1978; Ehrlén and Lehtila 2002; von Arx and Dietz 2006; de Witte and Stoecklin 2010) or life histories that include belowground phases (Whigham 2004). The few studies that exist, however, suggest that forest perennials can be relatively long-lived (Whigham 2004), and such longevity can help buffer populations from variations in size through time (Garcia et al. 2008). Bierzychudek (1982a) calculated the mean lifespans of shade-tolerant taxa of the temperate zone to be 14.5 ± 2.72 yr (mean ± standard error, n = 18) with sexual maturity reached after several years. Examples of taxa with long-lived individuals are *Panax quinquefolius* and species of *Trillium* that live for up to 20 years (Anderson et al. 1993; Webster and Jenkins 2008). A lifespan of 15–25 years has been estimated for *Arisaema triphyllum* (Bierzychudek 1982b). Many of the rare taxa listed in appendices 6.1 and 6.2 can also be long-lived. Twenty of the taxa live at least 5–10 years (Schweinitz's sunflower, *Helianthus schweinitzii* Torr. & A. Gray, and some of the orchids), particularly if clonal

(*Asclepias quadrifolia* Jacq., *Asplenium scolopendrium* L. var. *americanum* (Fernald) Kartesz & Gandhi, *Panax quinquefolius*, *Sarracenia* spp., and *Trillium* spp.). Although data are limited, shorter-lived rare perennials appear to be those of high light (*Dalea foliosa* (A. Gray) Barneby) or fire-associated habitats (e.g., the rare endemics of Florida rosemary scrub).

Although managers may have interest in the temporal persistence of individuals, the effect of longevity on reproductive success is secondary to that of size, particularly at the population level. For most species with indeterminate growth, increases in fecundity and thus reproductive value are associated with increases in size. Franco and Silvertown (1996) found that for 83 species of perennial plants, there was no expected covariation between longevity (or age at first reproduction or life expectancy at sexual maturity) and demographic traits related to reproduction (the intrinsic rate of natural increase, the net reproductive rate, or the average rate of decrease in the intensity of natural selection on fecundity).

BREEDING BIOLOGY, MATING SYSTEMS, AND POLLINATION

Generalizations about breeding biology and mating systems in herbs of forests of eastern North America are made at one's peril. Bierzychudek (1982a) stated with caution that most shade-tolerant temperate taxa are bisexual with hermaphroditic flowers. She found that herbs with partial or complete self-incompatibility are just as frequent as those that are self-compatible. However, determinations of mating systems are often inaccurate (Griffin et al. 2000 for the widely distributed *Aquilegia canadensis* L.), and some taxa differ through their range (Whigham 2004). For this reason, any blanket statement about mating systems of the 100 listed rare taxa could be spurious. Thorough information on plant breeding systems is largely lacking for many listed taxa; most are hermaphroditic (appendix 6.2), with rare occurrences of monoecy (*Carex lutea* LeBlond), dioecy (*Euphorbia telephioides* Chapm., *Sisyrinchium dichotomum* E. P. Bicknell, and *Thalictrum cooleyi* Ahles), or other breeding systems in Britton's beargrass, *Nolina brittoniana* Nash, *Oxypolis canbyi* (J. M. Coult. & Rose) Fernald, *Paronychia chartacea* Fernald, *Polygala smallii* R. R. Smith & Ward, and *Polygonella basiramia* (Small) G. L. Nesom & V. M. Bates. The breeding biology of most taxa remains unknown, even though mating system may be a trait associated with rarity. Of the slightly more than two dozen taxa in appendix 6.2 that have been sufficiently studied, self-compatibility dominates (31 out of 42). Relatively few taxa have cleistogamous flowers (e.g., pigeon wings, *Clitoria fragrans* [Weekley and Menges 2003] and *Polygala lewtonii* Small [Weekley and Brothers 2006]). The significance of the differences in flower forms on the same plant may not always be obvious (i.e., insurance of seed production and proximity to the maternal safe-site through selfing of cleistogamous flowers). In *Oxalis acetosella* L. (= *O. montana* Raf.), a common perennial herb of forests in Sweden, seeds from cleistogamous flowers were dispersed significantly farther than those from chasmogamous organs. Other studies suggest that chasmogamous flowers of some rare plants may not always be outcrossed (Berg 2000; Eckstein and Otte 2005).

The majority of the listed understory herbs in appendix 6.2 have mixed mating systems; however, again, only a small proportion has been studied adequately (see chapter 5, this volume). The predominance of mixed mating systems among these taxa parallels angiosperms in general (Goodwillie et al. 2005; chapter 5, this volume). Self-incompatibility has been suggested or documented only for 11 taxa including *Asclepias quadrifolia* Jacq., *Echinacea laevigata* (C. L. Boynt. & Beadle) S. F. Blake, *Galactia smallii* H. J. Rogers ex Herndon, *Iliamna corei, Symphyotrichum* spp., and the fern *Asplenium scolopendrium* L. var.*americanum* (Fernald) Kartesz & Gandhi (Wubs et al. 2010).

Quantitative or qualitative information on pollination of herbs of wooded landscapes is sparse; however, most observations have suggested that pollination of most species is insect-mediated (Cain et al. 1998). We found information on pollination biology for slightly more than half of the rare flowering taxa in appendix 6.2 (56 out of 100, 56 percent). At least one of those taxa use wind as a pollen vector: *Plantago cordata* Lam., as probably do the other graminoids such as *Carex lutea* LeBlond (R. LeBlond, pers. comm.). Our limited knowledge of the breeding biology of rare plants is more critical as we face associated precipitous declines of insect abundance (Cane and Tepedino 2001; Ashman et al. 2004; Vamosi et al. 2006; Alonso et al. 2010; Eckert et al. 2010). Pollen failure may be particularly acute for rare species (Larson and Barrett 2000; Wilcock and Neiland 2002; Ashman et al. 2004; Knight et al. 2005). While some herbs of the understory may be pollen-limited (e.g., the typical woodland herbs, *Hepatica acutiloba* DC., Murphy and Vasseur 1995, *Linnaea borealis* L., Wilcock and Jennings 1999), others are not (*Polemonium vanbruntiae* Britton, Hill et al. 2008). Some rare understory species have a high pollination rate and large numbers of seeds. The federally threatened *Isotria medeoloides* Rafin. produces fewer mature fruits and more capsules than its widely distributed congener, *I. verticillata* Rafin (Mehrhoff 1983). One of us (DFW) has yet to find a flowering plant in *I. verticillata* in four populations that have been monitored for four years. Other factors, in addition to pollination, further limit reproductive success (varying levels of sterility, S allele diversity, and ecesis in *Lysimachia asperulifolia* Poir. (Franklin et al. 2006).

VEGETATIVE AND SEED DISPERSAL

Forest herbs demonstrate a variety of dispersal and germination strategies (Silvertown and Lovett Doust 1993; chapter 1, this volume). Long-distance dispersal can have significant consequences for demography and genetic structure (Silvertown and Lovett Doust 1993; Kalisz et al. 1999; Cain et al. 2000) and be a significant trait associated with plant rarity. Spread of forest herbs can be limited by seed abundance (Jacquemyn et al. 2010a), as well as dispersal (Peterken and Game 1984; Matlack 1994b, Brudvig et al. 2011), and many species have no obvious means for long-distance dispersal (Bierzychudek 1982a). Some dispersal is a function of ant-plant mutualisms whose role in forested eastern North American may rival that of tropical systems (Handel et al 1981; Ness et al. 2009), yet dispersal via such modes is strictly on a local scale (Cain et al. 1998; Sorrells and Warren 2011).

In general, localized dispersal of forest herbs is often less than 1 m and rarely greater than 10 m (Bierzychudek 1982a; Matlack 1994b; Cain et al. 1998; Cheplick 1998). In an exhaustive review, Cain et al. (1998) included 14 herbaceous taxa of wooded eastern North America for which dispersal distances appeared in the literature. The maximum dispersal for the ant-dispersed common understory herb *Asarum canadense* L. was 35 m (Cain et al. 1998). The maximum dispersal distance for the 14 selected taxa averaged less than 9 m; typical dispersal distances averaged 1.23 ± 2.81 ($\bar{x} \pm$ SE). Successful establishment of forest herbs, however, may be a function of the availability of suitable habitat in space and time. For example, the spring ephemeral annual *Floerkea proserpinacoides* Willd. of deciduous forests on St. Lawrence River islands is capable of long-distance dispersal at the northern limits of its range. There, it is rare in low woods; however, the infrequency of such long-distance events may not coincide with the creation of potential microsites (McKenna and Houle 2000a). The interaction between seed dispersal and niche-based ecological filtering (e.g., spatial and temporal variation in disturbance such as fire or resource availability) also plays a role in community assembly, particularly for diverse habitats with many rare species, such as long-leaf pine savannas (Flinn et al. 2010; Myers and Harms 2011).

Despite limited seed dispersal, most (at least 57 of 100) of the listed perennial taxa (appendix 6.2) demonstrate some type of vegetative spread by structures such as rhizomes, offshoots, stolons, bulbs, corms, or xylopodium (of the Orchidaceae). Vegetative spread is a form of asexual reproduction, but it also enables genotypes to live for long periods of time even though individual ramets may be short-lived (Tanner 2001; Huber et al. 2004; Shefferson et al. 2011). Recent empirical evidence and modeling suggest that dispersal through clonal spread may be as great or greater than that by sexual propagules (Cain and Damman 1997), but there is also evidence that patches of understory herbs are composed of many genotypes even though clonal propagation is responsible for most of the patch development (Kudoh et al. 1999). Empirical calibration of models for *Asarum canadense* yielded dispersal estimates of 10–11 km during the last 16,000 years (Cain et al. 1998). In actuality, *A. canadense* moved over an order of magnitude longer distances during this time (100s of km). Cain et al. 1998 concluded that such occasional events were responsible for long-distance dispersal of this species during the Holocene epoch.

Biotic interactions also affect the success of sexual reproduction of forest herbs. Mutualisms between forest herbs and ants can affect dispersal and even influence germination success (Handel 1978; Heithaus 1981; Kjellsson 1985; Casper 1987; Levey and Byrne 1993). Ants disperse 30 percent of spring-flowering herbs in deciduous forests of eastern North America (Lanza et al. 1992). Their preferences appear to be related to the mass and chemical composition of the elaiosome (e.g., Lanza et al. 1992 on *Trillium* spp.). There is little consistent evidence that removal of the elaiosome by ants enhances germination success (Culver and Beattie 1980; Lobstein and Rockwood 1993). It is more likely that ants move seeds to a site more favorable for germination, either environmental or genetic (Handel 1976 for *Carex pedunculata*; Culver and Beattie 1980 for *Viola*).

Long-distance dispersal of both seed and pollen can figure significantly in the geographic migration and phylogeny of forest herbs (Griffin and Barrett 2004). Ants have been implicated in dispersal of many plant species at risk in forests: *Carex juniperorum* Catling, Reznicek & Crins, *Chamaesyce deltoidea* spp. *deltoidea* (Engelm. ex Chapm.) Small, *C. garberi* (Engelm. ex Chapm.) Small, *Hexastylis naniflora* H. L. Blomq., *Iris lacustris* Nutt., *Polygala lewtonii* Small, *P. smallii* Smith & Ward, *Stylophorum diphyllum* Nutt., *Symphyotrichum praealtum* (Poir.) G. L. Nesom, *Trillium flexipes* Raf., *T. persistens* W. H. Duncan, *T. reliquum* J. D. Freeman, and *Viola pedata* L. Disperser communities can be significant, variable across the landscape yet dominated by very few species (Zelikova et al. 2008). These plant-animal interactions may be antagonistic, involving herbivory, as well as dispersal (Vellend et al. 2006). Dispersal mutualisms can be disrupted by invasives and global change (e.g., ant invaders in pine savannas and mature forests, Stuble et al. 2009; 2010; Guérnard and Dunn 2010; organization of frugivores by *Lonicera* spp. in woodlands, Gleditsch and Carlo 2011; flowering-disperser asynchrony, Warren et al. 2010). Our empirical knowledge and theoretical understanding of dispersal will determine our ability to predict the response of rare herbs to global change (Iverson et al. 2004; Franklin 2010). While seed dispersal and clonal propagation are undoubtedly important, the establishment of populations of woodland herbs is determined by the background (i.e., environmental) characteristics of sites at the microscale, and not all microenvironments are equal in their ability to support the successful establishment of seedlings. A series of studies of species of *Carex* clearly demonstrated the importance of spatial heterogeneity in the maintenance of species diversity in understory herbs (e.g., Vellend et al. 2000a, b).

SEED BANKS, DORMANCY, AND GERMINATION

Silvertown and Lovett Doust (1993) remind us that only two things matter to seeds: the risk of death and the chance to germinate. They noted the irony that the chance to germinate also risks death. Persistence as a seed bank is one way to minimize that risk until conditions are favorable for successful germination. Few dispute the importance of the seed bank in population and community dynamics of forests (Leck et al. 1989; Fenner and Thompson 2005); however, the specifics of the role of the seed bank for most plant taxa may be unclear or virtually unknown (Pickett and McDonnell 1989; Honnay et al. 2008). Pickett and McDonnell (1989) reviewed the literature on seed banks in temperate deciduous forests and concluded that (1) seed bank composition usually differs from that of the extant vegetation; (2) seed densities are higher near the soil surface, with fewer seeds in organic or low pH soils; and (3) most seed banks in deciduous forests are small and largely composed of shade-intolerant species. Buried seeds are not necessarily abundant in the soils of coniferous forests (Archibold 1989), but can be extensive in some forest soils (Blood et al. 2010). Seed densities are lowest in primary forests (e.g., 100 to 1000 seeds/m² in coniferous or deciduous forests [Olmstead and Curtis 1947; Bicknell 1979] or subarctic pine/birch forests of Canada where no viable seed were present in the soil [Silvertown 1987]). Secondary forests of North Carolina housed 1,200–3,000 seeds/m², largely arable weeds and early successional species (Oosting and Humphreys 1940).

Baskin and Baskin (1998) reviewed the germination ecology of hundreds of vascular taxa worldwide and demonstrated that most forest herb taxa have seeds that demonstrate some dormancy at dispersal, largely physiological or morphophysiological dormancy. Requirements for breaking dormancy differ between life histories, and there is considerable variation in germination even within spring ephemerals, with profound implications for species distributions along microtopographic gradients (Albrecht and McCarthy 2009). Winter annuals typically require warm stratification (*Corydalis flavula* DC., Baskin and Baskin 1994) compared to short periods of cold stratification for biennials and perennials. Warmer temperatures averaging 20°C are typically required for germination after dormancy is broken. The light:dark photoperiod requirements are largely unknown for most taxa, but in general, light is required or at least enhances germination. Only two of 23 herbaceous species of the deciduous forest with physiological dormancy germinated at higher percentages in darkness. Understory herbs may be responsive to R:FR ratios of light. Jankowska-Blaszczuk and Daws (2007) suggested that small-seeded taxa are less responsive to R:FR light ratios, less likely to germinate under overtopping vegetation, and thus may be more likely to have a seed bank.

Twenty-one of the 59 taxa studied (36 percent) listed in appendix 6.2 have seeds that are part of the seed bank or seeds that require overwintering or chilling for germination. Examples of species with those characteristics are *Arabis serotina* L. (Baskin and Baskin 2002), *Astragalus bibullatus* Barneby & Bridges (Baskin and Baskin 2005), *Bonamia grandiflora* (A. Gray) Hallier, *Carex lupuliformis* Sartwell ex Dewey, *Crotalaria avonensis* DeLaney & Wunderlin, *Dalea foliosa*, *Eryngium cuneifolium* Small, *Hydrastis canadensis* (Albrecht and McCarthy 2011), *Hypericum cumulicola* (Small) P. Adams (Dolan et al. 2008), *Iliamna corei*, *Lesquerella lyrata*, *Lupinus aridorum* (McGarlin ex Beckner) Isley, *Scirpus ancistrochaetus* Schuyler, *Warea carteri* (Weekley et al. 2007), and *Xyris tennesseensis* Kral (Baskin and Baskin 2003). Recent work suggests that we may grossly underestimate the role of seed dormancy, particularly for taxa of concern such as orchid species (Whigham et al. 2006), and some orchid species will not successfully germinate or will germinate less successfully unless they are in the presence of an appropriate mycorrhizal fungus (Whigham et al. 2006, 2008; McCormick et al. 2012). Individual fitness can be affected by seed dispersal and dormancy through their influences on the timing of germination. Time of dispersal may delay germination or affect the temperatures required for it (Baskin and Baskin 1984, 1985). Seeds produced by adults in recent "good years" will dominate the seed bank (Silvertown and Lovett Doust 1993). Most seeds are buried too deeply to enter the population; thus, most recruitment occurs near the surface from recent additions to the seed pool. Rates and magnitude of dispersal into and recruitment from the seed pool remain unknown, although the genetic and population-level implications are profound ("evolutionary inertia" of Templeton and Levin 1979; Kalisz and McPeek 1993; Wilbur and Rudolf 2006).

We are just beginning to understand the details of how environmental factors influence germination, particularly for rare plants. Lambert and Menges (1996) reported higher germination of federally endangered Florida golden aster (*Chrysopsis floridana* Small) in disturbed soils and when litter was removed, suggesting light requirements for germination. *Iliamna corei*, federally endangered and known from one site in Virginia, has physical dormancy due to impermeability of the seed coat to water. Germination increased from 13–71 percent if seeds were heated to fire temperatures (Baskin and Baskin 1997). Despite significant mortality of seedlings during burns, fire can promote turnover in the seed bank without significant changes in population size, help maintain genetic variability, and become an important management tool (*Bonamia grandiflora*, a rare endemic of upland white sand scrub of central Florida, Hartnett and Richardson 1989; *Warea carteri*, Evans et al. 2000). Fire can be an important management tool for seedling recruitment and the forest understory in general (Collins et al. 2001; Gray et al. 2003; Bowles et al. 2007; Glasgow and Matlack 2007; Royo, Collins et al. 2010; Schafer et al. 2010; Slapcinsky et al. 2010). Knowledge of reproductive biology, particularly seed ecology, is critical for recovery of rare taxa (e.g., *Arabis serotina*, Baskin and Baskin 2002).

In contrast to the abundance of seeds in some forest soils, seedlings are rarely observed aboveground (*Aster acuminatus*, Winn and Pitelka 1981; Hughes et al. 1988), although some taxa produce abundant seedlings in some years, including rare species such as *Arabis perstellata* E. L. Braun (appendix 6.2). Instead, clonal growth occurs in most forest herbs, as is true of most perennials (Cain et al. 1998). The architecture of clonal growth is influenced by genotype and microsite differences (Bell and Tomlinson 1980) and was suggested to be analogous to foraging (e.g., increased frequency of branching in areas of high resource availability [Angevine and Handel 1986 for *Clintonia borealis* Rafin.]). The importance of vegetative growth for forest perennials cannot be underestimated (Campbell and Husband 2005). For example, asexual reproduction via ramet production maintains colonies of *Aster acuminatus* under intact canopies (Hughes et al. 1988). Vegetative propagation is key to the persistence and expansion of patches of *Uvularia perfoliata*, even though successful sexual reproduction results in the development of genetically diverse patches (Kudoh et al. 1999).

Negative correlations between clonal growth and fecundity (sexual reproduction and seed set) for clonal plants suggest a tradeoff between the two modes (Silvertown et al. 1993), although empirical and theoretical work challenges previous paradigms. Silvertown et al. (1993) modeled data from a combination of woody and herbaceous species and found a negative relationship between fecundity and clonal growth. In *Asarum canadense*, experimental removals of flowers resulted in a decrease in rhizome and ramet size (Muir 1995); however, Cain and Damman 1997 found no reduction in probabilities of flowering after production of lateral shoots, and thus little evidence for a tradeoff between vegetative and sexual reproduction. They also found that survivorship of seedlings could equal that of vegetatively produced ramets (Cain and Damman 1997). A negative relationship between sexual reproduction and growth has been demonstrated for *Tipularia discolor* (Snow and Whigham 1989; Zimmerman and Whigham 1992), but the relative costs may depend on the level of reproductive success for *Tipularia* (Snow and Whigham 1989) and the quality of the habitat, such as light conditions, for other orchids like *Orchis purpurea* (Jacquemyn et al. 2010a,b).

POPULATION DYNAMICS

An understanding of population dynamics is pivotal for understanding the ecology of woodland herbs, as the same abiotic and biotic factors that affect population change also determine population size, age structure, and genetic composition (Watkinson 1986; Araki et al. 2009). However, generalizations from empirical and theoretical efforts are complicated by variability among the few taxa that have been studied. Densities, size-age relationships, age-specific mortality, and probabilities of asexual and sexual reproduction vary both within a taxon among sites and between closely related taxa. Population sizes and their changes through time are also highly dynamic. Although relatively stable population sizes through time have been reported (e.g., *Aster acuminatus*, Hughes et al. 1988), more often than not, most population sizes are quite variable temporally (*Arisaema triphyllum*, Bierzychudek 1982b, 1999; Alvarez-Buylla and Slatkin 1994; Shefferson et al. 2011, as well as *Arabis serotina*, *Astragalus robbinsii* var. *jesupii* Eggl. & Sheldon, *Geocarpon minimum*, *Helianthus schweinitzii*, *Hydrastis canadensis, Hypericum cumulicola, Isotria medeoloides, Jacquemontia reclinata* House, *Pedicularis furbishiae,* and *Scirpus ancistrochaetus* of our appendix 6.1).

In discussing the lack of generalizations about life histories of forest herbs, Bierzychudek (1982a) noted the need for more study of age-dependent effects (life tables) and stage-dependent effects (lifecycles), pointing to the transition matrix model as a promising approach for studying plant demography. Of the rare taxa that we surveyed, more studies dealt with some aspect of population dynamics or structure than any other topic. We here overview recent approaches to demography and population dynamics, with emphasis on the threatened and endangered species of eastern North America forests. Population structure and changes in size through time of these forest herbs have been studied using new empirical and theoretical approaches, although again, very few taxa have been examined.

Demography

In their review of plant demography for 585 species, Franco and Silvertown (1990) found only 73 of 250 taxa (29 percent) were of forested systems, and iteroparous perennials of eastern North American forests were underrepresented. Since the 2003 version of this chapter was published, a significant number of studies, including a few on the rare taxa considered here, have expanded the use of stage-based life tables and their analysis, including elasticity analysis, sensitivity analysis, loop analysis, meta-population dynamics, and population viability analysis.

Size- and Stage-Based Projection Matrices

In 1982, Bierzychudek and others saw great promise in approaches pioneered by Tamm (1948, 1956, 1972a, 1972b) (i.e., following the fates of individually marked plants) and in the use of mathematical demographic models, such as the Lefkovitch and Leslie matrix models, to analyze long-term census data. Matrix projection methods involve taking censuses of mapped plants in permanent plots to construct a matrix and summarizing transition probabilities among life history stages/classes to predict future population size n_{t+1} from the vector n_t and the matrix A. Such methods usually also require experiments with seeds to determine germination and seedling transitions. Size-based projection matrices (Lefkovitch 1965) have been used for herbs, which are more readily classified by size than age. For some plants, including rare taxa, a combined size/stage model may be best (Gregg and Kery 2006).

With such models, one can compute population growth rates (λ). At the time of Bierzychudek's (1982a) writing, very few studies had quantified the population dynamics of forest herbs to allow predictive inferences: *Arisaema triphyllum* (Bierzychudek 1982b) and *Chamaelirium luteum* A. Gray (Meagher 1978). Since then, although some estimates of population growth rates have been calculated for plants (Menges 2000a; Crone et al. 2011), few exist for herbs of forested eastern North America, particularly rare taxa. Some estimates of λ suggest proximity to the equilibrium value of 1.0, typical of long-lived perennials and some short-lived species of relatively stable habitats (*Panax quinquefolius,* Nault and Gagnon 1993). Other plant populations have periods of exponential growth (*Danthonia sericea* Nutt., Moloney 1988; *Viola fimbriatula* Small (= *V. sagittata* Aiton var. *ovata* (Nutt.) Torr. & A. Gray), Solbrig et al. 1988), while others can increase rapidly one year and decline the next (*Collinsia verna* Nutt., λ = 1.80–0.41, Kalisz and McPeek 1992). An increasing number of studies use matrix models and calculate deterministic or stochastic growth rate. Of the 34 North America taxa treated in the Crone et al. (2011) review of 214 herbs, all except three present at least one estimate of λ.

Models based on transition matrices can also identify vulnerable stages particularly sensitive to selection, allowing comparison with other species. These matrices can be extended to forecast population sizes through time, project the fate of populations and species, and help select different management strategies. Similar analyses have evaluated the effects of sexual versus asexual reproduction and seed banks (Damman and Cain 1998; Piqueras and Klimes 1998; Adams et al. 2005), disturbance and succession (Cipollini et al. 1994; Valverde and Silvertown 1995, 1997a, 1997b, 1998; Damman and Cain 1998; Petru and Menges 2004), herbivores (Bullock et al. 1994; Bastrenta et al. 1995; Ehrlén 1995; Hori and Yokoi 1999; Maron and Kauffman 2006; Knight 2007; Knight 2009a, b), and invasives and biocontrol agents (Jongejans et al. 2006) on population growth rates. Transition matrices have been used to predict population size through time for species at risk, including impacts from fire (Hawkes and Menges 1995; Gross et al. 1998; Menges and Dolan 1998; Menges and Hawkes 1998; Silvertown et al. 1996; Satterthwaite et al. 2002; Menges and Quintana-Ascencio 2004; Kesler 2008; Quintana-Ascencio et al. 2011), habitat fragmentation (Alvarez-Buylla and Slatkin 1994; Lennartsson 2002; Brys et al. 2005; Colling and Matthies 2006), trampling (Gross et al. 1998), weather (Rose et al. 1998; Menges et al. 2011), global climate change (Doak and Morris 1999; Maschinski et al. 2006; Noel et al. 2010), and harvest or other management practices (Molnar and Bokros 1996; Nantel et al. 1996; Oostermeijer et al. 1996; Silvertown et al. 1996; Degreef et al. 1997; Emery et al. 1999; Endels et al. 2005; Ramula et al. 2008; Colas et al. 2008; Vitt et al. 2009).

Matrix population models are still the most commonly used technique for population projections, calculation of population growth rates, vital rates, comparisons across years, populations, species, life histories, and in response to other environmental factors, including management (Crone et al. 2011). Crone and her colleagues reviewed 397 published studies on modeling of populations; 214 dealt with annuals or herbaceous perennials. From their data accessible on the Web (http://knb.ecoinformatics.org/knb/metacat/nceas.961.\nceas), we found 70 that dealt with rare taxa. Only 19 dealt with herbaceous understory taxa, common or rare, in eastern North America. Of those 19, a mere four occur in appendix 6.1. In another recent review of variation in vital rates and population growth, Buckley et al. (2010) used data for 49 perennial plant species. Among those 49 taxa, the average number of populations studied was 4 and the mean duration of study was 4.5 years, as noted by others (Menges 2000b; Crone 2010), about the duration of a dissertation. Of those 49 taxa, again, a mere eight were herbs of forested eastern North America, and only five are listed taxa in appendix 6.1. Rare taxa in appendix 6.1 for which we have matrix models include *Eriogonum longifolium* Nutt. var.*gnaphalifolium* Gand. (Satterthwaite et al. 2002), *Eryngium cuneifolium* (Menges and Quintana-Ascencio 2004), *Hypericum cumulicola* (Small) P. Adams (Quintana-Ascencio et al. 1998, 2003, 2011), *Panax quinquefolius* L. (Charron and Gagnon 1991; Nantel et al. 1996; McGraw and Furedi 2005; Mooney and McGraw 2006; van der Voort et al. 2006), and *Pedicularis furbishiae* S. Watson (Menges 1990). The other forested understory herbs with matrices but lacking USFWS or COSEWIC status are *Actaea spicata* (Fröborg and Eriksson 2003), *Allium tricoccum* (Nault and Gagnon 1993; Nantel et al. 1996; Rock 2004), *Arisaema triphyllum*

(Bierzychudek 1982b; 1999), *Asarum canadense* (Damman and Cain 1998), *Boltonia decurrens* (Torr. & A. Gray) Alph. Wood (Smith et al. 2005), *Chamaelirium luteum* (Meagher 1982), the sub-shrub *Chamaecrista lineata* (Sw.) Greene var. *keyensis* (Pennell) Irwin and Barneby (= *Chamaecrista keyensis* (Pennell) Britton and Rose (Liu et al. 2005), *Cleistes divaricata* L. Ames (Gregg et al. 1991), *Collinsia verna* (Kalisz and McPeek 1992), *Cynoglossum virginianum* L. (Cipollini et al. 1993), *Cypripedium calceolus* L. (Nicolé et al. 2005), *Danthonia sericea* (Moloney 1988), *Froelichia floridana* (Nutt.) Moq. (McCauley and Ungar 2002), *Impatiens capensis* Meerb. (Steets et al. 2007), the barely woody evergreen *Linnaea borealis* (Eriksson 1992), *Oxalis montana* Raf. (Berg 2002), *Pinguicula ionantha* Godfrey (Kesler et al. 2008), *Sarracenia alata* Alph. Wood (Brewer 2001), *Sarracenia purpurea* L. (Gotelli and Ellison 2002), *Trillium grandiflorum* (Michx.) Salisb. (Knight et al. 2008, 2009a,b), and *Viola fimbriatula* (= *V. sagittata* Aiton var. *ovata* (Nutt.) Torr. & A. Gray, (Solbrig et al. 1988). `

Elasticity, Sensitivity, and Loop Analysis

Demographic perturbation analyses, including prospective (e.g., elasticity and sensitivity analyses) and retrospective analyses (e.g., variance decomposition), are a recent addition to the ecologist's toolbox to help predict how populations change through time (Caswell 2000; Zuidema and Franco 2001; Morris and Doak 2002, 2005). These analyses aim to identify those life stages or transitions during the lifecycle, such as survival and fecundity, that most affect population dynamics (van Groenendael et al. 1994; van Tienderen 2000).

Elasticities ($\partial\log \lambda/\partial\log a_{ij}$) are proportional changes in the population growth rate (λ), and thus are measures of fitness that result from proportional changes in population parameters (vital rates) related to survival, growth, and reproduction, again presented as matrix entries or elements (de Kroon et al. 1986, 2000; Heppell et al. 2000b; Menges 2000a). Loop analysis extends elasticity analysis and decomposes the population growth rate into the contributions made by lifecycle pathways (van Groenendael et al. 1994; de Kroon et al. 2000; Claessen 2005). In contrast, sensitivities ($\partial\lambda/\partial a_{ij}$), mathematically and biologically distinct from elasticities, estimate the absolute effects of changes in demographic parameters on λ (Caswell 1978; de Kroon et al. 1986; Horvitz et al. 1997; de Kroon 2000; van Tienderen 2000). These parameters reflect the relative contributions of the matrix elements or transitions to the population growth rate, and thus the "importance" of certain life stages and their associated demographic rates for management and research (Heppell et al. 2000b; de Kroon et al. 2000).

Elasticity and sensitivity analyses have been presented for dozens of plant taxa (see summaries in Silvertown et al. 1993; Pfister 1998; Reed et al. 2002), often weeds of open habitats or woody plants. A promising number of long-lived herbs associated with wooded habitats of eastern North America do have sufficient demographic data to allow construction of matrices and either elasticity or sensitivity analyses of the elements. Of the 397 sources surveyed by Crone et al. (2011), 249 of the studies calculated sensitivities of herbs. Of those, 25 studies presented sensitivity analyses for herbs of the forested understory, 15 of eastern North America. A few listed taxa in appendices 6.1 and 6.2 have elasticity or sensitivity analyses: *Eriogonum longifolium* var. *gnaphalifolium* and *Eryngium cuneifolium* of the Lake Wales Ridge (Satterthwaite et al. 2002; Menges and Quintana-Ascencio 2004), *Panax quinquefolius* (Charron and Gagnon

1991; Nantel et al. 1996; Van der Voort and McGraw 2006), and *Pedicularis furbishiae* (Menges 1990; de Kroon et al. 2000).

These relative contributions to population growth can be grouped in biologically meaningful ways (e.g., growth, reproduction, and stasis) to compare across taxa (Silvertown et al. 1993, 1996; Franco and Silvertown 2004) and can provide general categorizations of populations based on their responses during different phases of the lifecycle (Heppell et al. 2000a). As of yet, too few elasticity analyses have been performed to allow strong inferences about those phases of the life history of forest herbs that most affect population processes; although it is clear from what we know about the ecology of forest herbs that the role of vegetative modes should not be underestimated. In their 1993 review, Silvertown et al. noted that of 66 herbs, iteroparous forest taxa were associated with their "survival-growth axis," reflecting a range of survivorship and growth, but limited fecundity elasticities. Even for taxa with stable or increasing population sizes, the elasticities were highly variable among taxa (Silvertown et al. 1993). The most variable transitions contributing to the lifecycle were those involved in sexual reproduction (seed recruitment, seedling recruitment, and fecundity) and retrogression (decrease in size or reversion from flowering to vegetative or dormant phase). Sexual recruitment (a seed bank, germination, early seedling success) can play significant roles in long-term population growth rates, particularly for populations in temporally variable environments (Moloney 1988; Kalisz and McPeek 1992; Sletvold and Rydren 2007; Weekley et al. 2007; Torang et al. 2010).

Other analyses suggest that it is the vegetative modes that play major roles in population growth, although few projection matrices include both sexual and asexual reproduction. Growth and survival have been reported to affect population dynamics more than fecundity in common forest taxa (e.g., *Allium tricoccum*, Nault and Gagnon 1993; *Danthonia sericea*, Moloney 1988; *Potentilla anserina* L., Eriksson 1988) and some rare taxa of appendices 6.1 and 6.2. Howe and Miriti (2004) note that for long-lived plants, the highly variable transition from seed to juvenile is associated with low elasticity and thus can have little effect on population dynamics. Despite these analyses of those phases of the lifecycle most likely to affect λ, some initial evidence suggests that variable life history stages contribute little to population growth rates (Pfister 1998). Long-lived herbaceous perennial populations can be particularly sensitive to fecundity, as well as growth and survival elements. Thus, it becomes important to analyze individual vital rates including retrogression or shrinkage; use of fewer, smaller matrices may lead to erroneous inferences (Ramula and Lehtila 2005; Salguero-Gomez and Plotkin 2010). Recent theoretical work has emphasized that elasticity analysis can still be a simple first step in answering important questions in evolutionary and population ecology, conservation biology, and management (Enright et al. 1995; Silvertown et al. 1996; Benton and Grant 1999; Grant and Benton 2000; Smith et al. 2005; Gotelli and Ellison 2006a; Ramula et al. 2008; Bermingham 2010).

The use of elasticities is not without controversy (i.e., their summation for interpretation of life history theory has been debated; Silvertown et al. 1993; Franco and Silvertown 1994; Shea et al. 1994; Franco and Silvertown 1996; Oostermeijer et al. 1996). Authors have cautioned against use of mean values for several matrices through time and interpretation of the largest elasticities for conservation decisions. Instead, analysis of the range of variation for different demographic rates is encouraged

(Oostermeijer et al. 1996; Pfister 1998; Mills et al. 1999). Recent developments include evaluation of variation in vital rates, including temporal autocorrelation of rates (Buckley et al. 2010), the influence of exogenous environmental factors (climate, fire) on vital rates, and a focus on other phrases of the lifecycle in addition to sexual recruitment that have important implications for rare species management (Bruna et al. 2009; Evans et al. 2010).

Metapopulation Dynamics

A metapopulation was defined by Levins (1970) as a population of populations; "local dynamics and the regional processes of migration, extinction, and colonization" produce the ecology and genetics of populations (Olivieri et al. 1990; Husband and Barrett 1996). To understand the population biology of rare forest herbs, we must expand our study of demography and genetics of plant populations to a landscape-scale. To do so requires estimation of patch occupancy and extinction and colonization rates, both spatially and temporally (Husband and Barrett 1996), all facets of a metapopulation approach. Although plants appear appropriate for metapopulation analyses (i.e., immobility, strong spatial structure, restricted dispersal per Husband and Barrett 1996), few studies adopt this approach, especially theoretical work, due to the difficulty of measuring the critical parameters of extinction, colonization, and migration

Metapopulation dynamics are a promising approach for plant species in declining habitats, but empirical data that can be used to address the predictions of metapopulation dynamics are relatively scarce (Husband and Barrett 1996; Ouborg and Eriksson 2004). Again, bias is demonstrated toward annuals in ephemeral environments, and few herbs of forest or wooded ecotones have been evaluated for metapopulation dynamics (*Boltonia decurrens*, Mettler-Cherry et al. 2006; *Collinsia verna*, Kalisz and McPeek 1993; *Pedicularis furbishiae*, Menges 1990; and *Plantago cordata* Lam., Meagher et al. 1978; Husband and Barrett 1996). Demographic data sufficient for transition matrices or metapopulation analyses are available for some of the listed forest taxa here in appendices 6.1 and 6.2, notably the work by Menges and his colleagues on the rare flora of the Lake Wales Ridge of Florida (Boyle et al. 2003; Menges and Quintana-Ascencio 2004; Menges 2007; Quintana-Ascencio et al. 2007). *Agalinis gattingeri* Small in Britton & A. Br., listed as endangered in Canada, may be sufficiently abundant in the U.S. for extensive population study, as done with other members of the genus (Vitt et al. 2009).

Studies of isolated plants or those in unevenly distributed patches, over the full range of spatial scales of their occurrence, are needed, as is the development of more spatially explicit models (Czárán and Bartha 1992; Perry and Gonzalez-Andujar 1993; Perry 1998; Winkler et al. 1999). Understanding dispersal among patches, patch quality, and patch dispersion is critical for appropriate metapopulation analyses in general, and for forest herbs in particular (Eriksson 1997; Bullock et al. 2006).

Variation in size and spatial arrangement of patches influences population dynamics and persistence of metapopulations. "Analytically tractable" models of metapopulations assume that all patches are identical, but recent empirical and theoretical developments suggest local heterogeneity can impact metapopulation growth and species persistence (Gilpin 1991; Hanski 1991; Lande 1993; Olivieri et al. 1995). Valverde and Silvertown (1997b, 1998) demonstrated that variation among populations influences metapopulation dynamics. In their study, changing environmental conditions during canopy closure influenced demography of the common woodland herb *Primula vulgaris*; notably, fecundities and population growth rates were higher in patches under an open canopy with more light availability.

POPULATION VIABILITY ANALYSIS AND CONSERVATION BIOLOGY

Threats to populations, particularly small ones, include (1) demographic stochasticity, (2) environmental stochasticity, (3) systematic trends, and (4) catastrophes (Menges 2000a). Managers are often faced with the question of how long a rare plant species can persist in face of these threats. Population viability analysis (PVA) uses empirical data and modeling to predict the finite rate of increase (λ), extinction probability, time to extinction, or future population size or structure (Menges 2000b).

While PVA can be used to estimate a minimum viable population (MVP), the smallest population size that will persist given some maximum level of risk of extinction, such methods are limited, particularly for plants (Reed et al. 2002; Munzbergova and Ehrlén 2005; Traill et al. 2007). Most published plant PVA studies deal with one species, using just over three populations on average and data collected for about four years (Menges 2000a,b; Crone et al. 2011). Only 15 understory herbs that occur in forested communities of North America have been used in PVA studies or estimation of extinction risk (Menges 2000a, Crone et al. 2011). These herbs are *Allium tricoccum* (Nault and Gagnon 1993; Nantel et al. 1996; Rock et al. 2004), *Arisaema triphyllum* (Bierzychudek 1982b), *Asarum canadense* (Damman and Cain 1998), *Cypripedium calceolus* (Nicolé et al. 2005), *Chamaelirium luteum* (Meagher 1982), *Cynoglossum virginianum* (Cipollini et al. 1993), *Collinsia verna* (Kalisz and McPeek 1992), *Eryngium cuneifolium* (Menges and Quintana-Ascencio 2004), *Hypericum cumulicola* (Quintana-Ascencio et al. 1998; Quintana-Ascencio et al. 2003), the barely woody evergreen *Linnaea borealis* (Eriksson 1992), *Panax quinquefolius* (Nantel et al. 1996; Mooney and McGraw 2006; van der Voort et al. 2006), *Pedicularis furbishiae* (Menges 1990), *Sarracenia purpurea* (Gotelli and Ellison 2002), *Trillium grandiflorum* (Knight et al. 2008, 2009a), and *Viola fimbriatula* Small (Solbrig et al. 1988).

PVA is not without its challenges. Although increasing use is associated with increasing misuse, as is the case with any technique, one of the most effective uses of PVA may be to compare management strategies (Reed et al. 2002). Quantitative modeling of population sizes using metapopulation dynamics, and PVA is underutilized for forest herbs of eastern North America. Such modeling, however, can provide insight into various management practices including interactions with herbivores (Ehrlén 1995; McGraw and Furedi 2005; Knight et al. 2009a), fire management (Menges and Dolan 1998; Brewer 2001; Satterthwaite et al. 2002; Evans et al. 2008, 2010), or harvest (Nantel et al. 1996; Rock et al. 2004; van der Voort and McGraw 2006).

The finite population growth rate (λ) calculated from a projection matrix is only validly applied to a population with a stable age or size distribution. If age or size distributions are not stable, we cannot use these population growth rates to predict future population sizes (Bierzychudek 1982a, 1999; Coulson et al. 2001). Thus, predictions of long-term population growth that use the Lefkovitch transition matrix model depend on the assumption that demographic parameters do not vary through time (Caswell 1978). Considerable work demonstrates that demographic parameters are highly variable among populations, both spatially and temporally, including transient dynamics (Stott et al. 2010). Recent experimental approaches caution against the use of purely descriptive techniques and a limited portion of the plant lifecycle (Ramula and Buckley 2009; Waser et al. 2010). Use of "proxies" (more common or even sympatric plant models to approximate population trajectories and thus management for rare taxa) also can produce spurious conclusions about limiting factors (see Fox 2007 for two rare California annuals).

Integral Projection Models and Life Table Response Experiments

Some size categories may be underrepresented in populations or simply not obvious for many plant species. Integral projection modeling (IPM) can incorporate the virtues of matrix projection models (simple structures that can provide estimates of λ, stable distribution, reproductive value, and sensitivities of λ to changes in life history parameters), yet IPM does not require division of individuals into discrete size classes (Easterling et al. 2000). Classes can be defined by a continuous variable, such as measures of length or mass. Easterling et al. (2000) used their model with the federally endangered northern monkshood (*Aconitum noveboracense* A. Gray), with stem diameter as the class variable. Continuous state variables such as dispersal have recently been given spatial reference in the development of spatial integral projection models (SIPMs) for invasive plants (Neubert-Caswell models, Neubert and Caswell 2000; Jongejans et al. 2011). Studies based on time-variant population demography (stochastic matrices) hold promise for some (Moloney 1988), and theoretical considerations have increased (Tuljapurkar 1984; Caswell 2007). Despite the challenges of the theory, since 2003, the use of temporal variation in matrix-based analyses (i.e., non-stationary matrix or non-deterministic models) has increased (Gotelli and Ellison 2006 for *Sarracenia purpurea*; Lehtila et al. 2006 for *Primula veris* L. of European grasslands). Again, the application of promising theory is contingent upon the strength of the supporting empirical data.

Long-term demographic data are important for many rare taxa. Such datasets can be particularly valuable for tests of new approaches, as well as conservation (e.g., integral projection models for *Aconitum noveboracense* [Easterling et al. 2000; Mabry et al. 2009]). Recent extensions of life-stage transitions include construction of demographic models from common garden and life table response experiments (LTREs) to compare common versus rare taxa (Endels et al. 2007), invasive versus noninvasive species (Lambrecht-McDowell and Radosevich 2005; Burns 2008; Ramula et al. 2008), response to herbivory (Farrington et al. 2009; Knight et al. 2009a; Schutzenhofer et al. 2009), fire (Kesler et al. 2008), and other habitat changes (Nordbakken et al. 2004; Brys et al. 2005; Lehtila et al. 2006; Endels et al. 2007; Jacquemyn and Brys 2008; Bremer and

Jongejans 2010; Tomimatsu and Ohara 2010; Schmidt et al. 2011). LTREs decompose contributions to the population growth rate (λ) in an analytical way, similar to linear models in analysis of variance. Such approaches analyze vital rates under different conditions or treatments to quantify the effect of different environmental factors on population response (Caswell 1989, 2010). Such approaches hold promise as a way to evaluate the effect of management on population growth and viability (e.g., fire for *Pinguicula ionantha* [Kesler et al. 2008] and deer herbivory for *Trillium grandiflorum* [Knight et al. 2009a]).

CONCLUSIONS AND FUTURE DIRECTIONS

Bierzychudek (1982a) posed three woodland herb-related questions for future research: (1) What factors regulate population sizes of forest herbs? (2) How stable are population sizes of forest herbs? (3) How much site-to-site variation occurs in population behavior? The first edition of this chapter (Jolls 2003) evaluated the progress that had been made on the three questions and provided suggestions for future research. Whigham (2004) resonated many of the same issues found in the Bierzychudek and Jolls reviews and expanded on the themes and issues that needed further examination. After an additional decade of research and publications, we recognize that progress has been made on a number of the topics covered in the earlier reviews, but we also recognize that many challenges remain and new ones have been identified. We conclude this review by first addressing the three broad questions posed by Bierzychudek in 1982. We then provide an update on the "research needs" described by Jolls (2003) and Whigham (2004). We end with our thoughts and suggestions for future research on the ecology of woodland herbs.

What Factors Regulate Population Sizes of Forest Herbs?

Jolls (2003) and Whigham (2004) found that progress has been made in our understanding of the factors that regulate populations of woodland herbs. For rare species, however, much remains to be discovered. Too few species have been studied in detail under natural and experimental conditions to provide the information that is needed to identify broad patterns among species, let alone identify factors that are critically important for species for which recovery plans are needed. Little has been accomplished since Jolls (2003) noted that few recovery plans include information about key factors that regulate populations (Tear et al. 1995). Factors such as nutrients (Baeten, Hermy, et al. 2010; Baeten, Vanhellemont et al. 2010) and disturbance influence populations, but for most woodland herbs, light is a key factor. Critical light levels needed for population maintenance and expansion need to be elaborated for rare species (Vandepitte et al. 2010). Jacquemyn et al. (2010b) provide an example that demonstrates the importance of combining field-based monitoring data with modeling to show the importance of light conditions to the maintenance of herb populations. Light and temperature may become increasingly more important as microhabitat conditions change in concert with global changes (De Frenne, Brunet et al. 2011). Baeten, De Frenne et al. (2010) have demonstrated, for example, that individual species are likely to be impacted by multiple threats, and thus the responses by individual species are likely to be complex.

The relationships between woodland herbs and mycorrhizal fungi are another realm of plant-environment interactions that remains poorly understood even though it appears that almost all woodland herbs are mycorrhizal (Whigham 2004). An example of the importance of mycorrhiza was demonstrated recently by McCormick et al. (2012) who showed that to be successful, orchid populations require not only the presence of an appropriate fungus but also the right amount of the fungus, which may be as important as its presence or absence.

In the future, habitat fragmentation (Digiovinazzo et al. 2010), competition by nonnative plants and animals (Bauer et al. 2010; Royo, Collins et al. 2011; Royo, Stout, et al. 2011), and changes in habitat management also will be increasingly important factors that influence populations of rare woodland herbs; yet little is known about how these factors influence individual species. Isolation of populations by habitat fragmentation may expose woodland herbs to competition by invasive species, and fragmentation may also result in changes in assemblages of pollinators that are required by rare taxa (Schmucki and de Blois 2009b).

How Stable Are Population Sizes of Forest Herbs?

Since the 1986, 2003, and 2004 reviews, there have not been any significant changes in the number of studies in which populations of woodland herbs have been monitored or modeled for periods of time that are long enough to determine whether or not they are stable. The studies that have been published that shed light on this questions are of three forms: (1) surveys of herbs in forests after many years of recovery from disturbance (Baeten, De Frenne et al. 2010; Dyer 2010; Wyatt and Silman 2010); (2) studies of the distribution and, at times, aging of plants to infer the status of populations (Jenkins and Webster 2009; Araki et al. 2010); and (3) predictive models based on various sorts of population data (Bermingham 2010; Burton et al. 2011). When available, growth rates of many plant populations vary among years and sites (Valverde and Silvertown 1998; Crone et al. 2011). The recovery plans of many taxa note that populations are highly variable among years (*Isotria medeoloides*, United States Fish and Wildlife Service 1992), even though some populations are predicted to increase (*Polemonium vanbruntiae*, Bermingham 2010). For populations at risk, trajectories are also highly variable among populations, and by definition, negative (e.g., $r = -0.0040$ for *Panax quinquefolius* [Charron and Gagnon 1991]).

How Much Site-to-Site Variation Occurs in Population Behavior?

It is now clear that habitat heterogeneity is an important determinant of the abundance and dynamics of woodland herbs, but we do not yet know if the factor or suite of factors responsible for populations dynamics at one site are the same or different for the same species or suite of species at other sites. Lacking the enormous and complex datasets that would be needed to assess this question, which is critical in the context of issues related to habitat fragmentation and global change, we have to rely on the few studies that shed light on these issues. We know, for example, that variability in demography from one population to another can increase extinction probabilities of local populations at their distribution limits (Nantel and Gagnon 1999 for *Helianthus divaricatus* L.). Presumably, such variability should have equally critical impacts on rare plants at their distributional limits (small population size or habitat). Experimental studies such as those reported by (De Frenne, Graae et al. 2011) are essential if we are to understand how rare species will respond to environmental changes and variability. Given the relatively small number of scientists studying the ecology of woodland herbs and the difficulty of obtaining resources for long-term and large-scale experimental research, approaches such as megamatrix analysis hold promise (Pascarella and Horvitz 1998), but the approach has been very limited in its application (Dostal 2007).

Knowledge about individual woodland herbs or woodland herbs as a group has expanded at a glacial pace. Many of the issues raised by Whigham (2004) remain unanswered, resulting in our ability to do little more than offer broad generalities about the ecology of woodland herbs. The challenges, opportunities, and "calls to arms" described by Jolls (2003) remain.

The focus in this review has been on woodland herbs that could be categorized as rare. Much of the available data on the ecology of woodland herbs, however, come from studies of species that would not be considered rare. The challenge, therefore, is to evaluate the existing data in the context of the conservation and, where appropriate, restoration of rare taxa. In essence, the critical question posed by Schemske et al. (1994) remains salient for conservation biologists today and will be relevant into the future: "Is this taxon declining, and if so, why?" Regrettably, the information needed to answer this question is lacking for most rare forest herbs, as is basic biological information in the recovery plans for the vast majority of rare plant and animal taxa (Tear et al. 1995). The datasets for the few species that have been examined since our earlier reviews in 2003 and 2004, whether common or rare, are the results of commitments of individual researchers to long-term, extensive datasets for these taxa: for example, *Arisaema triphyllum* (Bierzychudek 1982b, 1999), *Asarum canadense* (Damman and Cain 1998), *Panax quinquefolius* (Nantel et al. 1996; McGraw et al. 2003; van der Voort et al. 2003; Wixted and McGraw 2009), *Pedicularis furbishiae* (Menges 1990), *Trillium grandiflorum* (Knight 2004, 2007; Knight et al. 2008, 2009a,b), and Eric Menges, Pedro Quintana-Ascencio, Carl Weekley, and their colleagues for the flora of the Lake Wales Ridge (Menges 2000a,b; Menges and Quintana-Ascencio 2004).

Even though there have been a few additional long-term studies of species, the point raised by Menges (2000a) is probably more important today. We need additional studies, experimental or observational, on how species response to disturbances that are one-time events, as well as recurrent ones; we also need to know more about how species respond to environmental stochasticity. Clearly, advancement in modeling will be needed to address many of these issues. Models are only as good as the data that they use; thus our renewed call for more long-term studies of woodland herbs.

New Techniques, Genetic Considerations, Demographic Information, and Conservation Biology

The development of molecular tools as almost-standard analytical procedures provides the opportunity to focus on other critical aspects of woodland herbs—genetic diversity (Godt and Hamrick 2001; Hamrick et al. 2006; Tomimatsu 2006; Van Rossum 2008; Jacquemyn et al. 2009; Walker et al. 2009). If rare species conservation is to be successful, it will be important to quantify the genetic diversity of species over the entire range and, most important, at the local and regional scales to assure that conservation efforts successfully incorporate the range of genetic diversity of the taxa. Research has shown that most clonal woodland herbs are genetically diverse, and species that are apomictic or autogamous also differ genetically among populations. One of us (DFW) and his colleagues are examining the genetic diversity of *Isotria medeoloides*, the rarest orchid in eastern North America, and they have found that, while overall genetic diversity may be low, populations are unique across the range of distribution of the species (Devlin 2007; Crystal 2009; McCormick et al. 2011). Such information is essential if restoration efforts are to be successful and ecologically meaningful. Once the levels of genetic diversity are known, other new techniques in conservation such as in vitro culture, cryopreservation, and molecular markers have the potential to complement preservation and restoration efforts of rare taxa (Yordanov et al. 2002; Kauth and Kane 2009), including the assessment of ecotypic variation on restoration outcomes (Kauth et al. 2008). Other approaches include the potential use of nonnative pollinators (Pemberton and Liu 2008).

Genetic knowledge must, however, complement rather than subordinate sound demography and population biology (Oostermeijer et al. 2003). Studies of the population biology of forest understory taxa, even the rare ones, can expand our understanding of major ecological and evolutionary paradigms. Recent work with *Asplenium scolopendrium* documented a mixed mating system and its importance in colonization and population persistence in ferns (Wubs et al. 2010). Other new approaches include use of plant demographic analyses within a phylogenetic context or what Kokko and Lopez-Sepulcre (2007) termed an "ecogenetic link." Buckley et al. (2010) demonstrated that phylogeny has a "minimal influence" on interspecies variation in population growth rates from their survey of matrix models, yet a phylogenetic signal was detected in sensitivities, with important implications for our study of life history evolution (Burns et al. 2010). Demographic and selection analyses can be combined to predict evolutionary, as well as ecological, population dynamics (Knight et al. 2008 for *Trillium grandiflorum*).

Call to Arms: Experimentation, Restoration, Determination of Declines, and Conservation Partnerships

In addition to more extensive empiricism, development of theory, knowledge of genetics, and the development of more sophisticated approaches to modeling, the use of carefully designed experimental manipulations in the field linked to modeling efforts offers a way forward to greatly expand our knowledge base about forest herbs, particularly rare taxa (Bierzychudek 1982a; Ashmun and Pitelka 1985; Schemske et al. 1994; Bevill and Louda 1999; Vellend et al. 2000b; Hale et al. 2006; Knight et al. 2009a). Such experimental approaches are even more challenging for rare plants with protected status, for which critical knowledge of basic biology, ecology, and propagation is lacking. For those with protected status, the regulatory process may make experimentation a bureaucratic hurdle that few of us could or would care to surmount. Yet, many rare taxa are extremely tractable in culture (e.g., *Justicia cooleyi* Monach. & Leonard, *Panax quinquefolius*, *Solidago shortii*) and offer information that is a result from or a contribution to restoration efforts.

If we are able to reach the point where we have enough information to develop and implement effective restoration and conservation plans, what will be the backdrop upon which those efforts are supported? Obviously, efforts will continue to focus on individual species to develop the knowledge base to assure the survival of species like *Isotria medeoloides*, a species for which state and federal agencies are working (Sara Cairns, pers. comm.).

Broader-scale efforts at many levels, however, will be needed to move the conservation effort forward. The focus of the Center for Plant Conservation on the collection of seeds of rare taxa and subsequent efforts to learn how to germinate them as part of conservation efforts represent a major advance and one that needs to be expanded and emulated. A related approach is currently being developed in an attempt to conserve the more than 200 orchid taxa in the U.S. and Canada. In 2012, the Smithsonian Institution and the United States Botanic Garden launched the North American Orchid Conservation Center (NAOCC). The establishment and success of this program will require a long-term and sustained effort, but if successful, NAOCC will represent a model system that could be adapted for use in conserving rare herbs of forested ecosystems.

NAOCC will be a private-public partnership with a mission to conserve orchids native to North America, and it will lead a broad-based effort focused on all native orchid species, including development of protocols for their cultivation, conservation, and restoration. Success will be determined by the eventual ability of NAOCC and its partners to cultivate all native orchids for purposes of displaying them in botanic gardens around the country. This living collection will conserve the genetic diversity of the native species. Development of seed and mycorrhizal fungi collections will support the efforts to determine the specific requirements of all native species for growing them in culture and natural habitats for conservation and restoration. The initial goals of NAOCC are to (1) partner with the Center for Plant Conservation to establish and manage a collection of seeds that is representative of the genetic diversity of all native orchids (the seeds will be used for long-term storage and propagation of orchids for research); (2) establish and maintain a national collection of orchid mycorrhizal fungi for use in research and conservation; (3) develop techniques on a species-by-species basis to cultivate all native orchids in botanic gardens in the United States and Canada; (4) provide specialized training focused on research, conservation, cultivation, and restoration of native orchids; and (5) develop website-based materials to educate the public about orchid identification, ecology, management, and propagation. NAOCC will have to make considerable effort to develop the financial basis for success, but success will also depend on the ability of the organization to focus on key elements of a meaningful conservation strategy.

At a basic level, the elements of a successful conservation strategy remain unchanged; however, approaches have changed and projections for conservation outcomes are more critical. Schemske and colleagues advocated a three-factor framework for species recovery that remains valid today: (1) Determine the biological status of a species, (2) identify the life history stages critical to population growth, and (3) determine the underlying biological causes of variation in critical life history stages (Schemske et al. 1994). Similarly, Montalvo et al. (1997) presented five research areas of importance that will all be essential elements of a successful NAOCC or any other conservation effort involving restoration. They include (1) the role of abundance and genetic variation in colonization, establishment, growth, and evolutionary potential, (2) the influence of local adaptation and life history traits in the success of restored populations, (3) the role of spatial arrangement of landscape elements on metapopulation dynamics and population processes such as migration, (4) the effects of genetic drift, gene flow, and selection on population persistence, and (5) the influence of interspecies interactions on population dynamics and community development. These questions and challenges posed for the conservation of rare plants are strikingly similar to the most basic ecological questions we ask of more common taxa.

Of late, ecology has sought to identify the role of plant functional traits, traits correlated with resource use. These quantifiable traits (growth rate, habit or leaf lifespan, leaf mass or area, nutrient or defensive compounds content, life history, dispersal ability) have been used to evaluate invasive species (i.e., their ability to capitalize on high resource availability, such as nitrogen; Suding et al. 2005). These resource use traits also are being extended to native taxa to (1) help evaluate potential success of restoration strategies (Aubin et al. 2007; Myers and Harms 2011 and references therein), (2) evaluate patterns of species loss at the community level (Wiegmann and Waller 2006; Farnsworth and Ogurcak 2006; Dolan et al. 2011), and (3) assess species response to global change (Tessier 2008). Such approaches hold promise for evaluation and restoration of individual rare species (Kooyman and Rossetto 2008; Hegazy et al. 2010), particularly when knowledge suggests that factors other than population size and abundance affect extinction risk (Cole 2003; Baeten et al. 2010). Larger ecological questions about the role of ecological filtering, including seed dispersal, spatial variation in disturbance regimes, and temporal variation in resources in community assembly may help illuminate causes of species rarity and maintenance of diversity in the herbaceous understory (Harrelson and Matlack 2006; Flinn 2007; Sutton and Morgan 2009; Myers and Harms 2011). For global issues like climate change, integration of ecological and evolutionary approaches at the population, community, and landscape level is required, what some call "evolutionary community ecology" (Lavergne et al. 2010). All evidence confirms, however, that successful conservation of herbs of the forest understory must also be firmly grounded in a solid understanding of their basic and often highly species-specific biology, even at the landscape level (Valdes and Garcia 2011).

Four decades later, we still agree with Bierzychudek (1982a) that variation among populations of forest herbs precludes generalizations about their life histories, growth rates, and stability of population sizes or structures, despite Goethe's expression of faith in the order of nature that opened this chapter. Yet, we still lack sufficient information, particularly for rare forest herbs, to embrace Margaret Fuller's view and simply admit we have sampled the exceptions to the rules. Despite limited generalizations, evidence from forest herbs, even the rare ones, has challenged previous paradigms about tradeoffs between reproductive modes and growth, including the relative primacy of sexual reproduction for population maintenance and dispersal. While these taxa may not be widely dispersed or abundant, they have demonstrated the dangers of underestimating the roles and significance of stochastic events, vegetative spread, and temporal and spatial variation in population size and recruitment.

For those of us who might regard our progress in the past decades since Bierzychudek's (1982a) review as "limited," we again consider Holsinger's (1999) perspective on the difference between population biology and conservation biology:

Population biologists choose a particular species for study, at least in part because they think that the species they have chosen will allow them to address broad, general issues of conceptual importance in population biology. Conservation biologists have the species chosen for them by circumstances—the circumstances of endangerment. One consequence of this difference is that it may be much more difficult for conservation biologists to get complete demographic information. Population biologists choose species that allow them to get the information they need. Conservation biologists have to figure out how to get the information they need from often-recalcitrant species. Population biologists are generally satisfied with discovering the factors that limit population size, population growth rate, or species distribution. Conservation biologists use that information to project the fate of populations/species and to decide among management strategies.

In a time of unprecedented loss of biodiversity, the dichotomy between population biologist and conservation biologist becomes dangerously artificial and semantic. We are all called upon to be both.

ACKNOWLEDGMENTS

This work would not have been possible without the efforts of Lindsay D. Leverett and Emily R. Stewart on update and critical review of the rare species information in the appendices. Other colleagues shared invaluable information: Larry Barden and Jim Matthews (*Helianthus schweinitzii*); Misty Franklin Buchanan, Paul Martin Brown, and Lawrence Zettler (Orchidaceae); Kay Kirkman (*Schwalbea americana*); Mike Kunz, Richard LeBlond, and Johnny Randall (*Carex lutea*); Eric S. Menges (Florida scrub endemics); Anton A. Reznicek (Cyperaceae); Dale Suiter and Jeffrey L. Walck (*Echinacea tennesseensis* and *Solidago shortii*); and Donna Herendeen and the Lenhardt Plant Science Library at Chicago Botanic Garden. Sincere yet insufficient thanks for patience, helpful comments, insightful discussion, and unflagging support are extended to Paulette Bierzychudek, Monica Burton, Hal J. Daniel, Karl Faser, Frank Gilliam, Carol Goodwillie, John Kartesz, Julie Marik, Jeff McKinnon, Eric Menges, Ron Newton, Steve Norton, Bob Peet, Mark Roberts, and to other researchers whose efforts make reviews possible, as well as those students, colleagues, friends, and family who thrive on benign neglect during the process. Nancy Tuchman, Kay Havens Young, and the Chicago Botanic Garden were gracious hosts to CLJ during the writing of this review.

APPENDIX 6.1

Endangered (E) or threatened (T) herbaceous vascular plants of the forested communities of eastern North America. Information is compiled from recovery plans, USFWS Five Year Reviews, USFWS Environmental Conservation Online System (ECOS) (http://ecos.fws.gov/ecos/indexPublic.do), COSEWIC Species-at-Risk (SARA), USDA Natural Resources Conservation Service Plants Database (www.plants.usda.gov), and the Center for Plant Conservation (www.centerforplantconservation.org). Changes in listing status since 2000 are noted in parentheses.

Appendix 6.1. Endangered [E] or threatened [T] herbaceous vascular plants of the forested communities of eastern North America.

Binomial	Common Name	Family	Status	Status Range	Habitat	Threats
Aconitum noveboracense A. Gray ex Coville	Northern wild monkshood	Ranunculaceae	T	IA, NY, OH, WI	Cold woods	Habitat loss/degradation, contamination and filling of sinkholes, grazing, trampling, logging, right-of-way (ROW) maintenance, pesticides, quarrying, road building, collection, flooding
Agalinis gattingeri (Small) Small	Gattinger's agalinis	Scrophulariaceae	E	Canada MA, ON	Dry open woodlands, glades	Habitat loss, human encroachment, increase in soil moisture
Agalinis skinneriana (Alph. Wood) Britton	Skinner's agalinis	Scrophulariaceae	E	Canada ON	Open woods, rocky open glades	Habitat loss, human disturbances, changes in water levels, invasives, fire suppression
Aletris farinosa L.	Colicroot	Liliaceae	T	Canada ON	Forest edges, rich sandy woods	Agriculture, development
Apios priceana B.L. Rob.	Price's potato-bean	Fabaceae	T	AL, IL, KY, MS, TN	Forest openings	Cattle grazing and trampling, clearcutting, ROW herbicides, lack of disturbance
Arabis perstellata E.L. Braun	Braun's shale barren rock-cress	Brassicaceae	E	KY, TN	Wooded steep slopes, limestone outcrops	Habitat loss/degradation, invasives (*Alliaria petiolata* (M. Bieb.) Cavara and Grande), trampling, logging, ROW maintenance
Arabis serotina Steele	Shale barren rock-cress	Brassicaceae	E	VA, WV	Mid-Appalachian shale barrens	Habitat loss/degradation, invasive plants (*Alliaria petiolata*, *Lonicera maackii* (Rupr.) Herder), grazing, trampling, logging
Asclepias quadrifolia Jacq.	Four-leaved milkweed	Asclepiadaceae	E (2010)	Canada (ON)	Dry to mesic, relatively open deciduous forest, often on rocky soils and steep slopes of limestone escarpments	Habitat loss/degradation, shading by invasive *Rhamnus cathartica* L, fire suppression, development

(Continued)

(Continued)

Binomial	Common Name	Family	Status	Status Range	Habitat	Threats
Asplenium scolopendrium L. var. americanum (Fernald) Kartesz & Gandhi	Hart's tongue fern	Aspleniaceae	T	AL, MI, NY, TN, Canada (ON)	Deep shade, limestone outcrops	Habitat degradation, trampling, development, logging, quarrying, infestations of defoliating insects, collecting (commercial trade)
Astragalus bibullatus Barneby & Bridges	Pyne's ground-plum	Fabaceae	E	TN	Cedar glades	Habitat destruction, development, shading by competitors and woody plants, grazing, ROW maintenance, off-road vehicles (ORVs), dumping, drought
Astragalus robbinsii (Oakes) A. Gray var. jesupii Eggl. & Sheldon	Jessup's milk-vetch	Fabaceae	E	NH, VT	Calcareous bed outcrops; ice scour with alders, willows, elms on banks above	invasives, climate change, low genetic diversity, flooding, collecting
Baptisia arachnifera Duncan	Hairy rattleweed	Fabaceae	E	GA	Pine woods, mixed woods	Clearcutting, reforestation
Bonamia grandiflora (A. Gray) Hallier f.	Florida bonamia	Convolvulaceae	T	FL	Sand pine scrub, evergreen oaks and sand pine (*Pinus clausa*)	Habitat destruction, development, trash dumping, invasive plants, ORVs, fire
Camassia scilloides (Raf.) Cory	Atlantic camas	Liliaceae	SC to T (2002)	Canada (ON)	Open hackberry or mixed species forests	Habitat loss, development, Double-crested Cormorant nesting
Cardamine micranthera Rollins	Streambank bittercress	Brassicaceae	E	NC, VA	Stream banks, moist woods near streams	Habitat loss, development, agriculture, impoundment, channelization, flooding, drought, invasives, scarcity of populations, small population sizes

Scientific name	Common name	Family	Status	Location	Habitat	Threats
Carex juniperorum Cating, Reznicek & Crins	Juniper sedge	Cyperaceae	E	Canada (ON)	Cedar glades (alvars)	Habitat fragmentation, alvar quarrying, grazing, development, ROW maintenance, ORVs, dumping, invasives
Carex lupuliformis Sartwell ex Dewey	False hop sedge	Cyperaceae	E	Canada (ON, QC)	Grassland/scrubland areas of maple-hickory forest, swamps, marshes forest edges/clearings; wet floodplain forests	Canopy closure, climate, development, agricultural drainage, water level control, competition
Carex lutea LaBlond	Golden sedge	Cyperaceae	E (2002)	NC	Long-leaf pine flats, pond pine, pocosin; tree-shaded ecotone, with scattered shrubs and a moderate to dense herb layer	Habitat loss, fire suppression, succession, timbering, development, hydrological impacts, herbicides
Chamaesyce deltoidea (Engelm. ex Chapm.) Small ssp. deltoidea	Deltoid spurge; Wedge sandmat	Euphorbiaceae	E	FL	Pine rocklands	Fire suppression, invasive plants, fragmented distribution
Chamaesyce garberi (Engelm. ex Chapm.) Small	Garber's spurge	Euphorbiaceae	E	FL	Transitions between hardwood hammocks and rock pinelands	Habitat loss, development, storms, fire suppression, exotic plant invasion, sea level rise
Chimaphila maculata (L.) Pursh	Spotted wintergreen	Pyrolaceae	T	Canada (ON)	Sandy habitats in dry-mesic oak-pine woods	Habitat loss, trail use, forest operations, ORVs
Chrysopsis floridana Small	Florida golden aster	Asteraceae	E	FL	Open areas of sand pine-evergreen oak scrub; beach dunes	Habitat loss, development, mowing, dumping, grazing, ORVs

(Continued)

(Continued)

Binomial	Common Name	Family	Status	Status Range	Habitat	Threats
Clitoria fragrans Small	Pigeon wings	Fabaceae	T	FL	Sandhill and scrub	Habitat loss (citrus groves, development), fire suppression, canopy closure
Crotalaria avonensis DeLaney & Wunderlin	Avon Park rattlebox	Fabaceae	E	FL	Open areas of sand pine-evergreen oak scrub, beach dunes	Habitat loss (development), ROW stabilization, dumping, ORVs, potential overutilization for scientific purposes
Dalea foliosa (A. Gray) Barneby	Leafy prairie-clover	Fabaceae	E	AL, IL, TN	Prairie cedar glades, limestone barrens; full sun	Habitat loss, drought
Drosera filiformis Raf.	Threaded-leaved sundew	Droseraceae	E	Canada (NS)	Swamps	Habitat loss through drainage of bogs; human activities
Echinacea laevigata (C.L. Boynt. & Beadle) S.F. Blake	Smooth coneflower	Asteraceae	E	GA, NC, SC, VA	Open woods, cedar barrens	Collecting, development, encroachment by woody vegetation, ROW maintenance, fire suppression
Enemion biternatum Raf.	Eastern false rue anemone	Ranunculaceae	from SC to T (2005)	Canada (ON)	Open wooded slopes, river floodplains, rich woods and thickets	Habitat loss, ORVs, compaction, trampling, exotic grasses and invasive plants, woodcutting, erosion, agriculture, use of herbicides and pesticides, road salting
Eriogonum longifolium Nutt. var. *gnaphalifolium* Gandog.	Scrub buckwheat	Polygonaceae	T	FL	Scrub and high pine (sandhills)	Development, inadequate or incorrectly-timed fire
Eryngium cuneifolium Small	Snakeroot	Apiaceae	E	FL	Sand pine-evergreen oak scrub, FL rosemary scrub	Development, ORVs, trampling, fire suppression

Scientific name	Common name	Family	Status	Location	Habitat	Threats
Erythronium propullans A. Gray	Minnesota dwarf trout lily	Liliaceae	E	MN	Rich deciduous/mixed woods	Development, logging, expanded agriculture, conversion of floodplains to cropland, disturbance of uplands
Euphorbia telephioides Chapm	Telephus spurge	Euphorbiaceae	T	FL	Savanna	Habitat loss, development, silvicultural practices, fire timing, ROW maintenance, fire suppression, exotic plant invasion
Eurybia divaricata (L.) G.L. Nesom	White wood aster	Asteraceae	T	Canada (ON, QC)	Deciduous forests	Habitat loss, insect grazing, invasive garlic-mustard (*Alliaria petiolata*)
Frasera caroliniensis Walter	American columbo	Gentianaceae	SC to E (2006)	Canada (ON)	Open deciduous forested slopes, thickets and clearings.	Habitat loss/degradation (agriculture, development); invasives, disturbance from trails, dumping, logging
Galactia smallii H.J. Rogers ex Herndon	Smalls' milkpea	Fabaceae	E	FL	Rock pineland	Habitat loss, fire suppression, invasion by exotic plants, overcollecting
Geocarpon minimum Mack.	Tinytim	Caryophyllaceae	T	AR, LA, MO	Sandstone glades	Succession, fire suppression, forestry practices, ORVs, grazing
Harrisia fragrans Small ex Britton & Rose	Fragrant prickly-apple	Cactaceae	E	FL	Sand pine (*Pinus clausa* (Chapm. ex Engelm.) Vasey ex Sarg.) scrub	Habitat loss/fragmentation, windthrow, development, ORVs, collection, occasionally hurricanes, vandalism, over-shading, herbicide damage, insect damage
Helianthus schweinitzii Torr. & A. Gray	Schweinitz's sunflower	Asteraceae	E	NC, SC	Clearings and edges of moist woods; roadside and power line ROWs	Habitat fragmentation, ROW maintenance, mowing, lack of disturbance (fire, native grazers), development, invasion by exotics, deer browsing

(Continued)

(Continued)

Binomial	Common Name	Family	Status	Status Range	Habitat	Threats
Helonias bullata L.	Swamp pink	Orchidaceae	T	DE, GA, MD, NC, NJ, NY, SC, VA	Swampy forested wetlands, often evergreens	Habitat loss to development, off-site water withdrawal, discharge, siltation, nutrient addition, succession, collecting, limited genetic variability, limited dispersal, survival, growth rate, and flowering
Hexastylis naniflora Blomquist	Dwarf-flowered heartleaf	Aristolochiaceae	T	NC, SC	Creek bluffs or slopes in oak-hickory forests	Timber harvesting, development, conversion of woodland to pasture, reservoir/pond construction
Hydrastis canadensis L.	Goldenseal	Ranunculaceae	T	Canada (ON)	Moist areas of deciduous woods and floodplain forests	Habitat loss (timber production, development, agriculture), harvesting, lack of disturbance (fire, flooding, wildlife)
Hypericum cumulicola (Small) P. Adams	Highlands scrub hypericum	Hypericaceae	E	FL	Open oak and rosemary scrub	Fire suppression, development, ranches, citrus groves
Iliamna corei Sherff	Peter's mountain mallow	Malvaceae	E	VA	Oak-mixed hardwoods	Fire suppression, collecting, vandalism, competition with weedy species, predation (insects feral goats)
Iris lacustris Nutt.	Dwarf lake iris	Iridaceae	T	MI, WI, Canada (ON)	Transition between boreal forest and lakeside	Development, road-construction, chemical spraying and salting, ORVs, collection, increasing human disturbance
Isotria medeoloides (Pursh) Raf.	Small-whorled pogonia	Orchidaceae	T (E, Canada)	CT, DE, GA, IL, MA, ME, MI, NC	Transition between boreal forest and lakeside	Habitat destruction, timbering, development, collection, trampling, habitat loss, ORVs

Scientific name	Common name	Family	Status	Location	Habitat	Threats
Isotria verticillata Raf.	Large-whorled pogonia	Orchidaceae	E	Canada (ON)	Open deciduous woods, damp mixed woods	Habitat loss, beaver activity (flooding), logging, trampling, collection
Jacquemontia reclinata House	Beach jacquemontia	Convolvulaceae	E	FL	Tropical maritime hammock	Urbanization, habitat loss, invasive plants, mowing, herbicides, park maintenance, recreation, limited and small populations
Justicia cooleyi Monachino & Leonard	Cooley's water-willow	Acanthaceae	E	FL	Hardwood forests, wet hammocks, swamps	Urbanization, habitat loss, conversion of forested habitats to pasture, silviculture, limestone mining, invasion by exotic plant species, ROW maintenance, alterations in hydrology
Lesquerella lyrata Rollins	Lyrate bladderpod	Brassicaceae	T	AL	Cedar glades	Small population sizes, herbicides, road improvement, quarrying, development
Liatris ohlingerae (S.F. Blake) B.L. Rob.	Scrub blazingstar	Asteraceae	E	FL	FL scrub, scrubby flatwoods	Development, conversion to citrus groves and agriculture, dumping
Liparis liliifolia (L.) Rich. ex Ker Gawl.	Purple twayblade	Orchidaceae	E	Canada (ON)	Open oak savanna, secondary successional deciduous/mixed forest	Habitat loss due to control of natural disturbances and conversion to agriculture; pesticides, collection
Lupinus aridorum McFarlin ex Beckner; *Lupinus westianus* Small var. *aridorum* (McFarlin ex Beckner) Isley	Scrub lupine	Fabaceae	E	FL	Sand pine scrub	Habitat loss, fire suppression, development, ROW construction/maintenance, conversion to pastureland, traffic, collection

(Continued)

(Continued)

Binomial	Common Name	Family	Status	Status Range	Habitat	Threats
Lysimachia asperulifolia Poir.	Rough-leaved loosestrife	Primulaceae	E	NC, SC	Long-leaf pine-pocosin ecotone	Fire suppression, drainage, development
Macbridea alba Chapm.	White birds-in-a-nest	Lamiaceae	T	FL	Savanna with long-leaf pine and/or runner oaks (mesic flatwoods)	Habitat loss, development, silvicultural practices, timing of fire
Marshallia mohrii Beadle & F.E. Boynt.	Mohr's Barbara button	Asteraceae	T	AL	Moist prairie-like openings in woodlands	Agricultural development, ROW maintenance/expansion, conversion to pasture/agriculture, drainage, seeding with forage grasses, woody succession
Mimulus michiganensis (Pennell) Posto & Prather; *Mimulus glabratus* Kunth var. *michiganensis* (Pennell) Fassett	Michigan monkey-flower	Scrophulariaceae	E	MI	Eastern white cedar (*Thuja occidentalis*) openings	Habitat loss/degradation, hydrologic disruption, invasives, climate change
Nolina brittoniana Nash	Britton's beargrass	Agavaceae	E	FL	FL scrub, high pine, hammocks	Habitat loss, fire suppression
Oxypolis canbyi (J.M. Coult. & Rose) Fernald	Canby's dropwort	Apiaceae	E	GA, MD, NC, SC	Wet pineland savannas	Habitat loss/alteration, lowering water tables, ditching, draining, road construction, swallow-tail herbivory?, unnecessary collecting
Panax quinquefolius L. (*P. quinquefolium* L.)	American ginseng	Araliaceae	E	Canada (ON, QC)	Rich, moist, mature deciduous woods	Habitat loss/degradation, small population size, logging, overharvesting

Paronychia chartacea Fernald	Papery whitlow-wort	Caryophyllaceae	T	FL	FL scrub, scrubby flatwoods	Development, ORVs, trampling, fire suppression
Pedicularis furbishiae S. Watson	Furbish's lousewort	Scrophulariaceae	E	ME, Canada (NB)	Where mixed forest and river meet; shaded	Habitat loss, lack of disturbance, small population sizes, dumping, litter, damming, gravel pit operations, forestry practices, recreation
Pilosocereus polygonus (Lam.) Byles & Rowley;Pilosocereus robinii (Lemaire) Byles & Rowley	Key tree cactus	Cactaceae	E	FL, Cuba	Tree-like cactus; tropical hammock	Habitat destruction from development, unique habitat specificity, small population sizes, herbivory, salt-water intrusion
Pinguicula ionantha Godfrey	Godfrey's butterwort	Droseraceae	T	FL	Depressions in pine flatwoods	Habitat degradation due to lack of prescribed burning, shading by planted pines; fire suppression, historic overcollecting
Plantago cordata Lam.	Heart-leaved plantain	Plantaginaceae	E	Canada (ON)	Streams running through heavily wooded areas, silver maple (Acer saccharinum L.) swamps	Habitat destruction/modification, water quality (eutrophication, siltation), needs shade from wooded buffer; conversion to agriculture, alteration of natural streams, cattle grazing/trampling
Polemonium vanbruntiae Britton	van Brunt's Jacob's ladder	Polemoniaceae	T	Canada (NB, QC)	Riparian meadows, swamps, partially-shaded with seasonal flooding	Habitat destruction, hydrologic alternation, road/residential construction (development), agriculture, plant succession, ORVs, alterations that produce permanent flooding, herbicides, mowing, grazing

(Continued)

(Continued)

Binomial	Common Name	Family	Status	Status Range	Habitat	Threats
Polygala lewtonii Small	Lewton's polygala	Polygonaceae	E	FL	scrub, high pine sandhills	Habitat loss, ROW maintenance, development, fire suppression, invasives
Polygala smallii R.R. Smith & Ward	Tiny milkwort	Polygonaceae	E	FL	Open areas in pine rocklands	Habitat loss, ROW maintenance, development, fire suppression, invasion by exotics
Polygonella basiramia (Small) G.L. Nesom & V.M. Bates	Florida jointweed	Polygonaceae	E	FL	FL scrub, scrubby flatwoods	Development, ORVs, trampling, fire suppression
Pycnanthemum incanum (L.) Michx.	Hoary mountain mint	Lamiaceae	E	Canada (ON)	Open, dry, sandy clay habitats in open deciduous woods	Habitat loss, invasion by shrubs, shoreline erosion and slumping
Sarracenia oreophila (Kearney) Wherry	Green pitcherplant	Sarraceniaceae	E	AL, GA, NC	Mixed oak or pine flatwoods	Collection for commercial sale, development, fire suppression
Sarracenia rubra Walter ssp. *alabamensis* (F.W. Case & R.B. Case) Schnell	Alabama pitcherplant	Sarraceniaceae	E	AL	Swamps	Agricultural development, fire suppression and growth of woody competitors, ROW herbicide use, water table alteration, invasives
Schwalbea americana L.	Chaffseed	Scrophulariaceae	E	FL, GA, LA, MS, NC, NJ, SC	Open moist pine flatwoods	Fire suppression, development, agricultural and forestry practices

Scientific name	Common name	Family	Status	States	Habitat	Threats
Scirpus ancistrochaetus Schuyler	Barbedbristle bulrush	Cyperaceae	E	MA, MD, NH, PA, VA, VT, WV	Forested wetlands	Lack of fluctuating water levels
Scutellaria floridana Chapm.	Florida skullcap	Scrophulariaceae	T	FL	Scrubby oak vegetation	Development, silvicultural practices, timing of burns (wildfires), woody plant encroachment, grazing, small pop size
Scutellaria montana Chapm.	Largeflower skullcap	Scrophulariaceae	E to T (2002)	GA, TN	Canopy of mature hardwoods	Development, silvicultural practices, timing of burns (wildfires), woody plant encroachment, grazing, small pop size
Silene polypetala (Walter) Fernald & B.G. Schub.	Eastern fringed catchfly	Caryophyllaceae	E	FL, GA	Deciduous hardwoods, ravines	Residential development, logging, invasives (Lonicera japonica Thunb., Lygodium japonicum (Thunb.) Sw.)
Sida hermaphrodita (L.) Rusby	Virginia fanpetals	Malvaceae	E (2010) Canada (ON)		Open, moist to partly shaded riparian habitats	Habitat destruction, invasive common reed, quarry expansion and pipeline maintenance
Sisyrinchium dichotomum E.P. Bicknell	White irisette	Iridaceae	E	NC, SC	Clearings and edges of upland woods	ROW/road maintenance, residential development, fire suppression, elimination of large native grazers, aggressive exotics (Pueraria lobata (Willd.) Ohwi, Lonicera japonicum, Microstegium vimineum (Trin.) A. Camus)

(Continued)

(Continued)

Binomial	Common Name	Family	Status	Status Range	Habitat	Threats
Solidago shortii Torr. & A. Gray	Short's goldenrod	Asteraceae	E	KY	Cedar glades, oak-hickory openings	Restricted distribution, limited numbers, development, inadvertent trampling, habitat alteration, overcollecting, destructive fires, fire suppression
Solidago speciosa Nutt.; *S. s.* var. *rigidiuscula* Torr. & A. Gray	Showy goldenrod	Asteraceae	E	Canada (ON)	Prairie-like areas under oak canopy	Habitat destruction through agricultural and residential development
Spigelia gentianoides Chapm. ex A. DC.	Gentian pinkroot	Loganiaceae	E	AL, FL	Mixed pine-hardwood	Habitat loss/degradation, timbering, disruption of fire regimes; development
Stylophorum diphyllum (Michx.) Nutt.	Wood-poppy	Papaveraceae	E	Canada (ON)	Rich woods in deciduous forest ravines, slopes, along streams, base of bluffs	Habitat destruction, development, invasive plants, trampling, forest clearing
Symphyotrichum anticostense (Fernald) G.L. Nesom	Anticosti aster	Asteraceae	T	Canada NS, QC	Banks of fast rivers through boreal forest	Habitat destruction, ORVs, development, regulation of water levels
Symphyotrichum praealtum (Poir.) G.L. Nesom	Willowleaf aster	Asteraceae	SC 1999 to T 2003	Canada (ON, NB)	Oak savannas, open woods or thickets, meadows, prairies	Habitat loss due to construction or agriculture
Symphyotrichum prenanthoides (Muhl. ex Willd.) G.L. Nesom	Crooked-stem aster	Asteraceae	SC to T (2002)	Canada (ON)	along the banks of streams and creeks, rich sandy soil, at edge of woods, in partial to full shade	Habitat loss due to stream and river modification, agriculture, chemical run-off, logging, road building

Scientific name	Common name	Family	Status	Distribution	Habitat	Threats
Symphyotrichum sericeum (Vent.) G.L. Nesom	Western silver aster	Asteraceae	T	Canada (MN, ON)	Open oak savanna	Habitat loss (development), recreation, quarrying, fire suppression, pasture enhancement, haying, invasion of grasslands by aliens and woody taxa; seed loss to weevil
Tephrosia virginiana (L.) Pers.	Virginia tephrosia	Fabaceae	E	Canada (ON)	Open oak and pine woods on ridges	Fire suppression and resultant natural canopy growth; ROW maintenance (sand removal, herbicides), weevils
Thalictrum cooleyi H.E. Ahles	Cooley's meadow-rue	Ranunculaceae	E	FL, NC	Savannas, woodland clearings	Fire suppression, agricultural development, small populations, ROW maintenance, logging, low genetic variability?
Thelypteris pilosa (M. Martens and Galeotti) Crawford var. *alabamensis* Crawford	Alabama maiden fern	Aspleniaceae	T	AL	Rock surfaces, crevices along streams, cove-type hemlock-hardwoods	Bridge construction, dam construction and resultant flooding; logging, canopy loss, vandalism, limited range, small population sizes
Trichophorum planifolium (Spreng.) Palla	Bashful bulrush	Cyperaceae	E	Canada (ON)	Open canopied, deciduous/mixed forests	Habitat loss, urbanization, erosion control, trampling, shading by woody taxa
Trifolium stoloniferum Muhl. ex Eaton	Running buffalo clover	Fabaceae	E	AR, IN, KY, MO, OH, WV	Open forest-prairie ecotones	Disappearance of large herbivores in woodlands
Trillium flexipes Raf.	Nodding wakerobin	Liliaceae	E	Canada (ON)	Deciduous woodlands	Habitat destruction, collecting, disease, deer grazing
Trillium persistens Duncan	Persistent wakerobin	Liliaceae	E	GA, SC	Deciduous or mixed woods of ravines or gorges	Limited range and distribution; overcollecting, logging

(Continued)

(Continued)

Binomial	Common Name	Family	Status	Status Range	Habitat	Threats
Trillium reliquum J.D. Freeman	Confederate wakerobin	Liliaceae	E	AL, GA, SC	Undisturbed hardwoods	Logging, road construction, agricultural conservation, development, urbanization, stone quarrying, invasives (*Lonicera japonicum, Pueraria lobata*)
Triphora trianthophora (Sw.) Rydb.	Threebirds	Orchidaceae	E	Canada (ON)	Rich, humid, deciduous woodlands	Trampling, soil compaction, collection, storm damage to humus layer; grazing, logging
Viola pedata L.	Birdfoot violet	Violaceae	T to E (2002)	Canada (ON)	Savannas with deciduous forests	Habitat loss (agriculture), competition from woody taxa, fire suppression, mowing, herbicides
Warea amplexifolia (Nutt.) Nutt.	Wide-leaf warea	Brassicaceae	E	FL	Dry long-leaf pine (*Pinus palustris* Mill.) and scrub	Habitat loss, development (citrus, residential), collecting, disturbance, limited genetic variability
Warea carteri Small	Carter's mustard	Brassicaceae	E	FL	High pine (sandhills), scrubby flatwoods	Development, ORVs, trampling, fire suppression
Woodsia obtusa (Spreng.) Torr.	Blunt-lobed woodsia	Aspleniaceae/ Dryopteridaceae	T to E (2000)	Canada (ON, QC)	Sugar maple (*Acer saccharum* Marshall) forests, extensive rock outcropping	Habitat loss/alteration, invasive *Rhamnus cathartica* L., recreation
Xyris tennesseensis Kral	Tennessee yelloweyed grass	Xyridaceae	E	TN, AL, GA	Thinly-wooded habitat, seep-slopes, springy meadows or gravelly shallows of small streams	Habitat loss, agricultural development, logging, quarrying, road construction, woody plant encroachment (natural succession), diversion of seeps or ground water

APPENDIX 6.2

Summary of biological characteristics of 100 threatened or endangered herbs of forest habitats of eastern North America from recovery plans, species accounts, and the published literature. A = annual, B = biennial, P = perennial. Phenology is presented as months of flower; months of fruiting. Terminology on mating system reflects that of the original reference (autogamy = transfer of pollen within the same flower; geitonogamy = transfer between flowers of the same genet; xenogamy = transfer of pollen between different genets—outcrossing). SC = self-compatible, SI = self-incompatible, CH = chasmogamous, CL = cleistogamous. *USFWS Recovery Plan, USFWS Five Year Review, or COSEWIC Assessment and Update Status Report not reviewed or not available.

Appendix 6.2. Summary of biological characteristics of 94 threatened or endangered herbs of forest habitats of eastern North America from recovery plans, species accounts and the published literature

Binomial	Habit	Phenology Flowering; Fruiting	Longevity	Vegetative Modes	Mating System	Pollination	Dispersal	Seed	Germination	Seed Dormancy
Aconitum noveboracense	P	Jun-Sep; late summer-fall		Tubers	Protandry	Bumblebees		8 per follicle; disperse late summer-fall	50% when collected in Oct	Seed bank
*Agalinis gattingeri	A; hemi parasitic	Aug-Sep; Sep-Oct		None		Insects, bees	Wind	Produces a seed bank		
*Agalinis skinneriana	A; hemi-parasitic	Mid-Aug-Sep; Sep-Oct		None?	SC	Lasioglossum sp., Hylaeus affinis, Megachile brevis, M. mendica, Bombus pennsylvanicus, B. impatiens				
*Aletris farinosa	P	Jun-Jul		Rhizome buds		Bumblebees, beeflies	Wind	Many small		
Apios priceana	P	Mid-Jul-mid-Aug; Aug-Sep		Large single tuber	Some populations selfing	Long-tailed skipper, honey bees, bumblebees				
Arabis perstellata	P	Mar-May; May-Jun	Veg. for 2 yr; 5 yr		Unknown	Probably insects; unknown	Wind; gravity		Seedlings can be abundant	Seed bank?

Arabis serotina	Facultative biennial	Jul-frost	< 5 yr	Rhizomes?	SC;	*Pyrgus wyandot*, Syrphidae		12-730 (14,000)	90% in controlled conditions	Broken by low temperatures; seed bank
Asclepias quadrifolia	P	May-Jun; Aug	> 5-10 yr	none	SI; young or small plants function as males	Hymenoptera, Lepidoptera; pollen-limited; pollen dispersal > 1 km	Wind; beyond 50-150 m is rare	1-3 follicles/pl, 35 sds/follicle	71% after 5 yr dry storage	Seed bank 1-5 yr (<2 yr)
Asplenium scolopendrium var. *americanum*	P	One-yr-old fronds; May-Aug (MI)		None	Fern				Spores on cool, calcareous beds among bryophytes	
Astragalus bibullatus	P	Apr-May; May-Jun					Gravity, water			Long-lived seed bank
Astragalus robbinsii var. *jesupii*	P	May-Jun; Jun-Jul				*Bombus* sp.			Low (33%) in controlled conditions; mortality high; rates peak after 1 yr cold storage	

(Continued)

(Continued)

Binomial	Habit	Phenology Flowering; Fruiting	Longevity	Vegetative Modes	Mating System	Pollination	Dispersal	Seed	Germination	Seed Dormancy
*Baptisia arachnifera	P	Jun-Jul; Aug-Sep							Reduced tolerance to high temp., contrary to congeners	
Bonamia grandiflora	P vine	Fire-dependent		Taproot; connections below-ground	Mixed; Occasionally apomictic				30-35% with scarification and soaking; viability decreases with age	Seed bank
Camassia scilloides	P	Late-mid-spring	2-4 yr?	Bulbs?	Corolla color polymorphism	Butterflies, various bees, bee flies, Syrphidae	Local based on clumping of plants			
Cardamine micranthera	A	Apr-May	< 1 yr	None		Ants?				
*Carex juniperorum	P	Apr-Jun	> 10 yr	Densely caespitose	Mostly selfing	Wind	Ants			
*Carex lupuliformis	P?	Jun-Oct; Jul-Sep	Indefinite?	Rhizomes		Wind	Gravity, water, animals (esp. ducks), flooding			Seed bank

Carex lutea	P	Mid-Apr-early May; May-Jun	> 4 yr	Short rhizomes	Monoecious	Probably wind	Precipitation sheet flow, animals	Trigonous nutlet	Low in controlled conditions and *in situ*
Chamaesyce deltoidea ssp. *deltoidea*	P	May-Nov	Long-lived from root system		Mono ecious; highly variable	Hymenoptera, Diptera	Explosively dehiscent, ants	Production strongly affected by rainfall amount	
Chamaesyce garberi	P	Largely wet summer months	Short-lived			Hymenoptera, Diptera	Explosively dehiscent, ants		Winter-early spring; 25-70%
*Chimaphila maculata	P	Jul-Aug; Sep-Oct		Shoots off larger stems		Insects	Wind		
Chrysopsis floridana	P	Late Nov.-Dec; Dec onward	Short-lived	Rosettes at end of rhizomes?				Storage > 2 yrs. increases fungal outbreak	Best in bare sand and cold chamber
Clitoria fragrans	P	CH: May-Jun; CL: late Sep	Long-lived	Fire-stimulated or clonal	CH, CL; inverted anthers and stigmas	CH: insects			Fire stimulated; few seedlings found

(Continued)

(Continued)

Binomial	Habit	Phenology Flowering; Fruiting	Longevity	Vegetative Modes	Mating System	Pollination	Dispersal	Seed	Germination	Seed Dormancy
Crotalaria avonensis	P	Mid-Mar-June		Substantial taproot; resprouts post-fire		Insects, mostly bees; required but infrequent		18 seeds per legume, very few mature	Seedlings rarely found; scarification not necessary	Persistent, but germ < 1% after 1 yr
Dalea foliosa	P	Jul-Aug; Oct	Short-lived	none	Strongly exserted anthers	Bees, syrphid flies		1 seed per fruit	March-April	Persistent seed bank
*Drosera filiformis	P	Mid-Jul				Insects		8 capsules/pl; 70 sd/cap		
Echinacea laevigata	P	May-Jul; late Jul-Sep		Rhizomes	SI; predominantly outcrossing	Generalist insects (butterflies, moths, beetles, bees); large bees most effective	Birds, small mammals, wind dispersed < 3 m	Poor reproductive success		
Enemion biternatum	P	Mar-Jun; May-Jun	> 3 yr	Tuberous rootstock	SC, not autogamous; protogynous	Bees, Syrphidae, other flies, beetles	Passive dispersal		Fall; requires high temp.	
Eriogonum longifolium var. gnaphalifolium	P	May-mid-Oct	Unknown; high post-fire survival	Woody taproot		Hymenoptera	Seedlings observed close to parent		In summer in open sand	

Species		Flowering	Vegetative/Longevity	Breeding system	Pollinators	Dispersal	Fecundity	Germination	Seed bank
Eryngium cuneifolium	P	Aug–Oct;	Short-lived; Very weak resprouter after fire	Mixed; SC	Generalist insects (bees, syrphid flies)	Limited; mostly gravity	Fecundity can be high (20–30/fruit); small and therefore susceptible to soil microclimate	0–20%; related to rainfall (winter and spring); inhibited by leaf litter and allelopathic compounds	Persistent seed bank > 6 yr; post-fire recruitment
*Erythronium propullans	P		Bulb offshoots				Rare		
Euphorbia telephioides	P	Apr–Jul	Stout storage root	Functionally dioecious; cyathium					
Eurybia divaricata	P	Fall; fall-winter	Rhizomes						
*Frasera caroliniensis	P	May–Jul; Oct–Nov	Long-lived, 7–15+ (30) yr; monocarpic		Honeybees, bumblebees	Gravity		Dormant until water absorption at 5°C	Fall dispersal with spring germination
Galactia smallii	P	All year (most abundant during dry season)		Most flowers do not produce fruit; SI	Bees, wasps, *Leptotes* sp., *Cassius* sp.		Small storage difficult; several months to mature	Often in response to fire	

(Continued)

(Continued)

Binomial	Habit	Phenology Flowering; Fruiting	Longevity	Vegetative Modes	Mating System	Pollination	Dispersal	Seed	Germination	Seed Dormancy
Geocarpon minimum	A	Late Feb-early Jun	(3-4) 4-6 wk				Surface water flow	November		
Harrisia fragrans	P	Apr-Sep (2 peaks); May and Sep		Fragmentation		Night blooming	Birds, rodents, tortoises	~1400/fruit; germination in situ 12-24 mo	Seedlings in open desiccate in a few yrs; room temp. better than cold storage (0-78 vs. 16-50 %, resp.)	Viability to 19 mo; 64-100% germination
Helianthus schweinitzii	P	Aug-frost	Long-lived; decades	Rhizomes; tubers			Limited or unknown		Readily in greenhouse	
Helonias bullata	P	Apr-May; late Jun-Jul		Clonal root growth	6-12% of plants flower		Limited; passive, animals		Seedlings rare; > 95% mortality in culture; can exceed 90%	
Hexastylis naniflora	P	Apr-Jun				Flies, thrips	Ants		Spring	Broken by cold stratification

Species		Phenology		Breeding system	Pollinator	Dispersal	Germination/Seedling	Seed bank/Other
Hydrastis canadensis	P	Apr-May; Jul-Aug	Rhizomes		Polylectic bees, syrphid flies; not pollen limited	Non-limiting vertebrates	3.4% in 2 yr; slow seedling development, one true leaf 1-2 yr	10 mo
Hypericum cumulicola	P	Apr (June)-Sep (Oct) 1-several yr	No post-fire resprouting	SI: 10% autogamy, reduced fruit set; herkogamy	Small native solitary bees	Passive, gravity, limited; 4000 fruit/pl	<6% in field, 10-90% in culture; (Nov) Dec-Feb (Jun)	Seed bank
Iliamna corei	P	Late June-early Aug.; Jul-Sep	Rhizomes	SI, protandrous	*Halictus*		Scarification; heat stimulated	Overwinters; no cold stratification requirement in congeners; long-lived seed bank
Iris lacustris	P	May-Jun (Oct); mid-Jul-Aug	Rhizomes, most repro.	SC	Halictid bees?	Ants; water dispersal of rhizomes	Small; 80-90% seed set from selfing, 70-71% from outcrossing	Low (5/192 plots had seedlings), late May-Jul	Overwinters; no cold requirement in genus

(Continued)

(Continued)

Binomial	Habit	Phenology Flowering; Fruiting	Longevity	Vegetative Modes	Mating System	Pollination	Dispersal	Seed	Germination	Seed Dormancy
Isotria medeoloides	P	Apr-Jun	Dormancy 4-(10-20) yr	Infrequent rootstock	SC; Autogamous	Mechanical; solitary bees (Andrenidae, Anthophoridae, Halictidae)	Wind	Low to moderate production; "dust-like," thousands per < 2 capsules/ plant	Likelihood low	Overwinters; short-lived seed
*Isotria verticillata	P	End (Feb) May-Jun; Sep-Oct	Clones > 40 yr	Extensive clones	SC; geitonogamous, xenogamous	Solitary bees	Wind	Poor, < 1% of population	Require a specific fungus	Overwinters; short-lived seed
Jacquemontia reclinata	P vine	Nov-May; Aug-Dec		Rhizomatous	Mixed;greater fruit set with outcross pollen	Small bees, flies, Lepidoptera	Gene flow between populations	Prolific but few seedlings in nature	Related to winter rainfall; low in field; up to 90% in culture	> 2 yr seed longevity, little or no seed bank
Justicia cooleyi	P	Aug-Sep (Mar);		Rhizomes			Insects		Low in field, "readily" in greenhouse	

Species		Flowering	Longevity	Fire/disturbance response	Breeding system	Pollination	Dispersal	Ex situ	Germination/notes
Lesquerella lyrata	A	Apr-May; Apr-Jun	< 1 yr	In response to disturbance					High temps required to break dormancy; low temperatures can cause dormancy; light 30/15 °C; long-lived seed bank
Liatris ohlingerae	P	May-Oct	Probably decades	Moderate post-fire resprouter from corm	All perfect disks; SI	Butterflies (skippers); pollen limited	Wind, secondary along sand	Easily grown from seeds	Low rates of recruitment from post-dispersal seed predation and micro-site; >60% germination in field and lab
*Liparis liliifolia	P	May-Jul	> 10 yr	Pseudobulb		Insects	Wind, water		

(Continued)

(Continued)

Binomial	Habit	Phenology Flowering; Fruiting	Longevity	Vegetative Modes	Mating System	Pollination	Dispersal	Seed	Germination	Seed Dormancy
Lupinus aridorum; Lupinus westianus var. aridorum	P	Mid-Mar-May; Jun	1-several yr; declines after 1st flowering	Susceptible to root rot					Fire-induced	Little to 50 yr seed bank
Lysimachia asperulifolia	P	Mid-May-Jun; July-Oct		Highly clonal	Xenogamous	Solitary bees; pollen limited				
Macbridea alba	P	May-Jul;		Fleshy rhizomes	Self- and outcrossing			Seedlings rare in nature		None; no seed bank; viability of stored seeds low
Marshallia mohrii	P	Mid-May-Jun; Jul-Aug			Protandrous; obligately outcrossing					
Mimulus michiganensis; Mimulus glabratus var. michiganensis	P; semi-aquatic	Mid-Jun-Aug (Oct);		Stolons	SC; autogamous, xenogamous	Pollen viability <1%; inbreeding depression; fruit set resource-limited		Very viable, resource limited	In light, 23 °C	

Species										
Nolina brittoniana	P	Mar–May; summer	Leaves live several yr; flowering annually	Clonal spread, bulb-like rootstock	Polygamodioecious; outcrossing very low genetic variation	Widely dispersing generalist pollinators	Wind, gravity; limited	Abundant	Easily	
Oxypolis canbyi	P	(May–early Aug) mid-Aug–Oct;		Stoloniferous rhizomes	Bisexual and/or unisexual; protandrous; self- and outcrossing	Black swallowtail butterflies	Strong winged schizocarp			
Panax quinquefolius; P. quinquefolium	P	June–Aug; Aug–Sep	Long-lived	Rhizome fragmentation; largely seed	Autogamous, xenogamous	Syrphidae, Halictidae	Close to parent, farther by birds	0.55% chance of reaching maturity; high seed predation and seedling mortality; extensive propagation protocols	Extensive propagation protocols	18–24 mo
Paronychia chartacea (P. c. ssp. chartacea and P. c. ssp. minima)	P (ssp. chartacea); A (ssp. minima)	Jun–Oct; Jul–Sep	Short-lived, 1–several yr	None	Gynodioecious or subdioecious; reduced fruit set in hermaphrodites				Post-fire, low to < 40%; removal of biotic crusts	Probably persistent seed bank

(Continued)

(Continued)

Binomial	Habit	Phenology Flowering; Fruiting	Longevity	Vegetative Modes	Mating System	Pollination	Dispersal	Seed	Germination	Seed Dormancy
Pedicularis furbishiae	P	Mid-Jul-mid Aug; Sep		None; root hemiparasite	SC; little genetic variation	Obligate insect; bumblebees (Bombus vagans); not pollinator limited	Wind, water; beneath or close to parent	Seeds per capsule variable; pre-dispersal herbivory	Stratification; seedlings late Jun-Aug obligately hemiparasitic; 23-39% with GA$_3$	1 yr viability; little evidence of seed bank
Pilosocereus polygonus; Pilosocereus robinii	P	Yr-rd., Jul-Oct; Aug		Mostly veg.; wind-thrown branches	SC; fruit set in absence of large pollinators	Flowering ~ 25 yr; night flowering; sets fruit in absence of large pollinators (sphingid moths, bats)	Ants, birds (Cardinalis cardinalis)	Encased in white pulp; viability ~58% in lab (10-90% in field); fruit set ~22%	Fresh seed readily germinate (87-95%)	
Pinguicula ionantha	P	Mid-Feb-Apr;		Carnivorous						Lack of a seed bank?
*Plantago cordata	P	Mid-Apr;			Strongly protogynous yet can self; little within- and high among-population genetic variation in US populations	Wind	Wind, water	86 cap/pl	Seedlings appear a few wks after dispersal; maximal at 16/8 L/D 30/16°C	None

Polemonium vanbruntiae	P	Jun-Jul; Aug-Sep		Horizontal rhizome; importance varies among sites	Mixed; strongly protandrous and herkogamous; outcrossing	Honeybees, bumblebees; not pollen limited	Winter winds; spring flooding; not ants	3-20 sds/fruit; 165 sds/pl		Congeners require winter dormancy
Polygala lewtonii	P	Feb.-May;	5-10 yr	None	SC, autogamous; CH and two types of small cleistogamous flowers (CL)	Lepidoptera, Diptera, Hymenoptera	Ants	Aril-like growths on capsule	Positive response to fire smoke; two germination periods (June and September-January)	Innate and conditional dormancy; seeds may persist for 10 yrs or more when slightly buried
Polygala smallii	B	Yr-rd. (peaks in summer); yr-rd	short-lived; < 1 yr	Taproot	SC, autogamous	Not observed	Ants, water	Pair of aril-like growths	Fire required, faster in response to smoke	> 2 yr persistent seed bank

(Continued)

(Continued)

Binomial	Habit	Phenology Flowering; Fruiting	Longevity	Vegetative Modes	Mating System	Pollination	Dispersal	Seed	Germination	Seed Dormancy
Polygonella basiramia	P	Sep–Oct; late Nov–Dec	Short-lived, 3 yr from seed to seed set	No post-fire resprouting	Gynodioecious, 1:1 F:H	Small halictid bees, Perdita polygonellae (a bee specific to Polygonella), Eumenidae wasps, Glabellula spp. (Bombyliidae)	Limited	Production by female plants > perfect plants	Seed/plant 30 times the average plant density; could replace population with 3% ecesis; 6–42% germination in field	Innate and conditional
Pycnanthemum incanum	P	Late Jun–Aug; Sep–Oct		Rhizomes; largely by seed in Ontario		Butterflies				
Sarracenia oreophila	P	Mid-Apr–early Jun; late Sep	Rhizomes live for decades	Rhizomes; root stocks; princi-pal mode		Ants, beetles, bees (Bombus), Sarracenia flies		Valvate capsule responds negatively to humidity	Germinable in greenhouse	
Sarracenia rubra ssp. alabamensis	P	Apr–May; Jun–Jul		Rhizomes				High seed set, germinability (~73%)	Seedling recruitment very low; not increased by fire or thinning	

Species		Flowering	Vegetative reproduction	Breeding system	Pollinator	Dispersal	Seed production	Germination	Seed bank / dormancy
Schwalbea americana	P	Apr-Jun (South), Jun-mid-Jul (North) fire induced flowering; mid-summer-Oct	Hemiparasite	Autogamous	Bees, esp. *Bombus*	Wind, ants unlikely	Numerous, enclosed in sac-like structure	90% in wet-cold vs. < 2.5% dry-cold stratification	Not capable of long-term dormancy within soil; plants in soil can remain in a dormant state for > 1 yr
Scirpus ancistrochaetus	P	Mid-Jun-Jul; Jul-Sep	Bulblets or nodal shoots from nodes and culms of recumbent stems; bulblets in inforescence	Autogamous?	Wind	Animals, water, wind	Spring and fall germination recruitment by seed is rare	March; 80% when dry storage followed by stratification at 3 or 8°C for 8-12 wk	Seed bank
Scutellaria floridana	P	May-June;	Swollen storage roots or rhizomes		Bumblebees, megachilid and halictid bees				
Scutellaria montana	P	Mid May-early Jun; mid Jun-mid Jul	Perennation as rootstocks	SC	Apoideae bees	< 1.5 km	10-40% fruit set, pollen limited		Overwinters
Silene polypetala	P	Late Mar-May; Apr-June	Stolon-like rhizomes; leafy offshoots		Hummingbirds				

(Continued)

(Continued)

Binomial	Habit	Phenology Flowering; Fruiting	Longevity	Vegetative Modes	Mating System	Pollination	Dispersal	Seed	Germination	Seed Dormancy
Sida hermaphrodita	P	Aug-frost;		Rhizomes			Water	Several thousand viable sds/pl	Early spring; high if scarified	Increased germination after 6-8 mo storage
Sisyrinchium dichotomum	P	Late May-Jul		From nodes and culms of recumbent stems				Low; 4-6 flowers/stem; 3-6 sds/cap		
Solidago shortii	P	Mid-Aug-early Nov; late Sep-Nov	Individuals required 3-9 yr to flower	Rhizomes	SI; xenogamous	Halicitidae, goldenrod soldier beetle, blister beetles (Meloidae)	Mud in the hair of passing bison, wind, gravity	~250-1700 sds/stem	Similar to more widespread congeners, up to 66% in field;	Conditional dormancy broken by cold stratification; smaller seed bank than congeners
Solidago speciosa; S. s. var. rigidiuscula	P	Aug-Oct		Short rhizomes from parental caudex		Hymenoptera, Diptera Lepidoptera	Wind	> 50% of stems bear flowers		
Spigelia gentianoides	P	Mid-Apr-Jun;	Can be propagated vegetatively		Secondary pollen presentation; self- and outcross; stamens stay inserted		Explosively dehiscent	Single-stemmed, few-flowered	Low, enhanced by GA$_3$ or cold stratification	

Stylophorum diphyllum	P	Apr-early Jun	Rhizomes		Green swallowtail (Battus philenor), bees, ants, moths, Halictidae bees	Ants			In subsequent spring
*Symphyotrichum anticostense	P	Aug-Sep	Creeping rhizome				Can mature to flowering on 1 yr		In spring
*Symphyotrichum praealtum	P	Early spring; early summer	Stoloniferous rhizomes	SI, xenogamous? facultative out-breeder with low selfing possible?	Coleoptera, Hemiptera	Ants	27.7 ± 1.46 sds/fruit (range 7–70)	Low immediately after harvest; 33.3 to 83.3% across sites (56.9 ± 3.9%)	Double dormancy, two cold periods and one warm period required
Symphyotrichum prenanthoides		Aug-Sep; late Jul- mid-Sep	Elongated rhizomes and stolons	Semi-obligate outbreeder, self-ing possible	Bees, Lepidoptera; Halictus quadri-maculatus; each flower remains open and viable 1 d or 3-4 if not pollinated	Wind		Improved by moist cold stratification	
*Symphyotrichum sericeum	P	Early Aug-mid-Sep; 3-4 wk after pollination	Rhizomes		Bees, insects		Main repro. mode; low set esp. in dry yrs		

(Continued)

(Continued)

Binomial	Habit	Phenology Flowering; Fruiting	Longevity	Vegetative Modes	Mating System	Pollination	Dispersal	Seed	Germination	Seed Dormancy
*Tephrosia virginiana	P	May-Aug;		Rhizomes					100% germination	
Thalictrum cooleyi	P	Late May-Jun; Aug-Oct	Several yr in culture	Rhizome	Dioecious; 3:1 M:F	No male plants at one site in 8 yr	Wind and/or insects?	Low	20% if stratified	Short-lived seed
Thelypteris pilosa var. alabamensis	P; evergreen	Spores year-round?	5 yr in culture	Rhizomes						
Trichophorum planifolium	P	Spring; late Jul-Aug	Indefinite?	Short rhizomes		Wind				
Trifolium stoloniferum	P	Mid-Apr-Jun;		Long stolons; rhizobia				"Good" on favorable sites	100% if scarified	
Trillium flexipes	P	May-Jun	Flower @ 10 yr	yes	SC (low) and autogamous (predominant)	Flying insects	Ants, white-tailed deer			
Trillium persistens	P	Mid-Mar-mid-Apr; Jul	> 6 yr			Bees, wasps, flies, ants, butterflies, beetles	Ants	eliasome	First spring, produce root and no stem	
Trillium reliquum	P	Early spring; early summer		Tuberous rhizome	Self- and outcrossing possible apomixis	Coleoptera, Hemiptera; not pollen limited	Ants	27.7 ± 1.46 sds/fruit (range 7-70)	33.3 to 83.3% across sites (56.9 ± 3.9%)	Double dormancy; two cold periods and one warm period required

Species										
Triphora trianthophora	P	Aug-Sep; late Jul- mid-Sep	Colony > 100 yr	Tuberous rooted		Insects, *Halictus quadrimaculatus*; each flower remains open and viable 1 d or 3-4 if not pollinated	Wind	Dry conditions limit flowering; 1-7 flowers, open 1-2 at a time; thousands of sds/cap	Contact with a specific fungus	
Viola pedata	P	Mid-May-mid-June and again end Sep-mid-Oct		Rhizome	SI?	Butterflies, bumblebees	Projected 25-510 cm, ants			
Warea amplexifolia	A	Mid-Aug-early Oct; late Sep-mid-Nov	< 1 yr	None	Exclusively sexual	Bumblebees, butterflies	Near parent, released by wind	12-43% in field		Possible seed bank (< 2-4 yr)
Warea carteri	A	Sep-Oct; Oct-Nov	Annual, < 1 yr	None	Protandrous; SC, autogamous, not agamospermous	Diversity of insects; can limit seed set	Passive release; potential travel is 1.89 m in wind	Numerous siliques	Fall/winter /spring season following > 2 yr production; not fire-stimulated; light	Persistent seed bank;

(Continued)

Binomial	Habit	Phenology Flowering; Fruiting	Longevity	Vegetative Modes	Mating System	Pollination	Dispersal	Seed	Germination	Seed Dormancy
Woodsia obtusa	P	Spores mature by late Jul	Several decades?	Rhizomes	Bisexual gametophyte	Water	Water, wind; may be limiting	High spore production; all gametophytes produced a sporophyte in culture	8.4% germination of spores in culture	Spores can be found in large quantities in the soil with high survival *in situ*
Xyris tennesseensis	P	Jul-Sep;		Bulbous bases; lateral buds in crown leaf axils	Apomixis?	Flowers wither in an afternoon		Thin-walled capsules with numerous small seeds	High, light;open wet areas needed; high spring and low fall cycle of germination	Initial conditional dormancy; tolerate 39.5-month burial in unheated greenhouse

PART THREE
COMMUNITY DYNAMICS OF THE HERBACEOUS LAYER ACROSS SPATIAL AND TEMPORAL SCALES

7 The Herbaceous Layer of Eastern Old-Growth Deciduous Forests

Brian C. McCarthy

The study of old-growth forests has long been a fascination of plant ecologists. In all likelihood, this was an outgrowth of the Clementsian view of succession (Clements 1936; Weaver and Clements 1938) in which communities were perceived to change in an orderly and predictable way and culminate in a terminal climax community (chapter 10, this volume). Throughout much of eastern North America, old-growth forests were the epitome of the climax community (Braun 1950; Whitney 1987). Old-growth forests have been of continued interest in the study of plant ecology in large part because they are generally free of the myriad of disturbances caused by humans, thereby allowing the study of natural processes. This unique quality has generated an enormous research database on many aspects of eastern old-growth forests (Nowacki and Trianosky 1993). Due to the massive disturbances associated with European settlement, the landscape in eastern North America underwent enormous change (M. Williams 1989; Whitney 1994; Irland 1999). Lumbering, agriculture, grazing, and anthropogenic wildfires all altered the landscape such that now, most deciduous old-growth forest exists only as small relicts. More recently, some have argued that no forest in eastern North America is free of anthropogenic disturbance (direct or indirect). There is certainly a need to better understand the ecology of human-dominated ecosystems (Vitousek et al. 1997; Grimm et al. 2000); however, natural systems will always be needed to serve as the controls or benchmarks in such studies.

The Clementsian concept of succession and the notion of a terminal old-growth climax have now been largely disputed; few ecologists currently accept this as a viable concept (McIntosh 1985), although the notion continued to be propagated in the biological literature throughout the early 1980s and remains in some introductory ecology textbooks. Likewise, few, if any, communities exhibit an orderly and predictable pattern of development, and communities rarely if ever achieve a stable equilibrium due to natural disturbances (White 1979). Concomitant with changing ideas about community succession, ecosystem ecology began to flourish and generated a renewed interest in old-growth forest ecosystems (Franklin et al. 1972). These ecosystems provided considerable information about ecosystem development. Moreover, they provided permanent benchmarks in the landscape that could be used to evaluate management and conservation activities.

Faced with the recognition of an emerging biodiversity crisis in the 1980s, there was a large, albeit uncoordinated, effort instituted throughout the eastern United States to develop criteria for the identification of old-growth forests, to find these relicts in the landscape, and to establish some form of preservation for their continued survival and study (e.g., T. L. Smith 1989). Forest managers were becoming increasingly aware of the need to manage forests for multiple reasons, including biological diversity. This period led to a focus on the characteristics of old-growth forests and what made them different from second-growth forests. Oddly, it was not until the early 1990s with the controversial work of Duffy and Meier (1992) that we began to gain a heightened concern regarding the effects of forest management activities on the forest herb layer. In spite of its shortcomings (chapter 14, this volume), this landmark contribution spurred an interest in community-level understanding of the herb layer, which had before then been largely population-based. The relative lack of attention to the herb layer relative to the overstory is curious given that it is the layer of greatest diversity in most hardwood forests throughout eastern North America (Braun 1950).

My focus in this chapter is fourfold: (1) to clarify the factors that constitute old-growth forests in most mesic eastern deciduous forests; (2) to describe what we know about composition, structure, and diversity of the herb layer in old-growth forests; (3) to evaluate the differences between old-growth and second-growth forests with respect to the herb layer; and (4) to assess the linkages among stability, diversity, and habitat invasibility. Although the herb layer contains both woody and herbaceous species (chapter 1, this volume), I restrict my focus to the herbaceous component only.

THE NATURE OF EASTERN MESIC OLD-GROWTH FORESTS

Before European settlement, forest vegetation of eastern North America could hardly be considered free from anthropogenic disturbance (Denevan 1992). Native Americans have been clearing hardwood forests since at least the last ice age (at least 10,000 years; Dickens 1976). However, Native American settlement appears to have been largely restricted to floodplain areas, and the long-term effects are questionable (M. Williams 1989). Evidence of the influence of Native Americans on the upland vegetation of the eastern deciduous forest, particularly with respect to fire, is conflicting (Day 1953; Russell 1983; Patterson and Sassaman 1988). Observations suggest that Native Americans did clear some portion of the uplands for various purposes using a slash (girdle) and burn technique that the early European settlers subsequently adopted. Regardless, the influence of Native Americans in the uplands pales in comparison to the subsequent land clearing and land conversion associated with European settlement. Early descriptions of pre-settlement eastern hardwood forest from the late 1700s and early 1800s suggest a composition and structure very different from today's forests (Walker 1983). Many forests were cleared by Europeans for grazing pasture or crop agriculture. Catastrophic fires frequently followed logging activities. Today, large parts of the land base are being converted for development. As a result, there is a paucity of primary hardwood forest left in eastern North America. Those stands that continue to exist today were preserved by a family lineage, were not easily accessible to loggers, or were the result of surveying errors (Auten 1941; McCarthy 1995). Recent concerns regarding the biodiversity crisis have pointed to old-growth forests as potential reservoirs of genetic material and possible rare species reserves. Moreover, old-growth forests as an ecosystem are generally considered endangered in much of the eastern landscape.

Whitney (1987), Hunter (1989), Parker (1989), Martin (1992), and McCarthy (1995) all provide technical definitions and descriptions of old-growth hardwood forest in the eastern United States. A simple definition is difficult, if not impossible, to employ. Different authors have adopted different criteria for designation. Some use a functional definition associated with stand dynamics (e.g., Oliver and Larson 1996). Others use a historical criterion such as lack of evidence of direct human impact (i.e., logging; Duffy and Meier 1992). Martin (1992) and others have designated a suite of structural criteria for mesic forests. These criteria relate to species identity, structure, coarse woody debris, and forest floor characteristics, among others. Keddy and Drummond (1996) espouse this criteria-based approach and provide a summary of features that should be monitored, and potentially managed for, in eastern deciduous forests.

Although all approaches have their merits, I strongly endorse the use of specific, quantifiable criteria in old-growth designations to reduce unproductive semantic debates. For example, Martin (1992) argues that mesic forests should contain most of the following attributes in order to be considered old-growth: a moderate to high richness and diversity (S and H, respectively) of tree species ($S > 20$; $H > 3.0$); uneven ages with a wide distribution of size and age classes (reverse J distribution); some large (> 75cm dbh) canopy tree species; some large, high-quality merchantable trees (i.e., of high economic importance suggesting no logging or high-grading); some trees older than 200 years; overstory density > 250 trees/ha (for stems > 10 cm dbh); overstory basal area > 25.0 m^2/ha; strong presence of coarse woody debris (logs and snags) in multiple age and decay classes; tree-fall gaps from windthrow along with pit-and-mound topography; plants and animals that prefer or reach their optimum in old growth; undisturbed soils with a thick organic layer and presence of soil macropores; and little or no evidence of human disturbance (e.g., stumps, skid trails, wire fencing, cultivated plants, foundations).

Although an abundant and diverse spring herbaceous flora is one of the hallmarks of temperate deciduous forests, this feature has not been widely used in the old-growth designation debate. Keddy and Drummond (1996) make specific recommendations regarding spring ephemerals (sensu Givnish 1987) of mature deciduous forest (table 7.1). They note that, given the variability in herb communities associated with latitude and environment, it would be inappropriate to use the presence of specific indicator species for the designation of high-quality old-growth forests. But a number (richness) of indicator species from the local spring ephemeral guild may be useful in assessing stand quality (table 7.1): > 6 for high-quality (old-growth), 2–5 for intermediate, < 2 for poor (Keddy and Drummond 1996). Although this approach seems useful, additional studies are necessary to include a broader subset of vegetation types (beyond *Fagus-Acer*) and guilds (functional groups) in the herbaceous flora

Table 7.1 Spring ephemerals from seven old-growth forests, predominantly Fagus-*Acer*, located throughout the Kentucky, Ohio, Pennsylvania, and Michigan region.

Species	KY	PA	OH	OH	OH	MI
				Locale		
Allium tricoccum			*	*	*	
Caulophyllum thalictroides	*	*		*		*
Claytonia virginica	*		*	*	*	*
Dentaria diphylla	*	*		*		
Dentaria laciniata	*		*		*	*
Dicentra canadensis			*	*	*	*
Dicentra cucullaria			*	*	*	
Erythronium americanum	*			*		*
Maianthemum canadense						*
Podophyllum peltatum	*		*	*	*	
Polygonatum biflorum	*	*	*	*	*	
Sanguinaria canadensis	*		*		*	
Tiarella cordifolia	*	*		*		
Trillium grandiflorum	*	*	*	*		*
Total number of species	10	5	9	11	8	7

(i.e., summer species). Moreover, simple observation in the central Appalachians indicates that six of these ephemeral species are present in even the most degraded second-growth deciduous forests of the region (McCarthy, pers. obs.).

Six species have been proposed as a minimum target number in this functional group to indicate the old-growth condition or quality. Presence or absence of an individual species is probably unimportant (Keddy and Drummond 1996). Nomenclature follows Gleason and Cronquist (1991).

COMPOSITION, STRUCTURE, AND DYNAMICS OF THE HERB LAYER

Beyond simple descriptions of vegetation (e.g., Oosting 1942; Wistendahl 1958), the composition, structure, and dynamics of species in the herbaceous layer of mesic old-growth forests only began to receive significant attention in the early 1980s. Most foresters, land managers, and ecologists have historically ignored the understory layer in favor of the more economically important overstory. Indeed, most definitions and characteristics of old growth (as the ones presented here) are rooted primarily in tree species composition and forest structure or disturbance characteristics. There is an important need to understand the factors affecting herb layer dynamics in old-growth forests. Historic views of succession (i.e., climax concept) would suggest that forest understories should be largely stable over long periods. Modern views of succession would suggest that the understory is quite dynamic and not in equilibrium. However, long-term temporal studies of the herb layer are few (Brewer 1980; Davison and Forman 1982), as are geographically broad studies of spatial pattern (Rogers 1981,

1982). The relationships between temporal and spatial pattern (scale) in forest herb communities are only recently attracting attention (McCarthy et al. 2001; Small and McCarthy 2002), even though these notions have been around in ecology for some time. In fact, Small and McCarthy (2002) suggest that previous studies of the herb layer in species-rich forests may have been undersampled by at least an order of magnitude, thus making inferences about patterns weak.

Brewer (1980) provided one of the first long-term (50-year) studies of herb community dynamics in an old-growth *Fagus-Acer* stand (Warren Woods) in southern Michigan. Warren Woods was found to have a luxuriant (i.e., dense cover) but a relatively species-poor herb layer. Some species decreased and some increased over the study period. Brewer concluded that changes were not related to exogenous factors (e.g., climate) but rather to changes in overstory dynamics stemming from a major disturbance more than 150 years before (believed to be a catastrophic fire). Indeed, what was being observed were long-term successional changes associated with old-growth development. Species with the greatest increase (> 200 percent) during this time included *Asarum canadense* L., *Boehmeria cylindrical* L., *Epifagus virginiana* L., *Laportea canadensis* L., *Osmorhiza claytoni* (Michx.) C. B. Clarke, *Polygonatum pubescens* (Willd.) Pursh., and *Viola* species, many of which are slow-growing perennials and tolerant of deep shade. He did not find windthrow to be a major influence with respect to diversity.

Davison and Forman (1982) also provided one of the few long-term studies of forest herb community dynamics. They conducted a 30-year study of herb and shrub dynamics in an old-growth oak forest (Hutcheson Memorial Forest; HMF) in central New Jersey. Their goal was to evaluate the stability of the understory layer over the 30 years and assess patterns of community change. They hypothesized that a stable climax forest should have a stable understory. They found that the herb layer declined from 33 species in 1950 to 24 in

1969 and 26 in 1979. Moreover, cover increased dramatically from 8 percent to 60 percent. *Podophyllum peltatum* L. increased in cover by 700 percent; Circaea *quadrisculcata* L. by 500 percent. The sharp increase in the former species was a partial explanation for the decrease in diversity. *Podophyllum* has a strong clonal nature and can displace other species. In addition, *Lonicera japonica* Thunb., an introduced vine, increased substantially and was believed to negatively influence the native species diversity. Davison and Forman also noted that a long period of fire suppression might have influenced the observed species composition. Increasing canopy gaps were believed to influence the understory by increasing light and moisture conditions.

McCarthy et al. (2001) established a long-term study of forest herb dynamics in an old-growth mesophytic forest dominated by white oak in southeastern Ohio (Dysart Woods; DW). Dysart Woods is comparable to HMF (Davison and Forman 1982) in many ways, including history, composition, structure, diversity, and natural disturbance regimes. Perhaps most important, DW is also experiencing a decline of white oak in the overstory. Many of the DW oaks are in excess of 85 cm dbh and 400 years of age (Rubino and McCarthy 2000) and are in a disease decline spiral (Manion 1991) associated with multiple predisposing and inciting agents (e.g., acidic deposition, drought stress, *Armillaria* root rot). This will likely result in dramatic long-term changes in the understory, but these patterns will only be revealed in the context of long-term permanent plot-type ecosystem data where both biological and environmental components are examined.

Within-year variability in the herb community is familiar to everyone who has worked in the eastern deciduous forest. McCarthy et al. (2001) provided a quantitative example of these short-term temporal (phenological) differences and local spatial differences. The vegetation varied dramatically among early spring, early summer, and late summer samples. Certainly, this would be expected between the vernal herbs and the summer species, but the differences between the two summer samplings were somewhat unexpected. Curiously, the phenological differences within seasons have only been rarely quantified in old-growth stands (Goebel et al. 1999). Most studies (e.g., McCarthy and Bailey 1996; Olivero and Hix 1998) use only a single sample period in midsummer that may not be representative. Further, McCarthy et al. (2001) also discovered a dramatic topographical aspect effect. Highly dissected topographies, like those found in much of the central Appalachians, may have dramatically different floras on north- and south-facing slopes (fig. 7.1). The interplay between spatial and temporal dynamics at various scales remains largely unexplored.

Rogers (1981, 1982) evaluated the understory layer of old-growth forests throughout Ohio, Indiana, Michigan, Wisconsin, and Minnesota. He noted that there had been few studies of the herb layer that were both quantitative and geographically extensive. He found that soil fertility, not climate, was the most important difference in explaining regional patterns of spring ephemerals. Within stands, soil drainage and microtopography had the most important influence on vernal herb diversity and abundance (higher on soil mounds than pits). Species with large perennial organs tended to be uncommon in forests that were relatively recently disturbed (Rogers 1982). Among the summer herbs, Rogers (1981) found 23 percent to be widespread and common (present in > 30 percent of stands), another 23 percent to be common but distributed unevenly, 15 percent uncommon but widely distributed, and the remaining 40 percent

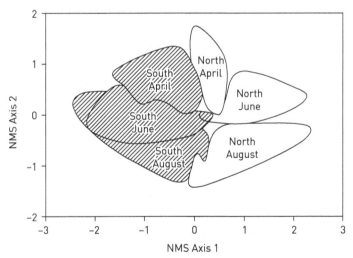

FIGURE 7.1 A nonmetric multidimensional scaling (NMS) ordination of 2-m² quadrats used to sample the herbaceous vegetation of Dysart Woods, an old-growth mesophytic forest in southeastern Ohio (*n* = 210). The first two NMS ordination axes account for 33.0 percent and 24.1 percent of the variability, respectively. Axis I separates quadrats on the north-facing slope from those on the south-facing slope. Axis II is a temporal gradient separating spring, early summer, and late summer floras. Individual points are omitted for visual clarity; isopleths are drawn to encompass all sample points.

to be both uncommon and highly restricted. This suggests that species-specific generalizations will be difficult or impossible to make and that current and future studies should focus on life-history types or guilds in analyzing community data.

Interest in spatial and temporal variation has returned the concept of diversity to center stage in understory ecological research (Wilson et al. 1998). However, few studies have explored the relationship of scale to patterns of understory diversity in eastern deciduous forests. In fact, the method of assessing, interpreting, and reporting understory diversity is less than clear. An objective evaluation of impending parameters is critical because many estimators of diversity are very sensitive to sample size, area measured, species rarity, grain of the environment, and so on. We recently explored the relationship between micro- (2 m^2) and mesoscale (70 m^2) herb diversity in DW (Small and McCarthy, 2002). We examined standard estimators of richness, evenness, and diversity, as well as species area curves and more recent techniques such as SHE (richness [S], diversity [H], and evenness [E]) analysis (Hayek and Buzas 1997, 1998) and species richness estimators (E. P. Smith and van Belle 1984; Palmer 1990; Colwell and Coddington 1994; Chazdon et al. 1998). Although scale clearly had an effect on the reporting and interpretation of diversity, we found the species area curves and species richness estimators to be the most enlightening (fig. 7.2). We sampled 35 2-m^2 plots on one northeast- and one southwest-facing slope—a relatively large sample compared to most studies. Each plot was sampled three times during the growing season to assess phenological variability (fig. 7.1). Based on the diversity patterns in this oak-dominated mesophytic old-growth forest and bootstrapped 95 percent confidence intervals around our estimators, we determined our sampling to be inadequate in this species-rich stratum. In fact, sample size estimation equations suggest that 100–300 2-m^2 quadrats are necessary to describe

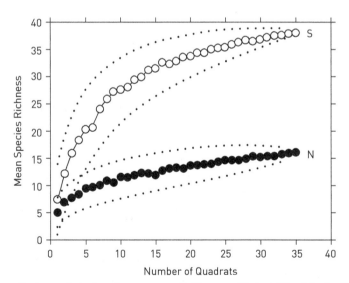

FIGURE 7.2 Bootstrap-derived species area curves (± 95 percent CI, dotted lines) for the 35 2-m^2 understory sampling quadrats established on north-facing (N) and south-facing (S) slopes at Dysart Woods for the June (early summer) sampling period. These data suggest that 70-m^2 (35 plots) is a minimum sampling area; however, sample size estimation equations indicated that > 200-m^2 (100 plots) would be necessary under most conditions to capture 95 percent of the species.

and estimate species richness within any one stand. This sampling intensity is dramatically higher than anything published in the literature. This suggests that previous studies of the herb layer in temperate hardwood forests need to be reconsidered. The likelihood that representative samples were obtained is low, and the strength of inference is potentially quite weak.

OLD-GROWTH VERSUS SECOND-GROWTH HERB LAYER DYNAMICS

In the absence of anthropogenic disturbance, the factors that affect herb distribution and abundance are numerous and include topographic and soil features such as elevation, aspect, soil quality (Bratton 1976; Elliott et al. 1997), overstory composition (Hicks 1980), stand structure attributes such as basal area and cover (Ford et al. 2000), herbivory (Alverson et al. 1988; van Deelan et al. 1996; Brown and Parker 1997; Rooney and Dress 1997a), and timing or size of gap disturbance (Collins and Pickett 1987; Clebsch and Busing 1989; Reader and Bricker 1992a). The relationship between disturbance, particularly anthropogenic disturbance in the form of logging, and herb community structure is still not well understood and has only recently begun to be explored in detail (Duffy and Meier 1992; Gilliam and Turrill 1993; Bratton et al. 1994, Gilliam et al. 1995; Meier et al. 1995, 1996; Goebel et al. 1999; Ford et al. 2000; Gilliam 2002; Roberts and Zhu 2002; chapters 11 and 14, this volume; others reviewed in Battles et al. 2001). Duffy and Meier (1992) argued that second-growth stands approaching 90 years since disturbance still did not exhibit a similar flora to paired old-growth stands. Old-growth stands had significantly greater cover and species density in all nine pairs of stands. They suggested that the explanations could include the following: (1) Recovery was so slow that 87 years was an insufficient time to observe change; (2) logged forests may never recover to match primary forest because of different climate conditions now relative to the past; and (3) many herbaceous species require the microtopography generated by pit-and-mound dynamics, so recovery must await the death and decay of the overstory.

The influence of landscape factors, such as slope aspect, is known to have an important effect on vegetation (Wolfe et al. 1949), yet the few studies that examine this component are not in agreement. Olivero and Hix (1998) examined the ground flora in second-growth and old-growth stands in southeastern Ohio. Half the plots were located on mesic, northeast-facing slopes and the other half on dry, southwest-facing slopes. First, they found significant differences in both of the main effects (i.e., between old-growth and second-growth stands and between mesic and dry stands). However, they also discovered an interactive effect in that species richness and Hill's diversity differed between old-growth and second-growth on northeast-facing plots but did not differ on southwest-facing plots. McCarthy et al. (2001) found the exact opposite pattern within DW. In this old-growth forest, all measures of diversity were greater on the southwest-facing slope compared to the northeast-facing slope (but abundance was greater on the latter). Goebel et al. (1999) conducted another study comparing an old-growth forest and second-growth forest in southeastern Ohio; however, they restricted the study to two stands in each study area on southwest-facing slopes only, but sampled both spring and summer vegetation. In contrast to the study of Olivero and Hix (1998), Goebel et al. did find differences in southwest-facing slope floras in old-growth versus second-growth forests.

From an experimental design standpoint, all of the previous studies (Olivero and Hix 1998; Goebel et al. 1999; McCarthy et al. 2001) are problematic in one way or another, particularly in the context of pseudoreplication (Hurlbert 1984). Olivero and Hix (1998) sampled only once in midsummer and then only eight 2-m² plots were sampled in each of 32 study areas. Goebel et al. (1999) sampled both the spring and summer herb vegetation but pseudoreplicated at the forest level so they had only one replicate treatment (primary versus secondary) and then only a relatively small sampling effort within any one time period. Based on data from Small and McCarthy (in press), considerably more sampling is required to describe within-stand herb communities in species-rich forests. McCarthy et al. (2001), while maintaining a moderate within-stand sample size to explore phenological patterns, pseudoreplicated at the stand level and thus had only one of each of the representative slope aspects in the one forest. In all likelihood, the limitations of time, money, and energy impinge on the scale of any one study. Investigators need to draw boundaries within the limits of their questions and available resources. The necessity to sample large numbers of plots multiple times within one season is very resource-intensive, particularly when the flora are so phenologically dynamic that complete species turnover can occur within weeks. Clearly, many more studies are needed over a larger geographical area for longer periods of time before we can begin to draw conclusions or conduct informative meta-analyses.

Several studies have now used successional chronosequences examining understory diversity recovery after major disturbances such as logging (Gilliam et al. 1995; Ford et al. 2000). Using this approach, neither Gilliam et al. (1995) nor Ford et al. (2000) were able to demonstrate any clear pattern in herb diversity with respect to stand age. These results could suggest that clearcutting mature second-growth stands does not significantly impact understory herb diversity. However, as Duffy and Meier (1992) and Meier et al. (1995) point out, several centuries may be required to develop the characteristics associated with old-growth outlined previously in this chapter. Thus, there may be a long time between stand maturity after clearcutting (75–100 years) and the old-growth condition (300–400 years) whereby herb community structure returns to its primary condition (chapters 11 and 14, this volume).

After disturbance, community composition and structure will be initially directed largely by propagule dispersal. Spatial properties such as patch isolation (landscape connectivity) and microenvironment (chapter 14, this volume) along with temporal factors such as seed banks, will be important determinants in the rates of recolonization. Unfortunately, most of the old-growth forest patches in the eastern deciduous forest exist in a nonforest matrix. For example, both DW in Ohio and HMF in New Jersey are surrounded by agriculture and/or suburban development. Without connectivity, disturbed forests will be slow to regenerate the previous community structure. Unfortunately, studies of temperate old-growth forest seed banks are uncommon. In contrast to general successional patterns found in the seed bank literature (e.g., Roberts and Vankat 1991), Leckie et al. (2000) found that weedy aliens of adjacent disturbed landscapes did not dominate the seed bank in an old-growth hardwood forest in Quebec. In fact, the seed bank was found to be fairly diverse and contained many shade-tolerant species. Leckie et al. also found that many of the species in the aboveground vegetation were also present in the seed bank. McCarthy et al. (unpublished data) found a similar pattern at DW. Many shade-tolerant forest species were found in the seed bank, and this could serve as an important propagule source after

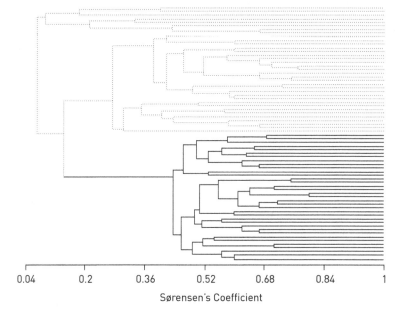

FIGURE 7.3 Unweighted pair group mean analysis, using Sørenson's coefficient of similarity, to compare the seed bank (solid lines) with the aboveground vegetation (dotted lines) in the 35 quadrats on the north-facing slope (June vegetation data shown) at Dysart Woods, Ohio.

disturbance. However, unlike Leckie et al. (2000), McCarthy et al. (unpublished data) found little similarity (< 20 percent in most sample periods) between aboveground and belowground species constituencies (fig. 7.3).

STABILITY, DIVERSITY, AND HABITAT INVASIBILITY

Concern over biodiversity loss with respect to ecosystem function has regenerated interest in the links among stability, diversity, and habitat invasibility (Levine and D'Antonio 1999). The notion of stability can be traced to early ideas about the development of the community as espoused by Clements and his followers. According to early thinking, at some point, all communities achieved a homeostatic equilibrium (the climax community). This idea continues today in many respects under the rubric "balance of nature." A community or ecosystem is often seen as stable when no change can be detected in species over time. However, as Connell and Sousa (1983) point out, it is important to distinguish between the degree of constancy of the numbers of organisms versus the constancy of species (presence or absence). The former is quantitative, the latter qualitative. Quantitative issues include both the *resistance* of a system to disturbance (the ability to remain at equilibrium when faced with potentially disturbing forces), as well as the *resilience* of a system (the ability to return to equilibrium after being disturbed). Qualitative issues focus on *persistence* (the ability of a species to not become locally extinct). Thus, both qualitative and quantitative features of a system must be examined.

Old-growth forests have been, and will continue to be, a critical component of our development of ecological theory, particularly with respect to issues of system stability. My observations in the central and southern Appalachians suggest that old-growth herb layers exhibit all three forms of stability: resistance, resilience, and persistence.

This is confirmed by at least one empirical field study (Brothers and Spingarn 1992). But long-term data in forests that have been perturbed are needed before this notion can be better assessed. In this regard, old-growth forests will remain invaluable benchmarks to compare against a predominantly managed (perturbed) forest landscape now existing in eastern North America. The predominant disturbance in most eastern old-growth forests, with the advent of fire suppression in the 20th century, is gap disturbance. However, empirical tests of the effects of gap disturbance on the understory community in second-growth forests have not been particularly revealing. Collins and Pickett (1987) found that small (single-tree) and large (multi-tree) gap openings in a northern hardwood forest had little influence on species richness or cover. This suggests that the herb community is resistant to the disturbance regime most prevalent in eastern old-growth forests and therefore relatively stable. In a similar study, Reader and Bricker (1992a) were unable to show a positive relationship between gap size and perennial herb abundance over a two-year period in hardwood forests of southern Ontario. They concluded that herbs might be under too much competition with advanced regeneration in larger gaps to allow increases in herb abundance.

For years, there has been the tacit assumption that there is a link between stability and diversity, probably first proposed by Elton (1958), who stated that "the balance of relatively simple communities of plants and animals is more easily upset than that of richer ones" (145). However, the empirical evidence for this notion is less than apparent (McNaughton 1988), particularly in communities of vascular plants. Tilman (1996) recently examined this relationship using long-term plot data in grasslands and concluded that diversity did stabilize community and ecosystem processes (e.g., biomass), but not population processes (e.g., individual species abundance). However, the ultimate interpretation of these results is difficult due to confounding effects found in many ecological experiments (Huston 1997). Huston (1994) suggests that in a dynamic equilibrium context (assuming low levels of disturbance), high-diversity communities are likely to occur under conditions of low population growth rates, whereas low-diversity communities are likely to be found under conditions with high population growth rates. But the relationship between stability and complexity may simply be a consequence of the type of environment in which high-diversity communities exist, rather than an inherent property of diversity and complexity (Huston 1994). Many old-growth relicts are found on relatively high-quality sites. Empirical tests of the diversity–stability hypothesis are lacking for old-growth forests. More recently, biologists have become concerned about the prevalence of biological invasions and their impact on natural systems (Mooney and Drake 1986; McKnight 1993; Williamson 1996; Luken and Thieret 1997; chapter 13, this volume). *Invasibility* is defined as the ease with which new members become established in a community. It is widely believed that high native diversity decreases the invasibility of communities (Lodge 1993). The origins and rationale for this notion have been summarized well by Levine and D'Antonio (1999). Constructed community studies where diversity has been directly manipulated have produced both positive and negative relationships with invasibility, both in field (Palmer and Maurer 1997) and microcosm (McGrady-Steed et al. 1997) experiments. As far as I am aware, there has been no empirical test of this notion in forest understory communities. Simple observations of old-growth forests are conflicting. HMF and DW described earlier are two interesting case examples. Both are old-growth forests dominated by white oak, have similar disturbance histories, and are of similar composition and structure. Yet, HMF has been plagued with invading species in the understory (Davison and Forman 1982; McCarthy, pers. obs.), and DW has not. In a recent vegetation study of DW, McCarthy et al. (2001) found no nonindigenous species in the herbaceous layer! But clearly, the woods are surrounded by many nonindigenous species, some quite invasive (e.g., *Lonicera japonica, Alliaria petiolata*). A key difference may have been the profound effect of gypsy moth (*Lymantria dispar* L.) attacks at HMF in the early 1980s, whereas DW has not yet been reached by the gypsy moth. A biological disturbance by one invasive organism may govern the invasibility of the entire community, depending on the strength of the disturbance. Under normal disturbance regimes and climatic fluctuations, old-growth forests may contain stable understories. Considerably more observations and experimental work are needed in this area.

SUMMARY

I have reviewed and explored several features of the herbaceous layer in eastern old-growth deciduous forests. After many years of debate, we are now coming to consensus on how to define old-growth forest. Technical definitions with specific quantifiable criteria are now available, but the herb layer has not commonly been included in these definitions. It is important to incorporate the herb layer in these definitions because this is usually the most diverse vegetative layer in these ecosystems. More research is needed to understand the herbaceous layer diversity patterns along chronosequences that include old growth. The use of functional groups (in place of species) may be helpful in setting targets for preservation or conservation. This will permit better standards to emerge and ultimately assist with land management decisions.

Because of the temporal variability of forest understory communities, single samplings of the vegetation are inappropriate in most cases; yet many examples remain in the literature. There also appears to be a large emphasis on the spring vernal herbs (perhaps because of their lower diversity), apparently at the expense of the rest of the summer flora. In fact, we know little of the complete herbaceous flora and its phenology in most forests. As I have described, given the high diversity in this layer, we need to better study the sampling methods and sample sizes required to capture at least 95 percent of the species. Furthermore, if we are to ever understand spatial and temporal patterns in the understory, we must expand our observations beyond the level of the stand and the single-year study. As far as forest herb communities are concerned, I cannot overemphasize the need for long-term, permanent plot studies arranged in a stratified fashion throughout the landscape.

Finally, in recent years, biologists have become acutely aware of the threat of invasive, nonindigenous species to many natural ecosystems. However, our understanding of the relationships among diversity, stability, and invasibility are still weak and confined to specific types of microcosms or ecosystems. Forest systems have not been carefully examined in this light, especially old-growth forests. Despite a shifting emphasis toward a better understanding of the managed forest landscape, old-growth forests will remain an important component in our understanding of forest patterns and processes. These systems serve as the benchmarks in our heavily disturbed eastern forest landscape.

8 Habitat Heterogeneity and Maintenance of Species in Understory Communities

Susan W. Beatty

What determines species distributions and richness in forested communities? This question has been debated for decades. Rather than ruling out possible explanations, we have continued to propose new hypotheses. Four explanatory factors often appear in the literature: disturbance, patterns in physical factors (soils, microclimate), biological processes (e.g., competition, dispersal, colonization, and extinction), and history (land use, anthropogenic impacts, and successional age). In this chapter, I address the effects of all four factors in determining the species composition and richness of northeastern deciduous forest communities in the context of spatially and temporally heterogeneous environments.

Disturbance in plant communities has been connected with the maintenance of species richness, community stability, and a variety of life history strategies (Watt 1947a; Whittaker 1969; F. E. Smith 1972; Drury and Nisbet 1973; Grubb 1977; Platt and Weis 1977; Whittaker and Levin 1977; Connell 1978; Grime 1979; Huston 1979; Denslow 1980, 1985; Pickett 1980; Collins and Pickett 1987; Foster 1988a; Foster and Boose 1992; Cooper-Ellis et al. 1999). Current disturbance theory includes the two following hypotheses: (1) Richness is maintained in communities where the disturbance is more frequent than the time required for competitive exclusion to operate; and (2) communities with the highest richness should be those affected by moderate disturbance intensity and/or frequency (intermediate disturbance hypothesis) (Huston 1979; Pickett and White 1985). Numerous studies have indicated that there is a complex interaction between controls exerted by fine-scale local processes and those exerted by coarse-scale regional processes (Glitzenstein et al. 1986; Pastor and Broschart 1990; Beatty 1991; Lertzman 1992; Frelich and Reich 1995; Lertzman and Fall 1998). We need to establish the interaction between potential controls on richness and the scales at which they operate within the spatial heterogeneity inherent to many communities (Wilson et al. 1999).

Variation in the physical environment has long had the attention of plant ecologists in explaining species distributions and, more recently, species diversity (Kupfer and Malanson 1993; Allen and Walsh 1996; Parker and Bendix 1996; Bendix 1997; Clark et al. 1999; Pitman et al. 1999). In forested ecosystems, individual tree falls may be responsible for maintaining spatial habitat heterogeneity and for supporting gap-phase species within a mature community (Stephens 1956; Lyford and MacLean 1966; Veblen et al. 1979; White 1979; Runkle 1981, 1982). However, Hubbell et al. (1999) argued that a recruitment limitation (lack of widespread dispersal to gaps) in tropical forests "appears to decouple the gap disturbance regime from control of tree diversity" (554) and said that we need to reexamine the gap dynamic models elsewhere. In glaciated regions of forested North America, tree fall disturbance creates a remnant microrelief on the forest floor that can affect spatial heterogeneity for hundreds of years after the direct disturbance gap effect has disappeared (Lyford and MacLean 1966; Beatty and Stone 1986; Schaetzl et al. 1989; Schaetzl and Follmer 1990). This mound-pit micro-topography is responsible, in part, for determining understory species distributions at the micro-scale (Beatty 1984, 1991; Canham 1984; Beatty and Sholes 1988; Peterson et al. 1990) and is discussed here as a "disturbance legacy" rather than as a direct disturbance effect.

A crucial question in plant-community ecology continues to be whether species composition results from assembly rules (e.g., dominance–diversity relations) that limit the number of species in an area through interactions among species and with the environment, or from dispersal/colonization dynamics that limit whether a species reaches a site (Wilson 1999a). Many studies have shown the importance of biological interactions in determining species composition and richness of communities (Grace and Tilman 1990; Tilman 1994; Hubbell 1997; Malanson 1997a,b; Dalling et al. 1998; Duncan et al. 1998). Explanations of species distributions have frequently invoked competition as a driving force (Lack 1947; Hutchinson 1959; Daubenmire 1966; Werner and Platt 1976; Grace and Wetzel 1981; Tilman 1982; Schoener 1983), but some have argued that stable communities have evolved so that competition is minimal or absent (Connell 1980; Givnish 1982; Parrish and Bazzaz 1982). With respect to under-story layer interactions, one of the few experimental studies with forest herbs that demonstrated competitive segregation of congeneric forest herbs used a transplantation technique (W. G. Smith 1975). Using nonexperimental studies in forests, Rogers (1983) found neither evidence of spatial interference competition between functionally similar spring ephemeral taxa nor evidence of temporal interference competition between spring ephemeral and summer species groups (Rogers 1985). In moist forest understory communities, distributional patterns may result from differences in species' colonizing abilities, longevity (as in clonal integration), and/or space preemption on available microsites (Harper et al. 1961; Drury and Nisbet 1973; Grubb 1977; Rogers 1982). Tree fall gaps in closer proximity to old field/forest edges were found to have higher species richness, yet also contained more exotic species (Goldblum and Beatty 1999). In the deciduous forests of the northeastern United States, Beatty (1991) found that active seed dispersal corresponded more closely to microsite species composition than did the buried seed component.

History of a site can also be important in determining the trajectory of community development (Hibbs 1983; Foster 1988b; Whitney 1990; Peterson and Carson 1996;

Nekola 1999). Understory species composition and richness may vary depending on the age of the stand, prior land-use treatment (plowed or not), and types of surrounding communities supplying a colonization source during the successional development. The clearing of forests since the 1800s for exploitation of wood resources and creation of agriculture/livestock grazing land has been widespread (Delcourt and Delcourt 1996). As a result, nearly all old-growth forests in some areas have been logged at some time since European settlement. The patterns of forest regeneration are patchy in the landscape, giving rise to a mosaic of stands abandoned at different times (Odum 1943; Russell 1958). Adjacent land cover has been identified as a factor in determining species richness for birds (Cubbedge and Nilon 1993; Green et al. 1994; Parish et al. 1994), as well as for floodplain tree species (Everson and Boucher 1998). Matlack (1994b) investigated the relationship between species composition and distance from nearby older stands that were sources of dispersal propagules. He found that the migration rates of plant species depended on distance from source populations, as well as on dispersal mode.

The importance of scale in ecological systems has been known for decades (Greig-Smith 1952; Stommell 1963; Schumm and Lichty 1965; Pielou 1969; Meentemeyer and Box 1987; Meentemeyer 1989), but we are still seeking a synthesis (O'Neill and King 1998). Fine-scale habitat heterogeneity is commonly overlooked in the study of coarser-scale vegetation processes (Beatty 1984). In this chapter, I consider the importance of micro-scale dynamics of herbaceous and woody species (dispersal, colonization, and persistence) in determining forest community pattern and process.

STUDY SITE

Over the last 20 years, I have been conducting a combination of observational and experimental studies in eastern deciduous forests of east-central New York State, at the Edmund Niles Huyck Preserve and Biological Field Station (42° 31' latitude, 74° 09' longitude). The preserve is 2,000 ha in area today and consists of parcels of land acquired intermittently since 1931 when it was established. Before settlement in 1781, some land was cleared for low-intensity agriculture, sheep grazing, haying, and logging for sawmill production. There are also areas thought to be old-growth hemlock forest (Odum 1943). The oldest second-growth deciduous forests are now about 150 years old. Mature deciduous forest in which much of my research has been conducted is second-growth forest located on east-facing upland slopes around Lake Myosotis (elevation 450–500 m). This area was part of the original preserve land acquisition and has been undisturbed by anthropogenic manipulations since that time.

The forest communities at the preserve are representative of deciduous and mixed forests throughout much of the northeastern United States. The dominant tree species are sugar maple (*Acer saccharum* Marsh.) and American beech (*Fagus grandifolia* Ehrh.), but white ash (*Fraxinus americana* L.), red oak (*Quercus rubra* L.), hop-hornbeam (*Ostrya virginiana* [Mill.] K. Kock), striped maple (*Acer pensylvanicum* L.), and occasionally eastern hemlock (*Tsuga canadensis* [L.] Carr.) are also found in the forests (see also Beatty 1984). The understory consists of a few shrub species, seedlings of tree species, and about 85 species of herbs, forbs, and bryophytes. The acid mull soils are moderately well-drained silt loams (Lordstown series) with glacial till parent material overlaying shale bedrock (1–5 m depth). Other vegetation types on and around the preserve include old fields of varying ages, young successional forest (ca. 25–50 years old), old-growth hemlock stands, spruce/pine plantations (Goldblum 1998), floodplain forest, lake-edge marsh, fen, and residential gardens.

METHODOLOGY

In 1978, I established 144 microsite plots on mounds, pits, and undisturbed forest floor and have monitored them on a yearly basis. Each plot is circular (to fit the shape of the microsite features) and 0.65 m² (average size of features). Since that time I initiated several additional studies and experiments, a summary of which is given here. In all cases, I preserved the initial sampling design, using the same-sized plots and usually stratifying the sampling by microsite. Plant species composition (density and coverage) was measured for all sample sites; I segregated data into finer categories on occasion, such as differentiating between first-year seedlings (identifying cotyledons) and established plants for both herbaceous and woody species. I also included bryophytes in the vegetation composition data, using only coverage as a measure of species importance in a plot. As of 2000, I had a total of 447 monitored microsite plots in these forest communities. Generally, I also monitored soil and microenvironmental parameters for plots (e.g., soil temperature, moisture, pH, extractable cations and nitrate, summer rainfall amounts, air temperature, photosynthetically active radiation, canopy coverage, recent tree fall activity, and standing tree mortality within 30 m of a plot), although not every year in every plot.

Experimental studies have included (1) a removal experiment to test for competitive interactions (n 80 experimental and control plots), (2) a leaf litter removal experiment to determine the impacts on establishment and survivorship (n 40 experimental and control plots), (3) a seed trap study that quantified dispersal pathways by which microsites are colonized (n 100 sample points), (4) an environmental variability experiment to test hypotheses about species shifting under extreme environmental conditions (n 80 experimental and control plots), and (5) an experiment creating mound and pit microsites to determine micro-successional changes in new microsites (n 40 experimental and control plots). In the competition experiment, I removed *Aster divaricatus* L. (dominant mound species) from replicate microsites using two techniques: clipping only aboveground parts and applying herbicide to cut stems after clipping. Clipping was repeated biweekly throughout the growing season for the four years of the study; herbicide killed plants in the first year, after which cotyledons were removed each year. In the leaf litter removal experiment (Beatty and Sholes 1988), we removed litter by hand and kept litter out of sites using wire-mesh cages for eight years. In the seed trap study, I used a nondrying spray-on adhesive on filter paper in petri plates located on the soil surface or buried down to the surface, and then either covered or not covered with a fine-mesh cage that allowed light and moisture input but no seed rain. This partitioned seed input into aerial versus overland flow. Buried seed was also germinated in the greenhouse (Beatty 1991). The environmental variability experiment was designed to either increase or decrease the available moisture to a microsite by a factor of two. Based on measured rainfall in the forest communities, collected rainfall was added to some microsites to mimic a wetter year. Other microsites had canopy covers that allowed PFD penetration but prevented direct input of ambient rainfall to mimic a drier year. Soil moisture was monitored to assess how effective the treatments were over the three years of the experiment. Finally, in 1979, I created 10 pairs of mounds and pits by digging up a 0.65 m² area of soil and depositing it to mimic a tree fall (some burial of A horizon, some mixing with B horizon; sensu Beatty and Stone 1986). These artificial microsites have been monitored since 1979, along with nearby control mound-pit pairs.

DISTURBANCE LEGACY EFFECTS ON UNDERSTORY

Tree fall is a common disturbance in northeastern deciduous forest. As a complement to the literature on the canopy regeneration dynamics that happen as a result of gap formation, my work has followed the longer-term effects of the soil disturbance created by the uprooting of the trees. This process creates persistent mound and pit microsites, which I estimated to be on the order of 200–300 years old (created before old-growth clearing). Thus, microtopography becomes a significant feature of the forest floor in these communities, representing a legacy of disturbance that has little to do with the original tree fall effect (Nakashizuka 1989). In my study sites, mounds and pits together compose 60 percent of the forest floor area. Previous work (Beatty 1984) established that many understory species populations are concentrated in one main microsite, with some species being distributed among all microsites. This creates a pattern of segregation such that the mounds have almost twice the species richness as the pits, with little spatial overlap in many of the species distributions. Spatial heterogeneity has been suggested to be important in maintaining species richness in communities (Whittaker and Levin 1977) by allowing for species segregation among microsites and providing some buffering against extreme environmental conditions. One of the major questions my research has addressed is whether the presence of this microsite heterogeneity is a benefit or a liability to the community in terms of species richness. As a benefit, it could provide a range of environmental conditions available to species so that some portion of a species population is likely to survive in even extremely stressful years. It may decrease competitive interactions via spatial segregation. It may enhance species richness by providing a variety of microsites to support species of widely varying environmental tolerances. As a liability, it may limit space available to species, possibly increasing competition in the microsites to which some species are restricted, and even limit species richness through exclusion or lack of space to support a viable population. To gain some understanding of what kind of role heterogeneity plays in deciduous forests, I experimentally tested several hypotheses about dynamics within and between mound and pit microsites.

HETEROGENEITY AS A LIABILITY?

Competitive Effects

Since mound microsites have higher richness than pit microsites, a valid question is whether the species packing is subject to competitive interactions that may exclude species from these sites. In the competition experiment, *A. divaricatus* was removed (aboveground and belowground removal gave the same results), and responses of species were monitored in subsequent years. Before any manipulation, microsites were monitored for two years in all plots, establishing that there were no significant differences between pretreatment experimental and control plots (fig. 8.1). In the first year

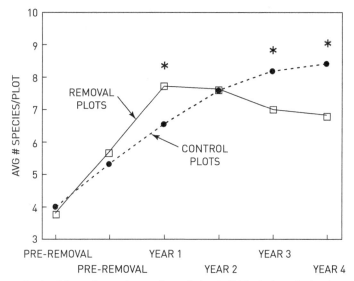

FIGURE 8.1 Species richness changes in experimental plots (solid line) where the dominant herb was removed versus changes in control plots (dashed line). Pre-removal years had no manipulations; years one to four had continuous removal in experimental plots. *Significant difference between richness in control and experimental plots in that year (paired *t* test, $p < .05$).

after removal, no significant changes in species cover were seen in 75 percent of species in control plots. However, in experimental plots, 83 percent of the species changed significantly, and the majority of these declined. Experimental sites also had new colonization in the first year, which increased richness significantly over controls. However, by the third year, many of those declining species became locally extinct, and richness was significantly lower than in control sites (fig. 8.1).

My conclusion is that, although mounds may support twice as many species as pits, the continued coexistence of these species is mediated by the presence of the dominant *A. divaricatus.* I believe this dominant species may be acting as a keystone competitor. This effectively counters the liability factor of competitive exclusion by a dominant in spatially limited microsites because its presence instead promotes coexistence of a number of species, albeit with lower population sizes.

Environmental Limitations

Pit microsites have many fewer species than mounds, yet seem to have more favorable environmental conditions, such as higher available moisture and nutrients, higher pH, more moderate temperature fluctuations, and a better developed A horizon (Beatty 1984; Beatty and Stone 1986). Pits also have much greater accumulation of leaf litter, which may act as physical and chemical limiting factors to establishment, particularly for small seeded species (Koroleff 1954; McPherson and Thompson 1972; Al-Mufti et al. 1977; Sydes and Grime 1981a,b). We tested the hypothesis that leaf litter limits pit species composition by removing leaf litter from experimental pits after leaf drop in 1983 (mounds do not have appreciable litter and so were not manipulated) (Beatty and Sholes 1988). Plots were sampled for species composition during the growing

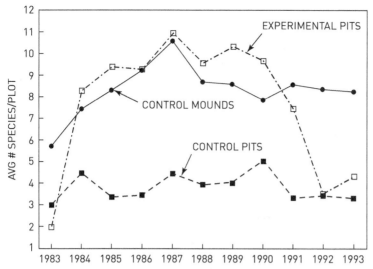

FIGURE 8.2 Species richness in mounds and pits in an experimental litter removal study. The 1983 data are prior to any manipulations; litter was eliminated in experimental pits (open squares) for years 1984–91; litter was allowed to reaccumulate after 1991. Control pits (filled squares) and control mounds (filled circles) are shown for comparison. Control mounds are significantly different from control pits for all years (paired *t* test, $p < .05$). Experimental pits are significantly different from control pits ($p < .05$) for years 1984–91.

season before removing litter. The litter was not allowed to accumulate in these sites for eight years, after which I monitored the effects of reaccumulation of litter.

Before litter removal (1983), plots to be used for experimental and control pits were not significantly different in species richness (paired *t* tests). However, in the first year after removal of leaf litter, pits significantly increased in species richness to the point of being the same as adjacent mounds (fig. 8.2). During the eight years of the experiment, species richness in litterless pits fluctuated in the same manner as in mounds, remaining not significantly different from mounds. In 1991, leaf litter was allowed to reaccumulate in experimental pits at the end of the growing season. During the 1992 season, species richness in experimental pits declined to levels seen in the control pits and remained at that level.

The mechanism behind such dramatic changes in species richness (and composition) was the successful germination and establishment in litterless pits. Even before litter removal, seed rain added many species to the pit seed pools that were not found in the flora of pits (Beatty 1991). However, these species either did not germinate or did not survive long enough to emerge above the litter layer. In the absence of litter, these species successfully established and survived the course of the experiment. The species that established in litterless pits were largely species that typically occurred on mounds (Beatty and Sholes 1988). Upon allowing litter to reaccumulate, almost all of these species were lost. Therefore, the leaf litter not only prevents establishment but also survivorship of adults.

Pit microsites do appear to be liabilities in the community, potentially limiting species richness by restricting space available to many species not able to tolerate the extreme conditions created by deep leaf litter accumulation. However, although the richness of pits increased due to non-pit species colonizing the experimental sites, the existing pit species declined (Beatty and Sholes 1988). By the end of the experiment, about 25 percent of the sites had lost one or two pit species, while maintaining the invaders (and thus a high richness). Thus, instead of limiting richness in the forest understory, unmanipulated pits allow the persistence of species that would otherwise not compete favorably in the understory community where many other species are present.

Succession in New Microsites

Both of the previous experiments examined dynamics on old, well-established mound and pit microsites. What are the dynamics on newly formed soil disturbances, and how do they differ from those in the mature microsites? Are newly created microsites rapidly colonized by forest species, or do exotic invaders preempt the space and delay establishment of mature forest species? On a more philosophical level, what is the quality of richness when it is enriched by species exotic to the forest community?

In 1978, I created pairs of artificial mounds and pits by digging up soil and redepositing it adjacent to the pit, as would happen in an uprooting event. Nearby natural mound-pit pairs were marked as controls. By monitoring species composition over the years, I found that there was an initial rapid colonization of new microsites by nonforest herbaceous species (e.g., *Eupatorium rugosum* Houtt., *Geum canadense* Jacq., *Solidago juncea* Ait., *Rubus allegheniensis* Porter), followed by a gradual increase in species more typical of the older forest microsites (controls). By the seventh year after creation (1985), the species richness and composition of new mounds were not significantly different from that of control mounds (fig. 8.3). The micro-successional process took longer in pits, which only reached richness and compositional similarity to controls in year 14 (1992).

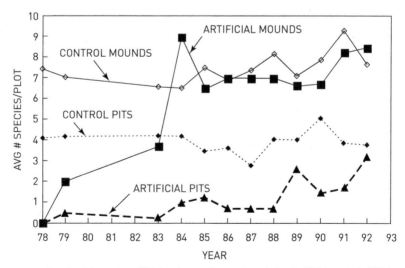

FIGURE 8.3 Species richness in artificial and control mounds and pits. Artificial mounds (filled squares) and pits (filled triangles) were created in 1979 and are compared with control mounds (open diamonds) and control pits (filled diamonds). Artificial mounds are significantly different from control mounds (paired *t* test; $p <.05$) in 1978–84. Artificial pits are significantly different from control pits ($p <.05$) for all years except 1992.

Although, initially, new microsites are largely occupied by species exotic to the mature forest community, there is a fairly rapid replacement of these species by forest understory species. The initial pulse of exotic species is accentuated in tree fall gaps, where newly forming mounds and pits are also in a higher light environment (Goldblum 1997; Goldblum and Beatty 1999) and are unstable substrates for several years as the root mass disintegrates (Beatty and Stone 1986; Nakashizuka 1989). As with tree fall gap dynamics in general, new soil microsites provide a temporary space for exotic species colonization, but these species are lost to the understory community as the site recovers. Thus, overall richness is increased in space (fugitive persistence among new sites) but not in time, and there appears to be no limitation to mature forest species as a result.

HETEROGENEITY AS A BENEFIT? BUFFERING AGAINST ENVIRONMENTAL VARIABILITY

It has been established that species composition and richness of the forest understory are affected by the heterogeneity of microsites. Species on mounds coexist in a seemingly high-competition environment tempered by dominance, whereas species in pits persist by tolerating limiting conditions deleterious to other species. The liability of spatial constriction into microsites is offset by the benefit of providing conditions where more species can persist and coexist. However, what happens when environmental conditions fluctuate? How do the microsites change, and what effect does this have on the dynamics of species maintenance in the forest community?

Using long-term data collected on control microsite plots over a 20-year period, I looked at the variability in species population sizes in the forest community (fig. 8.4). The variance in species density was used as a measure of change in population size from year to year. Species were first grouped into two main categories, based on their spatial distribution among microsites: Ubiquitous species occurred in more than one microsite (although usually concentrating in a particular one); restricted species were found only in one microsite (i.e., only on mounds or only in pits). Species were then placed in subcategories, based on the specific microsite (mounds or pits) in which they mainly or exclusively occurred. The question was whether species with more limited spatial distributions show a greater variation in population size over time. The answer is yes: The average variance among species in the ubiquitous category was considerably less than that for the restricted species (fig. 8.4). In the 20-year period, there were several drought years (e.g., 1980, 1985, 1987–88) and several very wet years (e.g., 1979, 1984, 1986), during which species restricted to one microsite may have experienced greater losses if conditions were stressful enough in the microsite. In contrast, I hypothesized that species with some individuals in more than one microsite may have differential survivorship in different microsites, thus ensuring that a greater number of individuals survive the stressful years. I consider these species to be "shifters" because their survivorship shifts between microsites depending on environmental conditions, similar to the shifting microsite mosaic hypothesis of Whittaker and Levin (1977). This suggests that the presence of different microsites provides many species with the opportunity for greater survivorship in the face of environmental variation, thus serving as a benefit to the maintenance of richness in the forest community.

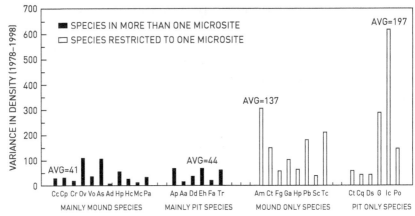

FIGURE 8.4 Variance in species density, 1978–98; higher values indicate greater variation in population density over the 20-year period. Species abbreviations are (1) mainly mound species: Cc = *Carex convoluta* Mackenz., Cp = *Carex pedunculata* Muhl., Cr = *Carex retrorsa* Schwein., Ov = *Ostrya virginiana*, Vo = *Veronica officinalis* L., As = *Acer saccharum*, Ad = *Aster divaricatus*, Hp = *Hieracium pratense* Tausch, Hc = *Hypnum curvifolium* Hedw., Mc = *Maianthemum canadense* Desf., Pa = *Prenanthes altissima* L.; (2) mainly pit species: Ap = *Acer pensylvanicum* L., Aa = *Arisaema atrorubens* (Ait.) Blume, Dd = *Dentaria diphylla* Michx., Eh = *Epipactus helleborine* (L.) Crantz, Fa = *Fraxinus americana*, Tr = *Trillium erectum* L.; (3) mound-only species: Am = *Aster macrophyllus* L., Ct = *Carya tomentosa* Nutt., Fg = *Fagus grandifolia*, Ga = *Galium aparine* L., Hp = *Hypericum punctatum* Lam., Pb = *Polygonatum biflorum* (Walt.) Ell., Sc = *Solidago caesia* L., Tc = *Tsuga canadensis*; (3) pit-only species: Ct = *Caulophyllum thalictroides* (L.) Michx., Cq = *Circaea quadrisulcata* (Maxim.) Franch. & Sav., Ds = *Dryopteris spinulosa* (O. F. Muell.) Watt, Gm = *Geranium maculatum* L., Ic = *Impatiens capensis* Meerb., Pa = *Polystichum acrostichoides* (Michx.) Schott.

Because my conclusion was based on observational data, I decided to experimentally test aspects of this microsite shifting hypothesis in the field by experimentally manipulating moisture regimes for replicate sets of microsites (refer to Methods section for details). I hypothesized that extreme conditions should have opposite effects on richness in mound versus pit microsites (a wet year might be good for mounds and bad for pits), which should affect survivorship. In experimental mound sites, the species richness in wet and dry treatments fluctuated almost inversely (fig. 8.5a). The wet treatment increased in richness during the experiment and the dry treatment had no change, while controls declined in richness. The year after treatments were stopped, wet mounds declined in richness, while dry mounds increased, as did controls. Similarly, experimental pit sites had slightly inverse responses to wet versus dry treatments (fig. 8.5b). Wet pits did not change in richness, whereas dry pits increased in richness during the experiment, and controls declined. The effect of simulating drought conditions in a pit gave similar results to that of the leaf litter removal experiment, with new colonization by non-pit species. Although I expected exaggerated wet conditions in pits and exaggerated dry conditions in mounds to both lead to species decline, I found instead that the extreme environmental conditions (of the experiment) promoted colonization (wet mounds and dry pits increased in richness) but had little liability for survivorship of existing species. This result helps explain the success of ubiquitous species that may colonize additional microsites in favorable years but not lose individuals in their main microsites in bad years. Restricted species are

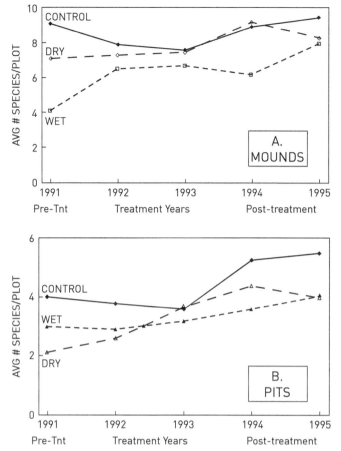

FIGURE 8.5 Species richness in experimental plots, with wet (twice ambient precipitation) and dry (half ambient precipitation) treatments. Results are shown for (A) mound microsites and (B) pit microsites. Data from 1991 are pretreatment; data from 1992 to 1993 are treatment applications; data from 1994 to 1995 are posttreatment.

not likely to colonize other microsites, so they do not have this population buffering capacity. It is certainly possible that the moisture conditions of my experiment did not reach levels sufficiently extreme to adequately test the hypothesis that survivorship would be affected in stressful years. However, the result that ubiquitous species can expand their distributions in moderate wet-dry years was a complementary finding. Thus, microsite heterogeneity does offer some buffering against environmental fluctuation, whether extreme or moderate.

In looking at fluctuations of some of the ubiquitous species over a 10-year period, it is apparent that there is often an inverse response in species density in mounds versus pits in a given year (fig. 8.6). For the two species shown in fig. 8.6, an increase in density in mounds is often accompanied by a decrease in density in pits in the same year, and vice versa. The observational data support the experimental data in suggesting that ubiquitous species can withstand environmental variation and maintain more stable forest-level population sizes by taking advantage of the microsite heterogeneity.

Because local microsite colonization and extinction are mechanisms by which species richness and population sizes fluctuate from year to year, an examination of

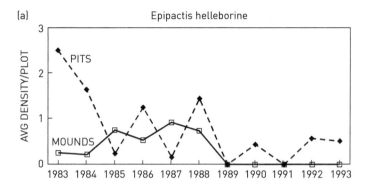

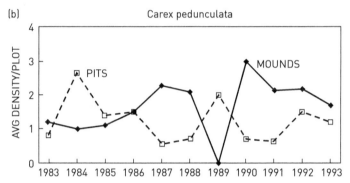

FIGURE 8.6 Individual species fluctuations in average density per plot over a 10-year period. Species density is given for mound (solid lines) and pit (dashed lines) microsites. (A) *Epipactis helleborine* is mainly found in pit microsites; (B) *Carex pedunculata* is mainly found in mound microsites. Variance in density values over a 20-year period is shown for these species in fig. 8.4.

these events over a similar time period is useful. The data in fig. 8.7 are from control microsites (for the litter removal experiment) that were monitored from 1984 to 1993. Species colonization and extinction rates (species/plot/year) often varied inversely over this 10-year period, in a pattern similar to that of fluctuations in individual species density in mounds and pits in fig. 8.6. If colonization rates are high in a given microsite (mound or pit), extinction rates are often low (favorable conditions). In stressful years for a given microsite, extinction rates go up, while colonization rates go down (more so in pits than on mounds). This supports the idea that the mechanism of the individual species fluctuations in density in a given microsite are partly a result of new colonization or extinction events as environmental conditions vary from favorable to unfavorable over the years. Finally, to further reinforce this pattern, the fluctuation in average richness for all control mound and pit microsites shows the same inverse trend (fig. 8.3, control curves). Often, an increase in richness in one microsite is accompanied by a decrease in the other microsite. This also buffers richness fluctuations in the forest as a whole, given that a local extinction of a species on a mound is likely to be balanced by a local colonization by that same species in a pit. Although not all species in the forest community are shifters, the proportion (~ 50 percent) is high enough to have an impact on forest richness and population sizes.

In conclusion, heterogeneity appears to be more of a benefit to the forest community than a liability. It serves to segregate species that might otherwise out-compete one another. It provides a range of environmental conditions that may be exploited

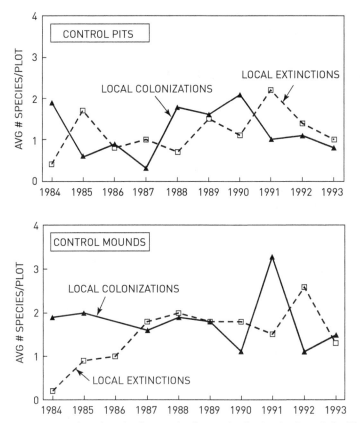

FIGURE 8.7 Average number of species disappearing from a plot (local extinctions; dashed lines) or appearing newly in a plot (local colonizations; solid lines) for control microsites over a 10-year period.

as climatic conditions vary from year to year, therefore serving as a spatial buffer to extreme environmental change. Those species able to grow in more than one microsite are less likely to become locally extinct, thus maintaining a higher species richness in the forest community.

MODELS FOR THE FUTURE

The various studies in this chapter differ from most studies in disturbance ecology in terms of the scale at which the data are collected and in the stratification by known microsites in the community. Rather than averaging across space, this work seeks to identify sources of variability at the fine scale. It is my hope that this approach can be applied in numerous other community types, seeking some common ground for testing hypotheses about species richness dynamics. To that end, I have developed two hypotheses relating to the function of heterogeneity in space and time. To determine the generality of these hypotheses, they need to be tested in as many communities and geographic regions as possible. The "intermediate heterogeneity hypothesis" presents the idea that heterogeneity can be both a benefit and a liability to a community, depending on scale and intensity of that heterogeneity. The "heterogeneity cycle hypothesis" proposes a model of heterogeneity in forest communities that relates to land use and successional age of a stand.

Intermediate Heterogeneity Hypothesis

For the forest communities I have been studying, as summarized here, it is clear that spatial heterogeneity in the form of mound and pit microtopography does not pose a limitation to species richness but enhances richness on several levels. Other work, however, has found that extreme microsites create conditions limiting to many species (Falinski 1978). Therefore, it seems that the degree or intensity of heterogeneity may be important in gauging its impact in a community. Based on limited sampling in areas at the Huyck Preserve that had been cleared and plowed, I found that this activity completely eliminated the mound-pit microtopography, leaving a homogeneous forest floor compared to the mature forest communities. Without mound and pit microsites, the forest had fewer total numbers of species (~ 15 percent fewer than average richness in adjacent forest of similar age), a higher proportion of species with large population sizes, and fewer rare species. A current research project is addressing whether this decline in richness might be due to lack of propagules to colonize the site, lack of specific microsites for some species (such as pit obligates that are poor competitors), or greater dominance by several species (similar to the results of my *A. divaricatus* removal experiment on mounds).

In 1977, I undertook some preliminary sampling before initiating the stratified microtopography design used in the work reported in this chapter. I wanted to test the hypothesis that greater heterogeneity correlated positively with higher richness. I sampled 40 belt transects (10 m × 1 m), measuring species composition and micro-elevational variability (deviation above or below the average slope for the transect). All transects were in mature forest with a range of mound heights and pit depths in microtopography. No flat sites were sampled at the time. The results did not support the hypothesis (fig. 8.8). Instead, there was a peak in richness at an intermediate level

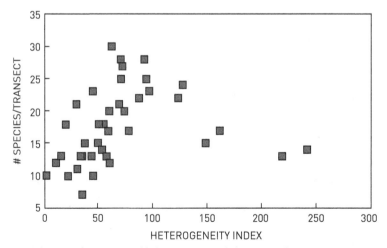

FIGURE 8.8 Species richness in 10-m² belt transects sampled in mature forest communities. Heterogeneity index is the variance of deviation in microelevation above and below the average slope of the transect. A high value indicates greater height and depth to mound and pit microsites, respectively.

of heterogeneity and a decline for areas having more extreme differences in mound-pit relative height (which would give a greater variance in micro-elevational departures from the average slope). At extreme levels of heterogeneity, physical limitations may exclude many species (i.e., heterogeneity as a liability). For instance, pits may accumulate litter to a much greater depth, retain moisture to the point of saturation for longer into the summer, and maintain much cooler soil temperature, all of which would affect germination and survivorship even for pit obligates. Coupled with the finding that forests with a lack of microtopography may tend toward lower richness, it appears that an intermediate spatial heterogeneity presents the condition where sufficient microsite differentiation exists to both support and segregate species, allowing coexistence and higher richness. In addition to continued work in the forests that I have been studying for 23 years, there is a need for datasets from other communities to support or refute this hypothesis.

Heterogeneity Cycle Hypothesis

Land-use history and stand successional age may also explain species richness dynamics. In all the mature stands that I have sampled, there is a well-developed microtopography, the stand ages are between 85 and 125 years, and each was grazed (not plowed) before abandonment with subsequent successional development. However, in the mosaic of forests and old fields of the Huyck Preserve, there are stands that vary in age from very young stands (~ 25 years) to much older stands (150 years or more) and that vary in land-use history. Plowing versus grazing creates different scales and intensities of heterogeneity in these forests. Plowing obliterates microtopography, leaving a much more uniform soil surface with lower heterogeneity. Grazing preserves much of the previous microtopography, so that a young successional forest will have some degree of spatial heterogeneity. In both cases, as the forest regrows, trees will reach sufficient age and size to uproot and begin creating new mound-pit microsites. This process accumulates with stand age, adding to and often reworking the microtopography and degree of heterogeneity. However, the stand regenerating on a plowed surface begins with very low heterogeneity, whereas the one on a grazed surface initially has a moderate to high heterogeneity (a legacy from previous forests before clearing). It may take several generations of tree fall activity for the plowed site to redevelop the heterogeneity of the grazed sites. In contrast, a truly old-growth stand would have possibly the greatest development of microtopography and degree of heterogeneity.

For the northeastern U.S. landscape, I propose three pathways that are important in the development of spatial heterogeneity in forests (fig. 8.9). The old-growth model (center box in fig. 8.9) continuously generates and accumulates microtopography through the process of tree fall and gap regeneration. These mounds and pits likely last centuries (Lyford and MacLean 1966). A land-use disturbance cycle involving clearing and/or grazing followed by abandonment (lower portion of fig. 8.9) could lead to a period of decreased heterogeneity with redevelopment through the successional recovery process. This should produce an intermediate level of heterogeneity compared to the old-growth stand. Finally, a land-use disturbance cycle that involved plowing and complete loss of microtopography (upper portion of fig. 8.9) would result in a successional stand with little or no heterogeneity initially, and a long process of reaccumulation of microrelief to follow. This stand would have the lowest level of

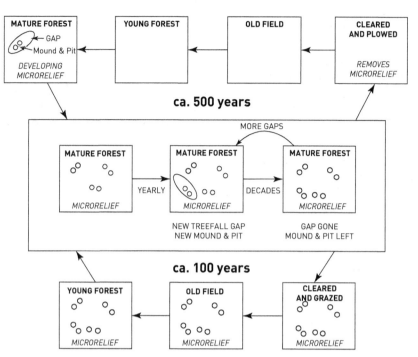

FIGURE 8.9 Cycles of change in northeastern deciduous forest landscapes. Microsite heterogeneity is generated internally within mature forests via the tree fall uprooting process. Exogenous anthropogenic disturbances initiate longer term cycles of regrowth and can alter the fine-scale nature of the soil substrate.

spatial heterogeneity. If there were repeated forest-clearing activities, a cycle of declining heterogeneity could result, depending on the nature of the land use. In addition, when assessing the effect of stand age on composition and richness, this effect of land use on heterogeneity may play a role that is independent of succession. Chapter 14 (this volume) discusses other land-use practices and their effects on substrates.

Based on studies in deciduous forest communities, I propose a general heterogeneity cycle hypothesis, which states that many communities may have persistent forms of spatial heterogeneity that come about through cycles of creation and destruction of heterogeneity and that the position of a community in this cycle may impact how or whether heterogeneity has any effect on richness. In work I have done in chaparral ecosystems in the Mediterranean climate of southern California (Beatty 1987a), I discovered a cycle of heterogeneity related to shrub effects on soil and the fire cycle. Different chaparral shrub species affect soils differently, creating a strong pattern of heterogeneity in physical and chemical properties that intensifies as a stand becomes older (Beatty 1987b). However, fire acts to reset the heterogeneity level to almost zero (very homogeneous surface) (Beatty 1989). Therefore, the fire return interval is important not only to species adaptations to fire recovery, but to the degree of generation of surface soil heterogeneity. In addition, those chaparral communities on the channel islands, which have much longer fire intervals (well over 150 years for Santa Cruz Island), may have a much better developed soil heterogeneity, which may play a role in understory species dynamics (this needs to be tested). These older island stands are up to 30 m in height, have a more open canopy, and have a substantial understory (Beatty and Licari 1992). I suggest that investigation of fine-scale heterogeneity in soils of coniferous forests, which also have fire cycles, might be another community in which to test the heterogeneity cycle hypothesis. As for deciduous forests in the eastern United States, just looking at stand age and species richness relationships may give an unrealistic view of a successional process, if the land use and heterogeneity are confounding factors not taken into account. Because heterogeneity may indeed be important in maintaining species richness of communities, knowing how the land-use history interacts with the development of heterogeneity can be a useful management, conservation, and restoration tool.

CONCLUSIONS

The species richness of forest understory communities can be affected by numerous spatial and temporal factors. Depending on the geographic location of the forested community, factors operating at a coarse scale, such as disturbance (tree fall, massive blowdown, fire, insect outbreak, land-use change), can substantially alter the successional development of a community (chapter 21, this volume). On a finer scale and usually a shorter timeframe, an underlying spatial heterogeneity within a community can affect local distributions, richness, and yearly variation in population sizes. At an even finer scale, dynamics within microsites themselves (competition, colonization, and extinction events) can determine the presence or absence of species or affect species reproductive success and productivity. A landscape mosaic exists because of the stand-destroying or perturbing effects at the coarser scale, and this mosaic can also affect the finer-scale, within-community dynamics by providing varying sources of species for colonization of new and existing microsites. The heterogeneity in a landscape and within a community is an important feature affecting species richness in understory communities.

The results and predictions made in this chapter have great potential for management, conservation, and restoration, as well as preservation. Because communities chosen (obtained) for preservation are often patches within mosaic landscapes (lots of edge effect, little interior), the exogenous factors (physical and biological) are likely to be very important. Knowing whether target forest species have suitable microsites may be crucial to their maintenance in a spatially limited community. In addition, how do exogenous factors affect these microsites (e.g., colonization by exotics, overland flow deposition or erosion, wind redistribution of leaf litter, browsing or herbivory effects that might shift competitive interactions in a microsite)? In a restoration plan, one could consider whether producing additional microsites might promote species maintenance. An important consideration is whether an increase in species richness is always a positive development. Many factors can increase richness in the understory of a forest community, but often this increase is due to the addition of species exotic to the forest community or geographic region (chapters 7, 13, and 21 this volume). In many cases in the arid western United States, exotic species exploit conditions or microsites not occupied by natives and gain a foothold in a community, with negative impacts for many natives. However, in the moist deciduous forest of the northeast, the few exotic species are usually considered naturalized and an established part of the forest community. None of the naturalized species in my study sites are aggressive colonizers, nor do they appear to affect other forest species distributions. The non-forest exotics that colonize new mound-pit formations do not persist beyond 15 years (in my experimental study), so disturbance does not facilitate permanent invasion of exotics.

Because much attention has been paid to the importance of maintaining a natural disturbance regime in conservation efforts, I suggest we also pay attention to whether we need to maintain a certain heterogeneity regime (intensity and cycle), and what impacts this might have on native and nonnative species composition.

SUMMARY

This chapter has explored some of the mechanisms by which heterogeneity may act as a liability and as a benefit to maintaining species in the community. In most cases, for the deciduous forest communities in the northeastern United States that I have studied, spatial heterogeneity (mound-pit microrelief) appears to provide a means by which species are maintained in the community. This maintenance may be a result of the presence of a specialized microsite in which a species finds a tolerable environment with minimal competition (pits), or the presence of a keystone competitor in a rich microsite (mounds) that allows coexistence of numerous species with lower population sizes by preventing other potential dominants from exerting greater influence. Those species whose spatial distributions include multiple microsites also have the added benefit of being buffered against moderate to severe environmental fluctuations. Colonization increases in years when conditions are favorable in a given site. Even though localized extinction may also result in unfavorable years, the loss is not uniform among microsites, thus ensuring that some individuals survive. Those species restricted to one microsite, however, suffer a greater variability in population size with environmental fluctuation and have a higher risk of local extinction. For these species, the heterogeneity may limit available space and serve as a liability.

Given the role of heterogeneity in these forest communities and the prevalence of land-use changes over the past 200 years in the northeastern United States, the interaction of these factors should be taken into account in any study of richness of a community. The proposed intermediate heterogeneity hypothesis suggests that an intermediate level of heterogeneity will promote greater species richness in a community. Extreme microsites may shift the balance toward a liability effect, restricting species composition. Lack of microsites may increase overall competition with greater species overlap and may not provide necessary safe sites for some species. The proposed heterogeneity cycle hypothesis suggests that the current level of heterogeneity in a community is likely the result of past events that either create/enhance the number of microsites or destroy/obliterate microsites. Plowing and intense compaction from overgrazing obliterate mounds and pits so that a second-growth forest on such land will have a much lower spatial heterogeneity for the understory. An old second-growth stand on land not plowed will retain microtopography from the original stand and continue to create new tree fall mounds and pits with age. This stand will have a higher spatial heterogeneity. Therefore, stand age alone should not necessarily be used to predict richness patterns through succession, as there are other confounding factors affecting that richness.

9 Interactions between the Herbaceous Layer and Overstory Canopy of Eastern Forests

A Mechanism for Linkage

Frank S. Gilliam and Mark. R. Roberts

The concept of linkage among strata of forest vegetation has received increasing attention in the ecological literature (e.g., Gilliam 2007; Barbier et al. 2008; Martin et al. 2011; Vockenhuber et al. 2011), and understanding the reciprocating effects of overstory and herbaceous layers offers important insights into the structure and function of forest ecosystems (Bump et al. 2009; McEwan and Muller 2009; Burton et al. 2011; Peterson and Drewa 2011; Bartels and Chen 2012), including implications for both basic and applied studies in forest ecology. For example, community mapping studies may rely on the dominant overstory strata as interpreted from aerial photographs or satellite imagery to represent the entire community. Conversely, site classification systems may use herbaceous layer vegetation to represent communities and their relationships to environmental factors (Cajander 1926; Rowe 1956; Pregitzer and Barnes 1992; Gazol and Ibáñez 2009). In such studies, an understanding of relationships between vegetation strata is necessary if interpretations are to be made concerning the entire community.

This information is generally lacking in disturbed stands because site classification studies are usually carried out in mature stands. As increasing proportions of forested areas become disturbed, it is a critical to know whether the same overstory-understory relationships that occur in mature stands are also found in disturbed stands. Also, the need to manage for biodiversity, a need now recognized by national and global forestry organizations (Burton et al. 1992; Roberts and Gilliam 1995a), requires a shift in focus away from the small number of commercially important tree species toward all plant species, including noncommercial tree and herbaceous species. Thus, the nature of interactions among forest strata and their response to forestry practices need to be understood to maintain biodiversity (Gilliam and Roberts 1995).

In this chapter, we have three primary objectives. First, we determine via literature review what is known of interaction among forest strata, with a specific focus on overstory-herbaceous layer interactions in eastern deciduous forests. We present contrasting views of the nature of these interactions, from one that sees a quantifiable linkage among strata to one that sees little true interaction occurring. Second, we develop a mechanistic explanation for patterns of linkage in forest ecosystems, with emphasis on eastern deciduous forests. Finally, we examine data from two different forest types, a central Appalachian hardwood forest and a successional aspen forest of northern lower Michigan, for evidence supporting or refuting this explanation.

THE NATURE OF LINKAGE AMONG FOREST STRATA

Studies of secondary succession have often emphasized changes in only dominant species in a single stratum of vegetation. For example, studies of old-field succession in the North Carolina Piedmont (e.g., Oosting 1942; Keever 1950, 1983; Christensen and Peet 1984; De Steven 1991b) have focused on the shift from herb-dominated communities early in succession to pine-dominated and then hardwood-dominated communities later and thus have not examined the herbaceous layer that develops beneath the woody overstory during these later stages of old-field succession (but see chapter 11, this volume). Indeed, despite the increasing number of studies of the herbaceous layer in forest communities (see fig. 1.2), few consider interactions among strata in any forest type.

Influence of the Overstory on the Herbaceous Layer

There is little argument that the forest overstory and herbaceous layer exert reciprocating influences on each other. The forest overstory has a direct effect on the availability of resources to herb layer species, the most obvious being to decrease the quantity and alter the quality of light reaching the forest floor (chapter 3, this volume). Other effects would include decreasing nutrient and moisture availability by competitive uptake by fine roots of trees. Although he did not speculate about mechanisms, Rogers (1981) found nearly 20 percent higher species richness and around 70 percent higher cover for the herb layer of mature mesophytic stands (Minnesota to Michigan) with little or no *Fagus grandifolia* Ehrh. compared to that of stands with *F. grandifolia* codominance in the overstory. Crozier and Boerner (1984) reported tree species-specific differences in microhabitat conditions (e.g., different levels of soil nutrients caused by differences in stemflow chemistry) that resulted in spatial variation in cover of dominant herb species. Hill and Silander (2001) found that spatial dynamics of dominant ferns of mixed hardwoods-hemlock stands of Connecticut varied significantly among dominant tree canopy species (i.e., there was a species-specific effect of individual trees on distribution of ferns). They ascribed these differences in fern species dynamics to different light regimes among contrasting stand types.

Other studies have emphasized the importance of detrital inputs to the forest floor by overstory species. Whitney and Foster (1988) found substantial differences in percent occurrence of numerous herb layer species in conifer and hardwood stands in New England, suggesting that, in addition to variation in soil moisture and light regimes, such differences resulted from contrasts in physical and chemical characteristics of litter of conifer versus hardwood species. Nemati and Goetz (1995) made similar conclusions for herb layer differences in stands of *Pinus ponderosa* Dougl. ex Laws. versus *Quercus gambelii* Nutt. Saetre et al. (1997) found that abundance of herb layer species was lower under pure *Picea abies* (L.) Karst. stands than under mixed *P. abies/Betula* stands. They proposed that foliar litter from *Betula* (and associated higher fertility) was the most important cause of such pronounced stand-related differences in the herb layer. McGee (2001) determined that decaying logs of dead overstory species provided sites for early establishment critical for some, but not all, herb layer species, suggesting an additional influence of the overstory on species composition of the herbaceous layer.

Influence of the Herbaceous Layer on the Overstory

Although the influence of the herbaceous layer on the overstory of forests may not be as obvious as that of the overstory on the herb layer, it is potentially as profound (Maguire and Forman 1983). In chapter 1, we discussed the temporal and spatial dynamics of resident and transient species of the herb layer, with resident species being the truly herbaceous (non-woody) annual, biennial, and perennial component of the herb layer, and transient species being predominantly seedlings and sprouts of tree species. Although resident and transient species exhibit contrasting life histories, they share common resources when co-occurring in the herb layer. Maguire and Forman (1983) demonstrated that cover and composition of herbaceous species (residents) determined, in part, the density and distribution of seedlings of dominant tree species (transients) in an old-growth hemlock-hardwood forest.

Because of their typical growth characteristics that often include a dense spreading of fronds, fern species can have a particularly profound effect on survivorship and growth of juveniles of forest overstory species. Horsley (1993a) demonstrated a species-specific interference of *Dennstaedtia punctilobula* (Michx.) limiting growth of seedlings of *Prunus serotina* Ehrh. in hardwood forests of the Allegheny region of Pennsylvania. George and Bazzaz (1999a,b) showed that high fern cover in a New England hardwood forest can function as a species-specific filter, affecting emergence and survival of tree species. This has particular ecological significance in the context of response of eastern hardwood forests to disturbance (chapter 14, this volume).

Linkage as Reported in the Literature

Several studies have reported significant relationships between species' patterns in overstory and herbaceous strata. Using canonical correlations between principal component axes, Gagnon and Bradfield (1986) concluded that tree and herb strata of coastal Vancouver Island forests were linked via their response to predominant site gradients. Roberts and Christensen (1988) combined canonical correlation analysis (CCA) with detrended correspondence analysis (DCA) to examine vegetation strata of successional aspen stands of northern lower Michigan; they attributed significant correlations between strata to soil factors and disturbance regime. Hermy (1988) demonstrated correlations between strata in deciduous forests of Belgium, concluding that the degree of correspondence between compositional patterns was directly proportional to β-diversity. Working in upland hardwood forests of northwestern lower Michigan, Host and Pregitzer (1992) determined that significant tree-herb linkages resulted from similar responses of strata to environmental and historical factors, citing moisture availability as especially predominant. Nemati and Goetz (1995) described a linkage between *Pinus ponderosa/Quercus gambelii* overstory and herbaceous understory by correlating canonical variable scores of the overstory to those for the herb layer. They concluded that linkage resulted from a variety of factors, but emphasized the importance of canopy-mediated changes in environmental conditions for herb layer species, such as light availability and soil acidity. Gilliam et al. (1995) studied interactions between the overstory and herb layer in second-growth hardwood forests of West Virginia. They found evidence of linkage for mature stands, but not for young (20-year old, even-aged) stands, and concluded that linkage changes through secondary succession, becoming tighter over time after disturbance.

Other studies, however, have concluded that forest strata do not form significant linkages. Looking at β-diversity in undisturbed *Fagus grandifolia* communities of the Great Smoky Mountains National Park, North Carolina, Bratton (1975) also found significant responses of species diversity to a moisture gradient. In contrast to Host and Pregitzer (1992), however, Bratton determined that overstory and herbaceous understory strata responded to this gradient in a manner that was neither linear nor parallel between strata.

Sagers and Lyon (1997) found that species associations in riparian forests of the Buffalo National River, Arkansas, were strongly influenced by gradients of pH and elevation. They concluded that forest strata largely responded to these gradients independently. They referred to this independent response as "incongruence" and suggested several possible reasons for its occurrence, including (1) environmental gradients appearing continuous at the landscape scale may be discontinuous at the local scale; and (2) each forest stratum may respond to a disturbance (in this case, largely flooding of riparian zones) in ways distinct from other strata (Lyon and Sagers 1998).

One of the more compelling arguments against the existence of linkage among forest strata was presented by McCune and Antos (1981). They reviewed earlier work in Europe (e.g., Lippmaa 1939) and North America (e.g., Cain 1936) that rejected the notion of linkage and instead urged a "synusial approach" to studying forest communities—taking a view that each stratum of a forest comprises a community (synusia) to be considered a distinct unit of vegetation (Oosting 1956). More important, McCune and Antos (1981) tested for linkage among five strata in forest stands of Swan Valley, Montana, using correlation of dissimilarity matrices, Bray-Curtis polar ordination, and cluster analysis. The different strata changed in composition across environmental gradients at neither the same rate nor in the same pattern (McCune and Antos 1981). They further concluded that apparent linkages, when found, can be artifacts of diversity across large sample areas. By sampling over large areas, it might be possible to encounter, for example, a conifer stand with its associated herbaceous component and a hardwood stand with its contrasting associated herbaceous component. Ordination of such data would produce two discontinuous clusters of plots and might lead to a spurious conclusion that the herbaceous and overstory components are closely linked.

Thus, part of the debate over the existence of linkage among forest strata appears to have arisen from studies that have addressed the question at different spatial scales.

Those working at the landscape scale (e.g., McCune and Antos 1981) have not found linkage to occur. We suggest that linkage is a phenomenon that does indeed occur in forest ecosystems, but that it operates at spatial scales smaller than the landscape.

Linkage may arise in two ways: (1) from similarities among strata in response to the same environmental factors (e.g., Gagnon and Bradfield 1986; Hermy 1988; Roberts and Christensen 1988; Host and Pregitzer 1992), or (2) from direct and reciprocating influences of the overstory and the understory on each other. The second mechanism has been documented for many forest types at fine spatial scales (e.g., 1-m² plots) as the influence of individual canopy trees on herbaceous layer species (Everett et al. 1983; Turner and Franz 1986; Joyce and Baker 1987; Tyler 1989; Nemati and Goetz 1995; Berger and Puettmann 2000; Hill and Silander 2001) via various mechanisms including changes in soil acidity and fertility, light availability, or physical effects of litter under canopy trees.

More recent literature has supported these mechanisms to explain linkage in temperate and conifer forests alike (Barbier et al. 2008; Chandy and Gibson 2009; Chávez and Macdonald 2010), with several emphasizing the importance of disturbance (chapter 14, this volume) in altering overstory/herb layer interactions (Ellum et al. 2010; Belote and Jones 2009; Belote et al. 2009; Fleming and Baldwin 2008; Durak 2012).

A MECHANISM FOR LINKAGE BETWEEN FOREST STRATA

It is notable that the reciprocating effects between overstory and herbaceous layer suggested in studies such as Maguire and Forman (1983) and Gilliam et al. (1995) occurred in mature forests. However, up through the thinning phase of secondary forest succession (chapter 11, this volume), the overstory and herb strata respond to different sets of environmental factors. Overstory composition at this time in succession is governed largely by competition for light (described by Bormann and Likens [1979] as the exploitive strategy), whereas herb layer growth and composition are determined largely by availability of moisture and nutrients (Gilliam and Turrill 1993; Morris et al. 1993; Wilson and Shure 1993). As the stand approaches a steady state, the overstory becomes dominated by shade-tolerant species that were able to survive beneath the initial canopy of intolerant species. The new canopy is more closed and stratified and alters light conditions for herb layer species (chapter 3, this volume; Brown and Parker 1994). Seedlings and sprouts of woody species often increase (relative to herbaceous species) in the herb layer because of more light-limited conditions (Wilson and Shure 1993; Gilliam et al. 1995; Walters and Reich 1997). Woody species also exhibit greater relative abundance at this time because of an increase in the number of juveniles from late successional overstory species that are typically prolific seed producers. The result of successional change, then, is that the two strata start responding to similar environmental gradients, establishing and intensifying the linkage between overstory and herbaceous layer (Gilliam et al. 1995). This leads us to pose the following hypothesis as a mechanism of linkage between forest strata: Linkage among forest strata arises from parallel responses of strata to similar environmental gradients.

One of the challenges of testing such a mechanism is establishing the appropriate environmental gradients to which species may be responding. Direct gradient

techniques are possible by stratifying sampling along a known gradient, such as elevation in a forested watershed (Barbour et al. 1999). This, however, has the limitation
of presuming that the chosen gradient (e.g., elevation) is indeed an overriding factor
influencing both species composition and gradients of other important environmental factors (e.g., moisture and soil nutrients). Indirect gradient techniques are also
possible, wherein a multivariate method, such as DCA, is used to generate ordination axis scores for plots. Axis scores are then correlated to environmental variables
measured at each plot (McCarthy et al. 1987; Roberts and Christensen 1988; Gilliam
et al. 1993; Sagers and Lyon 1997). This has the obvious limitation of presuming that
ordination axis scores and environmental variables are related in an inherently linear
fashion.

Palmer (1993) assessed the advantages of yet another multivariate analytical
approach, CCA (ter Braak 1986). In addition to pointing out the numerous improve-
ments of CCA over DCA, Palmer (1993) showed that the output from CCA contains
an important feature that is germane to testing our gradient-based hypothesis of linkage. Because CCA performs a least-squares regression of plot scores (species' weighted
averages) as dependent variables onto environmental variables as independent variables, CCA is a form of direct gradient analysis (Palmer 1993). In addition to generating
ordination diagrams with plot and species locations, CCA also generates environmental vectors originating from the center of the ordination space. The lengths of these
vectors represent the gradient lengths of each measured environmental variable, such
that vector length is proportional to the importance of an environmental gradient in
explaining species' patterns. Thus, shorter lines represent gradients of lesser importance, and longer lines represent gradients of more importance. Accordingly, whether
the herbaceous layer and overstory are responding to environmental gradients in a
similar fashion may be assessed by performing CCA on each stratum separately for a
given stand age and then comparing vector lengths of herb layer versus overstory on a
gradient-by-gradient basis.

Using such an approach, we examined two datasets for evidence of whether herbaceous and overstory layers respond to similar gradients. The datasets are each from
a different site and study: the Fernow Experimental Forest (FEF) in Tucker County,
West Virginia, and the University of Michigan Biological Station (UMBS) in northern
lower Michigan. Because these were carried out as unrelated studies, they were not
done using identical sampling methods. Nonetheless, the important environmental
gradients thought to control species distributions were quantified as appropriate in
each study, including stand structural variables, as well as soil nutrient and moisture
variables.

STUDY SITES

Fernow Experimental Forest

FEF, an approximately 1900 ha area of largely montane hardwood forests in the
Allegheny Mountain section of the unglaciated Allegheny Plateau, is located in Tucker
County, north-central West Virginia. Mean annual precipitation is approximately
1,430 mm, with most precipitation occurring during the growing season (Gilliam
and Adams 1996a). Four contiguous watersheds were selected for this study: WS7 and
WS3 were about 20 year-old, even-aged stands that developed following clearcutting

Table 9.1 Important overstory (live woody stems ≥ 2.5 cm diameter at 1.3 m height) species of young versus mature stands of FEF. Data are mean importance values (sum of relative basal area and relative density) for two watersheds per age class. Nomenclature follows Gleason and Cronquist (1991).

Species	Stand Age Class	
	Young[1]	Mature[2]
Acer pensylvanicum L.	5	5
A. saccharum	33	90
Betula lenta	19	–
Fagus grandifolia	5	14
Fraxinus americana	10	2
Liriodendron tulipifera	16	5
Prunus serotina	76	20
Quercus prinus L.	–	12
Q. rubra	7	30
Robinia pseudoacacia L.	6	–
Sassafras albidum (Nutt.) Nees	6	–

[1] Young—20 yrs (FEF), 1–20 yrs (UMBS)

[2] Mature—> 80 yrs (FEF), 55–167 yrs (UMBS)

(hereafter "young" stands); WS13 and WS4 were uneven-aged stands (> 80 years old, hereafter "mature" stands).

Study watersheds at FEF support primarily mixed hardwood stands, with dominant trees varying with stand age. Early successional species, such as *Betula lenta* L., *Prunus serotina*, and *Liriodendron tulipifera* L. are dominant in young stands, whereas late successional species, such as *Acer saccharum* Marshall and *Quercus rubra* L., are dominant in mature stands (table 9.1). Dominant herbaceous layer species vary less with stand age and include *Laportea canadensis* (L.) Wedd., *Viola* spp., and several ferns, including *Dryopteris marginalis* L. Gray and *Polystichum acrostichoides* Michx. Schott. (table 9.2).

Soils are similar among study watersheds. These are relatively thin (< 1m in depth), acidic, sandy-loam Inceptisols of two series: Berks (loamy-skeletal, mixed, mesic Typic Dystrochrept) and Calvin (loamy-skeletal, mixed, mesic Typic Dystrochrept) (Gilliam et al. 1994). Soils of the study watersheds are generally acidic, but are high in organic matter, resulting in high cation exchange capacity (table 9.3).

University of Michigan Biological Station

The UMBS study was conducted within a five-county (Cheboygan, Emmet, Charlevois, Otsego, Montmorency) region of northern lower Michigan. Climatic conditions are relatively uniform throughout the area, with an average annual precipitation of 770 mm and an average annual temperature of 6.2–6.7°C. Precipitation is distributed relatively evenly throughout the year (Albert et al. 1986).

Soils of the study area are Spodosols derived from parent materials of contrasting glacial origin. Study sites encompass a broader range of soil conditions than FEF, from

Table 9.2 Important herbaceous layer (vascular plants ≤ 1m tall) species of young versus mature stands of FEF. Data are mean importance values (sum of relative cover and relative frequency) for two watersheds per age class. Nomenclature follows Gleason and Cronquist (1991).

Species	Stand Age Class	
	Young[1]	Mature[2]
Acer pensylvanicum L.	7	17
Dryopteris marginalis	30	6
Laportea canadensis	17	27
Polygonatum biflorum (Walter) Elliot	–	10
Polystichum acrostichoides	9	15
Prunus serotina	9	5
Rubus spp.	12	4
Sassafras albidum (Nutt.) Nees	8	–
Smilax rotundifolia L.	14	9
Viola spp.	20	20

[1] Young—20 yrs (FEF), 1–20 yrs (UMBS)

[2] Mature—> 80 yrs (FEF), 55–167 yrs (UMBS)

dry mesic sites with soils of the Rubicon series (sandy, mixed, frigid Entic Haplorthods) derived from glacial outwash deposits, to mesic soils of the Montcalm series (sandy, mixed, frigid Alfic Haplorthods) derived from glacial till (Roberts and Richardson 1985; Roberts and Christensen 1988). In general, these soils are acidic and low in organic matter, with extractable nutrients supplied largely from organic constituents (table 9.3).

The pre-settlement forests within the region were predominantly northern hardwoods such as *Fagus grandifolia* and *A. saccharum* on mesic sites and coniferous species including *Pinus resinosa* Aiton, *P. strobus* L., and *Tsuga canadensis* (L.) Carriere on the dry mesic sites (Kilburn 1957). From 1850 to 1920, extensive logging of the pine and hardwood forests occurred, followed by wildfires (Gates 1930; Kilburn 1957). Thus, the mature stands (55–167 years old) in the present study are second-growth stands that originated from cutting and burning. The young stands (≤ 20 years old) originated from clearcutting (without burning) of these mature second-growth stands.

In our sample, *Populus grandidentata* Michx. had the highest importance value for trees in young stands, in contrast to mature stands where *Acer rubrum* L. and *A. saccharum* shared dominance with *P. grandidentata*. Mature stands contained a greater variety of secondary species than young stands, including *Fagus grandifolia*, *Quercus rubra*, *Fraxinus americana* L., *Pinus strobus*, and *P. resinosa* (table 9.4).

Herbaceous layer dominants in young stands included several early successional species, such as *Pteridium aquilinum* (L.) Kuhn, *Rubus ideaus* L., *R. allegheniensis* T. C. Porter, and *Fragaria virginiana* Duchesne (table 9.5). Dominant species in the herb layer in mature stands included seedlings of shade-tolerant to mid-tolerant tree species, such as *A. saccharum*, *Fagus grandifolia*, *Ostrya virginiana* (Miller) K. Koch, *Fraxinus americana*, and shade-tolerant herbaceous species like *Maianthemum canadense* Desf.

Table 9.3 Means of environmental variables used in CCA of young versus mature stands at FEF and UMBS. Means of all measured variables, except for elevation, are compared between stand age classes with a t-test. Asterisk indicates significant difference between age classes for a given variable at $p < 0.05$; NS indicates no significant difference at $p < 0.05$. Data summarized from previous studies at FEF (Gilliam 2002) and UMBS (Roberts and Gilliam 1995b).

Variable		Stand Age Class (FEF)			Stand Age Class (UMBS)		
		Young[1]		Mature[2]	Young[1]		Mature[2]
Elevation (range in m)		725–860		735–870			
Tree basal area (m²/ha)		22.5	*	42.8	10.8	*	22.8
Tree density (stems/ha)		2099	*	854			
Texture (%)	Sand	67.3	NS	65.7			
	Clay	10.8	NS	9.0			
	Silt	22.0	NS	25.4			
BD (g/cm³) [3]					1.06	*	1.13
WAI (%)[4]					2.62	NS	2.93
Organic matter (%)		13.8	NS	12.6	5.1	*	3.8
C.E.C. (μmol$_c$/g)		45.5	NS	40.1			
pH		4.39	NS	4.32	5.04	*	4.58
Nutrients (μg/g)	NO$_3$	1.3	NS	0.9			
	NH$_4$	2.1	NS	1.9			
	PO$_4$	0.8	NS	0.4	6.0	NS	4.3
	Ca	12.6	NS	6.4	826	NS	496
	Mg	2.1	NS	2.4	60.8	NS	41.0
	K	2.3	NS	2.2	54.3	*	33.4

[1] Young—20 yrs (FEF), 1–20 yrs (UMBS)

[2] Mature—> 80 yrs (FEF), 55–167 yrs (UMBS)

[3] Bulk density (disturbed)

[4] Water availability index (water content by weight between –0.033 MPa and –1.5 MPa moisture potential)

FIELD SAMPLING

Fernow Experimental Forest

Fifteen circular 0.04 ha sample plots were established in each watershed. In each plot, all woody stems > 2.5 cm diameter at about 1.3 m in height (dbh) were tallied, identified, and measured for diameter at breast height to the nearest 0.1 cm. The herbaceous layer was sampled by identifying and estimating cover of all vascular plants 1 m in height within ten 1-m² circular subplots in each sample plot, using a visual estimation method as described in Gilliam and Turrill (1993). Subplots were located within sample plots using a stratified random polar coordinates method (Gaiser 1951).

Methods for sampling mineral soil also have been described previously (Gilliam and Turrill 1993; Gilliam et al. 1994). Briefly, two 10-cm-deep samples were taken from each plot and placed into separate bags; thus, values for each plot represent the average of two soil samples. Each sample was sieved (2-mm screen), air-dried, and

Table 9.4 Important overstory (live woody stems ≥ 2.5 cm diameter at 1.3 m height) species of young versus mature stands of UMBS. Data are mean importance values (sum of relative basal area and relative density) for 25 (young age class) and 36 (mature age class) stands. Nomenclature follows Gleason and Cronquist (1991).

Species	Stand Age Class	
	Young[1]	Mature[2]
Acer pensylvanicum	–	4
A. rubrum	26	46
A. saccharum	10	33
Amelanchier spp.	6	–
Fagus grandifolia	–	10
Fraxinus americana	–	6
Ostrya virginiana	–	4
Pinus resinosa	–	6
P. strobus	–	5
Populus grandidentata	60	40
P. tremuloides	–	21
Quercus rubra	6	15

[1] Young—20 yrs (FEF), 1–20 yrs (UMBS)

[2] Mature—> 80 yrs (FEF), 55–167 yrs (UMBS)

Table 9.5 Important herbaceous layer (vascular plants ≤ 1m tall) species of young versus mature stands of UMBS. Data are mean importance values (sum of relative cover and relative frequency). Nomenclature follows Gleason and Cronquist (1991).

Species	Stand Age Class	
	Young[1]	Mature[2]
Pteridium aquilinum	43	9
Acer saccharum	13	45
Rubus ideaus	10	–
Fragaria virginiana	9	–
Rubus allegheniensis	8	–
Fraxinus americana	7	12
A. rubrum	6	14
Ostrya virginiana	5	15
Maianthemum canadense	3	20
Fagus grandifolia	1	15

[1] Young—20 yrs (FEF), 1–20 yrs (UMBS)

[2] Mature—> 80 yrs (FEF), 55–167 yrs (UMBS)

analyzed for pH (1:1 weight:volume, soil:water), 1 N KCl-extractable calcium, potassium, magnesium, and phosphorous (with plasma emission), 1 N KCl-extractable NO_3 and NH_4 (with flow-injection colorimetry), and organic matter (loss-on-ignition method). Particle size (texture) was determined for each soil sample using the hydrometer method.

Data were taken from 0.1 ha (20 × 50 m) plots, one plot located in each of 61 stands. Stands were selected that were at least 0.5 ha and were relatively undisturbed since the last disturbance. A single plot was located near the center of each stand in an area that was representative of the stand composition and soil conditions. In each plot, trees (woody stems > 1 m tall) were sampled as described in Roberts and Christensen (1988). Importance values for tree species (IVT) were calculated as relative density + relative basal area. Percent cover of species in the herbaceous layer (all vascular plants < 1 m in height) was visually estimated in 25 0.5 × 2.0 m contiguous quadrats extending along the plot center line. Percent cover and frequency (proportion of quadrats in a plot in which a given species was found) were combined to generate importance values for herb layer species (IVH; relative cover + relative frequency). Species that occurred within the 0.1 ha plot but not sampled in the 0.5 × 2.0 m quadrats were assigned an IVH of 0.001.

Four replicate soil samples were taken from the A1 horizons, one sample from a soil pit adjacent to each plot and the other three at random points along the plot center line. Soil variables (see below) were calculated as mean values ($n = 4$) for each plot. Details of sample preparation and laboratory analysis can be found in Roberts and Christensen (1988). Briefly, after drying and sieving (2-mm screen), soil samples were analyzed for bulk density, water availability (% moisture content, by weight, between -0.033 and -1.5 MPa moisture potential), pH (1:1 soil:H_2O, glass electrode), and organic carbon. After extraction with a dilute acid solution (0.05 M HCl with 0.0125M H_2SO_4), extractable PO_4 was determined by molybdenum blue colorimetry, and extractable calcium, potassium, and magnesium were determined by atomic absorption spectrophotometry.

DATA ANALYSIS

Fernow Experimental Forest

Data for overstory and herbaceous layer species have been reported previously for each watershed separately (Gilliam et al. 1995). Because of minor differences between the two watersheds of each stand age and because of the focus of this chapter on stand age-related comparisons, we combined data into two stand age classes: young (~ 20 years, even age) and mature (> 90 years, mixed age). Stand age means of environmental variables were subjected to t tests between the two age classes.

Gradient lengths of the environmental variables shown in table 9.3 were determined for the herbaceous and overstory strata separately in each age class using CCA. CCA was performed with the computer program CANOCO version 3.10 (ter Braak 1990), a version of the Cornell Ecology program DECORANA (Hill 1979; ter Braak 1987); all program defaults were used. Unlike DCA, CCA focuses on the relationships between plant species and measured environmental variables; thus, it provides direct interpretation of axes in the ordination (ter Braak 1986). All data were ln-transformed before ordination, according to suggestions of Palmer (1993).

Of importance in this chapter is CCA output in the form of trajectories of environmental gradients. CCA yields one trajectory for each environmental factor, the length of which is indicative of the importance of that environmental gradient in explaining species' patterns. We determined gradient lengths for all environmental factors by measuring the length of the lines in the trajectory figure. The focus of this chapter is on the relative importance, as measured by vector length, of environmental factors in influencing species' patterns in young and mature stands. Gradient lengths for herbaceous layer versus overstory ordinations were subjected to Spearman rank correlation for each stand age class (Zar 1996).

University of Michigan Biological Station

Site-dependent changes in soil nutrients and vegetation in these plots have been described elsewhere (Roberts and Gilliam 1995a; Roberts and Christensen 1988). The dry mesic and mesic sites sampled in this study represent the typical variation in site conditions and vegetation composition found in upland forests of the region; thus, we combined stands from both site types for this analysis. Stands were then subdivided into two age classes: young (1–20 years, 25 stands) or mature (55–167 years, 38 stands). These age classes correspond roughly to those used at FEF, although there is clearly a wider range of ages within each of the two age classes at UMBS than at FEF.

Data from UMBS were subjected to CCA, using the same defaults and ln-transformations as used at FEF. The t test (PROC TTEST; SAS Institute Inc. 1985) was used for comparisons of stand and soil variables between stand ages. Gradient lengths of the environmental variables from the herbaceous layer and overstory were measured in a manner identical to that used at FEF.

STAND AGE COMPARISONS OF ENVIRONMENTAL VARIABLES USED IN CCA

Fernow Experimental Forest

The two stand structural variables measured at FEF (tree basal area and stem density) varied significantly ($p < .05$) with stand age (table 9.3). Basal area for the mature stands was nearly twice that of the basal area for the young stands. Conversely, stem density for the young stands was nearly 2.5 times that for the mature stands. Such differences are typical of young versus mature forests: numerous, small stems early in succession followed by competitive thinning, which gives rise to fewer, but much larger, stems later in succession (Yoda et al. 1963; Christensen and Peet 1984). The other environmental data used in CCA for FEF were soil variables, including texture, organic matter, cation exchange capacity (CEC), pH, and extractable (exchangeable) nutrients, none of which varied significantly ($p < .05$) with stand age (table 9.3), confirming conclusions of earlier studies that general soil characteristics varied little across watersheds of sharply contrasting stand ages and histories (Gilliam 2002).

University of Michigan Biological Station

Although overstory basal area was lower at UMBS than at FEF, stand age contrasts were similar among the two study sites. Basal area of the mature stands was just more than twice that of the young stands at UMBS (table 9.3), consistent with the successional thinning process that has been described for this forest type (Roberts and Richardson

1985). In contrast to the results of stand age comparisons for FEF, several soil variables varied significantly with stand age at UMBS. In general, soils of mature stands were more acidic and less fertile than young stands, with soil fertility being largely a function of soil organic matter, which was significantly lower ($p < .05$) in mature stands than in young stands (table 9.3).

CANONICAL CORRESPONDENCE ANALYSIS OF VEGETATION DATA

Individual CCA ordinations were run for both of the vegetation strata (herb layer and overstory) in both stand ages (young and mature) separately, resulting in four ordinations for each site. Original ordination figures (i.e., X-Y graphs of axis 1 by axis 2 scores for sample plots) for these analyses are not given; rather, the axis scores were used to make correlations between strata. In all cases, axis 1 explained the greatest amount of variability in species data; thus, axis 1 scores were used in comparisons between strata. The correlation diagrams produced give a measure of the similarities in the ordering of plots along the first axis in the herbaceous and overstory vegetation ordinations.

Fernow Experimental Forest

Correlations between overstory and herbaceous layer varied with stand age at FEF. The correlation for young stands was not significant at ($p < .05$), whereas that for mature stands was highly significant ($p < .001$; fig. 9.1). Accordingly, we conclude that, although the two strata are not linked in the young stands, they are linked in the mature stands. Another way of viewing this conceptually is to consider the proximity

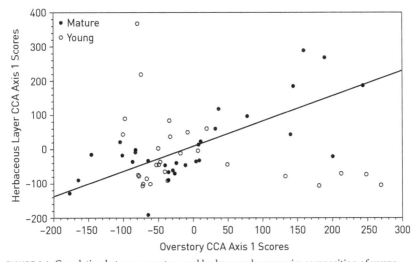

FIGURE 9.1 Correlation between overstory and herbaceous layer species composition of young stands (open symbols) and mature stands (filled symbols) for FEF. Overstory is represented on the X-axis as axis 1 scores from CCA of overstory species data. Herbaceous layer is represented on the Y-axis as axis 1 scores from CCA of herbaceous layer species data. Correlation for young stand plots was not significant ($p < .05$). The line shown is for mature stand plots only ($y = 9.51 + 0.73x$; $r^2 = .54$; $p < .001$).

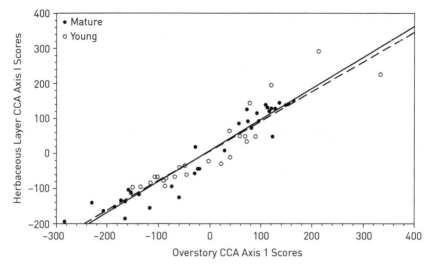

FIGURE 9.2 Correlation between overstory and herbaceous layer species composition of young stands (open symbols) and mature stands (filled symbols) for UMBS. Overstory is represented on the X-axis as axis 1 scores from CCA of overstory species data. Herbaceous layer is represented on the y-axis as axis 1 scores from CCA of herbaceous layer species data. Solid line represents mature stands (y 7.02 + 0.88x; r^2 = .93; p <.001). Dashed line represents young stands (y 5.21 + 0.85x; r^2 = .86; p <.001).

of points in the ordination diagrams. Points that are close to each other in ordination space represent sample plots that have similar species composition; conversely, points distant from each other represent plots that are dissimilar. Thus, a significant correlation between axis 1 scores from each stratum should indicate close similarity in the pattern and degree of spatial variation of species composition (sometimes referred to as *species turnover*) of the two strata. Once again, this degree of linkage appears to be related to stand age at FEF.

University of Michigan Biological Station

In contrast to results for FEF, overstory/herb layer correlations were highly significant (p <.0001) for both young and mature stands at UMBS (fig. 9.2). In fact, regression lines calculated to fit the data are nearly coincidental, with slopes of 0.85 and 0.88 for young and mature stands, respectively. Accordingly, we may conclude that the two strata are linked in these successional aspen forests, but that this occurs in a way that is independent of stand age (or certainly less dependent) than was found in stands at FEF.

ENVIRONMENTAL TRAJECTORIES

As discussed previously, CCA output presents environmental data in the form of trajectories or vectors, one per environmental variable, the length of which is proportional to the importance of that factor (variable) in explaining species' patterns. Each line, along with the arrow, indicates the positive direction of the vector (i.e., increasing values).

CCA ordinations for this part of our discussion (e.g., figs. 9.3–9.10) are presented with vectors only (i.e., without the plot data discussed previously) because (1) the result is an ordination diagram with less clutter, and (2) the environmental trajectories are of primary importance in testing the mechanistic hypothesis for linkage of forest strata. Finally, because these are true vectors (ter Braak 1987, 1990; Palmer 1993), the direction of each line (originating from the center of ordination space) is also important in interpreting the meaning of CCA ordinations. Accordingly, vectors that point in similar directions represent environmental factors that are closely related to each other.

Fernow Experimental Forest

Some of the more important environmental factors for the overstory in young stands at FEF were elevation, stand density, and extractable NO_3 (which was of equal importance with sand content and extractable PO_4); some of the less important factors were cation exchange capacity and extractable calcium and magnesium (fig. 9.3). In addition, elevation and extractable NO_3 were closely related, along with soil organic matter (OM). This suggests that extractable NO_3 and soil OM increase with elevation in a way that is significant in influencing tree species' patterns in young stands. Furthermore, it links OM with the production of NO_3 in the soil, a relationship that has been demonstrated for this site using in situ incubations (Gilliam et al. 1996, 2001).

Environmental trajectories for the herb layer in young stands appeared to contrast sharply with those for the overstory in young stands, especially for extractable PO_4 (fig. 9.4). The most important environmental factors were, in descending order, extractable NO_3, soil OM, and extractable potassium, whereas the least important were, in ascending order, extractable PO_4, pH, and extractable NH_4 (fig. 9.4). The

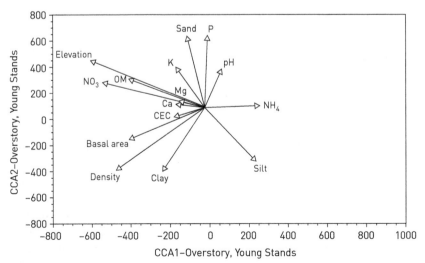

FIGURE 9.3 Environmental trajectories for the overstory of young stands for FEF, resulting from CCA. The length of each line is proportional to the importance of the associated environmental factor in explaining species' patterns among sample plots within stands. CEC, cation exchange capacity; OM, organic matter.

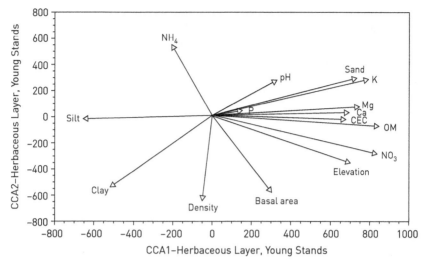

FIGURE 9.4 Environmental trajectories for the herbaceous layer of young stands for FEF, resulting from CCA. The length of each line is proportional to the importance of the associated environmental factor in explaining species patterns among sample plots within stands. CEC, cation exchange capacity; OM, organic matter.

relative importance of both extractable NO_3 and potassium (and lack of importance of extractable NH_4) for the herb layer in young stands supports conclusions of Gilliam et al. (1996) that NO_3 is the predominant form of nitrogen taken up by plants of the herb layer at FEF and that NO_3 is taken up with potassium from these soils. This also confirms findings of numerous studies demonstrating the close correlation between nitrogen uptake and potassium availability (Barber 1995; Marschner 1995).

Environmental factors of importance for the overstory of mature stands differed somewhat from those for the overstory of young stands, suggesting a temporal (successional) shift in responses of tree species to variables such as soil resource availability. In descending order, the more important factors were stand density, soil clay content, soil OM, silt content, and extractable calcium, whereas the less important factors, in ascending order, were CEC, sand content, stand basal area, and extractable magnesium (fig. 9.5).

In contrast to comparisons of overstory versus herb layer for young stands, environmental vectors for the herb layer in mature stands appeared to be quite similar to those for the overstory in mature stands (fig. 9.6). The important factors were, in descending order, extractable NO_3, clay, and stand density, and the unimportant factors were, in ascending order, CEC, stand basal area, sand, and extractable magnesium. In short, the two strata in mature stands showed considerable overlap for environmental factors that were both important and unimportant in explaining species' patterns. Finally, patterns of correlation among environmental variables were similar between strata for mature stands, in contrast to those between strata for young stands. For example, vectors for clay (%) and stand density showed close overlap, as did extractable NO_3 and phosphorus, for both strata in mature stands (figs. 9.5 and 9.6) but not in young stands (figs. 9.3 and 9.4).

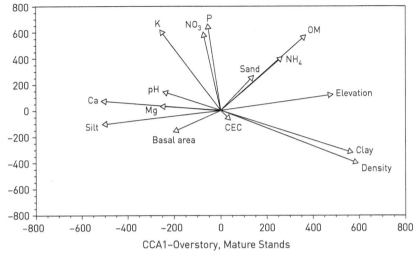

FIGURE 9.5 Environmental trajectories for the overstory of mature stands for FEF, resulting from canonical CCA. The length of each line is proportional to the importance of the associated environmental factor in explaining species patterns among sample plots within stands. CEC, cation exchange capacity; OM, organic matter.

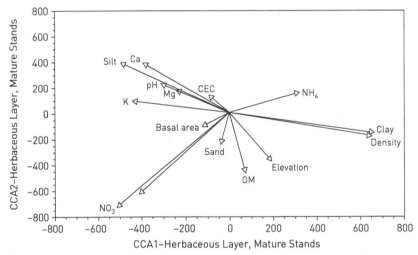

FIGURE 9.6 Environmental trajectories for the herbaceous layer of young stands for FEF, resulting from canonical correspondence analysis (CCA). The length of each line is proportional to the importance of the associated environmental factor in explaining species patterns among sample plots within stands. CEC, cation exchange capacity; OM, organic matter.

University of Michigan Biological Station

The more important environmental factors for the overstory in young stands at UMBS were soil pH and extractable soil calcium, with less important factors being extractable soil potassium and tree basal area (fig. 9.7). In fact, pH and calcium were closely related, each with vectors essentially superimposed on one another, indicating that soil pH is determined in large part by levels of calcium in these soils. Also highly correlated

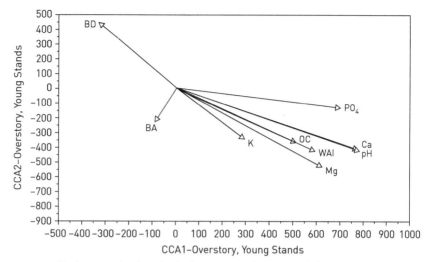

FIGURE 9.7 Environmental trajectories for the overstory of young stands for UMBS, resulting from CCA. The length of each line is proportional to the importance of the associated environmental factor in explaining species patterns among sample plots within stands. BA, basal area; BD, bulk density; OC, organic carbon; WAI, water availability index.

were water availability index and OM, suggesting that OM is important in determining water availability in these coarse-textured, well-drained sandy soils.

Similar to the results for the overstory in young stands at UMBS, the more important environmental factors for the herb layer in young stands were pH and calcium, whereas soil potassium was of lesser importance; however, unlike the overstory, PO_4 was of equally high importance as calcium for the herb layer, and soil bulk density was the least important of all environmental variables (fig. 9.8). Thus, early in succession in these aspen stands, spatial patterns of soil pH, as influenced by soil calcium, appear to exert a pronounced influence on the spatial patterns of composition of both overstory and herb layer species.

Soil calcium was by far the dominant environmental factor influencing species composition of the overstory in mature stands at UMBS, with extractable PO_4 and magnesium of secondary importance (fig. 9.9). Of minor importance were tree basal area and soil potassium, similar to results found for the overstory of young stands (fig. 9.7). As described previously (see Study Sites), these soils are generally acidic and low in fertility and OM, with available nutrients supplied largely from organic constituents; this is seen in the close coincidence of the OM vector with vectors of all extractable nutrients except potassium (fig. 9.9).

Finally, the more important environmental factors for the herb layer in mature stands at UMBS were soil calcium and magnesium, with extractable soil potassium and tree basal area being of minor importance (fig. 9.10), similar to the results found for the overstory of mature stands. In addition, the clustering of OM along with extractable nutrients (other than potassium) for the herb layer in mature stands was similar to that for the overstory in mature stands (fig. 9.9).

CORRELATIONS BETWEEN STRATA

The preceding discussion essentially has been a visual inspection of environmental vector lengths to determine a gradient of importance of specific factors in explaining

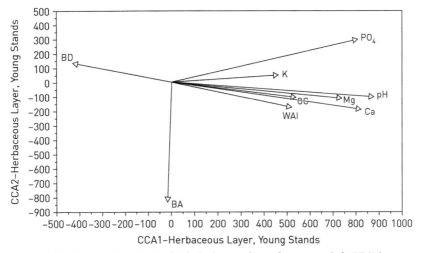

FIGURE 9.8 Environmental trajectories for the herbaceous layer of young stands for UMBS, resulting from CCA. The length of each line is proportional to the importance of the associated environmental factor in explaining species patterns among sample plots within stands. BA, basal area; BD, bulk density; OC, organic carbon; WAI, water availability index.

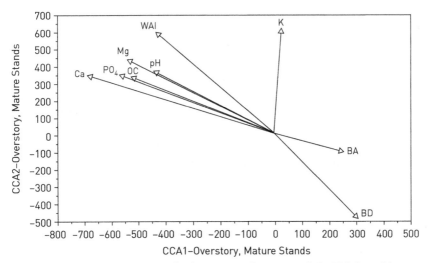

FIGURE 9.9 Environmental trajectories for the overstory of mature stands for UMBS, resulting from CCA. The length of each line is proportional to the importance of the associated environmental factor in explaining species patterns among sample plots within stands. BA, basal area; BD, bulk density; OC, organic carbon; WAI, water availability index.

species patterns for each strata and stand age combination. Quantitative evidence relevant to our mechanistic explanation of linkage can be provided by statistically determining whether the herbaceous layer and overstory are responding to environmental gradients in a parallel fashion. As described earlier in this chapter, because CCA performs a least-squares regression of species-based plot scores as dependent variables onto environmental factors as independent variables (Palmer 1993), it provides a direct quantitative assessment of these responses.

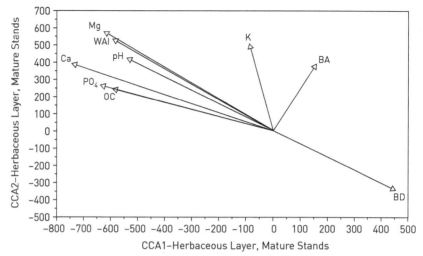

FIGURE 9.10 Environmental trajectories for the herbaceous layer of young stands for UMBS, resulting from CCA. The length of each line is proportional to the importance of the associated environmental factor in explaining species patterns among sample plots within stands. BA, basal area; BD, bulk density; OC, organic carbon; WAI, water availability index.

Accordingly, we can examine the evidence by comparing the rank order of environmental variables (from the most to the least important as determined by vector length) of herb layer versus overstory. Significant correlations in vector lengths between the herb layer and overstory would indicate that the two strata are responding to the same environmental factors to a similar degree. Consequently, considering our previous conclusions about stand age-related linkage at FEF (i.e., strata are not linked early in succession, but become linked later in succession), our mechanistic explanation would be supported only if rank-order correlation is not significant for young stands at FEF but is significant for mature stands. Regarding UMBS, our explanation would be supported only if rank-order correlation is significant for both stand age classes.

Fernow Experimental Forest

The herb layer-overstory correlation for young stands was not significant ($r = .02$, $p <.95$). In contrast, it was highly significant ($r = .92$, $p <.001$) for mature stands (table 9.6). Such stand age-related contrasts in these comparisons support our hypothesis of linkage between forest strata. For FEF, there appears to be a temporal (successional) shift in the degree of linkage. The lack of significant correlation between environmental vector lengths for herb layer and overstory in young stands indicates that the lack of linkage shown in fig. 9.1 is the result of differences in response of these strata to environmental gradients at this point in successional time. The overstory appeared to respond to elevation and stand density, whereas the herb layer responded to factors related to soil fertility, such as soil OM and extractable NO_3 and potassium. Such results for the herb layer are consistent with conclusions of Gilliam and Turrill (1993) at FEF and those of other studies (e.g., Morris et al. 1993; Wilson and Shure 1993) that herb layer development early in forest succession is influenced strongly by competition for soil nutrients.

The significant correlation between environmental vector lengths for herb layer and overstory in mature stands indicates that the high degree of linkage shown in

Table 9.6 Spearman rank correlation coefficients for importance of environmental factors for the herbaceous layer versus overstory of young and mature stands at FEF and UMBS. Importance was measured as length of environmental vector for CCA of each stratum and stand age for the two study sites.

Site	Age Class	Correlation Coefficient	P
FEF	Young[1]	0.02	0.95
FEF	Mature[2]	0.92	0.001
UMBS	Young[1]	0.90	0.01
UMBS	Mature[2]	0.97	0.0001

[1] Young—20 yrs (FEF), 1–20 yrs (UMBS)

[2] Mature—> 80 yrs (FEF), 55–167 yrs (UMBS)

fig. 9.1 is the result of the similar responses of these strata to environmental gradients, including factors related to stand characteristics, such as stand density, and to soil conditions, such as texture and nutrient availability. This supports conclusions of the herb layer study by Gilliam and Turrill (1993) at FEF that herb layer development may become more influenced by stand characteristics in later stages of forest succession.

University of Michigan Biological Station

In contrast to results for FEF, the correlation of herb layer versus overstory vector length for UMBS was highly significant for young stands ($r = .90$, $p < .01$); this correlation was even more significant ($r = .97$, $p < .0001$) for mature stands (table 9.6). As with results for FEF, these results for UMBS support our hypothesis that linkage arises from parallel responses of vegetation strata to environmental factors. Although it is not immediately clear why the two forest types contrasted with respect to stand age-related changes in linkage, we suspect that it may be related to (1) the distinctness of the ecology of aspen-dominated successional stands of northern lower Michigan compared to the mixed dominance of central Appalachian hardwood stands, and (2) a greater degree of soil heterogeneity at UMBS relative to FEF. That is, although soils of forest stands studied at UMBS are all Spodosols, they are derived from parent materials of widely varying glacial origin, including glacial outwash deposits (coarse-textured, sandy materials) and glacial till (mixtures of sand, silt, and clay). As we noted previously, there is a tendency to conclude that linkage occurs in studies that include a broader range of environments and β-diversity. Thus, at UMBS, even the young stands showed linkage (although weaker than the mature stands). To adequately test the influence of diversity on linkage would require running ordinations of the total dataset, along with ordinations of each site class separately. Our datasets were not large enough to allow this type of analysis.

Soil calcium is clearly an overriding environmental variable determining spatial patterns of species composition of both the herbaceous layer and the overstory in both young and mature stands at UMBS. Although additional factors, such as pH or soil OM, vary in importance among strata and stand ages, calcium is consistently the factor of greatest importance. In this region, calcareous substrates (indicated by high calcium concentrations) are associated with clay lenses or clay till within or underlying the sandy outwash surface deposits (Spurr and Zumberge 1956; Roberts and

Christensen 1988). Van Breemen et al. (1997) found significant correlation between soil calcium and overstory species composition in southern New England forests. Thus, soil calcium may serve as an indicator for a suite of co-related soil nutrient and moisture variables at UMBS.

SUMMARY

We have provided evidence that supports our mechanistic explanation of linkage in forest communities. Linkage among forest strata appears to arise from similarities among strata of forest vegetation in the responses of their respective species to environmental gradients. In central Appalachian hardwood stands of West Virginia, these responses may change through secondary forest succession and thus may be a function of stand age. Early in succession, spatial variation in species composition of the overstory appears largely related to the density of the stand, whereas variation in herb composition is related more to soil fertility. This changes later in succession when variation in herb composition responds more to stand structure (i.e., tree density) at a time when overstory variability is also related to density.

In successional aspen forests of northern lower Michigan, where correlations between strata were significant for both young and mature stands, these responses may be much less related to stand age. The degree to which linkage between strata is the result of higher β-diversity in the Michigan sample is not clear. We believe, however, that it is not an artifact of simply sampling across two extremes of environmental conditions (see McCune and Antos 1981), given the continuum of points along axis 1 for both vegetation strata, as depicted in fig. 9.2.

Although the concept of linkage among vegetation strata of forest communities likely will continue to be debated among vegetation scientists, we believe that it is a concept with a high degree of importance and application. It furthers our understanding of and appreciation for the complexities underlying the structure and function of forest ecosystems (e.g., responses to disturbance [chapter 13, this volume] and mechanisms of secondary succession [chapter 11, this volume]). It may also be applied toward landscape-level investigations of forest cover types and remote sensing.

In the previous edition of this book, we invited further testing of this mechanism as a predictive hypothesis in other forest types and over a wider range of stand ages (Gilliam and Roberts 2003), including studies examining linkage across different breadths of diversity and spatial scales. Interesting findings have emerged among such studies, generally supporting our predictions for temperate forests (e.g., Huebner et al. 2007; Barbier et al. 2008; Rollinson and Kaye 2012; Jackson et al. 2012). Notably, these predictions were not supported in tropical forests (Both et al. 2011), despite the much higher woody species (e.g., tree seedling) component of the herb layer of many tropical forests (Lu et al. 2010). Future work examining strata interactions should include linkages of forest vegetation with belowground communities, including soil micro- and macro-invertebrates and soil microbial groups (Eisenhauer et al. 2011, Gilliam et al. 2011).

10 Herbaceous Layer Species Richness of Southeastern Forests and Woodlands

Patterns and Causes

Robert K. Peet, Kyle A. Palmquist, and Samantha M. Tessel

Numerous factors have been shown or asserted to influence the species richness of natural plant communities. Species richness has variously been suggested to be high where propagule supply is high, competition is low, disturbance is intermediate or low, or soils are of intermediate to high fertility (e.g., Grime 1973; Huston 1979, 1994; Shmida and Wilson 1985). However, attempts to test the generality of these broad hypotheses have generally met with inconclusive or inconsistent results (e.g., Adler et al. 2011; Willig 2011). Part of the challenge is that the dominant patterns and processes vary with environmental and ecological context, as well as spatial scale. Moreover, the dominant patterns and processes may be system-specific. In this chapter, we explore the patterns in herbaceous layer species richness of forests and woodlands of southeastern North America, identify their likely drivers, and examine how these fit into a global context.

Numerous patterns have been reported for understory species richness in southeastern forests and woodlands. The upland forests of the southern Appalachian Mountains are famous for their herb-rich cove forests. Species richness in these systems has been widely reported to vary with elevation and topographic position (the work of Whittaker [1956] being best known), but subsequent work (e.g., Newell and Peet 1998; Newell et al. 1999; Peet et al. 2003; Wheeler 2011) has added a third gradient of increasing species richness with increasing soil nutrient status. The fire-maintained pine woodlands of the southeastern Coastal Plain, extending from southeastern Virginia south to southern Florida and west to eastern Texas, look superficially monotonous with mostly one tree species and a grass-dominated herbaceous layer, but previous studies have shown small-scale (1 m^2) and plot-scale (1,000 m^2) species richness to range from trivially low to among the highest reported for temperate North America, despite the generally infertile soils and lack of topographic diversity (Walker and Peet 1983; Peet 2006). Piedmont forests occupy an ancient landscape of highly weathered soils that is widely ignored by ecologists because it lacks the charismatic taxa and dramatic topography that characterize the Coastal Plain and Blue Ridge Mountains respectively. The herbaceous layer in these forests and woodlands exhibits a striking signature of underlying rock type evidenced by species richness showing a strong positive correlation with soil cation content and basic parent material (Peet and Christensen 1980b, 1988). Finally, riparian forests and woodlands are quite different from upland systems of the Southeast due to the important role of water in dispersal of propagules by flowing water, episodic flooding, and redistribution and supply of soil particles and nutrients. Species richness in these systems at the 1,000 m^2 scale has been reported to range from very low in chronically flooded swamps to among the highest levels reported for temperate North America in scour areas along Blue Ridge Mountain rivers (175 species / 1000 m^2; Brown and Peet 2003).

Previous reports of specific patterns of species richness largely result from independent and spatially isolated studies that largely fail to address variation in these patterns across the landscape and region, or their broader generality. In addition, these studies have been conducted at a range of different spatial scales, leaving uncertainty as to whether different species richness patterns might have been observed under different scales of observation. Various authors have argued that species richness should be studied in the context of multiple potential determinants and across a range of spatial scales (e.g., Shmida and Wilson 1985; Stohlgren et al. 1995; Brown et al. 2007; Dengler 2009). Giladi et al. (2011) have gone as far as to conclude that species richness is determined by the combined effect of multiple determinants acting at multiple scales and that conclusions from studies that do not employ multi-scale sampling across the range of potential drivers are restricted and likely misleading.

We draw on a large, multi-scale plot database to explore patterns of herbaceous layer diversity and the processes likely maintaining those patterns across contrasting sets of vegetation types. We use data from a set of > 5,000 vegetation plots collected across the Southeast and sampled at multiple scales (0.01 m^2 to 1,000 m^2) following the Carolina Vegetation Survey (CVS) protocol (Peet et al. 1998; Peet et al. 2012). These plots have full floristic inventories at each scale and thus capture the diversity and composition of the herbaceous layer. This is currently the largest vegetation plot dataset in the world that spans six orders of magnitude in subplot size.

We compare the results from four cohesive subsets of our data to provide greater clarity and synthesize general patterns in richness in southeastern forests and woodlands. The forests and woodlands of southeastern North America are often broken into subsets based on composition, history, and ecology. For our study area in the Carolinas, and more broadly across the Southeast, Braun (1950) recognized three major forest regions of the Eastern Deciduous Forest Formation corresponding to the southern Appalachian Mountains (Oak, Chestnut Forest), the Piedmont (Oak, Pine Forest), and the Coastal Plain (Southeastern Evergreen Forest). The EPA level-3 Ecoregion Map (fig. 10.1; Omernik 1987; USEPA 2011) makes similar divisions recognizing the

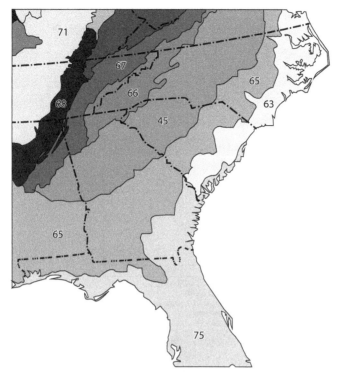

FIGURE 10.1 Ecoregions of the southeastern United States (U.S. EPA 2011). The three focal regions for this chapter are the Blue Ridge Mountains (Ecoregion 66), the Piedmont (Ecoregion 45), and the Southeastern Coastal Plain (Ecoregion 63: Middle Atlantic Coastal Plain, 65 Southeastern Plains, and 75 Southern Coastal Plain).

Blue Ridge Mountains, the Piedmont, and the Coastal Plain, albeit with the Coastal Plain divided into three sections. Here we recognize the Blue Ridge Mountains, the Piedmont, and the Coastal Plain as regions with distinct flora, climate, and geology, suggesting that patterns of plot-scale species richness might well differ among regions, and we examine their patterns and drivers separately. In addition, we look at brown-water riparian forests of North Carolina as a fourth focal vegetation type likely dominated by different ecological processes than upland forests and woodlands.

DATA AND METHODS

In this chapter, we identify patterns in species richness in the herbaceous layer vegetation of forests and woodlands of southeastern North America. We define forests and woodlands as areas with greater than 10 percent cover of trees, consistent with the definitions used by F.A.O. (2001), the U.S. Forest Service Forest Inventory and Analysis Program (Gray et al. 2012), and the U.S. National Vegetation Classification (U.S. FGDC 2008). We include in our analysis all vascular plant species present in the herbaceous layer, regardless of whether they are herbaceous or woody (chapter 1, this volume). We define species richness as the count of all vascular plant species rooted in a quadrat of fixed area.

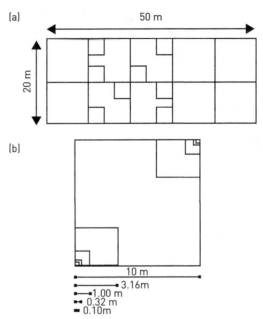

FIGURE 10.2 Vegetation plot design of the Carolina Vegetation Survey (Peet et al. 1998). (a) The 0.1 ha plots of 20 × 50 m typically include 10 modules of 10 × 10 m, with four intensive modules each containing two sets of smaller nested subplots. (b) An intensive module, 10 × 10 m, with nested subplots sized 0.01–10 m².

We use vegetation plot data drawn from the CVS database (Peet et al. 2012) that comply with the CVS protocol (Peet et al. 1998) and have intensive sampling down to 0.01 m². The standard plot (fig. 10.2) is 1,000 m² and consists of ten 10 × 10 m modules arranged as a 20 × 50 m rectangle. Typically, a square of four contiguous modules is designated as containing intensive modules, and each intensive module contains two sets of nested square subplots with areas of 0.01, 0.1, 1, and 10 m². Thus, in a typical plot we have eight species counts at scales of 0.01 m², 0.1 m², 1 m², and 10 m²; four counts at 100 m²; and one count each at 400 m² and 1,000 m². Occasionally, when there is insufficient homogeneous vegetation for a 1,000 m² plot, fewer modules are recorded. Thus, while our analysis is organized around seven plot sizes, occasionally the two largest sizes are not available. When only one intensive module is recorded, four sets of nested quadrats are recorded to assure that no plot has fewer than four sets of subplots less than or equal to 10 m². This is important because small plots are much more sensitive to chance variation in species occurrences. In total, we initially examined 5,051 CVS plots, of which 2,703 contained the full set of seven plot sizes. Our final analysis employs four subsets of plots spread across a total of 3,264 plots drawn from across North Carolina, South Carolina, Georgia, and Florida.

In addition to information on species composition across a range of spatial scales, CVS plot data include location, slope, aspect, elevation, and topographic position (including for the Blue Ridge Mountain dataset McNab's terrain shape index [TSI] and land form index [LFI]; McNab 1989, 1993). Soil samples were collected from the top 10 cm of mineral soil in the center of each intensively sampled module. Total cation exchange capacity (meq/100g), pH, percent humic matter, estimated N release, easily extractable P, exchangeable cations (Ca, Mg, K, Na in ppm), percent base saturation, extractable micronutrients (B, Fe, Mn, Cu, Zn, Al in ppm), soluble sulfur, and bulk density values were determined for each subsample. Extractions were carried out using the Mehlich III method (Mehlich 1984), and percent humic matter was determined by loss on ignition. Texture analysis employed the Bouyoucos hydrometer method (Patrick 1958) with a composite sample of the four subsamples from each plot. All soil values for a plot (typically four) were averaged to obtain a single value per plot.

Many of the vegetation plots in the CVS database were placed subjectively to represent a particular place or range of composition variation. Ideally, all plots would be selected objectively, but this is not practical when trying to capture more than the most common vegetation types. Roleček et al. (2007) have explained that while simple random sampling, systematic sampling, and stratified random sampling better meet certain statistical assumptions, preferential sampling yields datasets that cover a broader range of vegetation variability and allow inclusion of rare types that might otherwise be missed. Michalcová et al. (2011) further considered the problems inherent in using large plot databases wherein many of the plots are likely to represent preferential sampling. In their analysis, they found that preferentially sampled datasets contain more endangered species and have higher beta diversity, whereas estimates of species richness are not consistently different between preferentially and stratified randomly sampled datasets.

Vegetation plot databases often contain unbalanced representations of the range of compositional variation encountered in nature. In the CVS database, a few common vegetation types are represented by nearly 200 plots, whereas uncommon types are in some cases represented by just a few plots. Care must be taken not to allow the attributes of the most heavily represented types to dominate the analysis. Lengyel et al. (2011) have proposed that plot databases be sampled to provide even coverage in geographically broad studies. Knollová et al. (2005) proposed several methods for stratified resampling of vegetation databases where some of their methods divide the database into groups according to geography or according to environmental variables expected to influence between-plot variation in species composition. As a way of comparing across a broad range of communities with uneven sampling, we summarize our data as community types recognized at the association level in the U.S. National Vegetation Classification (NVC). Nationally, approximately 6,500 associations are currently recognized (see http://usnvc.org), and the CVS database contains plots assigned to over 500 NVC types that occur in the Carolinas. The types recognized in the NVC have been defined to be roughly equivalent in terms of their distinctiveness in composition and setting (Jennings et al. 2009). By summarizing plot data by NVC types, we minimize the problem of uneven sample size. For riparian vegetation, in some cases, we use new community classifications designed to replace the current NVC types, but which are not yet incorporated in the system (Brown 2002 for the Blue Ridge Mountains, Matthews et al. 2011 for the Piedmont, and Faestel 2012 in part for the Coastal Plain).

To determine the important drivers that structure plant communities in each of the four focal areas, we conducted principle components analysis (PCA) on 28 environmental variables: soil nutrients (N, P, Al, B, Ca, Cu, Fe, H, K, Mg, Mn, Na, S, Zn), bulk density, aspect, slope, elevation, base saturation, cation exchange capacity, pH, Ca/Mg ratio, soil texture (% sand, silt, clay), organic matter, latitude, and longitude. Also included for the Blue Ridge Mountains analysis were LFI and TSI. Each environmental variable was averaged across all plots within each NVC type prior to analysis. PCA was used because many of the pertinent soil variables were strongly correlated and were proxies for larger potential drivers of richness (e.g., nutrient and water availability). Prior to analysis, soil nutrient content variables measured in parts per million (ppm) were log-transformed to normalize the data. After we ran PCA on the environmental matrix, we examined which axes explained the most variation in species richness across the various scales of observation. Pearson correlations were calculated to assess the degree to which PCA axes represented the observed environmental variables.

Median richness values were calculated at seven spatial scales (.01 m², 0.1 m², 1 m², 10 m², 100 m², 400 m², and 1,000 m²) for each community type. We used Pearson correlations to identify the strength and direction of influence of all potential environmental drivers of species richness and the latent variables represented by PCA axes. Linear models were used to calculate variation in species richness explained by environmental variables or PCA axes, and to test the significance of these relationships. To visualize relationships between the important PCA axes and richness most effectively, we $\log_2$ transformed richness. For some vegetation associations, the median richness at .01 m² was 0; therefore, to avoid undefined values when taking the $\log_2$ of 0, we added 1 to median richness values across all spatial scales. To examine latitudinal patterns of species richness in Coastal Plain pine woodlands, we extracted richness values at 1,000 m² for each plot and tabulated a mean richness value for each of five major longleaf pine vegetation types recognized in Peet 2006 (see fig. 10.7).

REGIONAL PATTERNS IN SPECIES DIVERSITY

Local studies have reported sometimes similar and sometimes conflicting patterns in herbaceous layer species diversity. Here we discuss richness across four specific subsets of southeastern North American vegetation types.

Upland Forests and Woodlands of the Blue Ridge Mountains

The subset of data representing upland forests and woodlands of the Blue Ridge Mountains contains 1,184 vegetation plots distributed across 56 NVC associations in North Carolina and South Carolina. The first PCA axis of the site variables associated with those 56 associations was strongly correlated with pH ($r = 0.92$), percent base saturation (0.92), cation exchange capacity (0.75), calcium (0.79), magnesium (0.84), and manganese (0.80). This gradient, which we refer to as base cation availability, shows a strong positive correlation with species richness at all spatial scales from 0.01 to 1,000 m² (fig. 10.3), though the strength of the signal drops off below 1 m² where larger plant size damps the increase in species richness on rich sites (see Fridley et al. 2004).

The importance of base cation availability for prediction of species richness in this region has been underappreciated in the broader literature and is not evident in Whittaker's (1956) seminal work on the Great Smoky Mountains where he described elevation and topographic position as predictors of richness. However, subsequent work (e.g., Newell et al. 1999; Ulrey 2002; Peet et al. 2003; Wheeler 2011) has shown that when Blue Ridge Mountain forests are examined over a broad geographic extent, rather than from just one study area where parent rock can be relatively homogeneous, pH and soil cation availability are strong predictors of richness. The extent to which this pattern is a consequence of higher resource availability on high-base sites

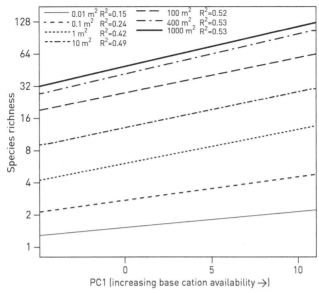

FIGURE 10.3 In upland forests and woodlands of the Blue Ridge Mountains, base cation availability correlates strongly with species richness at all spatial scales (0.01, 0.1, 1.0, 10, 100, 400, 1,000 m²). The base cation availability gradient represents 30 percent of the variation in site attributes and is strongly positively correlated with base saturation ($r = 0.92$), soil pH ($r = 0.92$), Mg ($r = 0.84$), Mn ($r = 0.80$), Ca ($r = 0.79$), exchange capacity ($r = 0.75$). All R^2 values reported are significant at $\alpha = 0.01$.

versus a larger species pool size (*sensu* Eriksson 1993) is difficult to assess, though a region-wide analysis for the Blue Ridge Mountains by Peet et al. (2003) showed high pH sites to have generally larger species pools.

Species richness did not show a strong relationship to PCA axes other than axis 1, with the exception that there is a negative correlation at the two smallest plot sizes (0.01 and 0.1 m²; $r = -0.51$ and -0.40 respectively) with axis 3 (PC3), but this relationship fades with increasing plot size and reverses to become modestly positive at large scales. PC3 is correlated with a broad range of variables including terrain shape index ($r = 0.51$), land form index ($r = 0.49$), and elevation ($r = -0.46$), indicating a connection to topographic position. The lower richness at small scales in topographic lows is likely a consequence of the larger mean plant size in these sites, limiting the number of species that can be packed into a very small area (Fridley et al. 2004).

The richest herb communities of the Blue Ridge Mountain forests and woodlands are often reported to occur in coves and valley bottoms, though not all coves and valley bottoms have high species richness. One reason Whittaker's (1956) interpretation of species richness in the Great Smoky Mountain forests did not include soil cations was likely because he examined compositional variation relative to a complex topographic position gradient that he referred to as "moisture." As soils weather, water-soluble nutrients tend to be transported downhill, accumulating in coves and valleys. Thus, Whittaker's moisture gradient combines a range of variables including temperature, moisture availability, and cation availability. Interestingly, we found that some of the most species-rich herbaceous layers are found in areas of moderately high base cation availability, but in an intermediate topographic position. As a case study, rich oak-hickory communities of mid-slopes are generally more species rich than the rich cove community types found in topographic lows, despite a similar pool of relatively high pH herb species (Schafale 2012). This may be attributed to asymmetric competition for light by species in the lush herb layer of rich coves with high soil moisture, whereas the herb cover is lower and richness higher on the somewhat higher and drier mid-slope oak forests.

We attempted to separate the contributions of soil cation availability from topographic position by graphing richness simultaneously against base saturation (representing cation availability) and McNab's Land Form Index (mean percent slope of an azimuth to the horizon), which ranges from zero at a local topographic high to a high value deep in a cove. Fig. 10.4 shows the results for 1 m² and 1,000 m² plots. Species number is strongly correlated with base saturation as already described, the signal being slightly stronger at 1,000m². However, the higher richness values at 1,000 m² usually occur on sites with high LFI values (i.e., coves and valley bottoms), but not all sites with high LFI values have high richness. This reflects the very low diversity that can occur in low base-availability coves ("acidic coves" *sensu* Schafale 2012) dominated by evergreen shrubs such as great laurel (*Rhododendron maximum* L.), which can limit herb development through both decreased light availability (Wheeler 2011) and allelopathic impacts (Nilsen et al. 1999). The base cation signal is not as strong at 1 m² because of the limitation of how many lush herbs can fit into a small plot.

Although elevation is known to constitute a strong environmental gradient that accounts for much of the variation in species composition in the southern Appalachian Mountains (e.g., Whittaker 1956; Newell et al. 1999) and is often correlated with soil pH and nutrients, it is only a weak determinant of species richness in our dataset (fig. 10.5). Elevation shows a weak negative relationship with species richness at large scales and a weak positive (though non-significant) relationship at small scales. The negative correlation with elevation at large scales may result from mass effects (Shmida and Wilson 1985) because at low elevations, multiple habitats are in close proximity, and propagules from plants in neighboring habitats frequently arrive and survive short periods in suboptimal community types (see Grime 1998), whereas the restricted area and isolation of higher elevation forests results in a more limited species pool (sensu Eriksson 1993). The small-scale, weak positive relationship may result

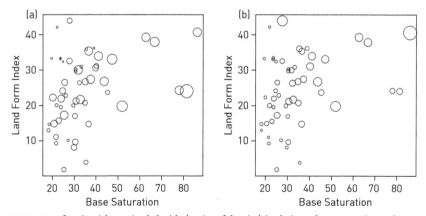

FIGURE 10.4 Species richness (scaled with the size of the circle) relative to base saturation and topographic position (Land Form Index sensu McNab 1989, high levels being in more sheltered locations) for (a) 1 m², and (b) 1,000 m² plots. Maximum richness values shown are 137 species for 1,000m² and 13 species for 1 m².

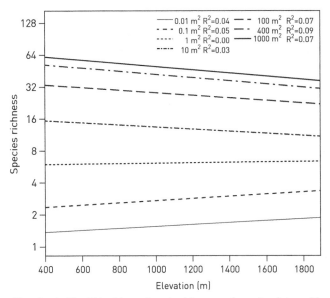

FIGURE 10.5 Elevation in Blue Ridge Mountain upland forests and woodlands is weakly negatively correlated with species richness at large scales, but weakly positively correlated at small scales. R^2 values for scales 100–1,000 m^2 are significant at $\alpha = 0.05$.

from a fairly high number of individuals per unit area in the generally mesic habitats of higher elevation forests, whereas the number of individuals in lower elevation forests varies more strongly as a function of topographic position.

Another factor known to significantly influence species richness in Blue Ridge Mountain forests and woodlands is fire (chapter 14, this volume). However, only limited data were available in our dataset for recently burned sites. Oak forests of eastern North America are widely appreciated to have developed in the context of chronic fire (e.g., Abrams 1992), and there are frequent reports in the literature of increased species richness with frequent fire, especially at small scales (e.g., Hutchinson et al. 2005). In two cases, Blue Ridge Mountain forests previously sampled using the CVS protocol have been resampled after fire. In 2003, Reilly et al. (2006a,b) resampled 20 plots from Linville Gorge Wilderness previously sampled by Newell and Peet (1998) in 1992 and examined the vegetation change at 0.01, 0.1, 1, 10, 100, and 400 m^2. While there was considerable variation in the impact of the fire, species richness increased across all scales and across four broad community types, roughly doubling in number. The increase at 400 m^2 ranged from a few species to 60. In a second study, Marx (2007) resampled six plots established on a serpentine barren community after 10 years and approximately three fires. She observed at the 100 m^2 scale a decline in woody species, but an increase in density and richness of herbaceous species. In both cases, a major contributor to increased plant establishment appeared to be the removal of the litter layer, allowing seedlings to become established in exposed soil.

Piedmont Upland Forests

The subset of data representing upland forests and woodlands of the Piedmont contains 851 vegetation plots distributed across 53 NVC associations and two states

(North Carolina and northern South Carolina). PCA revealed two important axes that may structure plant species richness in Piedmont uplands: base cation availability (PC1) and soil moisture (PC2). The variables that strongly load on PC1 and their respective correlations include base saturation ($r = 0.95$), pH (0.94), calcium (0.97), and magnesium (0.90). Thus, PC1 represents a base cation availability gradient across Piedmont upland forest associations. Compared to the other PCA axes, base cation availability has the strongest correlation with richness in the herbaceous layer, a result consistent with the findings of Peet and Christensen (1980b). Base cation availability and species richness are positively correlated across all scales; however, the strength of this relationship increases with increasing spatial scale (fig. 10.6). The extent to which the higher species richness on high-base sites is a consequence of greater resource availability or greater species pool size is unclear, but we expect that species pool size is important, at least at larger scales.

We identified PC2 as a soil moisture axis based on strong loading of nitrogen ($r = 0.88$), organic matter ($r = 0.63$), and sulfur ($r = 0.53$). This reflects, in part, the increased accumulation of organic matter in anaerobic soils and the storage of nitrogen and sulfur in organic matter in anaerobic soils. Thus, as soil moisture increases, organic matter, nitrogen, and sulfur increase. Soil moisture (PC2) is the second most important driver of richness patterns in Piedmont uplands; as soil moisture increases, species richness increases. This relationship is especially prominent at small spatial scales ($r = 0.35$ at .01 m² versus $r = 0.18$ at 1,000 m²).

In addition to the environmental axes described above, human modifications of the landscape (e.g., agriculture, tree harvest, urbanization, fragmentation, and climate change) impact diversity patterns in the Piedmont region. Peet (1992) and Peet and Christensen (1988) (chapter 11, this volume) report that during old-field succession on the Piedmont, the strength of the correlation between species richness and pH varies with stand development. The correlation first increases through the natural thinning phase as species become more strongly sorted relative to environment and

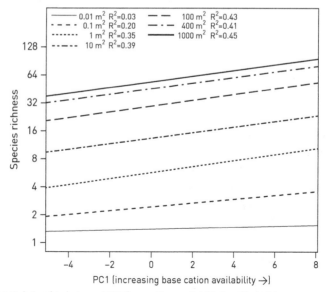

FIGURE 10.6 Relationship between PC1 (base cation availability) and $\log_2$ richness across seven spatial scales in Piedmont upland forests and woodlands of southeastern North America.

uncommon species have time to arrive. The correlation subsequently declines during the breakup of the original pine population owing to decreased competitive sorting, but then increases again into the mature hardwood phase with renewed competitive sorting. However, further work is needed to examine the importance of the various human impacts relative to environmental drivers of richness.

Disturbance in the form of heavy grazing and browsing also has important consequences for plant species richness in the Piedmont region. With the removal of predators and the decline in hunting, the white-tailed deer population has increased dramatically in many areas with severe negative impacts on plant community structure and diversity (Israel 2012; Cote et al. 2004; chapter 16, this volume), which is consistent with patterns documented in heavily grazed systems throughout the world (Fleischner 1994; chapter 14, this volume). Taverna et al. (2005) and Israel (2012) resampled permanent vegetation plots in the Duke Forest (in the Piedmont region of North Carolina) after 22 and 33 years during a period of dramatic increase in deer populations. They found that species richness declined steadily and significantly at both the 1 m² and 1,000 m² scale.

Coastal Plain Pine Woodlands

At the time of European settlement, fire-maintained longleaf pine (*Pinus palustris* P. Miller) woodlands and savannas dominated much of the southeastern Coastal Plain from southern Virginia south to south-central Florida and west to eastern Texas. Here we use a comprehensive sample of the remaining fire-maintained pine woodlands and savannas from northern North Carolina south to central Florida and west to the western edge of the Florida Panhandle. Our dataset contains 785 vegetation plots distributed across 58 NVC associations (see Peet 2006; Carr et al. 2009).

PCA revealed three potentially important environmental factors structuring plant species richness in Coastal Plain pine woodlands: soil moisture (PC2), soil texture (PC3), and base cation availability (PC1). The correlation strength of these three predictors with herbaceous layer richness varies across the spatial scales examined, but soil moisture is the most important driver, regardless of scale (table 10.1). Individual environmental variables that load on the soil moisture PCA axis and their respective correlations with the axis include bulk density ($r = -0.70$), sulfur (0.73), and organic matter (0.71). Linear models revealed that soil moisture is a highly significant predictor of species richness across all spatial scales examined (table 10.1). As soil moisture increases, richness increases in the herbaceous layer.

Soil texture is the second most important predictor in structuring species richness patterns in coastal plain pine woodlands after soil moisture. Environmental variables that load on the soil texture axis (PC3) and their respective correlations include aluminum ($r = 0.84$), iron (0.72), clay (0.64), sand (−0.63), and silt (0.57). As fine-textured soil components increase (clay % and silt %), richness increases significantly across all spatial scales (table 10.1). Fine-textured soils have greater water- and nutrient-holding capacity, which increases the number of species that can be supported in a given area.

The third PCA axis represents a base cation gradient across the Coastal Plain woodland community types with pH ($r = 0.89$), base saturation (0.88), and calcium (0.90) loading strongly on PC1. However, unlike Piedmont and Blue Ridge Mountain upland forests and riparian forests, base cation availability is only weakly correlated with richness, and the correlations shift from negative at small scales to positive at

Table 10.1 Correlations of species richness in Coastal Plain pine woodlands with axes of soil moisture, soil texture, and soil cation availability. * indicates significant relationships (p =.01 to.05), and ** indicates highly significant relationships (p < .01).

Richness	Soil Moisture	Soil Texture	Cation Availability
.01 m²	0.50 **	0.29 *	−0.32 *
.1 m²	0.55 **	0.36 **	−0.25
1 m²	0.55 **	0.39 **	−0.09
10 m²	0.54 **	0.43 **	0.06
100 m²	0.53 **	0.45 **	0.13
400 m²	0.56 **	0.44 **	0.17
1000 m²	0.57 **	0.44 **	0.18

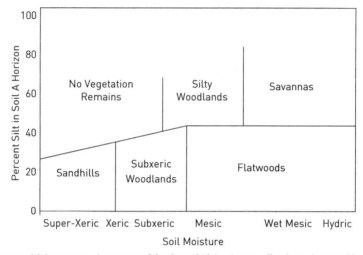

FIGURE 10.7 Major community groups of the Coastal Plain pine woodlands can be sorted by soil moisture and soil texture (after Peet 2006).

large scales (table 10.1). At small scales, the more infertile sites can contain more small plants as competition for space is relatively modest, whereas at large scales, competition for space is less important and more species can persist on the more fertile soils. Interestingly, some of the highest species richness values reported for North America at small scales (e.g., 52/1 m²) have been reported for infertile longleaf pine savannas (Walker and Peet 1983), whereas some of the highest species richness values reported for North America at large spatial scales (1,000 m²) have been reported for longleaf woodlands on relatively fertile soils (161/1,000 m²; see Orzell and Bridges 2006; Platt et al. 2006; Gilliam 2007).

In addition to the environmental drivers of richness, there is a geographic trend in species richness across latitude in Coastal Plain pine woodlands (Peet 2006). Species richness increases with decreasing latitude in four of the five major vegetation types, with the pattern especially strong for the xeric longleaf community types (fig. 10.8). This geographic signal is likely due to a combination of climatic factors and biogeographic history. The length of the growing season and average mean temperature

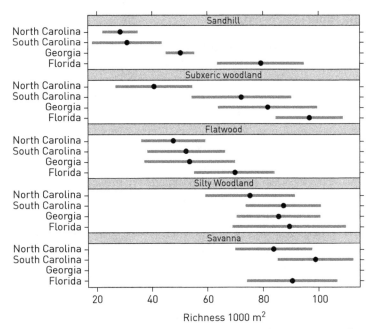

FIGURE 10.8 Comparison of average richness at 1,000 m² for longleaf community types by state reveals a latitudinal gradient. Gray bars indicate the inner quartile of the variation.

increase with decreasing latitude in southeastern North America; this may allow for the persistence of a larger suite of species. During the last glacial maximum (~ 18 ka), species refugia were concentrated on the Gulf Coastal Plain and in parts of peninsular Florida, and as climate warmed, species migrated eastward and northward to their current locations. Hence, the southern portion of the Coastal Plain pine woodlands may be more species rich due to fewer drastic fluctuations in climate, more speciation events, and less extinction over geologic and evolutionary time (Sorrie and Weakley 2001). Interestingly, species richness of Coastal Plain pine woodlands drops off again as one descends the Florida peninsula (Carr et al. 2009), probably owing to a smaller species pool resulting from the intrinsic isolation of communities on islands and peninsulas.

Fire history and current fire regimes (fire frequency, fire return interval, time since fire, season of fire) are also extremely important for the maintenance of plant species richness in Coastal Plain pine woodlands (Walker and Peet 1983; Glitzenstein et al. 2003; Kirkman et al. 2004). Historically, Coastal Plain pine woodlands burned every one to five years, depending on site productivity, topographic position, and landscape context, with annual fire on the flat outer Coastal Plain and less frequent fire in the dissected and topographically complex inner Coastal Plain (Frost 2006). Frequent fire maximizes species richness by reducing the density of litter and the abundance of dominant species and by increasing resource availability in the form of light, space, and nutrients (Sparks et al. 1998; Kirkman et al. 2004). Without fire, species richness decreases rapidly (Glitzenstein et al. 2003), especially in mesic to wet community types where competitive exclusion by bunch grasses eliminates the small-statured species that constitute the bulk of biodiversity.

Carolina Riparian Forests

Riparian forests may have different patterns of herbaceous layer richness compared to upland forests and woodlands because of the movement and persistence of water. We look only at rivers that originate in the Blue Ridge Mountains or the Piedmont, thereby excluding the smaller, black-water rivers of the Coastal Plain, which have very different hydrologic, geomorphic, and edaphic attributes. The subset of data representing brown-water riparian forests and woodlands of North Carolina includes 444 plots spanning 44 NVC or equivalent association units.

Analysis of all 44 riparian, brown-water forest community types across the Blue Ridge Mountains, Piedmont, and Coastal Plain revealed strong geographic, elevation, soil nutrient, and soil texture gradients, with montane riparian forests generally richer in species, base cations, and percentage of sand in the soil (fig. 10.9). It is difficult to interpret ecological drivers of species richness when there is such a strong geographic trend, other than to observe that Blue Ridge Mountain riparian forest community types, which are among the most species-rich communities in the region at large scales (100–1,000 m²), are likely to be richer in species because of propagule pressure from the wide variety of communities in close proximity and the limited duration of flooding events on these steep-gradient streams (Brown and Peet 2003). We therefore split the communities in this dataset into three subgroups, where each community in the full dataset was assigned to a dominant physiographic province. This resulted in 11 Blue Ridge Mountain riparian forest communities, 13 Piedmont

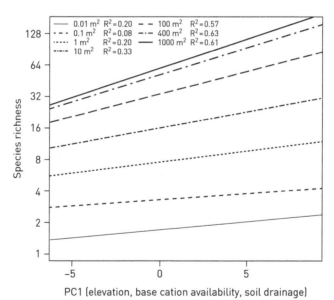

FIGURE 10.9 PCA axis 1 for explanatory variables of riparian brown-water forest community richness. PC1 represents 43 percent of the variation in environmental conditions and shows a strong geographic trend in richness, as well as environmental variables, where Blue Ridge Mountain riparian plots are richest in species, base cations, and percent sand. Variables strongly correlated with PC1 include elevation ($r = 0.75$), longitude ($r = -0.81$), pH ($r = 0.76$), base saturation ($r = 0.76$), cation exchange capacity ($r = -0.82$), nitrogen ($r = -0.86$), percent sand ($r = 0.88$), percent silt ($r = -0.76$), percent clay ($r = -0.86$), bulk density ($r = 0.81$), and soil organic matter ($r = -0.75$). R^2 values for all scales have $p < 0.01$ except 0.1 m² with $p < 0.05$.

riparian communities, and 20 Coastal Plain riparian communities. Species richness patterns were analyzed separately for these three subgroups.

Soil calcium and magnesium are very important determinants of species richness in Blue Ridge Mountain riparian forests, especially at smaller scales (r = 0.80 for Ca and 0.76 for Mg at 0.1 m^2, p < 0.01). Base saturation and pH, often correlated with calcium and magnesium, are not as strong predictors (r up to 0.55 for base saturation and 0.54 for pH, not significant). Higher species richness in areas with more base nutrients is a common pattern in plant community ecology (e.g., Peet et al. 2003), and similar relationships were detected for upland forests of the Piedmont and Blue Ridge Mountains. Terrain Shape Index (TSI) was another strong determinant of species richness at small scales (r up to –0.74, p < 0.05 for scales 0.01 m^2 to 100 m^2, not significant at larger scales); sites with high richness occur predominantly on local topographic high points such as ridges and levees, while low flats and depressions have lower richness. Sites that had concave local topography (high TSI) probably have fewer species because of greater duration of flooding and local dominance of flood-tolerant species.

The predictive power of most environmental variables at large scales in Blue Ridge Mountain riparian habitats is low. This is likely because propagule pressure is the dominant driver in this system, with stream-facilitated disturbance and seed dispersal allowing temporary occurrence of many species that would not otherwise be competitive. The highest known species richness values for the Carolinas and possibly temperate North America at scales of 100 to 1,000 m^2 (table 10.2) have been reported for scour woodlands along Blue Ridge Mountain rivers where chronic disturbance decreases competition and frequent, brief flooding provides a steady supply of propagules from throughout the adjacent watershed (Brown and Peet 2003).

In Piedmont brown-water forests, soil nutrients and texture, probably reflecting flooding regime and moisture, were strong determinants of species richness. Phosphorous was the strongest predictor at all scales (r ranges –0.60 to –0.85, p < 0.05 at all scales) and

Table 10.2 Highest values of species richness recorded for the Carolinas at different scales. At larger scales, scour zones along Blue Ridge Mountain rivers have the highest richness values reported, whereas at small scales, the most species-rich communities are moist, fire-maintained longleaf pine savannas.

Scale-m^2	Richness	USNVC Name
1,000	175	*Alnus serrulata—Xanthorhiza simplicissima* Shrubland
400	146	*Alnus serrulata—Xanthorhiza simplicissima* Shrubland
100	129	*Alnus serrulata—Xanthorhiza simplicissima* Shrubland
10	72	*Pinus palustris/Arundinaria tecta—Liquidambar/Andropogon glomeratus—Sarracenia minor* Woodland
10	72	*Liquidambar—Liriodendron—(Platanus)/Carpinus—Halesia tetraptera/Amphicarpaea* Forest
1	52	*Pinus palustris—Pinus serotina/ Sporobolus pinetorum—Aristida stricta—Eryngium integrifolium* Woodland
0.1	35	*Pinus palustris—Pinus serotina/ Sporobolus pinetorum—Aristida stricta—Eryngiumintegrifolium* Woodland
0.01	15	*Pinus palustris—Pinus serotina/ Ctenium aromaticum—Muhlenbergia expansa—Rhynchospora latifolia* Woodland

was strongly correlated with sulfur and iron, suggesting that flood events have resulted in storage of organic matter in swamps behind levees. In addition, soil clay was a strong negative predictor of species richness at larger spatial scales ($r = -0.72$ at 400 m^2, $p < 0.05$), again indicating swamps with poor drainage and sediment accumulation.

In Coastal Plain brown-water river forests, there is again a geographic trend in species richness, with species richness higher in more southerly areas and in the community types more common in the inner Coastal Plain ($r = -0.45$ with latitude and -0.51 with longitude at 100 m^2, $p < 0.05$). Distance to coast is an insignificant determinant of species richness, and though latitude, longitude, and elevation are among the few predictors of species richness, their contribution is weak or insignificant at most scales. Elevation is the strongest predictor of species richness at the scale of 100 m^2 ($r = 0.54$, $p < 0.05$), and it also primarily reflects river distance from the coast, as sites further inland tend to be higher in elevation. The richest community types in the Coastal Plain brown-water riparian forest data subset were (1) point bars with many vagrant, ephemeral species due to propagule pressure; and (2) herb-rich bottomlands and low slopes with good to moderate drainage. These community types were sampled mostly from the Cape Fear and Neuse River basins, whereas community types with geographic centroids along the Roanoke River more often had saturated soil, thereby supporting fewer individuals and species.

Differences in abundances of community types across river basins may arise from variation between rivers in hydrologic processes. The Cape Fear River, for instance, is entrenched due to geologic uplift in the Cape Fear Arch region resulting in a larger levee-to-swamp ratio and infrequent flooding. In contrast, the Roanoke River meanders broadly because of a history of crustal subsidence in the region. The river also has a history of altered hydrology over the last 50 years due to dam construction. Management of these dams has resulted in longer-lasting but less dramatic flooding events, which may have homogenized community composition along the river (Townsend 2001; Pearsall et al 2005). Annual variability in flooding may also affect species richness in the herb layer of riparian forests. A 2009 resurvey of Roanoke River plots originally sampled in the wet year of 1994 had consistently higher species counts than in the original sample (J. White, unpublished data). It is therefore possible that perceived differences in species richness between river basins may also be caused by annual hydrologic variability between rivers sampled in different years.

SYNTHESIS

Numerous hypotheses have been proposed to explain patterns in plant species richness and coexistence (see Whittaker 1972; Huston 1994; Palmer 1994; Wilson 2011). Here we examine several that seem to have particular relevance to the forests and woodlands of southeastern North America and that appeared with varying importance in our discussion of the four groups of plots considered above. Our intent is not to catalogue proposed mechanisms, something already done by Palmer (1994) and others, but to examine how the most important factors vary with ecological context and scale of observation.

Environmental Favorableness and Plant Size

Herbaceous richness has been linked to numerous factors that might best be collectively referred to as environmental favorableness. For example, richness peaks in moist but well-drained sites and drops off in very wet and very dry sites. In our data, we observed riparian sites with chronic inundation to have lower richness than better drained sites, and we observed that Coastal Plain pine woodlands, Piedmont upland forests, and Blue Ridge Mountain upland forests on moist soils support higher richness than those on xeric sites. Whittaker (1956) reported richness to decline with elevation in the Blue Ridge Mountains, and in our data we see a decline with elevation, at least at large scales. Of variables that might be considered components of favorableness, soil cation availability is most consistently correlated with species richness across our vegetation subsets. In general, as soil fertility increases, so does richness, especially at the larger spatial scales examined. Greater cation availability allows more species to coexist as nutrients are less limiting.

Although species richness increases with soil cation availability at large scales for all four subsets of our data, the highest richness values at small scales occur consistently in Coastal Plain pine woodlands, which are characterized by low cation availability and pH in comparison to the sites with high small-scale richness in the other subsets of our data. This reflects the smaller size of plants in fire-maintained Coastal Plain pine woodlands and the number of species that can be packed into a small area. In fact, for small scales in Coastal Plain pine woodlands, the normal pattern between species richness and soil cation availability is reversed (negatively correlated), whereas in all other regions, there is a consistent positive correlation. Plant size and density are also important in the Piedmont, Blue Ridge Mountain, and Riparian datasets as indicated by the generally weaker correlation between soil cation availability and richness at small scales than at large scales for each of these datasets.

Species Pool and History

Species richness increases with decreasing latitude in Coastal Plain pine woodlands (fig. 10.8) and at least weakly along a northeast-to-southwest axis down the spine of the Blue Ridge Mountains. These gradients are likely a consequence of geographic variation in the available species pool. The number of species available at a site, or the "species pool" (sensu Pärtel et al. 1996), generally reflects evolutionary history, historical events, and local context. For example, the pool is generally larger in or near areas where species persisted during the Pleistocene epoch or is larger because of conditions that are more prominent on the landscape. Within refugial areas, species richness may be higher due to fewer extinctions over geologic time and a longer period for evolutionary divergence in isolated habitats. Consistent with this, the species pool for Coastal Plain pine woodlands appears to vary with proximity to places of Pleistocene persistence, such as the Apalachicola region of Florida and, to a lesser extent, the Florida Peninsula and the Cape Fear Arch (located in southeastern North Carolina; see Sorrie and Weakley 2001). Similarly, the southwest end of the Blue Ridge Mountains has somewhat higher richness than in northern North Carolina, probably because of Pleistocene persistence along the southern edge of the Blue Ridge escarpment. An anomaly relative to the expectation that larger areas should have larger species pools (Pärtel 2002) is the observation of Peet et al. (2003) that species richness in Appalachian forests increases consistently with pH, despite most of the landscape having low-pH soils. This seeming anomaly likely results from the generally more favorable conditions for plant growth on high-cation sites.

Propagule Pressure and Mass Effect

Ever since MacArthur and Wilson (1967) proposed their classic theoretical framework for island biogeography, community assembly has been widely appreciated to represent a balance between immigration and extinction. Numerous papers have emphasized the importance of the immigration side of the equation, documenting how high species arrival rates can lead to high species richness. For example, Brown and Peet (2003) found that riparian vegetation of the Blue Ridge Mountains is sometimes exceptionally species rich because of propagules carried by water from throughout the adjacent watershed.

Grime (1998) noted that a large proportion of species occurring in plant communities are waifs, species that we should not expect to persist, but which simply dropped in via dispersal and generally persist for only a modest period. Shmida and Wilson (1985) referred to this process as spatial mass effect and also noted that proximity to other environmental conditions can increase species number through increased chance arrival. In regions of rapid environmental turnover, such as in mountain ranges, mass effects can be particularly important as species more frequently have propagules land and become established in habitats inadequate for long-term persistence. Thus, landscape context alone can be an important driver of species richness and could explain why Blue Ridge Mountain vegetation is generally more species rich than equivalent Piedmont vegetation.

Disturbance

Disturbance, both human-mediated and natural, represents an important set of processes that influence herbaceous richness patterns across all four data subsets. Recurrent scouring by floods maintains species richness in riparian forests of the Blue Ridge region (Brown and Peet 2003) through the removal of dominant species and the arrival of waifs. Fire is an essential process for the maintenance of biodiversity in several Piedmont and Blue Ridge Mountain community types, including both oak and pine woodlands (e.g., Reilly et al. 2006a,b). In the fire-maintained Coastal Plain pine woodlands, a reduction in fire frequency rapidly leads to decreased species richness at all scales for all except the most xeric sites, first owing to increased accumulation of litter and ultimately to increased growth of woody plants (Walker and Peet 1983; Glitzenstein et al. 2003; Kirkman et al. 2004).

Disturbances ranging from episodic canopy gaps following wind disturbance in closed forests to the frequent fires of the Coastal Plain pine woodlands create areas of temporary availability of resources and space that can be exploited by colonizing species, allowing persistence until the next disturbance event. This represents an example of the temporal mass effect of Shmida and Wilson (1985), a mechanism that explains local perpetuation of a species that cannot become established under current conditions. Consistent with this interpretation is the phenomenon that flowering in Coastal Plain pine woodlands increases by an order of magnitude following a fire, probably a consequence of selection for maximum reproduction when conditions for establishment are optimal.

Productivity

Herbaceous layer richness has been reported to increase, decrease, or show a bell-shaped curve along gradients of productivity, these typically being gradients of soil chemistry and especially gradients of nitrogen and phosphorus supply (e.g., Grime 1973; Huston 1979; Adler et al. 2011). Most studies where richness has been reported to exhibit a bell-shaped curve were conducted in relatively nutrient-poor grassland systems, essentially the same situation encountered in Coastal Plain pine woodlands. In contrast, many studies conducted in forested systems report a nearly monotonic positive correlation between production and species richness, as suggested by soil moisture and cation availability in our Piedmont and Blue Ridge Mountain datasets. However, Graves et al. (2006) observed that forest herbaceous layer richness will drop at the most productive extreme of a soil-fertility gradient. This is consistent with our observation that cove forests in the Blue Ridge Mountains are somewhat less species rich than equally fertile mid-slope sites.

Peet and Christensen (1988) suggested that the explanation for the relationship between productivity and small-scale richness in grasslands can be found in the changing character of competition across the fertility gradient. For grasslands at low levels of fertility, competition is symmetric (*sensu* Schwinning and Weiner 1998) in the sense that ability to capture resources is proportional to size (essentially, amount of root surface area). In this situation, many plant species can coexist. However, at higher fertility levels, the larger individuals overtop and preempt light from the smaller ones (see Lamb et al. 2009). Thus, when productivity is high, the taller plants win at competition and the smaller ones are excluded. At both a regional and a global scale, the most species-rich plant communities at scales on the order of 1 m² are infertile grasslands (sometimes with in excess of 40 species/m²) that are subject to chronic disturbance from some factor like mowing, grazing, or fire that removes the tops of the plants on a regular basis (Peet and Christensen 1988; Sykes et al. 1994; Wilson et al. 2012), reducing the degree of competition for light (asymmetry of competition) and allowing high species richness to occur on more fertile sites than would be the case in the absence of such disturbance (fig. 10.10). De Bello et al. (2007) observed, in a synthetic evaluation of the impact of grazing on richness, that grazing increases species richness of Spanish grasslands at all spatial scales except on arid sites. This is consistent with

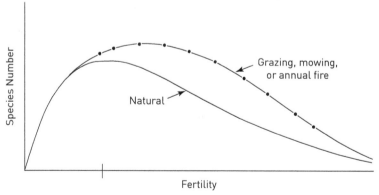

FIGURE 10.10 Species richness has frequently been reported to peak at low to intermediate levels along a gradient of fertility or primary productivity in grasslands and open savannas, after which competition for light becomes important and the shorter species are lost, reducing richness. Grasslands with very high richness are chronically disturbed by some factor such as fire or grazing or mowing that reduces plant height and thus reduces competition for light, allowing richness to increase along a fertility gradient longer before the asymmetric competition for light becomes a factor.

Community Dynamics across Spatial and Temporal Scales

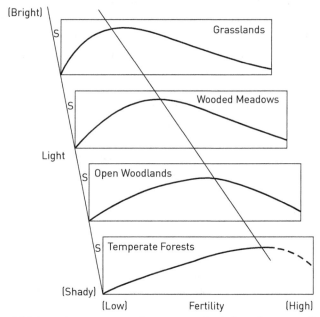

**Species number vs. Fertility relationships
at differing light levels**

FIGURE 10.11 With increasing canopy cover from open grasslands through open woodlands to closed canopy temperate forests, the light available to the herbaceous layer steadily declines. As the available light declines, it takes greater fertility for the herbaceous layer to become sufficiently robust for asymmetric light competition to become important, with the consequence that the peak in richness shifts progressively toward more fertile sites.

grazing increasing richness where competition is asymmetric, but decreasing richness where competition is symmetric. This interpretation is also consistent with our observation that fire does not have a significant influence on the richness of the most xeric Coastal Plain pine woodlands, whereas it does on all other sites.

The mechanism behind the shift in the peak of richness encountered along the fertility gradient in forests relative to grasslands can again be explained in terms of a shift from symmetric to asymmetric competition. With increasing cover of woody plants, the amount of light penetrating to the herbaceous layer declines. This allows for richness to keep increasing with fertility until the lushness of the herbaceous layer becomes such that competition for light within the herbaceous layer becomes important. At this point, richness starts to decline. Thus, one can envision a sequence from grassland to open woodland to closed forest with the peak in richness moving progressively toward the more fertile conditions (fig. 10.11).

Scale

One way of searching for general patterns in and drivers of richness across datasets is to examine which sites have the highest richness at each scale. In table 10.2, we report for each scale the NVC community type for which we have the highest species richness in our southeastern database. At large scales (100–1,000 m²), the scour zones of Blue Ridge Mountain riparian areas have by far the highest species number. At small scales

(0.01–1 m²), moist, infertile longleaf pine savannas on silty substrate have the highest richness values. At the intermediate scale of 10 m² the honors are split between Blue Ridge Mountain alluvial forests and somewhat fertile, moist, and silty longleaf pine savannas. Thus, we see the large-scale records driven by propagule pressure, fertility, and chronic but brief flooding, and the small-scale records driven by chronic fire on moist sites with low nutrient status and low productivity. A comparison with other records from the United States reveals no examples with higher values, but some close contenders for the most at 1,000 m² in cation-rich, fire-maintained longleaf savannas and prairies of Florida and Louisiana (e.g., 161 sp. in loess soil longleaf in Louisiana, William Platt pers. comm.; Orzell and Bridges 2006; Gilliam 2007). Globally, we find higher richness at small scales in oligotrophic, chronically grazed European grasslands (27 per 0.01 m², 43 per 0.1 m²; van der Maarel and Sykes 1993; Dengler et al. 2009) and in oligotrophic, grazed montane tropical grasslands in South America (89 per 1 m²; Cantero et al. 1999).

The first clear synthesis of changes in the processes driving richness with change in spatial scale appeared in two overlapping papers by Shmida (Shmida and Ellner 1984; Shmida and Wilson 1985). These papers proposed niche relationships (i.e., competition) as most important at smallest scales, habitat diversity and mass effects at intermediate scales, and ecological equivalency (i.e., species pool) at larger scales. These predictions fit well with our observations in southeastern North America. At smallest scales, we found plant interactions via space preemptions (size) and competition for light as mediated by chronic disturbance as critical. At larger scales, mass effects (propagule pressure) and species pool size appeared to be the critical drivers.

CONCLUSIONS

Examination of species richness patterns of the herbaceous layer of southeastern forests and woodlands reveals the changing importance of various drivers of species richness across environmental and geographic gradients and across vegetation types, and shows how the relative importance of those drivers varies with scale of observation. The most important processes structuring species diversity patterns in southeastern forests and woodlands appear to be cation availability (environmental favorableness), disturbance (flooding, fire, grazing), mass effects, and the relative size of the species pool.

Numerous previous studies have examined species richness, but typically in the context of a single spatial scale, and for a single region, vegetation type, or environmental gradient. Different community assembly processes operate at different spatial scales, with biotic interactions and local environmental filtering operating at smaller spatial scales, and dispersal and species pool size becoming increasingly important at broader spatial scales. By looking at richness across a broad range of regions, community types, and spatial scales, we show that to understand patterns in richness, a holistic approach that examines all of these components concurrently must be taken.

ACKNOWLEDGMENTS

Thomas Wentworth, Alan Weakley, and Michael Schafale have been longtime collaborators in organizing the Carolina Vegetation Survey (see Peet et al. 2012), and Susan

Carr collaborated in collection of data from longleaf pine sites in Florida. Without their continued dedication to building our dataset, this project would not have been possible. We are pleased to thank the 900+ persons who have participated in the collection of the vegetation plots in the CVS database. Collection of these data was supported by the Ecosystem Enhancement Program of the state of North Carolina, the U.S. Forest Service, and numerous other groups, programs, and persons. Michael Lee and Forbes Boyle provided invaluable assistance with data management and analysis.

11 Temporal Patterns in Herbaceous Layer Communities of the North Carolina Piedmont

Robert K. Peet, Norman L. Christensen, and Frank S. Gilliam

The questions ecologists, especially those who study plant communities, choose to ask are necessarily influenced by the character of landscapes immediately available for study. Thus, it is not surprising that researchers at mid-Atlantic universities in the first half of the 20th century—individuals such as B. W. Wells, H. J. Oosting, W. D. Billings, and M. F. Buell, who established some of the first American doctoral training programs in plant ecology—chose to focus much of their attention on the process of vegetation change that derives from the abandonment of farmland. Land degradation and a welter of economic factors resulted in massive abandonment of agricultural land across the mid-Atlantic region for the century that started with the Civil War, and set in motion a process of reforestation on an unprecedented regional scale. The region was awash in old fields and early successional forests. A unified theory of succession envisioned by many ecologists (e.g., Clements 1916, 1936) as a central element in our understanding of the distribution and structure of plant communities provided additional incentive to study these landscapes. The revegetation of old fields of the North Carolina Piedmont region was destined to become the community ecologists' equivalent of the fruit fly or *E. coli*—the "model system" for the study of succession.

Although abandoned agricultural fields are now comparatively rare, and human actions associated with urban development have begun to reverse decades of forest spread, much of the landscape available to those of us who have succeeded those ecological pioneers retains the unmistakable imprint of old-field succession (chapter 19, this volume). Furthermore, we are the beneficiaries of research carried out over a period that begins to have real relevance to successional processes. Although ecologists no longer see succession as the integrated, unifying process envisioned by Clements, disturbance and the processes that derive from it continue to shape our understanding of the distribution and abundance of organisms on landscapes. This body of work, which has accumulated over nearly a century, provides unique opportunities to explore the nature of change in a rapidly changing landscape.

Succession on forested landscapes is often depicted as a process that progresses from plant assemblages dominated by herbaceous species, to even-aged forests, and finally to uneven-aged, late successional or old-growth forests, with an almost-implied decline in the ecological significance of herb species. Certainly, herbs in old fields have received more study than their counterparts at other stages of succession. The herbaceous component is important in each successional stage; indeed, its diversity generally increases at most spatial scales as succession proceeds. Although most would agree that the factors that structure herb communities change with time, our understanding of the nature and mechanisms of such changes remains limited.

Over the past few decades, it has become obvious that successional trends associated with old-field abandonment are occurring against a backdrop of chronic and directional change of other sorts. The dominant oak and hickory species of the mature hardwood forests of the region are not reproducing sufficiently to maintain their current role (Abrams 2003; Nowacki and Abrams 2008). Open field and forested landscapes are becoming ever more dissected and fragmented by urban development (Tilman et al. 1994; Murcia 1995; Ries et al. 2004). These changes, as well as other factors, have resulted in explosive growth in populations of white-tailed deer, which thrive on herbs and seedlings of woody plants (Cote et al 2008; Rooney 2009; chapter 16, this volume). Exotic insect pests and pathogens are changing the character and understory environment of many forests through their impact on the canopy species (Lovett et al. 2006). Nonnative herbaceous species appear to be inexorably increasing in abundance at the expense of their native counterparts (chapter 15, the volume). Changes in climate, most notably increases in temperature and the length of growing seasons, are well documented for the mid-Atlantic Piedmont, although their specific effect on the herbaceous layer is not yet understood (chapters 3 and 21, this volume).

Our primary goal in this chapter is to explore variations in and dynamics of herb layer assemblages across the North Carolina Piedmont landscape. We are particularly interested in three questions: (1) What are the key environmental factors influencing herb distributions at various stages in the succession following land abandonment? (2) What do these patterns tell us with respect to the mechanisms that underlie the dynamics of herb populations? (3) Are Piedmont forest herbaceous communities changing in ways not related to old-field plant succession? To address these questions, we draw on several strands of research carried out over the last 80 years to provide a more comprehensive picture of the successional patterns and mechanisms of change in herb-layer communities of the forested landscapes of the Piedmont region of North Carolina.

Early studies of old-field succession were concerned more with describing the specific patterns of change in species composition over time than with determining the processes (i.e., mechanisms) that caused those changes. After nearly a century of study, debate continues regarding the nature of the underlying processes. Because of this, we provide here a brief historical chronology of some of the more influential hypotheses regarding successional change. We then apply these to the specific case of Piedmont old-field succession.

The pioneering work of Cowles on dune succession (Cowles 1899, 1901, 1911) was described by Tansley (1935) as "the first thorough working out of a strikingly complete and beautiful successional series." It was Cowles who led the way in "chronosequence" or "space-for-time" approaches to the study of succession. Cowles also recognized that early invading organisms typically modify their environments in ways that affect establishment of successors. Although Cowles reckoned that this leads to generally predictable patterns of change, he was also aware of the dynamic nature of plant communities in response to a variable abiotic environment. This awareness is captured in his characterization of succession as "a variable approaching a variable, not a constant" (see Olson 1958).

Clements (1916, 1928) saw succession as much more predictable and directional, converging (regardless of starting conditions) inexorably toward a stable climax community determined largely by climate. In Clements's view, the biotic reactions of dominant pioneer species determine the sequence of vegetation types leading to that climax—a process later dubbed "relay floristics" (Egler 1954).

In his then-controversial paper, Gleason (1926) rejected virtually all of Clements's ideas on succession and, especially, the nature of plant communities. Gleason reasoned that the principal mechanism driving succession was an interaction between migration of plant species (rates and modes of which vary greatly among species) and environmental selection. Acknowledging that successional change might be described as occurring in stages dominated by physiognomic types (e.g., herbs being replaced by shrubs and then trees), he argued that the sequence of invasion of species is highly individualistic and determined by their ability to disperse to a site and subsequently compete. This theme was reiterated by Drury and Nisbet (1973), who emphasized the importance of life history traits of successional species. They suggested that most of what happens during succession is best understood as a consequence of differential growth, survival, and colonizing ability of species adapted to conditions along environmental gradients.

In contrast to Drury and Nisbet (1973), Egler (1954) argued in his initial floristic composition model of succession that, in many circumstances, succession is driven by patterns of early establishment and that subsequent change is largely a matter of differential longevity. Because early establishment would be variable owing to potentially random variations (e.g., in climate and seed rain), he posited that successional change is neither fixed nor predictable, in contrast to what would be expected from Clements's relay floristics model. Mechanisms driving succession include stochastic migration of propagules to the disturbed site and differential longevity of plants. All pioneer species, many seral species, and some climax species are initially present after disturbance. Some of these germinate, becoming quickly established, whereas others germinate quickly but grow more slowly and for a longer period; still others become established later. Major changes in community dominance occur when larger, longer-lived, and slower-growing species out-compete smaller pioneer species.

A common failing of early studies of succession was lack of consideration of mechanisms that might be responsible for the observed changes. The work of Egler (1954) and Drury and Nisbet (1973) represented progress in that they suggested mechanisms for observed patterns, but they fell short of providing a conceptual framework for thinking about the multiple patterns observed in nature. The lack of scientific rigor in earlier studies of succession caught the attention of Connell and Slatyer (1977), who recognized that successional mechanisms need to be "stated in the form of hypotheses testable by controlled field experiments." To facilitate this approach, they proposed three models of succession, which they called facilitation, tolerance, and inhibition. While these do not really represent distinct mechanisms (i.e., various combinations could apply at any one time), they did help ecologists organize their thinking about the processes that drive succession and how they vary with environmental and disturbance context. The facilitation model most closely fits the Clementsian vision of succession in which early invaders alter the environment in such a way as to make it more habitable for successors than for themselves. The tolerance model captures the key elements of Gleason's framework in proposing that succession is largely determined by patterns of dispersal and differences in life history and physiology. The inhibition model depicts succession as a process in which early invaders establish, usurp resources, and thereby competitively exclude would-be successors, ideas similar to those introduced by Egler. In this final model, succession only proceeds when the populations of the current occupants decline due to their inability to reestablish.

An alternative approach to understanding succession is to examine traits of individual species and the progression of those traits through the successional sequence. For example, Grime (1977, 1979) proposed that spatial and temporal patterns could be understood in terms of three primary plant strategies: ruderal (ephemeral), competitor, and stress-tolerant, reflecting basic tradeoffs in life history traits. Ruderal species are generally easily dispersed and reproduce quickly, but they are not effective competitors, with the consequence being that they are most important early in the successional sequence. Competitors increase during the initial succession sequence owing to their greater ability to grow quickly and out-compete other species for light, but because they are depressed under low soil resource levels, they tend to be less important in climax communities. Stress-tolerant species are generally poor competitors in a context of rapid community development, but do well in the resource-limited later stages of succession. In a similar conceptual framework, Tilman (1985) proposed that temporal and spatial variation in species composition through succession could be understood in terms of variation in relative growth (and reproductive) rates of species in response to varying proportions of resources. Succession results from a gradient through time in the relative availabilities of limiting resources. Tilman argued that succession should thus be repeatable or directional only to the extent that the resource-supply trajectories are repeatable or directional. He proposed that succession often involves a gradient from habitats with resource-poor soils but high available light at the soil surface to habitats with resource-rich soils but low light availability.

Peet (1992) explained that most examples of secondary succession can viewed as driven by a combination of two models or sets of linked processes: a gradient-in-time model where biological characteristics of species can be used to explain their distributions along temporal gradients (Whittaker 1953; Pickett 1976), and a competitive sorting model where population interactions, particularly competition, cause a temporal gradient in the level of community organization and predictability (Margalef 1963, 1968). These models are neither mutually exclusive nor all encompassing, but it is possible to view autochthonous community change as variously representing the contributions of these two sets of mechanisms. In much the same fashion as different adaptations of species result in their being arrayed as an overlapping series along a resource or physical environment gradient, so too might they be expected to form a successional sequence representing a sequence of physiological or life history adaptations. This model captures the core ideas of Grime (1979), Tilman (1985), and Smith and Huston (1989). The competitive sorting model applies to the case where all species can readily disperse to a site, but they sort out over time through competition to ultimately match the specifics of the site, with composition becoming more predictable from site variables over time, and beta diversity increasing.

OLD-FIELD HERBS

In his 1932 description of the vegetation of North Carolina, Wells described the mosaic of old-fields as the "melting pot where foreigners and natives mingle." Wells described the general sequence of change, noting that the "foreigners" are relatively more important in the early years; indeed, many were weeds during cultivation, such as *Digitaria sanguinalis* (L.) Scop. [Botanical nomenclature follows Weakley et al. 2012] (crabgrass) and *Cynodon dactylon* (L.) Pers. (Bermuda grass). Wells (1932) and Crafton and Wells (1934) observed that the sequence of change in herbaceous dominance during the first three to four years was highly predictable, interpreting this as a process consistent with facilitation as subsequently described by Connell and Slatyer (1977).

Oosting (1942) provided a synthesis based on quantitative sampling of abandoned fields of varying age (i.e., years after abandonment), paying particular attention to replicating each age with fields as similar as possible in physical features (e.g., soil type and texture, slope, aspect). Keever's (1950) classic study of the early stages of old-field development provided even more detail. One-year-old fields sampled early in the summer after abandonment had a total of roughly 35 annual and perennial herbaceous species. Although these fields were not identical in species composition, they consistently had two species with highest density and frequency: *D. sanguinalis* and *Conyza canadensis* (L.) Cronq. (horseweed). Almost all first-year species, including *D. sanguinalis* and *C. canadensis*, were also found in two-year-old fields. The Sørensen community coefficient of similarity for first- as compared to second-year fields was high (0.63) despite 26 new species appearing in the second year. At this time, however, there was a pronounced shift in dominance to *Symphyotrichum pilosum* (Willd.) G. L. Nesom (hairy aster), which was absent from first-year fields, and *Ambrosia artemisifolia* L. (ragweed), a minor component of first-year fields (except those abandoned in the spring, a time when horseweed is not dispersing). Species richness dropped sharply in the third year after abandonment, corresponding to a rapid increase in dominance of the perennial grass *Andropogon virginicus* L. *s.l.* (broomsedge), which maintained dominance for several years.

Keever's (1950) experimental work showed little evidence for facilitation. Rather, she showed that the changes in species dominance could be understood in terms of modes of species dispersal and life histories (annuals replaced by biennials, subsequently replaced by longer-lived perennials). She suggested that the shift to dominance by broomsedge resulted from superior ability to compete for resources, a mechanism consistent with the gradient-in-time model. Keever (1983) later marveled, after a few decades on the faculty of the more northern Millersville College in Pennsylvania, at the uniqueness of these changes compared to the process of succession on abandoned land elsewhere:

"...the sequence of species and the timing of these changes in old-field succession in the Piedmont of the Southeast are not typical of such succession elsewhere. Nowhere else is there such a fast and distinct change in species dominance. In most places there is a gradual overlapping of species dominance often extended over a much longer time."

Keever's observation foreshadowed the subsequent work of Wright and Fridley (2010; Fridley and Wright 2012) where they document an eastern North American latitudinal gradient in the speed of woody plant invasion during old-field succession.

Much of the attention toward old-field vegetation has been devoted to understanding general patterns of change, with little study of the variability in those patterns. Schafale and Christensen (1986) examined variation among herb communities in three-to-seven-year-old fields. They found that species richness varied widely among such fields (14 to > 50 species/1,000 m^2) and was positively correlated with soil pH and cation availability. These same factors were also highly correlated with trends in species composition, suggesting that by year three, significant competitive sorting had already occurred. Standing crop and productivity, however, were more highly correlated with soil organic matter and may reflect other variables associated with the conditions of the field at abandonment or water availability. This suggests that there are multiple, independent factors influencing variation in old-field species composition that are independent of those that influence production.

During the early years of succession, seedlings of wind-dispersed *Pinus echinata* Miller (shortleaf pine) and *P. taeda* L. (loblolly pine) (in the 1930s and earlier, largely *P. echinata*, but by the 1950s, almost exclusively *P. taeda*) and hardwood species, such as *Fraxinus americana* L. (white ash), *Ulmus alata* Michx. (slippery elm), *Liquidambar styraciflua* L. (sweetgum), *Liriodendron tulipifera* L. (yellow poplar), and *Acer rubrum* L. (red maple), became established. Pines are generally favored in an environment of high light availability and nutrient and water stress, and typically form a closed canopy by the 10th year. On moister sites, sweetgum and tulip popular may share dominance with pine. The suite of herb species typical of old fields is virtually absent thereafter, because of the reduced light and soil resources under the closed forest canopy. In addition, there is ample evidence that the dominant old-field herbs significantly influence the patterns of early tree establishment. For example, most pine seedlings become established during the first three years after abandonment, before the development of an herbaceous thatch, which inhibits pine seedling growth (Oosting 1942). This accentuates the even-aged structure of the old-field pine stands.

De Steven (1991a,b) experimentally evaluated the role of dominant old-field herbs (and the animals that associate with them) with regard to the invasion of loblolly pine and the five previously mentioned early successional hardwood species common in the North Carolina Piedmont. De Steven found that competition from herbs, along with rodent herbivory, had significant effects on seedling emergence and the growth of many, though not all, of these species. Loblolly pine exhibited the highest levels of seedling emergence, seedling survival, and seedling height growth in all treatment combinations. Accordingly, her data help explain why, although all of these species produce wind-dispersed seeds that arrive at old-field sites in potentially large numbers, loblolly pine usually initiates the woody species stage of old-field succession.

Although the North Carolina Piedmont provides the primary model system for old-field succession in eastern North America, a number of other areas have received intensive study, such as the Buell plots in New Jersey (e.g., Myster and Pickett 1992). Wright and Fridley (2010) conducted a meta-analysis of these various old-field systems and found a strong inverse latitudinal gradient in the speed of woody plant invasion. These results beg the question of what drives this gradient and how typical the North Carolina Piedmont old fields might be when placed in a broader context. Fridley and Wright (2012) subsequently examined three hypotheses for the cause of the gradient: climate, species pool, and soil fertility. Their experimental study provided convincing evidence that soil fertility was the primary driver. Thus, whereas the North Carolina Piedmont retains its place as the primary model system, one should keep in mind that it represents the low-fertility end of a gradient of old-field study systems ranging geographically from Florida to New England.

SUCCESSIONAL CHANGE IN THE FOREST HERB LAYER

Although we focus primarily on temporal patterns of change in the herbaceous layer following old-field abandonment, it is important that we first provide an overview of successional change in woody species, as these plants greatly influence the environment in which the herbaceous layer occurs. The general pattern of change among woody species during succession is captured in the models proposed by Bormann and Likens (1979), Peet (1981), and Oliver (1982). The changes from old-field abandonment to the formation of an even-aged, closed-canopy forest constitute the establishment phase of development. During this period, species composition is heavily affected by dispersal and spatial processes influencing seed availability. The duration of the establishment phase varies from less than 10 years to several decades in some cases, and outside the Piedmont region, it can be significantly longer (Peet 1992; Wright and Fridley 2010). Peet and Christensen (1988) (fig. 11.1) suggested that the actual length of time appears to be directly related to factors that influence the initial stocking of woody stems (e.g., seed rain and early seedling survivorship), competition from herbaceous species, and site productivity (i.e., tree growth is faster and canopy closure often occurs earlier on productive sites, provided fertility is not sufficient for a dense herbaceous layer to develop and preclude tree establishment).

Canopy closure marks the initiation of the thinning phase. During this period, vegetation pattern and composition are affected heavily by limited light and intense competition for soil resources. Little tree establishment occurs during this period; rather, trees get larger and decline significantly in density (Peet and Christensen 1980a; Knox et al. 1989; Peet 1992). The duration of this phase is also inversely related to tree density and site productivity. Thinning progresses more rapidly on productive sites and where growth rates are high.

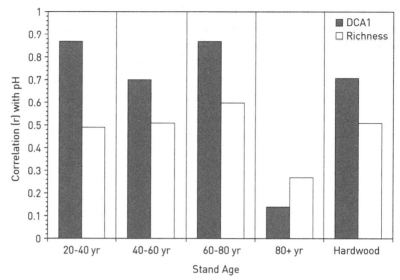

FIGURE 11.1 Spearman rank correlation comparisons of stand first-axis detrended correspondence analysis (DCA 1) ordination scores and species richness (number of species/0.1 ha) with soil pH. Data from Christensen and Peet 1984, Peet and Christensen 1988.

The transition phase begins as tree mortality becomes less driven by natural thinning and begins to create obvious canopy gaps (i.e., surviving trees are no longer able to close the canopy after a mortality event). This phase is marked by considerable small-scale (1–50 m) spatial heterogeneity. It is during this period that shade-intolerant pioneer trees (e.g., pines) are replaced in the understory by more shade-tolerant successors. In the Piedmont region, initiation of this stage can begin as early as 50 years after field abandonment in densely stocked stands, but 70–80 years is more typical. Of course, disturbance events such as hurricanes and tornadoes can dramatically alter the timing (see Xi et al. 2008).

The equilibrium (mature) phase is characterized by an uneven-aged stand structure. Vegetation patterns are determined by key environmental variables (e.g., gradients of moisture and soil properties) and gap-phase transients (Watt 1947a). It has generally been presumed that the broadleaved hardwood stands of the Piedmont are typical of this phase and represent the endpoint of the old-field successional process (Billings 1938; Oosting 1942; Braun 1950). However, Peet and Christensen (1987, 1988) provide clear evidence that most of these forests are experiencing considerable thinning as a consequence of a variety of historic disturbances (e.g., timber high-grading, livestock grazing, and elimination of chronic, low-intensity fire). Furthermore, few of these stands actually originated as old fields (Christensen and Peet 1984).

During the growing seasons of 1977 and 1978, Peet and Christensen sampled the herbaceous layer (cover below 1 m height) with 252 1,000-m² plots in Piedmont forest stands representing a wide range of stand ages, site conditions, and other landscape variables (Peet and Christensen 1980a,b; Christensen and Peet 1981, 1984). They also measured a suite of more than 20 environmental features in each sample plot. They then divided the dataset into 20–40, 40–60, 60–80, and 80+ year-old pine stands and all-aged hardwood stands for comparison. After exclusion of 20 hardwood forest stands located in bottomlands and on rock outcrops, the range of environmental variation represented within each age class was very nearly equivalent (Christensen and Peet 1984).

At the scale of 1,000 m², herb layer diversity varied considerably among these stands, with some stands having fewer than 20 and others having well in excess of 100 species in the herb layer. However, the average number of species was remarkably constant among stand age classes at ~ 50 species/1,000 m². That said, only 203 species were sampled among all of the pine stands, compared to 328 species among a smaller number of hardwood stands. As these results suggest, the range of variability in species composition among stands (Whittaker's β-diversity; 1960) was greater among hardwoods than among pine stands.

Both species composition (represented by the first axis of a detrended correspondence analysis; see Peet and Christensen 1980b, 1988; also see chapter 10, this volume) and herb layer richness were highly correlated with a number of soil variables, most notably pH and soil cations (fig. 11.2). Recall that Schafale and Christensen (1986) observed similar trends among much younger old-field herb communities. These relationships were strong among the early and intermediate-age pine stands, as well as in the mature hardwoods, but weaker (indeed, non-significant) in the 80+ year-old pines. These weak correlations in the older, transition-phase pine stands suggest significant differences in the factors affecting diversity and species composition, and potentially relaxation of competition due to fewer trees competing for resources. Fig. 11.2 shows that diversity increases with stand age at sites with the lowest and highest soil cation levels. It also shows less change with change in cations for the old pine stands than for any other age class.

These results suggest significant temporal changes in the factors affecting the distribution of herb-layer species during succession. In particular, they indicate a significant change in the relationship between species distributions and soil chemistry in transitional pine stands. High correlation between compositional variation and a factor such

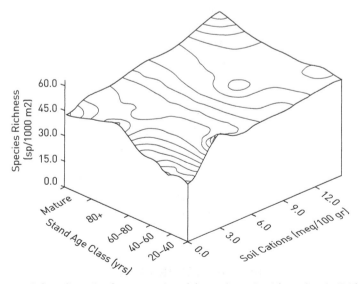

FIGURE 11.2 A three-dimensional representation of changes in species richness (species/0.1 ha with contours of three species) with stand age, and soil cation availability (sum of Ca, Mg, and K meq; highly correlated with pH) among Piedmont forests. Reproduced from Peet and Christensen 1988.

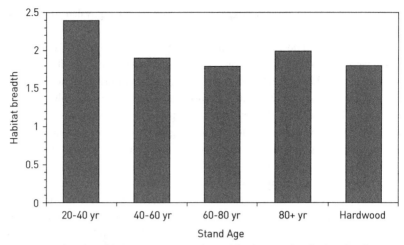

FIGURE 11.3 Habitat breadth (i.e., importance value-weighted species distributions in relation to pH) among different-age forest stands, showing a decline during the thinning phase, followed by an increase in the breakup phase and a decline again into the mature hardwoods. Data from Christensen and Peet 1984.

as pH implies that the range of conditions over which a typical species occurs is more constrained than when the correlation is lower. To test this, Christensen and Peet (1984) calculated the habitat breadth (abundance-weighted standard deviation of pH for stands within which a species occurs) for all species occurring in more than five stands with respect to soil pH. The results indicated that habitat breadth with regard to soil pH is greatest in the youngest pine stands, diminishes in intermediate- age stands (where competition is intense and there has been time for competitive sorting), and increases slightly among transitional pine stands (with relaxation of competition for soil resources because of canopy breakup; fig. 11.3). It is lowest for species in mature hardwood stands.

If convergence in species composition were to occur as conceived by Clements (1936), we would predict that the variance in composition among stands (β-diversity) should diminish through time. Christensen and Peet (1984) found just the opposite; β-diversity was higher in hardwood stands as compared to pine stands of various age classes. A more sophisticated approach to the convergence question implied in Whittaker (1956) is the extent to which vegetation gradients in successional stands resemble those in hardwood stands. Christensen and Peet (1984) pursued this by comparing (using canonical correspondence analysis [CCA]) the first three detrended correspondence analysis (DCA) axis scores of species in common between a particular pine age class and hardwood stands (fig. 11.4). This similarity generally increases with increasing pine stand age, but abruptly decreases in the transition-stage pines. This suggests that the distribution of species relative to one another becomes more like the distribution in hardwoods, but those relationships are altered considerably in transition-stage forests when canopy breakup relaxes competition for soil resources.

NON-SUCCESSIONAL CHANGE IN FOREST HERBS

Chronosequence studies, observations of different-age forests at a single point in time, assume that the environmental context (e.g., climate, landscape features) remains

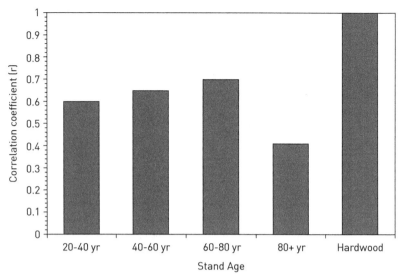

FIGURE 11.4 Comparison of species detrended correspondence analysis ordination scores on the first three axes, with scores in the mature hardwood stands using canonical correlation analysis. Species sorting gradually approaches that of the hardwood stands through competitive sorting, but then declines with breakup of the canopy in the old pine stands. Data from Christensen and Peet 1984.

constant across successional time and differences among different-age plots are due to succession alone (Pickett 1989; Foster and Tilman 2000). Given the extent of directional, non-successional environmental changes like fragmentation, mesophication (Nowacki and Abrams 2008), invasion of nonnative species (chapter 15, this volume), increased deer browse (chapters 16 and 17, this volume), increased deposition of nitrogen (chapter 20, this volume), and climatic change on the Piedmont landscape over the past century (chapters 3 and 21, this volume), this is almost certainly not the case.

A large number (83) of the 1977 Peet and Christensen permanent plots were resampled in 2000 (±1; Taverna et al. 2005) and again (72) in 2010 ((±1; Israel 2012). The wide range of successional ages represented in this dataset provided an opportunity to assess the impacts of non-successional change as separate from changes directly associated with succession over a 33-year timespan.

Taverna et al. (2005) presented the 2000 resampling results for 36 hardwood-dominated stands distributed across a wide range of site conditions. As expected, soil variables such as pH and cation concentration appear responsible for a considerable portion of the variation in herb composition in these stands as represented by first-axis ordination scores (Nonmetric multidimensional scaling; fig. 11.5). However, the vectors of compositional change over the 1977–2000 period in individual stands were consistently aligned and pointed in the same direction along the second ordination axis. This was even true for several stands that had been significantly damaged by Hurricane Fran in 1996. Nearly all of these stands were changing in composition in a consistent manner away from their 1977 composition. Israel (2012) examined change in these plots again in 2010 and found the trends continuing, but with the rate of change having more than doubled from the previous resample.

Schwartz (2007) observed a similar pattern of herb layer compositional change in 47 pine-dominated stands (fig. 11.6). Ages of pines in 1977 ranged from < 20 to >

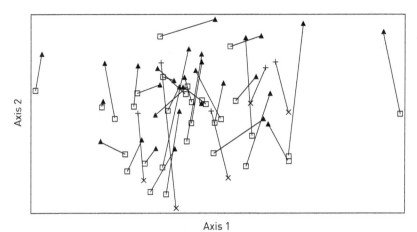

FIGURE 11.5 Nonmetric multidimensional scalilng ordination of 36 hardwood plots in species space with paired-plot vectors from the 1977– 2000 plot observation. Symbols are plots coded for year: closed diamond = 1977, open square = 2000, + = 1977 hurricane plot, × = 2000 hurricane plot. Reproduced from Taverna et al. 2005.

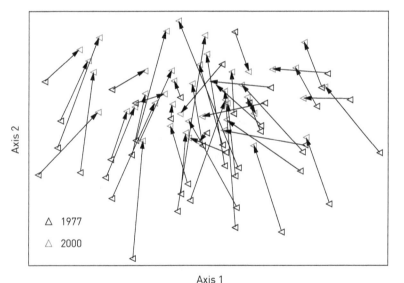

FIGURE 11.6 Nonmetric multidimensional scaling ordination of 47 pine-dominated plots in species space with paired-plot vectors from the 1977–2000 plot observation. Symbols are plots coded for year: black diamond = 1977, gray diamond = 2000. Reproduced from Schwartz 2007.

100 years. The first ordination axis was again correlated with soil pH and cation concentration, and the second axis was correlated with compositional change between 1977 and 2000. This was true regardless of successional age, indicating that much of the directional change in herb layer composition was not related to forest succession, but instead to non-successional changes. Israel (2012) followed up on this analysis by again resampling the plots in 2010. The trend away from the range of 1977 composition continued, but the changes were much greater between 2000 and 2010 than during the much longer period of 1977–2000. She then projected the 2010 composition

of the 1977 stands based on the differences in plot composition associated with age in 1977 (the classic space-for-time approach advocated by Pickett 1989) and compared this projected composition with the observed composition. She observed that all of the plots had changed dramatically away from the projected change and in a consistent direction within ordination space. These studies make it clear that Piedmont forests are changing dramatically in ways unrelated to old-field succession.

The herb-layer censuses described above included species of true herbs, as well as low (< 1 m tall) shrubs and tree seedlings. At the scales of 1,000, 25, and 1 m², Schwartz (2007) found that species richness of herbs alone significantly decreased between sample dates, whereas richness of herb layer woody species increased in both pines and hardwoods. The net effect of these changes was that herb-layer species richness at all three scales remained relatively constant between sampling intervals in both hardwood and pine stands. However, when Israel (1912) resampled these same plots in 2010, she found that species richness had declined significantly in both pine and hardwood plots, and across the pH gradient.

Schwartz (2007) reported that total species richness across all plots showed a net decline between 1977 and 2000 of 7.3 percent in the hardwood plots and 1.8 percent in the pine plots. Furthermore, there was considerable turnover in species composition. For example, among the hardwoods, 70 herb-layer species disappeared between 1977 and 2000, and all of these were natives. A total of 49 new species appeared in 2000, and of these, 42 were natives and seven were exotic. Species that were less common in 1977 were more likely to disappear. Sixty-one percent (89 out of 145) of herb species that occurred in 10 or fewer plots in 1977 declined in plot frequency, and more than half of those that declined (52 species) were not recorded at all in 2000. Schwartz (2007) observed similar patterns of species turnover and net increase in nonnative herb species in successional pine stands. This overall loss of herb-layer species richness is consistent with other studies showing regional losses of species (e.g., Tilman et al. 1994; Pimm et al. 1995).

Although it is not possible to pinpoint the precise cause of these non-successional changes, closer examination of compositional change during the 1977–2000 period suggests that three factors were especially important: hurricane disturbance, grazing by white-tailed deer, and increased abundance of exotic species. Two native weedy herbs, *Phytolacca americana* L. and *Erechtites hieraciifolia* (L.) Raf. ex de Candolle, increased dramatically in hurricane-damaged pine and hardwood stands for a period of two years, suggesting a temporary relaxation in the competitive environment of the herbaceous layer that would facilitate establishment of other species. Browsing by white-tailed deer likely accounts for a significant amount of the observed changes in herb-layer composition and species richness. Exact numbers are not available for the 1970s, but deer populations in the North Carolina Piedmont were quite sparse at that time (fewer than 1/km²) and in our study area remained so until after 1990. Today, deer populations exceed 16/km² in many places, including the vicinity of the Peet and Christensen study plots. In both pines and hardwoods, significant declines in the frequency and abundance of preferentially browsed species, including all legumes, *Chimophila maculata* (L.) Pursh., *Goodyera pubescens* (Willd.) R. Brown, and *Euonymus americana* L., are almost certainly due to deer. Legume cover declined by 40 percent during 1977–2000, and by 2010, had declined by over 70 percent in all plots compared to 1977, and in hardwood plots in 2010, it was at less than 20 percent the level of cover exhibited in 1977. By 2010, orchids had nearly disappeared. Vine cover, largely composed of such charismatic species as *Lonicera japonica* Thunberg (Japanese honeysuckle), *Toxicodendron radicans* (L.) Kuntze (poison ivy), *Smilax* spp. L. (greenbriar), *Muscadinia rotundifolia* (Michaux) Small (muscadine), and *Vitis spp.* L. (grape), had declined by 70 percent in 2000 and by over 90 percent in 2010. The only family that showed a large increase was the Poaceae, due to the spread of the exotic *Microstigeum vimineum* (Trinius) A. Camus, which increased across all plots by a factor of eight between 1977 and 2000, but by a factor of 24 between 1977 and 2010. Despite the increase in deer browse, other exotic species continued to invade and increase in this landscape with their total cover having increased by a factor of 10 over the 33-year period.

Increased abundance of woody species in the herb layer between 1977 and 2000 was contrary to the expected effects of deer browsing, but likely a response to the canopy being opened in many stands by the occurrence of Hurricane Fran in 1996. However, between 2000 and 2010, this pattern reversed, perhaps because of canopy closure and the large-scale elimination of herbaceous food for deer, which then fed more intensively on woody species.

One pattern widely observed in Piedmont hardwood stands (e.g., McDonald et al. 2002; Taverna et al. 2005) has been the steady increase in *Acer rubrum* L. (red maple) and *Fagus grandifolia* Ehrh. (American beech) at the expense of the canopy oaks (*Quercus* spp.) and hickories (*Carya* spp.), species traditionally viewed as the climax species of the region (Oosting 1942; Braun 1950). The steady decline in the importance of oaks and hickories relative to maples and beech over the 33 years of observation suggests a long-term trend in canopy composition consistent with the hypothesis of mesophication of eastern forests (Nowacki and Abrams 2008). Abrams (1998) describes *Acer rubrum* as a "supertree," able to compete under varied conditions, the only conspicuous exception being in the presence of recurrent fire. The consistent decline of oaks and hickories, particularly evident in plots dating back to the early 1930s and now spanning 80 years (McDonald et al. 2002), is consistent with the loss of low-intensity fire early in the 20th century, though deer herbivory, which has become a factor only since the early 1990s, may now be accelerating the process due to preferential feeding on oak (Waller and Alverson 1997; Wakeland and Swihart 2009). Regardless of the mechanism, this mesophication is resulting in much denser canopies and consequent lower light levels to support the herbaceous layer.

Other changes in this landscape during the period 1977–2010 have likely influenced change in forest herb layer composition and diversity, but their effects are more difficult to diagnose from these data. The human population of this region increased by over 70 percent during the interval 1977–2010 (U.S. Census Bureau), and this growth was accompanied by similar increases in urban development and land fragmentation. McDonald and Urban (2006) examined the herbaceous layer near urban and suburban edges in Piedmont forests and found large increases in exotics and significant increases in temperature associated with these edges. Subsequent unpublished work by Sexton and Urban has documented increases of up to 10°C in temperature within Piedmont forests near urban heat islands (see White et al. 2002; Carreiro and Tripler 2005; Imhoff et al. 2010).

CONCLUSIONS

To conclude, we return to the questions posed in the introduction. First, what are the key environmental factors influencing herb distribution at various stages in the succession following abandonment of agricultural land on the North Carolina Piedmont?

Although there are major changes in species dominance and community composition during succession and across environmental gradients, these patterns are best understood as a consequence of responses of individual species related to their opportunities to disperse and their competitive abilities at particular sites. A few individuals of woody plant species that will dominate late in succession may arrive early and simply outlive pioneers, supporting Egler's initial composition hypothesis; however, this is most certainly not the case for herbs. Virtually none of the herb species common in pine and hardwood stands is found in old fields.

At every stage of succession, a significant proportion of the variability in herbaceous species composition tracks soil variation. Across the entire landscape, soil chemistry and moisture conditions (determined by parent material, topography, and proximity to streams) account for much of the variation. Furthermore, these same variables are highly correlated with variation in overall species richness. It is important to note, however, that the strength of the correlations vary considerably with successional stage, as does the relative importance of other factors. Whereas soil factors are correlated with variation in vegetation among old fields, and the correlation increases in the competitive environment of the thinning phase of forest development, the strength of those correlations is not nearly as strong among old, transitional pine stands. Although difficult to quantify, it is clear that old-field composition is heavily influenced by landscape effects, such as proximity to other fields and disturbed areas that provide important sources of seeds. Much of the variation among old-field soils is due to variation in farming practices (e.g., liming and fertilizer applications), whereas such variation among forest stands is generally tied to the chemical character of the parent rock. Thus, sites that might be considered to be rich in soil resources due to practices before land abandonment may become less so as those historical effects diminish through time (see Satterson 1985; chapter 19, this volume).

The significant decline in correlation between soil site variables and species composition among late-stage pine stands is noteworthy. Christensen and Peet (1984) suggested that this is a consequence of changes in the physical structure of these stands (such as the existence of canopy gaps) that produce considerable heterogeneity in the light environment and reduce competition for soil resources. Put another way, understory light availability is uniformly low among pine stands at earlier stages and becomes highly variable at this stage, whereas soil resources are extremely limiting in successional stands, but likely become more available with reduced competition from canopy trees.

Variation in species richness through this successional sequence is considerably more complex than Odum's (1969) expectation that richness increases with increasing successional age and more in keeping with the competition-driven hypotheses of Peet and Christensen (1988). At the spatial scale of a 1,000 m^2 sample, the average number of herbaceous species encountered is remarkably similar (i.e., about 50 species) among successional ages. However, when comparing the total list of species encountered across the full range of environments among ages, species number consistently increases, suggesting increased beta diversity and increased competitive sorting with time.

Our second question was what do these patterns tell us regarding the mechanisms that underlie the dynamics of herb populations? Among the successional mechanisms proposed by Connell and Slatyer (1977), the tolerance and inhibition models seem to provide the most explanatory power for old-field succession in the North Carolina Piedmont. Keever's (1950) observations and experiments demonstrated clearly that variation in life history account for much of the change observed early in the successional process (e.g., the succession from annuals to biennials to perennials). Longer-lived herbaceous dominants, such as broomsedge, severely limit light at the soil surface and thereby prevent the subsequent invasion of many other herb species (inhibition). Similarly, it appears that usurpation of resources by pines prevents invasion of later successional species until the pine canopy begins to deteriorate.

There is no evidence for facilitation in its most simplistic form (i.e., a species directly prepares the way for another species). However, when one considers the full array of interspecies interactions (e.g., competition, dispersal, herbivory) occurring during succession, invasion of particular species is often facilitated by other species. Pines may limit light and soil nutrients (inhibition), but in so doing, influence the outcome of competition among potential successors. Thus, the successful competitors depend on the pines (Connell and Slatyer's operational definition of facilitation). Similarly, structural features in old fields influence the dispersal of later successional species, which could be viewed as a form of facilitation.

It is clear that changes in the relative availability of resources are important for explaining successional patterns, and that they are probably responsible for shifts in the relative abundance of species. That said, it is also true that designations like "competitive," "stress-tolerant," and "ruderal" are comparative and relativistic and cannot be defined operationally in a rigid fashion. Furthermore, as Tilman (1985) suggests, shifts in relative importance of resources need not be linear or directional; when they are not, then species shifts may be complex as well.

Finally, we asked whether Piedmont forest herbaceous communities are changing in ways not related to old-field plant succession. It is clear that dramatic changes are taking place and the speed of these changes is accelerating. Piedmont forests indeed are moving toward some unknown future composition, something Gilliam (2007) referred to as an "ecological moving target." This is driven by multiple factors including increased deer populations, increasing abundance of exotic species, landscape fragmentation, proximity to urban areas, climate change, and replacement of the original canopy species of the mature hardwood forest with more shade-tolerant species like red maple and beech. Other factors may be responsible as well, and this will likely be an active area of future research.

Much effort to explain variability in the distribution of herbs in successional landscapes has been focused on the importance of competitive interactions in the context of changes in resource availability. If such interactions were the only factors shaping the distributions of herbs in time and space, we would expect to see very high correlations between compositional variation and patterns of environmental variation. Although such correlations do explain significant amounts of variation in composition, they leave large amounts unexplained. It is fitting in closing this chapter to note that other mechanisms are likely to be equally important and that they may defy our attempts to create a unified theory of change. Christensen (1989) described the array of historical effects that influence vegetation composition, including pre- and post-abandonment land use and landscape effects such as context and patch spatial scale. Grubb (1977) presented compelling arguments that the distributions of many species are best understood in regard to the conditions required for their establishment. When this is the case, competition among mature plants may be limited in its explanatory power, and the extant pattern may be in large part a consequence of history. Such problems provide ample opportunity for future research.

ACKNOWLEDGMENTS

We gratefully acknowledge the many contributions of Dean Urban, who has been a long-term collaborator in explorations of succession in the Piedmont region and in the maintenance of the Duke Forest succession plots. We thank Kristin Taverna and Laura Phillips who conducted the 2000 resample of the Duke Forest plots, and Kimberly Israel who conducted the 2010 resample. Taverna and Israel took the leads, respectively, in the analyses of the 2000 and 2010 data. Miguel Schwartz also contributed significantly to the analysis of the 2000 data. The U.S. National Science Foundation funded much of the work in the Duke Forest through grants DEB-7708743, DEB-7804043, DEB-8102775, BSR-8314655, BSR-8502430, BSR-8905926, BSR-9107357, and DEB97-07551.

12 Composition and Dynamics of the Understory Vegetation in the Boreal Forests of Quebec

Louis De Grandpré, Yves Bergeron, Nicole J. Fenton, Thuy Nguyen, Catherine Boudreault, and Pierre Grondin

The boreal forest of Quebec extends from the 48th to the 58th northern parallels (fig. 12.1). It can be subdivided into four forest domains (from south to north): the *Abies balsamea* (Mill.) and *Betula papyrifera* (Marsh.) domain; the *Picea mariana* (Mill.) and feathermoss domain; the *Picea mariana* lichen woodland; and the forest-tundra domain (Grondin et al. 1996; Saucier et al. 1998). This chapter is restricted to the *Abies balsamea-Betula papyrifera* and the *Picea mariana*-feathermoss domains, which extend from 48° to 52° north latitude and include much of the closed-canopy, commercial boreal forest in Quebec. In this zone, average annual temperatures range between 1° and -2.5°C, and average annual precipitation is between 600 and 1,400 mm. Temperature and precipitation decrease toward the north, and precipitation increases from west to east. The main tree species are *Picea mariana*, *Picea glauca* (Moench), *Abies balsamea*, *Pinus banksiana* (Lamb.), *Larix laricina* (Du Roi), *Populus tremuloides* (Michx.), and *Betula papyrifera*.

In addition to the south-north transition from *Abies balsamea*-dominated forests to *Picea mariana* forests, there is a strong east-west gradient that mainly relates to topography and forest fire frequency. In the east, a low fire frequency associated with higher altitude and a more pronounced topography allows for the dominance of late successional stands of *Abies balsamea* and *Picea mariana*, while a relatively flat topography

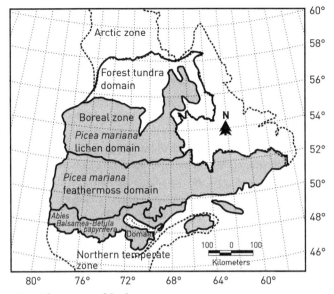

FIGURE 12.1 Boreal forest zones of Quebec.

and frequent fires are responsible for the abundance of post-fire stands dominated by deciduous species and *Pinus banksiana* in the west. The boreal ecosystem is strongly controlled by disturbances such as fire, insect outbreaks, and windthrow (Bergeron et al. 1998). Although fire is present in all of the boreal forest, there is a decrease in fire activity toward its eastern part. Since *Abies balsamea* is a late successional species, the impact of spruce budworm outbreaks, which cause significant mortality of *Abies balsamea*, increases toward the east (Grondin et al. 1996; Bergeron and Leduc 1998). Major windstorms are also reported in the eastern part of the boreal forest (Ruel 2000). Forest canopy composition is also strongly associated with local site conditions. With the exception of its western part, which belongs to the northern Clay Belt where clay and organic soils are abundant, the area is located on the Canadian Shield and is characterized by tills of various depths and fluvio-glacial coarse deposits. The northern Clay Belt of Ontario and Quebec south of James Bay is a vast physiographic region created by lacustrine deposits left after maximal extension of proglacial lakes (Vincent and Hardy 1977).

The total vascular flora is estimated to contain less than 1,000 species, including only 22 tree species. It is mainly represented by species with boreal affinities, with few intrusions from temperate-deciduous or arctic regions. Forest species compose a small part of this diversity with less than 300 common species. Although it is species poor, the boreal forest is characterized by understory dominants that vary from forbs and ericaceous shrubs to feathermosses, or *Sphagnum*. The variability in the composition of the understory layers has been recognized by many boreal ecologists and is the foundation of many classification systems using indicator species (Cajander and Ilvessalo 1921; Jurdant et al. 1977; Bergeron and Bouchard 1984).

The composition of the understory can be explained by several nonexclusive factors. It may be controlled by species' individualistic responses to regional climate, local site conditions (Whittaker and Levin 1975), and canopy cover composition (chapter 9, this volume). Disturbances also exert a strong influence on understory community composition and species distribution. Boreal plant species present various adaptive strategies to persist in the context of disturbance. The species can be classified into different functional groups according to their ability to tolerate disturbance, their successional status, their reproductive strategy, and their competitive ability (Noble and Slatyer 1980; Rowe 1983; Halpern 1989; Noble and Gitay 1996). Rowe (1983) identified five major groups of species in boreal forest ecosystems based on their reproductive strategies: pioneer species with high seed production and highly dispersed (*invaders*); species able to resprout following fire from buried vegetative organs (*endurers*); species surviving fire from protective organs such as thick bark (*resisters*); species evading fire by storing seeds in the humus or mineral layers (*evaders*); and late successional species more common in unburned areas and not adapted to maintain themselves in the context of recurrent fires (*avoiders*). The abundance of each of these groups over the landscape or in a plant community is largely determined by the fire frequency (Johnson 1979). At one end of the spectrum with frequent fires, invaders are more abundant, while at the other end, avoiders dominate the landscape. Thus, a regional variation in the fire regime characteristics would have repercussions on the composition and diversity of the understory. In addition, forest management has recently contributed to changing understory composition and consequently has to be considered as a factor responsible for species distribution (chapter 13, this volume). In this chapter, we discuss the factors that control the composition and dynamics of the understory community of the Quebec boreal forest. In the first section, the influence of fire recurrence, site type, and cover type on understory community composition are analyzed throughout the range of the commercial boreal forest. The second section focuses on the role of forest management in understory community dynamics.

INFLUENCE OF FIRE RECURRENCE, SITE, AND COVER TYPE ON UNDERSTORY COMMUNITY COMPOSITION AND DYNAMICS

Methods

We used data from the ecological survey of the Ministère des Ressources naturelles du Quebec to study the distribution of understory species (Bergeron et al. 1992). The ecological survey is based on an extensive uniform sampling including 15,000 plots well distributed in the southern boreal zone (Saucier et al. 1994). Sampling was designed to be representative of the distribution of physical features (soil type and hydric regime) and cover types present in each ecological region of the boreal forest. Trees, shrubs, herbs, ferns, and nonvascular species were sampled in circular plots of 400 m². Only forests with a dominant canopy of 7 m and more were sampled. Early post-fire communities with an opened canopy were not sampled. The percent cover of all species was estimated over the whole area based on cover classes ("+" for the presence of one individual, 1–5 percent, 6–25 percent, 26–40 percent, 41–60 percent, 61–80 percent, 81–100 percent). The environment of each plot was described in terms of hydric regime, type of soil deposit, geographical position, altitude, and many more variables (Ministe`re des Ressources naturelles du Quebec 1994).

We estimated fire recurrence using the forest fire data of the last 30 years and the forest age-class distribution based on the last provincial forest surveys. Fire recurrence was calculated for each ecological region (characterized by uniform association

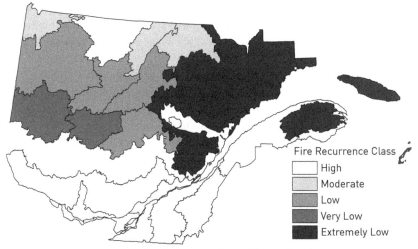

FIGURE 12.2 Fire recurrence map for the commercial boreal forest of Quebec. Fire recurrence was estimated within each ecological region. Ecological regions with similar fire recurrence were then grouped (high: 50–100 years, moderate: 101–150 years, low: 151–200 years, very low: 201–250 years, and extremely low: > 250 years).

of dominant vegetation under uniform regional climate; fig. 12.2). For the analysis, five qualitative fire recurrence classes were considered: high (50–100 years), moderate (101–150 years), low (151–200 years), very low (201–250 years), and extremely low (> 250 years, fig. 12.2). Fire recurrence is thus based on the current forest age-class distribution over an ecological region. The site type is a combination of the surficial deposit and the hydric regime of each plot. To simplify the interpretations, we created five site type classes based on the soil descriptions of each plot: organic deposit with hydric moisture regime, fine-textured with subhydric moisture regime, medium-textured deposits with mesic hydric regime, coarse-textured deposit with mesic-xeric moisture regime, and thin soils with xeric-mesic moisture regime. Finally, the cover type for each plot was assigned based on the dominant tree species (one or two) using the species cover data. We identified six dominant cover types: deciduous canopy, mixture of deciduous and coniferous species, canopy dominated by *Picea mariana*, mixture of *Picea mariana* and *Abies balsamea*, canopy dominated by *Abies balsamea*, and canopy dominated by *Pinus banksiana*.

Data Analyses

Data analyses were performed at two levels. First, we grouped plots with similar fire recurrence, site type, and cover type and used multivariate analyses to evaluate the effect of physical and ecological factors on understory species distribution and community composition. Second, understory species with similar life history traits in the context of fire were grouped. The richness and cover patterns of these groups were interpreted along the fire recurrence gradient and in relation to cover type and site type.

Understory community dynamics were then described using a correspondence analysis (CA). To perform this analysis, the size of the dataset had to be reduced, and plots were grouped. Each group represented a combination of fire recurrence, site type, and cover type (5 × 5 × 6 combinations). For each combination, we calculated the mean species cover based on the number of 400 m² plots. Although 150 groups were possible, only 108 were used for further analyses. Some combinations had no or too few observations (plots) to be used (only groups with more than five plots were used for further analyses). The CA was performed on the vegetation dataset of 108 groups (considered as stands) and 189 species. The compositional gradient was interpreted using fire recurrence, site type, cover type, latitudinal and longitudinal gradients, altitude and richness of the different components of the understory (total richness, herbs [including ferns, *Lycopodium*, grasses, and sedges], shrubs, ericaceous shrubs, moss, lichens, and *Sphagnum* richness). These variables are shown in the ordination diagram (fig. 12.3). Quantitative variables are represented by vectors in the ordination diagram (Spearman correlation, $p < .05$), and class variables are represented by their centroids.

More than 13,500 plots were used for further analyses. To evaluate the effects of fire recurrence on understory community dynamics, we classified the understory species according to Rowe's (1983) reproductive strategies. Only the most common herb, fern, ericaceous, and shrub species were classified (species with a weight of 10 or more given by the CA were retained: 87 species out of 170 excluding lichen, mosses, and *Sphagnum*). Lichens, mosses, and *Sphagnum* species were not considered because they behave differently from vascular species along the successional sequence (see appendix 12.1 for a complete list of species). This would have obscured the interpretations of the patterns of the different groups.

The invaders were characterized by 14 species, including *Epilobium angustifolium* (L.) and *Rubus idaeus* (L.). The most common reproductive strategy for boreal species

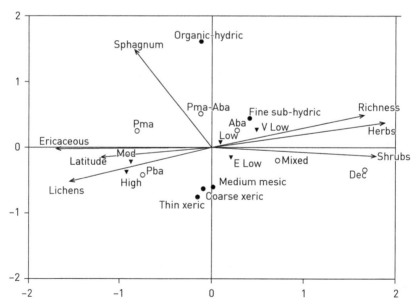

FIGURE 12.3 Scores of the environmental and ecological factors on the first two axes of the correspondence analysis of the 109 groups by 189 species. Centroids of fire recurrence classes, site and cover types with correlation coefficients of latitude and the richness of different species groups are shown in the diagram. Only significant correlations are shown on the graph. Fire recurrence classes: moderate, Mod; very low, V Low; extremely low, E Low. Cover types: *Abies balsamea*, Aba; deciduous, Dec; *Piceamariana*, Pma; *Picea mariana-Abies balsamea*, Pma-Aba; *Pinus bankasiana*, Pba.

is resprouting after fire from belowground organs (endurers). The endurers composed close to 60 percent of the understory community and were separated in two subgroups: ericaceous endurers (7 species) and endurers (43 species). *Ledum groenlandicum* (Retzius), *Vaccinium myrtilloides* (Michx.), and *Kalmia angustifolia* (L.) are ericaceous endurers; *Aralia nudicaulis* (L.), *Betula glandulosa* (Michx.), and *Pteridium aquilinum* (L.) are typical endurers. The evaders were represented by seven species in the *Ribes* and *Viburnum* genus. The avoiders comprised 16 late successional species including *Taxus canadensis* (Marsh.), *Circaea alpina* (L.), and *Goodyera repens* (L.). None of the species were classified as resisters.

FIRE RECURRENCE AND UNDERSTORY COMMUNITY COMPOSITION

The first two axes of the CA explained 26 percent and 18 percent, respectively, of the variance in the species matrix (Eigenvalues: 0.364 and 0.241). The variation in understory composition along axis 1 is mainly related to a latitudinal gradient (fig. 12.3). As latitude increases, ericaceous and lichen species are more dominant in the understory (appendix 12.1), and the richness of these groups is higher. Both these species groups are associated with *Picea mariana* and *Pinus banksiana* cover types, as well as high and moderate fire recurrence (fig. 12.3). As latitude decreases, on the right portion of axis 1, total richness of understory increases. Herbs and shrubs are more dominant (appendix 12.1) and are represented by more species. This higher richness is associated with the presence of deciduous and mixed dominated stands. At lower latitudes, a decrease in fire recurrence is observed, and *Abies balsamea* cover types are more frequently encountered (fig. 12.3). The second ordination axis is associated with hydric regime. On the upper part of the axis, organic-hydric sites are found, and they are characterized by a dominance of *Sphagnum* species (both in cover and richness; fig. 12.3 and appendix 12.1). Herb richness is higher on fine-textured soils with a subhydric regime, and lichen richness is highest on sites with xeric moisture regimes (fig. 12.3).

With increasing latitude, the successional sequence associated with *Picea mariana* (with or without *Pinus banksiana*) dominates the landscape. Although climate is related to the increased dominance of *Picea mariana*, fire recurrence also exerts a strong influence on species distribution. Regions with high and moderate fire frequency are dominated by *Picea mariana* and *Pinus banksiana* (table 12.1). Both species are adapted to fire, although *Pinus banksiana* is more restricted to regions that burn frequently. As fire recurrence decreases, *Abies balsamea* becomes more dominant in the landscape. The distribution and abundance of the different site types over the landscape (see table 12.1) will also contribute to influencing the distribution of tree species and probably affect fire recurrence (if the probability of burning decreases along with an increasing moisture regime). *Pinus banksiana* is usually more abundant on sandy soils with a xeric moisture regime. *Picea mariana* can also be dominant on this type of soil, but it is more associated with organic soils with a hydric moisture regime (table 12.2). Deciduous species and *Abies balsamea* usually dominate on the mesic-xeric moisture regime (table 12.2). These factors will interact in space and time to influence understory community composition and species distribution. Succession not only has to be interpreted along a time gradient (variation in cover type) but has to consider the physical setting of the landscape and the disturbance regime. In

Table 12.1 Proportion of site types and cover types in the fire recurrence classes

Recurrence	Site types (%)					Cover types (%)					
	O	FS	MM	CX	TX	Dec	Mix	Aba	Pba	Pma	Pma-Aba
Frequent	10.5	3.7	67.2	16.6	2.0	5.1	9.1	3.1	37.5	44.9	0.3
Moderate	10.7	2.2	77.1	8.2	1.8	2.3	8.5	7.4	14.6	59.4	7.8
Low	20.0	16.6	47.9	11.6	3.9	9.8	18.4	6.1	15.0	46.5	4.2
Very low	20.2	16.5	40.1	17.7	5.5	18.9	25.4	8.4	18.0	25.5	3.8
Extremely low	7.9	17.7	57.7	7.6	9.1	10.2	13.1	29.7	2.9	29.6	14.5

*Cover types: deciduous canopy (Dec), mixture of deciduous and coniferous species (Mix), canopy dominated by *Picea mariana* (Pma), mixture of *Picea mariana* and *Abies balsamea* (Pma-Aba), canopy dominated by *Abies balsamea* (Aba), and canopy dominated by *Pinus Banksiana* (Pba).

Site types: organic deposit with hydric moisture regime (O), fine-textured with subhydric moisture regime (FS), medium-textured deposits with mesic hydric regime (MM), coarse-textured deposits with mesic-xeric moisture regime (CX), and thin soils with xeric-mesic moisture regime (TX).

Table 12.2 Proportion of cover types in the different site types

Site type	Cover types (%)					
	Dec	Mix	Aba	Pba	Pma	Pma-Aba
Organic-hydric	2.2	5.1	13.0	1.6	69.5	8.6
Fine subhydric	12.4	16.4	32.1	6.7	23.2	9.3
Medium mesic	13.0	18.5	17.9	7.8	32.3	10.5
Coarse xeric	7.8	12.6	8.8	36.2	29.4	5.2
Thin xeric	8.7	19.3	17.3	6.0	37.1	11.6

*Cover types: deciduous canopy (Dec), mixture of deciduous and coniferous species (Mix), canopy dominated by *Picea mariana* (Pma), mixture of *Picea mariana* and *Abies balsamea* (Pma-Aba), canopy dominated by *Abies balsamea* (Aba), and canopy dominated by *Pinus banksiana* (Pba).

the following section, we address the impact of these factors on the understanding of boreal forest understory community dynamics using Rowe's (1983) reproductive strategies.

SUCCESSIONAL SEQUENCES

Understory Changes in the *Abies balsamea-Betula papyrifera* Domain

In the Abies balsamea-Betula papyrifera domain (fig. 12.1), the most common successional sequence observed, involve the early dominance of *Betula papyrifera* and *Populus tremuloides* after fire. In the absence of fire, the deciduous canopy will be replaced by a coniferous one and will be dominated by *Abies balsamea* (Bergeron and Charron 1994; Bergeron 2000; De Grandpré et al. 2000; Gauthier et al. 2000). As changes are observed in canopy composition with time elapsed since fire, the understory communities are also dynamic through time (De Grandpré et al. 1993). After canopy closure, pioneer species such as *Epilobium angusltifolium*, *Solidago rugosa* (L.), and *Rubus idaeus* disappear from the understory and are replaced by more shade-tolerant species including *Aster macrophyllus* (L.), *Acer spicatum* (Lam.), and *Aralia nudicaulis*. These species may persist for a long time in the understory by vegetative growth. Some changes in species composition do occur after canopy closure, but understory community dynamics are mostly characterized by shifts in community dominance, associated with changes in the composition of the canopy (Carleton and Maycock 1978; Hart and Chen 2008). Species richness and overall abundance are higher under a deciduous canopy and decline with the increasing dominance of *Abies balsamea* in the overstory (Foster and King 1986; De Grandpré et al. 1993). As conifers increase their dominance in the canopy, light penetration to the forest floor decreases, and the understory is dominated by even more shade-tolerant species like *Taxus canadensis*. These successional changes of the understory can be predicted from species life history strategies, such as establishment ability and shade tolerance (Noble and Slatyer 1980; Halpern 1989; De Grandpré et al. 2011). As *Abies balsamea* becomes a major component of the landscape, disturbances such as windthrow and spruce budworm outbreaks will affect community dynamics. Gap creation resulting from these disturbances will contribute to an increase in richness and allow many early successional understory species to remain longer in post-fire communities. Thus, understory community succession does not operate in a linear fashion with time elapsed since fire. De Grandpré and Bergeron (1997) hypothesized that openings of the canopy resulting from spruce budworm outbreaks allow for the reestablishment or the increase in cover of some early successional species, a situation that makes the understory more resistant to change after other disturbances.

Understory Changes in the *Picea mariana*-Feathermoss Domain

In the *Picea mariana*-feathermoss domain (fig. 12.1), succession after fire is characterized by the immediate establishment of a mixture of *Pinus banksiana* and *Picea mariana*. In the absence of fire for long time intervals, *Picea mariana* will dominate the canopy (St-Pierre et al. 1992). *Picea mariana* often dominates throughout the successional sequence, and few changes occur in canopy composition with time elapsed since last fire (Cogbill 1985; Foster 1985; Morneau and Payette 1989; Gauthier et al. 2000).

Several studies have shown that understory successional changes for vascular plants along the *Picea mariana* chronosequence occur before canopy closure (Dix and Swan 1971; Shafi and Yarranton 1973; Black and Bliss 1978; Foster 1985; Taylor et al. 1987; Sirois and Payette 1989). Most understory species in the *Picea mariana* boreal forest can survive fire and resprout afterward (Ahlgren 1960; Archibold 1979; Carleton and Maycock 1980; Rowe 1983), although depth of burn will affect post-fire succession. Foster (1985) observed that all species present before fire were present in the post-fire community, with the exception of *Empetrum nigrum* (L.). Furthermore, only few invading species were part of the post-fire community. Beside these minor changes in early post-fire succession, few compositional changes will occur in later stages. For bryophytes, depth of burn influences not only to what degree the existing community is killed, but also the conditions available for post-disturbance colonization (i.e., thickness of the humus layer). However, these characteristics vary not only among fires, but also within some fires depending on a variety of factors such as topography, weather, and season (see Ryan 2002 for a review). The impact of disturbance severities on bryophyte community dynamics can remain throughout the life of the forest stand.

Here we describe three stages in bryophyte community dynamics after fire. Immediately after fire, bryophytes and lichens rapidly colonize the burnt forest floor (Black and Bliss 1978; Van Cleve and Viereck 1981). This early community is very heterogeneous, as the species that are able to colonize vary with the thickness of the remnant humus layer (Shafi and Yarranton 1973; Foster 1985), which sometimes varies over very small scales (Ryan 2002; Shetler et al. 2008). In areas where mineral soil is exposed, several crustose and foliose lichen species (*Ceratodon pupureus, Polytrichum juniperinum, Bryum pseudotriquestrus,* and *Marchantia polymorpha*) have been identified as early post-fire colonizers (Black and Bliss 1978; Foster 1985; Van Cleve and Viereck 1981). These species could be classified as invaders using Rowe's 1983 classification. In contrast, in areas where a thick layer of moist peat remains after fire, some *Sphagnum* species can resprout from the peat, resulting in a rapid domination of *Sphagnum* spp (Clymo and Duckett 1986). Other *Sphagnum* spp. (*S. fallax, S. angustifoliuim, S. palustre, S. warnstorfii, S. capillifolium*) also take advantage of the moist, nutrient, and light-rich conditions to rapidly colonize the exposed peat post-fire resulting in a *Sphagnum*-dominated community in these areas (Shafi and Yarranton 1973; Fenton et al. 2005; Benscotter and Vitt 2008). *Sphagnum* spp. in these conditions could be considered as either endurers or invaders.

As the canopy closes, feathermosses (*Pleurozium schreberi, Hylocomium splendens, Ptilium crista-castrensis*), which frequently establish initially beneath small *Picea mariana* trees, colonize the forest floor and can frequently reach 100 percent cover in mineral soil sites after severe fire (Foster 1985; Taylor et al. 1987). In sites with a thick remnant peat layer, feathermoss cover is approximately 50 percent, with the balance covered by previously established *Sphagnum* spp. (Fenton et al. 2005; Benscotter and Vitt 2008). In these conditions, both species can be considered perennial stayers (sensu During 1992) and avoiders (sensu Rowe 1983); however, the latter description does not take into account the high dispersal capacity of many bryophyte species. The distribution of the different humicolous species (e.g., feathermosses, *Dicranum* spp., *Ptilidium ciliare*) across the forest floor in mineral sites is difficult to explain, and while some minor habitat differentiation is evident (Vellak et al. 2003; Frego and Carleton 1995), the bulk of the evidence points to the importance of patterns developed during colonization and the ability of species to maintain cover within their own colonies even after minor disturbances (e.g., rodent damage; Frego 1996).

Coarse, woody debris and other microhabitats (sensu Frisvoll 1997) created by the last fire, as well as microhabitats created by secondary disturbances and stand succession result, represent a diversity of habitats for smaller bryophytes. These smaller species are frequently the most species-rich components of the flora in boreal forests (LaRoi and Stringer 1976; Frisvoll 1997), and the number of species present is largely dependent on the number of microhabitats available (Mills and Macdonald 2004). While these species may be considered avoiders (sensu Rowe 1983) as they do not survive fire in situ and do not rapidly colonize the post-fire environment, they typically have a high reproductive output and are frequently classified as pioneers.

In the extended absence of fire, coniferous forests on mesic to moist sites accumulate thick organic layers (> 20 cm) over the mineral soil (Bonan 1989) due to a positive evapotranspiration budget and the low rates of decomposition of many conifer needles (Moore et al. 1999) and bryophytes (Turetsky et al. 2008). This process is accentuated in the significant areas of the boreal forest prone to successional paludification (i.e., the transformation of a forest on mineral soil into a peatland via forest succession [Simard et al. 2007]). In these sites, *Sphagnum* spp., particularly shade-tolerant and drought-resistant hummock species (e.g., *S. capillifolium* and *S. subtile*; Hayward and Clymo 1983), establish in the feathermoss carpet (Foster 1985; Taylor et al. 1987; Fenton and Bergeron 2006) and eventually expand their colonies over the humicolous species (Foster 1984; Fenton et al. 2007). The faster growth rate (Silvola 1991) and slower decomposition (Turetsky et al. 2008; Fenton et al. 2010) of the sphagna, compared to the feathermosses, result in the accumulation of an even thicker organic layer (20–40 cm), which reduces fluctuations in humidity. This along with the concurrent opening of the canopy (St-Denis et al. 2010) permits light-demanding, desiccation-intolerant *Sphagnum* spp. (*S. magellanicum, S. russowii, S. fallax*; Hayward and Clymo 1983) to establish on the forest floor. As these species have faster growth rates than the hummock sphagna (Rochefort et al. 1990), the heliotrophic species overtop the hummock sphagna and become dominant. Finally, in the extreme absence of fire, the organic layer can be sufficiently thick and the forest dominated by gaps (St-Denis et al. 2010) such that *S. fuscum* becomes an important part of the community. As such, three stages can be recognized during the paludification process: mature black spruce forest, paludified black spruce forest, and forest peatland. After low severity fires, the mature black spruce forest stage does not exist, and succession begins with forested peatland (Fenton et al. 2005).

FIRE RECURRENCE AND COVER TYPES

Along the *Abies balsamea* successional sequence, the variations in cover and richness of the functional groups are similar along the fire recurrence gradient (figs. 12.4 and 12.5). With the exception of the landscapes with high fire recurrence, where ericaceous endurers dominate the understory, typical endurers are dominant and tend to increase in dominance with decreasing fire recurrence. The richness pattern of the understory communities along the fire recurrence gradient is mainly associated with this group of species (fig. 12.5). Both the richness and the cover of the typical endurers group are highest under the deciduous cover type and decrease as *Abies balsamea* increases in the canopy. The species part of the invaders group increases in cover as fire becomes less common in the landscape. Although the relationship is strongest under deciduous canopy, it can still be observed under mixed and *Abies balsamea* cover types (fig. 12.4). Richness of this group also follows a similar pattern (fig. 12.5). Species belonging to the evaders and avoiders groups are present with extremely low cover in landscapes with high to moderate fire recurrence, no matter what the cover type is (fig. 12.4). As fire becomes less frequent, these species groups increase in mean cover. Although present with low cover in the high to moderate fire recurrence landscapes, the richness of these groups is almost comparable to that observed in lower fire recurrence landscapes.

Along the fire recurrence gradient, understory vascular plant composition for the *Picea mariana* successional sequence is characterized by the dominance of endurers. Ericaceous endurers are dominant in terms of cover in both *Picea mariana-* and *Pinus banksiana*-dominated stands (fig. 12.4). The richness of the ericaceous endurers group

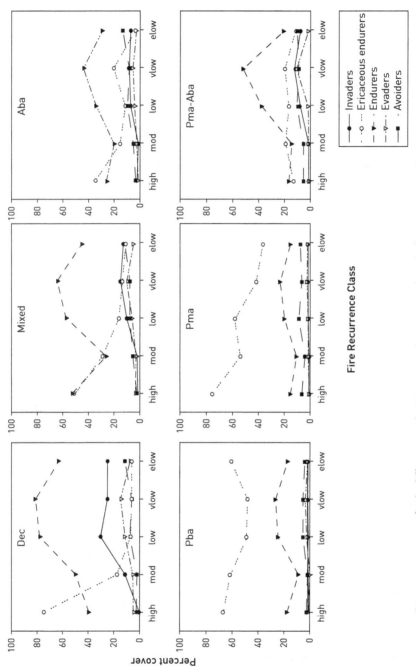

FIGURE 12.4 Percent cover patterns for the different reproductive strategies by cover type along the fire recurrence gradient (high, moderate, low, very low, extremely low). Cover types: deciduous canopy (Dec); mixture of deciduous and coniferous species (Mix); canopy dominated by *Picea mariana* (Pma); mixture of *Picea mariana* and *Abies balsamea* (Pma-Aba); canopy dominated by *Abies balsamea* (Aba); and canopy dominated by *Pinus banksiana* (Pba).

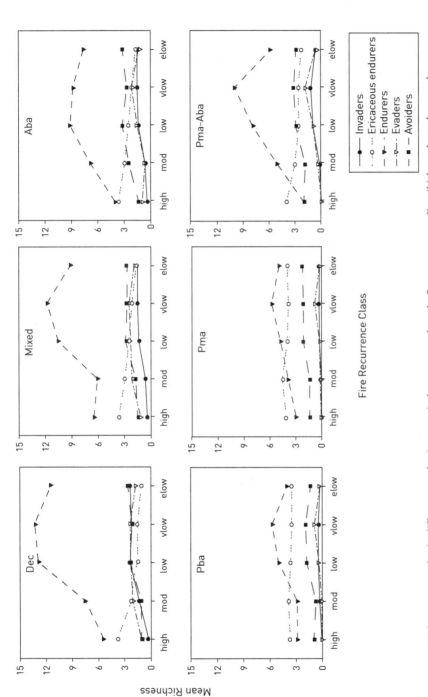

FIGURE 12.5 Richness patterns for the different reproductive strategies by cover type along the fire recurrence gradient (high, moderate, low, very low, extremely low). Cover types: deciduous canopy (Dec); mixture of deciduous and coniferous species (Mix); canopy dominated by *Picea mariana* (Pma); mixture of *Picea mariana* and *Abies balsamea* (Pma-Aba); canopy dominated by *Abies balsamea* (Aba); and canopy dominated by *Pinus banksiana* (Pba).

is not influenced by fire recurrence under both cover types (fig. 12.5). However, the mean cover of this group decreases almost linearly with decreasing fire recurrence under *Picea mariana* cover types, while it remains similar under *Pinus banksiana* cover types (fig. 12.4). In stands with a mixed composition of *Picea mariana* and *Abies balsamea*, typical endurers dominate the understory both in richness and cover along the recurrence gradient, with the exception of landscapes subject to high fire recurrence, where ericaceous endurers have the highest richness. The typical endurer species group is characterized by an increase in both richness and cover as fire recurrence decreases. After reaching a peak when fire recurrence is very low, richness and cover decrease (figs. 12.4 and 12.5). The same pattern is observed under the *Picea mariana-Abies balsamea* cover type. The species parts of the invaders and evaders groups are almost absent along the fire recurrence gradient in *Picea mariana-* and *Pinus banksiana*-dominated stands (figs. 12.4 and 12.5). Some invaders and shade-tolerant evaders are present under the *Picea mariana-Abies balsamea* cover type but only in regions with low to extremely low fire recurrences. Finally, avoiders are able to remain at comparable richness levels along the recurrence gradient, except under the *Pinus banksiana* cover type, where richness slightly increases as fire recurrence decreases. The cover of the avoiders increases as fire recurrence decreases (fig. 12.4), and this tendency is stronger in *Picea mariana-Abies balsamea*-dominated stands.

FIRE RECURRENCE AND SITE TYPES

As they are dominant under the different cover types, endurers also dominate in the different site types. In landscapes with high to moderate fire recurrences, ericaceous endurers dominate the understory communities in terms of cover on all site types (fig. 12.6). As fire recurrence decreases, the cover of this group also decreases. The richness of ericaceous endurers decreases as fire becomes less frequent (fig. 12.7). The richness and cover patterns for typical endurers along the fire recurrence gradient show some differences depending on the site type. The richness and cover of this group are highest on fine-textured soils with subhydric moisture regimes. Avoiders do not vary much in richness and cover along the fire recurrence gradient on organic and fine subhydric site types. For site types with a more xeric hydric regime, avoiders show an increase in richness and cover with decreasing fire recurrence (figs. 12.6 and 12.7). As for invaders and evaders, the patterns vary according to site type, but in general, there is a tendency for richness and cover to increase with decreasing fire recurrence (figs. 12.6 and 12.7).

UNDERSTORY COMMUNITY COMPOSITION AND SPECIES DISTRIBUTION

Carleton and Maycock (1981) studied the affinities between understory and canopy. They concluded that the majority of the understory species (75 percent) did not show any specificity for single canopy classes. The lack of specificity between cover type and understory species has been associated with the nature of regeneration after fire (Carleton and Maycock 1981). Because most species have developed reproductive strategies to cope with fire, recurrence should have more influence on understory species distribution and community composition than cover type. Cover type distribution is also influenced by the fire recurrence gradient, as tree species also have strategies to cope with fire. Species distribution and understory community composition

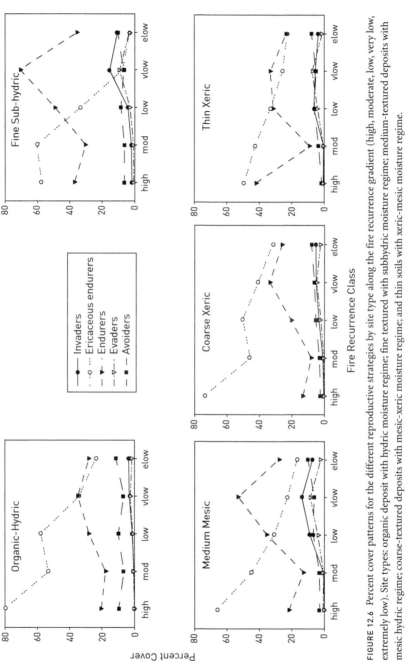

FIGURE 12.6 Percent cover patterns for the different reproductive strategies by site type along the fire recurrence gradient (high, moderate, low, very low, extremely low). Site types: organic deposit with hydric moisture regime; fine textured with subhydric moisture regime; medium-textured deposits with mesic hydric regime; coarse-textured deposits with mesic–xeric moisture regime; and thin soils with xeric–mesic moisture regime.

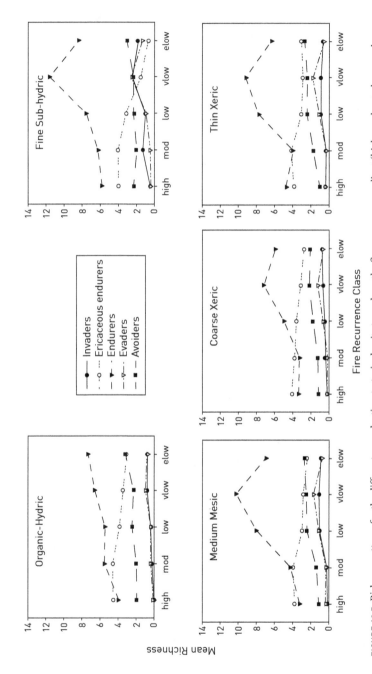

FIGURE 12.7 Richness patterns for the different reproductive strategies by site type along the fire recurrence gradient (high, moderate, low, very low, extremely low). Site types: organic deposit with hydric moisture regime; fine textured with subhydric moisture regime; medium-textured deposits with mesic hydric regime; coarse-textured deposits with mesic-xeric moisture regime; and thin soils with xeric-mesic moisture regime.

are largely influenced by site conditions (site type). Carleton et al. (1985) showed that 67 percent of the variance in understory species composition in the boreal forest of northern Ontario was explained by soils. Although site type influences the composition of the understory, our results showed that for the same site type, fire recurrence has an impact on the abundance and distribution of the species groups.

Only 17 percent of the stands sampled in the landscape subject to high fire recurrence are characteristic of the *Abies balsamea* successional sequence (table 12.1). In these stands, understory community composition does not correspond to the typical successional sequence described for *Abies balsamea* forests. Ericaceous endurers are dominant in deciduous, mixed, and *Abies balsamea* cover types in this landscape. The high fire recurrence contributes to the dominance of *Picea mariana* and *Pinus banksiana* cover types and ericaceous species. Even on the different site types, ericaceous endurers dominate. This observation confirms the hypothesis of Carleton and Maycock (1981) that the lack of specificity between the canopy and the understory is related to the reproductive strategies of the understory species in relation to fire. Ericaceous endurers thrive as resprouters where fire recurrence is high (Rowe 1983). There is a definite impact of fire recurrence on the composition of the understory and on species distribution. In contrast, the understories of deciduous, mixed, and *Abies balsamea* cover types support a higher mean species richness for the typical endurers group than in all other cover types where fire recurrence is high or moderate (figs. 12.4 and 12.5). In such landscapes, these stands could act as reservoirs for understory species that are usually found in the southern section of the commercial boreal forest, where *Abies balsamea* is dominant and fires are less frequent. In these stands, species like *Aralia nudicaulis*, *Clintonia borealis* (Ait.), *Cornus canadensis* (L.), and *Trientalis borealis* (Raf.) are found more frequently than in stands dominated by *Picea mariana* or *Pinus banksiana*. These species are typical endurers characteristic of the *Abies balsamea* forests of the south. Site type appears to play a similar role, and the presence of avoiders and some typical endurers in landscapes subject to high or moderate fire recurrence could be related to site types with hydric to subhydric moisture regimes. The mean richness of avoiders on organic and fine subhydric site types is almost twice that observed on other site types. Although these site types represent less than 15 percent of the landscapes, their contribution to the biodiversity over the landscape may well surpass their representation. A study in a two ha old-growth swamp forest in Sweden revealed that 33 percent of the bryophytes found throughout the country were found in this forest (Ohlson et al. 1997).

The richness patterns are in accordance with Connell's (1978) intermediate disturbance hypothesis, which predicts that diversity will be higher under intermediate disturbance. The argument behind this hypothesis is that intermediate frequency of disturbance will allow the coexistence of species with different competitive strategies (Huston 1979; Huston and Smith 1987).

The increase in richness observed in all of the functional groups as fire recurrence decreases supports this hypothesis (fig. 12.5). Although the richness and cover patterns of the avoiders and the shade-tolerant evaders are easy to relate to the recurrence gradient (figs. 12.4 and 12.5), this is not the case for the invaders group. Richness and cover of invaders should have been higher in the landscape subject to high fire recurrence since this group is characterized by r-selected species such as *Epilobium angustifolium* and *Hieracium* sp. (Rowe 1983). The absence of the invaders where recurrence is high to moderate may be related to the fact that only closed forests were sampled. Understory successional changes in *Picea mariana*-dominated forests occur before canopy closure for vascular plant species; invaders could only be present in open forests. Foster (1985) observed that the only invading species to colonize the recently burned black spruce forests of southeastern Labrador was *Epilobium angustifolium*. In similar forests in northern Minnesota and western Canada, species such as *Geranium bicknelii, Aralia hispida*, and *Polygonum cilinode* were noted in recently burned areas among other shade-intolerant species, which were absent from the prefire communities. These species have been identified as shade-intolerant evaders with a persistent seed bank (Rowe 1983). The absence of these species in the early post-fire community in southeastern Labrador is probably related to the extremely low fire recurrence. A fire rotation of 500 years has been suggested for this part of the boreal forest (Heinselman 1981; Foster 1985).

Invaders are more abundant with decreasing fire frequency, and a deciduous canopy could act as a reservoir from which these species could invade burned areas in regions where fire recurrence is low to extremely low. The increase in the abundance of invaders under lower fire recurrence could, however, be explained by the higher recurrence of other types of disturbances like spruce budworm outbreaks. De Grandpré and Bergeron (1997) and De Grandpré et al. (1993) have shown that in the *Abies balsamea-Betula papyrifera* domain, openings in the canopy resulting from spruce budworm outbreaks help maintain some early successional species.

RESPONSE OF THE UNDERSTORY LAYER TO FOREST MANAGEMENT

Until recently, the Canadian boreal forest has often been perceived as a simple and rather homogeneous system whose natural dynamics were mainly driven by the high recurrence of wildfires (Dix and Swan 1971; Carleton and Maycock 1978; Cogbill 1985). This idea was based on the frequent dominance of pioneer tree species like *Populus tremuloides, Betula papyrifera, Pinus banksiana*, and *Picea mariana* in the overstory of many boreal stands. As a result, even-aged stand management is being applied over most of the territory covered by the boreal forest. However, recent studies have shown that stand structures of increasing complexity and/or replacement of pioneer species by more late successional species, such as *Abies balsamea* and *Thuja occidentalis* (L.), are also observed with the prolonged absence of major fire events (Bergeron and Dubuc 1989; Gauthier et al. 2000). With the increasing integration of sustainable forest management into forestry policies, the pertinence of a generalized application of the even-aged management strategy over most of the boreal forest has also been questioned (Bergeron and Harvey 1997; Bergeron et al. 1999). We have shown in this chapter that significant spatial and temporal variation in composition and structure can be observed for the understory vegetation. It is also increasingly recognized that the understory vegetation greatly contributes to the diversity and nutrient dynamics of forest ecosystems of eastern North America (chapters 2 and 4, this volume). Given that a great proportion of the commercial timber that is now being harvested in eastern Canada originates from the boreal forest, the identification of the impact of generalized even-aged forest management on the understory layer of the boreal forest is important in assessing the sustainability of current forest practices.

In general terms, even-aged forest management in the boreal forests of Quebec consists of regeneration cuts that bring the forest stand back to an early seral stage, and it usually entails the complete removal of the overstory (Doucet et al. 1996). Adequate tree regeneration of the forest stand is ensured by the practice of careful logging on sites where advance tree regeneration is sufficient before harvesting, and by site preparation and/or planting on sites deficient in advance regeneration. As seen in chapters 2 to 4 (this volume) and in previous sections of this chapter, the composition and structure of the understory forest vegetation are mainly determined by the light and soil environments encountered at this stand level. The changes observed in the composition and structure of the understory layer after harvesting mostly result from the modifications this disturbance brings about in terms of these two environments. The increased amount of light reaching the forest floor often leads to a rise in soil temperatures, favoring soil microbial activity and increasing decomposition rates and nutrient availability (Keenan and Kimmins 1993). The impact of harvesting on the soil's physical properties (compaction, structure, mineral soil exposure, residual humus depth) will vary with site type, season of harvesting, type of machinery used, machinery circulation patterns, and subsequent silvicultural treatments. The amount of change in the soil's structural characteristics thus depends on the intensity of harvesting activities and is best expressed in terms of severity (chapter 13, this volume). Given the predominance of cryptograms in the *Picea mariana*-feathermoss domain of the Quebec boreal forest and the resulting influence they exert through the build-up of a significant forest floor layer, the severity of forest floor disturbance will be more crucial for post-harvest regeneration patterns of this domain compared to those of the *Abies balsamea-Betula papyrifera* domain.

The recurrent nature of wildfires in the boreal forest has led to the development of a variety of regeneration strategies by boreal understory plants. These strategies differ in their capacity to cope with different levels of forest floor disturbance severity (Rowe 1983) and to exploit the environmental resources (light and nutrients) available after the disturbance (Chapin and Van Cleve 1981). Thus, many understory pioneer plant species (invaders) quickly establish on a site after a disturbance by seeding from the surrounding areas or germinating from a dormant soil seed bank (evaders). These species generally prefer mineral soil or shallow humus seedbeds and are shade-intolerant plants with rapid growth rates that take advantage of the light- and nutrient-rich environment usually found after disturbance. These species are often observed after forest floor disturbances of moderate to high severity. Many understory species present in mature forests maintain their presence on a site after a disturbance by resprouting from undamaged underground organs (endurers). Most of these species are usually observed after forest floor disturbances of low to moderate severity and possess a certain degree of plasticity in their capability to exploit the light and nutrient resources of their environment. Finally, some species tend to be restricted to later seral stages of the boreal forest. These species often require establishment or growth conditions associated with older forests, such as lower light availability, cooler soil temperatures, or higher soil moisture levels (avoiders). These plant species do not persist after disturbance or do so only if the severity of the forest floor disturbance is low. Although these different strategies have developed as a response to the natural variability in forest floor disturbance severity, they can also serve as a basis to explain the regeneration patterns observed after harvesting (Nguyen-Xuan et al. 2000).

EFFECTS OF CLEARCUTTING ON DIVERSITY

As seen in the previous sections of this chapter, the understory vegetation of the forests of the *Abies balsamea-Betula papyrifera* domain is mainly characterized by various associations of herbs and shrubs. The majority of the species are endurers that take advantage of the improved light and soil conditions found after disturbance. Thus, clearcut harvesting with a low to moderate level of forest floor disturbance should not significantly affect the diversity of the understory vegetation. Indeed, a study conducted by Harvey et al. (1995) in recently harvested stands of the mixed-wood forest of western Quebec showed that low-intensity harvesting resulted in the release of pre-established understory herbs like *Clintonia borealis*, *Cornus canadensis*, *Linnaea borealis* (L.), *Maianthemum canadensis* (Desf.), *Aralia nudicaulis*, and *Rubus pubescens* (Raf.). Harvesting of higher intensity favored the establishment and/or development of a number of grasses, sedges, and introduced species (e.g., *Calamagrostis canadensis* [Michx.], *Scirpus atrocinctus* [Fern.], *Carex stipata* [Mu¨ hl.], *Galeopsis tetrahit* [L.], *Taraxacum officinale* [Weber], *Cirsium vulgare* [Savi], and *Phleum pratense* [L.]). Some of these species, especially grasses and sedges, can spread aggressively over a significant portion of the disturbed area, resulting in a decrease in post-disturbance plant diversity (Abrams and Dickman 1982). Harvey et al. (1995) observed that disturbance severity was mostly determined by site type and season of harvesting. Finally, it has also been noted that in mixed-wood stands, clearcut harvesting tends to favor a conversion to a predominantly deciduous canopy cover (Harvey and Bergeron 1989). The conversion of mixed stands to deciduous stands over extensive areas may have profound implications for the diversity of understory species present at the landscape level.

The previous sections of this chapter have shown the importance of mosses, *Sphagnum*, lichens, and ericaceous endurers in the characterization of the understory plant associations observed in the *Picea mariana*-feathermoss domain of the Quebec boreal forest. The majority of low shrubs are able to withstand disturbances of low to moderate severity through the persistence of underground organs in the forest floor. The bryophytes and lichens usually persist only if the forest floor disturbance severity is low. In a study conducted by Brumelis and Carleton (1989) in the spruce-dominated forests of northeastern Ontario, low-intensity logging promoted the development of many pre-established ericaceous endurers, such as *Cassandra calyculata* (L.), *Gaultheria hispidula* (L.), *Ledum groenlandicum*, and *Vaccinium myrtilloides*, or the persistence of many bryophytes, such as *Dicranum polysetum* (Sw.), *Hylocomium splendens* (Hedw.), *Pleurozium shreberi*, *Ptilium crista-castrensis* (Hedw.), *Sphagnum angustifolium* (C. Jens.), *S. magnellanicum* (Brid.), *S. nemoreum* (Braithw.), and *S. wulfianum* (Girg.). High-intensity logging favored the establishment of a number of grasses, sedges, herbs, and tall shrubs (*Calamagrostis canadensis*, *Carex canescens* (L.), *C. tenuiflora* [Wahl.], *C. trisperma* [Dewey], *Scirpus cyperinus* (L.), *Epilobium angustifolium*, *Hieracium aurantiacum* (L.), *Typha latifolia* (L.), *Salix discolor* [Mu¨ hl], all part of the invaders group). A conversion from conifer-dominated toward a mixed and deciduous cover type was also observed with increasing severity of forest floor disturbance in the *Picea mariana*-feathermoss domain (Carleton and MacLellan 1994).

Thus, similar tendencies are observed for the impact of harvesting on species diversity for this forest domain as for the *Abies balsamea-Betula papyrifera* domain: The diversity of the post-disturbance vegetation tends to decrease with increasing forest floor disturbance severity. Johnston and Elliott (1996) also noted that, after harvesting, the persistence of species associated with older stands contributed to an increased post-disturbance diversity of *Picea mariana*-dominated stands.

Canopy removal results in significantly more sunlight reaching the forest floor and a decreased interception of precipitation. In mesic to dry forests, this results in hotter and drier forest floors (Fenton and Frego 2005). Consequently, humidity-dependant humicolous bryophytes have reduced cover after forest harvest (Brumelis and Carleton 1989; Schmalholz and Hylander 2009). However, *Pleurozium schreberi* shows a remarkable resilience and frequently remains dominant on the forest floor in areas that have not been physically disturbed (Fenton and Frego 2005; Schmalholz and Hylander 2009). The drier post-harvest microclimate also reduces the richness of small species in microhabitats, particularly liverworts (Söderström 1988, Frisvoll and Prestø 1997, Hylander et al. 2005). Several studies have shown that the intensity of this effect is modulated by the amount of residual canopy post-harvest (Fenton and Frego 2005, Dynesius and Hylander 2007).

In contrast to mesic and dry forests, wet forest types are generally hotter and wetter, as the increased insolation does not counteract the decreased interception and evapotranspiration. In many of these wet forest types, removal of the forest canopy simply permits the *Sphagnum* spp. present in the understory to grow faster (Fenton and Bergeron 2007; Fenton et al. in prep).

In addition to these indirect microclimatic changes, bryophyte colonies are physically disrupted and mineral or organic soils are also exposed during forest harvest. These changes liberate space, which is generally the limiting resource in boreal environments for bryophytes (Slack 1990). In a light-saturated environment, species typical of disturbed habitats are able to establish themselves, either from the diaspore bank or via dispersal from previously established colonies (Dynesius and Hylander 2007; Caners et al. 2009). However, some longer-term studies suggest that these changes are short-lived when the canopy closes as the regenerating stand grows (Brumelis and Carleton 1989; Dynesius and Hylander 2007).

Finally, over the longer term, forest harvest affects bryophytes by reducing the input of woody debris in the ecosystem. Woody debris is one of the most important substrates for bryophytes in the boreal forest, and the lack of woody debris in managed forests has been for many years identified as one of the key threats to bryophytes in managed landscapes (Gustafsson and Hallingbäck 1988; Esseen et al. 1997; Frisvoll and Prestø 1997). The woody debris availability is further decreased when harvest residue (i.e., slash, tops, branches, stumps) is further harvested, reducing microhabitat availability (Åström et al. 2005; Olsson and Staaf 1995).

EFFECTS OF HARVESTING ON ECOSYSTEM NUTRIENT CYCLING

The understory vegetation often exerts a significant influence on ecosystem-level nutrient cycling (chapters 2 to 4, this volume). For example, during early succession, many pioneer herbs and shrubs play an important role in the immobilization of the nutrients released after a disturbance (Marks and Bormann 1972). Similarly, the dominance of bryophytes and their significant contribution to the accumulation of a thick forest floor in older stands of the boreal forest also illustrate the important influence of this vegetation layer on ecosystem nutrient cycling (Heilman 1966, 1968; Van Cleve et al. 1981; Weber and Van Cleve 1981, 1984). However, in the former case, the nutrients immobilized in the biomass of the pioneer species tend to be returned to the system's pool of available nutrients as this vegetation gradually dies off with the closure of the overstory canopy and produces a readily decomposable litter. In the latter case, the nutrients immobilized by the bryophyte layer tend to be sequestered in the forest floor and removed from the system's pool of available nutrients as a consequence of the low decomposition rates observed in this compartment of the boreal forest ecosystem. Thus, through its influence on the composition of post-disturbance understory vegetation, harvesting exerts a certain influence on the ecosystem's nutrient cycling. In a study where we examined the relationships that exist between post-disturbance vegetation composition and soil fertility, we observed that post-harvest stands with a greater proportion of graminoids, herb, and/or deciduous shrub species demonstrated greater levels of nutrient cycling (Nguyen-Xuan et al. 2000). Post-harvest stands with a greater proportion of mosses and *Sphagnum* demonstrated lower levels of nutrient cycling. Consequently, the severity of the disturbance directly influences post-harvest understory vegetation composition and indirectly affects post-harvest nutrient cycling. This observation yields more profound implications for the *Picea mariana*-feathermoss domain than for the *Abies balsamea-Betula papyrifera* domain because of the predominance of bryophytes in the former.

CONCLUSION

The variability in the disturbance regime influences the distribution of understory species of the boreal forest. The richness and the abundance of the different groups of species vary according to fire recurrence. High fire recurrence will favor ericaceous and terricolous lichen species, whereas a lower recurrence is associated with a higher richness of herbs and shrubs species. Because boreal understory and tree species have developed strategies to maintain in a context of fire, their regional distribution is closely linked to fire recurrence. Thus, the specificity between cover types and understory may only reflect similar responses to a particular disturbance regime (Carleton and Maycock 1981; Gilliam et al. 1995; chapter 8, this volume). As for fire recurrence, the proportion of the different site types over a landscape will affect both understory and tree species distribution. Although the canopy cover can modify the abiotic conditions of a stand, thus affecting the composition of the understory, many understory species are not restricted to a specific canopy, but rather to specific abiotic conditions.

Understory species composition and distribution are directly influenced by the disturbance regime. Understory diversity at the landscape level is highest with intermediate frequency of fire. This is true under any cover types and on all site types. The data fit Connell's (1978) intermediate disturbance hypothesis. Understory species have developed different reproductive strategies to maintain in a context of fire, and understory richness and abundance relationships between the different groups will be directly affected by disturbance characteristics. When we change the predominant disturbance regime from fire to forest harvesting, we are imposing a new disturbance for which species do not present any particular adaptive traits. Clearcutting alone is not a threat to the diversity of understory vascular plant species; however, it will change the relationships among species in the communities and contribute to a changed community composition. Brumelis and Carleton (1989) observed that under particular abiotic conditions, the effect of logging on community development had completely altered the successional processes. Understory communities are not only part of the biodiversity heritage, but they can also play important roles in boreal forest dynamics (De Grandpré and Bergeron 1997; Hart and Chen 2008).

ACKNOWLEDGMENTS

We acknowledge the Ministe`re des Ressources naturelles du Quebec for allowing us to use the ecological survey data. We are also grateful to Sylvie Gauthier for her comments on an earlier version of the manuscript. We thank Pamela Cheers for editing the English and Diane Paquet for correcting the manuscript.

APPENDIX 12.1

List of understory species, with their scores on the first two axes of the ordination and their reproductive strategies according to Rowe (1983).

Species name	Species code	Axis 1	Axis 2	Group	Repro. strategy
Empetrum nigrum	EMN	−0.49	0.27	Ericaceous	Avoider
Circaea alpina	CIA	1.00	0.32	Herb	Avoider
Coptis groenlandica	COG	0.32	0.02	Herb	Avoider
Cypripedium acaule	CYA	0.04	−0.70	Herb	Avoider
Gaultheria hispidula	CHH	−0.19	0.17	Herb	Avoider
Goodyera repens	GOR	0.35	0.04	Herb	Avoider
Linaea borealis	LIB	0.44	−0.07	Herb	Avoider
Mitella nuda	MIN	0.88	0.62	Herb	Avoider
Monese uniflora	MOU	0.54	−0.04	Herb	Avoider
Monotropa uniflora	MON	0.70	−0.42	Herb	Avoider
Oxalis montana	OXM	0.86	0.03	Herb	Avoider
Pyrola elliptica	PYE	0.70	−0.15	Herb	Avoider
Pyrola secunda	PYR	0.22	−0.06	Herb	Avoider
Rubus chamaemorus	RUC	−0.67	0.92	Herb	Avoider
Trilium undulatum	TRU	0.33	−0.50	Herb	Avoider
Cladina stellaris	CLT	−1.02	−0.69	Lichen	Avoider
Bazzania trilobata	BAT	0.12	−0.09	Moss	Avoider
Hylocomnium splendens	HYS	0.06	0.10	Moss	Avoider
Mnium punctatum	MNP	0.81	0.60	Moss	Avoider
Mnium sp.	MNS	0.70	0.51	Moss	Avoider
Pleurozium schreberi	PLS	−0.34	−0.24	Moss	Avoider
Ptilidium ciliare	PTI	−0.69	−0.16	Moss	Avoider

(Continued)

Species name	Species code	Axis 1	Axis 2	Group	Repro. strategy
Ptilium crista–castrensis	PTC	−0.38	−0.15	Moss	Avoider
Rythidiadelphus triquetus	RYT	0.81	0.30	Moss	Avoider
Taxus canadensis	TAC	1.29	−0.20	Shrub	Avoider
Sphagnum fuscum	SPF	−0.59	0.65	Sphagnum	Avoider
Sphagnum squarrosum	SPQ	0.30	1.07	Sphagnum	Avoider
Sphagnum girgensohnii	SPG	−0.15	0.78	Sphagnum	Avoider
Sphagnum sp.	SPS	−0.27	0.91	Sphagnum	Avoider
Cassandra calyculata	CAL	−0.76	0.69	Ericaceous	Endurer
Kalmia angustifolia	KAA	−0.63	−0.48	Ericaceous	Endurer
Ledum groenlandicum	LEG	−0.63	0.16	Ericaceous	Endurer
Rhododendron canadense	RHC	−0.25	0.13	Ericaceous	Endurer
Vaccinium angustifolium	VAA	−0.36	−0.38	Ericaceous	Endurer
Vaccinium myrtilloides	VAM	−0.28	−0.36	Ericaceous	Endurer
Vaccinium uliginosum	VAU	−0.43	0.21	Ericaceous	Endurer
Actaea rubra	ACR	1.45	0.26	Herb	Endurer
Aralia nudicaulis	ARN	1.02	−0.39	Herb	Endurer
Aster macrophyllus	ASM	1.39	0.02	Herb	Endurer
Atirium filix–femina	ATF	0.90	0.56	Herb	Endurer
Clintonia borealis	CLB	0.74	−0.32	Herb	Endurer
Comandra livida	COL	−0.54	0.03	Herb	Endurer
Cornus canadensis	CON	0.45	−0.24	Herb	Endurer
Dryopteris disjuncta	DRD	0.68	0.41	Herb	Endurer
Dryopteris noveboracensis	DRN	1.14	0.30	Herb	Endurer
Dryopteris phegopteris	DRP	1.02	0.09	Herb	Endurer
Dryopteris spinulosa	DRS	1.07	−0.06	Herb	Endurer
Epigaea repens	EPI	−0.36	−0.45	Herb	Endurer
Equisetum sp.	EQY	−0.08	0.81	Herb	Endurer
Equisetum sylvaticum	EQS	0.27	1.32	Herb	Endurer
Gaultheria procumbens	GAP	−0.18	−0.61	Herb	Endurer
Kalmia polifolia	KAP	−0.75	0.53	Herb	Endurer
Lycopodium annontinum	LYA	0.44	0.27	Herb	Endurer
Lycopodium clavatum	LYC	0.98	−0.48	Herb	Endurer
Lycopodium complanatum	LYP	0.68	−0.53	Herb	Endurer
Lycopodium lucidulum	LYL	1.24	−0.37	Herb	Endurer
Lycopodium obscurum	LYO	0.97	−0.44	Herb	Endurer

Species name	Species code	Axis 1	Axis 2	Group	Repro. strategy
Maianthemum canadense	MAC	0.64	−0.32	Herb	Endurer
Osmunda cinnamomea	OSC	1.05	0.18	Herb	Endurer
Petasites palmatus	PES	0.40	0.67	Herb	Endurer
Pteridium aquilinum	PTA	1.01	−0.82	Herb	Endurer
Rubus pubescens	RUP	1.00	0.68	Herb	Endurer
Smilacina trifolia	SMT	−0.39	1.20	Herb	Endurer
Streptopus amplexifolius	STA	0.76	−0.02	Herb	Endurer
Streptopus roseus	STR	1.23	−0.31	Herb	Endurer
Trientalis borealis	TRB	0.69	−0.10	Herb	Endurer
Vaccinium oxycoccos	VAO	−0.71	0.85	Herb	Endurer
Vaccinium vitis-idaea	VAV	−0.56	−0.22	Herb	Endurer
Viola spp.	VIS	1.13	0.39	Herb	Endurer
Alnus crispa	AUC	0.01	−0.45	Shrub	Endurer
Alnus rugosa	AUR	0.43	0.90	Shrub	Endurer
Amelanchier sp.	AME	0.28	−0.34	Shrub	Endurer
Betula glandulosa	BEG	−0.80	−0.30	Shrub	Endurer
Cornus stolonifera	COR	1.08	0.13	Shrub	Endurer
Corylus cornuta	COC	1.67	−0.56	Shrub	Endurer
Diervilla lonicera	DIE	1.31	−0.64	Shrub	Endurer
Lonicera canadensis	LON	1.37	−0.27	Shrub	Endurer
Lonicera vilosa	LOV	−0.66	0.54	Shrub	Endurer
Prunus pensylvanica	PRP	1.08	−0.47	Shrub	Evader
Ribes glandulosum	RIG	0.91	0.31	Shrub	Evader
Ribes lacustre	RIL	0.98	0.35	Shrub	Evader
Ribes triste	RIT	1.04	0.68	Shrub	Evader
Sambucus pubens	SAP	1.19	−0.09	Shrub	Evader
Viburnum cassinoides	VIC	0.68	−0.41	Shrub	Evader
Viburnum edule	VIE	0.80	0.18	Shrub	Evader
Vaccinium cespitosum	VAC	−0.84	−0.58	Ericaceous	Invader
Anaphalis margaritacea	ANM	1.19	−0.30	Herb	Invader
Aster accuminatus	ASA	1.25	0.22	Herb	Invader
Epilobium angustigolium	EPA	0.72	0.04	Herb	Invader
Fragaria spp.	FRG	1.07	0.61	Herb	Invader
Galium triflorum	GAT	0.86	0.96	Herb	Invader
Hieracium spp.	HIS	1.48	0.26	Herb	Invader
Melampyrum lineare	MEI	0.83	−0.71	Herb	Invader
Osmunda claytoniana	OSY	0.76	−0.09	Herb	Invader
Prenanthes spp.	PRS	1.17	0.06	Herb	Invader
Solidago macrophylla	SOM	0.80	−0.25	Herb	Invader

(Continued)

Species name	Species code	Axis 1	Axis 2	Group	Repro. strategy
Thalictrum polygamum	THP	0.73	1.52	Herb	Invader
Cladina mitis	CLM	−0.47	−0.39	Lichen	Invader
Cladina rangiferina	CLR	−0.70	−0.34	Lichen	Invader
Cladonia sp.	CLS	−0.19	−0.18	Lichen	Invader
Acer spicatum	ERE	1.32	−0.47	Shrub	Invader
Prunus virginiana	PRV	1.29	0.66	Shrub	Invader
Rubus idaeus	RUI	0.98	0.35	Shrub	Invader
Sphagnum magellanicum	SPM	−0.14	1.54	*Sphagnum*	Invader

PART FOUR
COMMUNITY DYNAMICS OF THE HERBACEOUS LAYER AND THE ROLE OF DISTURBANCE

13 Response of the Herbaceous Layer to Disturbance in Eastern Forests

Mark R. Roberts and Frank S. Gilliam

Forests are exposed to a wide variety of both natural and anthropogenic disturbances, variously defined (see below). The herbaceous layer is not only potentially quite sensitive to these events, but such effects also vary considerably among forests and types of disturbance. The dynamic response of the herb layer to disturbance has been of increasing interest to plant ecologists in recent decades (fig. 13.1), which is likely responsible for the increased attention paid to the herb layer in the ecological literature.

Several definitions of disturbance have been proposed, some restricted to discrete events (White and Pickett 1985) and others with long-term environmental fluctuations (Ryan 1991). We restrict our discussion to relatively discrete events because these are more readily tractable, and most types of direct management interventions (e.g., forest harvesting) are discrete in time and space. Accordingly, we adopt the definition of White and Pickett (1985) as our working definition of disturbance: "any relatively discrete event in time that disrupts ecosystem, community, or population structure and changes resources, substrate availability, or the physical environment" (7). We recognize the admonition of Pickett et al. (1989) that disturbance affects all levels of organization differently, from individuals to ecosystems and landscapes, and that most empirical work focuses on effects of disturbance on community structure rather than on ecological processes.

Although ecologists generally recognize that disturbances of various kinds strongly influence the structure and function of plant communities (e.g., White 1979; Pickett and White 1985), most attention has focused on disturbance size and frequency, with little explicit consideration of severity (Malanson 1984; Peterson and Pickett 1991; Peterson 2000). If more attention were given to the severity aspect of the disturbance

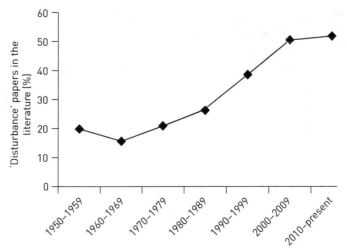

FIGURE 13.1 Relative (%) number of herb layer papers with focus on effects of disturbance by decade, from 1950 to present. Based on a literature search by Google Scholar™.

regime, our understanding of ecosystem dynamics and our ability to predict consequences of management actions would be greatly refined. Thus, we emphasize disturbance severity and give due consideration to size and frequency when appropriate. We modify Oliver and Larson's (1996) definition of *disturbance severity* as the amount of forest overstory removed and the amount of understory vegetation, forest floor, and soil destroyed. With disturbance severity quantified in this manner, we are able to evaluate disturbances that vary in degree of overstory and understory destruction. Quantifying overstory and understory disturbance independently is particularly important with respect to forest harvesting because different degrees of overstory removal and different harvesting systems can be combined with a variety of understory treatments, creating numerous combinations of overstory and understory disturbance conditions.

The herbaceous layer is simultaneously exposed to and responds to many forest disturbances, ranging from microscale disturbances such as frost heaving and trampling by large vertebrates (McCarthy and Facelli 1990) to more extensive and intensive disturbances resulting from herbivory (Rooney and Dress 1997a,b), tree mortality (Beatty 1984; Collins et al. 1985; Moore and Vankat 1986; Stone and Wolfe 1996; Goldblum 1997), inundation (Lyon and Sagers 1998; C. E. Williams et al. 1999b), periodic fire (Gilliam and Christensen 1986; De Granpre´ and Bergeron 1997), catastrophic wind damage (Peterson et al. 1990; Castelli et al. 1999; Peterson 2000), and forest management practices, including timber harvesting and use of herbicides (Duffy and Meier 1992; Roberts and Dong 1993; Gilliam et al. 1995; Halpern and Spies 1995; Hammond et al. 1998; Falk et al. 2008).

This chapter provides a conceptual overview of many of these disturbances. In addition, subsequent chapters address specific disturbances in more detail, including invasive species (chapter 15, this volume), deer herbivory (chapters 16 and 17, this volume), timber harvesting/agricultural practices (chapters 18 and 19, this volume), nitrogen pollution (chapter 20, this volume), and global warming (chapter 21, this volume).

Natural Disturbances that Primarily Affect the Forest Canopy

Using the above definition of disturbance severity, the principal types of relatively discrete natural disturbances in eastern forests can be generally categorized into those that primarily affect the overstory and those that primarily affect the understory. Insect defoliation, wind, and ice storms are the most common types of disturbances affecting the forest canopy. Outbreaks of the defoliating insect spruce budworm (*Choristoneura fumiferana* [Clem.]) are common throughout the range of balsam fir (*Abies balsamea* (L.) Mill.) in eastern forests (Blais 1983). Balsam fir is the most susceptible species to damage by spruce budworm defoliation, although the spruces (*Picea* spp.) are the preferred host for the insect. Severity of defoliation can range from light (partial removal of current foliage) to severe (complete shoot destruction with widespread tree mortality). The spruce budworm prefers large, mature overstory trees, but at extremely high larval densities, the insect may also defoliate understory saplings and seedlings (Pardy 1997). Numerous studies have addressed growth responses of defoliated trees and stands (e.g., Peine 1989), tree regeneration (e.g., Osawa 1994) and succession of woody species (e.g., Ghent et al. 1957; Batzer and Popp 1985) after insect attack. Overstory mortality typically results in growth release of advance regeneration of balsam fir and spruces and establishment of shade-intolerant and mid-tolerant deciduous species such as *Betula papyrifera* Marsh., *B. alleghemiensis* Britt., *Populus* spp., and *Acer rubrum* L. (Ghent et al. 1957; Batzer and Popp 1985). Studies of herbaceous layer response to spruce budworm defoliation are lacking.

The gypsy moth (*Lymantria dispar* L.) is another important canopy-defoliating insect in eastern forests, affecting hardwood forests throughout the northeastern and mid-Atlantic states of the United States (USDA Forest Service 1993). Like the spruce budworm, the gypsy moth preferentially selects certain tree species over others, such as *Quercus* spp., *Betula* spp., *Tilia* spp., and *Populus* spp. (Muzika and Liebhold 1999), and larger size classes of trees, principally those in the forest canopy (Campbell and Sloan 1977). The overall effect of moderate to severe defoliation by insect larvae is to release understory individuals, thereby altering species composition and initiating a new cohort of woody seedlings and saplings (Collins 1961; Fajvan and Wood 1996).

Mattson and Addy (1975) pointed out that plant-eating insects help maintain high primary productivity in forest communities by consuming less vigorous plants and opening the canopy for more vigorous plants. In addition to increased light in the understory, nutrient and moisture levels in the understory also increase because of removal of transpiring foliage in the overstory and additions of frass and debris to the forest floor (Eshleman et al. 1998). Several studies have documented increases in the abundance and growth of shrub species after insect attack (Ghent et al. 1957; Batzer and Popp 1985), but few have addressed changes in the herbaceous layer. Ehrenfeld (1980) found no significant differences in herb cover and no obvious changes in species composition between gap and control sites in a gypsy moth-defoliated forest. She concluded, however, that the spatial pattern and relative densities of plants in the forest understory, in combination with the size and pattern of gaps, are the critical factors determining the pattern of forest understory response to canopy gaps created by insect defoliation.

Wind damage in forests has been the subject of considerable study (see review by Everham and Brokaw 1996). As with insect defoliation, the severity of wind disturbance can vary from small gaps created by broken branches or the fall of individual canopy trees (Moore and Vankat 1986) to catastrophic removal of the majority of the canopy (Dunn et al. 1983; Foster 1988a; Merrens and Peart 1992; Peterson and Pickett 1995; others cited in Everham and Brokaw 1996). The severity of damage is related to wind intensity in combination with a number of biotic and abiotic factors, including tree species, stem size, canopy evenness, previous weakening by pathogens, and topographic exposure (Everham and Brokaw 1996). Wind influences conditions for understory herbaceous vegetation by increasing light, altering substrate (snapped trees versus uprooted), and depositing litter (Everham and Brokaw 1996). It is likely that the frequency of uprooted trees, and likewise the frequency of pits and mounds, is generally higher after wind disturbance than after insect defoliation.

Several studies (e.g., Beatty 1984; Peterson et al. 1990) have documented differences in species composition in pits and on mounds and have demonstrated the importance of pit and mound microsites in maintaining the species diversity of understory vegetation (chapter 8, this volume). Others have found subtle changes in understory composition after creation of individual tree windthrow gaps in mature forests (Brewer 1980; Moore and Vankat 1986). Moore and Vankat (1986) studied the portions of the gaps where soil had not been disturbed by uprooting and found significantly higher solar radiation and soil moisture within one-to-two-year-old gaps compared to older gaps and intact forest. They concluded that higher total herbaceous cover in the young gaps was related to increases in species that were present under the intact canopy before gap creation as opposed to invasion of new species. It is likely that invasion increases in importance with increasing soil disturbance and canopy removal.

Ice or glaze storms are common recurring disturbances in forests throughout eastern North America, with the exception of Florida (Oliver and Larson 1996; Rebertus et al. 1997; Lautenschlager and Nielsen 1999). Lemon (1961) showed that major ice storms occur more frequently in northeastern forests than do large wind storms or fires. Most studies of forest recovery after ice storm damage have focused on the canopy layer (e.g., Lemon 1961; Siccama et al. 1976; Bruederle and Stearns 1985; De Steven 1991b) and have concluded that the effects depend on storm intensity, landscape position, wind, and forest type and structure. Succession of forest tree species may be accelerated or retarded depending on the degree of damage and current successional stage; removal of early successional canopy dominants may allow late successional understory trees to fill canopy gaps, whereas extensive canopy damage might allow reproduction of early successional species (Whitney and Johnson 1984).

Little information is available on the response of the herbaceous layer to ice storms. Given that storm damage typically occurs from breakage of limbs or whole trees (Runkle 1985; Oliver and Larson 1996), we would predict that (1) canopy gaps would be created, favoring shade-tolerant shrubs and herbs in smaller gaps and shade-intolerant species in larger gaps; (2) there would be relatively little uprooting and disruption of the forest floor with little mineral soil exposure, resulting in (3) growth stimulation of preexisting plants with relatively little invasion of new individuals (as compared to wind disturbance, for example); and (4) the input of coarse, woody debris to the forest floor can be substantial (Bruederle and Stearns 1985), eventually providing substrate for herbaceous plants.

The ice storm of 1998, which affected Ontario, Quebec, and the Maritime Provinces of Canada, as well as portions of New England in the United States (Irland 1998), was widespread. This storm was unprecedented in terms of the total area affected (603,654 ha in Ontario alone), as well as the duration and the amount of freezing rain that was deposited (Lautenschlager and Nielsen 1999; Van Dyke 1999). More than 80 hours of freezing rain and drizzle occurred between January 5 and January 10 in Ontario, producing 73–108 mm of precipitation. This was twice the duration and amount of previous ice storms. The amount of woody litter (19.9 metric tons/ha) produced by the 1998 ice storm in an old-growth forest at Mont St. Hilaire, Quebec, was the greatest of any ice storm on record and approached amounts produced by the most power-ful hurricanes (Hooper et al. 2001). Such damage was found by Jones et al. (2001) to be predominantly a function of tree size for a mature, deciduous forest in eastern Ontario; that is, large stems in the canopy experienced much greater damage than did smaller stems in the subcanopy. Whether there are significant effects on the herba-ceous layer after this and other ice storms will likely depend on stand structure and species composition, in addition to storm intensity (Van Dyke 1999). The magnitude of the response of herbs is likely to be greater where canopy openings are large and shade-tolerant tree seedlings, saplings, or shrubs are sparse.

Natural Disturbances that Affect Only the Forest Floor or Both Floor and Canopy

The natural fire return interval (before European settlement) in eastern forests varies from two to 1,000 years, depending on climate, site, species, stand growth patterns, and influences of other disturbances (Oliver and Larson 1996 and studies reviewed therein). The forest types exhibiting the shortest return intervals are the longleaf and loblolly pine forests of the southeastern U.S. coastal plain and the jack pine forests in the Lake States. Upper-elevation conifer forests and mixed forests of northeast-ern Maine show the longest return intervals (Lorimer 1977; Wein and Moore 1977), whereas the eastern boreal forest, northern hardwoods of central New England, spruce/hemlock/pine types of eastern Canada, and the aspen/birch and birch/maple/hemlock types of the Lake States have intermediate return intervals of 50–350 years (Oliver and Larson 1996).

Various authors have emphasized the autecological characteristics of plant species in examining the response of plants to fire. We would expect plant species to have developed a wide range of adaptations, given the historical role of fire in eastern for-ests. Rowe (1983) cautioned, however, that there is considerable variability in the selec-tion process, resulting in only very broad, overlapping strategies among species for coping with fire. Correlations between the historical occurrence of fire and specific life history adaptations are likely to be weakest within broad regions containing mostly wide-ranging species, such as the boreal forest (Rowe 1983).

The effects of fires on vegetation are generally correlated with fire intensity and duration (Rowe 1983; Oliver and Larson 1996; Hutchinson et al. 2005). The heat from fires remains principally above the soil surface, except where soils are extremely dry, fuel is very concentrated, or fires burn in underground roots (Oliver and Larson 1996). Depth of heat penetration can be expected to affect regeneration from buried propa-gules (Moore and Wein 1977). Martin (1955) found that all of the herbaceous and shrub species two years after a severe burn survived the fire either as underground stems or dormant seeds. The resprouting plants originated from underground stems buried 2.5 cm in the humus and occurred only in parts of the burn where the humus was not completely consumed. In response to the temporal and spatial variability of the fire regime, species have evolved a variety of strategies for survival or regeneration after fire. Skutch (1929) noted that *Pteridium aquilinum* (L.) Kuhn resprouted from deep-seated rhizomes even where the humus had been burned away on a severely burned site in Maine. He also observed sprouting of *Epilobium angustifolium* L. from the primary and secondary roots within the first year, a phenomenon that has also been documented for *Rubus ideaus* L. (Roberts and Dong 1993). The cryptogams *Marchantia polymorpha* L., *Polytrichum commune* Hedw., and *P. juniperinum* Hedw. were in high abundance on burned sites in Maine (Skutch 1929) and Nova Scotia (Martin 1955). The early establishment of these species on burned sites has been attributed to their widely dispersed spores and preference for high light environments (Skutch 1929).

Ahlgren (1960) classified plants into three types regarding fire: (1) species found only on unburned sites, consisting of shade-loving perennials reproducing mostly by shallow or surface rhizomes or bulbs; (2) species found only on burned-over sites (mostly those that reproduce by seed); and (3) species occurring on both burned and unburned sites, including both seed and vegetatively reproduced species. Based on Noble and Slatyer's (1980) modes of persistence, Rowe (1983) proposed a classification of plant strategies in the context of fire. The first division in the classification is based on method of regeneration and reproduction, being either disseminule-based or vegetative-based. Disseminule-based species were subdivided into *invaders* (highly dispersive, pioneering fugitives with short-lived propagules), *evaders* (species with long-lived propagules stored in the soil or canopy), and *avoiders* (shade-tolerant, late successional species, often with symbiotic requirements). Vegetative-based species were subdivided into *resisters* (shade-intolerant species that can survive low-severity fires in the adult stage) and *endurers* (resprouting species with buried perennating buds). Lyon and Stickney (1976) also provided a classification of plants based on their autecological characteristics. They found that most plant species on a site before intense fires in the northern Rocky Mountains survived or reestablished by virtue of on-site surviving parts and seeds or the transport of seeds from adjacent, unburned communities. McLean (1969) found that fire resistance was related to rooting depth.

Another line of research has focused on changes in the physical environment caused by burning in explaining herbaceous layer response. Ahlgren (1960) attributed differences in species composition on lightly and severely burned sites to seedbed characteristics. He also noted that some species requiring open conditions might be limited by competition with resprouting species on light burns. Martin (1955) noted higher species richness and more luxuriant growth in plots under shade cloth than in open plots two years after burning. He attributed the difference to higher moisture in the shaded plots. Gilliam and Christensen (1986) found higher species richness and total cover of the herbaceous layer after burning on infertile sites in the southeastern coastal plain of the United States. This effect was found only after winter burns and disappeared after two years. They attributed the result to decreased shading and increased nutrient availability immediately after burning. Indeed, the fertilization effect of burning has been well documented (e.g., Ahlgren 1960; Wilbur and Christensen 1983; Skre et al. 1998), although the possible counterbalancing losses of nutrients to volatilization, leaching, and overland flow must also be considered (MacLean et al. 1983). Gilliam (1991) suggested that some fire-prone ecosystems may depend on fire to maintain the availability of essential resources that would otherwise be growth-limiting.

Although consumption of herb layer plants can occur via invertebrate herbivores (Hahn et al. 2010), herbivory by mammals is a common understory disturbance that has been frequently documented in the forests of eastern North America (chapters 4, 16, and 17, this volume). Because of dramatic increases in populations of white-tailed deer (*Odocoileus virginianus* Zimmermann) and moose (*Alces alces* L.) in specific regions throughout the 1900s, damage from these two animals is often cited. Crawley (1983) stresses that herbivores have both direct and indirect effects on plant species richness and community dynamics. Plants may be affected directly by being eaten to extinction or by being favored if they are unpalatable. Indirect effects operate by altering the relative competitive abilities of plants. Both categories of effects are clearly evident in studies that have documented browsing in eastern forests. As with other types of disturbances, most browsing studies have focused on the tree layer or tree regeneration; effects on the herbaceous layer have been seldom described.

Studies of moose browsing suggest that the effects on the herbaceous layer are mostly indirect. On Isle Royale, Michigan, moose browsing reduced the cover of canopy trees, particularly *Abies balsamea* and *Populus tremuloides* Michx., and promoted a well-developed understory of shrubs and herbaceous species (McInnes et al. 1992). The herbs, in general, were not browsed and became a greater proportion of total community biomass. Thompson et al. (1992) documented reduced densities of *Abies balsamea*, *Prunus pensylvanica* L.f., *Viburnum trilobum* Marsh., and *Amelanchier* spp., and increased densities of *Kalmia angustifolia* L. in response to moose browsing in Newfoundland. Although the herbaceous layer was not assessed in this study, one would expect the number and cover of herbaceous species to be low in areas where *Kalmia angustifolia* is dominant. Snyder and Janke (1976) found twice as much herbaceous layer cover on moose-browsed sites as on unbrowsed sites, which they attributed to increased light.

Populations of white-tailed deer began to increase throughout much of eastern North America in the early 20th century after enactment of numerous game laws (Marquis and Brenneman 1981). Heavy browsing of preferred species by deer has resulted in regeneration failures of many commercially important forest tree species, as well as noticeable changes in understory composition (Marquis and Brenneman 1981; Horsley and Marquis 1983). Preferred species of browse in northwestern Pennsylvania included *Prunus serotina* (Ehrh.), *P. pensylvanica*, *Acer rubrum*, *A. saccharum* (Marsh.), *Fraxinus americana* (L.), *Betula* spp., and *Rubus* spp. (Horsley and Marquis 1983). Species favored in areas that are heavily browsed included *Fagus grandifolia* (Ehrh.), *Acer pensylvanicum* (L.), ferns, grasses, *Solidago* spp., and *Aster* spp. (Marquis and Brenneman 1981). Horsley and Marquis (1983) documented an interaction between browsing and interference from ferns and grasses that caused regeneration failures of commercially important tree species in Pennsylvania. Deer browsing on *Rubus* spp. and tree seedlings promoted increases in cover of *Dennstaedtia punctilobula* (Michx.), *Thelypteris novaboracensis* (L.), and *Brachyelytrum erectum* (Schreb.), thereby reducing densities of preferred tree species. Any surviving tree seedlings that grew above the herb layer were browsed by deer. It is likely that richness and cover of other herbaceous species are low in areas with high abundance of the interfering ferns and grasses.

Heinen and Currey (2000) documented changes in tree species composition after browsing by introduced Rocky Mountain elk (*Cervus elaphus nelsonii* L.) and deer in Michigan. *Populus grandidentata* Michx. and *Acer rubrum* decreased in abundance, and *Populus tremuloides* increased in browsed areas. Approximately half of the browsed area was dominated by non-tree vegetation, predominantly *Pteridium aquilinum* and *Rubus* spp.

Unlike moose, deer browse directly on herbaceous species. Deer forage on herbs during the spring and summer, and then switch to woody browse in the winter months (Balgooyen and Waller 1995). Skinner and Telfer (1974) found that species of the lily family (Liliaceae), principally *Clintonia borealis* (Aiton) Raf. and *Maianthemum canadense* Desf., supplied 29 percent of the spring diet for white-tailed deer in New Brunswick, Canada. Other commonly browsed herbaceous species included *Gaultheriaprocumbens* L., *Erythronium americanum* Ker Gawler, grasses (Poaceae) in the spring, and *Cornus canadensis* L. in the fall (Skinner and Telfer 1974). Among woody species, *Acer spicatum* Lam., *Betula allegheniensis*, *Sorbus decora* (Sarg.) C. K. Schneider, and *Taxus canadensis* Marshall were reduced in abundance in areas with high deer densities in northern Wisconsin (Balgooyen and Waller 1995). Several herbaceous species, including *Aralia nudicaulis* L., *Maianthemum canadense*, and *Clintonia borealis*, also had decreased frequency and cover in areas with high densities of deer relative to areas with low densities. Other commonly grazed herbaceous species included *Aster macrophyllus* L., *Habenaria orbiculata* (Pursh) Torr., *Sanguinaria canadensis* L., *Smilacina racemosa* L. (Desf.), *Streptopus roseus* Michx., *Trillium cernuum* L., *T. grandiflorum* (Michx.) Salisb., and *Uvularia sessilifolia* L. (Balgooyen and Waller 1995). R. C. Anderson (1994) found that *Trilliumgrandiflorum*, *Erythronium americanum*, and *Claytonia virginica* L. were preferentially browsed in Illinois.

In some cases, herbaceous species have been used as indicators of deer browsing intensity. For example, percent cover, number of leaves/plant, scape height, and number of pedicels/umbel of *Clintonia borealis* were negatively correlated with deer densities in the study by Balgooyen and Waller (1995). R. C. Anderson (1994) found the height of *Trillium grandiflorum* to be a useful indicator of deer browsing intensity.

Deer browsing may also produce indirect effects on the herbaceous layer if the shrub, seedling, or sapling layers are heavily browsed. One example of the indirect effects of browsing is provided by Balgooyen and Waller (1995), who found greater herb diversity and cover in areas where *Taxus canadensis* was more heavily browsed.

Anthropogenic Disturbances: Agriculture and Forestry

The combined forces of clearing for agriculture and lumbering transformed eastern North America from a forested to a predominantly agricultural landscape in the two centuries following European settlement (Flinn and Vellend 2005; Baeten et al. 2011; chapter 19, this volume). Agriculture is the most severe form of these disturbances and has the greatest effect on the herbaceous layer because of the removal of vegetative propagules and seed banks associated with annual cultivation and the dramatic change in microenvironment (Runkle 1985; Vellend 2004; Fraterrigo et al. 2006). Grazing by pigs, sheep, and cattle can also dramatically affect woody and herbaceous vegetation composition in woodlands (Whitney 1994). The effects of forest harvesting depend on a number of factors, including type of harvesting system, equipment used, season of year, site conditions, soil type, subsequent treatments, and others.

Forest management approaches common in the eastern deciduous forest can be viewed as a gradient of disturbance intensity, varying from the least intense with single tree selection to the most intense with clearcutting (Gilliam and Roberts 1995; Hammond et al. 1998; Moola and Vasseur 2008; von Oheimb and Härdtle 2009). Recent research has looked at the direct effects of harvesting alone, as well as in combination with other management techniques, on herb layer composition and diversity (Reader and Bricker 1992a,b; Halpern and Spies 1995; Roberts and Gilliam 1995b; Elliott et al. 1997; Hammond et al. 1998; Thomas et al. 1999; He and Barclay 2000; Elliott and Knoepp 2005). Other work has examined herb layer recovery after more extreme treatments not associated with forest management, such as deforestation and regrowth suppression with repeated herbicide applications (Kochenderfer and Wendel 1983; Reiners 1992). Still others have provided valuable information on species dynamics of the herb layer by comparing patterns in second-growth forest stands to those in old-growth stands (Qian et al. 1997; Goebel et al. 1999; chapter 7, this volume). The lack of consistency in findings of these studies demonstrates the site-specific nature of herb layer responses to anthropogenic disturbances to forests (Roberts and Gilliam 1995b), precluding broad generalizations and underlining the importance of in-depth study of these responses for different forest types and harvest techniques.

Several studies have looked at post-harvest responses of herb layer vegetation to clearcutting either alone or in combination with other silvicultural treatments. Halpern and Spies (1995) found that changes in herb layer diversity were short-lived after clearcutting and slash-burning of Douglas fir forests of western Oregon and Washington and that herb diversity returned to pre-harvest conditions before canopy closure (10–20 years). Roberts and Gilliam (1995b) found that responses of the herb layer to clearcutting were highly site-dependent in mesic and dry mesic aspen stands. Harvested stands approximately 15 years old had higher diversity and richness than mature stands on mesic sites, whereas there were no significant differences on dry mesic sites. De Grandpre´ and Bergeron (1997) found that site dependence of herb response to disturbance might be related to the age of the stand at the time of disturbance in southern boreal forests of Quebec (i.e., younger communities changed less after clearcutting than did more mature communities). Fredericksen et al. (1999) concluded that only the most intense levels of harvesting measurably affected herb layer richness, diversity, composition, and cover in northern hardwood and oak-hickory forests of Pennsylvania.

Several lines of evidence suggest that forest harvesting may have long-term detrimental effects on the composition and diversity of herbaceous plants (Wyatt and Silman 2010; chapter 18, this volume). Based on direct comparisons of harvested and old-growth stands in southern Appalachian forests, Duffy and Meier (1992) argued that the harvested stands are impoverished even after 150 years. Because of methodological problems, the accuracy of the results of this study has been questioned (Elliott and Loftis 1993; Johnson et al. 1993). Replies to these criticisms (Duffy 1993a,b) and further work (Meier et al. 1995) by these authors failed to resolve the problems (see chapter 7, this volume, for further discussion). Although similar findings have been reported for a variety of European and North American forest communities (e.g., Hill 1979b, Scanlan 1981, Peterken and Game 1984, Whitney and Foster 1988, Dzwonko and Loster 1989, and others reviewed in Matlack 1994a), all have compared second-growth

Table 13.1 Effects of clearcut harvesting on herbaceous layer species diversity in selected forests of eastern North America.

Study and forest type or site type	Type of comparison	Treated			Control			Effect on herbaceous species diversity
		H'	S	Age (years)	H'	S	Age (years)	
Yorks and Dabydeen (1999)	Clearcuts and mature second-growth reference stands							No effect on H'
Frostburg Watershed		3.14[a]		2	3.42		90	
		3.91		13–14				
		3.93		19				
Savage R. (NW aspect)		2.25		2	4.23		75	
		3.63		13				
		3.79		17				
		2.80		26				
Savage R. (SE aspect)		4.49		2	3.26		80	
		3.96		13				
		3.16		26				
Jenkins and Parker (1999)	Clearcuts and mature second-growth reference stands							S and H' significantly greater on mesic slopes
Dry mesic slopes		2.20	28	9–15	2.40	27	> 80	No differences in S or H' with clearcut age; S and H' not different from control
		2.10	30	16–24				
Mesic slopes		2.50	38	9–15	2.40	27	> 80	No differences
		2.20	39	16–24				

Study	Description	H′	S	Age	H′	S	Age	Comments
Gilliam (2002)	Clearcuts and mature second growth reference stands	1.64	14[b]	20	1.53	13[b]	>70	No differences in S or H′; variations in H′ related more to changes in evenness than richness
Goebel et al. (1999)	Second growth compared to old growth	2.12[c]	14	70–79	2.54	19	>150	No significant differences in S or H′
Elliott et al. (1997)	Clearcut harvest vs. mature forest before harvest							Sustained decreases in S and H′ after harvest compared to precut forest
Cove hardwoods		2.19	22	2	2.52[d]	27	>70[e]	
		0.82	20	16				
Mixed-oak hardwoods		2.04	18		3.14	49	>70[e]	
		1.32	16	16				
Hardwood-pines		2.28	25	2	2.40	45	>70[e]	
		1.90	27	16				
Roberts and Zhu (2002)	Clearcut harvest vs. mature forest before harvest							Significantly greater S and H′ after harvest compared to precut forest
Clearcut only		0.80[f]	13[b]	2	0.60[f]	12[b]	>80	
Clearcut and planted		0.88[f]	19[b]	2	0.79[f]	16[b]	>80	
Roberts and Gilliam (1995b)	Clearcuts and mature second-growth reference stands							
Mesic sites		3.76	35	3–14	3.34	26	57–82	S and H′ significantly greater in young clearcuts
Dry mesic sites		3.04	24	3–12	2.76	23	55–80	No significant differences in S or H′

(Continued)

Table 13.1 (Continued)

Study and forest type or site type	Type of comparison	Treated			Control			Effect on herbaceous species diversity
		H'	S	Age (years)	H'	S	Age (years)	
Meier et al. (1995)	Clearcut and old-growth reference stand		10[b]	5		14[b]	?	S significantly greater in control
Roberts (2002)	Plantations and mature reference stands	1.73	27	5–16	1.75	24	> 90	No significant differences in S or H'

[a] Average of June and August sampling periods.

[b] Mean no. species/plot.

[c] Average of late spring and summer sampling periods.

[d] Pre-harvest inventory.

[e] Originated from cutting and burning, followed by selective logging.

[f] Mean H'/plot.

stands or plantations on abandoned agricultural fields to natural forests. It is not clear from these studies what the effects of harvesting on the herbaceous layer would have been independent from the effects of agriculture. Thus, further research is needed to determine the influence of harvesting on herbaceous layer composition and diversity. Long-term studies along gradients of disturbance type and severity would be of particular value.

Evidence from early botanical descriptions and herbarium records suggests that many species have declined in abundance or have become extinct in North America as a result of the combined effects of European settlement. Indeed, the impact of historical land use on forest floras has been frequently documented (Matlack 1994a); however, the extent to which these changes can be attributed to forest management activities, as distinct from other land uses, remains unknown.

Other studies have also found that the forest understory remains impoverished for long periods (perhaps centuries) after natural disturbances such as wildfires (Spies 1991; MacLean and Wein 1977). Thus, the effects of harvesting must be balanced against the natural patterns of succession (Roberts and Gilliam 1995a). It is not clear whether harvesting would cause more severe effects than natural disturbances, but any differences would likely be related to the intensity of the disturbance. Without doubt, more research is needed to identify patterns and mechanisms of herbaceous layer response to harvesting.

Published results of harvesting effects on herbaceous layer diversity of forest types throughout North America were reviewed by Battles et al. (2001). We have taken a similar approach with a narrower focus on studies in northeastern forests. We present the actual values as calculated in the various studies for species richness (S; usually the average number of species per plot) and the Shannon-Wiener index (H'; table 13.1). It was not possible to compare results among studies because of differences in methods; rather, we compared the treated condition to the reference condition within each study and noted the direction of change in S and H' for each case. Only treatments that involved clearcutting (with or without plantation management) were included because clearcutting constitutes the most severe management disturbance (Roberts and Zhu, 2002). Thus, if clearcutting shows no significant effect on species richness or diversity, it is unlikely that a less severe management treatment, such as selection harvest, would show a significant effect in that forest type.

The studies in eastern forests that we reviewed showed diverse patterns, including no differences in S or H' between clearcuts and controls (Goebel et al. 1999; Yorks and Dabydeen 1999; Gilliam 2002; Roberts, 2002), greater S or H' in clearcuts than in controls (Jenkins and Parker 1999; Roberts and Zhu 2002), and lower S or H' in clearcuts than in controls (Meier et al. 1995; Elliott et al. 1997; table 13.1). Roberts and Gilliam (1995b) found that the patterns depended on site type, with no difference on dry mesic sites and greater S and H' in clearcuts compared to controls on mesic sites in northern lower Michigan (table 13.1). Neither type of control (second growth versus old growth) nor age of treated stand appeared to explain any trends in S or H'. For example, Goebel et al. (1999) compared mature clearcuts (70–79 years) to old-growth reference stands, whereas Yorks and Dabydeen (1999), Gilliam (2002), and Roberts (2002) studied young clearcuts (2–26 years) in relation to mature second-growth reference stands, yet all found no significant differences between treatments and controls.

In the studies that included a chronosequence of treated stands, conflicting patterns were reported. Yorks and Dabydeen (1999) found no statistically significant differences with stand age but noted that S and H' peaked in recent clearcuts (3–4 years) and controls (90 years) on the moister northwestern aspects but tended to decrease over time on drier southwestern aspects. Jenkins and Parker (1999) also found no significant differences with stand age, although there was a slight tendency for H' to decrease and S to increase with age (9–15 year age class versus 16–24 year age class; table 13.1). In Elliott et al. (1997), two community types on moister sites (cove hardwoods and mixed-oak hardwoods) showed significantly lower H' in 1993 than in 1979, but the drier hardwood-pines site did not have significant differences with stand age (table 13.1). Certainly, changes in diversity over time are influenced by site conditions, as noted elsewhere (e.g., Roberts and Gilliam 1995b), along with a complex of additional factors, making generalizations difficult.

Without doubt, more research is needed to identify patterns and mechanisms of herbaceous layer response to harvesting. In the next section, we present a summary of theories that can be applied to this problem.

COMMUNITY PATTERNS AND MECHANISMS OF SUCCESSIONAL CHANGE IN UNDERSTORY COMMUNITIES

Hypothesized Changes in Species Diversity with Succession

Peet and Christensen (1988) hypothesized that diversity would wax and wane during stand development according to the changing intensity of competition (chapter 11, this volume). For example, species richness is initially high after disturbance, then decreases to a minimum during the stem exclusion stage (sensu Oliver and Larson 1996), when competition among the overstory trees is at a maximum. Subsequently, richness should increase again during the transition to the old-growth stage. During the old-growth stage, richness should either decline slightly due to the loss of early successional species or reach a new peak as slowly dispersed climax-specialist species invade. Beta (between-habitat) diversity should increase during the periods of most intense competition because of a decrease in niche breadth induced by competition (Peet and Christensen 1988). Gilliam et al. (1995) suggested that the link between forest strata becomes tighter as competition increases after the establishment phase. We hypothesize that different strata show increasingly similar responses to environmental gradients with successional time (chapter 9, this volume). Certainly, patterns of change in herbaceous layer diversity are related to the intensity of the disturbance as determined by the management regime.

Mechanisms of Change in Understory Communities during Succession: Initial Effects

Halpern and Spies (1995) have suggested that we separate disturbance effects into two broad classes: initial effects on existing plant populations and long-term effects on recovering plant populations. We follow this convention because different mechanisms are involved in each case (Roberts and Gilliam 1995a). The *initial effects* influence plant community response through destruction of vegetative stems and propagules, effects on propagule availability and species invasion, and modification of habitats, including seedbed conditions, light, temperature, and moisture. Initial effects could vary widely depending on the type and severity of disturbance. For example, management treatments such as clearcutting with mechanized site preparation influence early vegetation response quite differently from clearcutting alone (Roberts and Zhu, 2002). The type of disturbance in terms of its effects on the vegetation and environment is the important consideration here.

The *long-term effects* are manifested as changes in species composition, rate of stand development, and competitive interactions. Control of competing vegetation with herbicides is a typical example of a management treatment that has all of these long-term effects (e.g., Horsley 1994). Other long-term effects include composition and density of planting, timing and intensity of thinning, and length of harvest rotation (Halpern and Spies 1995). The analogues in natural disturbances are variations in initial stand density and stand structure, as well as the occurrence of minor disturbances during stand development.

One of the most important factors controlling the initial effects of disturbance on the herbaceous understory is the nature of the disturbance. As discussed above, characterizing the disturbance in terms of amount of forest canopy removed, amount of forest floor vegetation, forest floor, and soil removed (severity), and the frequency, size, and shape (Oliver and Larson 1996) captures the processes involved in understory recovery. Classifying disturbances in this fashion eliminates the need to exhaustively assess each individual disturbance event. This approach allows us to accurately categorize each disturbance in terms of its effects on the physical environment and the forest community and to examine understory response to these factors. Many studies have documented the changes in light (e.g., Jackson 1959; Berry 1964), soil temperature, moisture (e.g., Minckler et al. 1973; Fowler 1974; Hungerford and Babbitt 1987; McInnis and Roberts 1995), and nutrient availability (Johnson and Schultz 1999) that occur after disturbances of varying severities. Others have related disturbance severity to differences in vegetation response (Halpern 1988; Roberts and Dong 1993).

Taken in conjunction with disturbance characteristics, the life history characteristics (principally reproductive and survival strategies) provide the means for predicting initial vegetation response (Roberts and Gilliam 1995a). Various plant classifications based on functional (life history) characteristics have been proposed, including life forms (Raunkiaer 1934), competitor/stress tolerator/ruderal strategies (Grime 1977, 1979), assembly/response rules (Keddy 1992), vital attributes (Noble and Slatyer 1980; Rowe 1983), functional types (reviewed in T. M. Smith et al. 1997), or subsets of specific life history traits (Matlack 1994b; McIntyre et al. 1995). Numerous studies have demonstrated the importance of species' life histories in long-term successional community dynamics (e.g., Drury and Nisbet 1973; Sousa 1980; Roberts and Richardson 1985; Peet and Christensen 1988; Halpern 1989; others reviewed in McCook 1994). Different life history traits have been found to be relevant depending on the nature of the disturbance (Kirchner et al. 2011). Malanson (1984) pointed out the fundamental difference in regeneration mechanisms between light (survival in situ or vegetative regeneration) and severe disturbance (invasion). In the case of harvesting disturbance, we would expect to find correlations between species composition and a suite of life history traits including rooting habit, shade tolerance, ability to reproduce vegetatively, seed storability, seed production, seed size, and dispersal mechanism.

Species in the herbaceous layer may reappear following disturbance via one or more of four basic mechanisms:

1. Survival in situ. Depending on the disturbance severity, plants may survive in the vegetative form. Given the patchy nature of many types of disturbance and the low severity of others, considerable numbers of individual plants may survive the disturbance.

2. Vegetative regeneration. In situations where aboveground vegetation is damaged or killed, new individuals may reappear by vegetative means (Zobel and Antos 2009). Vegetative regeneration is the primary means of reproduction for many deciduous forest herbs (chapters 5 and 6, this volume). Rhizome growth rates may approach 1 m/year in some species (Sobey and Barkhouse 1977). Through a combination of these first two mechanisms, early vegetation composition often closely resembles the pre-disturbance composition (Lyon and Stickney 1976).

3. Regeneration from the seed bank. There is a potential for some species of the herbaceous layer to regenerate from the seed bank. Typically, however, buried seed reserves are modest in coniferous forests and are dominated by early successional species (Archibold 1989). Seed bank composition tends to greatly differ from the aboveground vegetation in most forest types (Pickett and McDonnell 1989).

4. Regeneration by dispersed propagules. Most temperate forest herbs flower and produce seeds regularly, and regeneration from seed may be the most important reproductive mechanism for many of these species (Bierzychudek 1982a; Cain et al. 1998; chapters 5 and 6, this volume). Seeds may be dispersed from individuals surviving in adjacent patches within the disturbed area or from nearby undisturbed communities.

Mechanisms of Change in Understory Communities during Succession: Long-Term Effects

After the initial effects of disturbance and the immediate response of the herbaceous layer, we must consider the long-term influences of the disturbance on the successional recovery of the herbaceous layer. Spies (1991) notes four factors that contribute to successional change:

1. The microclimate becomes more cool and humid during the dry season in old forests, and soil moisture may be higher because of litter accumulation.

2. There is an increase in horizontal spatial heterogeneity of resources and environments, relating to the development of canopy gaps in a matrix of closed forest. Some species survive in deep shade but require gaps for long-term survival.

3. An increase in vertical environmental diversity occurs (e.g., increase in height and number of canopy layers). This may be more important in habitat for foliose lichens and epiphytes than for forest herbs.

4. Sensitivity to disturbance (e.g., fire) and slow rates of reestablishment and growth after the disturbance are important. In addition to affecting initial vegetation response, the type and intensity of the disturbance also have long-term consequences by influencing the initial mix of species, propagule availability, environmental conditions, competitive relationships, and individual growth rates.

These factors help explain the changes in species richness with stand development hypothesized by Peet and Christensen (1988), Oliver and Larson (1996), and others.

These patterns correspond to an invasion of shade-intolerant herbs and shrubs into the surviving community of shade-tolerant forest species soon after disturbance, followed by a decrease in diversity during the stem-exclusion stage of stand development, and then higher diversity in the old-growth stage in which the increases in horizontal and vertical heterogeneity and changes in microclimate are expressed.

A number of factors may modify this idealized pattern of successional change. Site conditions, such as soil moisture and fertility, may exert an overriding control on successional patterns of species diversity as noted by Auclair and Goff (1971), Roberts and Christensen (1988), and Roberts and Gilliam (1995b). Auclair and Goff (1971) hypothesized that a more nearly linear increase in species diversity with increasing stand age would occur on xeric, hydric, or infertile sites as compared to mesic, fertile sites. Disturbance-related influences on resource availability may affect the rate and direction of succession, depending on the type and severity of disturbance. Indeed, several resource-mediated models of succession are based on the assumption that resource availability changes as a result of disturbance and continues to change with time (Grime 1977; Tilman 1985; Vitousek 1985). The competitive balance among species can vary as a consequence of differences in disturbance type and severity or chance factors (e.g., seed production, weather) controlling initial plant densities, resulting in different successional trajectories (Oliver and Larson 1996).

Conceptual Models of Herbaceous Layer Response to Disturbance

The factors discussed in the previous section have been incorporated into general conceptual models that attempt to capture the essential processes controlling response of the herbaceous layer to variations in disturbance severity in both the short term and long term (figs. 13.2 and 13.3). Disturbance affects forest structure in terms of overstory and understory density and cover, presence and relative densities of different vegetation layers (vertical stratification), and abundance of standing snags and coarse, woody debris. These effects depend on disturbance severity (overstory and understory). In turn, forest structure affects the environment and substrate for the herbaceous layer through modifications in microclimate (light intensity, relative humidity, temperature, surface moisture) and substrate (abundance of coarse, woody-debris and stages of decay). Forest structure, of course, changes over successional time, with resulting changes in levels of competition between the herbaceous layer and overtopping vertical strata. Disturbance also affects the forest floor directly by creating or destroying pits and mounds, creating mineral soil substrates, and modifying abundance and condition of coarse, woody debris substrates. Finally, disturbance affects the preexisting plant community by damaging or killing individual plants and changing propagule availability by modifying seed banks and seed rain. Using this framework, we are able to make improved predictions of the effects of disturbance on the herbaceous layer in eastern forests.

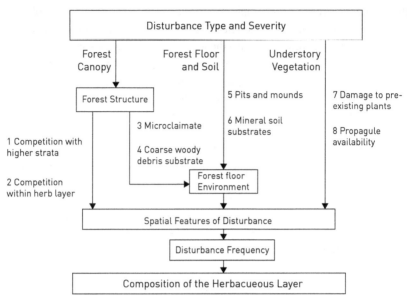

FIGURE 13.2 Mechanisms proposed for the effects of disturbance on structure and composition of the herbaceous layer in forests. Taken from Roberts (2004).

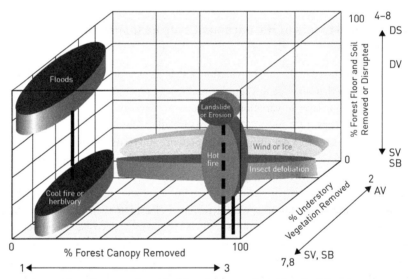

FIGURE 13.3 A three-dimensional model of disturbance severity, with each of three forest vegetation strata (forest canopy, understory vegetation, forest floor and soil) on separate axes. Labeled shapes represent the ranges in conditions on these axes created by the common natural disturbances in North American forests. Numbered arrows adjacent to axes represent the eight key factors controlling herbaceous layer response (see fig. 13.2). Letter codes adjacent to the arrows represent species' regeneration mechanisms: DV, deep-seated vegetative (deep rhizomes, root sprouts, bulbs); SV, surficial vegetative (shallow rhizomes, stolons); AV, aboveground vegetative (lateral extension, runners); SB, seed bank; DS, widely dispersed seed. Increasing importance of the particular factors and regeneration mechanisms is indicated by direction of arrow. Taken from Roberts (2004).

CONCLUSIONS AND RECOMMENDATIONS

Many studies have documented effects of disturbance on eastern forests, but surprisingly few have looked at the herbaceous layer. In assessing the nature of disturbance and its effects on the herbaceous layer, it is useful to characterize disturbance severity in terms of the amount of destruction of both the overstory and understory. Insect defoliation, wind, and ice storms are typical natural disturbances in eastern forests that primarily affect the forest canopy. Their effects on the herbaceous layer and forest floor are expressed largely through changes in environment (increased light) and substrate (additions of litter, frass, and coarse, woody debris to the forest floor and creation of pits and mounds). In contrast to canopy disturbances, fire and herbivory by mammals exert their greatest effects on the understory layers. The herbaceous layer is affected by these disturbances by direct mortality and damage of plants, alteration of propagule availability (reduction or destruction of the seed bank and changes in composition of the seed rain), and changes in competitive relationships among plant species. Forest harvesting and other anthropogenic disturbances can vary greatly in disturbance severity and in their relative effects on canopy and understory, depending on the types of treatment and how they are applied.

Characterizing disturbance in terms of severity at both the canopy and understory levels allows us to examine the effects of disturbance based on its impact on the ecosystem independent of the causal agent. Thus, we are able to focus more clearly on processes that control ecosystem response. This is particularly useful in characterizing the nature of anthropogenic disturbances and evaluating their effects on the ecosystem. With our current emphasis on ecosystem management and the need to pattern forest management after natural disturbance regimes, it is important to be able to compare disturbances on a common basis.

In characterizing the effects of disturbance on the herbaceous layer, it is useful to recognize two general types of effects: direct effects, which include direct damage to preexisting plants and alterations in propagule availability, and indirect effects, comprising changes in microclimate and forest floor substrates, as well as modification of competitive relationships with other plants in all forest strata. In addition, there are initial effects and long-term effects, the former including direct and indirect effects of the disturbance on preexisting plants, propagule availability, microclimate and substrates, and the latter including the development of competitive relationships, propagule availability, microclimate, and substrates over succession time. The interaction of species' life history characteristics with these disturbance factors determines the direction and outcome of forest succession.

14 The Herbaceous Layer as a Filter Determining Spatial Pattern in Forest Tree Regeneration

Lisa O. George and Fakhri A. Bazzaz

Although small in stature and seemingly ephemeral in nature, herbaceous understory communities have the potential to exert a strong influence on the dynamics of forest tree regeneration. Through the study of fern-dominated understory communities in central Massachusetts mixed-deciduous forests, we have found that this understory stratum can act as a selective filter of tree seedling species in their earliest life stages. All trees, first as seeds, must penetrate this layer to reach the forest floor and then germinate and grow under the "canopy" of the herbaceous stratum. The microenvironment at and near the forest floor is dictated largely by the nearby herbs and shrubs above. Tree seedlings that are able to germinate, survive, and grow in this environment will ultimately emerge from this stratum and become potential successors to the forest canopy. Tree seedling species performance may vary considerably under the particular rigors of a well-developed understory, and it is this variability that enables the understory to filter tree seedlings.

Because the tree seedling bank represents the starting capital for forest regeneration, pre-disturbance interactions between the understory and tree seedlings that shape the nature of the seedling bank will influence the rate and trajectory of post-disturbance forest regeneration (Brokaw and Scheiner 1989; Connell 1989). The presence of a well-developed understory stratum composed of herbs and/or shrubs generally reduces the density of tree seedlings and saplings beneath its canopy (Horsley 1977a,b; Phillips and Murdy 1985; McWilliams et al. 1995; Hill 1996; George and Bazzaz 1999a,b). A low density of advance regeneration may slow forest regeneration after canopy disturbance (Nakashizuka 1987; Taylor and Qin 1992; McWilliams et al. 1995). In stands that lack abundant advance regeneration, it may be possible for widely dispersed pioneer tree species to invade, and with little competition from advance regeneration, become an important component of the next generation of forest (Veblen 1989; Taylor and Qin 1992). In extreme cases, understory interference with tree regeneration has prevented forest regeneration and has led to the formation of permanent shrub communities (Niering and Egler 1955). In the Allegheny Plateau region of northwestern Pennsylvania, competition from herbs has contributed to the formation of savannas and orchard stands, which were previously forested stands, logged heavily in the early 1900s, that have failed to regenerate for more than 50 years (Horsley 1977a,b).

Although the invasion of tree seedlings into herbaceous and shrubby old-field communities has been well studied and provides insight into competitive interactions between tree seedlings and herbs (e.g., De Steven 1991a,b; Gill and Marks 1991; Putz and Canham 1992; Burton and Bazzaz 1995; chapter 10, this volume), we restrict our discussion to tree regeneration in forest communities. Our studies in central New England at the Harvard Forest in Massachusetts have dealt primarily with tree regeneration in closed-canopy *Quercus rubra-Acer rubrum* forests with well-developed fern understories. Some of our work has included the study of shrubs in the understory stratum when present, such as *Viburnum* species and *Corylus cornuta* Marsh. (beaked hazel), a well-studied understory dominant in the western Lake States (Kurmis and Sucoff 1989). One fern species that we have focused on, *Dennstaedtia punctilobula* (Michx.) Moore (hayscented fern), has also been studied extensively in the Allegheny Plateau region of Pennsylvania and New York from the perspective of commercial forestry (Horsley 1977a,b, 1988, 1993a,b; Horsley and Marquis 1983; Bowersox and McCormick 1987; Drew 1988; Kolb et al. 1989, 1990; McWilliams et al. 1995). This body of literature concentrates on the link between dense herbaceous understory vegetation and regeneration failure, which is the failure of a forest stand to be restocked after commercial timber harvest with appropriate densities of tree seedlings of commercially valued species in an acceptable period of time (Grisez and Peace 1973). Other understory species that have been observed to interact with Appalachian hardwood regeneration include clonal ferns such as *Thelypteris noveboracensis* (L.) Nieuwl. (New York fern), *Pteridium aquilinum* (L.) Kuhn. (bracken fern), *Onoclea sensibilis* L. (sensitive fern), and *Osmunda claytoniana* L. (interrupted fern) (Horsley 1988). Several grass species such as *Brachyelytrum erectum* Schreb. (short husk grass), *Danthonia compressa* Aust. (wild oat grass), and *Danthonia spicata* (L.) Beauv. (poverty oat grass) are important constituents of the understory and seed bank in the Appalachian hardwood region and have also been reported to interfere with tree regeneration (Horsley 1977a,b; Bowersox and McCormick 1987).

In the southern Appalachian region, the most prominent members of the understory stratum are the evergreen shrubs *Rhododendron maximum* L. (rosebay rhododendron) and *Kalmia latifolia* L. (mountain laurel). These species have expanded since the chestnut blight to cover an estimated 2.5 million ha in the Appalachians (Monk et al. 1985) and have been implicated in changes in forest succession (Baker and van Lear 1998). Although the focus of this book is on herbs, we discuss these well-studied shrub species because they contribute to the general discussion of understory filtering of tree regeneration and because they provide a useful counterpoint to the effects of herbaceous understory vegetation on tree regeneration. Just as the concept of the understory filter is not confined to herbaceous species, it is not confined to forests of the eastern United States. The processes of understory filtering are being recognized in a diversity of temperate and tropical forests that are characterized by dense or aggressive understory vegetation. Well-studied examples include Costa Rican tropical rainforest where the understory is characterized by palms and cyclanths (Denslow et al. 1991), Chilean subalpine forests where the understory is characterized by *Chusquea* bamboo (Veblen 1982; 1989), and the giant panda reserves in China where the understory is characterized by dwarf bamboo species (Taylor and Qin 1992; Taylor et al. 1995).

Before becoming a tree, an individual must pass through several life stages under or within the herbaceous stratum, each of which is a potential winnowing point for the understory filter. We first discuss the influence of the understory filter on dispersal, germination, and survival of tree seeds and seedlings individually and then discuss the effects of the understory filter on tree seedling community attributes such as tree seedling distribution, species composition, and diversity. The influence of the understory filter on seedling growth will then be addressed, followed by a discussion of the role of the understory in determining the size structure of tree seedling communities. The filtering activity of the understory is complex not only because of its activity at multiple life stages of a tree, but also because the understory itself is a complex and changing mosaic of understory plants. In conclusion, we discuss the spatial and temporal distribution of understory plants and how the mosaic nature of the understory affects the complexity of the understory filter.

THE UNDERSTORY MICROENVIRONMENT

Plant growth in the understory is commonly limited by the light environment, which is determined by a complex of variables including site topography, seasonal solar patterns, and overstory structure and composition (chapter 3, this volume). The herbaceous layer further reduces the quantity and quality of light reaching the forest floor. The fern understory in closed-canopy forests in Massachusetts reduces midsummer light levels approximately 70 percent—from an average of 3.5 percent full sun above ferns to 1 percent full sun below ferns (George and Bazzaz 1999a). The understory stratum of partially thinned Allegheny forest stands dominated by *Dennstaedtia punctilobula* reduces light from about 20 percent full sun above the fern stratum to less than 0.5 percent full sun below ferns; the fern understory also decreases the red/far-red ratio from 0.50–1.10 above ferns to 0.04–0.07 below ferns (Horsley 1993a). Forest understory communities dominated by *Rhododendron maximum* in the southern Appalachians have a similarly dramatic impact on the light environment. Midsummer light levels, which range from 4 percent to 8 percent of full sun above the *Rhododendron maximum* canopy, are reduced below the canopy to 1–2 percent of full sun (Clinton 1995; Beckage et al. 2000). In contrast to herbaceous ferns that senesce aboveground at the end of the growing season, *Rhododendron maximum*, an evergreen shrub, dramatically reduces light levels even in the early spring when the deciduous overstory has not yet fully leafed out. Peak forest light levels (measured at 1 m above the forest floor) occur in the southern Appalachians during mid-April and can reach 50 percent full sun in the absence of *Rhododendron maximum* compared to a peak of only 15 percent of full sun below *Rhododendron maximum* (Clinton 1995).

In our Massachusetts study sites, average litter depth was greater below the fern understory, and a greater area of mineral soil was exposed where ferns were absent. This effect was particularly dramatic in sloped sites, which have the potential for high levels of soil exposure (George and Bazzaz 1999a). Similarly, in a deciduous forest in the Blue Ridge Mountains, litter biomass beneath a *Rhododendron maximum* understory was 20 percent higher than in areas without *Rhododendron maximum* cover (Beckage et al. 2000). In our Massachusetts sites, soil water content, soil organic material content, and pH did not differ between fern and fern-free areas (George and Bazzaz 1999a). Similarly, in an Allegheny forest with a dense *Dennstaedtia punctilobula* understory, no differences were detected between soil moisture, soil nitrogen or phosphorus concentrations, soil ammonium and nitrate concentrations, and net ammonium and nitrate production between fern and fern-removal treatment plots (Horsley 1993a). There is some evidence, however, that soil moisture is reduced below a *Rhododendron maximum* understory due to evapotranspirational loss and high interception (Clinton and Vose 1996; Beckage et al. 2000). Additionally, the potential importance of allelopathy of *Dennstaedtia punctilobula* and *Rhododendron maximum* leachates has been investigated and found not to be of importance in field environments (Horsley 1993b; Nilsen et al. 1999).

THE INFLUENCE OF THE UNDERSTORY FILTER

Tree Seed Dispersal and Predation

In New England, fern fronds senesce by the time of autumn seed dispersal of most tree species and therefore do not represent a physical barrier for seeds being dispersed to the forest floor. We observed that spring-dispersed *Acer rubrum* L. seeds land on fern fronds, where they were held for several days before the seeds dropped to the forest floor. In dispersal trials in which *Acer rubrum* seeds were dropped over the canopies of *Osmunda claytoniana* and *Dennstaedtia punctilobula*, more seeds were caught by *Osmunda claytoniana* fronds (45 percent) than by the more fragile and vertically oriented fronds of *Dennstaedtia punctilobula* (31 percent) (George and Bazzaz unpublished data). All seeds were ultimately recovered, however, from the ground under the fern fronds. Whether seed-catching by the understory plays an important role in subsequent predation rates or secondary dispersal has not been well studied. We do expect, however, that the understory stratum may be a more important barrier to seed dispersal in other systems where the understory is characterized by woody or evergreen species. In addition to leaves of understory plants being potential impediments to seed dispersal, the thick litter layer that develops below a *Rhododendron maximum* understory has been reported to act as a physical barrier, preventing seeds from reaching the soil where moisture conditions are more favorable for germination (Clinton and Vose 1996).

Although we did not observe the fern understory to be a direct physical impediment to seed dispersal, we observed higher rates of seed predation under fern cover. In our experimental studies, acorns of *Quercus rubra* L. (northern red oak) experienced a 66 percent removal rate under ferns compared to a 45 percent removal rate in fern-removal plots (George and Bazzaz 1999a). Wada (1993) found even more dramatic acorn (*Quercus serrata* and *Quercus mongolica*) predation rates under the canopy of *Sasa* species (dwarf bamboos) in a Japanese temperate forest. Wada not only documented higher numbers of rodents under the bamboo understory, but he observed complete removal of all acorns experimentally placed below the bamboo understory. Higher rodent predation rates of seeds of *Acer rubrum* (red maple), *Pinus strobus* L. (white pine), *Rhamnus cathartica* L. (common buckthorn), and *Cornus race-mosa* (gray dogwood) have also been observed under herb cover in New York old fields (Gill and Marks 1991). It appears in all of these cases that understory plants provide valuable cover for rodents from their own predators.

Seed Germination and Emergence

Several dominant understory species such as *Dennstaedtia punctilobula, Aster acuminatus* Michx. (whorled wood aster), and *Rhododendron maximum* decrease the germination of individual tree species (Drew 1988; Clinton and Vose 1996). We investigated the germination of a suite of tree species below the understory stratum to determine whether understory filtering at the germination stage varied among tree species. Fig. 14.1 compares the patterns of spring seedling emergence in plots with and without a well-developed fern understory in mixed hardwood stands in Massachusetts. Response of seedling emergence to understory cover was either neutral or negative and, more important, emergence patterns were variable among species. Spring emergence of *Acer rubrum* and *Fraxinus americana* L. (white ash) was not affected by fern cover, but emergence of *Pinus strobus, Quercus rubra,* and *Betula lenta* L., and *B. alleghaniensis* Britt. (black birch and yellow birch) was reduced under the fern understory to varying degrees. Although absolute values of seedling emergents varied annually and from site to site due to variability of seed rain, the qualitative response of each tree species to fern cover remained the same (George and Bazzaz 1999a).

Not only does germination response to understory cover vary among tree species, but species responses seem to be mediated by different environmental factors. The aggregation of *Betula lenta* and *B. alleghaniensis* germinants in areas of exposed soil,

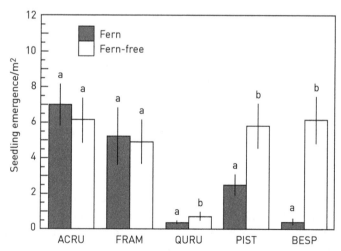

FIGURE 14.1 Density of emergent natural recruitment in fern and fern-free experimental plots. Each bar represents mean seedling emergence per square meter across six sites in central Massachusetts (± 1 SE, *n* = 60). Letters indicate significantly different treatment means within seedling species (Fisher's Protected LSD, *p* <.01). Seedling species: ACRU = *Acer rubrum* (red maple); FRAM = *Fraxinus americana* (white ash); QURU = *Quercus rubra* (northern red oak); PIST = *Pinus strobus* (white pine); BESP = *Betula alleghaniensis* and *B. lenta* (yellow and black birch, species combined). Figure modified from George and Bazzaz (1999a).

which were more common in fern-free areas, led to experiments that determined that the depth of litter and lack of exposed soil were the primary impediments to the germination of *Betula* species under ferns (George and Bazzaz 1999a). Further evidence indicated that low light under ferns limited summer germination of *A. rubrum* but did not affect spring germination of *A. rubrum* or *Fraxinus americana* because spring germination occurred before leaf-out of the fern canopy. The emergence pattern of oak appeared to be a function of differential seed predation as discussed above, rather than of differential germination. Seedling recruitment below *Rhododendron maximum* understories has been reported to be limited primarily by the same means: light attenuation, inhibition by a thick litter layer, and higher seed predation rates under *R. maximum* (Beckage et al. 2000).

Tree Seedling Survival

The understory continues to selectively filter tree seedlings through its influence on seedling survival during establishment and early growth phases (Horsley and Marquis 1983; Phillips and Murdy 1985; George and Bazzaz 1999a,b). Tree seedlings of five species were followed through their first full year of growth, and their survival rates are displayed in fig. 14.2. Understory cover negatively affected the survivorship of all species to varying degrees and precluded the establishment of any *Betula* seedlings below ferns.

Although understory interference with seed germination and emergence is mediated by several factors, the understory primarily influences seedling survival through aboveground interactions, particularly competition for light (Denslow et al. 1991; Pacala et al. 1994, 1996; George and Bazzaz 1999b). Herbivory is another important

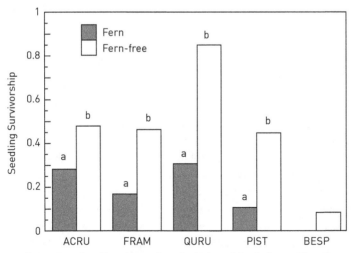

FIGURE 14.2 Proportion of seedling cohorts from fig. 14.1 surviving in fern and fern-free experimental plots for one year. Letters indicate whether survivorship of each species differed between fern manipulations (chi-square test, $p < .05$). No *Betula* seedlings survived for one year under ferns. Seedling species: ACRU = *Acer rubrum* (red maple); FRAM = *Fraxinus americana* (white ash); QURU = *Quercus rubra* (northern red oak); PIST = *Pinus strobus* (white pine); BESP = *Betula alleghaniensis* and *B. lenta* (yellow and black birch, species combined). Figure modified from George and Bazzaz (1999a).

factor that can contribute to seedling mortality, although the identity and specific behavior of a herbivore will determine whether predation rates are higher or lower beneath the understory stratum. High levels of insect herbivory under a palm understory in a Costa Rican rainforest decreased seedling survival beneath the understory (Denslow et al. 1991); however, we found that fern cover protected *Quercus rubra* seedlings from high levels of insect herbivory in fern-free areas in Massachusetts (George and Bazzaz 1999b).

Tree Seedling Community Characteristics

Because the understory stratum can differentially affect predation, germination, and survival rates of tree seedling species beneath its canopy, the pattern of understory plant distribution will strongly influence patterns of tree seedling distribution. Even at the earliest stages in the lifecycle of a tree, the understory has already begun a filtering process that leads to a characteristic distribution of new tree seedling germinants over the forest floor.

Because of the selective influence of the fern filter on seedling emergence in our New England study sites (fig. 14.1), *Betula lenta* and *B. allegheniensis* germinants were highly concentrated in fern-free areas, *Pinus strobus* and *Quercus rubra* germinants were more common in fern-free areas, and *Acer rubrum* germinants were more common in fern-free areas or nearly randomly distributed depending on the predominance of spring versus summer germination. *Fraxinus americana* germinants were distributed randomly over the forest floor with respect to understory cover.

Although survival patterns beneath the understory also varied among tree species (fig. 14.2), species did not necessarily follow the same patterns of response for survival as for emergence. The compounding of emergence patterns (fig. 14.1) and patterns of first-year mortality (fig. 14.2) produced the distribution patterns at the end of one year as displayed in fig. 14.3. *Acer rubrum* seedlings were more common in fern-free areas by a 1.5:1 ratio, as were *Fraxinus americana* seedlings (2.6:1). *Quercus rubra* seedlings were strongly concentrated in fern-free areas (6:1), and *Pinus strobus* seedlings were very concentrated (10:1). *Betula* seedlings, at least in this sampling pool, had been eliminated under fern cover.

Because tree species distributions varied individually with respect to understory cover, the attributes of the tree seedling community in areas of high understory cover varied widely from the seedling community attributes of areas within the same stand with low understory cover. Because of the generally neutral or negative effect of the understory on tree seedlings, total seedling density is reduced beneath the understory stratum. The seedling bank below the understory also exhibits a shift in species composition when compared to areas with little understory cover. Fig. 14.4 compares the species composition of the pool of one-year-old seedlings between areas with and without a prominent fern understory in Massachusetts forests. Under ferns, *Acer rubrum* is the most dominant contributor to the seedling bank, followed by *Fraxinus americana*, and *Betula* species are absent. In fern-free areas, *Acer rubrum*, *Fraxinus americana*, and *Pinus strobus* are codominant, and there is a strong representation of *Betula* species and *Quercus rubra*.

In the Blue Ridge Mountains of North Carolina, the selectivity of the *Rhododendron maximum* understory also causes a shift in the species composition of tree regeneration. Sapling density of *Quercus prinus* L. (chestnut oak) and *Quercus alba* L. (white

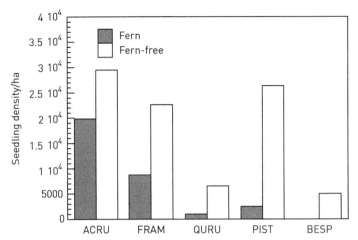

FIGURE 14.3 Density of surviving seedlings (from cohorts in fig. 14.1) in fern and fern-free experimental plots one year after seedling emergence. Data values are a combination of emergence values (fig. 14.1) and survivorship values (fig. 14.2) in fern and fern-free plots. Seedling species: ACRU = *Acer rubrum* (red maple); FRAM = *Fraxinus americana* (white ash); QURU = *Quercus rubra* (northern red oak); PIST = *Pinus strobus* (white pine); BESP = *Betula alleghaniensis* and *B. lenta* (yellow and black birch, species combined).

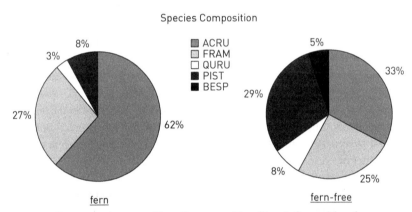

FIGURE 14.4 Percent species composition of one-year-old seedlings in fern and fern-free experimental plots. Total cohort seedling density in fern plots = 32,150 seedlings/ha; total cohort seedling density in fern-free plots = 89,691 seedlings/ha (seedling densities as in fig. 14.3). Seedling species: ACRU = *Acer rubrum* (red maple); FRAM = *Fraxinus americana* (white ash); QURU = *Quercus rubra* (northern red oak); PIST = *Pinus strobus* (white pine); BESP = *Betula alleghaniensis* and *B. lenta* (yellow and black birch, species combined).

oak) was depressed by high *Rhododendron maximum* cover, whereas regeneration of *Acer rubrum* was not affected by *R. maximum* cover. In contrast, greater regeneration of *Tsuga canadensis* (L.) Carr. (eastern hemlock) was associated with abundance of *R. maximum* (Phillips and Murdy 1985). This pattern of selective filtering resulted in a sapling bank beneath *R. maximum* in which *A. rubrum* and *Tsuga canadensis* were codominant, with a low representation of *Quercus* saplings. The sapling bank in areas of low *R. maximum* cover was dominated by *A. rubrum*, followed by *Quercus* species, with a low representation of *T. canadensis*.

In addition to reducing overall seedling density and shifting species composition of seedling communities, the understory filter may reduce the diversity of tree regeneration beneath its canopy (Drew 1988; Beckage et al. 2000). Where the understory of a stand is dominated by a single understory species of high density and aerial coverage such as *Rhododendron maximum*, stand-level diversity is generally reduced (Baker and van Lear 1998; Drew 1988). Diversity of herbaceous and woody regeneration may reach a fourfold difference between areas of scarce and high *R. maximum* cover (Baker and van Lear 1998). When the Shannon-Weiner index of diversity ($H' = -p_i \ln p_i$) is calculated for the Massachusetts tree seedling communities (fig. 14.4), greater diversity is found in fern-free areas ($H' = 1.41$) compared to areas beneath the fern canopy ($H' = 0.96$). Not only is species richness higher in fern-free areas, but tree species are more evenly represented.

Seedling Growth

Growth rates of tree seedlings beneath the understory stratum are generally depressed and have been most strongly correlated with low light availability (Horsley 1993a; George and Bazzaz 1999b). Because tree seedling species vary in their growth response to light availability, the presence of understory cover can differentially influence seedling growth. Differential tree seedling growth in areas with and without dense understory cover will lead to different size structures in their respective seedling communities.

The selective influence of the understory on seedling growth has been well demonstrated in the Allegheny Plateau region of Pennsylvania. Understories of both *Danthonia spicata* (poverty oat grass) and *Dennstaedtia punctilobula* (hayscented fern) reduce seedling height growth of several timber species (Kolb et al. 1989, 1990). After one year of seedling growth, herbaceous interference had reduced the height of *Fraxinus americana* by 65 percent, *Liriodendron tulipifera* L. (yellow poplar) by 60 percent, and *Quercus rubra* by 29 percent but did not affect the height growth of *Pinus strobus*. After two years of growth in herb-free environments, seedlings of *F. americana* were taller (49 cm) than those of *Q. rubra* (40 cm), which were taller than *P. strobus* (10 cm). In contrast, in areas with herbaceous cover, seedlings of *Q. rubra* were taller (22 cm) than those of *F. americana* (11 cm) and *P. strobus* (8 cm) (Kolb et al. 1990).

The influence of the understory on the size structure of seedling communities will influence the outcome of tree–tree competition after release. For example, in the Allegheny community described above, *Quercus rubra* seedlings will have a size advantage upon release in areas with a well-developed understory, and *Fraxinus americana* seedlings will have a size advantage in areas lacking understory cover. Where the understory has a dampening effect on the growth of all seedling species (see Bowersox and McCormick 1987), the understory may tend to equalize competitive status among individuals and among species.

Whether a tree seedling emerges above the understory stratum depends on species growth rates tempered by their survivorship rates. In our studies in Massachusetts, the relative growth rate of *Betula alleghaniensis* was higher than *Quercus rubra* and *Acer rubrum* beneath ferns and in fern-free areas (fig. 14.5). Although *Betula alleghaniensis* possessed the highest growth rate of all species in all treatments, it also had the lowest survivorship rates, particularly beneath ferns (see fig. 14.2). Conversely, the lower growth rates of *Q. rubra* and *A. rubrum* were balanced by higher rates of survivorship.

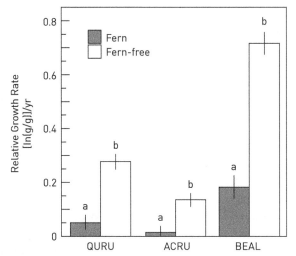

FIGURE 14.5 Relative growth rate (RGR) in terms of biomass, [ln(g/g)]/year of three-year-old seedlings growing in fern and fern-free experimental plots. Values represent the average relative growth rates over the second and third years of growth. Each bar represents the mean of the manipulation (± 1 SE, $n = 60$). Means with different letters are significantly different among manipulations within seedling species (Fisher's Protected LSD, $p < .05$). Manipulations: fern = control plots where ferns were left intact; fern-free = plots where ferns were removed. Seedling species: ACRU = *Acer rubrum* (red maple); QURU = *Quercus rubra* (northern red oak); BEAL = *Betula allegheniensis* (yellow birch). Figure modified from George and Bazzaz (1999b).

In fern-free areas, the high growth rates of *B. allegheniensis* result in its seedlings quickly becoming the tallest of all species of a given cohort. In spite of the relatively high growth rates of *B. allegheniensis* under ferns, its seedlings generally do not emerge above the understory stratum because of low survivorship rates under ferns. They generally do not even survive long enough to overtop other seedling species that have an initial size advantage at emergence. Because of this well-recognized tradeoff between traits that enhance persistence in low light and traits that promote maximum growth response to light (Pacala et al. 1994; Bazzaz 1996), it is often the slow growers that win the race to emerge above the understory canopy.

SPATIAL HETEROGENEITY OF THE UNDERSTORY STRATUM

Thus far, we have discussed only the influence of individual species of understory plants on the microenvironment and on tree seedling performance. The understory stratum, however, is a complex mosaic of many species that differ phenologically, morphologically, and physiologically. The influence of a single understory species can be very concentrated from the size perspective of a tree seedling, but from a stand-level perspective, tree seedling populations may be influenced by a number of different understory species of varying densities.

Typical understory communities in eastern forests can range in structure from nearly monospecific communities with uniformly dense cover to mixed-species communities with more patchy distributions. Many clonal understory plants form nearly monospecific patches that can range in size from a few meters to nearly 100 m in the case of *Rhododendron maximum* thickets (Baker and van Lear 1998). In our six Massachusetts study sites, the understory stratum was dominated by *Dennstaedtia punctilobula* and *Osmunda claytoniana* (interrupted fern), and commonly included *Osmunda cinnamomea* L. (cinnamon fern) and *Thelypteris noveboracensis* (New York fern). Because of their clonal growth form, these ferns formed relatively dense patches ranging in diameter from 2 to 20 m and in height from 30 to 70 cm. The ferns created an intergrading patchwork among which less densely distributed herbs and shrubs were interspersed. The patchwork was also punctuated with "holes" or areas with sparse understory cover. Although local cover could range up to 100 percent, average understory cover for individual stands was more typically around 60 percent.

Different understory species have the potential to alter the microenvironment in variable ways below their canopies (Burton and Bazzaz 1991; George 1996). For example, a species with a characteristically more open morphology or clonal density may permit greater light transmission through its canopy. Evergreen plants such as *Rhododendron maximum* and understory plants that leaf out in early spring will subject seedlings to a longer duration of reduced light levels than summer-green species. Differences in stature among understory species are also important to the activity of the understory filter because plant height will determine the length of time tree seedlings are subject to shading before a seedling is potentially able to overtop the understory canopy (Hill et al. 1994). Understory species drop litter of varying quantity and quality, and woody species may trap and hold more litter near their bases throughout the year when compared to deciduous herbaceous species (George and Bazzaz, pers. obs.). Understory species may also potentially capture or utilize belowground resources differently.

Whereas there is evidence that tree seedlings respond to the specific identity and density of the understory, the presence or absence of understory cover of any species may be more important than understory species identity (Berkowitz et al. 1995; George and Bazzaz 1999a,b). Holes in the understory stratum, places that are favorable for tree seedling growth but have not yet been colonized by understory plants, are therefore an important spatial component of the understory mosaic.

Studies comparing seedling densities among different types of understory cover suggest that understory species can contribute to differential tree seedling performance within and among seedling species (Horsley 1977a,b; Hill et al. 1994; George 1996). In a study of tree seedling density in gaps in the southern Appalachians, greater seedling densities were found in gaps with understory cover of *Kalmia latifolia* (1.6 seedlings/m^2) when compared to gaps with *Rhododendron maximum* cover (0.5 seedlings/m^2) (Clinton et al. 1994). These differences were ascribed to the higher leaf area of *R. maximum* compared to *K. latifolia*. After partial overstory removal in an Allegheny hardwood forest, greater seedling densities of *Prunus serotina* Ehrh. (black cherry) and *Acer saccharum* Marshall (sugar maple) were observed in areas with cover of *Brachyelytrum erectum* (short husk grass) compared to areas with *Dennstaedtia punctilobula* cover (Horsley and Marquis 1983). When grass or ferns were removed in experimental plots, *P. serotina* seedling growth and survival rates were similar in grass-removal and fern-removal plots, which indicates that *P. serotina* seedling performance varied due to the identity of understory plant species. The understory mosaic of patches of grass and ferns imposed a layer of environmental heterogeneity on initial site conditions to which *P. serotina* and other tree seedlings responded differentially.

Understory species may or may not segregate along easily detectable environmental gradients such as light or soil moisture (see Horsley 1993a). When they do, microsites occupied by different understory species may inherently have different potentials for tree seedling performance. In a New York northern hardwood forest, germination, growth, and survival of *Prunus serotina* seedlings differed between areas with *Dennstaedtia punctilobula* cover and areas with an understory of *Aster acuminatus* (Drew 1988). *P. serotina* height growth was lower under ferns compared to under asters but was also lower in fern-removal plots compared to aster-removal plots. Observed differences in seedling performance despite the removal of understory plants suggest that growth differences beneath the two types of understory were more associated with the microsites occupied by ferns and asters rather than with direct effects of the species of understory cover. Heterogeneity in site conditions were actually dampened or buffered in this case by the understory.

Heterogeneity in the local light environment beneath the overstory canopy may also be buffered by changes in local density of understory species. For example, *Dennstaedtia punctilobula* can cover large expanses of the forest floor, particularly in stands in which the overstory has been partially thinned (see Horsley and Marquis 1983; Drew 1988; Kolb et al. 1989). *D. punctilobula* density increases locally with light availability, and increased frond density reduces light transmission beneath the fern canopy (Hill 1996; Hill and Silander 2001). Therefore, *D. punctilobula* has been viewed as an equalizer of the variability in the spatial light environments of forests (Hill 1996).

The filtering influence of the understory can result in the aggregation of seedlings of the same species into certain areas defined by the type or density of understory cover. The grain of this aggregation will mirror the spatial structure of the understory stratum and will determine the future competitive and genetic neighborhood of trees during and after disturbance (Bazzaz 1996). The mosaic nature of the understory can provide different areas or niches in which regeneration of certain species is relatively more successful. In a Massachusetts forest with a structurally diverse understory stratum, we characterized the tallest seedling species of plots of four different understory types (fig. 14.6, George 1996). *Quercus rubra*, which has a tall initial seedling height, was well represented in all understory types. Successful *Acer rubrum* regeneration was proportionally best represented in *Corylus cornuta* plots, and regeneration of *Betula* species was nearly exclusively represented in plots with sparse understory cover. *Carya glabra* (Miller) Sweet and *C. ovata* (Miller) K. Koch (pignut hickory and shagbark hickory) seedlings were the tallest seedlings only in plots with well-developed understory cover, particularly cover of *Dennstaedtia punctilobula*. *Fraxinus americana* regeneration was well represented in areas of *Osmunda claytoniana* and *D. punctilobula* cover.

When seedling species are aggregated in certain patch types, intraspecific competition may predominate within patch types, and spatial aggregation into monospecific neighborhoods may lead to coexistence of species at the community level (Hibbs 1982; Pacala 1986; Silvertown and Law 1987; Pacala et al. 1993). The spatial structure of the understory stratum of this community appears to have contributed to the spatial aggregation of tree seedling species and promoted diversity of advance regeneration at the stand level. If this community lacked areas of open understory, successful *Betula* regeneration would have been drastically reduced. If the understory was entirely open, however, successful *Carya* regeneration would have been eliminated. The spatial segregation of advance regeneration by understory patches may be particularly important

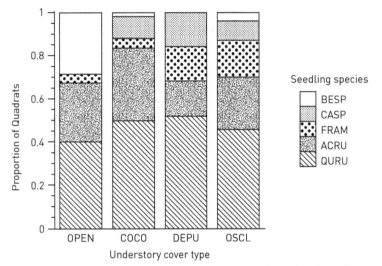

FIGURE 14.6 Proportion of quadrats in four understory cover types in which each seedling species is represented by the tallest seedling in the quadrat ($n = 50$ quadrats for each cover type). Understory cover types: OPEN = quadrats with 50 percent total understory cover; COCO = quadrats dominated by *Corylus cornuta* (beaked hazel); DEPU = quadrats dominated by *Dennstaedtia punctilobula* (hayscented fern); OSCL = quadrats dominated by *Osmunda claytoniana* (interrupted fern). Seedling species: BESP = *Betula alleghaniensis* and *B. lenta* (yellow and black birch, species combined); CASP = *Carya glabra* and *C. ovata* (pignut and shagbark hickory, species combined); FRAM = *Fraxinus americana* (white ash); ACRU = *Acer rubrum* (red maple); QURU = *Quercus rubra* (northern red oak). Figure from George (1996).

for preserving the representation of less common tree species such as *Carya*, *Betula*, and *Fraxinus americana* in the canopy.

TEMPORAL DYNAMICS OF THE UNDERSTORY FILTER

The understory filter can be a consistent as well as powerful force that structures the community of advance regeneration. Many clonal understory plants, including those we have discussed as important components of the understory filter in their respective communities, have extremely long lifespans, which may even exceed the lifespans of canopy trees (Watt 1947b; Knight 1964; McGee and Smith 1967; Oinonen 1967a,b; J. P. Anderson and Egler 1988). Once established, they may persist many years in the understory in closed forest conditions (McGee and Smith 1967; Kurmis and Sucoff 1989; Gilliam and Turrill 1993; Gilliam et al. 1995; Hill and Silander 2001), and they may also persist through conditions of extreme canopy disturbance (Horsley 1988; Halpern 1989; Hughes and Fahey 1991). Clones of *Osmunda claytoniana* in one of our Massachusetts study sites are 150–200 years old and spread only an average of 1.1 cm per year (Knight 1964). This temporal stability, coupled with low mobility, enable these plants to create an imprint on the microenvironment that will be experienced year after year by the same tree seedling individuals.

    In deciduous forests of the eastern United States, some degree of canopy disturbance is necessary for most species of advance regeneration to grow to canopy height (Canham 1985, 1988). To understand tree seedling and sapling response to canopy disturbance, we must understand the response of understory plants and how the activity of the understory filter will change in the new context of altered resource flux. In response to overstory canopy disturbance, established understory plants have often been observed to increase in density (Huenneke 1983; Moore and Vankat 1986; Mladenoff 1990), compensating for canopy opening by reducing resource flux to tree seedlings below the understory stratum. For example, light levels at the forest floor did not increase significantly after experimental canopy gap formation in mixed-oak forest of the southern Appalachians where *Rhododendron maximum* cover was present and undisturbed (Beckage et al. 2000). Small canopy gaps may promote increased understory plant density where plants are already present but do not necessarily provide opportunities for their establishment. Density of *Dennstaedtia punctilobula* increases with light availability due to canopy opening (Hill and Silander 2001); however, we have observed many areas in our study sites with favorable light availability where no ferns are present. Others have also found differences in the understory layer between gaps and intact forest to be primarily expressed as changes in plant abundance rather than as species presence (Ehrenfeld 1980; Mladenoff 1990).

Although many understory plants increase in density in response to canopy disturbance, this is by no means a universal response. Several understory species show little response to single or multiple canopy tree gaps (Collins and Pickett 1987, 1988; Mladenoff 1990) and, less commonly, others may show a density decrease (Veblen 1982; Mladenoff 1990). In a New Jersey oak forest where single and multiple tree gaps had been formed by gypsy moth defoliation, Ehrenfeld (1980) reported an increase in relative density of *Cornus florida* L. (eastern flowering dogwood) but little change in the herbaceous species *Osmunda cinnamomea Onoclea sensibilis* (sensitive fern) and *Maianthemum canadense* (Canada mayflower). The mode of canopy gap formation will also affect the level of disturbance to the understory stratum. Standing tree death due to drought, disease, or herbivory will have much less of a destructive impact on the understory stratum than windthrow or commercial harvesting (see chapter 14, this volume).

More extensive canopy opening used in commercial thinning of the overstory in the Allegheny Plateau region stimulates growth of understory plants such as *Dennstaedtia punctilobula* and grasses (Horsley and Marquis 1983; Drew 1988; Horsley 1988). Concomitant disturbance to the litter layer may promote establishment of new individuals of understory species that require mineral soil for establishment (Groninger and McCormick 1992), and these plants may cover virtually the entire area of the forest floor after canopy thinning. Light beneath ferns in stands with a relatively open overstory can be lower than levels experienced beneath the understory in closed forests (Horsley 1993a). In clearcut areas, however, where high insolation reduces soil moisture, fern cover can improve the moisture environment of seeds and improve germination levels (Kolb et al. 1989).

When forest stands experience large-scale disturbance such as hurricanes or clearcutting, understory herbs and shrubs can persist from underground structures, as well as from new recruitment. In areas of the Harvard Forest that have been subject to simulated hurricane, reestablished fern cover reduced light levels to approximately 6–10 percent of full sun (Carlton and Bazzaz 1998). In this case, these levels were a substantial improvement compared to the light environment tree seedlings experienced in adjacent closed forest stands under fern cover (1 percent full sun) or even outside of fern cover (3 percent full sun).

In areas of large-scale disturbance, forest understory plants may persist but may decrease in density due to competition with other invading species. After partial thinning of the canopy, *Dennstaedtia punctilobula* has been reported to increase in cover value up to 90 percent, but after complete harvest of canopy trees, *D. punctilobula* cover has been observed to decrease to 60 percent due to competition with *Rubus alleghheniensis* Porter and *R. occidentalis* L. (Horsley and Marquis 1983). Although the density of *D. punctilobula* varies over time, it is a good example of a forest understory herb that can persist throughout the whole disturbance cycle. Because of its persistence, an understory of *D. punctilobula* will likely continue to filter tree seedlings throughout the post-disturbance regeneration phase and into the next generation of forest. The extent of change in the filter's activity before, during, and after a disturbance event will depend on the extent to which understory plant growth preempts, neutralizes, and/or modifies available resources.

SUMMARY

Because the understory stratum can differentially influence seed predation, germination, and seedling growth and survival, the understory acts as an ecological filter that can structure the nature and composition of the tree seedling bank. The tree seedling bank represents the starting capital for future forest regeneration, so forces that structure this community will influence the rate and trajectory of regeneration and ultimately help determine the composition of future forests.

Understory communities that we expect to be the most important filters of tree seedling regeneration are those in which the understory plants commonly reach high densities, at least locally, and cover large areas, as well as those that are temporally persistent. Although the three study systems in eastern forests on which we have focused, New England forests characterized by mixed-fern understories (George and Bazzaz 1999a,b); southern Appalachian forests characterized by evergreen shrub understories (Beckage et al. 2000); and Allegheny forests characterized by a dense understory of *Dennstaedtia punctilobula* (Horsley 1993a), differ in overstory and understory structure and composition, they all demonstrate the substantial impact of the understory stratum on the light environment near the forest floor that tree seeds and seedlings experience. Important effects of the understory stratum on quantity and quality of litter have been repeatedly demonstrated, in contrast to the absence of significant understory effects on soil nutrient resources. Understories of *Rhododendron maximum* may influence tree seedling performance by decreasing soil moisture, but soil moisture has not been demonstrated to be an important mechanism of understory filtering in other systems, except in cases where an intact understory stratum conserves soil moisture in areas of high insolation after canopy opening.

The mechanisms by which the understory filters tree seedlings vary from tree species to species and even within a tree species at different life stages. We have found little evidence that the understory interferes directly with seed dispersal of trees in eastern forests; however, the presence of understory cover may play a more important role in influencing the secondary dispersal or predation of seeds by animals. The understory canopy often provides cover for seed predators, which leads to higher seed predation rates below the understory, particularly of large-seeded species such as *Quercus* spp. Primarily through the understory's influence on litter structure and light attenuation, it is able to differentially influence tree seedling germination and emergence. Low light levels beneath the understory and the behavior of herbivores affect seedling survival and growth, and these factors further enable the understory to filter tree seedlings. The seedling bank below the understory may be lacking in seedlings of relatively shade-intolerant species, but because the activity of the understory filter involves so many additional factors, including seed predation, seedling herbivory, and alteration of the litter layer, it is not always possible to predict the composition of the seedling bank beneath a well-developed understory based on shade tolerance alone.

The generally neutral or negative activity of the understory filter results in decreased tree seedling density below the understory stratum. Depending on post-disturbance conditions, reduced density of advance regeneration may increase the time necessary for forest regeneration, or in extreme cases, it may prevent forest regeneration. Selective filtering of tree regeneration by the understory during dispersal, germination, and early growth phases most commonly shapes the species composition and diversity of the tree seedling bank below the understory canopy by eliminating or decreasing representation of certain species. The species composition, as well as the density of the seedling bank, will influence the trajectory of regeneration directly by determining which species are available for post-disturbance release and indirectly by determining the competitive environment for species that seed in after disturbance.

The differential influence of the understory filter on tree seedling growth leads to a typical size structure among seedling species that will influence the outcome of future tree–tree competition. The compounded influence of the understory filter on tree seedlings over all of the life stages discussed leads to a characteristic distribution of tree seedlings over the forest floor with different species commonly aggregated to various degrees in patches defined by understory type or density. The degree of spatial structuring of the tree seedling community will mirror the spatial structure of the understory community, and the degree of seedling aggregation will define future competitive and genetic neighborhoods and may have important implications for future forest diversity.

The effects of the understory on future forest composition and structure must be interpreted in the context of both pre- and post-disturbance conditions. The understory, if intact, will continue to filter tree regeneration after a disturbance event, although the activity of the filter may be altered in the context of new resource levels. Understory plant populations may grow in size and density in response to disturbance and may neutralize canopy recruitment opportunities for trees by preempting available light resources. Where a well-developed understory stratum interferes strongly with tree regeneration, a relatively large-scale canopy disturbance may be required for significant release of advance regeneration. The presence of a well-developed understory stratum may require that certain types of disturbance that directly damage the understory, such as windthrow or fire, are necessary to regenerate the forest canopy. Because interactions between the understory filter and tree seeds and seedlings determine the density, species composition, diversity, and size structure of the pool of advance regeneration within a stand, exploring these pre-disturbance processes will expand our understanding of post-disturbance tree regeneration.

15 Forest Invasions
Perceptions, Impacts, and Management Questions

James O. Luken

The inception of modern plant invasion ecology in North America can be traced to the late 1980s when research began focusing on species typically associated with agricultural enterprise (Bazzaz 1986). As such, much of the early work in this discipline was in frequently disturbed, high light environments, and the species of interest were nonindigenous, typically of Eurasian origin (i.e., weeds). Quickly, however, invasion ecologists broadened their scope, and the study of pastures, road verges, and fields gave way to the study of forests. This shift revealed that the less disturbed, low light environment of forests is also susceptible to additions of nonindigenous species of Eurasian origin, although the number of successful invaders is small (Luken 2003).

Forest invasions by nonindigenous species are noteworthy because they offer unique opportunities to understand how plants arrive in new habitats, establish, and eventually persist vis-à-vis the filter of the tree layer and disturbances affecting the tree layer. In this sense, invasion ecology applied to forests, seeking explanations for distribution and abundance of species, is simply an extension of traditional ecology. However, invasion ecology, not by plan but by origin, retains the strong influence of agriculture, as well as certain cultural attitudes toward nonindigenous species (Luken and Seastedt 2004). Although forests are fundamentally different from agricultural fields in many ways, it is interesting to observe that the basic tenet of invasion ecology (i.e., nonindigenous species are anomalous system components) is still intact. As such, much of the forest invasion research assumes that management will follow, provides management suggestions, or more directly, focuses on management approaches.

Most recently, the basic tenet of invasion ecology has been questioned from various directions (Simberloff 2010). This questioning is generally relevant in the conservation arena and is specifically relevant when we attempt to determine the best paths for pre-serving, restoring, and sustaining forest communities. For example, Davis et al. (2011) diminished the utility of basing management decisions solely on whether or not a species is indigenous or nonindigenous. They argued that management should be based on measured impacts of species rather than on origins (Davis et al. 2011). Larson (2010) placed the basic tenet of invasion ecology in a broader philosophical context and argued that nonindigenous species need to be reevaluated in terms of how we (i.e., North American ecologists) view the interaction between humans and nature. And finally, Coates (2006) described an infatuation with species origin as the inevitable outcome of the unique cultural history of North America.

The purpose of this chapter is to evaluate forest invasion when certain criticisms of invasion ecology are given and accepted. Although this may seem daunting, the fact remains that invasion research tells us much about population, community, and ecosystem ecology of forests even when focused solely on nonindigenous species. Furthermore, an examination of the assumptions and values of invasion ecology tells us what work needs to be done so that human ecology can be more deeply included in the models and narratives that emerge from ecological research (Simberloff 2010).

THE TERMS OF INVASION ECOLOGY

Discussions of invasions have been obfuscated by the use of many poorly defined terms (Luken 1994). Most of these terms refer either to the site of evolutionary origin or original range (e.g., indigenous versus nonindigenous), the ability to establish in a disturbance or to enter intact vegetation (e.g., colonizer versus invader) (Bazzaz 1986; Pysek 1995; Schwartz 1997), or the human perception of problems associated with a species (e.g., weed) (Randall 1997; Larson 2005). Recognizing the need for standardization, Davis and Thompson (2000) proposed two types of events that can be considered as colonizations: species entering new regions and species occupying discrete disturbances. They developed a dichotomous classification scheme for plant species based on dispersal distance, uniqueness to the region, and impact. Their scheme yielded eight types of organisms, all of which could be component species of forests (table 15.1). The purpose of this exercise was to reinforce the point that both nonindigenous species and indigenous species function as colonizers and that these colonizations can be understood without invoking special status for nonindigenous species, an idea reiterated by Davis et al. (2011).

The scheme presented in table 15.1 raises provocative issues. Uniqueness to a region has spatial and temporal components. Thus, nonindigenous species that are now locally common could be categorized with other common, indigenous species. Traditionally, the status of a plant species is determined by referring to published floras where information on origin (e.g., introduced from Eurasia) is provided. This status is developed without consideration of whether or not the species is common. From the perspective of understanding the invasion processes, it is cogent to first know if a species is locally established, as this will determine propagule pressure and potential for colonizing disturbances in forest stands. At the spatial scale of forests that now occur throughout the eastern U.S., nonindigenous species may be novel or common; the same can be said for indigenous species. In keeping with the suggestion of Davis and Thompson (2000), the terms *invasion* or *invader* should be used in situations

Table 15.1 A classification of colonizers based on dispersal distance, uniqueness to the region, and environmental impact as defined by Davis and Thompson (2000).

Type	Dispersal distance	Uniqueness to region	Environmental impact	Example
1	Short	Common	Small	Indigenous annual herb present in the forest understory colonizes a gap for one season.
2	Short	Common	Great	Indigenous perennial herb present in the forest colonizes a gap and dominates the gap for many years.
3	Short	Novel	Small	Nonindigenous annual herb present as a founder population at the forest edge colonizes the gap and occupies the gap for one season.
4	Short	Novel	Great	Nonindigenous perennial herb present as a founder population at the forest edge colonizes a gap and dominates the gap for many years.
5	Long	Common	Small	Indigenous annual herb growing in a local field is dispersed into a forest gap and occupies the gap for one year.
6	Long	Common	Great	Indigenous perennial herb present in a local field is dispersed into a forest gap and dominates the gap for many years.
7	Long	Novel	Small	Nonindigenous annual herb is dispersed into a forest by hiker's boots. It establishes a small population and persists for one season.
8	Long	Novel	Great	Nonindigenous perennial herb is dispersed into a forest by hiker's boots. It establishes in a forest gap and dominates the gap for many years.

where species have large measured impacts. Species new to a forest patch but with high impacts would be referred to as novel *invasive* colonizers. Species new to a forest patch but with minimal impacts would be referred to as novel *noninvasive* colonizers. The terms *colonizer* or *colonization* should be used generally to refer to situations where plants occupy new areas.

Even when explicitly defined by ecological parameters, terms such as invader and colonizer can be criticized as too militaristic, thus codifying a negative or adversarial relationship between plants and people (Larson 2005). Alternatively, Larson (2005) suggested that we develop new terms that better reflect the synergistic relationship between people and nonindigenous species. This suggestion leaves open the idea that such species can be embraced, accepted, or rejected, but are still recognized as fundamental components of human-influenced landscapes (Larson 2007).

COLONIZERS AND INVADERS OF FORESTS

Invasion ecology is for the most part the study of invaders and potential invaders. As such, it is not surprising that a general model of invader impact on forest development has not emerged from the invasion arena (Simberloff 2010). Rather, assessments of impacts of plant invaders on forests have focused on coverage or biomass of nonindigenous species, simply the presence of nonindigenous species, experiments where a nonindigenous species is removed and responses of indigenous species are measured, or management to eradicate invaders (Luken 2003). See, however, Hartman and McCarthy (2007). In contrast, when the issue of plant impact in the forest understory is removed from the philosophical influence of invasion ecology and is placed in the context of forest management, a wider narrative emerges, one that involves establishment of dominance by resident indigenous species, the formation of dense understory layers, and subsequent cascading effects on various aspects of forest development (Royo and Carson 2006). This dichotomy of thought and action between invasion ecology as applied to forests and forest management as applied to forests is a salient starting point for finding common strengths that will allow new directions for both better forest conservation and improved forest management in the future.

Regardless of whether one is tasked with studying, conserving, restoring, or managing forests, the impact of common concern is the emergence of what Royo and Carson (2006) have termed a *recalcitrant understory layer* (RUL). A RUL is characterized by one or more of the following: high vegetation coverage and low diversity, the ability to alter succession due to interaction with tree seedlings, and persistence. A RUL forms when key environmental changes allow resident indigenous species to gain dominance and then hold it. Royo and Carson (2006) conclude that formation of a RUL is identical to the concept of forest invasion in numerous ways, except that invasions involve novel species (i.e., new additions to the system), while formation of a RUL involves resident common species. Clearly, the distinction between indigenous and nonindigenous species has created a conceptual boundary that is not necessary, at least when we are assessing the mechanism of impact in a forest system.

The *presence* of nonindigenous species may tell us more about the human connection to forests than it tells us about impacts. Stapanian et al. (1998) described results of the Forest Health Monitoring Program (FHMP) where cover of ground layer and understory species was assessed on a national scale. They found that different regions of the eastern U.S. supported nonindigenous species of different origins. Southeast forests had mostly nonindigenous species from eastern Asia, while northeast forests had nonindigenous species mostly from Eurasia, a pattern that may reflect selection in the introduction process. Forests in nature preserves may have relatively fewer nonindigenous species (Lonsdale 1999), a characteristic that is likely linked to less human impact, while human disturbances within nature preserves (e.g., roads) may facilitate forest entry of nonindigenous species (Huebner and Tobin 2006).

Luken (2003) examined 10 floristic surveys from 16 distinct forest communities in eastern North America (fig. 15.1). The communities ranged from savannas ($n = 3$) to mixed mesophytic forests ($n = 4$) to floodplain/bottomland forests ($n = 6$) to pine forests ($n = 3$). There were 144 nonindigenous forest species listed of which 44 percent were perennial herbs, 23 percent were annual herbs, 14 percent were shrubs, and the remaining 19 percent were evenly distributed among biennial herbs, graminoids, and vines. The set of floristic studies suggests that pine forests in the southeast generally support fewer nonindigenous species than adjacent hardwood communities (Easley and Judd 1990; Herring and Judd 1995; Crouch and Golden 1997). See, however, a different conclusion for New York forests (Howard et. al 2004). The highest number of nonindigenous species (56) recorded for a floodplain forest was in Rock Creek Park in Washington, D.C. (Fleming and Kanal 1995), while floodplain forests in relatively isolated preserves of the southeast had few nonindigenous species (Carpenter and Chester 1987; Herring and Judd 1995; Basinger et al. 1997). Relatively open savanna-like forests may also be more suitable to a larger pool of nonindigenous species due to higher light availability (Tester 1996; Laatsch and Anderson 2000). Several recent papers have suggested that hot spots of biodiversity are also more susceptible to additions of nonindigenous species (Wiser et al. 1998; Levine and D'Antonio 1999; Stohlgren et al. 1999), and this relationship appears to hold for forests of the eastern U.S. (Howard

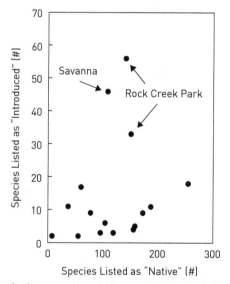

FIGURE 15.1 Numbers of indigenous and nonindigenous plant species in 16 eastern U.S. forest sites. Data were taken from the following floristic inventories: Basinger et al. 1997; Carpenter and Chester 1987; Crouch and Golden 1997; Easley and Judd 1990; Fleming and Kanal 1995; Herring and Judd 1995; Joyner and Chester 1994; Kearsley 1999; Reznicek and Catling 1989; Swanson and Vankat 2000. Rock Creek Park sites are urban mesic and floodplain forests.

et al. 2004; Huebner and Tobin 2006), suggesting once again that indigenous and non-indigenous species are not different.

Floristic surveys typically do not include information on the importance of individual species, except for an occasional qualitative assessment of frequency. Indeed, many nonindigenous species recorded in floristic surveys exist as single populations and would be considered novel or noninvasive colonizers. However, theories from invasion ecology that provide possible explanations why species moved outside the native range may express advantages in new habitats (Hierro et al. 2005), and Royo and Carson (2006) suggest that as forests are changed due to human impacts, then any species in the understory may emerge to form a RUL. As such, it is informative to examine how frequently the noninvasive colonizers become invaders, and more important, to determine what types of human impacts might stimulate such invasions.

I reviewed published literature on forests in an effort to extract those nonindigenous species that are documented as true invaders. I assumed that species with large impacts in the forest community were those capable of forming a RUL. Most commonly, published studies describe the ground layer and understory communities in terms of coverage, biomass, production, or importance, and thus it is necessary to make an inferential assessment of impact (e.g., a species with relatively high coverage must usurp a relatively large share of the resource base). Table 15.2 lists some invaders of forests as inferred from relatively high coverage or importance.

The list of species documented as invaders of forests (table 15.2) is brief when compared to the list of 144 nonindigenous species recorded in the floristic studies. The fact that few nonindigenous species have large impacts has been noted elsewhere, with the suggestion that in most situations, potential invaders and resident species are not

Table 15.2 Invasive plant species of eastern forests.

Species	Community	Criteria for invasive status	Associated invasive species	References
Alliaria petiolata	Lowland and mesic forests	Coverage, importance	Eupatorium rugosum Parthenocissus quinquefolia Rhus radicans Impatiens spp. Stellaria media Galium aparine	Nuzzo et al. 1996, McCarthy 1997, Luken and Shea 2000
Glechoma hederacea	Floodplain forest	Coverage	Alliaria petiolata	Pyle 1995
Lonicera japonica	Mesic forests	Coverage	Ligustrum sinense	Stapanian et al. 1998
Lonicera maackii	Mesic forests	Importance	Alliaria petiolata Impatiens biflora	Luken et al. 1997, Vankat and Snyder 1991
Lonicera tatarica	Mesic forests	Coverage	Impatiens biflora Hydrophyllum virginianum	Woods 1993
Stellaria media	Mesic forests	Coverage	Carex jamesii	Gibson et al. 2000

fundamentally different (Levine and D'Antonio 1999) and that the ability to form a RUL is the result of a unique match between species and environment. Similarly, Royo and Carson (2006) reviewed the literature and found only nine indigenous species forming RULs in eastern forests. Gordon (1998), however, examined nonindigenous plant species in a variety of Florida habitats and concluded that many of these species do have large impacts.

In forests, the ability to function as an invader may be shared by more than one species, and even in invaded communities, high importance is not solely within the domain of nonindigenous species. For example, as importance of *Alliaria petiolata* declined in Kentucky forests, the importance of *Stellaria media* increased (Luken and Shea 2000). Prescribed fire to manage *A. petiolata* was associated with more than a twofold increase in the importance of *Eupatorium rugosum* Houtt. (Nuzzo et al. 1996). When McCarthy (1997) removed *A. petiolata* from experimental plots, importance of *Impatiens* spp. increased. Interestingly, the northeast forests not heavily invaded by *A. petiolata* had extremely high importance of *Impatiens biflora* Walt. (Woods 1993). The extensive database on forests invaded by *A. petiolata* suggests the presence of an invasion window (sensu Johnstone 1986; Davis et al. 2000) that can temporarily open for several species, not just nonindigenous species.

Two of the invaders listed in table 15.2 have been well studied in terms of characteristics that contribute to success in the ground layer and understory. *Alliaria petiolata* rises to invader status as a result of an autogamous breeding system, high seed production, rapid growth, phenotypic plasticity, and production of allelopathic chemicals (Meekins and McCarthy 1999; Prati and Bossdorf 2004; Burke 2008; Rodgers et al. 2008). Recent research suggests that *A. petiolata* may be losing invasion potential as natural selection reduces phytotoxin production (Lankau et al. 2009). *Lonicera maackii* is an invader due to rapid growth, extended leaf display, allelopathic chemicals, and phenotypic plasticity (Luken and Mattimiro 1991; Hutchinson and Vankat 1997; Luken et al. 1997b; Gorchov and Trisel 2003; Dorning and Cipollini 2006). These two forest invaders share many traits with colonizers of successional communities (Bazzaz 1986). However, early successional communities and forests differ dramatically in light availability, and colonizers of forests must overcome light limitation to reach invader status. Among successful nonindigenous invaders, high plasticity and acclimation ability confer an advantage in low light environments (Luken et al. 1997b; Byers and Quinn 1998; Meekins and McCarthy 2000). Finally, Schierenbeck et al. (1994) compared growth of *Lonicera sempervirens* L. and *Lonicera japonica* in response to herbivory. They concluded that the nonindigenous *L. japonica* was less susceptible to herbivore damage and was better able to compensate for lost tissue than the indigenous *L. sempervirens* (Schierenbeck et al. 1994). The suite of traits allowing indigenous species to form RULs in eastern forests is identical to that noted for nonindigenous invaders: rapid growth, phenotypic plasticity, and production of allelopathic chemicals (Royo and Carson 2006).

Finally, I noted some correspondence between the nonindigenous species documented as invasive in table 15.2 and the nonindigenous species documented in three or more floristic surveys. The suggestion is that those species most frequently encountered throughout the eastern U.S. will also be the ones most likely to emerge as invaders. In a search for characteristics that predict invasiveness of woody species, Reichard (1997) suggested that those with large ranges in the native region were more likely to invade in a new region. Also, species shown to be invasive in one place are likely to be invasive in other places (Reichard and Hamilton 1997). Invaders listed in table (15.2) are also commonly found growing outside of forests and in some instances actually participate in early successional communities (Luken 1988). Thus, the ability to invade forests may not be linked to a single identifiable trait, but rather the ability to express different traits across a wide range of environments (i.e., phenotypic plasticity).

INVASION AND THE FOREST ENVIRONMENT

Through systematic sampling of North American forests, Stapanian et al. (1998) measured mean proportional coverage of nonindigenous species. The results, 1.5 percent in northeastern forests and 13 percent in southeastern forests, are remarkable due to the relatively low total coverage of nonindigenous species in eastern forests and the observed regional difference. Relatively low total coverage of nonindigenous species in forest understories suggests that the forest environment is a strong filter of potential invaders. Filtering by the forest environment could be a limitation to growth, a limitation to dispersal, or some combination of the two factors. Light limitation is apparently due to the fact that most nonindigenous species in the U.S. were originally introduced into high light environments while movement into low light environments was secondary (see, e.g., Luken and Thieret 1996). Forest edges support a rich assemblage of nonindigenous species, but most of these species do not invade forest interiors (Brothers and Spingarn 1992; Goldblum and Beatty 1999) presumably because of light limitation. In contrast to high light environments where soil disturbance is an important factor for invasion success, invasions of the forest understory appear to be linked to light availability and propagule availability. For example, canopy gaps may (Hutchinson and Vankat 1997; Luken et al. 1997a; Goldblum and Beatty 1999) or may not (Moore and Vankat 1986; Hughes and Fahey 1991) lead to species additions, depending on whether or not potential colonizers are near the gaps. Martin et al. (2009) concluded that the potential for forest invasion is high due to the introduction of many shade-tolerant plant species, but the evidence of impact for many of these species was weak.

Considering that light limitation and availability of potential invaders are important factors in determining which forests will be invaded, it has been argued that riparian forests are more susceptible because of flood-induced canopy gaps, soil disturbance, and relatively greater availability of potential invaders (DeFerrari and Naiman 1994; Pysek and Prach 1993). However, results from eastern riparian forests are not conclusive (Pyle 1995; Williams et al. 1999) and at best, we can conclude that disturbance increases the pool of potential invaders (Zampella and Laidig 1997). Royo and Carson (2006) concluded that canopy disturbance caused by logging, fire, and herbivory is the primary factor leading to formation of RULs.

POTENTIAL INTERACTIONS BETWEEN INVADERS AND ASSOCIATED SPECIES

Woods (1997) provided an excellent review of community-level effects associated with plant invasions and showed that effects of plant invaders range from dramatic to insignificant. He included few examples from eastern U.S. forests, suggesting that few such studies exist. Commonly, invader impacts are inferred by examining the relationship between invader density and species richness of the associated community (Woods 1993; Hutchinson and Vankat 1997) or by comparing species richness between narrowly circumscribed invaded and non-invaded sites (Gordon 1998; Lockhart et al. 1999). Conclusions from these types of studies are invariably confounded by a lack of information on site characteristics at the time when the invasion was initiated, and it is not possible to separate the effects of invaders from the potential effects of disturbances that likely initiated the invasions (Woods 1997).

Two studies on forests in the eastern U.S., one in Florida and one in Ohio, demonstrate the types of research that are necessary to determine impacts of invaders (Gould and Gorchov 2000; Horvitz et al. 1998). Gould and Gorchov (2000) addressed the effects of *Lonicera maackii* on the demography of three species of annual plants growing in Ohio forests. At two sites of differing invader densities (historically disturbed and relatively undisturbed), they established three treatments: *Lonicera* removal, *Lonicera* present, and *Lonicera* absent. They transplanted seedlings of the target species to the study plots and monitored plants for one year. The results indicated a significant increase in fitness (combination of survival and fecundity) for all transplanted species in the removal treatment. Plant responses were more dramatic in the heavily invaded site. Presumably greater degrees of invasion were associated with greater environmental changes associated with the treatments. The heavily invaded site also had less tree basal area, so presumably when *Lonicera* was removed, light was more available than at the less invaded site. Gould and Gorchov (2000) suggested that the direct effect of *Lonicera* was light limitation, although they pointed out that the results could differ in another year with different environmental conditions.

Horvitz et al. (1998) assessed a disturbance by Hurricane Andrew to determine effects of colonizers in forest preserves of Metro-Dade County, Florida. They studied three sites with differing amounts of hurricane damage over a period of two years following the hurricane. Treatments included control areas allowed to recover in the absence of management and managed areas where nonindigenous vines were removed. The results clearly demonstrated that nonindigenous vines were competitively superior to many indigenous species. Rapid response of the nonindigenous vines was facilitated by the fact that the forests were invaded prior to the disturbance and invaders simply responded by various regeneration mechanisms. Horvitz et al. (1998) concluded that nonindigenous species in these urban forests maintained the functional roles that they expressed in the native habitats. These functional roles were presumably matched to the disturbance regimen of the urban forest environment and were particularly matched to the occasional catastrophic disturbance associated with a hurricane.

The two previously described studies (Horvitz et al. 1998; Gould and Gorchov 2000) provide glimpses of the unique approaches and opportunities required to assess interactions between invaders and associated species. Specifically, one needs to be able to manipulate invader effects, and one needs to understand the interacting impacts of disturbance. However, these approaches are primarily of value in understanding the interactions in retrospect and do not offer much for predicting community development beyond the dominance of the target invaders; both studies involved communities that had been invaded by nonindigenous species many years in the past, and it is unknown to what degree the invaders had already modified the invaded system. Studies predicting long-term effects on forests must inevitably focus on interactions of the understory and canopy (Gorchov and Trisel 2003; Royo and Carson 2006; Hartman and McCarthy 2007).

INVASION AND FOREST DEVELOPMENT

Long-term studies of forest succession in the eastern U.S. demonstrate that nonindigenous species are sorted along resource gradients that emerge with the developing tree layer. Typically, the number of nonindigenous species declines with site age, but a few key invaders may persist in the forest environment. For example, Vankat and Snyder (1991) studied a chronosequence of sites in Ohio that included a two-year-old field, a 10-year-old field, a 50-year-old field, a 90-year-old forest, and an old-growth forest. Analysis of the ground layer flora indicated 30–35 nonindigenous species in the old fields and 3–8 nonindigenous species in the forests (fig. 15.2). During succession, annual and biennial species declined as a percentage of the flora, while woody species increased as a percentage of the flora. Nonindigenous understory species included *Alliaria petiolata, Berberis thunbergii, Duchesnea indica* (Andr.) Focke, *Ligustrum vulgare* L., *Lonicera japonica, Lonicera maackii, Ornithogalum umbellatum* L., and *Rosa multiflora*. None of these species were common in the old-growth forest, but *L. maackii* shared dominance of the 90-year-old forest ground layer with the indigenous forest herb *Impatiens biflora*. Maximum species richness was found in the 50-year-old field, the site that also supported the greatest number of nonindigenous species. Gibson et al (2000) monitored changes in the understory of an abandoned recreation area in a mesic Illinois forest. Their data also indicated a decline in importance of nonindigenous species through time, but *Stellaria media* persisted as an important invader and shared dominance of the forest understory with the indigenous sedge *Carex jamesii* Schwein. A survey of Ontario woodlands suggested that more mature woodlands supported fewer nonindigenous species, but the few nonindigenous species persisting in

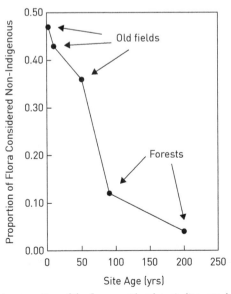

FIGURE 15.2 Changes in proportion of the flora considered nonindigenous during forest succession in Ohio. Adapted from Vankat and Snyder (1991).

mature forest were more invasive (Francis et al. 2000). Occasionally, a nonindigenous species in eastern forests may express such strong dominance that forest development is diverted. Fike and Niering (1999) showed that invasion by the woody vine *Celastrus orbiculatus* had diverted the typical path of old field to forest succession in Connecticut.

Royo and Carson (2006) presented a conceptual model explaining how formation of a RUL can affect successional development of forests. They proposed that a RUL interferes with tree regeneration through competition, allelopathy, litter accumulation, seed destruction, and mechanical damage, thus altering gap phase processes of forests.

CAN/SHOULD WE MANAGE NONINDIGENOUS FOREST SPECIES?

The presence of nonindigenous species in forest preserves poses dilemmas for resource managers and stewards of nature. Invasion by nonindigenous species is inevitable, and this may even be facilitated by the mere visitation of a preserve as visitors and their vehicles disperse seeds (Lonsdale 1999). Colonization of forests by nonindigenous species may be concurrent with local extirpations of other species (Robinson et al. 1994; Rooney and Dress 1997). Thus, the potential flora of a preserve is dynamic and will not likely conform to any conservation plans that focus on maintaining a relatively stable plant community (Pickett et al. 1992).

Another dilemma is the paucity of information on impacts of nonindigenous species in forest understories. In response, resource managers have crafted lists of problem species based on human perceptions of impacts, group consensus, and other means. For example, the Tennessee Chapter of the Exotic Pest Plant Council has placed species in categories ranging from severe threat to lesser threat. Hiebert (1997) discussed the shortcomings of such an approach when developing resource management policies as indigenous species are seldom examined in terms of their abilities to function as invaders. Species placed in "severe threat" or similar categories will likely be targeted for some type of control. However, in forests as in other types of plant communities, any effort to remove established plants is itself a type of disturbance that may create opportunities for new colonizations to occur (Hobbs and Huenneke 1992; Luken 1997; Provencher et al. 2000). Thus, resource managers may be placed in situations where they are managing species with unknown impacts and where the outcomes of the management process are highly unpredictable.

There are few examples of successful management of nonindigenous species in forests (Mack et al. 2000; Davis et al. 2011). Generally, management experiments elucidate the regeneration mechanisms that invaders possess (Horvitz et al. 1998); they show that responses to management are species-specific (Laatsch and Anderson 2000) or that restoration of indigenous species is necessary following removal of an invader (Vidra et al. 2007). Luken et al. (1997a) created gaps in dense thickets of *Lonicera maackii* to determine whether this might contribute to restoration of the ground layer in an urban Kentucky forest. Removal of the dense shrub canopy increased light availability, and species richness of the ground layer increased, but the responding species were generally not the targets, and some plots were quickly invaded and dominated by *Alliaria petiolata* and seedlings of *L. maackii*. Attempts to control *Alliaria petiolata* have been well documented. Burning either increases *A. petiolata* or has no effect (Nuzzo et al. 1996; Schwartz and Heim 1996; Luken and Shea 2000). Anderson et al.

(1996) reviewed the literature on *A. petiolata* and concluded that "it may be unrealistic to expect to eliminate the plant from many habitats it has already invaded." Perhaps the best approach for management of nonindigenous species is the elimination of founder populations (Hobbs and Humphries 1995). This is realistic in small forest preserves, but likely not possible over large areas.

Through time, forests in eastern North America have experienced both additions and losses of species mostly due to human impacts (Robinson et al. 1994; Reader and Bricker 1992; Rooney and Dress 1997); continued human impacts will likely allow a special subset of both indigenous and nonindigenous species to increase in importance and eventually form RULs. As such, the decision to manage should be predicated on the measurement of impacts and statements of clear management goals. With regard to the idea that the status of a plant species (i.e., indigenous versus nonindigenous) is by itself a reason for management, Larson (2007, 2010) provides the suggestion that nonindigenous species should be recast in terms of positive interactions between people and plants. His suggestions, if accepted by the research enterprise and the management arena, would entail changes in how we interpret forests, particularly in urban settings, and might also lead to better understanding of how humans interact with the systems where they live.

SUMMARY

Whereas it is clear that the structure and composition of the ground layer and understory are changing in many forests throughout the eastern U.S. as a result of additions *and* losses of species, the causes are not well understood. Human impacts are both overt and subtle. Specifically, humans add to the pool of potential forest invaders; and human-generated disturbance of forests apparently increases light availability and thus forest invasibility. Although the pool of nonindigenous species now occurring in forests is large, the number of species actually documented as invaders is relatively small. The proven invaders show a wide range of invasion success across the eastern U.S. that is apparently linked to limiting environmental factors and canopy disturbances, but further work is needed to assess invasion along environmental gradients that are associated with human impact.

Low light availability is a key limitation to forest invasion. Many nonindigenous species can establish in forest edges but cannot invade forest interiors. Those species that do invade forest interiors show a high degree of phenotypic plasticity, can respond quickly to changes in light availability, and can produce seed under a wide range of light conditions. Most successful forest invaders are generalists that also grow well outside the forest environment. Although previous research suggests that riparian forests are more susceptible to invasion as a result of the disturbance regimen, this has not been fully tested with forests of the eastern U.S. Forests located in urban areas will have a larger pool of potential invaders.

Impacts of invaders on community- and ecosystem-level processes in eastern U.S. forests are not well understood. Removal experiments, however, indicate that once a site is invaded, resilience of invaders may be high due to various mechanisms for population regeneration. Removal experiments also suggest the existence of an invasion window that can open not just for nonindigenous species, but for a larger subset of potential colonizers that includes indigenous species. This may allow the formation of a RUL that can affect future forest development. It is now clear that most nonindigenous species are not fundamentally different from indigenous species, and thus a complete understanding of changes in the ground layer and understory will come from research where arrival, establishment, and persistence are assessed relative to changing environmental factors.

Although forest invaders are often managed, few studies can demonstrate the utility of this activity. Instead, some have suggested that invasion should be viewed as the positive end result of humans forming synergistic relationships with some plant species.

16 Effects of Deer on Forest Herb Layers

Donald M. Waller

Most people delight at the sight of deer as pretty, often delicate ungulates. They are a highly popular wildlife and game species and the only large mammal we are likely to see in most North America forests. It thus seems natural to many to feed deer to get better views of them, concentrate them near hunting blinds, or support hungry animals through the winter. Unfortunately, such well-intentioned supplemental feeding is contributing to an overabundance of deer with repercussions for the forest communities that sustain them. Until recently, most assumed that deer acted only as a natural component of forest ecosystems and thus could not pose a serious threat to these systems. The public and even many ecologists are surprised to learn how deer were driven extinct, or nearly extinct, over much of their range in the eastern United States and how strongly they have rebounded since then in response to favorable habitat conditions, scarce predators, strong game laws, and mild winters. They are even more surprised to learn how deer are having dramatic impacts on forest ecosystems, not only by eating plants known to be sensitive to deer herbivory, but by decimating forest understories generally to the point of altering canopy dynamics or even preventing forest regeneration altogether (fig. 16.1). While we should celebrate the recovery of deer as a conservation success, we must also face the problems this recovery has brought in terms of increased crop damage, vehicle accidents, failed tree regeneration, impacts on a wide array of understory plants and ecosystem processes, and outbreaks of Lyme disease in humans and Chronic Wasting Disease in deer.

Despite all the attention deer have received as an important game animal, serious scientific studies of how deer affect forest ecosystems only began in recent decades – with the conspicuous exception of Aldo Leopold. Leopold noted clear evidence of overbrowsing in German and Austrian forests in the 1930s (Leopold 1936) and on the Kaibab Plateau north of the Grand Canyon (Flader 1974). He was also the first to warn the public of the dangers of deer overabundance and the consequent value of retaining deer predators like wolves (Leopold 1938, 1946; Flaspohler and Meine 2006). His efforts also led

FIGURE 16.1 Conspicuous effects of excluding deer from an upland mixed forest in northern Wisconsin. Although cover by woody plants, broadleaf herbs, and ferns became 150-fold, 63-fold, and 20-fold greater in such exclosure plots, cover by sedges and grasses became 3.8-fold and 2.2-fold greater in nearby control plots (Rooney, 2009). Photo by the author.

to the first regional survey of deer damage to forests (Swift 1948). Despite these efforts, the public and many game biologists largely ignored deer impacts in following decades. Some ecologists argued that it was unlikely that deer populations could be controlled by wolf predators (Caughley 1970). More recently, evidence has accumulated to suggest that ungulates indeed do have dramatic impacts on plant communities and that top-down effects of predators on ungulates may often be important in ameliorating these impacts (Karr et al. 1992; Williams et al. 2004; Binkley et al. 2006; Estes et al. 2011). For example, wolves reintroduced into Yellowstone National Park are reducing the impacts of elk on vegetation, particularly along rivers (Ripple and Beschta 2003, 2004 a,b). Such effects probably reflect both direct predation on elk and the indirect effects that wolves have on elk movement and wariness (the "ecology of fear"). Créte (1999) estimates that deer biomass has increased fivefold in the absence of wolves in North America, imposing historically unprecedented browsing pressures on plants eaten by deer.

Deer and other ungulates can have both positive and negative impacts on forest understory plant diversity and abundance depending on how their density, selectivity, and consumption rates affect the relative performance of trees, shrubs, and herbs. For example, moose can favor shrubs and herbs by maintaining more open understory conditions on Isle Royale (McInnes et al. 1992). On islands in Lake Superior where deer are absent, Canada yew (*Taxus canadensis*) dominates many areas, limiting herb cover and diversity (Judziewicz and Koch 1993). Similarly, low to intermediate densities of deer can promote herb diversity by preferentially browsing fast-growing pioneer species (Royo et al. 2010). Thus, ungulates may enhance or diminish plant diversity depending on their density, distribution, and behavior relative to the system they occupy.

In this chapter, I explore what is known about how deer (here, mostly white-tailed deer, *Odocoileus virginianus* Boddaert) affect forest understory plants and ultimately forest community dynamics. Let us first examine factors that nearly caused deer to go extinct through the eastern U.S. and then consider the factors that boosted deer populations so forcefully through the 20th century. I then review the evidence that deer now represent an overabundant "keystone herbivore" in much of the region. Because deer management is contentious, ecologists have special roles to play in assessing deer impacts and recommending policies to ameliorate these. Ecologists assess impacts using a variety of methods aimed at measuring both short- and longer-term effects of browsing. These methods form the primary focus for this chapter and provide an opportunity to explore what is known about how deer affect both woody and herbaceous plants in forest understories. This evidence reinforces the idea that deer are radically changing ecological conditions in many forests. I also seek to identify the traits that make plants vulnerable or resistant to deer and explore what is known about how deer impacts vary over time, space, and communities of varying composition. This variation presents challenges regarding how best to monitor the impacts deer have and the potential we have to help forest understories recover from those impacts.

Our methods for assessing deer impacts are still developing, having yet to be tested, standardized, and applied to their potential (Waller et al. 2009). In the final section on Management Challenges, I discuss these uncertainties and their corollary: that research into the methods used to monitor deer impacts should become part of an "adaptive monitoring" network to improve and apply these methods in more extensive networks. In this domain, it would also be foolish to ignore the complicated issues involved with practical deer and forest management, both of which are subject to diverse social and economic forces. Rather than trying to provide a comprehensive review of these complex issues, I conclude by considering how we might use science to improve our ability to manage both deer and forests as a coupled system.

The focus here is on understory plants, where most forest diversity resides (chapter 1, this volume; Gilliam 2007) and the methods we use to study deer impacts. I particularly focus on eastern and Midwestern forests and white-tailed deer, the dominant ungulate in these regions. However, most of the ideas and many results also pertain to other regions and ungulate species. Although browsing strictly applies to herbivory on woody stems and leaves, I use the term loosely here to refer to herbivory on herbaceous plant parts as well. The examples presented are intended to be illustrative rather than exhaustive. For more comprehensive reviews of deer impacts, see Alverson and Waller (1988), Miller et al. (1992), Waller and Alverson (1997), Russell et al. (2001), Rooney (2001), Rooney and Waller (2003), Côté et al. (2004), and Waller et al. (2009).

BACKGROUND

Why Have Deer Increased So Much in Abundance?

Ancestors of modern deer and elk migrated into North America about 20 million years ago and so represent native herbivores that have long coevolved with extant plant communities in a dynamic equilibrium. Deer populations likely remained at relatively low levels for much of this period due to relatively sparse food in mature forest understories and being hunted by a broad spectrum of large predators through the Miocene and Pleistocene epochs. After the last glaciation about 14,000 years ago, humans swept through the Americas, likely contributing to the demise of most of the larger ungulates and predators – with the conspicuous exception of deer (Martin and Klein 1984). As Native Americans became a new predator, deer adjusted.

Before European settlement, deer are thought to have occurred at a density of two to five overwintering deer per square kilometer of suitable habitat across northern Wisconsin (McCabe and McCabe 1984, 1997). Densities now range from 8 to > 20 deer per km² through most this region (Garrott et al. 1993) and are higher in southern Wisconsin. Total deer populations in Wisconsin increased from 600,000 in 1960 to more than 1,600,000 by 2000, chronically exceeding target densities in most Deer Management Units. Similar increases have occurred in other states (e.g., Michigan, fig. 16.2). Deer now exist across the eastern and Midwestern U.S. at record densities (e.g., 32 / km² in Rock Creek Park in Washington, D.C.; Carroll 2009). How did these remarkable increases occur, and what factors drove them?

European settlement substantially affected deer populations. Initially, hunting with guns drastically reduced deer populations, extirpating them from broad parts of the eastern and Midwestern U.S. by the late 19th century. Nevertheless, they made a remarkable comeback in the 20th century to become the region's most abundant large mammal. Game managers often take credit for this recovery. There is no doubt that bag limits, restricted hunting seasons, buck-only hunting, reintroductions, and habitat improvement projects ("wildlife openings") contributed to the recovery of deer populations. However, radical shifts in habitat conditions also contributed to this turnaround. As Leopold (1933) first noted, deer (and other game species) thrive in landscapes where open and closed habitats lie adjacent to each other. The widespread conversions of forests, savannas, and prairies to agriculture, timber production, and urban and suburban development all increased the forage available to deer (Côté et al. 2004). In forested regions, deer thrive in early successional landscapes dominated by

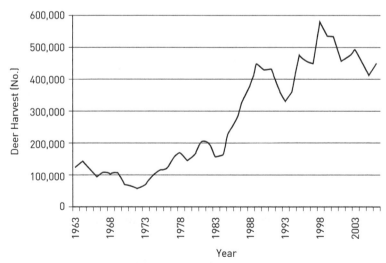

FIGURE 16.2 Deer populations increased greatly over much of the Midwestern, eastern, and southern U.S. through much of the 20th century. The curves give the total deer harvest in Michigan from 1963 to 2006. Wisconsin experienced similar trends. Source: Michigan DNR.

aspen and other fast-growing species that provide excellent browse, as well as plentiful edges and sunlit openings that support a thick growth of grasses and other herbaceous species. Such habitats dominated the cutover landscapes of the upper Midwest in the early 20th century. Since that time, game and forest managers have enjoyed a convenient partnership pursuing compatible goals on the same land base. Active timber management, especially for pulpwood, on both public and private forestland now sustains early successional stands and high deer densities across the "paper belt" of the upper Midwest (R. Doepker, Mich, DNR, pers. comm.).

Reductions in predation and increases in overwinter survival also contributed to the substantial increases in deer populations through the U.S. Wolves, mountain lions, wolverines, and other predators were all actively hunted as "varmints" through the 19th and much of the 20th century, often to local extinction. Native American populations and hunters declined and became more restricted to reservations. Deer near the northern limit of their historic range in the upper Midwest used to regularly face severe winters and starvation. Milder winters since 1990, however, have reduced overwinter mortality, helping to boost deer populations, as has the popularity of supplemental winter feeding (K. McCaffery, Wisc, DNR, pers. comm.). Thus, changes in habitat conditions, predation, and available food have all contributed to substantial increases in deer populations with consequent implications for forest herb layers (fig. 16.3).

How Do Deer Affect Forest Dynamics?

Plants occupying the understory of any forest are vulnerable to a host of threats. In addition to intermittent falling limbs and trunks, fires may consume them or floods

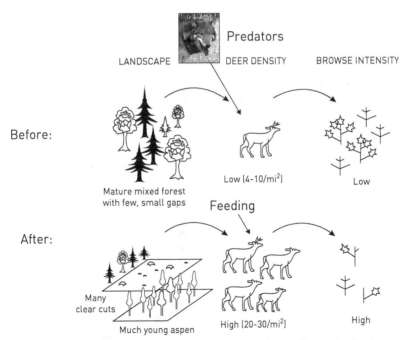

FIGURE 16.3 Diagram indicating some of the dominant habitat factors affecting the abundance of white-tailed deer before and after European settlement (left side) and consequent likely downstream impacts of these shifts in abundance on patterns of deer browsing on tree seedlings and forest herb layers (right side).

may submerge or wash them away. Plants also face hungry invertebrate and vertebrate herbivores, as well as ubiquitous microbes capable of infecting them and altering the availability of soil water and nutrients. In fact, much of the biochemical, genetic, and species diversity of plants is thought to reflect the diversifying selection imposed by herbivores and pathogens. The diversity of plant defenses, in turn, has fostered a co-evolutionary enhancement of strategies to attack plants. The significance of these interactions and the delicate balance they often represent become obvious when novel players invade a new system. Conspicuous examples include the Chestnut blight fungus (*Cryphonectria parasitica* [Murrill] Barr) devastating populations of the American chestnut (*Castanea dentata* [Marsh.] Borkh.) in the first half of the 20th century followed by invasions of European elm bark beetles (*Scolytus multistriatus* Marsham, 1802) and the Dutch Elm disease fungi (*Ophiostoma* spp.) that have largely eliminated American Elms (*Ulmus americana* L.). Here, we also see a co-evolutionary collaboration between a herbivorous insect and a fungus. Disease and decay organisms often depend on invertebrate and vertebrate vectors or hosts to reach, or provide, their next meal. These include birds, rodents, beetles, or slugs for the Chestnut blight (Scharf and DePalma 1981; Turchetti and Chelazzi 1984; Pakaluk 1997).

Interestingly, deer can shift forest composition and structure as much as these keystone pathogens and depend in similar ways on microbes in their ruminant guts to detoxify plant defenses and break down cellulose. Herbivory by deer also reinforces regional declines in hemlock forests due to the hemlock woolly adelgid, an exotic insect pest (Eschtruth and Battles 2008).

Deer alter the composition of forest plant communities because plants differ in their palatability and resistance or tolerance to browsing. Some are highly defended or have morphological or life history traits that allow them to avoid or physically resist browsing. Plant defenses include physical defenses (e.g., thorns and toughness) and chemical defenses (e.g., toxins, silica, and digestion inhibitors). Some plant species have low nutritional value (Hartley and Jones 1997). Plants also respond differently to the effects of browsing because they differ in life history traits like their ability to resprout after browsing or grow quickly to a height where leaves and meristems are out of the reach of deer. Because grasses and sedges grow continuously from low basal meristems, they can tolerate high levels of grazing. When deer are sufficiently abundant, though, even fast-growing, palatable species may not be able to thrive within the molar zone (i.e., 20–140 cm tall; Kitterage et al. 1995). Deer typically reduce both the height and density of seedlings and saplings (Opperman and Merenlender 2000). Where they have been abundant for many years, deer remove most shrubs and saplings, creating an open park-like structure. Some people see these areas as peaceful and attractive, allowing easy walking and long sightlines through the trees. A blanket of low-growing ferns may add to the effect (George and Bazzaz 1999; chapter 13, this volume). However, such open, shrub-free forests (fig. 16.4) are biologically impoverished (Rooney 2001) and not self-sustaining (Horsley et al. 2003). As overstory trees die and fall, no young trees replace them, allowing the canopy to eventually break up as the density of overstory trees declines. Deforestation occurs gradually, "from the bottom up" eventually creating a savanna (sometimes termed a "fern park" in Pennsylvania; Pedersen and Wallis 2004).

Slow-growing forest understory plants, including shade-tolerant herbs, shrubs, and tree seedlings, may be particularly vulnerable to deer browse. Small spring ephemeral and early summer forest herbs can lose all of their leaves or flowers in a single episode of herbivory, making regrowth difficult (Augustine and McNaughton 1998; Augustine

FIGURE 16.4 Sustained deer browsing in forest understories can lead to ground layer dominated by ferns or graminoids like *Carex pennsylvanica*. Photo by the author.

and DeCalesta 2003). Where deer are abundant, browsing-intolerant herbs tend to be smaller, less likely to flower, and less likely to survive relative to plants in exclosures (Anderson 1994; Augustine and Frelich 1998; Ruhren and Handel 2000; Fletcher et al. 2001a; Ruhren and Handel 2003a). Over time, the density of such intolerant plants tends to decline and populations may be extirpated (Rooney and Dress 1997).

Conversely, deer browsing tends to favor grasses and sedges and some exotic species in Wisconsin (Wiegmann and Waller 2006). Plants that lose only a small fraction of their leaves or flowers, store resources underground, and place their meristems low (as in grasses), or those that regrow quickly via indeterminate growth, tolerate deer herbivory better (Augustine and McNaughton 1998; Wiegmann and Waller 2006). Such species include many annuals, graminoids, deciduous trees and shrubs, and some herbs and forbs that mature in late summer. Thus, as local deer browsing increases in mixed coniferous–deciduous forest stands, understory herb community diversity and sensitive conifers decline, while ferns, grasses, sedges, and rushes increase in dominance.

Plants susceptible to deer browse often lack physical and chemical defenses to deter browsing or have life history traits that make them vulnerable. Some species either cannot resprout after being browsed once or cannot recover quickly enough from the amount of carbon lost from repeated browsing. In forest understories, shaded environments slow growth, stranding shade-tolerant species for many years in the vulnerable molar zone. Species that cannot tolerate or resist deer usually succumb. In addition, many long-lived understory herbs take a decade or more to grow before reproducing. Herbivory at any point during this long juvenile phase may doom plants to death before they can set seed. Even if they do survive, their maturing flowers and fruits are often conspicuous and vulnerable to being preferentially grazed. If such impacts are widespread and sustained, seed sources are eliminated, and populations decline. In contrast, well-defended and otherwise resistant or tolerant species will persist or increase under these conditions, further reducing opportunities for deer-sensitive species to recolonize these sites. In such cases, the continued presence of some plants belies the reproductive failures and ecological extinction of other species (Redford 1992). Once species decline to low population numbers, they also become more vulnerable to stochastic forces and possible Allee effects (negative population growth) associated with restricted pollination, dispersal, or seedling establishment. For example, before deer browse Canada yew (*Taxus canadensis* Marshall) down to the ground (fig. 16.5), they nibble off male cones, preventing reproduction (Allison 1990).

(a)

"Before" Deer Browse on York Island (2003)

(b)

"After" Deer Browse on York Island (2005)

FIGURE 16.5 Rapid decimation of Canada yew (*Taxus canadensis*) by deer on York Island, Apostle Islands National Lakeshore. (a) 2005: healthy yew cover before deer colonized York Island. (b) 2007: Remnant dying yew on York Island following deer colonization. Photos courtesy of J. VanStappen, Apostle Islands National Lakeshore.

A spate of research starting in the 1980s has revealed that deer have multiple, sustained, and substantial effects on many forest ecosystems through the eastern, Midwestern, and southern U.S. In particular, deer affect the distribution and abundance of many species, as well as the relative abundance of species within forest communities (as documented below). They also alter the abundance not only of plant species but also of animal species at higher trophic levels (Casey and Hein 1983; McShea and Rappole 1992; deCalesta 1994a,b; McShea and Rappole 2000; Fuller 2001; Allombert et al. 2005a; Ostfeld et al. 2006). Together, these criteria establish deer as keystone herbivores capable of substantially altering forest communities (McShea and Rappole 1992; Waller and Alverson 1997). We can define overabundant deer populations as those existing at a density above the point where other species within the system can persist indefinitely, eventually causing extensive impacts on vegetation and ecosystem function (McShea et al. 1997). In forested landscapes, overabundant deer strongly affect species composition, tree regeneration, vertical structure, understory species dynamics, species diversity, the prevalence of invasive plant species, and nutrient cycling.

Forest Tree Dynamics

Deer consume many foods including flowers, herbaceous plants, acorns, carrion, and fish but rely primarily on woody browse in winter (Johnson et al. 1995). Although deer are considered generalists, they clearly prefer some food plants. As a result, deer can have substantial impacts on preferred species even at moderate densities. For example, because deer like to eat acorns and oak seedlings, they can substantially reduce oak populations. In winter, deer prefer to eat conifers like northern white cedar (*Thuja occidentalis* L.), eastern hemlock (*Tsuga canadensis* (L.) Carrière), and Canada yew (*Taxus canadensis*). Although cedar and hemlock can eventually grow tall enough to escape browsing, this takes many years under shady conditions. Yew never outgrows its vulnerability to deer, making it particularly susceptible to heavy browsing. This sensitivity makes it one of the clearest indicators for discriminating between deer-dominated landscapes and habitats where deer are scarce or absent, as seen clearly in the Apostle Islands of Lake Superior (Judziewicz and Koch 1993).

Preferential browsing by deer shifts the tree composition of forests toward species that tolerate or resist browsing (Ross et al. 1970; Horsley et al. 2003). In the upper Great Lakes region, deer reduce the density of eastern hemlocks (*Tsuga canadensis*) in hemlock-dominated forests favoring sugar maple (*Acer saccharum* Marshall) and other hardwoods in their place (Davis et al. 1996). Although deer eat both species, deer prefer hemlock to sugar maple especially in winter. Hemlock's slower growth restricts its ability to rapidly exploit light gaps. In contrast, maple can resprout vigorously (Anderson and Loucks 1979). Such shifts in species composition affect forest dynamics and alter successional pathways. Abundant deer can stall succession, accelerate succession, or alter its pathways (Davidson 1993; Côté et al. 2004). In early successional grassy, old fields, deer remove pioneer tree species, delaying the time until a closed forest canopy develops (Inouye et al. 1994). In mid or late successional forests, moderate or severe disturbances typically permit pioneer species to regenerate and become established, but abundant deer can remove many of these pioneers allowing late successional deer-tolerant species to persist (Davidson 1993). In this case, late successional species can come to dominate sites sooner than if deer were scarce or there were no disturbance. In sum, deer populations can strongly affect plant communities and successional trajectories.

The largest impact deer have on trees is preventing some species from regenerating. Abundant deer in New England have the strongest impact on hemlock and black birch, but the regeneration of all species was curtailed when deer densities reached about 60/km^2 (Kitterage et al. 1995). Although deer can clearly reduce or eliminate tree regeneration, other factors also affect patterns of tree regeneration (Didier and Porter 2003). In Pennsylvania, Massachusetts, and Wisconsin, deer densities of 7–12 deer per km^2 prevent the regeneration of at least some tree species (deCalesta and Stout 1997). In Wisconsin, winter deer browsing depresses the regeneration of eastern hemlock (*Tsuga canadensis*) and northern white cedar (*Thuja occidentalis*), evergreens that are important winter foods for deer (Waller et al. 1996a; Rooney et al. 2000, 2002). Deer browse on hardwoods mostly in the spring. Deer browsing strongly limits the regeneration of northern red oak (*Quercus rubra* L.) and yellow birch (*Betula alleghaniensis* Britt.) seedlings (Rooney and Waller 2003). Anderson (1993) concluded that Wisconsin forests would need to be protected from deer for upward of 70 years for most shade-tolerant trees to achieve size class distributions that used to characterize mature forests in the region.

Herb Dynamics

Deer consume herbaceous species, as well as woody ones, particularly in spring and early summer when they quickly switch from woody diets to focus on more nutritious herbaceous plants (McCaffery et al. 1974; Skinner and Telfer 1974; Stormer and Bauer 1980). Herbaceous plants remain in the molar zone, making them especially susceptible to deer herbivory. Herb layers also support high plant diversity, allowing diet preferences to be expressed. The herbaceous layer is also highly dynamic spatially and temporally relative to the other forest layers (chapter 9, this volume; Gilliam 2007). Herbivory in the understory also affects overall forest dynamics, as even tree seedlings must pass through the herb layer's ecological filter. By influencing the composition and competitive dynamics among plants, herbivory affects patterns of forest succession (chapter 13, this volume).

The herb layer includes many highly palatable and preferred species. Deer particularly like to consume nutritious flowers and fruit. Thus, even when deer do not remove entire plants, they can depress reproduction. As a result, sensitive herb species become rare or absent (Rooney and Waller 2003; Rooney et al. 2004). Sensitive species typically lack effective anti-herbivore compounds and tend to be long lived with low annual reproduction. Such plants include pretty wildflowers like orchids, lobeliads, and lilies like *Trillium* (Miller et al. 1992). Abundant deer contribute to the declines we observe in many herbaceous species and overall herb diversity (Anderson 1994; Augustine et al. 1998; Patel and Rapport 2000; Rooney and Waller 2003; McGraw and Furedi 2005; Stockton et al. 2005).

As already noted, deer can create park-like conditions within forests by removing native shrubs, tree seedlings and saplings, and most herbaceous species. Under heavy deer herbivory, forests can come to have understories dominated by one or a few very abundant species that are tolerant of or resistant to deer herbivory. Such species include exotic invasives (e.g., garlic mustard, *Alliaria petiolata* [M. Bieb.] Cavara & Grande or Asian silt grass, *Microstegium vimineum* [Trin.] A. Camus); native herbaceous species (e.g., Jack-in-the-pulpit, *Arisaema triphyllum* L. enchanters nightshade, *Circaea lutetiana L.)*; woody natives like Virginia creeper (*Parthenocissus quinquefolia* L.); certain native shrubs (e.g., choke cherry, *Prunus virginiana* L.); and exotic shrub species like common and European buckthorn (*Rhamnus cathartica* L. and *Rhamnus frangula* L.). Interestingly, all these dominant species have increased dramatically in the Lake States over the last 50 years (Rooney et al. 2004; Wiegmann and Waller 2006a; Rogers et al. 2008). Concurrent with these increases for a few species has been a conspicuous decline in overall native plant diversity.

Remarkably, deer also appear to be having negative impacts even on unpalatable plant species in some forests. Heckel and Kalisz (2008) found that Jack-in-the-pulpit (*Arisaema triphyllum*) had reduced growth, plant size, flowering, and seed rain in proportion to deer impacts on favored browse species. They attributed these impacts to drier, more compacted soils, revealing that deer impacts may extend farther than previously thought.

Do Deer Facilitate Invasions?

Most exotic species are ruderal or weedy and maintain populations in disturbed areas such as roadsides or old fields. Perhaps 10 percent of introduced exotic species become invasive, frequently displacing native species via competition by being better able to exploit and use resources. Other invasives become abundant by producing toxic chemicals that reduce the abundances of other plant species or deter herbivory and disease (Callaway and Ridenour 2004). Invasive species have strong impacts on ecosystem processes and function (Shea and Chesson 2002). For example, invasive plants can alter fire return times and fire intensity, change microbial symbiont and detritus communities, and reduce tree regeneration.

Deer and invasive species can interact to produce a double-whammy effect on native plant communities. Deer can cause apparent competition when they selectively forage on native species while avoiding invasives. In such cases, natives are removed or reduced in abundance, expanding the resources available for less browsed invasives to use. Second, white-tailed deer can increase the spread of invasive species through the dispersal of their seeds. Deer disperse seeds of invasive species either by carrying seeds on their fur or by ingesting mature seeds and ripe fruit and depositing viable seeds in fecal scat piles (Myers et al. 2004). Third, the impacts of deer browsing depend on plant density, as well as deer density.

Most invasive species that thrive within the range of white-tailed deer have a trait in common: the ability to tolerate or resist white-tailed deer herbivory. Case in point: Garlic mustard and buckthorn, two of the most invasive species in the Lake States, are species that deer avoid consuming. A recent study in New Jersey and Pennsylvania hemlock forests found support for the enemy release hypothesis in that three exotic plants (*Microstegium vimineum, Alliaria petiolata*, and *Berberis thunbergii* DC.) gained a competitive advantage in the presence of more deer (Eschtruth and Battles 2009). Deer herbivory accelerated the invasion of these exotic plants, an effect they attributed to resisting herbivory (though trampling or soil nutrient mechanisms were not ruled out).

Do Deer Affect Nutrient Cycling?

Overabundant white-tailed deer may also alter nutrient cycling. To date, this subject is understudied, but there is direct and indirect evidence that abundant deer could have substantial effects, accelerating nutrient cycling by shifting carbon and nutrients from plant biomass into deer biomass, urine, and feces that enter the soil. In some areas with elevated deer populations, dung beetles are more prevalent than where deer are less abundant (Brian Pederson, pers. comm.). By converting plant biomass accumulating in the understory and midstory into soil biomass, deer may be shifting forest ecosystems from a primary production-based food web to a detritus-based food web.

Ungulate herbivory in the Serengeti is known to accelerate nutrient cycling (McNaughton 1976, 1985) by increasing tissue loss, which in turn increases plant uptake of nutrients. Richtie et al. (1998), however, found that herbivores including deer can decelerate nutrient cycling because deer feed on nutrient rich tissue, increasing the dominance of plants with nutrient-poor tissue and/or defense compounds. Such plant species have leaves with a higher lignin concentration, higher C:N ratio, or both (unpublished data). In this case, nutrients remain tied up in the leaf litter longer and mineralize more slowly than in species with less lignin and lower C:N ratios (Hobbs et al. 1996). Thus, nutrient cycling is altered, and site productivity may decline.

How Are Scientists Addressing Deer Overabundance?

After observing overbrowsed forests in Germany in the mid-1930s, Leopold (1936) began to speak out on the dangers of overabundant deer in the U.S. (Leopold 1943, 1946). He laid out the case that unconstrained ungulate populations could have severe and long-lasting impacts on forest plant communities, eventually compromising their ability to sustain healthy deer populations. Strong hunter opposition, however, largely stymied his efforts to reform deer management in Wisconsin (Meine 1988). Few ecologists or wildlife biologists pursued active research on deer impacts in the decades following, perhaps because severe winters and the popularity of hunting largely kept deer populations in check during this period. Deer populations continued to grow, however, as did their impacts, not only on forests, but also on crops, ornamental plantings, vehicle accident rates, and on outbreaks of Lyme and other human and animal diseases.

The scarcity of carefully controlled studies and long-term monitoring data allowed many to ignore the ecological threats posed by deer for many years. Even some ecologists questioned the extent of deer impacts until recently (e.g., Mladenoff and Stearns 1993). Now, however, the widening set of studies on deer impacts has led to more consensus on their nature and significance. Questions are now turning to whether chronically high densities of deer can be sustained without threatening natural values like species diversity. Despite this growing scientific consensus, public contention over issues regarding deer management continue even in states like Pennsylvania where such impacts have long been manifest (chapter 17, this volume; deCalesta 1994a,b; deCalesta and Stout 1997; Frye 2008). These public controversies indicate that we still have some way to go in translating our science into sound management (see Management Challenges section). They also provide an impetus to do additional research on deer impacts, to draw inferences carefully, and to share our results widely. To these ends, let us turn to the range of techniques that ecologists use to assess deer impacts.

HOW DO ECOLOGISTS STUDY DEER IMPACTS?

A wide array of methods has emerged for studying the impacts deer have on forest herb layers. The data these methods provide vary in type, amount, and level of quantitative detail. Broadly, these methods can be divided into two groups—those that provide snapshots of current patterns of deer browsing (i.e., in the current growing season) and those that assess the longer-term impacts of browsing by using data that integrate these effects over many years. Methods based on directly tallying browse on current stem and twig growth or this year's reproductive structures clearly reflect immediate and current patterns of browsing. These methods can often be extended back on woody stems (and some herbaceous stolons, corms, or rhizomes) to estimate browsing in the few years previous to the current one (assuming these twigs persist and that the characteristic deer-torn stems can be distinguished from hare browsing). More integrative measures of past browsing include observed browse lines, shifts in plant size or demographic structure of browse-sensitive species, and, over longer periods, shifts in overall community composition and/or structure (missing herb layers, as seen in long-browsed forests in Pennsylvania; chapter 17, this volume). Methods can also be divided between those that are based on field observations and surveys and those that employ experimental approaches as found in food-choice experiments, fenced enclosures and exclosures, and the "natural" experiments afforded by islands or other regions of the landscape that differ conspicuously in deer densities or their histories of deer use. We review these methods in turn in this section and conclude by comparing their utility and the potential to integrate data more effectively by standardizing methods and combining complementary approaches.

Methods to Assess Immediate Browse Impacts

Methods for estimating current browse impacts on forest herb layer plants are used to compare areas that differ in deer density or browsing levels such as fenced exclosures, different forest types, or regions with different management or ownership. To provide a basis for comparison, observational studies often seek to estimate deer abundance using scat group counts, deer trails, night surveys, or agency estimates. These methods vary in cost and efficacy and reviewing them is beyond the scope of this chapter.

Browsing Indexes for Woody Plants

Monitoring direct ungulate impacts on woody plants typically involves tracking either plant size or stature or the number of browsed twigs. Indirect inferences of browsing on woody plants are often based on demography (e.g., the relative proportions of individuals in various size or age classes). Browse levels can accurately characterize local recent impacts, while demographic approaches provide a longer-term or broader-scale picture that integrates ungulate impacts over time and space. Woody plants leave physical records of past growth and browsing that can often be read in terms of twig damage, extension, and branching (table 16.1). For example, the Sugar Maple Browse Index (SMBI) provides a simple method to estimate local deer browsing pressure from the proportion of browsed twigs on sugar maple (*Acer saccharum*) (Frelich and Lorimer 1985). The SMBI relies on the fact that sugar maple seedlings and saplings tend to be abundant and shade-tolerant, providing a convenient phytometer for estimating the local intensity of deer browsing. Other, more favored species have often become too scarce to provide adequate sample sizes (as do sparsely distributed species). The SMBI is based on the overall proportion of browsed terminal sugar maple twigs located 30–200 cm above the ground as judged from the ratio of browsed to total twigs on at least 12–20 maple saplings per site.

Rooney and Waller (2001) also tried using red oak seedlings (*Quercus rubra*) as phytometers but found that seedling densities drop precipitously as browsing pressure increases from low to intermediate. Thus, red oak regeneration appears to be strongly limited by deer but could be used as a phytometer for that lower range of browse intensities (or recently increased browsing). Other woody plants studied in connection to deer browse include *Taxus canadensis*, whose original high frequency in the region reflected low historic deer populations (Foster 1993; Balgooyen and Waller 1995). The SMBI is related to browsing on other species like hemlock (Rooney and Waller 1998).

Two indices of deer browsing have been developed in Europe to assess the impacts of roe deer (*Capreolus capreolus*). Both are unusual in being based on the browsing of all browse species present rather then particular species. Guibert (1997) developed the Index of browsing Pressure on the Flora (IPF) to track changes in browsing pressure through time at a site defining IPF as the ratio of the number of browsed woody plant species to the total number of woody plant species present at a site:

$$IPF = \frac{\Sigma_i \Sigma_j C_{ij}}{\Sigma_i \Sigma_j P_{ij}}$$

where C_{ij} refers to the browsing of woody plant species j on plot i and P_{ij} is the presence of this woody species j on plot i. The sums are over all species and plots. Guibert used plots 3.57 m in diameter (40 m^2) and restricted his surveys to woody species present in > 10 percent of the plots. He considered a species browsed if > 5 percent of its shoots in the molar zone (< 1.2 m) were eaten, with surveys typically occurring just before the resumption of vegetative growth in the spring (allowing browsing impacts to accumulate, much like scat groups, over the winter). Morellet et al. (2003) tested this index for its replicability across 14 sets of observers on 50 plots. Estimated IPF ranged from 15 percent to 46 percent with a highly significant observer x plot effect. Such large observer effects and bias handicap the use of this index. They also pointed out that the presence and browsing of various species are not independent of each other, possibly also causing bias.

As an alternative, Morellet et al. (2003) introduced a new, even simpler index for tallying browse damage on woody plants. This index is based on a statistical model calibrated against densities of roe deer in France (directly estimated) during a period when populations increased greatly. Their Browsing Index (BI) uses a Bayesean approach where the posterior distribution has the expected value:

$$BI = (1 + n_c)/(2 + n_p)$$

where n $_c$ is the number of plots with any evidence of browsing present and n $_p$ is the total number of plots with any woody twigs present < 1.2m tall. This index is also based on all available browse species present (they found *Rubus* sp. to be particularly widespread and useful). Although species-specific browsing rates differed widely, this browsing index closely tracked roe deer population size. They concluded that their index provides an efficient and reliable tool for monitoring deer impacts sensitive to changes in deer density. They recommend a sample size of at least 150 plots of 1 m^2 spaced evenly across a study area. As its statistical properties are well characterized, it is straightforward to make comparisons over space and time. This index deserves to be tried in North America as it shows promise for providing an index that could be employed widely with minimal expertise and compared easily among regions.

Herbaceous Indicators of Browsing

Although herbaceous plants leave few physical records of past herbivory (except, perhaps, small size), they can provide abundant and widespread phytometers to infer current deer impacts. We can, for example, tally browse damage on herbaceous species' leaves, stems, or reproductive organs, identifying the tears to infer deer impacts. Such measures are usually limited to the current growing season and often focus on particular indicator species known to attract ungulate herbivory (see table16.1). We can also use the presence, abundance, size (typically height), and/or flowering condition of these plants to infer the current and recent impacts of deer (Anderson 1994; Rooney 1997; Rooney and Waller 2001). Such approaches differ from studies of the direct impacts of browsing. Instead, the characteristics or densities of plants are compared to areas with higher or lower levels of deer herbivory (as inferred from deer access, population estimates, or another indicator—e.g., a woody browse index). Let us consider some examples.

Anderson (1994) first studied height in large-leaf trillium (*Trillium grandiflorum* [Michx.] Salisb., 1805) in Illinois and found this to vary inversely with deer browse as inferred from browsing on all herbs. He concluded that trillium height could serve as a useful indicator of deer browse. Webster et al. (2005a) found similar connections between trillium height and deer browse impacts in the Great Smoky Mountain National Park. Webster et al. (2001) also looked at height in sweet cicely (*Osmorhiza claytonii*), jack-in-the-pulpit (*Arisaema triphyllum*), and white baneberry (*Actaea pachypoda* Elliot). They found that these species also provide reasonable indicators of deer impacts as inferred from other measures of deer browse.

Several characters have been used to infer deer browsing in herbs. In the Allegheny region of Pennsylvania, Canada mayflower (*Maianthemum canadense* Desf.) grows to larger sizes, at three times the density, and flowers more frequently on top of tall boulders compared with nearby short boulders (Rooney 1997). These differences are clearly attributable to deer herbivory. Balgooyen and Waller (1995) studied blue-bead lily (*Clintonia borealis* Aiton [Raf.]), an important spring food for deer. They found that the frequency, scape height, leaf number, and pedicels per umbel decreased on islands with higher deer density, making blue-bead lily a good indicator for deer browsing. Fletcher et al. (2001a) examined a number of species and genera, including *Uvularia* sp., *Smilacina* sp., *Polygonatum* sp., *Orchis spectabilis* (L.) Raf., and *Arisaema triphyllum*, noting population and reproductive activity. In all cases, reproductive

Community Dynamics and the Role of Disturbance

Table 16.1 Range of deer impacts on plants and associated potential indicators.

Group or indicator	Number or density	Size or height	Reproductive condition	Direct Damage
Trees	Oak and hemlock seedlings (Rooney & Waller 2001)	Hemlock (Rooney and Dress 1997)		Sugar Maple Browse Index (Frelich and Lorimer 1985)Morellet Index, (Morellet et al. 2001)
Shrubs	Yew (*Taxus*)	Yew patch size or cover	Damage to male yew cones (Allison 1990)	Yew
Herbaceous Forbs	*Maianthemum canadensis* (Rooney 1997) *Laportea canadensis* (Augustine et. al 1998)	*Trillium grandiflorum* (Augustine and Frelich 1998; Anderson 1994) *Clintonia borealis* (Balgooyen and Waller 1995) *Maianthemum canadensis* (Rooney 1997) *Osmorhiza claytonii* (Webster et al. 2001) *Arisaema triphyllum* (Webster et al. 2001) *Actaea pachypoda* (Webster et al. 2001)	*Clintonia borealis* (Balgooyen and Waller 1995) *Maianthemum canadensis* (Rooney 1997) *Trillium grandiflorum* (Augustine and Frelich 1998) *Arisaema triphyllum* (Fletcher et al. 2001) *Uvularia* sp. (Fletcher et al. 2001) *Smilacina* sp. (Fletcher et al. 2001) I sp. (Fletcher et al. 2001) I (Fletcher et al. 2001)	*Chelone glabra* (Williams et al. 2000)

activity declined with increasing deer density. They conclude that reproductive activity provides a way to estimate deer impacts among these studied species and perhaps more generally (Fletcher et al. 2001b).

Sometimes, herbaceous species' height and reproductive activity are not well correlated with other measures of deer impacts. Kirschbaum and Anacker (2005) found that *Maianthemum canadensis* and *Trillium grandiflorum* heights and reproduction in Pennsylvania were affected by deer but did not correlate well with levels of woody browse. The authors concluded that while deer clearly consume herbaceous species, browsing on woody stems provides a better predictor of deer densities and impacts. Their result might also reflect the spotty nature of deer herbivory and associated high variance.

Herbaceous plants may also leave a demographic signature of past browsing in the form of smaller plants or missing flowers or fruit, as demonstrated in *Maianthemum* (Rooney 1997; Kirschbaum and Anacker 2005; Collard et al. 2010), *Clintonia* (Balgooyen and Waller 1995; Banta et al. 2003), *Trillium* (Anderson 1994, 1997; Augustine and Frelich 1998; Augustine and DeCalesta 2003; Rooney and Gross 2003; Knight 2004; Knight et al. 2009; Collard et al. 2010), and other species (Kraft et al. 2004). Such approaches can be very useful, particularly in allowing us to assess effects of deer browsing relative to other factors (e.g., human harvesting in American ginseng [*Panax quinquefolius*]; Farrington et al. 2005, 2009; McGraw and Furedi 2005).

Species in the genera *Trillium*, *Polygonatum*, *Clintonia*, and *Uvularia* provide candidates for observing the direct impacts of deer. All are easy-to-identify long-lived perennials. They also share a determinate pattern of flowering and must reach a minimum threshold size to flower, providing the opportunity to use several traits (abundance, size or height, clipped leaves or stems, and flowering or fruiting condition) to indicate deer herbivory. Williams et al. (2000) also suggested tracking herbivory in *Chelone glabra* L. (turtle-head), *Aster divaricatus* (*Eurybia divaricata* (L.) G.L. Nesom), *Symphyotrichum prenanthoides* (Muhl. ex Willd.) G. L. Nesom, and *Impatiens capensis* Meerb., all of which they found to be preferentially browsed by deer in the eastern U.S.

Using several species to indicate deer impacts makes sense as individual species are not always present and because more species give us a more reliable and complete picture of deer impacts (Waller et al. 2009). This would be particularly true if we could cross-calibrate deer effects among species and arrange species into a sequence of differential susceptibility (or preference) for use in areas with higher and lower impacts. More generally, methods should be tested against one another in various habitat types to determine when each is more accurate or efficient. This may depend on community type or composition as the availability of alternative food species will affect deer preferences.

Negative Indicators

To monitor indicators sensitive to deer herbivory (or rare species of conservation concern susceptible to herbivory), we face another dilemma. If deer consume most or all aboveground shoots, they may leave no visible record of herbivory. In addition, rare species, including indicators made scarce by browsing, present us with statistical concerns as their rarity makes it difficult to obtain sample sizes adequate to reliably infer impacts or differences among sites. In such cases, we can choose to include many indicators (perhaps combining them for statistical analysis), survey larger areas, or base our inferences on absences relative to suitable control areas that support these species (e.g., the islands or exclosures described below). We can also examine long-term shifts in community composition (see below).

Alternatively, we might simplify field sampling and gain statistical power by focusing instead on negative indicators of deer browse, that is, species that respond sensitively but positively to deer browsing. For example, we know that sustained deer browsing boosts the abundance of grasses, sedges, and some ferns (Horsley et al. 2003; Wiegmann and Waller 2006; Rooney 2009; Randall and Walters 2011). As these species increase in abundance, they are easier to find, and their abundance becomes easier to quantify. Such indicators thus become more useful as browse-sensitive plants decline.

Methods to Infer the History of Browsing

To complement direct measures of browsing, ecologists and wildlife biologists use a broad range of methods to infer the impacts of past browsing. These range from simply tallying the numbers of branches browsed in the preceding two to three years (counting back using bud-scale scars) to tracking shifts in demographic structure to monitoring half-century or longer shifts in overall community composition. Most of these methods rely on indirect associations to infer links between the variables measured and deer herbivory. Nevertheless, and particularly in combination, they can provide convincing evidence for the nature and range of deer impacts.

Anecdotes

Most simply, we can collect individual observations on whether a particular plant species or individual shows evidence of deer herbivory, or whether a species has declined or disappeared in some location in apparent response to deer browsing (as long done in deer "yards" under conifers where deer tend to congregate in winter particularly when the snow is deep). We can sometimes follow deer, noting which species or individuals are favored. One of the most obvious indicators of ungulate browse are the conspicuous browse lines that appear, particularly on sensitive conifers like northern white cedar (*Thuja occidentalis*) following browsing (fig. 16.6a). In areas with deep snow, we also see "sandwich" trees with low and high foliage surrounding a bare central trunk. Although easy to identify, these do not provide ideal indicators in that, by the time browse lines appear, impacts have probably been underway for years. Browse lines also persist for years after browsing may have ceased, providing a lagging indicator. Real-time indicators of browsing might instead involve tracking browse on living phytometers—newly planted seedlings, saplings, or shrubs that could provide immediate (and comparable) data on deer impacts.

Such anecdotal information is often traded informally among biologists and many amateur naturalists and hunters, contributing to the stock of information they draw on, consciously or unconsciously, in drawing conclusions about deer densities and impacts. These anecdotes have utility in being abundant, diverse, and involving many observers. Their disadvantages are also obvious to scientists: they are unverified, nonsystematic, and often pertain to only one location and time. Although scientists often criticize anecdotal information for these limitations, amassing a large number of observations of one or a few kinds from an organized network of participants could

FIGURE 16.6 Conspicuous effects of browsing by white-tailed deer on two trees, (a) northern white cedar (*Thuja occidentalis*, and (b) red maple (*Acer rubrum*), and (c) a twisted stalk lily (*Streptopus roseus*. Both (a) and (c) have declined conspicuously in the upper Midwest in apparent response to deer herbivory. Photos by the author.

provide the basis for systematic analysis. It would be particularly useful to have many such observations collected across a broad geographic area and for many years. Such a program would also afford opportunities to involve the public (including hunters) via "citizen science" programs which would bring additional benefits in terms of public education and constructive engagement. Although no such program yet exists, such programs deserve to be explored.

Woody Plant Demography

Demographic approaches to inferring sustained browsing impacts rely on characterizing the distribution of size or age classes within a population and comparing these to expectations based on how these would look with reduced or no browsing (as already discussed for herbaceous indicators above). As ungulate densities increase, medium sized plants tend to be hit hardest by browsing. Anderson and Loucks (1979) pioneered this approach by tallying the numbers of seedlings, saplings, and trees of various size to compile a demographic profile and using these to compare profiles among stands known or thought to differ in deer browse intensity. Similar methods have been used now to infer browse impacts on white pine in southwestern Wisconsin (Ziegler 1995). The method has now been extended using path analysis models to track the effects of several abiotic and biotic variables on the survival and growth of seedlings and saplings in progressively larger size classes (e.g., in eastern hemlock and northern white cedar) (Waller et al. 1996b; Rooney et al. 2000, 2002).

Vila et al. (2001, 2003) pioneered the use of a different technique—dendrochronology involving bud-scale scars, scars from antler scrapes, and historical variation in growth rates—to infer when particular stems were released from browsing on the Queen Charlotte Islands, Canada. These methods proved valuable for inferring a chronology of when past ungulate impacts occurred. However, they require some time and effort, preventing quick use in the field.

Island Studies and Other "Natural Experiments"

Landscapes differ considerably in deer density and impacts due to differences in history, management, or environmental conditions. Such variation can provide "natural experiments" for assessing the impacts of deer (Diamond, 1983). Perhaps the most obvious such experiments occur in archipelagos where islands differ in their history of deer occupancy and/or deer densities. For example, in the Apostle Islands in Lake Superior, deer are absent from some islands, abundant on others, have disappeared from some islands, and have recently invaded others. Deer quickly browse down clumps of Canada yew (*Taxus canadensis*) after being introduced while yew remains abundant on deer-free islands like Raspberry Island (fig. 16.5). Balgooyen and Waller (1995) documented that deer conspicuously reduce not only yew but also striped maple (*Acer spicatum* Larn.), yellow birch (*Betula allegheniensis*), mountain ash (*Sorbus decora* [Sarg.] C. K. Schneid.), blue-bead lily (*Clintonia borealis*), and wild sarsaparilla (*Aralia nudicaulis* L.). Furthermore, these impacts tracked deer abundance from 30+ years ago more closely than recent abundances, showing that these impacts have inertia and persist for decades.

Researchers in Haida Gwaii (the Queen Charlotte Islands) in British Columbia have also studied the impacts of introduced Sitka black-tailed deer on west coast forests. Impacts on the ericaceous shrub salal (*Gaultheria shallon* Pursch) there are as dramatic as impacts on yew in the Apostle Islands. Deer there greatly alter forest understories with subsequent cascading effects on invertebrates, nesting birds, and forest dynamics (Allombert et al. 2005a,b; Stockton et al. 2005). On the main island, hunting has some effect, partially ameliorating the strong effects of deer on seedlings of Western red cedar (*Thuja plicata* Donn ex D. Don) (Martin and Baltzinger 2002). Similarly dramatic evidence of overbrowsing and shifts in forest structure are evident on Anticosti Island in Quebec where white-tailed deer were introduced around 1900. There, foresters routinely employ huge exclosures (10–20 km2) to ensure regeneration, and deer must subsist mostly on balsam fir and bark lichens (Sauvé and Coté 2006).

Deer impacts are easy to document in such archipelagos where different islands provide dramatic evidence of deer impacts. However, the comparisons they provide are extreme—between areas with no deer and those with high densities. This tends to exaggerate deer effects relative to those found under more intermediate deer densities (perhaps more relevant to deer managers). It is therefore worth seeking out particular areas within a region that display more moderate differences in deer abundance and impacts. In the upper Midwest, such areas exist in the form of Indian reservations where differences in forest and wildlife management lead to significantly lower deer densities (e.g., about 10 per square mile in the Menominee reservation relative to 15–30 in nearby public lands in Wisconsin). These differences in ambient deer densities translate into conspicuous differences in the demographic profiles and patterns of regeneration in eastern hemlock (*Tsuga canadensis*) and northern white cedar (*Thuja occidentalis*) (Rooney et al. 2000, 2002). The broader range of variation in deer densities and impacts across the region can also be used to study deer impacts, as in our study of how hemlock regeneration varies among sites in response to contrasting summer deer densities (as inferred from the SMBI previously discussed) (Waller and Alverson 1997).

Experimental Enclosures and Exclosures

The most obvious way to evaluate whether deer are having impacts on plant communities is to build a fence. If the fence surrounds an area lacking deer, you have an exclosure that eliminates browsing impacts altogether, and you can monitor the differences in plant growth and survival between matched areas with zero and ambient deer densities and how these accumulate over time. If some deer occur within the fence, you can count them and use data from the enclosure to monitor the effects of that known density of deer. These, in turn, can be compared to areas lacking deer (inside an exclosure) or ambient deer densities (outside). Enclosures or exclosures generally involve a sustained investment of time, money, and effort but represent a valuable standard for judging other methods.

Enclosures allow one to assess deer impacts at levels other than zero and ambient densities (McShea and Rappole 1997). For example, McCullough's (1984) work in the George Reserve in southern Michigan used a fenced area to assess the dynamics of deer populations and impacts. Controlled experiments using known deer density in enclosures also provide realistic comparisons for inferring whole community responses to manipulated deer densities—provided they are large enough and cover relevant habitat types (Tilghman 1989; deCalesta 1994b; Hester et al. 2000; McShea and Rappole 2000; Coté et al. 2003; Horsley et al. 2003).

Fenced exclosures are also valuable for monitoring how deer impacts accumulate over time (outside the fence) and the potential for plant communities to recover from browsing (inside the fence). By maximizing the difference in deer densities, they are often able to provide clear results in a relatively short period of time. However, these extreme comparisons are also considered by some to be artificial in that areas with no deer were historically scarce. Placing exclosures in particular areas (e.g., conifer deer yards or upland deciduous stands) allows us to evaluate how deer impacts vary from place to place. Exclosures in a New Jersey national park doubled the survival of nine native herbaceous perennials over three years and allowed flowering and fruit dispersal in a manner that did not occur outside the fence (Ruhren and Handel 2003b). Such studies are clearly highly relevant for restoring forest understory communities.

We can also use exclosures to construct additional experiments (e.g., by fencing off individuals of particular species for a comparative study of their growth and demography). If suitable wild individuals are scarce, we can also plant seeds or seedlings as phytometers into and outside fenced areas to monitor their differential responses over time. Such studies have existed for more than 50 years and continue to be actively employed to assess deer impacts (Stewart and Burrows 1989; Allison 1990; Anderson and Katz 1993; Ruhren and Dudash 1996; Augustine and Frelich 1998). We use exclosures in this way to track the differential survival and growth of hemlock seedlings in response to hare and deer (Alverson and Waller 1997) and how deer impacts interact with those from garlic mustard, a weedy invasive (Waller and Maas 2013).

Data from exclosures gain value over time as differences in growth and survival accrue. They gain further value if the exclosures are replicated over a region and monitored regularly using a consistent sampling scheme both in- and outside the fence. To be most useful, exclosures should be large enough to provide suitable sampling areas. They should be securely built to block deer access and withstand accidents and falling branches. The aperture of the fencing can be adjusted to exclude only deer or deer and smaller mammals, allowing us to distinguish the effects of deer from those of other browsers like snowshoe hare. Finally, exclosures have great value for providing visually arresting demonstrations of how deer affect plant growth and density. Such demonstrations are of great value for convincing a skeptical public of the severity of deer impacts.

Exclosures also entail costs, including the initial cost of constructing a rugged fence and the continuing costs involved in monitoring plots and maintaining fences. These can be substantial for larger and/or replicated exclosures particularly when fences are placed into mature forests subject to falling branches and trees. Despite the insights that enclosure studies provide, they also have limitations. Most obviously, they provide an extreme comparison to the artificial situation of no deer (like islands lacking deer). Such conditions may be outside the historical range of variation and leave unclear just how deer at intermediate densities affect plants. Another source of uncertainty concerns the history of browsing before the fence was erected. Heavy past browsing may limit the local pool of species and propagules preventing even fenced plots from being able to recover from browsing (the "ghost of herbivory past"). This, plus slow growth, may explain why Kraft et al. (2004) found no significant difference in species richness and cover after five years in- and outside exclosures in the western Upper Peninsula of Michigan and why Webster et al. (2005b) found recovery within exclosures in the

Great Smoky Mountains National Park to be largely limited to species that could persist under intense herbivory. It would thus be useful to extend exclosure studies to explore how proximity to other forest patches and the dispersal characteristics of individual species affect the ability of herb communities to recover from browsing.

Food Choice Experiments

Another experimental approach for understanding the impacts of deer on particular plant species involves the use of "cafeteria" trials to determine which foods deer prefer to eat. Such trials allow us to experimentally determine deer preferences for key nutrients under various conditions (Schwartz et al. 1980; Berteaux et al. 1998). Such experiments also allow one to titrate deer food preferences versus accessibility (Renaud et al. 2003) and demonstrate genetic differences in chemical defense levels between plant populations subject to historic browsing and those isolated from browsing (Vourc'h et al. 2001).

Long-Term Shifts in Community Composition and Structure

Another valuable method for assessing deer impacts involves using baseline data on plant populations and/or communities from decades ago to assess changes over the intervening interval. If deer impacts have been substantial over this interval, we expect declines in plant species favored by deer and increases in species known to resist or tolerate browsing. We generally find two general trends after heavy deer herbivory: a decline in browse-sensitive forbs, woody shrubs, and seedlings and increases in browse-tolerant grasses, sedges, and ferns. Shifts from dense, diverse understories to open woodlands are also often reported, but how open a stand is often reflects a subjective determination by an observer. To translate these reports from anecdotes to science requires solid and ideally quantitative historical data. Without such data, we face the missing baseline problem.

Resurveys of upland forests in northern Wisconsin some 50 years after the classic vegetation surveys by J. T. Curtis and his colleagues reveal that local understory species richness has declined by nearly 20 percent, with sites also converging in composition (Rooney et al. 2004). A recent exclosure study confirms that many of these shifts reflect the effects of deer. More than 40% of the regional changes in abundance over the past 50 years in the more abundant plant species are accounted for by differential growth across exclosure fences (Frerker et al., in review). These changes reflect declines in lilies and other uncommon and conspicuous native species known to be favored by deer and dramatic increases in native grasses, sedges, and some ferns (Wiegmann and Waller 2006). These winning species typically display traits that allow them to tolerate herbivory (i.e., plants with high fiber and low nutrition content, low meristems, etc.) and may further act to limit tree seedling regeneration (chapter 13, this volume).

Using a simpler historical survey (based only on species lists), Rooney and Dress (1997) showed that beech stands in Pennsylvania lost most (59 percent and 80 percent) of their ground flora between 1929 and 1995. They attributed many of these losses to the direct and indirect effects of deer. A continental review reveals that 141 plant taxa are negatively affected by white-tailed deer, some 11 percent of the vascular plant species present in its range (Crête et al. 2001).

Shifts in Palatability

Declines in palatable species and increases in less nutritious species support the hypothesis that deer strongly affect forest understory communities. Can we quantify this and perhaps construct an index of community palatability to infer past deer impacts and/or track deer impacts over time? Such an index might be based on a combination of deterrents like the tannin or fiber content of plant tissues and/or nutrients like N or protein levels. Other plant traits, such as leaf toughness and height, also seem likely to affect plant susceptibility to browsing. If we could determine just which plant traits best predict changes in plant species abundance in response to deer herbivory, we could combine data on these traits into a composite indicator. As deer force declines in plant palatability, we should expect this indicator to shift. Such an approach reflects current interest in using plant functional traits to predict community composition and dynamics (Gondard et al. 2003; Cingolani et al. 2005; Suding et al. 2005; Williams et al. 2005; Mayfield et al. 2006; Roy and de Blois 2006).

Although no one has yet constructed a community indicator of cumulative deer impacts, the variation we observe among species and the changes in nutritional values in Wisconsin forests over time support its feasibility (Waller, unpubl. data). The first step would be to determine which traits best predict susceptibility or resistance/tolerance to deer (using either experiments or field observations) and to test how stable these rankings are over sites or community types. These traits might then be weighted to produce a composite palatability indicator for each species. Alternatively, we could compute a community average of the various trait values for all species present at a site, weighted by their abundance, and combine these community mean values into a composite index for the community. The advantage of this approach is that such an index could be readily computed from data for any plant community once the species trait values were known. Such an index thus has the potential to provide a simple and reliable tool that forest and wildlife managers could use to monitor and compare deer impacts (e.g., as forests recover following deer control efforts). This approach assumes that these trait values are species-specific and reliable indicators of susceptibility to deer. If this were not the case for some problematic species, they might be excluded from the index.

HOW SHOULD WE ASSESS AND COMBINE THESE APPROACHES?

Each of these methods has particular advantages and disadvantages in terms of assessing browse impacts. Ideally, we should study the sampling properties and error statistics associated with each approach under a variety of conditions. This would allow us to consider their relative efficiency and reliability. It would also help us to decide which methods to use under different circumstances (low versus high deer density, coniferous versus broad-leafed forests, or another circumstance). We should also cross-calibrate these methods by applying them side-by-side under similar conditions in the field to assess how comparable they are (Waller et al. 2009).

Although these methods were employed separately in the various studies cited, ecologists should also explore ways in which these different methods could complement each other (e.g., at different deer densities). Given the relevance of deer impact work for forest and wildlife management, we need metrics that are consistent and well tested. We should also seek to combine data from the different methods to produce composite indicators of browse intensity, combining the best qualities of each. Such composite indicators might combine data on direct browsing on woody species with trait or population data from herbaceous indicators. They might also encompass community data by combining data from many species at a site as with the palatability index proposed above. With suitable development and testing, such composite indicators could prove more reliable, accurate, and efficient than single variable indicators.

HOW DO DEER IMPACTS AND PATTERNS OF RECOVERY VARY?

Patterns of Browsing Are Patchy and Often Localized

The impacts of deer browsing are often local and patchy, particularly in forests that have not been browsed heavily and to the point of homogenization. This reflects local heterogeneity in where deer forage, which, in turn, reflects many factors including the availability, size, and condition of preferred food plants. Because female deer are philopatric, local patterns of deer distributions also have inertia and local reductions in deer may protect that area for 10–15 years (Porter et al. 1991; McNulty et al. 1997). Locally dense patches of woody debris can also provide local refugia to enhance the survival of otherwise vulnerable species (Ripple and Larsen 1991). Dense fir patches can protect hemlock seedlings, enhancing their survival (Borgmann et al. 1999). Regardless of its basis, such patchiness and its impacts can act to maintain overall diversity by enhancing local beta diversity and providing at least temporary refuges for browse-sensitive species. As noted earlier, the presence of deer can also prevent highly competitive species like Canada yew from dominating sites, also enhancing diversity.

Local variation in deer densities and impacts complicates our efforts to estimate deer densities and average levels of browse by inflating the sampling variance for metrics like scat group counts and the SMBI. These therefore typically require large sample sizes to perform reliably. This was part of the rationale for Morellet et al. (2003) to develop their browsing index based on simple scores of the presence or absence of browse and woody twigs across many sampling points. Composite indicators based on multiple species, traits, and sites could also average deer impacts over time and space so as to control sampling variance and improve reliability.

Deer Impacts Also Vary over Time

Deer densities and impacts also vary over time as deer populations fluctuate and as the plants they feed on experience either declines in abundance or periods of recovery. In the upper Midwest, these fluctuations appear to reflect levels of timber harvest (particularly pulpwood clearcuts), the severity of winters (in terms of both snow and extreme temperatures), and hunting intensity. As winters have become milder, local habitat features like timber cutting and hunting pressure have probably become more important. These fluctuations could provide refugia for browse-sensitive species, provided they lasted long enough for woody plants to outgrow their vulnerability or for smaller plants to complete their reproductive cycle. However, most shade-tolerant understory plants grow slowly and support limited seed dispersal, prolonging their period of vulnerability and diminishing their ability to persist or recolonize at a site. As mature forest stands become smaller and more isolated from one another, opportunities for local recolonization (the "rescue effect", Brown and Kodric-Brown 1977) decline further. This effect is already evident in southern Wisconsin upland forests (Rogers et al. 2009).

Deer Impacts Depend on Local Factors, Deer Density, and Plant Density

The impacts of deer browsing can also depend on complex interactions with other environmental factors. Across 60 aspen stands, the effects of higher deer density in reducing forbs while increasing bracken fern and sedges increased greatly at sites with a lower site index (a measure of site fertility and ability to support tree growth) (Randall and Walters 2011). Similar interactions appear to be prevalent in other studies of deer impacts (Martin and Baltzinger 2002; Ruhren and Handel 2003b; Morrison and Brown 2004; Eschtruth and Battles 2008; Collard et al. 2010, Royo et al. 2010).

Deer impacts depend on deer density in that more deer will clearly eat more plant tissue. However, deer impacts also depend on "prey" (food plant) density in a way that is not commonly understood. For example, when the native wood nettle *Laportea canadensis* (L.) Weddell was abundant in woodlots in southern Minnesota, deer browsing had little effect on its populations. In contrast, in forests where this species was less abundant, deer browsing sharply reduced its density (Augustine and Frelich 1998). Such nonlinear effects could quickly drive a species extinct once it dropped below a certain threshold, creating persistent alternative stable states that depend on the history of both deer and plant density.

Why Is Recovery from Deer Browsing Slow?

Over time, we expect forest herb layers to shift as they respond to both the direct effects of deer herbivory and the indirect effects of changing canopy conditions. Such changes in the canopy will themselves act to shift the composition of herb layers given the links between over- and understories (chapter 9, this volume; Gilliam 2007). Thus, we can expect forest herb layers to respond directly and quickly to sudden increases in browsing pressure, followed by slower responses to continued browsing as these species respond to declines in shrub and sapling cover but increases in browse-tolerant and resistant competitors including invasive species that may alter litter and soil conditions. Shifts in canopy composition and density will eventually force further changes. For reasons already elaborated, recovery from any and all of these impacts following reductions in browsing pressure could be slow and via an altogether different trajectory, a phenomenon sometimes referred to as "ecological hysteresis" (Sternberg 2001).

It should now be clear why deer browse impacts can be so persistent. Slow-growing, shade-tolerant plants are by their nature slow to recover from any disturbance. Short growing seasons in more northern latitudes may further limit growth. *Erythronium americanum* and *Maianthemum canadense* exhibited limited recovery within exclosures in Quebec remaining at the single-leaf stage after eight years of protection (Collard et al. 2010). Even low-level browsing may also eliminate chances for pollination and/or dispersal, further slowing or preventing recovery particularly when populations are low. These and other density-dependent Allee effects may limit the ability of populations to recover from low densities. As deer overabundance becomes more pervasive and chronic, populations of many of these species will decline further or disappear, further limiting opportunities for recolonization.

Another factor that can delay recovery from heavy browsing in many forests are the "recalcitrant understory layers" of sedges, hay-scented or bracken fern, or exotic invasive plants that often come to dominate the understory vegetation when deer herbivory is high (De La Cretaz and Kelty 2002b; Royo and Carson 2006). These layers have been noted in forests around the world (e.g., in the Quabbin reservoir area of western Massachusetts where a thick layer of hay-scented fern covered 4,000 ha of oak-pine forest [De La Cretaz and Kelty 2002a]). About 15 years of intensive browsing after canopy thinning allowed the ferns to form this layer with densities of > 90 fronds/m^2 at a height of 60–80 cm (De La Cretaz and Kelty 2002b). The species that dominate these recalcitrant layers tend to be clonal, fast growing, fairly intolerant of shade, but tolerant of fire and tolerant of, or resistant to, herbivores (Royo and Carson 2006). They act to suppress the growth of many native forbs and tree seedlings, reducing both plant diversity and forest tree regeneration (De La Cretaz and Kelty 2002a). Such layers also raise the specter that deer are driving forests into alternate stable states that are difficult or impossible to reverse (Stromayer and Warren 1997).

Given that plant populations and communities can be slow to recover from deer impacts, we may need to employ active recovery and restoration efforts to accelerate this process. Efforts to restore native plant diversity following sustained deer herbivory face several difficulties. First, adequate seed sources and conditions suitable for their germination must be present. Prior dense deer populations and heavy invasions of exotic weedy plants and earthworms may have substantially altered soil conditions (nutrients, structure, and allelochemic levels). Thus, reducing deer densities alone may not suffice to ensure recovery. Second, the impacts from renewed deer herbivory must be reduced to levels that will allow survival, growth, and reproduction for long enough to allow recovery, which may be many years. Finally, such plants must be present in sufficient numbers and densities to ensure adequate pollination and dispersal opportunities once they reach reproductive maturity. The viability of populations may be threatened at any of these stages. Other threats to diversity, aside from and in addition to deer, may also be present. Many of these processes may be cryptic or act in combination with deer (as previously discussed). Thus, our ability to perceive what the true limiting factors are in particular situations will often be limited. Again, we see the value of exploring the effects of multiple factors, particularly when this can be done under experimental conditions where outcomes can be monitored over time.

MONITORING AND MANAGEMENT

The many studies of deer impacts over the past 30 years cited above expose a complex mix of factors affecting our forests via herbivory. We understand that deer have a remarkably broad range of impacts and that these impacts interact with site conditions, disturbances, and other species to modify the outcomes we observe. Although deer impacts can be severe and long-lasting, our current knowledge should allow us to adaptively monitor and manage them to avert further widespread declines in biotic diversity and promote the restoration of this diversity.

The number, range, complexity, and significance of deer impacts on forest plant communities make it vital that we monitor these and devise management strategies to mitigate them when they cause serious declines in plant diversity or tree regeneration. However, the complexity of deer impacts and the diverse ways in which herb layers respond to browsing create substantial challenges. My goal here is to emphasize their importance and the uncertainties we face. Interested readers should also consult the excellent edited volume by McShea et al. (1997), the issue of the Wildlife Society Bulletin dedicated to these topics (1997, Vol. 25), and websites covering ongoing debates regarding deer management.

Great Needs, Many Challenges, Few Resources

As we have seen in this chapter, we have learned a lot in recent decades about how deer affect both individual species and forest community composition and dynamics. Given the number and significance of deer impacts on forest communities, we should expect state and federal agencies to dedicate time and resources to address these challenges by collecting extensive data, sharing useful ideas, developing standardized and reliable methods for monitoring deer impacts, and integrating their research and monitoring data into effective regional networks to manage deer in a coordinated and effective way. Unfortunately, this is not yet the case. We still lack comprehensive surveys of the extent, severity, and longevity of deer impacts across forests of various types. We also lack an integrated understanding of how deer herbivory acts, alone and in combination with invading species, recalcitrant layers, climate change, and other factors over years, to restructure forest herb layers. These interactions are significant in individual studies, but we have yet to test their generality or form a complete picture of how they play out. We do not yet base deer management on deer impacts on their environment. Agencies have yet to develop coordinated approaches or to enlist hunters and the public in helping them to collect data. And game biologists have yet to apply our current knowledge of deer-habitat dynamics to manage deer conservatively so as to sustain habitat quality for both deer and other species. To achieve these goals, academic and agency specialists will need to forge new networks and bridge the gaps between research, monitoring, and management.

Why and How Should We Monitor Deer Herbivory?

We need better and more extensive monitoring of deer impacts for several reasons including *early detection*—to detect and respond to increases in deer herbivory that may threaten biodiversity, particularly in protected natural areas. Because they have historically restricted hunting, many state and national parks have ironically suffered particularly acute impacts from deer (Bratton 1979; Warren 1991; Hadidian 1993; Webster and Parker 1997; Porter and Underwood 1999; Webster et al. 2005b; Brown and Parker 2009). If monitoring systems had been in place in these parks, the problem would have been detected sooner, allowing for earlier remedies. An early detection network would also allow us to track how forests respond to shifts in logging practices or hunting regulations in real time, facilitating true adaptive management (Holling and Meffe 1996).

Another reason to expand routine monitoring is to *track levels of deer herbivory and overall community responses over time*. Student theses and research grants rarely support on-going monitoring and agencies have been remiss in establishing these. This has left conspicuous gaps in our knowledge regarding the longer-term dynamics of how forest herb layers simplify over time in response to continued or increased browsing and how they recover once browsing pressure declines. Only sustained and widespread monitoring programs will allow us to assess the short- and longer-term ecological impacts of deer browsing. While some populations and species appear resilient and able to recover quickly from browsing, other populations and species are sensitive to browsing and slow to recover, particularly in fragmented habitats. The data accumulated in monitoring programs would allow us to evaluate not only how browsing affects particular plant species and communities but also the conditions that favor their recovery.

To monitor deer impacts in a comprehensive and sustained way is neither simple nor cheap. Nevertheless, such efforts are cheaper and arguably more useful than expending resources to try to accurately estimate and track deer populations. Estimating deer densities is notoriously labor-intensive and subject to error. Agency estimates like the sex-age-kill model used in Wisconsin apply only to large regions, rely on sometimes questionable assumptions, and are not trusted by many hunters. In general, assessing the impacts of deer browsing using methods like those reviewed in this chapter would be cheaper and more useful for managing deer. Encouragingly, Pennsylvania has recently moved toward basing their deer management activities directly on the results of forest vegetation monitoring rather than trying to monitor deer populations (Latham et al. 2009).

Monitoring could take any of several forms but should be designed carefully to maximize the value of the data returned, given limited monitoring funds. Any such program should be efficient in terms of time and money, simple to administer, sustained, and capable of delivering reliable results soon enough to allow timely adjustments in deer and forest management. This is particularly important for public lands where hunters may compete keenly for limited hunting opportunities.

Given that herb layers respond to increased levels of browsing faster than forest overstories, we should focus monitoring on understory plant communities. The more direct measures of browse like Morellet's index give us a picture of contemporary browsing impacts, but also one that may often reflect effects of past browsing pressure if the composition of woody browse in the molar zone has already shifted toward browse-tolerant or resistant species. In areas where ungulate pressure has been high for a long time, tree composition changes due to browse can reduce or altogether eliminate tree species sensitive to browsing (Blewett 1976). More integrative measures of cumulative browsing impacts, including shifts in demographic profiles and community composition, are better suited for assessing the longer-term impacts of browsing. With suitable baseline data, we can use these to plan our tactics for restoring forest herb layers and track their success.

Ideally, we should seek to build an extensive and coordinated network to monitor deer across multiple regions. Coordinated state agencies or federal leadership could facilitate the use of standardized and reliable methods. The Forest Inventory and Analysis (FIA) program of the USDA Forest Service (http://www.fia.

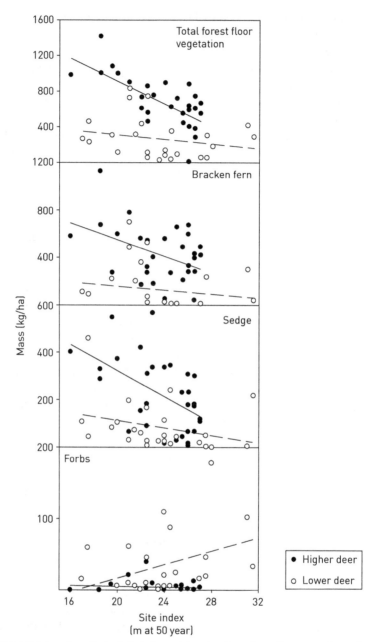

FIGURE 16.7 Interacting effects of site index and deer density on forest floor vegetation and particular plant groups across 60 aspen stands in Michigan. Note contrasting effects on ferns and sedges versus forbs. From Randall et al. (2011) with permission of the author and Elsevier.

fs.fed.us/) holds promise for such a program in already employing a dispersed grid of repeated vegetation surveys across all forestlands of the U.S. The program was originally designed to estimate standing timber volumes and growth rates, but is now being used to track shifts in forest composition (e.g., Rentch and Hicks 2005). More recently, it was extended to monitor forest health and understory conditions. Although the scanty understory sampling (12 x 1m² quadrats) limits the inferences we can make about understory composition and change at individual sites (Johnson et al. 2008), it could be extended to include more quadrats and tallies of woody plant browsing (fig. 16.7).

Management Issues

Professional wildlife managers face a complex social and political landscape and must make important and timely decisions with limited data at hand. They hear often from vocal constituencies of hunters and animal lovers, but rarely from disinterested scientists or the public. They also know that most of their funding derives from hunting license fees. They have little time and few incentives to develop coordinated programs to monitor deer impacts. Lacking reliable data and models on impacts and facing pressure to appease hunters, they find it difficult to coax hunters away from their strong preferences for hunting bucks rather than does and limiting harvests so as to maintain abundant deer. Additional factors like declining hunter numbers and restricted access to private lands further restrict their ability to curtail deer numbers via management.

In response to our growing understanding of deer impacts, many wildlife managers are seeking ways to reformulate game management by expanding hunting opportunities, favoring doe hunting, and limiting baiting and feeding. However, such efforts in Wisconsin met vehement opposition by many hunters who bypassed professional managers altogether by taking their concerns directly to state legislators. Such a climate makes many game biologists reluctant to launch new initiatives to monitor or control deer.

Given the social and political minefield that game managers and state agencies face in struggling to address deer overabundance, we need to forge stronger links between academic ecologists and wildlife professionals. In particular, we need to share ideas and resources both to augment scientific research on deer impacts and to implement monitoring programs to provide managers with timely information. Solid science and monitoring data will also be needed to alert the public to the nature and severity of deer impacts and the consequent need to support deer control efforts. Creating a "citizen science" monitoring program would be particularly valuable here for expanding public interest in deer impacts and broadening the basis for deer management decisions. The popularity of deer and forests could allow public agencies to save dollars while accumulating valuable information, provided these systems were well designed to provide useful and high-quality data. Involving hunters would improve their knowledge of deer impacts and ecological dynamics. Involving high school teachers and students would broaden public understanding of these issues and demonstrate how field surveys and simple experiments (like exclosures with plant phytometers) can enhance our ability to draw important inferences about complex ecological phenomena. We should also discuss deer impacts in hunter training courses so that hunters appreciate their significance and the key role they play as human predators. By injecting science and data more effectively into deer and forest management, such programs could greatly enhance our ability to manage deer and forests as a coupled system.

17 A Pox on our Land

A Case Study of Chronic Deer Overbrowsing throughout the Allegheny National Forest Region of Pennsylvania

Walter P. Carson, Alejandro A. Royo, and Chris J. Peterson

In a recent article in *Science*, Estes et al. (2011) reported on the deleterious consequences of the loss of apex consumers in biomes worldwide. This is especially true for Pennsylvania where the extirpation of mountain lions and wolves in the early 20th century and lax game management have led to overabundant populations of white-tailed deer since at least the 1930s (Redding 1995; Latham et al. 2005). For decades, herd sizes in the Allegheny National Forest Region (ANFR) have been more than twice as high as specific goals that were historically set by the state agency responsible for wildlife management, the Pennsylvania Game Commission (PGC), and almost always higher than levels compatible with healthy forest regeneration (Redding 1995; Horsley et al. 2003). The situation in 2001 caused the National Audubon Society and the Pennsylvania Habitat Alliance to appoint a panel of experts to address this issue. Their lengthy and thorough report strongly recommended reductions in the size of the state's deer herd (Latham et al. 2005).

Shortly before this group convened, the PGC in 1999 chose a highly respected wildlife biologist, Dr. Gary Alt, to head the section responsible for statewide deer management. Alt concluded that the "lack of science-based management" at the PGC was harming forests, as well as the sport of hunting, and that deer populations had to come down statewide (Marshall 2005). Alt's message was often so unpopular that he received death threats leading him to wear a bulletproof vest during hostile meetings with sportsmen's groups (Gary Alt, pers. comm.). In 2003, Dr. Alt received the Quality Deer Management Association's Professional Deer Manager of the Year Award in specific recognition of his work to bring the Pennsylvania deer herd into balance with its habitat. Unfortunately, Dr. Alt was forced out of his leadership position in the PGC in 2004, and despite some progress, the problems of deer overabundance and the degraded habitat they create remain a significant challenge in many parts of the state including the ANFR.

While the practice of wildlife management does not always garner widespread attention from diverse stakeholders, it often does in Pennsylvania. Indeed, Frye (2006) devoted an entire book to the bitter politics of deer management in Pennsylvania, and MacDonald (2005) addressed similar issues within the ANFR. Sportsmen decry forests with "too few deer" and loudly press for stricter bag limits while a broad spectrum of stakeholders from farmers to foresters to conservationists plead for sound deer management that puts forest health first (Diefenbach et al. 1997; Frye 2006). While such politics lie outside the scope of this chapter, decades of lax deer management combined with the loss of large carnivores seriously threaten the herbaceous layer statewide, and this is particularly true in the ANFR. In spite of overwhelming empirical evidence that overbrowsing threatens forest biodiversity and degrades habitat, the politics surrounding deer management impede attempts at mitigation (for Pennsylvania, see Diefenbach et al. 1997; Frye 2006; MacDonald 2005; Latham et al. 2005; and for broader regions, see Levy 2006; Waller 2012; chapter 14, this volume).

In this chapter, we quantify the demise of herbs and shrubs throughout the ANFR as a consequence of long-term deer mismanagement. This region lies in northwestern Pennsylvania on the unglaciated Allegheny Plateau and encompasses well over 200,000 ha of forested land, most of which is made up of the Allegheny National Forest, although the Pennsylvania Bureau of Forestry, the PGC, and private logging concerns also manage large parcels. The forest is part of the hemlock-northern hardwoods association and includes two well-known tracts of old-growth forest, Heart's Content and the Tionesta Scenic Area. For details of climate, soils, topography, and history, see Marquis (1975) and Bjorkbom and Larson (1977).

Our goals here are to (1) quantify the deleterious impact that overbrowsing has on both herbs and shrubs focusing entirely on the ANFR; (2) describe how overbrowsing has led to recalcitrant understory layers that are inimical to the recovery of a diverse herb layer (legacy effects); (3) quantify the long-term changes in herb abundance following a tornado that destroyed the canopy of a large old-growth forest, the Tionesta Scenic Area; and (4) report preliminary results of a large-scale study (~ 32,000 ha) designed to mitigate the impact of overbrowsing and evaluate the potential for the recovery of herbaceous species.

THE IMPACT OF OVERBROWSING ON THE DIVERSITY AND ABUNDANCE OF HERBS AND SHRUBS

Fully evaluating the degree that browsing has changed vegetation is difficult because deer have been regionally overabundant for decades, thus reference or control sites are rare. Indeed Dr. Susan Stout, a U.S. Forest Service scientist working in the ANFR for more than 25 years concluded, "We think we know our forests. But in Pennsylvania and many other parts of the northeast, deer overabundance has changed our forests so much and for so long that we truly don't know how our forests would look without too many deer" (Stout and Horsley 2004). Here, we try to quantify how our forests might look in the understory without a plague of deer (sensu Levy 2006). We do this using three types of data from the ANFR: retrospective studies, natural deer refugia, and deer fences.

Retrospective Studies

Rooney and Dress (1997a) compared changes in herb and shrub species richness between 1929 and 1995 in 160 1 m² plots within a 50 ha old-growth forest remnant (Heart's Content) containing two forest types (hemlock and hemlock-beech, see Lutz 1930). The same exact plots were not resampled but were the same size and arrayed in a similar randomized fashion. They found an 80 percent (33 total) and 59 percent (16 species) loss of species in the hemlock-beech and hemlock types, respectively, by 1995. The least common species (< 1 percent) present in 1929 were the most likely to disappear. Family richness declined from 27 in 1929 to 10 in 1995 while two fern species (*Dennstaedtia punctilobula* [Michx.] T. Moore and *Dryopteris intermedia* [Muhl. Ex Willd.] A. Gray syn = *D. carthusiana*) increased significantly in abundance.

A second resurvey was conducted in 2000 where Lutz's (1930) original 160 plots were relocated and all herbs and shrubs were tallied visually throughout the stand (Ristau unpubl. data; Latham et al. 2005). All but seven of the species originally found by Lutz were relocated. Nonetheless, many of these species were far less common and thus vulnerable to local extinction. For example, the shrub *Viburnum alnifolium* Marsh. was found in 50 percent of the original plots in 1929, but none were found in 2000. Still, a small number of suppressed individuals of *V. alnifolium* were found at the site. This suggests vulnerable or preferred browse species may persist at low densities perhaps because they become less conspicuous to browsers or are hidden within dense patches of unpalatable species (e.g., Borgmann et al. 1999).

Overall, these studies demonstrate significant reductions in both species richness and abundance. It is difficult of course to attribute all changes solely to overbrowsing because other factors may have changed during the period between surveys. Still, the fact that the species lost are typically preferred browse species (Latham et al. 2005) leaves little doubt that browsing is responsible. Indeed, Rooney and Dress (1997a) attributed the loss of species solely to overbrowsing, as did Hough (1965), who 30 years earlier documented understory collapse at the nearby Tionesta old-growth remnant using repeated photographs over 20 years. Hough warned in the final sentence of his paper, "Unless some way is found to keep animal populations, such as deer, in balance in this particular forest stand, the objectives of scientific study, public education, and historic value will inevitably be lost." A walk through Heart's Content or the Tionesta Scenic Area today confirms Hough's prescient predictions.

Natural Deer Refugia

In some cases, natural obstacles preclude deer access, and these areas serve as refugia from browsing. These include large tree tip-up mounds, slash piles, and perhaps most importantly, boulders that are large (often > 100 m² on top) and flat enough to support vegetation (Grisez 1960; Rooney 1997; Long et al. 1998; Banta et al. 2005; Comisky et al. 2005; Krueger and Peterson 2006, 2009). Other potential refugia include urban habitats with small forest patches lacking deer, steep slopes, cliffs, and dry hummocks enmeshed within wet areas. For example, in southeastern Pennsylvania, Loeffler and Wegner (2000) found that dry hummocks were a likely refuge from browsing for the globally rare glade spurge *Euphorbia purpurea* (Raf.) Fernald.

The diversity, abundance, and performance of herbs and shrubs in refugia may provide a picture of how understories might have appeared prior to decades of over-browsing. For example, Comisky et al. (2005) quantified the number of herbs that produced an inflorescence on the tops of 12 tall boulders (inaccessible to deer), on short boulders, and on adjacent areas of the same size on the soil surface (total area ~ 375 m²). Forbs on tall boulders produced 1,338 flowering individuals whereas adjacent areas produced only 6 flowering individuals. Mean species richness was nine times higher on these refugia versus off (tall boulder = 4.6 per m², small boulder = 0.5 per m², $p < 0.001$).

Rooney (1997) found that the frequency of flowering of the forest herb *Maianthemum canadense* Desf. was 48 percent on tall boulders versus 5 percent on short boulders. Individuals of *M. canadense* on boulders were five times denser and also larger. The density and performance of the unpalatable species *Oxalis montana* Raf. (= *Oxalis acetosella* L. ssp. *montana* [Raf.] Hultén ex D. Löve) did not differ on and off the boulders. Because both Comisky et al. (2005) and Rooney (1997) used short boulders accessible to deer, as well as tall boulders, community and species level responses were unlikely due to environmental differences between the two locations.

Banta et al. (2005) found sharply contrasting communities in refugia versus non-refugia habitats; forbs and shrubs dominated boulder tops (~ 70 percent cover), whereas adjacent areas had no shrubs and were dominated by ferns, club mosses, and graminoids (~ 75 percent cover). These boulder tops have been called rock refugia gardens (Comisky et al. 2005) and demonstrate that overbrowsing has created under-stories dominated by ferns and graminoids as opposed to shrubs and forbs.

Deer Exclosures and Enclosures

Replicated, long-term fenced deer exclosures (or enclosures) are perhaps the most rig-orous way to evaluate the long-term impact of overbrowsing; however, these fences are costly and require year-round maintenance. Thus, there are only a few long-term exclusion studies in the ANFR. Marquis (1981) used exclosures to evaluate the degree that deer browsing was the cause of regeneration failures following logging in the 1970s. Though focused primarily on tree regeneration, he found that browsing created an understory dominated by grasses and ferns. The response of forbs and shrubs was not reported.

Horsley et al. (2003) used a dose-response design to evaluate how increases in deer density (4, 8, 15, and 25 deer per km²) inside fenced enclosures (65 ha) caused changes in understory vegetation over a 10-year period at four locations scattered around the ANFR. The four doses represented densities spanning pre-settlement times to the present (Horsley et al. 2003). Within each enclosure, part of the canopy was clearcut, another part thinned, and the remainder left intact as a control, thus allowing the evaluation of understory response following contrasting silvicultural treatments. After 10 years in both the clearcut and thinned areas, the percent cover of ferns and graminoids increased from ~ 20 percent at the lowest deer density to ~ 50 percent or more at the highest density. Where the canopy was left intact inside the enclosures, increases in deer density did not significantly increase fern abundance but did cause a significant increase in graminoids. Thus, increases in deer density increased the abundance of ferns and graminoids, though this response was less pronounced beneath intact canopies.

Goetsch et al. (2011) compared the abundance and diversity of forbs and shrubs between a 60-year-old exclosure (0.4 ha, McKean County) and an adjacent reference site within a stand of intact forest. This is the oldest exclosure in the eastern deciduous forest. Browsing caused a biodiversity collapse creating a depauperate understory dominated by a single fern (*Dennstaedtia punctilobula*) and reduced the percent cover of forbs from 43 percent to less than 0.2 percent. Five species of shrubs were found inside the exclosure but none outside. Mean species richness at the plot scale (1 m² plots) was five times higher inside the fence. A survey of the entire site revealed 25 herb and shrub species inside the fence versus 10 outside. Browsing reduced the height of two indicator forb species (*Trillium erectum* L. and *Medeola virginiana* L.) by 40 percent. These findings for *Trillium* were nearly identical to those of Kirschbaum and Anaker (2005) who evaluated *Trillium* height and density in the Latham plot five years earlier. Overall, these types of depauperate herb layers have been documented elsewhere in the ANFR (Collins and Picket 1982; Peterson and Pickett 1995; Rooney and Dress 1997a), as well as in forests elsewhere (chapter 16, this volume).

Clearly, browsing has devastated the understory in this region. Some have argued that because fences exclude deer entirely, they do not provide an accurate image of what a natural understory would look like. Indeed, recent work by Royo, Collins et al. (2010) demonstrated that when deer are closer to pre-settlement levels, they promote forb diversity by reducing the abundance and competitive effects of fast-growing pioneer trees and shrubs. Thus, with small herd sizes, deer may promote herbaceous species diversity rather than decreasing it.

The Indirect Impact of Overbrowsing Has Led to Recalcitrant Understory Layers that Are Inimical to the Recovery of a Diverse Herb Layer

In the ANFR, the indirect effects of overbrowsing often create a dense and depauperate understory layer characterized by species that are both browse-tolerant (or unpalatable) and, to some degree, shade-tolerant. Royo and Carson (2006) termed this type of vegetation a recalcitrant understory layer because once established, it tends to persist for decades, is difficult to eradicate, and is highly browse-tolerant or unpalatable. For example, in the ANFR, overbrowsing has led to the spread of an unpalatable, native, rhizomatous fern (hay-scented *Dennstaedtia punctilobula*) that now forms dense layers in more than 60 percent of the understory throughout the ANFR (Royo and Carson 2006). Fern cover is negatively correlated with herb richness (Rooney and Dress 1997a; Krueger and Peterson 2009) because a dense fern layer provides a refuge for seed-eating rodents and casts deep shade, which together severely inhibit plant species establishment, growth, and survival (Horsley and Marquis 1983; Horsley 1993; George and Bazzaz 1999a, b; Royo and Carson 2008).

Overbrowsing has also indirectly led to the development of an understory woody layer that, like the fern layer, appears to be inimical to herbaceous species. This layer is typically composed of striped maple (*Acer pensylvanicum* L.) and saplings of American beech (*Fagus grandifolia* Ehrh.) (Bjorkbom and Larson 1977; Whitney 1984; Peterson and Pickett 1995; Banta 2005; Runkle 2007; Kain et al. 2011). Deer prefer neither of these species but will consume both when they have eliminated more preferred species (Horsley et al. 2003; Whitney 1984). In the case of beech, beech bark disease has caused high adult mortality (Runkle 2007); this in combination with browsing has stimu- lated the production of numerous root suckers, thereby creating a dense sapling layer that casts deep shade (mean = 6 stems per m²) (Peterson and Pickett 1995; see also Whitney 1984; Runkle 2007). Because these root suckers are clonally attached to larger saplings above the reach of deer, they continue to receive carbon from belowground connections (Jones and Raynal 1987) and thus are highly browse-tolerant (Kain et al. 2011). Striped maple appears to survive browsing because its stems are photosynthetic, and even heavy defoliation allows individuals to retain some photosynthetic tissue (Kain et al. 2011). Thus, two recalcitrant understory layers characterize many parts of the ANFR, one woody and one herbaceous. Both are likely to persist for decades and retard the reestablishment of a rich herbaceous layer; this makes immediate action even more imperative to reduce deer herds so the process of recovery can begin.

LONG-TERM RESPONSE OF THE HERB LAYER TO A LARGE-SCALE BLOWDOWN

Catastrophic canopy disturbances typically facilitate abundant regeneration of trees and shrubs, and establishment or expansion of herbaceous species that were rare or absent prior to the disturbance (Dunn et al. 1983; Rumbaitis del Rio 2006; Nelson et al. 2008; Turner 2010). Such responses are facilitated, at least in part, by increases in resource availability following canopy destruction (e.g., Royo et al. 2010a). Large-scale disturbances may also enhance herb layer vegetation by creating piles of woody debris and tip-up mounds, which provide vulnerable species with a refuge from browsing (Long et al. 1998; de Chantal and Granstrom 2007; Relva et al. 2009; Krueger and Peterson 2006; but see Krueger et al. 2009). Below, however, we report the results of the impact of a catastrophic disturbance within primary forest that had only a very modest impact on the herb and shrub layer, most likely due to legacy effects of decades of overbrowsing.

The Tionesta Scenic Area, along with the contiguous Tionesta Research Natural Area, form a large tract (1,673 ha) of primary forest near the center of ANFR that was free of large-scale disturbance for at least 350 years (Hough and Forbes 1943). On May 30, 1985, a category F4 tornado tracked across the center of ANFR, creat- ing a swath of near-complete canopy destruction over nearly 400 ha of the Tionesta Scenic Area (Peterson and Pickett 1991; Peterson and Carson 1996). Beginning in 1986, 344 vegetation quadrats (0.5 m²) were placed in a stratified random arrangement along three transects that ran perpendicular across the tornado swath; 289 were in the disturbed area itself (Peterson and Pickett 1991). Percent cover of all vascular plants and counts of woody seedlings (< 2 m tall) were recorded each August from 1986–1991 (Peterson and Pickett 1995). Woody regeneration was resurveyed in 1993, 1997, 2000, and 2004. In 2010, 149 of the original disturbed-area quadrats, as well as 10 quadrats within the intact forest, were resurveyed for all woody and herbaceous species. We have classified all herb layer species (sprawling shrubs, forbs, graminoids, ferns, and mosses) into preferred/intolerant versus not preferred/tolerant based on published findings (e.g., Horsley et al. 2003; Latham et al. 2005) and our collective experience with the natural history of the area. Note that here we use "tolerant" or "intolerant" in reference to browsing, not shade tolerance. We considered the following to be unpalatable or not sensitive: all mosses, grasses, sedges, ferns, *Viola* spp. L., *Oxalis montana*, and *Erechtites hieraciifolia* (L.) Raf. ex DC. Conversely, we considered the following to be palatable or browse sensitive: *Rubus allegheniensis* Porter, *Arisaema triphyllum* (L.) Schott, *Maianthemum canadense*, *Medeola virginiana*, *Trillium* spp. L., *Impatiens capensis* Meerb., *Chelone glabra* L., and *Aster* spp. L.

We quantified changes in abundances of common species and species richness for 25 years post-disturbance (1985–2010; figs. 17.1–17.4). Canopy destruction greatly enhanced light availability and should have fostered substantial increases in many plant species; however, increases were limited to a single shrub (*Rubus allegheniensis*) and a fern (*Dennstaedtia punctilobula*) (figs. 17.1 and 17.2) and although species richness increased following the disturbance, it remained low throughout the study and was low at the outset (fig. 17.3; see also Peterson and Pickett 1995). Overall, the only herbaceous species that increased substantially after disturbance was a species not eaten by deer, and only browse-tolerant species as a group showed increases in cover (fig. 17.4). In addition, browsing likely constrained the response of *Rubus allegheniensis*, which often can reach high abundance (> 60 percent cover) following large-scale disturbances in the ANFR, but only when browsing is low (e.g., Marquis 1981; Horsley et al. 2003). Evidence suggests that browsing was heavy within the blowdown. For example, Peterson and Pickett (2000) demonstrated experimentally that browsing caused substantial decreases in the growth and survivorship of *Acer rubrum* L. seedlings, and Krueger and Peterson (2006) found that hemlock seedlings (*Tsuga canadensis* (L.) Carrière) thrived only on tip-up mounds that served as a refuge from browsing (see also Long et al. 1998). Thus, our results suggest that decades of overbrowsing both before and after a catastrophic disturbance seriously constrained herbaceous species responses and thus created the pattern of post-disturbance succession within the herb layer.

Overall, these results suggest that even a catastrophic disturbance is not sufficient to overcome a legacy of overbrowsing because the disturbance occurred over a depauperate herb layer (see above) where subsequent browsing further constrained herb layer responses. Even 25 years after the disturbance, two fern species (*Dennstaedtia punctilobula* and *Dryopteris carthusiana* [Vill.] H. P. Fuchs [= *Dryopteris spinulosa* (O. F. Müll.) Watt]) remain the only herbs with mean cover greater than 1.5 percent. Our conclusions suggest a reinterpretation of past research on the impact of disturbances within the ANFR. In the Kane Experimental Forest several km from Tionesta Scenic Area, Collins and Pickett (1987, 1988a,b) created artificial tree fall gaps of differing sizes to examine the effects of small gaps on herb layer vegetation. They found that

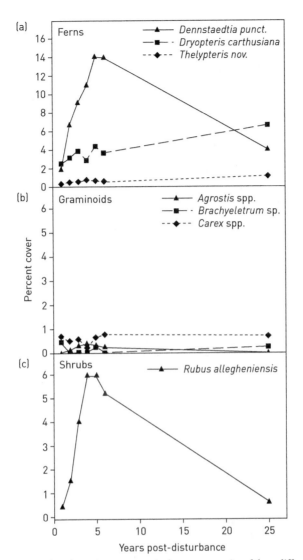

FIGURE 17.1 Change in abundance (percent cover) of common species of three different growth forms following a catastrophic blowdown in the Tionesta Scenic Area, Pennsylvania: (a) ferns (b) graminoids, (c) shrubs. Data from first six years based on N = 289 quadrats within the blowdown; data from year 25 based on N = 149 quadrats that are a subset of the original. *R. allegheniensis* was the only common shrub.

the herb layer barely responded and concluded that "modal and mean gap sizes elicit little response in forest herb populations on the Allegheny Plateau" and that "future research should focus on larger gap sizes" (Collins and Pickett 1988). We offer an alternative explanation, specifically that past and current browsing during the years they conducted their studies seriously constrained herb responses. Indeed, the herb assemblage in their study was depauperate and composed almost entirely of slow-growing browse-tolerant species (Collins and Pickett 1982, 1988) that may not have been capable of taking advantage of the enhanced light levels that occur beneath canopy gaps. Further studies will be required that simultaneously exclude deer, enhance light via canopy gaps (e.g., Royo, Collins et al. 2010), and account for legacy effects whereby

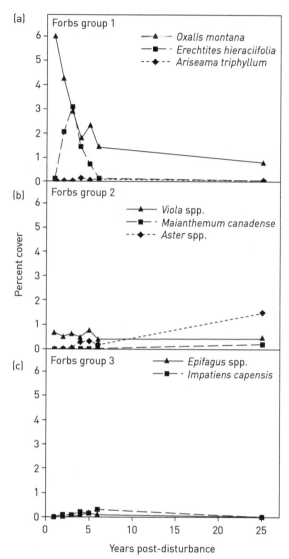

FIGURE 17.2 Change in abundance (percent cover) of common forb species following a catastrophic blowdown in the Tionesta Scenic Area, Pennsylvania. The eight forb species were separated into three panels for clarity. Data from first six years based on N = 289 quadrats within the blowdown; data from year 25 based on N = 149 quadrats that are a subset of the original.

browsing has driven faster-growing and palatable herb species to extremely low densities. Royo, Collins et al. (2010) found that the herb layer not only responded to canopy gaps but that moderate to low levels of browsing promoted herb diversity by reducing the abundance of fast-growing woody pioneers. This leaves little doubt that herb responses to canopy gaps and larger disturbances will depend upon current and historical browsing regimes within a given region.

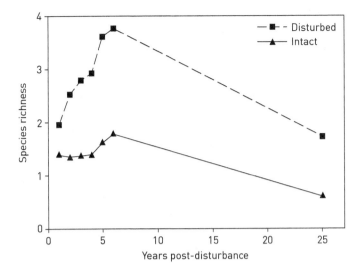

FIGURE 17.3 Change in species richness both within a catastrophic blowdown and the adjacent undisturbed forest in the Tionesta Scenic Area, Pennsylvania. Data from the first six years based on N = 289 quadrats (149 in year 25) within the blowdown and 51 outside within the intact forest (10 in year 25).

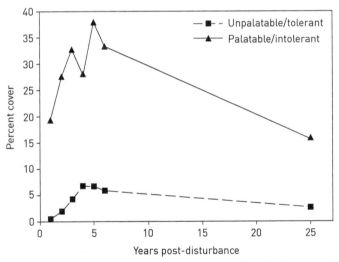

FIGURE 17.4 Change in abundance (percent cover) of palatable and unpalatable species (see text) following a catastrophic blowdown in the Tionesta Scenic Area, Pennsylvania. Palatable and unpalatable species grouped as described in the text. Data from first six years based on N = 289 quadrats within the blowdown; data from year 25 based on N = 149 quadrats that are a subset of the original.

MITIGATING OVERBROWSING VIA REDUCTIONS IN DEER HERDS: PRELIMINARY RESULTS OF A LANDSCAPE-SCALE STUDY

Above, we demonstrated how chronic overbrowsing drastically altered understory diversity, species composition, and abundance, and that even a large-scale canopy replacement disturbance did not lead to substantial changes in the herb layer, most likely due to a long legacy of overbrowsing, as well as contemporary browsing. This, however, does not address the degree to which forest understories can recover if herd sizes and browsing are reduced. Resolving this issue requires sustained reductions in deer populations across broad areas, coupled with repeated vegetation surveys over many years. This has only been attempted a few times because it typically requires coordination among diverse stakeholders including various public and private landowners and state and federal management agencies (see e.g., Kuiters and Slim 2002; Virtanen et al. 2002; Tanentzap et al. 2009; Tanentzap et al. 2011).

Within the ANFR, the Kinzua Quality Deer Cooperative (KQDC) is conducting a sustained landscape-level (30,628 ha) reduction in deer herd sizes to evaluate the rate and degree of understory plant community recovery (Reitz et al. 2004). The KQDC is a partnership between private and public land management agencies with the goal of providing information to hopefully influence forest and wildlife management actions and outcomes. Initiated in 2001, the KQDC project provides data from a set of 26, 259 ha blocks (1.609 km × 1.609 km) randomly allocated throughout the study area. The vegetation within large permanent subplots (1,250 m²) within each block was censused in 2001, 2003, 2007, and 2011, and deer densities were determined annually using pellet group surveys (N = 26 blocks × 7 plots = 192; for details, see Kirschbaum and Anacker 2005; Anacker and Kirschbaum 2006). Beginning in 2003, deer populations within the study region were aggressively culled primarily through a PGC deer management assistance program (DMAP), which provided additional antlerless licenses, thereby allowing hunters to harvest more deer. Deer populations averaged ~ 10.4 deer per km² from 2002–2004 and declined to ~ 5.4 deer per km² from 2005–2011.

Preliminary results from this ongoing study showed that browse-sensitive phytoindicator forbs responded quickly to lowered deer densities. For example, heights of *Trillium* spp. and *Medeola virginiana* doubled, *Trillium* flowering frequency increased by 165 percent, *Trillium* density increased by 76 percent, and *Maianthemum canadense* cover increased by 200 percent. In stark contrast to these encouraging results, the overall plant community remained depauperate. Species richness within the plots did not increase over time, and nearly two-thirds of the total understory vegetation cover remains dominated by three fern species (*Dennstaedtia punctilobula*, *Dryopteris* spp. Adans., and *Thelypteris noveboracensis* (L.) Nieuwl.) and American beech saplings (Royo et al. 2010b; Royo unpubl. data). In fact, of the approximately 300 species found in the vegetation surveys, the vast majority (91.5 percent) were found in fewer than 10 percent of the plots, and most forb species comprised far less than 1 percent of the total vegetation cover due primarily to the direct and indirect effects of decades of overbrowsing (Anacker and Kirschbaum 2006; Royo et al. 2010b).

These results suggest that even if deer herds are brought under control for multiple years, the process of augmenting herb layer diversity (i.e., increased browse-sensitive herb abundance, decreased browse-resistant plant dominance, or both) may require decades. Banta et al (2005) termed this phenomenon the "ghost of herbivory past" and argued that in regions with a long legacy of overbrowsing, recovery will likely be delayed because of dominance by unpalatable species coupled with the fact that many forbs are now sparsely distributed, have short dispersal distances, do not form a seed bank, are slow-growing, and may suffer from Allee effects (chapter 16, this volume). Thus, it is not surprising that the small number of studies evaluating vegetation recovery after large-scale deer herd reductions in various forest ecosystems generally find that recovery is slow and often indiscernible (Kuiters and Slim 2002; Virtanen et al. 2002; Tanentzap et al. 2009; Tanentzap et al. 2011; reviewed by Tanentzap et al. 2012). We predict long-term legacy effects of deer overabundance even if the PGC enacts a sound policy of deer management.

Although we found limited recovery within the herbaceous layer, this was not the case for woody species. Indeed, prior to the KQDC initiative, regenerating diverse woody seedling cohorts following clearcuts in the ANFR often required costly investments, including deer exclosures to protect seedlings and control of recalcitrant vegetation layers with herbicides (Marquis and Ernst 1992). However, following herd reductions, land managers reported that clearcuts rarely required fences, and diverse woody seedling carpets occurred where recalcitrant layers were controlled or absent (deCalesta 2011). While these reports did not address herbaceous responses, in sites within and adjacent to the KQDC study area, Ristau et al. (2011) found tree harvesting and herbicide application increased herbaceous diversity by mitigating recalcitrant layer dominance without any collateral species losses. Elsewhere, Royo et al. (2010a) found that moderate deer herds promoted herb diversity, but only in areas with co-occurring disturbances (i.e., fire and/or gaps). These results suggest targeted silvicultural actions along with strategies that address existing propagule limitations (e.g., protecting populations in refugia, transplanting desired species) may accelerate the restoration process (see Tanentzap et al. 2012).

CONCLUSIONS

Perhaps no broad region in the United States has suffered as much from over-browsing as has Pennsylvania, where the "Deer Wars" have been ongoing for more than 50 years (Frye 2006). In the Allegheny National Forest Region of Pennsylvania, overbrowsing has created a depauperate and structurally simple herbaceous stratum that was once composed of a rich layer of wildflowers but is now dominated by a small number of browse-tolerant grasses and ferns that form recalcitrant layers that are inimical to herbaceous species recovery. Even large-scale canopy replacement disturbances cause little change in the herbaceous layer, apparently because these disturbances now occur over a species-poor herbaceous layer where the species capable of responding are absent or in very low density. Novel and long-term landscape-level efforts at reducing deer herd sizes suggest that mitigation efforts may take decades. Regardless, there is now overwhelming evidence that deer herds in Pennsylvania and elsewhere are incompatible with healthy and diverse forest understories, and the only responsible course of action is long-term and sustained reductions in the deer herd throughout regions where they are overabundant.

18 Long-Term Effects of Clearcutting in the Southern Appalachians

Julie L. Wyatt and Miles R. Silman

Every spring, thousands of visitors flock to southern Appalachian parks to witness the spectacular wildflower displays of the diverse understory herbaceous layer of deciduous forests (Meier et al. 1995). Early explorers and naturalists of these forests commented on the widespread and abundant occurrence of wildflowers in the understory (Bartram 1792; Gray 1841), painting an image similar to Muir's (1894) description of the vast "bee gardens" of California. Over the past century, Appalachian forests have undergone extensive clearcutting (Meier et al. 1996), with old-growth forests now covering less than 1 percent of the original forested landscape (Davis 1993). The dramatic decrease in old-growth forest and the similarly dramatic increase in secondary forests beg the question of how the herb layer in previously logged forests compares to what early explorers observed, and whether the spring displays are as spectacular now as they were before anthropogenic disturbance. The impacts of logging on the understory herb community became a concern after Duffy and Meier (1992) first reported reduced species richness even 87 years after logging compared to old-growth forests.

With logging rotations rarely exceeding 150 years, understanding long-term recovery and resilience in terms of not just diversity but also the processes structuring the herb layer is necessary for conserving this species-rich community. What are the forces that determine its community structure, especially in response to disturbance? When disturbed, is the community resilient? What aspects of the community change? How long does it take to recover from past disturbances? And, finally, are recovering communities structured similarly to undisturbed communities? We address these questions in this chapter, focusing on the herbaceous layer in southern Appalachian cove forests.

LOGGING DISTURBANCE

Natural small-scale disturbances are common in temperate forests, creating canopy gaps that are rapidly recolonized (Thompson 1980; Beatty 1984). Humans have increased the size, frequency, and intensity of disturbances through timber extraction on vast spatial scales (Brunet and von Oheimb 1998). In 1923, 822 million acres in eastern North America were covered with old-growth forests (Leverett 1996). Over the past century, these forests have undergone widespread logging (Meier et al. 1996), and today old-growth forests are estimated to cover 750,000 acres (0.09 percent of the original area) due to harvesting and clearcutting (Davis 1993). No large tracts of continuous old-growth forest remain, though there are numerous remnants that have been reduced to small tracts of 10 to 100 acres.

Most logging of old-growth in the southern Appalachians took place at the turn of the 20th century by private lumber companies, with approximately 50 percent of the timberlands being privately owned in 1901 (Yarnell 1998). In the 20 years that followed, the scale and prevalence of disturbance expanded greatly due to narrow-gauge logging railroads and overhead cables that enabled timber to be recovered from even remote mountains (Lambert 1961). Harvesting methods also caused extensive damaged to the understory by massive logs being dragged out of the forests, as well as increased nutrient export through soil leaching and erosion. Fire frequency also increased due to the abundance of slash, increased solar penetration to the understory, and widespread sources of human ignition (Mastran and Lowerre 1983).

The majority of logged forests experienced natural regeneration after harvesting (USDA 1994). Today, these forests have been recovering for over a century and are referred to as "mature forests" by the United States Forest Service. Importantly, studies often compare recently harvested areas to mature forests, despite the fact that mature forests may still be recovering from previous disturbance. Mature forests may also differ greatly in species composition and ecosystem function from old-growth forests, which have return times for large disturbances that are an order of magnitude longer than the age of mature forests (Ford et al. 2000). Indeed, mature forests may represent a relatively early stage in Appalachian forest succession, and recommendations for timber harvesting based on mature forests may not give an adequate representation of patterns and processes in the herbaceous layer in the absence of anthropogenic disturbance.

OLD-GROWTH FORESTS

Old-growth forests are those forests that have never been harvested for timber and show little evidence of anthropogenic disturbance (Meier et al. 1995), and, while reduced to small relicts in eastern North America, they serve as important controls for studying natural processes (chapter 6, this volume). Old-growth forests contain massive living trees over 200 years old and average basal areas ranging from 35 m²/ha to more than 75 m²/ha (Busing and White 1993; Jackson 2006; Elliot et al. 2008). In a study of southern Appalachian forests in the Great Smoky Mountains National Park, Busing and White (1993) found old-growth forests to have a mean basal area of 52.4 m²/ha and an average biomass of 440 Mg/ha. Canopy structure is uneven due to natural tree regeneration (Martin 1992). Old-growth forests are characterized by gap-phase dynamics that increase light availability in the understory and cause an uneven canopy structure (Martin 1992; Busing 1998; Bellemare et al. 2002). Natural tree mortality results in standing snags and downed logs at varying stages of decay and creates micro-topography in the understory with the formation of pits and mounds (Beatty 1984; Hardt and Swank 1997; Miller et al. 2002; Christie and Armesto 2003) These characteristics distinguish old-growth forests from mature forests and may have important implications for the patterns and processes occurring in the understory herb layer.

HERB LAYER

The understory herb community is the major component of overall forest species diversity, provides habitats for many species, plays an important role in nutrient cycling, and has been used as an indicator of forest site quality (Collins et al. 1985; Gilliam 2007). Knowing the impact of logging on the herb community is therefore important for the health of the forest ecosystem. Characteristics of the herb layer such as life history, phenology, dispersal ability, and clonal growth are important for understanding the complexities of this system and the multifaceted ways logging disturbance can impact it.

Life History

Life history characteristics of understory herbs make them susceptible to disturbance, thus the herb layer acts as an indicator of forest site quality (chapter 6, this volume). Most woodland herbs are perennial (94 percent) and exhibit clonal growth (chapter 3, this volume; Whigham 2004). Lifespans can range from 1 – > 50 years (Bender et al. 2000, 2002; Whigham 2004). Many of these species are slow-growing, taking years to reach reproductive maturity (Bierzychudek 1982), and frequent disturbance can therefore disrupt the reproductive success of herb species, as well as spatial patterning and competitive interactions among species. For example, *Trillium* species take at least seven years to go from germination to producing first flower (Patrick 1973).

Phenology

When addressing the impact of logging disturbance on herbs, it is important to distinguish patterns occurring within different phenologies. Seasonal variation in light levels and temperature throughout the year is utilized by different temporal guilds in the understory. These temporal guilds include spring ephemerals, summer-greens, winter-greens, and evergreens. Each phenology has a unique strategy for surviving and gaining carbon in the understory layer, so the effects of logging may differ.

Spring ephemerals are those species that leaf out in early spring and senesce prior to canopy closure. They are shade-intolerant, but can tolerate low temperatures by staying close to the soil surface. To take advantage of this early growing season, they photosynthesize as soon as their leaves expand with high photosynthetic rates and low shade acclimation (Lapointe 2001). Low soil temperatures restrict water absorption, which is necessary for high photosynthetic rates. Optimal temperature for photosynthesis in spring ephemerals is ~ 20°C, which has been attributed to high protein content in leaves to offset low enzymatic activity (Mamushina and Zubkova 1996).

Most of the understory species in temperate deciduous forests are summer-greens (Uemura 1994). These species usually emerge prior to canopy closure, but only after temperatures have increased. However, unlike spring ephemerals, they retain their leaves throughout the summer with leaf senescence occurring in late summer or fall (chapter 3, this volume). Temperatures generally rise high enough for adequate carbon gain during the period before canopy closure (Graves 1990), and summer-greens gain more than half of their total annual carbon during this brief window of adequate temperature and high sunlight (Rothstein and Zak 2001). Summer-greens, unlike spring ephemerals, can tolerate the shade and assimilate some carbon in the low light conditions beneath a closed canopy. Due to light competition after canopy closure, summer-greens are the tallest of the phenological guilds (chapter 3, this volume).

Two leaf phenologies, winter-greens and evergreens, have leaves present during the winter when both spring ephemerals and summer-greens are dormant. Winter-greens have overwintering leaves that are produced in late summer or fall and are lost the following late spring or summer (Uemura 1994). Evergreens are those species that retain their leaves for more than one year (chapter 3, this volume). Even though both evergreens and winter-greens have leaves present in early spring, their photosynthetic capacity is much lower than spring ephemerals (Gonzalez 1972; McCarron 1995). Evergreens gain limited amounts of carbon during the shaded summer months when winter-greens are dormant. Both phenologies gain most of their carbon during spring and fall when temperatures are moderate and light levels are highest (chapter 3, this volume).

Dispersal

Dispersal limitation can be an impediment to recovery from logging disturbance. Seed production varies greatly among herbaceous species, with some species failing to produce seeds for several years (Whigham 2004) and others producing copious amounts (Kawano 1975). Most understory herbaceous species invest more in asexual reproduction than sexual reproduction, limiting the distance they can colonize (Whigham 2004). Herbaceous species seed weights range from 0.03 mg for *Desmodium glutinosum* (Muhl. ex Willd.) Wood to 34.4 mg for *Arisaema triphyllum* (L.) Schott, with a median of 1.8 mg (Bierzychudek 1982). Dispersal distances are known for few herbaceous species (Cain et al. 1998). For those species that have been studied, dispersal includes ant, bird, wind, and ballistic vectors with dispersal distances often < 1 m and occasionally > 10 m (Bierzychudek 1982; Matlack 1994; Cain et al. 1998). Long-distance dispersal by deer occurs, although little is known about this vector for forest herb species (Myers et al. 2004).

Clonal Growth

Many woodland herbs have clonal growth with varying degrees of patch size and physiological integration (Jonsdottir and Watson 1997). Species range from having small to large patches with either short- or long-lived connections between ramets (Whigham 2004). *Podophyllum peltatum* L. is an example of an herb with large patches that are highly integrated with long-lived connections (Landa et al.

1992). Clonal growth provides a competitive edge in high-density communities (Stoll and Prati 2001) and allows species to forage for resources (Hutchings and Dekroon 1994).

Logging Disturbance

The impact of logging on the understory herb community was first addressed by Duffy and Meier (1992) who discovered reduced species richness 87 years after logging. The impact of logging on the understory herb layer in rich cove forests of the southern Appalachians has been a focus of several subsequent studies (Brewer 1980; Meier et al. 1995; Ford et al. 2000; Gilliam 2002; Scheller and Mladenoff 2002; Kraft et al. 2004; Aubin et al. 2007; Vellend et al. 2007), but conclusions remain contentious because key studies suffer from different confounding factors that make results hard to reconcile. Since herb communities vary in composition, and individual species abundances vary with elevation, aspect, soil, and forest type (Gilliam and Turrill 1993; Ohtsuka et al. 1993; McCarthy et al. 2001; De Keersmaeker et al. 2004), failure to account for these confounding intersite factors was a major criticism of Duffy and Meier (1992). Ford et al (2000) took into account intersite heterogeneity, but neglected long-term recovery by comparing recently logged sites to "mature" forests that were as young as 85 years old, finding little differentiation between the herb communities. Since stand initiating events require hundreds of years, herb communities in forests termed mature may be early in their successional trajectory (Lorimer 1980). Strategies for conserving the high biodiversity in these communities require understanding the full trajectory of herb layer recovery and developing logging rotations and landscape management plans that take the potential long-term successional cycles into account.

PROCESSES

Understanding the long-term patterns that emerge in the herbaceous layer due to logging is important, but it is also critical to know the processes that assemble the community. The species that make up any given local community come from a regional species pool. For a species to occur in a given community, it must go through multiple filters. First, species must be able to disperse into a habitat. Once species arrive, there are environment filters that determine whether a species can survive within a habitat (Keddy 1992). In addition, there are biotic filters such as competition and predation that can limit membership in a community. Dispersal combined with environmental and biotic filters determine which species comprise the local community. The relative role of each of these filters may vary among communities and across spatial and temporal scales and with disturbance.

Not all species that disperse into a local community can survive and become part of the community because of abiotic conditions present. Environmental filters act by removing species that lack the traits necessary to survive in the habitat from the pool (Booth and Swanton 2002). Environmental filters such as soil nutrients, light, and moisture can limit the establishment and survival of species within a community (Facelli and Pickett 1991; Adkison and Gleeson 2004; Bellemare et al. 2005). Logging changes the environmental conditions of soil nutrients, light availability, and moisture (Covington 1981; Brown and Parker 1994; Small and McCarthy 2005; Fraterrigo et al.

2006). These changes in the environment may translate into differences in the herb layer community.

An important question to address is whether alterations in community assembly filters due to disturbance result in changes in species composition. Community composition has an important role in ecosystem functioning (Wedin and Tilman 1993; Hobbie 1996; Tilman 1999). In addition, species differ in their traits and how they function in the environment in terms of water, nutrients, and light use, which impact ecosystem processes (Hooper and Vitousek 1998). Nutrient dynamics, productivity, and invasibility have all been tied to species composition (Tilman 1999). Changes in species composition due to anthropogenic disturbance can alter ecosystem processes, so it is critical to understand whether communities are resilient to disturbance.

STUDY SITES

Within the temperate zone, rich cove forests of the southern Appalachians harbor some of the highest plant diversity (Cain 1943; Whittaker 1956). Coves are mesic forests that occur in sheltered concave stream drainages with north-facing slopes (Braun 1950; Whittaker 1956; Glenn-Lewin 1977; Whittaker and Levin 1977; Hicks 1980). In the southern Appalachians, cove forests are found primarily at low to mid-elevations (700–1,200 m) and represent a small fraction of the land area (Ford et al. 2000). The topography of a cove reduces both the duration and intensity of light, providing a shady environment when the canopy is leafed out. The shape of a cove brings in runoff moisture from all sides that is collected in the depression (Parker 1987). Cove hardwood forests receive 80–300 cm of rain annually (Olano and Palmer 2003). As a result, these forests are very moist habitats and have rich, deep soil that acts as a catchment for the buildup of organic matter. Coves are pockets of high nutrients in the highly eroded slopes of the southern Appalachians where low cation availability is the norm (Ulrey 2002).

The abiotic and topographic conditions of rich coves create an ideal habitat for a diverse array of species. Cove forests are characterized by high diversity of plant species in both the overstory and understory due to the abundant moisture and nutrients. The overstory is dominated by mesic shade-tolerant species. Characteristic tree species of cove forests include *Acer saccharum* Marshall, *Aesculus octandra* Aiton, *Betula alleghaniensis* Britton var. *alleghaniensis*, *Fagus grandifolia* Ehrhart, *Halesia carolina* L., *Liriodendron tulipifera* L., and *Tilia heterophylla* L. var. *heterophylla* (Vent.) Loudon (Schafale and Weakly 1990). However, most of the diversity is found in the understory herb layer. On average, for every tree species, there are six herb species in the understory (Gilliam 2007). The understory herbaceous layer is characterized by *Actaea pachypoda* Ell., *Asarum canadense* L., *Caulophyllum thalictroides* (L.) Michx., *Viola canadensis* L., *Hepatica acutiloba* (DC.) G. Lawson, *Laportea canadensis* (L.) Weddell, *Polygonatum biflorum* (Walter) Elliott, and *Tiarella cordifolia* L. (Schafale and Weakly 1990).

Within the southern Appalachians, cove forests comprise 25 percent of the forest. These forests are highly susceptible to anthropogenic disturbance because they contain quality timber for harvesting and fertile soils for agriculture sites (Beck 1988; Turner et al. 2003). We selected sites of similar slope, aspect (0°–90°), elevation (700–1,200 m), in rich cove hardwood forest in the southern Appalachians of North Carolina in the Nantahala National Forest (NNF) based on U.S. Forest

Service Continuous Inventory and Stand Condition (CISC) data and USGS digital elevation models (ArcGIS 8.0, USGS digital elevations models, and USFS CISC). The underlying geology in this area is composed of metamorphosed rocks with mostly Dystrochrepts and Hapludults soils (Pittillo et al. 1998). Annual temperatures range from $-13.2°C$ to $33.2°C$, with an average temperature of $13.6°C$. Rainfall averages 82.6 cm annually (www.ncdc.noaa.gov).

Six sites were chosen with paired old-growth and mature forest sites using CISC data. Logging rotation times are 100 to 150 years in the southern Appalachians (USFS), so these mature forests represent the amount of recovery that is likely to occur before a subsequent logging. Data from the CISC layers indicate that these forests were logged between 1864–1906. This time period coincided with intensive clearcut logging of the southern Appalachians prior to Forest Service ownership (Western North Carolina Alliance 1995). Since harvesting a century ago, these forests have undergone natural regeneration (United States Department of Agriculture 1994).

PATTERNS: SPECIES RICHNESS, ABUNDANCE, AND COMPOSITION

To establish a thorough baseline understanding of the herb community, we combined diversity, abundance, and species composition across spatial scales while taking into account phenological groups. This multifaceted approach better addresses persistence in the herb community (Symstad et al. 1998; Loreau et al. 2001). Spatial dependency of diversity can occur at a range of scales (Whittaker 1960; Levin 1992). Large-scale spatial processes include landscape-level land use history and heterogeneity between forest sites (Gering et al. 2003). High turnover in diversity at landscape scales is generally a signature of dispersal limitation (Freestone and Inouye 2006; Vellend et al. 2007). At smaller spatial scales, intraspecific aggregation through clonal growth or environmental processes, such as patchy distribution of light, nutrients in the understory, and forest floor microtopography, can affect diversity (Miller et al. 2002; Barbier et al. 2008). Diversity surveys often provide a snapshot of diversity at the plot scale, which is only one component of total diversity (Clough et al. 2007). Using multiple spatial scales to address diversity provides a more comprehensive view of the community and can indicate underlying processes based on the scales at which diversity accumulates (Miller et al. 2002; Gering et al. 2003; Barbier et al. 2008).

Plant communities are dynamic on an annual cycle with species having temporal niches based on leaf phenology. This is an often overlooked, but important, component of diversity. Three primary phenologies in the understory (spring ephemerals, summer-greens, and evergreens) differentiate in the timing and duration of their carbon gain (chapter 3, this volume). These phenologies utilize resources and habitats at different times, and this contributes to greater diversity by allowing more species to coexist over an annual cycle (Chesson 2000). Combining phenology with spatial scales in old-growth forests provides a comprehensive baseline of the plant community that can be used to assess recovery in previously logged forests. By comparing mature forests to old-growth forests, we extend our understanding of herb layer recovery across a longer trajectory of succession to provide better data for landscape management plans.

DIVERSITY AND PARTITIONING SAMPLING

At each study site, 12 transects consisting of five 0.25 m² plots spaced 5 m apart and running perpendicular to the cove drainage were established following Ford et al. (2000) (fig. 18.1). Presence/absence of understory herbaceous species was surveyed for each of these 360–0.25m² plots to assess overall diversity. For diversity partitioning, a subset of the diversity plots was used for abundance sampling. Ten randomly chosen 0.25 m² plots at each site were expanded to 1 m² quadrats (fig. 18.1). The four 0.25 m² subplots within each quadrat comprise the lowest spatial scale with 40 subplots per site for a total of 240–0.25 m² subplots across all forest sites. Abundance of individual ramets was surveyed within each subplot during the same time intervals as the diversity sampling. The 1 m² quadrats make up the second spatial scale with a total of 60–1 m² quadrats followed by the site scale (six forest sites) and the highest hierarchy (age) with two forest ages (fig. 18.1). Details of methods and analysis can be found in Wyatt and Silman (2010).

Species richness was partitioned within and among the four scales (subplots, quadrats, sites, and forest age) to determine the contribution of various spatial scales to total diversity. The four 0.25 m² subplots within each quadrat are level 1, quadrats are the second level, followed by third- level site scale, and fourth-level age, corresponding to the two forest age categories (old-growth and mature forests). We determined whether the observed diversity at any given spatial scale differs from a random distribution of individuals among samples at all scales using partition v2 (Veech et al. 2002; Crist et al. 2003; Gering et al. 2003). Three measurements of diversity were used: species richness (N_0), Shannon's index (H'), and Simpson's index (λ). Within1 is the mean diversity in subplots, and among1 is the diversity that accumulates among subplots. Among2 is the diversity that accumulates among quadrats, among3 is turnover in species across forest sites, and among4 is across old-growth and mature forests. To test the null hypothesis that the observed within and among diversity values are due to a random distribution of species among samples at all scales, we compared the null distribution to the scale-specific values. We determined statistical significance by the

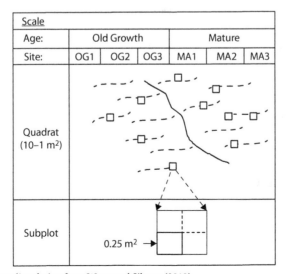

FIGURE 18.1 Sampling design from Wyatt and Silman (2010).

proportion of null values greater (or less) than the estimate. Details of the analysis can be found in Wyatt and Silman (2010).

Phenology

Species were categorized according to their phenological guilds: spring ephemerals, summer-greens, winter-greens, and evergreens (table 18.1). Spring ephemerals are those species that leaf out in early spring and senesce prior to canopy closure. Summer-greens can leaf out before, during, or after canopy closure, but retain their

Table 18.1 Binomial, phenological groups and number of plots present at each old-growth (OG) and mature (MA) site sampled.

Binomial	Phenology	OG1	OG2	OG3	MA1	MA2	MA3
Allium tricoccum Aiton	spring ephemeral			12			
Anemone quinquefolia L.	spring ephemeral	23	12		23	3	44
Claytonia caroliniana Michaux	spring ephemeral	57	46	23	17	3	35
Dicentra sp Berhn	spring ephemeral	56		19	4		
Erythronium americanum Ker	spring ephemeral	55	11	27	17	1	3
Thalictrum thalictroides (L.) Boivin	spring ephemeral		11	2	4	4	1
Actaea pachypoda Ell.	summer-green	5	14	4	3	3	2
Adiantum pedatum L.	summer-green		2	1			
Arisaema triphyllum (L.) Schott	summer-green		2	2	22	26	7
Aruncus dioicus (Walter) Fernald	summer-green		1	1	1		
Asarum canadense L.	summer-green		15	2	1		
Aster sp L.	summer-green				7	3	
Botrychium virginianum (L.) Sw.	summer-green	1	2			6	1
Botrypus virginiana (L.) Michx.	summer-green		3				
Cardamine clematitis Shuttleowrth ex A. Gray	summer-green	42	2		3	7	37
Cardamine diphylla (Michaux) Alph. Wood	summer-green	13	38	25			5
Caulophyllum thalictroides (L.) Michaux	summer-green	1	2	13	12	6	1
Conopholi s americana (L.) Wallroth	summer-green		1	2			

Table 18.1 (Continued)

Binomial	Phenology	OG1	OG2	OG3	MA1	MA2	MA3
Cryptotaenia Canadensis (L.) DC.	summer-green		1			8	
Desmodium nudiflorum (L.) DC.	summer-green		4	2			
Dioscorea villosa L.	summer-green		4	2			2
Diphylleia cymosa Michaux	summer-green			5			
Disporum lanuginosum (Michx.) D. Don	summer-green	1	1	8	8		3
Eupatorium rugosum Houttuyn	summer-green	13	1	2	1		
Eupatorium sp L.	summer-green		1			1	
Eurybia divaricate (L.) G. L. Nesom	summer-green	17	21	5	5	2	36
Galearis spectabilis (L.) Rafinesque	summer-green		1		1		
Galium aparine L.	summer-green	11	2	2		3	
Galium circaezans Michx.	summer-green	2	7	2		2	1
Geranium maculatum L.	summer-green		17				
Hydrophyllum virginianum L.	summer-green		4	2	19	1	
Impatiens sp L.	summer-green	23	11	38	26	23	3
Iris cristata Solander ex. Aiton	summer-green		5				
Laportea canadensis (L.) Weddell	summer-green	32	26	32	3	39	6
Luzula sp Woodrush	summer-green						1
Maianthemum racemosum (L.) Link	summer-green		1	9	24	4	
Medeola virginiana L.	summer-green		5			4	2
Melanthium parviflorum (Michaux) S. Watson	summer-green		6	4	3		9
Monarda sp L.	summer-green	11	3	17			1
Osmorhiza longistylis (Torr.) DC.	summer-green	6	17	3	16	16	
Osmunda claytoniana L.	summer-green	6	1	1			
Osmunda sp L.	summer-green			7			1
Panax trifolius L.	summer-green	2					8
Poa sp L.	summer-green	21	6	5		5	4
Podophyllum peltatum L.	summer-green	3	2	2	11	1	9
Polygonatum biflorum (Walter) Elliott	summer-green	1	4			1	
Potentilla sp L.	summer-green					1	2

(Continued)

Table 18.1 (Continued)

Binomial	Phenology	OG1	OG2	OG3	MA1	MA2	MA3
Prenanthes sp L.	summer-green		13	2		8	7
Ranunculus hispidus Michaux.	summer-green		2				
Ranunculus sp L.	summer-green	11	13	7	12	26	1
Sanguinaria Canadensis L.	summer-green		11	6	16	11	
Solidago sp L.	summer-green	16	2	33	9	5	8
Stellaria pubera (Michaux) Britton	summer-green	5	31	42	37	21	38
Thalictrum dioicum L.	summer-green		9	6	7	1	
Thaspium barbinode (Michaux) Nuttall	summer-green		6				
Thelypteris noveboracensis (L.) Nieuwland	summer-green		14	2		6	9
Tradescantia subaspera Ker Gawler	summer-green		1	1	1		
Trillium cuneatum Rafinesque	summer-green		22				
Trillium erectum L.	summer-green		2	1	4		1
Trillium grandiflorum (Michaux) Salisbury	summer-green		11		2	6	1
Trillium luteum (Muhlenberg) Harbison	summer-green		2		15		
Trillium sp L.	summer-green	5	33	8	46	12	1
Trillium vaseyi Harbison	summer-green				2		
Unknown aster	summer-green			3			
Uvularia grandiflora Smith	summer-green		9	3	2	1	9
Uvularia sp L.	summer-green		6		5	3	9
Viola blanda Willdenow	summer-green	6	3	18			
Viola Canadensis L.	summer-green	7	5	2	3	19	23
Viola hastate Michaux	summer-green		26	2	2	12	
Viola palmate L.	summer-green		1			7	5
Viola papilionacea Pursh.	summer-green	16	3	2	2	2	2
Viola pubescens Aiton	summer-green	1	2		4	6	16
Viola rotundifolia Michaux	summer-green		3				
Carex plantaginea Lamarck	evergreen			3			
Dryopteris cristata (L.) Gray	evergreen			3			
Dryopteris intermedia (Muhlenbery ex Willdenow) Gray	evergreen	18	8	8	6	3	11
Hepatica acutiloba DC.	evergreen		1	1	17	16	2
Hexastylus arifolium (Michaux) Small	evergreen						1
Polystichum acrostichoides (Michaux) Schott	evergreen	1	6	12	11	14	7
Tiarella cordifolia L.	evergreen	44	41	2	21	2	23

Table 18.1 (Continued)

Binomial	Phenology	OG1	OG2	OG3	MA1	MA2	MA3
Tipularia discolor (Pursh) Nuttall	evergreen					1	
Goodyera pubescens (Willdenow) R. Brown	evergreen					1	5
Total number of species		**30**	**63**	**48**	**39**	**44**	**41**

leaves throughout the summer. Summer-greens generally senesce their leaves in late summer or fall (chapter 3, this volume). Winter-greens have overwintering leaves that are produced in late summer or fall and are lost the following late spring or summer (Uemura 1994). Evergreens retain leaves for more than one year (chapter 3, this volume). Due to the small number of winter-green species, they were categorized with the evergreen species as those species that have overwintering leaves.

Diversity, Abundance, and Composition

Previously logged forests are not equivalent to remnant old-growth stands after a century of recovery in terms of species richness, abundance, and composition when intersite heterogeneity is taken into account. Old-growth forests have greater species richness and abundance than previously logged forests, along with a distinct species composition (table 18.2; fig.18.2). An indicator species analysis demonstrates that several species are more likely to be found in old-growth forests, while one species, *Anemone quinquefolia* L., is a significant indicator species of mature sites (table 18.3).

Table 18.2 Species richness and abundance per plot (0.25 m²) for all species, spring ephemerals, summer-greens, and evergreens at old-growth and mature forest sites. Reporting average per plot, standard deviation, and p-value based on randomization tests where species richness or abundance was randomly assigned to the 360 0.25m² plots. The null probability distribution was based on 10,000 random permutations, and the p-value was calculated as the proportion of sampled permutations where the absolute difference between means was greater than or equal to the absolute value of the difference between the observed means using R 2.6.2.

Species Richness	OG Average	MA Average	OG Stdev	MA Stdev	p-value
All species	9.8	7.4	2.8	3.1	< 0.001
Spring ephemerals	2.0	1.0	1.2	1.1	< 0.001
Summer-greens	6.9	5.6	2.3	2.4	< 0.001
Evergreens	0.9	0.8	0.8	0.9	0.11
Abundance	OG Average	MA Average	OG Stdev	MA Stdev	p-value
All species	117.8	75.3	66.8	60.0	< 0.001
Spring ephemerals	40.6	27.2	48.4	41.3	< 0.001
Summer-greens	56.7	42.9	35.0	27.2	< 0.001
Evergreens	11.9	12.5	5.2	6.9	< 0.001

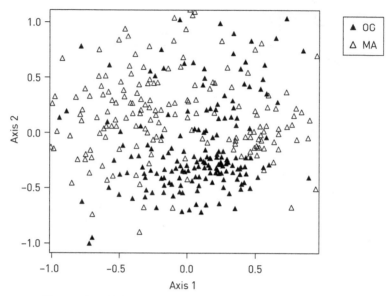

FIGURE 18.2 Non-metric multidimensional scaling biplot axes 1 and 2 for forest age x herb layer community composition sampled in 360 plots across six rich cove forests for all species. The ordination of all species yielded a three-dimensional solution that explained 64.4 percent of the variation in plot species composition. Species composition forms significant groups according to forest age (A = 0.08 [chance-corrected within group agreement], $p < 0.001$), with forest age explaining 18.6 percent of variation in species composition along axis 1. Figure from Wyatt and Silman (2010).

Table 18.3 Indicator species for mature and old-growth forests for the top five species with indicator values → 25 percent.

Forest Age	n	Indicator Species	Indicator Value (%)
Mature	3	Anemone quinquefolia	26.3
Old-growth	3	Claytonia caroliniana	49.0
		Tiarella cordifolia	40.8
		Dicentra spp.	40.0
		Cardamine diphylla	40.0
		Stellaria pubera	38.1

These results support previous arguments that timber harvesting alters the herb layer (Brewer 1980; Peterken and Game 1984; Duffy and Meier 1992; Bratton and Miller 1994) and refutes conclusions that timber extraction retains species richness and composition (Ford et al. 2000; Gilliam 2002; Scheller and Mladenoff 2002; Kraft et al. 2004; Aubin et al. 2007). Recovery of the understory may take centuries and may never reach the same baseline found in undisturbed forest (Brewer 1980; Peterken and Game 1984). Previous studies in the southern Appalachians show a lack of recovery after 45–87 years (Duffy and Meier 1992), and similar conclusions have been made in systems with much shorter harvesting intervals (Decocq et al. 2004). Timber harvesting intervals of 100–150 years are more frequent than herb layer recovery time in rich cove

Table 18.4 Average species richness, Shannon (H') and Simpson (λ) diversity indices partitioned within subplots (within1), and the turnover among subplots (1), among quadrats (2), among sites (3), and among ages (4) for all species, spring ephemerals, summer-greens, and evergreens. Partitioning of diversity is shown for all sites and within old-growth and mature forests alone. The randomization process determined whether the diversity partitioned at each level is more or less than what would be expected by comparing to null estimates for all forest ages, old-growth forests alone, and mature forests alone. The randomization process was conducted for all species and each phenological group. Significance was determined at the 0.05 level; * indicates significantly greater than expected.

	All Species			Spring Ephemerals			Summer-Greens			Evergreens		
All Ages	N_o	*H'*	λ	N_o	*H'*	λ	N_o	*H'*	λ	N_o	*H'*	λ
within 1	10.0	1.67	0.76	1.5	0.35	0.63*	7.2	1.42	0.71	1.2	0.29	0.57
among 1	6.8	0.24	0.03*	0.6	0.12*	-0.06*	5.5	0.28	0.03*	0.6	0.13	-0.12*
among 2	28.9	0.76*	0.09	2.1*	0.59	0.04	24.5	0.81*	0.12	2.5*	0.62	0.11
among 3	28.3*	0.39*	0.03*	1.3*	0.13*	0.04	24.8*	0.34*	0.02*	2.2*	0.50*	0.18*
among 4	11.0*	0.24*	0.02*	0.5*	0.27*	0.10*	9.0*	0.17*	0.01*	1.5*	0.39*	0.09*
Mature	N_o	*H'*	λ	N_o	*H'*	λ	N_o	*H'*	λ	N_o	*H'*	λ
within 1	8.8	1.54	0.76	1.2	0.25	0.61*	6.7	1.38	0.73	0.9	0.21	0.65*
among 1	6.4	0.24	0.02*	0.7	0.13*	-0.10*	5.2	0.25	0.02*	0.6	0.12	-0.15*
among 2	26.5	0.90*	0.10	2.1*	0.56	0.04	21.8	0.83*	0.11	3.2*	0.68	0.03
among 3	26.3*	0.31*	0.03*	1.0*	0.26*	0.09*	24.3*	0.36*	0.03*	1.3*	0.28*	0.14*
Old-growth	N_o	*H'*	λ	N_o	*H'*	λ	N_o	*H'*	λ	N_o	*H'*	λ
within 1	11.2	1.78	0.77	1.7	0.44	0.65*	7.7	1.46	0.69	1.4	0.36	0.49
among 1	7.1	0.24	0.03	0.6	0.11*	-0.02*	5.8	0.31	0.04	0.7	0.14	-0.10
among 2	31.4*	0.63*	0.08*	2.0*	0.62	0.05	27.2*	0.78*	0.12*	1.9*	0.57*	0.19
among 3	30.3*	0.47*	0.04*	1.7*	0.01	-0.01	25.3*	0.32*	0.02*	3.0*	0.72*	0.21*

forests. After a century of undisturbed recovery, logged stands are not equivalent to remnant old-growth stands.

Spatial Partitioning

In the debate over whether herb layer diversity recovers from timber harvesting, spatial scale has not been taken into account despite the importance of scale for determining conservation practices (Meier et al. 1995; Ford et al. 2000; Whittaker et al. 2005). We demonstrate that there is greater species turnover than expected at large spatial scales (among sites and among forest ages; table 18.3). Most of the herb layer diversity accumulates at the forest site scale among quadrats (34 percent) and among forest sites (33.3 percent; table 18.4; fig. 18.3). Diversity between forest ages accounted for 12.9 percent of the total species richness, and there was greater diversity than expected in the old-growth forests. Despite the fact that diversity differs between old-growth and mature forests, the partitioning of diversity across spatial scales is similar within mature and old-growth forests. Diversity among forest sites and among quadrats

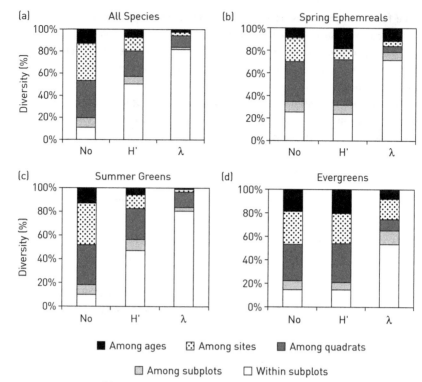

FIGURE 18.3 Percent of diversity partitioned into within and among components using species richness (N_o), Shannon's diversity index (H'), and Simpson's index (λ) for all species and each phenological group. Figure from Wyatt and Silman (2010).

contributed the most toward total species richness for both forest ages (fig. 18.4). High diversity among forest sites demonstrates the importance of landscape scale variation in preserving diversity and conserving multiple forest stands is required to maximize species richness.

Dispersal limitation, habitat heterogeneity, and intraspecific aggregation drive patterns of how diversity is partitioned across space (Jacquemyn et al. 2001; Small and McCarthy 2002; Freestone and Inouye 2006). Species turnover at large scales (between sites and ages) was greater than expected, which could be due to dispersal limitation or environmental differences from logging disturbance. Previous studies give evidence for dispersal limitation in forests recovering from disturbance (Verheyen et al. 2006; Tessier 2007) with species recovery constrained by characteristics of the disturbed forest such as isolation and size (Honnay et al. 2002). In addition, the majority of understory herbs have limited dispersal abilities (Bierzychudek 1982; Whigham 2004). Most of the total herb diversity occurs at the site scale among quadrats (fig. 18.3), which suggests finer-scale intraspecific aggregation due to clonal growth and species sorting along fine-scale environmental gradients (Condit et al. 2002; Legendre et al. 2005).

Previous studies have addressed partitioning of diversity for several taxa across landscape and ecoregion scales (Wagner et al. 2000; Gering et al. 2003; Roschewitz et al. 2005; Chandy et al. 2006; Clough et al. 2007). Previous studies support our results of plant species accumulating mostly at the landscape scale (Wagner et al. 2000); though other studies found that larger scales contribute more to diversity (Roschewitz et al. 2005). One study in a forested landscape found that intermediate scales similar to

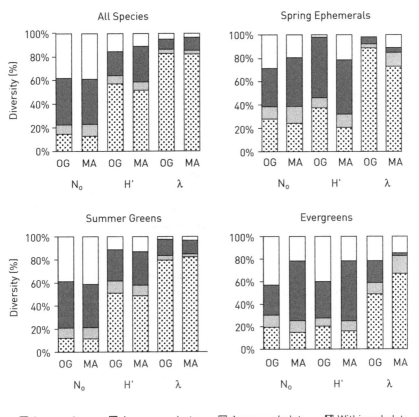

□ Among sites   ■ Among quadrats   ▨ Among subplots   ▨ Within subplots

FIGURE 18.4 Percent of diversity partitioned into within and among components within old-growth (Og) and mature (Ma) forests based on species richness (N_o), Shannon's index (H'), and Simpson's index (λ) for all species and each phenological group. Figure from Wyatt and Silman (2010).

the quadrat scale of our study contributed the most to diversity (Chandy et al. 2006), though they focused on trees and woody understory species, excluding the herbaceous layer. We found that herbaceous layer diversity was partitioned primarily at the intermediate scale (among quadrats) and landscape scale (among forest sites).

Diversity Indices

Using multiple diversity indices that take into account proportional abundance of species allows for understanding how abundant and rare species are distributed across spatial scales. Shannon's index is more sensitive to rare species richness than Simpson's index (Chandy et al. 2006). Simpson's index is more sensitive to changes in common species and is the probability of drawing two individuals of the same species at random from a sample, which is why the percent of total diversity explained was highest for the Simpson's index within subplots (Gering et al. 2003). Contrasting partitions between species richness and Shannon's index for all species and summer-green species indicate that abundant species are widespread and rare species occur in a single subplot (fig. 18.3). Similar contrasting partitioning patterns have been observed for both beetles (Gering et al. 2003) and plants (Wagner et al. 2000). Contrasting partitions between species richness and Shannon's index were not seen for spring ephemerals or evergreens. These phenologies are more evenly distributed across the landscape at all spatial scales irrespective of abundance.

Phenology

All phenologies are affected by past timber harvesting based on species richness or abundance. Mature forests have lower spring ephemeral and summer-green species richness, along with decreased ramet abundance for all phenologies (table 18.2). In addition, more turnover of spring ephemeral and summer-green species occurs among forest ages than expected (table 18.4). Differences between old-growth and mature forests are not random, but rather can be traced to life histories. In mature forests, spring ephemerals and summer-greens occur in fewer plots, fewer species occur in a single plot, and total site abundance is lower. These differences result from slow growth rates and limited dispersal that make them more susceptible to logging (Meier et al. 1995). For example, *Erythronium americanum* Ker Gawler and *Allium tricoccum* Solander take seven to eight years to go from seed to reproducing, with high mortality at the young life history stages (Holland 1981; Nault and Gagnon 1993). Reproduction occurs via clonal growth or by sexual reproduction with dispersal distances generally less than a meter (Bierzychudek 1982; Nault and Gagnon 1993; Whigham 2004).

Only evergreens differed in their partitioning of diversity across space with land use history. Species turnover in evergreens occurs at larger scales in old-growth forests than mature forests (table 18.3; fig. 18.4). Small-scale processes of clonal growth and unassisted dispersal could be limiting the spread of evergreens across a site even after over a hundred years of recovery (Handel et al. 1981; Bierzychudek 1982; Whigham 2004). Patterns in old-growth sites demonstrate that landscape-scale processes rather than the spread of species within a site are more important for evergreens. Large-scale environmental heterogeneity between old-growth forest sites and limited dispersal among sites plays a more defining role in old-growth forests.

Conservation Implications

Logging affects forests worldwide, and understanding the successional trajectory of recovery is critical for conservation. We demonstrate that century-old forests should not be used as the benchmark for understanding herb layer diversity. Rather, remnant old-growth forests need to be the standard by which recovery is assessed. A century is not enough time for the herb layer to recover from timber harvesting in a diverse community. Species richness, abundance, and composition in mature forests have not recovered to old-growth levels. Spring ephemeral and evergreen phenologies are the hardest-hit by harvesting, but they respond in different ways due to life history characteristics, with evergreens having altered spatial patterns and spring ephemerals differing in species richness and composition.

Turnover in species across a site and between forest sites contributes the greatest amount to diversity and should be the focus for conservation. Multiple forest stands need to be preserved to maximize herb layer diversity in rich cove forests of the southern Appalachians. Species turnover across a forest site needs to be further addressed to determine whether differences in environmental heterogeneity or intraspecific aggre-gation through dispersal limitation or clonal growth drive these patterns.

429

Effects of Clearcutting in the Southern Appalachians

PROCESSES: ENVIRONMENTAL AND SPATIAL FILTERS

After establishing that previously logged forests are not equivalent to remnant old-growth stands after a century of recovery in terms of species richness, abundance, and composition, the next step is to understand the processes that structure com-munities. The species observed in a given area arise from a two-part process: species first arriving at sites and then establishing and surviving given the biotic and abiotic environmental filters they encounter (Tilman 1994; Chase and Leibold 2003; Ricklefs 2004). Dispersal into sites creates spatial patterns independent of the local environ-ment and plays a critical role in determining plant community composition (Tilman 1994; Hubbell 2001; Bolker et al. 2003; Clark et al. 2004). The spatial pattern is modi-fied as species abundances change given their responses to the environment and biotic interactions (Tilman 1994; Harrelson and Matlack 2006). Species responding to the environment create a coupling between composition and environmental vari-ables, causing sorting along environmental gradients in relation to their traits (Ford et al. 2000; Huebner et al. 2007). Anthropogenic disturbance can alter both disper-sal and subsequent environment, changing the successional trajectory of communi-ties (Bellemare et al. 2002; Fraterrigo et al. 2006; Wiegmann and Waller 2006; Vellend et al. 2007).

A central debate in community ecology has been the degree to which communi-ties bear the mark of history in their composition and structure. Foster et al. (1998) found that historical records of tree species distributions showed strong correla-tions with environmental variables. Post-European tree distributions, however, have broken the correlation between species distributions and environmental variables, effectively increasing the niche breadth of Eastern tree species. This has resulted in modern forests with distinct species compositions that are largely decoupled from gradients in temperature, precipitation, and soil types. Similar patterns of a weakened species-environment relationship have been found for former agricultural fields in North America and Europe (Vellend et al. 2007). Dispersal plays a more prominent role in structuring these previously disturbed communities (Bellemare et al. 2002). While composition has been shown to reflect historical events, we do not know how long it will take or if the relationship between species composition and the environ-ment will return.

Human disturbance differs from natural disturbance in both scale and intensity. Logging is a large-scale and widespread human disturbance that has been demon-strated to alter species composition for many organisms in forest communities (Nowacki and Abrams 1994; Hardt and Swank 1997; Miller et al. 2002; Thompson et al. 2002; Hamer et al. 2003; Selmants and Knight 2003; Kavanagh and Stanton 2005; Kreyling et al. 2008). However, knowing that composition changes with logging dis-turbance does not shed light on how the processes that determine communities have changed, as logging can alter dispersal, environment, and biotic interactions. Logging changes environmental conditions of soil nutrients, light availability, and moisture (Covington 1981; Brown and Parker 1994; Small and McCarthy 2005; Fraterrigo et al. 2006). Dispersal of species at both the local and landscape scales can also be altered by logging. Recovery of species composition in logged forests has been linked to dispersal limitation based on the distance from old-growth species pools and connectivity between forest patches (Donohue et al. 2000; Ford et al. 2000; Graae et al. 2003; Verheyen et al. 2003).

DISTURBANCE INTENSITY

The intensity of disturbance may affect the time it takes for environmental coupling to return. On former agricultural land, intense soil disturbance caused by tilling homogenizes the soil and has been demonstrated to weaken environmental filtering (Vellend et al. 2007). Logging disturbance may have a lesser impact on the environment than agriculture. Average soil nutrients remain unchanged after logging; however, the variance and spatial structure of the soil changes (Fraterrigo et al. 2006). Forests of Eastern North America were extensively logged and clearcut at the turn of the 20th century, with more of the landscape altered by logging than agriculture (Davis 1996). Forests ranging from 100–150 years old now dominate forested landscapes and are referred to as "mature" in terms of forest management (USDA 1994). These mature forests have been used as the standard for assessing recovery of younger forests (Ford et al. 2000; Gilliam 2002; Selmants and Knight 2003; Small and McCarthy 2005). Though logging is a lower-intensity disturbance, and these communities have had 100–150 years of recovery time, it remains unknown whether environmental coupling and dispersal limitation play an equal role in the herb community of old-growth and previously logged forests, even though designing effective conservation and management strategies relies crucially on the relative strengths of these factors (Keddy and Drummond 1996; McLachlan and Bazely 2001, 2003). With large-scale logging, most of the species are kept, but the connections between species composition and ecosystem processes may take much longer to recover.

We used the diverse understory herb community of rich cove forests in old-growth and 100–150-year-old stands in the southern Appalachians to assess the effects of logging disturbance by clearcutting over a century ago. We ask: What is the relative role of dispersal and environmental coupling in determining composition in a diverse old-growth community? Do previously logged forests that have been recovering for over a century exhibit the same processes?

ENVIRONMENTAL MONITORING

Ten randomly chosen 0.25 m^2 plots at each site were expanded to 1 m^2 plots for a total of 60 1 m^2 quadrats (fig. 18.1). In each quadrat, all ramets were mapped, identified, and counted once monthly between March and August. Surveys among all sites were conducted in the same week to minimize any variations in phenology among sites.

We analyzed 24 environmental factors at each site that have been shown in previous studies to be predictors of herb composition and diversity (Ford et al. 2000; Adkison and Gleeson 2004; Burrascano et al. 2008). Canopy cover was measured in the center of the 10 1 m^2 plots (Ford et al. 2000; Adkison and Gleeson 2004; Burrascano et al. 2008) at each site in both early spring and summer when the canopy was fully leafed

Table 18.5 Summary of the environmental variables reporting the median and range in old-growth and mature forests. *P*-values based on randomization tests with 10,000 permutations.

Environmental Variable	Old-growth		Mature		p-value
	Median	Range	Median	Range	
Aluminium (ppm)	1234	388–1569	1328	640–1721	1.97
Ammonium (NH4) (ppm)	25.7	6.4–93.2	13.2	3.3–73.8	0.11
Boron (ppm)	0.47	0.32–0.98	0.45	0.32–0.81	0.12
Calcium (ppm)	1104	278–3268	1060	415–2911	0.44
Copper (ppm)	1.13	0.71–1.970	1.254	0.75–1.62	1.72
Estimated nitrogen release (ENR)	128	125–130	127	125–130	**0.006**
Iron (ppm)	135	80–223	90	54–201	**< 0.001**
Litter depth (cm)	4.5	3.0–9.0	5.5	0.0–13.0	1.88
Magnesium (ppm)	158	50–310	112	63–213	0.06
Manganese (ppm)	43	24–113	43	38–94	1.59
Nitrate (NO3) (ppm)	117.1	88.5–258.1	74.7	26.8–127.3	**< 0.001**
Organic matter	16.82	10.53–52.79	13.93	10.56–19.04	**0.001**
pH	4.6	3.6–5.6	4.6	4.0–6.3	1.77
Phosphorus (ppm)	27	17–50	22	15–33	**0.001**
Potassium (ppm)	126	88–200	112	67–188	0.22
SMP buffer	6	5.3–6.5	6	5.5–7.2	1.905
Sodium (ppm)	21	13–45	18	12–36	**0.03**
Soluble sulfur	28	25–40	28	21–40	0.38
Spring canopy cover (%)	36.49	10.82–53.93	39.28	25.32–60.62	1.94
Summer canopy cover (%)	66.3	43.93–78.25	68.04	51.30–90.60	1.61
Total exchangeable cations	21.03	6.77–42.23	15.77	11.75–25.93	**0.02**
Tree basal area	97.33	75.4–201.85	65.47	27.25–119.96	**< 0.001**
Tree species richness	5	4.0–7.0	4.93	3.0–8.0	0.32
Zinc (ppm)	4.18	2.66–15.05	2.82	1.34–6.2	**< 0.001**

out using hemispherical photographs analyzed in Image J (Rasband 2008). Litter depth was measured from litter layer top to soil surface in the center of each plot. In five randomly selected plots, total tree basal area and tree species richness were surveyed for a 10-meter radius surrounding each site. Soil samples were collected (8 cm diameter, 4 cm depth) from the center of the five 1 m² plots. Samples were analyzed for total exchangeable cations (TEC), pH, lime requirement, organic matter, macronutrients, micronutrients, ammonium, and nitrate by Brookside Laboratories, New Knoxville, Ohio (table 18.5).

The percent of species composition explained by environmental parameters alone, space alone, and the interaction of space and environment was partitioned out (fig. 18.5). The percent of species composition explained by environmental variables and spatial variables was determined in old-growth and previously logged forests separately using partial canonical correspondence analysis (CCA). Details of methods and analysis can be found in Wyatt (2009).

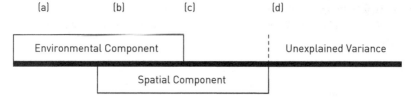

FIGURE 18.5 Adapted from Borcard et al. (1992) showing how the variation in species composition is partitioned through CCA. Variation is partitioned into the environmental component alone (a), the spatial component alone (b), the intersection of the environmental and spatial components (c), and the unexplained variance in species composition (d).

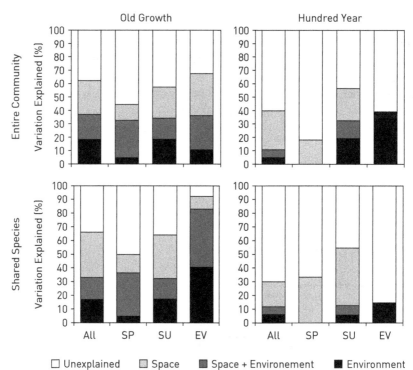

FIGURE 18.6 Partitioning species composition into space, environment, combined environmental and spatial components, along with unexplained components for all species (ALL), spring ephemerals (SP), summer-greens (SU), and evergreens (EV) in old-growth and mature forests. The first row shows the percent variation explained for the entire community, and the second row includes only shared species that are found in both old-growth and mature forests. Figure from Wyatt (2009).

Logging a century ago results in decoupling of species composition from the environment. Environmental filtering is an important component for determining species composition in old-growth forests, and this process is reduced in mature forests (fig. 18.6). Our results support previous conclusions that human land use disrupts existing biotic-environmental relationships (Foster et al. 1998; Vellend et al. 2007), while demonstrating that less intense logging disturbance also disrupts this relationship. Nine of the 24 environmental variables differed significantly between old-growth and mature forests (table 18.5), with old-growth forests having greater macronutrients

(P and estimated N released), micronutrients (Fe, Na, and Zn), tree basal area, total exchangeable cations (TEC), organic matter (OM), and NO_3.

An alternative hypothesis may be that logging causes changes in species composition and that different composition, rather than disturbance per se, is responsible for the difference in importance of environment in community structure. However, differences in environmental filtering were not due to intrinsic differences in the species that inhabit each aged forest. When including only those species that occur in both aged forests, species composition in old-growth forests was coupled to the environment in ways not evident in logged sites, even though the logging occurred 100–150 years ago (fig. 18.6).

THE ROLE OF THE ENVIRONMENT

The environment plays a larger role in determining species composition in old-growth forests than in mature forests. In mature forests, only zinc explains any significant portion of the variation in species composition and only a small percentage (5.1 percent; table 18.6). This is a site-specific phenomenon with one site having higher Zn concentrations than the other two sites. Excessive zinc concentrations from mining can cause distinct species composition (Brown 1994; Szarek-Lukaszewska et al. 2007); however, concentrations found at this site do not indicate excessive amounts and are likely due to differences in parent rock material (table 18.5).

In old-growth forests, species sort along a fertility gradient based on total exchangeable cations and Mg (table 18.7). Species composition does not sort along a fertility gradient in previously logged forests. The fertility gradient differs between old-growth and mature forests with a larger gradient present in old-growth forests compared to mature forests (table 18.5). The fertility gradient may be due to input of nutrients from plants, and the plants themselves may alter the environment (Facelli and Pickett 1991; Xiong and Nilsson 1999). Input material from plants differs depending on species composition of both the herb and canopy layer (Muller 2003). Decomposition is driven by moisture, temperature, carbon availability, and manganese concentrations that can vary with forest age (Berg 2000; Knoepp et al. 2005). In old-growth forests, plants have input nutrients into the soil over a longer time. In previously logged forest, a hundred years is not enough time for environmental coupling to occur, which may be due to changes in the decomposition process, differences in the input plant material because of species composition, or species spatial patterning. Within mature forests, species have not had enough time for species interactions to play out and establish spatial patterns with pronounced environmental gradients.

Manganese concentration (tables 18.5 and 18.7) is also a significant predictor of species composition in old-growth forests. Although the concentrations do not differ between old-growth and mature forests, the Mn gradient is greater in old-growth forests compared to mature forests. Positive correlations have been found between Mn concentration and herb layer diversity and abundance in the southern Appalachians (Newell and Peet 1998; chapter 10, this volume). The enzyme manganese peroxidase (MnP) is produced by the majority of wood-degrading fungi and has an important role in lignin breakdown. Wood-inhabiting fungi have been shown to have greater species richness in old-growth forests compared to forests logged 60–80 years ago (Lindblad 1998). This suggests that species composition in old-growth forests may be coupled with a decomposition gradient due to wood-degrading fungi as indicated by

Table 18.6 Top 10 highest-scoring species along each axis of the partial canonical correspondence analysis in mature forests based on the environment model and three significant spatial parameters showing whether the species is positively or negatively correlated with each axis. The Env 1 model included one significant predictor (Zn) that explained 11.1 percent of community variation. In the spatial models, two of the significant variables model broad-scale patterns (14–19 km; Space 1 and Space 2), while the third spatial variable describes spatial patterns between plots (← 0.1 km; Space 3).

Species	Env 1	Space 1	Space 2	Space 3
Actaea sp	+			+
Asarum canadense				+
Capsella bursa pastoris				+
Cardamine diphylla			-	
Cryptotaenia canadensis				+
Desmodium nudiflorum		-		
Disporum lanuginosum				+
Dryopteris intermedia		+		
Eupatorium rugosum	+		-	
Eupatorium sp		+	+	
Eurybia divaricata	+		-	
Galium aparine				+
Galium circaezans	-	+	+	
Geranium maculatum	-			
Goodyera pubescens	-			
Hydrophyllum virginianum				+
Medeola virginiana		+		
Osmunda spp			-	
Panax trifolius		+		
Poa sp				+
Polygonatum biflorum				+
Potentilla sp	+		-	
Prenanthes sp		+		
Thelypteris noveboracensis		+	+	
Trillium erectum			-	
Trillium vaseyi		-		
Uvularia grandiflora				+
Viola blanda	+		-	
Viola palmata	-			
Viola rotundifolia	+	+		

Mn concentrations, but confirmation would require direct measurements of MnP or other indicators of fungal action.

Logging disturbance can alter the environmental gradient by changing the availability and distribution of soil nutrients and light availability. Soil nutrients vary in concert with changes in biogeochemical cycling due to mechanical disturbance during

Table 18.7 Top 10 highest-scoring species along each axis of the partial canonical correspondence analysis in old-growth forests based on the environment model along with three significant spatial parameters showing whether the species is positively or negatively correlated with each axis. The environmental model resulted in three constrained axes that explained 37.2 percent of the variation in species composition. The first environment axis explains 18.1 percent of the variation in species composition with Mn concentrations correlating with this axis. Environment axis 2 correlates negatively with TEC and Mg and explains 10.0 percent, while the third constrained environmental axis is negatively correlated with TEC and explains 9.2 percent of the variation. The first significant spatial variable describes broad spatial patterns across the landscape (29–32 km). The second significant spatial variable models patterns between forest sites (5–10 km), while the third significant spatial variable describes between-plot patterns (← 0.1 km) at two of the sites.

Species	Env 1	Env 2	Env 3	Space 1	Space 2	Space 3
Aruncus dioicus	+				-	
Botrychium virginianum			-			
Cardamine clematitis			-			-
Carex sp						+
Caulophyllum thalictroides			+			+
Conopholis Americana	+					
Cryptotaenia canadensis						-
Disporum lanuginosum			+			+
Galearis spectabilis	+					
Galium circaezans						-
Goodyera pubescens		+		+	+	
Hydrophyllum virginianum	-					
Iris cristata					-	
Panax trifolius		-				
Platanthera sp		+		+	+	
Podophyllum peltatum		+				
Polystichum acrostichoides						+
Thalictrum dioicum	+					
Thaspium barbinode	+					
Thelypteris noveboracensis	+		-			
Tipularia discolor				+		
Trillium cuneatum	+			+		
Trillium erectum		+	+	+	+	
Trillium grandiflorum	+			-		
Trillium luteum	+			+		
Trillium vaseyi	+			+		
Uvularia grandiflora		+				-
Uvularia sessilifolia		+	+	+	+	
Viola blanda		+	+	+	+	
Viola Canadensis			+			+
Viola palmate		+		+	+	
Viola pubescens	-	+				+
Viola rotundifolia					-	

harvesting, as well as nutrient export through log removal and runoff (Likens et al. 1970; Martin et al. 2000). Logging reduces the amount of carbon and nitrogen available (Covington 1981; Small and McCarthy 2005). Our data demonstrate more nitrogen and organic matter in old-growth forests and a larger environmental gradient compared to previously logged forests (table 18.5). Logging disturbance also alters the light environment with maximum light transmittance in 50-year-old forests and decreasing with age due to the increase of shade-tolerant canopy species that intersect more light (Brown and Parker 1994). Although the light environment did not differ between mature forests and old-growth forests (table 18.5), gap-phase dynamics in old-growth forests create a patchy and heterogeneous understory light environment that may not be captured when measuring canopy cover (Martin 1992; Busing 1998; Miller et al. 2002).

THE ROLE OF SPACE

Spatial processes contribute the most to explaining species composition in mature forests (35 percent) with between-site scales (2–10 km) the main significant contributor (fig. 18.6). We interpret this as indicating landscape-level dispersal limitation. In old-growth forests, each site has high diversity, and the species composition is explained by within-site gradients. In mature forests, within-site gradients do not explain species composition, and species vary due to vagaries of dispersal (fig. 18.6). Noted dispersal distances are known for few herbaceous species (Cain et al. 1998). For those species that have been studied, dispersal includes ant, bird, wind, and ballistic vectors with dispersal distances often < 1 m and occasionally > 10 m (Bierzychudek 1982; Matlack 1994; Cain et al. 1998). Potential long-distance dispersal by deer is possible, but little is known about this vector for forest herb species (Myers et al. 2004). Dispersal limitation at the scales of 2–10 km is shown in this study to be the primary predictor of species composition in mature forests.

PHENOLOGY

In mature forests, the environment does not explain any of the variability in spring ephemeral species composition, while in old-growth forests the interaction between space and environment explains most of the composition (fig. 18.6). Spring ephemerals disperse either by ants or lack dispersal vectors (Beattie and Culver 1981; Handel et al. 1981; Singleton et al. 2001), which can make these species slow to reoccupy sites (Meier et al. 1995). Composition and abundance of seed-dispersing ants may also be altered by logging disturbance. Evidence for this has only been determined in highly and continually disturbed habitats (Heithaus and Humes 2003). However, comparisons between old-growth forests and century-old forests have not been conducted for ant communities.

Partitioning summer-green variation within mature and old-growth sites showed similar patterns. Most of the variation was explained by space alone or environment alone (fig. 18.6). Several environmental parameters were significant predictors (old-growth: Mg, Mn, and TEC; mature: Mg, Zn, and Ca). Using only shared species, partitioning of summer-green composition in mature forests had little variation explained by environment alone (5.7 percent), with Zn the only significant variable. Old-growth partitioning patterns using shared summer-green species were similar to patterns observed for the entire community (fig. 18.6).

Evergreen composition is only explained by the environment in mature forests with no contribution from spatial processes, while in old-growth forests, both environment and space contribute to explaining species composition (fig. 18.6). Evergreen composition is explained by a summer light gradient along with available nitrogen in mature forests. Evergreen carbon gain occurs primarily in spring and fall, but additional carbon may be gained during the summer (chapter 3, this volume). In addition, nitrogen is an important component for many photosynthetic compounds (Lambers et al. 2000). A photosynthetic gradient appears to explain the largest proportion of evergreen composition in mature forests. In old-growth forests, Mn and Ca were the important predictors for evergreen species composition. Soil calcium and species richness and composition in North Carolina Piedmont forests have previously been found to be correlated with foliar calcium concentrations (Peet and Christensen 1980; Palmer 1991; Falkengren-Grerup et al. 2006).

DISTURBANCE INTENSITY AND CONSERVATION

Despite the reduced intensity of logging disturbance in comparison to agricultural land use, logging leaves a legacy on the understory community. Large-scale logging disturbance decouples species composition from the environment even after a century of recovery. Dispersal limitation between sites (2–10 km) explains most of the variation in species composition in mature sites, while environmental gradients within sites explain old-growth species composition. To conserve and manage these diverse communities, arrival of species into recovering forests needs to be addressed. In addition, more time is needed to determine whether and how long the environmental gradients that species sort along in old-growth forests will take to return in logged forests.

CONCLUSIONS

Clearcutting has long-term and persistent effects on the diverse herbaceous layer. We addressed both long-term recovery of an understory herbaceous community and accounted for intersite heterogeneity by comparing paired sites of old-growth forest and forest logged over a century ago. These studies also included seasonal variation according to phenology within the community, which has been absent from most previous studies. In agreement with Duffy and Meier (1992), we show that understory herb communities do not return to their pre-disturbance states even after 100–150 years of recovery according to both patterns and processes. Both species richness and abundance were greater in old-growth forests than mature forests, and species composition differed significantly between the two. Importantly, this study showed that diversity in the herb layer varies with spatial scales. Most of the understory herb species accumulate when going across a single forest cove and between forest coves. We also show that species composition in old-growth forests is largely explained by environmental variables. In mature forests, the pattern of species composition was decoupled from the environment. Environmental variables related to soil fertility and decomposition largely explain species composition across old-growth forest landscapes, while dispersal limitation between sites (2–10 km) explains most of the variation in species composition in mature sites. These results demonstrate that 100–150 years of recovery are inadequate for species to reach equilibrium with the environment.

19 Agricultural Legacies in Forest Herb Communities

Kathryn M. Flinn

Forests growing on former farmlands may show the effects of their agricultural heritage for hundreds and even thousands of years (e.g.,, Foster 1992; Dupouey et al. 2002). Some of the strongest and most lasting legacies of past agriculture are changes in the diversity and composition of herbaceous plant communities (Flinn and Vellend 2005). Here I review these changes and examine the mechanisms underlying them, paying particular attention to the evidence supporting the mechanisms of dispersal limitation and recruitment limitation or environmental sorting. I illustrate the patterns and processes of herbaceous plant community responses to agriculture with examples from the literature and case studies from forests in central New York State.

WHY ARE AGRICULTURAL LEGACIES IN FOREST HERB COMMUNITIES IMPORTANT?

Post-agricultural forests are very prevalent in many landscapes of eastern North America and Europe, often more prevalent than forests that were never cleared for agriculture (e.g.,, Grashof-Bokdam and Geertsema 1998; Bellemare et al. 2002; Gerhardt and Foster 2002). In central New York State, for example, forests covered 54 percent of the land area in 1995, and 66 percent of these forests were growing on abandoned agricultural lands (Flinn et al. 2005). In landscapes like this, histories of changing land use have wholly transformed patterns of biological diversity. Herbaceous plant communities, which represent the majority of plant diversity in temperate forests (chapter 1, this volume; Gilliam 2007), show especially strong and lasting effects, in part due to species' life history traits (Whigham 2004). In fact, agriculture may be considered the most severe disturbance to affect herbaceous plant communities (chapters 13 and 14, this volume). As forests regrow, then, any strategy for preserving native herbaceous plant communities in these landscapes must take community recovery in post-agricultural forests into account. In fact, post-agricultural forests represent a large reservoir of potential for restoring native herbaceous plant communities. To inform conservation plans, we need to know:

1. How are herbaceous plant communities recovering in post-agricultural forests?
2. What ecological mechanisms drive this recovery?

The literature on post-agricultural forests generally divides the ecological mechanisms driving recovery into two categories (e.g.,, Honnay et al. 2002). Since clearing forests for agriculture completely destroys herbaceous plant communities, including seed and spore banks, part of recovery simply requires time for seeds and spores of forest plants to arrive at the site again. If the number or identity of species in a post-agricultural forest is limited by the time it takes to disperse in, then this is commonly called *dispersal limitation*. Agriculture may also leave legacies in forest environments (e.g., Dzwonko 2001; De Keersmaeker et al. 2004; Flinn and Marks 2007). If the number or identity of species in a post-agricultural forest is limited by differential performance at any life stage, then this may be called *recruitment limitation* or *environmental sorting*. Distinguishing between these mechanisms is critical not only to understanding ecological interactions within post-agricultural communities, but also to developing any restoration plans.

DEFINITIONS AND CAVEATS

The North American literature has commonly used the terms *primary* and *secondary* to distinguish forests that have never been cleared (i.e., primary forests) from forests that grew up on abandoned agricultural lands (i.e., secondary forests). It is important to note that primary forests are not necessarily old-growth; most have been selectively cut and possibly grazed. They have simply remained forests rather than being converted into other land uses. In Europe, where it is often impossible to know whether a forest was cleared prior to the earliest records, forests tend to be classified as *ancient*— forests that have existed continuously since the oldest maps—or *recent*—forests that originated more recently on abandoned agricultural lands.

Specific agricultural uses may impact the subsequent recovery of forests once the land is no longer used for agriculture. In particular, former pastures and croplands tend to have slightly different successional trajectories (Stover and Marks 1998). Thus, it is important to distinguish between them in any analysis. Another crucial caveat is that clearing and abandonment decisions are often strongly biased by topography and soils, such that primary forests tend to be located on different types of lands than secondary forests (Flinn et al. 2005). Focusing on the consequences of land clearing and abandonment requires finding similar, preferably paired, stands that share similar topography and soils.

HOW ARE HERBACEOUS PLANT COMMUNITIES RECOVERING IN POST-AGRICULTURAL FORESTS?

It is abundantly clear that agricultural land use has a strong and lasting influence on plant diversity and distributions. Legacies in species richness and composition can last as long as 2,000 years (Dupouey et al. 2002). One of the most consistent changes in the herbaceous plant communities of post-agricultural forests is a reduction in the species richness of native forest species (Peterken and Game 1984; Dzwonko and Loster 1989; Matlack 1994; Bossuyt et al. 1999; Singleton et al. 2001; Vellend 2004). In central New York State, secondary forests 70–100 years old contained on average 65 percent of the number of forest herb species in primary forests (Flinn and Marks 2004). This pattern is not universal, and it depends on the definition of the species pool; secondary forests can sometimes be richer in weedy or early successional species (Motzkin et al. 1996). However, among studies that consider native forest species, lower diversity in secondary forests compared to primary forests is remarkably consistent. This only makes sense given that herbaceous communities in post-agricultural forests were completely destroyed and must reassemble from new colonists; it points to dispersal limitation as a major factor in recovery at this stage.

Changes in species composition are also common (Peterken and Game 1984; Dzwonko and Loster 1989; Matlack 1994; Motzkin et al. 1996; Graae 2000; Singleton et al. 2001; Bellemare et al. 2002; Wulf 2004). To illustrate the shifts in species composition that occurred due to past agriculture in central New York State, I used data from herbaceous plant communities in 20 adjacent pairs of primary and secondary forests (Singleton et al. 2001; Flinn 2011). The secondary forests had established 85–100 years before on plowed fields. Flinn and Marks (2007) provide more information on the sites' land use history and characteristics, including latitude, longitude, elevation, slope, aspect, and soil type. Herbaceous plant communities were sampled by recording species' occurrences in 60 1.5 × 2 m plots along three parallel transects through each stand (Singleton et al. 2001). Nomenclature follows the PLANTS database (USDA, NRCS 2011). To summarize variation in species composition, I conducted an NMS ordination of species' frequencies in each site. The ordination used Sørensen (Bray-Curtis) similarities. I compared 50 iterations with real data and 50 iterations with randomized data to select an appropriate dimensionality, and then performed 200 iterations with the chosen dimensionality to find a stable solution with minimal stress (McCune and Grace 2002). I also used the indicator species analysis of Dufrêne and Legendre (1997) to highlight species associated with each forest type. This method calculates indicator values for each species in each type as the product of the species' mean abundance in that type relative to other types and the proportion of sites in that type where it is present. The indicator values thus represent the degree to which species distinguish among types in both relative frequency and relative abundance. I evaluated the statistical significance of the indicator values using Monte Carlo tests with 1,000 randomizations. These analyses were conducted in PC-ORD (McCune and Mefford 2006).

The ordination indicates that whereas primary and secondary herbaceous plant communities overlap in composition, secondary communities clearly show a consistent directional shift (fig. 19.1). Secondary communities tend to be represented by *Maianthemum canadensis* Desf., *Trientalis borealis* Raf., *Aralia nudicaulis* L., *Lycopodium obscurum* L., *Mitchella repens* L., and *Lycopodium clavatum* L. Interestingly, a number of the species associated with secondary communities are commonly considered acidophilic (Flinn 2011). Primary forest communities were also characterized by particular species, as demonstrated by indicator values (table 1). *Eurybia divaricata* (L.) G. L. Nesom, *Polystichum acrostichoides* (Michx.) Schott, *Dryopteris intermedia* (Muhl. ex Willd.) A. Gray, *Prenanthes* L. spp., and *Trillium grandiflorum* (Michx.) Salisb. were among the strongest indicators of primary forests, corroborating previous work (Singleton et al. 2001; Flinn and Marks 2004; Vellend 2004; Flinn 2007). These clear

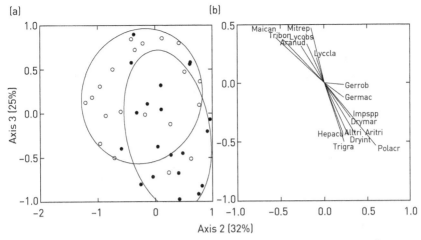

FIGURE 19.1 NMS ordination of herbaceous plant species composition in 40 primary and secondary forests in central New York State. A scatter plot of the sites (a) has 68 percent confidence ellipses around primary forests (closed circles) and secondary forests (open circles). A joint plot (b) shows Pearson correlations between the axes and the species frequencies. Axis 1, which explained 21 percent of the variation in species composition, is not shown. Abbreviations are the first three letters of genus and species names. The species include (left to right): *Maianthemum canadensis* Desf., *Trientalis borealis* Raf., *Aralia nudicaulis* L., *Lycopodium obscurum* L., *Mitchella repens* L., *Lycopodium clavatum* L., *Hepatica acutiloba* DC., *Trillium grandiflorum* (Michx.) Salisb., *Allium tricoccum* Aiton, *Dryopteris intermedia* (Muhl. ex Willd.) A. Gray, *Polystichum acrostichoides* (Michx.) Schott, *Arisaema triphyllum* (L.) Schott, *Dryopteris marginalis* (L.) A. Gray, *Impatiens* L. spp., *Geranium maculatum* L., and *Geranium robertianum* L.

Table 19.1 Indicator values for herbaceous plant species in primary and secondary forests (Dufrêne and Legendre 1997). The table shows species with significant indicator values, in order of their indication of primary forest. The values range from 0 to 100.

Species	Primary	Secondary	P
Eurybia divaricata (L.) G. L. Nesom	77	7	0.001
Polystichum acrostichoides (Michx.) Schott	66	11	0.004
Dryopteris intermedia (Muhl. ex Willd.) A. Gray	64	10	0.013
Prenanthes L. spp.	51	1	0.003
Trillium grandiflorum (Michx.) Salisb.	49	2	0.014
Thelypteris noveboracensis (L.) Nieuwl.	47	3	0.015
Solidago caesia L.	41	2	0.023
Actaea L. spp.	39	4	0.040
Hepatica acutiloba DC.	25	0	0.043
Lycopodium digitatum Dill. ex A. Braun	2	44	0.007

associations between individual species and forests of different land use history raise questions about the mechanisms driving colonization. Are certain species more common in post-agricultural forests because they have greater dispersal ability, or because they flourish once they arrive?

Patterns at the community level are also suggestive of ecological mechanisms. Secondary forests tend to be compositionally more similar to each other than primary forests, with weakened relationships between species distributions and environmental gradients (Vellend et al. 2007). Vellend et al. (2007) attributed this pattern to a process of "selective dispersal assembly," in which better dispersers become consistently overrepresented in post-agricultural forests. A widely held paradigm for community recovery holds that species composition in secondary forests will gradually grow to resemble species composition in primary forests. In a rare resurvey study, however, Baeten et al. (2010) showed that over 30 years, species richness in secondary forests did not increase, and species composition in secondary forests did not become more similar to primary forests. Hopefully, more studies like this will help make clear the mechanisms behind these counterintuitive results.

WHAT ECOLOGICAL MECHANISMS DRIVE THE RECOVERY OF HERBACEOUS PLANT COMMUNITIES?

The evidence that dispersal limits the number and identity of species in post-agricultural forests is strong. Probably the clearest forms of evidence are positive relationships between species richness and time since abandonment (Matlack 1994; Flinn and Marks 2004; Brunet 2007) and negative relationships between species richness and geographical isolation (Peterken and Game 1984; Matlack 1994; Honnay et al. 2002; Flinn and Marks 2004; Brunet 2007). (Note that, in contrast to the results of Baeten et al. [2010], species richness indeed increased over time when longer time scales were considered.) Attempts to relate colonization success to dispersal ability have produced less clear results. Whereas some studies relate species' frequency in post-agricultural forests to their dispersal traits (e.g., Matlack 1994; Verheyen et al. 2003), this relationship is inconsistent (Mabry et al. 2000; Singleton et al. 2001; Flinn and Marks 2004; Ito et al. 2004; Wulf 2004). Clearly, much of the variation among species in colonization success cannot be explained by dispersal alone. The ferns form an instructive example here because they share similarly high dispersal abilities, yet differ in the extent to which they occur in post-agricultural forests (Flinn 2007).

Variation among species unexplained by dispersal suggests a role for recruitment limitation or environmental sorting. Evidence for this mechanism controlling the recovery of herbaceous plant communities in post-agricultural forests has accumulated in recent years. It includes studies that found that particular species perform better or worse in secondary forests compared to primary forests (Donohue et al. 2000; Endels et al. 2004; Vellend 2005; Fraterrigo et al. 2006; Flinn 2007; Baeten, Hermy et al. 2009). Some species appear to perform better in post-agricultural habitats (e.g., *Gaultheria procumbens*, Donohue et al. 2000; *Polystichum acrostichoides*, Flinn 2007); some perform worse (e.g., *Trillium grandiflorum*, Vellend 2005). Experimental introductions have also been useful (Verheyen and Hermy 2004; Graae et al. 2004; Flinn 2007; Baeten, Hermy et al. 2009; Baeten, Jacquemyn et al. 2009). Some, though certainly not all, differences in recruitment and performance between primary and secondary forests have been attributable to soil differences (Endels et al. 2004; Vellend 2005; Fraterrigo et al. 2006; Baeten, Hermy et al. 2009). In fact, the performance of certain species could be enhanced by fertilization in secondary but not primary forests (Fraterrigo et al. 2009). A few studies have compared the demographic rates of herbaceous plants between primary and secondary forests (Donohue et al. 2000; Flinn 2007; Jacquemyn and Brys 2008). These studies specified the life stages that limit population growth in different forest types. For several fern species, establishment clearly limited population growth and colonization, and some microsites for establishment were less common on post-agricultural forest floors (Flinn 2007). Thus the lack of microtopography in previously plowed stands may play a key role in limiting the colonization of some herbaceous species; it may take generations of tree-fall activity to recover (chapter 7, this volume). At the genetic level, several studies have found reduced genetic diversity in post-agricultural forests (Jacquemyn et al. 2004; Vellend 2004).

Recently, investigators have begun to examine interactions between herbaceous plants and the biotic environment in post-agricultural forests, including microbial communities, seed-dispersing ants, exotic earthworms, and exotic and invasive plants. Fraterrigo et al. (2006) found that microbial community composition varied with past land use, potentially affecting ecosystem processes. It remains to be seen whether mycorrhizal partners are differently available in primary and secondary forests. Since many forest herbs are ant-dispersed (Handel et al. 1981), a lack of seed-dispersing ants in post-agricultural forests could constrain colonization. However, results so far suggest that ant activity does not vary with past land use (Mitchell et al. 2002; Ness and Morin 2008). Earthworm invasion, which can have strong effects on herbaceous plant communities (Bohlen et al. 2004), may occur more intensively in forests recovering from agriculture or logging than in older forests (Crow et al. 2009). In central New York State, however, earthworm occurrence was similar in primary and secondary forests (Flinn and Marks 2007). A number of studies have found exotic and invasive plant species to be more abundant in secondary than in primary forests (Lundgren et al 2004; McDonald et al. 2008; Mosher et al 2009; Parker et al. 2010; Kuhman et al. 2011). This effect may be mediated in part by soil enrichment (e.g., McDonald et al. 2008). In Europe, there is particular concern about *Urtica dioica*, a native species differentially common in post-agricultural forests that can competitively exclude other native plants (De Keersmaeker et al. 2004; Endels et al. 2004). One important biotic interaction that has not yet been investigated in post-agricultural forests is pollination: Do pollinator richness, abundance, or composition differ between primary and secondary forests? In addition, it remains unknown whether deer prefer post-agricultural habitats (chapter 16, this volume).

CONCLUSION

A comprehensive picture is emerging of the ecology of herbaceous plants in post-agricultural forests, from the genetic level to the ecosystem level. Dispersal limitation is an important factor controlling the recolonization process, but it is by no means the only factor; in fact, recolonization is more subtle and complex. Whereas several studies have set in opposition the forces of dispersal limitation versus recruitment limitation or environmental sorting, these forces appear to operate in concert as herbaceous plant communities in post-agricultural forests reassemble. It is obvious that dispersal limitation must play a major role, especially in the early development of post-agricultural forests. It may then become less important as seeds and spores accumulate. There is reason to think it will never completely be relieved, because many forest herb populations are dispersal-limited in any context (Turnbull et al. 2000; Ehrlén and Eriksson 2000). Likewise, recruitment limitation or environmental sorting is likely to be extreme in the early stages of forest regrowth, then moderate as the environment of post-agricultural forests approaches that of never-cleared forests. However, subtle environmental legacies of agriculture can persist for 100 (Flinn and Marks 2007) or even 2,000 years (Dupouey et al. 2002). So the interplay between these two forces is likely to continue even in mature post-agricultural stands.

20 Effects of Excess Nitrogen Deposition on the Herbaceous Layer of Eastern North American Forests

Frank S. Gilliam

The response of plant species of the herbaceous layer of forest ecosystems to excess nitrogen (N) availability can arise from N-mediated changes in several processes, including competition, herbivory, mycorrhizal infection, disease, and species invasions. This chapter discusses how these processes respond to excess N and how such responses affect the herb layer of forests, reviewing recent pertinent literature from both North America and Europe. There is compelling evidence that all processes potentially respond sensitively to N deposition and that this response generally leads to drastic shifts in species composition and decreases in biodiversity of forest herb communities. A recently suggested hypothesis—*the N homogeneity hypothesis*—predicts a loss of biodiversity in forest ecosystems experiencing chronically elevated N deposition. The hypothesized mechanism for this response is a decrease in spatial heterogeneity of N availability that is typically high in forest soils under N-limited conditions. A great majority of studies on effects of N on plant diversity have been carried out in herb-dominated communities, with few in forest herb layer communities. Accordingly, more studies are needed, using both field gradient and manipulative approaches, in forest ecosystems, particularly in eastern North America where far fewer studies have been done.

NATURE OF EXCESS N IN THE ENVIRONMENT

Given the high rates of N deposition currently experienced in many parts of the biosphere, and its projected further increases in the future (Bobbink et al. 2010), it is not surprising that there has been a notable recent rise in the number of studies investigating the effects of N on terrestrial ecosystems in general (De Schrijver et al. 2011; Goodale et al. 2011). On the other hand, there has been a rich history of experimental studies investigating the effects of N on species diversity in plant communities. The first and likely best-known of these is the Park Grass Experiment in Rothamsted, England (see Richardson 1938 and Silvertown et al. 2006 as early and recent references, respectively), initially established in 1856 to assist English farmers in enhancing forage production for cattle. Ongoing investigations at the Cedar Creek Natural Area in Minnesota (e.g., Clark and Tilman 2008) confirm results of this earlier work—excess N can profoundly alter species composition and decrease species diversity of plant communities. To date, N effects research has still been predominantly directed toward herb-dominated communities, with far fewer studies in forested ecosystems (Bobbink et al. 1998; Gilliam 2006; Clark et al. 2007; Stevens et al. 2010; De Schrijver et al. 2011). This is an unfortunate discrepancy, however, considering that forests often occupy areas receiving high rates of atmospheric deposition of N (e.g., eastern U.S. and central Europe) and generally display considerable structural complexity relative to herb-dominated systems. Indeed, despite the prominence of the overstory, most plant species diversity of forests is associated with the vegetation of greatest sensitivity to the effects of excess N—the herbaceous layer (Gilliam 2007).

The N_2 gas that comprises 78 percent of our atmosphere is inert to virtually all living organisms and enters into few non-anthropogenic, abiotic chemical reactions. Consequently, it is often referred to as non-reactive N (N_{nr}), in sharp contrast to other forms of N, such as NH_3, NH_4^+, NO_3^-, NO, and NO_2, collectively referred to as reactive N (N_r), that do enter into biological or photochemical transformations. Increases in both high-energy combustion associated with fossil fuel consumption and use of the Haber-Bosch process for production of inorganic N fertilizers have enhanced otherwise naturally low rates of conversion of N_{nr} to N_r, chronically increasing amounts of N_r in the biosphere. Based on estimates from Galloway et al. (2004), total atmospheric deposition of NH_4^+ and NO_3^- in terrestrial ecosystems has increased from 17 Tg N yr^{-1} in 1860 to 64 Tg N yr^{-1} in the early 1990s, with projected further increases to 125 Tg N yr^{-1} by 2050. Thus, the projection over this 190-year period is that atmospheric deposition of N_r will increase nearly 10-fold. It is notable that, whereas N_r from vehicles and power plants in the eastern United States has decreased ~ 30 percent in the past decade in response to Clean Air Act regulations, N_r from fertilizer production and use has increased during this period (Pinder et al. 2011).

N LIMITATION VERSUS N SATURATION: INTERFACE OF BIOGEOCHEMISTRY AND VEGETATION SCIENCE

Although net primary productivity of most terrestrial ecosystems of the biosphere is still predominantly limited by availability of N (*N limitation*), anthropogenically enhanced atmospheric deposition of N in some regions of the biosphere has increased available N to levels that exceed the biotic demand for N (*N saturation*). Global patterns of increased atmospheric deposition of N_r are far from homogeneous, and highest rates understandably co-occur with areas of high human population density. In North America, these are also spatially coincidental with the distribution of forests, especially in the eastern United States (Gilliam et al. 2011). As a result, most N-saturated ecosystems are forests.

The phenomenon of N saturation represents an intriguing interface between biogeochemistry and vegetation science, as many of the biogeochemical consequences of N saturation are directly relevant to the structure and function of plant communities (Gilliam 2006). Primarily, these consequences are related to a notable change in the N cycle toward increasing dominance of nitrate (NO_3^-). Ammonium (NH_4^+) typically dominates in N-limited systems because NH_4^+ generated by ammonifying microbes is rapidly taken up by plant roots and immobilized by other microbial populations, leaving little for oxidation by nitrifying bacteria (autotrophic nitrification). However, during the sequence of stages leading to N saturation, NH_4^+ becomes increasingly available to nitrifier populations, as ammonification exceeds uptake and immobilization by plants and microbes, respectively. Increasing predominance of NO_3^- as the available form of N in forest soils may cause potentially rapid change in herb layer composition because (1) preferential use of NH_4^+ versus NO_3^- can be highly species-specific among plants, particularly among forest herbs (chapter 2, this volume; Boudsocq et al. 2012), and (2) increases in soil NO_3^- pools can increase invasibility by exotic species (chapter 13, this volume; Fargione and Tilman 2005). Increases in levels of NO_3^- in forest soils have also been shown to increase mobility and decrease availability of base cations, such as Ca^{2+} and Mg^{2+} (Gilliam et al. 2001).

N-SENSITIVE PROCESSES POTENTIALLY AFFECTING THE HERB LAYER

As suggested, several processes are sensitive to change mediated by enhanced atmospheric deposition of N that potentially influence herb layer dynamics. It is coincidental that the primary geographic scope of this book—eastern North America—experiences some of the higher rates of N deposition in the world (Gruber and Galloway 2008; Bobbink et al. 2010). Thus, understanding herb layer dynamics in this highly N-impacted region has broad application over other impacted areas. Moreover, such understanding is also important in application of knowledge toward effective conservation policies (see Critical Loads for N Deposition below).

The principal N-mediated change in soil N processing is the simultaneous increase in N availability and increasing predominance of NO_3^- as the available form of N uptake. Because nitrification in excess of NO_3^- uptake results in net H^+ production, in some cases, chronic excess N can increase soil acidity (Kelly et al. 2011). Thus, one of the immediate changes in herb layer composition is an increase in the predominance of species that are nitrophilic, preferential NO_3^--uptake species, acidophilic, or some combination of these.

I suggest the following as a general pattern of response of the herbaceous layer of temperate deciduous forests of eastern North America, with the degree to which this occurs being largely influenced by antecedent N conditions in the soil (Hurd et al. 1998). Initially, there should be an overall increase in biomass of the herb layer as the forest shifts from N limitation toward N saturation (i.e., a fertilizer effect). This will be followed by a loss of N-efficient species and a general decrease in species richness, which can represent a rapid decline in plant biodiversity because of the relative high numbers of such species (fig. 20.1). The next stage will be an increasing predominance of nitrophilic species. As there are far fewer of these species in N-limited forests (fig. 20.1), this will further negatively impact forest biodiversity by decreasing species

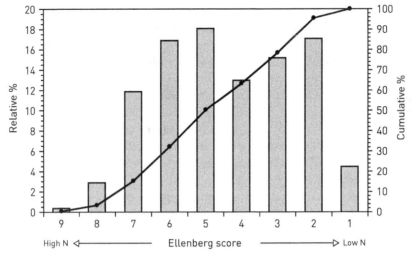

FIGURE 20.1 Relative and cumulative percentages of number of species within Ellenberg N groups, with N demand being highest for 9 and lowest for 1, for ~ 1,900 vascular plant species of Great Britain.

equitability (evenness). It has been further suggested that decreases in evenness can be further exacerbated by the clonal nature of many of these nitrophilic species (Eilts et al. 2011).

MECHANISMS FOR N-MEDIATED RESPONSE OF HERB LAYER

In a previous synthesis and review (Gilliam 2006), I developed a conceptual model (fig. 20.2) to articulate several processes sensitive to N deposition that have the potential to alter herb layer composition and dynamics, ultimately resulting in N-mediated declines in forest biodiversity. Because of their relevance to the discussion of this chapter, I summarize these here.

Interspecific Competition

Most work on the effects of additions of N on the outcomes of interspecific competition has been carried out on herb-dominated plant communities and has demonstrated notable N-mediated changes in success of dominant species. Early work at Cedar Creek demonstrated that N-efficient species (e.g., *Schizachyrium scoparium*) outcompeted high N-requiring species (e.g., *Poa pratensis* and *Agropyron scabra*) under N-limited conditions by taking up inorganic N to the extent that it was below the requirement of the high-N species (i.e., R*, the resource reduction model for competition—Wedin and Tilman 1993).

In contrast to herb-dominated communities wherein nutrients, especially N, can be particularly limiting to herbaceous species, closed-canopied forests are generally light-limited. Direct light only reaches the forest understory in discrete patches called *sunflecks* (chapter 3, this volume), creating a *dynamic mosaic*, in which the size and distribution of sunflecks vary widely across temporal and spatial scales (Gilliam and

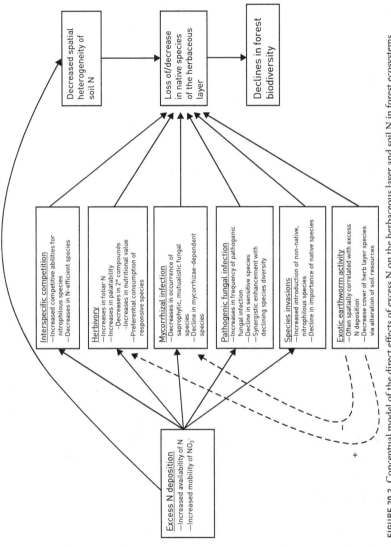

FIGURE 20.2 Conceptual model of the direct effects of excess N on the herbaceous layer and soil N in forest ecosystems (Gilliam 2006, used by permission). Note that although "exotic earthworm activity" is part of the original model of Gilliam (2006), it is not discussed in this chapter.

Roberts 2003). Nitrogen availability can exhibit considerable spatial heterogeneity (patchiness) in which plant roots compete interspecifically and with soil microbes (Hodge et al. 2000). Although temporal variation in nutrient availability is usually much less than availability of light, high spatial heterogeneity of soil resources is important in maintaining species diversity of the herb layer (chapter 8, this volume).

Given that the resource reduction model for competition (Wedin and Tilman 1993) predicts that plants gain competitive superiority by usurping essential soil resources and decreasing availability to other plants, high inputs of N to a forest should give a competitive disadvantage to N-efficient plants because these plants will be decreasingly able to deplete available soil N constantly resupplied via atmospheric deposition. Price and Morgan (2007) demonstrated this process experimentally for an herb-rich forest in Australia. They concluded that increased soil N promoted competitive exclusion of species adapted to low N availability, resulting in declines in species initially dominant prior to treatment.

Herbivory

Herbivory by vertebrate and invertebrate animals can exert a profound influence on the herbaceous layer of forests (chapters 13, 16, and 17, this volume; Roberts 2004). Intensity of herbivory is influenced by numerous factors, particularly nutritional value and palatability of plant—especially foliar—tissue. Chronically elevated N deposition can stimulate herb layer species to undergo luxury uptake of N (chapter 2, this volume), which increases foliar N concentrations and creates the potential to alter herbivore activity. Hartley and Mitchell (2005) found that additions of N increased grazing consumption of species adapted to low-N soils and did so in a way that shifted herb community composition.

In their synthesis and review of research on effects of N deposition on insect herbivory, Throop and Lerdau (2004) found a great degree of variability among studies, but concluded that the most likely mechanisms explaining N-enhanced herbivory were via deposition-mediated changes in quality and availability of forage plant tissue, especially those related to tissue chemistry. This included increases in content of amino acids, such as glutamine and arginine, and simultaneous decreases in carbon-based defensive secondary compounds, including condensed tannins and phenolics. Ultimately, increases in herbivory from excess N deposition potentially result in profound shifts in species composition/dominance of the herb layer through preferential consumption of those plants most sensitive to increased N availability.

Mycorrhizae

The well-known mutualistic relationships between vascular plant roots and fungal symbionts known as mycorrhizae are very common among herbaceous layer species (Whigham 2004). Plants get considerable benefits from the fungus, including increased access to nutrients, protection from pathogens, and increased water-use efficiency (Smith and Read 1997). Also, relative to non-mycorrhizal plants, mycorrhizal plants are superior competitors in nutrient-limited soils, primarily because of their fungal-enhanced abilities to take up nutrients, such as N (Read and Perez-Moreno 2003). Conversely, excess N can alter this competitive dynamic.

Several studies (e.g., Lilleskov et al. 2002, 2008; van Diepen et al. 2011) have found notable change in fungal sporocarp (aboveground) communities in response to increased

N, suggesting the likelihood of similar N-mediated alteration in ectomycorrhizal diversity. Dighton et al. (2004) used both an ambient N deposition gradient and an experimental greenhouse approach in demonstrating that ectomycorrhizae declined significantly with increased N in soils from New Jersey pine barren forests. Thus, it is likely that for forests receiving elevated levels of N deposition, herb layer composition and diversity may be negatively impacted via declines/loss of numerous mycorrhizal plant species.

Disease

Excess N has been shown to increase occurrence and degree of pathogenic fungal infections in a variety of plant species (Mitchell et al. 2003). Strengbom et al. (2006) found that the host plant *Vaccinium myrtillus* was more susceptible to the parasitic fungus *Valdensia heterodoxa* when exposed to 12.5 and 50 kg N ha^{-1} yr^{-1} compared to untreated control plots, and that the incidence of disease was significantly and positively correlated with summer precipitation. Nordin et al. (2006) reported a species-specific plant response to added N in boreal forests, one that contrasted with effects on pathogenic fungi. Plant species discriminated between the forms of added N: High-N-requiring species responded primarily to NO_3^-, and bryophytes responded to NH_4^+, whereas N-efficient species exhibited no response. In contrast, frequency of pathogenic fungi increased in response to all additions of N, regardless of the form in which it was added.

Mitchell et al. (2003) examined interactions of elevated CO_2 and decreased plant species diversity with effects of excess N on pathogenic fungal infection of several herbaceous species. They developed a metric called "pathogen load"—relative (%) leaf area infected by fungi—to quantify responses. All variables (elevated CO_2, decreased diversity, and increased N) increased pathogen load on several herb species, often interactively. Response to N was particularly pronounced for N-efficient species, but the most pronounced response of pathogen load was not to N, but to diversity. Plots with one or four species had > 2 times the pathogen load as plots with nine or 16 species. This finding has important relevance for long-term indirect effects of N on herb layer communities. That is, N-mediated declines in herb diversity may make forest herb communities more susceptible to pathogenic fungi.

Invasive Species

Although invasion of nonnative species in undisturbed forests with closed canopies are generally rare (chapter 15, this volume), considerable work has shown that species invasions can be facilitated by increasing N supply. These studies suggest that N limits the invasibility of the herbaceous layer of both conifer and hardwood forests (Gurevitch et al. 2008). Thus, N-saturated forests would be particularly susceptible to introduction of exotic species (Ehrenfeld 2010).

It is further likely that positive feedbacks can reinforce increases in invasions of forest herbaceous layers by exotic species via excess soil NO_3^-. Ehrenfeld et al. (2001) examined invasion of the herb layer of New Jersey hardwood stands by two exotic species—*Berberis thunbergii* and *Microstegium vimineum*—and found that soil in which these species grew had higher pH and net N mineralization/nitrification than soil occupied by native species. Higher pH in impacted soil was largely the result of preferential uptake of NO_3^- by the exotic species (Marschner 1995; Ehrenfeld et al.

2001). Ehrenfeld (2003) provided a synthesis of studies of this phenomenon and concluded that most of the 56 invasive species reviewed had the ability to drastically alter the N cycle of forest soils, particularly by increasing N availability, altering rates of N fixation, and producing litter of lower C/N ratios that decomposes more rapidly than that of co-occurring native species. Thus, a precarious feedback can develop when (i) excess N deposition increases N availability in forest soils that (ii) enhances the success of exotic species invading the herbaceous layer that (iii) further alter N dynamics of forest soil by maintaining high levels of available NO_3^- that (iv) simultaneously gives a competitive advantage to invasive species themselves and (v) a disadvantage to native species. As a result, there is substantial change in species composition and decrease in biodiversity of the herb layer following N-mediated increases in species' invasions.

SYNTHESIS OF N-RESPONSE STUDIES IN FORESTS

Research Approaches

As with most studies of effects of atmospheric deposition on terrestrial plant communities, research approaches toward determining the response of plant biodiversity to increasing N deposition can generally be divided into two broad categories: observational versus manipulative studies (Dunne et al. 2004). Each of these approaches has innate strengths and weaknesses that are largely mutually exclusive. Observational studies tend to be more common in Europe (Brunet et al. 1998; Strengbom et al. 2003; Stevens et al. 2010; Verheyen et al. 2012), whereas manipulative studies are generally more common in North America (Gilliam et al. 1994, 2006; Hurd et al. 1998; Rainey et al. 1999), South America (Siddique et al. 2010; Ochoa-Hueso et al. 2011), and Asia (Lu et al. 2010, 2011).

Observational, or gradient, studies to examine the potential effects of excess N on plant biodiversity typically lack experimental manipulations, instead characterizing variation in plant species composition over a given region experiencing widely varying amounts of N deposition. Among the scientific strengths associated with gradient studies, perhaps the most important is the ability to examine plant response to N under unaltered, ambient conditions, including cyclical processes related to seasonal change. In addition, N deposition occurs in these studies (1) without the "pulse" phenomenon associated with experimentally added N, and (2) in an ambient balance of forms of reactive N (including NH_4^+, NO_3^-, and organic N) via both wet and dry processes. Weaknesses of the N deposition gradient approach are primarily related to the fact that it is essentially a variation of space-for-time substitution often used in studies of plant succession (chapter 11, this volume). As such, these studies carry with them the unavoidable confounding effects of other environmental factors/gradients, including soil properties and microclimatic variables. Despite any limitations, gradient studies offer excellent insight into effects of N on plant biodiversity.

Manipulative, or experimental, approaches to studying the effects of excess N on plant biodiversity involve controlled addition of N in various forms and amounts to plots and, much more rarely, entire watersheds. A strength of this approach, especially for studies employing experimental plots (often 10 m × 10 m, but also as small as 1 m × 1 m), includes greater statistical power in data analysis related to use of replicated treatments. In addition, because of the more controlled nature of these experiments, they lack the problems of confounding of other environmental factors inherent in gradient studies. However, the weaknesses of manipulative studies arise out of their limitations in simulating natural processes. Thus, their form (usually NH_4^+, NO_3^-, or both) of N addition and timing/amount of N addition often poorly resemble ambient atmospheric N deposition processes. For example, the amount of N added will almost invariably represent a "pulse" of N not normally experienced under ambient conditions. As with gradient-based approaches, these manipulative studies have greatly enhanced our understanding of plant diversity responses to excess N. In addition, synoptic-scale analyses and meta-analyses of plot-based experiments have yielded still further insights (Suding, et al. 2005; Pennings et al. 2005; De Schrijver et al. 2011).

Temperate Forests

Gilliam (2006) reviewed the literature on effects of N on herbaceous layer dynamics of temperate forests of both eastern North America and Europe, the principle regions wherein this work was being conducted, with the main focus having been on effects on species diversity. The purpose of this section is to examine work published since that time.

EASTERN NORTH AMERICA

Regrettably, few, if any, eastern North American studies of the effects of N on herb layer dynamics published since 2006 have focused explicitly on responses of herb layer species composition and diversity to added N. However, studies have examined other facets of N response, such as interactions with patterns of land use and light availability and effects on invasive species that are directly relevant to influencing herb layer species composition and maintaining biodiversity.

Fraterrigo et al. (2009) studied responses of six herb taxa to N fertilization in forests of contrasting land use history in western North Carolina, with an emphasis on whether forests developed on former agricultural land. By adding three levels of N to paired plots in native (reference) versus post-agricultural stands, they found a significant interaction between N and land use for three taxa (*Arisaema triphyllum*, *Osmorhiza* spp., and *Cimicifuga racemosa*). In general, responses to N were more pronounced in post-agricultural stands. They concluded that post-agricultural forests may have been more N-limited, whereas native stands were approaching N saturation.

Focusing on the potential for N to influence invasions of exotic species (chapter 12, this volume), Gurevitch et al. (2008) determined interactive effects of light (via experimental gap formation) and N on establishment of seedlings of native and exotic woody species (i.e., transient species, chapter 1, this volume) in forests of Long Island, New York. Consistent with predictions of Gilliam and Turrill (1993), they found that light was more profound in its effect than was added N; however, they also found that invasive species responded more sensitively than did native species to N. They concluded that the response of invasive forest species to excess N is complex and, therefore, often unpredictable.

Also addressing the potential for invasive species to exhibit different growth response to N than native species, Ross et al. (2011) examined effects of adding different forms of available N (i.e., NH_4^+ versus NO_3^-) on native and exotic herb layer species from forests of New Jersey. They found a highly species-specific response to added N, largely but not solely related to invasiveness status. Invasive species *Microstegium vimineum* responded significantly via increases in stem height/relative growth rate and biomass to both forms of N. Surprisingly, native *Hamamelis virginiana* and invader *Berberis thunbergii* exhibited N-response patterns similar to each other, responding to both forms of added N, whereas native *Vaccinium pallidum* responded only to NH_4^+. Their conclusions supported those of Gurevitch et al. (2008) that the complexity of plant-environment interactions of invasive species precludes broad generalizations regarding the response, and subsequent effects, of species invasions to excess N.

Gilliam (2014) summarized ecosystem responses to N as part of an ongoing, watershed-based experimental study in north-central West Virginia. Whole-watershed studies are far less common than plot-based studies, due largely to the greater logistical challenges associated with carrying out experimental treatments on such a broad scale. These studies lack the statistical advantage of plot experiments, and in fact are subject to the problem of pseudoreplication (Hurlbert 1984). However, they have the advantage of examining responses on a more realistic spatial scale. Most watershed-scale manipulations have focused on responses to disturbances, such as forest harvesting, whereas those that have employed experimental N additions generally have examined only biogeochemical responses.

One watershed (WS3) at the Fernow Experimental Forest (FEF), West Virginia, has received aerial applications (via helicopter/airplane) of N since 1989. Gilliam et al. (1994) reported no response of the herb layer following two years of application, and Gilliam et al. (2006) reported similar lack of response following six years of N treatment. However, repeated sampling in 2003 indicated a substantial decline of species diversity of the herbaceous layer in response to aerial N additions, a decrease that appears to be related to loss of species and increased total cover (Gilliam 2014). Most of this has arisen from increases in cover of shade-intolerant *Rubus* spp. from < 1 percent in 1991 to ~ 15 percent in 2003. In fact, *Rubus* spp. cover was 5 percent of total herb layer in cover on WS3 and increased to > 35 percent of total herb cover by 2003. These increases have come at the expense of one of the more diverse taxa in these forests—*Viola* spp.

EUROPE

Working in forests of central Sweden, Strengbom and Nordin (2008) took advantage of N fertilization treatments initially designed for enhancing tree growth to experimentally examine residual (long-lived) effects of excess N on herb layer cover and diversity measures, with their treatment plots having received 150 kg N ha^{-1} over 20 years prior to their study. They found that the herb layer of the N-fertilized stand had significantly higher cover, lower evenness, and lower biodiversity, and concluded that excess N can exert long-term negative effects on the herb layer. Strengbom and Nordin (2012) followed their 2008 study with a field experiment to determine the interactive effects of forest harvesting and N additions in these same stands. Using a harvesting x fertilization factorial design, they found that species of the herb layer were more sensitive to N additions in harvested than in non-harvested stands.

Because herb layer dynamics can directly influence development of seedlings/juveniles of overstory species (chapter 14, this volume), it is important to determine how N-mediated changes in herb layer cover/composition might mitigate this influence. Diwold et al. (2010) investigated this by using soil C/N ratios as a surrogate for N processing and availability in forest soils of the Northern Limestone Alps of Austria to examine relationships with herb cover, with focus on effects on tree seedlings. They found that N availability was not only positively correlated with herb cover, but that increases in herb cover had a negative effect on recruitment and growth rate of seedlings of one of the dominant hardwood species, *Acer pseudoplatanus* (L.).

Hedwall et al. (2011) studied the effects of frequency of N fertilization on herb layer species composition and diversity in forests of southern Sweden, including bryophyte species, which can be quite prominent in these forests, in their analysis. Although the plots receiving N treatments exhibited altered species composition and decreased diversity, relative to control plots for vascular, there was no significant response found for bryophyte species. All responses increased with increasing frequency of N additions. Hedwall et al. (2011) concluded that increased N will lead to long-term change in herb layer dynamics at the scale of individual stands and possibly that of the landscape.

N HOMOGENEITY HYPOTHESIS

There is increasing evidence that spatial variability (heterogeneity) in soil resources, such as essential nutrients, exerts a profound influence in creating and maintaining high species diversity in plant communities, including the herb layer of forest ecosystems (Hutchings et al. 2003; Lundholm 2009; Costanza et al. 2011; García-Palacios 2012; chapter 8, this volume). In a synthesis paper, Bartels and Chen (2010) reviewed 130 relevant studies from the peer-reviewed literature and found that both resource supply (quantity) and heterogeneity were important in maintaining herb layer diversity, but that heterogeneity was more important in disturbed forests, a condition that characterizes most forests of eastern North America. Costanza et al. (2011) analyzed data from 150 nested vegetation plots from North and South Carolina and found consistently positive relationships between heterogeneity and herb species richness, independent of spatial scale.

One of the early observations in the ongoing whole-watershed N experiment at Fernow Experimental Forest, West Virginia, wherein N is added aerially three times per year at a rate of 35 kg N ha^{-1} yr^{-1}, was that the N treatment increased extractable soil NO$_3^-$ and soil solution NO$_3^-$. A more novel finding, however, was that the treatment also substantially decreased the spatial heterogeneity of these variables in the 35 ha treatment watershed (Gilliam et al. 2001). This observation led to the development of the *N homogeneity hypothesis* (Gilliam 2006).

Assumptions and Predictions

The primary assumptions of the N homogeneity hypothesis arise from the previously discussed relationship between spatial heterogeneity of soil resources and diversity of plant communities, focusing on spatial heterogeneity of available N in forest ecosystems. Relatively undisturbed forests typically display a high degree of spatial heterogeneity, with spatially discrete areas of high and low rates of N mineralization in soils. High heterogeneity of soil N should maintain high diversity, particularly at the landscape scale, by creating a patchwork of areas of high soil N—referred to as "islands of fertility" by Schlesinger et al. (1996) and as "hot spots" by McClain et al. (2003)—that support nitrophilous species, and areas of low soil N that support non-nitrophilous, low-N-requiring species. A final assumption of the hypothesis is that high rates of atmospheric N deposition will decrease spatial heterogeneity (increase homogeneity)

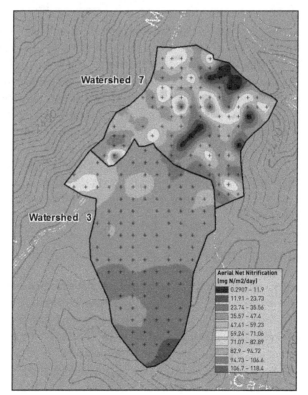

FIGURE 20.3 Spatial patterns of net nitrification in soils of reference (WS7) and N-treated (WS3) watersheds at Fernow Experimental Forest, West Virginia. See text for description of N treatments. Figure used with permission of William Peterjohn, West Virginia University, Morgantown, WV.

of N by increasing N availability of the low-N matrix. These assumptions are supported by work carried out at the Fernow Experimental Forest, West Virginia (fig. 20.3).

Accordingly, the N homogeneity hypothesis predicts that excess N deposition will lead to decreases in spatial heterogeneity of N availability and that such N-mediated decreases will lead to decreases in biodiversity of the herb layer of impacted forests. By homogenizing patterns of N availability (i.e., maintaining high levels of soil N throughout the landscape), increased excess N in atmospheric deposition will give a competitive advantage to the relatively few nitrophilous species (see fig. 20.1) that will outcompete non-nitrophilous plant species.

Tests of Hypotheses in Literature

Since its original appearance in 2006, the N homogeneity hypothesis has been reviewed in synthesis papers (e.g., Lu et al. 2008; Fujimaki et al. 2009; García-Palacios 2012) and addressed, either explicitly or implicitly, in several studies. All but one study (Bernhardt-Römermann et al. 2010) provided evidence either in direct support of or consistent with predictions of the N homogeneity hypothesis (e.g., Eilts et al. 2011). Hülber et al. (2008) sampled > 120 plots throughout the ~ 90 ha Northern Limestone Alps in Austria and found results indicating that homogenization of site conditions from long-term high levels of N deposition leads to a homogenization of forest floor vegetation. They concluded that these limestone areas with such diverse soil conditions at the broader landscape scale are negatively affected by airborne N deposition, supporting predictions of the hypothesis. Combining a plant function type (PFT) and non-manipulative N gradient (soil N 0.6–1.1 percent) approach, Bernhardt-Römermann et al. (2010) sampled 20 relevés in a ~ 24 ha deciduous forest of southern Germany to test the N homogeneity hypothesis. Of the seven PFTs they identified (based on leaf persistence, height of plant, seed mass, and flowering phenology), they found that the greatest numbers were associated with high-N plots, inconsistent with predictions of the hypothesis. Hedwall et al. (2011) examined fertilized and unfertilized plots in forest stands of middle and southern Sweden to assess effects of N on herb layer composition and species richness. Fewer vascular plant species were observed on fertilized plots than on control plots, although numbers of bryophyte species remained unchanged. These authors reported support for the N homogeneity hypothesis, finding that fertilized plots also showed a lower variance in species composition and a lower Shannon's diversity index than unfertilized plots. Indeed, fertilized plots were more similar to each other than unfertilized plots were to each other over the geographical range (Hedwall et al. 2011). García-Palacios et al. (2012) added another dimension to this response—belowground processes—in a synthesis study that strongly supported the N homogeneity hypothesis.

In contrast to the lack of herb layer response at Fernow Experimental Forest, West Virginia, following two and six years of N additions to WS3 (Gilliam et al. 1994, 2006;

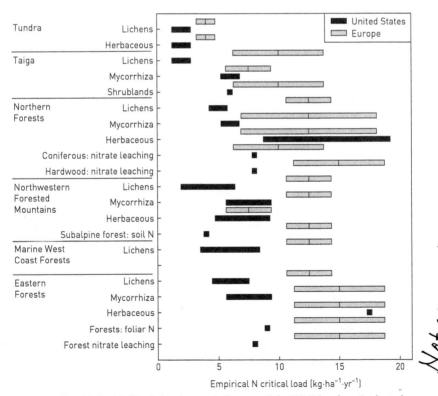

FIGURE 20.4 Empirical critical loads for nitrogen in Europe and the U.S. Taken from Pardo et al. (2011); used by permission.

(a)

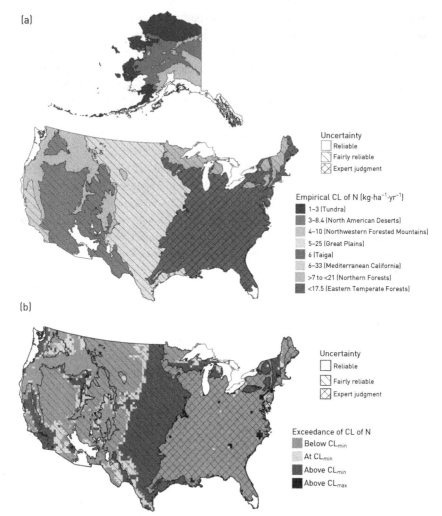

Uncertainty
☐ Reliable
▨ Fairly reliable
▧ Expert judgment

Empirical CL of N (kg·ha⁻¹·yr⁻¹)

Empirical CL of N (kg·ha^{-1}·yr^{-1})
■ 1–3 (Tundra)
■ 3–8.4 (North American Deserts)
▨ 4–10 (Northwestern Forested Mountains)
□ 5–25 (Great Plains)
■ 6 (Taiga)
▨ 6–33 (Mediterranean California)
▨ >7 to <21 (Northern Forests)
■ <17.5 (Eastern Temperate Forests)

(b)

Uncertainty
☐ Reliable
▨ Fairly reliable
▧ Expert judgment

Exceedance of CL of N
■ Below CL$_{min}$
▨ At CL$_{min}$
■ Above CL$_{min}$
■ Above CL$_{max}$

FIGURE 20.5 Maps of (a) critical loads of N for herbaceous plants and shrubs by ecoregion in the U.S., and (b) exceedances of N for herbaceous plants and shrubs by ecoregion in the U.S. Taken from Pardo et al. (2011); used by permission.

respectively), Gilliam (2014) reported reductions in species diversity—related both to decreased richness and evenness—following 14 years of treatment. This was primarily related to increases in cover of clonal *Rubus* spp., which was initially (1991) a minor component (~ 1 percent relative cover) of the herb layer, but was ~ 15 percent of the herb layer in 2003. Contemporaneously with these increases in cover, spatial variability of cover of *Rubus* spp. has decreased on WS3, consistent with declines in spatial variability of soil N (Gilliam and Adams 2011), supporting the N homogeneity hypothesis. Other studies (e.g., Strengbom and Nordin 2008; Hedwall et al. 2011) have found excess N-mediated increases in *Rubus* spp. Furthermore, the clonal nature of species, such as *Rubus* spp., has been shown to contribute measurably to increases in homogeneity of herb layer composition. For example, Eilts et al. (2011) found strongly consistent negative effects of clonal plants on species richness of herb-dominated communities, effects that were greatest at high fertility and when soil resources were applied at a scale at which rhizomatous clonal species could integrate across resource patches.

Clonal Plants

Recent integrative models to study the effects of N on plant diversity are being incorporated into determination of *critical loads* for N deposition. This is a concept developed originally in Europe, but it is now being used in North America (Pardo et al. 2011). By definition, the critical load for N is the level of N deposition below which there are no harmful ecological effects of excess N. Critical load is distinguished from *target load*, which is the level of N deposition established by policymakers to protect sensitive ecosystems, considering such criteria as economic costs for reduction of N emissions. Critical loads are generally determined via three approaches: empirical (based on observations, such as those reviewed above), simple mass balance (using inputs/outputs of N), and dynamic models (expanding the steady-state models by incorporating internal feedbacks, including ecosystem N accumulation). Until recently, critical load approaches have been largely based on N biogeochemistry (e.g., examining effects on base cations, soil fertility, and foliar chemistry). However, more recent studies have begun to include effects of N on plant biodiversity as a major response variable and critical load criterion (Nordin et al. 2005; Bobbink et al. 2010; Posch et al. 2011; Pardo et al. 2011). Based on results taken from Pardo et al. (2011), examples of critical load determinations are given in figs. 20.4 and 20.5. From these data, it appears that much of the eastern U.S. is below critical loads for N.

CONCLUSIONS

It is clear that excess N has the potential to substantially alter species composition and decrease biodiversity of the herbaceous layer of forests of eastern North America, and to do so in ways that are distinctive from other forms of forest disturbance. The literature is replete with studies confirming that increasing N in forests from N limitation to N saturation can not only alter soil N biogeochemistry and deplete nutrient cations, but it can also (1) alter competition to give advantages to fewer nitrophilous species, (2) increase intensity and degree of herbivory, (3) increase frequency of mycorrhizal infection, (4) increase occurrence and severity of fungal pathogens, and (5) enhance species invasions. Such responses of all these processes can contribute to N-mediated changes in forest herb layer community dynamics.

The N homogeneity hypothesis that predicts loss of biodiversity in forest ecosystems experiencing chronically elevated N deposition has largely been supported in the literature, as several studies have reported increased soil N heterogeneity—coupled with declines of herb layer diversity—with increasing N supply, particularly at the stand and landscape scales. As this is a hypothesis that is easily tested through manipulative field studies, I suggest that more studies be carried out to examine its application in a variety of forest types, particularly in eastern North America, where rates of N deposition can be notably high. Indeed, given the dearth of studies within this region on the effects of N on herb layer diversity, especially relative to more numerous studies carried out in Europe, I strongly urge that more emphasis be placed on such investigations in general, both by biogeochemists and vegetation scientists.

21 Climate Change and Forest Herbs of Temperate Deciduous Forests

Jesse Bellemare and David A. Moeller

Climate change is projected to be one of the top threats to biodiversity in coming decades (Thomas et al. 2004; Parmesan 2006). In the Temperate Deciduous Forest (TDF) biome, mounting climate change is expected to become an increasing and long-term threat to many forest plant species (Honnay et al. 2002; Skov and Svenning 2004; Van der Veken et al. 2007a), on par with major current threats to forest plant biodiversity, such as high rates of deer herbivory, intensive forestry, habitat fragmentation, and land use change (chapters 4, 14, 15, and 16, this volume). At the broadest scale, changing climate regimes are predicted to cause major shifts in the geographic distribution of the climate envelopes currently occupied by forest plants, with many species' ranges projected to shift northward or to higher elevations to track these changes (Iverson and Prasad 1998; Schwartz et al. 2006; Morin et al. 2008; McKenney et al. 2011). In parallel, these climate-driven range dynamics are likely to include population declines or regional extinctions for many plant species, particularly in more southerly areas and along species' warm-margin distribution limits (Iverson and Prasad 1998; Hampe and Petit 2005; Schwartz et al. 2006; Svenning and Skov 2006; Morin et al. 2008).

Among the plant species characteristic of TDF, forest herbs may be especially vulnerable to climate change for several reasons. First, many forest herbs have biological and ecological traits that may limit the rate at which they are capable of migrating in response to changing climate (e.g., species with seed dispersal mechanisms adapted primarily to local movement rather than long-distance dispersal; Van der Veken et al. 2007a). Second, the fragmentation and limited connectivity of forest areas due to agriculture, roads, and development in the modern landscape may exacerbate the innate challenges of long-distance dispersal and colonization for these species (Honnay et al. 2002; chapter 4 this volume). Finally, the geographic distributions of some forest herbs may still be impacted by past climate change (e.g., marginalization to southern areas by Pleistocene glaciations; Skov and Svenning 2004; Van der Veken et al. 2007a), making their rapid response to modern climate change less likely. Although the magnitude of the threat to forest herb biodiversity posed by climate change is not yet fully understood, several fields are providing important new insights into the relationship between temperate forest plants and climate change, including paleoecological (e.g., Williams et al. 2004) and phylogeographic research (e.g., Gonzales et al. 2008), comparative studies (e.g., Van der Veken et al. 2007a), and bioclimatic modeling approaches (e.g., Skov and Svenning 2004), as well as field-based experimentation (e.g., Van der Veken et al. 2007b; Warren et al. 2011). A synthetic view combining insights from these various fields will be key to understanding the challenges posed by modern climate change and developing effective conservation strategies for vulnerable plant species.

Although the rate and eventual magnitude of modern climate change are projected to differ qualitatively from climate dynamics in the recent geologic past (e.g., glacial cycles of the late Quaternary Period), important insights into the nature of threats to forest plant biodiversity and to the types of species most likely to be severely impacted by rapid climate change may be drawn from historical and biogeographic perspectives (Delcourt 2002; Svenning 2003; Van der Veken et al. 2007a; Petit et al. 2008; Willis et al. 2010). In this chapter, we review what is known about the long-term, large-scale range dynamics of forest herbs in response to past climate change and present a new biogeographic analysis investigating how contemporary distribution and diversity patterns among a subset of rare forest herbs may relate to these past climate dynamics. We also discuss how forest herb species may be affected by contemporary climate change and consider options for species conservation.

TEMPERATE DECIDUOUS FORESTS AND CLIMATE CHANGE: DEEP TIME PERSPECTIVES

The plant lineages that comprise the modern TDF biome have a deep and dynamic history in the Northern Hemisphere, inextricably linked to climate change over millions of years (Davis 1983; Donoghue and Smith 2004; Graham 2011). Almost all major temperate forest plant lineages have histories extending back 10s of millions of years into the Tertiary and upper Cretaceous periods, spanning climatic conditions that have been both significantly warmer and colder than at present (Graham 2011). For example, many of the angiosperm forest tree lineages that provide the structural foundation for modern TDF plant communities, including Aceraceae, Fagaceae, and Juglandaceae, trace their origins and rise to prominence to the upper Cretaceous (~ 100–65 million years ago; Manchester 1999; Willis and McElwain 2002; Wang et al. 2009). Similarly, characteristic forest herb lineages, such as the Aristolochiaceae, Berberidaceae, Ranunculaceae, and Liliaceae, emerged relatively early in the evolutionary diversification of angiosperms and include many genera that have apparently been closely associated with temperate forest habitats for millions of years since (i.e., phylogenetic niche conservatism; Ricklefs and Latham 1992; Wen 1999; Patterson and Givnish 2002).

During much of the upper Cretaceous and Tertiary, relatively warm and wet climatic conditions, combined with greater connectivity among landmasses in the Northern Hemisphere, allowed TDF-like vegetation to extend across large portions of North America and Eurasia, including many high latitude areas now occupied by boreal forest, tundra, and arctic desert (Manchester 1999; Wen 1999; Tiffney and Manchester 2001; Willis and McElwain 2002). With the onset of climatic cooling and drying in the Pliocene Epoch (~ 5.3–2.6 million years ago), and the advent of extensive continental glaciations in the Quaternary (~ 2.6 million years ago to present), the geographic distributions of TDF plant species were forced southward in a series of climate-driven range contractions during glacial maxima (Davis 1983; Latham and Ricklefs 1993; Delcourt 2002). Paleoecological studies, focused primarily on the pollen record from during and after the Last Glacial Maximum (LGM; ~ 21,500 years ago), have provided an important window on recent range dynamics, documenting large-scale shifts in the distributions of many forest plant species during periods of rapid climate change (Davis 1983; Prentice et al. 1991; Williams et al. 2004). Consistent with evolutionary research suggesting long-term niche conservatism in forest herbs (e.g., Ricklefs and Latham 1992; Wen 1999), these paleoecological studies tend to document migration or altitudinal shifts in response to past climate change, rather than substantial *in situ* evolution of species climatic tolerances (Huntley and Webb 1989; Martínez-Meyer and Peterson 2006; but see Davis et al. 2005).

Past climate change has also been linked to the extinction or regional extirpation of numerous TDF plant taxa (Davis 1983; Latham and Ricklefs 1993; Svenning 2003). Although relatively few plant extinctions are documented from the final glacial cycles of the Pleistocene Epoch (Bennett 1997; but see Jackson and Weng 1999), the initial shift to colder and drier climate in the Pliocene and the onset of extensive glaciations in the early Quaternary have been linked to the regional extinction of large numbers of characteristic TDF plant lineages in Europe, including *Carya, Hamamelis, Liriodendron, Magnolia, Tsuga*, and upward of 80 other woody plant genera (Davis 1983; Latham and Ricklefs 1993; Svenning 2003). Fewer forest plant extinctions are documented for eastern North America, but this period did see the regional extirpation of at least eight woody plant genera, including *Dendropanax, Platycarya, Pterocarya*, and *Sciadopitys* (Latham and Ricklefs 1993; Manchester 1999; Tiffney and Manchester 2001). In contrast, species from many of the plant lineages extirpated in Europe and eastern North America persist to this day in the TDF of eastern Asia, where species losses appear to have been buffered by the region's greater topographic heterogeneity and lack of extensive continental glaciations (Huntley 1993; Latham and Ricklefs 1993; Qian and Ricklefs 1999). Notably, the severe Pliocene and early Quaternary species losses in Europe appear to underlie the striking differences in contemporary species diversity seen when contrasting European TDF with similar forests in eastern North America or eastern Asia (Davis 1983; Huntley 1993; Latham and Ricklefs 1993; Svenning 2003). These deep-time biogeographical patterns underscore the potential for long-lasting impacts of anthropogenic climate change on plant diversity and distribution in the TDF biome (Delcourt 2002; Thomas et al. 2004; Petit et al. 2008).

WHICH FOREST HERBS MAY BE MOST VULNERABLE TO CLIMATE CHANGE?

It is clear from past episodes of climate change and future projections that not all species are equally threatened by changing climate (Svenning 2003; Thomas et al. 2004; Thuiller et al. 2005; Schwartz et al. 2006; Willis et al. 2007). For example, the ongoing poleward range shifts of many bird, mammal, and insect taxa suggest that some relatively vagile species are already adjusting their distributions in response to anthropogenic climate change (Parmesan and Yohe 2003; Hickling et al. 2005; Zuckerberg et al. 2009; Breed et al. 2012). Although similar range shifts in response to modern climate change have not yet been well documented for forest plants, the paleoecological record suggests that some species may be capable of relatively rapid range adjustments (e.g., Clark 1998; Williams et al. 2004). Nevertheless, the substantial numbers of forest plant extirpations and extinctions linked to the onset of a qualitatively new climatic regime during the late Tertiary and early Quaternary suggest that not all forest plants are equally resilient to abrupt climate change (Latham and Ricklefs 1993; Svenning 2003).

Of greatest concern in the face of modern climate change are species with limited geographic distributions, such as endemics and other small-ranged species (Thomas et al. 2004; Parmesan 2006; Schwartz et al. 2006; Thomas 2011). The increased risk of extinction projected for small-ranged species traces to a number of ecological and biogeographical factors. For example, macroecological studies have frequently detected a positive correlation between range size and local abundance, such that small-ranged species are often characterized by lower abundances and smaller population sizes than widespread species (Gaston 2003), a result that has been apparent in several plant-focused studies (Thompson et al. 1998; Murphy et al. 2006; Pocock et al. 2006). This characteristic, combined with the geographic clustering of populations, may expose small-ranged species to greater risk of extinction due simply to stochastic population processes or to chance regional events (e.g., drought, introduction of novel pathogens; Gaston 2003). In addition to risk factors that may be inherently linked to small range size, modern climate change poses a significant new threat to many small-ranged, endemic species (Thomas et al. 2004; Thomas 2011). Specifically, substantial geographic disjunctions are likely to develop between the locations of many small-ranged species' current ranges and the locations of climatically similar areas in the future (Thomas et al. 2004; Schwartz et al. 2006). Such disjunctions between present and future habitat areas are less likely for widespread species, where at least some portions of these broadly distributed species' ranges are likely to remain climatically suitable into the future, buffering against climate-driven threats (Thomas et al. 2004; Schwartz et al. 2006). Without successful long-distance dispersal to track shifting climate zones as they move poleward, populations of small-ranged species may soon be exposed to novel climatic regimes that fall outside the range of climatic conditions they exist under currently; for some species this is likely to result in population declines or extinction (Thomas et al. 2004).

WHY MIGHT SMALL-RANGED SPECIES HAVE SMALL RANGES?

Ecologists have long recognized that the restricted distributions of small-ranged endemic plant species may be the outcome of a variety of causes (Willis 1922; Wherry 1944; Stebbins and Major 1965; Daubenmire 1978). Among potential drivers of endemism, the most commonly cited are species' innate biological or ecological characteristics (e.g., competitive inferiority or association with uncommon habitats; Daubenmire 1978; Baskin and Baskin 1989; Lavergne 2004), their recent evolutionary origin (Stebbins and Major 1965; Levin 2000; Lesica et al. 2006), or endemism due to the contraction of a formerly more extensive range (Daubenmire 1978). These three general classes of endemic species have been termed "ecological endemics," "neoendemics," and "paleoendemics," respectively (Stebbins and Major 1965; Daubenmire 1978; Estill and Cruzan 2001). In addition to these traditional explanations for the small ranges of endemic plant species, studies have increasingly raised the possibility that seed dispersal limitation may also be a factor contributing to the restricted geographic distributions of many small-ranged plants (Kropf et al. 2002; Rossetto and Kooyman 2005; Svenning and Skov 2007a; Van der Veken et al. 2007a; Rossetto et al. 2008). In the case of ecological endemics whose distributions are linked to unusual habitats (e.g., serpentine bedrock), suitable habitat patches are often widely scattered in a matrix of unsuitable habitat, likely making inter-site seed dispersal and range expansion difficult. For neoendemics, evidence suggests that some recently evolved species may simply have had limited time to disperse and expand their ranges (Lesica et al. 2006). Dispersal limitation has also been suggested as a key factor involved in the restricted distributions of some paleoendemics (Rossetto and Kooyman 2005; Rosetto et al. 2008). Although considerations of paleoendemics frequently focus on the dynamics of range fragmentation and decline leading to these species' restricted distributions (Daubenmire 1978; Levin 2000), it is also evident that the limited expansion of paleoendemics' ranges after conditions have ameliorated could be linked to dispersal limitation (Svenning and Skov 2007a; Van der Veken et al. 2007a; Hampe and Jump 2011). In general, the potential for dispersal limitation to be a key historical factor influencing the small range size of many endemic plants suggests that these species will have limited ability to track modern climate change.

Dispersal limitation of range size for endemic forest herbs could be traced to innate species characteristics, as well as aspects of regional landscape structure and biogeographic history. For example, studies have shown that factors such as low seed production, a lack of morphological adaptations for long-distance seed dispersal, and the absence of suitable dispersal agents may lead to significant dispersal limitation for many forest herbs (e.g., Matlack 1994; Bellemare et al. 2002; Verheyen et al. 2003; Van der Veken et al. 2007a; chapter 16, this volume). Although most studies investigating seed dispersal limitation in forest herbs have focused on local scales over relatively short timeframes (e.g., post-agricultural recolonization of secondary forests; Matlack 1994; chapter 16, this volume), evidence is increasing from studies at larger geographic scales that dispersal limitation may also contribute to limited range size in some forest herbs (e.g., Skov and Svenning 2004; Van der Veken et al. 2007a; Bellemare 2010). For example, Van der Veken et al. (2007a) found that European forest herbs with seeds adapted to local dispersal (e.g., via ants) and those lacking morphological adaptations for dispersal had significantly smaller geographic ranges than related species with seeds exhibiting adaptations for longer-distance dispersal (e.g., via wind or vertebrates). These studies have highlighted the potential for key climate change risk factors, like small range size and dispersal limitation (Thomas et al. 2004), to be causally linked in forest herbs (Van der Veken et al. 2007a).

WHERE ARE SMALL-RANGED FOREST HERBS IN EASTERN NORTH AMERICA?

Given that small-ranged species are expected to be at increased risk from climate change, what do we know about the current distributions of small-ranged forest herbs in eastern North America? To date, there have been no comprehensive reviews of the distribution of small-ranged forest plants (i.e., endemics) or analyses of patterns of endemism focused specifically on the TDF biome. Prior studies by Stein et al. (2000) and Estill and Cruzan (2001) have surveyed patterns of endemism in portions of eastern North America, but neither focused on forest habitats in detail. These investigations highlighted numerous "hotspots" of endemism in non-forest habitats (e.g., scrub and sand hill vegetation in central Florida, open cedar glade habitats in central Tennessee), in addition to a limited number of hotspots in TDF (e.g., the southern Appalachian Mountains; Estill and Cruzan 2001). Although these earlier studies have been key to mapping the distribution and diversity of plant endemics in general, a biome-centered survey focusing specifically on small-ranged plants associated with TDF has not been conducted. Such a study will be crucial in the context of climate change, as the unique ecology and biogeographic history of forest plants may predispose them to climate-related vulnerabilities. Further, conservation options for small-ranged forest plants may include some approaches (e.g., assisted colonization) that may be less feasible for species associated with other, more unusual and spatially limited habitats where endemics are often found, such as serpentine barrens or limestone glades.

In the analysis presented here, we have focused specifically on the distribution of small-ranged forest herbs associated with TDF habitats in eastern North America. To identify appropriate species for inclusion in this survey, we visually inspected all plant species distribution maps developed by the Biota of North America Program (BONAP; Kartesz 2010) for species with geographic ranges centered in eastern North America. These maps are available online (www.bonap.org) and are updated on a continuing basis as new records become available; the distribution maps used in the present analysis were accessed from BONAP in 2010. For the purposes of this survey, we defined "small-ranged" plant species as those with distributions including 70 or fewer U.S. counties. Although many plant species with small ranges are classified as endangered or threatened at the federal or state level, our species selection process did not consider current listed status as a criterion; rather, we consider range size as an important correlate of future risk in the face of climate change, regardless of species' current legal status (cf. Harris and Pimm 2008; also see chapter 4, this volume, for a review of population biology and threats to federally listed forest herbs).

For each small-ranged herbaceous species with a distribution centered in eastern North America, we reviewed habitat information to identify those that were associated with deciduous forest habitats using the *Flora of North America* (Flora of North America editorial committee 1993+) and key regional references (e.g., Radford et al. 1968; Gleason and Cronquist 1991; Yatskievych 1999; Wunderlin and Hansen 2003; Weakley 2011). Species were selected for inclusion if their habitat descriptions included deciduous forest or woodland, or mixed deciduous-coniferous forest (e.g., hardwood-hemlock or oak-pine forest). Species were also included if their habitat was more specialized but still typically situated within a deciduous forest matrix (e.g., shaded ledges, woodland clearings, forest edges, forested seeps and stream banks). A subset of the forest herb species included was also described as occasionally occurring outside forest habitats in meadows, open rocky areas, wetlands, or along roadsides. Of note, BONAP distribution data for plant species in Canada are provided at a coarser scale (i.e., province level) than within the U.S. (county level); however, this did not become a significant issue in quantifying species distributions as almost all forest herbs with small ranges were distributed substantially south of the Canadian border.

In total, the criteria outlined above resulted in a set of 189 small-ranged forest herb species native to deciduous forests in eastern North America (appendix 21.1). These species represent taxa from 38 families and 87 genera, with four of these families accounting for ~ 50 percent of the species included: Asteraceae (34 spp., ~ 18 percent), Lamiaceae (21 spp., ~ 11 percent), Melanthiaceae (21 spp., ~ 11 percent), and Cyperaceae (20 spp., ~ 11 percent). Notably, representatives of the latter two were drawn almost entirely from *Trillium* and *Carex*, with 21 and 18 small-ranged forest species, respectively. Pteridophytes and lycophytes contributed only two small-ranged species to the final analysis (*Botrychium mormo* W. H. Wagner and *Gymnocarpium appalachianum* Pryer), as most ferns and lycophytes associated with forest habitats in eastern North America are relatively widespread.

To provide quantitative estimates of range size and geographic position for the 189 small-ranged forest herbs, the BONAP county-level distribution maps were digitized into a geographic information system (GIS). The total range area occupied by each species was calculated as the summation of the areas of all the counties occupied by that species; additionally, a centroid was estimated for each range based on these county-level distributions. Range sizes exhibited a positively skewed distribution, with a median range size of ~ 61,448 km^2 (fig. 21.1). Minimum range size was ~ 1,600 km^2 for *Onosmodium decipiens* J. Allison, a narrow endemic native to open woodland and glade habitats on dolomite bedrock in Bibb County, Alabama. Maximum range size was ~ 280,000 km^2 for the relatively more widespread *Meehania cordata* (Nutt.) Britton, a species native to mountain woods in the mid-Appalachians from western North Carolina to southwestern Pennsylvania. Notably, even the range sizes of the most widespread small-ranged species included in our analysis, such as *M. cordata*, are still almost an order of magnitude smaller than the ranges of large-ranged forest herbs like *Podophyllum peltatum* L., *Asarum canadense* L., or *Sanguinaria canadensis* L. (estimated range areas ~ 2.3, 2.7, and 3.5 million km^2, respectively).

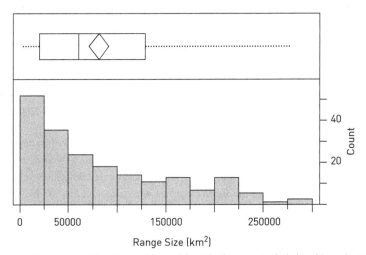

FIGURE 21.1 Range sizes of the 189 small-ranged forest herb species included in this study. Range sizes were estimated as the total area of U.S. counties occupied by each species, as determined from Biota of North America Program (BONAP) county-level species distribution maps accessed in 2010. Box plot (top) depicts mean range size (diamond), median range size (vertical line), the 25th and 75th quantiles (outer edges of box), and dashed "whisker" lines mark the range of data beyond these quantiles.

To assess overall patterns of small-ranged forest herb distribution and diversity in eastern North America, range maps for the 189 species were compiled in a GIS to create a map of small-ranged species richness (no. of small-ranged species per county). The results of this analysis show that the distribution and diversity of small-ranged forest herbs across eastern North America exhibit marked biogeographical patterning, with both pronounced hotspots and coldspots of endemic species richness (fig. 21.2). At the broadest scale, small-ranged forest herbs are relatively common in the southeastern U.S. and lower Midwest, but are almost entirely absent from TDF areas north of the Last Glacial Maximum (LGM) in the Northeast, upper Midwest, and adjacent Canada (figs. 21.2 and 21.3). Although these northern areas often include well-developed forest herb communities, almost all of the species found north of the LGM have relatively large geographic ranges when compared to the small-ranged forest herb species that were the focus of this analysis.

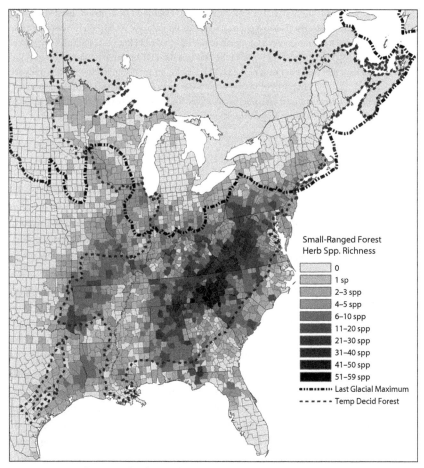

FIGURE 21.2 Distribution and richness of 189 small-ranged forest herb species in eastern North America relative to the distribution of the Temperate Deciduous Forest biome (TDF; dashed line) and the Last Glacial Maximum (LGM; dash-dot line). County-level richness of small-ranged forest herbs ranges from a high of 59 species in western North Carolina to a low of zero species recorded across much of the formerly glaciated northern portion of the TDF biome, and some counties in the southeastern U.S. along the Coastal Plain and Mississippi Embayment. Boundaries of TDF biome follow Ricketts et al. (1999); the LGM boundary was derived from state-level surficial geology maps.

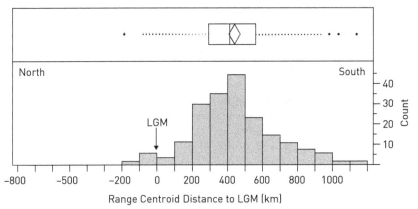

FIGURE 21.3 Range centroid distances to the LGM boundary for 189 small-ranged forest herb species in eastern North America. Positive values indicate range centroids that are situated south of the LGM, outside formerly glaciated regions; negative values indicate centroids located north of the LGM, within formerly glaciated regions; the LGM boundary is set to 0 on the distance axis. The mean distance from range centroids north to the LGM was 438 km (± 224 SD). The distance axis extends to –800 km, or 800 km north of the LGM, as the TDF biome extends northward into areas of Canada ~ 800–900 km north of the LGM; however, no small-ranged species centroids are located further than 186 km north of the LGM (i.e., –186 km on x axis in this figure). In contrast, the centroids of 16 small-ranged forest herb species are found near or beyond the southern boundaries of the TDF biome in the southeastern U.S., ~ 800–1,200 km south of the LGM.

Among the 189 species included in this analysis, almost all (183 spp., ~ 97 percent) have range centroids situated substantially south of the LGM (mean distance: 438 km ± 224 SD; fig. 21.3). Of the six species with range centroids falling north of the LGM boundary, only *Botrychium mormo* (a pteridophyte native to sugar maple forests in northern Minnesota, Wisconsin, and Michigan) has a range situated substantially north of the LGM (centroid located 186 km inside LGM boundary); the remaining five species have ranges that straddle the LGM boundary (centroids < 100 km inside LGM; fig. 21.3). This pattern of low richness of endemic forest herbs in formerly glaciated regions emerged despite the large spatial extent of the TDF biome in areas north of the LGM. In fact, portions of the TDF biome extend 800–900 km north of the LGM into Canada, but no small-ranged species distributions approached this limit. In contrast, some areas along the southern margins of the TDF biome, lying 800–1,200 km south of the LGM, have high concentrations of small-ranged forest herb species (fig. 21.2). Indeed, 16 of the small-ranged species (~ 8 percent) included in this analysis have range centroids located on or outside of the southern boundary of the TDF biome; these outlying species tend to be associated with patches of TDF-like habitat in cooler and more mesic sites on the coastal plain in the southeastern U.S., such as north-facing slopes or bluffs along rivers.

In contrast to the general absence of small-ranged forest herbs from most north-ern portions of the TDF biome, the southeastern U.S. and lower Midwest include sev-eral geographically distinctive hotspots of small-ranged forest herb diversity, as well as a more heterogeneous background pattern of low to moderate levels of endemism across much of the region (fig. 21.2). Although the criteria for defining and delineating hotspots can be somewhat subjective when confronted with the complex diversity pat-terns evident in our results, we focus here on three prominent areas that stand out due to their geographic distinctiveness and relatively high diversity of small-ranged forest herbs: the *Southern Appalachians*, the *Apalachicola River* region in the Florida panhandle and adjacent Georgia, and the *Interior Highlands* of Arkansas and Missouri (fig. 21.2).

The Southern Appalachian Hotspot

Previous studies have highlighted the southern Appalachian Mountains as a major center of plant diversity and endemism in eastern North America (e.g., Stein et al. 2000; Estill and Cruzan 2001). This trend clearly holds for small-ranged forest herbs, with counties in western North Carolina, eastern Tennessee, southwestern Virginia, and extreme northern Georgia and western South Carolina including the highest richness of small-ranged forest herbs anywhere in eastern North America (peaking at 59 species with overlapping distributions in western North Carolina; fig. 21.2). In total, 119 of the 189 small-ranged species (63 percent) reviewed in this survey have distributions that overlap the Southern Appalachian hotspot; among these 119 species, 18 have ranges that are entirely restricted to this region (i.e., 15 percent of the species occurring in the hotspot). For example, *Diphylleia cymosa* Michx. is found only in cool, mesic forests at high elevations in the southern Appalachian Mountains, while *Shortia galacifolia* Torr. & A. Gray is a well-known narrow endemic native to just six counties in the region (Weakley 2011). The spatial extent of this hotspot also seems remarkable: Beyond the core area of high diversity and endemism in the southern Appalachian Mountains of western North Carolina, a broader zone of high diversity extends along most of the mid- to southern Appalachian Mountains, from West Virginia and western Virginia, south to the southern edges of the Appalachian Plateau in northeastern Alabama (fig. 21.2).

The Apalachicola River Hotspot

The Apalachicola River area of the Florida panhandle and adjacent southeastern Alabama and southwestern Georgia is the region with the next highest richness of small-ranged forest herbs, peaking at 21 species with overlapping distributions in both Gadsden County, Florida, and Decatur County, Georgia. Overall, 29 small-ranged forest herb species have distributions that include counties in and around the Apalachicola River area. Importantly though, this hotspot is comprised primarily of species for which the Apalachicola River area represents a southernmost extension or disjunct station in geographic ranges that also include counties farther to the north in central Alabama, the southern Appalachian Mountains, or the adjacent Piedmont. Of the 29 small-ranged forest herbs in this area, only two (7 percent) are narrow endemics restricted entirely to the Apalachicola River hotspot (*Carex thornei* Naczi and *Liatris gholsonii* L. C. Anderson); one additional species, *Matelea alabamensis* (Vail) Woodson, occurs in this area, as well as in one county in eastern Georgia. Notably though, the Apalachicola River hotspot does also include several narrow endemics in its woody flora, such as *Magnolia ashei* Weatherby, *Taxus floridana* Nuttall ex Chapman, and *Torreya taxifolia* Arnott.

The Interior Highlands Hotspot

The Interior Highlands hotspot, including parts of the Ouachita Mountains and Ozark Plateau in Arkansas, Missouri, and extreme eastern Oklahoma, has received considerably less attention in the botanical and ecological literature on forest plant diversity than areas further to the east; however, it stands out in this analysis as a key hotspot of small-ranged forest herb diversity, with 28 species co-occurring in the region. Although characterized by a slightly lower peak of small-ranged forest herb richness (19 species in Montgomery County, Arkansas) than the Apalachicola River hotspot, it is nonetheless a distinct and important area. First, it is geographically and physiographically isolated from the other major hotspots of forest herb diversity in eastern North America. Second, narrow endemics comprise a substantially larger component of the regional flora than in the other two hotspot regions: Seven of the 28 small-ranged species (25 percent) associated with the Interior Highlands hotspot are narrow endemics restricted to just this region. These include species such as *Carex latebracteata* Waterfall, *Delphinium newtonianum* D. M. Moore, and *Solidago ouachitensis* C. E. S. Taylor & R. J. Taylor, as well as recently described forest herb species such as *Hydrophyllum brownei* Kral & V. M. Bates (Kral and Bates 1991), *Polymnia cossatotensis* Pittman & V. M. Bates (Pittman and Bates 1989), and *Stachys iltisii* J. Nelson (Nelson 2008).

Secondary Hotspots

In addition to the three geographically distinctive hotspots described above, a number of secondary hotspots with lower peaks of diversity (e.g., 10–15 overlapping distributions) are also apparent in other parts of the southeastern U.S. and lower Midwest. Among these, an area around Tuscaloosa County in central-western Alabama emerges as a hotspot for regional and local endemics that is distinct from the Southern Appalachian hotspot to the northeast. Further to the east, in the Piedmont region, several South Carolina counties along the upper Savannah River watershed also exhibit relatively high densities of small-ranged forest herbs, including some narrow endemics, like *Trillium discolor* Wray ex Hook. and *T. persistens* Duncan. Further to the north, a number of small-ranged forest herb species have ranges centered along the Ohio River Valley in southern Ohio, Indiana, Illinois, and adjacent northern Kentucky (e.g., *Oxalis illinoiensis* Schwegm., *Penstemon deamii* Pennell). Finally, two coastal plain counties, Pender County, North Carolina, and Berkeley County, South Carolina, also stand out as areas with relatively high numbers of small-ranged forest herbs.

Trends in Range Size

In addition to overall patterns in the distribution and diversity of small-ranged forest herbs, we also analyzed correlations between range size and three geographical and historical factors: range centroid longitude, centroid latitude, and centroid distance to the LGM boundary. Among the 189 species, no trend in range size relative to longitude was apparent, despite expectations that decreased rainfall and water availability to the west in our study area might influence range size for forest herbs (fig. 21.4a, $p > 0.05$). In contrast, a highly significant positive correlation was apparent between range size and latitude (fig. 21.4b; $F_{1,187} = 11.5$, $p = 0.0009$, $R^2 = 0.06$). This correlation is consistent with the commonly observed biogeographic trend of increasing range size with increasing latitude, often referred to as Rapoport's Rule (Lomolino et al. 2006). Although a number of hypotheses have been advanced to explain this pattern (e.g., increases in species niche breadths with latitude; Stevens 1989), the relatively

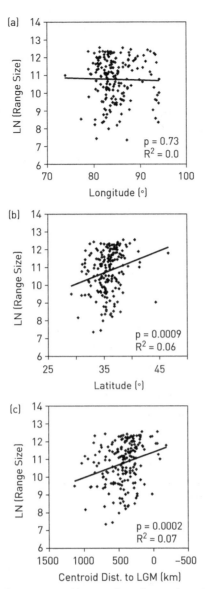

FIGURE 21.4 Correlations between natural log-transformed range size and species' range centroid longitude (panel A), latitude (B), and distance to the LGM boundary (C) for 189 small-ranged forest herbs in eastern North America. Among the small-ranged forest herbs included in this study, range size varied from ~ 1,600 km² to ~ 280,000 km². The p-values and R^2 indicated in each panel are derived from simple linear regression; the associated F statistics are as follows: $F_{1,187}$ = 0.1 for panel A; 11.5 for B; 14.0 for C.

abrupt truncation in the distribution and richness of small-ranged species near the LGM boundary, rather than a more continuous decline tracking latitude north of the LGM, suggests an important historical component to the pattern in our study area (cf. Cowling and Samways 1994; Dynesius and Jansson 2000; Jansson 2003). Consistent with this possibility, the trend in range size is fit more closely by a regression on range centroid distance to the LGM boundary ($F_{1,187}$ = 14.0, p = 0.0002, R^2 = 0.07; fig. 21.4c), an analysis that takes into account the irregular border and major southward lobes of the last glacial advance (fig. 21.2). Overall, these results show that the range sizes of small-ranged forest herbs tend to increase toward the LGM, even while very few of these species have distributions that actually extend north of this boundary.

FROM PATTERN TO PROCESS: INSIGHTS INTO THREATS POSED BY MODERN CLIMATE CHANGE

The absence of small-ranged forest herbs from most formerly glaciated portions of eastern North America is consistent with observations on patterns of endemism in other areas of the Northern Hemisphere and suggests that past climate change and glaciation have had a major effect on the distributions of endemic species (Cowling and Samways 1994; Dynesius and Jansson 2000; Jansson 2003; Finnie et al. 2007; Sandel et al. 2011). Similarly, the concentration of many small-ranged species in distinct hotspots of endemism far to the south of the LGM, as seen in the results of this survey, has frequently been taken as indirect evidence for the locations of Pleistocene-era glacial refugia (Estill and Cruzan 2001; Médail and Diadema 2009). Such hotspots are thought to have developed when the ranges of temperate zone species contracted south to small areas of suitable habitat during the LGM (Estill and Cruzan 2001; Svenning and Skov 2007a). With the amelioration of climate in the late Pleistocene and early Holocene eras, the distributions of many temperate plant species expanded out of these southern areas (Davis 1983; Prentice et al. 1991; Cain et al. 1998; Williams et al. 2004), but the ranges of a subset of forest plant species appear to have remained restricted to regions in or around these former glacial refugia (Svenning and Skov 2007a).

All three of the major hotspots identified in this study correspond to areas previously suggested as important Pleistocene-era refugia in eastern North America. For example, the Apalachicola River area has long been hypothesized as a glacial refugium (Thorne 1949; Estill and Cruzan 2001). Similarly, increasing population genetic evidence points to the southern Appalachian Mountains as an area where populations of some temperate forest plant species may have persisted during the LGM (McLachlan et al. 2005; Gonzales et al. 2008). The Interior Highlands hotspot identified in this study has also been described as a Pleistocene-era refugium (Ricketts et al. 1999), although most recent research has focused on biogeographic and phylogeographic evidence from animal species native to the region (e.g., Carlton and Robison 1998; Near et al. 2001). One notable exception to this pattern of correspondence between putative glacial refugia and small-ranged forest herb diversity hotspots is seen in the Lower Mississippi River Valley: This region has frequently been mentioned as a likely refugium for temperate forest species (e.g., Delcourt and Delcourt 1975; Cain et al. 1998; Jackson et al. 2000), but exhibits low diversity of small-ranged forest herbs (fig. 21.2).

It is also clear from the results of this study that not all small-ranged forest herbs are restricted exclusively to the limited number of hotspots described above. Indeed, the low-to-moderate levels of small-ranged forest herb diversity apparent across much of the southeastern U.S. and lower Midwest are surprising, particularly when contrasted to the absence of small-ranged forest herbs from most areas north of the LGM (figs. 21.2 and 21.3). This pattern may be suggestive of several interesting processes bearing on post-glacial migration rates and so-called cryptic refugia. First, at the broadest geographic scale, it is apparent that very few small-ranged forest herbs have substantially expanded or shifted their distributions into formerly glaciated regions in the north; only six of the 189 species (3 percent) included in this analysis had range centroids situated north of the LGM, and most species range centroids were situated substantially south of this boundary (mean distance to LGM = 438 km; fig. 21.3). This pattern emerges despite nearly ~ 15,000 years since widespread deglaciation and seems to stand in marked contrast to the relatively rapid northward range expansion inferred for other temperate forest plant species (e.g., Cain et al. 1998; Clark 1998; Williams et al. 2004).

In particular, the dispersal and range dynamics suggested by the results of the present survey appear to diverge most strikingly from conclusions drawn by Cain et al. (1998) regarding forest herb migration in response to climate change. Cain et al. (1998) reviewed literature on the dispersal ability of 28 forest herbs and highlighted the mismatch between the limited seed dispersal distances reported in the field for these species and the substantial distances many must have migrated during the Holocene to reach current range boundaries in the north. Based on these discrepancies, Cain et al. (1998) concluded that rare long-distance dispersal events likely enable rapid migration and range shifts in forest herbs (cf. Clark 1998), even for species that otherwise appear to be severely dispersal-limited based on field observations (e.g., Matlack 1994). Notably though, almost all of the forest herbs considered by Cain et al. (1998) were common large-ranged species with distributions extending well into formerly glaciated regions (e.g., *Asarum canadense, Sanguinaria canadensis, Geranium maculatum* L.). Rare long-distance dispersal events clearly need to be invoked to account for the distribution patterns seen among these wide-ranging species, and subsequent studies have documented potential mechanisms (e.g., *Trillium* seeds dispersed by deer; Vellend et al. 2003). However, in contrast to the species considered by Cain et al. (1998), the present study focused on small-ranged endemics, a group that has typically been overlooked in the plant dispersal and paleoecological literature, even though it is among such species where long-term dispersal limitation of range size is a reasonable hypothesis (Skov and Svenning 2004; Van der Veken et al. 2007a).

Prior studies have linked small range size in forest herbs to biological and ecological traits like limited seed production and dispersal ability (Van der Veken et al. 2007a). We have not formally reviewed the life history traits of the 189 species included in the present study, as little published data is available on these relatively rare, range-restricted species. However, it is striking that a large number of these forest herbs come from families or genera known to include species with limited dispersal ability (e.g., species with ant-dispersed seed or no obvious mechanism of dispersal: *Carex* spp., *Hexastylis* spp., *Trillium* spp., various Lamiaceae and Ranunculaceae spp.). Similarly, the presence of only two ferns and lycophytes (i.e., taxa that typically produce large quantities of wind-dispersed spores) in the set of small-ranged species identified for the analysis seems telling. In contrast, the large number of small-ranged Asteraceae (34 spp.), a family often characterized by wind-dispersed propagules, was surprising. Clearly, further research on the trait characteristics of these small-ranged species is needed, especially in a comparative phylogenetic context including wide-ranging congeners or confamilials (cf. Lavergne et al. 2004; Van der Veken et al. 2007a).

The second pattern evident in our results with implications for estimating migration capacity of forest herbs was the close proximity of some small-ranged species distributions to the LGM boundary. Specifically, 43 of the small-ranged forest herbs (23 percent of total) had range centroids ≤ 300 km from the LGM, well outside the major hotspots identified in the southeastern U.S. (fig. 21.3). This pattern may suggest that the geographic ranges of this subset of species have shifted or expanded substantially northward during the Holocene Epoch, a dynamic that would be consistent with the larger range size exhibited by species distributed closer to the LGM (fig. 21.4). However, this finding may also indicate that some small-ranged forest herbs persisted through the LGM in cryptic northern refugia, outside the areas traditionally cited as major glacial refugia in the southeastern U.S. (e.g., the Gulf Coast and the Lower Mississippi River Valley; Delcourt and Delcourt 1975, 1987; Davis 1983).

Increasing genetic evidence points to the existence of such cryptic northern refugia during the LGM, as recent phylogeographic studies have documented unique haplotypes in temperate forest plant populations well to the north of the Gulf Coast and the Lower Mississippi River Valley (McLachlan et al. 2005; Hu et al. 2009). These divergent genetic lineages are believed to represent the descendants of populations that were isolated in distinct glacial refugia during the LGM or earlier glacial maxima (Gonzales et al. 2008). For example, Gonzales et al. (2008) documented *Trillium cuneatum* Raf. haplotypes in areas of Kentucky and Tennessee, as well as in the southern Appalachians, that were divergent relative to those seen farther south in the species' range. Similar associations between unique haplotypes and the southern Appalachian Mountains have been detected for *Acer rubrum* L. and *Fagus grandifolia* Ehrh. (McLachlan et al. 2005). More strikingly, Beatty and Provan (2011) presented genetic evidence of a glacial refugium for *Monotropa hypopitys* L. in the unglaciated "Driftless Area" of southwestern Wisconsin and southeastern Minnesota, a region that also emerged in our analysis as a northern area with a relatively high richness of small-ranged forest herbs (fig. 21.2).

The northern refugia inferred from these genetic data are referred to as "cryptic" in that paleoecological studies focused on the pollen record have generally not detected the presence of TDF plant species in these areas during the LGM, likely due to small population sizes, low density, and isolation (McLachlan et al. 2005; Beatty and Provan 2011). Regardless, most forest herbs are missing from the pollen record because they produce only limited quantities of insect-dispersed pollen, as compared to the more abundant wind-dispersed pollen of many trees, grasses, and sedges. As such, prior to these recent genetic studies, forest herbs have largely been invisible to paleoecological studies based on the pollen record, and their range dynamics were typically extrapolated from those of better-documented TDF tree species (e.g., Cain et al. 1998).

The new evidence for cryptic northern refugia during the LGM may have significant implications for estimates of post-glacial migration rates (McLachlan et al. 2005). Specifically, the persistence of temperate forest plant populations within a few 100 km of the LGM boundary would imply that post-glacial migration rates may have been substantially lower than what has previously been inferred based on models assuming long-distance dispersal from the Gulf Coast or Lower Mississippi River Valley (e.g., Cain et al. 1998; Clark 1998; see also MacLachlan et al. 2005). As such, the high migration potential originally estimated for many forest plant species based on the pollen record is now being reevaluated, with critical implications for how rapidly species can be expected to migrate in response to modern climate change (McLachlan et al. 2005). Indeed, some studies have projected that plant migration rates will need to approach 1,000 m/yr or more to keep pace with modern climate change, but even the fastest migrations of the late Pleistocene and early Holocene now appear to have been on the order of 100 m/year or less (McLachlan et al. 2005; Petit et al. 2008).

CONSERVATION IMPLICATIONS

Although the co-occurrence of many small-ranged forest herbs in regional hotspots in the southeastern U.S. would likely facilitate conservation planning under more stable climatic conditions, the rapid climate change projected for coming decades may substantially complicate this goal. In particular, because hotspots of endemism and diversity tend to be localized to southern areas where TDF species survived climatic *cooling* in the past, their ranges may now be poorly positioned to withstand future climatic *warming* (Delcourt 2002; Hampe and Petit 2005; Wilson et al. 2005; Ashcroft 2010). Consistent with this prediction, relict populations of a number of boreal and TDF plant species already exhibit limited or failing recruitment at their southern range edges in Europe (e.g., García et al. 1999; Hampe and Arroyo 2002; Mejías et al. 2002, 2007; Castro et al. 2004; Beatty et al. 2008). In eastern North America, few studies have focused on the population dynamics of small-ranged forest plants at the southern margins of the TDF biome, but some researchers have suggested that the severe decline of one narrow endemic, *Torreya taxifolia*, native to the Apalachicola River hotspot, may be linked in part to climate change (Barlow and Martin 2004; Schwartz 2004).

Interestingly, there is evidence that hotspots of endemism tend to occur in areas that have historically permitted some resilience to climate change (Jansson 2003; Ashcroft 2010; Sandel et al. 2011). For example, regions with substantial topographic heterogeneity may allow species to survive via local elevational shifts rather than large-scale migration; similarly, the presence of microhabitats that may moderate climatic stress, such as mesic sites, river valleys, and north-facing slopes, may allow for local persistence despite changing climate (Jansson 2003; Ashcroft 2010; Sandel et al. 2011). Consequently, it is possible that the hotspots and small-ranged species identified in this analysis may be associated with areas that exhibit some resilience to near-term climate change; however, the magnitude of modern climate change may eventually overwhelm such environmental buffering. In this context, small-ranged forest herbs native to areas with limited topographic heterogeneity (e.g., Gulf Coastal Plain, portions of midwestern U.S.) may be at increased risk relative to those in mountainous areas, as successful tracking of climate envelopes for the former species will likely require larger latitudinal displacement of ranges (cf. Sandel et al. 2011). At the other extreme, small-ranged species linked to high elevation habitats in the southern Appalachian Mountains may also face severe habitat loss due to upward elevational shifts in regional climate zones, with the potential for some habitats to disappear entirely off the tops of southern mountains (i.e., the so-called escalator effect; see also Delcourt and Delcourt 1998).

In the face of such climate-driven threats, conservationists have traditionally stressed the importance of habitat corridors and landscape connectivity to facilitate natural dispersal and range shifts (Hunter et al. 1988; Hannah et al. 2002; Hunter 2007). Unfortunately, this approach may prove ineffectual for species that are severely dispersal-limited, or for those whose present ranges and potential future habitat are separated by large expanses of unsuitable habitat (Thomas et al. 2004; Thomas 2011; chapter 4, this volume). Given these challenges, some researchers have begun to consider the potential for assisted colonization or managed relocation to avoid species extinctions due to rapid climate change (Barlow and Martin 2004; McLachlan et al. 2007; Hoegh-Guldberg et al. 2008; Thomas 2011). Assisted colonization proposes intentionally translocating species to regions where they have not occurred historically, but where they are expected to survive as self-sustaining, naturalized populations as climate changes in the future (McLachlan et al. 2007; Hoegh-Guldberg et al. 2008; Thomas 2011). This unconventional approach to ex situ conservation may be necessary for the long-term preservation of some species, as reintroduction into climatically compromised former ranges may be impossible, and the indefinite maintenance of species (and the genetic diversity within them) in botanic gardens and arboreta may be impractical (MacLachlan et al. 2007; Oldfield 2009; Thomas 2011). Long-term seed storage in seed banks (e.g., via cryopreservation) also offers some potential to preserve rare and climate-threatened species (Li and Pritchard 2009), but using this technique alone might consign species to extinction in the wild and reduce the potential for future adaptive evolution in response to climate change (Davis et al. 2005).

Nevertheless, the possibility of assisted colonization has sparked vigorous debate among ecologists and conservationists, particularly regarding the potential for invasiveness among translocated species (e.g., Mueller and Hellmann 2008; Ricciardi and Simberloff 2009; Minteer and Collins 2010). However, to date, most discussions of assisted colonization have been largely hypothetical in nature or illustrated with a range of extreme examples drawn from around the globe; as such, these discussions have tended to lack clear grounding in the ecology, biogeographic history, and likely candidate species of any particular region or biome. In the final sections of this chapter, we discuss assisted colonization as a potential conservation tool for small-ranged forest herbs that may be threatened by modern climate change.

WOULD ASSISTED COLONIZATION OF SMALL-RANGED FOREST HERBS BE FEASIBLE?

Even if evidence indicated the climate-driven decline of a small-ranged forest herb, what is the likelihood that self-sustaining populations of such a species could be successfully established beyond its current range boundaries? Most species distribution models in ecology, biogeography, and paleoecology are premised on the assumption that contemporary range edges represent a dynamic equilibrium between environmental conditions, principally climate, and population growth rates (Webb 1986; Woodward 1987; Gaston 2003). Similarly, evolutionary theory on species' ranges typically assumes that range margins are in equilibrium with current environments in order to examine the role of various evolutionary forces in limiting adaptation (e.g., Kirkpatrick and Barton 1997; Holt 2003; Case et al. 2005; Holt and Barfield 2011). Overall, these "equilibrial" range models would typically predict that species translocated beyond their range edges would likely fail to establish populations due to abiotic or biotic limits. Even with anthropogenic climate change, equilibrial range models would tend to suggest that shifts in the distribution of suitable habitat might occur only incrementally, limiting the potential for the types of large-scale translocations envisioned to ensure long-term species survival under new climatic regimes (Thomas 2011).

However, the applicability of equilibrial range models to small-ranged TDF plant species appears increasingly tenuous (e.g., Svenning and Skov 2004, 2007a,b; Schwartz et al. 2006; Van der Veken et al. 2007a). Specifically, for plant species with significant dispersal limitation, current range boundaries might not reflect fixed limits determined by environmental factors, but rather slow-moving colonization fronts influenced largely by species' dispersal rates, time since amelioration of past climatic stress, and the geographic locations of former refugia (Holt et al. 2005; Svenning and Skov 2007a,b; Bellemare 2010). Although the potential for long-term dispersal limitation of geographic ranges is not widely acknowledged by paleoecologists (e.g., Webb 1986; Prentice et al. 1991; Williams et al. 2001; but see Davis 1986), empirical evidence for this type of range "disequilibrium" (sensu Davis 1986) is increasing among TDF plant species (e.g., Holland 1980; Skov and Svenning 2004; Svenning and Skov 2004; Van der Veken et al. 2007b; Bellemare 2010). For example, Bellemare (2010) found that seeds of the ant-dispersed forest herb *Jeffersonia diphylla* (L.) Pers. germinated and successfully established over a five-year period in forest habitats 200 km beyond the species' natural range edge in the northeastern U.S. Similarly, Van der Veken et al. (2007b) presented data on an extra-range transplant experiment initiated almost 50 years earlier that showed long-term survival and expansion of *Hyacinthoides non-scripta* (L.) Chouard ex Rothm. populations in areas up to ~ 100 km beyond its natural range edge in northwestern Europe. These empirical studies suggest that the extent of potentially suitable habitat for many dispersal-limited forest herbs may greatly exceed the area actually occupied (cf. Skov and Svenning 2004). Consequently, assisted colonization efforts for such species might be feasible over substantially greater spatial scales than would be predicted by standard equilibrial range models.

Other sources of information on plant species' climatic tolerances and the potential geographic scale of assisted colonization efforts are the many accidental or unplanned "experiments" evident in horticulture, where the climatic limits on numerous native plant species' distributions are routinely tested (Van der Veken et al. 2008; Sax et al. 2013). In particular, the horticultural trade includes numerous small-ranged forest species that are commonly grown many 100s to 1,000 km or more north of their natural ranges in eastern North America (Dirr 1998; Cullina 2000, 2002; Sax et al. 2013). Similarly, a review by Van der Veken et al. (2008) found that native plants were grown, on average, ~ 1,000 km north of their natural range edges in the horticultural trade in Europe. Although horticultural observations do not provide reliable information on the role that biotic factors (e.g., competitors, pollinators, pathogens, herbivores) might play in limiting the distributions of small-ranged plant species in the wild, they do demonstrate that climate per se is not limiting for many range-restricted species.

Even more strikingly, numerous incidences of small-ranged forest plant species escaping from horticulture and naturalizing in forest communities well beyond their range limits have been documented (Gleason and Cronquist 1991; Skov and Svenning 2004; Kartesz 2010). In Europe, a number of plant species endemic to areas around Pleistocene-era glacial refugia in southern and south-central Europe have been observed to readily naturalize in TDF forests of northwestern Europe (e.g., *Aesculus hippocastanum* L., *Aruncus dioicus* (Walter) Fernald, *Eranthis hyemalis* (L.) Salisb., *Lilium martagon* L., *Rhododendron ponticum* L.; Lid and Lid 1994; Stace 1997; Skov and Svenning 2004). Although such patterns have not been as extensively documented for forest plants in eastern North America, notable cases of small-ranged forest herbs and woody species naturalizing in areas far to the north of their natural ranges have been observed (e.g., *Aristolochia macrophylla* Lam., *Catalpa bignonioides* Walter, *Dicentra eximia* (Ker. Gawl.) Torr., *Leucothoe fontanesiana* (Steud.) Sleumer, *Torreya taxifolia*, *Trillium luteum* (Muhl.) Harbison; Gleason and Cronquist 1991; Case and Case 1997; Barlow and Martin 2004; Kartesz 2010). These various lines of evidence suggest that large-scale dispersal limitation may be a relatively common phenomenon among small-ranged TDF plants and, as a result, assisted colonization could be both a necessary and effective conservation strategy for some species.

OPEN QUESTIONS AND RESEARCH OPPORTUNITIES

It is evident that considerable research is still needed to better understand the magnitude of threat posed by modern climate change to forest herb biodiversity. Likewise, unconventional responses to these new conservation challenges, such as assisted colonization, will require substantial investigation before they should be considered for implementation (McLachlan et al. 2007; Minteer and Collins 2010; Sax et al. 2013). Here we outline what we see as some of the key open questions relating to small-ranged forest herbs, rapid climate change, and conservation.

First and foremost, a major research effort is needed to document and monitor existing populations of small-ranged TDF plant species in order to establish a baseline against which future population dynamics could be gauged. Because any attempts at intervention and translocation should be limited to species demonstrating clear evidence of climate-driven decline, basic descriptive research is needed on substantial numbers of plant species (e.g., species listed in appendix 21.1, as well as numerous woody TDF endemics). We are not aware of any demographic studies of forest herb populations, small-ranged species or otherwise, that have demonstrated declining population growth rates (i.e., $\lambda < 1$) at southern range margins in eastern North America, even though the biogeographic patterns detected in this and other studies suggest that such declines may be likely. Because these studies would be technically simple to conduct, albeit time-consuming, they could potentially be run simultaneously on multiple small-ranged TDF species to determine which, if any, should be considered as candidates for management, translocation, or other ex situ conservation options.

Second, in contrast to field-based demographic studies, molecular population genetic studies provide an opportunity to examine evidence of population dynamics across geographic ranges over substantially longer time scales (e.g., 100s–1,000s of years; reviewed in Moeller et al. 2011). If populations have expanded at northern range margins, but declined at southern range margins, these contrasting demographic histories should leave distinct signatures in samples of DNA sequences drawn from these populations. Although some forest plants have been the focus of phylogeographic studies using cpDNA haplotypes and population genetic studies focused on allozyme diversity (e.g., Griffin and Barrett 2004; MacLachlan et al. 2005; Gonzales et al. 2008), large datasets on nuclear DNA would be a substantially more powerful tool for uncovering demographic history. We are not aware of any studies that have yet used this approach to test hypotheses about demographic history in forest herbs.

Third, given that most analyses projecting plant species' responses to future climate change are based on models presuming distributional equilibrium with current climate (Huntley et al. 1995; Guisan and Thuiller 2005; Schwartz et al. 2006), there is a great need for more experimental research to directly test this assumption in forest herbs. Most notably, such efforts might include experimental seed-sowing within and beyond current range boundaries to assess plant performance and its relationship to environmental factors (e.g., Eckhart et al. 2004; Angert and Schemske 2005; Geber and Eckhart 2005; Griffith and Watson 2006; Van der Veken et al. 2007b; Bellemare 2010). Although northern range edges are a clear target for this type of investigation in light of the probable direction of future migration or assisted colonization efforts, there is also a significant need for further insight to the nature of species' southern, warm-margin distribution limits. If, as predicted by some ecological theory (MacArthur 1972), warm-margin range edges are determined primarily by biotic factors (e.g., competition, herbivory), rather than climate, there may actually be limited response to moderate levels of climate change, or species responses could be confounded or accelerated by complex biotic interactions (Van der Putten et al. 2010).

Fourth, whether forest herbs migrate naturally in response to climate change or threatened species are moved intentionally via assisted colonization, many forest plant communities will be colonized by new species in coming decades. Such intracontinental movements have received relatively little attention in the invasion biology literature, which has been focused primarily on invaders of intercontinental origin (e.g., Mack et al. 2000; chapter 12, this volume). It is not yet clear if intra- versus intercontinental invasions are directly comparable, but some evidence indicates that intracontinental movement of plants does not commonly lead to invasive behavior (Mueller and Hellman 2008; Simberloff et al. 2012). This difference might be due to a range of factors, for example, escape from natural enemies (e.g., pathogens, herbivores) is a key factor that has been linked to invasiveness among intercontinental exotics (Mitchell and Power 2003; Carpenter and Cappuccino 2005), but this ecological phenomenon may be less likely with intracontinental movements. An important focus for the types of forest herb seed-sowing experiments described above will be documentation of such biotic interactions within and beyond species' natural range limits. Insight into these biotic dynamics will be key to predicting species' migration potentials and evaluating risks associated with assisted colonization.

Finally, it has become clear that historical post-glacial range expansion has involved evolutionary change, not simply migration (Davis and Shaw 2001; Davis et al. 2005), and that populations migrating in response to modern climate change will likely experience natural selection on ecologically important traits (Geber and Dawson 1993; Etterson and Shaw 2001; Davis et al. 2005). For example, northward migration will involve substantial shifts in photoperiod (an important cue for development, dormancy, and flowering in many species), even if migrating populations were to perfectly track a particular set of climatic factors. It is important, then, to understand what genetic variation is currently harbored within and among populations in species' native ranges and how different genotypes may perform in novel northern environments. Identifying such genetic variation (e.g., through common garden experiments; cf. Fournier-Level et al. 2011) may be key to designing successful conservation efforts and preserving valuable intra-specific diversity in the future (Hampe and Petit 2005; McLachlan et al. 2007).

SUMMARY

Research increasingly indicates that dispersal limitation may be a major factor controlling the geographic distribution of numerous forest plant species and that the current distributions of many range-restricted species may still be strongly influenced by past episodes of climate change. The biogeographic patterns emerging from our survey of small-ranged forest herbs are highly consistent with this possibility, suggesting that many endemic species have exhibited relatively limited migration and range expansion during the Holocene. As many of these endemic species would be predicted a priori to be at increased risk from modern climate change due to small range size, the added challenge of long-term, large-scale dispersal limitation may significantly compound this risk (Thomas et al. 2004). Given these findings, modern climate change is likely to be a significant threat to forest herb biodiversity, and unconventional conservation options, like assisted colonization, may need to be considered for some particularly vulnerable forest herb species.

ACKNOWLEDGMENTS

Numerous colleagues provided valuable comments on earlier versions of this man-uscript, including Monica Geber, Anurag Agrawal, Jens-Christian Svenning, Peter Marks, Paul Somers, Mark Vellend, Martin Hermy, and Kris Verheyen. The biogeo-graphic analysis presented here would not have been possible without the detailed plant distribution data compiled through the efforts of the Biota of North America Program (BONAP) and John Kartesz. Valuable assistance with the GIS components of this project was provided by Lilly Dalton and Jon Caris in the Smith College Spatial Analysis Lab.

APPENDIX 21.1

Range area, range centroid latitude and longitude, and habitat for 189 small-ranged forest herbs associated with Temperate Deciduous Forest in eastern North America. Nomenclature follows Kartesz (2010). Range statistics were derived from county-level distribution maps developed for each species by Kartesz (2010) and the Biota of North America Program (BONAP; see www.bonap.org). Habitat information was drawn from the *Flora of North America* for species covered by published volumes and from various regional sources (e.g., Radford et al. 1968; Gleason and Cronquist 1991; Case and Case 1997; Yatskievych 1999; Wunderlin and Hansen 2003; Weakley 2011).

Species	Family	Range Area (km2)	Range Centroid Latitude (°)	Range Centroid Longitude (°)	Habitat Description
Aconitum reclinatum A. Gray	Ranunculaceae	43681	37.736	80.554	Rich cove forests, seeps & shaded ravines, mtn woods
Aconitum uncinatum L.	Ranunculaceae	167349	37.011	81.422	Mesic woods, seeps & clearings
Actaea podocarpa DC	Ranunculaceae	107768	37.649	81.176	Moist, rich wooded slopes & coves
Actaea rubifolia (Kearney) Kartesz	Ranunculaceae	38063	36.564	85.945	Rich cove forests over calcareous bedrock
Ageratina luciae-brauniae (Fernald) King & H. Rob.	Asteraceae	11840	36.728	84.539	Shaded wet ledges, sandstone cliffs, "rockhouses"
Anemone lancifolia Pursh	Ranunculaceae	164761	36.171	80.675	Damp rich woods
Apios priceana B.L. Rob.	Fabaceae	48167	35.295	87.156	Rocky limestone woods
Astilbe biternata (Vent.) Britton	Saxifragaceae	90349	35.968	83.680	Rich woods, north-facing banks & seeps
Boechera perstellata (E.L. Braun) Al-Shehbaz	Brassicaceae	6767	36.855	85.985	Calcareous bluffs, wooded hillsides
Botrychium mormo W.H. Wagner	Ophioglossaceae	130069	46.635	91.286	Rich basswood & sugar maple forest
Boykinia aconitifolia Nuttall	Saxifragaceae	71430	36.256	83.296	Moist woodland, water edges
Cardamine flagellifera O.E. Schulz	Brassicaceae	29109	35.852	82.736	Moist wooded slopes, ravines, seeps
Cardamine micranthera Rollins	Brassicaceae	3770	36.412	80.239	Moist woods, along streams & seeps
Carex acidicola Naczi	Cyperaceae	11721	32.576	85.805	Dry to mesic deciduous forest
Carex austrocaroliniana L.H. Bailey	Cyperaceae	58524	35.339	84.677	Rich moist deciduous and mixed forest

(Continued)

(Continued)

Species	Family	Range Area (km2)	Range Centroid Latitude (°)	Range Centroid Longitude (°)	Habitat Description
Carex basiantha Steudel	Cyperaceae	153979	31.691	89.115	Mesic to wet-mesic deciduous forests
Carex biltmoreana Mackenzie	Cyperaceae	20185	35.001	82.627	Rocky woods, moist ledges, granite balds
Carex brysonii Naczi	Cyperaceae	8677	33.541	87.709	Mesic deciduous forest, slopes above streams
Carex impressinervia Bryson Kral & Manhart	Cyperaceae	21699	32.604	86.166	Mesic deciduous forest, slopes above streams
Carex latebracteata Waterfall	Cyperaceae	22384	34.489	94.140	Steep shaded slopes, mesic to dry-mesic forest
Carex manhartii Bryson	Cyperaceae	26810	35.654	82.765	Moist deciduous and mixed forest
Carex ouachitana Kral Manhart & Bryson	Cyperaceae	19719	34.709	93.815	Mesic, dry-mesic rocky deciduous or mixed forest
Carex picta Steudel	Cyperaceae	106445	35.079	86.973	Forests & forest openings
Carex pigra Naczi	Cyperaceae	33105	34.541	85.530	Mesic to wet-mesic deciduous forests
Carex purpurifera Mack.	Cyperaceae	91720	36.981	84.201	Moist deciduous forests, often near limestone ledges
Carex radfordii Gaddy	Cyperaceae	6738	34.908	82.832	Moist deciduous forests on calcareous soil
Carex roanensis F.J. Herm.	Cyperaceae	25391	37.632	80.928	Rich moist soil under beech trees
Carex socialis Mohlenbr. & Schwegm.	Cyperaceae	138778	34.543	87.543	Lowland deciduous forests, clay soils
Carex superata Naczi, Reznicek & B.A. Ford	Cyperaceae	56149	33.926	84.342	Moist to dry-mesic open deciduous forests, ravines
Carex thornei Naczi	Cyperaceae	12881	31.586	84.898	Mesic deciduous forests, slopes & floodplains
Carex timida Naczi & B.A. Ford	Cyperaceae	30531	37.221	87.338	Mesic deciduous or mixed woods, calcareous soil
Chelone lyonii Pursh	Scrophulariaceae	48756	35.430	83.152	Rich coves, stream banks

Collinsonia tuberosa Michx.	Lamiaceae	84.845	33.890	156125	Moist woods, calcareous soils
Collinsonia verticillata Baldw.	Lamiaceae	83.558	34.640	104793	Wooded slopes, low woods
Corallorhiza bentleyi Freudenstein	Orchidaceae	80.285	37.931	4972	Deciduous forest & disturbed forest edges
Coreopsis delphinifolia Lam.	Asteraceae	81.577	33.195	57448	Woodlands, thickets & swamps
Coreopsis latifolia Michx.	Asteraceae	82.818	35.293	37579	Shaded slopes in rich moist woods
Coreopsis pulchra Boynt.	Asteraceae	86.160	33.938	15001	Forest openings, outcrops
Croomia pauciflora (Nutt.) Torr.	Stemonaceae	86.422	32.445	118397	Mesic wooded slopes & bottoms, circumneutral soils
Cymophyllus fraserianus (Ker Gawl.) Kartesz & Gandhi	Cyperaceae	81.412	37.209	161869	Rich mesic shaded slopes in deciduous or mixed forest
Delphinium exaltatum Aiton	Ranunculaceae	80.962	38.378	150440	Rocky slopes in rich woods or barrens, calcareous soil
Delphinium newtonianum D.M. Moore	Ranunculaceae	93.320	35.210	15456	Slopes in deciduous forest
Desmodium humifusum (Muhl. Ex Bigelow) Beck	Fabaceae	73.884	41.435	60252	Dry woods, sandy soils
Desmodium ochroleucum M.A. Curtis ex Canby	Fabaceae	82.393	36.163	68327	Dry open woods, sandy or rocky soils
Dicentra eximia (Ker Gawl.) Torr.	Fumariaceae	80.477	38.533	113533	Dry to moist rocky mountain woods, cliffs & crevices
Diphylleia cymosa Michx.	Berberidaceae	82.732	35.653	30681	Moist slopes, seeps & stream banks in deciduous forest

(Continued)

(Continued)

Species	Family	Range Area (km2)	Range Centroid Latitude (°)	Range Centroid Longitude (°)	Habitat Description
Dodecatheon amethystinum (Fassett) Fassett	Primulaceae	77954	41.491	88.342	Moist hillsides & limestone cliffs in deciduous forest
Dodecatheon frenchii (Vasey) Rydb.	Primulaceae	33569	36.935	88.144	Moist shaded flats in woods under cliffs, near streams
Draba ramosissima Desv.	Brassicaceae	189985	36.897	82.298	Rocky wooded areas, limestone cliffs, shale barrens
Elymus svensonii Church	Poaceae	15901	36.556	85.829	Woods on limestone bluffs, slopes & ledges
Erythronium propullans A. Gray	Liliaceae	8469	44.329	92.825	Mesic floodplain woods
Eupatorium godfreyanum Cronquist	Asteraceae	206635	37.821	80.203	Woods and disturbed open sites, forest edges
Euphorbia mercurialina Michx.	Euphorbiaceae	154614	34.917	84.759	Rich soil on wooded slopes, ravines
Euphorbia purpurea (Raf.) Fernald	Euphorbiaceae	65719	38.408	79.312	Dry or moist woods
Eurybia furcata (Burgess) G.L. Nesom	Asteraceae	144841	41.253	89.021	North-facing slopes, moist deciduous woods
Eurybia mirabilis (Torr. & A. Gray) G.L. Nesom	Asteraceae	36392	34.616	81.526	Deciduous & mixed woods, slopes or alluvial plains
Eutrochium steelei (E.E. Lamont) E.E. Lamont	Asteraceae	53807	36.108	82.830	Open woods, gravelly banks, thickets
Gentiana decora Pollard	Gentianaceae	147285	36.058	82.497	Wooded slopes, coves, streambanks
Geum geniculatum Michx.	Rosaceae	4251	36.105	81.832	Balds and wooded coves at high elevation
Gymnocarpium appalachianum Pryor & Haufler	Dryopteridaceae	63167	39.360	79.509	Maple-birch-hemlock woods, tallus w/ cold air seepage

Species	Family				Habitat
Helianthus glaucophyllus D.M. Sm.	Asteraceae	31974	34.361	84.283	Moist forests, woodland edges
Heuchera longiflora Rydb.	Saxifragaceae	120569	36.636	83.826	Rich woods and roadcuts over limestone
Heuchera pubescens Pursh	Saxifragaceae	223208	37.923	81.327	Shaded circumneutral rock outcroppings in woods
Hexastylis contracta Blomquist	Aristolochiaceae	35994	36.444	83.544	Acid soils in deciduous woods
Hexastylis heterophylla (Ashe) Small	Aristolochiaceae	220495	35.921	82.539	Deciduous & mixed forests
Hexastylis lewisii (Fernald) Blomquist & Oosting	Aristolochiaceae	84708	36.178	78.893	Upland & lowland forests, floodplains
Hexastylis minor (Ashe) Blomquist	Aristolochiaceae	118466	36.385	79.880	Slopes & bluffs along streams in deciduous woods
Hexastylis naniflora Blomquist	Aristolochiaceae	13875	35.342	81.773	Acidic soils on bluffs & ravines in deciduous woods
Hexastylis rhombiformis Gaddy	Aristolochiaceae	5571	35.381	82.665	Deciduous woods on sandy river bluffs, ravines
Houstonia serpyllifolia Michx.	Rubiaceae	68074	35.968	82.651	Rich woods, stream margins, road cuts, pastures
Hydrophyllum brownei Kral & V.M. Bates	Hydrophyllaceae	14729	34.463	93.601	Rich deciduous forests
Liatris gholsonii L.C. Anderson	Asteraceae	3622	30.303	84.994	Slopes in deciduous woods, open xeric woods
Lilium grayi S. Watson	Liliaceae	27634	37.260	80.417	Moist forests, openings, bogs, seeps & wet meadows
Listera smallii Wiegand	Orchidaceae	137443	37.341	81.060	Damp humus in shady forests, under *Rhododendron*

(Continued)

(Continued)

Species	Family	Range Area (km2)	Range Centroid Latitude (°)	Range Centroid Longitude (°)	Habitat Description
Lysimachia tonsa (Alph. Wood) Alph. Wood ex Pax & R. Knuth	Primulaceae	188779	35.454	83.082	Moist hardwood forests, pine-oak woods, bluffs
Matelea alabamensis (Vail) Woodson	Asclepiadaceae	12680	30.963	84.563	Slopes in deciduous forest
Matelea baldwyniana (Sweet) Woodson	Asclepiadaceae	91821	34.289	90.614	Open rocky woods, thickets
Matelea flavidula (Chapm.) Woodson	Asclepiadaceae	28298	32.215	83.229	Forested slopes & alluvial woods
Meehania cordata (Nutt.) Britton	Lamiaceae	280290	38.502	81.341	Rich mountain woods
Monotropsis odorata Schwein. Ex Elliott	Monotropaceae	117575	35.895	81.484	Mixed deciduous or coniferous forests
Napaea dioica L.	Malvaceae	144997	41.233	87.559	Moist alluvial woods
Onosmodium decipiens J. Allison	Boraginaceae	1595	32.997	87.124	Dolomite outcrops in rocky woods & glades
Orbexilum onobrychis (Nutt.) Rydb.	Fabaceae	211639	36.834	85.907	Open woods, prairies
Oxalis illinoiensis Schwegm.	Oxalidaceae	18788	37.076	86.559	Mesic to dry-mesic forests
Penstemon deamii Pennell	Scrophulariaceae	14461	38.374	87.972	Moist open woods, prairies
Penstemon smalli A. Heller	Scrophulariaceae	67622	35.223	84.115	Woodlands, cliffs, banks & forest edges
Penstemon tenuis Small	Scrophulariaceae	226272	32.491	92.333	Wet woodland soils, bottomlands
Phacelia covillei S. Watson	Hydrophyllaceae	18121	37.690	78.988	Rich soil of floodplains & alluvial woods
Phacelia fimbriata Michx.	Hydrophyllaceae	18475	35.225	84.269	Streambanks and alluvial woods
Phacelia gilioides Brand	Hydrophyllaceae	203809	36.851	93.099	Woodland openings, low rich woods, forest edges

Species	Family				Habitat
Phacelia ranunculacea (Nutt.) Constance	Hydrophyllaceae	86316	36.495	89.531	Mesic alluvial forests
Platanthera integrilabia (Torr.)	Orchidaceae	71905	34.626	85.345	Wet wooded flats, seeps, wetlands
Polymnia cossatotensis Pittman & V.M. Bates	Asteraceae	4264	34.518	93.949	Upland rocky woods & tallus, chert outcrops
Polymnia laevigata Beadle	Asteraceae	32810	34.956	86.666	Damp shaded sites, calcareous soils
Prenanthes crepidinea Michx.	Asteraceae	214423	39.023	87.680	Moist rich deciduous woods, thickets, prairies
Prenanthes roanensis (Chickering) Chickering	Asteraceae	64373	36.042	82.453	Spruce-hardwood forests, wooded slopes & balds
Prosartes maculata (Buckley) A. Gray	Liliaceae	133520	36.723	83.839	Rich moist deciduous woods, slopes & ravines
Pycnanthemum beadlei (Small) Fernald	Lamiaceae	9218	36.036	82.318	Forests, woodland borders
Pycnanthemum curvipes (Greene) E. Grant & Epling	Lamiaceae	11002	35.505	83.566	Dry rocky woodlands, rock outcrops
Pycnanthemum loomisii Nutt.	Lamiaceae	167430	36.288	83.308	Forests, woodland borders
Pycnanthemum montanum Michx.	Lamiaceae	60612	36.036	82.721	Balds, woodlands, forests & forest edges
Pycnanthemum pycnanthemoides (Leavenworth) Fernald	Lamiaceae	224378	35.977	83.790	Forests, woodland borders
Pycnanthemum torrei Benth.	Lamiaceae	118144	38.117	80.876	Dry rocky woodlands
Ranunculus alleghroniensis Britton	Ranunculaceae	228781	39.716	78.869	Moist or dry woods, pastures
Ranunculus harveyi (A. Gray) Britton	Ranunculaceae	181241	35.757	90.860	Acid soils on rocky wooded slopes, ridges, open areas

(Continued)

(Continued)

Species	Family	Range Area (km2)	Range Centroid Latitude (°)	Range Centroid Longitude (°)	Habitat Description
Rudbeckia heliopsidis Torr. & A. Gray	Asteraceae	30072	34.134	82.963	Mesic to wet woodlands, meadows
Ruellia purshiana Fernald	Acanthaceae	96854	35.755	82.650	Dry woodlands over calcareous rock
Rugelia nudicaulis Shuttlw. ex Chapm.	Asteraceae	8435	35.416	83.423	High elevation spruce-fir & northern hardwood forest
Salvia urticifolia L.	Lamiaceae	222452	35.074	83.547	Rocky woodlands on circumneutral soils
Scirpus flaccidifolius (Fernald) Schuyler	Cyperaceae	5145	36.680	77.301	Wooded bottomlands
Scutellaria arguta Buckley	Lamiaceae	8601	37.422	82.573	Mesic woods and boulderfields at high elevation
Scutellaria montana Chapm.	Lamiaceae	11465	35.125	84.912	Open deciduous woods on mesic soil
Scutellaria pseudoserrata Epling	Lamiaceae	25289	34.273	85.258	Rich rocky forests
Scutellaria saxatilis Riddell	Lamiaceae	134303	37.039	82.940	Rocky forests, moist cliffs
Scutellaria serrata Andrews	Lamiaceae	160329	37.415	81.183	Rich deciduous forests
Sedum glaucophyllum R.T. Clausen	Crassulaceae	70801	36.266	80.519	Shaded cliffs, rocky slopes
Shortia galacifolia Torr. & A. Gray	Diapensiaceae	16960	35.255	82.715	Moist forest slopes & stream banks in deep shade
Silene catesbaei Walter	Caryophyllaceae	13101	32.253	84.080	Mesic deciduous forests along streams or slopes
Silene nivea (Nutt.) Muhl. Ex Otth	Caryophyllaceae	278558	40.581	86.336	Rocky or flood-scoured alluvial woodlands
Silene ovata Pursh	Caryophyllaceae	94821	33.975	86.367	Woodlands & forests on circumneutral soil
Silphium brachiatum Gattinger	Asteraceae	14651	35.098	86.501	Open forests on calcareous soil, roadcuts

Species	Family		Latitude	Longitude	Habitat
Silphium wasiotense M. Medley	Asteraceae	7680	36.852	83.588	Dry open sites in mesic forests
Sisyrinchium dichotomum E.P. Bicknell	Iridaceae	6560	35.282	82.132	Dry to mesic oak-hickory forests
Solidago arenicola B,R, Keener & Kral	Asteraceae	4422	35.138	85.582	Mesic woods in deep sandy alluvium
Solidago auriculata Shuttlw. ex S.F. Blake	Asteraceae	132792	32.712	88.619	Rocky wooded slopes, alluvial soils
Solidago brachyphylla Chapman	Asteraceae	50576	32.068	84.767	Open woodlands, bluff forests
Solidago buckleyi Torrey & A. Gray	Asteraceae	46291	38.199	89.896	Open oak woods on ridges, slopes & bluffs
Solidago curtisii Torrey & A. Gray	Asteraceae	199625	36.086	83.685	Shaded mesic woods & thickets
Solidago drummondii Torrey & A. Gray	Asteraceae	5268	35.384	93.380	Limestone ledges & bluffs in rocky woods
Solidago faucibus Wieboldt	Asteraceae	27460	36.378	83.214	Mesic deciduous forests & hardwood-hemlock
Solidago flaccidifolia Small	Asteraceae	65118	34.581	85.173	Mesic woods & clearings
Solidago lancifolia (Torrey & A. Gray) Chapman	Asteraceae	4481	36.214	82.168	Rich woods, mountain slopes, road embankments
Solidago ouachitensis C.E.S. Taylor & R.J. Taylor	Asteraceae	12521	34.697	94.053	Woods on north-facing slopes
Solidago roanensis Porter	Asteraceae	166235	36.793	82.307	Forests, woodlands, roadbanks, edges of mtn balds
Solidago sphacelata Rafinesque	Asteraceae	210540	36.501	84.152	Open woods & rocky places, calcareous soils
Spigelia loganioides (Torr. & A. Gray ex Endl. & Fenzl) A. DC.	Loganiaceae	13586	29.101	82.055	Wet calcareous hammocks & woods

(Continued)

(Continued)

Species	Family	Range Area (km2)	Range Centroid Latitude (º)	Range Centroid Longitude (º)	Habitat Description
Stachys clingmanii Small	Lamiaceae	22374	37.965	86.496	Cove forests & boulderfields at high elevation
Stachys cordata Riddell	Lamiaceae	205560	37.270	83.244	Moist forests, alluvial soils or over calcareous rock
Stachys eplingii J.B. Nelson	Lamiaceae	31266	36.409	82.080	Mtn woods, mesic forests, bogs & wet meadows
Stachys iltisii J.B. Nelson	Lamiaceae	29848	35.582	93.084	Rich soil in open upland woods
Stachys latidens Small ex Britton	Lamiaceae	55908	36.708	81.645	Mesic forests in coves, forest edges
Stellaria corei Shinners	Caryophyllaceae	127557	37.891	84.276	Mesic cove forests & seeps at mid- to high-elevation
Symphyotrichum anomalum (Engelm.) G.L. Neson	Asteraceae	245731	37.523	91.701	Rocky open deciduous woods, dry ridges, cliffs, bluffs
Symphyotrichum phlogifolium (Muhl. ex Willd.) G.L. Nesom	Asteraceae	229281	37.520	82.037	Rich mesic mixed hardwood forests, roadsides
Symphyotrichum retroflexum (Lindl. ex DC.) G.L. Nesom	Asteraceae	64470	34.405	83.084	Moist woodlands, meadows, open pine or oak woods
Synandra hispidula (Michx.) Britton	Lamiaceae	121940	38.105	84.694	Rich mesic woods
Thalictrum clavatum DC.	Ranunculaceae	105376	36.293	83.545	Rich moist woods, cliffs, seeps, stream banks
Thalictrum coriaceum (Britton) Small	Ranunculaceae	92381	37.382	81.760	Rocky or mesic open deciduous woods, thickets
Thalictrum debile Buckley	Ranunculaceae	28466	33.444	87.312	Rich, rocky woods on limestone, wet alluvial soil
Thalictrum macrostylum Small & A. Heller	Ranunculaceae	81502	34.951	80.734	Rich wooded slopes, cliffs, swamp forests, meadows
Thalictrum mirabile Small	Ranunculaceae	15112	35.523	86.089	Moist bluffs, wet sandstone cliffs, sinks

Species	Family		Latitude	Longitude	Habitat
Thaspium pinnatifidum (Buckley) A. Gray	Apiaceae	15560	36.586	84.752	Forests & woodlands over calcareous rock
Thermopsis fraxinifolia Nutt. ex M.A. Curtis	Fabaceae	42342	34.942	83.022	Dry slopes, ridges & clearings
Thermopsis mollis (Michx.) M.A. Curtis ex A. Gray	Fabaceae	80831	35.746	82.320	Dry slopes, open woods & clearings
Thermopsis villosa (Walter) Fernald & B.G. Schub.	Fabaceae	37056	35.877	82.885	Mesic forest openings, floodplains & roadbanks
Tragia cordata Michx.	Euphorbiaceae	172584	33.632	89.576	Rich woods over limestone, rocky hillsides
Trifolium stoloniferum Muhl. ex Eaton	Fabaceae	102702	38.140	87.699	Moist disturbed forests, streams, open woods, lawns
Trillium decipiens J.D. Freeman	Melanthiaceae	41712	31.828	84.671	Rich woods & river bluffs in mixed deciduous forests
Trillium decumbens Harbison	Melanthiaceae	38956	33.870	85.463	Rocky slopes in open deciduous woodlands
Trillium discolor Wray ex Hook.	Melanthiaceae	15733	34.339	82.551	Forested slopes & stream banks
Trillium foetidissimum J.D. Freeman	Melanthiaceae	71867	31.105	92.228	Rich woods on river bluffs, floodplains, roadsides
Trillium gracile J.D. Freeman	Melanthiaceae	47927	31.009	94.179	Mature pine & hardwood forests, slopes near streams
Trillium lancifolium Raf.	Melanthiaceae	68672	33.317	85.249	Floodplain forests, rocky upland woods & thickets
Trillium ludovicianum Harbison	Melanthiaceae	61448	31.552	92.487	Mixed deciduous floodplain woods & adj. slopes
Trillium luteum (Muhl.) Harbison	Melanthiaceae	71780	34.354	83.826	Rich deciduous forest & open woods, calcareous soils

(Continued)

(Continued)

Species	Family	Range Area (km2)	Range Centroid Latitude (°)	Range Centroid Longitude (°)	Habitat Description
Trillium maculatum Raf.	Melanthiaceae	92959	31.660	83.938	Rich mesic forests, river banks & bluffs, floodplains
Trillium oostingii Gaddy	Melanthiaceae	1742	34.352	80.583	Rich bottomland forests
Trillium persistens Duncan	Melanthiaceae	2970	34.755	83.198	Mixed deciduous & pine woodlands, stream flats
Trillium pusillum Michx.	Melanthiaceae	92822	36.115	85.434	Dry to mesic forests, along streams, swampy woods
Trillium reliquum J.D. Freeman	Melanthiaceae	26511	32.315	84.163	Rich mixed forest, slopes, bluffs & stream flats
Trillium rugelii Rendle	Melanthiaceae	91092	35.133	83.850	Rich deciduous forests, calcareous or mafic bedrock
Trillium simile Gleanon	Melanthiaceae	26375	35.307	83.421	Forested coves, slopes & seeps with rich soil
Trillium stamineum Harbison	Melanthiaceae	97060	33.645	87.520	Upland deciduous forest over limestone, floodplains
Trillium sulcatum Patrick	Melanthiaceae	99413	38.779	80.968	Coves & moist slopes, rich mesic woodlands
Trillium underwoodii Small	Melanthiaceae	75918	31.587	85.220	Dry to mesic rich deciduous forests, stream edges
Trillium vaseyi Harbison	Melanthiaceae	36463	33.210	84.492	Steep wooded slopes, rich coves & ravines
Trillium viride Beck	Melanthiaceae	41016	38.471	90.572	Rich woods, bluffs & rocky hillsides
Trillium viridescens Nutt.	Melanthiaceae	120456	34.685	93.618	Rich deciduous forests, bluffs & floodplains
Uvularia floridana Chapm.	Liliaceae	48386	32.203	84.840	Rich hardwood forests, floodplains & moist ravines
Valeriana pauciflora Michx.	Valerianaceae	213927	38.998	84.412	Rich mesic woods

Species	Family				Habitat
Veratrum latifolium (Desr.) Zomlefer	Liliaceae	164689	36.651	81.255	Moist to dry forests
Veratrum parviflorum Michx.	Liliaceae	110403	35.900	83.904	Moist wooded slopes, dry forests
Veratrum woodii J.W. Robbins ex Alph. Wood	Liliaceae	183745	37.339	87.774	Rich woods on circumneutral soil
Vernonia arkansana DC.	Asteraceae	188301	39.133	93.390	Low woods, streambanks, roadsides
Viola tripartita Elliott	Violaceae	214221	35.650	83.407	Rich woods, moist slopes, bottomlands
Viola villosa Walter	Violaceae	251059	33.182	88.085	Moist sandy or rocky soil, hardwood hammocks
Waldsteinia lobata (Baldw.) Torr. & A. Gray	Rosaceae	16248	33.792	83.900	Forests, streambanks
Xerophyllum asphodeloides (L.) Nutt.	Liliaceae	86181	36.641	81.026	Forests on dry ridges & slopes, pine barrens
Zizia trifoliata (Michx.) Fernald	Apiaceae	228512	34.441	83.091	Mesic forest, woodlands, forest edges

PART FIVE
SYNTHESIS

22 The Dynamic Nature of the Herbaceous Layer

A Brief Synthesis

Frank S. Gilliam

It is likely that the lion's share of plant ecologists over the past ~ 100 years have been inspired by the work and writings of Henry Chandler Cowles, particularly his extensive fin-de-siècle opus on the vegetation of the Indiana Dunes. His succinct and often-quoted description of succession as "a variable approaching a variable, not a constant" (Cowles 1901, 81) defined the dynamic nature of plant communities more clearly than any other ecologist before him or since. Indeed, his view has been adopted for this book to highlight the spatially and temporally dynamic nature of the herbaceous layer of forests.

One of the reasons I related my experience as a young graduate student at Duke University with the term "step-overs" as a collective synonym for the herbaceous layer (chapter 1, this volume) was to emphasize the low regard that those in the forestry profession have commonly and traditionally had for the lower vascular strata of forests. In this final chapter, I would like to bring back into focus several of the various conclusions brought out in previous chapters to demonstrate how unfortunate such a view is.

As is becoming increasingly apparent, the herb layer is an integral component in maintaining the structure and function of forest ecosystems (Gilliam 2007). Just as apparent, however, is that one of the consequences of ignoring the ecological significance of herb layer species is their demise, particularly as a result of land-use practices that fail to take into account the essential role these species play in forests. Although it is clear that, relative to shrub, hardwood, and conifer species, herbaceous species have the highest rates of natural extinction (Levin and Levin 2001; chapter 1, this volume), it is less clear what the specific effects of land-use practice are on herb layer biodiversity. The debate concerning the effects of forest harvesting practices on species diversity continues (Noble and Dirzo 1997; Reich et al. 2001) and has been presented in several forms throughout this book (chapters 7, 8, 13, and 18, this volume). This is an area worthy of much more intensive research, and it is particularly encouraging to note that research focusing on disturbance ecology of the herb layer has been increasing in recent decades (fig. 13.1, chapter 13, this volume).

In addition to attempting to convey new knowledge regarding the ecology of the herbaceous layer of eastern North American forests, a major impetus behind this book was to bring together in a single volume, to the extent possible, what is known of herb layer ecology. Thus, I conclude this book with a brief synthesis of the major points brought out in the preceding chapters. As with the first edition (Gilliam and Roberts 2003), this will be done using the sections of the book, rather than simply providing summaries chapter by chapter, as a basis for the synthesis: "The Environment of the Herbaceous Layer" (part I), "Population Dynamics of the Herbaceous Layer" (part II), "Community Dynamics of the Herbaceous Layer across Spatial and Temporal Scales" (part III), and "Community Dynamics of the Herbaceous Layer and the Role of Disturbance" (part IV).

SYNTHESIS

Research on the forest herbaceous layer has increased dramatically in the past several decades (fig. 1.2, chapter 1, and fig. 13.1, chapter 13, this volume). This increase has been as timely as it has been essential, given the naturally high diversity of the herb layer and the ongoing concern over loss of biodiversity. Indeed, this work has done much to increase our understanding of functional roles of herb species in forest ecosystems.

Plant ecologists with an interest in the ecology of the herb layer should expect to find a wide variety of synonyms for this vegetation stratum in the literature. Vegetation scientists of North America tend to use *herbaceous/herb layer* more than other terms, whereas those of Europe tend to use *ground vegetation* more often. Rather than being a call for strict uniformity in use of terminology, this is an opportunity to advise researchers what to expect among published studies, particularly when carrying out literature searches.

Similarly, the literature contains numerous definitions of the herb layer, reflecting the considerable variation in vegetation structure and composition among forest types. Most definitions of the herbaceous layer focus on its physical aspects, especially height, rather than on growth form. Although a commonly used definition of the herb layer is the forest stratum composed of all vascular species that are < 1 m in height, the maximum height limit and exclusion/inclusion of nonvascular plant species vary substantially in the literature, with most height limits generally falling between 0.5 and 1.5 m.

Once again, this is not a call for a uniform definition of the herb layer. Vegetation scientists should have the freedom to adapt their definitions in ways that are appropriate for the particular forest type being studied. Because the literature contains several studies that do not provide a clear definition of the herb layer, researchers should explicitly state their working definition of the herb layer and base such definition on the biological and physical structure of the forest system.

I presented a simple conceptual framework for the forest herbaceous layer comprising two functional groups: resident species and transient species. *Resident species* are those with life history characteristics that confine them to maximum aboveground heights of no more than about 1.5 m. *Transient species* are those with the potential to develop and emerge into higher strata, and thus their existence in the herb layer is temporary, or transient. Juveniles of overstory species compete as transient species with resident species and either pass through this layer or die.

Thus, as a stratum of forest vegetation, the herb layer is the intimate spatial and temporal coincidence of resident and transient species—two otherwise disparate plant groups. In addition to the more obvious differences between them in growth habit and form, they differ in the factors that determine their distribution, patterns of reproduction, and respective mechanisms of seed dispersal. Whereas wind and vertebrate herbivores are predominant mechanisms for transient species, invertebrates are predominant dispersal vectors for resident species (especially myrmecochory, seed dispersal by ants). Such differences between resident and transient species in the herbaceous layer of forest ecosystems create a forest stratum with impressive spatial and temporal variability.

The Environment of the Herbaceous Layer

The microenvironment of the forest floor, the one that most closely influences plants of the herbaceous layer, provides stark contrast to that of an open field or that above in the forest canopy. Forest overstory species alter the quality and/or quantity of virtually all aspects of the environment that are essential to the survivorship and growth of herb layer species. The focus here is on nutrient and light availability.

Foliar concentrations of essential nutrients are generally much higher in herbaceous species than in woody overstory species, with spring ephemeral herbs having particularly high foliar concentrations of nitrogen, emphasizing yet another important contrast between resident and transient species of the herb layer (chapter 2, this volume). Surprisingly, foliar nutrient concentrations exhibit little variation within herb species occupying contrasting forested sites, possibly the result of shifting carbon sinks (i.e., whereas enhanced foliar growth would occur on nutrient-rich sites, increased mycorrhizal support would occur on nutrient-poor sites). There is evidence that herbaceous species are capable of rapid uptake and temporary storage of nutrients during periods of high nutrient availability; this is followed by retranslocation of these nutrients to support growth during periods of active biomass accumulation. Therefore, although herbaceous species do not exhibit luxury uptake of nutrients in the more traditional sense (i.e., as evidenced in intersite variation), they do exhibit seasonal patterns of luxury uptake supporting subsequent growth during periods of limited nutrient availability (chapter 2, this volume).

Clearly, the most spatially and temporally variable component of the environment of the forest floor is light availability. The light environment to which herb layer species are exposed varies at many levels of scale over space and over time. Accordingly, this environment can be envisioned as a *dynamic mosaic*, for light penetrates the forest canopy to reach the forest floor in a mosaic of discrete patches of varying size (i.e., sunflecks), the size and distribution of which vary at time scales from the diurnal to the seasonal. Time-lapse photography would reveal the constant dance of these sunflecks across the forest floor.

The presence of herbs in the understory of temperate deciduous forests depends greatly on their ability to grow in this dynamic mosaic of light environment. In turn, variations in irradiance can influence other microclimatic factors, including temperature, relative humidity, and water availability. Adaptations to the dynamic nature of this environment are expressed physiologically and morphologically at multiple scales—from subcellular to leaf to whole plant (chapter 3, this volume).

There is a selective advantage for herb species that are physiologically active during the warmer portions of the year when temperatures are more favorable for photosynthesis and nutrient uptake. Other selective advantages among forest herbs include adaptations to increase light absorption in the forest understory, such as a well-developed spongy mesophyll to scatter light, reflective lower leaf surface to direct light back into the leaf, and adaxial surface cells that are concavely shaped to direct light toward cells containing chloroplasts (chapter 3, this volume). Among the many challenges in understanding the complex ecophysiology of forest herb species are the various changes that are occurring, and will continue to occur, in the context of global change (chapter 3, this volume).

Despite the fact that the importance of nutrients in influencing plant growth and survivorship is often considered independent of the importance of light, the two factors exert their influences simultaneously and synergistically. Thus, although the nutrient environment of the herbaceous layer of deciduous forests may be relatively rich, the light environment may affect herbaceous species' ability to exploit available nutrients (chapter 4, this volume). Severe light limitation may decrease demand for nutrients because nutrient uptake may be limited by accumulation of biomass by individual plants and their specific nutrient saturation points. Efficiency of nutrient resorption may also decrease in herb layer plants in an environment of nutrient availability that is high relative to demand.

Population Dynamics of the Herbaceous Layer

An appreciation of the highly variable nature of the environment in which species of the herbaceous layer have evolved is essential to understand the complexity of life history strategies that govern population dynamics of herb layer species. This is particularly pronounced for forest herbs and their light environment. The distinct seasonality of the light environment has resulted in the evolution of diverse phenological patterns among herb species—spring ephemerals, summer-greens, winter-greens, evergreens, heteroptics, and parasitic and saprophytic plants. In addition to their obvious contrasts in temporal variation in growth characteristics, these phenological groups exhibit contrasting reproductive modes.

Because many forest herbs are cryptophytes, vegetative reproduction is commonly considered the predominant reproduction mode for forest herbs. Sexual reproduction, however, plays a major role in the persistence of these species, many, if not most, of which are relatively long-lived (e.g., 15–25 years). Still, it is difficult to generalize about breeding biology and mating systems of forest herbs because current estimates of breeding systems are often inaccurate. Pollination is often insect-mediated. Population spread can be limited by seed dispersal, with rates of spread often < 1 m per year and rarely > 10 m per year. Vegetative spread may equal or exceed spread by seed dispersal. The role of the seed bank for most taxa is unknown. Most species exhibit some type of seed dormancy (largely physiological or morphological) at dispersal, which can reduce the risk of extinction (chapter 5, this volume).

Numerous vascular taxa of the forests of eastern North America have been identified as endangered and threatened. Demographic studies have been conducted on only a limited number of species. In spite of the usefulness of matrix projection models, few have been used for herbs of forested eastern North America, especially rare taxa. Newer methods, including elasticity and sensitivity analysis and variance decomposition, are potentially useful for predicting population changes through time. The metapopulation approach that uses measures of site occupancy, recruitment, and extinction is potentially useful for community-wide surveys of species in declining habitats, but unfortunately, it has seldom been used. Furthermore, adequate demographic data for transition matrices or metapopulation analyses are not widely available for many species.

Despite its importance, quantitative modeling of population sizes using metapopulation dynamics and population viability analysis (PVA) has been underutilized for forest herbs of eastern North America. Indeed, only nine herbaceous species that occur in forests of eastern North America have been used in notable PVA studies (chapter 6, this volume).

After 30 years, the questions originally posed in the seminal paper by Bierzychudek (1982a) are still relevant today and warrant further attention in the future: What factors regulate population sizes of forest herbs? How stable are population sizes of forest herbs? How much site-to-site variation occurs in population behavior?

Community Dynamics of the Herbaceous Layer across Spatial and Temporal Scales

Land-use practices and natural disturbances have created a complex patchwork within the landscape of eastern North America. Beginning at the time of the first European settlers, agriculture and logging throughout this region, once essentially covered with pristine forests, eliminated much of the primeval forest, resulting in limited coverage of what is often called *old-growth forest*. Although this term has been the subject of much debate, consensus is growing as to how to define old-growth forest. Unfortunately, the herbaceous layer is generally not included in these definitions, a serious omission considering the high species diversity of this stratum. Preservation or conservation efforts using functional groups, rather than individual species, within the herb layer should allow better standards to emerge for assessing old-growth status, ultimately assisting with land management decisions (chapter 7, this volume).

Likely because of the logistical demands of field sampling, studies based on one-time samples of the herb layer are prevalent in the literature. Unfortunately, this approach does not lead to an appreciation of the great temporal variability of forest understory communities. A large emphasis on the spring vernal herbs often occurs at the expense of studies of the flora throughout the rest of the growing season. Certainly, observations should be expanded beyond the level of the stand and single-year study to fully understand spatial and temporal patterns in the understory.

Current emphases on sustainable use for forest ecosystems have focused on management questions. In spite of this, old-growth forests will remain an important component in our understanding of the structure and function of forest ecosystems. These will serve as benchmark ecosystems in the heavily disturbed landscape of forests of eastern North America (chapter 7, this volume).

One characteristic of older forest stands, whether true old growth or mature secondary growth, is the high degree of spatial heterogeneity in microtopography (also called *microrelief*) that naturally results when overmature trees die and tip over, creating paired, contrasting conditions of mounds (the vertically displaced root system and associated soil) and pits (the space formerly occupied by the root system). This spatial heterogeneity in microrelief provides a means by which many species are maintained in the community (chapter 8, this volume). Those species with spatial distributions across multiple microsites have the advantage of being buffered against moderate to severe environmental fluctuations. Those species restricted to one microsite, however, suffer a greater variability in population size with environmental fluctuation and have a higher risk of local extinction. For these species, microtopographic heterogeneity may limit available space, placing such species at a disadvantage.

Given the role of spatial heterogeneity and long-term, on-going changes in land use in forest communities of eastern North America, the interaction of these environmental factors should be taken into account in any study of herb layer communities. It has been proposed that an intermediate level of heterogeneity will promote greater species richness in a community (chapter 8, this volume). Extreme microsites may shift the balance to restrict species composition, whereas lack of microsites may increase overall competition with greater species overlap, eliminating safe sites necessary for some species. It has also been suggested that the current level of heterogeneity in a given forest community is likely the result of past events that either minimize or maximize microsites (chapter 8, this volume). Because these confounding factors can influence community richness, stand age alone is likely a poor predictor of patterns of species richness through succession.

Pit and mound microtopography represents only one of several ways in which the forest overstory can directly and indirectly influence the herbaceous layer. Through competitive interactions, however, the herb layer can, in turn, influence the composition of the overstory. In addition, species of both strata respond to spatial and temporal shifts in a suite of environmental factors. These reciprocating effects and responses to environmental gradients can lead to a measurable spatial correlation of the occurrence of plant species between the overstory and the herb layer. When this condition develops, the strata are said to be *linked*. It has been suggested that such linkage arises from similarities among forest strata in the responses of their respective species to environmental gradients (chapter 9, this volume). These responses may change through secondary forest succession and thus may be a function of stand age.

Although the concept of linkage among vegetation strata of forest communities has been the subject of considerable debate among vegetation scientists in the past, it is gaining wider acceptance and exhibits great potential as a concept with a high degree of ecological importance and practical application. That is, it furthers our understanding of and appreciation for the complexities underlying the structure and function of forest ecosystems (e.g., responses to disturbance and mechanisms of secondary succession). In addition, it may be applied toward landscape-level investigations of forest cover types and remote sensing.

The herbaceous layer of southeastern forests and woodlands not only often displays impressive species richness, but also does so in ways that vary greatly with the scale of observation (chapter 10, this volume). Among the dominant processes driving patterns of species diversity in this region are cation availability, natural and anthropogenic disturbance, mass effects, and the relative size of the species pool. The various processes that govern community assembly function at different spatial scales, with biotic interactions and local environmental filtering operating at finer spatial scales, and dispersal and species pool size becoming more important at broader spatial scales (chapter 10, this volume).

A particularly intense disturbance that severely disrupts overstory–herbaceous layer interactions is that involving clearing of forests for agricultural practices, the agricultural practices themselves, and abandonment of agricultural fields. The response of vegetation following this abandonment is called *old-field succession*. In the Piedmont of North Carolina, where old-field succession has been studied in greatest detail, the sequence begins with a complex assemblage of herbaceous species and ends with pine and, finally, hardwood dominance. Patterns associated with this response are best understood as a consequence of individualistic responses of species related to their ability and opportunities to disperse to and compete at particular sites (chapter 11, this volume). Although a few of the individuals of woody plant species that will dominate late in succession may arrive early and simply outlive pioneers, virtually none of the herb species common in pine and hardwood stands is found in old fields initially after abandonment.

A significant proportion of the variability in herbaceous species composition of old fields is correlated with soil variables, regardless of successional stage. At the landscape scale, soil moisture conditions, a function of topography and proximity to streams, account for much of the variation. Soil chemistry is also highly correlated with herb species distributions and overall species richness. The correlation between soil site variables and species composition diminishes sharply among late-stage pine stands, a decline that has been suggested to be a consequence of changes in stand structure (e.g., creation of canopy gaps from increased pine mortality) that increase variability of the light environment (chapter 11, this volume).

Although it is clear that changes in the relative availability of resources are important in explaining successional patterns, much effort to explain variability in the distribution of herbs on successional landscapes has focused on the importance of competitive interactions in the context of changes in resource availability. If such interactions were the only factors shaping temporal and spatial variability of herb species, high correlations between compositional variations and patterns of environmental variation should be expected. Although such correlations do explain significant amounts of variation in composition, often the majority of such variation remains unexplained. Other mechanisms are likely equally important, precluding the creation of a unified theory of change (chapter 11, this volume).

The combination of forest clearing and agricultural practices that ultimately leads to old-field succession represents an extremely intense form of disturbance. Forests of the boreal region (often called taiga) also experience intense, often frequent, disturbances of a very different nature—fire and forest management practices. It is not surprising that variability in disturbance regime influences the distribution of herbaceous layer species of boreal forests (chapter 12, this volume).

Whereas high fire frequencies favor the presence of ericaceous species and terricolous lichens, lower frequencies are associated with higher richness of herb and shrub species. Because boreal species have evolved to persist in a context of fire, their spatial distribution is closely linked to fire frequency. Thus, the apparent co-occurrence of overstory cover types and herb layer species may only reflect similar responses to a particular disturbance regime. Although the canopy cover can modify the abiotic conditions of a stand, thus affecting the composition of the understory, many understory species are not restricted to a specific canopy, but rather to specific abiotic conditions (chapter 12, this volume). Herbaceous layer diversity at the boreal landscape level is generally highest with intermediate frequency of fire, independent of cover and site type, supporting the intermediate disturbance hypothesis.

It is clear that herb layer species of boreal forests have developed different reproductive strategies to persist under particular fire regimes. It is not surprising, then, that patterns of herb layer richness and abundance will be directly affected by disturbance characteristics. Accordingly, when the predominant disturbance regime shifts from fire to forest harvesting, herb species are exposed to a very different disturbance regime for which they lack particular adaptive traits. Clearcutting does not necessarily have a direct negative impact on the diversity of vascular herb species; however, it does change the relationships among species in boreal communities and contributes to change in community composition. Clearcutting has been observed to greatly alter the successional processes under certain abiotic conditions. Herbaceous layer communities are not only part of the rich biodiversity of boreal forests; they can also play important roles in boreal forest dynamics (chapter 12, this volume).

Community Dynamics of the Herbaceous Layer and the Role of Disturbance

Although disturbances are often regarded only in terms of their initial effects, it is important to consider the long-term effects of the disturbance on herbaceous layer recovery. Our ultimate goal is to predict herbaceous layer response over the long term to disturbances from both natural and anthropogenic sources and to apply this knowledge to the wise conservation and management of the forests of eastern North America (chapter 13, this volume). Disturbance-mediated changes in environmental conditions often make forests more habitable for invasive species, which are most likely to appear in forest habitats that have higher light availability, such as light gaps or along forest edges, and that are proximate to a seed source. Invasion susceptibility should increase in areas with higher degrees of anthropogenic disturbance, especially those close to populated areas. Using the categorization of disturbance severity as the degree of disruption of the overstory and understory/forest floor (chapter 13, this volume), greater invasions should occur in environments where both understory and overstory disturbance is severe.

The life history characteristics of species interact with disturbance characteristics to determine herbaceous layer response. For example, whether the disturbance primarily affects the overstory canopy or the understory, along with the severity of those effects in each canopy layer, will control in situ survival, vegetative regeneration, regeneration from the seed bank, or regeneration from dispersed propagules (chapter 14, this volume). In addition to the direct effects of disturbance on the herbaceous layer, there are also indirect effects, like herbivory on trees and shrubs, that influence the microenvironment for the understory. Most forms of agriculture constitute the extreme in disturbance severity for the herbaceous layer because of the outright destruction of preexisting plants and the removal of propagules of forest species. Forestry practices typically engender less dramatic changes in the herbaceous layer than do agricultural practices, although treatments that severely disturb both the canopy and understory (e.g., whole-tree harvesting with heavy mechanical site preparation) can greatly modify the herbaceous layer. Our knowledge of the long-term effects of forestry practices on the herbaceous layer is limited by the lack of long-term studies addressing forestry practices in isolation from other anthropogenic disturbances such as agriculture.

Although the community dynamics and response of the herbaceous layer to disturbance have long been popular and important avenues of inquiry, the appreciation of the importance of *novel species* (nonindigenous species) in the forests of eastern North America is more recent (chapter 15, this volume). The presence of novel species in eastern forests is increasingly being noted, and it is apparent that temperate forests may be more susceptible to invasions of novel species than other types of communities. Indeed, different regions of eastern forests support different novel species, with species often emerging as invasive only in subsections of their range.

The impacts of novel species can be better understood when categorized by their degree of invasiveness rather than painting them all with a broad brush as invaders (e.g., capable of high impacts). Novel species may not be fundamentally different from indigenous species in terms of their ability to colonize. Although invaders of forest communities share traits of colonizers of successional communities, they must also be adapted to low light. In addition, some are either less susceptible or more resilient to herbivory, or both, compared to native species. The ability to invade may be linked more closely with phenotypic plasticity than with a single trait.

Novel species may be competitively superior to indigenous species and better able to respond to disturbance. In the long term, novel species can change the composition of the bank of potential colonizers, thereby reducing the ability of indigenous species to respond. The implication for management is that removal of novel species may lead to further invasions. Thus, novel species add another dimension to the process of community recovery following disturbance. The influence of novel species may result in a very different post-disturbance composition of the herbaceous layer. As a result, invasion by novel species may be not only an immediate response to disturbance, but also a chronic disturbance itself (chapter 15, this volume).

Identifying the nature of understory–overstory interactions is one of the keys to understanding herbaceous layer dynamics; indeed, it has been one of the main themes of this book. Again, using the terminology set forth in the opening chapter and summarized at the beginning of this chapter, transient species influence the microclimate and competitive relationships in the understory and control the composition and spatial distribution of understory plants. There may also be an element of passive linkage among understory and overstory canopy strata that results from similar responses of different strata to the physical environment (chapter 9, this volume). Another important form of interaction occurs when resident species exert control over the germination, survival, and growth of transient species. Indeed, the influence of herbaceous plants on tree seedlings can be highly selective (i.e., species-specific), with long-term consequences for the composition of tree species (chapter 14, this volume).

The microenvironment under the herbaceous layer is characterized by lower light, more litter (under some ferns and shrub species), and in some cases, increased seed predation. These conditions decrease seed germination for some tree species, as well as decreasing seedling survival and reducing overall seedling density. Shifts in tree species composition occur under some herbaceous layer species, such as ferns and shrubs. Species-selective reductions in seedling growth alter the competitive relationships among the trees (chapter 14, this volume).

Different understory species alter the microenvironment below their canopies to varying degrees, depending on leaf morphology and area, clonal density, phenology, stature (height), litter quantity and quality, and belowground resource capture. The clonal growth habit of many understory species and the segregation of understory species in different microsites lead to spatial heterogeneity in the intensity of the selective filtering influence on tree seedlings. The understory mosaic, then, can result in the aggregation of seedlings of different tree species into patches. Once these distinct patches of transient species emerge from the herbaceous layer and become the overtopping canopy, they can be expected to have their own reciprocating influence on the herbaceous layer through their effects on forest structure and the forest floor microenvironment (fig. 13.1, chapter 13, this volume). Thus, extending the concept of the selective filter (chapter 14, this volume) to multiple canopy layers, it is likely that the resident species of the herbaceous layer and the transient species do exert selective filtering effects on each other in turn as dominance shifts from one group of species to the other.

Another disturbance that threatens the herbaceous layer of forests is overconsumption of foliar and woody material (overbrowsing) by vertebrate herbivores. In contrast to western North American forests, where this commonly results from introduced herbivores, in eastern North American forests, the problem is largely a function of overpopulation of native species, such as white-tailed deer, caused by the removal of top carnivores, such as wolves and mountain lions (chapter 16, this volume). Evidence clearly demonstrates that the diversity of herbaceous communities in forests throughout eastern North America has declined substantially in areas with high densities of white-tailed deer (chapters 16 and 17, this volume), with some browsing-sensitive species (e.g., *Trillium* spp.) being used as indicators of browsing intensity. In extreme cases, many of which exist in northeastern United States, overbrowsing by deer can severely retard forest regeneration following intense canopy-removing disturbances, including windthrow and timber harvesting (chapter 17, this volume).

Timber harvesting and other management practices can represent both acute and legacy forms of disturbance. Although there is evidence that harvesting of second growth can allow rapid recovery of forest herb communities (chapter 13, this volume), recent work has demonstrated that recovery to "pristine" (old-growth) pre-harvest levels requires more time than typical harvest rotations allow (chapter 18, this volume). A likely more profound legacy effect than harvesting is agriculture. Much of the currently forested landscape of eastern North America arose from conversion of primal forest to agriculture, followed by forest regrowth after abandonment of farms (chapters 11 and 19, this volume). Such historical events have created long-lived influences on the species composition and diversity of the herbaceous layer. Herb layer communities of forests that have recovered following agricultural abandonment are typically depleted in native species, compared to non-cleared forests (chapter 19, this volume).

Total atmospheric deposition of N to terrestrial ecosystems is predicted to increase greatly as a result of a variety of human activities. Recent research has shown that such increases in N loading to forests may alter forest species composition and species diversity of the herbaceous layer. Although sensitivity to N deposition varies widely among sites, declines in species richness often follow several stages: (a) initial increases in herb layer cover; (b) decreases in species richness, caused by the loss of numerous species that are efficient under low-N conditions; (c) decreases in species evenness, caused by the increasing dominance of relatively few species that require high N availability; and (d) loss of forest biodiversity as a result of these decreases in species richness and evenness. The N homogeneity hypothesis predicts that as excess N inputs reduce the naturally high spatial heterogeneity in soil, N availability (i.e., patchiness) that helps to maintain the species diversity of the herbaceous layer of affected forests will decline (chapter 20, this volume).

Current increases in concentrations of CO_2 can have direct influences on plant ecophysiology, eliciting novel responses among herb layer species (chapter 3, this volume). Simultaneously, increasing CO_2 contributes greatly to global change in general and global warming in particular. The current distributions of herb layer species, especially those considered range-restricted endemic species, may still be profoundly affected by historical patterns of climate change. Many of such endemic species would be predicted to be at increased risk from modern climate change due to small range size, compounded by long-term, broad-scale dispersal limitation (chapter 21, this volume). Thus, current patterns of climate change are likely to significantly threaten forest herb biodiversity (chapter 21, this volume).

SUMMARY

It should be clear from this chapter that, to paraphrase a well-known line from Alfred Lord Tennyson's "Ulysses" ("Tho' much is taken, much abides"), although much has been learned about the ecological dynamics of the herbaceous layer in forests of eastern North America, much remains to be learned. Our awareness of what lies ahead for future research in herb layer ecology remains in spite of the increasing amount of work that is being done. Some of this awareness, however, is also because of the work being done. That is, just like in any field of scientific endeavor, new knowledge begets new questions.

A great deal of the impetus behind the first edition of this book (Gilliam and Roberts 2003) was the belief that the time had come to synthesize our understanding of the basic ecology of the herb layer. A theme that seemed to emerge from that initial compilation, however, was the conservation ecology of the herb layer. In this regard, the book entered the realm of applied ecology. Certainly, given the spatial coincidence of high population densities with the distribution of eastern North American forests, both basic and applied approaches are relevant and essential to studying and understanding the spatial and temporal dynamics of the herbaceous layer. Conservation ecology is now firmly established as a prominent ecological subdiscipline. Although it has been broadly defined, it generally focuses on the nature and extent of deviations of anthropogenically altered ecosystems from minimally altered states. Among the many challenges facing conservation ecologists is that, as discussed in chapter 7, examples of such minimally altered states (i.e., old-growth stands) are all too infrequent in eastern North America

Thus, it is not surprising that this second edition further delves into the disturbance ecology of the herb layer of forest ecosystems. The final observations of the first edition merit repetition here. First, existing old-growth stands of the region must be preserved, both as ecological legacies and as benchmarks for conservation ecologists, especially for studies of the herbaceous layer; this is a call for the preservation of such areas. Second, the remaining forest stands of eastern North America represent a variety of responses to myriad types and intensities of disturbances over many spatial and temporal scales. In short, if there were ever a case of a variable approaching a variable, this would be it. Thus, researchers, particularly those working on the landscape scale, should bear this in mind when conducting their studies.

The highly disturbed nature of eastern North American forests will not change in the future. Rather, projected increases in human populations in the region will place an even greater demand on forested areas. The authors who have contributed to this book have provided ample evidence that responsible use of our forest resources is not necessarily inconsistent with protection of the herbaceous layer. It is imperative that all embrace the concept of sustainable use of natural resources, such as forests, that will allow continued use of those resources by future generations. Forest ecosystems have indeed always been essential to the survival, success, and well-being of human civilization. At the foundation of these forests is the diminutive herbaceous layer—the forest between the trees.

References

Abrahamson, W.G. 1980. Demography and vegetative reproduction. Pages 89–106 in O.T. Solbrig, editor. Demography and evolution in plant populations. University of California Press, Berkeley, CA.

Abrams, M.D. 1992. Fire and the development of oak forests. BioScience 42:346–353.

Abrams, M.D. 1998. The red maple paradox. BioScience 48:355–364.

Abrams, M.D. 2003. Where has all the white oak gone? BioScience 53:927–939.

Abrams, M.D., and D.I. Dickmann. 1982. Early revegetation of clear-cut and burned jack pine sites in northern lower Michigan. Canadian Journal of Botany 60:946–954.

Adams, M.S. 1970. Adaptations of *Aplectrum hyemale* to the environment: Effects of pre-conditioning temperature on net photosynthesis. Bulletin of the Torrey Botanical Club 97:219–224.

Adams, V.M., D.M. Marsh, and J.S. Knox. 2005. Importance of the seed bank for population viability and population monitoring in a threatened wetland herb. Biological Conservation 124:425–436.

Adkison, G.P., and S.K. Gleeson. 2004. Forest understory vegetation along a productivity gradient. Journal of the Torrey Botanical Society 131:32–44.

Adler, P.B., et al. 2011. Productivity is a poor predictor of plant species richness. Science 333:1750–1753

Aerts, R. 1996. Nutrient resorption from senescing leaves of perennials: are there general patterns? Journal of Ecology 84:597–608.

Ågren, J., and M.F. Willson. 1992. Determinants of seed production in *Geranium maculatum*. Oecologia 92:177–182.

Aguilar, R., M. Quesada, L. Ashworth, Y. Herrerias-Diego, and J. Lobo. 2008. Genetic consequences of habitat fragmentation in plant populations: Susceptible signals in plant traits and methodological approaches. Molecular Ecology 17:5177–5188.

Ahlgren, C.E. 1960. Some effects of fire on reproduction and growth of vegetation in northeastern Minnesota. Ecology 41:431–445.

Ahlgren, I.F., and C.E. Ahlgren. 1960. Ecological effects of forest fires. Botanical Review 26:483–533.

Aide, T. 1986. The influence of wind and animal pollination on variation in outcrossing rates. Evolution 40:434–435.

Aizen, M.A., L. Ashworth, and L. Galetto. 2002. Reproductive success in fragmented habitats: do compatibility systems and pollination specialization matter? Journal of Vegetation Science 13:885–892

Albert, D.A., S.A. Denton, and B.V. Barnes. 1986. Regional landscape ecosystems of Michigan. School of Natural Resources, University of Michigan, Ann Arbor, MI.

Albert, L.P., L.G. Campbell, and K.D. Whitney. 2011. Beyond simple reproductive assurance: cleistogamy allows adaptive plastic responses to pollen limitation. International Journal of Plant Sciences 172:862–869.

Albrecht, M.A, and B.C McCarthy. 2006. Seed germination and dormancy in the medicinal woodland herbs *Collinsonia canadensis* L. (Lamiaceae) and *Dioscorea villosa* L. (Dioscoreaceae). Flora 201:24–31.

Albrecht, M.A., and B.C. McCarthy. 2009. Seedling establishment shapes the distribution of shade-adapted forest herbs across a topographical moisture gradient. Journal of Ecology 97:1037–1049.

Albrecht, M.A., and B.C. McCarthy. 2011. Variation in dormancy and germination in three co-occurring perennial forest herbs. Plant Ecology 212:1465–1477.

Allen, J.A., C.S. Brown, and T.J. Stohlgren. 2009. Non-native plant invasions of United States national parks. Biological Invasions 11:2195–2207.

Allen, T.R., and S.J. Walsh. 1996. Spatial and compositional pattern of alpine treeline, Glacier National Park, Montana. Photogrammetric Engineering and Remote Sensing 62:1261–1268.

Alliance, W.N.C. 1995. Nantahala-Pisgah national forests old growth survey: Citizen involvement in old growth protection. Asheville, North Carolina.

Allison, T.D. 1990. The influence of deer browsing on the reproductive biology of Canada Yew (*Taxus canadensis* marsh.). I. Direct effect on pollen, ovule, and seed production. Oecologia 83:523–529.

Allombert, S., A. J. Gaston, and J.-L. Martin. 2005a. A natural experiment on the impact of overabundant deer on songbird populations. Biological Conservation 126:1–13.

Allombert, S., S. Stockton, and J.-L. Martin. 2005b. A natural experiment on the impact of overabundant deer on forest invertebrates. Conservation Biology 19:1917–1929.

Al-Mufti, M.M., C.L. Sydes, S.B. Farness, J.P. Grime, and S.B. Band. 1977. A quantitative analysis of shoot phenology and dominance in herbaceous vegetation. Journal of Ecology 65:759–791.

Alonso, C., J.C. Vamosi, T.M. Knight, J.A. Steets, and T.-L. Ashman. 2010. Is reproduction of endemic plant species particularly pollen limited in biodiversity hotspots? Oikos 119:1192–1200.

Alpert, P., and H.A. Mooney. 1986. Resource sharing among ramets in the clonal herb, *Fragaria chiloensis*. Oecologia 70:227–233.

Alvarez-Buylla, E.R., and M. Slatkin. 1994. Finding confidence limits on population growth rates: three real examples revisited. Ecology 75:255–260.

Alverson, W.S., and D.M. Waller. 1997. Pages 280–297 in W. McShea and J. Rappole, editors. Deer populations and the widespread failure of hemlock regeneration in northern forests. The science of overabundance: deer ecology and population management. Washington, DC: Smithsonian Institution Press.

Alverson, W.S., D.M. Waller, and S.L. Solheim. 1988. Forests too deer: edge effects in northern Wisconsin. Conservation Biology 2:348–358.

Amthor, J.S., P.J. Hanson, R.J. Norby, and S.D. Wullschleger. 2010. A comment on "Appropriate experimental ecosystem warming methods by ecosystem, objective, and practicality" by Aronson and McNulty. Agricultural and Forest Meteorology 150:497–498.

Anacker, B.L., and C.D. Kirschbaum. 2006. Vascular flora of the Kinzua Quality Deer Cooperative, northwestern Pennsylvania, USA. Bartonia 63:11–28.

Anderson, J.P., Jr., and F.E. Egler. 1988. Patch studies in the stability of non-diversity: *Dennstaedtia, Solidago, Spiraea, Kalmia*. Phytologia 64:349–364.

Anderson, J.V., W.S. Chao, and D.P. Horvath. 2001. A current review on the regulation of dormancy in vegetative buds. Weed Science 49:581–589.

Anderson, M.C. 1964. Studies of the woodland light climate. I. The photographic computation of light conditions. Journal of Ecology 52:27–41.

Anderson, R.C. 1994. Height of white-flowered trillium (*Trillium grandiflorum*) as an index of deer browsing intensity. Ecological Applications 4:104–109.

Anderson, R.C. 1997. Pages 117–134 in M.W. Schwartz, editor. Native pests: the impact of deer in highly fragmented landscapes. Conservation in Highly Fragmented Landscapes. New York: Chapman & Hall.

Anderson, R,C., and M.H. Beare. 1983. Breeding system and pollination ecology of *Trientalis borealis* (Primulaceae). American Journal of Botany 70:408–415.

Anderson, R.C., J.S. Fralish, J.E. Armstrong, and P.K. Benjamin. 1993. The ecology and biology of *Panax quinquefolium* L. (Araliaceae) in Illinois. American Midland Naturalist 129:357–372.

Anderson, R.C., and A.J. Katz. 1993. Recovery of browse-sensitive tree species following release from white-tailed deer (*Odocoileus viginianus* Zimmerman) browsing pressure. Biological Conservation 63:203–208.

Anderson, R.C., S.S. Khillion, and T.M. Kelley. 1996. Aspects of the ecology of an invasive plant, garlic mustard (*Alliaria petiolata*), in central Illinois. Restoration Ecology 4:181–191.

Anderson, R.C., and O.L. Loucks. 1973. Aspects of the biology of *Tridentalis borealis*. Ecology 54:798–808.

Anderson, R.C., and O.L. Loucks. 1979. White-tail deer (*Odocoileus virginianus*) influence on the structure and composition of *Tsuga canadensis* forests. Journal of Applied Ecology 16:855–861.

Anderson, R.C., O.L. Loucks, and A.M. Swain. 1969. Herbaceous response to canopy cover, light intensity and through fall precipitation in coniferous forests. Ecology 50:235–263.

Anderson, W.B. 1998. The role of spring ephemeral herbs in deciduous forest nutrient cycling, with special reference to *Claytonia virginica* L. (Portulacaceae). Ph.D. dissertation, Vanderbilt University, Nashville, TN.

Anderson, W.B., and W.G. Eickmeier. 1998. Physiological and morphological responses to shade and nutrient additions of *Claytonia virginica* (Portulacaceae): implications for the "vernal dam" hypothesis. Canadian Journal of Botany 76:1340–1349.

Anderson, W.B., and W.G. Eickmeier. 2000. Nutrient resorption in *Claytonia virginica* L.: Implications for deciduous forest nutrient cycling. Canadian Journal of Botany 78:832–839.

Andersson, T. 1992. Significance of foliar nutrient absorption in nutrient-rich low-light environments—as indicated by *Mercurialis perennis*. Flora 187:429–433.

Andersson, T. 1997. Seasonal dynamics of biomass and nutrients in *Hepatica nobilis*. Flora 192:185–195.

Angert, A.L., and D.W. Schemske. 2005. The evolution of species' distributions: reciprocal transplants across the elevation ranges of *Mimulus cardinalis* and *M. lewisii*. Evolution 59:1671–1684.

Angevine, M. 1983. Variation in the demography of natural populations of the wild strawberries *Fragaria vesca* and *F. virginiana*. Journal of Ecology 71:959–974.

Angevine, M.W., and S.N. Handel. 1986. Invasion of forest floor space, clonal architecture, and population-growth in the perennial herb Clintonia borealis. Journal of Ecology 74:547–560.

Anonymous. 2000. Program and abstracts. Ice Storm 1998 Forest Research Conference, Ottawa, Ontario, CN.

Antonovics, J., and R.B. Primack. 1982. Experimental ecological genetics in Plantago. VI. The demography of seedling transplants of *P. lanceolata*. Journal of Ecology 70:55–75.

Antos, J.A., and D.B. Zobel. 1984. Ecological implications of belowground morphology of 9 coniferous forest herbs. Botanical Gazette 145:508–517.

Araki, K., K. Shimatani, M. Nishizawa, T. Hoshizane, and M. Ohara. 2010. Growth and survival patterns of *Cardiocrinum cordatum* var. *glehnii* (Liliaceae) based on a 13-year monitoring study: life history characteristics of a monocarpic perennial herb. Botany 88:745–752.

Araki, K., K. Shimatani, and M. Ohara. 2009. Dynamics of distribution and performance of ramets constructing genets: A demographic-genetic study in a clonal plant, *Convallaria keiskei*. Annals of Botany 104:71–79.

Archibold, O.W. 1979. Buried viable propagules as a factor in postfire regeneration in northern Saskatchewan. Canadian Journal of Botany 57:54–58.

Archibold, O.W. 1989. Seed banks and vegetation processes in coniferous forests. Pages 107–122 in M.A. Leck, V.T. Parker, and R.L. Simpson, editors. Ecology of soil seed banks. Academic Press, New York.

Armbruster, W.S., C.P.H. Mulder, B.G. Baldwin, S. Kalisz, B. Wessa, and H. Nute. 2002. Comparative analysis of late floral development and mating-system evolution in Tribe Collinsieae (Scrophulariaceae *s.l.*). American Journal of Botany 89:37–49.

Armesto, J.J., G.P. Cheplick, and M.J. McDonnell. 1983. Observations on the reproductive biology of *Phytolacca americana* (Phytolaccaceae). Bulletin of the Torrey Botanical Club 110:380–383.

Arnold, S.E.J., S. Faruq, V. Savolainen, P.W. OcOwan, and L. Chittka. 2010. FReD: the floral reflectance database—a web portal for analyses of flower color. PLoS ONE 5(12): e14287. doi:10.1371/journal.pone.0014287[.

Arnold, S.E.J., S.C. Le Comber, and L. Chittka. 2009. Flower color phenology in European grassland and woodland habitats, through the eyes of pollinators. Israel Journal of Plant Sciences 57:211–230.

Ashcroft, M.B. 2010. Identifying refugia from climate change. Journal of Biogeography 37: 1407–1413.

Ashman, T.-L., T. Knight, J. Steets, P. Amarasekare, M. Burd, D. Campbell, M. Dudash, M. Johnston, S. Mazer, R. Mitchell, M. Morgan, and W. Wilson. 2004. Pollen limitation of plant reproduction: Ecological and evolutionary causes and consequences. Ecology 85:2408–2421.

Ashmun, J.W, and L.F. Pitelka. 1984. Light-induced variation in the growth and dynamics of transplanted ramets of the understory herb, *Aster acuminatus*. Oecologia 64:255–262.

Ashmun, J.W., R.J. Thomas, and L.F. Pitelka. 1982. Translocation of photoassimilates between sister ramets in two rhizomatous forest herbs. Annals of Botany 49:403–416.

Asshoff, R., G. Zotz, and C. Korner. 2006. Growth and phenology of mature temperate forest trees in elevated CO_2. Global Change Biology 12:848–861.

Åström, M., M. Dynesius, K. Hylander, and C. Nilsson. 2005. Effects of slash harvest on bryophytes and vascular plants in southern boreal forest clear-cuts. Journal of Applied Ecology 42:1194–1202.

Aubin, I., S. Gachet, C. Messier, and A. Bouchard. 2007. How resilient are northern hardwood forests to human disturbance? An evaluation using a plant functional group approach. Ecoscience 14:259–271.

Auclair, A.N., and F.G. Goff. 1971. Diversity relations of upland forests in the western Great Lakes area. American Naturalist 105:499–528.

Augspurger, C.K. 2009. Spring 2007 warmth and frost: phenology, damage and refoliation in a temperate deciduous forest. Functional Ecology 23:1031–1039.

Augustine, D.J., and D. DeCalesta. 2003. Defining deer overabundance and threats to forest communities: From individual plants to landscape structure. Ecoscience 10:472–486.

Augustine, D.J., and L.E. Frelich. 1998. Effects of white-tailed deer on populations of an understory forb in fragmented deciduous forests. Conservation Biology 12:995–1004.

Augustine, D.J., L.E. Frelich, and P.A. Jordan. 1998. Evidence for two alternative stable states in an ungulate grazing system. Ecological Applications 8:1260–1269.

Augustine, D.J., and S.J. McNaughton. 1998. Ungulate effects on the functional species composition of plant communities: herbivore selectivity and plant tolerance. Journal of Wildland Management 62:1165–1183.

Auten, J. 1941. Notes on old-growth in Ohio, Indiana, and Illinois. U.S.D.A. Forest Service. Tech. Note 49. Columbus, OH.

Awmack, C.S., E.B. Mondor, and R.L. Lindroth. 2007. Forest understory clover populations in enriched CO_2 and O_3 atmospheres: Interspecific, intraspecific, and indirect effects. Environmental and Experimental Botany 59:340–346.

Axelrod, D.I. 1966. Origin of deciduous and evergreen habits in temperate forests. Evolution 20:1–15.

Badri, M.A., P.E.H. Minchin, and L. Lapointe. 2007. Effects of temperature on the growth of spring ephemerals: *Crocus vernus*. Physiologia Plantarum 130:67–76.

Baeten, L., P. De Frenne, K. Verheyen, B.J. Graae, and M. Hermy. 2010. Forest herbs in the face of global change: a single-species-multiple-threats approach for *Anemone nemorosa*. Plant Ecology and Evolution 143:19–30.

Baeten, L., M. Hermy, S. Van Daele, and K. Verheyen. 2010. Unexpected understory community development after 30 years in ancient and post-agricultural forests. Journal of Ecology 98:1447–1453.

Baeten, L., M. Hermy, and K. Verheyen. 2009. Environmental limitation contributes to the differential colonization capacity of two forest herbs. Journal of Vegetation Science 20:209–223.

Baeten, L., H. Jacquemyn, H. Van Calster, E. Van Beek, R. Devlaeminck, K. Verheyen, and M. Hermy. 2009. Low recruitment across life stages partly accounts for the slow colonization of forest herbs. Journal of Ecology 97:109–117.

Baeten, L., M. Vanhellemont, P. De Frenne, A. De Schrijver, M. Hermy, and K. Verheyen. 2010. Plasticity in response to phosphorus and light availability in four forest herbs. Oecologia 163:1021–1032.

Baeten, L., M. Vanhellemont, P. De Frenne, M. Hermy, and K. Verheyen. 2010. The phosphorus legacy of former agricultural land use can affect the production of germinable seeds in forest herbs. Ecoscience 17:365–371.

Baeten, L., G. Verstraeten, P. De Frenne, M. Vanhellemont, K. Wuyts, M. Hermy, and K. Verheyen. 2011. Former land use affects the nitrogen and phosphorus concentrations and biomass of forest herbs. Plant Ecology 212:901–909.

Baird, W.V., and J.L. Riopel. 1986. Life history studies of *Conopholis americana* (Orobanchaceae). American Midland Naturalist 116:140–151.

Baker, T.T., and D.H. Van Lear. 1998. Relations between density of rhododendron thickets and diversity of riparian forests. Forest Ecology and Management 109:21–32.

Baldocchi, D.D., and S. Collineau. 1994. The physical nature of solar radiation in heterogeneous canopies: spatial and temporal attributes. Pages 21–72 in M.M. Caldwell and R.W. Pearcy, editors. Exploitation of Environmental Heterogeneity by Plants: Ecophysiological Processes Above- and Belowground. Academic Press, San Diego, CA.

Baldocchi, D.D., B. Hutchison, D. Matt, and R. McMillen. 1984. Seasonal variations in the radiation regime within an oak-hickory forest. Agricultural and Forest Meteorology 33:177–191.

Baldocchi, D.D., S.B. Verma, and D.R. Matt. 1986. Eddy correlation measurements of CO_2 efflux from the floor of a deciduous forest. Journal of Applied Ecology 23:967–976.

Balgooyen, C.P., and D.M. Waller. 1995. The use of *Clintonia borealis* and other indicators to gauge impacts of white-tailed deer on plant communities in northern Wisconsin, USA. Natural Areas Journal 15:308–318.

Bandeff, J.M., K.S. Pregitzer, W.M. Loya, W.E. Holmes, and D.R. Zak. 2006. Overstory community composition and elevated atmospheric CO_2 and O_3 modify understory biomass production and nitrogen acquisition. Plant and Soil 282:251–259.

Banks, J.O. 1980. The reproductive biology of *Erythronium propullans* Gray and sympatric populations of *E. albidum* Nutt. (Liliaceae). Bulletin of the Torrey Botanical Club 107:181–188.

Banner, I.C. 1998. Leaf folding and photoprotective responses in *Oxalis acetosella* (L.). Ph.D. dissertation, University of Newcastle upon Tyne, UK.

Banta, J.A., A.A. Royo, C. Kirschbaum, and W.P. Carson. 2005. Plant communities growing on boulders in the Allegheny National Forest: evidence for boulders as refugia from deer and as a bioassay of overbrowsing. Natural Areas Journal 25:10–18.

Bao, Y., and E.T. Nilsen. 1988. The ecophysiological significance of leaf movements in *Rhododendron maximum*. Ecology 69:1578–1587.

Barber, S.A. 1995. Soil nutrient bioavailability: a mechanistic approach. Second edition. John Wiley & Sons, Inc., New York.

Barbier, S., F. Gosselin, and P. Balandier. 2008. Influence of tree species on understory vegetation diversity and mechanisms involved—A critical review for temperate and boreal forests. Forest Ecology and Management 254:1–15.

Barbour, M.G., J.H. Burk, W.D. Pitts, F.S. Gilliam, and M.W. Schwartz. 1999. Terrestrial plant ecology. Third edition. Benjamin/Cummings, Menlo Park, CA.

Bard, G.E. 1945. The mineral nutrient content of the foliage of forest trees on three soil types of varying limestone content. Proceedings, Soil Science Society of America 10:419–422.

Bard, G.E. 1949. The mineral nutrient content of the annual parts of herbaceous species growing on three New York soil types varying in limestone content. Ecology 30:384–389.

Barker Plotkin, A., and P.B. Tomlinson. 2010. The flowering of botany at the Harvard Forest. Plant Science Bulletin 56:78–84.

Barlow, C., and P.S. Martin. 2004. Bring *Torreya taxifolia* north—now. Wild Earth, Fall/Winter 2004–2005.

Barrett, S.C.H. 1990. The evolution and adaptive significance of heterostyly. Trends in Ecology and Evolution 5:144–148.

Barrett, S.C.H., and C.G. Eckert. 1990. Current issues in plant reproductive ecology. Israel Journal of Botany 39:5–12.

Barrett, S.C.H., L.D. Harder, and A. Worley. 1996. The comparative biology of pollination and mating in flowering plants. Philosophical Transactions of the Royal Society of London Series B–Biological Sciences 351:1271–1280.

Barrett, S.C.H,, and K. Helenurm. 1987. The reproductive biology of boreal forest herbs. 1. Breeding systems and pollination. Canadian Journal of Botany 65:2036–2046.

Barriault, I., D. Barabe, L. Cloutier, and M. Gibernau. 2010. Pollination ecology and reproductive success in jack-in-the-pulpit (*Arisaema triphyllum*) in Quebec (Canada). Plant Biology 12:161–171.

Bartels, S.F., and H.Y.N. Chen. 2010. Is understory plant species diversity driven by resource quantity or resource heterogeneity? Ecology 91:1931–1938.

Bartels, S.F., and H.Y.H. Chen. 2012. Interactions between overstory and understory vegetation along an overstory compositional gradient. Journal of Vegetation Science 23.

Bartomeus, I., J.S. Ascher, D. Wagner, B.N. Danforth, S.R. Colla, S. Kornbluth, and R. Winfree. 2011. Climate-associated phenological advances in bee pollinators and bee-pollinated plants. Proceedings of the National Academy of Sciences USA 108:20645–20649.

Basinger, M.A., J.S. Huston, R.J. Gates, and P.S. Robertson. 1997. Vascular flora of Horseshoe Lake Conservation Area, Alexander County, Illinois. Castanea 62:82–99.

Baskauf, C.J., and J.M. Burke. 2009. Population genetics of *Astragalus bibullatus* (Fabaceae) using AFLPs. Journal of Heredity 100:424–431.

Baskin, C. C., and J. M. Baskin. 1998. Seeds: ecology, biogeography, and evolution of dormancy and germination. New York: Academic Press.

Baskin, C.C., and J.M. Baskin. 2002. Studies on the seed germination and flowering stages of the life cycle of the shale barren endemic *Arabis serotina* Steele (Brassicaceae). Natural Areas Journal 22:270–276.

Baskin, C.C., and J.M. Baskin. 2003. Seed germination and propagation of *Xyris tennesseensis*, a federal endangered wetland species. Wetlands 23:116–124.

Baskin, J.M., and C.C. Baskin. 1984. The ecological life cycle of *Campanula americana* in northcentral Kentucky. Bulletin of the Torrey Botanical Club 111:329–337.

Baskin, J.M., and C.C. Baskin. 1985. Role of dispersal date and changes in physiological responses in controlling timing germination in achenes of *Geum canadense*. Canadian Journal of Botany 63:1654–1658.

Baskin, J.M., and C.C. Baskin. 1994. Nondeep simple morphophysiological dormancy in seeds of the mesic woodland winter annual *Corydalis flavula* (Fumariaceae). Bulletin of the Torrey Botanical Club 121:40–46.

Baskin, J.M., and C.C. Baskin. 1997. Methods of breaking seed dormancy in the endangered species *Iliamna corei* (Sherff) Sherff (Malvaceae), with special attention to heating. Natural Areas Journal 17:313–323.

Baskin, J.M., and C.C. Baskin. 2005. Ecology of two geographically restricted *Astragalus species (Fabaceae), A. bibullatus and A. tennesseensis*, of the eastern United States. Brittonia 57:345–353.

Bauer, J.T., R.C. Anderson, and M.R. Anderson. 2010. Competitive interactions among first-year and second-year plants of the invasive biennial garlic mustard (*Alliaria petiolata*) and native ground layer vegetation. Restoration Ecology 18: 720–728

Bazzaz, F.A. 1986. Life history of colonizing plants: some demographic, genetic, and physiological features. Pages 96-110 in H. A. Mooney and J. A. Drake, editors, Ecology of biological invasions of North America and Hawaii. Springer-Verlag, New York.

Bazzaz, F.A. 1996. Plants in changing environments. Linking physiological, population, and community ecology. Cambridge University Press, Cambridge, UK.

Bazzaz, F.A., and W.E. Williams. 1991. Atmospheric CO_2 concentrations within a mixed forest: implications for seedling growth. Ecology 72:12–26.

Beattie, A.J., and D.C. Culver. 1981. The guild of myrmecochores in the herbaceous flora of West Virginia forests. Ecology 62:107–115.

Beatty, G.E., P.M. McEvoy, O. Sweeney, and J. Provan. 2008. Range-edge effects promote clonal growth in peripheral populations of the one-sided wintergreen *Orthilia secunda*. Diversity and Distributions 14:546–555.

Beatty, G.E., and J. Provan. 2011. American populations of the parasitic herbaceous plant *Monotropa hypopitys* L. reveals a complex history of range expansion from multiple late glacial refugia. Journal of Biogeography 38:1585–1599.

Beatty, S.W. 1984. Influence of microtopography and canopy species on spatial patterns of forest understory plants. Ecology 65:1406–1419.

Beatty, S.W. 1987a. Spatial distributions of *Adenostoma* species in southern California chaparral: an analysis of niche separation. Annals of the Association of American Geographers 77:255–264.

Beatty, S.W. 1987b. Origin and role of soil variability in southern California chaparral. Physical Geography 8:1–17.

Beatty, S.W. 1989. Fire effects on soil heterogeneity beneath chamise and redshanks chaparral. Physical Geography 10:44–52.

Beatty, S.W. 1991. Colonization dynamics in a mosaic landscape: the buried seed pool. Journal of Biogeography 18:553–563.

Beatty, S.W., and D.L. Licari. 1992. Invasion of fennel (*Foeniculum vulgare* Mill.) into shrub communities on Santa Cruz Island, California. Madroño 39:54–66.

Beatty, S.W., and O.D.V. Sholes. 1988. Leaf litter effect on plant species composition of deciduous forest treefall pits. Canadian Journal of Forest Research 18:553–559.

Beatty, S.W., and E.L. Stone. 1986. The variety of soil microsites created by treefalls. Canadian Journal of Forest Research 16:539–548.

Beaubien, E., and A. Hamann. 2011. Spring flowering response to climate change between 1936 and 2006 in Alberta, Canada. BioScience 61:514–524.

Beckage, B., J.S. Clark, B.D. Clinton, and B.L. Haines. 2000. A long-term study of tree seedling recruitment in southern Appalachian forests: the effects of canopy gaps and shrub understories. Canadian Journal of Forest Research 30:1617–1631.

Becker, P., and A.P. Smith. 1990. Spatial autocorrelation of solar radiation in a tropical moist forest understory. Agricultural and Forest Meteorology 52:373–379.

Beerling, D.J., and C.K. Kelly. 1997. Stomatal density responses of temperate woodland plants over the past seven decades of CO_2 increase: A comparison of Salisbury (1927) with contemporary data. American Journal of Botany 84:1572–1583.

Beier, C. 2004. Climate change and ecosystem function—full-scale manipulations of CO_2 and temperature. New Phytologist 162:243–251.

Bellemare, J. 2010. Biogeographical and evolutionary processes influencing the assembly of deciduous forest plant communities. Ph.D. dissertation, Cornell University, Ithaca, NY.

Bellemare, J., G. Motzkin, and D.R. Foster. 2002. Legacies of the agricultural past in the forested present: an assessment of historical land-use effects on rich mesic forests. Journal of Biogeography 29:1401–1420.

Bellemare, J., G. Motzkin, and D.R. Foster. 2005. Rich mesic forests: Edaphic and physiographic drivers of community variation in western Massachusetts. Rhodora 107:239–283.

Belote, R.T., and R.H. Jones. 2009. Tree leaf litter composition and nonnative earthworms influence plant invasion in experimental forest floor mesocosms. Biological Invasions 11:1045–1052.

Belote, R.T., N.J. Sanders, and R.H. Jones. 2009. Disturbance alters local–regional richness relationships in Appalachian forests. Ecology 90:2940–2947.

Belote, R.T., J.F. Weltzin, and R.J. Norby. 2003. Response of an understory plant community to elevated $[CO_2]$ depends on differential responses of dominant invasive species and is mediated by soil water availability. New Phytologist 161:827–835.Bell, A.D., and P.B. Tomlinson. 1980. Adaptive architecture in rhizomatous plants. Botanical Journal of the Linnean Society 80:125–160.

Bender, M.H., J.M. Baskin, and C.C. Baskin. 2000. Ecological life history of *Polymnia canadensis*, a monocarpic species of the North American Temperate Deciduous Forest: Demography. Plant Ecology 147:117–136.

Bender, M.H., J.M. Baskin, and C.C. Baskin. 2002. Flowering requirements of *Polymnia canadensis* (Asteraceae) and their influence on its life history variation. Plant Ecology 160:113–124.

Bendix, J. 1997. Flood disturbance and the distribution of riparian species diversity. Geographical Review 87:468–483.

Bennett, K.D. 1997. Evolution and ecology: the pace of life. Cambridge University Press, Cambridge, UK.

Bennington, C.C., and J.B. McGraw. 1995. Natural-selection and ecotypic differentiation in *Impatiens pallida*. Ecological Monographs 65:303–323.

Benscotter, B.W., and D.H. Vitt. 2008. Spatial patterns and temporal trajectories of the bog ground layer along a post-fire chronosequence. Ecosystems 11:1054–1064.

Benton, T.G., and A. Grant. 1999. Elasticity analysis as an important tool in evolutionary and population ecology. Trends in Ecology and Evolution 14:467–471.

Berg, B. 2000. Litter decomposition and organic matter turnover in northern forest soils. Forest Ecology and Management 133:13–22.

Berg, H. 2000. Differential seed dispersal in *Oxalis acetosella*, a cleistogamous perennial herb. Acta Oecologica-International Journal of Ecology 21:109–118.

Berg, H. 2002. Population dynamics in *Oxalis acetosella*: The significance of sexual reproduction in a clonal, cleistogamous forest herb. Ecography 25:233-243.

Berg, H., and P. Redbo-Torstensson. 1998. Cleistogamy as a bet-hedging strategy in *Oxalis acetosella*, a perennial herb. Journal of Ecology 86:491–500.

Berger, A., and K.J. Puettmann. 2000. Overstory composition and stand structure influence herbaceous plant diversity in the mixed aspen forest of northern Minnesota. American Midland Naturalist 143:111–125.

Bergeron, J.-F., J.-P. Saucier, A. Robitaille, and D. Robert. 1992. Québec forest ecological classification program. Forestry Chronicle 68:53–63.

Bergeron, Y. 2000. Species and stand dynamics in the mixed woods of Quebec's southern boreal forest. Ecology 81:1500–1516.

Bergeron, Y., and A. Bouchard. 1984. Use of ecological groups in analysis and classification of plant communities in a section of western Québec. Vegetatio 56:45–63.

Bergeron, Y., and D. Charron. 1994. Postfire stand dynamics in a southern boreal forest (Québec): A dendroecological approach. Écoscience 1:173–184.

Bergeron, Y., and M. Dubuc. 1989. Succession in the southern part of the Canadian boreal forest. Vegetatio 79:51–63.

Bergeron, Y., O. Engelmark, B. Harvey, H. Morin, and L. Sirois. 1998. Key issues in disturbance dynamics in boreal forests: introduction. Journal of Vegetation Science 9:464–468.

Bergeron, Y., and B. Harvey. 1997. Basing silviculture on natural ecosystem dynamics: an approach applied to the southern boreal mixed-wood forest of Québec. Forest Ecology and Management 92:235–242.

Bergeron, Y., B. Harvey, A. Leduc, and S. Gauthier. 1999. Forest management guidelines based on natural disturbance dynamics: stand- and forest-level considerations. Forestry Chronicle 75:49–54.

Bergeron, Y., and A. Leduc. 1998. Relationships between change in fire frequency and mortality due to spruce budworm outbreak in the southeastern Canadian boreal forest. Journal of Vegetation Science 9:492–500.

Berkowitz, A.R., C.D. Canham, and V.R. Kelly. 1995. Competition vs. facilitation of tree seedling growth and survival in early successional communities. Ecology 76:1156–1168.

Bermingham, L.H. 2010. Deer herbivory and habitat type influence long-term population dynamics of a rare wetland plant. Plant Ecology 210:359–378.

Bernatchez, A., and L. Lapointe. 2012. Cooler temperatures favour growth of wild leek (*Allium tricoccum*), a deciduous forest spring ephemeral. Botany 90:1125–1132.

Bernhardt-Römermann, M., C. Römermann, V. DeP. Pillar, T. Kudernatsch, and A. Fischer. 2010. High functional diversity is related to high nitrogen availability in a deciduous forest—evidence from a functional trait approach. Folia Geobot 45:111–124.

Berry, A.B. 1964. Effect of strip width on proportion of daily light reaching the ground. Forestry Chronicle 40:130–131.

Berteaux, D., M. Crête, J. Huot, J. Maltais, and J.-P. Ouellet. 1998. Food choice by white-tailed deer in relation to protein and energy content of the diet: a field experiment. Oecologia 115:84–92.

Bertin, R.I. 2001. Life cycle, demography, and reproductive biology of herb Robert (*Geranium robertianum*). Rhodora 103:96–116.

Bever, J.D. 1994. Feedback between plants and their soil communities in an old field community. Ecology 75:1965–1977.

Bever, J.D., K.M. Westover, and J. Antonovics. 1997. Incorporating the soil community into plant population dynamics: the utility of the feedback approach. Journal of Ecology 85:561–573.

Bevill, R.L., and S.M. Louda. 1999. Comparisons of related rare and common species in the study of plant rarity. Conservation Biology 13:493–498.

Bicknell, S.H. 1979. Pattern and process of plant succession in a revegetating northern hardwood ecosystem. Ph.D. dissertation, Yale University, New Haven, CT.

Bidartondo, M.I. 2005. The evolutionary ecology of myco-heterotrophy. New Phytologist 167:335–352.

Bierzychudek, P. 1981. Pollen limitation of plant reproductive effort. American Naturalist 117:838–840.

Bierzychudek, P. 1982a. Life histories and demography of shade-tolerant temperate forest herbs: a review. New Phytologist 90:757–776.

Bierzychudek, P. 1982b. The demography of jack-in-the pulpit, a forest perennial that changes sex. Ecological Monographs 62:335–351.

Bierzychudek, P. 1999. Looking backwards: assessing the projections of a transition matrix model. Ecological Applications 9:1278–1287.

Billings, W.D. 1938. The structure and development of old field short-leaf pine stands and certain associated physical properties of the soil. Ecological Monographs 8:437–499.

Binkley, D., M.M. Moore, and W. H. Romme. 2006. Was Aldo Leopold right about the Kaibab deer herd? Ecosystems 9:227–241.

Birch, C.P.D., and M.J. Hutchings. 1994. Exploitation of patchily distributed soil resources by the clonal herb *Glechoma hederacea*. Journal of Ecology 82:653–664.

Bisbee, K.E., S.T. Gower, J.M. Norman, and E.V. Nordheim. 2001. Environmental controls on ground cover species composition and productivity in a boreal black spruce forest. Oecologia 129:261–270.

Bjorkbom, J.C., and R.G. Larson. 1977. The Tionesta Scenic and Research Natural Areas. U.S. Forest Service General Technical Report NE-31.

Björkman, O. 1981. Responses to different quantum flux densities. Pages 57–107 in O.L. Lange, P.S. Nobel, C.B. Osmond, and H. Ziegler, editors. Physiological plant ecology I. Encyclopedia of plant physiology, NS, Vol. 12A. Springer-Verlag, Berlin.

Björkman, O., and B. Demmig-Adams. 1995. Regulation of photosynthetic light energy capture, conversion, and dissipation in leaves of higher plants. Pages 17–47 in E.D. Schulze and M.M. Caldwell, editors. Ecophysiology of photosynthesis, Springer-Verlag, Berlin.

Björkman, O., and S.B. Powles. 1981. Leaf movement in the shade species *Oxalis oregana*. I. Response to light level and light quality. Carnegie Institute of Washington Yearbook 80:59–62.

Black, R.A., and L.C. Bliss. 1978. Recovery sequence of *Picea mariana–Vaccinium ulginosum* forests after burning near Inuvik, Northwest Territories, Canada. Canadian Journal of Botany 56:2020–2030.

Blackman, G.E., and A.J. Rutter. 1946. Physiological and ecological studies in the analysis of plant environment. I. The light factor and the distribution of the bluebell (*Scilla non-scripta*) in woodland communities. Annals of Botany 10:361–390.

Blais, J.R. 1983. Trends in the frequency, extent, and severity of spruce budworm outbreaks in eastern Canada. Canadian Journal of Forest Research 13:539–547.

Blank, J.L., R.K. Olson, and P.M. Vitousek. 1980. Nutrient uptake by a diverse spring ephemeral community. Oecologia 47:96–98.

Blewett, T.J. 1976. Structure and dynamics of the McDougall Springs lowland forest. M.S. thesis, University of Wisconsin–Madison, WI.

Blood, L.E., J.H. Pitoniak, and J.H. Titus. 2010. Seed bank of a bottomland swamp in western New York. Castanea 75:19–38.

Bloom, A.J., F.S. Chapin, and H.A. Mooney. 1985. Resource limitation in plants: an economic analogy. Annual Review of Ecology and Systematics 16:363–392.

Boardman, N.K. 1977. Comparative photosynthesis of sun and shade plants. Annual Review of Plant Physiology 28:355–377.

Bobbink, R., K. Hicks, J. Galloway, T. Spranger, R. Alkemade, M. Ashmore, M. Bustamante, S. Cinderby, E. Davidson, F. Dentener, B. Emmett, J.-W. Erisman, M. Fenn, F. Gilliam, A. Nordin, L. Pardo, and W. de Vries. 2010. Global assessment of nitrogen deposition effects on terrestrial plant diversity effects of terrestrial ecosystems: a synthesis. Ecological Applications 20:30–59.

Bobbink, R., M. Hornung, and J.G.M. Roelofs. 1998. The effects of air-borne nitrogen pollutants on species diversity in natural and semi-natural European vegetation. Journal of Ecology 86:717–738.

Boerner, R.E.J. 1986. Seasonal nutrient dynamics, nutrient resorption, and mycorrhizal infection intensity of two perennial forest herbs. American Journal of Botany 73:1249–1357.

Boetsch, J., F. Van Manen, and J. Clark. 2003. Predicting rare plant occurrence in Great Smoky Mountains National Park, USA. Natural Areas Journal 23:229–237.

Bohlen, P.J., S. Scheu, C.M. Hale, M.A. McLean, S. Migge, P.M. Groffman, and D. Parkinson. 2004. Non-native invasive earthworms as agents of change in northern temperate forests. Frontiers in Ecology and the Environment 2:427–435.

Bolker, B.M., S.W. Pacala, and C. Neuhauser. 2003. Spatial dynamics in model plant communities: What do we really know? American Naturalist 162:135–148.

Bolmgren, K., and K. Lönnberg. 2005. Herbarium data reveal an association between fleshy fruit type and earlier flowering time. International Journal of Plant Science 166:663–670.

Bonan, G., and H. Shugart. 1989. Environmental factors and ecological processes in boreal forests. Annual Review of Ecological Systematics 20:1–28.

Booth, B.D., and C.J. Swanton. 2002. Assembly theory applied to weed communities. Weed Science 50:2–13.

Borgmann, K.L., D.M. Waller, and T.P. Rooney. 1999. Does balsam fir (*Abies balsamea*) facilitate the recruitment of eastern hemlock (*Tsuga canadensis*)? American Midland Naturalist 141:391–397.

Bormann, F.H., and G.E. Likens. 1979. Pattern and process in a forested ecosystem. Springer-Verlag, New York.

Bossuyt, B., M. Hermy, and J. Deckers. 1999. Migration of herbaceous plant species across ancient-recent forest ecotones in central Belgium. Journal of Ecology 87:628–638.

Both, S., T. Fang, M. Böhnke, H. Bruelheide, C. Geißler, P. Kühn, T. Scholten, S. Trogisch, and A. Erfmeier. 2011. Lack of tree layer control on herb layer characteristics in a subtropical forest, China. Journal of Vegetation Science 22:1120–1131.

Boudsocq, S., A. Niboyet, J.C. Lata, X. Raynaud, N. Loeuille, J. Mathieu, M. Blouin, L. Abbadie, and S. Barot. 2012. Plant preference for ammonium versus nitrate: a neglected determinant of ecosystem functioning? American Naturalist 180:60–69.

Boufford, D.E., and S.A. Spongberg. 1983. Eastern Asia–Eastern North American phytogeographical relationships—A history from the time of Linnaeus to the twentieth century. Annals of the Missouri Botanical Garden 70:423–439.

Bowersox, T.W., and L.H. McCormick. 1987. Herbaceous communities reduce the juvenile growth of northern red oak, white ash, yellow poplar, but not white pine. Proceedings of the Sixth Central Hardwood Forestry Conference, University of Tennessee, Knoxville, TN.

Bowles, M.L., K.A. Jacobs, and J.L. Mengler. 2007. Long-term changes in an oak forest's woody understory and herb layer with repeated burning. Journal of the Torrey Botanical Society 134:223–237.

Boyle, O.D., E.S. Menges, and D.M. Waller. 2003. Dances with fire: Tracking metapopulation dynamics of *Polygonella basirania* in Florida scrub (USA). Folia Geobotanica 38:255–262.

Brach, A.R., and D.J. Raynal. 1992. Effects of liming on *Oxalis acetosella* and *Lycopodium lucidulum* in a northern hardwood forest. Journal of Applied Ecology 29:492–500.

Bradley, N., A. Leopold, J. Ross, and W. Huffaker. 1999. Phenological changes reflect climate change in Wisconsin. Proceedings of the National Academy of Sciences of the United States of America 96:9701–9704.

Bratton, S.P. 1975. A comparison of the beta diversity functions of the overstory and herbaceous understory of a deciduous forest. Bulletin of the Torrey Botanical Club 102:55–60.

Bratton, S.P. 1976. Resource division in an understory herb community: Responses to temporal and microtopographic gradients. American Naturalist 110:679–693.

Bratton, S.P. 1979. Impacts of white-tailed deer on the vegetation of Cade Cove, Great Smoky Mountains National Park. Proc. Ann. Conf. Southeastern Assoc. of Fish & Wildlife Agencies 33:305–312.

Bratton, S.P., J.R. Hapeman, and A.R. Mast. 1994. The lower Susquehanna River gorge and floodplain (U.S.A.) as a riparian refugium for vernal, forest-floor herbs. Conservation Biology 8:1069–1077.

Bratton, S.P., and S.G. Miller. 1994. Historic field systems and the structure of maritime oak forests, Cumberland-Island National Seashore, Georgia. Bulletin of the Torrey Botanical Club 121:1–12.

Braun, E.L. 1950. Deciduous forests of eastern North America. Blakiston, Philadelphia.

Breed, G.A., S. Stichter, and E.E. Crone. 2012. Climate-driven changes in northeastern US butterfly communities. Nature Climate Change 3: 142-146.

Bremer, P., and E. Jongejans. 2010. Frost and forest stand effects on the population dynamics of *Asplenium scolopendrium*. Population Ecology 52:211–222.

Brewer, J.S. 2001. A demographic analysis of fire-stimulated seedling establishment of *Sarraenia alata* (Sarraceniaceae) 1. American Journal of Botany 88:1250–1257.

Brewer, R. 1980. A half-century of changes in the herb layer of a climax deciduous forest in Michigan. Journal of Ecology 68:823–832.

Bridgham, S.D., J. Pastor, C.A. McClaugherty, and C.J. Richardson. 1995. Nutrient-use efficiency: A litterfall index, a model, and a test along a nutrient-availability gradient in North Carolina peatlands. American Naturalist 145:1–21.

Brodersen, C.R., and T.C. Vogelmann. 2010. Do changes in light direction affect absorption profiles in leaves? Functional Plant Biology 37:403–412.

Brodersen, C.R., T.C. Vogelmann, W.E. Williams, and H.L. Gorton. 2008. A new paradigm in leaf-level photosynthesis: direct and diffuse lights are not equal. Plant, Cell and Environment 31:159–164.

Brokaw, N.V.L., and S.M. Scheiner. 1989. Species composition in gaps and structure of a tropical forest. Ecology 70:538–541.

Brook, B., W. Tonkyn, J. O'Grady, and R. Frankham. 2002. Contribution of inbreeding to extinction risk in threatened species. Conservation Ecology 6:16.

Brooks, J.R., L.B. Flanagan, N. Buchman, and J.R. Ehleringer. 1997. Carbon isotope composition of boreal plants: functional grouping of life forms. Oecologia 110:301–311.

Brooks, P.D., M.W. Williams, and S.K. Schmidt. 1998. Inorganic nitrogen and microbial biomass dynamics before and during spring snowmelt. Biogeochemistry 43:1–15.

Brothers, T.S., and A. Spingarn. 1992. Forest fragmentation and alien plant invasion of central Indiana old-growth forests. Conservation Biology 6:91–100.

Brown, A.H.F. 1974. Nutrient cycles in oakwood ecosystems in NW England. Pages 141–161 in M.C. Morris and F.H. Perring, editors. The British oak. E.W. Classey, Farrington, UK.

Brown, G. 1994. Soil factors affecting patchiness in community composition of heavy metal-contaminated areas of Western Europe. Vegetatio 115:77–90.

Brown, J.H., and A. Kodric-Brown. 1977. Turnover rates in insular biogeography: effect of immigration on extinction. Ecology 58:445–449.

Brown, M.J., and G.G. Parker. 1994. Canopy light transmittance in a chronosequence of mixed-species deciduous forests. Canadian Journal of Forest Research 24:1694–1703.

Brown, M.J., G.G. Parker, and N.E. Posner. 1994. A survey of ultraviolet-B radiation in forests. Journal of Ecology 82:843–854.

Brown, R.L. 2002. Biodiversity and exotic species invasion in southern Appalachian riparian plant communities. Ph.D. dissertation University of North Carolina at Chapel Hill, North Carolina.

Brown, R.L., L.A. Jacobs, and R.K. Peet. 2007. Species richness: small scale. Encyclopedia of Life Sciences. http://onlinelibrary.wiley.com/doi/10.1002/9780470015902. a0020488/pdf.

Brown, R.L., and R.K. Peet. 2003. Diversity and invasibility of southern Appalachian plant communities. Ecology 84:32–39.

Brown, S.E., and G.R. Parker. 1997. Impact of white-tailed deer on forest communities within Brown County State Park, Indiana. Proceedings of the Indiana Academy of Science 106:39–51.

Broyles, S.B., S.L. Sherman-Broyles, and P. Rogati. 1997. Evidence of outcrossing in *Trillium erectum* and *Trillium grandiflorum* (Liliaceae). Journal of Heredity 88:325–329.

Brudvig, L.A., C.M. Mabry, and L.M. Mottl. 2011. Dispersal, not understory light competition, limits restoration of Iowa woodland understory herbs. Restoration Ecology 19:24–31.

Bruederle, L.P., and F.W. Stearns. 1985. Ice storm damage to a southern Wisconsin mesic forest. Bulletin of the Torrey Botanical Club. 112:167–175.

Brumelis, G., and T.J. Carleton. 1989. The vegetation of post-logged black spruce lowlands in central Canada. II. Understorey vegetation. Journal of Applied Ecology 26:321–339.

Bruna, E.M., I.J. Fiske, and M.D. Trager. 2009. Habitat fragmentation and plant populations: is what we know demographically irrelevant? Journal of Vegetation Science 20:569–576.

Brundrett, M.C., and B. Kendrick. 1988. The mycorrhizal status, root anatomy, and phenology of plants in a sugar maple forest. Canadian Journal of Botany 66:1153–1173.

Brundrett, M.C, and B. Kendrick. 1990. The roots and mycorrhizas of herbaceous woodland plants. I. Quantatitve aspects of morphology. New Phytologist 114:457–468.

Bruneau, A., and G.J. Anderson. 1988. Reproductive biology of diploid and triploid *Apios americana* (Leguminosae). American Journal of Botany 75:1876–1883.

Brunet, J. 2007. Plant colonization in heterogeneous landscapes: an 80-year perspective on restoration of broadleaved forest vegetation. Journal of Applied Ecology 44:563–572.

Brunet, J., and G. von Oheimb. 1998. Migration of vascular plants to secondary woodlands in southern Sweden. Journal of Ecology 86:429–438.

Brunet, J., and H.R. Sweet. 2006. Impact of insect pollinator group and floral display size on outcrossing rate. Evolution 60:234–346.

Brunet, J., M. Diekmann, and U. Falkengren-Grerup. 1998. Effects of nitrogen deposition on field layer vegetation in south Swedish forests. Environmental Pollution 102:35–40.

Brys, R., H. Jacquemyn, P. Endels, G. De Blust, and M. Hermy. 2005. Effect of habitat deterioration on population dynamics and extinction risks in a previously common perennial. Conservation Biology 19:1633–1643.

Brys, R., R.P. Shefferson, and H. Jacquemyn. 2011. Impact of herbivory on flowering behaviour and life history trade-offs in a polycarpic herb: a 10-year experiment. Oecologia 166:293–303.

Buchanan, M.R., and J. Padgett. 2007. Crabtree Creek Site Survey Report, North Carolina, Raleigh, North Carolina: Natural Heritage Program, Office of Conservation, Planning, and Community Affairs, Department of Environment and Natural Resources.

Buckley, Y.M., S. Ramula, S.P. Blomberg, J.H. Burns, E.E. Crone, J. Ehrlén, T.M. Knight, J. Pichancourt, H. Quested, and G.M. Wardle. 2010. Causes and consequences of variation in plant population growth rate: A synthesis of matrix population models in a phylogenetic context. Ecology Letters 13:1182–1197.

Buell, M.F., and R.E. Wilbur. 1948. Life form spectra of the hardwood forests of the Itasca Park region, Minnesota. Ecology 29:352–359.

Bullock, J. M., B.C. Hill, and J. Silvertown. 1994. Demography of *Cirsium vulgare* in a grazing experiment. Journal of Ecology 82:101–111.

Bullock, J.M., K. Shea, and O. Skarpaas. 2006. Measuring plant dispersal: an introduction to field methods and experimental design. Plant Ecology 186:217–234.

Bump, J.K., C.R. Webster, J.A. Vucetich, R.O. Peterson, J.M. Shields, and M.D. Powers. 2009. Ungulate carcasses perforate ecological filters and create biogeochemical hotspots in forest herbaceous layers allowing trees a competitive advantage. Ecosystems 12: 996–1007.

Burd, M. 1994. Bateman's principle and plant reproduction: the role of pollen limitation in fruit and seed set. Botanical Review 60:83–139.

Burke, D.J. 2008. Effects of *Alliaria petiolata* (garlic mustard; Brassicaceae) on mycorrhizal colonization and community structure in three herbaceous plants in a mixed deciduous forest. American Journal of Botany 95:1416–1425

Burke, D.J., J.C. Lopez-Gutierrez, K.A. Smemo, and C.R. Chan. 2009. Vegetation and soil environment influence the spatial distribution of root-associated fungi in a mature beech-maple forest. Applied and Environmental Microbiology 75:7639–7648.

Burkey, K.O., H.S. Neufeld, L. Souza, A.H. Chappelka, and A.W. Davison. 2006. Seasonal profiles of leaf ascorbic acid metabolism in ozone-sensitive wildflowers. Environmental Pollution 143:427–434.

Burns, J.H. 2008. Demographic performance predicts invasiveness of species in the Commelinaceae under high-nutrient conditions. Ecological Applications 19:335–346.

Burns, J.H., S.P. Blomberg, E.E. Crone, J. Ehrlén, T.M. Knight, J. Pichancourt, S. Ramula, G.M. Wardle, and Y.M. Buckley. 2010. Empirical tests of life-history evolution theory using phylogenetic analysis of plant demography. Journal of Ecology 98:334–344.

Burrascano, S., F. Lombardi, and M. Marchetti. 2008. Old-growth forest structure and deadwood: Are they indicators of plant species composition? A case study from central Italy. Plant Biosystems 142:313–323.

Burton, J.I., D.J. Mladenoff, M.K. Clayton, and J.A. Forrester. 2011. The roles of environmental filtering and colonization in the fine-scale spatial patterning of ground-layer plant communities in north temperate deciduous forests. Journal of Ecology 99: 764–776.

Burton, P.J., A.C. Balisky, L.P. Coward, S.G. Cumming, and D.D. Kneeshaw. 1992. The value of managing for biodiversity. Forestry Chronicle 68:225–237.

Burton, P.J., and F.A. Bazzaz. 1991. Tree seedling emergence on interactive temperature and moisture gradients in patches of old-field vegetation. American Journal of Botany 78:131–149.

Burton, P.J., and F.A. Bazzaz. 1995. Ecophysiological responses of tree seedlings invading different patches of old-field vegetation. Journal of Ecology 83:99–112.

Busing, R.T. 1998. Composition, structure and diversity of cove forest stands in the Great Smoky Mountains: a patch dynamics perspective. Journal of Vegetation Science 9:881–890.

Busing, R.T., and P.S. White. 1993. Effects of area on old-growth forest attributes—Implications for the equilibrium landscape concept. Landscape Ecology 8:119–126.

Byers, D.L. 1995. Pollen quantity and quality as explanations for low seed set in small populations exemplified by *Eupatorium* (Asteraceae). American Journal of Botany 82:1000–1006.

Byers, D.L., and J.A. Quinn. 1998. Demographic variation in *Alliaria petiolata* (Brassicaceae) in four contrasting habitats. Journal of the Torrey Botanical Society 125:138–149.

Cabin, R.J. 1996. Genetic comparisons of seed bank and seedling populations of a perennial desert mustard, *Lesquerella fendleri*. Evolution 50:1830–1841.

Cain, M.L., and H. Damman. 1997. Clonal growth and ramet performance in the woodland herb, *Asarum canadense*. Journal of Ecology 85:883–887.

Cain, M.L., H. Damman, and A. Muir. 1998. Seed dispersal and the Holocene migration of woodland herbs. Ecological Monographs 68:325–347.

Cain, M.L., D.A. Dudle, and J.P. Evans. 1996. Spatial models of foraging in clonal plant species. American Journal of Botany 83:76–85.

Cain, M.L., B.G. Milligan, and A.E. Strand. 2000. Long-distance seed dispersal in plant populations. American Journal of Botany 87:1217–1227.

Cain, S.A. 1936. Synusiae as a basis for plant sociological fieldwork. American Midland Naturalist 17:665–725.

Cain, S.A. 1943. The tertiary character of the cove hardwood forests of the Great Smoky Mountains National Park. Bulletin of the Torrey Botanical Club 70:213–235.

Cain, S.A. 1950. Life forms and phytoclimate. Botanical Review 16:1–32.

Cajander, A.K. 1926. The theory of forest types. Acta Forestalia Fennica 29:1–108.

Cajander, A.K., and Y. Ilvessalo. 1921. Uber Waldtypen II. Acta Forestalia Fennica 20:1–77.

Callahan, H.S., and D.M. Waller. 2000. Phenotypic integration and the plasticity of integration in an amphicarpic annual. International Journal of Plant Sciences 161:89–98.

Callaway, R.M., and W.M. Ridenour. 2004. Novel weapons: invasive success and the evolution of increased competitive ability. Frontiers in Ecology and the Environment. 2:436–443.

Callaway, R.M., S.L. Miao, and Q. Guo. 2006. Are trans-Pacific invasions the new wave? Biological Invasions 8:1435–1437.

CamachoB, S.E., A.E. Hall, and M.R. Kaufmann. 1974. Efficiency and regulation of water transport in some woody and herbaceous species. Plant Physiology 54:169–172.

Campbell, L.G., and B.C. Husband. 2005. Impact of clonal growth on effective population size in *Hymenoxys herbacea* (Asteraceae). Heredity 94:526–532.

Campbell, R.W., and R.J. Sloan. 1977. Forest stand responses to defoliation by the gypsy moth. Forest Science Monograph 19:1–34.

Cane, J.H., and V.J. Tepedino. 2001. Causes and extent of declines among native North American invertebrate pollinators: detection, evidence, and consequences. Conservation Ecology 5(1):1 [http://www.consecol.org/vol5/iss1/art1].

Caners, R.T., S.E. Macdonald, and R.J. Belland. 2009. Recolonization potential of bryophyte diaspore banks in harvested boreal mixed-wood forest. Plant Ecology 204:55–68.

Canham, C.D. 1984. Canopy recruitment in shade tolerant trees: The response of *Acer saccharum* and *Fagus grandifolia* to canopy openings. Ph.D. dissertation, Ecology and Systematics, Cornell University, Ithaca, NY.

Canham, C.D. 1985. Suppression and release during canopy recruitment in *Acer saccharum*. Bulletin of the Torrey Botanical Club 112:134–145.

Canham, C.D. 1988. Growth and canopy architecture of shade-tolerant trees: response to canopy gaps. Ecology 69:786–795.

Canham, C.D., J.S. Denslow, W.J. Platt, J.R. Runkle, T.A. Spies, and P.S. White. 1990. Light regimes beneath closed canopies and tree-fall gaps in temperate and tropical forests. Canadian Journal of Forest Research 20:620–631.

Canham, C.D., A.C. Finzi, S.W. Pacala, and D.H. Burbank. 1994. Causes and consequences of resource heterogeneity in forests: interspecific variation in light transmission by canopy trees. Canadian Journal of Forest Research 24:337–349.

Canner, J.E., and M. Spence. 2011. A new technique using metal tags to track small seeds over short distances. Ecological Research 26:233–236.

Cantero, J.J., M. Pärtel, and M. Zobel. 1999. Is species richness dependent on the neighbouring stands? An analysis of the community patterns in mountain grasslands of central Argentina. Oikos 87:346–354.

Cantlon, J.E. 1953. Vegetation and microclimate of north and south slopes of Cushetunk Mountain, New Jersey. Ecological Monographs 23:241–270.

Cantlon, J.E., E.J.C. Curtis, and W.M. Malcolm. 1963. Studies of *Melampyrum lineare*. Ecology 44:466–474.

Carlton, C.E., and H.W. Robison. 1998. Diversity of litter-dwelling beetles in the Ouachita Highlands of Arkansas, USA. Biodiversity and Conservation 7:1589–1605.

Carlton, G.C., and F.A. Bazzaz. 1998. Resource congruence and forest regeneration following an experimental hurricane blowdown. Ecology 79:1305–1319.

Carleton, T.J., R.K. Jones, and G.F. Pierpoint. 1985. The prediction of understory vegetation by environmental factors for the purpose of site classification in forestry: an example from northern Ontario using residual ordination analysis. Canadian Journal of Forest Research 15:1099–1108.

Carleton, T.J., and P. MacLellan. 1994. Woody vegetation responses to fire versus clear-cutting logging: a comparative survey in the central Canadian boreal forest. Écoscience 1:141–152.

Carleton, T.J., and P.F. Maycock. 1978. Dynamics of the boreal forest south of James Bay. Canadian Journal of Botany 56: 1157–1173.

Carleton, T.J., and P.J. Maycock. 1980. Vegetation of the boreal forests south of James Bay: non-centered component analysis of the vascular flora. Ecology 61:1199–1212.

Carleton T.J., and P.F. Maycock. 1981. Understorey-canopy affinities in boreal forest vegetation. Canadian Journal of Botany 59:1709–1716.

Carlisle, A., A.H.F. Brown, and E.J. White. 1967. The nutrient content of tree stem flow and ground flora litter and leachates in a sessile oak (*Quercus petraea*) woodland. Journal of Ecology 55:615–627.

Carpenter, D., and N. Cappuccino. 2005. Herbivory, time since introduction and the invasiveness of exotic plants. Journal of Ecology 93:315–321.

Carpenter, J.S., and E.W. Chester. 1987. Vascular flora of the Bear Creek Natural Area, Stewart County, Tennessee. Castanea 52:112–128.

Carr, S.C., K.M. Robertson, W.J. Platt, and R.K. Peet. 2009. A model of geographic, environmental and regional variation in vegetation composition of pyrogenic pinelands of Florida. Journal of Biogeography 36:1600–1612.

Carreiro, M.M., and C.E. Tripler. 2005. Forest remnants along urban-rural gradients: examining their potential for global change research. Ecosystems 8:568–582. 73:S1316–S1324.

Carroll, C. 2009. Deer invade the district. American Stories. Washington, DC: American University Press, pp. 3–5.

Carroll, G. 1995. Forest endophytes—pattern and process. Canadian Journal of Botany 73:S1316–S1324.

Case, A.L., and T.-L. Ashman. 2009. Resources and pollinators contribute to population sex-ratio bias and pollen limitation in *Fragaria virginiana* (Rosaceae). Oikos 118:1250–1260.

Case, F.W., Jr., and R.B. Case. 1997. Trilliums. Timber Press, Portland, OR.

Case, M.A., and Z.R. Bradford. 2009. Enhancing the trap of lady's slippers: a new technique for discovering pollinators yields new data from *Cypripedium parviflorum* (Orchidaceae). Botanical Journal of the Linnean Society 160:1–10.

Case, M.A., K.M. Flinn, J. Jancaitis, A. Alley, and A. Paxton. 2007. Declining abundance of American ginseng (*Panax quinquefolius* L.) documented by herbarium specimens. Biological Conservation 134:22–30.

Casey, D., and D. Hein. 1983. Effects of heavy browsing on a bird community in a deciduous forest. Journal of Wildlife Management 47:829–836.

Casper, B.B. 1987. Spatial patterns of seed dispersal and post-dispersal seed predation of *Cryptantha flava* (Boraginaceae). American Journal of Botany 74:1646–1655.

Castelli, J.P., B.B. Casper, J.J. Sullivan, and R.E. Latham. 1999. Early understory succession following catastrophic wind damage in a deciduous forest. Canadian Journal of Forest Research 29:1997–2002.

Castro, J., Zamora, R., Hódar, J.A., and Gómez, J.M. 2004. Seedling establishment of a boreal tree species (*Pinus sylvestris*) at its southernmost distribution limit: consequences of being in a marginal Mediterranean habitat. Journal of Ecology 92: 266–277.

Caswell, H. 1978. A general formula for the sensitivity of population growth rate to changes in life history parameters. Theoretical Population Biology 14:215–230.

Caswell, H. 1989. The analysis of life table response experiments. I. Decomposition of treatment effects on population growth rate. Ecological Modelling 46: 221-237.

Caswell, H. 2000. Prospective and retrospective perturbation analyses: their roles in conservation biology. Ecology 81:619–627.

Caswell, H. 2007. Sensitivity analysis of transient population dynamics. Ecology Letters 10:1–15.

Caswell, H. 2010. Life table response experiment analysis of the stochastic growth rate. Journal of Ecology 98:324-333.

Caswell, H., and P.A. Werner. 1978. Transient behavior and life-history analysis of teasel (*Dipsacus sylvestris* Huds). Ecology 59:53–66.

Caughley, G. 1970. Eruption of ungulate populations, with special emphasis on Himalayan Thar of New Zealand. Ecology 51:53–72.

Chabot, B.F., and D.J. Hicks. 1982. The ecology of leaf life spans. Annual Review of Ecology and Systematics 13:229–259.

ChalkerScott, L. 1999. Environmental significance of anthocyanins in plant stress responses. Photochemistry and Photobiology 70:1–9.

Chandy, S., and D.J. Gibson. 2009. Scale dependency of species composition and environmental variables in the strata of a deciduous forest. Community Ecology 10:121–130.

Chandy, S., D.J. Gibson, and P.A. Robertson. 2006. Additive partitioning of diversity across hierarchical spatial scales in a forested landscape. Journal of Applied Ecology 43:792–801.

Chapin, F.S., III. 1980. The mineral nutrition of wild plants. Annual Review of Ecology and Systematics 11:233–260.

Chapin, F.S., III, K. Autumn, and F. Pugnaire. 1993. Evolution of suites of traits in response to environmental stress. American Naturalist 142:S78–S92.

Chapin, F.S., III, and K. Van Cleve. 1981. Plant nutrient absorption and retention under differing fire regimes. Pages 301–321 in Fire regimes and ecosystem properties. U.S. Department of Agriculture, Forest Service, Gen. Tech. Rep. WO-26.

Chapman, S.K., J.A. Langley, S.C. Hart, and G.W. Koch. 2006. Plants actively control nitrogen cycling: uncorking the microbial bottleneck. New Phytologist 169:27–34.

Chappelka, A.H., H.S. Neufeld, A.W. Davison, and G.L. Somers. 2003. Evaluation of ozone injury on foliage of cutleaf coneflower (*Rudbeckia laciniata*) and crownbeard (*Verbesina occidentalis*) in Great Smoky Mountains National Park. Environmental Pollution 125:53–59.

Charlesworth, D., 1989. Why do plants produce so many more ovules than seeds? Nature 338:21–22.

Charlesworth, D., and B. Charlesworth. 1987. Inbreeding depression and its evolutionary consequences. Annual Review of Ecology and Systematics 18:237–268.

Charron, D., and D. Gagnon. 1991. The demography of northern populations of *Panax quinquefolium* (American ginseng). Journal of Ecology 79:431–445.

Chase, J.M., and M.A. Leibold. 2003. Ecological niches: linking classical and contemporary approaches. University of Chicago Press, Chicago.

Chávez, V., and S.E. Macdonald. 2010. The influence of canopy patch mosaics on understory plant community composition in boreal mixed-wood forest. Forest Ecology and Management 259:1067–1075.

Chazdon, R.L. 1988. Sunflecks and their importance to forest understory plants. Advances in Ecological Research 18:1–63.

Chazdon, R.L., R.K. Colwell, J.S. Denslow, and M.R. Guariguata. 1998. Statistical methods for estimating species richness of woody regeneration in primary and secondary rain forests of northeastern Costa Rica. Pages 285–309 in F. Dallmeier and J.A. Comiskey, editors. Forest biodiversity research, monitoring and modeling. Unesco and Parthenon Publishing Group.

Chazdon, R.L., and N. Fetcher. 1984. Photosynthetic light environments in a lowland tropical rainforest in Costa Rica. Journal of Ecology 72:553–564.

Chazdon, R.L., and R.W. Pearcy. 1986a. Photosynthetic responses to light variation in rainforest species. I. Induction under constant and fluctuating light conditions. Oecologia 69:517–523.

Chazdon, R.L., and R.W. Pearcy. 1986b. Photosynthetic responses to light variation in rainforest species. II. Carbon gain and photosynthetic efficiency during lightflecks. Oecologia 69:524–531.

Chazdon, R.L., and R.W. Pearcy. 1991. The importance of sunflecks for forest understory plants. BioScience 41:760–766.

Chen, B.M., G.X. Wang, and S.L. Peng. 2009. Role of desert annuals in nutrient flow in arid area of Northwestern China: a nutrient reservoir and provider. Plant Ecology 201:401–409.

Cheng, Z. 1983. A comparative study of the vegetation in Hubei Province, China, and in the Carolinas of the United States. Annals of the Missouri Botanical Garden 70:571–575.

Cheplick, G. P. 1998. Seed dispersal and seedling establishment in grass populations. Pages 84–105 in G. P. Cheplick, editor. Population ecology of grasses. Cambridge University Press, Cambridge, UK.

Cheplick, G.P. 2008. Growth trajectories and size-dependent reproduction in the highly invasive grass *Microstegium vimineum*. Biological Invasions 10:761–770.

Cheptou, P. 2007. Why should mating system biologists be demographers? Trends in Ecology and Evolution 22:562–563.

Cheptou, P., and D.J. Schoen. 2007. Combining population genetics and demographical approaches in evolutionary studies of plant mating systems. Oikos 116:271–279.

Chesson, P. 2000. Mechanisms of maintenance of species diversity. Annual Review of Ecology, Evolution, and Systematics 31:343.

Chittka, L., A. Shmida, N. Troje, and R. Menzel. 1994. Ultraviolet as a component of flower reflections, and the colour perception of *Hymenoptera*. Vision Research 34:1489–1508.

Christensen, N.L. 1989. Landscape history and ecological change. Journal of Forest History 33:116–124.

Christensen, N.L., and R.K. Peet. 1981. Secondary forest succession on the North Carolina Piedmont. Pages 230–245 in D. West, H. Shugart, and D. Botkin, editors. Forest Succession: Concept and applications. New York: Springer-Verlag.

Christensen, N.L., and R.K. Peet. 1984. Convergence during secondary forest succession. Journal of Ecology 72:25–36.

Christie, D.A., and J.J. Armesto. 2003. Regeneration microsites and tree species coexistence in temperate rain forests of Chiloe Island, Chile. Journal of Ecology 91:776–784.

Cid-Benevento, C.R. 1987. Relative effects of light, soil-moisture availability and vegetative size on sex-ratio of two monoecious woodland annual herbs—*Acalypha rhomboidea* (Euphorbiaceae) and *Pilea pumila* (Urticaceae). Bulletin of the Torrey Botanical Club 114:293–306.

Cingolani, A.M., G. Posse, and M.B. Collantes. 2005. Plant functional traits, herbivore selectivity and response to sheep grazing in Patagonian steppe grasslands. Journal of Applied Ecology 42:50–59.

Cipollini, M.L., D.A. Wallace-Senft, and D.F. Whigham. 1994. A model of patch dynamics, seed dispersal, and sex-ratio in the dioecious shrub *Lindera benzoin* (Lauraceae). Journal of Ecology 82:621–633.

Cipollini, M L., D.F. Whigham, and J. O'Neill. 1993. Population growth, structure, and seed dispersal in the understory herb *Cynoglossum virginianum*: a population and patch dynamics model. Plant Species Biology 8:117–129.

Claessen, D. 2005. Alternative life-history pathways and the elasticity of stochastic matrix models. American Naturalist 165:E27–E35.

Clark, C.M., E.E. Cleland, S.L. Collins, J.E. Fargione, L. Gough, K.L. Gross, S.C. Pennings, K.N. Suding, and J.B. Grace. 2007. Environmental and plant community determinants of species loss following nitrogen enrichment. Ecology Letters 10:596–607.

Clark, C.M., and D. Tilman. 2008. Loss of plant species after chronic low-level nitrogen deposition to prairie grasslands. Nature 451:712–715.

Clark, D.B., D.A. Clark, P.M. Rich, S. Weiss, and S.F. Oberbauer. 1996. Landscape-scale evaluation of understory light and canopy structure: methods and application in a neotropical lowland rain forest. Canadian Journal of Forest Research 26:747–757.

Clark, D.B., M.W. Palmer, and D.A. Clark. 1999. Edaphic factors and the landscape-scale distributions of tropical rain forest trees. Ecology 80:2662–2675.

Clark, J.S. 1991. Disturbance and population structure on the shifting mosaic landscape. Ecology 72:1119–1137.

Clark, J.S. 1998. Why trees migrate so fast: confronting theory with dispersal biology and paleorecord. American Naturalist 152:204–224.

Clark, J.S., S. LaDeau, and I. Ibanez. 2004. Fecundity of trees and the colonization-competition hypothesis. Ecological Monographs 74:415–442.

Clark, J.S., M. Lewis, and L. Horvath. 2001. Invasion by extremes: population spread with variation in dispersal and reproduction. American Naturalist 157:537–554.

Clarke, R.T., J.A. Thomas, G.W. Elmes, and M.E. Hochberg. 1997. The effects of spatial patterns in habitat quality on community dynamics within a site. Proceedings of the Royal Society of London, Series B-Biological Sciences 264:347–354.

Clay, K. 1984. The effect of the fungus *Atkinsonella hypoxylon* (Clavicipitaceae) on the reproductive system and demography of the grass *Danthonia spicata*. New Phytologist 98:165–175.

Clebsch, E.C., and R.T. Busing. 1989. Secondary succession, gap dynamics, and community structure in southern Appalachian cove forest. Ecology 70:728–735.

Clegg, M.T. 1980. Measuring plant mating systems. BioScience 30:814–818.

Cleland, E.E., I. Chuine, A. Menzel, H.A. Mooney, and M.D. Schwartz. 2007. Shifting plant phenology in response to global change. Trends in Ecology and Evolution 22:357–365.

Clements, F.E. 1916. Plant succession: an analysis of the development of vegetation. Carnegie Institute of Washington Publication 242.

Clements, F.E. 1928. Plant succession and indicators. H.W. Wilson, New York.

Clements, F.E. 1936. Nature and structure of the climax. Journal of Ecology 24:252–284.

Clinton, B.D. 1995. Temporal variation in photosynthetically active radiation (PAR) in mesic Southern Appalachian hardwood forests with and without rhododendron understories. Pages 534–540 in K.W. Gottschalk and S.L.C. Fosbroke, editors. Proceedings of the Tenth Central Hardwood Forest Conference, Morgantown, WV, Gen. Tech. Rep. NE-197, Department of Agriculture, Forest Service, Northeastern Forest Experiment Station, Radnor, PA.

Clinton, B.D., L.R. Boring, and W.T. Swank. 1994. Regeneration patterns in canopy gaps of mixed-oak forests of the Southern Appalachians: Influences of topographic position and evergreen understory. American Midland Naturalist 132:308–319.

Clinton, B.D., and J.M. Vose. 1996. Effects of *Rhododendron maximum* L. on *Acer rubrum* L. seedling establishment. Castanea 6:38–45.

Coates, P. 2006. American perceptions of immigrant and invasive species, strangers on the land. University of California Press.

Cochrane, M. E., and S. Ellner. 1992. Simple methods for calculating age-based life history parameters for stage-structured populations. Ecological Monographs 63:345–365.

Cogbill, C.V. 1985. Dynamics of the boreal forests of the Laurentian highlands, Canada. Canadian Journal of Forest Research 15:252–261.

Colas, B., F. Kirchner, M. Riba, I. Olivieri, A. Mignot, E. Imbert, C. Beltrame, D. Carbonell, and H. Freville. 2008. Restoration demography: a 10-year demographic comparison between introduced and natural populations of endemic *Centaurea corymbosa* (Asteraceae). Journal of Applied Ecology 45:1468–1476.

Colautti, R., S. Bailey, C. van Overdijk, K. Amundsen, and H. MacIsaac. 2006. Characterised and projected costs of nonindigenous species in Canada. Biological Invasions 8:45–59.

Cole, C. 2003. Genetic variation in rare and common plants. Annual Review of Ecology, Evolution, and Systematics 34:213–237.

Colla, S.R., and S. Dumesh. 2010 The bumble bees of southern Ontario: notes on natural history and distribution. Journal of the Entomological Society of Ontario 141:39–68.

Collard, A., L. Lapointe, J.-P. Ouellet, M. Crêtec, A. Lussierd, C. Daiglee, and S.D. Côté. 2010. Slow responses of understory plants of maple-dominated forests to white-tailed deer experimental exclusion. Forest Ecology and Management 260:649–662.

Colling, G., and D. Matthies. 2006. Effects of habitat deterioration on population dynamics and extinction risk of an endangered, long-lived perennial herb (*Scorzonera humilis*). Journal of Ecology 94:959–972.

Collins, B.S., K.P. Dunne, and S.T.A. Pickett. 1985. Response of forest herbs to canopy gaps. Pages 218–234 in S.T.A. Pickett and P.S. White, editors. The ecology of natural disturbance and patch dynamics. Academic Press, Orlando, FL.

Collins, B.S., and S.T.A. Pickett. 1982. Vegetation composition and relation to environment in an Allegheny hardwoods forest. American Midland Naturalist 108:117–123.

Collins, B.S., and S.T.A. Pickett. 1987. Influence of canopy opening on the environment and herb layer in a northern hardwoods forest. Vegetation 70:3–10.

Collins, B.S., and S.T.A. Pickett. 1988a. Demographic responses of herb layer species to experimental canopy gaps in a northern hardwoods forest. Journal of Ecology 76:437–450.

Collins, B.S., and S.T.A. Pickett. 1988b. Response of herb layer cover to experimental gaps. American Midland Naturalist 119:282–290.

Collins, B., P. White, and D. Imm. 2001. Introduction to ecology and management of rare plants of the southeast. Natural Areas Journal 21:4–11.

Collins, S. 1961. Benefits to understory from canopy defoliation by gypsy moth larvae. Ecology 42:836–838.

Colwell, R.K., and J.A. Coddington. 1994. Estimating terrestrial biodiversity through extrapolation. Philosophical Transactions of the Royal Society 345:101–118.

Comisky, L., A.A. Royo, and W.P. Carson. 2005. Deer browsing creates rock refugia gardens on large boulders in the Allegheny National Forest, Pennsylvania. American Midland Naturalist 154:201–206.

Condit, R., N. Pitman, E.G. Leigh, J. Chave, J. Terborgh, R.B. Foster, P. Nunez, S. Aguilar, R. Valencia, G. Villa, H.C. Muller-Landau, E. Losos, and S.P. Hubbell. 2002. Beta-diversity in tropical forest trees. Science 295:666–669.

Connell, J.H. 1978. Diversity in tropical rainforests and coral reefs. Science 199:1302–1310.

Connell, J.H. 1980. Diversity and coevolution of competitors, or the ghost of competition past. Oikos 35:131–138.

Connell, J.H. 1989. Some processes affecting the species composition in gaps. Ecology 70:560–562.

Connell, J.H., and R.O. Slatyer. 1977. Mechanisms of succession in natural communities and their role in community stability and organization. American Naturalist 111:1119–1144.

Connell, J.H., and W.P. Sousa. 1983. On the evidence needed to judge ecological stability or persistence. American Naturalist 121:789–824.

Constabel, A.J., and V.J. Lieffers. 1996. Seasonal patterns of light transmission through boreal mixed-wood canopies. Canadian Journal of Forest Research 26:1008–1014.

Constable, J.V.H., B. Peffer, and D.M. DeNicola. 2007. Temporal and light-based changes in carbon uptake and storage in the spring ephemeral *Podophyllum peltatum* (Berberidaceae). Environmental and Experimental Botany 60:112–120.

Cook, R.A. 1979. Asexual reproduction: a further consideration. American Naturalist 113:769–772.

Coomes, D.A., and P.J. Grubb. 2000. Impacts of root competition in forests and woodlands: a theoretical framework and review of experiments. Ecological Monographs 70:171–207.

Cooper-Ellis, S., D.R. Foster, G. Carlton, and A. Lezberg. 1999. Forest response to catastrophic wind: results from an experimental hurricane. Ecology 80:2683–2696.

Costanza, J.K., A. Moody, and R.K. Peet. 2011. Multi-scale environmental heterogeneity as a predictor of plant species richness. Landscape Ecology 26:851–864.

Cote, M., J. Ferron, and R. Gagnon. 2003. Impact of seed and seedling predation by small rodents on early regeneration establishment of black spruce. Canadian Journal of Forest Research 33:2362–2371.

Cote, S.D., T.P. Rooney, J.P. Trembly, C. Dussault, and D.M. Waller. 2004. Ecological impacts of deer overabundance. Annual Review of Ecology, Evolution, and Systematics 35:113–147.

Coulson, T., G.M. Mace, E. Hudson, and H. Possingham. 2001. The use and abuse of population viability analysis. Trends in Ecology and Evolution 16:219–221.

Courty, P., M. Buee, A.G. Diedhiou, P. Frey-Klett, F. Le Tacon, F. Rineau, M. Turpault, S. Uroz, and J. Garbaye. 2010. The role of ectomycorrhizal communities in forest ecosystem processes: new perspectives and emerging concepts. Soil Biology and Biochemistry 42:679–698.

Covington, W.W. 1981. Changes in forest floor organic-matter and nutrient content following clear cutting in northern hardwoods. Ecology 62:41–48.

Cowles, H.C. 1899. The ecological relations of the vegetation on the sand dunes of Lake Michigan. Botanical Gazette 27:95–117, 167–202, 281–308, 361–391.

Cowles, H.C. 1901. The physiographic ecology of Chicago and vicinity: a study of the origin, development, and classification of plant societies. Botanical Gazette 31:73–108, 145–182.

Cowles, H.C. 1911. The causes of vegetation cycles. Botanical Gazette 51:161–183.

Cowling, R.M., and M.J. Samways. 1994. Predicting global patterns of endemic plant species richness. Biodiversity Letters 2:127–131.

Crafton, W.M., and B.W. Wells. 1934. The old field prisere: an ecological study. Journal of the Elisha Mitchell Science Society 49:225–246.

Crawford, R.M.M. 1989. Survival on the forest floor. Chap. 7 in Studies in plant survival. Blackwell Scientific, Oxford, UK.

Crawley, M.J. 1983. *Herbivory: The dynamics of animal-plant interactions*. University of California Press, Berkeley, CA.

Crawley, M.J. 1989. Insect herbivores and plant population dynamics. Annual Review of Entomology 34:531–564.

Crête, M. 1999. The distribution of deer biomass in North America supports the hypothesis of exploitation ecosystems. Ecology Letters 2:223–227.

Crête, M., J.-P. Ouellet, and L. Lesage. 2001. Comparative effects on plants of caribou/reindeer, moose and white-tailed deer herbivory. Arctic 54:407–417.

Crick, J.C., and J.P. Grime. 1987. Morphological plasticity and mineral nutrient capture in two herbaceous species of contrasted ecology. New Phytologist. 107:403–414.

Crist, T.O., J.A. Veech, J.C. Gering, and K.S. Summerville. 2003. Partitioning species diversity across landscapes and regions: A hierarchical analysis of alpha, beta, and gamma diversity. American Naturalist 162:734–743.

Critchley, C. 1998. Photoinhibition. Pages 264–272 in A.S. Raghavendra, editor. Photosynthesis: a comprehensive treatise. Cambridge University Press, Cambridge, UK.

Cromack, K., and C.D. Monk. 1975. Litter production, decomposition, and nutrient cycling in a mixed hardwood watershed and a white pine watershed. Pages 609–624 in F.G. Howell, J.B. Gentry, and M.H. Smith, editors. Mineral cycling in southeastern ecosystems. ERDA Symposium Series (CONF-740513).

Crone, E.E., E.S. Menges, M.M. Ellis, T. Bell, P. Bierzychudek, J. Ehrlén, T.N. Kaye, T.M. Knight, P. Lesica, W.F. Morris, G. Oostermeijer, P.F. Quintana-Ascencio, A. Stanley, T. Ticktin, T. Valverde, and J.L. Williams. 2011. How do plant ecologists use matrix population models? Ecology Letters 14:1–8.

Crouch, V.E., and M.S. Golden. 1997. Floristics of a bottomland forest and adjacent uplands near the Tombigbee River, Choctaw County, Alabama. Castanea 62:219–238.

Crow, S.E., T.R. Filley, M. McCormick, K. Szlávecz, D.E. Scott, D. Gamblin, and G. Conyers. 2009. Earthworms, stand age, and species composition interact to influence particulate organic matter chemistry during forest succession. Biogeochemistry 92:61–82.

Crozier, C.R., and R.E.J. Boerner. 1984. Correlations of understory herb distribution patterns with microhabitats under different tree species in a mixed mesophytic forest. Oecologia 62:337–343.

Cruse-Sanders, J., and J. Hamrick. 2004. Genetic diversity in harvested and protected populations of wild American ginseng, *Panax quinquefolius* L. (Araliaceae). American Journal of Botany 91:540–548.

Crystal, P. 2009. Estimation of population reduction and gene flow in the rare orchid Isotria medeoloides. Honors thesis, Colby College, Waterville, Maine.

Cubbedge, A.W., and C.H. Nilon. 1993. Adjacent land use effects on the flood-plain forest bird community of Minnesota valley national wildlife refuge. Natural Areas Journal 13:220–230.

Cui, M., and M.M. Caldwell. 1997. Shading reduces exploitation of soil nitrate and phosphate by *Agropyron desertorum* and *Artemisia tridentata* from soils with patchy and uniform nutrient distributions. Oecologia 109:177–183.

Culley, T.M. 2000. Inbreeding depression and floral type fitness differences in *Viola canadensis* (Violaceae), a species with chasmogamous and cleistogamous flowers. Canadian Journal of Botany 78:1420–1429.

Culley, T.M. 2002. Reproductive biology and delayed selfing in *Viola pubescens* (Violaceae), an understory herb with chasmogamous and cleistogamous flowers. International Journal of Plant Sciences 163:113–122.

Culley, T.M., and M.R. Klooster. 2007. The cleistogamous breeding system: a review of its frequency, evolution, and ecology in angiosperms. Botanical Review 73:1–30.

Cullina, W. 2000. The New England Wildflower Society guide to growing and propagating wildflowers of the United States and Canada. Boston: Houghton Mifflin.

Cullina, W. 2002. Native trees, shrubs, and vines: A guide to using, growing and propagating North American woody plants. Boston: Houghton Mifflin.

Culver, D.C., and A.J. Beattie. 1980. The fate of *Viola* seeds dispersed by ants. American Journal of Botany 67:710–714.

Currie, W.S., and J.D. Aber. 1997. Modeling leaching as a decomposition process in humid montane forests. Ecology 78:1844–1860.

Curtis, W.F., and D.T. Kincaid. 1984. Leaf conductance responses of *Viola* species from sun and shade habitats. Canadian Journal of Botany 62:1268–1272.

Czaran, T., and S. Bartha. 1992. Spatiotemporal dynamic models of plant populations and communities. Trends in Ecology and Evolution 7:38–42.

Dalling, J.W., S.P. Hubbell, and K. Silvera. 1998. Seed dispersal, seedling establishment and gap partitioning among tropical pioneer trees. Journal of Ecology 86:674–689.

Damman, H., and M.L. Cain. 1998. Population growth and viability analyses of the clonal woodland shrub, *Asarum canadense*. Journal of Ecology 86:13–26.

Darwin, C.R. 1876. The effects of cross and self-fertilization in the vegetable kingdom. London: John Murray.

Daubenmire, R.F. 1966. Vegetation: identification of typal communities. Science 151:291–298.

Daubenmire, R. 1978. Plant Geography. Academic Press, New York.

Davidson, D.W. 1993. The effects of herbivory and granivory on terrestrial plant succession. Oikos 68:23–35.

Davis, M.A., M.K. Chew, R.J. Hobbs, A.E. Lugo, J.J. Ewel, G.J. Vermeij, J.H. Brown, M.L. Rosenzweig, M.R. Gardener, S.P. Carroll, K. Thompson, S.T.A. Pickett, J.C. Stromberg, P. Del Tredici, K.N. Suding, J.G. Ehrenfeld, J.P. Grime, J. Mascaro, and J.C. Briggs. 2011. Don't judge species on their origins. Nature 474:153–154.

Davis, M.A., J.P. Grime, and K. Thompson. 2000. Fluctuating resources in plant communities: a general theory of invasibility. Journal of Ecology 88:528–534.

Davis, M.A., and K. Thompson. 2000. Eight ways to be a colonizer; two ways to be an invader: a proposed nomenclature scheme for invasion ecology. Bulletin of the Ecological Society of America 81:226–230.

Davis, M.A., K.J. Wrage, and P.B. Reich. 1998. Competition between tree seedlings and herbaceous vegetation: support for a theory of resource supply and demand. Journal of Ecology 86:652–661.

Davis, M.A., K.J. Wrage, P.B. Reich, M.G. Tjoelker, T. Schaeffer, and C. Muermann. 1999. Survival, growth, and photosynthesis of tree seedlings competing with herbaceous vegetation along a multiple resource gradient. Plant Ecology 145:341–350.

Davis, M.B. 1993. Old growth in the East: A survey. Cenozoic Society, Richmond, VT.

Davis, M.B., ed. 1996. Eastern old-growth forests: prospects for rediscovery and recovery. Island Press, Washington, DC.

Davis, M.B., T.E. Parshall, and J.B. Ferrari. 1996. Landscape heterogeneity of hemlock-hardwood forest in northern Michigan. Pages 291–304 in M.B. Davis, editor. Northeastern old-growth forest. Washington, DC: Island Press.

Davis, M.B. 1983. Quaternary history of deciduous forests of eastern North America and Europe. Annals of the Missouri Botanical Garden 70:550–563.

Davis, M.B. 1986. Climatic instability, time lags, and community disequilibrium. 269–284 269–284 in J. Diamond and T.J. Case, editors. Community ecology. New York: Harper and Row.

Davis, M.B., R.G. Shaw, and J.R. Etterson. 2005. Evolutionary responses to changing climate. Ecology 86:1704–1714.

Davison, A.W., H.S. Neufeld, A.H. Chappelka, K. Wolff, and P.L.Finkelstein. 2003. Interpreting spatial variation in ozone symptoms shown by cutleaf coneflower, *Rudbeckia laciniata* L. Environmental Pollution 125:61–70.

Davison, S.E., and R.T.T. Forman. 1982. Herb and shrub dynamics in a mature oak forest: a thirty-year study. Bulletin of the Torrey Botanical Club 109:64–73.

Day, G.M. 1953. The Indian as an ecological factor in the northeast forest. Ecology 34:329–346.

Day, J.R., and H.P. Possingham. 1995. A stochastic metapopulation model with variability in patch size and position. Theoretical Population Biology 48:333–360.

DeAngelis, D.L., R.H. Gardner, and H.H. Shugart. 1981. Productivity of forest ecosystems studied during the IBP: the woodlands data set. Pages 567–672 in D.E. Reichle, editor. Dynamic properties of forest ecosystems. International Biological Programme 23. Cambridge University Press, Cambridge, UK.

de Araújo, A.C., B. Kruijt, A.D. Nobre, A.J. Dolman, M.J. Waterloo, E.J. Moors, and J.S. de Souza. Nocturnal accumulation of CO2 underneath a tropical forest canopy along a topographical gradient. Ecological Applications 18:1406–1419.

De Bello, F., J. Lepš, and M.T. Sebastia. 2007. Grazing effects on the species-area relationship: Variation along a climatic gradient in NE Spain. Journal of Vegetation Science 18:25–34.

De Boeck, H.J., T. De Groote, and I. Nijs. 2012. Leaf temperatures in glasshouses and open-top chambers. New Phytologist 194:1155–1164.

deCalesta, D. S. 1994a. Effect of white-tailed deer on songbirds within managed forests in Pennsylvania. Journal of Wildlife Management 58:711–717.

deCalesta, D. S. 1994b. Impact of deer and silvicultural treatments on small mammals in northwestern Pennsylvania. Journal of Mammalogy.

deCalesta, D. S. 2011. Kinzua quality deer cooperative report: 2001–2010. Wildlife Analysis Consulting, Hammondsport, NY.

deCalesta, D.S. and S.L. Stout. 1997. Relative deer density and sustainability: a conceptual framework for integrating deer management with ecosystem management. Wildlife Society Bulletin 1997:252–258.

de Castro, F. 2000. Light spectral composition in a tropical forest: measurements and model. Tree Physiology 20:49–56.

De Chantal, M., and A. Granstrom. 2007. Aggregations of dead wood after wildfire act as browsing refugia for seedlings of *Populus tremula* and *Salix caprea*. Forest Ecology & Management 250:3–8.

Decocq, G., M. Aubert, F. Dupont, D. Alard, R. Saguez, A. Wattez-Franger, B. De Foucault, A. Delelis-Dusollier, and J. Bardat. 2004. Plant diversity in a managed temperate deciduous forest: understory response to two silvicultural systems. Journal of Applied Ecology 41:1065–1079.

DeFerrari, C.M. and R.J. Naiman. 1994. A multi-scale assessment of the occurrence of exotic plants on the Olympic Peninsula, Washington. Journal of Vegetation Science 5:247–258.

de Freitas, C.R., and N.J. Enright. 1995. Microclimatic differences between and within canopy gaps in a temperate rainforest. International Journal of Biometeorology 38:188–193.

De Frenne, P., J. Brunet, A. Shevtsova, A. Kilb, B.J. Graae, O. Chabrerie, S.A. Cousins, G. Decocq, A. De Schrijver, M. Diekmann, R. Bruwez, T. Heinken, M. Hermy, C. Nilsson,

S. Stanton, W. Tack, J. Willaert, and K. Verheyen. 2011. Temperature effects on forest herbs assessed by warming and transplant experiments along a latitudinal gradient. Global Change Biology 17:3240–3253.

De Frenne, P., A. De Schrijver, B.J. Graae, R. Gruwez, W. Tack, F. Vandelook, M. Hermy, and K. Verheyen. 2010. The use of open-top chambers in forests for evaluating warming effects on herbaceous understory plants. Ecological Research 25:163–171.

De Frenne, P., B.J. Graae, A. Kolb, J. Brunet, O. Chabrerie, S.A.O. Cousins, G. Decocq, R. Dhondt, M. Diekmann, O. Eriksson, T. Heinken, M. Hermy, Ü. Jõgar, R. Saguez, A Shevtsova, S. Stanton, R. Zindel, M. Zobel, and K. Verheyen. 2010. Significant effects of temperature on the reproductive output of the forest herb *Anemone nemorosa* L. Forest Ecology and Management 259:809–817.

De Frenne, P., B.J. Graae, A. Kolb, A. Shevtsova, L. Baeten, J. Brunet, O. Chambrerie, S.A. Cousins, G. Decocq, R. Dhondt, M. Diekmann, R. Gruqez, T. Heinken, M. Hermy, M. Oster, R. Saguez, S. Stanton, W. Tack, M. Vanhellemont, and K. Verheyen. 2011. An intraspecific application of the leaf-height-seed ecology strategy scheme to forest herbs along a latitudinal gradient. Ecography 34:132–140.

De Grandpré, L., and Y. Bergeron. 1997. Diversity and stability of understory communities following disturbance in the southern boreal forest. Journal of Ecology 85:777–784.

De Grandpré, L., D. Boucher, Y. Bergeron, and D. Gagnon. 2011. Effects of small canopy gaps on boreal mixed-wood understory vegetation dynamics. Community Ecology 12:67–77.

De Grandpré, L., D. Gagnon, and Y. Bergeron. 1993. Changes in the understory of Canadian southern boreal forest after fire. Journal of Vegetation Science 4:803–810.

De Grandpré, L., J. Morissette, and S. Gauthier. 2000. Long-term post-fire changes in the northeastern boreal forest of Quebec. Journal of Vegetation Science 11:791–800.

Degreef, J., J.P. Baudoin, and O.J. Rocha. 1997. Case studies on breeding systems and its consequences for germplasm conservation. 2. Demography of wild Lima bean populations in the Central Valley of Costa Rica. Genetic Resources and Crop Evolution 44:429–438.

de Jong, J.H., N.M. Waser, and P.G.L. Klinkhamer. 1993. Geitonogamy: the neglected side of selfing. Trends in Ecology and Evolution 8:321–325.

De Keersmaeker, L., L. Martens, K. Verheyen, M. Hermy, A. De Schrijver, and N. Lust. 2004. Impact of soil fertility and insolation on diversity of herbaceous woodland species colonizing afforestations in Muizen forest (Belgium). Forest Ecology and Management 188:291–304.

de Kroon, H., B. Fransen, J.W.A. van Rheenen, A. van Dijk, and R. Kreulen. 1996. High levels of inter-ramet water translocation in two rhizomatous *Carex* species, as quantified by deuterium labelling. Oecologia 106:73–84.

de Kroon, H., A. Plaisier, J. van Groenendael, and H. Caswell. 1986. Elasticity: The relative contribution of demographic parameters to population growth rate. Ecology 67:1427–1431.

de Kroon, H., J. van Groenendael, and J. Ehrlén. 2000. Elasticities: a review of methods and model limitations. Ecology 81:607–618.

De La Cretaz, A.L., and M.J. Kelty. 2002a. Development of tree regeneration in fern-dominated forest understories after reduction of deer browsing. Restoration Ecology 10:416–426.

De La Cretaz, A.L., and M.J. Kelty. 2002b. Establishment and control of hay-scented fern: A native invasive species. Biological Invasions 1:223–236.

Delcourt, H. 2002. Forests in peril: tracking deciduous trees from ice-age refuges into the greenhouse world., Blacksburg, VA: McDonald and Woodward.

Delcourt, H.R., and P.A. Delcourt. 1975. The blufflands: Pleistocene pathway into the Tunica Hills. American Midland Naturalist 94:385–400.

Delcourt, H.R., and P.A. Delcourt. 1996. Eastern deciduous forests. Pages 357–395 in M.G. Barbour and D.W. Billings, editors. North American Terrestrial Vegetation. Cambridge University Press, Cambridge, UK.

Delcourt, P.A., and H.R. Delcourt. 1987. Long-term forest dynamics of the temperate zone. New York: Springer-Verlag.

Delcourt, P.A., and H.R. Delcourt. 1998. Paleoecological insights on conservation of biodiversity: a focus on species, ecosystems, and landscapes. Ecological Applications 8: 921–934.

DeLuca, T.H., D.R. Keeney, and G.W. McCarty. 1992. Effect of freeze-thaw events on mineralization of soil nitrogen. Biology and Fertility of Soils 14:116–120.

DeLucia, E.H., H.D. Shenoi, S.L. Naidu, and T.A. Day. 1991. Photosynthetic symmetry of sun and shade leaves of different orientations. Oecologia 87:51–57.

DeLucia, E.H., K. Nelson, T.C. Vogelmann, and W.K. Smith. 1996. Contribution of internal reflectance to light absorption and photosynthesis of shade leaves. Plant, Cell and Environment 19:159–170.

DeLucia, E.H., H.D. Shenoi, S.L. Naidu, and T.A. Day. 1991. Photosynthetic symmetry of sun and shade leaves of different orientations. Oecologia 87:51–57.

DeMars, B.G. 1996. Vesicular-arbuscular mycorrhizal status of spring ephemerals in two Ohio forests. Ohio Journal of Science 96:97–99.

DeMars, B.G., and R.E.J. Boerner. 1997. Foliar phosphorus and nitrogen resorption in three woodland herbs of contrasting phenology. Castanea 62:43–54.

Demmig-Adams, B., W.W. Adams, D.H. Barker, B.A. Logan, D.R. Bowling, and A.S. Verhoeven. 1996. Using chlorophyll fluorescence to assess the fraction of absorbed light allocated to thermal dissipation of excess excitation. Physiologia Plantarum 98:253–264.

Denevan, W.M. 1992. The pristine myth, the landscape of the Americas in 1492. Annals of the Association of American Geographers 34:329–346.

Dengler, J. 2009. A flexible multi-scale approach for standardised recording of plant species richness patterns. Ecological Indicators 9:1169–1178.

Dengler, J., E. Ruprecht, A. Szabó, D. Turtureanu, M. Beldean, E. Uğurlu, H. Pedashenko, C. Dolnik, and A.Jones. 2009. EDGG cooperation on syntaxonomy and biodiversity of *Festuco-Brometea* communities in Transylvania (Romania): report and preliminary results. Bulletin of the European Dry Grassland Group 4:13–19, Hamburg.

Denslow, J.S. 1980. Patterns of plant species diversity during succession under different disturbance regimes. Oecologia 46:18–21.

Denslow, J.S. 1985. Disturbance-mediated coexistence of species. Pages 309–323 in S.T.A. Pickett and P.S. White, editors. The ecology of natural disturbance and patch dynamics. New York, Academic Press.

Denslow, J.S., E. Newell, and A.M. Ellison. 1991. The effect of understory palms and cyclanths on the growth and survival of *Inga* seedlings. Biotropica 23:225–234.

DePamphilis, C.W., and H.S. Neufeld. 1989. Phenology and ecophysiology of *Aesculus sylvatica*, a vernal understory tree. Canadian Journal of Botany 67:2161–2167.

DePamphilis, C.W., N.D. Young, and A.D. Wolfe. 1997. Evolution of plastid gene rps2 in a lineage of hemiparasitic and holoparasitic plants: Many losses of photosynthesis and complex patterns of rate variation. Proceedings of the National Academy of Sciences of the United States of America 94:7367–7372.

De Schrijver, A., P. De Frenne, E. Ampoorter, L. Van Nevel, A. Demey, K. Wuyts, and K. Verheyen. 2011. Cumulative nitrogen inputs drive species loss in terrestrial ecosystems. Global Ecology and Biogeography 20:803–816.

De Steven, D. 1991a. Experiments on mechanisms of tree establishment in old-field succession: seedling emergence. Ecology 72:1066–1075.

De Steven, D. 1991b. Experiments on mechanisms of tree establishment in old-field succession: seedling survival and growth. Ecology 72:1076–1088.

Devlin, E. 2007. Geographic distribution of genetic variation in the rare orchid Isotria medeoloides. Honors thesis, Colby College, Waterville, ME.

de Witte, L.C., and J. Stoecklin. 2010. Longevity of clonal plants: Why it matters and how to measure it. Annals of Botany 106:859–870.

Diamond, J.M. 1989. Overview of recent extinctions. Pages 37–330 in D. Western and M.C. Pearl, editors. Conservation for the twenty-first century. Wildlife Conservation International, New York Zoological Society. New York: Oxford University Press.

Díaz, S., and M. Cabido. 1997. Plant functional types and ecosystem function in relation to global change. Journal of Vegetation Science 8:463–474.

Dickens, R.S. 1976. Cherokee prehistory: the Pisgah phase in the Appalachian summit region. University of Tennessee Press, Knoxville, TN.

Didier, K.A., and W.F. Porter. 2003. Relating spatial patterns of sugar maple reproductive success and relative deer density in northern New York State. Forest Ecology & Management 181:253–266.

Diefenbach, D.R., W.L. Palmer, and W.K. Shope. 1997. Attitudes of Pennsylvania sportsmen towards managing white-tailed deer to protect the ecological integrity of forests. Wildlife Society Bulletin 25:244–251.

Dieringer, G. 1992. Pollinator limitation in populations of *Agalinis strictifolia* (Scrophulariaceae). Bulletin of the Torrey Botanical Club 119:131–136.

Diez, J.M. 2007. Hierarchical patterns of symbiotic orchid germination linked to adult proximity and environmental gradients. Journal of Ecology 95:159–170.

Dighton, J., A.R. Tuininga, D.M. Gray, R.E. Huskins, and T. Belton. 2004. Impacts of atmospheric deposition on New Jersey pine barrens forest soils and communities of ectomycorrhizae. Forest Ecology and Management 201:131–144.

Digiovinazzo, P., G.F. Ficetola, L. Bottoni, C. Andreis, and E. Padoa-Schioppa. 2010. Ecological thresholds in herb communities for the management of suburban fragmented forests. Forest Ecology and Management 259:343–349.

Dirr, M.A. 1998. Manual of Woody Landscape Plants. Stipes Publishing, Champagne, IL.

Diwold, K., S. Dullinger, and T. Dirnböck. 2010. Effect of nitrogen availability on forest understory cover and its consequences for tree regeneration in the Australian limestone Alps. Plant Ecology 209:11–22.

Dix, R.L., and J.M.A. Swan. 1971. The roles of disturbance and succession in upland forest at Candle Lake, Saskatchewan. Canadian Journal of Botany 49:657–676.

DNR, W. 2005. Deer abundance records, http://dnr.wi.gov/org/land/wildlife/hunt/deer.

Doak, D.F., and W. Morris. 1999. Detecting population-level consequences of ongoing environmental change without long-term monitoring. Ecology 80:1537–1551.

Dolan, R.W., M.E. Moore, and J.D. Stephens. 2011. Documenting effects of urbanization on flora using herbarium records. Journal of Ecology 99:1055–1062.

Dolan, R.W., P.F. Quintana-Ascencio, and E.S. Menges. 2008. Genetic change following fire in populations of a seed-banking perennial plant. Oecologia 158:355–360.

Dolan, RW., R. Yahr, and E.S. Menges. 2004. Population genetic structure in *Nolina brittoniana* (Agavaceae), a plant endemic to the central ridges of Florida. Southeastern Naturalist 3:25–36.

Donoghue, M.J., and S.A. Smith. 2004. Patterns in the assembly of temperate forests around the Northern Hemisphere. Philosophical Transactions of the Royal Society of London, B: 359:1633–1644.

Donohue, K., D.R. Foster, and G. Motzkin. 2000. Effects of the past and the present on species distribution: land-use history and demography of wintergreen. Journal of Ecology 88:303–316.

Dorning, M., and D. Cipollini. 2006. Leaf and root extracts of the invasive shrub, *Lonicera maackii*, inhibit seed germination of three herbs with no autotoxic effects. Plant Ecology 184:287–296.

Dostal, P. 2007. Population dynamics of annuals in perennial grassland controlled by ants and environmental stochasticity. Journal of Vegetation Science 18:91–102.

Doucet, R., M. Pineau, J.-C. Ruel, and G. Sheedy. 1996. Sylviculture appliquée. Pages 965–1004 in J.A. Bérard and M. Côté, editors. Manuel de Foresterie. Presses de l'Université Laval, Sainte-Foy.

Dragoni, D., and A.F. Rahman. 2012. Trends in fall phenology across the deciduous forests of the eastern USA. Agricultural and Forest Meteorology 157:96–105.

Drew, A.P. 1988. Interference of black cherry by ground flora of the Allegheny uplands. Canadian Journal of Forest Research 18:652–656.

Drury, W.H. and I.C.T. Nisbet. 1971. Inter-relations between developmental models in geo-morphology, plant ecology and animal ecology. General Systems 16:57–68.

Drury, W.H., and I.C.T. Nisbet. 1973. Succession. Journal of the Arnold Arboretum 54:331–368.

Dudash, M. 1990. Relative fitness of selfed and outcrossed progeny in a self-compatible, protandrous species, *Sabatia angularis* L (Gentianaceae): a comparison in three environments. Evolution 44:1129–1139.

Dudash, M.R., and C.B. Fenster. 1997. Multiyear study of pollen limitation and cost of reproduction in the iteroparous *Silene virginica*. Ecology 78:484–493.

Dudash, M., and C. Fenster. 2001. The role of breeding system and inbreeding depression in the maintenance of an outcrossing mating strategy in *Silene virginica* (Caryophyllaceae). American Journal of Botany 88:1953–1959.

Duffy, D.C. 1993a. Letter: Herbs and clearcutting: reply to Elliot and Loftis and Steinbeck. Conservation Biology 7:221–223.

Duffy, D.C. 1993b. Seeing the forest for the trees: response to Johnson et al. Conservation Biology 7:436–439.

Duffy, D.C., and A.J. Meier. 1992. Do Appalachian herbaceous understories ever recover from clearcutting? Conservation Biology 6:196–201.

Dufrêne, M., and P. Legendre. 1997. Species assemblages and indicator species: The need for a flexible asymmetrical approach. Ecological Monographs 67:345–366.

Duncan, R.P., H.L. Buckley, S.C. Urlich, G.H. Stewart, and J. Geritzlehner. 1998. Small-scale species richness in forest canopy gaps: the role of niche limitation versus the size of the species pool. Journal of Vegetation Science 9:455–460.

Dunham, A.E., H.R. Akçakaya, and T.S. Bridges. 2006. Using scalar models for precautionary assessments of threatened species. Conservation Biology 20:1499–1506.

Dunn, C.P., G.R. Gutenspergen, and J.R. Dorney. 1983. Catastrophic wind disturbance in an old-growth hemlock-hardwood forest. Canadian Journal of Botany 61:211–217.

Dunne, J.A., S.R. Saleska, M.L. Fischer, and J. Harte. 2004. Integrating experimental and gradient methods in ecological climate change research. Ecology 85:904–916.

Dupouey, J.L., E. Dambrine, J.D. Laffite, and C. Moares. 2002. Irreversible impact of past land use on forest soils and biodiversity. Ecology 83:2978–2984.

Durak, T. 2012. Changes in diversity of the mountain beech forest herb layer as a function of the forest management method. Forest Ecology and Management 276:154–164.

During, H.J. 1992. Ecological classification of bryophytes and lichens. Pages 1–31 in J. Bates and A. Farmer, editors. Bryophytes and lichens in a changing environment. Oxford, UK: Clarendon Press.

Dwyer, L.M., and G. Merriam. 1984. Decomposition of natural litter mixtures in a deciduous forest. Canadian Journal of Botany 62:2340–2344.

Dyer, J.M. 2010. Land-use legacies in a central Appalachian forest: differential response of trees and herbs to historic agricultural practices. Applied Vegetation Science 13:195–206.

Dynesius, M., and K. Hylander. 2007. Resilience of bryophyte communities to clear-cutting of boreal stream-side forests. Biological Conservation 135:423–434.

Dynesius, M., and R. Jansson. 2000. Evolutionary consequences of changes in species geographical distributions driven by Milankovitch climate oscillations. Proceedings of the National Academy of Sciences 97:9115–9120.

Dzwonko, Z. 2001. Assessment of light and soil conditions in ancient and recent woodlands by Ellenberg indicator values. Journal of Applied Ecology 38:942–951.

Dzwonko, Z., and S. Loster. 1989. Distribution of vascular plant species in small woodlands on the Western Carpathian foothills. Oikos 56:77–86.

Easley, M.C., and W.S. Judd. 1990. Vascular flora of the southern upland property of Paynes Prairie State Preserve, Alachua County, Florida. Castanea 55:142–186.

Easterling, M.R., S.P. Ellner, and P.M. Dixon. 2000. Size-specific sensitivity: Applying a new structured population model. Ecology 81:694–708.

Eckert, C.G., and C.R. Herlihy. 2004. Using a cost-benefit approach to understand the evolution of self-fertilization in plants: the perplexing case of *Aquilegia canadensis* (Ranunculaceae). Plant Species Biology 19:159–173.

Eckert, C.G., S. Kalisz, M.A. Geber, R. Sargent, E. Elle, P. Cheptou, C. Goodwillie, M.O. Johnston, J.K. Kelly, D.A. Moeller, E. Porcher, R.H. Ree, M. Vallejo-Marin, and A.A. Winn. 2010. Plant mating systems in a changing world. Trends in Ecology and Evolution 25:35–43.

Eckert, C.G., B. Ozimec, C.R. Herlihy, C.A. Griffin, and M.B. Routley. 2009. Floral morphology mediates temporal variation in the mating system of a self-compatible plant. Ecology 90:1540–1548.

Eckert, C.G., and A. Schaefer. 1998. Does self-pollination provide reproductive assurance in *Aquilegia canadensis* (Ranunculaceae)? American Journal of Botany 85:919–924.

Eckhart, V.M., M.A. Geber, and C.M. McGuire. 2004. Experimental studies of adaptation in *Clarkia xantiana*. I. Sources of trait variation across a subspecies border. Evolution 58: 59–70.

Eckstein, R.L., and A. Otte. 2005. Effects of cleistogamy and pollen source on seed production and offspring performance in three endangered violets. Basic and Applied Ecology 6:339–350.

Edens-Meier, R.M., N. Vance, Y. Luo, P. Li, E. Westhus, and P. Bernhardt. 2010. Pollen-pistil interactions in North American and Chinese *Cypripedium* L. (Orchidaceae). International Journal of Plant Sciences 171:370–381.

Edwards, J., and J.R. Jordan. 1992. Reversible anther opening in *Lilium philadelphicum* (Liliaceae): a possible means of enhancing male fitness. American Journal of Botany 79:144–148.

Egler, F.E. 1954. Vegetational science concepts. I. Initial floristic composition, a factor in old-field vegetation development. Vegetatio 4:412–417.

Ehleringer, J.R., and H.A. Mooney. 1978. Leaf hairs: Effects on physiological activity and adaptive value to a desert shrub. Oecologia 37:183–200.

Ehleringer, J.R., and K.S. Werk. 1986. Modifications of solar radiation absorption patterns and implications for carbon gain at the leaf level. Pages 57–82 in T.J. Givnish, editor. On the economy of plant form and function. London, Cambridge University Press.

Ehrenfeld, J.G. 1980. Understory response to canopy gaps of varying size in a mature oak forest. Bulletin of the Torrey Botanical Club 107:29–41.

Ehrenfeld, J.G. 2003. Effects of exotic plant invasions on soil nutrient cycling processes. Ecosystems 6:503–523.

Ehrenfeld, J.G. 2010. Ecosystem consequences of biological invasions. Annual Review of Ecology, Evolution, and Systematics 41:59–80.

Ehrenfeld, J.G., P. Kourtev, and W. Huang. 2001. Changes in soil functions following invasions of exotic understory plants in deciduous forests. Ecological Applications 11:1287–1300.

Ehrlén, J. 1995. Demography of the perennial herb *Lathyrus vernus*. II. Herbivory and population dynamics. Journal of Ecology 83:297–308.

Ehrlén, J. 1996. Spatiotemporal variation in predispersal seed predation intensity. Oecologia 108:708–713.

Ehrlén, J. 2002. Assessing the lifetime consequences of plant-animal interactions for the perennial herb *Lathyrus vernus* (Fabaceae). Perspectives in Plant Ecology, Evolution, and Systematics 5:145–163

Ehrlén, J., and O. Eriksson. 2000. Dispersal limitation and patch occupancy in forest herbs. Ecology 81:1667–1674.

Ehrlén, J., and K. Lehtila. 2002. How perennial are perennial plants? Oikos 98:308–322.

Eickmeier, W.G., and E.E. Schussler. 1993. Responses of the spring ephemeral *Claytonia virginica* L. to light and nutrient manipulations and implications for the "vernal-dam" hypothesis. Bulletin of the Torrey Botanical Club 120:157–165.

Eilts, J.A., G.G. Mittelbach, H.L. Reynolds, and K.L. Gross. 2011. Resource heterogeneity, soil fertility and species diversity: impacts of clonal species on plant communities. American Naturalist 177:574–588.

Eisenhauer, N., K. Yee, E.A. Johnson, M. Maraun, D. Parkinson, D. Straube, and S. Scheu. 2011. Positive relationship between herbaceous layer diversity and the performance of soil biota in a temperate forest. Soil Biology and Biochemistry 43:462–465.

Eliáš, P. 1981. Some ecophysiological leaf characteristics of components of spring synuzium in temperate deciduous forests. Biológia Plantarum 36:841–849.

Eliáš, P. 1983. Water relations pattern of understory species influenced by sunflecks. Biologia Plantarum 25:68–74.

Eliáš, P., and E. Masaroviová. 1986a. Chlorophyll content in leaves of spring geophytes in two temperate deciduous forest. Biologica (Bratislava) 41:477–485.

Eliáš, P., and E. Masaroviová. 1986b. Seasonal changes in leaf chlorophyll content of *Mercurialis perennis* growing in deciduous and coniferous forests. Photosynthetica 20:181–186.

Elliott, K.J., L.R. Boring, W.T. Swank, and B.R. Haines. 1997. Successional changes in plant species diversity and composition after clearcutting a Southern Appalachian watershed. Forest Ecology and Management 92:67–85.

Elliott, K.J., and J.D. Knoepp. 2005. The effects of three regeneration harvest methods on plant diversity and soil characteristics in the southern Appalachians. Forest Ecology and Management 211:296–317.

Elliott, K.J., and D.L. Loftis. 1993. Letter: Vegetation diversity after logging in the southern Appalachians. Conservation Biology 7:220–221.

Elliott, K.J., J.M. Vose, J.D. Knoepp, D.W. Johnson, W.T. Swank, and W. Jackson. 2008. Simulated effects of sulfur deposition on nutrient cycling in class I wilderness areas. Journal of Environmental Quality 37:1419–1431.

Elliott, N.B., and L.M. Elliott. 1994. Recognition and avoidance of the predator *Phymata americana* Melin on *Solidago odora* Ait. by late-season floral visitors. American Midland Naturalist 131:378–380.

Ellis, J.R., C.H. Pashley, J.M. Burke, and D.E. McCauley. 2006. High genetic diversity in a rare and endangered sunflower as compared to a common congener RID B-7897-2009. Molecular Ecology 15:2345–2355.

Ellum, D.S., M.S. Ashton, and T.G. Siccama. 2010. Spatial pattern in herb diversity and abundance of second growth mixed deciduous-evergreen forest of southern New England, USA. Forest Ecology and Management 259:1416–1426.

Elton, C.S. 1953. The ecology of invasions of animals and plants. Methuen, London.

Emery, K.M., P. Beuselinck, and J.T. English. 1999. Evaluation of the population dynamics of the forage legume *Lotus corniculatus* using matrix population models. New Phytologist 144:549–560.

Endels, P., D. Adriaens, K. Verheyen, and M. Hermy. 2004. Population structure and adult plant performance of forest herbs in three contrasting habitats. Ecography 27:225–241.

Endels, P., H. Jacquemyn, R. Brys, and M. Hermy. 2005. Rapid response to habitat restoration by the perennial *Primula veris* as revealed by demographic monitoring. Plant Ecology 176:143–156.

Endels, P., H. Jacquemyn, R. Brys, and M. Hermy. 2007. Genetic erosion explains deviation from demographic response to disturbance and year variation in relic populations of the perennial *Primula vulgaris*. Journal of Ecology 95:960–972.

Enright, N., and J. Ogden. 1979. Application of transition matrix models in forest dynamics: *Araucaria* in Papua New Guinea and *Nothofagus* in New Zealand. Australian Journal of Zoology 4:3–23.

Enright, N.J., M. Franco, and J. Silvertown. 1995. Comparing plant life histories using elasticity analysis: the importance of lifespan and the number of life cycle stages. Oecologia 104:79–84.

Eriksson, O. 1988. Ramet behavior and population growth in the clonal herb *Potentilla anserina*. Journal of Ecology 76:522-536.

Eriksson, O. 1992. Population structure and dynamics of the clonal dwarf-shrub *Linnaea borealis*. Journal of Vegetation Science 3:61–68.

Eriksson, O. 1993. The species-pool hypothesis and plant community diversity. Oikos 68:371–374.

Eriksson, O. 1995. Asynchronous flowering reduces seed predation in the perennial forest herb *Actaea spicata*. Acta Oecologica-International Journal of Ecology 16:195–203.

Eriksson, O. 1997. Colonization dynamics and relative abundance of three plant species (*Antennaria dioica, Hieracium pilosella* and *Hypochoeris maculata*) in dry semi-natural grassland. Ecography 20:559–568.

Eriksson, O., and J. Ehrlén. 1992. Seed and microsite limitation of recruitment in plant populations. Oecologia 91:360–364.

Eriksson, O., and A. Jakobsson. 1998. Abundance, distribution and life histories of grassland plants: a comparative study of 81 species. Journal of Ecology 86:922–933.

Eriksson, O., and K. Kiviniemi. 1999. Site occupancy, recruitment and extinction thresholds in grassland plants: an experimental study. Biological Conservation 87:319–325.

Eschtruth, A.K., and J.J. Battles. 2008. Deer herbivory alters forest response to canopy decline caused by an exotic insect pest. Ecological Applications 18:360–376.

Eschtruth, A.K., and J.J. Battles. 2009. Acceleration of exotic plant invasion in a forested ecosystem by a generalist herbivore. Conservation Biology 23:388–399.

Eshleman, K.N., R.P. Morgan II, J.R. Webb, F.A. Deviney, and J.N. Galloway. 1998. Temporal patterns of nitrogen leakage from midAppalachian forested watersheds: Role of insect defoliation. Water Resources Research 34:2017–2030.

Esseen, P.A., B. Ehnström, L. Ericson, and K. Sjöberg. 1997. Boreal forests. Ecological Bulletins 46:16–47.

Estes, J.A., J. Terborgh, J.S. Brashares, M.E. Power, J. Berger, W.J. Bond, S.R. Carpenter, T.E. Essington, R.D. Holt, J.B.C. Jackson, R.J. Marquis, L. Oksanen, T. Oksanen, R.T. Paine, E.K. Pikitch, W.J. Ripple, S.A. Sandin, M. Scheffer, T.W. Schoener, J.B. Shurin,

A.R.E. Sinclair, M.E. Soulé, R. Virtanen, and D.A. Wardle. 2011. Trophic downgrading of planet earth. Science 333:301–306.

Estill, J.C., and M.B. Cruzan. 2001. Phytogeography of rare plant species endemic to the southeastern United States. Castanea 66:3–23.

Ethier, G.J., N.J. Livingston, D.L. Harrison, T.A. Black, and J.A. Moran. 2006. Low stomatal and internal conductance to CO_2 versus Rubisco deactivation as determinants of the photosynthetic decline of ageing evergreen leaves. Plant, Cell and Environment 29: 2168–2184.

Etterson, J.R., and R.G. Shaw. 2001. Constraint to adaptive evolution in response to global warming. Science 294:151–154.

Evans, G.C. 1956. An area survey method of investigating the distribution of light intensity in woodlands, with particular reference to sunflecks. Journal of Ecology 44:391–428.

Evans, J.R. 1986. A quantitative analysis of light distribution between the two photosystems, considering variation in both the relative amounts of the chlorophyll-protein complexes and the spectral quality of light. Photobiochemistry and Photobiophysics 10:135–147.

Evans, J.R. 1996. Carbon dioxide profiles do reflect light absorption profiles in leaves. Australian Journal of Plant Physiology 22:79–84.

Evans, J.R. 1999. Leaf anatomy enables more equal access to light and CO_2 between chloroplasts. New Phytologist 143:93–104.

Evans, L.S., J. H. Adamski, and J. R. Renfro. 1996a. Relationships between cellular injury, visible injury of leaves, and ozone exposure levels for several dicotyledonous plant species at Great Smoky Mountains National Park. Environmental and Experimental Botany 36:229–237.

Evans, L.S., K. Albury, and N. Jennings. 1996b. Relationships between anatomical characteristics and ozone sensitivity of leaves of several herbaceous dicotyledonous plant species at Great Smoky Mountains National Park. Environmental and Experimental Botany 36:413–420.

Evans, M.E.K., R.W. Dolan, E.S. Menges, and D.R. Gordon. 2000. Genetic diversity and reproductive biology in *Warea carteri* (Brassicaceae), a narrowly endemic Florida scrub annual. American Journal of Botany 87:372–381.

Evans, M.E.K., K.E. Holsinger, and E.S. Menges. 2008. Modeling the effect of fire on the demography of *Dicerandra frutescens* ssp. *frutescens* (Lamiaceae), an endangered plant endemic to Florida scrub. Population Ecology 50:53–62.

Evans, M.E.K., K.E. Holsinger, and E.S. Menges. 2010. Fire, vital rates, and population viability: a hierarchical Bayesian analysis of the endangered Florida scrub mint. Ecological Monographs 80:627–649.

Everett, R.L., S.H. Sharrow, and R.O. Meeuwig. 1983. Pinyon-Juniper woodland understory distribution patterns and species associations. Bulletin of the Torrey Botanical Club 110:454–463.

Everham, E.M., III, and N.V.L. Brokaw. 1996. Forest damage and recovery from catastrophic wind. Botanical Review 62:114–185.

Everson, D.A., and D.H. Boucher. 1998. Tree species-richness and topographic complexity along the riparian edge of the Potomac River. Forest Ecology and Management 109:305–314.

Ewel, J., D. O'Dowd, J. Bergelson, C. Daehler, C. D'Antonio, L. Gomez, D. Gordon, R. Hobbs, A. Holt, K. Hopper, C. Hughes, M. LaHart, R. Leakey, W. Lee, L. Loope, D. Lorence, S. Louda, A. Lugo, P. McEvoy, D. Richardson, and P. Vitousek. 1999. Deliberate introductions of species: research needs—benefits can be reaped, but risks are high. BioScience 49:619–630.

F.A.O. (Food and Agriculture Organization). 2001. Global Forest Resources Assessment 2—Main Report. FAO Forestry Paper 140. Food and Agriculture Organization of the United Nations, Rome [N01FAO01ICEC].

Facelli, J.M., and S.T.A. Pickett. 1991. Plant litter—its dynamics and effects on plant community structure. Botanical Review 57:1–32.

Faegri, K., and L. van der Pijl. 1979. The principles of pollination ecology. New York: Pergamon Press.

Faestel, M. 2012. Classification and description of alluvial plant communities of the North Carolina coastal plain. M.S. thesis, University of North Carolina at Chapel Hill, NC.

Fajvan, M.A., and J.M. Wood. 1996. Stand structure and development after gypsy moth defoliation in the Appalachian Plateau. Forest Ecology and Management 89:79–88.

Falinski, J.B. 1978. Uprooted trees, their distribution and influence in the primeval forest biotope. Vegetatio 38:175–183.

Falk, D.A., and K.H. Holsinger, editors. 1991. Genetics and conservation of rare plants. Center for Plant Conservation. Oxford University Press, Oxford, UK.

Falk, K.J., D.M. Burke, K.A. Elliott, and S.B. Holmes. 2008. Effects of single-tree and group selection harvesting on the diversity and abundance of spring forest herbs in deciduous forests in southwestern Ontario. Forest Ecology and Management 255:2486–2494.

Falkengren-Grerup, U., D.J. ten Brink, and J. Brunet. 2006. Land use effects on soil N, P, C and pH persist over 40–80 years of forest growth on agricultural soils. Forest Ecology and Management 225:74–81.

Fangmeier, A. 1989. Effects of open-top fumigations with SO_2, NO_2 and ozone on the native herb layer of a beech forest. Environmental and Experimental Botany 29:199–213.

Fargione, J.E., and D. Tilman. 2005. Diversity decreases invasion via both sampling and complementarity effects. Ecology Letters 8:604–611.

Farnsworth, E.J., J. Nunez-Farfan, S.A. Careaga, and F.A. Bazzaz. 1995. Phenology and growth of three temperate forest life forms in response to artificial soil warming. Journal of Ecology 83:967–977.

Farnsworth, E.J., and D.E. Ogurcak. 2006. Biogeography and decline of rare plants in New England: Historical evidence and contemporary monitoring. Ecological Applications 16:1327–1337.

Farnsworth, E.J., and D.E. Ogurcak. 2008. Functional groups of rare plants differ in levels of imperilment. American Journal of Botany 95:943–953.

Farrington, S.J., R.M. Muzika, T.M. Knight, and D.G. Drees. 2005. Effects of deer herbivory on population dynamics of American ginseng (*Panax quinquefolius* L.). Missouri Natural Resources Conference.

Farrington, S.J., R. Muzika, D. Drees, and T.M. Knight. 2009. Interactive effects of harvest and deer herbivory on the population dynamics of American ginseng. Conservation Biology 23:719–728.

Felsenstein, J. 1985. Phylogenies and the comparative method. American Naturalist 125:1–15.

Fenner, M., and K. Thompson. 2005. The ecology of seeds. Cambridge, UK: Cambridge University Press.

Fenster, C.B., W.S. Armbruster, P. Wilson, M.R. Dudash, and J.D. Thomson. 2004. Pollination syndromes and floral specialization. Annual Review of Ecology and Systematics 35:375–403.

Fenton, N.J., C. Béland, S. De Blois, and Y. Bergeron. 2007. Sphagnum establishment and expansion in black spruce (*Picea mariana*) boreal forests. Canadian Journal of Botany 85:43–50.

Fenton, N.J. and Y. Bergeron. 2006. Facilitative succession in a boreal bryophyte community driven by changes in available moisture and light. Journal of Vegetation Science 17:65–76.

Fenton, N.J. and Y. Bergeron. 2007. Sphagnum community change after partial harvest in black spruce boreal forests. Forest Ecology and Management 242:24–33.

Fenton, N.J. and K.A. Frego. 2005. Bryophyte (moss and liverwort) conservation under remnant canopy in managed forests. Biological Conservation 122:417–43

Fenton, N., N. Lecomte, S. Légaré, and Y. Bergeron. 2005. Paludification in black spruce (*Picea mariana*) forests of eastern Canada: Potential factors and management implications. Forest Ecology and Management 213:151–159.

Ferguson, W.S., and E.R. Armitage. 1944. The chemical composition of Bracken (*Pteridium aquilinum*). Journal of Agricultural Science 34:165–171.

Fike, J., and W.A. Niering. 1999. Four decades of old field vegetation development and the role of *Celastrus orbiculatus* in the northeastern United States. Journal of Vegetation Science 10:483–492.

Finnie, T.J.R., C.D. Preston, M.O. Hill, P. Uotila, and M.J. Crawley. 2007. Floristic elements in European vascular plants: an analysis based on Atlas Florae Europaeae. Journal of Biogeography 34:1848–1872.

Fisher, J., and K. Jayachandran. 2002. Arbuscular mycorrhizal fungi enhance seedling growth in two endangered plant species from South Florida. International Journal of Plant Sciences 163:559–566.

Fitter, A.H., and R.S.R. Fitter. 2002. Rapid changes in flowering time in British plants. Science 296:1689–1691.

Fitter, A.H., R.S.R. Fitter, I.T.B. Harris, and M.H. Williamson. 1995. Relationships between first flowering date and temperature in the flora of a locality in central England. Functional Ecology 9:55–60.

Flader, S.L. 1974. Thinking like a mountain: Aldo Leopold and the evolution of an ecological attitude toward deer, wolves, and forests. Madison, WI: University of Wisconsin Press.

Flanagan, L.B., and W. Moser. 1985. Flowering phenology, floral display and reproductive success in dioecious, *Aralia nudicaulis* L. (Araliaceae). Oecologia 68:23–28.

Fleischner, T.L. 1994. Ecological costs of livestock grazing in western North America. Conservation Biology 8:629–644.

Fleming, P., and R. Kanal. 1995. Annotated checklist of vascular plants of Rock Creek Park, National Park Service, Washington D.C. Castanea 60:283–316.

Fleming, R.L., and K.A. Baldwin. 2008. Effects of harvest intensity and aspect on a boreal transition tolerant hardwood forest. I. Initial postharvest understory composition. Canadian Journal of Forest Research 38:685–697.

Fletcher, J.D., W.J. McShea, L.A. Shipley, and D. Shumway. 2001a. Use of common forest forbs to measure browsing pressure by white-tailed deer (*Odocoileus virginianus* Zimmerman) in Virginia, USA. Natural Areas Journal 21:172–176.

Fletcher, J.D., L.A. Shipley, W.J. McShea, and D.L. Shumway. 2001b. Wildlife herbivory and rare plants: the effects of white-tailed deer, rodents, and insects on growth and survival of Turk's cap lily. Biological Conservation 101:229–238.

Flinn, K.M. 2007. Microsite-limited recruitment controls fern colonization of post-agricultural forests. Ecology 88:3103–3114.

Flinn, K.M. 2011. Why are acidophilic plants abundant in post-agricultural forests? Journal of the Torrey Botanical Society 138:73–76.

Flinn, K.M., T.C. Gouhier, M.J. Lechowicz, and M.J. Waterway. 2010. The role of dispersal in shaping plant community composition of wetlands within an old-growth forest. Journal of Ecology 98:1292–1299.

Flinn, K.M., and P.L. Marks. 2004. Land-use history and forest herb diversity in Tompkins County, New York, USA.Pages 81–95 in O. Honnay, K. Verheyen, B. Bossuyt, and M. Hermy, editors. Forest Biodiversity: Lessons from History for Conservation. Wallingford, UK: CABI.

Flinn, K.M., and P.L. Marks. 2007. Agricultural legacies in forest environments: Tree communities, soil properties, and light availability. Ecological Applications 17:452–463.

Flinn, K.M., and M. Vellend. 2005. Recovery of forest plant communities in post-agricultural landscapes. Frontiers in Ecology and the Environment 3:243–250.

Flinn, K.M., M. Vellend, and P.L. Marks. 2005. Environmental causes and consequences of forest clearance and agricultural abandonment in central New York, USA. Journal of Biogeography 32:439–452.

Flint, A.L., and S.W. Childs. 1987. Calculation of solar radiation in mountainous terrain. Agricultural and Forest Meteorology 40:233–249.

Flora of North America editorial committee. 1993+. Flora of North America north of Mexico. 16+ vols. New York and Oxford, UK: Oxford University Press.

Ford, W.M., R.H. Odom, P.E. Hale, and B.R. Chapman. 2000. Stand-age, stand characteristics, and landform effects on understory herbaceous communities in southern Appalachian cove-hardwoods. Biological Conservation 93:237–246.

Formann, R.T.T., and M. Godron. 1986. Landscape ecology. J. Wiley & Sons, New York

Foster, B.L., and D. Tilman. 2000. Dynamic and static vies of succession: testing the descriptive power of the chronosequence approach. Plant Ecology 146:1–10.

Foster, D.K. 1993. *Taxus canadensis* marsh. Its range, ecology, and prospects in the state of Wisconsin. M.S. thesis, University of Wisconsin–Madison, WI.

Foster, D.R. 1984. The dynamics of Sphagnum in forest and peatland communities in southeastern Labrador, Canada. Arctic 37:133–140

Foster, D.R. 1985. Vegetation development following fire in *Picea mariana* (black spruce)–*Pleurozium* forests of south-eastern Labrador, Canada. Journal of Ecology 73:517–534.

Foster, D.R. 1988a. Species and stand response to catastrophic wind in central New England, U.S.A. Journal of Ecology 76:135–151.

Foster, D.R. 1988b. Disturbance history, community organization and vegetation dynamics of the old-growth Pisgah Forest, southwestern New Hampshire, U.S.A. Journal of Ecology 76:105–134.

Foster, D.R. 1992. Land-use history (1730–1990) and vegetation dynamics in central New England, USA. Journal of Ecology 80:753–772.

Foster, D.R., and E.R. Boose. 1992. Patterns of forest damage resulting from catastrophic wind in central New England, U.S.A. Journal of Ecology 80:79–98.

Foster, D.R., and G.A. King. 1986. Vegetation pattern and diversity in S.E. Labrador, Canada: *Betula papyrifera* (Birch) forest development in relation to fire history and physiography. Journal of Ecology 74:465–483.

Foster, D.R., G. Motzkin, and B. Slater. 1998. Land-use history as long-term broad-scale disturbance: Regional forest dynamics in central New England. Ecosystems 1:96–119.

Fournier-Level, A., A. Korte, M.D. Cooper, M. Nordborg, J. Schmitt, and A.M. Wilczek. 2011. A map of local adaptation in *Arabidopsis thaliana*. Science 334:86–89.

Fowler, D. 1999. The global exposure of forests to air pollution. In Forest Growth Responses to the Pollution Climate of the 21st Century, L.J. Sheppard and J.N Cape, eds. Lancaster, UK: Kluwer Academic Publishers, pp. 5–32.

Fowler, W.B. 1974. Microclimate. Pages N1 to N18 in O.P. Cramer, editor. Environmental effects of forest residues management in the Pacific Northwest: a state of knowledge compendium. United States Forest Service, Pacific Northwest Forest Experiment Station, General Technical Report PNW-24. Portland, OR.

Fox, G.A., and C.K. Kelly. 1993. Plant phenology: Selection and neutrality. Trends in Ecology and Evolution 8:34–55.

Fox, L.R. 2007. Climatic and biotic stochasticity: Disparate causes of converence demographies in rare, sympatric plants. Conservation Biology 6:1556–1561.

Francis, C.M., M.J.W. Austen, J.M. Bowles, and W.B. Draper. 2000. Assessing floristic quality in Southern Ontario woodlands. Natural Areas Journal 20:66–77.

Franco, M., and J. Silvertown. 1990. Plant demography: What do we know? Evolutionary Trends in Plants 4:74–76.

Franco, M., and J. Silvertown. 1994. On trade-offs, elasticities and the comparative method—A reply to Shea, Rees and Wood. Journal of Ecology 82:958–958.

Franco, M., and J. Silvertown. 1996. Life history variation in plants: An exploration of the fast- slow continuum hypothesis. Philosophical Transactions of the Royal Society of London Series B-Biological Sciences 351:1341–1348.

Franco, M., and J. Silvertown. 2004. Comparative demography of plants based upon elasticities of vital rates. Ecology 85:531–538.

Frank, E.C., and R. Lee. l966. Potential solar beam irradiation on slopes: tables for 30° to 50° latitude. U.S.D.A. for Serv. Rocky Mt. For. Range Exp. Sta. Res. Pap. RM-18.

Franklin, J. 2010. Moving beyond static species distribution models in support of conservation biogeography. Diversity and Distributions 16:321–330.

Franklin, J.F., R.E. Jenkins, and R.M. Romancier. 1972. Research natural areas: contributors to environmental quality programs. Journal of Environmental Quality 1:133–139.

Franklin, M.A., J.M. Stucky, T.R. Wentworth, C. Brownie, and T. Roulston. 2006. Limitations to fruit and seed production by *Lysimachia asperulifolia* Poir. (Primulaceae), a rare plant species of the Carolinas. Journal of the Torrey Botanical Society 133:403–411.

Fraterrigo, J.M., T.C. Balser, and M.G. Turner. 2006. Microbial community variation and its relationship with nitrogen mineralization in historically altered forests. Ecology 87:570–579.

Fraterrigo, J.M., S.M. Pearson, and M.G. Turner. 2009. The response of understory herbaceous plants to nitrogen fertilization in forests of different land-use history. Forest Ecology and Management 257:2182–2188.

Fraterrigo, J.M., M.G. Turner, and S.M. Pearson. 2006a. Interactions between past land use, life-history traits and understory spatial heterogeneity. Landscape Ecology 21:777–790.

Fraterrigo, J.M., M.G. Turner, and S.M. Pearson. 2006b. Previous land use alters plant allocation and growth in forest herbs. Journal of Ecology 94:548–557.

Fredericksen, T.S., B.D. Ross, W. Hoffman, M.L. Morrison, J. Beyea, B.N. Johnson, M.B. Lester, and E. Ross. 1999. Short-term understory plant community responses to timber-harvesting intensity on non-industrial forestlands in Pennsylvania. Forest Ecology and Management 116:129–139.

Freestone, A.L., and B.D. Inouye. 2006. Dispersal limitation and environmental heterogeneity shape scale-dependent diversity patterns in plant communities. Ecology 87:2425–2432.

Frego, K.A. 1996. Regeneration of four boreal bryophytes: colonization of experimental gaps by naturally occuring propagules. Canadian Journal of Botany 74:1937–1942.

Frego, K.A., and T.J. Carleton. 1995. Microsite conditions and spatial pattern in a boreal bryophyte community. Canadian Journal of Botany 73:544–551.

Frelich, L.E., C.M. Hale, S. Scheu, A.R. Holdsworth, L. Heneghan, P.J. Bohlen, and P.B. Reich. 2006. Earthworm invasion into previously earthworm-free temperate and boreal forests. Biological Invasions 8:1235–1245.

Frelich, L.E., and C.G. Lorimer. 1985. Current and predicted long-term effects of deer browsing in hemlock forests in Michigan, USA. Biological Conservation 34:99–120.

Frelich, L.E., and P.B. Reich. 1995. Spatial patterns and succession in a Minnesota southern-boreal forest. Ecological Monographs 65:325–356.

Fridley, J.D., R.L. Brown, and J.F. Bruno. 2004. Null models of exotic invasion and scale-dependent patterns of native and exotic species richness. Ecology 85:3215–3222.

Fridley, J.D., and J.P. Wright. 2012. Drivers of secondary succession rates across temperate latitudes of the eastern USA: climate, soils, and species pools. Oecologia 168:1069–1077.

Frisvoll, A. 1997. Bryophytes of spruce forest stands in central Norway. Lindbergia 22:83–97.

Frisvoll, A.A., and T. Prestø. 1997. Spruce forest bryophytes in central Norway and their relationship to environmental factors including modern forestry. Ecography 20:3–18.

Fritz, R., and G. Merriam. 1994. Fencerow and forest edge vegetation structure in eastern Ontario farmland. Ecoscience 1:160–172.

Fritz-Sheridan, J.K. 1988. Reproductive biology of *Erythronium grandiflorum* varieties *grandiflorum* and *candidum*. American Journal of Botany 75:1–14.

Fröborg, H., and O. Eriksson. 2003. Predispersal seed predation and population dynamics in the perennial understorey herb *Actaea spicata*. Canadian Journal of Botany 81:1058–1069.

Frost, C. 2006. History and future of the longleaf pine ecosystem. In S. Jose, E. Jokela, and D. Miller, eds. Longleaf pine ecosystems: ecology, management, and restoration. New York: Springer-Verlag, pp. 9–48.

Frye, B. 2006. Deer wars: science, tradition, and the battle over managing whitetails in Pennsylvania. University Park, PA: Pennsylvania State University Press.

Fujimaki, R., A. Sakai, and N. Kaneko. 2009. Ecological risks of anthropogenic disturbance of nitrogen cycles in natural terrestrial ecosystems. Ecological Research 24:955–964.

Fukai, S., R. Kanechika, and A. Hasegawa. 2006. Effect of low temperature on breaking dormancy and flowering of *Arisaema sikokianum* (Araceae). Scientia Horticulturae 111:97–100.

Fuller, H.J. 1948. Carbon dioxide concentration of the atmosphere above Illinois forest and grassland. American Midland Naturalist 39:247–249.

Fuller, R.J. 2001. Responses of woodland birds to increasing numbers of deer: a review of evidence and mechanisms. Forestry 74:289–298.

Gagnon, D., and G.E. Bradfield. 1986. Relationships among forest strata and environment in southern coastal British Columbia. Canadian Journal of Forest Research 16:1264–1271.

Gagnon, D., A. LaFond, and L.P. Amiot. 1958. Mineral nutrient content of some forest plant leaves and the humus layer as related to site quality. Canadian Journal of Botany. 36:209–220.

Gaiser, R.N. 1951. Random sampling within circular plots by means of polar coordinates. Journal of Forestry 49:916–917.

Galen, C., R.C. Plowright, and J.D. Thomson. 1958. Floral biology and regulation of seed set and seed size in the lily, *Clintonia borealis*. American Journal of Botany. 72:1544–1552.

Garcia, M.B., F.X. Pico, and J. Ehrlén. 2008. Life span correlates with population dynamics in perennial herbaceous plants. American Journal of Botany. 95:258–262.

Gardner, R.H., and K.A.M. Engelhardt. 2008. Spatial processes that maintain biodiversity in plant communities. Perspectives in Plant Ecology, Evolution, and Systematics 9:211–228.

Garrett, H.E., G.S. Cox, and J.E. Roberts. 1978. Spatial and temporal variations in carbon dioxide concentrations in an oak-hickory forest ravine. Forest Science 24:180–190.

Garrott, R.A., P.J. White, and C.A.V. White. 1993. Overabundance: an issue for conservation biologists? Conservation Biology 7:944–949.

Garten, C.T. 1976. Correlations between concentrations of elements in plants. Nature 261:686–688.

Garten, C.T. 1978. Multivariate perspectives ion the ecology of plant mineral element composition. American Naturalist 112:533–544.

Gaston, K.J. 2003. The Structure and Dynamics of Geographic Ranges. Oxford, UK: Oxford University Press.

Gates, F.C. 1930. Aspen association in northern lower Michigan. Botanical Gazette 90:233–259.

Gauthier, S., L. De Grandpré, and Y. Bergeron. 2000. Differences in forest composition in two boreal forest ecoregions of Quebec. Journal of Vegetation Science 11:781–790.

Gazol, A., and R. Ibáñez. 2009. Different response to environmental factors and spatial variables of two attributes (cover and diversity) of the understory layers. Forest Ecology and Management 258:1267–1274.

Geber, M.A., and T.E. Dawson. 1993. Evolutionary responses of plants to global change. In P.M. Kareiva, J.G. Kingsolver, and R.B. Huey, eds. Biotic Interactions and Global Change., Sunderland, MA: Sinauer Associates, pp. 179–197.

Geber, M.A., and V.M. Eckhart. 2005. Experimental studies of adaptation in *Clarkia xantiana*. II. Fitness variation across a subspecies border. Evolution 59:521–531.

Geber, M.A., H. de Kroon, and M.A. Watson. 1997a. Organ preformation in mayapple as a mechanism for historical effects on demography. Journal of Ecology 85:211–223.

Geber, M.A., M.S. Watson, and H. de Kroon. 1997b. Organ preformation, development, and resource allocation in perennials. Pages 113–142 in F.A. Bazzaz and J. Grace, editors. Plant resource allocation. Academic Press, San Diego, CA.

Gehlhausen, S.M., Schwartz, M.W., and C.K. Augspurger. 2000. Vegetation and microclimatic edge effects in two mixedmesophytic forest fragments. Plant Ecology 147:21–35.

George, L.O. 1996. The understory as an ecological filter. Ph.D. dissertation, Harvard University, Cambridge, MA.

George, L.O., and F.A. Bazzaz. 1999a. The fern understory as an ecological filter: Emergence and establishment of canopy-tree seedlings. Ecology 80:833–845.

George, L.O., and F.A. Bazzaz. 1999b. The fern understory as an ecological filter: Growth and survival of canopy tree seedlings. Ecology 80:846–856.

Gerhardt, F., and D.R. Foster. 2002. Physiographical and historical effects on forest vegetation in central New England, USA. Journal of Biogeography 29:1421–1437.

Gering, J.C., T.O. Crist, and J.A. Veech. 2003. Additive partitioning of species diversity across multiple spatial scales: Implications for regional conservation of biodiversity. Conservation Biology 17:488–499.

Gerloff, G.C., D.D. Morre, and T.T. Curtis. 1964. Mineral content of native plants of Wisconsin. University of Wisconsin. College of Agriculture, Experiment Station. Research Report No. 14.

Germino, M.J., and W.K. Smith. 2000. High resistance to lowtemperature photoinhibition in two alpine, snowbank species. Physiologia Plantarum 110:89–95.

Ghent, A.W., D.A. Fraser, and J.B. Thomas. 1957. Studies of regeneration in forest stands devastated by the spruce budworm. I. Evidence of trends in forest succession during the first decade following budworm devastation. Forest Science 3:184–208.

Gibson, D.J., E.D. Adams, J.S. Ely, D.J. Gustafson, D. McEwan, and T.R. Evans. 2000. Eighteen years of herbaceous layer recovery of a recreation area in a mesic forest. Journal of the Torrey Botanical Society 127:230–239.

Gibson, D.J., J.S. Ely, and S.L. Collins. 1999. The core-satellite species hypothesis provides a theoretical basis for Grime's classification of dominant, subordinate, and transient species. Journal of Ecology 87:1064–1067.

Giladi, I., Y. Ziv, F. May, and F. Jeltsch. 2011. Scale-dependent determinants of plant species richness in a semi-arid fragmented agro-ecosystem. Journal of Vegetation Science 22:983–996.

Gildner, B.S., and D.W. Larson. 1992. Seasonal changes in photosynthesis in the desiccation-tolerant fern *Polypodium virginianum*. Oecologia 89:383–389.

Gill, D.S., and P.L. Marks. 1991. Tree and shrub seedling colonization of old fields in central New York. Ecological Monographs 61:183–205.

Gilliam, F.S. 1988. Interactions of fire with nutrients in the herbaceous layer of a nutrient-poor coastal plain forest. Bulletin of the Torrey Botanical Club 115:265–271.

Gilliam, F.S. 1991. The significance of fire in an oligotrophic forest ecosystem. In S.C. Nodvin and T.A. Waldrop, editors. Fire and the environment: ecological and cultural perspectives: Proceedings of an international symposium. March 20–24, 1990. Knoxville, TN. United States Forest Service, Southeastern Forest Experiment Station, General Technical Report SE-69. Asheville, NC.

Gilliam, F.S. 2002. Effects of harvesting on herbaceous layer diversity of a central Appalachian hardwood forest. Forest Ecology and Management 155:33–43.

Gilliam, F.S. 2006. Response of the herbaceous layer of forest ecosystems to excess nitrogen deposition. Journal of Ecology 94:1176–1191.

Gilliam, F.S. 2007. The ecological significance of the herbaceous layer in forest ecosystems. BioScience 57:845–858.

Gilliam, F.S. 2014. Nitrogen biogeochemistry research at Fernow Experimental Forest, West Virginia, USA: soils, biodiversity, and climate change. In M.A. Sutton, et al., editors. Nitrogen Deposition, Critical Loads and Biodiversity: Proceedings of the INI/ CLRTAP/CBD Expert Workshop, November 16–18, 2009. New York: Springer-Verlag.

Gilliam, F.S., and M.B. Adams. 1996a. Wetfall deposition and precipitation chemistry for a central Appalachian forest. Journal of the Air and Waste Management Association 46:978–984.

Gilliam, F.S., and M.B. Adams. 1996b. Plant and soil nutrients in young versus mature central Appalachian hardwood stands. Pages 109–118 in K.W. Gottschalk and S.L.C. Fosbroke, editors. 10th Central Hardwood Forest Conference. U. S. Forest Service, Northeastern Forest Experiment Station. General Technical Report NE-197.

Gilliam, F.S., and M.B. Adams. 2011. Effects of nitrogen on temporal and spatial patterns of nitrate in streams and soil solution of a central hardwood forest. ISRN Ecology, Article ID 138487, doi:10.5402/2011/138487.

Gilliam, F.S., M.B. Adams, and B.M. Yurish. 1996. Ecosystem nutrient responses to chronic nitrogen inputs at Fernow Experimental Forest, West Virginia. Canadian Journal of Forest Research 26:196–205.

Gilliam, F.S., and N.L. Christensen. 1986. Herb-layer response to burning in pine flatwoods of the lower Coastal Plain of South Carolina. Bulletin of the Torrey Botanical Club 113:42–45.

Gilliam, F.S., A.W. Hockenberry, and M.B. Adams. 2006. Effects of atmospheric nitrogen deposition on the herbaceous layer of a central Appalachian hardwood forest. Journal of the Torrey Botanical Society 133:240–254.

Gilliam, F.S., R.L. McCulley, and J.A. Nelson. 2011. Spatial variability in soil microbial communities in a nitrogen-saturated hardwood forest watershed. Soil Science Society of America Journal 75:280–286.

Gilliam, F.S., W.J. Platt, and R.K. Peet. 2006. Natural disturbances and the physiognomy of pine savannas: a phenomenological model. Applied Vegetation Science 9:83–96.

Gilliam, F.S., and M.R. Roberts. 1995. Impacts of forest management on plant diversity. Ecological Applications 5:911–912.

Gilliam, F.S., and M.R. Roberts. 2003a. Interactions between the herbaceous layer and overstory canopy of eastern forests. In F. S. Gilliam and M. R. Roberts, eds. The Herbaceous Layer in Forests of Eastern North America. New York: Oxford University Press, pp. 198–223.

Gilliam, F.S., and M.R. Roberts. 2003b. The dynamic nature of the herbaceous layer: synthesis and future directions for research. In F.S. Gilliam and M.R. Roberts, eds. The herbaceous layer in forests of eastern North America. New York: Oxford University Press, pp. 323–337.

Gilliam, F.S., and N.L. Turrill. 1993. Herbaceous layer cover and biomass in a young versus a mature stand of a central Appalachian hardwood forest. Bulletin of the Torrey Botanical Club 120:445–450.

Gilliam, F.S., N.L. Turrill, and M.B. Adams. 1995. Herbaceous-layer and overstory species in clear-cut and mature central Appalachian hardwood forests. Ecological Applications 5:947–955.

Gilliam, F.S., N.L. Turrill, S.D. Aulick, D.K. Evans, and M.B. Adams. 1994. Herbaceous layer and soil response to experimental acidification in a central Appalachian hardwood forest. Journal of Environmental Quality 23:835–844.

Gilliam, F.S., B.M. Yurish, and M.B. Adams. 2001. Temporal and spatial variation of nitrogen transformations in nitrogen-saturated soils of a central Appalachian hardwood forest. Canadian Journal of Forest Research 31:1768–1785.

Gilliam, F.S., B.M. Yurish, and L.M. Goodwin. 1993. Community composition of an old-growth longleaf pine forest: relationship to soil texture. Bulletin of the Torrey Botanical Club 120:287–294.

Gilpin, M.S. 1991. The genetic effective size of a metapopulation. Biological Journal of the Linnean Society 42:165–175.

Gilpin, M.S., and I. Hanski. 1991. Metapopulation dynamics: empirical and theoretical investigations. Academic Press, London.

Gitzendanner, M.A., and P.S. Soltis. 2000. Patterns of genetic variation in rare and widespread plant congeners. American Journal of Botany 87:783–792.

Givnish, T.J. 1982. On the adaptive significance of leaf height in forest herbs. American Naturalist 120:353–381.

Givnish, T.J. 1986. Biomechanical constraints on crown geometry in forest herbs. Pages 525–583 in T.J. Givnish, editor. On the economy of plant form and function. Cambridge University Press, London.

Givnish, T.J. 1987. Comparative studies of leaf form: assessing the relative roles of selective pressures and phylogenetic constraints. New Phytologist 106:131–160.

Givnish, T.J., and G.J. Vermeij. 1976. Sizes and shapes of liana leaves. American Naturalist 110:743–778.

Glasgow, L.S., and G.R. Matlack. 2007. Prescribed burning and understory composition in a temperate deciduous forest, Ohio, USA. Forest Ecology and Management 238:54–64.

Gleason, H.A. 1926. The individualistic concept of the plant association. Bulletin of the Torrey Botanical Club 53:1–20.

Gleason, H.A., and A. Cronquist. 1991. Manual of vascular plants of the northeastern United States and adjacent Canada, 2nd ed. New York Botanical Garden, New York.

Gleditsch, J.M., and T.A. Carlo. 2011. Fruit quantity of invasive shrubs predicts the abundance of common native avian frugivores in central Pennsylvania. Diversity and Distributions 2:244–253.

Glenn-Lewin, D.C. 1977. Species diversity in North American temperate forests. *Vegetatio* 33:153–162.

Glennon, K.L., J.T. Donaldson, and S.A. Church. 2011. Evidence for hybridization between the endangered roan mountain bluet, *Houstonia purpurea* var. *montana* (Rubiaceae) and its common congener. *Journal of the Torrey Botanical Society* 138:272–286.

Gliessman, S.R. 1976. Allelopathy in a broad spectrum of environments as illustrated by bracken. Botanical Journal of the Linnean Society 73:95–104.

Glitzenstein, J.S., P.A. Harcombe, and D.R. Streng. 1986. Disturbance, succession, and maintenance of species diversity in an east Texas forest. Ecological Monographs 6:243–258.

Glitzenstein, J.S., D.R. Streng, and D.D. Wade. 2003. Fire frequency effects on longleaf pine (*Pinus palustris* P. Miller) vegetation in South Carolina and northeast Florida, USA. Natural Areas Journal 23:22–37.

Glover, G.R., J.L. Creighton, and D.H. Gjerstad. 1989. Herbaceous weed control increases loblolly pine growth. Journal of Forestry 87:47–50.

Godt, M J.W., and J.L. Hamrick. 1996. Genetic structure of two endangered pitcher plants, *Sarracenia jonesii* and *Sarracenia oreophila* (Sarraceniaceae). American Journal of Botany 83:1016–1023.

Godt, M.J., B.R. Johnson, and J.L. Hamrick. 1996. Genetic diversity and population size in four rare southern Appalachian plant species. Conservation Biology 10: 796–805.

Godt, M.J.W., and J.L. Hamrick. 1998a. Allozyme diversity in the endangered pitcher plant *Sarracenia rubra* ssp. *alabamensis* (Sarraceniaceae) and its close relative *S. rubra* ssp. *rubra*. American Journal of Botany 85:802–810.

Godt, M.J.W., and J.L. Hamrick. 1998b. Low allozyme diversity in *Schwalbea americana* (Scrophulariaceae), an endangered plant species. Journal of Heredity 89:89–93.

Godt, M., and J. Hamrick. 2001. Genetic diversity in rare southeastern plants. Natural Areas Journal 21:61–70.

Godt, M.J.W., J.L. Hamrick, and S. Bratton. 1995. Genetic diversity in a threatened wetland species, *Helonias bullata* (Liliaceae). Conservation Biology 9:596–604.

Godt, M., J. Walker, and J. Hamrick. 2004. Allozyme diversity in *Macbridea alba* (lamiaceae), an endemic florida mint. Journal of Heredity 95:244–249.

Goebel, P.C., D.M. Hix, and A.M. Olivero. 1999. Seasonal ground-flora patterns and site factor relationships of second-growth and old-growth south-facing forest ecosystems, southeastern Ohio, USA. Natural Areas Journal 19:12–21.

Goetsch, C., J. Wigg, A.A. Royo, T. Ristau, and W.P. Carson. 2011. Chronic overbrowsing and biodiversity collapse in a forest understory in Pennsylvania: results from a 60 year-old deer exclusion plot. Journal of the Torrey Botanical Society 138: 220–224.

Goldblum, D. 1997. The effects of treefall gaps on understory vegetation in New York, USA. Journal of Vegetation Science 8:125–132.

Goldblum, D. 1998. Regeneration in unmanaged conifer plantations, upstate New York. Northeastern Naturalist 5:343–358.

Goldblum, D., and S.W. Beatty. 1999. Influence of an old field/forest edge on a northeastern United States deciduous forest understory community. Journal of the Torrey Botanical Society 126:335–343.

Gondard, H., J. Sandrine, J. Aronson, and S. Lavorel. 2003. Plant functional types: a promising tool for management and restoration of degraded lands. Applied Vegetation Science 6:223–234.

Gonzales, E., and J. Hamrick. 2005. Distribution of genetic diversity among disjunct populations of the rare forest understory herb, *Trillium reliquum*. Heredity 95:306–314.

Gonzales, E., J.L. Hamrick, and S. Chang. 2008. Identification of glacial refugia in southeastern North America by phylogeographical analyses of a forest understorey plant, *Trillium cuneatum*. Journal of Biogeography 35:844–852.

Gonzalez, V.C. 1972. The ecology of Hexastylis arifolia, an evergreen herb in the North Carolina deciduous forest. Ph.D. dissertation, Duke University, Durham, NC.

Goodale, C.L., N.B. Dise, and M.A. Sutton. 2011. Special issue on nitrogen deposition, critical loads, and biodiversity. Environmental Pollution 159:2211–2213.

Goodwillie, C., S. Kalisz, and C. Eckert. 2005. The evolutionary enigma of mixed mating systems in plants: occurrence, theoretical explanations, and empirical evidence. Annual Review of Ecology, Evolution, and Systematics 36:47–79.

Goodwillie, C., R.D. Sargent, C.G. Eckert, E. Elle, M.A. Geber, M.O. Johnston, S. Kalisz, D.A. Moeller, R.H. Ree, M. Vallejo-Marin, and A.A. Winn. 2010. Correlated evolution of mating system and floral display traits in flowering plants and its implications for the distribution of mating system variation. New Phytologist 185:311–321.

Gorchov, D.L., and D.E. Trisel. 2003. Competitive effects of the invasive shrub, *Lonicera mackii* (Rupr.) Herder (Caprifoliaceae), on the growth and survival of native tree seedlings. Plant Ecology 166:13–24.

Gordon, D.R. 1998. Effects of invasive, non-indigenous plants species on ecosystem processes: lessons from Florida. Ecological Applications 8:975–989.

Goryshina, T.K. 1972. Recherches écophysiologiques sur les plantes éphéméroïdes printaniéres dans les chénaies de la zone, forét-steppe de la Russie central. Oecologia Plantarum 7:241–258.

Gosz, J.R., G.E. Likens, and F.H. Bormann. 1973. Nutrient release from decomposing leaf and branch litter in the Hubbard Brook forest, New Hampshire. Ecological Monographs 43:173–191.

Gotelli, N.J., and A.M. Ellison. 2002. Nitrogen deposition and extinction risk in the northern pitcher plant, *Sarracenia purpurea*. Ecology 83:2758–2765.

Gotelli, N.J., and A.M. Ellison. 2006. Forecasting extinction risk with nonstationary matrix models. Ecological Applications 16:51–61.

Gotmark, F., H. Paltto, B. Norden, and E. Gotmark. 2005. Evaluating partial cutting in broadleaved temperate forest under strong experimental control: Short-term effects on herbaceous plants. Forest Ecology and Management 214:124–141.

Gould, A.M.A., and D.L. Gorchov. 2000. Effects of the exotic invasive shrub *Lonicera maackii* on the survival and fecundity of three species of native annuals. American Midland Naturalist 144:36–50.

Gould, K.S., K.R. Markham, R.H. Smith, and J.J. Goris. 2000. Functional role of anthocyanins in the leaves of *Quintinia serrata* A. Cunn. Journal of Experimental Botany 51:1107–1115.

Gould, K.S., and B.D. Quinn. 1999. Do anthocyanins protect leaves of New Zealand native species from UV-B? New Zealand Journal of Botany 37:175–178.

Graae, B.J. 2000. The effect of landscape fragmentation and forest continuity on forest floor species in two regions of Denmark. Journal of Vegetation Science 11:881–892.

Graae, B.J., P. De Frenne, A. Kolb, J. Brunet, O. Chabrerie, K. Verheyen, N. Pepin, T. Heinken, M. Zobel, A. Shevtsova, I. Nijs, and A. Milbau. 2012. On the use of weather data in ecological studies along altitudinal and latitudinal gradients. Oikos 121:3–19.

Graae, B.J., T. Hansen, and P.B. Sunde. 2004. The importance of recruitment limitation in forest plant species colonization: a seed sowing experiment. Flora 199:263–270.

Graae, B.J., A. Kolb, S. Van Der Veken, T. Heinken, O. Chabreie, M. Diekmann, K. Valtinat, R. Zindel, E. Karlsson, L. Strom, G. Decocq, M. Hermy, and C.C. Baskin. 2009. Germination requirements and seed mass of slow- and fast-colonizing temperate forest herbs along a latitidunal gradient. Ecoscience 16:248–257.

Graae, B.J., P.B. Sunde, and B. Fritzboger. 2003. Vegetation and soil differences in ancient opposed to new forests. Forest Ecology and Management 177:179–190.

Grace, J., and D. Tilman. 1990. Perspectives in Plant Competition. Academic Press, New York.

Grace, J.B., and R.G. Wetzel. 1981. Habitat partitioning and competitive displacement in cattails (*Typha*): experimental field studies. American Naturalist 118:463–474.

Grace, S.C., B.A. Logan, and W.W. Adams. 2002. Seasonal differences in foliar content of chlorogenic acid, a phenylpropanoid antioxidant, in *Mahonia repens*. Plant, Cell and Environment 21:513–521.

Graham, A. 2011. A natural history of the new world: the ecology and evolution of plants in the Americas. Chicago: University of Chicago Press.

Grant, A., and T.G. Benton. 2000. Elasticity analysis for density-dependent populations in stochastic environments. Ecology 81:680–693.

Grant, R.H. 1997. Partitioning of biologically active radiation in plant canopies. International Journal of Meteorology 40:26–40.

Grashof-Bokdam, C.J., and W. Geertsema. 1998. The effect of isolation and history on colonization patterns of plant species in secondary woodland. Journal of Biogeography 25:837–846.

Gratani, L. 1997. Canopy structure, vertical radiation profile and photosynthetic function in a *Quercus ilex* evergreen forest. Photosynthetica 33:139–149.

Gravatt, D.A., and C.E. Martin. 1992. Comparative ecophysiology of five species of *Sedum* (Crassulaceae) under well-watered and drought-stressed conditions. Oecologia 92:532–541.

Graves, J.D. 1990. A model of the seasonal pattern of carbon acquisition in two woodland herbs, *Mercurialis perennis* L. and *Geum urbanum* L. Oecologia 83:479–484.

Graves, J.H., R.K. Peet, and P.S. White. 2006. The influence of carbon-nutrient balance on herb and woody plant abundance in temperate forest understories. Journal of Vegetation Science 17:217–226.

Gray, A. 1841. Notes on a botanical excursion to the mountains of North Carolina, with some remarks on the botany of the higher Allegheny Mountains. American Journal of Science 42:1–49.

Gray, A.N., T.J. Brandeis, J.D. Shaw, W.H. McWilliams, and P.D. Miles. 2012. Forest inventory and analysis database of the United States of America (FIA). Biodiversity and Ecology 4: 225–232.

Gray, J.B., T.R. Wentworth, and C. Brownie. 2003. Extinction, colonization, and persistence of rare vascular flora in the longleaf pine-wiregrass ecosystem: responses to fire frequency and population size. Natural Areas Journal 23:210–219.

Green, R.E., P.E. Osborne, and E.J. Sears. 1994. The distribution of passerine birds in hedgerows during the breeding-season in relation to characteristics of the hedgerow and adjacent farmland. Journal of Applied Ecology 31:677–692.

Gregg, K.B. 1991a. Reproductive strategy of *Cleistes divaricata* (Orchidaceae). American Journal of Botany 78:350–360.

Gregg, K.B. 1991b. Variation in behaviour of four populations of the orchid *Cleistes divaricata*, an assessment using transition matrix models. Pages 139–159 in T.C.E. Wells and J.H. Willems, editors. Population ecology of terrestrial orchids. The Hague, NL: SPB Publishing.

Gregg, K.B., and M. Kery. 2006. Comparison of size vs. life-state classification demographic models for the terrestrial orchid *Cleistes bifaria*. Biological Conservation 129:50–58.

Greig-Smith, P. 1952. The use of random and contiguous quadrats in the study of the structure of plant communities. Annals of Botany 16:293–316.

Greller, A.M., D.C. Locke, V. Kilanowski, and G.E. Lotowycz. 1990. Changes in vegetation composition and soil acidity between 1922 and 1985 at a site on the North Shore of Long Island, New York. Bulletin of the Torrey Botanical Club 117:450–458.

Grewel, J.S., and S.N. Singh. 1980. Effect of potassium nutrition on frost damage and yield of potato plants on alluvial soils of the Punjab (India). Plant and Soil 57:105–110.

Griffin, S.R., and S.C.H. Barrett. 2004. Post-glacial history of *Trillium grandiflorum* (Melanthiaceae) in eastern North America: inferences from phylogeography. American Journal of Botany 91:465–473.

Griffin, S.R., K. Mavraganis, and C.G. Eckert. 2000. Experimental analysis of protogyny in *Aquilegia canadensis* (Ranunculaceae). American Journal of Botany 87:1246–1256.

Griffith, T.M., and M.A. Watson. 2006. Is evolution necessary for range expansion? Manipulating reproductive timing of a weedy annual transplanted beyond its range. American Naturalist 167:153–164.

Grigal, D.F., and L.F. Ohmann. 1980. Seasonal change in nutrient concentrations in forest herbs. Bulletin of the Torrey Botanical Club 107:47–50.

Grime, J.P. 1973. Competitive exclusion in herbaceous vegetation. Nature 242:344–347.

Grime, J.P. 1977. Evidence for the existence of three primary strategies implants and its relevance to ecological and evolutionary theory. American Naturalist 11:1169–1194.

Grime, J.P. 1979. Plant strategies and vegetation processes. John Wiley & Sons, Chichester, UK.

Grime, J.P. 1998. Benefits of plant diversity to ecosystems: immediate, filter and founder effects. Journal of Ecology 86:902–910.

Grimm, N.B., M. Grove, S.T.A. Pickett, and C.L. Redman. 2000. Integrated approaches to long-term studies of urban ecological systems. BioScience 50:571–584.

Grisez, T.J. 1960. Slash helps protect seedlings from deer browsing. Journal of Forestry 58:385–387.

Grisez, T.J., and M.R. Peace. 1973. Requirements for advance reproduction in Allegheny hardwoods—an interim guide. USDA Forest Serv. Res. Note NE-180.

Groffman, P.M., D.R. Zak, S. Christensen, A. Mosier, and J.M. Tiedje. 1993. Early spring nitrogen dynamics in a temperate forest landscape. Ecology 74:1579–1585.

Grondin, P. et al. 1996. Écologie forestière. Pages 134–279 in J.A. Bérard and M. Côté, editors. Manuel de Foresterie. Presses de l'Université Laval, Sainte-Foy.

Groninger, J.W., and L.H. McCormick. 1992. Effects of soil disturbance on hayscented fern establishment. Northern Journal of Applied Forestry 9:29–31.

Groom, M.J. 1998. Allee effects limit population viability of an annual plant. American Naturalist 151:487–496.

Gross, K., J.R. Lockwood, C.C. Frost, and M.F. Morris. 1998. Modeling controlled burning and trampling reduction for conservation of *Hudsonia montana*. Conservation Biology 12:1291–1301.

Grubb, P.J. 1977. The maintenance of species-richness in plant communities: the importance of the regeneration niche. Biological Review 52:107–145.

Gruber, N., and J.N. Galloway. 2008. An Earth-system perspective of the global nitrogen cycle. Nature 451:293–296.

Guénard, B., and R.R. Dunn. 2010. A new (old) invasive ant in the hardwood forests of eastern North America and its potentially widespread impacts. PLoS One 5:e11614.

Guisan, A. and Thuiller, W. 2005. Predicting species distribution: offering more than simple habitat models. Ecology Letters 8:993–1009.

Gurel, F., A. Gosterit, and O. Eren. 2008 Life-cycle and foraging patterns of native *Bombus terrestris* (L.) (Hymenoptera, Apidae) in the Mediterranean region. Insectes Sociaux 55:123–128.

Gurevitch, J., T.G. Howard, I.W. Ashton, E.A. Leger, K.M. Howe, E. Woo, and M. Lerdau. 2008. Effects of experimental manipulation of light and nutrients on establishment of seedlings of native and invasive woody species in Long Island, NY forests. Biological Invasions 10:821–831.

Gutjahr, S., and L. Lapointe. 2008. Carbon dioxide enrichment does not reduce leaf longevity or alter accumulation of carbon reserves in the woodland spring ephemeral *Erythronium americanum*. Annals of Botany 102:835–843.

Haberlandt, G. 1914. Physiological plant anatomy. Macmillan, London.

Hackney, E.E., and J.B. McGraw. 2001. Experimental demonstration of an Allee effect in American ginseng. Conservation Biology 15:129–136.

Hadidian, J. 1993. Science and management of white-tailed deer in the U.S. National Parks. In W.E. Brown and J.S.D. Veirs, eds. Partners in Stewardship: Proceedings of the 7th conference on research and resource management in parks and on public lands. Hancock, MI: George Wright Society, pp. 77–85.

Hahn, P.G., M.L. Draney, and M.E. Dornbush. 2010. Exotic slugs pose a previously unrecognized threat to the herbaceous layer in a Midwestern woodland. Restoration Ecology 19:786–794.

Hale, C.M., L.E. Frelich, and P.B. Reich. 2006. Changes in hardwood forest understory plant communities in response to European earthworm invasions. Ecology 87:1637–1649.

Hale, C.M., L.E. Frelich, P.B. Reich, and J. Pastor. 2005. Effects of European earthworm invasion on soil characteristics in northern hardwood forests of Minnesota, USA. Ecosystems 8:911–927.

Halpern, C.B. 1988. Early successional pathways and the resistance and resilience of forest communities. Ecology 69:1703–1715.

Halpern, C.B. 1989. Early successional patterns of forest species: interactions of life history traits and disturbance. Ecology 70:704–720.

Halpern, C.B., and T.A. Spies. 1995. Plant species diversity in natural and managed forests of the Pacific Northwest. Ecological Applications 5:913–934.

Hamer, K.C., J.K. Hill, S. Benedick, N. Mustaffa, T.N. Sherratt, M. Maryati, and V.K. Chey. 2003. Ecology of butterflies in natural and selectively logged forests of northern Borneo: the importance of habitat heterogeneity. Journal of Applied Ecology 40:150–162.

Hamilton, M.B. 1994. Ex-situ conservation of wild plant species: time to reassess the genetic assumptions and implications of seed banks. Conservation Biology 8:39–49.

Hammond, D.N., D.W. Smith, S.M. Zedaker, D.K. Wright, and J.W. Thompson. 1998. Floral diversity following harvest on southern Appalachian mixed oak sites. Pages 461–465 in Proceedings of the Ninth Southern Biennial Silvicultural Res. Conf. Clemson, SC. U.S.D.A. Forest Service General Technical Report SRS20.

Hampe, A., and Arroyo, J. 2002. Recruitment and regeneration in populations of an endangered South Iberian Tertiary relict tree. Biological Conservation 107:263–271.

Hampe, A., and A.S. Jump. 2011. Climate relicts: past, present and future. Annual Review of Ecology, Evolution, and Systematics 42:313–333.

Hampe, A., and R.J. Petit. 2005. Conserving biodiversity under climate change: the rear edge matters. Ecology Letters 8:461–467.

Hamrick, J.L., M.J.W. Godt, and E. Gonzales. 2006. Conservation of genetic diversity in old-growth forest communities of the southeastern United States. Applied Vegetation Science 9:51–58.

Handel, S.N. 1976. Dispersal ecology of Carex pedunculata (Cyperaceae), a new North American myrmecochore. American Journal of Botany 63:1071–1079.

Handel, S.N. 1978. The competitive relationship of three woodland sedges and its bearing on the evolution of ant-dispersal of Carex pedunculata. Evolution 32:151–163.

Handel, S.N., S.B. Fisch, and G.E. Schatz. 1981. Ants disperse the majority of herbs in a mesic forest community in New York State. Bulletin of the Torrey Botanical Club 108:430–437.

Hannah, L., G.F. Midgley, T. Lovejoy, W.J. Bond, M. Bush, J.C. Lovett, D. Scott, and F.I. Woodward. 2002. Conservation of biodiversity in a changing climate. Conservation Biology 16:264–268.

Hannan, G.L., and H.A. Prucher. 1996. Reproductive biology of Caulophyllum thalictroides (Berberidaceae), an early flowering perennial of eastern North America. American Midland Naturalist 136:267–277.

Hanski, I. 1991. Single species metapopulation dynamics: concepts, models and observation. Biological Journal of the Linnean Society 42:17–38.

Harcombe, P.A., and P.L. Marks. 1977. Understory structure of a mesic forest in southeast Texas. Ecology 58:1144–1151.

Harder, L.D., and S.C.H. Barrett. 1995. Mating cost of large floral displays in hermaphrodite plants. Nature 373:512–515.

Harder, L.D., M.B. Cruzan, and J.D. Thomson. 1993. Unilateral incompatibility and the effects of interspecific pollination for *Erythronium americanum* and *Erythronium albidum* (Liliaceae). Canadian Journal of Botany 71:353–358.

Hardt, R.A., and W.T. Swank. 1997. A comparison of structural and compositional characteristics of southern Appalachian young second-growth, maturing second-growth, and old-growth stands. Natural Areas Journal 17:42–52.

Harper, J.L. 1977. Population biology of plants. Academic Press, London.

Harper, J.L., J.N. Clatsworthy, I.H.M. Naughton, and G.R. Sagar. 1961. The evolution and ecology of closely related species living in the same area. Evolution 15:209–227.

Harrelson, S.M., and G.R. Matlack. 2006. Influence of stand age and physical environment on the herb composition of second-growth forest, Strouds Run, Ohio, USA. Journal of Biogeography 33:1139–1149.

Harris, G., and S.L. Pimm. 2008. Range size and extinction risk in forest birds. Conservation Biology 22:163–171.

Harris, W.F., P. Sollins, N.T. Edwards, B.E. Dinger, and H.H. Shugart. 1975. Analysis of carbon flow and productivity in a temperate deciduous forest ecosystem. In D.E. Reichle, J.F. Franklin, and D.W. Goodall, editors. Productivity of World Ecosystems. Natl. Acad. Sci., Washington, DC.

Harrison, S. 1991. Local extinction in a metapopulation context—an empirical evaluation. Biological Journal of the Linnean Society 42:73–88.

Harrison, S., and E. Bruna. 1999. Habitat fragmentation and large-scale conservation: what do we know for sure? Ecography 22:225–232.

Harrison, S., and J.F. Quinn. 1989. Correlated environments and the persistence of metapopulations. Oikos 56:1–6.

Hart, S.A., and H.Y.H. Chen. 2006. Understory vegetation dynamics of North American boreal forests. Critical Reviews in Plant Science 25:381–397.

Hart, S.A., and H.Y.H. Chen. 2008. Fire, logging, and overstory affect understory abundance, diversity, and composition in boreal forest. Ecological Monographs 78:123–140.

Hartley, S.E., and C.G. Jones. 1997. Pages 284–324 in M.J. Crawley, editor. Plant Chemistry and Herbivory, or why the world is green. In M.J. Crawley, ed. Plant Ecology. Oxford, UK: Blackwell.

Hartley, S.E., and R.J. Mitchell. 2005. Manipulation of nutrients and grazing levels on heather moorland: changes in *Calluna* dominance and consequences for community composition. Journal of Ecology 93:990–1004.

Hartman, K.M., and B.C. McCarthy. 2007. A dendro-ecology study of forest overstory productivity following the invasion of the non-indigenous shrub *Lonicera mackii*. Applied Vegetation Science 10:3–14.

Hartnett, D.C., and D.R. Richardson. 1989. Population biology of *Bonamia grandiflora* (Convolvulaceae)—effects of fire on plant and seed bank dynamics. American Journal of Botany 76:361–369.

Hartshorn, G.S. 1975. A matrix model of tree population dynamics. Pages 41–51 in F.B. Golley and E. Medina, editors. Tropical ecological systems. Springer-Verlag, New York.

Havens, K., K. Preston, C. Richardson, and L. Delph. 1995. Nutrients affect allocation to male and female function in *Abutilon theophrasti* (Malvaceae). American Journal of Botany 82:726–733.

Harvey, B.D., and Y. Bergeron. 1989. Site patterns of natural regeneration following clear-cutting in northwestern Quebec. Canadian Journal of Forest Research 19:1458–1469.

Harvey, B.D., A. Leduc, and Y. Bergeron. 1995. Early postharvest succession in relation to site type in the southern boreal forest of Quebec. Canadian Journal of Forest Research 25:1658–1672.

Harvey, G.W. 1980. Seasonal alteration of photosynthetic unit sizes in three herb layer components of a deciduous forest community. American Journal of Botany 67:293–299.

Hawkes, C.V., and E.S. Menges. 1995. Density and seed production of a Florida endemic, *Polygonella basiramia*, in relation to time since fire and open sand. American Midland Naturalist 113:138–148.

Hayek, L.C., and M.A. Buzas. 1997. Surveying natural populations. Columbia University Press, New York.

Hayek, L.C., and M.A. Buzas. 1998. SHE analysis: an integrated approach to the analysis of forest biodiversity. Pages 311–321 in F. Dallmeier and J.J. Comiskey, editors. Forest biodiversity research, monitoring, and modelling: conceptual background and old-world case studies. Smithsonian Institution, Washington, DC.

Hayward, P.M. and R.S. Clymo. 1983. The growth of sphagnum: experiments on, and simulation of, some effects of light flux and water-table depth. Journal of Ecology 71:845–863.

He, F., and H.J. Barclay. 2000. Long-term response of understory plant species to thinning and fertilization in a Douglas-fir plantation on southern Vancouver Island, British Columbia. Canadian Journal of Forest Research 30:566–572.

Heckel, C.D., N.A. Bourg, W.J. McShea, and S. Kalisz. 2010. Nonconsumptive effects of a generalist ungulate herbivore drive decline of unpalatable forest herbs. Ecology 91:319–326.

Hedwall, P.-O., J. Brunet, A. Nordin, and J. Bergh. 2011. Decreased variation of forest understory is an effect of fertilisation in young stands of *Picea abies*. Scandinavian Journal of Forest Research 26:46–55.

Hegazy, A.K., H.F. Kabiel, L. Boulos, and O.S. Sharashy. 2010. Functional traits and life history diversity of the North Africa endemic *Ebenus pinnata* aiton. Flora 205:666–673.

Heilman, P.E. 1966. Change in distribution and availability of nitrogen with forest succession on north slopes in interior Alaska. Ecology 47:825–831.

Heilman, P.E. 1968. Relationship of availability of phosphorus and cations to forest succession and bog formation in interior Alaska. Ecology 49:331–336.

Heinen, J.T., and R.C.D. Currey. 2000. A 22-year study on the effects of mammalian browsing on forest succession following a clearcut in northern lower Michigan. American Midland Naturalist 144:243–252.

Heinselman, M.L. 1981. Fire and succession in the conifer forests of northern North America. Pages 374–406 in D.C. West and D.B. Botkin, editors. Forest succession: concepts and application. Springer-Verlag, New York.

Heithaus, E.R. 1981. Seed predation by rodents on three ant-dispersed plants. Ecology 63:136–145.

Heithaus, E.R., and M. Humes. 2003. Variation in communities of seed-dispersing ants in habitats with different disturbance in Knox County, Ohio. Ohio Journal of Science 103:89–97.

Helvey, J.D., J.D. Hewlett, and J.E. Douglass. 1972. Predicting soil moisture in the southern Appalachians. Soil Science Society of America Proceedings 36:954–959.

Henry, D.G. 1973. Foliar nutrient concentrations of some Minnesota forest species. Minnesota Forestry Research Notes No. 241.

Heppell, S.S., H. Caswell, and L.B. Crowder. 2000a. Life histories and elasticity patterns: perturbation analysis for species with minimal demographic data. Ecology 81:654–665.

Heppell, S.S., C.A. Pfister, and H. de Kroon. 2000b. Elasticity analysis in population biology: methods and applications. Ecology 81:605–606.

Herlihy, C.R., and C.G. Eckert. 2002. Genetic cost of reproductive assurance in a self-fertilizing plant. Nature 416:320–323.

Herlihy, C.R., and C.G. Eckert. 2004. Experimental dissection of inbreeding and its adaptive significance in a flowering plant, *Aquilegia canadensis* (Ranunculaceae). Evolution 58:2693–2703.

Herlihy, C.R., and C.G. Eckert. 2005. Evolution of self-fertilization at geographical range margins? A comparison of demographic, floral and mating system variables in central versus peripheral populations of *Aquilegia canadensis* (Ranunculaceae). American Journal of Botany 92:746–753.

Hermy, M. 1988. Correlation between forest layers in mixed deciduous forests in Flanders (Belgium). Pages 77–85 in H.J. During, M.J.A. Werger, and J.H. Willems, editors. Diversity and pattern in plant communities. SPB Academic Publishing, The Hague, NL.

Herrera, C.M. 1995. Microclimate and individual variation in pollinators: flowering plants are more than their flowers. Ecology 76:1516–1524.

Herrera, J.M., D. Garcia, and J.M. Morales. 2011. Matrix effects on plant-frugivore and plant-predator interactions in forest fragments. Landscape Ecology 26:125–135.

Herring, B.J., and W.S. Judd. 1995. A floristic study of Ichetucknee Springs State Park, Suwannee and Columbia counties, Florida. Castanea 60:318–369.

Hester, A.J., L. Edenius, R.M. Buttenschon, and A.T. Kuiters. 2000. Interactions between forests and herbivores: the role of controlled grazing experiments. Forestry 73:381–391.

Hibbs, D.E. 1982. White pine in the transition hardwood forest. Canadian Journal of Botany 60:2046–2053.

Hibbs, D.E. 1983. Forty years of forest succession in central New England. Ecology 64:1394–1401.

Hickling, R., D.B. Roy, J.K. Hill, R. Fox, and C.D. Thomas. 2006. The distributions of a wide range of taxonomic groups are expanding polewards. Global Change Biology 12:450–455.

Hickling, R., D.B. Roy, J.K. Hill, and C.D. Thomas. 2005. A northward shift of range margins in British Odonata. Global Change Biology 11:502–506.

Hicks, D.J. 1980. Intrastand distribution patterns of southern Appalachian cove forest herbaceous species. American Midland Naturalist 104:209–222.

Hicks, D.J., and B.F. Chabot. 1985. Deciduous forest. Pages 257–277 in B.F. Chabot and H.A. Mooney, editors. Physiological Ecology of North American Plant Communities. Chapman and Hall, New York.

Hicks, D.J., R. Wyatt, and T.R. Meagher. 1985. Reproductive biology of distylous partridgeberry, *Mitchella repens*. American Journal of Botany 72:1503–1514.

Hiebert, R.D. 1997. Prioritizing invasive plants and planning for management. In J.O. Luken and J.W. Thieret, editors. Assessment and management of plant invasions. Springer-Verlag, New York.

Hierro, J.L., J.L. Maron, and R.M. Callaway. 2005. A biogeographical approach to plant invasions: the importance of studying exotics in their introduced and native range. Journal of Ecology 93:5–15.

Hickling, R., D.B. Roy, J.K. Hill, R. Fox, and C.D. Thomas. 2006. The distributions of a wide range of taxonomic groups are expanding polewards. Global Change Biology 12:450–455.

Hikosaka, K., Y. Kawauchi, and T. Kurosawa. 2010. Why does *Viola hondoensis* (Violaceae) shed its winter leaves in spring? American Journal of Botany 97:1944–1950.

Hill, J.D. 1996. Population dynamics of hayscented fern (Dennstaedtia punctilobula) and its effects on the composition, structure, and dynamics of a northeastern forest. Ph.D. dissertation, University of Connecticut, Storrs, CT.

Hill, J.D., C.D. Canham, and D.M. Wood. 1994. Patterns and causes of resistance to tree invasion in rights-of-way. Ecological Applications 5:459–470.

Hill, J.D., and J.A. Silander, Jr. 2001. Distribution and dynamics of two ferns: *Dennstaedtia punctilobula* (Dennstaedtiaceae) and *Thelypteris noveboracensis* (Thelypteridaceae) in a northeast mixed hardwoods-hemlock forest. American Journal of Botany 88:894–902.

Hill, L.M., A.K. Brody, and C.L. Tedesco. 2008. Mating strategies and pollen limitation in a globally threatened perennial *Polemonium vanbruntiae*. Acta Oecologica-International Journal of Ecology 33:314–323.

Hill, M.O. 1979. DECORANA: A FORTRAN program for detrended correspondence analysis and reciprocal averaging. Section of Ecology and Systematics, Cornell University, Ithaca, NY.

Hill, M.O. 1979. The development of a flora in even-aged plantations. Pages 175–192 in E.D. Ford, D.C. Malcolm, and J. Atterson, editors. The ecology of even-aged forest plantations. Institute of Terrestrial Ecology, Cambridge, UK.

Hobbie, S.E. 1996. Temperature and plant species control over litter decomposition in Alaskan tundra. Ecological Monographs 66:503–522

Hobbs, N.T., D.L. Baker, G.D. Bear, and D.C. Bowden. 1996. Ungulate grazing in sagebrush grassland: mechanimsms of resource competition. Ecological Applications 6:200–217.

Hobbs, R.J., and L.F. Huenneke.1992. Disturbance, diversity and invasion: implications for conservation. Conservation Biology 6:324–337.

Hobbs, R.J., and S.E. Humphries. 1995. An integrated approach to the ecology and management of plant invaders. Conservation Biology 9:761–770.

Hodge, A., J. Stewart, D. Robinson, B.S. Griffiths, and A.H. Fitter. 2000. Competition between roots and soil micro-organisms for nutrients from nitrogen-rich patches of varying complexity. Journal of Ecology 88:150–164.

Hoegh-Guldberg, O., L. Hughes, S. McIntyre, D.B. Lindenmayer, C. Parmesan, H.P. Possingham, and C.D. Thomas. 2008. Assisted colonization and rapid climate change. Science 321: 345–346.

Holland, P.G. 1980. Trout lily in Nova Scotia: an assessment of the status of its geographic range. Journal of Biogeography 7:363–381.

Holland, P.G. 1981. The demography of trout lily (*Erythronium-Americanum* Ker) in Nova Scotia. Vegetatio 45:97–106.

Holling, C.S., and G.K. Meffe. 1996. Command and control and the pathology of natural resource management. Conservation Biology 10:328–337.

Holsinger, K. 1999. Population viability analysis (http://darwin.eeb.uconn.edu/ eeb310/lecture-notes/pva/pva.html).

Holt, R.D., and M. Barfield. 2011. Theoretical perspectives on the statics and dynamics of species' borders in patchy environments. American Naturalist 178:S6–S25.

Holt, R.D., and R. Gomulkiewicz. 1997. How does immigration influence local adaptation? A reexamination of a familiar paradigm. American Naturalist 149:563–572.

Holt, R.D., T.H. Keitt, M.A. Lewis, B.A. Maurer, and M.L. Taper. 2005. Theoretical models of species' borders: single species approaches. Oikos 108:18–27.

Holtum, J.A.M., and K. Winter. 2001. Are plants growing close to the floors of tropical forests exposed to markedly elevated concentrations of carbon dioxide? Australian Journal of Botany 49:629–636.

Holub, P., and I. Tůma. 2010. The effect of enhanced nitrogen on aboveground biomass allocation and nutrient resorption in the fern *Athyrium distentifolium*. Plant Ecology 207:373–380.

Honnay, O., and B. Bossuyt. 2005. Prolonged clonal growth: escape route or route to extinction. Oikos 108:427–432.

Honnay, O., B. Bossuyt, H. Jacquemyn, A. Shimono, and K. Uchiyama. 2008. Can a seed bank maintain the genetic variation in the aboveground plant population? Oikos 117:1–5.

Honnay, O., B. Bossuyt, K. Verheyen, J. Butaye, H. Jacquemyn, and M. Hermy. 2002. Ecological perspectives for the restoration of plant communities in European temperate forests. Biodiversity and Conservation 11:213–242.

Honnay, O., and H. Jacquemyn. 2007. Susceptibility of common and rare plant species to the genetic consequences of habitat fragmentation. Conservation Biology 21:823–831.

Honnay, O., H. Jacquemyn, B. Bossuyt, and M. Hermy. 2005. Forest fragmentation effects on patch occupancy and population viability of herbaceous plant species. New Phytologist 166:723–736.

Honnay, O., K. Verheyen, J. Butaye, H. Jacquemyn, B. Bossuyt, and M. Hermy. 2002. Possible effects of habitat fragmentation and climate change on the range of forest plant species. Ecology Letters 5:525–530.

Hommels, C.H., P.J.C. Kuiper, and O.G. Tanczos. 1989. Luxury uptake and specific utilization rates of three macroelements in two *Taraxacum* microspecies of contrasting mineral ecology. Physiologia Plantarum 77:569–578.

Hooper, D.U., and P.M. Vitousek. 1998. Effects of plant composition and diversity on nutrient cycling. Ecological Monographs 68:121–149.

Hooper, M.C., K. Arii, and M.J. Lechowicz. 2001. Impact of a major ice storm on an old-growth hardwood forest. Canadian Journal of Botany 79:70–75.

Hoppes, W.G. 1988. Seedfall pattern of several species of bird-dispersed plants in an Illinois woodland. Ecology 69:320–329.

Hörandl, E., C. Dobeš, J. Suda, P. Vít, T. Urfus, E.M. Temsch, A.C. Cosendai, J. Wagner, and U. Ladinig. 2011. Apomixis is not prevalent in subnival to nival plants of the European Alps. Annals of Botany 108:381–390.

Hori, Y., and T. Yokoi. 1999. Population structure and dynamics of an evergreen shade herb, *Ainsliaea apiculata* (Asteraceae), with special reference to herbivore effects. Ecological Research 14:39–48.

Horibata, S., S.F. Hasegawa, and G. Kudo. 2007. Cost of reproduction in a spring ephemeral species, *Adonis ramosa* (Ranunculaceae): Carbon budget for seed production. Annals of Botany 100:565–571.

Horn, H.S. 1971. The adaptive geometry of trees. Princeton University Press, Princeton, NJ.

Horn, H.S. 1975. Forest Succession. American Scientist 232:90–98.

Horsley, S.B. 1977a. Allelopathic inhibition of black cherry by fern, grass, goldenrod, and aster. Canadian Journal of Forest Research 7:205–216.

Horsley, S.B. 1977b. Allelopathic inhibition of black cherry. II. Inhibition by woodland grass, ferns, and club moss. Canadian Journal of Forest Research 7:515–519.

Horsley, S.B. 1988. How vegetation can influence regeneration? Pages 38–55 in H.C. Smith, A.W. Perkey, and W.E. Kidd, editors. Guidelines for Regenerating Appalachian Hardwood Stands. United States Department of Agriculture, Forest Service, Morgantown, WV.

Horsley, S.B. 1993a. Mechanisms of interference between hayscented fern and black cherry. Canadian Journal of Forest Research 23:2059–2069.

Horsley, S.B. 1993b. Role of allelopathy in hayscented fern interference with black cherry regeneration. Journal of Chemical Ecology 19:2737–2755.

Horsley, S.B. 1994. Regeneration success and plant species diversity of Allegheny hardwood stands after Roundup application and shelterwood cutting. Northern Journal of Applied Forestry 11:109–116.

Horsley, S.B., and D.A. Marquis. 1983. Interference by weeds and deer with Allegheny hardwood reproduction. Canadian Journal of Forest Research 13:61–69.

Horsley, S.B., S.L. Stout, and D.S. deCalesta. 2003. White-tailed deer impact on the vegetation dynamics of a northern hardwood forest. Ecological Applications 13:98–118.

Horton, J.L., and H.S. Neufeld. 1998. Photosynthetic responses of *Microstegium vimineum* (Trin.) A. Camus, a shade-tolerant, C4 grass, to variable light environments. Oecologia 114:11–19.

Horvitz, C.C., and A. Koop. 2001. Removal of nonnative vines and post-hurricane recruitment in tropical hardwood forests of Florida. Biotropica 33:268–281.

Horvitz, C.C., J.B. Pascarella, S. McMann, A. Freedman, and R.H. Hofstetter. 1998. Functional roles of invasive non-indigenous plants in hurricane-affected subtropical hardwood forests. Ecological Applications 8:947–974.

Horvitz, C.C., D.W. Schemske, and H. Caswell. 1997. The relative "importance" of life-history stages to population growth: prospective and retrospective analyses. Pages 247–271 in S. Tuljapurkar and H. Caswell, editors. Structured population models in marine, terrestrial and freshwater systems. Chapman and Hall, New York.

Host, G.E., and K.S. Pregitzer. 1992. Geomorphic influences on ground-flora and overstory composition in upland forests of northwestern lower Michigan. Canadian Journal of Forest Research 22:1547–1555.

Hough, A.F. 1965. A twenty-year record of understory vegetational change in a virgin Pennsylvania forest. Ecology 46:379–373.

Hough, A.F., and R.D. Forbes. 1943. The ecology and silvics of forests in the high plateaus of Pennsylvania. Ecological Monographs 13:299–320.

Howard, T.G., J. Gurevitch, L. Hyatt, M. Carreiro, and M. Lerdau. 2004. Forest invisibility in communities in southeastern New York. Biological Invasions 6:393–410.

Howe, H., and M. Miriti. 2004. When seed dispersal matters. BioScience 54:651–660.

Hu, F.S., A. Hampe, and R.J. Petit. 2009. Paleoecology meets genetics: deciphering past vegetational dynamics. Frontiers in Ecology and the Environment 7:371–379.

Hubbell, S.P. 1997. A unified theory of biogeography and relative species abundance and its application to tropical rain forests and coral reefs. Coral Reefs, Suppl. 16:S9–S21.

Hubbell, S.P. 2001. The unified neutral theory of biodiversity and biogeography. Princeton, NJ: Princeton University Press.

Hubbell, S.P., R.B. Foster, S.T. O'Brien, K.E. Harms, R. Condit, B. Wechsler, S.J. Wright, and S. Loo de Lao. 1999. Light-gap disturbances, recruitment limitation, and tree diversity in a neotropical forest. Science 283:554–557.

Huber, H., D.F. Whigham, and J. O'Neill. 2004. Timing and disturbance changes the balance between growth and survival of parent and offspring ramets in the clonal forest understory herb *Uvularia perfoliata*. Evolutionary Ecology 18:521–539.

Huebner, C.D., and P.C. Tobin. 2006. Invasibility of mature and 15-year-old deciduous forests by exotic plants. Plant Ecology 186:57–68.

Huebner, C.D., S.L. Stephenson, H.S. Adams, and G.W. Miller. 2007. Short-term dynamics of second-growth mixed mesophytic forest strata in West Virginia. Castanea 72:65–81.

Huenneke, L.F. 1983. Understory response to gaps caused by the death of *Ulmus americana* in central New York. Bulletin of the Torrey Botanical Club 110:170–175.

Hufkens, K., M.A. Friedl, T.F Keenan, O. Sonnentag, A. Bailey, J. O'Keefe, and A.D. Richardson. 2012. Ecological impacts of a widespread frost event following early spring leaf-out. Global Change Biology 18:2365–2377.

Hughes, J.W., and T.J. Fahey. 1991. Colonization dynamics of herbs and shrubs in a disturbed northern hardwood forest. Journal of Ecology 79:605–616.

Hughes, J.W., T.J. Fahey, and F.H. Bormann. 1988. Population persistence and reproductive ecology of a forest herb: *Aster acuminatus*. American Journal of Botany 75:1057–1064.

Hughes, N.M. 2011. Winter leaf reddening in 'evergreen' species. New Phytologist 190:573–581

Hughes, N.M., H.S. Neufeld, and K.O. Burkey. 2005. Functional role of anthocyanins in high-light winter leaves of the evergreen herb *Galax urceolata*. New Phytologist 168:575–587.

Hughes, N.M., and W.K. Smith. 2007. Attenuation of incident light in *Galax urceolata* (Diapensiaceae): Concerted influence of adaxial and abaxial anthocyanic layers on photoprotection. American Journal of Botany 94:784–790.

Hughes, N.M., T.C. Vogelmann, and W.K. Smith. 2008. Optical effects of abaxial anthocyanin on absorption of red wavelengths by understory species: revisiting the back-scatter hypothesis. Journal of Experimental Botany 59:3435–3442.

Hülber, K., T. Dirnböck, I. Kleinbauer, W. Willner, S. Dullinger, G. Karrer, and M. Mirtl. 2008. Long-term impacts of nitrogen and sulphur deposition on forest floor vegetation in the Northern limestone Alps, Austria. Applied Vegetation Science 11:395–404.

Hull, J.C. 2001. Photosynthetic responses to sunflecks of deciduous forest understory herbs with different phenologies. International Journal of Plant Science.

Hungerford, R.D., and R.E. Babbitt. 1987. Overstory removal treatments affect soil surface, air, and soil temperature: implications for seedling survival. USDA Forest Service Research Paper INT-377.

Hunter, M.L. 1989. What constitutes an old-growth stand? Journal of Forestry 87:33–35.

Hunter, M.L., Jr. 2007. Climate change and moving species: Furthering the debate on assisted colonization. Conservation Biology 21:1356–1358.

Hunter, M.L., Jr., G.L. Jacobson, Jr., and T. Webb, III. 1988. Paleoecology and the coarse-filter approach to maintaining biological diversity. Conservation Biology 2:375–385.

Huntley, B. 1993. Species-richness in north-temperate zone forests. Journal of Biogeography 20: 163–180.

Huntley, B., P.M. Berry, W. Cramer, and A.P. McDonald. 1995. Modeling present and potential future ranges of some European higher plants using climate response surfaces. Journal of Biogeography 22:967–1001.

Huntley, B., and T. Webb, III. 1989. Migration: species' response to climatic variations caused by changes in Earth's orbit. Journal of Biogeography 16:5–19.

Hurd, T.M., A.R. Brach, and D.J. Raynal. 1998. Response of understory vegetation of Adirondack forests to nitrogen additions. Canadian Journal of Forest Research 28:799–807.

Hurlbert, S.H. 1984. Pseudoreplication and the design of ecological field experiments. Ecological Monographs 54:187–211.

Husband, B.C., and S.C.H. Barrett. 1996. A metapopulation perspective in plant population biology. Journal of Ecology 84:461–469.

Husband, B.C., and D.W. Schemske. 1996. Evolution of the magnitude and timing of inbreeding depression in plants. Evolution 50:54–70.

Huston, M. 1979. A general hypothesis of species diversity. American Naturalist 113:81–101.

Huston, M., and T. Smith. 1987. Plant succession: life history and competition. American Naturalist 130:168–198.

Huston, M.A. 1994. Biological diversity: the coexistence of species on changing landscapes. Cambridge University Press, Cambridge, UK.

Huston, M.A. 1997. Hidden treatments in ecological experiments: re-evaluating the ecosystem function of biodiversity. Oecologia 110:449–460.

Hutchings, M.J., and J.P. Barkham. 1976. An investigation of shoot interactions in *Mercurialis perennis* L., a rhizomatous perennial herb. Journal of Ecology 64:723–743.

Hutchings, M.J., and H. Dekroon. 1994. Foraging in plants—the role of morphological plasticity in resource acquisition. Advances in Ecological Research 25:159–238.

Hutchings, M.J., E.A. John, and D.K. Wijesinghe. 2003. Toward understanding the consequences of soil heterogeneity for plant populations and communities. Ecology 84:2322–2334.

Hutchinson, G.E. 1959. Homage to Santa Rosalia, or why are there so many kinds of animals? American Naturalist 93:145–459.

Hutchinson, T.F., R.E.J. Boerner, S. Sutherland, E.K. Sutherland, M. Ortt, and L.R. Iverson. 2005. Prescribed fire effects on the herbaceous layer of mixed-oak forests. Canadian Journal of Forest Research 35:877–890.

Hutchinson, T.F., and J.L. Vankat. 1997. Invasibility and effects of Amur honeysuckle in southwestern Ohio forests. Conservation Biology 11:1117–1124.

Hutchison, B.A., and D.R. Matt. 1976. Beam enrichment of diffuse radiation in a deciduous forest. Agricultural Meteorology 17:93–110.

Hutchison, B.A., and D.R. Matt. 1977. The distribution of solar radiation within a deciduous forest. Ecological Monographs 47:185–207.

Hutchison, B.A., D.R. Matt, R.T. McMillen, L.J. Gross, S.J. Tajchman, and J.M. Norman. 1986. The architecture of a deciduous forest canopy in eastern Tennessee. Journal of Ecology 74:635–646.

Hylander, K. 2009. No increase in colonization rate of boreal bryophytes close to propagule sources. Ecology 90:160–169.

Ida, T.Y., and G. Kudo. 2008. Timing of canopy closure influences carbon translocation and seed production of an understorey herb, Trillium apetalon (Trilliaceae). Annals of Botany 101:435–446.

Ida, T.Y., and G. Kudo. 2009. Comparison of light harvesting and resource allocation strategies between two rhizomatous herbaceous species inhabiting deciduous forests. Journal of Plant Research 122:171–181.

Ida, T.Y., and G. Kudo. 2010. Seasonal patterns of carbon assimilation and allocation of a summer-green forest herb, Parasenecio auriculata (Senecioneae; Asteraceae). Plant Ecology 210:181–193.

Igic, B., and J.R. Kohn. 2006. The distribution of plant mating systems: study bias against obligately outcrossing species. Evolution 60:1098–1103.

Imhoff, M.L., P. Zhang, R.E. Wolfe, and L. Bounoua. 2010. Remote sensing of the urban heat island effect across biomes in the continental USA. Remote Sensing of Environment 114: 504–513.

Inouye, R.S., T.D. Allison, and N.C. Johnson. 1994. Old field succession on a Minnesota sand plain: Effects of deer and other factors on invasion by trees. Bulletin of the Torrey Botanical Club 121:266–276.

IPCC. 2007. Climate Change 2007: The Physical Science Basis. Contributions of Working Group I to the Fourth Assessment Report of the Intergovernmental Panel on Climate Change. S. Solomon, D. Qin, M. Manning, Z. Chen, M. Marquis, K.B. Averyt, M. Tignor, and H.L. Miller, eds. New York and Cambridge, UK: Cambridge University Press.

Ingvarsson, P.K., and S. Lundberg. 1995. Pollinator functional response and plant population dynamics—pollinators as a limiting resource. Evolutionary Ecology 9:421–428.

Irland, L.C. 1998. Ice storm 1998 and the forests of the Northeast: A preliminary assessment. Journal of Forestry 96:32–40.

Irland, L.C. 1999. The northeast's changing forest. Harvard University Press, Petersham, MA.

Irwin, R.E. 2000. Morphological variation and female reproductive success in two sympatric trillium species: evidence for phenotypic selection in Trillium erectum and Trillium grandiflorum (Liliaceae). American Journal of Botany 87:205–214.

Irwin, R.E. 2001. Field and allozyme studies investigating optimal mating success in two sympatric spring-ephemeral plants, Trillium erectum and T. grandiflorum. Heredity 87:178–189.

Ishii, H.S., and L.D. Harder. 2006. The size of individual Delphinium flowers and the opportunity for geitonogamous pollination. Functional Ecology 20:1115–1123.

Isogai, N., Y. Yamamura, S. Mariko, and T. Nakano. 2003. Seasonal pattern of photosynthetic production in a subalpine evergreen herb, Pyrola incarnata. Journal of Plant Research 116:199–206.

Israel, K. 2012. Vegetation change in the Duke Forest, 1977–2010. M.S. thesis, University of North Carolina, Chapel Hill, NC.

Ito, S., R. Nakayama, and G.P. Buckley. 2004. Effects of previous land-use on plant species diversity in semi-natural and plantation forests in a warm-temperate region in southeastern Kyushu, Japan. Forest Ecology and Management 196:213–225.

Iverson, L., M. Schwartz, and A. Prasad. 2004. Potential colonization of newly available tree-species habitat under climate change: an analysis for five eastern US species. Landscape Ecology 19:787–799.

Iverson, L.R., and A.M. Prasad. 1998. Predicting abundance of 80 tree species following climate change in the eastern United States. Ecological Monographs 68:465–485.

Iverson, L.R., D. Ketzner, and J. Karnes. 1999. Illinois Plant Information Network. Database at http://www.nrs.fs.fed.us/data/il/ilpin/. Illinois Natural History Survey and USDA Forest Service.

Ives, A.R., M.G. Turner, and S.M. Pearson. 1998. Local explanations of landscape patterns: can analytical approaches approximate simulation models of spatial processes? Ecosystems 1:35–51.

Jackson, B.C. 2006. Vegetation differences in neighboring old growth and second growth rich coves in the Joyce Kilmer Wilderness Area: a thirty-two-year perspective. Raleigh, NC: North Carolina State University.

Jackson, M.M., M.G. Turner, S.M. Pearson, and A.R. Ives. 2012. Seeing the forest and the trees: multilevel models reveal both species and community patterns. Ecosphere 3:1–16 (article 79).

Jackson, L.W.R. 1959. Relation of pine forest overstory opening diameter to growth of pine reproduction. Ecology 40:478–480.

Jackson, S.T., and C. Weng. 1999. Late Quaternary extinction of a tree species in eastern North America. Proceedings of the National Academy of Sciences 96:13847–13852.

Jackson, S.T., R.S. Webb, K.H. Anderson, J.T. Overpeck, T. Webb III, J.W. Williams, and B.C.S. Hansen. 2000. Vegetation and environment in eastern North America during the Last Glacial Maximum. Quaternary Science Reviews 19:489–508.

Jacquemyn, H., and R. Brys. 2008. Effects of stand age on the demography of a temperate forest herb in post-agricultural forests. Ecology 89:3480–3489.

Jacquemyn, H., R. Brys, D. Adriaens, A.O. Honnay, and I. Roldan-Ruiz. 2009. Effects of population size and forest management on genetic diversity and structure of the tuberous orchid *Orchis mascula*. Conservation Genetics 10:161–168.

Jacquemyn, H., R. Brys, and E. Jongejans. 2010a. Size-dependent flowering and costs of reproduction affect population dynamics in a tuberous perennial woodland orchid. Journal of Ecology 98:1204–1215.

Jacequemyn, H., R. Brys, and E. Jongejans. 2010b. Seed limitation restricts population growth in shaded populations of a perennial woodland orchid. Ecology 91:119–129.

Jacquemyn, H., J. Butaye, and M. Hermy. 2001. Forest plant species richness in small, fragmented mixed deciduous forest patches: the role of area, time and dispersal limitation. Journal of Biogeography 28:801–812.

Jacquemyn, H., O. Honnay, P. Galbusera, and I. Roldán-Ruiz. 2004. Genetic structure of the forest herb *Primula elatior* in a changing landscape. Molecular Ecology 13:211–219.

Jahnke, L.S., and D.B. Lawrence. 1965. Influence of photosynthetic crown structure on potential productivity of vegetation, based primarily on mathematical models. Ecology 46:319–326.

Jain, S.K. 1976. The evolution of inbreeding in plants. Annual Review of Ecology and Systematics 7:69–95.

Jandl, R., H. Kopeszki, and G. Glatzel. 1997. Effect of a dense *Allium ursinum* (L.) ground cover on nutrient dynamics and mesofauna of a *Fagus sylvatica* (L.) woodland. Plant and Soil 189:245–255.

Jankowska-Blaszczuk, M., and M.I. Daws. 2007. Impact of red: far red ratios on germination of temperate forest herbs in relation to shade tolerance, seed mass and persistence in the soil. Functional Ecology 21:1055–1062.

Jansson, R. 2003. Global patterns in endemism explained by past climatic change. Proceedings of the Royal Society B 270:583–590.

Jenkins J.C., and G. Motzkin. 2009. Harvard Forest flora database. Harvard Forest Data Archive: HF116.

Jenkins, J.C., G. Motzkin, and K. Ward. 2008. The Harvard Forest Flora. An Inventory, Analysis and Ecological History. Harvard Forest Paper 28:266.

Jenkins, M.A., and C.R. Webster. 2009. Spatial patterning and population structure of a common woodland herb, *Trillium erectum*, in primary and post-logging secondary forests. Forest Ecology and Management 258:2569–2577.

Jenkins, M.A., C.R. Webster, and J.H. Rock. 2009. Effects of chronic herbivory and historic land use on population structure of a forest perennial, *Trillium catesbaei*. Applied Vegetation Science 10:442–450.

Jennings, M.D., D. Faber-Langendoen, O.L. Loucks, R.K. Peet, and D. Roberts. 2009. Characterizing associations and alliances of the U.S. National Vegetation Classification. Ecological Monographs 79:173–199.

Jeong, S.J., C.H. Ho, H.J. Gim, and M.E. Brown. 2011. Phenology shifts at start vs. end of growing season in temperate vegetation over the Northern Hemisphere for the period 1982–2008. Global Change Biology 17:2385–2399.

John, E., and R. Turkington. 1995. Herbaceous vegetation in the understorey of the boreal forest: does nutrient supply or snowshoe hare herbivory regulation species composition and abundance? Journal of Ecology 83:581–590.

Johnson, A.S., W.M. Ford, and P.E. Hale. 1993. The effects of clearcutting on herbaceous understories are still not fully known. Conservation Biology 7:433–435.

Johnson, A.S., P.E. Hale, W.M. Ford, J.M. Wentworth, J.R. French, O.F. Anderson, and G.B. Pullen. 1995. White-tailed deer foraging in relation to successional stage, overstory type, and management of southern Appalachian forests. American Midland Naturalist 133:18–35.

Johnson, D.W., and B. Schultz. 1999. Responses of carbon and nitrogen cycles to disturbance in forests and rangelands. Pages 545–569 in L.R. Walker, editor. Ecosystems of disturbed ground. Elsevier, Amsterdam: NL.

Johnson, E.A. 1979. Fire recurrence in the subarctic and its implications for vegetation composition. Canadian Journal of Botany 57:1374–1379.

Johnson, S.E., E.L. Mudrak, and D.M. Waller. 2008. Comparing power among three sampling methods for monitoring forest vegetation. Canadian Journal of Forest Research 38:143–156.

Johnston, M.O. 1991. Pollen limitation of female reproduction in *Lobelia cardinalis* and *L. siphilitica*. Ecology 72:1500–1503.

Johnston, M.H., and J.A. Elliott. 1996. Impacts of logging and wildfire on an upland black spruce community in northwestern Ontario. Environmental Monitoring and Assessment 39:283–297.

Johnstone, I.M. 1986. Plant invasion windows: a time-based classification of invasion potential. Biological Review 61:369–394.

Jolls, C.L. 2003. Populations of and threats to rare plants of the herb layer: more challenges and opportunites for conservation biologists. Pages 105–159 in F.S. Gilliam and

and M.R. Roberts, editors. The herbaceous layer in forests of eastern North America. New York: Oxford University Press.

Jones, J., J. Pither, R.D. DeBruyn, and R.J. Robertson. 2001. Modeling ice storm damage to a mature, mixed-species hardwood forest in eastern Ontario. Ecoscience 8:513–521.

Jongejans, E., K. Shea, O. Skarpaas, D. Kelly, and S.P. Ellner. 2011. Importance of individual and environmental variation for invasive species spread: a spatial integral projection. Ecology 92:86–97.

Jongejans, E., A.W. Sheppard, and K. Shea. 2006. What controls the population dynamics of the invasive thistle *Carduus nutans* in its native range? Journal of Applied Ecology 43:877–886.

Jonsdottir, I.S., and M.A. Watson. 1997. Extensive physiological integration: an adaptive trait in resource-poor environments? In H. de Kroon and J.M. Van Groenendael, eds. The ecology and evolution of clonal plants. Leiden, NL: Backhuys, pp. 109–136.

Joyce, L.A., and R.L. Baker. 1987. Forest overstory-understory relationships in Alabama forests. Forest Ecology and Management 18:49–59.

Joyner, J.M., and E.W. Chester. 1994. The vascular flora of Cross Creeks National Wildlife Refuge, Stewart County, Tennessee. Castanea 59:117–145.

Judziewicz, E.J., and R.G. Koch. 1993. Flora and vegetation of the Apostle Islands National Lakeshore and Madeline Island, Ashland and Bayfield Counties, Wisconsin. The Michigan Botanist 32:43–189.

Jules, E.S., and B.J. Rathcke. 1999. Mechanisms of reduced *Trillium* recruitment along edges of old-growth forest fragments. Conservation Biology 13:784–793.

Junkys, R., K. Žeimavičius, G. Sujetovienė, and J. Gustainytė. 2012. Response of tree seasonal development to climate warming. Polish Journal of Environmental Studies 21:107–113.

Jurdant, M., J.-L. Bélair, V. Gérardin, and J.-P. Ducruc. 1977. L'inventaire du capital nature: méthode de classification et de cartographie du territoire (3e approximation). Service des Études écologiques régionales, Dir. Gén. des Terres, Environnement Canada.

Jurik, T.W., and B.F. Chabot. 1986. Leaf dynamics and profitability in wild strawberries. Oecologia 69:296–304.

Kain, M., L. Battaglia, A. Royo, and W.P. Carson. 2011. Over-browsing in Pennsylvania creates a depauperate forest dominated by an understory tree: results from a 60-year old deer exclosure. Journal of the Torrey Botanical Society 138:322–326.

Kalisz, S., and M. McPeek. 1992. Demography of an age-structured annual: resampled projection matrices, elasticity analyses, and seed bank effects. Ecology 73:1082–1093.

Kalisz, S., and M.A. McPeek. 1993. Extinction dynamics, population growth and seedbanks. Oecologia 95:314–320.

Kalisz, S., F.M. Hanzawa, S.J. Tonsor, D.A. Thiede, and S. Voigt. 1999. Ant-mediated seed dispersal alters pattern of relatedness in a population of *Trillium grandiflorum*. Ecology 80:2620–2634.

Kalisz, S., and D.W. Vogler. 2003. Benefits of autonomous selfing under unpredictable pollinator environments. Ecology 84:2928–2942.

Kalisz, S., D. Vogler, B. Falls, M. Finer, E. Shepard, T. Herman, and R. Gonzales. 1999. The mechanism of delayed selfing in *Collinsia verna* (Scrophulariaceae). American Journal of Botany 86:1239–1247.

Kallunki, J.A. 1981. Reproductive biology of mixed-species populations of *Goodyera* (Orchidaceae) in northern Michigan. Brittonia 33:137–155.

Karnofsky, D.F., D.R. Zak, K.S. Pregitzer, C.S. Awmack, J.G. Bockheim, R.E. Dickson, G.R. Hendrey, G.E. Host, J.S. King, B.J. Kopper, E.I. Kruger, M.E. Kubiske, R.L. Lindroth, W.J. Mattson, E.P. McDonald, A. Noormets, E. Oksanen, W.F.J. Parsons, K.E. Percy, G.K. Podila, D.E. Riemenschneider, P. Sharma, R. Thakur, A. Sober, J. Sober, W.S. Jones, S. Anttonen, E. Vapaavuori, B. Mankovska, W. Heilman and J.G. Isebrands. 2003. Tropospheric O_3 moderates responses of temperate hardwood forests to elevated CO_2: a synthesis of molecular to ecosystem results from the Aspen FACE project. Functional Ecology 17:289–304.

Karr, J.R., M. Dionne, and I. Schlosser. 1992. Bottom-up versus top-down regulation of vertebrate populations: lessons from birds and fish. In M.D. Hunter, T. Ohgushi, and P.W. Price, eds. Effects of resource distribution on animal-plant interactions. New York: Academic Press, pp. 244–286.

Karron, J.D., R.T. Jackson, N.N. Thumser, and S.L. Schlicht. 1997. Outcrossing rates of individual *Mimulus ringens* genets are correlated with anther-stigma separation. Heredity 79:365–370.

Kartesz, J.T. 2010. The Biota of North America Program (BONAP). North American Plant Atlas (http://www.bonap.org/MapSwitchboard.html). Chapel Hill, NC.

Kauth, P.J., and M.E. Kane. 2009. *In vitro* ecology of *Calopogon tuberosus* var. *tuberosus* (Orchidaceae) seedlings from distant populations: implications for assessing ecotypic differentiation. Journal of the Torrey Botanical Society 136:433–444.

Kauth, P.J., M.E. Kane, and W.A. Vendrame. 2011. Chilling relieves dormancy in *Calopogon tuberosus* (Orchidaceae) from geographically distant populations. Environmental and Experimental Botany 70:283–288.

Kauth, P.J., M.E. Kane, W.A. Vendrame, and C. Reinhardt-Adams. 2008. Asymbiotic germination response to photoperiod and nutritional media in six populations of *Calopogon tuberosus* var. *tuberosus* (Orchidaceae): evidence for ecotypic differentiation. Annals of Botany 102:783–793.

Kavanagh, R.P., and M.A. Stanton. 2005. Vertebrate species assemblages and species sensitivity to logging in the forests of northeastern New South Wales. Forest Ecology and Management 209:309–341.

Kawano, S. 1970. Species problems viewed from productive and reproductive biology. I. Ecological life histories of some representative members associated with temperate deciduous forests in Japan. Journal of the College of Liberal Arts, Toyama University, Natural Sciences 3:181–213.

Kawano, S. 1975. The productive and reproductive biology of flowering plants. II. The concept of life history strategy in plants. Journal of the College of Liberal Arts, Toyama University, Natural Sciences 8:51–86.

Kawano, S., and J. Masuda.1979. The productive and reproductive biology of flowering plants. VI. Assimilation behavior and reproductive allocation of *Coptis japonica* (Thunb.) Makino (Ranunculaceae). Journal of the College of Liberal Arts, Toyama University, Natural Sciences 12:49–63.

Kawano, S., H. Takasu, and Y. Nagai. 1978. The productive and reproductive biology of flowering plants. IV. Assimilation behavior of some temperate woodland herbs. Journal of the College of Liberal Arts, Toyama University, Natural Sciences 11:33–60.

Kaye, J.P., and S.C. Hart. 1997. Competition for nitrogen between plants and soil microorganisms. Trends in Ecology amd Evolution 12:139–143.

Kearns, C.A., and D.W. Inouye. 1993. Techniques for pollination biologists. Boulder, CO: University of Colorado Press.

Kearns, C.A., D.W. Inouye, and N.M. Waser. 1998. Endangered mutualisms: The conservation of plant-pollinator interactions. Annual Review of Ecology, Evolution, and Systematics 29:83–112.

Kearsley, J.B. 1999. Inventory and vegetation classification of floodplain forest communities in Massachusetts. Rhodora 101:105–135.

Keddy, P.A. 1992. Assembly and response rules: two goals for predictive community ecology. Journal of Vegetation Science 3:157–164.

Keddy, P.A., and C.G. Drummond. 1996. Ecological properties for the evaluation, management, and restoration of temperate deciduous forest ecosystems. Ecological Applications 6:748–762.

Keenan, R.J., and J.P. Kimmins. 1993. The ecological effects of clear-cutting. Environmental Reviews 1:121–144.

Keever, C. 1950. Causes of succession on old fields of the Piedmont, North Carolina. Ecological Monographs 20:229–250.

Keever, C. 1983. Retrospective view of old-field succession after 35 years. American Midland Naturalist 110:397–404.

Kelly, C.N., S.H. Schoenholtz, and M.B. Adams. 2011. Soil properties associated with net nitrification following watershed conversion from Appalachian hardwoods to Norway spruce. Plant and Soil 344:361–376.

Kesler, H.C., J.L. Trusty, S.M. Hermann, and C. Guyer. 2008. Demographic responses of *Pinguicula ionantha* to prescribed fire: A regression-design LTRE approach. Oecologia 156:545–557.

Kevan, P.G. 1978. Floral coloration, its colorimetric analysis, and significance in anthecology. Pages 51–78 in A.J. Richards, ed. The pollination of flowers by insects. London: Academic Press.

Kevan, P.G., and H.G. Baker. 1983. Insects as flower visitors and pollinators. Annual Review of Entomology 28:407–453.

Kikuzawa, K. 1984. Leaf survival of woody plants in deciduous broad-leaved forests. 2. Small trees and shrubs. Canadian Journal of Botany 62:2551–2556.

Kikuzawa, K. 1991. A cost-benefit analysis of leaf habit and leaf longevity of trees and their geographical pattern. American Naturalist 138:1250–1263.

Kikuzawa, K., and D. Ackerly. 1999. Significance of leaf longevity in plants. Plant Species Biology 14:39–45.

Kilburn, P.D. 1957. Historical development and structure of the aspen, jack pine, and oak vegetation types on sandy soils in northern lower Michigan. Ph.D. dissertation, University of Michigan, Ann Arbor, MI.

Kilkenny, F.F., and L.F. Galloway. 2008. Reproductive success in varying light environments; direct and indirect effects of light on plants and pollinators. Oecologia 155:247–255.

Killingbeck, K.T. 1996. Nutrients in senesced leaves: Keys to the search for potential resorption and resorption proficiency. Ecology 77:1716–1727.

Kimball, B.A. 2011. Comment on the comment by Amthor et al. on "Appropriate experimental ecosystem warming methods" by Aronson and McNulty. Agricultural and Forest Meteorology 151:420–424.

Kimmins, J.P. 1996. Forest ecology: a foundation for sustainable management. 2nd ed. Prentice-Hall, Upper Saddle River, NJ.

Kinerson, R.S. 1979. Studies of photosynthesis and diffusion resistance in paper birch (*Betula papyrifera* Marsh) with synthesis through computer simulation. Oecologia 39:37–49.

Kirchner, F., J. Ferdy, C. Andalo, B. Colas, and J. Moret. 2003. Role of corridors in plant dispersal: an example with the endangered *Ranunculus nodiflorus*. Conservation Biology 17:401–410.

Kirkman, L.K., M.G. Drew, and D. Edwards. 1998. Effects of experimental fire regimes on the population dynamics of *Schwalbea americana* L. Plant Ecology 137:115–137.

Kirkman, L.K., P.C. Goebel, and B.J. Palik. 2004. Predicting plant species diversity in a long-leaf pine landscape. Ecoscience 11: 80–93.

Kirchner, K., S. Kathke, and H. Bruelheide. 2011. The interaction of gap age and microsite for herb layer species in a near-natural spruce forest. Journal of Vegetation Science 22:85–95.

Kirkman, L.K., M.G. Drew, and D. Edwards. 1998. Effects of experimental fire regimes on the population dynamics of *Schwalbea americana* L. Plant Ecology 137:115–137.

Kirkman, L.K., P.C. Goebel, and B.J. Palik. 2004. Predicting plant species diversity in a long-leaf pine landscape. Ecoscience 11: 80–93.

Kirchner, K., S. Kathke, and H. Bruelheide. 2011. The interaction of gap age and micro-site for herb layer species in a near-natural spruce forest. Journal of Vegetation Science 22:85–95.

Kirschbaum, C.D., and B.L. Anacker. 2005. The utility of *Trillium* and *Maianthemum* as phyto-indicators of deer impact in northwestern Pennsylvania, USA. Forest Ecology and Management 217:54–66.

Kitterage, D.B., P. Mark, and S. Ashton. 1995. Impact of deer browsing on regeneration in mixed stands in southern New England. Northern Journal of Applied Forestry 12:115–120.

Kjellsson, G. 1985. Seed fate in a population of *Carex pilulifera* L. II. Seed predation and its consequences for dispersal and seed bank. Oecologia 67:424–429.

Kliber, A., and C.G. Eckert. 2004. Temporal decline in reproductive investment among flowers in a sequentially blooming plant *Aquilegia canadensis* (Ranunculaceae): proximate mechanisms and adaptive significance. Ecology 85:1675–1687.

Klooster, M.R., and T.M. Culley. 2009. Comparative analysis of the reproductive ecology of *Monotropa* and *Monotropsis*: two mycoheterotrophic generals in the Monotropoideae (Ericaceae). American Journal of Botany 96:1337–1347.

Knight, G.J. 1964. Distribution of *Osmunda cinnamomea* L. and *Osmunda claytoniana* L. in relation to natural soil drainage. M.S. thesis, Harvard University, Cambridge, MA.

Knight, T.M. 2003. Effects of herbivory and its timing across populations of *Trillium grandiflorum* (Liliaceae). American Journal of Botany 90:1207–1214.

Knight, T.M. 2004. The effect of herbivory and pollen limitation on a declining population of *Trillium grandiflorum*. Ecological Applications 14:915–928.

Knight, T.M. 2007. Population-level consequences of herbivory timing in *Trillium grandiflorum*. American Midland Naturalist 157:27–38.

Knight, T.M., M. Barfield, and R.D. Holt. 2008. Evolutionary dynamics as a component of stage-structured matrix models: an example using *Trillium grandiflorum*. American Naturalist 172:375–392.

Knight, T.M., H. Caswell, and S. Kalisz. 2009a. Population growth rate of a common under-story herb decreases non-linearly across a gradient of deer herbivory. Forest Ecology and Management 257:1095–1103.

Knight, T.M., J.L. Dunn, J. Davis, and S. Kalisz. 2009b. Deer facilitate invasive plant success in a Pennsylvania forest understory. Natural Areas Journal 29:110–116.

Knight, T.M., J.A. Steets, and T.-L. Ashman. 2006. A quantitative synthesis of pollen supple-mentation experiments highlights the contribution of resource reallocation to estimates of pollen limitation. American Journal of Botany 93:271–277.

Knight, T.M., J.A. Steets, J.C. Vamosi, S.J. Mazer, M. Burd, D.R. Campbell, M.R. Dudash, M.O. Johnston, R.J. Mitchell, and T.-L. Ashman. 2005. Pollen limitation of plant repro-duction: pattern and process. Annual Review of Ecology, Evolution, and Systematics 36:467–497.

Knoepp, J.D., B.C. Reynolds, D.A. Crossley, and W.T. Swank. 2005. Long-term changes in forest floor processes in southern Appalachian forests. Forest Ecology and Management 220:300–312.

Knollová, I., M. Chytrý, L. Tichý, and O. Hájek. 2005. Stratified resampling of phytosocio-logical databases: some strategies for obtaining more representative data sets for clas-sification studies. Journal of Vegetation Science 16:479–486.

Knox, R.G., R.K. Peet, and N.L. Christensen. 1989. Population dynamics in loblolly pine stands: changes in skewness and size inequality. Ecology 70: 1153–1166.

Knudsen, J.T., and J.M. Olesen. 1993. Buzz-pollination and patterns in sexual traits in north European Pyrolaceae. American Journal of Botany 80:900–913.

Knuth, P. 1906–1909. Handbook of flower pollination based upon Herman Müller's work "The fertilization of flowers by insects" translated by J.R. Ainsworth Davis. London: Clarendon Press.

Kochenderfer, J.N., and G.W. Wendel. 1983. Plant succession and hydrologic recovery on a deforested and herbicided watershed. Forest Science 29:545–558.

Köelreuter, J.G. 1761–1766. Vorläufige Nachrich von einegn das Geschlecht der Pflanzen betreffenden Versuchen und Boebachtungen. Leipzig, DE: Leipzig in der Gleditschischen Handlung.

Koizumi, H. 1985. Studies on the life history of an evergreen herb, *Pyrola japonica*, population on a forest floor in a warm temperate region. 1. Growth, net production and matter economy. Botanical Magazine of Tokyo 98:383–392.

Koizumi, H. 1989. Studies on the life history of an evergreen herb, *Pyrola japonica*, population on a forest floor in a warm temperate region. 2. Photosynthesis, respiration and gross production. Botanical Magazine of Tokyo 102:521–532.

Koizumi, H., and Y. Oshima. 1985. Seasonal changes in photosynthesis of four understory herbs in deciduous forest. Botanical Magazine of Tokyo 98:1–13.

Koizumi, H., and Y. Oshima. 1993. Light environment and carbon gain of understory herbs associated with sunflecks in a warm temperate deciduous forest in Japan. Ecological Research 8:135–142.

Kokko, H., and A. Lopez-Sepulcre. 2007. The ecogenetic link between demography and evolution: can we bridge the gap between theory and data. Ecology Letters 10:773–782.

Kolb, A., and M. Diekmann. 2005. Effects of life-history traits on responses of plant species to forest fragmentation. Conservation Biology 19:929–938.

Kolb, T.E., T.W. Bowersox, and L.H. McCormick. 1990. Influences of light intensity on weed-induced stresses of tree seedlings. Canadian Journal of Forest Research 20:503–507.

Kolb, T.E., T.W. Bowersox, L.H. McCormick, and K.C. Steiner. 1989. Effects of shade and herbaceous vegetation on first-year germination and growth of direct-seeded northern red oak, white ash, white pine, and yellow-poplar. Proceedings of the Seventh Central Hardwood Conference, Southern Illinois University, Carbondale, IL.

Königer, M., G.C. Harris, A. Virgo, and K. Winter. 1995. Xanthophyll-cycle pigments and photosynthetic capacity in tropical forest species: a comparative field study on canopy, gap and understory plants. Oecologia 104:280–290.

Körner, C. 1994. Scaling from species to vegetation: the usefulness of functional groups. Pages 117–140 in E.-D. Schulze and H.A. Mooney, editors. Biodiversity and ecosystem function. Springer-Verlag, Berlin: DE.

Körner, C., J.A. Scheel, and H. Bauer. 1979. Maximum leaf diffusive conductance in vascular plants. Photosynthetica 13:45–82.

Kooyman, R., and M. Rossetto. 2008. Definition of plant functional groups for informing implementation scenarios in resource-limited multi-species recovery planning. Biodiversity and Conservation 17:2917–2937.

Körner, C., J.A. Scheel, and H. Bauer. 1979. Maximum leaf diffusive conductance in vascular plants. Photosynthetica 13:45–82.

Koroleff, A. 1954. Leaf litter as a killer. Journal of Forestry 52:178–187.

Koyama, H., and S. Kawano. 1973. Biosystematic studies on *Maianthemum* (Liliaceae-Polygonatae). VII. Photosynthetic behavior of *M. dilatatum* under changing temperate woodland environments and its biological implications. Botanical Magazine of Tokyo 86:89–101.

Kraft, L.S., T.R. Crow, D.S. Buckley, E.A. Nauertz, and J.C. Zasada. 2004. Effects of harvesting and deer browsing on attributes of understory plants in northern hardwood forests, Upper Michigan, USA. Forest Ecology and Management 199:219–230.

Kral, R., and V. Bates. 1991. A new species of *Hydrophyllum* from the Ouachita Mountains of Arkansas. Novon 1:60–66.

Kreyling, J., A. Schmiedinger, E. Macdonald, and C. Beierkuhnlein. 2008. Slow understory redevelopment after clearcutting in high mountain forests. Biodiversity and Conservation 17:2339–2355.

Kriebitzsch, W.U. 1984. Seasonal course of chlorophyll content in leaves of *Mercurialis perennis* L. Flora 175:111–115.

Kriebitzsch, W.U. 1992a. CO_2 and H_2O gas exchange of understory plants in a submontane beech forest on limestone. I. Seasonal changes of the photosynthetic response to light. Flora 186:67–85.

Kriebitzsch, W.U. 1992b. CO_2 and H_2O gas exchange of understory plants in a submontane beech forest on limestone. II. Influence of temperature and air humidity. Flora 186:87–103.

Kriebitzsch, W.U. 1992c. CO_2 and H_2O gas exchange of understory plants in a submontane beech forest on limestone. III. CO_2 balances and net primary production. Flora 187:135–158.

Kriebitzsch, W.U. 1993. Der Wasserumsatz von Pflanzen in der Krautschicht eines Kalkbuchenwaldes. Phytocoenologia 23:35–50.

Kriebitzsch, W.U., and J. Regel. 1982. Bestimmung der Netto-Primärproduktion von Mercurialis perennis über die CO_2-Bilanz bzw. über die Ernte-Methode—Ein Methodenvergleich. Kurzmtlg. SFB 135 1:9–16.

Kriedeman, P.E., T.F. Neales, and D.H. Ashton. 1964. Photosynthesis in relation to leaf orientation and light interception. Australian Journal of Biological Science 17:591–600.

Kropf, M., J.W. Kadereit, and H.P. Comes. 2002. Late Quaternary distributional stasis in the submediterranean mountain plant *Anthyllis montana* L. (Fabaceae) inferred from ITS sequences and amplified fragment length polymorphism markers. Molecular Ecology 11: 447–463.

Krueger, L.M., and C.J. Peterson. 2006. Effects of white-tailed deer on *Tsuga canadensis* regeneration: evidence of microsites as refugia from browsing. American Midland Naturalist 156:353–362.

Krueger, L.M., and C.J. Peterson. 2009. Effects of woody debris and ferns on herb-layer vegetation and deer herbivory in a Pennsylvania forest blowdown. Ecoscience 16:461–469.

Kudo, G., and T.Y. Ida. 2010. Carbon source for reproduction in a spring ephemeral herb, *Corydalis ambigua* (Papaveraceae). Functional Ecology 24:62–69.

Kudo, G., T.Y. Ida, and T. Tani. 2008. Linkages between phenology, pollination, photosynthesis, and reproduction in deciduous forest understory plants. Ecology 89:321–331.

Kudo, G., Y. Nishikawa, T. Kasagi, and S. Kosuge. 2004. Does seed production of spring ephemerals decrease when spring comes early? Ecological Research 19:255–259.

Kudoh, H., H. Shibaike, H. Takasu, D.F. Whigham, and S. Kawano. 1999. Genet structure and maintenance of clonal diversity in a temperate deciduous forest herb, *Uvularia perfoliata*. Journal of Ecology 84: 244–257.

Kuhman, T.R., S.M. Pearson, and M.G. Turner. 2011. Agricultural land-use history increases non-native plant invasion in a southern Appalachian forest a century after abandonment. Canadian Journal of Forest Research 41:920–929.

Kuiters, A.T., and P.A. Slim. 2002. Regeneration of mixed deciduous forest in a Dutch forest-heathland, following a reduction of ungulate densities. Biological Conservation 105:65–74.

Kupfer, J.A., and G.P. Malanson. 1993. Structure and composition of a riparian forest edge. Physical Geography 14:154–170.

Küppers, M. 1994. Canopy gaps: Competitive light interception and economic space filling—A matter of whole-plant allocation. Pages 111–144 in M.M. Caldwell and R.W.

Pearcy, editors. Exploitation of environmental heterogeneity by plants: ecophysiological processes above- and belowground. Academic Press, San Diego, CA.

Küppers, M., H. Timm, F. Orth, J. Stegemann, R. Stöber, H. Schneider, K. Paliwal, K.S.T.K. Karunaichamy, and R. Ortiz. 1996. Effects of light environment and successional status on lightfleck use by understory trees of temperate and tropical forests. Tree Physiology 16:69–80.

Kurmis, V., and E. Sucoff. 1989. Population density and height distribution of *Corylus cornuta* in undisturbed forest of Minnesota: 1965–1984. Canadian Journal of Botany 67:2409–2413.

Kursar, T.A., and P.D. Coley. 1993. Photosynthetic induction times in shade-tolerant species with long- and short-lived leaves. Oecologia 93:165–170.

Laatsch, J.R., and R.C. Anderson. 2000. An evaluation of oak woodland management in northeastern Illinois, USA. Natural Areas Journal 20:211–220.

Lack, D. 1947. Darwinhs finches: an essay on the general biological theory of evolution. Cambridge University Press, Cambridge, UK.

Lamb, E.G., S.W. Kembel, and J.F. Cahill. 2009. Shoot, but not root, competition reduces community diversity in experimental mesocosms. Journal of Ecology 97:155–163.

Lambers, H. 1985. Respiration in intact plants and tissues: Its regulation and dependence on environmental factors, metabolism and invaded organisms. Pages 418–473 in R. Douce and D.A. Day, editors. Encyclopedia of plant physiology, N.S., Vol. 18. Springer-Verlag, Berlin.

Lambers, H., F.S. Chapin III, and T.L. Pons. 1998. Plant physiological ecology. Springer, New York.

Lambers, H., F.S. Chapin, and T.L. Pons. 2000. Plant Physiological Ecology. New York: Springer Science.

Lambert, B.B., and E.S. Menges. 1996. The effects of light, soil disturbance and presence of organic litter on the field germination and survival of the Florida golden aster, *Chrysopsis floridana* Small. Florida Scientist 59:121–137.

Lambert, R.S. 1961. Logging the Great Smokies, 1880–1930. Tennessee Historical Quarterly 20:350–363.

Lambrecht-McDowell, S., and S. Radosevich. 2005. Population demographics and trade-offs to reproduction of an invasive and noninvasive species of *Rubus*. Biological Invasions 7:281–295.

Landa, K., B. Benner, M.A. Watson, and J. Gartner. 1992. Physiological integration for carbon in mayapple (Podophyllum-Peltatum), a clonal perennial herb. Oikos 63:348–356.

Lande, R. 1988. Genetics and demography of biological conservation. Science 241:1455–1460.

Lande, R. 1993. Risks of population extinction from demographic and environmental stochasticity and random catastrophes. American Naturalist 142:911–927.

Lande, R., and D.W. Schemske. 1985. The evolution of self-fertilization and inbreeding depression in plants.1. Genetic models. Evolution 39:24–40.

Landhäusser, S.M., K.J. Stadt, and V.J. Lieffers. 1997. Photosynthetic strategies of summer-green and evergreen herbs of the boreal mixed-wood forest. Oecologia 112:173–178.

Lankau, R.A., V. Nuzzo, G. Spyreas, and A.S. Davis. 2009. Evolutionary limits ameliorate the negative impact of an invasive plant. Proceedings of the National Academy of Sciences 107:15362–15367.

Lanza, J., M.A. Schmitt, and A.B. Awad. 1992. Comparative chemistry of elaiosomes of three species of *Trillium*. Journal of Chemical Ecology 18:209–221.

Lapointe, L. 2001. How phenology influences physiology in deciduous forest spring ephemerals. Physiologia Plantarum 113:151–157.

Lapointe, L., and S. Lerat. 2006. Annual growth of the spring ephemeral *Erythronium americanum* as a function of temperature and mycorrhizal status. Canadian Journal of Botany 84:39–48.

Lapointe, L., and Molard, J. 1997. Cost and benefits of mycorrhizal infection in a spring ephemeral, *Erythronium americanum*. New Phytologist 135:491–500.

LaRoi, G.H., and M.H.L. Stringer. 1976. Ecological studies in the boreal spruce-fir forests of the North American taiga. II. Analysis of the bryophyte flora. Canadian Journal of Botany 54:619–643.

Larson, B.M.H. 2005. The war of the roses: demilitarizing invasion biology. Frontiers in Ecology and the Environment 3:495–500.

Larson, B.M.H. 2007. Who's invading what? Systems thinking about invasive species. Canadian Journal of Plant Science 87:993–999.

Larson, B.M.H. 2010. Reweaving narratives about humans and invasive species. Etudes Rurales 185:25–38.

Larson, B.M.H., and S.C.H. Barrett 2000. A comparative analysis of pollen limitation in flowering plants. Biological Journal of the Linnean Society 69:503–520.

Latham, R.E., J. Beyea, M. Benner, C.A. Dunn, M.A. Fajvan, R.R. Freed, M. Grund, S.B. Horsley, A.F. Rhoads, and B.P. Shissler. 2005. Managing white-tailed deer in forest habitat from an ecosystem perspective. Report by the Deer Management Forum for Audubon Pennsylvania and Pennsylvania Habitat Alliance, Harrisburg, PA.

Latham, R., M.D. Grund, S.B. Horseley, B.C. Jones, W.H. McWilliams, C.K. Nielsen, C.S. Rosenberry, R.S. Seymour, B.P. Shissler, and D.M.Waller. 2009. Monitoring deer effects on forest ecosystems in Pennsylvania State Forests. Pennsylvania Dept. of Conservation & Natural Resources, Bureau of Forestry, Harrisburg, PA.

Latham, R.E., and R.E. Ricklefs. 1993. Continental comparisons of temperate-zone tree species diversity. In R.E. Ricklefs and D. Schluter, eds. Species diversity in ecological communities. Chicago: University of Chicago Press, pp. 294–314.

Lau, R.R., and D.R. Young. 1988. Influence of physiological integration on survivorship and water relations in a clonal herb. Ecology 69:215–219.

Lautenschlager, R.A., and C. Nielsen. 1999. Ontario's forest science efforts following the 1998 ice storm. Forestry Chronicle 75:633–641.

Lavergne, S., N. Mouquet, W. Thuiller, and O. Ronce. 2010. Biodiversity and climate change: integrating evolutionary and ecological responses of species and communities. Annual Review of Ecology, Evolution, and Systematics, 41:321–350.

Lavergne, S., J. Thompson, E. Garnier, and M. Debussche. 2004. The biology and ecology of narrow endemic and widespread plants: a comparative study of trait variation in 20 congeneric pairs. Oikos 107:505–518.

Laverty, T.M. 1980. The flower-visiting behavior of bumble bees: floral complexity and learning. Canadian Journal of Zoology 58:1324–1335.

Lavoie, C., and D. Lachance. 2006. A new herbarium-based method for reconstructing the phenology of plant species across large areas. American Journal of Botany 93:512–516.

Lawton, R.O. 1990. Canopy gaps and light penetration into a wind-exposed tropical lower montane rain forest. Canadian Journal of Forest Research 20:659–667.

Leach, M.K., and T.J. Givnish. 1999. Gradients in the composition, structure, and diversity of remnant oak savannas in southern Wisconsin. Ecological Monographs 69:353–374.

Leakey, A.D.B., E.A. Ainsworth, C.J. Bernacchi, A. Rogers, S.P. Long, and D.R. Ort. 2009. Elevated CO_2 effects on plant carbon, nitrogen, and water relations: six important lessons from FACE. Journal of Experimental Botany 60:2859–2876.

Leck, M.A., V.T. Parker, and R.L. Simpson. 1989. Ecology of Soil Seed Banks. New York: Academic Press.

Leckie, S., M. Vellend, G. Bell, M.J. Waterway, and M.J. Lechowicz. 2000. The seed bank in an old-growth, temperate deciduous forest. Canadian Journal of Botany 78:181–192.

Lee, D.W., and R. Graham. 1986. Leaf optical properties of rainforest sun and extreme-shade plants. American Journal of Botany 73:1100–1108.

Lee, T.D. 1989. Patterns of fruit and seed production in a Vermont population of *Cassia nictitans* L (Caesalpiniaceae). Bulletin of the Torrey Botanical Club 116:15–21.

Lee, T.D., and F.A. Bazzaz. 1982. Regulation of fruit and seed production in an annual legume, *Cassia fasciculat*a. Ecology 63:1363–1373.

Leege, L.M., J.S. Thompson, and D.J. Parris. 2010. The responses of rare and common Trilliums (*Trillium reliquum*, *T. cuneatum*, and *T. maculatum*) to deer herbivory and invasive honeysuckle removal. Castanea 75:433–443.

Legendre, P., D. Borcard, and P.R. Peres-Neto. 2005. Analyzing beta diversity: Partitioning the spatial variation of community composition data. Ecological Monographs 75:435–450.

Lehtila, K., K. Syrjanen, R. Leimu, M. Garcia, and J. Ehrlén. 2006. Habitat change and demography of *Primula veris*: identification of management targets. Conservation Biology 20:833–843.

Lefkovitch, L.P. 1965. The study of population growth in organisms grouped by stages. Biometrics 21:1–18.

Lei, T.T., and T. Koike. 1998. Some observations of phenology and ecophysiology of *Daphne kamtschatica* Maxim. var. jezoensis (Maxim.) Ohwi, a shade deciduous shrub, in the forest of northern Japan. Journal of Plant Research 111:207–212.

Leicht-Young, S.A., N.B. Pavlovic, K.J. Frohnapple, and R. Grundel. 2010. Liana habitat and host preferences in northern temperate forests. Forest Ecology and Management 260:1467–1477.

Leimu, R, P. Mutikainen, J. Koricheva, and M. Fischer. 2006. How general are positive relationships between plant population size, fitness and genetic variation? Journal of Ecology 94:942–9452.

Lendzion, J., and C. Leuschner. 2009. Temperature forest herbs are adapted to high air humidity—evidence from climate chamber and humidity manipulation experiments in the field. Canadian Journal of Forest Research 39:2332–2342.

Lengyel, A., M. Chytrý, and L. Tichý. 2011. Heterogeneity-constrained random resampling of phytosociological databases. Journal of Vegetation Science 22:175–183.

Lennartsson, T. 2002. Extinction thresholds and disrupted plant-pollinator interactions in fragmented plant populations. Ecology 83:3060–3072.

Lemon, P.C. 1961. Forest ecology of ice storms. Bulletin of the Torrey Botanical Club 88:21–29.

Leopold, A. 1933. Game Management. New York: Charles Scribner's Sons.

Leopold, A. 1936. Deer and Dauerwald in Germany I. History. Journal of Forestry 34:366–375.

Leopold, A. 1943. The excess deer problem. Audubon 45:156–157.

Leopold, A. 1946. The deer dilemma. Wisconsin Conservation Bulletin 11:3–5.

Lerat, S., R. Gauci, J.G. Catford, H. Vierheilig, Y. Piché, and L. Lapointe. 2002. ^{14}C transfer between the spring ephemeral *Erythonium americanum* and sugar maple via arbuscular mycorrhizal fungi in natural stands. Oecologia 132:181–187.

Lertzman, K.P. 1992. Patterns of gap-phase replacement in a subalpine, old-growth forest. Ecology 73:657–669.

Lertzman, K.P., and J. Fall. 1998. From forest stands to landscapes: spatial scales and the roles of disturbances. Pages 339–368 in D.L. Peterson and V.T. Parker, editors. Ecological Scale: Theory and Applications. Columbia University Press, New York.

Lesica, P., R. Yurkewycz, and E.E. Crone. 2006. Rare plants are common where you find them. American Journal of Botany 93:454–459.

Leverett, R. 1996. Definitions and history. In M. B. Davis, ed. Eastern old-growth forests: Prospects for rediscovery and recovery. Washington, DC: Island Press, pp. 3–17.

Levey, D.J., and M.M. Byrne. 1993. Complex ant-plant interactions: rain-forest ants as secondary dispersers and post-dispersal seed predators. Ecology 74:1802–1812.

Levin, D.A. 2000. The origin, expansion, and demise of plant species. Oxford, UK: Oxford University Press.

Levin, D.A., and A.C. Wilson. 1976. Rates of evolution in seed plants: Net increase in diversity of chromosome numbers and species numbers through time. Proceedings of the National Academy of Sciences of the United States of America 73:2086–2090.

Levin, P.S., and D.A. Levin. 2001. The real biodiversity crisis. American Scientist 90:6–8.

Levin, S.A. 1992. The problem of pattern and scale in ecology. Ecology 73:1943–1967.

Levine, J.M., and C.M. D'Antonio. 1999. Elton revisited: a review of the evidence linking diversity and invasibility. Oikos 87:15–26.

Levins, R. 1968. Evolution in changing environments. Princeton University Press, Princeton, NJ.

Levins, R. 1970. Extinctions. Pages 75–107 in M. Gerstenhaber, editor. Lectures on Mathematics in the Life Sciences, Vol. 2. American Mathematical Society, Providence, RI.

Levy, F., and D. Moore. 1993. Population variation of sleep movements in Oxalis grandis (Oxalidaceae). American Journal of Botany 80:1482–1493.

Levy, S. 2006. A plague of deer. BioScience 56:718–721.

Lezberg, A., C. Halpern, and J. Antos. 2001. Clonal development of Maianthemum dilatatum in forests of differing age and structure. Canadian Journal of Botany 79:1028–1038.

Li, D.-Z., and H.W. Pritchard. 2009. The science and economics of ex situ plant conservation. Trends in Plant Science 14:614–621.

Liang, L., M.D. Schwartz, and S. Fei. 2012. Photographic assessment of temperate forest understory phenology in relation to springtime meteorological drivers. International Journal of Biometeorology 56:343–355.

Lid, J., and D.T. Lid. 1994. Norsk Flora. Oslo, NO: Det Norske Samlaget.

Likens, G.E., and F.H. Bormann. 1970. Chemical analyses of plant tissues from the Hubbard Brook Ecosystem in New Hampshire. Yale University School of Forestry Bulletin No. 79.

Likens, G.E., F.H. Bormann, N.M. Johnson, D.W. Fisher, and R.S. Pierce. 1970. Effects of forest cutting and herbicide treatment on nutrient budgets in the Hubbard Brook watershed-ecosystem. Ecological Monographs 40:23–47.

Likens, G.E., F.H. Bormann, R.S. Pierce, J.S. Eaton, and N.M. Johnson. 1977. Biogeochemistry of a forested ecosystem. Springer-Verlag, New York.

Lilleskov, E.A., T.J. Fahey, T.R. Horton, and G.M. Lovett. 2002. Belowground ectomycorrhizal fungal community change over a nitrogen deposition gradient in Alaska. Ecology 83:104–115.

Lilleskov, E.A., P.M. Wargo, K.A. Vogt, and D.J. Vogt. 2008. Mycorrhizal fungal community relationship to root nitrogen concentration over a regional atmospheric nitrogen deposition gradient in the northeastern US. Canadian Journal of Forest Research 38:1260–1266.

Lindblad, I. 1998. Wood-inhabiting fungi on fallen logs of Norway spruce: relations to forest management and substrate quality. Nordic Journal of Botany 18:243–255.

Lindenmayer, D.B., M.A. Murgman, H.R. Akcakaya, R.C. Lacy, and H.P. Possingham. 1995. A review of the generic computer-programs ALEX, RAMAS/SPACE and VORTEX for modeling the viability of wildlife metapopulations. Ecological Modelling 82:161–174.

Lippmaa, T. 1939. The unistratal concept of plant communities (the unions). American Midland Naturalist 21:111–143.

Lipscomb, M.V. 1986. The influence of water and light on the physiology and spatial distributions of three shrubs in the southern Appalachian Mountains. M.S. thesis, Virginia Polytechnic Institute and State University, Blacksburg, VA.

Lipscomb, M.V., and E.T. Nilsen. 1990a. Environmental and physiological factors influencing the natural distribution of evergreen and deciduous ericaceous shrubs on northeast and southwest slopes of the southern Appalachian Mountains. I. Irradiance tolerance. American Journal of Botany 77:108–115.

Lipscomb, M.V., and E.T. Nilsen. 1990b. Environmental and physiological factors influencing the natural distribution of evergreen and deciduous ericaceous shrubs on northeast and southwest slopes of the southern Appalachian Mountains. II. Water relations. American Journal of Botany 77:517–526.

Lipson, D.A., W.D. Bowman, and R.K. Monson. 1996. Luxury uptake and storage of nitrogen in the rhizomatous alpine herb, *Bistorta bistortoides*. Ecology 77: 1277–1285.

Liu, H., E.S. Menges, and P.F. Quintana-Ascencio. 2005. Population viability analyses of *Chamaecrista keyensis*: effects of fire season and frequency. Ecological Applications 15:210–221.

Lloyd, D.G. 1992. Self-fertilization and cross-fertilization in plants. 2. The selection of self-fertilization. International Journal of Plant Sciences 153:370–380.

Lobstein, M.B., and L.L. Rockwood. 1993. Influence of elaiosome removal on germination in five ant-dispersed plant species. Virginia Journal of Science 44:59–72.

Lockhart, C.S., D.F. Austin, W.E. Jones, and L.A. Downey. 1999. Invasion of carrotwood (*Cupaniopsis anacardioides*) in Florida natural areas (USA). Natural Areas Journal 19:254–262.

Lodge, D.M. 1993. Biological invasions: lessons for ecology. Trends in Ecology and Evolutionary Biology 8:133–137.

Loeffler, C.C., and B.C. Wegner. 2000. Demographics and deer browsing in three Pennsylvania populations of the globally rare glade spurge, *Euphorbia purpurea* (Raf.) Fern. Castanea 65:273–290.

Loehle, C. 2000. Strategy space and the disturbance spectrum: a life-history model for tree species coexistence. American Naturalist 156:14–33.

Loehle, C., and B.-L. Li. 1996. Habitat destruction and the extinction debt revisited. Ecological Applications 6:784–789.

Lofgren, A. 2002. Effects of isolation on distribution, fecundity, and survival in the self-incompatible *Achillea millefolium* (L.). Ecoscience 9:503–508.

Logan, B.A., D.H. Barker, W.W. Adams III, and B.D. Demmig-Adams. 1997. The response of xanthophyll cycle-dependent energy dissipation in *Alocasia brisbanensis* to sunflecks in a subtropical rainforest. Australian Journal of Plant Physiology 24:27–33.

Lomolino, M.V., B.R. Riddle, and J.H. Brown. 2006. Biogeography, 3rd ed. Sunderland, MA: Sinauer Associates.

Long, R.W. 1971. Floral polymorphy and amphimictic breeding systems in *Ruellia caroliniensis* (Acanthaceae). American Journal of Botany 58:525–531.

Long, Z.T., W.P. Carson, and C.J. Peterson. 1998. Can disturbance create refugia from herbivores: an example with hemlock regeneration on treefall mounds. Journal of the Torrey Botanical Society 125:165–168.

Lonn, M., H.C. Prentice, and K. Bengtsson. 1996. Genetic structure, allozyme habitat associations and reproductive fitness in *Gypsophila fastigiata* (Caryophyllaceae). Oecologia 106:308–316.

Lonsdale, W.M. 1999. Global patterns of plant invasions and the concept of invasibility. Ecology 80:1522–1536.

Loreau, M., S. Naeem, P. Inchausti, J. Bengtsson, J.P. Grime, A. Hector, D.U. Hooper, M.A. Huston, D. Raffaelli, B. Schmid, D. Tilman, and D.A. Wardle. 2001. Biodiversity and ecosystem functioning: Current knowledge and future challenges. Science 294:804–808.

Lorimer, C.G. 1977. The presettlement forest and natural disturbance cycle of northeastern Maine. Ecology 58:139–148.

Lorimer, C.G. 1980. Age structure and disturbance history of a southern Appalachian virgin forest. Ecology 61:1169–1184.

Louda, S., A. Arnett, T. Rand, and F. Russell. 2003. Invasiveness of some biological control insects and adequacy of their ecological risk assessment and regulation. Conservation Biology 17:73–82.

Louda, S., D. Kendall, J. Connor, and D. Simberloff. 1997. Ecological effects of an insect introduced for the biological control of weeds. Science 277:1088–1090.

Louda, S., R. Pemberton, M. Johnson, and P. Follett. 2003. Nontarget effects—the Achilles' heel of biological control? Retrospective analyses to reduce risk associated with biocontrol introductions. Annual Review of Entomology 48:365–396.

Louda, S., and P. Stiling. 2004. The double-edged sword of biological control in conservation and restoration. Conservation Biology 18:50–53.

Lovett, G.M., C.D. Canham, M.A. Arthur, K.C. Weathers, and R.D. Fitzhugh. 2006. Forest ecosystem responses to exotic pests and pathogens in eastern North America. BioScience 56:395–405.

Lovett, G.M., T.H. Tear, D.C. Evers, S.E.G. Findlay, B.J. Cosby, J.K. Dunscomb, C.T. Driscoll, and K.C. Weathers. 2009. Effects of air pollution on ecosystems and biological diversity in the eastern United States. Year in Ecology and Conservation Biology 1162:99–135.

Lu, X., J. Mo, and S. Dong. 2008. Effects of nitrogen deposition on forest biodiversity. Acta Ecologica Sinica 28:5532–5548.

Lu, X., J. Mo, F.S. Gilliam, G. Yu, W. Zhang, Y. Fang, and J. Huang. 2011. Effects of experimental nitrogen additions on plant diversity in tropical forests of contrasting disturbance regimes in southern China. Environmental Pollution 159:2228–2235.

Lu, X., J. Mo, F.S. Gilliam, G. Zhou, and Y. Fang. 2010. Effects of experimental nitrogen deposition on plant diversity in an old-growth tropical forest. Global Change Biology 16:2688–2700.

Lubbers, A.E., and M.J. Lechowicz. 1989. Effects of leaf removal on reproduction vs. belowground storage in *Trillium grandiflorum*. Ecology 70:85–96.

Luettge, U. 2000. Light stress and Crassulacean acid metabolism. Phyton 40:65–82.

Luken, J.O. 1988. Population structure and biomass allocation of the naturalized shrub *Lonicera maackii* (Rupr.) Maxim. in forest and open habitats. American Midland Naturalist 119:258–267.

Luken, J.O. 1994. Valuing plants in natural areas. Natural Areas Journal 14:295–299.

Luken, J.O. 1997. Management of plant invasions: implicating ecological succession. Pages 133–144 in J.O. Luken and J.W. Thieret, editors. Assessment and management of plant invasions. Springer-Verlag, New York.

Luken, J.O. 2003. Invasions of forests in the eastern United States. Pages 283–301.in F. S. Gilliam and M.R. Roberts, editors. The herbaceous layer in forests of eastern North America. New York: Oxford University Press.

Luken, J.O., L.M. Kuddes, and T.C. Tholemeier. 1997a. Response of understory species to gap formation and soil disturbance in *Lonicera maackii* thickets. Restoration Ecology 5:229–235.

Luken, J.O., L.M. Kuddes, T.C. Tholemeier, and D.M. Haller. 1997b. Comparative responses of *Lonicera maackii* (Amur honeysuckle) and *Lindera benzoin* (spicebush) to increased light. American Midland Naturalist 138:331–343.

Luken, J.O., and D.T. Mattimiro. 1991. Habitat-specific resilience of the invasive shrub Amur honeysuckle (*Lonicera maackii*) during repeated clipping. Ecological Applications 1:104–109.

Luken, J.O., and T.R. Seastedt. 2004. Management of plant invasions: the conflict of perspective. Weed Technology 18:1514–1517

Luken, J.O., and M. Shea. 2000. Repeated prescribed burning at Dinsmore Woods State Nature Preserve (Kentucky, USA): responses of the understory community. Natural Areas Journal 20:150–158.

Luken, J.O., and J.W. Thieret. 1996. Amur honeysuckle, its fall from grace. Bioscience 46:18–24.

Luken, J.O., and J.W. Thieret, editors. 1997. Assessment and management of plant invasions. Springer, New York.

Lundberg, S., and P.K. Ingvarsson. 1998. Population dynamics of resource limited plants and their pollinators. Theoretical Population Biology 54:44–49.

Lundegardh, H. 1921. Ecological studies in the assimilation of certain forest-plants and shore plants. Svensk Botanisk Tidskrift 15:45–95.

Lundgren, M.R., C.J. Small, and G.D. Dreyer. 2004. Influence of land use and site characteristics on invasive plant abundance in the Quinebaug Highlands of southern New England. Northeastern Naturalist 11:313–332.

Lundholm, J.T. 2009. Plant species diversity and environmental heterogeneity: spatial scale and competing hypotheses. Journal of Vegetation Science 20:377–391.

Lundmark, M., H. Vaughan, and L. Lapointe. 2009. Low temperature maximizes growth of *Crocus vernus* (L.) Hill via changes in carbon partitioning and corm development. Journal of Experimental Botany 60:2203–2213.

Lutz, H.J. 1930. The vegetation of Heart's Content, a virgin forest in northwestern Pennsylvania. Ecology 11:1–29.

Lyford, W.H., and D.W. MacLean. 1966. Mound and pit microrelief in relation to soil disturbance and tree distribution in New Brunswick, Canada. Harvard Forest Paper 15:1–18.

Lynch, R.L., H. Chen, L.A. Brandt, and F.J. Mazzotti. 2009. Old world climbing fern (*Lygodium microphyllum*) invasion in hurricane caused treefalls. Natural Areas Journal 29:210–215.

Lyon, J., and C.L. Sagers. 1998. Structure of herbaceous plant assemblages in a forested riparian landscape. Plant Ecology 138:1–16.

Lyon, L.J., and P.F. Stickney. 1976. Early vegetal succession following northern Rocky Mountain wildfires. Pages 355–375 in Proceedings of the Montana Tall Timbers Fire Ecology Conference and Fire and Land Management Symposium, No. 14. Tall Timbers Research Station, Tallahassee, FL.

Mabry, C., D. Ackerly, and F. Gerhardt. 2000. Landscape and species-level distribution of morphological and life history traits in a temperate woodland flora. Journal of Vegetation Science 11:213–224.

Mabry, C., C. Henry, and C. Dettman. 2009. Population trends in northern monkshood, *Aconitum noveboracense*, at four sample intervals over fifteen years. Natural Areas Journal 29:146–156.

MacArthur, R.H. 1972. Geographical Ecology. New York: Harper and Row.

MacArthur, R.H., and E.O. Wilson 1967. The theory of island biogeography. Princeton, NJ: Princeton University Press.

MacDonald, S. A. 2005. The agony of an American wilderness: loggers, environmentalists, and the struggle for control of a forgotten forest. Lanham, MD: Rowman and Littlefield.

MacDougall, A. 2001. Conservation status of Saint John River Valley hardwood forest in western New Brunswick. Rhodora 103:47–70.

Machado, J.L., and P.B. Reich. 1999. Evaluation of several measures of canopy openness as predictors of photosynthetic photon flux density in deeply shaded conifer-dominated forest understory. Canadian Journal of Forest Research 29:1438–1444.

Macior, L.W. 1968. Pollinator adaptation in *Pedicularis canadensis*. American Journal of Botany 555:1031–1035.

Mack, R.N., D. Simberloff, W.M. Lonsdale, H. Evans, M. Clout, and F.A. Bazzaz. 2000. Biotic invasions: causes, epidemiology, global consequences, and control. Ecological Applications 10:689–710.

MacLean, D., and R.W. Wein. 1977. Changes in understory vegetation with increasing stand age in New Brunswick forests: species composition, cover, biomass and nutrients. Canadian Journal of Botany 55:2818–2831.

MacLean, D.A., and R.W. Wein. 1978. Weight loss and nutrient changes in decomposing litter and forest floor material in New Brunswick forest stands. Canadian Journal of Botany 56:2730–2749.

MacLean, D.A., S.J. Woodley, M.G. Weber, and R.W. Wein. 1983. Fire and nutrient cycling. Pages 111–132 in R.W. Wein and D.A. MacLean, editors. The role of fire in northern circumpolar ecosystems. John Wiley & Sons, New York

Magbool, M., K.E. Cushman, R.M. Moraes, and P.D. Gerard. 2004. Overcoming dormancy of mayapple rhizome segments with low temperature exposure. HortScience 39:307–311.

Maguire, D.A., and R.T.T. Forman. 1983. Herb cover effects on tree seedling patterns in a mature hemlock-hardwood forest. Ecology 64:1367–1380.

Mahall, B.E., and F.H. Bormann. 1978. A quantitative description of the vegetative phenology of herbs in a northern hardwood forest. Botanical Gazette 139:467–481.

Malanson, G.P. 1984. Intensity as a third factor of disturbance regime and its effect on species diversity. Oikos 43:411–413.

Malanson, G.P. 1997a. Effects of feedbacks and seed rain on ecotone patterns. Landscape Ecology 12:27–38.

Malanson, G.P. 1997b. Simulated responses to hypothetical fundamental niches. Journal of Vegetation Science 8:307–316.

Malik, C.P., Gill, R.K., and M.B. Singh. 1983. Nonphotosynthetic carbon dioxide fixation in *Monotropa uniflora*, a colorless angiosperm. Indian Journal of Experimental Biology 21:405–407.

Mamushina, N.S., and E.K. Zubkova. 1996. Effect of temperature on potential photosynthesis and photosynthetic carbon metabolism in C-3-plants with different seasonal patterns of development. Russian Journal of Plant Physiology 43:313–318.

Manchester, S.R. 1999. Biogeographical relationships of North American Tertiary floras. Annals of the Missouri Botanical Garden 86:472–522.

Manion, P.D. 1991. Tree disease concepts. 2nd ed. Prentice-Hall, Englewood Cliffs, NJ.

Mann, L.K., A.W. King, V.H. Dale, W.W. Hargrove, R. Washington-Allen, L.R. Pounds, and T.L. Ashwood. 1999. The role of soil classification in geographic information system modeling of habitat pattern: threatened calcareous ecosystem. Ecosystems 2:524–538.

Mårell, A., F. Archauz, and N. Koroulewsky. 2009. Floral herbivory on the wood anemone (*Anemone nemorosa* L.) by roe deer (*Capreolus capreolus* L.) Plant Species Biology 24:209–214.

Margalef, R. 1963. On certain unifying principles in ecology. American Naturalist 97:357–374.

Margalef, R. 1968. Perspectives in ecological theory. Chicago: University of Chicago Press.

Marks, P.L., and F.H. Bormann. 1972. Revegetation following forest cutting: mechanisms for return to steady-state nutrient cycling. Science 176:914–915.

Marquis, D.A. 1975. The Allegheny hardwood forests of Pennsylvania. U.S. Forest Service General Technical Report NE-15.

Marquis, D.A., and R. Brenneman 1981. The impact of deer on forest vegetation in Pennsylvania. United States Forest Service General Technical Report NE-65. Broomall, PA.

Marquis, D.A., and R.L. Ernst. 1992. User's guide to SILVAH: stand analysis, prescription, and management simulator program for hardwood stands of the Alleghenies. U.S. Forest Service General Technical Report NE-162.

Marschner, H. 1995. Mineral nutrition of higher plants, 2nd ed. Academic Press, London.

Marshall, B. The deer wars: the battle over Pennsylvania whitetails is getting ugly. Field and Stream, July 2005, December 29, 2011 <http://www.fieldandstream.com / articles/gear/2005/07/deer-wars>.

Martin, C.W., J.W. Hornbeck, G.E. Likens, and D.C. Buso. 2000. Impacts of intensive harvesting on hydrology and nutrient dynamics of northern hardwood forests. Canadian Journal of Fisheries and Aquatic Sciences 57:19–29.

Martin, J.L. 1955. Observations on the origin and early development of a plant community following a forest fire. Forestry Chronicle 31:154–161.

Martin, J.-L., and C. Baltzinger. 2002. Interactions among deer browse, hunting, and tree regeneration. Canadian Journal of Forest Research 32:1254–1264.

Martin, K.L., D.M. Hix, and P.C. Goebel. 2011. Coupling of vegetation layers and environmental influences in a mature, second-growth central hardwood forest landscape. Forest Ecology and Management 261:720–729.

Martin, M.C. 1966. An ecological life history of *Geranium maculatum*. American Midland Naturalist 73:111–149.

Martin, P.H., C.D. Canham, and P.L. Marks. 2009. Why forests appear resistant to exotic plant invasions: intentional introductions, stand dynamics, and the role of shade tolerance. Frontiers in Ecology and the Environment 7:142–149.

Martin, P.S., and R.G. Klein, eds. 1984. Quaternary extinctions: A prehistoric revolution. Tucson, AZ: University of Arizona Press.

Martin, W.H. 1992. Characteristics of old-growth mixed mesophytic forests. Natural Areas Journal 12:127–135.

Martínez, E., and A.T. Peterson. 2006. Conservatism of ecological niche characteristics in North American plant species over the Pleistocene-to-recent transition. Journal of Biogeography 33:1779–1789.

Marx, E. 2007. Vegetation dynamics of the Buck Creek serpentine barrens, Clay County, North Carolina. B.S. thesis, University of North Carolina at Chapel Hill, NC.

Masarovičová, E., and P. Eliáš 1986. Photosynthetic rate and water relations in some forest herbs in spring and summer. Photosynthetica 20:187–195.

Maschinski, J., J.E. Baggs, P.E. Quintana-Ascencio, and E.S. Menges. 2006. Using population viability analysis to predict the effects of climate change on the extinction risk of an endangered limestone endemic shrub, Arizona cliffrose. Conservation Biology 20:218–228.

Maschinski, J., R. Frye, and S. Rutman. 1997. Demography and population viability of an endangered plant species before and after protection from trampling. Conservation Biology 11:990–999.

Mastran, S.S., and N. Lowerre. 1983. Mountaineers and rangers: A history of federal forest management in the Southern Appalachians, 1900–81. New Port Richey, FL: Maximum Publishing.

Matlack, G. 1994a. Plant demography, land-use history, and the commercial use of forests. Conservation Biology 8:298–299.

Matlack, G. 1994b. Plant species migration in a mixed-history forest landscape in eastern North America. Ecology 75:1491–1502.

Matthews, E.M., R.K. Peet, and A.S. Weakley. 2011. Classification and description of alluvial plant communities of the Piedmont region, North Carolina, USA. Applied Vegetation Science 14:485–505.

Matthies, D., I. Brauer, W. Maiborn, and T. Tscharntke. 2004. Population size and the risk of local extinction: empirical evidence from rare plants. Oikos 105:481–488.

Mattson, W.J., and N.D. Addy. 1975. Phytophagous insects as regulators of forest primary production. Science 190:515–522.

Mayfield, M.M., D. Ackerly, and G.C. Daily. 2006. The diversity and conservation of plant reproductive and dispersal functional traits in human-dominated tropical landscapes. Journal of Ecology 94:522–536.

McCabe, R.E., and T.R. McCabe. 1984. Of slings and arrows: An historical retrospective. In L. K. Halls, ed. White-tailed deer ecology and management. Harrisburg, PA: Stackpole Books, pp. 19–72.

McCabe, T.R., and R.E. McCabe. 1997. Recounting whitetails past. Pages 11–26 in W.J. McShea, H.B. Underwood, and J.H. Rappole, editors. The Science of Overabundance: Deer Ecology and Population Management. Washington DC: Smithsonian Institution Press.

McCaffery, K.R., J. Tranetzki, and J. Piechura. 1974. Summer foods of deer in Northern Wisconsin. Journal of Wildlife Management 38:215–219.

McCall, C., and R.B. Primack. 1985. Effects of pollen and nitrogen availability on reproduction in a woodland herb, Lysimachia quadrifolia. Oecologia 67:403–410.

McCarron, J.K., III. 1995. Ecophysiological adaptations of Galax aphylla to the understory of southern Appalachian forests. M.S. thesis, Appalachian State University, Boone, NC.

McCarthy, B.C. 1995. Eastern old-growth forests. Ohio Woodland Journal Winter:8–10.

McCarthy, B.C. 1997. Response of a forest understory community to experimental removal of an invasive nonindigenous plant (*Alliaria petiolata*, Brassicaceae). Pages 117–130 in J.O. Luken and J.W. Thieret, editors. Assessment and management of plant invasions. Springer-Verlag, New York.

McCarthy, B.C., and D.R. Bailey. 1996. Composition, structure and disturbance history of Crabtree Woods: an old-growth forest in western Maryland. Bulletin of the Torrey Botanical Club 123:350–365.

McCarthy, B.C., J.E. Brown, and C.J. Small. Unpublished. Seed bank of an old -growth mixed mesophytic forest in southeastern Ohio.

McCarthy, B.C., and J.M. Facelli. 1990. Microdisturbances in old fields and forests: implications for woody seedling establishment. Oikos 58:55–60.

McCarthy, B.C., C.A. Hammer, G.L. Kauffman, and P.D. Cantino. 1987. Vegetation patterns and structure of an old-growth forest in southeastern Ohio. Bulletin of the Torrey Botanical Club 114:33–45.

McCarthy, B.C., C.J. Small, and D.L. Rubino. 2001. Composition, structure, and dynamics of Dysart Woods, an old-growth mixed mesophytic forest of southeastern Ohio. Forest Ecology and Management 140:193–213.

McCauley, D.E., J. Raveill, and J. Antonovics. 1995. Local founding events as determinants of genetic structure in a plant metapopulation. Heredity 75:630–636.

McCauley, R.A., and I.A. Ungar. 2002. Demographic analysis of a disjunct population of *Froelichia floridana* in the mid-Ohio River Valley. Restoration Ecology 10: 348–361.

McClain, M.E., E.W. Boyer, C.L. Dent, S.E. Gergel, N.B. Grimm, P.M. Groffman, S.C. Hart, J.W. Harvey, C.A. Johnston, E. Mayorga, W.H. McDowell, and G. Pinay. 2003. Biogeochemical hot spots and hot moments at the interface of terrestrial and aquatic ecosystems. Ecosystems 6:301–312.

McCook, L.J. 1994. Understanding ecological community succession: Causal models and theories, a review. Vegetatio 110:115–147.

McCormick, M.K., K.L. Parker, K. Szlavecz, and D.F. Whigham. 2013. Native and exotic earthworms affect orchid seed loss. AoB Plants, doi:10.1093/aobpla/plt018.

McCormick, M.K., D.F. Whigham, and J.P. O'Neill. 2011. Restore the Federally Threatened Small Whorled Pogonia (*Isotria medeoloides*) in Three NPS Regions. Annual Report, November 2011. Edgewater, MD: Smithsonian Environmental Research Center.

McCormick, M.K., D.F. Whigham, J.P. O'Neill, J.J. Becker, S. Werner, H.N. Rasmussen, T.D. Bruns, and D.L. Taylor. 2009. Abundance and distribution of *Corallorhiza odontorhiza* reflects variations in climate and ectomycorrhizae. Ecological Monographs 79:619–635.

McCormick, M.K., D.F. Whigham, D. Sloan, K. O'Malley, and B. Hodkinson. 2006. Orchid-fungus fidelity: a marriage meant to last? Ecology 87:903–911.

McCormick, M.K., D.L. Taylor, K. Juhaszova, R.K. Burnett Jr., D.F. Whigham, and J.P. O'Neill. 2012. Limitations on orchid recruitment: not a simple picture. Molecular Ecology 21:1511–1523.

McCullough, D.R. 1984. Lessons from the George Reserve. In L.K. Halls, ed. White-tailed deer: Ecology and management. Harrisburg, PA: Stackpole Books.

McCune, B., and J.A. Antos. 1981. Correlations between forest layers in the Swan Valley, Montana. Ecology 62:1196–1204.

McCune, B., and J.B. Grace. 2002. Analysis of ecological communities. Gleneden Beach, OR: MjM Software Design.

McCune, B., and M.J. Mefford. 2006. PC-ORD. Multivariate Analysis of Ecological Data. Version 5.32. Gleneden Beach, OR: MjM Software Design.

McDonald, D., and D.A. Norton. 1992. Light environments in temperate New Zealand Podocarp rainforests. New Zealand Journal of Ecology 16:15–22.

McDonald, R.I., G. Motzkin, and D.R. Foster. 2008. Assessing the influence of historical factors, contemporary processes, and environmental conditions on the distribution of invasive species. Journal of the Torrey Botanical Society 135:260–271.

McDonald, R.I., Peet, R.K., and Urban, D.L. 2002. Environmental correlates of oak decline and red maple increase in the North Carolina Piedmont. Castanea 67:84–95.

McDonald, R.I., and D.L. Urban. 2006. Edge effects on species composition and exotic species abundance in the North Carolina Piedmont. Biological Invasions 8:1049–1060.

McDonnell, M.J. 1986. Old field vegetation height and the dispersal pattern of bird-disseminated woody plants. Bulletin of the Torrey Botanical Club 113:6–11.

McEvoy, P.B., and E.M. Coombs. 1999. Biological control of plant invaders: regional patterns, field experiments, and structured population models. Ecological Applications 9:387–401.

McEwan, R.W., R.J. Brecha, D.R. Geiger, and G.P. John. 2011. Flowering phenology change and climate warming in southwestern Ohio. Plant Ecology 212:55–61.

McEwan, R.W., and R.N. Muller. 2011. Dynamics, diversity, and resource gradient relationships in the herbaceous layer of an old-growth Appalachian forest. Plant Ecology 212:1179–1191.

McFarland, J.W., R.W. Ruess, K. Kielland, K. Pregitzer, R. Hendrick, and M. Allen. 2010. Cross-ecosystem comparisons of in situ plant uptake of amino acid-N and NH_4^+. Ecosystems 13:177–193.

McGee, C.E., and R.C. Smith. 1967. Undisturbed rhododendron thickets are not spreading. Journal of Forestry 65:334–336.

McGee, G.G. 2001. Stand-level effects on the role of decaying logs as vascular plant habitat in Adirondack northern hardwood forests. Journal of the Torrey Botanical Club 128:370–380.

McGrady-Steed, J., P.M. Harris, and P.J. Morin. 1997. Biodiversity regulates ecosystem predictability. Nature 390:162–165.

McGraw, J.B., and M.A. Furedi. 2005. Deer browsing and population viability of an understory plant. Science 307:920–922.

McGraw, J.B., S.M. Sanders, and M. Van der Voort. 2003. Distribution and abundance of *Hydrastis canadensis* L. (Ranunculaceae) and *Panax quinquefolius* L. (Araliaceae) in the central Appalachian region. Journal of the Torrey Botanical Society 130:62–69.

McGraw, J.B., S. Souther, and A.E. Lubbers. 2010. Rates of harvest and compliance with regulations in natural populations of American ginseng (*Panax quinquefolius* L.). Natural Areas Journal 30:202–210.

McInnes, P.F., R.J. Naiman, J. Pastor, and Y. Cohen. 1992. Effects of moose browsing on vegetation and litter of the boreal forest, Isle Royale, Michigan, USA. Ecology 73:2059–2075.

McInnis, B.G., and Roberts, M.R. 1995. Seedling microenvironment in full-tree and tree-length logging slash. Canadian Journal of Forest Research 25:128–136.

McIntosh, R.P. 1985. The background of ecology: concept and theory. Cambridge University Press, New York.

McIntyre, S., S. Lavorel, and R.M. Tremont. 1995. Plant life-history attributes: their relationship to disturbance response in herbaceous vegetation. Journal of Ecology 3:31–44.

McKenna, M., and G. Houle. 2000a. Under-saturated distribution of *Floerkea proserpinacoides* Willd. (Limnanthaceae) at the northern limit of its distribution. Ecoscience 7:466–473.

McKenna, M., and G. Houle. 2000b. Why are annual plants rarely spring ephemerals? New Phytologist 148:295–302.

McKenney, D.W., J.H. Pedlar, R.B. Rood, and D. Price. 2011. Revisiting projected shifts in the climate envelopes of North American trees using updated general circulation models. Global Change Biology 17:2720–2730.

McKinney, A.M., and K. Goodell. 2010. Shading by invasive shrub reduces seed production and pollinator services in a native herb. Biological Invasions 12:2751–2763.

McKnight, B.N., editor. 1993. Biological pollution: the control and impact of invasive exotic species. Indiana Academy of Science, Indianapolis, IN.

McLachlan, S.M., and B.R. Bazely. 2001. Recovery patterns of understory herbs and their use as indicators of deciduous forest regeneration. Conservation Biology 15:98–110.

McLachlan, S.M., and D.R. Bazely. 2003. Outcomes of long-term deciduous forest restoration in southwestern Ontario, Canada. Biological Conservation 113:159–169.

McLachlan, J., J.S. Clark, and P.S. Manos. 2005. Molecular indicators of tree migration capacity under rapid climate change. Ecology 86:2088–2098.

McLachlan, J., J.J. Hellmann, and M.W. Schwartz. 2007. A framework for debate of assisted migration in an era of climate change. Conservation Biology 21: 297–302.

McLean, A. 1969. Fire resistance of forest species as influenced by root systems. Journal of Range Management 22:120–122.

McLendon, J.H. 1992. Photographic survey of the occurrence of bundle sheath extensions in deciduous dicots. Plant Physiology 99:677–1699.

McMillen, C.G., and J.H. McClendon. 1979. Leaf angle: an adaptive feature of sun and shade leaves. Botanical Gazette 140:437–442.

McNab, W.H. 1989. Terrain Shape Index: quantifying effect of minor landforms on tree height. Forest Science 35:91–104.

McNab, W.H. 1993. A topographic index to quantify the effect of mesoscale landform on site productivity. Canadian Journal of Forest Research 23:1100–1107.

McNaughton, S.J. 1976. Serengeti migration wildebeest: facilitation of energy flow by grazing. Science 53:92–94.

McNaughton, S.J. 1985. Ecology of grazing cost: the Serengeti. Ecological Monographs 53:291–320.

McNaughton, S.J. 1988. Mineral nutrition and spatial concentrations of African ungulates. Nature 334:343–345.

McNulty, S.A., W.F. Porter, N.E. Mathews, and J.A. Hill. 1997. Localized management for reducing white-tailed deer populations. Wildlife Society Bulletin 25:265–271.

McPherson, J.K., and G.L. Thompson. 1972. Competitive and allelopathic suppression of understory by Oklahoma oak forests. Bulletin of the Torrey Botanical Club 99:293–300.

McShea, W.J., and J.H. Rappole. 1992. White-tailed deer as keystone species within forested habitats of Virginia. Virginia Journal of Science 43:177–186.

McShea, W.J., and J.H. Rappole. 1997. Herbivores and the ecology of forest understory birds. Pages 298–309 in W.J. McShea, H.B. Underwood, and J.H. Rappole, editors. The science of overabundance: deer ecology and population management. Washington, DC: Smithsonian Institution Press, pp.

McShea, W.J., and J.H. Rappole. 2000. Managing the abundance and diversity of breeding bird populations through manipulation of deer populations. Conservation Biology 14:1161–1170.

McShea, W.J., H.B. Underwood, and J.H. Rappole, eds. 1997. The science of overabundance: deer ecology and population management. Washington, DC: Smithsonian Institution Press.

McWilliams, W.H., S.L. Stout, T.W. Bowersox, and L.H. McCormick. 1995. Adequacy of advance tree-seedling regeneration in Pennsylvania's forests. Northern Journal of Applied Forestry 12:187–191.

Meagher, T.R. 1978. The evolutionary consequences of dioecy in *Chamaelirium luteum*, a perennial plant species. Ph.D. dissertation, Duke University, Durham, NC.

Meagher, T.R. 1982. The population biology of *Chamaelirium luteum*, a dioecious member of the lily family: two-sex population projection and stable population structure. Ecology 63:1701–1711.

Meagher, T. 1986. Analysis of paternity within a natural population of *Chamaelirium luteum*. 1. Identification of most-likely male parents. American Naturalist 128:199–215.

Meagher, T.R., J. Antonovics, and R. Primack. 1978. Experimental ecological genetics in Plantago. III. Genetic variation and demography in relation to survival of *Plantago cordata*, a rare species. Biological Conservation 14:242–257.

Médail, F., and K. Diadema. 2009. Glacial refugia influence plant diversity patterns in the Mediterranean Basin. Journal of Biogeography 36:1333–1345.

Meekins, J., and B.C. McCarthy. 1999. Competitive ability of *Alliaria petiolata* (garlic mustard, Brassicaceae), an invasive, nonindigenous forest herb. International Journal of Plant Sciences 160:743–752.

Meekins, J.F., and B.C. McCarthy. 2000. Responses of the biennial forest herb, *Alliaria petiolata*, to variation in population density, nutrient addition and light availability. Journal of Ecology 88:447–463.

Meentemeyer, V. 1989. Geographical perspectives of space, time, and scale. Landscape Ecology 3:163–173.

Meentemeyer, V., and E.O. Box. 1987. Scale effects in landscape studies. Pages 15–36 in M.G. Turner, editor. Landscape heterogeneity and disturbance. Springer-Verlag, New York.

Mehroff, L.A., III. 1983. Pollination in the genus, *Isotria* (Orchidaceae). American Journal of Botany 70:1444–1453.

Meier, A.J., S.P. Bratton, and D.C. Duffy. 1995. Possible ecological mechanisms for loss of vernal-herb diversity in logged Eastern deciduous forests. Ecological Applications 5:935–946.

Meier, A.J., S.P. Bratton, and D.C. Duffy. 1996. Biodiversity in the herbaceous layer and salamanders in Appalachian primary forests. Pages 49–64 in M.B. Davis, editor. Eastern old-growth forests. Island Press, Washington, DC.

Meine, C. 1988. Aldo Leopold: His life and work. Madison, WI: University of Wisconsin Press.

Mejías, J.A., J. Arroyo, and T. Marañóna. 2007. Ecology and biogeography of plant communities associated with the post Plio-Pleistocene relict *Rhododendron ponticum* subsp. *baeticum* in southern Spain. Journal of Biogeography 34:456–472.

Mejías, J.A., Arroyo, J., and Ojeda, F. 2002. Reproductive ecology of *Rhododendron ponticum* (Ericaceae) in relict Mediterranean populations. Botanical Journal of the Linnean Society 140:297–311.

Mehlich, A. 1984. Mehlich 3 soil test extractant: a modification of Mehlich 2 extractant. Communications in Soil Science and Plant Analysis 15:1409–1416.

Melillo, J.M., J.D. Aber, A.E. Linkins, A. Ricca, B. Fry, and K.J. Nadelhoffer. 1989. Carbon and nitrogen dynamics along the decay continuum: Plant litter to soil organic matter. Plant and Soil 115:189–198.

Melin, E. 1930. Biological decomposition of some types of litter from North American forests. Ecology 11:72–101.

Menge, J.A., D. Steirle, D.J. Bagyaraj, E.L.V. Johnson, and R.T. Leonard. 1978. Phosphorus concentrations in plants responsible for inhibition of mycorrhizal infection. New Phytologist 80:575–578.

Menges, E.S. 1987. Biomass allocation and geometry of the clonal forest herb *Laportea canadensis*: Adaptive responses to the environment or allometric constraints? American Journal of Botany 74:551–563

Menges, E.S. 1990. Population viability analysis for an endangered plant. Conservation Biology 4:41–62.

Menges, E.S. 2000a. Applications of population viability analyses in plant conservation. Ecological Bulletins 48:73–84.

Menges, E.S. 2000b. Population viability analyses in plants: Challenges and opportunities. Trends in Ecology and Evolution 15:51–56.

Menges, E.S. 2007. Integrating demography and fire management: an example from Florida scrub. Australian Journal of Botany 55:261–272.

Menges, E.S., and R.W. Dolan. 1998. Demographic viability of populations of *Silene regia* in midwestern prairies: Relationships with fire management, genetic variation, geographic location, population size, and isolation. Journal of Ecology 86:63–78.

Menges, E.S., and D.R. Gordon. 1996. Three levels of monitoring intensity for rare plant species. Natural Areas Journal 16:227–237.

Menges, E.S., and C.V. Hawkes. 1998. Interactive effects of fire and microhabitat on plants of Florida scrub. Ecological Applications 8:935–946.

Menges, E.S., and P.F. Quintana-Ascencio. 2004. Population viability with fire in *Eryngium cuneifolium*: deciphering a decade of demographic data. Ecological Monographs 74:79–99.

Menges, E.S., C.W. Weekley, G.L. Clarke, and S.A. Smith. 2011. Effects of hurricanes on rare plant demography in fire-controlled ecosystems. Biotropica 43:450–458.

Menzel, A., and P. Fabian. 1999. Growing season extended in Europe. Nature 397:659.

Merrens, E.J., and D.R. Peart. 1992. Effects of hurricane damage on individual growth and stand structure in a hardwood forest in New Hampshire, USA. Journal of Ecology 80:787–795.

Mettler-Cherry, P., M. Smith, and T. Keevin. 2006. Habitat characterization and geospatial metapopulation dynamics of threatened floodplain species *Boltonia decurrens* using a GIS. Wetlands 26:336–348.

Meyer, S., and G. Parker. 2003. Distribution and habitat classification of goldenseal (*Hydrastis canadensis* L.) in the Hoosier National Forest, Indiana, USA. Natural Areas Journal 23:332–340.

Michalcová, D., S. Lvončík, M. Chytrý, and O. Hájek. 2011. Bias in vegetation databases? A comparison of stratified-random and preferential sampling. Journal of Vegetation Science 22:281–291.

Miller, K., and D. Gorchov. 2004. The invasive shrub, *Lonicera maackii*, reduces growth and fecundity of perennial forest herbs. Oecologia 139:359–375.

Miller, S.G., S.P. Bratton, and J. Hadidian. 1992. Impacts of white-tailed deer on endangered plants. Natural Areas Journal 12:67–74.

Miller, T.F., D.J. Mladenoff, and M.K. Clayton. 2002. Old-growth northern hardwood forests: Spatial autocorrelation and patterns of understory vegetation. Ecological Monographs 72:487–503.

Miller, T.K., C.R. Allen, W.G. Landis, and J.W. Merchant. 2010. Risk assessment: simultaneously prioritizing the control of invasive plant species and the conservation of rare plant species. Biological Conservation 143:2070–2079.

Miller-Rushing, A.J., T.T. Hoye, D.W. Inouye, and E. Post. 2010. The effects of phenological mismatches on demography. Philosophical Transactions of the Royal Society B-Biological Sciences 365:3177–3186.

Miller-Rushing, A.J., and R.B. Primack. 2008. Global warming and flowering times in Thoreau's Concord: A community perspective. Ecology 89:332–341.

Miller-Rushing, A.J., R.B. Primack, D. Primack, and S. Mukunda. 2006. Photographs and herbarium specimens as tools to document phenological changes in response to global warming. American Journal of Botany 93:1667–1674.

Milligan, B.G., J. Leebensmack, and A.E. Strand. 1994. Conservation genetics: beyond the maintenance of marker diversity. Molecular Ecology 3:423–435.

Mills, L.S., D.F. Doak, and M.J. Wisdom. 1999. Reliability of conservation actions based on elasticity analysis of matrix models. Conservation Biology 13:815–829.

Mills, S.E., and S.E. MacDonald. 2004. Predictors of moss and liverwort species diversity of Minckler, L.S., J.D. Woerheide, and R.C. Schlesinger. 1973. Light, soil moisture, and tree reproduction in hardwood forest openings. United States Forest Service, North Central Forest Experiment Station Research Paper NC-89.

Ministère des Ressources naturelles du Québec. 1994. Le point d'observation écologique: normes techniques. Service de l'inventaire forestier.

Minteer, B.A., and J.P. Collins. 2010. Move it or lose it? The ecological ethics of relocating species under climate change. Ecological Applications 20:1801–1804.

Mitchell, C.E., and A.G. Power. 2003. Release of invasive plants from fungal and viral pathogens. Nature 421:625–627.

Mitchell, C.E., P.B. Reich, D. Tilman, and J.V. Groth. 2003. Effects of elevated CO_2, nitrogen deposition, and decreased species diversity on foliar fungal plant disease. Global Change Biology 9:438–451.

Mitchell, C.E., M.G. Turner, and S.M. Pearson. 2002. Effects of historical land use and forest patch size on myrmecochores and ant communities. Ecological Applications 12:1364–1377.

Mitchell, R.J., R.E. Irwin, R.J. Flanagan, and J.D. Karron. 2009. Ecology and evolution of plant-pollinator interactions. Annals of Botany 103:1355–1363.

Miyashita, A., D. Sugiura, K. Sawakami, R. Ichihashi, T. Tani and M. Tateno. 2012. Long-term, short-interval measurements of the frequency distributions of the photosynthetically active photon flux density and net assimilation rate of leaves in a cool-temperate forest. Agricultural and Forest Meteorology 152:1–10.Mladenoff, D.J. 1990. The relationship of the soil seed bank and understory vegetation in old-growth northern hardwood-hemlock treefall gaps. Canadian Journal of Botany 68:2714–2721.

Mladenoff, D.J., and F. Stearns. 1993. Eastern hemlock regeneration and deer browsing in the northern Great Lakes region: A re-examination and model simulation. Conservation Biology 7:889–900.

Moeller, D.A., M.A. Geber, and P. Tiffin. 2011. Population genetics and the evolution of geographic range limits in an annual plant. American Naturalist 178:S44–S61.

Mohan, J.E., L.H. Ziska, W.H. Schlesinger, R.B. Thomas, R.C. Sicher, K. George, and J.S. Clark. 2006. Biomass and toxicity responses of poison ivy (*Toxicodendron radicans*) to elevated atmospheric CO_2. Proceedings of the National Academy of Sciences 103:9086–9089.

Molnar, E., and S. Bokros. 1996. Studies on the demography and life history of *Taraxacum serotinum* (Waldst et Kit) Poir. Folia Geobotanica and Phytotaxonomica 31:453–464.

Moloney, K.A. 1988. Fine-scale spatial and temporal variation in the demography of a perennial bunchgrass. Ecology 69:1588–1598.

Monk, C.D. 1966. An ecological significance of evergreenness. Ecology 47:504–505.

Monk, C.D., D.T. McGinty, and F.P. Day Jr. 1985. The ecological importance of *Kalmia latifolia* and *Rhododendron maximum* in the deciduous forest of the southern Appalachians. Bulletin of the Torrey Botanical Club 112:187–193.

Montalvo, A.M., S.L. Williams, K.J. Rice, S.L. Buchmann, C. Cory, S.N. Handel, G.P. Nabhan, R. Primack, and R.H. Robichaux. 1997. Restoration biology: a population biology perspective. Restoration Ecology 5:277–290.

Montgomery, J.D., and D.E. Fairbrothers. 1970. A biosystematic study of *Eupatorium rotundifolium* complex (Compositae). Brittonia 22:134.

Moola, F., and L. Vasseur. 2008. The maintenance of understory residual flora with even-aged forest management: A review of temperate forests in northeastern North America. Environmental Review 16:141–155.

Moola, F.M., and L. Vasseur. 2009. The importance of clonal growth to the recovery of *Gaultheria procumbens* L. (Ericaceae) after forest disturbance. Plant Ecology 201:319–337.

Mooney, E.H., and J.B. McGraw. 2006. Alteration of selection regime resulting from harvest of American ginseng, *Panax quinquefolius*. Conservation Genetics 8:57–67.

Mooney, E.H., and J.B. Mcgraw. 2007. Effects of self-pollination and outcrossing with cultivated plants in small natural populations of American ginseng, *Panax quinquefolius* (Araliaceae). American Journal of Botany 94:1677–1687.

Mooney, E.H., and J.B. McGraw. 2009. Relationship between age, size, and reproduction in populations of American ginseng, *Panax quinquefolius* (Araliaceae), across a range of harvest pressures. Ecoscience 16:84–94.

Mooney, H.A., and J.A. Drake, editors. 1986. Ecology of biological invasions. Springer-Verlag, New York.

Moore, J.M., and R.W. Wein. 1977. Viable seed populations by soil depth and potential site recolonization after disturbance. Canadian Journal of Botany 55:2408–2412.

Moore, M.R., and J.L. Vankat. 1986. Responses of the herb layer to the gap dynamics of a mature beech-maple forest. American Midland Naturalist 115:336–347.

Moore, R.M., and J.L. Vankat. 1986. Responses of the herb layer to the gap dynamics of a mature beech-maple forest. American Midland Naturalist 115:336–347.

Moore, T.R., J.A. Trofymow, B. Taylor, C. Prescott, C. Camire, L. Duschene, J. Fyles, L. Kozak, M. Kranabetter, I. Morrison, M. Siltanen, S. Smith, B. Titus, S. Visser, R. Wein, and S. Zoltai. 1999. Litter decomposition rates in Canadian forests. Global Change Biology 5:75–82.

Morales, M.A., G.J. Dodge, and D.W. Inouye. 2005. A phenological mid-domain effect in flowering diversity. Oecologia 143:83–89.

Morellet, N., P. Ballon, Y. Boscardin, and S. Champeley. 2003. A new index to measure roe deer (*Capreolus capreolus*) browsing pressure on woody flora. Game and Wildlife Science 20:155–173.

Morellet, N., S. Champely, J.-J. Gaillard, P. Ballon, and Y. Boscardin. 2001. The browsing index: new tool uses browsing pressure to monitor deer populations. Wildlife Society

Bulletin 29:1243–1252.Morgan, M.D. 1968. Life history and energy relationships of *Hydrophyllum appendiculatum*. Ph.D. dissertation, University of Illinois, Urbana, IL

Morgan, M., D. Schoen, and T. Bataillon. 1997. The evolution of self-fertilization in perennials. American Naturalist 150:618–638.

Morgan, M.D. 1968. Life history and energy relationships of *Hydrophyllum appendiculatum*. Ph.D. dissertation, University of Illinois, Urbana, IL.

Morin, X., D. Viner, and I. Chuine. 2008. Tree species range shifts at a continental scale: new predictive insights from a process-based model. Journal of Ecology 96:784–794.

Morley, T. 1982. Flowering frequency and vegetative reproduction in *Erythronium albidum* and *E. propullans*, and related observations. Bulletin of the Torrey Botanical Club 109:169–176.

Morneau, C., and S. Payette. 1989. Postfire lichen-spruce woodland recovery at the limit of the boreal forest in northern Quebec. Canadian Journal of Botany 67:2770–2782.

Morris, L.A., S.A. Moss, and W.S. Garbett. 1993. Competitive interference between selected herbaceous and woody plants and *Pinus taeda* L. during two growing seasons following planting. Forest Science 39:166–187.

Morris, W.F., and D.F. Doak. 1998. Life history of the long-lived gynodioecious cushion plant *Silene acaulis* (Caryophyllaceae), inferred from size-based population projection matrices. American Journal of Botany 85:784–793.

Morris, W.F., and D.F. Doak. 2002. Quantitative conservation biology: theory and practice of population viability analysis. Sunderland, MA: Sinauer Associates.

Morris, W.F., and D.F. Doak. 2005. How general are the determinants of the stochastic population growth rate across nearby sites? Ecological Monographs 75:119–137.

Morrison, J.A., and L. Brown. 2004. Effect of herbivore exclosure caging on the invasive plant *Aliaria petiolata* in three southeastern New York forests. Bartonia 62:25–43.

Mosher, E.S., J.A. Silander Jr., and A.M. Latimer. 2009. The role of land-use history in major invasions by woody plant species in the northeastern North American landscape. Biological Invasions 11:2317–2328.

Mosse, B., and J.M. Phillips. 1971. The influence of phosphate and other nutrients on the development of vesicular-arbuscular mycorrhiza in culture. Journal of General Microbiology 69:157–166.

Motten, A.F. 1986. Pollination ecology of the spring wildflower community of a temperate deciduous forest. Ecological Monographs 56:21–42.

Motten, A.F., D.R. Campbell, D.E. Alexander, and H.L. Miller. 1981. Pollination effectiveness of specialist and generalist visitors to a North Carolina population of *Claytonia virginica*. Ecology 62:1278–1287.

Motzkin, G., D. Foster, A. Allen, J. Harrod, and R. Boone. 1996. Controlling site to evaluate history: vegetation patterns of a New England sand plain. Ecological Monographs 66: 345–365.

Mueller, J.M., and J.J. Hellmann. 2008. An assessment of invasion risk from assisted migration. Conservation Biology 22: 562–567.

Muir, A.M. 1995. The cost of reproduction to the clonal herb *Asarum canadense* (wild ginger). Canadian Journal of Botany 73:1683–1686.

Muir, J. 1894. The Mountains of California. New York: Penguin Books.

Mulder, C.P.H. 1999. Vertebrate herbivores and plants in the Arctic and subarctic: effects on individuals, populations, communities and ecosystems. Perspectives in Plant Ecology, Evolution, and Systematics 2:29–55.

Muller, R.N. 1978. The phenology, growth and ecosystem dynamics of Erythronium americanum in the northern hardwood forest. Ecological Monographs 48:1–20.

Muller, R.N. 1979. Biomass accumulation and reproduction in *Erythronium albidum*. Bulletin of the Torrey Botanical Club 106:276–283.

Muller, R.N. 1990. Spatial interrelationships of deciduous forest herbs. Bulletin of the Torrey Botanical Club 117:101–105.

Muller, R.N. 2003. Nutrient relations of the herbaceous layer in deciduous forest ecosystems. In F.S. Gilliam and M.R. Roberts, eds. *The herbaceous layer in forests of eastern North America*. Oxford, UK: Oxford University Press, pp. 15–37.

Muller, R.N., and F.H. Bormann. 1976. Role of *Erythronium amercanum* Ker. in energy flow and nutrient dynamics of a northern hardwood forest ecosystem. Science 193:1126–1128.

Munzbergova, Z., and J. Ehrlén. 2005. How best to collect demographic data for population viability analysis models. Journal of Applied Ecology 42:1115–1120.

Munzbergova, Z., M. Krivanek, A. Bucharova, V. Juklickova, and T. Herben. 2005. Ramet performance in two tussock plants: do the tussock-level parameters matter? Flora 200:275–284.

Muraoka, H., A. Takenaka, Y. Tang, H. Koizumi, and I. Washitani. 1998. Flexible leaf orientations of *Arisaema heterophyllum* maximize light capture in a forest understorey and avoid excess irradiance at a deforested site. Annals of Botany 82:297–307.

Murcia, C. 1995. Edge effects in fragmented forests: implications for conservation. Trends in Ecology and Evolution 10:5 8–62.

Murphy, H.T., J. VanDerWal, and J. Lovett-Doust. 2006. Distribution of abundance across the range in eastern North American trees. Global Ecology and Biogeography 15:63–71.

Murphy, S.D., and L. Vasseur. 1995. Pollen limitation in a northern population of *Hepatica acutiloba*. Canadian Journal of Botany 73:1234–1241.

Muzika, R.M., and A.M. Liebhold. 1999. Changes in radial increment of host and non-host tree species with gypsy moth defoliation. Canadian Journal of Forest Research 29:1365–1373.

Myers, J.A., and K.E. Harms. 2011. Seed arrival and ecological filters interact to assemble high-diversity plant communities. Ecology 92:676–686.

Myers, J.A., M. Vellend, S. Gardescu, and P. L. Marks. 2004. Seed dispersal by white-tailed deer: implications for long-distance dispersal, invasion, and migration of plants in eastern North America. Oecologia 139:35–44.

Myster, R.W., S.T.A. Pickett. 1992. Dynamics of associations between plants in ten old fields during 31 years of succession. Journal of Ecology 80:291–302.

Nakashizuka, T. 1987. Regeneration dynamics of beech forests in Japan. Vegetatio 69:169–175.

Nakashizuka, T. 1989. Role of uprooting in composition and dynamics of an old growth forest in Japan. Ecology 70:1273–1278.

Nantel, P., and D. Gagnon. 1999. Variability in the dynamics of northern peripheral versus southern populations of two clonal plant species, *Helianthus divaricatus* and *Rhus aromatica*. Journal of Ecology 87:748–760.

Nantel, P., D. Gagnon, and A. Nault. 1996. Population viability analysis of American ginseng and wild leek harvested in stochastic environments. Conservation Biology 10:608–621.

Nault, A., and D. Gagnon. 1987. Some aspects of the pollination ecology of wild leek, *Allium tricoccum* Ait. Plant Species Biology 2:127–132.

Nault, A., and D. Gagnon. 1988. Seasonal biomass and nutrient allocation patterns in wild leek (*Allium tricoccum* Ait.), a spring geophyte. Bulletin of the Torrey Botanical Club. 115:45–54.

Nault, A., and D. Gagnon. 1993. Ramet demography of *Allium tricoccum*, a spring ephemeral, perennial forest herb. Journal of Ecology 81:101–119.

Naumburg, E., and D.S. Ellsworth. 2000. Photosynthetic sunfleck utilization potential of understory saplings growing under elevated CO_2 in FACE. Oecologia 122:163–174.

Neal, P., A. Dafni, and M. Giurfa. 1998. Floral symmetry and its role in plant-pollinator systems: terminology, distribution, and hypotheses. Annual Review of Ecology and Systematics 29:345–373.

Near, T.J., L.M. Page, and R.L. Mayden. 2001. Intraspecific phylogeography of *Percina evides* (Percidae: Etheostomatinae): an additional test of the central highlands pre-Pleistocene vicariance hypothesis. Molecular Ecology 10:2235–2240.

Neiland, M., and C. Wilcock. 1995. Maximization of reproductive success by European Orchidaceae under conditions of infrequent pollination. Protoplasma 187:39–48.

Nekola, J.C. 1999. Paleorefugia and neorefugia: the influence of colonization history on community pattern and process. Ecology 80:2459–2473.

Nelson, J.B. 2008. A new hedge-nettle (*Stachys*: Lamiaceae) from the interior highlands of the United States, and keys to the southeastern species. Journal of the Botanical Research Institute of Texas 2:761–769.

Nelson, J.L., J.W. Groninger, L.L. Battaglia, and C.M. Ruffner. 2008. Bottomland hardwood forest recovery following tornado disturbance and salvage logging. Forest Ecology and Management 256:388–395.

Nemati, N., and H. Goetz. 1995. Relationships of overstory to understory cover variables in a Ponderosa pine/Gambel oak ecosystem. Vegetatio 119:15–21.

Ness, J.H., and D.F. Morin. 2008. Forest edges and landscape history shape interactions between plants, seed-dispersing ants and seed predators. Biological Conservation 141:838–847.

Ness, J.H., D.R. Morin, and I. Giladi. 2009. Uncommon specialization in a mutualism between a temperate herbaceous plant guild and an ant: are *Aphaenogaster* ants keystone mutualists? Oikos 118:1793–1804.

Neubert, M.G., and H. Caswell. 2000. Demography and dispersal: calculation and sensitivity analysis of invasion speed for structured populations. Ecology 81:1613–1628.

Neufeld, H.S., S.J. Peoples, A.W. Davison, A.H. Chappelka, G.L. Somers, J.R. Thomley, and F.L. Booker. 2012. Ambient ozone effects on gas exchange and total non-structural carbohydrate levels in cutleaf coneflower (*Rudbeckia laciniata* L.) growing in Great Smoky Mountains National Park. Environmental Pollution 160:74–81.

Neufeld, H.S., J.R. Renfro, W.D. Hacker, and D. Silsbee. 1992. Ozone in Great Smoky Mountains National Park: Dynamics and effects on plants. Pages 594–617 in Ronald L. Berglund. Tropospheric Ozone and the Environment II., Pittsburgh, PA: Air & Waste Management Association.

Newell, C.L., and R.K. Peet. 1998. Vegetation of Linville Gorge Wilderness, North Carolina. Castanea 63:275–332.

Newell, C.L., R.K. Peet, C.J. Ulrey, T.R. Wentworth, K.D. Patterson, and D.E. McLeod. 1999. Geographic variation in forest distribution across five landscapes in the southern Appalachian Mountains of North and South Carolina. In R.P. Eckerlin, ed. Proceedings of the Appalachian Biogeography Symposium, Special Pub., Virginia Museum of Natural History 7:19–34.

Newell, S.J., and E.J. Tramer. 1978. Reproductive strategies in herbaceous plant communities during succession. Ecology 59:228–234.

Nguyen-Xuan, T., Y. Bergeron, D. Simard, J.W. Fyles, and D. Paré. 2000. The importance of forest floor disturbance in the early regeneration patterns of the boreal forest of western and central Quebec: a wildfire versus logging comparison. Canadian Journal of Forest Research 30:1353–1364.

Nicolé, F., E. Brzosko, and I. Till-Bottraud. 2005. Population viability analysis of *Cypripedium calceolus* in a protected area: longevity, stability, and persistence. Journal of Ecology 93:716–726.

Nicolé, F., J.P. Dahlgren, A. Vivat, I. Till-Bottraud, and J. Ehrlén. 2011. Interdependent effects of habitat quality and climate on population growth of an endangered plant. Journal of Ecology 99:1210–1218.

Niering, W.A., and F.E. Egler. 1955. A shrub community of *Viburnum lentago*, stable for twenty-five years. Ecology 36:356–360.

Nilsen, E.T., and D.M. Orcutt. 1996. The physiology of plants under stress. J. Wiley & Sons, New York.

Nilsen, E.T., D.A. Stetler, and D.A. Gassman. 1988. Influence of age and microclimate on the photochemistry of *Rhododendron maximum* leaves: II. Chloroplast structure and photosynthetic light response. American Journal of Botany 75:1526–1534.

Nilsen, E.T., J.F. Walker, O.K. Miller, S.W. Semones, T.T. Lei, and B.D. Clinton. 1999. Inhibition of seedling survival under *Rhododendron maximum* (Ericaceae): Could allelopathy be a cause? American Journal of Botany 86:1597–1605.

Noble, I.R., and R. Dirzo. 1997. Forests as human-dominated ecosystems. Science 277:522–525.

Noble, I.R., and H. Gitay. 1996. A functional classification for predicting the dynamics of landscapes. Journal of Vegetation Science 7:329–336.

Noble, I.R., and R.O. Slatyer. 1980. The use of vital attributes to predict successional changes in plant communities subject to recurrent disturbances. Vegetatio 43:5–21.

Noda, H., H. Muraoka, Y. Tang, and I Washitani. 2007. Phenological changes in rate of respiration and annual carbon balance in a perennial herbaceous plant, *Primula sieboldii*. Journal of Plant Research 120:375–383.

Noel, F., S. Maurice, A. Mignot, S. Glemin, D. Carbonell, F. Justy, I. Guyot, I. Olivieri, and C. Petit. 2010. Interaction of climate, demography and genetics: a ten-year study of *Brassica insularis*, a narrow endemic Mediterranean species. Conservation Genetics 11:509–526.

Nordbakken, J., K. Rydgren, and R. Okland. 2004. Demography and population dynamics of *Drosera anglica* and *D. rotundifolia*. Journal of Ecology 92:110–121.

Nordin, A., J. Strengbom, and L. Ericson. 2006. Responses to ammonium and nitrate editions by boreal plants and their natural enemies. Environmental Pollution 141:167–174.

Nordin, A., J. Strengbom, J. Witzell, T. Näsholm, and L. Ericson. 2005. Nitrogen deposition and the biodiversity of boreal forests: implications for the nitrogen critical load. Ambio 34:20–24.

Nowacki, G.J., and M.D. Abrams. 1994. Forest composition, structure, and disturbance history of the Alan Seeger Natural Area, Huntington County, Pennsylvania. Bulletin of the Torrey Botanical Club 121:277–291.

Nowacki, G.J., and M.D. Abrams. 2008. The demise of fire and "mesophication" of forests in the eastern United States. BioScience 58:123–138.

Nowacki, G.J., and P.A. Trianosky. 1993. Literature on old-growth forests of eastern North America. Natural Areas Journal 13:87–107.

Nuñez, M. 1980. The calculation of solar radiation in mountainous terrain. Journal of Biogeography 7:173–186.

Nuzzo, V.A., W. McClain, and T. Strole. 1996. Fire impact on groundlayer flora in a sand forest 1990–1994. American Midland Naturalist 136:207–221.

Oberhuber, W., and H. Bauer. 1991. Photoinhibition of photosynthesis under natural conditions in ivy (*Hedera helix* L.) growing in an understory of deciduous trees. Planta 185:545–553.

Ochoa-Hueso, R., E.B. Allen, C. Branquinho, C. Cruz, T. Dias, M.E. Fenn, E.Manrique, M.E. Pérez-Corona, L.J. Sheppard, and W.D. Stock. 2011. Nitrogen deposition effects on Mediterranean-type ecosystems: An ecological assessment. Environmental Pollution 159:2265–2279.

Odum, E.P. 1943. Vegetation of the Edmund Niles Huyck Preserve, New York. American Midland Naturalist 29:72–88.

Odum, E.P. 1969. The strategy of ecosystem development. Science 164:262–270.

Ogle, K. 2003. Implications of interveinal distance for quantum yield in C4 grasses: a modeling and meta-analysis. Oecologia 136:532–542.

Ögren, E., and U. Sundin. 1996. Photosynthetic responses to variable light: a comparison of species from contrasting habitats. Oecologia 106:18–27.

Ohlson, M., L. Söderström, G. Hörnberg, O. Zackrisson, and J. Hermansson. 1997. Habitat qualities versus long-term continuity as determinants of biodiversity in boreal old-growth swamp forests. Biological Conservation 81:221–231.

Ohmann, L., and D.F. Grigal. 1979. Early revegetation and nutrient dynamics following the 1971 Little Sioux forest fire in northeastern Minnesota. Forest Science Monograph 21, Washington, DC.

Ohtsuka, T., T. Sakura, and M. Ohsawa. 1993. Early herbaceous succession along a topographical gradient on forest clear-felling sites in mountainous terrain, central Japan. Ecological Research 8:329–340.

Oinonen, E. 1967a. Sporal regeneration of bracken (*Pteridium aquilinum* (L.) Kuhn.) in Finland in light of the dimensions and the age of its clones. Acta Forestalia Fennica 83(1):1–96.

Oinonen, E. 1967b. Sporal regeneration of ground pine (*Lycopodium complanatum* L.) in southern Finland in the light of the size and the age of its clones. Acta Forestalia Fennica 83(3):76–85.

Oláh, R., and E. Masarovičová. 1997. Response of CO_2 uptake, chlorophyll content, and some productional features of forest herb *Smyrnium perfoliatum* L. (Apiaceae) to different light conditions. Acta Physiologiae Plantarum 19:285–293.

Olano, J.M., and M.W. Palmer. 2003. Stand dynamics of an Appalachian old-growth forest during a severe drought episode. Forest Ecology and Management 174:139–148.

Oldfield, S.F. 2009. Botanic gardens and the conservation of tree species. Trends in Plant Science 14:581–583.

Olesen, J.M. 1996. From naivete to experience: Bumblebee queens (*Bombus terrestris*) foraging on *Corydalis cava* (Fumariaceae). Journal of the Kansas Entomological Society 69:274-286.

Olesen, T. 1992. Daylight spectra (400–700 nm) beneath sunny, blue skies in Tasmania, and the effect of a forest canopy. Australian Journal of Ecology 17:451–461.

Oliver, C.D. 1982. Stand development—its uses and methods of study. In J.E. Means, ed. Forest succession and stand development research in the Northwest. Corvallis, OR: Forest Research Laboratory, Oregon State University, pp. 100–112.

Oliver, C.D., and B.C. Larson. 1996. Forest stand dynamics. Update ed. John Wiley & Sons, New York.

Olivero, A.M., and D.M. Hix. 1998. Influence of aspect and stand age on ground flora of southeastern Ohio forest ecosystems. Plant Ecology 139:177–187.

Olivieri, I., D. Couvert, and P.H. Gouyon. 1990. The genetics of transient populations: Research at the metapopulation level. Trends in Ecology and Evolution 5:207–210.

Olivieri, I., Y. Michalakis, and P.H. Gouyon. 1995. Metapopulation genetics and the evolution of dispersal. American Naturalist 146:202–228.

Ollerton, J., and A. Lack. 1992. Flowering phenology: an example of relaxation of natural selection? Trends in Ecology and Evolution 7:274–276.

Olmstead, N.W., and J.D. Curtis. 1947. Seeds of the forest floor. Ecology 28:49–52.

Olson, J.S. 1958. Rates of succession and soil changes on southern Lake Michigan sand dunes. Botanical Gazette 119:125–170.

Olson, M. 2001. Patterns of fruit production in the subdioecious plant *Astilbe biternata* (Saxifragaceae). Journal of Ecology 89:600–607.

Olsson, B.A., and H. Staaf. 1995. Influence of harvesting intensity of logging residues on ground vegetation in coniferous forests. Journal of Applied Ecology 32:640–654.

Olsson, M.O., and U. Falkengren-Grerup. 2003. Partitioning of nitrate uptake between trees and understory in oak forests. Forest Ecology and Management 179:311–320.

Omernik, J.M. 1987. Ecoregions of the conterminous United States, map (scale 1:7,500,000). Annals of the Association of American Geographers 77:118–125.

O'Neill, R.V., and A.W. King. 1998. Homage to St. Michael; or, Why are there so many books on scale? Pages 3–16 in D.L. Peterson and V.T. Parker, editors. Ecological Scale: Theory and Applications. Columbia University Press, New York.

Oostermeijer, J.G.B., M.L. Brugman, E.R. DeBoer, and H.C.M. DenNijs. 1996. Temporal and spatial variation in the demography of *Gentiana pneumonanthe*, a rare perennial herb. Journal of Ecology 84:153–166.

Oostermeijer, J., S. Luijten, and J. den Nijs. 2003. Integrating demographic and genetic approaches in plant conservation. Biological Conservation 113:389–398.

Oosting, H.J. 1942. An ecological analysis of the plant communities of Piedmont, North Carolina. American Midland Naturalist 28:1–126.

Oosting, H.J. 1956. The study of plant communities, 2nd ed. W.H. Freeman and Company, San Francisco, CA.

Oosting, H.F., and M.E. Humphreys. 1940. Buried viable seeds in successional series of old fields and forest soils. Bulletin of the Torrey Botanical Club 67:253–273.

Opperman, J.J., and A.M. Merenlender. 2000. Deer herbivory as an ecological constraint to restoration of degraded riparian corridors. Restoration Ecology 8:41–47.

Orwig, D.A., and D.R. Foster. 1998. Forest response to the introduced hemlock woolly adelgid in southern New England, USA. Journal of the Torrey Botanical Society. 125:60–73.

Orzell, S.L., and E.L. Bridges. 2006. Pages 136–175 in R.F. Noss, editor. Floristic composition and species richness of subtropical seasonally wet *Muhlenbergia sericea* prairies in portions of central and south Florida. Land of fire and water: the Florida dry prairie ecosystem. DeLeon Springs, FL: E.O. Painter Printing.

Osawa, A. 1994. Seedling responses to forest canopy disturbance following a spruce budworm outbreak in Maine. Canadian Journal of Forest Research 24:850–859.

Osborne, C.P., B.G. Drake, J. LaRoche, and S.P. Long. 1997. Does long-term elevation of CO_2 concentration increase photosynthesis in forest floor vegetation? Plant Physiology 114:337–344.

Oshima, K., Y. Tang, and I. Washitani. 1997. Spatial and seasonal patterns of microsite light availability in a remnant fragment of deciduous riparian forest and their implication in the conservation of *Arisaema heterophyllum*, a threatened plant species. Journal of Plant Research 110:321–327.

Ostfeld, R., C. Canham, K. Oggenfuss, R. Winchcombe, and F. Keesing. 2006. Climate, deer, rodents, and acorns as determinants of variation in Lyme-disease risk. PLoS Biology 4:1058–1068.

Ouborg, N.J. and O. Eriksson. 2004. Toward a metapopulation concept for plants. Pages 337–469 in Hanski and O.E. Gaggiotii, editors. Ecology, Genetics, and Evolution of Metapopulations. New York: Elsevier Academic Press.

Ovington, J.D. 1962. Quantitative ecology and the woodland ecosystem concept. Advances in Ecological Research 1:103–192.

Pacala, S.W. 1986. Neighborhood models of plant population dynamics. II. Multi-species models of annuals. Theoretical Population Biology 29:262–292.

Pacala, S.W., C.D. Canham, J. Saponara, J.A. Silander Jr., R.K. Kobe, and E. Ribbens. 1996. Forest models defined by field measurements: estimation, error analysis and dynamics. Ecological Monographs 66:1–43.

Pacala, S.W., C.D. Canham, and J.A. Silander Jr. 1993. Forest models defined by field measurements: I. The design of a northeastern forest simulator. Canadian Journal of Forest Research 23:1980–1988.

Pacala, S.W., C.D. Canham, J.A. Silander Jr., and R.K. Kobe. 1994. Sapling growth as a function of resources in a north temperate forest. Canadian Journal of Forest Research 24:2172–2183.

Pakaluk, J. 1997. *Acoptus suturalis* LeConte (Coleoptera: Curculionidae: Zygopinae), a potential vector of the chestnut blight fungus, *Cryphonectria parasitica* (Murrill) Barr, in the eastern United States. Proceedings of the Entomological Society of Washington 99:583–584.

Pakeman, R.J. 2001. Plant migration rates and seed dispersal mechanisms. Journal of Biogeography 28:795–800.

Paliwal, K., M. Küppers, and H. Schneider. 1994. Leaf gas exchange in lightflecks of plants of different successional range in the understorey of a central European beech forest. Current Science 67:29–34.

Palmer, M.W. 1990. The estimation of species richness by extrapolation. Ecology 71:1195–1198.

Palmer, M.W. 1991. Patterns of species richness among North-Carolina hardwood forests— Tests of 2 hypotheses. Journal of Vegetation Science 2:361–366.

Palmer, M.W. 1993. Putting things in even better order: the advantages of canonical correspondence analysis. Ecology 74:2215–2230.

Palmer, M.W. 1994. Variation in species richness: towards a unification of hypotheses. Folia Geobotanica 29:511–530.

Palmer, M.W., and T.A. Maurer. 1997. Does diversity beget diversity? A case study of crops and weeds. Journal of Vegetation Science 8:235–240.

Pardo, L.H., M.E. Fenn, C.L. Goodale, L.H. Geiser, C.T. Driscoll, E.B. Allen, J. Baron, R. Bobbink, W.D. Bowman, C. Clark, B. Emmett, F.S. Gilliam, T. Greaver, S.J. Hall, E.A. Lilleskov, L. Liu, J. Lynch, K. Nadelhoffer, S.S. Perakis, M.J. Robin-Abbott, J. Stoddard, K. Weathers, and R.L. Dennis. 2011. Effects of nitrogen deposition and empirical nitrogen critical loads for ecoregions of the United States. Ecological Applications 21:3049–3082.

Pardy, A.B. 1997. Forest succession following a severe spruce budworm outbreak at Cape Breton Highlands National Park. M.S. thesis, University of New Brunswick, Fredericton, New Brunswick, CA.

Parent, S., and C. Messier. 1996. A simple and efficient method to estimate microsite light availability under a forest canopy. Canadian Journal of Forest Research 26:151–154.

Parish, T., K.H. Lakhani, and T.H. Sparks. 1994. Modeling the relationship between bird population variables and hedgerow and other field margin attributes. 1. Species richness of winter, summer, and breeding birds. Journal of Applied Ecology 31:764–775.

Parker, G.G. 1995. Structure and microclimate of forest canopies. Pages 73–106 in M.D. Lowman and N.M. Nadkarni, editors. Forest Canopies. Academic Press, San Diego, CA.

Parker, G.G., and M.J. Brown. 2000. Forest canopy stratification—is it useful? American Naturalist 155:473–484.

Parker, G.R. 1989. Old-growth forests of the central hardwood region. Natural Areas Journal 9:5–11.

Parker, J.D., L.J. Richie, E.M. Lind, and K.O. Maloney. 2010. Land use history alters the relationship between native and exotic plants: the rich don't always get richer. Biological Invasions 12:1557–1571.

Parker, K.C., and J. Bendix. 1996. Landscape-scale geomorphic influences on vegetation patterns in four environments. Physical Geography 17:113–141.

Parker, P.G., A.A. Snow, M.D. Schug,.G.C. Booton, and P.A. Fuerst. 1998. What molecules can tell us about populations: choosing and using a molecular marker. Ecology 79:361–382

Parkhurst D.G., and O.L. Loucks. 1972. Optimal leaf size in relation to environment. Journal of Ecology 60:505–537.

Parmesan, C. 2006. Ecological and evolutionary responses to recent climate change. Annual Review of Ecology, Evolution, and Systematics 37:637–669.

Parmesan, C., and G. Yohe. 2003. A globally coherent fingerprint of climate change impacts across natural systems. Nature 421:37–42.

Parrish, J.A.D., and F.A. Bazzaz. 1982. Competitive interactions in plant communities of different successional ages. Ecology 63:314–320.

Pärtel, M. 2002. Local plant diversity patterns and evolutionary history at the regional scale. Ecology 83:2361–2366.

Pärtel, M., M. Zobel, K. Zobel, and E. van der Maarel. 1996. The species pool and its relation to species richness: evidence from Estonian plant communities. Oikos 75:111–117.

Pascarella, J.B., and C.C. Horvitz. 1998. Hurricane disturbance of the population dynamics of a tropical understory shrub: megametric elasticity analysis. Ecology 79:547–563.

Pastor, J., and S.D. Bridgham. 1999. Nutrient efficiency along nutrient availability gradients. Oecologia 118:50–58.

Pastor, J., and M. Broschart. 1990. The spatial pattern of a northern conifer-hardwood landscape. Landscape Ecology 4:55–68.

Patel, A., and D.J. Rapport. 2000. Assessing the effects of deer browsing, prescribed burns, visitor use, and trails on an oak-pine forest: Pinery Provincial Park, Ontario. Natural Areas Journal 20:250–260.

Patrick, T.S. 1973. Observations on the life history of Trillium grandiflorum (Michaus) Salisbury. M.A. thesis, Cornell University, Ithaca, NY.

Patrick, W.H. 1958. Modification of particle size analysis. Soil Science Society of America Proceedings 22:366–367.

Patterson, T.B., and T.J. Givnish. 2002. Phylogeny, concerted convergence, and phylogenetic niche conservatism in the core Liliales: insights from rbcL and ndhF sequence data. Evolution 56:233–252.Patterson, W.A., III, and K.E. Sassaman. 1988. Indian Fires in the Prehistory of New England. Pages 107–135 in G. P. Nicholas, editor. Holocene human ecology in northeastern North America. Plenum Press, New York.

Payette, S. 1992. Fire as a controlling process in the North American boreal forest. Pages 44–169 in H.H. Shugart, R. Leemans, and G. Bonan, editors. A systems analysis of the global boreal forest. Cambridge, UK: Cambridge University Press.

Pearcy, R.W. 1983. The light environment and growth of C3 and C4 tree species in the understory of a Hawaiian forest. Oecologia 58:19–25.

Pearcy, R.W. 1987. Photosynthetic gas exchange responses of Australian tropical forest trees in canopy, gap and understory microenvironments. Functional Ecology 1:169–178.

Pearcy, R.W. 1988. Photosynthetic utilization of lightflecks by understory plants. Australian Journal of Plant Physiology 15:223–238.

Pearcy, R.W. 1998. Acclimation to sun and shade. Pages 250–263 in A.S. Raghavendra, editor. Photosynthesis: A comprehensive treatise. Cambridge University Press, Cambridge, UK.

Pearcy, R.W. 1999. Responses of plants to heterogeneous light environments. Pages 269–314 in F.I. Pugnaire and F. Valladares, editors. Handbook of functional plant ecology. Marcel Dekker, New York.

Pearcy, R.W., O. Bjorkman, M.M. Caldwell, J.E. Keeley, R.K. Monson, and B.R. Strain. 1987. Carbon gain by plants in natural environments. Bioscience 37:21–29.

Pearcy, R.W., R.L. Chazdon, L.J. Gross, and K.A. Mott. 1994. Photosynthetic utilization of sunflecks: A temporally patchy resource on a time scale of seconds to minutes. Pages 175–208 in M.M. Caldwell and R.W. Pearcy, editors. Exploitation of environmental heterogeneity by plants: ecophysiological processes above- and belowground. Academic Press, San Diego, CA.

Pearcy, R.W., and W.A. Pfitsch. 1991. Influence of sunflecks on the δ13C of *Adenocaulon bicolor* plants occurring in contrasting forest understory microsites. Oecologia 86:457–462.

Pearcy, R.W., J.S. Roden, and J.A. Gamon. 1990. Sunfleck dynamics in relation to canopy structure in a soybean (*Glycine max* (L.) Merr.) canopy. Agricultural and Forest Meteorology 52:359–372.

Pearcy, R.W., and D.A. Sims 1994. Photosynthetic acclimation to changing light environments: scaling from the leaf to the whole plant. Pages 223–234 in M.M. Caldwell and R.W. Pearcy, editors. Exploitation of environmental heterogeneity by plants: ecophysiological processes above- and belowground. Academic Press, San Diego, CA.

Pearcy, R.W., and W. Yang. 1996. A three-dimensional shoot architecture model for assessment of light capture and carbon gain by understory plants. Oecologia 108:1–12.

Pearcy, R.W., and D.A. Way. 2012. Two decades of sunfleck research: looking back to move forward. Tree Physiology 32:1059–1061.

Pearsall, S.H., B.J. McCrodden, and P.A. Townsend. 2005. Adaptive management of flows in the lower Roanoke River, North Carolina. Environmental Management 35:353–367.

Pedersen, B.S., and A.M. Wallis. 2004. Effects of white-tailed deer herbivory on forest gap dynamics in a wildlife preserve, Pennsylvania, USA. Natural Areas Journal 24:82–94.

Peet, R.K. 1981. Forest vegetation of the northern Colorado front range: Composition and dynamics. Vegetatio 45:3–75.

Peet, R.K. 1992. Community structure and ecosystem function. In D.C. Glenn-Lewin, R.K. Peet, and T.T.Veblen, eds. Plant Succession: Theory and Prediction. London: Chapman and Hall, pp. 103–151.

Peet, R.K. 2006. Ecological classification of longleaf pine woodlands. In S. Jose, E. Jokela, and D. Miller, eds. Longleaf pine ecosystems: ecology, management, and restoration. New York: Springer-Verlag, pp. 51–94.

Peet, R.K., and N.L. Christensen. 1980a. Succession: A population process. Vegetatio 43:131–140.

Peet, R.K., and N.L.Christensen. 1980b. Hardwood forest vegetation of the North Carolina Piedmont. Veröffentlichungen Geobotanik Institut ETH. Stiftung Rübel, 69:14–39.

Peet, R.K., and N.L. Christensen. 1987. Competition and tree death. BioScience 37:586–595.

Peet, R.K., and N.L. Christensen. 1988. Changes in species diversity during secondary forest succession on the North Carolina Piedmont. Pages 233–245 in H.J. During, M.J.A. Werger, and J.H. Willems, editors. Diversity and pattern in plant communities. SPB Academic Publishing, The Hague, NL.

Peet, R.K., J.D. Fridley, and J.M. Gramling. 2003. Variation in species richness and species pool size across a pH gradient in forests of the southern Blue Ridge Mountains. Folio Geobotanica 38:391–401.

Peet, R.K., M.T. Lee, M.F. Boyle, T.R. Wentworth, M.P. Schafale, and A.S. Weakley. 2012. Vegetation-plot database of the Carolina Vegetation Survey. Biodiversity and Ecology 4: 243–253.

Peet, R.K., T.R. Wentworth, and P.S. White. 1998. A flexible, multipurpose method for recording vegetation composition and structure. Castanea 63:262–274.

Peine, H. 1989. Spruce budworm defoliation and growth loss in young balsam fir: recovery of growth in spaced stands. Canadian Journal of Forest Research 19:1616–1624.

Pellmyr, O. 1985. The pollination biology of *Actaea pachypoda* and *Actaea rubra* (including *Actaea erythrocarpa*) in northern Michigan and Finland. Bulletin of the Torrey Botanical Club 112:265–273.

Peloquin, R.L., and R.D. Hiebert. 1999. The effects of black locust (*Robinia pseudoacacia* L.) on species diversity and composition of black oak savanna/woodland communities. Natural Areas Journal 19:121–131.

Pemberton, R.W., and H. Liu. 2008. Potential of invasive and native solitary specialist bee pollinators to help restore the rare cowhorn orchid (*Cyrtopodium punctatum*) in Florida. Biological Conservation 141:1758-1764.

Pennings, S.C., C.M. Clark, E.E. Cleland, S.L. Collins, L. Gough, K.L. Gross, D.G. Milchunas, and K.N. Suding. 2005. Do individual plant species show predictable responses to nitrogen addition across multiple experiments? Oikos 110:547–555.

Peroni, P.A., and W.G. Abrahamson. 1985. A rapid method for determining losses of native vegetation. Natural Areas Journal 5:20–24.

Perry, J.N. 1998. Measures of spatial pattern for counts. Ecology 79:1008–1017.

Perry, J.N., and J.L. Gonzalez-Andujar. 1993. Dispersal in a metapopulation neighborhood model of an annual plant with a seedbank. Journal of Ecology 81:453–463.

Peterken, G.F., and M. Game. 1984. Historical factors affecting the number and distribution of vascular plant species in the woodlands of central Lincolnshire. Journal of Ecology 72:155–182.

Petersen, S.M., and P.B. Drewa. 2009. Are vegetation-environment relationships different between herbaceous and woody groundcover plants in barrens with shallow soils? Ecoscience 16:197–208.

Peterson, C.J. 2000. Damage and recovery of tree species after two different tornadoes at the same old growth forest: a comparison of infrequent wind disturbances. Forest Ecology and Management 135:237–252.

Peterson, C.J., and W.P. Carson. 1996. Generalizing forest regeneration models: the dependence of propagule availability on disturbance history and stand size. Canadian Journal of Forest Research 26:45–52.

Peterson, C.J., W.P. Carson, B.C. McCarthy, and S.T.A. Pickett. 1990. Microsite variation and soil dynamics within newly created treefall pits and mounds. Oikos 58:39–46.

Peterson, C.J., and S.T.A. Pickett. 1991. Treefall and resprouting following catastrophic windthrow in an old-growth hemlock-hardwoods forest. Forest Ecology and Management 42:205–217.

Peterson, C.J., and S.T.A. Pickett. 1995. Forest reorganization: a case study in an old-growth forest catastrophic blowdown. Ecology 76:763–774.

Peterson, C.J., and S.T.A. Pickett. 2000. Patch type influences on regeneration in a western Pennsylvania, USA, catastrophic windthrow. Oikos 90:489–500.

Peterson, C.J., and A.J. Rebertus. 1997. Tornado damage and initial recovery in three adjacent, lowland temperature forests in Missouri. Journal of Vegetation Science 8:559–564.

Peterson, D.L., and G.L. Rolfe. 1982. Nutrient dynamics of herbaceous vegetation in upland and floodplain forest communities. American Midland Naturalist 107:325–339.

Petit, R.J., F.S. Hu, and C.W. Dick. 2008. Forests of the past: a window to future changes. Science 320:1450–1452.

Petru, M., and E.S. Menges. 2004. Shifting sands in Florida scrub gaps and roadsides: Dynamic microsites for herbs. American Midland Naturalist 151:101–113.

Pfister, C.A. 1998. Patterns of variance in stage-structured populations: Evolutionary predictions and ecological implications. Proceedings of the National Academy of Sciences of the United States of America 95:213–218.

Pfitsch, W.A., and R.W. Pearcy. 1989a. Daily carbon gain by Adenocaulon bicolor, a redwood forest understory herb, in relation to its light environment. Oecologia 80:465–470.

Pfitsch, W.A., and R.W. Pearcy. 1989b. Steady-state and dynamic photosynthetic responses of *Adenocaulon bicolor* in its redwood forest habitat. Oecologia 80:471–476.

Pfitsch, W.A., and R.W. Pearcy. 1992. Growth and reproductive allocation of *Adenocaulon bicolor* following experimental removal of sunflecks. Ecology 73:2109–2117.

Pfitsch, W.A., and R.W. Pearcy. 1995. The consequences of sunflecks for photosynthesis and growth of forest understory plants. Pages 343–359 in E.-D. Schulze and M.M. Caldwell, editors. *Ecophysiology of photosynthesis*. Springer-Verlag, Berlin.

Phillips, D.L., and W.H. Murdy. 1985. Effects of rhododendron (*Rhododendron maximum* L.) on regeneration of southern Appalachian hardwoods. Forest Science 31:226–233.

Phillips, R.D., M.D. Barrett, K.W. Dixon, and S.D. Hopper. 2011. Do mycorrhizal symbioses cause rarity in orchids? Journal of Ecology 99:858–869.

Pickett, S.T.A. 1976. Succession: an evolutionary interpretation. American Naturalist 110:107–119.

Pickett, S.T.A. 1980. Non-equilibrium coexistence of plants. Bulletin of the Torrey Botanical Club 107:238–248.

Pickett, S.T.A. 1989. Space-for-time substitution as an alternatiave to long-term studies. In G.E. Likens, ed. Long-term studies in ecology: approaches and alternatives. New York: Springer-Verlag, pp. 110–135.

Pickett, S.T.A., and J.S. Kempf. 1980. Branching patterns in forest shrubs and understory trees in relation to habitat. New Phytologist 86:219–228.

Pickett, S.T.A., J. Kolasa, J.J. Armesto, and S.L. Collins. 1989. The ecological concept of disturbance and its expression at various hierarchical levels. Oikos 54:129–136.

Pickett, S.T.A., and M.J. McDonnell. 1989. Seed bank dynamics in temperate deciduous forest. Pages 123–148 in M. Allessio Leck, V.T. Parker, and R.L. Simpson, editors. Ecology of soil seed banks. Academic Press and Harcourt Brace Jovanovich, New York.

Pickett, S.T.A., V.T. Parker, and P.L. Fiedler. 1992. The new paradigm in ecology: implications for conservation biology above the species level. Pages 65–88 in P.L. Fiedler and S.K. Jain, editors. The theory and practice of nature conservation, preservation and management. New York: Chapman and Hall.

Pickett, S.T.A., and P.S. White. 1985. The ecology of natural disturbance and patch dynamics. Academic Press, New York.

Pielou, E.C. 1969. An introduction to Mathematical Ecology. Wiley-Interscience, New York.

Pimm, S.L., and M.E. Gilpin. 1989. Theoretical issues in conservation biology. Pages 287–305 in J. Roughgarden, R.M. May, and S.A. Levin, editors. Perspectives in ecological theory. Princeton University Press, Princeton, NJ.

Pimm, S.L., G.J. Russell, J.L. Gittleman, and T.M. Brooks. 1995. The future of biodiversity. Science 269:347–350.

Pinder, R.W., K.W. Appel, and R.L. Dennis. 2011. Trends in atmospheric reactive nitrogen for the eastern United States. Environmental Pollution 159:3138–3141.

Piqueras, J., and L. Klimes. 1998. Demography and modelling of clonal fragments in the pseudoannual plant *Trientalis europaea* L. Plant Ecology 136:213–227.

Pitelka, L.F., J.W. Ashmun, and R.L. Brown. 1985. The relationships between seasonal variation in light intensity, ramet size, and sexual reproduction in natural and experimental populations of *Aster acuminatus* (Compositae). American Journal of Botany 72:311–319.

Pitelka, L.F., and W.F. Curtis. 1986. Photosynthetic responses to light in an understory herb, *Aster acuminatus*. American Journal of Botany 73:535–540.

Pitelka, L.F., D.S. Stanton, and M.O. Peckenham. 1980. Effects of light and density on resource allocation patterns in a forest herb, *Aster acuminatus* (Compositae). American Journal of Botany 67:942–948.

Pitman, N.C.A., J. Terborgh, M.R. Silman, and P.V. Nunez. 1999. Tree species distributions in an upper Amazonian forest. Ecology 80:2651–2661.

Pittillo, J.D., R.D. Hatcher Jr., and S.W. Buol. 1998. Introduction to the environment and vegetation of the southern Blue Ridge province. Castanea 63:202–216.

Pittman, A.B., and V. Bates. 1989. A new species of *Polymnia* (Compositae: Heliantheae) from the Ouachita Mountain region of Arkansas. SIDA 13:481–486.

Plašilová, J. 1970. A study of the root systems and root ecology of perennial herbs in the undergrowth of deciduous forests. Preslia 42:136–152.

Platt, W.J., S.C. Carr, M. Reilly, and J. Fahr. 2006. Pine savanna overstory influences on ground-cover biodiversity. Applied Vegetation Science 9:37–50.

Platt, W.J., and I.M. Weis. 1977. Resource partitioning and competition within a guild of fugitive prairie plants. American Naturalist 111:479–513.

Pleasants, J.M., and J.F. Wendel. 1989. Genetic diversity in a clonal narrow endemic, *Erythronium propullans*, and in its widespread progenitor, *Erythronium albidum*. American Journal of Botany 76:1136–1151.

Pockman, W.T., and J.S. Sperry. 2000. Vulnerability to xylem cavitation and the distribution of Sonoran desert vegetation. American Journal of Botany 87:1287–1299.

Pocock, M.J.O., S. Hartley, M.G. Telfer, C.D. Preston, and W.E. Kunin. 2006. Ecological correlates of range structure in rare and scarce British plants. Journal of Ecology 94:581–596.

Polgar, C.A., and R.B. Primack. 2011 Leaf-out phenology of temperate woody plants: from trees to ecosystems. New Phytologist 191:926–941.

Pons, T.L. 1977. An ecophysiological study in the field layer of ash coppice. II. Experiments with *Geum urbanum* and *Cirsium palustre* in different light intensities. Acta Botanica Neerlandica 26:29–42.

Poorter, H. 1994. Construction costs and payback time of biomass: a whole plant perspective. Pages 111–127 in J. Roy and E. Garnier, editors. A whole-plant perspective on carbon-nitrogen interactions. SPB Academic Publishing, The Hague, NL.

Poorter, H., and J.R. Evans. 1998. Photosynthetic nitrogen-use efficiency of species that differ inherently in specific leaf area. Oecologia 116:26–37.

Poorter, L., and S.F. Oberbauer. 1993. Photosynthesis induction responses of two rainforest tree species in relation to light environment. Oecologia 96:193–199.

Popović, Z.S., and J.L. Lindquist. 2010. Evaluation of the INTERCOM model for predicting growth of forest herbs. Archives of Biological Science 62:175–183.

Porcar-Castell, A., and S. Palmroth. 2012. Modelling photosynthesis in highly dynamic environments: the case of sunflecks. Tree Physiology 32:1062–1065.

Porter, W.F., and H.B. Underwood. 1999. Of elephants and blind men: deer management in the U.S. National Parks. Ecological Applications 9:3–9.

Porter, W.F., N.E. Mathews, H.B. Underwood, R.W. Sage, and D.F. Behrend. 1991. Social organization in deer: Implications for localized management. Environmental Management 15:809–814.

Posch, M., J. Aherne, and J.-P. Hettelingh. 2011. Nitrogen critical loads using biodiversity-related critical limits. Environmental Pollution 159:2223–2227.

Powles, S.B. 1984. Photoinhibition of photosynthesis induced by visible light. Annual Review of Plant Physiology 35:15–44.

Prance, G.T., H. Beentje, J. Dransfield, and R. Johns. 2000. The tropical flora remains under-collected. Annals of the Missouri Botanical Garden 87:67–71.

Prati, D., and O. Bossdorf. 2004. Allelopathic inhibition of germination by *Alliaria petiolata* (Brassicaceae). American Journal of Botany 91:285–288.

Pregitzer, K.S., and B.V. Barnes. 1992. The use of ground flora to indicate edaphic factors in upland ecosystems of the McCormick Experimental Forest, Upper Michigan. Canadian Journal of Forest Research 12:661–672.

Prentice, I.C., P.J. Bartlein, and T. Webb, III. 1991. Vegetation and climate change in eastern North America since the last glacial maximum. Ecology 72:2038–2056.

Price, J.N., and J.W. Morgan. 2007. Vegetation dynamics following resource manipulations in herb-rich woodland. Plant Ecology 188:29–37.

Primack, R.B. 1980. Phenotypic variation of rare and widespread species of *Plantago*. Rhodora 82:87–96.

Primack, R.B., and P. Hall. 1990. Costs of reproduction in the pink lady's slipper orchid: a four-year experimental study. American Naturalist 136:638–656.

Primack, R.B., I. Ibanez, H. Higuchi, S.D. Lee, A.J. Miller-Rushing, A.M. Wilson, and J.A. Silander, Jr. 2009. Spatial and interspecific variability in phenological responses to warming temperatures. Biological Conservation 142:2569–2577.

Primack, R.B., and A.J. Miller-Rushing. 2009. The role of botanical gardens in climate change research RID D-5102-2009. New Phytologist 182:303–313.

Primack, R.B., A.J. Miller-Rushing, and K. Dharaneeswaran. 2009. Changes in the flora of Thoreau's Concord. Biological Conservation 142:500–508.

Proctor, M., P. Yeo, and A. Lack. 1996. The natural history of pollination. Portland, OR: TimberPress.

Provencher, L., B.J. Herring, D.R. Gordon, H.L. Rodgers, G.W. Tanner, L.A. Brennan, and J.L. Hardesty. 2000. Restoration of northwest Florida sandhills through harvest of invasive *Pinus clausa*. Restoration Ecology 8:175–185.

Putz, F.E., and C.D. Canham. 1992. Mechanisms of arrested succession in shrublands: root and shoot competition between shrubs and tree seedlings. Forest Ecology and Management 49:267–275.

Pykala, J. 2004. Immediate increase in plant species richness after clear-cutting of boreal herb-rich forests. Applied Vegetation Science 7:29–34.

Pyke, D.A., M.L. Brooks, and C. D'Antonio. 2010. Fire as a restoration tool: a decision framework for predicting the control or enhancement of plants using fire. Restoration Ecology 18:274–284.

Pyke, G.R., D.W. Inouye, and J.D. Thomson. 2011. Activity and abundance of bumble bees near Crested Butte, Colorado: diel, season, and elevation effects. Ecological Entomology 36:511–521.

Pyle, L.L. 1995. Effects of disturbance on herbaceous exotic plant species on the floodplain of the Potomac River. American Midland Naturalist 134:244–253.

Pysek, P. 1995. On the terminology used in plant invasion studies. Pages 71–81 in P. Pysek, K. Prach, M. Rejmanek, and M. Wade, editors. Plant invasions—general aspects and special problems. SPB Academic Publishing, Amsterdam.

Pysek, P., and K. Prach. 1993. Plant invasions and the role of riparian habitats: a comparison of four species alien to central Europe. Journal of Biogeography 20:413–420.

Qian, H., K. Klinka, and B. Sivak. 1997. Diversity of the understory vascular vegetation in 40 year-old and old-growth forest stands on Vancouver Island, British Columbia. Journal of Vegetation Science 8:773–780.

Qian, H., and R.E. Ricklefs. 1999. A comparison of the taxonomic richness of vascular plants in China and the United States. American Naturalist 154:160–181.

Quintana-Ascencio, P.F., R.W. Dolan, and E.S. Menges. 1998. *Hypericum cumulicola* demography in unoccupied and occupied Florida scrub patches with different time-since-fire. Journal of Ecology 86:640–651.

Quintana-Ascencio, R.F., and E.S. Menges. 1996. Inferring metapopulation dynamics from patch-level incidence of Florida scrub plants. Conservation Biology 10:1210–1219.

Quintana-Ascencio, P.F., E.S. Menges, and C.W. Weekley. 2003. A fire-explicit population viability analysis of *Hypericum cumulicola* in Florida rosemary scrub. Conservation Biology 17:433–449.

Quintana-Ascencio, P.F., E.S. Menges, C.W. Weekley, M.I. Kelrick, and B. Pace-Aldana. 2011. Biennial cycling caused by demographic delays in a fire-adapted annual plant. Population Ecology 53:131–142.

Quintana-Ascencio, R.F., and M. Morales-Hernandez. 1997. Fire-mediated effects of shrubs, lichens and herbs on the demography of *Hypericum cumulicola* in patchy Florida scrub. Oecologia 112:263–271.

Quintana-Ascencio, P.F., C.W. Weekley, and E.S. Menges. 2007. Comparative demography of a rare species in Florida scrub and road habitats. Biological Conservation 137:263–270.

Rabinowitz, D. 1981. Seven forms of rarity. In H. Synge, ed. The biological aspects of rare plant conservation. London: John Wiley & Sons, pp. 205–217.

Radford, A.E., H.E. Ahles, and C. Ritchie Bell. 1968. Manual of the flora of the Carolinas. University of North Carolina Press, Chapel Hill, NC.

Rafferty, N.E., and A.R. Ives. 2011. Effects of experimental shifts in flowering phenology on plant-pollinator interactions. Ecology Letters 14:69–74.

Raghavendra, A.A., J.M. Rao, and V.S.R. Das. 1976. Replaceability of potassium by sodium for stomatal opening in epidermal strips of *Commelina benghalensis*. Zurich Pflanzenphysiologie 80:36–42.

Rainey, S.M., K.J. Nadelhoffer, W.L. Silver, and M.R. Downs. 1999. Effects of chronic nitrogen additions on understory species in a red pine plantation. Ecological Applications 9:949–957.

Ramovs, B.V. 2001. Understory plant composition, microenvironment and stand structure of maturing plantations and naturally regenerated forests. M.S. thesis, University of New Brunswick, Fredericton, New Brunswick, CN.

Ramula, S., and Y.M. Buckley. 2009. Multiple life stages with multiple replicated density levels are required to estimate density dependence for plants. Oikos 118:1164–1173.

Ramula, S., T.M. Knight, J.H. Burns, and Y.M. Buckley. 2008. General guidelines for invasive plant management based on comparative demography of invasive and native plant populations. Journal of Applied Ecology 45:1124–1133.

Ramula, S., and K. Lehtila. 2005. Importance of correlations among matrix entries in stochastic models in relation to number of transition matrices. Oikos 111:9–18.

Randall, J.A., and M.B. Walters. 2011. Deer density effects on vegetation in aspen forest understories over site productivity and stand age gradients. Forest Ecology and Management 261:408–415.

Randall, J.M. 1997. Defining weeds of natural areas. Pages 18–25 in J.O. Luken and J.W. Thieret, editors. Assessment and management of plant invasions. Springer-Verlag, New York.

Randall, W. J. 1952. Interrelations of autoecological characteristics of forest herbs. Ph.D. dissertation, University of Wisconsin, Madison, WI.

Rasband, W.S. 2008. ImageJ. U.S. National Institutes of Health, Bethesda, MD.

Rasmussen, H., and D. Whigham. 2002. Phenology of roots and mycorrhiza in orchid species differing in phototrophic strategy. New Phytologist 154:797–807.

Rathcke B., and E.P. Lacey. 1985. Phenological patterns of terrestrial plants. Annual Review of Ecology and Systematics 16:179–214.

Raunkiaer, C. 1934. The life forms of plants and statistical plant geography. Clarendon Press, Oxford, UK.

Raven, J.A. 1989. Fight or flight: the economics of repair and avoidance of photoinhibition of photosynthesis. Functional Ecology 3:5–19.

Read, D.J., and J. Perez-Moreno. 2003. Mycorrhizas and nutrient cycling in ecosystems—a journey towards relevance? New Phytologist 157:475–492.

Reader, R.J., and B.D. Bricker. 1992a. Response of five deciduous forest herbs to partial canopy removal and patch size. American Midland Naturalist 127:149–157.

Reader, R.J., and B.D. Bricker. 1992b Value of selectively cut deciduous forest for understory herb conservation: an experimental assessment. Forest Ecology and Management 51:317–327.

Rebertus, A.J., S.R. Shifley, R.H. Richards, and L.M. Roovers. 1997. Ice storm damage to an old-growth oak-hickory forest in Missouri. American Midland Naturalist 137:48–61.

Redding, J.A. 1995. History of deer population trends and forest cutting on the Allegheny National Forest. In Proceedings of the 10th North-Central Hardwoods Conference. U.S. Forest Service Technical Report NE-197, pp. 214–224.

Redford, K.H. 1992. The empty forest. BioScience 42:412–422.

Reed, J.M., L.S. Mills, J.B. Dunning, E.S. Menges, K.S. McKelvey, R. Frye, S.R. Beissinger, M.C. Anstett, and P. Miller. 2002. Emerging issues in population viability analysis. Conservation Biology 16:7–19.

Reich, P.B., P. Bakken, D. Carlson, L.E. Frelich, S.K. Friedman, and D.F. Grigal. 2001. Influence of logging, fire, and forest type on biodiversity and productivity in southern boreal forests. Ecology 82:2731–2748.

Reichard, S.E. 1997. Prevention of invasive plant introductions on national and local levels. Pages 215–227 in J.O. Luken and J.W. Thieret, editors. Assessment and management of plant invasions. Springer-Verlag, New York.

Reichard, S.H., and C.W. Hamilton. 1997. Predicting invasions of woody plants introduced into North America. Conservation Biology 11:193–203.

Reid, A. 1964. Light intensity and herb growth in white oak forests. Ecology 45:396–398.

Reifsnyder, W.E., G.M. Furnival, and J.L. Horowitz. 1971. Spatial and temporal distribution of solar radiation beneath forest canopies. Agricultural Meteorology 9:21–37.

Reilly, M.J., M.C. Wimberly, and C.L. Newell. 2006a. Wildfire effects on plant species richness at multiple spatial scales in forest communities of the southern Appalachians. Journal of Ecology 94:118–130.

Reilly, M.J., M.C. Wimberly, and C.L. Newell. 2006b. Wildfire effects on ß-diversity and species turnover in a forested landscape. Journal of Vegetation Science 17:447–454.

Reiners, W.A. 1992. Twenty years of ecosystem reorganization following experimental deforestation and regrowth suppression. Ecological Monographs 62:503–523.

Reitz, S., A. Hille, and S.L. Stout. 2004. Silviculture in cooperation with hunters: the Kinzua Quality Deer Cooperative. Pages 110–126 in W.D. Shepperd and L.G. Eskew, editors. Silviculture in special places: proceedings of the National Silviculture Workshop RMRS-P-34. USDA Forest Service RMRS, Fort Collins, CO.

Relva, M.A., C.L. Westerholm, and T. Kitzberger. 2009. Effects of introduced ungulates on forest understory communities in northern Patagonia are modified by timing and severity of stand mortality. Plant Ecology 201:11–22.

Renaud, P.C., H. Verheyden, and B. Dumont. 2003. Damage to saplings by red deer (Cervus elaphus): effect of foliage height and structure. Forest Ecology and Management 181:31–37.

Renner, S.S., and R.E. Ricklefs. 1995. Dioecy and its correlates in the flowering plants. American Journal of Botany 82:596–606.

Rentch, J.S., and R.R. Hicks. 2005. Changes in presettlement forest composition for five areas in the central hardwood forest, 1784–1990. Natural Areas Journal 25:228–238.

Reznicek, A.A., and P.M. Catling. 1989. Flora of Long Point, Regiona Municipality of Haldimand-Norfolk, Ontario. Michigan Botanist 28:99–175.

Ricciardi, A., and D. Simberloff. 2009. Assisted colonization is not a viable conservation strategy. Trends in Ecology and Evolution 24:248–253.

Rich, P.M., D.D. Breshears, and A.B. White. 2008. Phenology of mixed woody-herbaceous ecosystems following extreme events: net and differential responses. Ecology 89:342–352.

Rich, P.M., D.B. Clark, D.A. Clark, and S.F. Oberbauer. 1993. Long-term study of solar radiation regimes in a tropical wet forest using quantum sensors and hemispherical photography. Agricultural and Forest Meteorology 65:107–127.

Richards, A.J. 1997. Plant breeding systems, 2nd ed. London: Chapman and Hall.

Richardson, A.D., A.S. Bailey, E.G. Denny, C.W. Martin, and J. O'Keefe. 2006. Phenology of a northern hardwood forest canopy. Global Change Biology 12:1174–1188.

Richardson, H.L. 1938. The nitrogen cycle in grassland soils: with especial reference to the Rothamsted Park Grass Experiment. Journal of Agricultural Science, 28:73–121.

Ricketts, T.H., E. Dinerstein, D.M. Olson, and C. Loucks. 1999. Who's where in North America? BioScience, 49:369–381.

Ricketts, T.H., E. Dinerstein, D.M. Olson, C.J. Loucks, W. Eichbaum, D. DellaSalla, K. Kavanagh, P. Hedao, P. Hurley, K. Carney, R. Abell, and S. Walters. 1999. Terrestrial ecoregions of North America: a conservation assessment. Washington, DC: Island Press.

Ricklefs, R.E. 2004. A comprehensive framework for global patterns in biodiversity. Ecology Letters 7:1–15.

Ricklefs, R.E., and R.E. Latham. 1992. Intercontinental correlation of geographical ranges suggests stasis in ecological traits of relict genera of temperate perennial herbs. American Naturalist 139:1305–1321.

Ries, L., J.R. Fletcher Jr., J. Battin, and T.D. Sisk. 2004. Ecological responses to habitat edges: mechanisms, models and variability explained. Annual Review of Ecology, Evolution, and Systematics 35:491–522.

Rinnan, R., and T. Holopainen. 2004. Ozone effects on the ultrastructure of peatland plants: *Sphagnum* mosses, *Vaccinium oxycoccus*, *Andromeda polifolia*, and *Eriophorum vaginatum*. Annals of Botany 94:623–634.

Ripple, W.J., and R.L. Beschta. 2003. Wolf reintroduction, predation risk, and cottonwood recovery in Yellowstone National Park. Forest Ecology and Management 184:299–313.

Ripple, W.J., and R.L. Beschta. 2004a. Linking wolves and plants: Aldo Leopold on trophic cascades. BioScience 55:613–621.

Ripple, W.J., and R.L. Beschta. 2004b. Wolves and the ecology of fear: Can predation risk structure ecosystems? BioScience 54:755–766.

Ripple, W.J., and E.J. Larsen. 1991. The role of postfire coarse woody debris in aspen regeneration. Western Journal of Applied Forestry 16:61–64.

Risser, P.G., and G. Cottam. 1967. Influence of temperature on the dormancy of some spring ephemerals. Ecology 48:500–503.

Risser, P.G., and G. Cottam. 1968. Carbohydrate cycle in the bulbs of some spring ephemerals. Bulletin of the Torrey Botanical Club 95:359–369.

Ristau, T.E., S.H. Stoleson, S.B. Horsley, and D.S. deCalesta. 2011. Ten-year response of the herbaceous layer to an operational herbicide-shelterwood treatment in a northern hardwood forest. Forest Ecology and Management 262:970–979.

Ritchie, M.E., D. Tilman, and J.N.H. Knops. 1998. Herbivore effects on plant and nitrogen dynamics in oak savannah. Ecology 79:1650177.

Roberts, M.R. 2004. Response of the herbaceous layer to natural disturbance in North American forests. Canadian Journal of Botany 82:1273–1283.

Roberts, M.R. 2007. A conceptual model to characterize disturbance severity in forest harvests. Forest Ecology and Management 242:58–64.

Roberts, M.R., and N.L. Christensen. 1988. Vegetation variation among mesic successional forest stands in northern lower Michigan. Canadian Journal of Botany 66:1080–1090.

Roberts, M.R., and H. Dong. 1993. Effects of soil organic layer removal on regeneration after clearcutting a northern hardwood stand in New Brunswick. Canadian Journal of Forest Research 23:2093–2100.

Roberts, M.R., and F.S. Gilliam. 1995a. Patterns and mechanisms of plant diversity in forested ecosystems: implications for forest management. Ecological Applications 5:969–977.

Roberts, M.R., and F.S. Gilliam. 1995b. Disturbance effects on herbaceous layer vegetation and soil nutrients in *Populus* forests of northern lower Michigan. Journal of Vegetation Science 6:903–912.

Roberts, M.R., and C.J. Richardson. 1985. Forty-one years of population change and community succession in aspen forests on four soil types, northern lower Michigan, U.S.A. Canadian Journal of Botany 63:1641–1651.

Roberts, M.R., and L. Zhu. 2002. Early response of the herbaceous layer to harvesting in a mixed coniferous-deciduous forest in New Brunswick, Canada. Forest Ecology and Management 155:17–31.

Roberts, T.L., and J.L. Vankat. 1991. Floristics of a chronosequence corresponding to old field-deciduous forest succession in southwestern Ohio. II. Seed banks. Bulletin of the Torrey Botanical Club 118:377–384.

Robertson, C. 1895. The philosophy of flower seasons, and the phaenological relations of the entomophilous flora and the anthrophilous insect fauna. American Naturalist 29:97–117.

Robichaux, R.H., E.A. Friar, and D.W. Mount. 1997. Molecular genetic consequences of a population bottleneck associated with reintroduction of the Mauna Kea silversword (*Argyroxiphium sandwichense* ssp. *sandwichense* (Asteraceae)). Conservation Biology 11:114–1146.

Robinson, G.R., M.E. Yurlina, and S.N. Handel. 1994. A century of change in the Staten Island flora: ecological correlates of species losses and invasions. Bulletin of the Torrey Botanical Club 121:119–129.

Robson, D.B. 2008. The structure of the flower-insect visitor system in tall-grass prairie. Botany 86:1266–1278.

Rochefort, L., D.H. Vitt, and S.E. Bayley. 1990. Growth, production and decomposition dynamics of Sphagnum under natural and experimentally acidified conditions. Ecology 71:1986–2000.

Rock, J., B. Beckage, and L. Gross. 2004. Population recovery following differential harvesting of *Allium tricoccum* Ait. in the Southern Appalachians. Biological Conservation 116:227–234.

Rockwood, L.L., and M.B. Lobstein. 1994. The effects of experimental defoliation on reproduction in four species of herbaceous perennials from northern Virginia. Castanea 59:41–50.

Rodgers, V.L., K.A. Stinson, and A.C. Finzi. 2008. Ready or not, garlic mustard is moving in: *Alliaria petiolata* as a member of eastern North American forests. BioScience 58:426–436.

Rogers, D.A., T.P. Rooney, and D.M. Waller. 2008. Fifty years of change in southern Wisconsin forests: Shifts in canopy and understory richenss, composition and heterogeneity. Ecology 89:2482–2492.

Rogers, D.A., T.P. Rooney, T.J. Hawbaker, V.C. Radeloff, and D.M. Waller. 2009. Paying the extinction debt: The increasing influence of patch size and landscape factors on vegetation community composition and dynamics in southern Wisconsin upland forests. Conservation Biology 23:1497–1506.

Rogers, R.S. 1981. Mature mesophytic hardwood forest: community transitions, by layer, from east-central Minnesota to southeastern Michigan. Ecology 62:1634–1647.

Rogers, R.S. 1982. Early spring herb communities in mesophytic forests of the Great Lakes region. Ecology 63:1050–1063.

Rogers, R.S. 1983a. Small-area coexistence of vernal forest herbs: does functional similarity of plants matter? American Naturalist 121:834–850.

Rogers, R.S. 1983b. Annual variability in community organization of forest herbs: Effect of an extremely warm and dry early spring. Ecology 64:1086–1091.

Rogers, R.S. 1985. Local coexistence of deciduous-forest groundlayer species growing in different seasons. Ecology 66:701–707.

Roleček, J., M. Chytrý, M. Háyek, S. Lvoncik, and L. Tichý, L. 2007. Sampling in large-scale vegetation studies: Do not sacrifice ecological thinking to statistical puritanism. Folia Geobotanica 42:199–208.

Rollinson, C.R., and M.W. Kaye. 2012. Experimental warming alters spring phenology of certain plant functional groups in an early successional forest community. Global Change Biology 18:1108–1116.

Rooney, T.P. 1997. Escaping herbivory: refuge effects on the morphology and shoot demography of the clonal forest herb, *Maianthemum canadense*. Journal of the Torrey Botanical Society 124:280–285.

Rooney, T.P. 2001. Impacts of white-tailed deer to forest ecosystems: a North American perspective. Forestry 74:201–208.

Rooney, T.P. 2009. High white-tailed deer densities benefit graminoids and contribute to biotic homogenization of forest ground-layer vegetation. Plant Ecology 202:103–111.

Rooney, T.P., and W.J. Dress. 1997a. Species loss over sixty-six years in the ground-layer vegetation of Heart's Content, an old-growth forest in Pennsylvania, USA. Natural Areas Journal 17:297–305.

Rooney, T.P., and W.J. Dress. 1997b. Patterns of plant diversity in overbrowsed primary and mature secondary hemlock northern hardwood forest stands. Journal of the Torrey Botanical Club124:43–51.

Rooney, T.P., and K. Gross. 2003. A demographic study of deer browsing impacts on *Trillium grandiflorum*. Plant Ecology 168:267–277.

Rooney, T.P., R.J. McCormick, S.L. Solheim, and D.M. Waller. 2000. Regional variation in recruitment of eastern hemlock seedlings in the Southern Superior Uplands section of the Laurentian Mixed Forest Province, USA. Ecological Applications 10:1119–1132.

Rooney, T.P., S.L. Solheim, and D.M. Waller. 2002. Factors influencing the regeneration of northern white cedar in lowland forests of the Upper Great Lakes region, USA. Forest Ecology and Management. 163:119–130.

Rooney, T.P., and D.M. Waller. 1998. Local and regional variation in hemlock seedling establishment in forests of the upper Great Lakes region, USA. Forest Ecology and Management 111:211–224.

Rooney, T.P., and D.M. Waller. 2001. How experimental defoliation and leaf height affect growth and reproduction in *Trillium grandiflorum*. Journal of the Torrey Botanical Society 128:393–399.

Rooney, T.P., and D.M. Waller. 2003. Direct and indirect effects of deer in forest ecosystems. Forest Ecology and Management 181:165–176.

Rooney, T.P., S.M. Wiegmann, D.A. Rogers, and D.M. Waller. 2004. Biotic impoverishment and homogenization in unfragmented forest understory communities. Conservation Biology 18:787–798.

Roschewitz, I., D. Gabriel, T. Tscharntke, and C. Thies. 2005. The effects of landscape complexity on arable weed species diversity in organic and conventional farming. Journal of Applied Ecology 42:873–882.

Rose, R.J., R.T. Clarke, and S.B. Chapman. 1998. Individual variation and the effects of weather, age and flowering history on survival and flowering of the long-lived perennial *Gentiana pneumonanthe*. Ecography 21:317–326.

Ross, B.A., J.R. Bray, and W.H. Marshall. 1970. Effects of long-term deer exclusion on *Pinus resinosa* forest in north-central Minnesota. Ecology 51:1088–1093.

Rossetto, M., and R.M. Kooyman. 2005. The tension between dispersal and persistence regulates the current distribution of rare palaeo-endemic rainforest flora: a case study. Journal of Ecology 93:906–917.

Rossetto, M., R. Kooyman, W. Sherwin, and R. Jones. 2008. Dispersal limitations, rather than bottlenecks or habitat specificity, can restrict the distribution of rare and endemic rainforest trees. American Journal of Botany 95:321–329.

Rossi, G., G. Parolo, and T. Ulian. 2009. Human trampling as a threat factor for the conservation of peripheral plant populations. Plant Biosystems 143:104–113.

Rothstein, D.E. 2000. Spring ephemeral herbs and nitrogen cycling in a northern hardwood forest: an experimental test of the vernal dam hypothesis. Oecologia 124:446–453.

Rothstein, D.E., and D.R. Zak. 2001a. Relationships between plant nitrogen economy and life history in three deciduous-forest herbs. Journal of Ecology 89:385–394.

Rothstein, D.E., and D.R. Zak. 2001b. Photosynthetic adaptation and acclimation to exploit seasonal periods of direct irradiance in three temperate, deciduous-forest herbs. Functional Ecology 15:722–731.

Routhier, M.C., and L. Lapointe. 2002. Impact of tree leaf phenology on growth rates and reproduction in the spring flowering species *Trillium erectum* (Liliaceae). American Journal of Botany 89:500–505.

Roy, V., and S. de Blois. 2006. Using functional traits to assess the role of hedgerow corridors as environmental filters for forest herbs. Biological Conservation 130:592–603.

Royo, A.A., and W.P. Carson. 2006. On the formation of dense understory layers in forests worldwide: consequences and implications for forest dynamics, biodiversity, and succession. Canadian Journal of Forest Research 36:1345–1362.

Royo, A.A., R. Collins, M.B. Adams, C. Kirschbaum, and W.P. Carson. 2010. Pervasive interactions between ungulate browsers and disturbance regimes promote temperate forest herbaceous diversity. Ecology 91:93–105.

Royo, A.A., S.L. Stout, D.S. deCalesta, and T.G. Pierson. 2010. Restoring forest herb communities through landscape-level deer herd reductions: is recovery limited by legacy effects? Biological Conservation 143:2425–2434.

Rowe, J.S. 1956. Uses of undergrowth plant species in forestry. Ecology 37:461–473.

Rowe, J.S. 1983. Concepts of fire effects on plant individual and species. Pages 134–154 in R.W. Wein and D.A. MacLean, editors. The role of fire in northern circumpolar ecosystems. John Wiley & Sons, New York.

Ruben, J.A., Bolger, D.T., Peart, D.R., and M.P. Ayres. 1999. Understory herb assemblages 25 and 60 years after clearcutting of a northern hardwood forest, USA. Biological Conservation 90:203–215.

Rubino, D.L., and B.C. McCarthy. 2000. Dendroclimatological analysis of white oak (*Quercus alba* L., Fagaceae) from an old-growth forest of southeastern Ohio, USA. Journal of the Torrey Botanical Society 127:240–250.

Ruel, J.-C. 2000. Factors influencing windthrow in balsam fir forests: from landscape studies to individual tree studies. Forest Ecology and Management 135:169–178.

Ruhren, S., and M. Dudash. 1996. Consequences of the timing of seed release of *Erythronium americanum* (Liliaceae), a deciduous forest myrmecochore. American Journal of Botany 83:633–640.

Ruhren, S., and S.N. Handel. 2000. Considering herbivory, reproduction, and gender when monitoring plants: A case study of Jack-in-the-pulpit (*Arisaema triphyllum* L. Schott). Natural Areas Journal 20:261–266.

Ruhren, S., and S.N. Handel. 2003. Herbivory constrains survival, reproduction, and mutu-alisms when restoring nine temperate forest herbs. Journal of the Torrey Botanical Society 130:34–42.

Rumbaitis del Rio, C.M. 2006. Changes in understory composition following catastrophic windthrow and salvage logging in a subalpine forest ecosystem. Canadian Journal of Forest Research 36:2943–2954.

Runkle, J.R. 1981. Gap regeneration in some old-growth forest of the eastern United States. Ecology 62:1041–1051.

Runkle, J.R. 1982. Patterns of disturbance in some old-growth mesic forests of eastern North America. Ecology 63:1533–1546.

Runkle, J.R. 1985. Disturbance regimes in temperate forests. Pages 17–33 in S.T.A. Pickett and P.S. White, editors. The ecology of natural disturbance and patch dynamics. Academic Press, Orlando, FL.

Runkle, J.R. 2007. Impacts of beech bark disease and deer browsing on the old-growth for-est. American Midland Naturalist 157:241–249.

Russell, E.W.B. 1983. Indian-set fires in the forests of the northeastern United States. Ecology 64:78–88.

Russell, F.L., D.B. Zippen, and N.L. Fowler. 2001. Effects of white-tailed deer (*Odocoileus virginianus*) on plants, plant populations and communities: a review. American Midland Naturalist 146:1–26.

Russell, N.H. 1958. Vascular flora of the Edmund Niles Huyck Preserve, New York. American Midland Naturalist 59:138–145.

Rust, R.W., and R.R. Roth. 1981. Seed production and seedling establishment in the may-apple *Podophyllum peltatum* L. American Midland Naturalist 105:51–60.

Rusterholz, H., M. Kissling, and B. Baur. 2009. Disturbances by human trampling alter the performance, sexual reproduction and genetic diversity in a clonal woodland herb. Perspectives in Plant Ecology, Evolution, and Systematics 11:17–29.

Ryan, K.C. 2002. Dynamic interactions between forest structure and fire behavior in boreal ecosystems. Silva Fennica 36:13–39.

Ryan, M.G. 1991. Effects of climate change on plant respiration. Ecological Applications 1:157–167.

Saetra, P., L.S. Saetra, P.-O. Brandtberg, H. Lundkvist, and J. Bengtsson. 1997. Ground vegetation composition and heterogeneity in pure Norway spruce and mixed Norway spruce-birch stands. Canadian Journal of Forest Research 27:1110–1116.

Sage, R.F. 1993. Lightdependent modulation of ribulose1,5bisphosphate carboxylase/oxy-genase activity in the genus *Phaseolus*. Photosynthesis Research 35:219–226.

Sage, R.F., and J.R. Seemann. 1993. Regulation of ribulose1,5bisphosphate carboxylase/oxygen-ase activity in response to reduced light intensity in C4 plants. Plant Physiology 102:21–28.

Sage, R.F., D.A. Wedin, and M. Li. 1999. The biogeography of C4 photosynthesis: Patterns and controlling factors. Pages 313–373 in R.F. Sage and R.K. Monson, editors. C4 Plant Biology. Academic Press, New York.

Sage, T.L., S.R. Griffin, V. Pontieri, P. Drobac, W.W. Cole, and S.C.H. Barrett. 2001. Stigmatic self-incompatibility and mating patterns in *Trillium grandiflorum* and *Trillium erectum* (Melanthiaceae). Annals of Botany 88:829–841.

Sagers, C.L., and J. Lyon. 1997. Gradient analysis in a riparian landscape: contrasts among forest layers. Forest Ecology and Management 96:13–26.

Sakai, A.K., F.W. Allendorf, J.S. Holt, D.M. Lodge, J. Molofsky, K.A. With, S. Baughman, R.J. Cabin, J.E. Cohen, N.C. Ellstrand, D.E. McCauley, P. O'Neil, I.M. Parker, J.N. Thompson, and S.G. Weller. 2001. The population biology of invasive species. Annual Review of Ecology and Systematics 32:305–332.

Salguero-Gomez, R., and J.B. Plotkin. 2010. Matrix dimensions bias demographic inferences: Implications for comparative plant demography. American Naturalist 176:710–722.

Salisbury, E.J. 1928. On the causes and ecological significance of stomatal frequency with special reference to the woodland flora. Philosophical Transactions of the Royal Society Series B 216:1–65.

Salomonson, A., M. Ohlson, and L. Ericson. 1994. Meristem activity and biomass production as response mechanisms in two forest herbs. Oecologia 100:29–37.

Sandel, B., L. Arge, B. Dalsgaard, R.G. Davies, K.J. Gaston, W.J. Sutherland, and J.-C. Svenning. 2011. The influence of late Quaternary climate-change velocity on species endemism. Science 334:660–664.

Sargent, R.D. 2004. Floral symmetry affects speciation rates in angiosperms. Proceedings of the Royal Society of London Series B-Biological Sciences 271:603–608.

Sarukhán, J., and M. Gadgil. 1974. Studies on plant demography: *Ranunculus repens* L., *R. bulbosus* L., and *R. acris* L. III. A mathematical model incorporating multiple modes of reproduction. Journal of Ecology 62:921–936.

SAS Institute. 1985. SAS user's guide: statistics. SAS Institute, Cary, NC.

Sassenrath-Cole, G.F., and R.W. Pearcy. 1992. The role of ribulose 1,5 bisphosphate regeneration in the induction requirement of photosynthetic carbon dioxide exchange under transient light conditions. Plant Physiology 99:227–234.

Sato, T., and A. Sakai. 1980. Phenological study of the leaf of pteridophyte in Hokkaido. Japanese Journal of Ecology 30:369–375.

Satterson, K. 1985. Nitrogen availability, primary production, and nutrient cycling during secondary succession in North Carolina Piedmont forests. Ph.D. dissertation, University of North Carolina, Chapel Hill, NC.

Satterthwaite, W.H., E.S. Menges, and P.F. Quintana-Ascencio. 2002. Assessing scrub buckwheat population viability in relation to fire using multiple modeling techniques. Ecological Applications 12:1672–1687.

Saucier, J.-P., J.-P. Berger, H. D'Avignon, and P. Racine. 1994. Le point d'observation écologique, normes techniques. Ministère des Ressources naturelles du Québec, Direction de la gestion des stocks, Service des inventaires forestiers, Québec.

Saucier, J.-P., J.-F. Bergeron, P. Grondin, and A. Robitaille. 1998. The land regions of southern Québec (3rd version): One element in the hierarchical land classification system developed by the Ministère des Ressources naturelles du Québec. Internal report, Ministère des Ressources naturelles du Québec.

Sauvé, D.G., and S.D. Coté. 2006. Winter forage selection in white-tailed deer at high density: balsam fir is the best of a bad choice. Journal of Wildlife Management 71:911–914.

Sawada, S., M. Yamashita, M. Kasai, A. Harada, and A. Hashimoto. 1997. Photosynthesis and micro-environmental factors in a spring ephemeral, *Erythronium japonicum*, from native and open habitats. Ecological Research 12:55–62.

Sawyer, N.W., and G.J. Anderson. 1998. Reproductive biology of the carrion flower, *Smilax herbacea* (Smilacaceae). Rhodora 100:1–24.

Sax, D.F., R. Early, and J. Bellemare. 2013. Niche syndromes, species extinction risks, and management under climate change. Trends in Ecology and Evolution 28: 517-523.

Scanlan, M.J. 1981. Biogeography of forest plants in the prairie-forest ecotone in western Minnesota. Pages 97–124 in R.L. Burgess and D.M. Sharpe, editors. Forest island dynamics in man-dominated landscapes. Springer-Verlag, New York.

Schaal, B.A., and W.G. Smith. 1980. The apportionment of genetic variation within and among populations of *Desmodium nudiflorum*. Evolution 34:214–221.

Schaetzl, R.J., S.F. Burns, D.L. Johnson, and T.W. Small. 1989. Tree uprooting: review of impacts on forest ecology. Vegetatio 79:165–176.

Schaetzl, R.J., and L.R. Follmer. 1990. Longevity of treethrow microtopography: implications for mass wasting. Geomorphology 3:113–123.

Schafale, M.P. 2012. Guide to the natural communities of North Carolina. Fourth approximation. North Carolina Natural Heritage Program. Department of Environment and Natural Resources.

Schafale, M.P. and N.L. Christensen. 1986. Vegetational variation among old fields in Piedmont North Carolina. Bulletin of the Torrey Botanical Club 113:413–420.

Schafer, J.L., E.S. Menges, P.F. Quintana-Ascencio, and C.W. Weekley. 2010. Effects of time-since-fire and microhabitat on the occurrence and density of the endemic *paronychia chartacea* ssp chartacea in Florida scrub and along roadsides. American Midland Naturalist 163:294–310.

Schafale, M.P., and A.S. Weakly. 1990. Classification of the natural communities of North Carolina: Third approximation. North Carolina Natural Heritage Program, Raleigh, NC.

Scharf, C.S., and N.K. DePalma. 1981. Birds and mammals as vectors of the chestnut blight fungus (*Endothia parasitica*). Canadian Journal of Zoology 59:1647–1650.

Scheller, R.M., and D.J. Mladenoff. 2002. Understory species patterns and diversity in old-growth and managed northern hardwood forests. Ecological Applications 12:1329–1343.

Schemske, D.W. 1978. Sexual reproduction in an Illinois population of *Sanguinaria canadensis* L. American Midland Naturalist 100:261–268.

Schemske, D.W., B.C. Husband, M.H. Ruckelshaus, C. Goodwillie, I.M Parker, and J.G. Bishop. 1994. Evaluating approaches to the conservation of rare and endangered plants. Ecology 75:584–606.

Schemske, D.W., and R. Lande. 1985. The evolution of self-fertilization and inbreeding depression in plants. 2. Empirical observations. Evolution 39:41–52.

Schemske, D.W., M.F. Willson, M.N. Melampy, L.J. Miller, L. Verner, K.M. Schemske, and L.B. Best. 1978. Flowering ecology of some spring woodland herbs. Ecology 59:351–366.

Scheu, S. 1997. Effects of litter (beech and stinging nettle) and earthworms (*Octolasion lacteum*) on carbon and nutrient cycling in beech forests on a basalt-limestone gradient: A laboratory experiment. Biology and Fertility of Soils 24:384–393.

Schiefthaler, U., A.W. Russell, H.R. Bolhár-Nordenkampf, and C. Critchley. 1999. Photoregulation and photodamage in *Schefflera arboricola* leaves adapted to different light environments. Australian Journal of Plant Physiology 26:485–494.

Schierenbeck, K.A., R.N. Mack, and R.R. Sharitz. 1994. Effects of herbivory on growth and biomass allocation in native and introduced species of *Lonicera*. Ecology 75:1661–1672.

Schlesinger, W.H., J.A. Raikes, A.E. Hartley, and A.F. Cross. 1996. On the spatial pattern of soil nutrients in desert ecosystems. Ecology 77:364–374.

Schmalholz, M., and K. Hylander. 2009. Succession of bryophyte assemblages following clear-cut logging in boreal spruce-dominated forests in south-central Sweden—Does retrogressive succession occur? Canadian Journal of Forest Research 39:1871–1880.

Schmidt, I.B., L. Mandle, T. Ticktin, and O.G. Gaoue. 2011. What do matrix population models reveal about the sustainability of non-timber forest product harvest? Journal of Applied Ecology 48:815–826.

Schmidt, S.K., E.K. Costello, D.R. Nemergut, C.C. Cleveland, S.C. Reed, M.N. Weintraub, A.F. Meyer, and A.M. Martin. 2007. Biogeochemical consequences of rapid microbial turnover and seasonal succession in soil. Ecology 88:1379–1385.

Schmidt, S.K., and D.A. Lipson. 2004. Microbial growth under the snow: Implications for nutrient and allelochemical availability in temperate soils. Plant and Soil 259:1–7.

Schmucki R., and S. de Blois. 2009a. Pollination and reproduction of self-incompatible forest herb in hedgerow corridors and forest patches. Oecologia 160:721–733.

Schmucki R., and S. de Blois. 2009b. Population structures and individual performances of *Trillium grandiflorum* in hedgerow and forest habitats. Plant Ecology 202: 67–78.

Schoener, T.W. 1983. Field experiments on interspecific competition. American Naturalist 122:240–285.

Schulz, K.E., and M.S. Adams. 1995. Effect of canopy gap light environment on evaporative load and stomatal conductance in the temperate forest herb *Aster macrophyllus* (Asteraceae). American Journal of Botany 82:630–637.

Schulz, K.E., M. Smith, and Y. Wu. 1993. Gas exchange of *Impatiens pallida* Nutt. (Balsaminaceae) in relation to wilting under high light. American Journal of Botany 80:361–368.

Schulze, E.D. 1972. Die Wirkung von Licht und Temperatur auf den CO2-Gaswechsel verschiedener Lebensformen aus der Krautschicht eines montanen Buchenwaldes. Oecologia 9:235–258.

Schumm, S.A., and R.W. Lichty. 1965. Time, space, and causality in geomorphology. American Journal of Science 263:110–119.

Schutzenhofer, M.R., T.J. Valone, and T.M. Knight. 2009. Herbivory and population dynamics of invasive and native lespedeza. Oecologia 161:57–66.

Schwartz, C.C., W.L. Regelin, and J.G. Nagy. 1980. Deer preference for juniper forage and volatile oil treated foods. Journal of Wildland Management 44:114–120.

Schwartz, M.D., R. Ahas, and A. Aasa. 2006. Onset of spring starting earlier across the Northern Hemisphere. Global Change Biology 12:343–351.

Schwartz, M.D., and B.E. Reiter. 2000. Changes in North American spring. International Journal of Climatology 20:929–932.

Schwartz, M.J., 2007. Vegetation change over decadal and century scales in the North Carolina Piedmont. Ph.D. dissertation, Duke University, Durham, NC.

Schwartz, M.W. 1997. Defining indigenous species: an introduction. Pages 7–17 in J.O. Luken and J.W. Thieret, editors. Assessment and management of plant invasions. Springer-Verlag, New York.

Schwartz, M.W. 2004. Conservationists should not move *Torreya taxifolia*. Wild Earth 2004–2005: 1-4.

Schwartz, M.W., and J.R. Heim. 1996. Effects of a prescribed fire on degraded forest vegetation. Natural Areas Journal 16:184–191.

Schwartz, M.W., L.R. Iverson, A.M. Prasad, S.N. Matthews, and R.J. O'Connor. 2006. Predicting extinctions as a result of climate change. Ecology 87:1611–1615.

Schwinning, S., and J. Weiner. 1998. Mechanisms determining the degree of size asymmetry in competition among plants. Oecologia 113:447–455.

Scott, D.R.M. 1955 Amount and chemical composition of the organic matter contributed by overstory and understory vegetation to forest soil. Yale University School of Forestry. Bulletin No. 62.

Selmants, P.C., and D.H. Knight. 2003. Understory plant species composition 30–50 years after clearcutting in southeastern Wyoming coniferous forests. Forest Ecology and Management 185:275–289.

Seybold, A., and K. Eagle. 1937. Lichtfeld und Blattfarbstoffe. I. Planta 26:491–515.

Shafi, M.I., and G.A. Yarranton. 1973. Vegetational heterogeneity during a secondary (post-fire) succession. Canadian Journal of Botany 51:73–90.

Shaver, G.R., and J.M. Melillo. 1984. Nutrient budgets of marsh plants: Efficiency concepts and relation to availability. Ecology 65:1491–1510.

Shea, K., and P. Chesson. 2002. Community ecology theory as a framework for biological invasions. Trends in Ecology and Evolution 17:170–176.

Shea, K., M. Rees, and S.N. Wood. 1994. Trade-offs, elasticities and the comparative method. Journal of Ecology 82:951–957.

Shefferson, R.P. 2009. The evolutionary ecology of vegetative dormancy in mature herbaceous perennial plants. Journal of Ecology 97:1000–1009.

Shefferson, R.P., M.K. McCormick, D.F. Whigham, and J.P. O'Neill. 2011. Life history strategy in herbaceous perennials: inferring demographic patterns from the aboveground dynamics of a primarily subterranean, myco-heterotrophic orchid. Oikos 120:1291–1300.

Shetler, G., M. R. Turetsky, E. Kane, and E. Kasischke. 2008. Sphagnum mosses limit total carbon consumption during fire in Alaskan black spruce forests. Canadian Journal of Forest Research 38:2328–2336.

Sheviak, C.J. 2001. A role for water droplets in the pollination of *Platanthera aquilonis* (Orchidaceae). Rhodora 103:380–386.

Shmida, A., and S. Ellner 1984. Coexistence of plants species with similar niches. Vegetatio 58:29–55.

Shmida, A., and M.V. Wilson. 1985. Biological determinants of species diversity. Journal of Biogeography 12:1–20.

Shugart, H.H. 1997. Plant and ecosystem functional types. Pages 20–43 in Plant functional types: their relevance to ecosystem properties and global change. Cambridge University Press, Cambridge, UK.

Siccama, T.G., F.H. Bormann, and G.E. Likens. 1970. The Hubbard Brook ecosystem study: productivity, nutrients and phytosociology of the herbaceous layer. Ecological Monographs 40:389–402.

Siccama, T.G., G. Weir, and K. Wallace. 1976. Ice damage in a mixed hardwood forest in Connecticut in relation to *Vitis* infection. Bulletin of the Torrey Botanical Club 103:180–183.

Siddique, I., I.C.G. Vieira, S. Schmidt, D. Lamb, C.J.R. Carvalho, R.O. Figueiredo, S. Blomberg, and E.A. Davidson. 2010. Nitrogen and phosphorus additions negatively affect tree species diversity in tropical forest regrowth trajectories. Ecology 91:2121–2131.

Silander, J.A., and R.B. Primack. 1978. Pollination intensity and seed set in evening primrose (*Oenothera fruticosa*). American Midland Naturalist 100:213–216.

Silva, J. 1978. Studies on the population biology of Maianthemum canadense Desf. Ph.D. dissertation, Harvard University, Boston.

Silvertown, J.W. 1987. Introduction to plant population ecology, 2nd ed. Longman Scientific and Technical and Jon Wiley & Sons, New York.

Silvertown, J.W. 1991. Dorothy's dilemma and the unification of plant population biology. Trends in Ecology and Evolution 6:346–348.

Silvertown, J., M. Franco, and E. Menges. 1996. Interpretation of elasticity matrices as an aid to the management of plant populations for conservation. Conservation Biology 10:591–597.

Silvertown, J., M. Franco, I. Pisanty, and A. Mendoza. 1993. Comparative plant demography and relative importance of life-cycle components to the finite rate of increase in woody and herbaceous perennials. Journal of Ecology 81:465–476.

Silvertown, J., and R. Law. 1987. Do plants need niches? Some recent developments in plant community ecology. Trends in Ecology and Evolution 2:24–26.

Silvertown, J.W., and J. Lovett Doust. 1993. Introduction to plant population biology. Blackwell Scientific Publications, Oxford, UK.

Silvertown, J., P. Poulton, A.E. Johnston, G. Edwards, M. Heard, and P.M. Biss. 2006. The Park Grass Experiment 1856–2006: its contribution to ecology. Journal of Ecology 94:801–814.

Silvola, J. 1991. Moisture dependance of CO_2 exchange and its recovery after drying in certain boreal forest peat mosses. Lindbergia 17:5–10.

Simard, M., N. Lecomte, Y. Bergeron, P.Y. Bernier, and D. Paré. 2007. Forest productivity decline caused by successional paludification of boreal soils. Ecological Applications 17:1619–1637.

Simberloff, D. 2010. Invasion of plant communities—more of the same, something very different, or both? American Midland Naturalist 163:220–233.

Simberloff, D., L. Souza, M.A. Nunez, M.N. Barrios-Garcia, and W. Bunn. 2012. The natives are restless, but not often and mostly when disturbed. Ecology 93: 598-607.

Simonovich, V. 1973. Study of the root biomass in the herb layer of an oak-hornbeam forest. Biologia 28:11–22.

Simons, A.M., and M.O. Johnston. 2000. Plasticity and the genetics of reproductive behaviour in the monocarpic perennial, *Lobelia inflata* (Indian tobacco). Heredity 85:356–365.

Sims, D.A., and R.W. Pearcy. 1993. Sunfleck frequency and duration affects growth rate of the understory plant, *Alocasia macrorrhiza*. Functional Ecology 7:683–689.

Sinclair, A., and P.M. Catling. 2004. Restoration of *hydrastis canadensis*: Experimental test of a disturbance hypothesis after two growing seasons. Restoration Ecology 12:184–189.

Singsaas, E.L., D.R. Ort, and E.H. DeLucia. 2001. Variation in measured values of photosynthetic quantum yield in ecophysiological studies. Oecologia 128:15–23.

Singleton, R., S. Gardescu, P.L. Marks, and M.A. Geber. 2001. Forest herb colonization of postagricultural forests in central New York State, USA. Journal of Ecology 89:325–338.

Sirois, L., and S. Payette. 1989. Postfire black spruce establishment in subarctic and boreal Quebec. Canadian Journal of Forest Research 19:1571–1580.

Skelly, J.M., T.S. Fredericksen, J.E. Savage, and K.R. Snyder. 1996. Vertical gradients of ozone and carbon dioxide within a deciduous forest in central Pennsylvania. Environmental Pollution 94:235–240.

Skillman, J.B., B.R. Strain, and C.B. Osmond. 1996. Contrasting patterns of photosynthetic acclimation and photoinhibition in two evergreen herbs from a winter deciduous forest. Oecologia 107:446–455.

Skinner, W.R., and E.S. Telfer. 1974. Spring, summer, and fall foods of deer in New Brunswick. Journal of Wildlife Management 38:210–214.

Skov, F., and J.-C. Svenning. 2004. Potential impact of climatic change on the distribution of forest herbs in Europe. Ecography 27:366–380.

Skre, O., F.E. Wielgolaski, and B. Moe. 1998. Biomass and chemical response of common forest plants in response to fire in western Norway. Journal of Vegetation Science 9:501–510.

Skutch, A.F. 1929. Early stages of plant succession following forest fires. Ecology 10:177–190.

Slack, N. 1990. Bryophytes and ecological niche theory. Botanical Journal of the Linnean Society 104:187–213.

Slapcinsky, J.L., D.R. Gordon, and E.S. Menges. 2010. Responses of rare plant species to fire in Florida's pyrogenic communities. Natural Areas Journal 30:4–19.

Sletvold, N., and K. Rydgren. 2007. Population dynamics in *Digitalis purpurea*: the interaction of disturbance and seed bank dynamics. Journal of Ecology 95:1346–1359.

Small, C.J., and B.C. McCarthy. 2002. Spatial and temporal variation in the response of understory vegetation to disturbance in a central Appalachian oak forest. Journal of the Torrey Botanical Society 129:136–153.

Small, C.J., and B.C. McCarthy. 2005. Relationship of understory diversity to soil nitrogen, topographic variation, and stand age in an eastern oak forest, USA. Forest Ecology and Management 217:229–243.

Small, C.J., and B.C. McCarthy. in press. The influence of spatial and temporal variability on understory diversity in an eastern deciduous forest. Plant Ecology.

Smith, D. 2000. The population dynamics and community ecology of root hemiparasitic plants. American Naturalist 155:13–23.

Smith, E.P., and G. van Belle. 1984. Nonparametric estimation of species richness. Biometrics 43:793–803.

Smith, F.E. 1972. Spatial heterogeneity, stability, and diversity in ecosystems. Transactions of the Connecticut Academy of Arts and Sciences 44:309–355.

Smith, M., H. Caswell, and P. Mettler-Cherry. 2005. Stochastic flood and precipitation regimes and the population dynamics of a threatened floodplain plant. Ecological Applications 15:1036–1052.

Smith, M., and S. Stocker. 1992. Effect of temperature on rhizome regrowth and biomass in *Muhlenbergia sobolifera*, a shadetolerant C4 grass. Transactions of the Illinois State Academy of Science 85:19–28.

Smith, M., and Y. Wu. 1994. Photosynthetic characteristics of the shade-adapted C4 grass *Muhlenbergia sobolifera* (Muhl.) Trin.: control of development of photorespiration by growth temperature. Plant, Cell and Environment 17:763–769.

Smith, S.E., and D.J. Read. 1997. Mycorrhizal symbiosis, 2nd ed. San Diego, CA: Academic Press.

Smith, T.L. 1989. An overview of old-growth forests in Pennsylvania. Natural Areas Journal 9:40–44.

Smith, T.M., and M.A. Huston. 1989. A theory of the spatial and temporal dynamics of plant communities. Vegetatio 83:49–69.

Smith, T.M., H.H. Shugart, and F.I. Woodward, editors. 1997. Plant functional types: their relevance to ecosystem properties and global change. Cambridge University Press, Cambridge, UK.

Smith, W.G. 1975. Dynamics of pure and mixed populations of *Desmodium glutinosum* and *D. nudiflorum* in natural oak-forest communities. American Midland Naturalist 94:99–107.

Smith, W.H. 1981. Air pollution and forests: Interactions between air contaminants and forest ecosystems. Springer-Verlag, New York.

Smith, W.K., and N.M. Hughes. 2009. Progress in coupling plant form and photosynthetic function. Castanea 74: 1–26.

Smith, W.K., A.K. Knapp, and W.A. Reiners. 1989. Penumbral effects on sunlight penetration in plant communities. Ecology 70:1603–1609.

Smith, W.K., T.C. Vogelmann, E.H. DeLucia, D.T. Bell, and K.A. Shepard. 1997. Leaf form and photosynthesis. Bioscience 47:785–793.

Snaydon, R.W. 1962. Micro-distribution of *Trifolium repens* L. and its relation to soil factors. Journal of Ecology 50:133–143.

Snellgrove, R.C., W.E. Splittstoesser, D.B. Stribley, and P.B. Tinker. 1982. The distribution of carbon and the demand of the fungal symbiont in leek plants with vesicular-arbuscular mycorrhizas. New Phytologist 92:75–87.

Snow, A.A., and D.F. Whigham. 1989. Costs of flower and fruit production in *Tipularia discolor* (Orchidaceae). Ecology 70:1286–1293.

Snyder, J.D., and R.A. Janke. 1976. Impact of moose browsing on boreal-type forests of Isle Royale National Park. American Midland Naturalist 95:79–92.

Snyder, K.M., J.M. Baskin, and C.C. Baskin. 1994. Comparative ecology of the narrow endemic *Echinacea tennesseensis* and two geographically widespread congeners: relative competitive ability and growth characteristics. International Journal of Plant Science 155:57–65.

Söderström, L. 1988. Sequence of bryophytes and lichens in relation to substrate variables of decaying coniferous wood in northern Sweden. Nordic Journal of Botany 8:89–97.

Sobey, D.G., and P. Barkhouse. 1977. The structure and rate of growth of the rhizomes of some forest herbs and dwarf shrubs of the New Brunswick-Nova Scotia border region. Canadian Field Naturalist 91:177–383.

Sohn, J.J., and D. Policansky. 1977. The costs of reproduction in the mayapple *Podophyllum peltatum* (Berberidaceae). Ecology 58:1366–1374.

Solbrig, O.T., R. Sarandon, and W. Bossuyt. 1988. A density-dependent growth model of a perennial herb, *Viola frimbriatula*. American Naturalist 17:385–400.

Sorrells, J., and R.J. Warren. 2011. Ant-dispersal herb colonization lags behind forest re-establishment. Journal of the Torrey Botanical Society 138:77–84.

Sorrie, B.A., and A.S. Weakley. 2001. Coastal plain vascular plant endemics: phytogeographic patterns. Castanea 66:50–82.

Souther, S., M.J. Lechowicz, and J.B. McGraw. 2012. Experimental test for adaptive differentiation of ginseng populations reveals complex response to temperature. Annals of Botany 110:829–837.

Sousa, W.P. 1980. The response of a community to disturbance: The importance of successional age and species' life histories. Oecologia (Berlin) 45:72–81.

Souza, L., R.T. Belote, P. Kardol, J.F. Weltzin, and R.J. Norby. 2010. CO_2 enrichment accelerates successional development of an understory plant community. Journal of Plant Ecology 3:33–39.

Souza, L., H.S. Neufeld, A.H. Chappelka, K.O. Burkey, and A.W. Davison. 2006. Seasonal development of ozone-induced foliar injury on tall milkweed (*Asclepias exaltata*) in Great Smoky Mountains National Park. Environmental Pollution 141:175–183.

Sparks, J.C., R.E. Masters, D.M. Engle, M.W. Palmer, and G.A. Bukenhofer. 1998. Effects of late growing-season and late dormant-season prescribed fire on herbaceous vegetation in restored pine-grassland communities. Journal of Vegetation Science 9:133–142Sparling, J.H. 1964. Ontario's woodland flora. Ontario Naturalist 2:18–25.

Sparling, J.H. 1967. Assimilation rates of some woodland herbs in Ontario. Botanical Gazette 128:160–168.

Sparling, J.H., and M. Alt. 1966. The establishment of carbon dioxide gradients in Ontario woodlands. Canadian Journal of Botany 44:321–329.

Sperduto, M.B., and R.G. Congalton. 1996. Predicting rare orchid (small whorled pogonia) habitat using GIS. Photogrammetric Engineering and Remote Sensing 62:1269–1279.

Sperry, J.S., J.R. Donnelly, and M.T. Tyree. 1988. A method for measuring hydraulic conductivity and embolisms in xylem. Plant, Cell and Environment 11:35–40.

Spies, T.A. 1991. Plant species diversity and occurrence in young, mature, and old-growth Douglas-fir stands in western Oregon and Washington. Pages 111–121 in L.F. Ruggiero, K.B. Aubry, A.B. Carey, and M.H. Huff, coordinators. Wildlife and vegetation of unmanaged Douglas-fir forests. United States Forest Service General Technical Report PNW-GTR-285. Portland, OR.

Spigler, R.B., and S. Chang. 2009. Pollen limitation and reproduction varies with population size in experimental populations of *Sabatia angularis* (Gentianaceae). Botany 87:330–338.

Spigler, R.B., J.L. Hamrick, and S. Chang. 2010. Increased inbreeding but not homozygosity in small populations of *Sabatia angularis* (Gentianaceae). Plant Systematics and Evolution 284:131–140.

Spira, T. 2001. Plant-pollinator interactions: a threatened mutualism with implications for the ecology and management of rare plants. Natural Areas Journal 21:78–88.

Sprengel, C.K. 1793. Das entdeckte Geheimnis der Natur in Bau und in der Befruchtung der Blumen. Berlin: Vieweg.

Spurr, S.H., and J.H. Zumberge. 1956. Late Pleistocene features of Cheboygan and Emmet Counties, Michigan. American Journal of Science 254:96–109.

Stace, C. 1997. New Flora of the British Isles. Cambridge, UK: Cambridge University Press.

St-Denis, A., D. Kneeshaw, and Y. Bergeron. 2010. The role of gaps and tree regeneration in the transition from dense to open black spruce stands. Forest Ecology and Management 259:469–476.

Stapanian, M.A., S.D. Sundberg, G.A. Baumgardner, and A. Liston. 1998. Alien plant species composition and associations with anthropogenic disturbance in North American forests. Plant Ecology 139:49–62.

Stebbins, G.L. 1974. Flowering plants: evolution above the species level. Harvard University Press, Cambridge, MA.

Stebbins, G.L., and J. Major. 1965. Endemism and speciation in the California flora. Ecological Monographs 35:1–35.

Steets, J.A., T.M. Knight, and T.-L. Ashman. 2007. The interactive effects of herbivory and mixed mating for the population dynamics of Impatiens capensis. American Naturalist 170:113–127.

Stein, B.A., L.S. Kutner, and J.S. Adams. 2000. Precious heritage. Oxford University Press, Oxford, UK.

Stein, B.A., L.S. Kutner, G.A. Hammerson, L.L. Master, and L.E. Morse. 2000. State of the states: Geographic patterns of diversity, rarity, and endemism. Pages. 119–157 in B.A. Stein, L.S. Kutner, and J.A. Adams, editors. Precious heritage: the status of biodiversity in the United States. New York: Oxford University Press.

Stephens, E.P. 1956. The uprooting of trees: a forest process. Soil Science Society of America Proceedings 20:113–116.

Sternberg, L. 2001. Savanna-forest hysteresis in the tropics. Global Ecology and Biogeography 10:369–378.

Steubing, L., A. Fangmeier, R. Both, and M. Frankenfeld. 1989. Effects of SO2, NO2 and O3 on population development and morphological and physiological parameters of native herb layer species in a beech forest. Environmental Pollution 58:281–302.

Steven, J.C., T.P. Rooney, O.D. Boyle, and D.M. Waller. 2003. Density-dependent pollinator visitation and self-incompatibility in upper Great Lakes populations of Trillium grandiflorum. Journal of the Torrey Botanical Society 130:23–29.

Steven, J.C., and D.M. Waller. 2007. Isolation affects reproductive success in low-density but not high-density populations of two wind-pollinated Thalictrum species. Plant Ecology 190:131–141.

Stevens, C.J., C. Duprè, E. Dorland, C. Gaudnik, D.J.G. Gowing, A. Bleeker, M. Diekmann, D. Alard, R. Bobbink, D. Fowler, E. Corcket, J.O. Mountford, V. Vandvik, P.A. Aarrestad, S. Muller, and N.B. Dise. 2010. Nitrogen deposition threatens species richness of grasslands across Europe. Environmental Pollution 158:2940–2945.

Stevens, G.C. 1989. The latitudinal gradient in geographical range: how so many species coexist in the tropics. American Naturalist 133:240–256.

Stewart, G.H., and L.E. Burrows. 1989. The impact of white-tailed deer Odocoileus virginianus on regeneration in the coastal forests of Stewart Island, New Zealand. Biological Conservation 49:275–293.

Stockton, S.A., S. Allombert, A.J. Gaston, and J.-L. Martin. 2005. A natural experiment on the effects of high deer densities on the native flora of coastal temperate rain forests. Biological Conservation 126:118-128.

Stohlgren, T.J., D. Binkley, G.W. Chong, M.A. Kalkhan, L.D. Schell, K.A. Bull, Y. Otsuki, G. Newman, M. Bashkin, and Y. Son. 1999. Exotic species invade hot spots of native plant diversity. Ecological Monographs 69:25–46.

Stohlgren, T.J., M.B. Falkner, and L.D. Schell. 1995. A modified-Whittaker nested vegetation sampling method. Vegetatio 117:113–121.

Stoll, P., and D. Prati. 2001. Intraspecific aggregation alters competitive interactions in experimental plant communities. Ecology 82:319–327.

Stommel, H. 1963. Varieties of oceanographic experience. Science 139:572–576.

Stone, E.L., and P.J. Kalisz. 1991. On the maximum extent of tree roots. Forest Ecology and Management. 46:59–102.

Stone, W.E., and M.L. Wolfe. 1996. Response of understory vegetation to variable tree mortality following a mountain pine beetle epidemic in lodgepole pine stands in northern Utah. Vegetatio 122:1–12.

Stormer, F.A., and W.A. Bauer. 1980. Summer forage use by tame deer in northern Michigan. Journal of Wildlife Management 44:98–106.

Stott, I., M. Franco, D. Carslake, S. Townley, and D. Hodgson. 2010. Boom or bust? A comparative analysis of transient population dynamics in plants. Journal of Ecology 98:302–311.

Stout, S.L., and S.B. Horsley. 2004. Canary in the coal mine—a short history of northern Pennsylvania forests and their deer herd. Forest Science Review Northeastern Research Station, USDA Forest Service, Issue 1, Winter.

Stoutjesdijk, P. 1974. The open shade as an interesting microclimate. Acta Botanica Neerlandica 23:125–130.

Stover, M.E., and P.L. Marks. 1998. Successional vegetation on abandoned cultivated and pastured land in Tompkins County, New York. Journal of the Torrey Botanical Society 125:150–164.

St-Pierre, H., R. Gagnon, and P. Bellefleur. 1992. Régénération après feu de l'épinette noire (*Picea mariana*) et du pin gris (*Pinus banksiana*) dans la forêt boréale, Québec. Canadian Journal of Forest Research 22:474–481.

Strengbom, J., G. Englund, and L. Ericson. 2006. Experimental scale and precipitation modify effects of nitrogen addition on a plant pathogen. Journal of Ecology 94: 227–233.

Strengbom, J., and A. Nordin. 2008. Commercial forest fertilization causes long-term residual effects in ground vegetation of boreal forests. Forest Ecology and Management 256:2175–2181.

Strengbom, J., and A. Nordin. 2012. Physical disturbance determines effects from nitrogen addition on ground vegetation in boreal coniferous forests. Journal of Vegetation Science 23:361–371.

Strengbom, J., M. Walheim, T. Näsholm, and L. Ericson. 2003. Regional differences in occurrences of understorey forest species reflect differences in N deposition. Ambio 32:91–97.

Stromayer, K.A.K., and R.J. Warren. 1997. Are overabundant deer herds in the eastern United States creating alternate stable states in forest plant communities? Wildlife Society Bulletin 25:227–234.

Struik, G.J. 1965. Growth patterns of some native annual and perennial herbs in southern Wisconsin. Ecology 46:401–420.

Struik, G.J., and J.T. Curtis. 1962. Herb distribution in an *Acer saccharum* forest. American Midland Naturalist 68:285–296.

Stuble, K.L., K.L. Kirkman, and C.C. Ronald. 2009. Patterns of abundance of fire ants and native ants in a native ecosystem. Ecological Entomology 34:520–526.

Stuble, K.L., K.L. Kirkman, and C.C. Ronald. 2010. Are red imported fire ants facilitators of native seed dispersal? Biological Invasions 12:1661-1669.

Stuefer, J.F., H.J. During, and H. de Kroon. 1994. High benefits of clonal integration in two stoloniferous species, in response to heterogeneous light environments. Journal of Ecology 82:511–518.

Suding, K.N., S.L. Collins, L. Gough, C. Clark, E.E. Cleland, K.L. Gross, D.G. Milchunas, and S. Pennings. 2005. Functional- and abundance-based mechanisms explain diversity loss due to N fertilization. Proceedings of the National Academy of Sciences 102:4387–4392.

Surrette, S.B., and J.S. Brewer. 2008. Inferring relationships between native plant diversity and *Lonicera japonica* in upland forests in north Mississippi, USA. Applied Vegetation Science 11:205–214.

Sutherland, S. 1986. Patterns of fruit-set: what controls fruit-flower ratio in plants? Evolution 40:117–128.

Sutton, F.M., and J.W. Morgan. 2009. Functional traits and prior abundance explain native plant extirpation in a fragmented woodland landscape. Journal of Ecology 97:718–727.

Suzuki, R.O., T. Kato, Y. Maesako, and A. Furukawa. 2009. Morphological and population responses to deer grazing for herbaceous species in Nara Park, western Japan. Plant Species Biology 24:145–155.

Svenning, J.-C. 2003. Deterministic Plio-Pleistocene extinctions in the European cool-temperate tree flora. Ecology Letters 6:646–653.

Svenning, J.-C., and F. Skov. 2007a. Ice age legacies in the geographical distribution of tree species richness in Europe. Global Ecology and Biogeography 16:234–245.

Svenning, J.-C., and F. Skov. 2004. Limited filling of the potential range in European tree species. Ecology Letters 7:565–573.

Svenning, J.-C., and F. Skov. 2006. Potential impact of climate change on the northern nemoral forest herb flora of Europe. Biodiversity and Conservation 15: 3341–3356.

Svenning, J.-C., and F. Skov. 2007b. Could the tree diversity pattern in Europe be generated by postglacial dispersal limitation? Ecology Letters 10:453–460.

Swanson, A.M., and J.L. Vankat. 2000. Woody vegetation and vascular flora of an old-growth mixed-mesophytic forest in southwestern Ohio. Castanea 65:36–55.

Sydes, C., and J.P. Grime. 1981a. Effects of tree leaf litter on herbaceous vegetation in decid-uous woodland. I. Field investigations. Journal of Ecology 69:237–248.

Sydes, C., and J.P. Grime. 1981b. Effects of tree leaf litter on herbaceous vegetation in decid-uous woodland. II. An experimental investigation. Journal of Ecology 69:249–262.

Sykes, M.T., E. van der Maarel, R.K. Peet, and J. Willems. 1994. High species mobility in species-rich plant communities: an intercontinental comparison. Folia Geobotanica and Phytotaxonomica. 29:439–448.

Symstad, A.J., D. Tilman, J. Willson, and J.M.H. Knops. 1998. Species loss and ecosystem functioning: effects of species identity and community composition. Oikos 81:389–397.

Syvertsen, J.P., and G.L. Cunningham 1979. The effects of irradiating adaxial and abaxial leaf surfaces on the rate of net photosynthesis of *Peresia nana* and *Helianthus annuus*. Photosynthetica 13:287–293.

Szarek-Lukaszewska, G., K. Grodzinska, and K. Grodzinska. 2007. Vegetation of a post-mining open pit (Zn/Pb ores): Three-year study of colonization. Polish Journal of Ecology 55:261–282.

Szlavecz, K., M. McCormick, L. Xia, J. Saunders, T. Morocol, D. Whigham, and T. Filley. 2011. Ecosystsem effects of non-native earthworms in Mid-Atlantic deciduous forests. Biological Invasions 13:1165–1182.

Tagaki, H. 2005. Rhizome dormancy and its breaking in *Polygonatum macranthum* (Maxim.) Koidz. Horticultural Research 4:213–218.

Taki, H., P.G. Kevan, and J.S. Ascher. 2007. Landscape effects of forest loss in a pollination system. Landscape Ecology 22:1575–1587.

Tamm, C.O. 1948. Observations on reproduction and survival of some perennial herbs. Botaniska Notiser, Hafte 3:305–321.

Tamm, C.O. 1956. Further observations on the survival and flowering of some perennial herbs. Oikos 7:274–292.

Tamm, C.O. 1972a. Survival and flowering of some perennial herbs: II. The behaviour of some orchids on permanent plots, Oikos 23:23–28.

Tamm, C.O. 1972b. Survival and flowering of some perennial herbs: III. The behaviour of *Primula veris* on permanent plots. Oikos 23:159–166.

Tanentzap, A.J., D.R. Bazely, S. Koh, M. Timciska, E.G. Haggith, T.J. Carleton, and D.A. Coomes. 2011. Seeing the forest for the deer: do reductions in deer-disturbance lead to forest recovery? Biological Conservation 144:376–382.

Tanentzap, A.J., L.E. Burrows, W.G. Lee, G. Nugent, J.M. Maxwell, and D.A. Coomes. 2009. Landscape-level vegetation recovery from herbivory: progress after four decades of invasive red deer control. Journal of Applied Ecology 46:1064–1072.

Tanentzap, A.J., K.J. Kirby, and E. Goldberg. 2012. Slow responses of ecosystems to reductions in deer (Cervidae) populations and strategies for achieving recovery. Forest Ecology and Management 264:159–166.

Tang, Y., I. Washitani, and H. Iwaki. 1992. Effects of microsite light availability on the survival and growth of oak seedlings within a grassland. Botanical Magazine of Tokyo 105:281–288.

Tang, Y., N. Kachi, A. Furukawa, and M.B. Awang.1999. Heterogeneity of light availability and its effects on simulated carbon gain of tree leaves in a small gap and the understory in a tropical rain forest. Biotropica 31:268–278.

Tani, T., and G. Kudo. 2006. Seasonal pattern of leaf production and its effect on giant summer-green herbs in deciduous forests in northern Japan. Canadian Journal of Botany 84:87–98.

Tanner, J.E. 2001. The influence of clonality on demography: Patterns in expected longevity and survivorship. Ecology 82:1971–1981.

Tansley, A.G. 1935. The use and abuse of vegetational concepts and terms. Ecology 16:284–307.

Taverna, K., R.K. Peet, and L. Phillips. 2005. Long-term change in ground-layer vegetation of deciduous forests of the North Carolina Piedmont, USA. Journal of Ecology 93:202–213.

Taylor, A.H., and Z. Qin. 1992 Tree regeneration after bamboo die-back in Chinese *Abies-Betula* forests. Journal of Vegetation Science 3:253–260.

Taylor, A.H., Z. Qin, and J. Liu. 1995. Tree regeneration in an *Abies faxoniana* forest after bamboo dieback, Wang Lang Natural Reserve, China. Canadian Journal of Forest Research 25:2034–2039.

Taylor, B.R., D. Parkinson, and W.F.J. Parsons. 1989. Nitrogen and lignin content as predictors of litter decay rates: a microcosm test. Ecology 70:97–104.

Taylor, G., G. Taylor, M.J. Tallis, C.P. Giardina, K.E. Percy, F. Miglietta, P.S. Gupta, B. Giolis, C. Calfapietra, B. Gielen, M.E. Kubiske, G.E. Scarascia-Mugnozza, K. Kets, S.P. Long, and D.F. Karnofsky. 2008. Future atmospheric CO_2 leads to delayed autumnal senescence. Global Change Biology 14:264–275.

Taylor, K. 2009. Biological flora of the British Isles: *Urtica dioica* L. Journal of Ecology 97:1436–1458.

Taylor, R.J., and R.W. Pearcy. 1976. Seasonal patterns of the CO2 exchange characteristics of understory plants from a deciduous forest. Canadian Journal of Botany 54:1094–1103.

Taylor, S.J., T.J. Carleton, and P. Adams. 1987. Understorey vegetation change in a *Picea mariana* chronosequence. Vegetatio 73:63–72.

Tear, T.H., J.M. Scott, P.H. Hayward, and B. Griffith. 1995. Recovery plans and the endangered-species-act—are criticisms supported by data? Conservation Biology 9:182–195.

Templeton, A.R., and D.A. Levin. 1979. Evolutionary consequences of seed pools. American Naturalist 114:232–249.

Teras, I. 1983. Estimation of bumblebee densities (*Bombus*: Hymenoptera, Apidae). Acta Entomologica Fennica 42:103–113.

ter Braak, C.J.F. 1986. Canonical correspondence analysis: a new eigenvector technique for multivariate direct gradient analysis. Ecology 67:1167–1179.

ter Braak, C.J.F. 1987. CANOCO—a FORTRAN program for community ordination by [partial] [detrended] [canonical] correspondence analysis, principal components analysis and redundancy analysis. Version 2.1. Agricultural Mathematics Group, Wageningen, NL.

ter Braak, C.J.F. 1990. Update notes: CANOCO version 3.10. Agricultural Mathematics Group, Wageningen, NL.

Teskey, R.O., and R.B. Shrestha. 1985. A relationship between carbon dioxide, photosynthetic efficiency and shade tolerance. Physiologia Plantarum 63:126–132.

Tessier, J.T. 2007. Re-establishment of three dominant herbaceous understory species following fine-scale disturbance in a Catskill northern hardwood forest. Journal of the Torrey Botanical Society 134:34–44.

Tessier, J.T. 2008. Leaf habit, phenology, and longevity of 11 forest understory plant species in Algonquin State Forest, northwest Connecticut, USA. Botany 86:457–465.

Tessier, J.T., S.J. McNaughton, and D.J. Raynal. 2001. Influence of nutrient availability and tree wildling density on nutrient uptake by *Oxalis acetosella* and *Acer saccharum*. Environmental and Experimental Botany 45:11–20.

Tessier, J.T., and D.J. Raynal. 2003. Vernal nitrogen and phosphorus retention by forest understory vegetation and soil microbes. Plant and Soil 256:443–453.

Tester, J.R. 1996. Effects of fire frequency on plant species in oak savanna in east-central Minnesota. Bulletin of the Torrey Botanical Club 123:304–305.

Thieret, J.W. 1969. Notes on *Epifagus virginiana* D. Castanea 34:397–402.

Thomas, C.D. 2011. Translocation of species, climate change, and the end of trying to recreate past ecological communities. Trends in Ecology and Evolution 26:216–221.

Thomas, C.D., A. Cameron, R.E. Green, M. Bakkenes, L.J. Beaumont, Y.C. Collingham, B.F.N. Erasmus, M.F. de Siqueira, A. Grainger, L. Hannah, L. Hughes, B. Huntley, A.S. van Jaarsveld, G.F. Midgley, L. Miles, M.A. Ortega-Huerta, A.T. Peterson, O.L. Phillips, and S.E. Williams. 2004. Extinction risk from climate change. Nature 427:145–148.

Thomas, S.C., C.B. Halpern, D.A. Falk, D.A. Liguori, and K.A. Austin. 1999. Plant diversity in managed forests: understory responses to thinning and fertilization. Ecological Applications 9:864–879.

Thompson, I.D., W.J. Curran, J.A. Hancock, and C.E. Butler. 1992. Influence of moose browsing on successional forest growth on black spruce sites in Newfoundland. Forest Ecology and Management 47:29–37.

Thompson, J.N. 1980. Treefalls and colonization patterns of temperate forest herbs. American Midland Naturalist 104:176–184.

Thompson, J., N. Brokaw, J.K. Zimmerman, R.B. Waide, E.M. Everham, D.J. Lodge, C.M. Taylor, D. Garcia-Montiel, and M. Fluet. 2002. Land use history, environment, and tree composition in a tropical forest. Ecological Applications 12:1344–1363.

Thompson, J.S., and L.M. Leege. 2011. A field study of seed germination in the endangered *Trillium reliquum* Freeman (Trilliaceae). Plant Species Biology 26:111–115.

Thompson, K., J.G. Hodgson, and K.J. Gaston. 1998. Abundance-range size relationships in the herbaceous flora of central England. Journal of Ecology 86:439–448.

Thomson, D. 2005. Measuring the effects of invasive species on the demography of a rare endemic plant. Biological Invasions 7:615–624.

Thomson, J.D. 1986. Pollen transport and deposition by bumblebees in *Erythronium*: influences of floral nectar and bee grooming. Journal of Ecology 74:329–341.

Thorne, R.F. 1949. Inland plants on the Gulf Coastal Plain of Georgia. Castanea 14: 88–97.

Throop, H.L., and M.T. Lerdau. 2004. Effects of nitrogen deposition on insect herbivory: implications for community and ecosystem processes. Ecosystems 7:109–133.

Thuiller, W., C. Albert, M.B. Araujo, P.M. Berry, M. Cabeza, A. Guisan, T. Hickler, G.F. Midgely, J. Paterson, F.M. Schurr, M.T. Sykes, and N.E. Zimmermann. 2008. Predicting global change impacts on plant species' distributions: future challenges. Perspectives in Plant Ecology, Evolution, and Systematics 9:137–152.

Thuiller, W., S. Lavorel, and M.B. Araújo. 2005. Niche properties and geographical extent as predictors of species sensitivity to climate change. Global Ecology and Biogeography 14: 347–357.

Tiffney, B.H., and S.R. Manchester. 2001. The use of geological and paleontological evidence in evaluating plant phylogeographic hypotheses in the northern hemisphere Tertiary. International Journal of Plant Sciences 162:S3–S17.

Tilghman, N.G. 1989. Impacts of white-tailed deer on forest regeneration in northwestern Pennsylvania. Journal of Wildlife Management 53:424–453.

Tilman, D. 1982. Resource competition and community structure. Princeton University Press, Princeton, NJ.

Tilman, D. 1985. The resource-ratio hypothesis of plant succession. American Naturalist 125:827–852.

Tilman, D. 1994.Competition and biodiversity in spatially structured habitats. Ecology 75:2–16.

Tilman, D. 1996. Biodiversity: population versus ecosystem stability. Ecology 77:350–363.

Tilman, D. 1999. The ecological consequences of changes in biodiversity: A search for general principles. Ecology 80:1455–1474.

Tilman, D., R.M. May, C.L. Lehman, and M.A. Nowak. 1994. Habitat destruction and the extinction debt. Nature 371:65–66.

Timonen, U., S. Huttunen, and S. Manninen. 2004. Ozone sensitivity of wild field layer plant species of northern Europe; a review. Plant Ecology 172:27–39.

Ting, S., S. Hartley, and K.C. Burns. 2008. Global patterns in fruiting seasons. Global Ecology and Biogeography 17:648–657.

Tinoco-Ojanguren, C., and R.W. Pearcy. 1993a. Stomatal dynamics and its importance to carbon gain in two rainforest *Piper* species. I. VPD effects on the transient stomatal response to lightflecks. Oecologia 94:388–394.

Tinoco-Ojanguren, C., and R.W. Pearcy. 1993b. Stomatal dynamics and its importance to carbon gain in two rainforest *Piper* species. II. Stomatal versus biochemical limitations during photosynthetic induction. Oecologia 94:395–402.

Tissue, D.T., J.B. Skillman, E.P. McDonald, and B.R. Strain. 1995. Photosynthesis and carbon allocation in *Tipularia discolor* (Orchidaceae), a wintergreen understory herb. American Journal of Botany 82:1249–1256.

Tomimatsu, H. 2006. Evaluating the consequences of habitat fragmentation: a case study in the common forest herb *Trillium camschatcense*. Population Ecology 48:189–198.

Tomimatsu, H., and M. Ohara. 2010. Demographic response of plant populations to habitat fragmentation and temporal environmental variability. Oecologia 162:903–911.

Tomimatsu, H., J. Yamagishi, I. Tanaka, M. Sato, R. Kondo, and Y. Konno. 2011. Consequences of forest fragmentation in an understory plant community: extensive range expansion of native dwarf bamboo. Plant Species Biology 26:3–12.

Tooke, F., and N.H. Battey. 2010. Temperate flowering phenology. Journal of Experimental Botany 61:2853–2862.

Torang, P., J. Ehrlén, and J. Ågren. 2010. Linking environmental and demographic data to predict future population viability of a perennial herb. Oecologia 163:99–109.

Townsend, P., and D. Levey. 2005. An experimental test of whether habitat corridors affect pollen transfer. Ecology 86:466–475.

Townsend, P.A. 2001. Relationships between vegetation patterns and hydroperiod on the Roanoke River Floodplain, North Carolina. Plant Ecology 156:43–58.

Traill, L.W., C.J.A. Bradshaw, and B.W. Brook. 2007. Minimum viable population size: A meta-analysis of 30 years of published estimates. Biological Conservation 139:159–166.

Travis, J. 1984. Breeding system, pollination, and pollinator limitation in a perennial herb, *Amianthium muscaetoxicum* (Liliaceae). American Journal of Botany 71:941–947.

Trenberth, K.E., P.D. Jones, P. Ambenje, R. Bojariu, D. Easterling, A. Klein Tank, D. Parker, F. Rahimzadeh, J.A. Renwick, M. Rusticucci, B. Soden, and P. Zhai. 2007. Observations: surface and atmospheric climate change. Pages 235–336 in S. Solomon, et al., editors. Climate Change 2007: The Physical Science Basis. Cambridge, UK: Cambridge University Press.

Tuljapurkar, S. 1984. Demography in stochastic environments. 1. Exact distributions of age structure. Journal of Mathematical Biology 9:335–350.

Turchetti, T., and G. Chelazzi. 1984. Possible role of slugs as vectors of the chestnut blight fungus. Forest Pathology 14:125–127.

Turetsky, M.R., S.E. Crow, R.J. Evans, D.H. Vitt, and R.K. Wieder. 2008. Trade-offs in resource allocation among moss species control decomposition in boreal peatlands. Journal of Ecology 96:1297–1305.

Turnbull, L.A., M.J. Crawley, and M. Rees. 2000. Are plant populations seed-limited? A review of seed sowing experiments. Oikos 88:225–238.

Turnbull, M.H., and D.J. Yates. 1993. Seasonal variation in the red/far-red ratio and photon flux density in an Australian sub-tropical rainforest. Agricultural and Forest Meteorology 64:111–127.

Turner, D.P., and E.H. Franz. 1986. The influence of canopy dominants on understory vegetation patterns in an old-growth cedar-hemlock forest. American Midland Naturalist 116:387–393.

Turner, M.G., S.M. Pearson, P. Bolstad, and D.N. Wear. 2003. Effects of land-cover change on spatial pattern of forest communities in the southern Appalachian Mountains (USA). Landscape Ecology 18:449–464.

Tyler, G. 1975. Soil factors controlling ion absorption in the wood anemone (*Anemone nemorosa*). Oikos 27:71–80.

Tyler, G. 1989. Interacting effects of soil acidity and canopy cover on the species composition of field-layer vegetation in oak/hornbeam forests. Forest Ecology and Management 28: 101–114.

Uemura, S. 1994a. Climatic preferences and frequent co-occurrence of boreal and temperate plants in Hokkaido Island, northern Japan. Vegetatio 112:113–126.

Uemura, S. 1994b. Patterns of leaf phenology in forest understory. Canadian Journal of Botany 72:409–414.

Ulrey, C.J. 2002. The relationship between soil fertility and the forests of the southern Appalachian region. Ph.D. dissertation. North Carolina State University, Raleigh, NC.

United States Department of Agriculture, FSSR. 1994. Land and resource management plan, Nantahala and Pisgah National Forests, amendment 5. Asheville, NC.

United States Department of Agriculture, NRCS. 2011. The PLANTS Database (http://plants.usda.gov, June 18, 2011). National Plant Data Team, Greensboro, NC.

United States Department of Agriculture, NRCS. 2012. The PLANTS Database (http://plants.usda.gov, May 17, 2012). National Plant Data Team, Greensboro, NC.

U.S. EPA (Environmental Protection Agency). 2011. Level III ecoregions of the continental United States. National Health and Environmental Effects Research Laboratory <ftp.epa.gov/wed/ecoregions/us/Eco_Level_III_US.pdf>.

U.S. FGDC (Federal Geographic Data Committee). 2008. National Vegetation Classification Standard. FGDC-STD-005-2008 (Version 2) <http://www.fgdc.gov/standards/projects/FGDC-standards-projects/vegetation/NVCS_V2_FINAL_2008-02.pdf>.

United States Fish and Wildlife Service. 1992. Small whorled pogonia (*Isotria medeoloides*) recovery plan. First revision. Newton Corner, MA.

United States Fish and Wildlife Service. 1993. Recovery plan for *Geocarpon minimum* Mackenzie. Atlanta, GA.

U.S.D.A. Forest Service. 1993. Forest health assessment for the Northeastern Area, NA-TP-01-95.

Valdes, A., and D. Garcia. 2011. Direct and indirect effects of landscape change on the reproduction of a temperate perennial herb. Journal of Applied Ecology 48:1422–1431.

Valladares, F. 1999. Architecture, ecology, and evolution of plant crowns. Pages. 121–194 in F.I. Pugnaire and F. Valladares, editors. Handbook of Functional Plant Ecology. New York: Marcel Dekker.

Vallejo-Marin, M., M.E. Dorken, and S.C.H. Barrett. 2010. The ecological and evolutionary consequences of clonality for plant mating. Annual Review of Ecology, Evolution, and Systematics 41:193–213.

Vallejo-Marin, M., and H.E. O'Brien. 2007. Correlated evolution of self-incompatibility and clonal reproduction in *Solanum* (Solanaceae). New Phytologist 173:415–421.

Valverde, T., and J. Silvertown. 1995. Spatial variation in the seed ecology of a woodland herb (*Primula vulgaris*) in relation to light environment. Functional Ecology 9:942–950.

Valverde, T., and J. Silvertown. 1997a. An integrated model of demography, patch dynamics and seed dispersal in a woodland herb, *Primula vulgaris*. Oikos 80:67–77.

Valverde, T., and J. Silvertown. 1997b. A metapopulation model for *Primula vulgaris*, a temperate forest understory herb. Journal of Ecology 85:193–210.

Valverde, T., and J. Silvertown. 1998. Variation in the demography of a woodland understorey herb (*Primula vulgaris*) along the forest regeneration cycle: projection matrix analysis. Journal of Ecology 86:545–562.

Vamosi, J., T. Knight, J. Steets, S. Mazer, M. Burd, and T.-L. Ashman. 2006. Pollination decays in biodiversity hotspots. Proceedings of the National Academy of Sciences of the United States of America 103:956–961.

van Breemen, N., A.C. Finzi, and C.D. Canham. 1997. Canopy tree–soil interactions within temperate forests: effects of soil elemental composition and texture on species distributions. Canadian Journal of Forest Research 27:1110–1116.

Van Calster, H., P. Endels, K. Antonio, K. Verheyen, and M. Hermy. 2008. Coppice management effects on experimentally established populations of three herbaceous layer woodland species. Biological Conservation 141:2641–2652.

Van Cleve, K., R. Barney, and R. Schlentner. 1981. Evidence of temperature control of production and nutrient cycling in two interior Alaska black spruce ecosystems. Canadian Journal of Forest Research 11:258–273.

Van Cleve, K., and L.A. Viereck. 1981. Forest succession in relation to nutrient cycling in the boreal forest of Alaska. Pages 185–211 in D. West, H. Shugart, and D. Botkin, editors. Forest Succession: Concepts and applications. New York: Springer-Verlag.

van Deelan, T.R., K.S. Pregitzer, and J.B. Haufler. 1996. A comparison of presettlement and present-day forests in two northern Michigan deer yards. American Midland Naturalist 135:181–194.

Vandepitte, K., O. Honnay, T. De Meyer, H. Jacquemyn, and I. Roldan-Ruiz. 2010. Patterns of sex ratio variaton and genetic diversity in the dioecious forest perennial *Mercurialis perennis*. Plant Ecology 206: 105–114.

van der Maarel, E., and M.T. Sykes. 1993. Small-scale plant species turnover in a limestone grassland: the carousel model and some comments on the niche concept. Journal of Vegetation Science 4:179–188.

van der Maarel, E., and M.T. Sykes. 1993. Small-scale plant species turnover in a limestone grassland: the carousel model and some comments on the niche concept. Journal of Vegetation Science 4:179–188.

Van der Putten, W.H., M. Macel, and M.E. Visser. 2010. Predicting species distribution and abundance responses to climate change: why it is essential to include biotic interactions across trophic levels. Philosophical Transactions of the Royal Society, B: 365:2025–2034.

Van der Veken, S., J. Bellemare, K. Verheyen, and M. Hermy. 2007a. Life-history traits are correlated with geographical distribution patterns of western European forest herb species. Journal of Biogeography 34:1723–1735.

Van der Veken, S., J. Rogister, K. Verheyen, M. Hermy, and R. Nathan. 2007b. Over the (range) edge: a 45-year transplant experiment with the perennial forest herb *Hyacinthoides non-scripta*. Journal of Ecology 95:343–351.

Van der Veken, S., M. Hermy, M. Vellend, A. Knapen, and K. Verheyen. 2008. Garden plants get a head start on climate change. Frontiers in Ecology and the Environment 6:212–216.

Van der Voort, M.E., B. Bailey, D.E. Samuel, and J.B. McGraw. 2003. Recovery of populations of goldenseal (*Hydrastis canadensis* L.) and American ginseng (*Panax quinquefolius* L.) following harvest. American Midland Naturalist 149:282–292.

Van der Voort, M.E., and J.B. McGraw. 2006. Effects of harvester behavior on population growth rate affects sustainability of ginseng trade. Biological Conservation 130: 505–516.

van Diepen, L.T.A., E.A. Lilleskov, and K.S. Pregitzer. 2011. Simulated nitrogen deposition affects community structure of arbuscular mycorrhizal fungi in northern hardwood forests. Molecular Ecology 20:799–811.

van Dorp, G., P. Schipper and J.M. van Groenendael. 1997. Migration rates of grassland plants along corridors in fragmented landscapes assessed with a cellular automation model. Landscape Ecology 12:39–50.

Van Dyke, O. 1999. A literature review of ice storm impacts on forests in eastern North America. Ontario Ministry of Natural Resources, Southcentral Sciences Section, Technical Report #112. North Bay, Ontario, CN.

Van Geert, A., F. Van Rossum, and L. Triest. 2010. Do linear landscape elements in farmland act as biological corridors for pollen dispersal? Journal of Ecology 98:178–187.

van Groenendael, J., H. de Kroon, S. Kalisz, and S. Tuljapurkar. 1994. Loop analysis: evaluating life history pathways in population projection matrices. Ecology 75:2410–2415.

Vankat, J.L., and G.W. Snyder. 1991. Floristics of a chronosequence corresponding to old field-deciduous forest succession in southwestern Ohio. II. Undisturbed vegetation. Bulletin of the Torrey Botanical Club 118:365–376.

van Kleunen, M. 2007. Adaptive genetic differentiation in life-history traits between populations of *Mimulus guttatus* with annual and perennial life cycles. Evolutionary Ecology 21:185–199.

Van Rossum, F. 2008. Conservation of long-lived forest herbs in an urban context: *Primula elatior* as case study. Conservation Genetics 9:119–128.

van Tienderen, P.H. 2000. Elasticities and the link between demographic and evolutionary dynamics. Ecology 81:666–679.

Veblen, T.T. 1982. Growth patterns of *Chusquea* bamboos in the understory of Chilean *Nothofagus* forests and their influences in forest dynamics. Bulletin of the Torrey Botanical Club 109:474–487.

Veblen, T.T. 1989. Tree responses to gaps along a transandean gradient. Ecology 70:541–543.

Veblen, T.T., D.H. Ashton, and F.M. Schlegel. 1979. Tree regeneration strategies in a lowland *Nothofagus*-dominated forest in south-central Chile. Journal of Biogeography 6:329–340.

Veech, J.A., K.S. Summerville, T.O. Crist, and J.C. Gering. 2002. The additive partitioning of species diversity: recent revival of an old idea. Oikos 99:3–9.

Vellak, K., J. Paal, and J. Liira. 2003. Diversity and distribution pattern of bryophytes and vascular plants in a boreal spruce forest. Silva Fennica 37:3–13.

Vellend, M. 2004. Parallel effects of land-use history on species diversity and genetic diversity of forest herbs. Ecology 85:3043–3055.

Vellend, M. 2005. Land-use history and plant performance in populations of *Trillium grandiflorum*. Biological Conservation 124:217–224.

Vellend, M., M.J. Lechowicz, and M.J. Waterway. 2000a. Environmental distribution of four *Carex* species (Cyperaceae) in an old-growth forest. American Journal of Botany 87: 1507–1516.

Vellend, M., M.J. Lechowicz, and M.J. Waterway. 2000b. Germination and establishment of forest sedges (*Carex*, Cyperaceae): Tests for home-site advantage and effects of leaf litter. American Journal of Botany 87:1517–1525.

Vellend, M., J.A. Myers, S. Gardescu, and P.L. Marks. 2003. Dispersal of *Trillium* seeds by deer: implications for long-distance migration of forest herbs. Ecology 84:1067–1072.

Vellend, M., K. Verheyen, K.M. Flinn, H. Jacquemyn, A. Kolb, H. Van Calster, G. Peterken, B.J. Graae, J. Bellemare, O. Honnay, J. Brunet, M. Wulf, F. Gerhardt, and M. Hermy. 2007. Homogenization of forest plant communities and weakening of species–environment relationships via agricultural land use. Journal of Ecology 95:565–573.

Vellend, M., K. Verheyen, H. Jacquemyn, A. Kolb, H. Van Calster, G. Peterken, and M. Hermy. 2006. Extinction debt of forest plants persists for more than a century following habitat fragmentation. Ecology 87:542–548.

Vellend, M., M.J. Lechowicz, and M.J. Waterway. 2000a. Environmental distribution of four *Carex* species (Cyperaceae) in an old-growth forest. American Journal of Botany 87: 1507–1516.

Vellend, M., M.J. Lechowicz, and M.J. Waterway. 2000b. Germination and establishment of forest sedges (*Carex*, Cyperaceae): Tests for home-site advantage and effects of leaf litter. American Journal of Botany 87:1517–1525.

Vellend, M., T.M. Knight, and J.M. Drake. 2010. Antagonistic effects for seed dispersal and herbivory on plant migration. Ecology Letters 9:316–323.

Verheyen, K., L. Baeten, P. De Frenne, M. Bernhardt-Römermann, J. Brunet, J. Cornelis, G. Decocq, H. Dierschke, O. Eriksson, R. Hédl, T. Heinken, M. Hermy, P. Hommel, K. Kirby, T. Naaf, G. Peterken, P. Petřík, J. Pfadenhauer, H. Van Calster, G.-R. Walther, M. Wulf, and G. Verstraeten. 2012. Driving factors behind the eutrophication signal in understorey plant communities of deciduous temperate forests. Journal of Ecology 100:352–365.

Verheyen, K., I. Fastenaekels, M. Vellend, L. De Keersmaeker, and M. Hermy. 2006. Landscape factors and regional differences in recovery rates of herb layer richness in Flanders (Belgium). Landscape Ecology 21:1109–1118.

Verheyen, K., and M. Hermy. 2001. The relative importance of dispersal limitation of vascular plants in secondary forest succession in Muizen Forest, Belgium. Journal of Ecology 89:829–840.

Verheyen, K., and M. Hermy. 2004. Recruitment and growth of herb-layer species with different colonizing capacities in ancient and recent forests. Journal of Vegetation Science 15: 125–134.

Verheyen, K., O. Honnay, G. Motzkin, M. Hermy, and D.R. Foster. 2003. Response of forest plant species to land-use change: a life-history trait-based approach. Journal of Ecology 91:563–577.

Vézina, P.E., and M.M. Grandtner. 1965. Phenological observations of spring geophytes in Quebec. Ecology 46:869–872.

Vico, G., S. Manzoni, S. Palmoth, and G. Katul. 2011. Effects of stomatal delays on the economics of leaf gas exchange under intermittent light regimes. New Phytologist 192:640–652.

Vidra, R.L., T.H. Shear, and J.M Stucky. 2007. Effects of vegetation removal on native understory recovery in an exotic-rich urban forest. Journal of the Torrey Botanical Society 134:410–419.

Viereck, L.A., and L.A. Schandelmeier. 1980. Effects of fire in Alaska and adjacent Canada: a literature review. Technical report 6. Bureau of Land Management, Alaska State Office.

Vierling, L.A., and C.A. Wessman. 2000. Photosynthetically active radiation heterogeneity within a monodominant Congolese rain forest canopy. Agricultural and Forest Meteorology 103:265–278.

Vincent, J.S., and L. Hardy. 1977. L'évolution et l'extinction des lacs glaciaires Barlow et Ojibway et territoires québécois. Géographie Physique Quaternaire 31:357–372.

Vingarzan, R. 2004. A review of surface ozone background levels and trends. Atmospheric Environment 38:3431–3442.

Virtanen, R., G.R. Edward,s and M.J. Crawley. 2002. Red deer management and vegetation on the Isle of Rum. Journal of Applied Ecology 39:572–583.Vitousek, P. 1982. Nutrient cycling and nutrient use efficiency. American Naturalist 119:553–572.

Vitousek, P.M. 1985. Community turnover and ecosystem nutrient dynamics. Pages 325–333 in S.T.A. Pickett and P.S. White, editors. The ecology of natural disturbance and patch dynamics. Academic Press, Orlando, FL.

Vitousek, P.M., D.M. D'Antonio, L.L. Loope, and R. Westbrooks. 1996. Biological invasions as global environmental change. American Scientist 84:468–478.

Vitousek, P.M., H.A. Mooney, J. Lubchenco, and J. Mellilo. 1997. Human domination of earth's ecosystem. Science 277:494–499.

Vitt, P., K. Havens, B.E. Kendall, and T.M. Knight. 2009. Effects of community-level grassland management on the non-target rare annual *Agalinis auriculata*. Biological Conservation 142:798–805.

Vockenhuber, E.A., C. Scherber, C. Langenbruch, M. Meißner, D. Seidel, and T. Tscharntke. 2011. Tree diversity and environmental context predict herb species richness and cover in Germany's largest connected forest. Perspectives in Plant Ecology, Evolution, and Systematics 13:111–119.

Vogelmann, T.C. 1993. Plant tissue optics. Annual Review of Plant Physiology and Plant Molecular Biology 44:231–251.

Vogelmann, T.C., J.F. Bornman, and D.J. Yates, 1996. Focusing of light by leaf epidermal cells. Physiologia Plantarum 98:48–56.

Vogler, D., and S. Kalisz. 2001. Sex among the flowers: the distribution of plant mating systems. Evolution 55:202–204.

Vogt, K.A., C.C. Grier, C.E. Meier, and M.R. Keyes. 1983. Organic matter and nutrient dynamics in forest floors of young and mature *Abies amabilis* stands in western Washington, as affected by fine-root input. Ecological Monographs 53:139–157.

von Arx, G., and H. Dietz. 2006. Growth rings in the roots of temperate forbs are robust annual markers. Plant Biology 8:224–233.

von Caemmerer, S., and R.T. Furbank. 1999. Modeling C4 photosynthesis. Pages 173–211 in R.F. Sage and R.K. Monson, editors. C4 plant biology. Academic Press, New York.

von Oheimb, G., and W. Härdtle. 2009. Selection harvest in temperate deciduous forests: impact on herb layer richness and composition. Biodiversity and Conservation 18:271–287.

Vourc'h, G., J.L. Martin, P. Duncan, J. Escarré, and T.P. Clausen. 2001. Defensive adaptations of *Thuja plicata* to ungulate browsing: a comparative study between mainland and island populations. Oecologia 126:84–93.

Wada, N. 1993. Dwarf bamboos affect the regeneration of zoochorous trees by providing habitats to acorn-feeding rodents. Oecologia 94:403–407.

Wagner, H.H., O. Wildi, and K.C. Ewald. 2000. Additive partitioning of plant species diversity in an agricultural mosaic landscape. Landscape Ecology 15:219–227.

Wakeland, B., and R.K. Swihart. 2009. Ratings of white-tailed deer preferences for woody browse in Indiana. Proceedings of the Indiana Academy of Science 118:96–101.

Walker, A.N., S.A. Fore, and B. Collins. 2009. Fine-scale structure within a *Trillium maclatum* (Liliaceae) population. Botany 87:223–230.

Walker, J., and R.K. Peet. 1983. Composition and species diversity of pine-wiregrass savannas of the Green Swamp, North Carolina. Vegetation 55:163–179.

Walker, J.E. 1983. The travel notes of Joseph Gibbons, 1804. Ohio History 92:96–146.

Waller, D.M., and W.S. Alverson. 1997. The white-tailed deer: a keystone herbivore. Wildlife Society Bulletin 25:217–226.

Waller, D.M., W.S. Alverson, and S.L. Solheim. 1996. Local and regional factors influencing the regeneration of eastern hemlock. In G. Mroz and J. Martin, eds. Hemlock Ecology and Management. Houghton, MI: Michigan Technological University.

Waller, D.M., S. Johnson, R. Collins, E. Williams. 2009. Threats posed by ungulate herbivory to forest structure and plant diversity in the Upper Great Lakes Region with a review of methods to assess those threats. National Resource Report NPS/GLKN/NRR-2009/102.

Waller, D.M. & L.I. Maas. 2013. Do white-tailed deer and the exotic plant, garlic mustard, interact to affect the growth and persistence of native forest plants? Forest Ecology and Management 304: 296–302.

Walters, B.B., and E.W. Stiles. 1996. Effect of canopy gaps and flower patch size on pollinator visitation of *Impatiens capensis*. Bulletin of the Torrey Botanical Club 123:184–188.

Walters, M.B., and P.B. Reich. 1997. Growth of *Acer saccharum* seedlings in deeply shaded understories of northern Wisconsin: effects of nitrogen and water availability. Canadian Journal of Forest Research 27:237–247.

Walther, G. 2004. Plants in a warmer world. Perspectives in Plant Ecology, Evolution, and Systematics 6:169–185.

Wang, B., and Y.-L. Qiu. 2006. Phylogenetic distribution and evolution of mycorrhizas in land plants. Mycorrhiza 16:299–363.

Wang, H., M.J. Moore, P.S. Soltis, C.D. Bell, S.F. Brockington, R. Alexandre, C.C. Davis, M. Latvis, S.R. Manchester, and D.E. Soltis. 2009. Rosid radiation and the rapid rise of angiosperm-dominated forests. Proceedings of the National Academy of Sciences 106: 3853–3858.

Waring, R.H., and W.H. Schlesinger. 1985. Forest ecosystems: concepts and management. Academic Press, New York.

Warren, C.R. 2006. Why does photosynthesis decrease with needle age in *Pinus pisaster*? Trees 20:157–164.

Warren, R.J. 1991. Ecological justification for controlling deer populations in Eastern National Parks. Trans. 56th N.A. Wildl. & Nat. Res. Conf. 56:56–66.

Warren, R.J., II. 2008. Mechanisms driving understory evergreen herb distributions across slope aspects: as derived from landscape position. Plant Ecology 198:297–308.

Warren, R.J., V. Bahn, and M.A. Bradford. 2011. Temperature cues phenological synchrony in ant-mediated seed dispersal. Global Change Biology 17:2444–2454.

Warren, R.J., II, and M.A. Bradford. 2010. Seasonal climate trends, the North Atlantic oscillation, and salamander abundance in the southern Appalachian Mountains. Journal of Applied Meteorology and Climatology 49:1597–1603.

Warren, R.J., II, and M.A. Bradford. 2011. The shape of things to come: woodland herb niche contraction begins during recruitment in mesic forest microhabitat. Proceedings of the Royal Society Section B 278:1390–1398.

Warren, R.J., II, I. Giladi, and M.A. Bradford. 2010. Ant-mediated seed dispersal does not facilitate niche expansion. Journal of Ecology 98:1178–1185.

Warren, R.J., II, and E. Mordecai. 2010. Soil moisture mediated interaction between *Polygonatum biflorum* and leaf spot disease. Plant Ecology 209:1–9.

Warren, R.J., II, J.P. Wright, and M.A. Bradford. 2011. The putative niche requirements and landscape dynamics of *Microstegium vimineum*: an invasive Asian grass. Biological Invasions 13:471–483.

Waser, N.M., D.R. Campbell, M.V. Price, and A.K. Brody. 2010. Density-dependent demographic responses of a semelparous plant to natural variation in seed rain. Oikos 119:1929–1935

Waser, N.M., L. Chittka, M.V. Price, N.M. Williams, and J. Ollerton. 1996. Generalization in pollination systems, and why it matters. Ecology 77:1043–1060.

Washitani, I., and Y. Tang. 1991. Microsite variation in light availability and seedling growth of *Quercus serrata* in a temperate pine forest. Ecological Research 6:305–316.

Waterman, J.R., A.R. Gillespie, J.M. Vose, and W.T. Swank. 1995. The influence of mountain laurel on regeneration in pitch pine canopy gaps of the Coweeta Basin, North Carolina, USA. Canadian Journal of Forest Research 25:1756–1762.

Watkinson, A.R. 1986. Plant population dynamics. Pages 137–185 in M.J. Crawley, editor. Plant ecology. Blackwell Scientific Publications, Oxford, UK.

Watkinson, A.R. 1998. The role of the soil community in plant population dynamics. Trends in Ecology and Evolution 13:171–172.

Watling, J.R., S.A. Robinson, I.E. Woodrow, and C.B. Osmond. 1997. Responses of rainforest understorey plants to excess light during sunflecks. Australian Journal of Plant Physiology 24:17–25.

Watson, L.E., W.J. Elisens, and J.R. Estes. 1991. Electrophoretic and genetic evidence for allopolyploid origin of *Marshallia mohrii* (Asteraceae). American Journal of Botany 78:408–416.

Watson, M., K. Scott, J. Griffith, S. Dieter, C. Jones, and S. Nanda. 2001. The developmental ecology of mycorrhizal associations in mayapple, *Podophyllum peltatum*, Berberidaceae. Evolutionary Ecology 15:425–442.

Watt, A.S. 1947a. Pattern and process in the plant community. Journal of Ecology 35:1–22.

Watt, A.S. 1947b. Contributions to the ecology of bracken (*Pteridium aquilinium*). IV. The structure of the community. New Phytologist 46:97–121.

Way, D.A., and R.W. Pearcy. 2012. Sunflecks in trees and forests: from photosynthetic physiology to global change biology. Tree Physiology 21:1066–1081.

Weakley, A.S. 2011. Flora of the Southern and Mid-Atlantic States. Chapel Hill, NC: University of North Carolina Herbarium, North Carolina Botanical Garden.

Weakley, A.S., J.C. Ludwig, and J.F. Townsend. 2012. Flora of Virginia. Williamsburg, VA: Foundation of the Flora of Virginia.

Weaver, J.E., and F.E. Clements. 1938. Plant ecology. 2nd ed. McGraw-Hill, New York.

Webb, T., III. 1986. Is vegetation in equilibrium with climate? How to interpret late-Quaternary pollen data. Vegetatio 67: 75–91.

Weber, J.A., T.W. Jurik, J.D. Tenhunen, and D.M. Gates.1985. Analysis of gas exchange in seedlings of *Acer saccharum*: integration of field and laboratory studies. Oecologia 65:338–347.

Weber, M.G., and K. Van Cleve. 1981. Nitrogen dynamics in the forest floor of interior Alaska black spruce ecosystems. Canadian Journal of Forest Research 11:743–751.

Weber, M.G., and K. Van Cleve. 1984. Nitrogen transformations in feather moss and forest floor layers of interior Alaska black spruce ecosystems. Canadian Journal of Forest Research 14:278–290.

Webster, C.R., M.A. Jenkins, and G.R. Parker. 2001. A field test of herbaceous plant indicators of deer browsing intensity in mesic hardwood forests of Indiana, USA. Natural Areas Journal 21:149–158.

Webster, C.R., M.A. Jenkins, and J.H. Rock. 2005. Long-term response of spring flora to chronic herbivory and deer exclusion in Great Smoky Mountains National Park, USA. Biological Conservation 125:297–307.

Webster, C.R., and M.A. Jenkins. 2008. Age structure and spatial patterning of *Trillium* populations in old-growth forests. Plant Ecology 199:43–54.

Webster, C.R., and G.R. Parker. 1997. The effects of white-tailed deer on plant communities within Indiana State Parks. Proceedings of the Indiana Academy of Science 106:213–231.

Wedin, D., and D. Tilman. 1993. Competition among grasses along a nitrogen gradient— Initial conditions and mechanisms of competition. Ecological Monographs 63:199–229.

Weekley, C.W., and A. Brothers. 2006. Failure of reproductive assurance in the chasmogamous flowers of *Polygala lewtonii* (Polygalaceae), an endangered sandhill herb. American Journal of Botany 93:245–253.

Weekley, C.W., and E.S. Menges. 2003. Species and vegetation responses to prescribed fire in a long-unburned, endemic-rich Lake Wales Ridge scrub. Journal of the Torrey Botanical Society 130:265–282.

Weekley, C.W., E.S. Menges, and P.F. Quintana-Ascencio. 2007. Seedling emergence and survival of *Warea carteri* (Brassicaceae), an endangered annual herb of the Florida scrub. Canadian Journal of Botany 85:621–628.

Wein, R.W., and J.M. Moore. 1977. Fire history and rotations in the New Brunswick Acadian Forest. Canadian Journal of Forest Research 7:285–294.

Welch, N.L., J.M. Belmont, and J.C. Randolph. 2007. Summer ground layer biomass and nutrient contribution to above-ground litter in an Indiana temperate deciduous forest. American Midland Naturalist 157:11–26.

Wells, B.W. 1932. The natural gardens of North Carolina. University of North Carolina Press, Chapel Hill, NC.

Wells, E.F. 1979. Interspecific hybridization in eastern North American *Heuchera* (Saxifragaceae). Systematic Botany 4:319–338.

Wen, J. 1999. Evolution of eastern Asian and eastern North American disjunct distributions in flowering plants. Annual Review of Ecology, Evolution, and Systematics 30:421–455.

Werger, M.J., and E.M. van Laar. 1985. Seasonal changes in the structure of the herb layer of a deciduous woodland. Flora 176:351–364.

Werner, P.A. 1978. Determination of age in *Liatris aspera* using cross-sections of corms—implications for past demographic studies. American Naturalist 112:1113–1120.

Werner, P.A., and H. Caswell. 1977. Population growth rates and age versus stage-distribution models for teasel (*Dipsacus sylvestris* Huds.). Ecology 58:1103–1111.

Werner, P.A., and W.J. Platt. 1976. Ecological relationships of co-occurring goldenrods. American Naturalist 110:959–971.

Wesselingh, R.A., and M.L. Arnold. 2003. A top-down hierarchy in fruit set on inflorescences in *Iris fulva* (Iridaceae). Plant Biology 5:651–660.

Wheeler, B.E. 2011.Species diversity of vegetation in the Carolinas: The influence and interaction of scale of observation, soil nutrients, and disturbance events. Ph.D. dissertation, University of North Carolina at Chapel Hill, NC.

Wheelwright, N.T., E.E. Dukeshire, J.B. Fontaine, S.H. Gutow, D.A. Moeller, J.G. Schuetz, T.M. Smith, S.L. Rodgers, and A.G Zink. 2006. Pollinator limitation, autogamy and minimal inbreeding depression in insect-pollinated plants on a boreal island. American Midland Naturalist 155:19–38.

Wherry, E.T. 1944. A classification of endemic plants. Ecology 25:247–248.

Whigham, D.F. 1974. An ecological life history study of *Uvularia perfoliata*. American Midland Naturalist 91:343–359.

Whigham, D.F. 1984. Biomass and nutrient allocation of *Tipularia discolor* (Orchidaceae). Oikos 2:303–313.

Whigham, D.F. 1990. The effect of experimental defoliation on the growth and reproduction of a woodland orchid, *Tipularia discolor*. Canadian Journal of Botany 68:1812–1816.

Whigham, D.F. 2004. Ecology of woodland herbs in temperate deciduous forests. Annual Review of Ecology, Evolution, and Systematics 35:583–621.

Whigham, D.F., and A.S. Chapa. 1999. Timing and intensity of herbivory: Its influence on the performance of clonal woodland herbs. Plant Species Biology 14:29–38.

Whigham, D.F., McCormick, M.K., and O'Neill, J.P. 2008. Specialized seedling strategies II: orchids, bromeliads, carnivorous plants, and parasites. Pages. 79–100 in M.A. Leck, V.T. Parker, and R.L. Simpson, editors. Seedling ecology and evolution. Cambridge, UK: Cambridge University Press.

Whigham, D.F., and M.M. McWethy. 1980. Studies on the pollination ecology of *Tipularia discolor* (Orchidaceae). American Journal of Botany 67:550–555.

Whigham, D.F., J.P. O'Neill, H.N. Rasmussen, B.A. Caldwell, and M.K. McCormick. 2006. Seed longevity in terrestrial orchids—Potential for persistent in situ seed banks. Biological Conservation 129:24–30.

Whisler, S.L., and A.A. Snow. 1992. Potential for the loss of self-incompatibility in pollen-limited populations of mayapple (*Podophyllum peltatum*). American Journal of Botany 79:1273–1278.

White, M.A., R.R. Nemani, P.E. Thornton, and S.W. Running. 2002. Satellite evidence of phenological differences between urbanized and rural areas of the eastern United States deciduous broadleaf forest. Ecosystems 5:260–277.

White, P.S. 1979. Pattern, process, and natural disturbance in vegetation. Botanical Review 45:229–299.

White, P.S., and S.T.A. Pickett. 1985. Pages 3–13 in S.T.A. Pickett and P.S. White, editors. The ecology of natural disturbance and patch dynamics. Academic Press, Orlando, FL.

Whitney, G.G. 1984. Fifty years of change in the arboreal vegetation of Heart's Content, an old-growth hemlock-white pine-northern hardwood stand. Ecology 65:403–408.

Whitney, G.G. 1990. The history and status of the hemlock-hardwood forests of the Allegheny plateau. Journal of Ecology 78:443–458.

Whitney, G.G. 1994. From coastal wilderness to fruited plain: a history of environmental change in temperate North America from 1500 to the present. Cambridge University Press, Cambridge, UK.

Whitney, G.G., and D.R. Foster. 1988. Overstorey composition and age as determinants of the understorey flora of woods of central New England. Journal of Ecology 76:867–876.

Whitney, G.W. 1987. Some reflections on the value of old-growth forests, scientific and otherwise. Natural Areas Journal 7:92–99.

Whitney, H.E., and W.C. Johnson. 1984. Ice storms and forest succession in southwestern Virginia. Bulletin of the Torrey Botanical Club 111:429–437.

Whittaker, R.H. 1953. A consideration of climax theory: The climax as a population and pattern. Ecological Monographs 23:41–78.

Whittaker, R.H. 1956. Vegetation of the Great Smoky Mountains. Ecological Monographs 26:1–80.

Whittaker, R.H. 1960. Vegetation of the Siskiyou Mountains, Oregon and California. Ecological Monographs 30:279–338.

Whittaker, R.H. 1969. Evolution of diversity in plant communities. Brookhaven Symposium in Biology 22:178–195.

Whittaker, R.H. 1972. Evolution and measurement of species diversity. Taxon 21:213–251.

Whittaker, R.H. 1975. Niche: theory and application. R.H. Whittaker, and S.A. Levin, editors. Dowden, Hutchinson & Ross, Stroudsburg, PA.

Whittaker, R.H., and S.A. Levin. 1977. The role of mosaic phenomena in natural communities. Theoretical Population Biology 12:117–139.

Whitten, W.M. 1981. Pollination ecology of *Monarda didyma*, *Monarda clinopodia*, and hybrids (Lamiaceae) in the southern Appalachian Mountains. American Journal of Botany 68:435–442.

Widden, P.M. 1996. The morphology of vesicular-arbuscular mycorrhizae in *Clintonia borealis* and *Medeola virginiana*. Canadian Journal of Botany 74:679–685.

Wiegmann, S.M., and D.M. Waller. 2006. Fifty years of change in northern upland forest understories: Identity and traits of "winner" and "loser" plant species. Biological Conservation 129:109–123.

Wijesinghe, D.K., and D.F. Whigham. 1997. Costs of producing clonal offspring and the effects of plant size on population dynamics of the woodland herb *Uvularia perfoliata* (Liliaceae). Journal of Ecology 85:907–919.

Wikberg, S., and B.M. Svensson. 2006. Ramet dynamics in a centrifugally expanding clonal sedge: a matrix analysis. Plant Ecology 183:55–63.

Wilbur, H.M., and V.H.W. Rudolf. 2006. Life-history evolution in uncertain environments: bet hedging in time. American Naturalist 168:398–411.

Wilbur, R.B., and N.L. Christensen. 1983. Effects of fire on nutrient availability in a North Carolina coastal plain pocosin. American Midland Naturalist 110:54–61.

Wilcock, C.C., and S.B. Jennings. 1999. Partner limitation and restoration of sexual reproduction in the clonal dwarf shrub *Linnaea borealis* L. (Caprifoliaceae). Protoplasma 208:76–86.

Wilcock, D., and R. Neiland. 2002. Pollination failure in plants: why it happens and when it matters. Trends in Plant Science 7:270–277.

Wilczek, A.M., J.L. Roe, M.C. Knapp, M.D. Cooper, C. Lopez-Gallego, L.J. Martin, C.D. Muir, S. Sim, A. Walker, J. Anderson, J.F. Egan, B.T. Moyers, R. Petipas, A. Giakountis, E. Charbit, G. Coupland, S.M. Welch, and J. Schmitt. 2009. Effects of genetic perturbation on seasonal life history plasticity. Science 323:930–934.

Wildman, H.E. 1950. Pollination of *Asarum canadense* L. Science 111:551–551.

Willems, J.H., and C. Melser. 1998. Population dynamics and life-history of *Coeloglossum viride* (L.) Hartm.: an endangered orchid species in the Netherlands. Botanical Journal of the Linnean Society 126:83–93.

Williams, C.E., W.J. Moriarity, and G.L. Walters. 1999a. Overstory and herbaceous layer of a riparian savanna in northwestern Pennsylvania. Castanea 64:90–97.

Williams, C.E., W.J. Moriarity, G.L. Walters, and L. Hill. 1999b. Influence of inundation potential and forest overstory on the ground-layer vegetation of Allegheny Plateau riparian forests. American Midland Naturalist 141:323–338.

Williams, C.E., E.V. Mosbacher, and W.J. Moriarity. 2000. Use of turtlehead (*Chelone glabra* L.) and other herbaceous plants to assess intensity of white-tailed deer browsing on Allegheny Plateau riparian forests, USA. Biological Conservation 92:207–215.

Williams, C.F., and R. Guries. 1994. Genetic consequences of seed dispersal in three sympatric forest herbs. 1. Hierarchical population genetic structure. Evolution 48:791–805.

Williams, J.W., B.N. Shuman, T. Webb, III, P.J. Bartlein, and P.L. Leduc. 2004. Late-quaternary vegetation dynamics in North America: scaling from taxa to biomes. Ecological Monographs 74:309–334

Williams, K., C.B. Field, and H.A. Mooney. 1989. Relationships among leaf construction cost, leaf longevity, and light environment in rain-forest plants of the genus *Piper*. American Naturalist 133:198–211.

Williams, L.D. 1998. Factors affecting growth and reproduction in the invasive grass *Microstegium vimineum*. M.S. thesis, Appalachian State University, Boone, NC.

Williams, M. 1989. Americans and their forests: a historical geography. Cambridge University Press, New York.

Williams, N.S.G., J.W. Morgan, M.J. McDonnell, and M.A. McCarthy. 2005. Plant traits and local extinctions in natural grasslands along an urban-rural gradient. Journal of Ecology 93:1203–1213.

Williams, T.M., J.A. Estes, D.F. Doak, and A.M. Springer. 2004. Killer appetites: Assessing the role of predators in ecological communities. Ecology 85:3373–3384.

Williamson, M. 1996. Biological invasions. Chapman & Hall, New York.

Williamson, M., and A. Fitter. 1996. The varying success of invaders. Ecology 77:1661–1666.

Willig, M.R. 2011. Biodiversity and productivity. Science 333:1709–1710.

Willis, J.C. 1922. Age and area: a study in geographical distribution and origin. Cambridge, UK: Cambridge University Press.

Willis, K.J., R.M. Bailey, S.A. Bhagwat, and H.J. Birks. 2010. Biodiversity baselines, thresholds and resilience: testing predictions and assumptions using palaeoecological data. Trends in Ecology and Evolution 25:583–591.

Willis, K.J., A. Kleczkowski, M. New, and R.J. Whittaker. 2007. Testing the impact of climate variability on European plant diversity: 320,000 years of water-energy dynamics and its long-term influence on plant taxonomic richness. Ecology Letters 10:673–679.

Willis, K.J., and J.C. McElwain. 2002. The evolution of plants., Oxford, UK: Oxford University Press.

Willmer, P. 2011. Pollination and floral ecology. Princeton, NJ: Princeton University Press.

Willmot, A. 1989. The phenology of leaf life spans in woodland populations of the ferns *Dryopteris filix-mas* (L.) Schott and *D. dilatata* (Hoffm.) A. Gray in Derbyshire. Botanical Journal of the Linnean Society 99:387–395.

Wilson, A.D., and D.J. Shure. 1993. Plant competition and nutrient limitation during early succession in the southern Appalachian Mountains. American Midland Naturalist 129:1–9.

Wilson, J.B. 1999. Assembly rules in plant communities. Pages 130–164 in E. Weiher and P. Keddy, editors. Ecological assembly rules: perspectives, advances, retreats. Cambridge University Press, Cambridge, UK.

Wilson, J.B. 1999. Guilds, functional types, and ecological groups. Oikos 86:507–522.

Wilson, J.B. 2011. The twelve theories of co-existence in plant communities: the doubtful, the important and the unexplored. Journal of Vegetation Science 22:184–195.

Wilson, J.B., H. Gitay, J.B. Steel, and W.M. King. 1998. Relative abundance distributions in plant communities: effects of species richness and of spatial scale. Journal of Vegetation Science 9:213–220.

Wilson, J.B., R.K. Peet, J. Dengler, and M. Pärtel. 2012. Plant species richness: the world records. Journal of Vegetation Science 23:796–802.

Wilson, J.B., J.B. Steel, W.M. King, and H. Gitay. 1999. The effect of spatial scale on evenness. Journal of Vegetation Science 10:463–468.

Wilson, R.J., D. Gutiérrez, D. Martínez, R. Agudo, and V.J. Monserrat. 2005. Changes to the elevational limits and extent of species ranges associated with climate change. Ecology Letters 8:1138–1146.

Winkler, E., M. Fischer, and B. Schmid. 1999. Modelling the competitiveness of clonal plants by complementary analytical and simulation approaches. Oikos 85:217–233.

Winn, A.A., and L.F. Pitelka. 1981. Some effects of density on the reproductive patterns and patch dynamics of *Aster acuminatus*. Bulletin of the Torrey Botanical Club 108:438–445.

Winter, C., S. Lehmann, and M. Diekmann. 2008. Determinants of reproductive success: A comparative study of five endangered river corridor plants in fragmented habitats. Biological Conservation 141:1095–1104.

Winter, K., M.R. Schmitt, and G.E. Edwards. 1982. *Microstegium vimineum*, a shade-adapted C4 grass. Plant Science Letters 24:311–318.

Wise, D.H., and M. Schaefer. 1994. Decomposition of leaf litter in a mull beech forest: comparison between canopy and herbaceous species. Pedobiologia 38:269–288.

Wiser, S.K., R.B. Allen, P.W. Clinton, and K.H. Platt. 1998. Community structure and forest invasion by an exotic herb over 23 years. Ecology 79:2071–2081.

Wistendahl, W.A. The flood plain of the Raritan River, New Jersey. Ecological Monographs 28:129–153.

Wixted, K., and J.B. McGraw. 2009. A *Panax*-centric view of invasive species. Biological Invasions 11:883–893.

Wolfe, J.N., R.T. Wareham, and H.T. Schofield. 1949. Microclimates and macroclimate of Neatoma, a small valley in central Ohio. Ohio State University, Columbus, OH.

Wolters, V. 1999. *Allium ursinum* litter triggering decomposition on a beech forest floor—the effect of earthworms. Pedobiologia 43:528–536.

Woods, K.D. 1993. Effects of invasion by *Lonicera tatarica* L. on herbs and tree seedlings in four New England forests. American Midland Naturalist 130:62–74.

Woods, K.D. 1997. Community response to plant invasion. Pages 56–68 in J.O. Luken and J.W. Thieret, editors. Assessment and management of plant invasions. Springer-Verlag, New York.

Woodward, F.I. 1987. Climate and Plant Distribution. Cambridge, UK: Cambridge University Press.

Woycicki, S. 1945. A note on the development of the lily of the valley by early forcing. Sprawozda Tow Nauk Warszawskiego Wydział IV Nauk Biol. 39:63–72.

Wright, J.P., and J.D. Fridley. 2010. Biogeographic synthesis of secondary succession rates in eastern North America. Journal of Biogeography 37:1584–1596.

Wu, B., and F.E. Smeins. 2000. Multiple-scale habitat modeling approach for rare plant conservation. Landscape and Urban Planning 51:11–28.

Wu, J., D. Guan, F. Yuan, H. Yang, A. Wang, and C Jin. 2012. Evolution of atmospheric carbon dioxide concentrations at different temporal scales recorded in a tall forest. Atmospheric Environment 61:9–14.

Wubs, E.R.J., G.A. de Groot, H.J. During, J.C. Vogel, M. Grundmann, P. Bremer, and H. Schneider. 2010. Mixed mating system in the fern *Asplenium scolopendrium*: implications for colonization potential. Annals of Botany 106:583–590.

Wulf, M. 2004. Plant species richness of afforestations with different former use and habitat continuity. Forest Ecology and Management 195:191–204.

Wunderlin, R.P., and B.F. Hansen. 2003. Guide to the Vascular Plants of Florida. Gainesville, FL: University of Florida Press.

Würth, M.K.R., K. Winter, and Ch. Körner. 1998. In situ responses to elevated CO_2 in tropical forest understory plants. Functional Ecology 12:886–895.

Wyatt, J.L. 2009. Recovery and resilience of Appalachian herbs. Ph.D. dissertation, Wake Forest University, Winston-Salem, NC.

Wyatt, J.L., and M.R. Silman. 2010. Centuries-old logging legacy on spatial land temporal patterns in understory herb communities. Forest Ecology and Management 260:116–124.

Wyatt, R. 1983. Pollinator-plant interactions and the evolution of breeding systems. Pages 51–108 in L. Real, editor. Pollination biology. Orlando, FL: Academic Press.

Wyatt, R. 1984. Evolution of self-pollination in granite outcrop species of *Arenaria* (Caryophyllaceae). 3. Reproductive effort and pollen-ovule ratios. Systematic Botany 9:432–440.

Wyatt, R., and S.B. Broyles. 1994. Ecology and evolution of reproduction in milkweeds. Annual Review of Ecology, Evolution, and Systematics 25:423–441.

Xi, W., R.K. Peet, J.K. DeCoster, and D.L. Urban. 2008. Tree damage risk factors associated with large, infrequent wind disturbances of Carolina forests. Forestry 81:317–334.

Xiong, S.J., and C. Nilsson. 1999. The effects of plant litter on vegetation: a meta-analysis. Journal of Ecology 87:984–994.

Yamamura, Y. 1984. Matter production processes of *Reineckia carnea* Kunth, an evergreen forest floor herb in the warm-temperate region of Japan. Botanical Magazine of Tokyo 97:179–191.

Yanhong, T., K. Hiroshi, S. Mitsumasa, and I. Washitani. 1994. Characteristics of transient photosynthesis in *Quercus serrata* seedlings grown under lightfleck and constant light regimes. Oecologia 100:463–469.

Yarie, J. 1980. The role of understory vegetation in the nutrient cycle of forested ecosystems in the mountain hemlock biogeoclimatic zone. Ecology 61:1498–1514.

Yarnell, S.L., ed. 1998. The Southern Appalachians: A history of the landscape. Asheville, NC: U.S. Department of Agriculture, Forest Service, Southern Research Station.

Yatskievych, G. 1999. Steyermark's Flora of Missouri, Vol. 1, revised ed. St. Louis, MO: Missouri Botanical Garden Press.

Yeh, D.M., Y.R. Lin, and J.G. Atherton. 2000. A thermal model for predicting time to aerial shoot elongation in variegated Solomon's Seal. Annals of Applied Biology 136:69–75.

Ying, T. 1983. The floristic relationships of the temperate forest regions of China and the United States. Annals of the Missouri Botanical Garden 70:597–604.

Yoda, K., T. Kira, H. Ogawa, and K. Hozumi. 1963. Self-thinning in overcrowded pure stands under cultivated and natural conditions. Journal of Biology, Osaka City University 14:107–129.

Yordanov, Y., E. Yordanova, and A. Atanassov. 2002. Plant regeneration from interspecific hybrid and backcross progeny of *Helianthus eggertii* x *Helianthus annuus*. Plant Cell Tissue and Organ Culture 71:7–14.

Yorks, T.E., and S. Dabydeen. 1999. Seasonal and successional understory vascular plant diversity in second-growth hardwood clearcuts of western Maryland, USA. Forest Ecology and Management 119:217–230.

Yoshie, F. 2008. Effects of growth temperature and winter duration on leaf phenology of a spring ephemeral (*Gagea lutea*) and a summergreen forb (*Maianthemum dilatatum*). Journal of Plant Research 121:483–492.

Yoshie, F., and S. Kawano. 1986. Seasonal changes in photosynthetic characteristics of *Pachysandra terminalis* (Buxaceae), an evergreen woodland chamaephyte, in the cool temperate regions of Japan. Oecologia 71:6–11.

Yoshie, F., and S. Yoshida. 1987. Seasonal changes in photosynthetic characteristics of *Anemone raddeana*, a spring-active geophyte, in the temperate region of Japan. Oecologia 72:202–206.

Young, A., T. Boyle, and T. Brown. 1996. The population genetic consequences of habitat fragmentation for plants. Trends in Ecology and Evolution 11:413–418.

Young, D.R., and W.K. Smith. 1979. Influence of sunflecks on the temperature and water relations of two subalpine understory congeners. Oecologia 43:195–205.

Yun, N.Y., Y.H. Rhie, H.H. Jung, and K.S. Kim. 2011. Chilling requirement for dormancy release of variegated Solomon's Seal. Horticulture Environment and Biotechnology 52:553–558.

Zak, D.R., P.M. Groffman, K.S. Pregitzer, S. Christensen, and J.M. Tiedje. 1990. The vernal dam: Plant-microbe competition for nitrogen in northern hardwood forests. Ecology 71:651–656.

Zak, D.R., and K.S. Pregitzer. 1988. Nitrate assimilation by herbaceous ground flora in late successional forests. Journal of Ecology 76:537–546.

Zak, D.R., K.S. Pregitzer, and G.E. Host. 1986. Landscape variation of nitrogen mineralization and nitrification. Canadian Journal of Forest Research 16:1258–1263.

Zampella, R.A., and K.J. Laidig. 1997. Effects of watershed disturbance on Pinelands stream vegetation. Journal of the Torrey Botanical Society 124:52–66.

Zar, J.H. 1996. Biostatistical analysis, 3rd ed. Prentice-Hall, Englewood Cliffs, NJ.

Zavitkovsky, J. 1976. Ground vegetation biomass, production, and efficiency of energy utilization in some northern Wisconsin forest ecosystems. Ecology 57:694–706.

Zelikova, T.J., R.R. Dunn, and N.J. Sanders. 2008. Variation in seed dispersal along an elevational gradient in Great Smoky Mountains National Park. Acta Oecological-International Journal of Ecology 34:155–162.

Zhang, D. 2000. Resource allocation and the evolution of self-fertilization in plants. American Naturalist 155:187–199.

Zhang, D., and X. Jiang. 2002. Size-dependent resource allocation and sex allocation in herbaceous perennial plants. Journal of Evolutionary Biology 15:74–83.

Zhang, Y., Q. Zhang, P. Luo, and N.Wu. 2009. Photosynthetic response of *Fragaria orientalis* in different water contrast clonal integration. Ecological Research 24:617–625.

Ziegler, S.S. 1995. Relict eastern white pine (*Pinus strobus* L.) stands in southwestern Wisconsin. American Midland Naturalist 133:88–100.

Zimmerman, J.K., and D.F. Whigham. 1992. Ecological functions of carbohydrates stored in corms of *Tipularia discolor* (Orchidaceae). Functional Ecology 6:575–581.

Zimmerman, M., and G.H. Pyke. 1988. Reproduction in *Polemonium*: assessing the factors limiting seed set. American Naturalist 131:723–738.

Zobel, D.B., and J.A. Antos. 2009. Species properties and recovery from disturbance: Forest herbs buried by volcanic tephra. Journal of Vegetation Science 20:650–662.

Zogg, G.P., D.R. Zak, D.B. Ringelber, N.W. MacDonald, K.S. Pregitzer, and D.C. White. 1997. Compositional and functional shifts in microbial communities due to soil warming. Soil Science Society of America Journal 61:475–481.

Zuckerberg, B., A.M. Woods, and W.F. Porter. 2009. Poleward shifts in breeding bird distributions in New York State. Global Change Biology 15:1866–1883.

Zuidema, P.A., and M. Franco. 2001. Integrating vital rate variability into perturbation analysis: An evaluation for matrix population models of six plant species. Journal of Ecology 89:995–1005.

Index